# Gallia County, Ohio

*Harrington Mill and Northup Bridge - near Gallipolis, Ohio*

*McCarley Grain Mill*

*Flood April 1948*

*Flood - December 1937*

Gallia County, Ohio

# GALLIA COUNTY OHIO

# HISTORY VOL. II

Bicentennial Edition - 2003

*Gallipolis Wharf 1870*

PUBLISHING COMPANY

Turner Publishing Company
Publishers of America's History

Copyright © 2003
Gallia County Historical Society

This book or any part thereof may not be
reproduced without the written consent of the Gallia
County Historical Society History Book
Committee and the Publisher.

The materials were compiled and produced using
available information; Turner Publishing Company and
the Gallia County History Book Committee regret they
cannot assume liability for errors or omissions.

Library of Congress
Control Number: 2003103440
ISBN: 978-1-68162-498-3

Limited Edition of 1000 copies of which
this book is number _____

# Contents

| | |
|---|---|
| Gallia County Historical Society | 4 |
| History | 5 |
| Churches | 47 |
| Clubs & Organizations | 81 |
| Schools | 93 |
| Memorials & Veterans | 101 |
| Businesses | 115 |
| Biographies | 145 |

*Aerial view of Gallipolis, Ohio*

# Gallia County
# 1803 - 2003
## Gallia County Historical Society
## Board Of Trustees - 2002

*1st row - left to right - Alice Kay Giles, Frank Braxton - President, Harold Thompson, Gail Smith - Vice-President, Becky Scott, Nancy Hood*
*2nd row - left to right - Doug Wetherholt, Robert Condee, Jerry Barnes, Charles Murray, Jim Clark - Treasurer, Marjorie Wood, Donald O'Rourke - Secretary Not pictured - Thomas Moulton, Barbara Scott and Dene Pellegrinon*

This book is dedicated to the people, businesses, churches and organizations of Gallia County as it celebrates, along with the great State of Ohio, the 200th anniversary of the year both became part of the United States of America. Our early history returns to a time of change for Ohio and this special part of Ohio playing a big role in the history of making it the great state it has become. The beautiful Ohio River and the ability to live with all the times it has brought us prosperity and, also, humbleness after floods and disaster, has made the citizens of this great county strong and resilient. It is the hope of this historical society for those that read this book now, and for generations to come, the realization of a great legacy we leave to future generations.

The following members of the Gallia County Historical Society have spent much time compiling this book. The board would like to acknowledge the following for their participation in preparing the book. Our Director, Mary Lee Marchi, was the catalyst behind this enormous task being completed. Many thanks to her typing committee partially composed of Alice Giles, Bobette Braxton, Margaret Myers, Christina Cogar, Maxie Oliver, Sonny Garnes, Marjorie Wood and Bertie Roush.

Proofreaders included Carolyn Cogar, Mr. and Mrs. Henry Myers, Myron and Barbara Jones, Vickie and Bob Powell, Wilma Brown, The Gallia County Genealogical Society, Doug and Janet Wetherholt, Jerry Barnes, Alice Giles, Nancy Hood, Annabelle Hagans, Annabelle Fellure, Irene Clark, Gail Smith, Christina Cogar, Marjorie Wood and others.

# Gallia County History

*Downtown, Gallipolis Ohio*

*Drugstore, Ewington Road, Ewington, OH ca. 1916*

# Introduction to Gallia County

By Charles A. Murray

Gallia County was established, in 1803. 500 French colonists had settled Gallipolis, its first major settlement, thirteen years earlier. They had left France because of the turmoil in that country. One of Gallipolis's earliest inns, "The Our House" still exists as a museum.

## Early Pioneers

In addition to the French settlers, other ethnic groups began to arrive. In 1818, Welsh pioneers arrived. They settled in the Tyn Rhos, Nebo, and Peniel areas of western Gallia County. In 1859 German families migrated to Walnut Township. Many of these were excellent craftsmen.

Black American citizens have lived in Gallia County since 1803. During the 1850s many made their way northward from the South via of the Underground Railroad. Around 1900, a group of Italians settled in Gallipolis. Many of them and their offspring have become successful merchants. The latest ethnic group to reside in Gallia County is the Amish. This religious group settled in the Gage and Patriot communities. They have lived here since the 1990s.

Gallia County is sub-divided into 15 townships. Among these are the present-day communities of Mice, Ewington, Vinton, Morgan Center, Glenn Summit, Eno, Kygerville, Little Kyger, Cheshire, Harrisburg, Centerville Thurman, Rio Grande, Adamsville, Bidwell, Porter, Evergreen, Kerr, Bulaville, Addison, Gallia, Center Point, Patriot, Gage, Cora, Rodney, Centenary, Northup, Hanerville, Kanauga, Cadmus, Mudsoc, Little Bullskin, Leaper, Yellowtown, Eureka, Mercerville, Crown City, Swan Creek, Peniel, and Chambersburg.

## Transportation

For many years Gallipolis was a major river port on the Ohio River. People traveled on steamboat packets to major river cities. From Gallipolis, ferryboats were used to transport vehicles across the Ohio River to West Virginia before the Silver Bridge was constructed in 1928. This bridge later collapsed on December 15, 1967, killing 46 people. The Silver Memorial Bridge replaced the ill-fated structure in 1969.

The earliest roadway in Gallia County was the Hannan Trace which connected present-day Charleston (WV) with Chillicothe, Ohio. It was not until 1818 that a road from Gallipolis to Chillicothe was built. At one time, covered bridges crossed the major streams. It was 1863, during the Civil War, when a rebel general named John Hunt Morgan and his men invaded Gallia County While in Vinton, these southern raiders burned the covered bridge over Raccoon Creek. Today State Route 35, a 4-lane highway, serves as the major transportation highway in the county.

Railway transportation arrived in 1880 when the first Hocking Valley Railway train began its operation. Because of the railway, several communities were developed including Mills Station, Kerr, Evergreen, Bidwell, Vinton, Glenn Summit and Alice. Passenger train service in Gallia County ended in 1949.

In 1934, the Holzer Airfield opened in Gallipolis along the strip of land between the Ohio River and State Route 7. Later this was discontinued, and presently a limited air-service at the Gallia-Meigs Regional Airport at Kanauga exists.

## Communication

Mail service via canoe was established between Marietta, Ohio's and Gallipolis in 1794. At the present time, the county has U.S. Postal offices located at Bidwell, Cheshire, Crown City, Gallipolis, Kerr, Patriot, Rio Grande, and Vinton.

The Gallia Gazette became Gallia County's first newspaper in 1818. Today the Gallipolis Daily Tribune and The Sunday Times Sentinel provide coverage of local, state, national, and world news. The Central Union Telephone Company established telephone service in Gallipolis in 1882. Today Ameritech provides the area telephone service. In 1950, Gallipolis aired its first radio program on station WJEH-990.

Now, it, as well as WRYV (101.5) provides this communication service to the area.

## Recreation

Kygerville, in Cheshire Township, once had a natural spa at Blue Sulfur Springs where people bathed and partook the medicinal effects of sulfur water. Around 1900, people in Gallipolis attended Lakewood Park, a resort where dancing, boating, and music were the main attractions. The Bidwell-Porter villages shared a park in the first half of the 1900s. During the days of steamboats on the Ohio River, showboats provided great entertainment. Gallipolis had several opera houses including the Betz Opera House, the Aleshire Hall, and the Ariel Theater, which still exists as the home of the Ohio Valley Symphony. Traveling circuses, Chatauqua meetings, spelling bees, pie socials and county fairs once provided great recreation for area residents. Today nature study can be enjoyed at the Raccoon Creek Park, Tycoon Lake, Wayne National Forest, Elizabeth Evans' Bird Sanctuary and the American Electric Power Wildlife.

## Education

By 1811, the seeds of education were planted in Gallipolis when Gallia Academy, then a private school, was established. Other private schools were established at Cheshire, Ewington and Porter during the 1800s. Gallia Academy, now a public school, has the largest enrollment of the local high schools. South Gallia and River Valley High Schools exist as well. The Buckeye Career Center serves a three county area. Public schools were established, first as one-room schools. Presently the Gallia County School System, the Gallipolis City Schools, and the Buckeye Hills School District exist. Among these are the following elementary schools: Addaville, Bidwell, Green, Hannan Trace, Kyger Creek Middle, Rio Grande, Southwestern, Vinton and Washington. The Ohio Valley Christian School, established in 1977, serves as a private educational institution K-12. The Rio Grande Community College joined the University of Rio Grande, first established as Rio Grande College in 1876, in 1974. Today's Rio Grande is a multi-faceted institution offering both undergraduate and graduate programs of learning. Its mission, since its beginning, is to provide high quality education to students and to serve all of the people who reside in Southern Ohio. The Gallipolis Career College is also another institution of higher learning located within the county.

## Religion

Religious societies have been important elements of Gallia County history. Most of its religious institutions in Gallia County have been Protestant denominations; however the French 500 first introduced Roman Catholicism in 1790. Historians recorded that a Baptist Church was organized in Cheshire Township as early as 1805. Methodism began in Addison Township in 1806. The first Religious Society of Gallipolis (The Presbyterians) was formed in 1815.

## Government

In 1808 the town of Gallipolis was incorporated. The first courthouse was built in the present-day public square just south of the Bandstand; consequently the nearest cross street was called Court Street. The courthouse was moved from the Public Square to Locust Street where it remains today. Several courthouses were destroyed by fire throughout the years, and the present facility was dedicated in 1985. Among the local governmental agencies in Gallia County is the Senior Citizens Center, located on Jackson Pike. This building was constructed in 1906. Another county agency is the Gallia County Children's Home constructed in 1885, making it the oldest standing original children's home in the State of Ohio. The villages of Centerville, Cheshire, Crown City and Vinton are also incorporated.

## Agriculture and Industry

Generally speaking, Gallia County has primarily existed as a rural area with agriculture providing a source of income for many of its residents. One of Gallia's historic farms, "The Homestead", built in 1820, is located on State Route 588 at Rio Grande. The Wood family pioneered this property, and at one time the house served as a stagecoach stop. Bob Evans, the founder of the Bob Evan's Restaurant chain, purchased the farm in 1953 and lived there with his family for many years. Today the Bob Evans Farm is a working farm as well as a historic landmark. Most of the southern townships produce tobacco as a money crop. In recent years local farmers have declined with poultry, sheep, and hog farming. Several farmers now grow peppers as a supplementary money crop. The young people in Gallia County have been active in 4H clubs and junior leadership activities. The Ohio State University maintains local extension service to the county with its headquarters located in the C.H. McKenzie Agriculture Building on Jackson Pike.

Throughout the past 200 years, the people of Gallia County have used their natural resources not only for transportation but also for power. Joseph Rife built one of the first gristmills in Gallia County on Campaign Creek at Bulaville in 1808. Waterpower was used to grind wheat and corn produced by the farmers into flour and cornmeal. Early gristmills once existed on about every major steam with Big Raccoon Creek having the greatest number. The villages of Ewington, Vinton, Harrisburg, Adamsville, Northup, Thevenir and Cora were established as former mill sites.

During Gallia County's history, major industries have been sparse. Once boat building and repair businesses existed along the river, as well as a brick factory, furniture factory, paper factory, stove factory, and buggy factory. Prior to the Civil War Era, iron ore was smelted at the Gallia Furnace (1847) and nearby Keystone Furnace (1848). The Welshmen who settled in the area had introduced the iron industry. In 1955 the Kyger Creek Power Plant began producing electricity near Cheshire, and later also did the Gavin Plant (1974). The Dan Evans Industrial Park is currently being developed on State Rt. 850.

## Health Care Services

Even as early as the Civil War Era, Gallipolis had a hospital facility called Camp Carrington. . In 1883 a marine hospital was established for riverboat workers. From 1884-1887, the Ohio Valley Medical and Surgical Institute existed in Gallipolis. In 1890 the Ohio Hospital for Epileptics was established. In 1910, Charles E. Holzer Sr. first introduced his own health-care facility, which consisted of a 7-bed Holzer Hospital on Second Avenue. The Holzer Hospital and Gallipolis Clinic moved to a new location northwest of the city, creating the Holzer Medical Center in 1972. Other health care centers include the Arbor, Scenic Hills, Wyngate and the Holzer Senior Care Center.

In 2002, the population of Gallia County was 32,820. Because of the county's location on the Ohio River and the early establishments of transportation, mercantilism, educational, religious, and healthcare institutions, a legacy of interesting history has developed over the past two centuries.

*Shirley Angel*
*County Commissioner*

*William J. "Bill" Davis*
*County Commissioner*

*Casby "Skip" Meadows,*
*III County Commissioner*

*Molly Plymale*
*Gallia County Recorder*

*Brent A. Saunders*
*Gallia County Prosecutor*

*Noreeen M. Saunders*
*Clerk of Courts*

*D. Dean Evans*
*Gallia County Common Pleas Judge*

*William Scott Medley*
*Gallipolis Municipal Court Judge*

*Glenn A. Smith*
*Gallia County Engineer*

*David L. Martin*
*Gallia County Sheriff*

## Gallia County Elected Officeholders 2002

Gallia County Trustees and Clerks - 2002
Addison Township Clerk - Deborah L. Hughes
Trustees - Charles E. Martin, Fred F. Burnett and Robert Rothgeb
Cheshire Township Clerk - Carolyn Holland
Trustees - Homer L. McCarty, Michael R. Conkle, and J. D. Taylor
Clay Township Clerk - Wanda K. Waugh
Trustees - Charles Lee Barcus, Jerry L. Haner and Ray Slone
Gallipolis Township Clerk - James R. Allen
Trustees - Lloyd E. Danner, Richard M. Bane and Clyde D. Burnett
Green Township Clerk - Howard Joseph Foster
Trustees - Tony L. Beck, Tom F. Woodward and Lonnie Boggs
Greenfield Township Clerk - Brenda S. Lewis
Trustees - Randall Lee Hammond, Roy McCarty and Henry D. Sheline
Guyan Township Clerk - Carolyn Halley
Trustees - James E. Swain, Monvil C. Swain and Roger A. Watson
Harrison Township Clerk - Terry E. Cremeens
Trustees - Ronald J. Slone, Margaret Adkins and Randy L. Cox
Huntington Township Clerk - Verna Easter
Trustees - Dick Neal, Bill L. Petrie and Roger Shadwick
Morgan Township Clerk - Paula Justus
Trustees - Randall Lee Adkins, Clarence R. Hash and Samuel O. Kemper
Ohio Township Clerk - Judy G. Wright
Trustees - Clarence Mooney, Todd M. Bowers and James D. Green
Perry Township Clerk - Nancy Ehman Tucker
Trustees - Larry Fallon, Jeffery A. Pope and Mark Hager
Raccoon Township Clerk - Ruth A. Millhone
Trustees - Charles W. Metzler, John Coffee and Dwight Rees
Springfield Township Clerk - Pamela Riley
Trustees - Scott L. Howell, Holzer Gregory and Mike Hager
Walnut Township - Jane Saunders Miller
Trustees - Thomas Stanley, Wanda L. Hively and Richard L. Ingles

*Daniel H. Whiteley*
*Gallia County Coroner*

*Larry M. Betz*
*Gallia County Auditor*

*Steve McGhee*
*Gallia County Treasurer*

*Thomas S. Moulton*
*Gallia County Probate Judge*

## Gallia County Local School Board 2002

Mike Polcyn
Jon P. Thompson
Mel Carter
John Payne
Sheila Regan

### Gallipolis City School Board Of Education 2002

Dannie Greene
Nancy A. Mullins
David A. Walker
Timothy V. Kyger
Lynn Angell Queen

### Gallipolis City Commission

Robert D. Gordon, City Manager
J. Gary Fenderbosch
Richard A. Moore
Robert L. Marchi
Celestine M. Skinner
Carroll K. Snowden

### Village Of Centerville Mayor

Ted Perroud
Clerk/Treasurer - David W. House
Council - Marlin Rose, Retha Naomi Beman, Virginia A. Daniels, Eugene T. Layton, Connie J. Miller and Robert H. Terry

### Village Of Cheshire Mayor

H. Thomas Reese
Clerk/Treasurer - Jennifer Lynn Harrison
Council - Charles Lee Bradbury, Claude Cornelius, Herbert Lee Clarke, Ronald L. Hammond, John S. Harrison and James R. Neal

### Village Of Crown City Mayor

Sampson Earl Johnson
Clerk/Treasurer - Lana J. Lane
Council - James E. Wolford, Elizabeth G. Woodyard, Paul Dillon, Keith Durst, Mike Klinger and Vickie I. Unroe

### Village Of Rio Grande Mayor

Donald B. Wothe
Council - Jean Curtis, Randall D. Skaggs, Robert W. Allen, Michelle L. Miller, Mark E. Neal, II and Patty Wetherholt
Board of Public Affairs - Curtis Clark

### Village Of Vinton Mayor

Donna Lynn Dewitt
Clerk/Treasurer - Kathryn E. Kelly
Council - Herbert Moore, Marvin L. Sallee, Charles Conley, Flem Meade and Samuel G. Sowards, Jr.

# Gallipolis Township

In October of 1787, Rev. Manasseh Cutler and Winthrop Sargant, acting as agents for the Ohio Company, signed a contract with the Board of Treasury for the purchase of land along the Ohio River. This was the land that was later to become Gallia County.

June of 1788, Joel Barlow arrived in Paris to sell the land in Ohio. Not being a salesman he was ready to leave by the summer of 1789 until he met William Playfair. Playfair was a good salesman and with the help of Joel Barlow and Jen de Soisson they began selling the land to Frenchmen wanting to leave France prior to the French Revolution.

By February of 1790 more that 100,000 acres of the Scioto Lands had been sold. in the same month about 500 Frenchmen boarded ships and set sail for their new homes in America. When they reached America at Alexandria, Virginia in May of 1790 there was no one to meet them and take them to their new land. June of 1790, agents of the Scioto Company arranged to take them to their new homeland on the Ohio River.

On October 17, 1790, the Frenchmen arrived in boats at "Gallipolis". They saw there four rows of log cabins paralleling the river. Each row was about 300 feet long and intervals of 100 feet there were open spaces for cross streets, blockhouses stood at each corner of the cabined area and nearby were a stockade, which enclosed a company store. A log breastwork stretched along the crest of the riverbank and on the other three sides was found a deep, almost impenetrable, forest that looked forbidding.

According to the "Records of the Township of Gallipolis, AD 1802", territory of the United States, Northwest of the Ohio River, Washington County at a meeting in the home of John Bing, on the first Monday in March, 1802, township officers were elected. It is interesting to that this was over a year before Gallia County was formed and about a year before the meeting of the first general assembly of the State. (March 1, 1803).

The first town, under the name of Fair Haven had been laid out by the Scioto Company, opposite the mouth of the Kanawha River and was intended as the point for the location of the French settlers. This ground was determined to be unsuitable, as the ground was considered low and liable to flood. It was then decided to move the site four miles downriver where the banks were well elevated above the high water mark. This is the site of present day Gallipolis. The earlier site is known as Kanauga.

A few years after the French arrival in 1790 the Welsh, English and Germans came to Gallipolis. As the Welsh and English were not to compatible, the Welsh moved to the western part of the County and into Jackson County where they started iron furnaces. This brought the railroad to Gallia County.

Industries active in the 19th century and into the 20th century were boat building, engine works, furniture factories, stove foundries, a broom factory, sand and gravel operations in the Ohio River and distilleries.

Farming was started and remains a major industry today. Gallipolis at one time had five produce houses, two creameries, a dairy, two flour mills and a meatpacking house.

Gallipolis was a medical center during and after the Civil War. Gallipolis was at one time the site of a Civil War camp and Union Hospital located in the area of the Gallipolis Developmental Center. In the late 19th century, the largest cottage-type hospital for epilepsy, the Ohio Hospital for Epileptics was established. It was the first of its kind in America and the pioneer of all others in the world in having its maintenance pledge by the state, and therefore, from public revenues. The Ohio Hospital for Epileptics later changed to the Gallipolis State Institution and today is known as the Gallipolis Developmental Center. The Ohio Hospital for Epileptics was located adjacent to the village and was annexed into it in order to have enough population to become a city.

Dr. Charles E. Holzer, Sr. founded Holzer Hospital prior to World War 1. It is now known as Holzer Medical Center and is located four miles outside of the city. Holzer Clinic was founded by his son Dr. Charles E. Holzer, Jr. now has over 100 doctors in a county of 24,000. Charles E. Holzer Sr.'s wife started the Holzer School of Nursing in Gallipolis and it is now part of the University of Rio Grande. The old Holzer Hospital has been transformed into apartments for the elderly. The home of the founder of Holzer Hospital, Charles Holzer, Sr., has been converted into the French Art Colony

Over the years Gallipolis Township has seen much growth. Gallipolis, the county seat has remained the center of activities, with the city growing upriver toward Kanauga. The Gallia County Courthouse is located in Gallipolis as is several other county and city government offices.

The Gallipolis Fire Department has one of the newest facilities and the Bossard Memorial Library has one of the finest research facilities and library in the area.

The City Park houses the bandstand, which is a memorial to all Civil War veterans in Gallia County. There are other monuments in the park honoring other Gallia County Soldiers from various wars and conflicts. The Gallia County Historical/Genealogical Society's building is located in the downtown area of Gallipolis and the start of a Gallia County Museum to be housed at this location in the near future.

The city of Gallipolis has a charter form of government with City Commissioners elected by the city voters. The City Commissioners then appoint a City Manager and City Solicitor who will be the legal advisor to the city. Also, the Municipal Judge will be the judge of the Municipal court in and for said City of Gallipolis.

*Robert L. "Bob" Marchi*

*Carroll Snowden*

Unavailable for Pictures
Gallipolis City Commissioners
Gary Fenderbosch
Richard "Dick" Moore
Celestine Skinner

# Green Township

Green Township has gone from agricultural to residential. Beginning in the 1900s, there were many dairies and farms where tobacco was raised. Now these farms have become large and many have gabled homes. Some tobacco is still grown since it is a cash crop. Most of the dairies have disappeared. Two such farms are the Reginald Ball farm and Pete McCormicks in the Fairfield community.

There are three villages; Centenary, Northup and Rodney. Northup and Rodney both had post offices but they were closed in the 1980s. Before the Ohio Bell Telephone Company put in modern phones, Rose Koontz had the switchboard in her home and there were party lines. They consisted of three or four families having certain rings - maybe one long ring and a short ring.

Centenary and Rodney had Grange - a farm organization.

In the 1930s, the one-room schools were abandoned and three-roomed grade schools were constructed at Centenary and Rodney. The one at Centenary was remodeled into a home and the Grange used both. The one at Rodney is now owned by the Methodist Church and used as a youth center. A modern brick school was built at Centenary to house one through junior high in 1947. Later it became one through 6 with the junior high attending the Gallipolis City Schools.

Route #35 went through Rodney until 1951 when the road with all its curves was straightened and the village of Rodney was by-passed. Soon after this, Paul Owen had a grocery and gas station on this new road. In the early 1940s Brady Graham had an egg candling business in Rodney and delivered eggs to larger cities. There were three small stores. Roscoe Fox had the post office and the oldest grocery with Standard Oil Products. John Bateman, Ray Simmons and later Grace Shriver had the other grocery stores. Now there is just the gas station and grocery on old Route #35. This road has been renamed Jackson Pike and U. S. Route 588 goes through Rodney.

In 1950 the Evans Grocery Company donated land near the Junction of Route #35 and #160 for a fair grounds. In August of 1999, the Gallia County Fair Board celebrated fifty years. It is known as one of the best Junior Fairs in the State of Ohio.

*Robert "Bob" Gordon Gallipolis City Manager*

*Bob Donnally Gallipolis Fire Chief*

*Roger Brandeberry Gallipolis Chief of Police*

Holzer Hospital relocated just across from the fair grounds in 1972. Presently there are over one hundred doctors in practice at this facility.

The Ohio State Patrol is just west of the hospital in new and larger headquarters.

There are several churches: two Methodist, one at Centenary and one at Rodney. Northup has a Baptist and one on Bob McCormick Road, a Christian church on #588 near Mitchell Road. A new Lutheran Church and Calvary Baptist Church is located on Jackson Pike.

Edwin R. "Pete" McCormick lived in the Fairfield Community and was a Boy Scout leader for over 50 years. He was also known as the weatherman. He had the official weather station for 40 years, reporting the temperature every morning at 6:00 a.m. He retired from this position in 1972.

Dr. Clay Priestly was a well-know veterinarian and was called all over to doctor sick livestock. He lived near Centenary.

Businessman, Joe D. Miller, had heavy equipment and lived near Rodney.

This area of Gallia County has shown much progress with new homes, businesses and updating of school facilities. As always, this township adapts to the needs of the future. *Submitted by Annabelle Fellure*

# Greenfield Township

This township was described in the History of Gallia County by Hardesty in 1882 in great detail and not much has changed since then. It still is greatly covered with forests even though there has been a lot of logging done there. The government has purchased from the owners some of the land that is part of the Wayne National Forest to try to preserve it for the future. There is an underground spring that comes to the surface and it has been providing water for some of the people there for untold number of years.

The population is down from the 1880s when the Gallia Furnace was in full use. It closed down in 1916 and the tracks were pulled up by the C. H. & D. Railroad. Rt. 233 follows the track route now. All that's left of the furnace and surrounding buildings is a hole in the hillside where the furnace itself was. Now there are under 500 people living in Greenfield Township. When the furnace closed down the post office that was there was eliminated too. We used to have both one room schools and bigger ones too but that too is gone. The children all go to Gallia Co. schools now. A few of the old schools are still in existence but not used as schools. We now have some Amish people living here also. Some of our younger people have gone to bigger cities to make a living. Some of the older people have moved back for the quiet living here. Greenfield Township was a big part of the Underground Railroad and a lot of the Black people stayed here and still have descendants living here.

The first crime watch meeting for Gallia Co. was started and held here in Greenfield Township in 1995. Since then almost all the rest of the townships have begun one too. They work hand in hand with the Sheriffs department to help curtail crime in our area. There is also a volunteer fire department that is adding to their buildings now.

# Guyan Township 1826-2002

The history of Guyan Township will be presented to the reader to show the township's formation and endurance. The township, being one of fifteen located in Gallia County, was the last to be organized. The township was organized on December 4, 1826. The settling of the township started much earlier.

The early history of the settlements in the Guyan township area started in 1814. The first permanent structure was a cabin erected by William Garlick and E. Hobbs. This would have been in 1814 at the present site of Crown City. A second early settlement was established on Indian Guyan Creek (Guyan) at the mouth of Little Creek.

The first individuals having to endure all the hardships of being the first settlers were mostly farmers. Among these first settlers are names that are still found prominent in the township today. The following individuals are original settlers; William Sheets, James Brumfield, William Johnson, John Williams, John Brumfield, Elijah Fowler, William Fowler, John and Brice Henry, John Sheets, J. Johnson, Samuel Holley, Henry Radford, A. Chapman, John Swindler, Humphrey Brumfield, John Bay, Hugh Clark, and Frances Blake.

The township contains twenty-eight full and two fractional sections of land. The Ohio River cuts off the southeastern corner of the township. Guyan Township is the most southern position township in Gallia County.

In April, 1827 the township held its first election in the home of John Swindler, at which time eleven votes were cast. The first elected officials were Elijah Fowler and John Swindler, Justices of the Peace; Henry Swindler, Constable and trustee; Samuel Holley, trustee and Guy Fry, one of the ministerial trustees.

The early government officials began performing duties very quickly. The first marriage was Seth Chase to Anna Garlick, with the ceremony performed by the Justice of the Peace, Elijah Fowler. The first child born in the township was a Blankenship.

The original settlements in the Guyan Township demanded the area to have growth. The area soon saw the construction of a grist-mill by William Janson in 1816. Located on Indian Guyan Creek, the mill was constructed from logs, contained one set of stones, and was powered by water. In 1820, Mr. Janson attached a saw mill to the mill. The area also realized the need for post offices and for communication and schools to educate the youth of the area.

The early settlers recognized the need for establishing an educational system. The first schooling was held in a small log cabin which stood one-half mile west of Crown City. The first school was taught by Elijah Fowler. The first building constructed for the sole purpose of schooling was built of logs in 1816, near the mouth of Georges Creek. This is just the beginning of a long educational history.

Guyan Township's first school under the direction of Elijah Fowler flourished quickly. G.H. Hardesty reports by 1882 "there are twelve good frame school houses in the township and the schools are well attended." A brief history of each of these very important schools will be addressed.

The Campbell school was located in section 10 on State Route 218. The original agreement for the establishment was entered into on February 19, 1862. The parties involved were Lewis

11

Campbell and the Board of Education for School District No. 6.

The Cofer School was located 1.5 miles west of Mercerville. The school was established with an agreement between C. B. Cofer and the Board of Education of Guyan Township. The property was sold to the township for the sum of $10. The school operated until it was discontinued at end of the 1923-24 school terms. The last teacher was Edward Evans.

The Crown City School was established in 1849. The agreement was between Ann Bay and the Directors of School District No. 3 of Guyan Township. The date of the agreement was December 10, 1849.

The George's Creek school located in section 27 on George's Creek Road now known as Wells Run. The original building was on the W. H. Haskins Farm. The list of teachers is very long for this school. The school term of 1911-1912 was taught by Isaac Fowler. The one room school was discontinued in 1929 due to the construction of a two room building.

The Gothord or Rocky Fork School was established in 1862. The school was located in section 22 and found on Fillinger Road. The agreement between the Board of Education and George A. Rice took place on April 21, 1862. The school was later reconstructed on the Tommy Daniel's Farm because of a fire. The school was discontinued at the end of the 1934-35 term.

The original Gregory school was established in the days of the Civil War. The land was purchased for $5 from Elizabeth Lewis on November 6, 1865. The land was located in section 31 in Guyan Township.

The Mercerville school is located in section 12 on State Route 218. The school was discontinued in 1922. The students of the Mercerville school attended the Cofer School

The Sardis school was located in section 14, on Sowards Road. The school was built by John Hill Hineman. The school had operated before 1900, but was closed at the end of the 1928-1929 school terms. The building is still standing.

The Siloam School was located in section 36, on Saunders Ridge. The school operated until the end of the 1935-36 school year. The students were then sent to Mercerville school.

The Snowball school was established in 1878. An agreement was made between Samuel Hesson and Guyan Township Board of Education on April 16, 1878. The cost of the land was $15. The land would be located on present day Fillinger Road in section 34. The school stopped operating at the end of the 1928-29 school term.

The Sowards Ridge School was located in section 15. The school was located on Sowards Ridge Road. The school terminated its operation in 1949. The last teacher was Mrs. Ruby Shockely.

The Stoney Point School was found in section 20 of Guyan Township. The school was established April 10, 1867. The agreement was between Harrison Fowler and The Board of Education. The land was sold for the sum of $6. The school was destroyed by fire in 1929. The students were then sent to Sowards Ridge or Gregory school.

The one room schools served the township community for many years. The location of most schools can be found easily by using the 1910 Plat Book map of Guyan Township. The reader will find a much more in depth and detailed history of one room schools in the book "Gallia County One Room Schools': The Cradle Years."

The educational system of Guyan Township and the southern part of Gallia County has gone through many changes. The one room schools were slowly replaced by methods of consolidation. The township soon saw the growth of schools not only serving Guyan Township, but surrounding townships. The unincorporated village of Mercerville soon found it would be the home of Mercerville High School. The name was changed in the early 1960's to Hannan Trace High School due to the construction of a new building. The school district was known as the Hannan Trace School District until 1974 when all four county schools formed Gallia County Local Schools. The Hannan Trace High School operated until 1991 when the schools were consolidated and formed River Valley High School. The building formally known as Hannan Trace High School was reopened in 1996 and became known as South Gallia High School. The school serves students in Guyan Township and the southern part of Gallia County.

Guyan Township witnessed the need for an increase in post offices, due to population growth. The first post office was located in Mercervile. The number grew to a total of five; Mercerville, Crown City, Saundersville, Chapman's Mill and Yoho. These post offices functioned for many years. They served as few as 75 families to as high as 200 families. The post offices closed as modern travel took place in the township. By the 1950's, the township had only two of the five post offices remaining, Crown City and Mercerville. The Mercerville office was discontinued June 20, 1952. Leaving the entire township and surrounding areas in the service of Crown City.

The old post offices are an important part of the township history. They not only represented a form of communication, but also represented community life that is only a memory today. The only building that served as a post office can be found on Buddy Joe Fowler's Farm. The farm includes what was once called Yoho. Ohio.

Guyan Township over the years has had two main villages. The two villages would be Crown City and Mercerville. The other small villages slowly disappeared because of changing business and educational needs or a combination of both.

The village of Crown City has a very colorful history. The village served as a port village on the Ohio River. The village existed in one form or another since the early 1800's. The village was first called Bay's Bottom after Thomas Bay, who owned the biggest piece of river frontage. The village had a name change in the 1870's and became Crown City. The village about the same time period petitioned the State of Ohio to be incorporated.

Crown City was laid out by Hiram Rankin and Vincent Daley. Mr. Rankin filed a petition in the Gallia County's recorders office December 18, 1873. The village would be comprised of the released land of residence and an adjacent farm land. Crown City would include land from the farms of William Knight, Isaac Rucker, Eijah Williams, Hiram Rankin, William Rankin, Thomas Bays, Franklin Fowler and Nelson Lane. The village was granted a municipal corporation

The village of Crown City has had many business, community and social functions. The village served as a port for steam boats and wharf boats. In the early days, the boats helped the local farmers and businesses transport goods and provided entertainment to local citizens. The village over the years had many businesses. These businesses included: Riley Cart's Florence Hotel, saloons, general stores, Redmond Rose blacksmith shop, Russell Hineman Garage, The Crown City Bank, the American Tobacco Company Warehouse, Fat Watt's beer joint and grill and doctor's offices to name only a few.

The village of Mercerville took a similar path in history. The village was never incorporated, but served the township in various ways. It was the sight of the first township post office, Stevens Funeral Home, mechanic shops and various gas stations over the years. The main business in the township was farming.

The township was dotted by many farms. The farmers in the township operated beef and dairy farms, but the main cash crop was tobacco. The farmers raised such large amounts of tobacco that a tobacco warehouse was located in Crown City. This was the crop that fed and clothed many people in the township.

The township, in its beginning had a strong sense of religion. The first religious society (Baptist) was formed in 1832. The founding members were Eijah Fowler and John Henry. The Rev. John Lee was the first Baptist minister; he preached his first sermon at the home of John Swindler. The township over the years had as high as nine different church organizations. The township today has five churches; Good Hope Baptist, Mercerville Baptist, Crown City United Methodist, Bethlehem Baptist and the Wesleyan Church.

The early settlers had natural resources they could call on. The hills of the township had limestone, coal and iron ore. The natural resources of coal were plentiful enough to supply local fuel to residence of the township for many years. The local residence many times could get their coal supply from local mines or "coal banks". This was a commonly used local term. The coal from the coal banks sometimes would find its way to other surrounding communities. Coal was so plentiful in the township that it lead to the development of Crown City Mining. Crown City Mining employed a large number of people and was comprised over 11,000 acre track of land. The mine was located on Rocky Fork Road, but encompassed large sections of land from other townships and Lawrence County. The mine operated from the 1970's into the 1980's. The land now is used by the State of Ohio as a wild life refuge.

The township in general was a farming area. A visitor to the area down through time could find a very industrial farming community. The agricultural history didn't change much over the years. A writer by the name of R.C. Hall, Ph.D. reported in 1938 included the production of cattle, dairy, tobacco and fruit growing. This same visitor could still find three of the four farming production; tobacco, cattle and dairy, but in a much smaller size.

The township over the years has evolved. The residence no longer looks for businesses inside the township to meet all their needs. The township lost the Eagle Rock Tavern which closed in 1988. This was the only surviving local tavern in the township. A few businesses still operate in Crown City or in the township; Dairy Boy, two filling stations/convenience stores, a pizza shop, Owsley's carry out and General Store and Hardware. The township is spotted with small family farms. These farms still mostly grow the golden leaf tobacco which is slowly fading away. The farmers now are turning to cattle or other alternative crops. The township only has one remaining post office, Crown City, but is protected by two Volunteer Fire Departments: Crown City and Guyan Township. The citizens still have many social functions supplied by the Masonic Lodge in Crown City, churches and schools. One such event is Old Timers Day in Crown City Village. If a visitor came to Guyan Township today they would still find some early settlers names; Sheets, Brumfield, Johnson, Williams, Holley and Fowler.

The writer of this short history is an example, I am the great-great-great-great grandson of Elijah Fowler and I too am a teacher.

This historical account would not have been possible without the help of local people. I would like to thank Max Hafflet, Jessie May Bills and the historical research of Danny Fulks.

# Harrison Township 1806-2002

Harrison Township is known to contain thirty full sections and is bordered by Green, Clay, Guyan and Walnut Townships. The township was laid out on December 10,1812 and later organized on March 6, 1816.Records show that the first settlement was made as early as 1806 with the first child being born to Mr. and Mrs.Isaac Dewitt. Her name was Hannah. William Trotter served as the first elected Justice of the Peace of the township.

The lay of the land of Harrison Township was broken with flatland, hillyland and consisted of black loamy soil, conducive for a high level of production. Settlers of Harrison Township were known to be very industrious and very much interested in educational matters.

Some of the early settlers were; Fredrick Bickel, Benjamin Williams, William Littleton, John Roadamour, Isaac Dewitt, Henry Iron, William Carter, James McCall, Jacob Loucks, Vernon Northup, William Trotter, Elijah Howell, Jefferson Ward, Gilbert Gibson, John Dewitt, Daniel Boster, Soloman Boster, John Boster, Johnathan Boster, Stephen Martin and Elkanah Cremeens.

Berry Angel, Henry Angel and Lawrence Washington Angel, sons of Reverend John L. Angel an American Revolutionary War Veteran of Surry County, North Carolina had settled in Harrison Township by 1816.

William Sheridan Angel, son of William Henry Angel, a Civil War Veteran was born in Harrison Township on May 30, 1870. William Sheridan Angel was the grandfather of Shirley Angel presently, serving a second term as Gallia County Commissioner.

Growth in Harrison Township was eminent. Soon in its history, the first Grist Mill was erected. George Waugh was accredited with building the mill, which was operated by waterpower on Raccoon Creek. About ten years later, Cornelius Waugh was successful in building the first Saw Mill on Big Bull Skin Creek.

In 1830, the first building was built in Section 7 for school purposes. It would become the Smith School House on Martin Road. It was built with round logs and had split logs for seats. The school house contained a five-foot fire place. It also had small openings for windows which were covered with oiled paper.

A school of twenty five pupils and taught by James McCall was located on Clay Lick Road in 1835.The school building was an old log house owned by Mr. McCall. It was furnished with seats made of small logs split in halves with legs added. Other one room - schools in Harrison Township were; Fairview, located in Section 25 and Lincoln School, located in Section 33.These schools were shown in the plat books of Harrison Township in 1870,1880,1890 and 1910.

Macedonia School was located in Section 17 on the Macedonia Road close to Macedonia Church. In 1910,the school was shown to be on the John Rose property, which was close to Macedonia Church. Macedonia School closed in 1935.The pu-

*Front Row: L: to R: Lucy Chandler Angel, Husband, William Henry Angel (Civil War Vetran) son, William Sheridian Angel Back Row L to R: Mae Angel Boyd, Daughter, Nettie Angel Shaw, Daughter, And John Sherman Angel, Son*

pils were transferred to the Little Bull Skin's three-room school, which had been in operation the previous year.

Martin School number 1 was located near the intersection of Johnson Road and in Section 24. It was a log school at the top of a hill and described as a school dating back to Pioneer Days. Henry Martin was stated as owning the land for which the school was named. The school is noted as being attended by John Bane's grandparents during the Civil War Era.

Located on the Cremeens Road in Section 29 was a second McCall School It was a framed building and had a porch with no railings. The school also closed at the end of the 1934-35 school term and the pupils would also go to the new Clay Lick School.

The Mt Carmel School was located in Section 21 on Little Bull Skin Road near Mt Carmel Church. The school closed at the end of the 1933-34 school year because of consolidation. Mt. Carmel's pupils would attend Little Bull Skin the following year.

The North Bend School was built in Section 12 of Harrison Township in the early 1900's and closed at the end of the 1930-31 school year. The pupils would attend Macedonia School the following school year, also.

Mr. Woodrow McCall was said to have purchased the North Bend School building and moved it to Section 16 on Lewis Road. The building was converted into a dwelling where Noel Lambert presently resides.

The Phillips School being named after the property owner, was located in Section 13. After the school closed, the property was returned to Mr. Roy Martin owner, at the time of the closing.

The Porter-Angel-Trotter School was located in Section 10 of Harrison Township on State Route 218 near Bailey Chapel Church. This area was known as Angeltown until the late 1930's. The new signs erected in 1999 in that area by the State Department of Highways renamed Angeltown as Angel, as shown in Section 10, on the plat map of Harrison Township.

The Porter School was referred to as the Angel School and also the Trotter School. At the close of the 1934-35 school year, the school closed and the pupils would then attend the three-room Little Bull Skin School. The old Porter School building was purchased by Jeff Perkins, moved to Burnt Run Road and remodeled into a dwelling where Mr. and Mrs. Elmer Fowler now resides.

Smokey Row, No 2 School was located in Section 35 on White Cemetery Road. After the 1929-30 school year, the pupils attended Macedonia School. The first Smokey Row School was in Section 30 on Smokey Row Road near the intersection of Dent Davis Road. The school burnt in 1926.

A mutual agreement seems to exist that the one-room schools in Harrison Township were too much of a part of a healthier livlihood for the early settlers to be forgotten. Its lessons seem to live on in hearts of surving students who learned and grew up to help shape a strong township, county and a strong nation.

Approximately, 80 % of Harrison Township's students now attend Hannan Trace Grade School and South Gallia High School in Guyan Township. Students in the out lying areas of the township have an option of attending a school of their choice in other school districts.

The first Post office in Harrison Township was on Big Bull Skin Creek and kept by Cornelius Holley serving as Postmaster. Other offices in the township were at Leaper, on Big Bull Skin, Moody, on Little Bull Skin and Lincoln, which provided deliveries three times a week for the Ironton and Gallipolis routes.

Reverend John Strait was an early Baptist Minister. He preached at homes of different citizens along Clay Lick Road. In 1833, Reverend Strait organized a Baptist Society at the residence of John Boster on Big Bull Skin Creek. Reverend Strait was known to be highly respected. He died at the age of 104 years and 3 months.

A Missionary Baptist and a Methodist Episcopal Church were soon organized. Mount Carmel Methodist, Macedoma Disciple Baptist Hopewell Missionary Baptist and Mount Pleasant United Brethern were flourishing with Sunday School being held in each church.

Bailey Chapel Church was built in 1906 on State Route 218 in Angeltown, currently known as Angel. At the present time the church has an active congregation. Services are held on Sunday and on Wednesday nights with Sunday School and Worship Service being held on Sundays. Bailey Chapel is known to have been named after the famous Ann Bailey.

Dickey Chapel Church was built in 1855 and is located on Hannan Trace Road. Currently worship services, are being held on Sunday mornings and on Sunday evenings. Sunday School is held on Sunday mornings and a mid-week service is also held.

Canaan Missionary Baptist Church established in 1977 is located on State Route 218 near the intersection of Little Bull Skin Road and S.R.218.The church has a growing congregation. Worship Service and Sunday School are held on Sunday mornings. Services are also held on Sunday nights and a mid-week service is held on Wednesday nights. The congregation has plans to add additional rooms to this church.

Ann Bailey, whose maiden name was Hennis, proved to be an interesting settler in Harrison

Township. Ann was born in Liverpool, England and married Richard Trotter at the age of thirty. She then came to the colonies with him. Richard's life became a sacrifice while serving under General Lewis in the summer of 1774 with Lord Dunnmore's forces.

From the time of the death of her husband, Ann is said to have possessed a strange and wild spirit and had a determination of revenge. Some believe that she abandoned the natural pursuits of a woman. She spent her time practicing with a riffle, a tomahawk and riding through the countryside attending every muster of soldiers. She dressed in a hunting skirt, leggings and moccasins.

Ann later married a man named Bailey and for several years followed a party of soldiers sent to garrison a fort at the Great Kanawha, where Charleston is now located. She became known for her skill with the riffle and later acted as a messenger between the Fort and Point Pleasant on her well trained companion named Liverpool. On one of these trips, Ann was being hotly perused by Indians and in danger of being captured when she slipped off her horse and took refuge in a hollow log with the horse keeping on course. Eventually, night fell and the Indians were slumbering. Ann then took possession of her horse, arousing the enemy, as she disappeared with a triumphal shout

After trouble with the Indians ceased, Ann Bailey returned to her habit of hunting wild game and fishing. She received the name of Mad Ann Bailey on account of her eccentric behavior which was regarded with great indulgence by the people for the service she had rendered during the war.

After the war, Ann Bailey came to Ohio and lived in Harrison Township. She enjoyed solitude and spent most of her time alone. Her neighbors would frequently, gather to persuade her to relate her stories of adventures to them. The date of death for this most interesting woman is given as 1825. Her original burial place was on her son's farm in Harrison Township. Ann's descendants are believed to be living in that area.

Jackson T. Smith, great grandfather of Carroll C. Smith, was instrumental in providing the early settlers of Harrison Township with access too much needed items that could be purchased in a General Store as early as 1844. The business was referred to as the Jackson T. Smith Co. of Harrison Township and was located at Leaper, Ohio and at the present time, near the area where Teens Run Road intersects with State Route 218. Frank Smith, son of Jackson T. Smith operated the store from the Post Civil War Period until the early 1900's.Later G. M. Smith, father of Carroll Smith took over the operation of the store. The early settlers of Harrison Township could have viewed the fact of having access to a store nearby and in the neighborhood as a blessing in disguise. Many of the early settlers were without means of transportation, traveling long distances was almost impossible for many people; therefore, having a General Store in the neighborhood became a welcomed reality.

In the 1930's business for Grover M. Smith seemed to be thriving and the Rolling Store was in operation. Once again, Mr. Smith was providing a much needed service for the people of Harrison Township as well as for people living in surrounding areas.

People in the area anticipated the day when the Rolling Store would come to stop where they could buy or sell items. Yes, the Rolling Store was referred to as the Peddlin Truck or as the Peddlin Wagon. Betty L. Angel Crouse recalled visits to the Peddlin Wagon, as her father Brady T. Angel called it of course, the little ones tagged along. Betty recalls her father's famous words, "Now you kids be good, if I have money left, I'll get you a poke of candy."

The G. C. Saunders General Store at Leaper, in Harrison Township was operated by the owner Glenny Saunders and wife Ruby from the period of 1930 -1960.After their death, Imogene Church and her sister Irene continued operating the store until January 6,2001.The G.C. Saunders General Store also provided needed items for people living in the area.

The original Homestead of Charles Price located on Little Bull Skin Road is still standing. The house is occupied by Mr. and Mrs. Dale Taylor. During a conversation, Dale shared that be had bought the home about ten years ago and the house is believed to be about 200 years old. Amazing! The outward appearance of the house showed it to be in good condition.

Currently, Harrison Township still continue to experience growth Loren and Jane Ann Clary Cox are owners and operators of Crown Excavating and Stone Yard. The business is located on State Route 218. Once again; the operators are people with a vision, providing needed materials and services for the community.

Jividen's Farm Equipment is located on Ingalls Road in Harrison Township. The business has been in operation for over twenty years. Kim Jividen Rose is owner and operator of the business.

The Rodney Roberts Construction has been in operation in Harrison Township for several years. The business is owned and operated by Mr. Rodney Roberts and he is a builder of homes.

Finally, Harrison Township's people will soon realize a dream coming true of having their own Harrison Township Fire Department. Construction is to begin by the middle of June, 2002 .The home of the new Fire Department will be on Little Bull Skin Road. Once again, progress in the making!

Jewel McKean Caldwell, daughter of Charles Morgan McKean and Nora B. Porter McKean was born and grew up in Harrison Township. Her view of life and growing up there was good. She portrayed a person with great satisfaction of having lived in Harrison Township. Jewel spoke of acquiring good work ethics, sharing and enjoying family members while living on the family farm. In her words, "Life was good." *Submitted by: Betty L. Angel Crouse*

# Huntington Township

Huntington Township is the extreme northwestern township of Gallia County. It was founded from Raccoon Township June 5 1810, organized June 2, 1812 and the first meeting for election purposes was held at the home of Stephen Holcomb on the last Saturday July of 1810.

Vinton is the oldest of the two main villages in Huntington Township.

# History Of The Village Of Vinton
## By Kevin E. Kelly

The village of Vinton in Huntington Township was incorporated in 1882, but can trace its beginnings back to 1815, when a grist mill was built by Enoch McNeal on the backs of the Raccoon Creek. It was the start of an unbroken link between the creek and the village as water-powered mills became the first business in what was to become known as Vinton.

The first sawmill in the community followed in 1819, erected by Stephen and Samuel R. Holcomb for John Adney, who operated the mill until1852. The business then went through several hands until it was destroyed in a 1919 fire. Rebuilt the following year, it continued in the grain business until the 1960's, and remained vacant until fire leveled it for good on April 28, 1976.

With the location of the mills and business, a settlement formed. The community itself was laid out in 1832 by Gen. Samuel R. Holcomb and former U. S. Representative and Gallia County attorney Samuel F. Vinton, although incorporation did not follow until a half-century later. That did not stop the community from growing, serving not only as a commercial center in northern Gallia County but also attracting residents.

Gallia County commissioners approved the petition of 30 residents to incorporate the village on June 7, 1882. The petition listed the town as having 300 residents, more than enough to justify its village status.

Vinton was not immune from the events of the day, and earned its spot in the history of the Civil War when it became one of a number of communities struck by Confederate Gen. John Hunt Morgan.

A maneuver to draw Union troops away from eastern Tennessee, "Morgan's Raid" saw 2,500 infantry sweep through southern Ohio, reaching Vinton on July 17, 1863. The town was plundered for supplies, and after crossing the covered bridge over the Raccoon, Morgan's men burned the span. No lives were lost during the raid. An Ohio Historical Society marker now stands at the Vinton Post Office commemorating the event, and a 140-foot suspension walk bridge was built in 1991 over the creek.

The bridge burning was the only known damage attributed to the raid in Gallia County. Anselm T. Holcomb, then 17, recalled that he was accused by the raiders of firing a shot at Morgan's officers, which another youth had done from the woods. Holcomb hid in a closet of the home of a minister, and waited out the raiders' foraging, in which they "consumed all of the patent medicine; especially those with any kind of alcoholic flavor, and all of the tobacco and cigars, he wrote."

Morgan's Raid continued in the area for several more days until his forces were defeated at Meigs County's Buffington Island on the Ohio River, the only known battle of the war fought on Ohio soil. Captured, Morgan escaped from the Ohio Penitentiary in Columbus to fight another day, only to die in a raid at Greenville, Tennessee, in September 1864.

Vinton's expansion got a boost in 1880 when it became a stop along the Columbus, Hocking Valley & Toledo Railroad, prompting a boom that lasted well into the 1920s Fears the railroad would drain the community of about 200 proved unfounded, as the Vinton correspondent for the Gallipolis Journal observed in 1881:

" The theory of these prophets was that everybody would go to Gallipolis to do their trading and consequently would leave our home merchants without customers. I am glad to say that results have proven this predictions false, and instead of a decrease in trade, it has increased over 25 percent within the past six months."

By 1904, in addition to the mills, the village boasted a brick plant, a spoke factory, a newspaper, -the Vinton Leader, which lasted until about 1916-, general stores, an opera house, doctors' offices and numerous other small business. By then, two churches were in existence— Vinton United Methodist, founded in 1881 and whose 1882 structure still exists on South Main Street, and Vinton Baptist, established in 1895. Today, Vinton also boasts Fellowship Chapel and Vinton Full Gospel among its churches. Services were last held in the Methodist Church in 1996, while a new Vinton Baptist is under construction on State Route 160 south of the village. Ground was broken for the new church in April 2001.

On September 25, 1893, an important step in the local educational scene was taken with the construction of the Vinton School on Clay Street for grades 1-8, with students attending the ninth and tenth grades at the George Glenn Building. Those planning to finish high school went to Ewington Academy.

Overcrowding at the new school, which replaced a number of one-room classrooms in the community, prompted the construction of a new building in 1915. The 1893 building was sold to the village on April 7, 1936, and it has served as the seat of village government ever since. Vinton Elementary School on Keystone Road still serves the community, and through a Gallia County Local Schools district-wide bond issue, was significantly renovated and dedicated in 1986. North Gallia High School, a combination of Vinton and Bidwell-Porter high schools, served the area from 1956 until its closing in 1992. Vinton students now attend River Valley High School after eighth grade.

The village suffered a setback on January 5, 1928, when a

*Vinton Town Hall, Clay Street Vinton, OH*

*Ewington Academy, Ewington Road April 17, 2002*

fire originating in the A.L. Stevens home on Main Street spread to McCarley Brothers Hardware, the Baptist church, the IOOF hall, and the Kerr Butler Funeral Home and garage. "Fortunately, there was little wind stirring or else nearly the entire village would have been swept away," the Gallia Times reported.

The church was rebuilt and dedicated on June 23, 1929. During the March 1997 flood, the worst in Vinton's history, the church served as base for emergency workers.

Flooding has not been a stranger to Vinton. Severe floods in 1937 and 1968 left their mark on the community, but the 1997 high water event, causing damage estimated in the millions, drew a brief visit from then Vice President Al Gore, who pledged federal assistance in rebuilding the village.

Today, Vinton still hosts what is considered one of the oldest Civil War-era bean dinners on the first Saturday of August, and is awaiting groundbreaking for a new sewer system, projected for completion in 2003. A flood mitigation project, involving purchase of flood-prone properties, elevations of residence and protection of home utilities was scheduled to begin in the summer of 2002.

The current mayor of Vinton is Donna Lynn DeWitt, and the clerk is Elizabeth Kelly. Council members as of April 2002 include Chuck Conley, William J. " Jack" Dempsey, Darryl Martin, Flem Meade, the Rev. Marvin Sallee and Sam Sowards.

Another short story in regards to Vinton by Mrs. Frank J. Long and submitted by Mary Scott reads as follows:

My great grandfather McGhee came over from Ireland and he built a big grist mill, woolen mill and planing mill in a little village that sat in a valley surrounded by big hills. It was named Vinton, Ohio on the banks on the Big Raccoon Creek. There was a big home built up above the mill which was John Matthews home. Ansel Holcomb built the first house which was later my home.

My grandpa Shack built a big store on the corner next to our house and there was a blacksmith just across from us. We had a big covered bridge across Raccoon Creek just below the mill. Steve Perkins had a big hardware store just as you came into town over the covered bridge. Jap James had a barber shop near the bridge. We had Feltmans big store on corner of Main and Jackson Street. Then Mr. Well had a store in the building next to us at one time. There were five stores in Vinton which carried shoes, yard goods, groceries of all kinds and men's clothing. There was a big iron structured bridge over the creek built by the railroad. On the other side of the creek was an engine house where Frank McGhee and his boys ran to keep an immense big tank full of creek water for all the trains that passed through. We had two passengers trains a day, several freights which hauled coal, lumber, machinery and whatever folks had to ship. We had local freight trains which ran from Toledo to Middleport and Pomeroy along the Ohio River. I used to ride passenger trains to Gallipolis . Sometimes we would drive in because it was just 15 miles from Vinton.

There were 60 some families who lived in town and a lot of farmers all around Vinton. It's pretty country down that way to the river. We had churches in Vinton. The men built the Baptist Church and I went with my grandfather Shack to that church and sang in the choir till I was 20 yr old. We had a Christian Church on Clay St. We had two cemeteries. The old Glenn Cemetery and the McGhee Cemetery were located on a big hill just above our street.

Vinton was a busy little place. So many folks coming in to the mill and to shop at the stores and they had their grist "flour" ground while they shopped. My father quit school when he was 14 yr old went into the mill to learn the trade. He was a wonderful miller. He made the grandest flour called Lily White, made buckwheat flour, graham flour and corn meal. They shipped it out to a lot of it to different places. The flour was bolted through silk costing $7.50 a yd. It made such a wonderful bread.

I was happiest when I was helping either my dear mother or my father at the mill. I would fill the wheat bins and the corn burr and could run the corn shucking machine. I'd sweep the

*Old George Ewing house*

floor and clean up the office room and helped my dad sack flour for hours. They shipped so much out to different towns. Kept my father busy. He used to run the mill day and night. At midnight I'd light the old lantern and mother would have a nice lunch and hot coffee. I'd take it to my dad at the mill. He would lie on a board padded and get a few hours rest. Had an alarm clock to waken him. Those were the busy days. They shipped out a lot flour and lumber also.

Jim McGhee worked for grandpa. He owned a strip of land around the old bayou. Jim would plant water melons and musk melons and corn, beans, beets, sweet potatoes and white one's, pickles, peas and celery. Jake Clark had a water melon patch up the creek a little ways. They would lay water melons in the creek and they would get so cold.

At the end of Vinton bridge was a hoop hole shop where they made wagon and buggy wheels and other implements. Steve Perkins had this big hardware store at the other end of the bridge.

Jap James had a barber shop across the road. That's where men folks loved to congregate to gossip. Vinton was a pretty little town. They had street lights and Joel Pugh would go all over lighting all the lamps in the evening. The young and older men had a band. My father played an alto horn. Uncle John Matthews played a big tuba. They would go over to the old saw mill and play and it would echo over the water. This could be heard it all over town.

My uncle John Matthews had a big tan house. He had big vats in the back of this place where they tanned the hides after processing them. Those were happy days. In those days folks "lived and loved thy neighbor." There was a closeness there I never felt anywhere else.

Morgan Raiders came through our town. They would go into the stores and would take bolts, yard goods and muslin and anything else they wanted. They stole all the good horses and took my grandfathers finest horse. They were going to burn down the mill but grandpa said they could take grain to feed their horses and coaxed them not to burn the mill. They made everyone who could, go to the hills and to hide until they had no food left. Walter Holcomb, a lad 12 years old, fired a canon down on them and they jumped their horses and tried to find him. He ran to Mrs. Donnelly's house and she pushed him up through a hatch hole in ceiling and he just made it. She was so cool and collected they didn't look up there. Walter was a happy boy to be saved by a dear old lady. Morgan's Raiders went to Jackson, Ohio then on north. My grandfather hid my Grandmother Shirley, Aunt Jennie, my daddy and Uncle John in Oiler's home up the creek. The raiders would open up bolts of cloth and let it trail in the dirt for miles. This was a dear old town I loved.

Onto Betty Cantrell's Story of Huntington Township.

The other town being Ewington. Abel Sargeant began a village called "Leafygenia", but nothing came of his labors.

Only five of Gallia County's political townships coincide with congressional townships. Huntington is one of the five.

Huntington Township's population was listed as being 972 people in its borders in 1840. Its inhabitants were predominately from Wales and the Middle Atlantic states. The 1990 population for Huntington Township was 1,445.

Vinton and Ewington were ever expanding friendly places.

Huntington Townships prominent names were Holcomb, Ewing, McCarley, Dodrill, McNeal (McNeil), Shade, Porter, and others.

The first settlement was near Vinton on Raccoon Creek, with George Tyler, the first settler. Joseph McKnight built the first log cabin, and the first child born in the township was John McDaniel, son of David and Elizabeth (McCarley) Daniels.

The township is composed of thirty-six sections, Shiloh was a settlement is Section 16 ( Land deed dated in the late 1840s). There was a school and cemetery in the settlement. It was a settlement of blocks brought in by their owners from Virginia. The owners bought each family a plot of forty acres. The names of the original people were: Anderson, Hawks, Pounds, Shaffer, Long, McDaniel, and Bunch.

*Old Stage Coach Stop, Hotel*

The first house was built in 1804 by George Tyler in Section 36. Next came the farm of Milton Kent 1805 and at that time the farm of John Wallace was in the township. In Section 35, was the farm of Lucy Woodruff, known as "Woodriff", on State Route 325, over Little Raccoon, three miles south of Vinton. Enoch Russell and John Dickerson built a house in Section 27 in the farm owned by Abraham Depree in 1808. In the spring of 1809, Mother Edmondson and William Wood moved to a farm in the Dodrill community. Dodrill was "Edmundon's Corner" ( old Edmondson place). William Ewing was located in Section 11, known as "The Rock" (the old Casto Place) in 1809. In Section 36 up the creek in the northwest corner, were the Ewing and Casto places, and due west, is Irish Ridge. In the southwest corner, one mile southwest, is Coal Valley Road, Hartsook, Coal Valley and Scott Scholl. Roy Spars in buried behind the house on the Turner place. William C. Huntley came from the state of New York .

Morgan's Raiders came to Gallia County in July 1863 when they came to Ewington. The Northern Militia surrendered to Morgan's men. The rebels were then fired upon by some farmers hiding in the woods, causing then to go back and surrender to the men who had just surrendered to them. This took place in the yard of the Ewington Academy. The rebel soldiers fired shots into the gaslight of the Ewington Academy.

Vinton today, has a volunteer fire department, which serves the township, as well. The present Huntington Township trustees are Dick Neal, Bill Petrie, and Roger Shadenck. Verne Easter is the clerk.

Huntington Township Crime Watch started by George Pendleton ( deceased); then Pauline McCoy; Charles Adkins and then it went to George Troyman, Sgt. Jae Browing was Chief Deputy Sheriff when it was started.

There were several one-room schools in Huntington Township: Adney, Alice, Bunker Hill, Coal Valley, Ewington, Fort Scott, Scott School, Ground Valley, Hartsook, Hickerson, Shiloh, Tomato Valley and Willow Grove. There schools were discontinued in the later 1920s and early 1930s.

There are several cemeteries located in the township: Anderson, Brush, Ewing, Ewington, Franklin, Glenn, Holcomb, Huntley, Jones, Long, Lower McCarley, Lucas, Martindale, McGhee, McGlothin, Mt. Tabor, Norman, Old Holcomb, Parker, Potter, Pendleton, Sheppard, Shiloh, Turner, Tyler, Vinton-Memorial, Wilcox, and Wood.

The Village of Ewington is two and one - half miles north of Vinton. It was laid out in 1852 by George Ewing. In the year 1880 the town contained a grand total of 85 residents.

John Collins owned a farm in Section 2, Huntington Township. This farm was located on Alice Road at the north end of Ewington, Ohio ( Ewington is on State Route # 160.) The first land deed found for John Collins was in 1829. It reverted to his son Joshua and he sold it to John M. Cherrington in 1856.

John M. Cherrington built a two story frame house in 1859 on the property .5 of a mile west on Alice Road. It still stands and known as the Cherrington House. Perhaps the house was planned and supervised by George Ewing as it is the same style of architecture of the Ewington Academy with the same style window tops. The Academy, built in 1859, was also planned and supervised by George Ewing.

William and Mary Hughes McNeil Ewing arrived here from Scotland in 1810.

Seven years later, they were ready to make a "city". It had unofficially been Ewington since they first settled there.

There were other Ewing's in the area at that time. William and Mary lived in a log cabin known as Calla House located behind the Ewington cemetery. They came over from Greenbrier County, Virginia. Alice Ewing was the first to be buried in the Ewing Cemetery land which was donated by Mary McNeil Ewing.

Sarah Ewing, daughter of " Indian John" Ewing ( William's brother) married Samuel Holcomb and they came to Vinton in 1803. Holcomb was General of the Ohio Militia among many other things. Frances Ewing, daughter of Isaac, married Wesley Earl Tilden.

The covered bridge in Ewington, which preceded the present concrete structure was built by one of the Ewing's in the middle 1800s. Some say ice collapsed the bridge. Others say it was caused by people floating timber down the creek. There were two mills at Ewington, both near the covered bridge. One was a cider mill and the other was a three- story flour mill located at the dam. The dam was located at the hill top on Alice Road. L. Cloud, Rose Glassburn's father ( she lived one mile southwest of Bidwell) had the flour mill. The road was in the same location as it is today, with the exception of a short stretch were the present bridge replaces the covered one.

*Vinton Main Street*

In 1889, Ewington had grown from its first population figure of 200 inhabitations. Dr. E. A. Edminston laid out as addition to the town, located along the road to Durgan, which is about a mile away, and where the Hocking Valley Railroad later had passenger and freight stations, The Hocking Valley Railroad later became the C & O (Chesapeake and Ohio Railroad.)

Ewington had quite a few establishments: There was a hotel run by W. R. Denney; a flour mill and a saw mill at that time owned by McCauley & Co.; a harness maker, H. D. Peden; a blacksmith, F. T. Sales; a store mason, C. Long; a druggist, G. A. Ewing; and a grocery run by A. E. McCarley, who in 1855 was the owner of a grist mill. In the newer addition there was later built the Ewington Academy, the small grade school, and the Methodist Church.

Some of the businesses were a furniture manufacturing factory store owned by James Burke and located on Main St. ( present State Route 160, directly across from store owned by A. Edminston). Another store, a drug store stood on the corner diagonally across from the furniture store. There was a harness shop in Ewington. Mr. Griggs owned a nursery of fruit trees, with Mr. Burke as his agent. Noble S. Matthews owned a dry goods store called the "Crystal Palace." James Macomber was a sawyer. Andrew McCarley came to the county in 1836, where he engaged in merchandising in Ewington. Richard D. Edwards was a builder and a contractor. The drugstore became a feed store, on Ewington Road ( it burned); L. C. Bobo had a general merchandise store. It was last owned by Jim Marr, known as the Marr's Store ( it burned). Later Milton Snyder owned a garage and welding shop.

A doctor in Ewington was Dr. Gilbert Alexander Ewing, son of George Ewing, who practiced in the area up until 1881.

In 1866 there was a rumor of oil found in the county. This excited people, while some were drilling for oil they came upon a well of very strong salt water, mixed with oil and gas. This was the salt well in Ewington. The idea was to use it as a spa and sell the water for medicinal purposes.

No businesses exist in Ewington at the present time. The last was an Ashland Service Station owned by James Hall in the 1980s, and then by Lucy Wolford. It has been closed for several years.

A Post Office was established in Ewington February 8, 1850 and has been discontinued. Alice Post Office began September 13, 1880 and converted to Ewington July 31, 1939. Chestnut Grove began December 31, 1870 and was discontinued November 30, 1895 in order to make the name Chestnutgrove. Under this name it began operations December 31, 1895 and was carried to Vinton December 31, 1905. Rural mail routes were established in 1903. Charles Robinson was postmaster in 1855.

Delbert Vance had the Post Office and store in Ewington. Also, Harry and Desta Palsley had the Post Office and store. It used to be that a Post Office was often in a store, or even a house ( the house /home of the postmaster or postmistress.)

Mrs. Roberts had the Ewington post office for years. Then Pearl Twyman took it over. The Ewington Post Office no longer exists - it was moved to Vinton.

The Ewington Academy was established in 1859. In 1859, the homesteaders established what was possibly the first teachers' college in Ohio, the Southern Ohio Normal College. Fremont Vale was the first principal around 1888. An addition was built onto the academy to house the first four grades. The fifth through the eighth grades were held downstairs in the academy, while high school classes were held upstairs. When the high school was changed to Vinton in 1917, the academy was used for plays by area schools. In 1928, the partitions were moved to make two rooms instead of three. The school building addition burned sometime in the 1920s. From then on until the last classes were held in 1944 - 45 the main part was used for all eight grades. It is still used for church dinners, American Legion meetings, 4-H and etc.

The academy was constructed in 1959, on three lots bought by the Ewington Citizens' Literary Institute from A. S. McCarley. The Ewington District School later stood beside the academy. The building of the academy was done by volunteers in the area. The people were anxious to use the building and so were using it before it was finished, a scaffold fell, killing a " Mr. Burke", injuring a Turner boy and at least two others.

Mr. George Ewing planned and supervised the building of the academy. The school was a co-educational private academy with tuition. Instructors were George Cherrington, Jordan Booth, Alex Baird, and Fremont Vale.

Frances Ewing, who married Wesley Earle Tilder, taught in the grade school next to the academy.

Abner Johnson Holcomb Tyler was elected school director in 1879. James Calhoun was school director for one year in 1882. Enoch R. Dickerson was elected school director in 1855 for three years. As of 1882 there were twelve school in this area.

The Methodist Episcopal Church was established in Ewington in 1856 (it was torn down). Brush Ridge Church was established in 1869. First, it was a Baptist Church; later it was called Brush Church ( in the next decade). This church was five miles out of Vinton on Keystone road. The church is gone now, but the cemetery is still called Brush Cemetery. The Mt. Tabor Methodist Church is now called Little Pearl Church. The cemetery is still called Mt. Tabor. The Ewington Church of Christ in Christian Union was established in the late 1800s. Rev. Mckibbon started the Church of Christ and David Marhoover was pastor for ten years. Mike Prickett is the present pastor.

Wesley Earle Tilder was a Methodist Circuit Rider, which included the Ewington Church. Bunker Hill Church was located on Keystone road . It was discontinued in 1934.

Huntington Township had five Free-Will Congregations.

Ewington once had a 4-H club ( from 1987-1992). Pauline McCoy and Margaret Denny were advisors.

The Village of Alice once had two stores. Earl Spires had one of the two stores and the post office was in the store until it (the post office) was moved to Ewington. Von Thompson owned the store, sold it to a Mr. Cooper and he sold it to Ben Kruskamp. Mr. Kruskamp sold it to George and Emma Montgomery. This was the last time it was used for a store. The store building is now a dwelling. The second store was owned by Henry Hoover and he had living quarters upstairs. This store was torn down.

Garnet Snyder Kiser's grandfather had a blacksmith shop in Alice. Alice also had a one-room school in the early days. The Columbus, Hocking Valley and Toledo Railroad which later became the C & O ( Chesapeake & Ohio ) ran through Alice. There was a side track called a "siding" where cross-tries were loaded onto freight cars, and cattle were loaded into "cattle cars" to send to the stockyards.

There was a big building where ice was kept . In the wintertime, ice was cut and layered with sawdust and hauled in wagons from Raccoon Creek. It was stored in sawdust in the ice-house for use in the summertime. Those were the days before electric refrigerators and icemakers!

The Fairview Church is located in Alice. Dorothy Jane Whittington was pastor for a year ( 1976-77) and Denver McCarty is the present pastor. Before the Fairview Church was built, services were held in the Alice School. Rev. Gidon McCoy ( Vernon McCoy's father) was preaching there at that time.

*This is the history of Huntington Township in Gallia County, Ohio as of the year 2003. Information and Stories Submitted By Betty Cantrell, Kevin E. Kelly and Mary Scott*

# Morgan Township's Historic Lambert Land

### By Charles A. Murray

The Lambert Land is one of Gallia County's historic landmarks. It started as an early black settlement in November 1843 when Frank Lambert from Virginia purchased 265.5 acres of land in Fraction No. 32 of Morgan Township. Stories about this segment of Gallia County's history were handed down by word-of-mouth for three generations before the true facts were discovered by members of the Lambert Land Preservation Society in 2002.

Deed Records at the Gallia County Courthouse show that Frank Lambert and 29 other individuals with the surname Lambert purchased three tracts of land in Ohio in November 1843. For years it was believed that Frank Lambert and brothers, Miller and Minnis freed their slaves and led them to Ohio where they could live in freedom. Researchers, Glenn and Corliss Miller and Ernestine Mundell traveled to Virginia and found the last will and testament of Charles Lambert, Jr. of Bedford County. Charles Lambert, a slaveholder died in 1839 and willed his blacks to be free. The will also disclosed the true surnames of each slave and gave a personal description, including age. The researchers found the slaveholder's tax list which presented the monetary value of each slave.

The authentic names of the Lambert slaves who settled in Gallia County 1843 are listed as follows:

Aggy Wingfield Lambert   Age 44
Matilda Wingfield   Age 5

Albert Jones Lambert   Age 24
Alice Burks Lambert   Age 19
Alvin Jones Lambert   Age 18
Amy Lambert   Age 65
Benjamin Sales Lambert   Age 23
Callohill Minnis Lambert   Age 18
Caroline Lambert   Age 38
Nancy Lambert   Age 4
David Jones Lambert   Age 55
Francis Jones Lambert   Age 9
Frank Jones Lambert   Age 51
Isham Miller Lambert   Age 40
James Burks Lambert   Age 36
Jordan Miller Lambert   Age 38
Lewis Wingfield Lambert   Age 8
Lucinda Lambert   Age 24
Milly Lambert   Age S
George Lambert   Age 3
Watson Lambert   Age 0
Mary Ann Jones Lambert   Age 14
Milly Leftwich Lambert   Age 24
Martha Ann Leftwich   Age 5
Nancy Jones Lambert   Age 36
Hawkins Jones   Age 6
Amanda Jones Lambert   Age 4
Caroline Jones Lambert   Age 2
Alexander Jones Lambert   Age 0
Robert Sales Lambert   Age 12
Perthena Wingfield Lambert   Age 10
Peter Read Lambert   Age 80
Robert Sales Lambert   Age 12
Thomas Randolph Lambert   Age 64
Thomas Randoph Jr. Lambert   Age 53
Spotswood Jones Lambert   Age 13
William Jones Lambert   Age 35

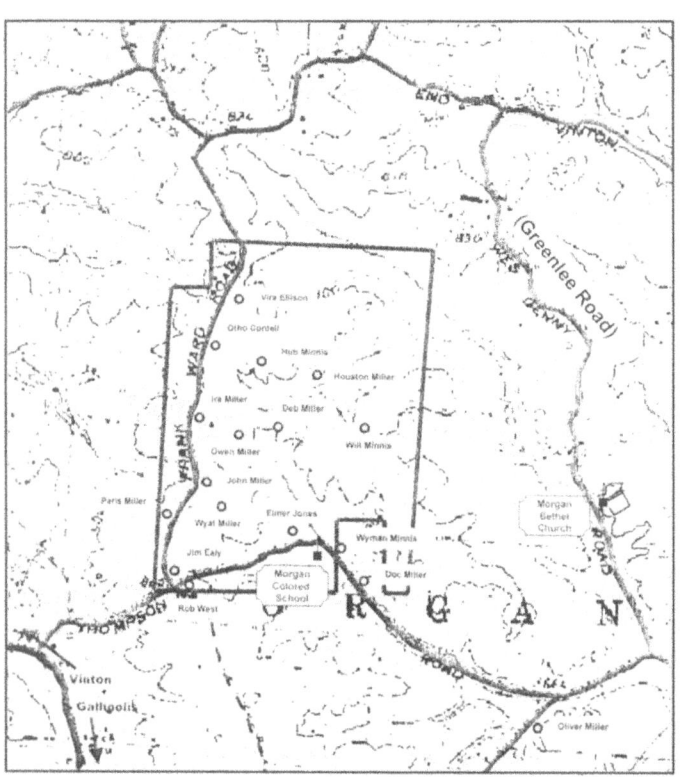

Shortly after the former Lambert slaves settled in Morgan Township, they began changing their Lambert surname back to their authentic names which included Burks, Jones, Leftwiches, Millers, Minnises, Randolphs, Reeds, Sales, and Wingflelds. In 1845, these former slaves aided in establishing the Morgan Bethel Church which is located a short distance east of the settlement on present-day Greenlee Rd. Their names appear in the early church records that are still in existence. At first the church members probably met in individual homes, and it was not until 1879 that land was purchased in Section 21 to erect a church building. In 1995 the Morgan-Bethel Church mysteriously burned, but it was replaced with a new structure. In 2002, Pastor Calvin Minnis, a descendant of Callohill Minnis, one of the original slaves, ministered at the church. Many of Charles Lambert's former slaves are buried in the church cemetery without markers.

Descendants of the Lambert land grantees continued to live on the land for two or three generations. Most of the dwellings, situated along hilltop ridges, were connected with walking paths. The land was communal, and each year the eldest person living on the property would collect money from the inhabitants to pay the property tax. This plan worked well until jobs became scarce and people moved to cities or other places to find work. By the 1960s most descendants had moved away; consequently on January 24, 1970, the land was sold on the courthouse steps for back taxes. This was the termination for the Lambert land settlement.

The 1908 Vinton Quadrangle topographical map shows the Lambert Land purchase and the home locations of the second and third generation inhabitants who lived there at some point in time.

For many years the children of the Lambert Land families attended a one-room school that existed on Thompson Rd. The Morgan Colored School served these families until August 1934 when it was closed. Some of the teachers who taught at this school were Ethel Bryant Anderson, Flossie Miller Bass, Edith Bryant, John Bowles, Henry Browner, T.D. Bunce, Flossie Miller Ford, Goldia Clark Games, Naomi Grover, Goldia Stevens Hogan, Bessie Norman, Mattie Clark Pounds, Ferney Payne, John F. Pound, Israel Roberts, I. C. Roberts, and Mary Viney. The black community first attended a log school, situated on a plateau adjacent to the Morgan-Bethel Church before the one on Thompson Rd. was built. It served several black families who lived in the area before the Lamberts settlers arrived.

In the summer of 2002, Mrs. Estivaun Matthews of Gallipolis spearheaded the formation of the Lambert Land Preservation

Society which pursued three primary goals: (1) to secure 16 monuments from the U.S. Government as memorials to the soldiers buried in the Morgan-Bethel Church cemetery; (2) to develop a map of the Lambert Land purchase showing the location of family homes of the slave descendants; (3) to purchase a memorial, consisting of three markers, one with a listing of original settlers and a brief history of the settlement, and two others inscribing the names of the 154 individuals known to be buried in the cemetery without grave markers. The preservation group elected the following officers: President Calvin Minnis, Vice President Glenn Miller, Secretary Buford Minnis, Treasurer Corliss Miller, and Chaplain Barbara Scott.

On Sept. 14, 2002 the Lambert Land Memorial was dedicated to commemorate the stamina and bravery of the "freedom-bound Lambert slaves." This group was able to migrate north of the Ohio River to live in freedom twenty years before Abraham Lincoln proclaimed his famous Emancipation Proclamation. Even though their lives are gone, their "spirit for freedom" lives eternally. Because of this memorial, the history of this early Gallia County settlement is now preserved in stone for future generations to see and learn about their heritage.

# Perry Township

Perry Township is an area of land located in the middle of the western edge of Gallia County in Southeastern Ohio. It is composed of 36 full sections and is sandwiched between Raccoon and Walnut Townships on its north and south and between Greenfield and Green Townships on its west and east. The topography is extremely hilly with hardwood forests and fertile valleys. Most valleys, although rich farm land, are subject to flooding. The township's watershed feeds the following streams and creeks: Raccoon, Symmes, Sandfork, Trace, Mud, Beaver, and Rocky Fork. Most of the smaller streams are tributaries of the two larger creeks, Raccoon and Symmes, which are both tributaries of the beautiful Ohio River.

The first known settler was Andrew Friend. He built a cabin along Raccoon Creek in 1803. The surnames of other early settlers are: Boggs, Beaver, Smith, Armstrong, Carter, Prose, Allison, Roadamour, Gates, Weis, Danner, Porter, Ripley and Campbell.

The township was formally organized in 1816.(Hardesty) By 1880 the population had grown to 1329 in number. The surnames of land owners in 1886 were: Amos, Anderson, Beardsley, Beck, Beman, Boggs, Bryan. Calloway, Campbell, Carter, Chick, Childers, Clark, Copeland, Danner, Davies, Drake, Erit, Evans, Ferrell, Fennell, Pry, Gates, Gilland, Green, Griffith, Grove, Hanson, Harbour, Harriger, Hashrarger, Hughes, Issacs, Ivey, James, Jenkins, Jones, Keller, Koontz, Lloyd, Love, Massie, McCall, McDaniel, McGath, McLoud, Moats, Morris, Morgan, Mossbarger, Noel, Norman, Owen, Parkins, Patterson, Perry, Pierce, Prose, Rees, Richards, Ripley, Roach, Rodgers, Samuals, Skinner, Slagle, Smith, Spear, Street, Swindler, Tanner, Thomas, Walters, Wafts, White, Wickline, Wigner, Wilson, Wiseman, Womeldorff, Wood, Wright, Zink. (source: 1886 platt map)

Early landowners sometimes owned large tracts of land, quarter to whole sections, but the land has been divided and sub-divided in to smaller tracts or small farms. Today few farms contain more than 200 acres.

Villages and communities evolving were Centerpoint (Wales). Cora, Gage, and Patriot. Most of these communities had post offices and/or stores at some point in their history. Most of the residents are now served by the Patriot Post Office. Another early post office was Holcomb, which was located along Symmes Creek in Greenfield Township. This post office once served a large area of Perry Township.

These early citizens of Perry Township built gristmills, sawmills, stores, schools, and churches. They were of varied faiths. Welsh, Methodist, and Baptist were the most dominant. At one point Perry Township had a ratio of 1 church for every 125.5 residents. One-room schools numbered 11. By the 1950s most I room schools had consolidated into larger schools and students were often bussed to neighboring townships. The only remaining public school within Perry Township borders at the present time is Southwestern Elementary. There are two or three private Amish schools. The Amish began buying farms in Perry Township in the early 1990s. It has become very picturesque to view their way of life. Horse-drawn buggies are now a common sight on the country roads and their method of farming is reminiscent of the past for many older residents.

The surnames of the present residents and registered voters in Perry Township are as follows: Adams, Adkins, Akers, Allie, Altizer, Apple, Armstead, Ashley, Ashworth, Atha, Baker, Baldwin, Barber, Barker, Barnette, Barry, Baxter, Beck, Bell, Berent, Bess, Black, Blair, Blauser, Blessing, Blevins, Bloomer, Boggs, Bonice, Born, Bowman, Boyd, Branham, Brannen, Brown, Bryant, Burgess, Burleson, Burnett, Burns, Bunside, Bush, Byer, Cable, Caldwell, Camden, Carpenter, Carr, Carter, Cemini, Chambers, Cheesebrew, Christian, Clagg, Clary, Cline, Clonch, Cochran, Colburn, Colley, Cooper, Coury, Cox, Crago, Crews, Crouse, Daft, Dailey, Dais, Danner, Darst, Davies, Davis, Davison, Deboard, Dellarco, Dillon, Dotson, Double, Doubleday, Doyle, Duke, Dmnmitt Duncan, Edwards, Ebman, Elkins Elliott, Ellis, Ellison, Evans, Fadley, Fallon, Fellure, Ferguson, Fife, Fisher, Flowers, Fountain, Fraley, Frantom, Frazee, Fry, Fulks, Gaither, Gilbert, Gill, Gilliam, Oilman, Gindlesberger, Goble, Golden, Goody, Grate, Gray, Green, Greene, Gregory, Hager, Haislop, Hall, Halley, Hammond, Hansen, Hanson, Harder, Harnetty, Harris, Harrison, Hatfield, Haynes, Heidari, Heinke, Henderson, Hershberger, Hill, Hobbs, Hoffman, Holcomb, Holstein, Hoover, Hopkins, Howard, Huffman, Humphreys, Hunt, Hunter, Hutchins, Irwin, Jackson, James, Jarrell, Jeffers, Jenkins, Jividen, Johnson, Jones, Jordan, Kaloust, Keefer, Kenney, King, Kirkhart, Kiser, Knapp, Kocher, Lakin, Lambert, Lawrence, Lear, Leffingwell, Lester, Lewis, Lively, Lloyd, Lovelace, Lucas, Lyles, Lynch Mabe, Martin, Massey, Mayes, McClellan, McCombs, McConnell, McCreedy, McDaniel, McGinnis, McGovern, McGuire, McNeal, Meadows, Mershon, Metzger, Meyer, Michael, Miles, Miller, Mitchell, Mobley, Mohler, Morgan, Mullins, Myers, Neal, Newberry, Nolan, Null, Nutter, Owens, Oxyer, Parker, Patrick, Patro, Pauley, Payne, Penwell, Perry, Petrie, Phillips, Pinkerman, Pitchford, Pope, Potts, Pratt, Prose, Provens, Puckett, Queen, Ramey, Randolph, Ratlifl Rawlins, Reynolds, Rice, Richie, Roberts, Rodgers, Rose, Rucker, Ruff, Rupe, Russell, Rustemeyer, Rutherford, Salisbury, Sanders, Saunders, Scarberry, Schuffer, Schuldt, Sexton, Shato, Sheets, Shelton, Shoemaker, Shriver, Shuler, Skaggs, Skidmore, Slack, Slaven, Sloan, Sloane, Smith, Snodgrass, Sowards, Spiers, Sprouse, Spurlock, Staley, Stanley, Stauffer, Stevens, Stayer, Straub, Stumbo, Surdyka, Swindler, Taylor, Terry, Thacker, Thomas, Thompson, Tirpak, Tisdale, Tope, Travis, Triplett, Trout, Tucker, Vanbibber, Vigue, Wade, Wagner, Walker, Walkup, Wallace, Walter, Ward, Waugh, Webb, Wedemeyer, Wellington, Wells, Wemyss, Whittaker, Whittington, Wilburn, Williams, Wiseman, Wood, Wooten, Yoder, and Yoho. (source: 2002 voter registration list) *Submitted by Marinelle Jeffers*

# Springfield Township

Springfield Township, composed of thirty-six full sections, six each way, is located northwest of Gallipolis, the county seat. Its wooded hills, natural springs, abundant streams, and rolling plains truly attracted the pioneers to the region for settlement. These early settlers organized Springfield Township on June 2, 1812, and their first election was held at the house of Charles Buck during the last week of September that year. They used waterpower provided by man-made dams in the major streams to saw virgin timber into logs. More and more log cabin homesteads began to dot the countryside as others crossed the mountains from the East. Samuel Denney built a gristmill upon Barren Creek on Section 27 in 1815. Other streams within the township include Chickamauga Creek, Campaign Creek and Trace Creek.

## Early Settlers

These pioneers are listed in Hardesty's History of Gallia County as being early settlers of Springfield Township: Charles Mills (1800), Michael Womeldorff (1801), Thomas Sawyer (1803), John Glassburn, (1804), David D. Varian (1807), William Watkins (1811), James D. Sprague (1812), Lewis Denney (1814), John N. Kerr (1817) Stephen Sisson (1819), Jacob Fee (1822), Peter Jarson (1824), John Cherrington (1825), Andrew Watts (1834), and Daniel Coverston (1835). David, a son of John and Mary (Richardson) Glassburn was the first child born in the township.

## Porter, The Township's Oldest Village

Porter, located in Section 24, was laid out on March 1, 1830, by Joseph Fletcher, a surveyor. Charles Russell owned the land. George J. Paine became the village's first postmaster in 1834. The post office, however, was known as the Pine Grove post office. During the 1840s, Porter became a prominent station of the Underground Railroad, a system where run-away slaves traveled northward incognito from the South seeking the freedom of the northern states. Paine was an abolitionist and local leader of this movement. He was also an entrepreneur who established a grocery within the town in 1860. In later years, this landmark was known as the E. L. Cottrell grocery store.

In 1843, three brothers, Frank, Minnis, and Miller Lambert, from the Richmond, Virginia area, purchased land about three miles north of Porter for their freed slaves to live. The descendants of these freed slaves, taking the names of their, former owners, have continued to live in the Bidwell-Porter area since that time. Another group of these Afro-Americans settled in Section 7 on Buck Ridge.

Dr. Nelson B. Sisson (1820-1903), may well be remembered as Porter's most civic-minded citizen. He not only provided medical care for the local citizenry but also assisted with the development of the Porter Methodist church. The first Porter Methodist church building, made of brick, was erected in 1842. When its walls weakened, church members built a new, wood-framed building. That building, dedicated in 1892, still remains at its initial location on Old Route 160, but it is no longer used for church services. The Trinity United Methodist church, situated on present-day Route 160, opened in 1991. It represents the consolidation of the Porter, Westerman and Vinton United Methodist churches.

In Section 11, about two miles southeast of Porter was the Laodicea Church, established in 1899. This church, along with an adjacent one-room school, initially served members of the Afro-American community who had settled in the area. In later years, it was called the Valley View Church. At the present time, it is the headquarters for a local motorcycle club.

Dr. Sisson's impact upon the community is also notable in the field of education. He initiated educational reform for both the Porter and Bidwell communities when he donated land located half the distance between the two villages for the purpose of erecting a new, consolidated school building. By his action, the Bidwell-Porter High School, built in 1902, became the first consolidated high school in the county.

At one time, the Porter Academy existed on Lots 47 and 48, of the village. Many students who studied at this select or private school became teachers and taught in the local one-room schools. Springfield Township had had as many as 16 one-room schools scattered across its landscape by the time Ohio began to pass mandatory consolidation school laws.

Near the beginning of the Twentieth Century, the residents of Porter and Bidwell were very privileged to share a public recreational facility. In 1906, some entrepreneurs developed an amusement park halfway between the two communities. The 24-acre Bidwell-Porter Park, located in the Dustin Grove, became the site for annual Fourth-of- July celebrations, bean dinners, and emancipation reunions. Large crowds, numbering as many as 7,000 visitors, came for these events. The grounds, also known as "The Bush Park" closed in 1965. Horse racing and semi-professional baseball competitions were common sights and sounds during the 1920s and 30s.

## The Evergreen Community

About three miles south of Porter is Evergreen, Springfield Township's second-oldest village. It is located in Section 15, along present-day State Route 160. The grove of "Pinus Rigida", commonly known as evergreens or pine trees, highlights this local landmark. In 1855, Henry Graham, a surveyor, laid out this quiet hamlet on land owned by John Cherrington.

In 1856, the settlers built the Westerman Methodist Church, which was named for one of the early circuit-riding preachers. This church building also served as a temporary grammar school. Shortly after the Civil War ended, the need for a schoolhouse arose, and a schoolhouse was erected. The Evergreen one-room school was located at the intersection of Old State Route 160 and the Evergreen-Prospect Rd. In 1935, the seventh and eighth grade pupils were transported to Bidwell for schooling. School continued for the younger children until the end of the 1940-41 school term. In later years the structure was sold and remodeled as a private residence.

A short distance from the former Evergreen schoolhouse, at the crest of the western horizon, lies the Pine Hill Cemetery. This cemetery is one of two burial grounds located in the Evergreen community. Another one exists adjacent to the former Westerman Methodist church, now known as the Countryside Baptist Church. The granite tombstones of both burial grounds now record the names of many residents who once witnessed the events of this community's past.

In 1880, the whistles of the Columbus, Hocking Valley trains became a familiar sound to the residents of Evergreen. Trains stopped at the public road crossing for passengers to embark or disembark, but no depot was ever established. The Denneys, Cherringtons, Hanks, Horgers, Phillips, Mossmans, Donnallys, Brookmans, Morrisons, Mossmans, Stephens, Siders, Dyers, Delilles, Ewings, Skidmores, and Kerrs are common family names associated with the history of this community.

At the present time, the township trustees hold their meetings in the Springfield Townhouse, which was once the former one-room Blosser School. This building was moved to Evergreen from Section 12 near Campaign Creek to its present location on Old 160. For many years the Springfield Grangers held meetings in the structure. It is also used today for public voting and for church services.

West of the village, located in Section 28, is the Springfield Baptist Church. This church was established in 1852, however the building itself was not completed until 1856. Today this church is a vivid reminder of the early fundamentalists and their puritan beliefs. The church facade still has two doors. In the early days, men and women had separate entrances and sat on separate sides of the church during the worship services. "Obe" Denney, Rube Bray, and Jacob Koontz were instrumental in the founding of the church. The Denney family cemetery is located a short distance north of the Springfield Baptist Church.

During the days of the Civil War, this brick structure was often used as a temporary jail when Confederate prisoners were kept overnight while moving them from Gallipolis to Oak Hill.

## The Kerr Community

Perhaps the greatest impact upon the history of Springfield Township was the advent of the Columbus, Hocking Valley and Toledo Railway in 1880. As the result of this business venture, at least three villages within the township were founded. One of these, called Ken, was developed in Section 8. By 1881, a train depot containing the Kerr post office was established at the intersection of Kerr-Harrisburg Rd. Charles W. Kerr became the first depot agent and postmaster. This railroad community not only offered passenger and freight service, but also facilities to market local produce and natural resources. A Gallipolis newspaper records that Kerr's railroad depot and adjacent store building were destroyed by a fire one night during a storm in 1904, but these were soon re-built.

In 1916, the Keener Sand and Clay Company purchased about 300 acres of land near the Kerr Depot. The surrounding hills contained an expansive deposit of sand and clay that was especially useful for molding steel products. The company built a tall drying building, a workshop, and a large open-sided storage shed to process the "Gallia Red" sand. Carloads of bagged clay were shipped by rail to foundries in Northern Ohio, Michigan, Canada, and even as far west as Iowa. In 1992, the Keener Sand and Clay Company closed its business at Kerr. Its land was then sub-divided into lots and sold for real estate development. A post office continues to serve the Kerr community.

In 1957, the Springfield Grange built a new grange hall along State Route 160. This building later became the Lighthouse Assembly of Church (Section 8). At the present time, other churches within the surrounding area include the following: The Church of Jesus Christ Latter Day Saints (Section 8), Living Water, built in 2000 (Section 14), French City Baptist (Section 1), Church of God of Prophecy (Section 8), Prospect Enterprise (Section 19), Providence, an Afro-American church, built in 1910 (Section 7), Rodney Church of God (Section 19), and the Cornerstone, built 2002 (Section 26).

About two miles south of Kerr, also on State Route 160, is the site of the Gallia County Children's Home (Section 1), established as an orphanage in 1885. Currently it is used as a home for abused, neglected and dependent children. The County School Board Office, the Holzer Senior Care Center, and Wyngate, an assisted living home, are also located in Section 1.

## Bidwell Community

The village of Bidwell, initially known as Porter Station, was surveyed in 1881 after the arrival of the Columbus, Hocking Valley, and Toledo Railroad. A depot (Porter Station) was built on the site for passenger and freight service. Since the new development needed a post office, John Kerr Powell, a local landowner applied to Congress. His request was honored, and in 1881, he became the first postmaster. The post office was named Heatly after Charles Heatly, another local proprietor. Powell built the first store in the village the same year and later sold it to E. T. Morrison in 1896. While the store was being built, William H. H. Frederick purchased a lot and built the first dwelling in Porter Station, also known as Heatly. His daughter, Maude Frederick, born July 19, 1883, was the first child born in the village. Several years later in 1892, some confusion involving the mail service occurred. As the result, the Heatly post office changed its name to Bidwell, in honor of John Bidwell from California, a Prohibitionist candidate running for the United States presidency.

John Kerr Powell (1854-1934) was Bidwell's most prominent land developer. He built the first Bidwell school, a 2-room building (Ca. 1890), Bidwell-Methodist Church (1892), the first Bidwell-Porter High School (1902), the Porter Methodist Church in 1888, and the Eno Methodist Church (1902), the Mt. Carmel Baptist, an Afro-American church (1903). He owned a brick and tile factory in Bidwell, but it was destroyed by fire in 1893. He later moved to Gallipolis in 1909 and served as the county treasurer (1909-13). Powell served as a trustee to Rio. Grande College from 1904-1919. He was elected as a state representative in 1915 and was re-elected the following year. He owned the Gallipolis Tile Factory from 1917- 1927.

By 1906, the thriving railroad business, coupled with the efforts of J. K. Powell, Charles Heatly, and E. T. Morrison, caused land speculation to boom. The area became a hub of several homes and businesses. A livery barn was built by Davis Moffitt in 1900. E.T. Morrison owned a general store. Charley Russell and Mason Grover had blacksmith shops. There was a flourmill, built in 1886, a creamery (1906), a hotel, and several grocery stores and restaurants. The Kents had a stave mill. The Bidwell Bank (1910), a branch of the Farmer's Bank of Gallipolis, was a short-lived financial institution of only eight months. The International Order of the Odd Fellows had a lodge building in 1920. Bill Reese operated a grocery in the building for several years. Cliff Fredrick,

"Pony" Borden, and Herbert Black operated gasoline stations. Grant Ward owned a general store. Two physicians, Dr. L. B. Turner and Dr. J. B. Dustin had offices in the village in 1906. Dan Glassburn and Floyd Ward were early undertakers. J. L. Coleman had a funeral home that closed in 1951.

Over the past 121 years, several businesses operated in the village, but many have disappeared. The Wickline Grocery, located on Market Street in Bidwell, established in 1944, continues to operate at this date. Passenger train service in Bidwell ended December 31, 1949, but freight trains continued for several years. When the railroad tracks were dismantled in 1992, a vital segment of Springfield's history came to an end.

At the present time, the following churches exist in Bidwell: the United Methodist Church, Mt. Carmel Baptist Church, Church of Christ, and the Apostolic Faith Church. A short distance west of the village is the Garden of My Heart Church, formerly known as the Fairview Church with a cemetery where several early residents are buried. About three miles northwest of Bidwell is the Mt. Olive Cemetery. The Mt. Olive Church was destroyed by fire in 1996.

In 1928, the first Bidwell-Porter High School was replaced with a new brick structure built at the same location. Since several Afro-American families lived within the local school district, a two-room segregated school building was built in 1934 on Midway Street to relieve the overcrowded conditions. Afro-American elementary students (Grades 1-6) attended the segregated building until 1954 when it closed. The Bidwell-Porter High School was always an integrated school. The last senior class to graduate from Bidwell-Porter High School was the Class of 1957. Springfield Township high school students then attended a new consolidated high school known as North Gallia. Elementary students continued to use the former Bidwell-Porter buildings until 1985 when the present-day Bidwell-Porter Elementary opened.

## Growth And Progress

In 2003, as the State of Ohio and County of Gallia simultaneously celebrate their 200th anniversaries, Springfield Township's economic growth is showing positive signs of improvement and progress. Its four highways including, State Route 35, State Route 160, State Route 554, and State Route 850 are becoming vital links to the economy of the county. One of the township's oldest and most successful industries is Bob Evans Sausage, located in Section 21 on Green Valley Rd. The company continues to process and ship its products to local and interstate markets. It has provided jobs and money for local people since 1948. The Gallia County Rural Water Association developed a rural water system throughout the township beginning in 1972.

Along State Route 850, is the Dan Evans Industrial Park, dedicated in 1998. With the addition of new buildings and businesses, it is presently showing signs of positive progress. In 1999, with the completion of the Bidwell-Porter Sewer Project, the health and living conditions of the township's population have greatly improved. As the present century progresses, the citizens of Gallia County must continue to elect leaders who are willing to create worthwhile community goals. The history of Springfield Township is a portrait of this image.
*By Charles A. Murray*

*German Ridge Cemetary*

# Walnut Township

This township is situated in the geological formation belonging to the carboniferous age. It contains thirty—eight full sections of land and is the largest township in the county. It is said by residents that Henry McDaniel caused this township to be larger because he wanted all of his land to be in Gallia County. The land is very rough, but, for the most part, fertile and is cultivated by a thrifty and industrious—class of people. The central part is settled largely by a class of Germans who are noted for their skill in farming. The timber is of fine quality, but growing scarce. Sandstone rock abounds along the streams and immense quantities of limestone and iron ore is found in the hills, but yet undeveloped, excepting the quarrying of stone to a limited extent. Veins five to seven feet thick, of the best coal in the State, (according to the report of the State Geologist,) are found underlying thousands of acres. It is being quite extensively worked in the Southwest part of the township, in the vicinity of Waterloo, Lawrence County. A railroad for which surveying was done was never built. In 1660 the township had a population of 1,692. At this time the population is 1924. The Wayne National Forest owns several acres here.

The first actual settler in the township was Henry McDaniel, who came in 1808, and built a cabin in Section Six on Symmes Creed near the mouth of Camp Creek. His son, Ephraim McDaniel, was the first child born in the township. Among other early settlers were John Louis, Giles Herrington, John Carter, Thomas Clark, Walter Neal, John Peoples, J. Mc Daniel, Charles Neal, John Lounds, William Williams, William Null, W. Long, Samuel Boggs, and Alexander McDaniel.

The township was organized April 13, 1819, and the first election was held on Sand Fork Creek when Henry McDaniel and Thomas Clark were elected justices of the peace. In the 1900s Otis Drummond was elected Auditor of Gallia County, and Joe Stewart was elected County Commissioner.

Symmes Creek is a large stream averaging fifty yards in width, in the township. It enters Section Five at the north, takes a crooked course southwesterly across the northwest corner of the township through Section Twelve. Very fertile bottom lands exist along this stream which have been in a high state of cultivation. Sand Fork Creek enters the southeast part of the township in Section Thirty—five, runs sluggishly northward through the eastern part, enters Perry township from section three and empties into Symmes Creek. This stream also contains very rich cultivated bottom lands and is noted for being the creek on which most of the old settlers located.

In 1812, John Coddington erected a grist mill, built of logs containing one run of stone, which was located upon Symmes Creek and run by water. In 1819 he added a saw mill.

In 1829 he sold the mills to Samuel Wiseman who sold the property to Wilson Sprinkles. Other owners of mills at Cadmus were a McAlister, Harvey McDaniel, John Barger, Christopher Mosier, William Mosier, Benjamin Mosier, William Wood, and Walter Pope. Pope closed the mill in 1973. During the mid 1900s cream testing was done at a small building in Cadmus.

Cadmus blacksmiths were Bill Hayes, Charles Weatherford, Bill Roberts, Charles Wickline, John S. Boggess, Esco Wiseman, and Clarence Drummond. Wickline's shop was between the mill and the Cadmus bridge.

Store owners in Cadmus include Samuel Drummond, Hattie Mae Barger, Willis I. Howard (He also ran a peddling route with basic groceries.), William Mosier, Benjamin Mosier,

Calvin W. Carter, John F. Null, Elliot Slagle, .John Everett Evans, Christopher Mosier, Orin Wiseman, Joe Carter, Elwin Willis, Walter Pope, Fred Null , and Ernie Null.

Cecil McDaniel also had a store and a peddling wagon in the Cross Roads area and on State Route 141 he later operated a store. Chester Howard also operated a store in the area. At one time there was also a blacksmith.

At Mudsoc, formerly known as Sand Fork, .Johnnie Davis had operated a store built in 1897 by James Luman and Brown for Monroe Drummond. Curtis Elliott and Cyrus Drummond purchased the store in 1918. The building still stands although no longer in business. Enoch Mahan and Sam Brown were blacksmiths at Mudsoc. There was a grist mill near Allison Road and at Sand Fork a stagecoach stop.

In 2002 businesses in the township include Pope and Pope Farm Supply; Trickling Springs Grocery (Mennonite); Amish bulk food, sawmill, lumber company; Cedar Knoll Bed and Breakfast; and Neal's Greenhouse.

Robert Armstrong, Mr. Petty, Thomas Ray, and Jacob Bosworth taught school commencing in 1818 in a round log building near Henry McDaniel's place. In 1822 the first building was erected for school purposes about one mile south of where Sylvester McDaniel now lives. It was made of round logs, with a puncheon floor and oiled paper windows.  There were several one-room schools in the township. They are Bethesda School (before 1890—1933—34), Boggs School (1854—1933—34), Cadmus Hill School (1887—1930—31), Flag Springs School (before 1870—1931—32), German Ridge School (before 1870—1931) , Low Gap School (discontinued in 1923) Luman School (1859—after 1879), McDaniel 's Crossroads (—1932), Mudsoc School (1857—1933—34), Myers Hollow School (1848—1916—17), Null School (1869—1916—17), Olive (Greenhorn) School (before 1870—1931—32), Pine Grove School (1917—16) made from Luman, White Hollow, Myers Hollow, Null, and Snowball schools; Snowball (before 1870—1916—17), and White Hollow School (before 1899—1916—17).

In 1918 a third grade high school was started in the Red Men's Lodge Hall at Cadmus and was used until a new building was built in 1926. The Red Men's Hall continued to house elementary students until the Southwestern High School opened in 1957. In 1985 the new Southwestern Elementary building opened which closed Cadmus Elementary. (The building is presently known as the Cadmus Community Center).  In 2002 the only schools in the township are the Mennonite on Hannan Trace Road and Amish schools near their residences.

The first post office established was the Flag Springs office kept by Charles Neal in 1839. There were four post offices located in the township in 1882: McDaniels established in 1852, Bowler established in 1888 also operating for seven years in the Flag Springs area, Sand Fork (1878), Boggs, McDaniel , and Sprinkle's Mills (established in 1872~ name changed to Cadmus in 1866). In 2002 there are no post offices located here; the mail is delivered in two routes beginning at Patriot Post Office.

In 1817 religious services were held at the residence of Walter Neal on Symmes Creek, near what is now Cadmus, conducted by William Kent, a Methodist minister. Also, the same year at the residence of Charles Neal , sermons were delivered by Rev. John Lee, a Baptist minister. The first religious society organized was a Methodist Episcopal at the residence of Benjamin Smith. Among its first members were Benjamin McDaniel and wife, Benjamin Smith and wife, James McDaniel and wife, and John Ray and wife.. The second society was organized at Flag Springs. In 1861 there were eight church buildings in the township which were nearly all frame and in good condition; Methodist, Baptist, and the Christian orders predominate..* During the last hundred years the following churches were established or continued for a time: Mt. Zion Methodist (1874-75-1990), Bethesda, Flag Springs, Walnut Ridge (1951— ),McDaniel Crossroads Pentecostal (1926) , Olive (1873) , Sandfork Baptist (1856—57—late 1900s), Fox Fairview (first established in 1854), Walnut M. E., St. Martin's Lutheran, and a Mennonite Church (established in late 1900s)

The first Sabbath-school in the township was organized in 1625 by John McDaniel.

 There were seven as recorded in 1862: Flag Springs, Sand Fork, Olive, Bethesda, Mount Zion, Pleasant Valley, and Fairview.

Flag Springs is noted for being the nucleus of the early population and the center from which extended to every part of the township. Representatives from this point are to be found in nearly every State in the Union.

John Lewis, one of the early settlers, made the first settlers, and sold it as an article of merchandise. The Amish and Mennonite families make furniture in 2002.

During the early 1900s a Red Man's Lodge was formed at Cadmus; later in the 1900s Grange membership met at Cadmus for a time. During the 1990s) the Floral Friends Garden Club was formed. *Information in the paragraphs with the asterisk was taken in large part from Hardesty's History dated 1882. Other information was gleaned from friends, relatives, and neighbors, and by reading Symmes Creek and Waterloo books as well as the Null Family History , Myers Family History, and the White Family History, and Gallia County One Room Schools. Pictures were donated by Opal and Bill Lloyd.*

# Cheshire

This is a tribute to Cheshire, to all current and past residents of our beloved little village. To all who have known her and loved her, before the media arrived.

AEP generously donated money to the Gallia County Historical Society to cover the cost of this history.

In the Ohio River Valley of Southeast Ohio lies hidden, a beautiful little village called Cheshire. Family homes with manicured lawns and beautiful flower beds on tree lined streets; the village overlooks the Ohio River. Descendants of pioneer families still reside in Cheshire today. Care free days of watching river traffic, hearing birds sing, playing with friends, chores, fruits and vegetables from the garden and church services on Sunday; envelopes the wonderful memories of childhood in Cheshire. Hard work and lean years during the depression, then the war, brought tough economic times to the village but did not diminish its beauty or sense of community. So many memories have been created over the years. Harold Mack remembers playing marbles outside, and his pet duck, Magnolia, who happened to eat his very favorite yellow marble. This one memory is probably seventy-five years old. Memories of bean dinners at Uri Swisher's and valentines passed at Cheshire School, back when you made your own valentines, have also been shared.

Some of Cheshire's children, grandchildren and great-grandchildren, have spanned the globe, some returned and others decided to move on to brighter lights and bigger cities. Cheshire residents have studied to become educators, doctors, lawyers, and politicians. Other residents served in the armed forces or labored in coal mines, or the railroad and ship yards. They have purchased war stamps, knitted socks and sweaters for the war effort, raised victory gardens and collected money for Red Cross Drives. Some straying residents have returned home for their retirement years or returned home to their final resting place at Gravel Hill Cemetery. Others are often drawn back to the village by the peacefulness, serenity and the beautiful river view.

*Cheshire Village Council July 2001. L: to R: Council Members: Jim Neal, Ron Hammond, Steve Harrison, Mayor Tom Reese, Teresa Mills of Buckeye Environmental Network, Chuck Bradbury. Clerk-Treasurer Jennifer Harrison, Council Member Randy Lucas. Missing Herb Clark.*

## Cheshire In Memory
### Author Unknown

In Loving memory of the Little Village of Cheshire, who was slain in the name of progress by the Purveyors of greed. Although, dear Cheshire, you were never big and famous, or you were never really beautiful, you overcame all these things, because to us you were home. You were a comfort to the elderly and a haven for your weary children, you were a source of girlhood fantasies and boyhood dreams. Although your children travelled the world over in war and peace, they always returned to you and your comforting rural ways. In years gone by you proudly withstood flood and disaster but this time, it was far too much even for you. So now as you lay torn and buried all the fond memories of you will live forever in our hearts. Rest in peace, Proud Cheshire. Sadly missed by Countless Survivors.

On April 16, 2002, American Electric Power (AEP) announced that an agreement in principal had been made to purchase the village of Cheshire for $20 million dollars. Lawyers hired by the village in 2001 approached the plant about purchasing the property from residents. Newspapers reported that there were approximately 90 homes and 220 residents inside the village limits. Some residents believed that there were health risks from living in such close proximity to the plant. Other residents did not share that fear. On September 24, 2002 the deal was completed. Some residents have decided to stay and special arrangements were made by AEP with older residents. Older residents were allowed to sell their property to AEP but remain there rent free, for the rest of their lives. Businesses will remain. Special arrangements were also made to accommodate the churches, allowing them to remain for the time being with the ability to sell at a later date.

C. L. Guthrie founded the village of Cheshire and Asa Bradbury founded the village of Kyger, which at one time boasted more residents than Cheshire. The first land purchase found for C. L. Guthrie occurred in 1837. The first recorded plat map of Cheshire was filed by Asa Bradbury. The land was surveyed in December of 1840 and results filed with a map of the village August 24, 1841.

C. L. Guthrie filed a plat map for Lots 1-26 of the Village of Cheshire and the record was dated October 20, 1851. By this time, the township population had increased to 1410 residents, occupying 243 households. In March of 1858, this plat record was amended and the lots were re-deeded from 26 lots to 21 lots, but covered the same acreage. These lots are now considered the original lots of the Village of Cheshire. On December 12, 1859, Lots 23-27 were added. These lots are considered Guthrie's 1st addition.

On August 19, 1863, Lots 28 through 48 were added and considered Guthrie's second addition. On May 17, 1867, Knopp's first addition, Lots 49-79 were added.

Cheshire was a thriving village with a strong sense of community, service and values. Nearly all of Cheshire's in-

*First Filling Station in Cheshire*

habitants attended either the Methodist or Baptist Church and supported the temperance or prohibition movement. Cheshire also had Presbyterians that met at the Academy building.

Members in the community were upset when in September of 1875; a whiskey saloon opened in the village. The barkeeper was referred to as the "benzine merchant" and the correspondent to *The Journal* suggested that residents should hold an "Indignation meeting." Residents elected a committee to circulate a petition to be presented to the proprietor. The petition stated that the residents of the village did not want, nor would they patronize a whiskey saloon. Unfortunately, others outside the village did visit the new establishment and sometimes behaved badly afterward. Cheshire continued to rally against the saloon and in May of 1876, it was announced that the "benzine merchant" was going to pull up stakes in Cheshire and relocate to Middleport.

Cheshire was the proud home of several businesses including: two stores, a barrel factory, flour mill, broom factory, drug store, barber shop, warehouse, hotel, telegraph office, carriage factory, whiskey saloon, millinery goods, post office and a train depot. William Symmes, Esq. sold his storehouse and goods to Mr. Sandford & Maddy. William Symmes retired as a dry goods merchant and in 1876, hauled coal from the coal mines at Arlington.

L. W. Mauck & Co. reorganized in 1876 and dissolved the partnership between L. W. Mauck and Daniel Mauck. The following was reported to the newspaper: "The Company partnership heretofore existing between L. W. Mauck and Daniel Mauck, under the firm name of L. W. Mauck and Company is this day dissolved by mutual consent. The business will be continued at the old stand by L. W. Mauck and D. B. Mauck under the firm name of L. W. & D. B. Mauck.

Hooper and Company Barrel Factory was in active operation but in April 1875, their partnership was dissolved and L. W. Mauck continued the business with 20 employees. Later that year, L. W. Mauck built a large addition in order to increase business. By December of that year, the business had increased and five more employees were hired. Mr. Mauck later purchased a steam engine for running the machinery in the shop. The improvements would increase production and L. W. Mauck stated that after the steam engine begins operation, they would be capable of producing one thousand barrels a week. The six machines in the barrel factory, run by steam, cut, bucked, planed and jointed the staves. The machines would also saw and round the heading, leaving little work to be done by hand.

Resener's & Sons Flour Mill were turning out "boat loads" of excellent flour. H. Resener purchased wheat from several places including 500 bushels of wheat from the Cincinnati Market. Resener's not only supplied flour, meal etc. in Cheshire and the surrounding area, they also sold and shipped to other markets.

T. R. Weed and Mr. Dunlap had broom factories. Brooms were made in Cheshire and shipped to other markets. Before leaving the broom business to engage in harness making, T. R. Weed went to Pittsburg with a shipment of 75 dozen brooms.

George W. Swanson was the druggist in Cheshire during this time and was the proprietor of the drug store. In January of 1875, he added on to his building because business was brisk. Regardless, Jno. Jackson of Anderson, Indiana came to Cheshire in early April to purchase G. W. Swanson's store. Mr. Jackson was met with a couple of mishaps while traveling on the Hudson. It is not known whether the transaction between Mr. Jackson and Mr. Swanson took place. By the end of the month it was announced that A. D. "Dunn" Guthrie was fitting up a neat storeroom for the reception of drugs. In September, the Cheshire correspondent reported that Cheshire once more had a drug store in active operation but the merchant was not mentioned.

Cheshire's barbershop was under the able direction of R. Long. Trichler's owned a warehouse in town and apples were mentioned to be stored there. The St. Charles Hotel reported good business, located on the river near flourmill landing.

In April 1875, A. D. "Dunn" Guthrie opened Cheshire's telegraph office and he "manipulated the electricity".

Coleman's had a carriage factory in town and in November of 1875 lost one of their long time employees. The Cheshire correspondent reported that Rickard Hackley, a colored man who had been employed by R. Coleman for the last seven years, died after a short illness of only twenty-six hours. Mr. Hackley died of apoplexy (a stroke). Many current residents of Cheshire Township never realized that Cheshire had a colored population but in 1875, they certainly did. Peaceful coexistence could be boasted in Cheshire and activities of all were supported.

Not to be left out of the business boom, in May of 1875, A. D. Guthrie's wife traveled to the city to purchase millinery goods with the intention of setting up business upon her return.

The following doctors served the residents of Cheshire Township: Dr. Barton of Addison, Dr. Johnson of Kyger and Dr. Watkins of Middleport.

Cheshire's main industry focused on farming and livestock. The news correspondent discussed corn, wheat, apples, potatoes, straw, pumpkins, melons, cabbage, beans, garden vegetables, clover and timothy hay. The weather conditions and progress of the growing crops weighed on the minds of many residents.

The Centennial holiday of the United States passed and Cheshire residents were hard at work. Residents were spotted with mattocks, spades and shovels, scattered all along Main Street, from the river to the Gravel Hill Cemetery, setting out forest trees. In May of 1876, it was reported that the trees lately set out along "Centennial Avenue" seem to be thriving.

That same month there was a little bit of excitement just outside of the village. The Cheshire correspondent to *The Journal* told the following tale: "Considerable excitement prevailed among the inhabitants in the valleys of the Little Kyger and Turkey Run a few days ago, for it was reported, and believed, that a wild animal (supposed to be a catamount or panther) was roaming at large in the woods, as a peculiar noise, sounding like the barking of some wild beast, could be heard every night. The people armed, turned out in mass, and it was soon reported that the animal had been seen, and a horrible description was given. The search continued every night for more than a week; hounds from all parts of the county were sent for, some of which it was reported got tore all to atoms. The chaps that had been making the noise by applying resin to a string and drawing it through a hole in a tin can, finally concluded that it might be safe to carry the joke no further; there was several parties of them, and when one would make the noise and get the hunter started in that direction, one of the others would start the music in another locality."

In May 1875, the news correspondent reported on another little town, "the new town in our suburbs, in which a couple of our young gents are so deeply interested, is christened "Dayton". It will contain one mill, one drug store and no more."

Cheshire residents enjoyed watching the river traffic. From the journal "At Cheshire, they all came out to see the Gazelle and Salt Valley pass. Cheshire has a decided 'weakness' in this direction." Later, "The war between the Hummingbird and Gazelle creates considerable excitement; we can never see less than about 50 people on the bank as they pass. Both boats have friends here."

Cheshire had a brass band that sponsored balls and gatherings in their hall. The brass band was reportedly one of the best in the county and they even attended events in other communities. Cheshire Brass Band made a trip on the Ohio No. 4 to attend the May Musical Festival.

An active Masonic Temple, Siloam Lodge No. 456 Free and Accepted Masons organized in Cheshire and purchased the old Academy Dormitory to use as their lodge. Samuel Rothgeb, died in January of 1880. In his memory, the lodge adopted a resolution to drape the lodge furniture in mourning for sixty days. Serving on the lodge committee were William Symmes, R. Coleman and George W. Bing.

Mr. Frank Wheeler, an artist from Belpre, Ohio pitched his photographic tent in Cheshire where you could get a "picter for your gal".

The "N. K. N. Association of Cheshire" was organized to raise funds to purchase a new organ for Academy Hall. Over one hundred people were present in May of 1876 for their first effort and over $18 was raised.

The Mauck Addition, Lots 80-110 were added to the Village of Cheshire and recorded on May 5, 1881.

In 1888, Jacob Gee was the village blacksmith and wagon maker but he also represented area residents in legal matters as a local esquire. At one time, he also served as Justice of the Peace. T. A. Weed had a store at the depot but later that year, moved his business to his lot on Main Street. J. E. "Fish" Fargo had a store in the old Mauck (Academy Dormitory) building on Second Street. "Fish" carried dried goods, groceries and notions.

For awhile in 1888, Cheshire had a saloon run by A. Ruble. The saloon burnt down and Mr. Ruble, determined to stay in business moved the saloon to his residence before finally surrendering. He moved his family to Middleport and not long after, the residents of Cheshire finally voted "her dry" and passed a local option.

Watson's Grove was an active place in Cheshire Twp. located west of the village of Cheshire. It was reportedly a beautiful and well cared for place and many events were held there, even events brought in from other communities. There were booths at the grove and rights could be purchased for concessions.

The Cheshire Flour Mill did a booming business and was still run by H. W. Resener and Sons. Ed Resener was the salesman for the flour mill and Robert Fulton, engineer. In 1888, the mill paid 75 cents for a bushel of wheat. Sometime before January of 1893 the Resener's mill burned and there was talk of building a new one. Resener's also had a big storeroom or building in Cheshire at the time where they sometimes stored hay. There was also talk of social events being held at Resener's Hall.

Hood & Wheeler ran an ice cream saloon in Cheshire during this time; Franklin Smith was the village druggist; Ben F. Warner, barber and T. R. Weed, Notary. Ed Good was a painter, L. D. Amos and Mr. Rife, butchers. Besides Jacob Gee, Esquires Bartlett Shuler and William Tate also handled legal business in the community. The firm Shuler & Company Steam Threshers ably assisted farmers.

Doctors found in town during this time were Dr. J. H. Pake, Dr. Charles Ely, Dr. Powell and later Dr. Ihle. Dr. Reed of Middleport was often found in Cheshire or the township assisting one of the doctors in an extreme case or serious accident.

Businesses south of town in an area referred to as "Cheshire Bottom" included Ben Warner's baker shop, Milo Guthrie's hardware store and a mill owned by James Murphy. Another legal mind was located in the "Bottoms" who served the community that was Esq. Symmes.

Of course farming and stock raising were still big in the area. Many individuals in the area owned farms. Other residents worked as horsemen or general farm hands on the bigger farms in the area. Popular farm crops during this period included wheat, grass for cow pastures, straw, hay, cabbage, potatoes, peaches, apples, corn, oats, blackberries, watermelon, wild goose plums, grapes, raspberries, strawberries and other garden vegetables. Crops were not only grown for home use but residents still sold or transported to southern and eastern markets.

Livestock raised in the area included: pigs, cows, sheep, chickens and horses. The types of horses, their usefulness and beauty was often discussed including a fine "Robin Hood " colt that someone had just acquired.

Cheshire played a large role in a nation-wide movement. A branch of the nation-wide Farmer's Alliance was organized in Cheshire sometime in May 1870. 22 members organized with George Bing, President. By December, 1890, there were thirty of these subordinate alliances in the county. Alva J. Agee of Cheshire served as president of the Gallia County Alliance. In 1891 the Alliance organized and placed before the electors of the county, a "Peoples" Party ticket. Though the organization had a very short existence, Gallia county was greatly honored when in 1891 Alva Agee, a young Cheshire farmer, aged 33, was elected to the presidency of the Ohio State Alliance.

During this time, Cheshire residents worked together to bring prosperity and culture to their community. A petition was passed to incorporate the village but for some reason, this was not realized until years later. A subscription was passed to raise money to erect a Baptist Church, money was being raised for a fruit-canning factory in Cheshire and 5,000 shares were being raised to erect a flouring mill near the railroad station. This flour mill was to supply a long felt need for custom work. Cheshire residents were enterprising citizens.

Social events included many plays, lectures and musical performances. Indian shows and different groups setup at Watson's Grove and some residents even ventured to the Worlds Fair in 1893. Residents of Cheshire organized a Lodge of the Knights of Pythias in May 1891. Members of visiting lodges assembled and performed the work of installing the Lodge and Cheshire's twenty members. Mrs. John Cregg, prepared the supper. Cheshire and Kyger both had an active GAR (Grand Army of the Republic).

Newspaper correspondents report often on the beauty and serenity of the village of Cheshire referring to Cheshire as a "daisy little town" and reporting "Cheshire floats along in its usual quiet way, with nothing occurring to disturb its harmony".

Gallia County suffered a severe flood in April 1913. The water mark was 31 inches higher than the flood of 1884. Not much is known about the damage in the village caused by the flood.

With the usual Cheshire style, residents organized a volunteer, Good Roads Association in March 1916. All work would be done by volunteer labor and Cheshire residents suspected that if work was done at the appropriate time, the overall condition of the roads would improve. A petition was presented to the township trustees and the association included that all work would be done under their supervision. Eli Hix, Charles Tipton, George Thompson, S. S. Anderson, F. M. Swisher and Orestus Roush signed the petition. The petition was well received and the trustees organized by electing Arthur Grover, President and Perry Swisher, Clerk. The other members were Taylor Gordon and Edmund Kail. They also selected the following representatives, one in each school district, to solicit their fellow-citizens for volunteer work: George Vanzant, Orestus Roush, Enos Story, Pearl Rife, Horace Kail, C. E. Fife, Samuel Halfhill, William Jacobs, Horton Roush, Alonzo Grover and Wilbur Butcher.

Cheshire residents at this time were also working toward a new school. A motion was passed in March that proposed a $30,000 Bond Issue, payable in 30 years at the rate of $1,000 per year be put before the voters by special election at the earliest possible date. The motion was made by M. W. Ralston and seconded by A. H. Kirby. A vote was called and Yea votes were cast by J. A. Swisher, A. H. Kirby and M. W. Ralston. N. R. Rothgeb cast the only Nay vote. In April 1916, the Bond Issue carried 79 Votes to 69. The next month a suit was filed by Mrs. Laura M. Luckey asking that the Bond Issue be declared null and void because proper procedures had not been followed in land transfers and the annexation of certain lands. Judge Roscoe J. Mauck ruled on the issue in July 1916 and annulled the election and prohibited the bond issue. In April 1917 the bond issue was put before the voters again and it won again by ten votes. The new bond issue was for $20,000. Plans were drawn in July by Webber & Webber, Columbus Architects and were approved by the Cheshire board. Mr. R. A. Miller of Middleport won the building contract.

During all of this work to build a new school, draft boards were opening and men were being called to serve in World War I. Cheshire residents busied themselves with Red Cross work and also the sale of War Bonds and War Savings Stamps. The Cheshire Red Cross Unit at one time had 130 members.

Electric light plants came to Cheshire as early as 1920. Mr. Bert Miller, B. F. Palmer and Glenn Chase were all found in Cheshire on business in 1920. Mr. Bert Miller was the Delco light man. B. F. Palmer, the furnace and light man of Eno, was the sales agent for the National Hot Air Furnace Company. Glenn Chase was the Willys electric light plant agent for Meigs, Gallia and Mason Counties. M. L. Guthrie had electric lights installed in his home by Emmett Ralston. J. Ed. Bing and C. A. Ralph also had electric lights installed and both purchased their Willys plants from Glenn Chase. C. A. Ralph had his furnace installed by Glenn Chase's father of Pomeroy. Alva Bing purchased a Delco light plant for his home from Bert Miller. George Briggs installed a hot air furnace from B. F. Palmer.

*Cheshire Academy ca. September 1910*

Harold Mack reports that electricity as we know it today came to Cheshire in 1927. Some residents still lived without electricity for several years. Renters may have lived in homes that were connected, but couldn't afford to pay for the service, especially during the depression.

By 1920, some residents were working in nearby Gallipolis and Middleport. In and around town it was reported that Vernie Roush clerked in the Rothgeb store, Harlan Athey raised apples, Roma Hern had an ice cream parlor, C. A. Ralph and J. H. Ewing worked as salesmen for the Cheshire Milling Company and Nellie McCarty worked as a telephone operator. That same year, a parent teacher organization for Cheshire School was organized and Mrs. Curt Ralph was elected president. Cheshire also had an active club called the "Cheshire Social Circle". Otto Rothgeb bought the residence and post office building from William Russell. Cheshire High School enrollment reported in 1920 was 43 including 17 students in the freshman class.

W. H. Trumbo and Pearl Ward were appointed to the Board of Education in 1921. Most social activities during this time centered on the churches and the school. Cheshire High School had a debate team, orchestra and active football, basketball and baseball teams. Cheshire even had a semi-pro basketball team known as the Cheshire All-Stars. Harold Mack and Helen Preston both remember having chapel at school. In high school, band music was played on the victrolla as they marched out of school. A Lyceum course was held at the high school, which included lectures, concerts and literary programs for the adults in the community. Lyceum (Lie-see-um) means to spread useful information in the community by means of lectures and debates. The Lyceum courses across the nation led to the creation of the federal extension service. .

Cheshire men previously laid off from the Hobson Railroad shops were called back to work. J. F. Winegar operated a garage and was Cheshire's Ford dealer. He sold several Ford Touring cars and also Ford Coupes and Runabouts. Mrs. Garnet Kirby coordinated the Girl's Food Club. In November of that year, Dr. Maag came to town and Cheshire then had at least two doctors. Dr. Ely's office was across the street from the school on the east side of his residence. Dr. Maag's was located in a room at George Thompson's store. Pearle Rothgeb operated an ice cream parlor and lunch counter. It was a treat to go to Pearle's for an ice cream cone. Ice cream cones were five cents.

Helen (Noble) Preston and Harold Mack both share memories of their childhoods in Cheshire. Helen was born in 1914 and Harold was born in 1918. Helen remembers the first automobile she saw as a child belonged to Mr. Haptonstall of Middleport. It was a big car and when he came to town the children gathered to hear him honk the horn. Mr. Haptonstall was a Riverboat Captain. Harold believes at one time Cheshire had three doctors but by the mid to late 1930's, Bob Little remembers there were no doctors in town. Some residents then went to Middleport to see Dr. Boice. It cost seventeen cents to ride to Middleport and back on the Hocking Valley Railroad. Potatoes and cattle were shipped out by train. Kids scoured the refrigerated railroad cars for pieces of ice. Ice found was then dragged home for the icebox. The Cheshire train depot was the gathering place back in those days. Ben Warner carried mail from the depot to the post office.

Traveling shows and entertainment were still popular during this era and Helen and Harold remember the showboat that used to come to town. The showboat the "Golden Rod" used to come to town. Residents described the showboat as a big barge with a calliope. The barge was pushed by a tugboat called the "Adaboy" and docked at the flour mill landing. The cost for the show was fifteen cents. Many activities were remembered at Watson's Grove and Uri Swisher's bean dinners. Uri would take people up in an airplane. Helen's father, George "Geo" Noble, belonged to the K of P (Knights of Pythias) Hall and many activities were held at that hall. Helen remembers a hypnotist coming to town and giving a show at the K of P Hall. He hypnotized Foster Little and while under hypnosis, Foster was instructed to eat the apple he was handed, when in reality, he was handed an onion! Clarence "Thumb" Little was also hypnotized and he was balanced on two chairs and then they smashed a rock on his chest.

*Foster Little Jr. Cheshire Football ca. 1951*

The river was still an active means of transportation and riverboats were still used to transport produce to market, especially the potato crop. The flour mill landing, where boats docked in town, was later a gathering place for children, meeting there to swim in the Ohio River. By the late 1930's, early 1940's, Bob Little doesn't remember riverboats docking at the landing anymore. Harold remembers the river back then was clear and there was a good beach. The river was for a time, Cheshire's only entertainment outside of school and church activities. The flour mill caught fire possibly in 1927 and burned for almost a month. The house next door caught fire initially and the mill could not be protected.

Harold's father, Fred Mack, purchased the hardware/general store from Frank and Idie Winegar around 1926 or 1927. They carried general merchandise. Harold remembers the big barrel of marbles in the front of the store. Marbles were one of the few toys back then.

Helen reminisces about P. O. Swisher's store. Perry and his wife Eve lived close to the Baptist Church. Perry ran a grocery in town and every year at Christmas time, his wife Eve would decorate the front window of the store. Eve had a Santa Claus bust that she would use and she filled the pouch of his jacket with all kinds of trinkets. In all of Helen's travels, especially New York City, Helen can't remember a store window as beautiful as Swisher's back home. Gifts for Christmas often consisted of fruit, especially oranges. Most families at that time couldn't afford presents like what we might receive today but holidays were filled with celebrations, family gatherings and special programs at the church.

P. O. Swisher sold bananas at his store and the bananas sold for five cents a pound. Helen remembers the bananas were shipped on the stalk in big baskets. Perry would hang the bananas in the storeroom. Later, Bob Little remembers that the bananas came in cardboard boxes packed in shredded paper. The un-ripened bananas were stored in a dark storeroom because they ripened when exposed to the light. P. O. also sold live chickens and Harold seemed to think that the chickens sold for fifty cents or so. Roberta (Allensworth) Kail writes that

P.O. Swisher's store was located on the southeast corner of Main and Second Streets where the car dealership is located today.

In the 1930's Roberta Kail writes, "there was a beer garden just south of Cheshire on Route 7 called The Midway". Later, the name was changed to New Villa and even later called the Merry-Go-Round. "At one time, the Merry-Go-Round housed a walking marathon and people walked around the hall until they were exhausted and collapsed. After that, there was a skating rink in that building called Dillons." Young people traveled some distance to the edge of Cheshire to skate at this skating rink and this is where Harold and Odella (Drummond) Mack first met. Around 1937, Roberta Kail remembers that Jim "Skipper" Shamblin built another beer parlor just north of the Merry-Go-Round and named it "The Pilot Wheel". Mr. Shamblin and his family lived in the same area and Mr. Shamblin was a riverboat captain. Mr. Shamblin's "Pilot Wheel" was a very popular establishment and was a draw for visitors from both Gallia and Meigs Counties. The Shamblin house became a retreat for some residents of Cheshire during the 1937 flood. Livestock was taken to Gravel Hill Cemetery and residents found refuge with relatives and friends.

Fred Mack, purchased the Sterling Station from Wash. Thomas around 1933 selling Sterling and Quaker State gas. Later, Victor Bradbury, then Bill Scott and finally Bennett Little operated the station. Bennett Little ran the station for several years and had a grocery store at the station. At one time, Cheshire had five grocery stores. Some of the stores over the years included: Hern's, Thompson's "Sack of Treats", P.O. Swisher's, Bill Scott's, Bennett Little's and probably others. Denny's took over from the Thompsons and P.O. Swisher's store later was a restaurant run by Bill Rader.

On the corner where the Community Action is now, Roberta Kail remembers that Everett and Freda Rife were the proprietors of a restaurant. Later, the restaurant was run by Pearle Rothgeb. "My first memory of the building which is now the Cheshire Food Mart is that Paul Martin operated a gas station there. Then in the 1950's he built a new one, one-half mile south on Route 7. Bess Vaughn took over the old station. Next door to the original gas station close to Rucker and Mary Jane Neal's, was a grocery store owned and operated by Bert and Loma Hern." There were also several other filling or gas stations in town including Pud Mulford's, Walter McCarty's, Bennett Little's (Mack's) and Johnny Russell's. Clarence "Pud" Mulford's station was in the building that now houses "VOTO". After Pud died, his son Junior ran the station. Fred Mulford ran a garage on Route 554 east of the railroad tracks, where he worked on cars. Deannie's Pizza, also used to be a gas station and in the 1930's was operated by Jack Robertson. Johnny Garrison and Ernest "Daddy" Ward took over from Mr. Robertson and then in the 1960's Mr. Gillenwater ran the station.

Cheshire had it's own marble shop and Harold remembers it was located at the corner of Roush Road and was owned by the Swanson family. Many of the stones in the older section of Gravel Hill Cemetery were made at Swanson's and the stones have the company name on them. This business was actually in the area for several years.

Helen remembers past Memorial Days from her youth. Memorial Days back then, were used to remember Civil War Soldiers. Cheshire residents would go around the village to collect flowers and they would take them to Martha Swisher's house where they would make bouquets to put on the soldier's graves.

Roberta Kail remembers Wink Long's poolroom was located on the northeast side of Main Street back from the traffic light. Billy Grape's blacksmith shop was behind Wink Long's. Later, Mrs. Fetty owned the poolroom.

Billy Grapes, the village blacksmith was very well liked and respected. Many residents remember how talented Billy was and how he could fix anything you could imagine. Billy even made his own false teeth. Bob Little remembers that Billy had a Model A Ford Coupe with a rumble seat and he put a heater in it. The blacksmith shop was located behind where the Community Action is now, close to the northwest corner of Locust. Billy lived right beside his shop.

Ben Warner was the village barber. Later Mrs. Grapes, Billy's wife, barbered in town as did Clarence "Thumb" Little and a colored gentleman named Bill Winston, who was from Middleport. Bill was well liked and came to Cheshire every day on the bus, returning to his home in Middleport every evening. Bob Little remembers that Mr. Winston charged 25 cents for a haircut.

Ed Swisher was the milkman in Cheshire and he and his wife Millie lived over by where the village park is now. Their fields were on the west side of Second Street and they walked over and milked twice a day. Harold and Odella Mack remember Ed milked by hand, run the milk through a separator and delivered the milk in quart jars. Ed made his deliveries in a Model T Ford. Besides milk, Ed and Millie also made cheese. Walter Bode Athey worked for the Swishers.

Many people called on Belle Thompson in times of crisis because Belle always knew just what to do. Apparently this was common practice during this time, especially for younger mothers who might not have the advantage to have their own mothers in close proximity. Betty Jo (Matthews) Clark tells similar stories about her own mother and their neighbor, Mary Little.

*Ladies Missionary Society, Cheshire Baptist Church December 1998 L: to R: Seated: Odella Mack, Helen Preston and Niki Tracewell. Back Row: Doris Zerkle, Georgia Hughes, Connie Palmer, Sue Thacker, Jinette Raike, Dee Tracewell, and Henrietta Shuler.*

*Cheshire High School May 2002. Now home to the Cheshire Village Offices, CHS Alumni Association and the Masons*

Raymond Thomas had the first television that anyone remembers in town and everyone went down to their house to see what it was all about. The first show that Odella Mack remembers was an old western. The Thomas brothers; Don, Marvin, Harold and Raymond constructed the building where the Pepsi plant is now in the late 1940's-early 1950's and it housed an auto body shop. The Pepsi plant is located near the point, on the north end of the village on St. Rt. 7 close to Riverside Drive.

Helen Preston remembers the first boys from Gallia County to volunteer for service in World War II. The memory comes to mind because one volunteer was her brother, George Robert Noble. Helen remembered that Lafe Rupe and Johnny Garrison were also among the group and the newspaper revealed that Ray Gardner, George Leo Gardner and Clair Spires were the others. Many activities at school were suspended because of the war and residents were busy with Red Cross Drives and scrap collection. Because of rationing, many of the men who worked across the river at Marietta Manufacturing met at the river and shared boat rides across to work. Harold Mack was one of those making this trek and he remembers as many as six row boats lined up. This allowed the men to save the toll paid twice a day to cross the Silver Bridge and to save money on gas. It also saved a lot of travelling time. One memory Bob Little has of the war was the fact that Chester Thivener never returned home. Chester's parents lived in the double by the station that now houses Deenie's Pizza. For a long time, Chester's car sat under the roof at the station, a constant reminder of the loss of a popular young man.

Cheshire residents traveled to Pt. Pleasant in September 1952 to here General Eisenhower speak. An estimated 5,000 people were on hand to greet the General and Mrs. Eisenhower during their stop. Those from Cheshire attending were Mr. and Mrs. Delbert Underwood, Mrs. Mary S. Plants, Mrs. Mae Casto, Mrs. Ruth Mack, Mrs. Elizabeth Mulford, Mrs. Odella Mack and Mrs. Mary Jane Neal.

Tragedy struck Gallia County again on December 15, 1967, when the Silver Bridge collapsed into the Ohio River during rush hour, just ten days before Christmas. Harold and Odella Mack went down to the bridge and discovered that the rescue efforts were being hampered because of lack of light. They quickly returned home and loaded their generator and lights to take back down to the site. Alonzo Luther Darst of Cheshire, was one of the 46 that perished that day. One of the survivors, Paul A. Scott of Middleport was born and raised in Cheshire. Most everyone in Gallia County either lost a family member or someone they knew. The Silver Memorial Bridge was dedicated on September 15, 1969, exactly two years after the tragedy.

Bill Scott was one of nine children born to Elsie and Ether Scott. Bill served in the Navy during World War II, along with two of his brothers. Bill's sister, Gertrude Scott (Hysell), also served in WWII as a nurse in England. She was a Lieutenant. Bill's wife, Mildred (Rice) Scott, shares memories of her husband and of Cheshire.

Wilbur Ward was the mail carrier for more then 30 years and her husband, Bill Scott, used to substitute for him. Bill also worked at the TNT plant across the river. He drove school bus for Cheshire schools as a full-time driver, then as a substitute driver before retiring. Bill and Mildred opened a grocery store in Cheshire around 1947. The grocery was located on Main St. where the beauty salon is now. The Scott's carried a full line of groceries, produce and animal feed. Scott's grocery closed around 1976 when prices were so high they could no longer remain competitive.

Cheshire remains the home of several businesses and descendants of original pioneers. Time may march on without our beautiful village but the memories will be forever in our hearts.

By: Shari Little-Creech

# Carlton

Carlton was located one mile north of the village of Cheshire. First known by the name of Carlsburg, then Henking, the village took the name of Carlton in 1893, when the post office was renamed. This community formed around the coal mines in the early 1870's. The mines were owned by Charles August Carl, Sr.

Charles Carl, Sr. was born in Kempheld, Prussia June 17, 1833 and he was raised in Germany. He married Caroline Wildermuth in May 1856 and arrived in Cincinnati, Ohio ca. 1858. He worked at his trade there for $12 per month before coming to Gallia County presumably before 1865. Children of C. A. and Caroline Carl were: Gottlieb Frederick, Charles, Alexander, Herman, Albert and Arthur. The boys would eventually marry in to the Rothgeb, Boice and Bing families, some of the most prominent families in Cheshire. As adults, they worked along side their father in the coal business.

Alexander Carl died in April 1882. He left Cheshire to visit relatives in Louisville and while he was there suddenly became ill and died in a few days. He was buried at Cave Hill Cemetery in Louisville, Ky.

By 1888 the Carl's had built a village and a booming business. They were very active in Cheshire society and in the community. Besides the coal business, they also owned a store in the village of Cheshire and in January 1888 brought what was possibly the first telephone to the village. The telephone was put up between their store and Cheshire Depot. Herman Carl ran for treasurer of Cheshire Twp. that year and won.

Gottlieb Frederick, moved to Gallipolis and in 1888 ran a coal business there. The youngest Carl son, Art was found in Gallipolis that year, helping his older brother with business.

The Carl's sold some of the mining homes to the miners in 1888. Miners were also able to purchase small amounts of acreage. Many of the individuals purchasing homes may not have otherwise been able to afford to own their own home. The Carl family was also busy building houses and making repairs on others already built. The care the properties received is an indication of the relationship between the mine owners and employees. Many mines supplied tenant houses for the coal miners but some homes were barely more than shacks. Miners were often forced to live in unsavory conditions, unable to afford their way to a better life.

By the next year, residents petitioned for a post office and the petition was allowed. The post office was located in the Carl's store and was named "Henking". C. A. Carl, Jr. was Carlton's first postmaster.

In 1889, the miners formed a Knights of Labor Lodge with 22 members. Unions during that time served more than just the financial interests of the miners. They also assisted their members when injured, ill or during times of strife like the death of a

Postmaster N.R. Rothgeb, wife Cora Rothgeb, Anna Mapes-Clerk, Will Thompson, Delivery man #1, Ben Warner-carrier from trains to Post Office and vise versa, Rinenldo Swisher, Rt. Delivery Man #2

family member. Officers of the Knights of Laborer elected were: William J. Blackburn, Grand Worker; Wesley Swisher, Treasurer and William Carrier, Secretary. Residents also formed their own Sabbath school and appointed the following officers: Jacob Blackburn, Superintendent; Thomas

Manley, Assistant Superintendent; Charles Little, Secretary and Arthur "Art" Carl, Librarian and Treasurer. A baseball club was organized and named the Henking Red Stockings. They played several games against other clubs and were very proud of their record. Residents were also busy raising money for a church, which was finally erected at Silver Run.

The Carl's maintained a good relationship with the miners and socialized among them. Cheshire and Carlton seemed to have always lacked the class distinction or separation that often existed in communities. The miners did occasionally fuss over wages and would briefly strike but the turmoil never lasted and no hard feelings ever seemed to be held on either side. Very few accidents occurred at the Carl mines which I believe adds to the character of this family and the manner in which they treated their workers. Workers were paid on a regular basis and paid in gold instead of coal mine scrip, which was often the case in the mines across the river. Carl's miners were paid per car load of coal and often when one became a father, they joked they would have to mine an "extra car load". Coal mine scrip was money made by the mines to be used at the company businesses. Often the scrip was marked for a specific mine, within a specific company. Businesses such as stores etc. were run by the mines and prices were often inflated. Miners, earning only scrip, were forced to conduct their business at these stores and pay the inflated prices for goods needed. This created situations where miners were constantly indebted to the company's they worked for.

In 1890, there was an accident of sorts in Carlton. Wilbur George, Arthur Carl and some other young men were out playing with Art's Flobert target gun. Wilbur who was standing about 200 yards from Art Carl told Art that he could shoot at him. One of the boys fired the gun and missed Wilbur, which you could guarantee Wilbur had already assumed. Unfortunately, Art took back the gun and asked Wilbur if he could try and Wilbur said yes. Arthur fired at him, also assuming the distance was too great to actually hit him but both boys were wrong and the ball entered the fleshy part of Wilbur's leg. The doctor was called and the newspaper correspondent spoke with Wilbur afterward. Wilbur said he attached no blame to Art and that they were the best of friends.

Charles A. Carl, Sr. sold the coal business and store at Carlton to his five sons in January 1890. The boys assumed all liabilities of the firm and vowed to vigorously push the business. C. A. Carl, Jr. and Art continued clerking in the store. Jacob Blackburn reported that C. A. Carl had charge of the mine for the last 15 years.

Business at this time depended on the water level in the river. Barges sometimes were stuck below the village of Cheshire because the water level was too low to support them. This often held up the shipment of coal and slowed the mining business for the workers. Often when this happened, homes were temporarily closed up and miners would go "down Kanawha" to other mines to work. The Carl boys were often found traveling up and down the river doing business for the coal firm.

In October 1890, the Carl's were making arrangements to open and operate another mine in addition to the current business. The new mine was located near Mr. Hanson's property in Meigs county.

Jacob Blackburn reported in February 1891 that Carlton had communication with the outside world. A pay station for the telephone was installed and Jacob said that "If the Carl boys had the means in proportion to their energy, they would build a city". By 1891, the Carl's were also able to ship coal out by rail instead of depending solely on the river to transport goods.

Allen Frazier was employed by the Carl's and worked as the blacksmith at the mines. Alexander and Edward Frazier were also employed by C. A. Carl, building a new residence for him in the village. Robert Little, a soldier of the late war, worked in Carlsburg; he was the village barber.

Miners who purchased homes were listed in the paper in 1891 and included: James and Albert Frazier, E. F. and John Mulford, Daniel Lynch, Isaac T. Manley, J. M. Rice, W. J. and J. H. Blackburn, John Thompson, William Carrier and Joseph Buttricks.

*Cheshire Village bought by Gavin Power Plant*

Jacob Blackburn reported in July 1891 that no spot in Cheshire township had improved in appearance more than Arlington Heights and Henking in the past five years. In that time, 21 new dwelling houses had been built and large tracts of land cleared and at the time, was in a high state of cultivation. It was also the coal region of Gallia county. The main business in that line was conducted by C. A. Carl's Sons and the firm of Roush & Casto. Arlington and Henking had one store, one blacksmith shop, one barbershop, two hay and grain merchants, one surveyor, one Justice of the peace, one constable and one or two gas machines. It was also the home of Jacob Blackburn. L. W. Swanson's marble shop was located near Carlsburg and Harold Mack remembers the business being located at the corner of Roush Rd. Carlsburg also had their own train depot and the track was also used (by foot) for residence to access Silver Run and as a short cut towards 1st Kyger Church. Presumably they walked the railroad tracks to the west side of Cheshire and then west to the church. Carlton also had a school which was called Carlton or Roush School house and was located on Roush Rd.

Bennie Hysell worked at the mines and was severely injured while driving. Apparently Bennie hit his head on slate at a low point in the bank. Mule teams were used at the Carl mines to haul coal out of the mine. John Drake was a boss and track layer at the mines.

In January 1893, the post office name was changed from Henking to Carlton and the name of the village also changed. Most residents remember the village only by the name of Carlton. A Carlton school was built in June 1893 and Jacob Blackburn wondered why it was built on the same site as the old school and not in the village.

Bad news came in June 1893. The Carls Coal Works was closed by order of the sheriff because of a debt due in Franklin County. Liability to the firm was estimated at $40,000 with assets only amounting to about $8,000. Many Cheshire residents and businesses were on the books at the mine and also miners who had not yet been paid. Many of the miners immediately left to go down the Kanawha in search of work. Sixty miners were employed by Carl's Coal Works when the closure took place. In August, it was announced that Carl Mack and G. W. Bing had purchased the business and would begin operation. By June of the next year, some of the miners down the Kanawha were forced to return because of mine strikes in West Virginia. Ed George, Charley Little, Al Frazier, Charley Carrier and Albert George walked from the Black Band mines, through to Carlton and Mr. Carrier reported that the crowd only had 35 cents when they started, a distance of some seventy miles. The miners returned home to find full time employment at Carlton.

C. A. Carl, Sr. died September 30, 1893. Some of the Carl boys continued in the coal business after Carl Mack and G. W. Bing took over. Albert Carl and then Carl Mack became the postmaster in 1893 and even with the tragedy of the closure, the post office was allowed to stay and was again in active operation. It is unknown how long this post office operated.

Another little village close by which has been long ago forgotten was "Pity Me". Not much has been recorded about this village but presumably it may have been another little mining community surrounding the Epitome Coal Works. *By: Shari Little-Creech*

# Cheshire Village Incorporation

Anticipating growth from the new Kyger Creek Power Plant, the village of Cheshire was incorporated on April 6, 1953 and the population was estimated at 300. Sherley Woods and Elwood Howard acted as agents for the village and Halliday and Sheets Law Firm, Warren F. Sheets, prosecuting attorney, served as attorney for the commissioners. The following residents petitioned for the incorporation:

Ralph Rife, Gladys Rife, Cornelius Rife, Clarence Peters, Goldia Peters, Wilma Fife, Clarence Mulford, Sr., Elizabeth Mulford, Lorena B. Reynolds, Leith Reynolds, Edward Preston, Helen Preston, Clara Howard, Elwood Howard, Clarence Mulford, Jr., Huldah Jenkins, Ivan Grover, Leanna Grover, Melvin Little, Harold Mack, Otto Rothgeb, Pearle Rothgeb, Ada Ward, William M. Fife, Raymond L. Zerkle, Doris Zerkle, Edgar Rucker, Garnett Rucker, Curtis Rice, Marcella Rice, John E. Russell, Violet Russell, Fred C. Mack, Catherine Woods, Sherley Woods, Delbert Underwood, Jay Hall, Wilbur Ward, W. J. Grapes, Mary Jane Neal, Rucker Neal, Ruth Mack, C. W. Swisher, Nellie McCarty F. Dale Allensworth, Donald E. Thomas, Willard Reese, Mrs. W. J. Grapes

On April 6, 1953 the Gallipolis Daily Tribune ran the following story: County Commission OK's Cheshire Incorporation

Men Unanimous Reaching Verdict Opposed by 36 Cheshire village is to be incorporated. The Gallia County commissioners unanimously voted in favor of the group's petitioning for the incorporation this morning at their regular meeting at the Court House.

A group of 23 representative women and men from Cheshire in favor of incorporating met with the commissioners and their enthusiasm and interest was keen.

Sheets Advisor

Prosecuting attorney Warren F. Sheets was there to advise the commissioners on the legal side of the question.

The group favoring incorporation have had a plot made of the proposed incorporation and have gone through all the legal requirements and their petition with 48 names had been filed with county auditor Bodimer for the legal required length of time.

A petition bearing 36 names opposing incorporating the village was filed Saturday in the auditor's office.

A committee appointed to do the preliminary work on incorporating has been working several weeks. Members of the committee are the Rev. Sherley Woods, Harold Mack, Elwood Howard, L. J. Reynolds and C. W. Swisher.

The plans to incorporate Cheshire are one of the many changes made in the area due to the coming of the new Kyger Creek plant.

Applause Greets Verdict

Harry Wilcox, chairman, said, "We want to be fair and do what the majority of the people want." When the commissioners returned their verdict there was a loud round of cheers and applause.

During the meeting, several of those present said they could get many more signers but they had only acquired the number needed to make the petition legal.

Signers Listed (see above). Signing the petition against incorporating were: G. M. Hawley, E. F. Long, Eulalia Long, F. R. Long, R. W. Grover, Bethel Grover, J. A. Grover, Mrs. J. A. Grover, Edward O. Yeauger, Mrs. Edward O. Yeauger, Orion Ward, Mabel Butcher, James Irion, Russell Eblin, Mrs. Russell Eblin, James Thompson, Pearlie W. Thompson, Delmar Rothgeb, Mrs. Delmar Rothgeb, Ada Thompson, Mina Amos, Levert Amos, Millie Swisher, Ray Lemley, Alice Lemley, Harold Martin, Emory Edwin Gordon, Mabel A. Gordon, Pansy Spires, John A. Martin, Colesta Yeauger, Sallie McCarty, Clarence Ebersbach, Edward Ebersbach, Cecil Hawley, Nellie Hawley. Curt Swisher was the 1st Marshall after Cheshire's incorporation in 1953.

The incorporation date recorded in the village minutes was June 20, 1953. The first village council meeting was held in the church social room and the first mayor was L. J. Reynolds. The first village council members were: Shirley Woods, Elwood Howard, Curt Swisher, Curt Rice, Edward Preston, and Harold Mack. Mary Jane Neal served as Treasurer and Doris Zerkle as Clerk.

Mayors of the Village: L. J. Reynolds (1953-1957), Elwood Howard (1958), Ada Ward (1959), Harold Mack (1960-1966), Robert Burchett (February 1966-June 1970), Walter "Scott" Lucas (June 1970-December 1997)Tom Reese (January 1998-Present)

The latest additions to the village included land for the village garage and baseball diamond which were annexed in September 1992 and the Swisher subdivision was annexed August 12, 1993.

In December 1997, Mayor Walter Scott Lucas announced he would retire as Mayor of the Village of Cheshire, after 27 years of service. He had been involved in the village council for more than 35 years. Mr. Lucas also retired earlier that year from his position as administrator of Veteran's Memorial Hospital in Pomeroy. Nearly a lifelong resident of Cheshire, Scott planned to spend time with family and enjoying activities he never allowed time for. He was very well liked and sentiments were, he would be difficult to replace. In January 1998, Councilman Tom Reese was appointed mayor to finish the term of retired mayor Scott Lucas. Tom Reese had been serving as council president and his position was filled by Herb Clarke. New council members that year were Steve Harrison and Ron Hammond. Returning members included Jim Neal and Herb Clarke.

The village council in May 2002 consisted of Tom Reese, Mayor and Councilman: Chuck Bradbury, Ron Hammond, Randy Lucas, Herb Clarke, Steve Harrison and Jim Neal. Jennifer Harrison serves as Village Clerk and Treasurer. *Information provided by Jennifer Harrison and Shari Little-Creech.*

# OLD BUSINESSES

## Commercial And Savings Bank

In September of 1908, six men met in the office of Dr. J. A. Lupton in Gallipolis. The result of the meeting was the signing of the articles of incorporation of the Gallipolis Commercial and Savings Bank. The men who met on that September day nearly a century ago were Dr. James A. Lipton, John R. McCormick, S. H. Eagle, W. Pres Beall, Jehu Eakins and Max Shober, all leading citizens of the county.

It was not until January 2. 1909, that the bank was installed in suitable rooms and opened for business with a capital stock of $35,000. (By 1965, the bank's assets stood at the $10,444,302 level.) Initial officers were: Dr. Lupton, president; Eakins, vice-president; A. P. Kerr, secretary and cashier; and Harry Maddy,

*The Commercial and Savings Bank, 25 Court Street.*

treasurer. At the first stockholders' meeting, E. N. Deardorff was chosen chairman and Jehu Eakins, Dr. J. A. Lupton, W. Pres Beall, J. R. McCormick, S. H. Eagle, E. N. Deardorff, Max Shober, W. R. Tanner, Simon Silverman, John W. Gills, L. R. Fletcher and James L. Haskins were named directors of the organization. Dr. Lupton, the leading personality in the organization, served as president for sixteen years. At his death in 1924, he was succeeded by Henry W. Cherrington, who served until his death in 1971. Three others have held the post of bank president: U. A. Cornett, Donald Crance and Scott Hinsch.

The bank's first location, in 1909, was in the Shober building in the 300 block of Second Avenue. It then moved to the Adams building in 1915, and to the Lupton Block a year later. In 1938, the bank moved into the Lafayette Hotel building. After the bank acquired the property at 25 Court Street, a new building was erected which opened in September 20 of 1965.

As in the case of the other financial institutions in Gallipolis, sound judgment and business ability of its' leaders kept the Commercial and Savings Bank solvent during the trying years of the depression and the hysteric hours of the 1932 bank holiday. According to minutes of the annual stockholders' meeting, the bank did feel the pressure of the depression years. The minutes stated that, "many members expressed their opinions of the dangerous financial situation of the country and stated their view on conservation of the bank's resources". It was one of three banks in all the cities of Ohio which did not restrict withdrawing of deposits in any manner.

The Commercial and Saving Bank, with the exception of the depression years, when even then, its' operation was superior to most of the nation's financial institutions, was a profitable business venture. In 1940, there was $55,000 worth of capital stock and total resources of the bank amounted to $1,100,000. The officers were Cherrington, president; F. C. Ghrist, cashier; and Dean H. Davis assistant cashier. Directors elected for the year 1940 were Cherrington, Resener, W. E. Spear, J. E. Gills, H. B. Ecker, C. E. Holzer, H. A. Wood and C. T. Robinson. Employees of the bank were: James Walker, teller, and Helen McNealey and Bernice Graham, bookkeepers.

Always a leader in community betterment, the bank in 1937 inaugurated a successful plan to increase the beef cattle herds in Gallia County. In three years, it placed 900 head of Hereford cows with various farmers. It also sold 20 registered bulls to local farmers, in addition to nine bulls which were the property of the bank. The program was developed to improve and increase the beef cattle in the county and to encourage boys and girls to engage in agricultural projects. The bank also introduced methods to facilitate the individual farmer in obtaining beef cattle.

In 1955, president of the bank was H. W. Cherrington; C. E. Holzer was vice-president; and G. C. Beard was cashier. Assistant cashiers were A. 0. Cotton and Mrs. Helen M. West.

*Employees of the C & S Bank taken circa 1949: left: Kay Haffelt, Gilbert Beard, Helen McNealey West, Jean Smith, Saunders Bernice Wood, Marietta Hively, Austin Cotton and Vance Campbell.*

Two years after the founding of the bank, the articles of incorporation were amended to provide for 15 members on the board of directors. The names of E. J. Resener, J. S. Biddle and J. C. Rue were added. Later the number of directors was changed again. Once in 1923 to nine and again in 1930 it was reduced to eight. In 1923, the board of directors included Lupton, Cherrington, Resener, Tanner. Fletcher, Gills, Biddle, Beall and Rue.

When the bank moved to its' new quarters in 1965, the directors were: Carl C. Myers, first elected in 1959; Gilbert C. Beard, 1957; U. A. Cornett, 1951; J.E. Gills, 1933 and Henry W. Cherrington, 1920. J. E. Gills succeeded his father, John W. Gills and Carl C. Myers succeeded his partner, the late Colonel H. B. Ecker. Henry W. Cherrington was president and Gilbert C. Beard was cashier.

On August 1, 1979, The First National Bank of Cincinnati purchased all of the capital stock of The Commercial and

Savings Bank. The bank continued to use the name of The Commercial and Savings Bank until July 1, 1988. The name was then changed to Star Bank.

## Drug Store Second & State

Throughout America's history people in large cities and small towns depended on the goods and services provided by the local Mom and Pop drug store. The people of Gallipolis were blessed with 5 such drug stores right in the heart of town on Second Avenue and they were: Rathburns, Kerrs, Neals, Gillinghams, and Walgreens.

While each served Gallipolis well, Walgreens began what would be a 50-year tradition of Pharmaceutical services provided on the corner of Second Avenue and State Street. On April 16, 1937 Howard K. Hughes and Warden Lewis opened the Walgreen agency drug store complete with an ice cream soda fountain, cards, cosmetics, over-the-counter drugs, and various sundries in addition to it's pharmacy department headed by Warden Lewis as Pharmacist and Manager.

January 10, 1949 marked a change when Pharmacist Orville Butler along with his wife Mary purchased the store changing the name to Butler Walgreen Pharmacy. In fact, the Butlers purchased the entire building at 400 Second Avenue from the Betz family. For the next 11 years the Butlers continued to serve Gallipolis at that location.

April 27, 1960 marked another change when the Butlers sold the Pharmacy as well as the building to Clyde and Margaret Price who renamed the store Price and Sons Pharmacy. The Price's remodeled the store removing the soda fountain and enlarging the pharmacy as well as incorporating the business with Clyde, President and Pharmacist D., Margaret, Bookkeeper, and Margaret's parents Ben and Leora Wright as Secretary and Treasurer. After the passing of the Wrights, Gil and Kent Price (the Sons of Price and Sons) took their place in the family business as they were appointed Secretary and Treasurer.

Price and Sons Pharmacy held it's place in history on the corner of Second Avenue and State Street for 22 years making it the longest of the 50 year history. It came to an end in 1982 when the Price's sold the Pharmacy to Frank and Jan Doolittle. The newly named Doolittle Pharmacy continued until 1987 when Frank sold the business to Rite Aid Pharmacies. Frank continues to work as a Pharmacist for the Rite Aid Pharmacies Corporation today.

While the business had been sold, the building was still owned by the Price's and as time had gone on the Sons had become Doctors. Margaret and her sons, Dr. Gil and Dr. Kent Price, sold the building in 1987 to Ed Bosworth thus ending the 50-year tradition of the local Mom and Pop drug store at the corner of Second Avenue and State Street, 1937-1987. *Submitted by Mrs. Clyde Price*

## Evans Packing Company

Evans Packing Company was established on July 4th, 1937 with brothers John Everette Evans, Jr. and Emerson E. Evans dividing duties. Emerson was the sales and business manager. John was the stock buyer. The first salesmen for southeast Ohio were another brother, Chauncey L. Evans and a nephew, Robert L. Evans. By 1945 Carroll MacKenzie and Harland Martin had joined the company.

*Evans Packing Co. 1950's*

A first fire, in 1940, destroyed the plant. The owners located a company that could rebuild and employees of the Evans Packing Company were used as laborers so they would have incomes until the company was rebuilt. With the help of other companies, such as Logans in Huntington and Davis Ice and Fuel of Middleport, Oh, the customers never missed a call. The Evans Packing Company bought their livestock over a wide area and then slaughtered them at their own plant. They featured wholesale fancy baby beef, veal, pork and lamb fresh meats, also Dixie tender smoked hams and Dixie Bacon, along with lunch meat loaves and their own brands, which won wide recognition for superb fine flavor.

The business prospered and in 1942 the company bought Green Valley Farm, just below Raccoon Creek on Route #7. John operated the farm and his son Tim Evans operated the dairy. They made a trip to Waukeesha WI to purchase the best dairy cows. During World War II, they raised approximately 72,000 tomatoes and several acres of cabbage each summer to feed the troops.

In 1953, Green Valley Farm was sold. John retired and Tim bought an interest in the Evans Packing Company. He worked there until the plant was sold to Landmark in 1972.

The plant passed through several companies before burning to the ground December 14, 1990. *Submitted by Bess Evans Grace Davis, Tim Evans, John Bostic and others.*

## Ewington Grist Mill

As I Remember!

The Ewington Grist Mill was located on Alice Road approximately one-fourth mile off State Route 160 on Raccoon Creek.

My memories are prior to and including 1935, the year I graduated from Vinton High School and moved to Columbus. However the Mill was still standing in 1940 as my husband remembered having been there and that was the year we married. I do not know what happened to the Mill after that. I was told that it was torn down after it was no longer in use, which is entirely possible as the road was very narrow—on a curve—with a very steep hill across the road and a spring flowing from the rock, this being a hindrance for vehicles.

*Ewington Grist Mill, Picture taken in teens or twenties*

My father, John Sherman Cottrill, began operating the Mill in 1921-22. He began by assisting Mr. Cloud who ran the Mill at that time. Mr. Cloud was an elderly gentleman who passed away not long after. I might add here that Mr. Cloud was the father of Harley Cloud who was a prominent educator in Gallia County, a principal as well as teacher at different schools in the county.

I really don't know who owned the property at that time, but I do know that Mr. Gordon Hammond bought the Mill and my father continued to operate it as long as it was in operation which was probably 1932-33.

I remember early in the mornings when horse and mule-drawn wagon loads of corn and wheat pulled up to the big front door and unloaded their grain and then leave for Vinton or Wilkesville, returning in the afternoon or evening to claim the finished products, feed, meal or flour.

I remember when it grew dark, early evening and I would carry a kerosene lantern around for my father as he finished his long days work.

Little did I realize at that time when the old Mill and that moment of my childhood spent with my father would become just a memory. My father passed away in 1939.

The mill was quite a large building, three stories, two above ground and a lower floor just above the water where a large engine was housed. It was for use when the water was too high or too low for regular mill operations. I do not remember ever having seen the engine in operation.

The first floor was where the corn was ground into corn meal or feed of different types. The shelled corn was dumped into a large hopper going from there to the large burr stone which was powered by a flat water wheel laying in a crib in the water directly underneath the mill. As I remember, flour-making machinery was on the second floor, a much more sophisticated operation than the processing of corn. As I remember the small dark wooden boxes or cabinets with doors that opened to check on the flow of the flour. The large tubes that fed the flour were made of silk as I remember. I recall very little about the flour-making at the Mill. Corn processing was the main operation there.

I have very recently been told by Ernestine Polsley, wife of Fred Polsley deceased, a member of a prominent old-time Ewington family that the Mill was torn down in the year 1945.
*by Mary Scott*

# First National Bank

On Friday October 9,1863 a meeting was held at the store of Edward Deletombe to organize the First National Bank of Gallipolis. Those attending were Charles Creuzet, Robert L. Stewart, James D. Thompson, Rueben Aleshire, Samuel C. Bailey, Robert Black, Lemuel Perry and Mr. Deletombe. Edward Deletombe was elected President, James D. Thompson, Vice President, and Robert L. Stewart, Secretary. Robert Black and James Harper were named tellers.

The Bank was chartered thirteen days later on October 22, 1863, being one of

*Edward Deletombe*

the first banks franchised by the United States under the National Banking Act signed by President Abraham Lincoln in February of that year. President Lincoln signed all official documents, "A. Lincoln". Whether this fact influenced the first president of the First National Bank is not known, but he always signed minutes of board meeting as "E. Deletombe".

Original holders of the 1,000 shares of stock were: Roman Menager 50, Rueben Aleshire 30, Isaac R. Calohan 10, Robert L. Stewart 20, Joseph Hunt 20, John Hutsinpiller 70, Lemuel Perry 70, Samuel C. Bailey 50, Charles Creuzet 40, Robert Black 40, John J. Blagg 80, James Harper 10, Daniel Mauck of Cheshire 50, Edward Deletombe 150, Francis Leclercq 10, Alice Jackson of Ironton 250, and James D. Thompson of Cincinnati 50.

The First National Bank of Gallipolis, after being approved by the United States Comptroller opened for business in the C. Henking Building, located on the site of the present Firstar Bank on Court Street, for annual rent of $125. In May of 1871 the institution moved to the Deletombe Building on the corner of Second Avenue and Court Street as larger quarters were needed to take care of the growing business. Again the demand for more space

*First National Bank November 20, 1897*

prompted another move in March of 1894 to the recently constructed building of Dr. John A. Lupton located on Second Avenue for an annual rent of $600.

The First National Bank signed a contract in March 1916 in the amount of $13,415.88 with John F. Danner to construct a three story brick structure at 352 Second Avenue to be used as their banking rooms, with rental office space and apartments on the upper floors. Womeldorff Thomas Company was given a contract for the plumbing and heating in the amount of $2,061.50 and H. E. Houck was awarded a contract to wire the structure. The Bank opened in the new offices January 1, 1917. In 1968, an Auto Bank was constructed at 349 Third Avenue with two drive thru lanes, and was enlarged to four lanes in 1978.

The First National Bank purchased the Vinton Banking Company in Vinton, Ohio during 1975. A new brick building with a drive thru was constructed on the corner where the Vinton Post Office now stands. The Vinton office was closed in October 1981 after the third armed robbery in 10 years.

Central Bancorporation, headquartered in Cincinnati, Ohio, and operated as the Central Trust Company N.A., purchased the First National Bank on October 5, 1979.

**PRESIDENTS OF THE FIRST NATIONAL BANK**

| | |
|---|---|
| Edward Deletombe | 1863-1891 |
| Horace R. Bradbury | 1892-1899 |
| John L. Vance, Jr. | 1899-1903 |
| Charles F. Stockhoff | 1903-1913 |
| Joe Moch | 1913-1967 |
| John F. Halliday | 1967-1978 |
| Clyde M. Ramsay | 1978-1979 |

# Little Kyger Grange No. 2074

The Little Kyger Grange No. 2074, located on Little Kyger Road, Addison, Ohio, was organized on April 17, 1916. The organizational meeting was held in the Union Hall school house with H.C. Skinner the officer attending. Some of the family community leaders attending were Shaver's, Kail's, Swisher's, Thomas', Briggs', Thompson's, Ralston's.

Below is a list of the first year Grange members as recorded in secretary's roll book: H.E. and Millie Shaver, Edmund and Nina Kail, Aaron and Laura Thomas, Hoarce and Mabel Kail, Jerry Shuler, Luna Thomas, Ida Thomas, George and Ora Kail, Grace Thomas, Oliver and Julia Shaver, Scott Mossman, George and Ann Briggs, Arthur and Louise Ralston, David and Carrie Briggs, Emmet and Mary Thompson, Deffie and Nora Swisher, George and Ruth Thompson, Erman and Vesta Swisher, Budd Swisher, James Swisher, James and Minnie Smyth, John M. and Myrtle Swisher, Don Grover, Melvin Coughenour, Burdella Kail, James Swisher, Ode and Sylvia Johnson, Gladys Caldwell, Oliver Roush, Chauncey Rife, Mina Roush, Ella Rothgeb, Lettie Swisher, Julia Swisher, John Scott, Savannah Russell, Ansel and Mary Hughes and Cora Schoonfeld. Many others joined during the seventy-five years existence of this order.

Soon the Grange decided it needed a home of its own and construction began. Emmet P. and Mary Thompson moved here from Meigs County where they were members at Star Grange. Thus the construction of the Little Kyger building was very similar to the Star Grange design. H.E. Shaver hauled lumber from Gallipolis with his horses and wagon. (I heard he also suffered from measles during that time). The chief construction foreman was Jim Hicks. The members were in such a hurry to move into the new building that they didn't wait for a stairway and used a ladder to climb to the second story. Some of the older matronly ladies had to have a little help-—much to the amusement of the men folks. The "fire escape" stairs was added a few years later and was built by Dan Kelly and sons. The new building was dedicated on May 26, 1917, with State Master Taber present.

*Little Kyger Grange Hall No. 2074*

Equipment for the hall was procured from various sources. The dining tables were donated by a store in Cheshire. Harlow Coughenour built and donated the stations and the altar table. Perry Bradbury constructed the hopefully "mouse—proof" box where the records, sashes, and other paraphernalia was stored. Erman and Vesta Swisher acquired a gas cook stove, and Vesta saved sales tax stamps to purchase metal chairs. George Thompson was responsible for securing gas heat for the building.

The Grange Hall was used for regular and special meetings and many other community activities for many years. Some of the events included showers for newly weds, short courses offered by agriculture teachers at Cheshire High School, 4-H club meetings, Farmer's Institutes with exhibits of farm produce, poster contests and local and state speakers, music by local bands, and scrumptious food where a fine time was enjoyed by all. The hall was always decorated with vines and berries by Ode Johnson, the chief decorator.

During the 1930's the grange sponsored a softball team who played in the county grange league. The members scoured the countryside for the best available ball players and initiated them in the four degrees of grange. (T.F. Burleson was one of those who was recruited and joined the grange about that time).

Many years of Juvenile Grange meetings were held downstairs.

Gladys Caldwell was one of the first Matrons and she held that position for many years. (One of her readings was "Cubby Bear" a story from the Comforter magazine). Some of the other Matrons were Georgia Burleson, Polly Thompson, Pauline Thompson, and Sophia Swisher.

Note: Since I, Polly Thompson, was a granger from the day I was born, the Grange has been a very important part of my life and I really miss the "Grange Glamorous Days". So many dedicated grangers kept the grange going for over 75 years that it would take many pages to write down all of their contributions. I would like to pay tribute to my sister, Georgia Burleson. She was always a Grange booster, filled many offices, and dearly loved the grange and the Little Kyger community.

By the way — the goat was kept in the small closet at the back of the hall. ???????

## Ohio Valley Laundry

The Ohio Valley laundry truck is being driven by Jake Brown who worked for the establishment for several years. With him are his daughter Mary, his son Charlie, and his father-in-law, Charles Saunders.

*Picture was taken about 1920. Submitted by Carol Robinson.*

## Old Dan Glassburn House

The five-room log cabin was probably built circa 1790. It is reported to be the oldest house in what is now Springfield Township, Gallia County, Ohio. Five frame rooms were added to the cabin later. It was the old Dan Glassburn Funeral Home. The large room with the bay was the funeral parlor. The log cabin had three rooms downstairs and two upstairs. There was an unfinished attic over the funeral parlor. The stairs went up from the windowless room, called the "dark room." The stairs were so narrow and the landing turns were so steep that large objects (furniture) had to be taken in through the attic window. The house had two unusual features - the middle board in the first stair landing slid out and revealed a space underneath where valuables could be hidden. The other feature was a little cabinet recessed into the chimney in the northwest downstairs rooms.

The kitchen had a recessed area (sunken into the wall) where the wall was joined onto the living room of the log cabin. This was used as a spice ("cupboard".

The house is presently located at the junction of State Route 554 and Fairview Road, on Section 34, Range 15. Daniel Glassburn owned land in Sections 28 and 29, also.

*Daniel Glassburn House, Bidwell, Ohio 1929*

*Daniel Glassburn House, Bidwell, Ohio 1993*

The old casket building still stands (a little sway-backed and leaning), on a rise southwest of the house. There is a cellar beneath the north section of the building

An article written by Dwight Wetherholt, which appeared in the Aril 15, 1966 issued of The Gallia Times, featuring Gallia County landmarks stated that the house was called the "Ben" Glassburn home. This was an error. It was the "Dan" Glassburn home. Ben owned land that joined the Dan Glassburn land. The article also stated that it "is the second house from Bidwell". This was an error also, it is the fourth house. "It has the most ancient appearance of any house in the county".

Morgan's Raiders were there July 23, 1863. The bulk of the forces stayed in the house overnight and it is reported that the women of the house cooked around the clock to provide the raiders with meals."

The book, Hardesty's History of Gallia County, 1882, provided the following information: "David Glassburn was born January 28, 1805 in Gallia County and was the first white child born in Springfield Township. His parents, John and Mary (Richardson ) Glassburn, were among the first settlers in Gallia County settling here in 1804. Their son, Daniel Glassburn was born June 24, 1837.

The book "David Glassburn, Virginia Pioneer, by Oma Richardson States that "Daniel Glassburn was in the undertaking business for fifty years and conducted 1,016 funerals. He died March 28, 1913.

It is possible that Dan's son, Melvin, owned the house and farm from the time of Dan's death until William Phillips purchased it. After William died in 1924, it reverted to his widow, Helen. After her death in 1925, it reverted to the Phillips' sons and grandchildren, William A., Charles R. (Ross) and Joseph (Joe) Phillips, and W. T. Hess (grandson) and Nellie Parks (granddaughter). Dan Glassburn owned land all the way to Heatley, now Bidwell, to Shade River Road, now Vale Road. Thomas and Zoie Butcher purchased the house and forty-three acre farm from the Phillips heirs.

There was a small building adjoining the cellar, called the "engine room". This room housed the Delco Pant that provided lights in the house and also powered the pump that pumped water from the spring into the kitchen. The pump was connected to the Delco Plant. There was also a sunken "pump house" beside the spring, that housed the pump. However, the Delco Plant was often "out of order", and when this occurred, there were no "electric lights" or water in the house. Kerosene lamps provided light and water was carried from the spring.

About 1949 or 1950, Buckeye Rural Electric came into the area. After that they had electricity!

There were eleven buildings on the farm in the 1940s and 1950s. Dan Glassburn had built a little house for his mother near the farm house. The Butchers used it as a "chicken house".

Edna Goodall and her daughter, Betty, lived with the Butchers in the 1940s and 1950s. Betty, her husband Charles Cantrell and their two daughters, Pearl and Mary also lived there. Pearl and Mary were born while the Cantrell's lived in the old house.

Thomas and Zoie Butcher sold sixteen acres to John and Pearl Denney in 1956.

After Thomas' death, Zoie sold the remaining land, house and buildings to Bertis (Thomas's half-sister) and her husband Virgil Halley in 1960. After Bertis and Virgil died, the house and farm reverted to their children, Linda Halley Criner, Diana Lintala and John Halley. They still own the farm and remaining buildings. They sold the log cabin to Ed Moore of Addison in the spring of 2001. He has torn down the frame structure of the house and is dismantling the five-room log cabin. He plans to reassemble the log cabin on his property on Addison Pike, Addison, Ohio. The house has been vacant since the Cantrells and Edna Goodall, Betty's mother, moved to Ewington, January 28, 1974. *Submitted by Betty Cantrell*

## Roach Electric

Founder - Chancey Hollis Roach - After marrying Ola (Miller) on 8/16/28, Hollis went to work at GE electric at 9th Avenue in Huntington, WV. He was the electrician involved in the building of the Gallipolis Locks and Dam. In early 1940, during the war and depression times he and his father, Charles Camden Roach, went to Texas and Washington to do electrical work.

In 1940, Hollis began the business of Roach Electric at the corner of Third Avenue and Spruce Street. His father, Charles, also worked there. Later they moved down the street into an office where the VFW parking lot now is and again a few more doors down the street into a building that also housed Tabor Flooring and Valley Bell Dairy.

In 1970, the business was moved for the last time. Virgil & Clem Trotter owned a house across the street. Upon their becoming ill they stated to John Trotter that the residence was to be sold to Hollis Roach. The new address was 123 Third Avenue.

*Roach Electric*

In 1948, Hollis partnered with Hambie (Abner) Pleasant and the business was changed to Roach & Pleasant Electric. Most people knew them by their nicknames, Lum & Abner.

Over the years there were several different family members and friends that worked at the business. His daughter, Doris worked in the office, but quit because of a fall injury; a nephew- Clinton Murphy; and friends Clarence Springer, Russell Bush, Herb McQuaid and others.

In 1952, Hollis's son, Richard (Dick) returned from the service and began working at the business. His wife, Clarabelle, worked in the office. Later on in years Hollis and Ab became ill. Hollis passed away 1/29/1974 and Abner became a sugar diabetic and had to have both legs amputated and also passed away a few years later.

Dick continued with the business. The name was changed back to Roach Electric. Dick has a son named Kevin who also grew up learning the business from his father and worked with him side by side serving the electrical needs of the community. Kevin also worked as a substitute postal carrier when not working with his father.

In 2001, Dick retired the business and the sign, Roach Electric, was taken down for the last time. Roach Electric has served the community of Gallipolis from 1936 to 2002 (66 years) with 4 generations of Roach men.

## U.S. Navy Warehouse

*This photo was taken Oct. 1944 during WW II in Gallipolis at the U.S. Navy Warehouse. This building was located on Sycamore St. between 3rd and 4th Ave. The building sat right by the railroad tracks. The gentlemen in the picture to the right of the doorway, is Samuel Jackson Tandy Walker. Mr. Walker was the father of Orva B., Etta Lorene, Marcella Ann, Mary Elizabeth, Jackson Tandy Jr. & Karen Linn Walker.*

# STORIES

## Burglar's Bungling Becomes Blood Bath

Over 100 years ago the front page headline of the January 31, 1902 *Gallipolis Tribune* read "Two New Faces In Hades". Two men from Athens, Ohio planned to rob Mary Priestly, the widow of James Priestley, who lived at 810 Second Avenue. They believed she kept a large amount of money in a basement safe. They made the mistake of confiding in a blacksmith in Athens by saying they would share the loot with him if he would make some safe cracking tools. The blacksmith did not like the idea so he contacted Sheriff Murphy of Athens County. Murphy had a conference with Sheriff McDaniel of Gallia County and agreed that blacksmith Swett should pretend to accept the burglars' offer and keep the officers advised of the date of the attempted robbery.

John Priestley, son of Henry Clay and Magdalene Morgan Priestley volunteered to dress as his Aunt Mary and occupy her favorite chair on that fateful night. While Mary Priestley, her sister and her maid hid on the second floor, the lead burglar was admitted by John disguised as his aunt. The thief was surprised to find he was dealing with a husky 28 year old man instead of a 70 year old woman. Officers came out from behind doors and the fire fight began.

When it was over the two robbers were dead and two officers were wounded, one seriously. As John was leaving the house to find a doctor, he was mistakenly fired upon but fortunately was not hit. He soon returned with Dr. L. C. Bean and Dr. J. B. Alcorn who cared for the wounded officers who eventually recovered from their wounds. This experience left its mark on John Priestley. Windows and doors were always locked day and night, the car was locked in the driveway and he kept two loaded guns on the bedpost.

Read more about this incident in the Friday, January 31, 1902 issue of the Gallipolis Tribune or the October 8, 1933 issue of the Columbus Sunday Star.

## Cholera Epidemic

Fate has not been kind to Gallia County, since Ohio became a State in 1803. Gallipolis was a little more than a decade old when the 19th Century began. Thirty-seven people died in the outbreak of Cholera in 1849. Although the epidemic was confined to an area of about only four miles. There were about 100 cases in Walnut and Harrison Townships. The first victim was William Clark, who died after being ill for about four hours. The deaths of his wife and daughter quickly followed. Local physicians were inexperienced and unable to cope with the horrible disease which rapidly spread.

William Martt of Walnut Township assisted in moving a family in Lawrence County. After returning home, he became desperately ill, but lived for more than a week. His friends and neighbors kindly assisted in his care. It was not until the disease spread to the families of those who had cared for him. That it was discovered to be Cholera of the most malignant type. Treating the disease was a Mr. Middlewarth, a Clay Township farmer. Although unskilled in Medicine, he had previously obtained a recipe from a physician in New Orleans, La. and being a skilled nurse, he volunteered and did good work in caring for the victims.

At one time, eight members of his family, including Mr. Middleswarth, lay dead in his home. Five of them were buried in one grave, since assistance could not be obtained to dig the sufficient number of graves. Due to the lack of coffins, many were buried without them. An excitement seldom witnessed in any community prevailed for some time. Many who had been exposed expected to die. Nothing of this kind had ever occurred before or has been experienced since in Gallia County.

## John Porter Yellow Fever

The only major disease epidemic that ever struck Gallia County and the Old French City of Gallipolis was in July of 1878. The towboat, John Porter, pushing 18 barges with a crew of 35 men, left New Orleans, La. Soon after departure, one of the firemen was stricken by Yellow Fever, followed by two others. All that were supposed to be afflicted were taken off at Vicksburg, Mississippi. But the epidemic broke out again and all patients were immediately sent ashore. Two young doctors came aboard at Cincinnati. By the time the boat reached Gallipolis, ten men were laid up with Yellow Fever.

Upon arrival at Gallipolis, the boat was quarantined. Seventeen deaths had occurred among those who were on the boat. When the John Porter left Gallipolis, headed upstream, her cylinder packing blew out and she drifted back down stream. This was soon repaired, and starting again, she broke her rocker arm and she came drifting back in a helpless condition. The Enos, Hill & Company's large foundry was put into action and a new shaft was forged for the boat. Then two or three of the crew died over night.

Captain Bickerstaff wired for money and one thousand dollars was wired for relief. As soon as some of the men received their money, they began deserting until none were left except the helpless ones who could not get away. The Porter lay here for some time guarded both day and night. After having been disinfected, many who thought there was no danger went aboard the boat. In a short time a number of these people were stricken with Yellow Fever.

During the reign of terror, lasting only a few weeks, there was an almost a total suspension of business. Hotels were closed, hundreds fled town and streets were almost deserted. Fires of coal tar were burned day and night at the corners of all principal streets and at each of the roads entering town. All people from the affected regions had to be fumigated. Happily, several brisk frosts occurred early which broke the epidemic.

About the middle of September with the Porter and her barges anchored two or three miles below Gallipolis, there was a heavy rise and drift in the river breaking loose the Porter's barges. The Porter, now being declared free of Yellow Fever obtained a new crew and started down the river securing all but three.

Thus ended the first and only visitation of the Yellow Fever to Gallipolis and it will long be remembered. Thirty-five local citizens lost their life in the terrible epidemic. One of these was Richard Blazer, a Captain in the Union Army during the Civil

War. Captain Blazer was in The 91st Ohio Volunteer Infantry, and later in the conflict headed The Scouts," a guerilla group, organized to capture Colonel John Singleton Mosby and his Confederate Partisan Rangers. It cost the town and county thousands of dollars carried away almost entire from some of the most respected families and for a period of about six weeks put a stop to all business.

# Silver Bridge Disaster

Tragedy struck the Gallipolis-Point Pleasant area just before Christmas in December 1967 when the Silver Bridge connecting Point Pleasant, WV. and Kanauga, OH, collapsed. The bridge was named the Silver Bridge because it was the first, and in the end, the only bridge in the area, painted with aluminum paint.

At approximately 4:58 p.m., Friday December 15, 1967, the bridge spanning the Ohio River between Point Pleasant, WV and Kanauga, Ohio collapsed killing 46 people. Bodies of two people were never recovered. The evening rush hour travelers had been going about their daily lives preparing for the Christmas holiday when the bridge collapsed beneath them.

*Silver Bridge, viewed from Ohio side of the river*

*Piers after collapse of bridge*

*Salvage operation*

Following the collapse, all Emergency units in Gallia and Meigs counties in Ohio and Mason County in West Virginia, were mobilized, along with Fire, County Sheriffs' Departments, and State Police. Hospitals on both sides of the Ohio River were placed on High Alert status. Temporary morgues were set up in local churches. The air was filled with sirens and traffic was heavy on all routes leading to the scene of the disaster.

Constructed in 1928, the bridge was an" eye-bar" suspension bridge, meaning that instead of wire cables like those found on the Golden Gate Bridge, the Silver Bridge used steel eye-bars which supported the deck or road bed of the bridge. An eye-bar resembles for all purposes and intent a dog bone with a hole or an "eye" in each end. These eye-bars rain in pairs, one on each side of the bridge, linked by massive pins.

In months following the collapse pieces of the bridge were recovered and laid out like a massive jigsaw puzzle in a field south of Point Pleasant. All but the deck or road bed were recovered. Final analysis conducted by the U.S. Department of Transportation ruled that failure of eye-bar No. 13, on the upriver or north side of the bridge had failed causing the down river or south side eye-bar chain to drop below the road bed. The down river or south eye-bar chain was unable to support the weight of the entire structure causing an immediate and complete failure of the span.

There were two twin structures of a similar type to the Silver Bridge ; one up the Ohio River at St. Mary's. WV and the other in Brazil, South America. The St. Mary's span was immediately closed, demolished and replaced by a new bridge.

In December 1969, two years to the day, a new bridge was completed and opened just south of Point Pleasant U.S. Route 35, was relocated to the south side of the Kanawha River. Former U.S. Route 35 on the north side of the Kanawha river, was redesignated WV State Route 62.

## Songs Of The Silver Bridge Disaster
### By Ivan Tribe

The article Discography appeared as follows:

1. The Collapse of the Silver Bridge by Billy Hill, Jr. This song was written December 15, 1967 and unrecorded.

2. The Silver Bridge Disaster by Ray Anderson, Ra Mac Music. This song written and recorded December 17, 1967 along with the assistance of the Roar Family.

3. Why Did It Happen? - The Silver Bridge Disaster by Ray Anderson. This was written and recorded ca 1968 by Ray Anderson.

4. The Great Silver Bridge by M. D. Ralph, recorded ca. 1968 by Charles Alexander and The Carolina Five, Mohawk

5. The Fate of the Silver Bridge by Cecil Pigote recorded ca. 1968-1969 Cecil Pigote, Silver Star

6. The Day the Silver Bridge Went Down by Mike Watson written by M.ike Watso ca. fall 1968 and unrecorded. (Tape copy by the Sunday Creek String Band, April 1969).

7. Silver Bridge History by Stan Lane, Tan-Lan Music BMI, recorded ca. 1968 by Jim Stout, GO-T203 Saddle 105.

8. Tragedy of the Silver Bridge by Wayne and Bobby Barnette, Jimmy Skinner Music, BMI recorded ca. 1968 by Barnette Brothers.

9. When the Silver Bridge Went Down by Opal Skaggs, Jacci Music, BMI, recorded ca. 1969 by Jim Wayne, Pacer

10. Silver Bridge Disaster (unknown) recorded ca. 1968 by The Three J's (local)

11. Silver Bridge Disaster (by Oleta Singleton) poem printed in the West Virginia Hillbilly, December 7, 1968

12. The Silver Bridge (by Howard M. Stocksdale, ASCAP, copyright by the author, 1974, unrecorded except for demo record by Howard M. Stocksdale and Kris Arden.

13. The Silver Bridge (by Buddy Starcher) recorded on Bear Family (formerly CMH) records and currently unreleased (tape copy provided through the courtesy of Richard Weize).

14. The Silver Bridge (by Varney, Horn and Marcus, Fayette Music BMI) recorded ca. 1968 by Lowell Varney and Jim Horn,

15. Tragedy of the Silver Bridge (by John W. and Eva White) Cedarwood Publishing Company, BMI) recorded ca. 1968 by Sunshine Twins, Sunshine.

16. A Silver Bridge song was recorded by Steve Chapman - this information was provided by Pearl Cantrell.

A program of Silver Bridge songs for the thirtieth anniversary of The Silver Bridge Disaster was done in December 1997 by Deanna and Ivan Tribe on their Hornpipe and Fugue program on WOUB radio, Athens, Ohio. Pearl Cantrell was their guest on the program and assisted the Tribes with the program. *Information submitted by Betty Cantrell*

# Welsh Immigrants

This story of some Welsh immigrants is a fascinating one. Imagine, if you can, selling everything you had to go to a strange and sometimes dangerous country to live. But, times were so bad that the Welsh people of the country of Wales in the British Isles, were going hungry and had little to look forward to except their religion. There were cathedrals in the large towns, but in the countryside, it was the small chapels that were filed by believing countrymen. These were the people who saved to come to this country for a better life. Anything seemed better than what they had.

From Wales came Ann Richards, Age 72. She brought with her daughters Nannie, Kathryn and Margaret and son Thomas Richards. They were all married and two had children. Evan Rees and Nannie found land settled near the Tyn Rhos Church. In fact, the Methodist Camp is on that same property. They all prospered and raised large families. Tyn Rhos Church and cemetery are known for their beautiful surroundings and view.

Evan and Nannie Rees are my great, great grandparents. They came from Talybont, Wales, which is in the central part of Wales.

My mother's maternal grandfather was also named Rees and came from southern Wales. Jane Daniels migrated to Licking County in the mid 1800s. Here she met and married John Aaron Rees. They came to Gallia County about 1900. Each family had several children who became school teachers, merchants and preachers. *Submitted by Bertha Elizabeth E. "Bess" Grace Davis*

*Tyn Rhos Church*

*City Park during 1937 flood*

**Ponn Covered Bridge near Ewington**

# Gallia County Churches

*Downtown, Gallipolis, Ohio*

*Cheshire Methodist Church*

# St. Louis Catholic Church

(From work documented by Harriet Davison in a book written for St. Louis Diamond Jubilee 1908 - 1983, and church history collected for the years 1980 -2002, available at the Gallia County Historical Society or St. Louis Catholic Church)

The Catholic Church began in Gallipolis with its founding fathers in 1790. In the midst of the French Revolution, the Scioto Company, an American Land Company, promised the unhappy Frenchmen a heaven on earth in America. The founders of the Colony of Gallipolis represented a cross section of French society at the outbreak of the Revolution. Besides professional men and well-to-do merchants of the middle class, together with some peasants and laborers, their ranks included noblemen who belonged to some of the leading families of France.

Following a landing at Alexandria, Virginia, the French 500 learned that the title to their lands was invalid. The indignant colonists set about trying to get the Scioto Company to make restitution. They petitioned President Washington and he assured them of the protection of the laws of the General Government of the United States. A contract was finally agreed to with the Scioto Company and most of the 500 began the journey overland to their new home. Instead of a city on the banks of the beautiful Ohio, they found a stockade with 80 log cabins. They began to suffer from the moment of landing but managed a prayer service and then a dance on the first night in Gallipolis.

After hearing plans of fellow Frenchmen leaving for Gallipolis, the Marquis Marnesia and d'Epremesnil, purchased 10,000 acres from the Scioto Company with a view of providing a refuge for the French Royalists in America. The colonists were required to bring letters from their Pastors stating that they were people who practiced their religion. D'Epremesnil suggested to Rome that a Bishop be appointed for Gallipolis. He also planned a charity hospital under the charge of the Lazarists Sisters to minister to sick colonists and also suggested a charity committee to provide for the needy. Provisions were also made to promote the intellectual life of the colony. A University was to be established as well as an Academy modeled after the Famous French institutions. The Press was to be represented by a newspaper printed in French and English.

The appointed Bishop, one Abbe Baisnautier (Boisnantier), a Canon of St. Denis in Paris, may have been recalled when Pope Pius VI learned of the great fraud perpetrated on the colonists. When Marnesia and his followers learned that Abbe Baisnautier would not be permitted to become the Bishop of Gallipolis, they again petitioned Rome that Father Peter Joseph Didier (Didur), a Benedictine Monk, be appointed Bishop of the new Colony. Although Rome did not appoint Father Didier Bishop, he was made the Spiritual Superior with the title of "Vicar General Spiritualibus." Father Didier was under the jurisdiction of Bishop Carroll of Baltimore. It is said that he was idealistic and impetuous and tried to get the colonists to practice their religion. He probably stayed in Gallipolis only until the summer of 1791, when he was obliged to report to Baltimore. He is known to have been in St. Louis, Mo. in 1794 and was believed to have died there. This fact has been refuted by Andrew Truslow, a descendant of one of the original French 500. Truslow reported that Didier accompanied his ancestor to New Orleans where they are both buried in the Cathedral of St. Louis.

After Father Didier left, there was no organized Catholic Religion in the colony for a number of years. By 1808, a Father Badin visited the community for a second time and reported he found a spark of Faith in the much declined settlement. He assured the Bishop that there were many Irish Catholic families in the vicinity.

In 1818 Father La Font arrived in Gallipolis and finding no church, made an effort to build one; but failed through want of support. However, he did teach school and ministered to the people for about two years, then left for New Orleans. By 1848, Bishop Purcell of Cincinnati visited and reported a feeling of sadness because it seemed God had forsaken Gallipolis. He said there was no facility there for offering Mass in a town where all were once, at least, baptized Catholics. He began planning to purchase land for a new church.

Bishop Purcell bought lot #43 on Grape Street. The property was purchased from J. G. (Jane) Devacht in 1852 for $350. Mrs. Devacht donated $50 toward the purchase. In 1854, Rev. David J. Kelly of Minerton (near Wilksville), wrote to Bishop Purcell that Father John Christopher Albrinck was willing to take charge of Gallipolis.

Following his appointment, he began plans for the church. It took until September 1856 to begin construction, which they hoped would be finished by winter and cost a little over a thousand dollars. The parish was dedicated by Bishop Purcell in 1858. Although enthusiasm was great, the few Catholics in Gallipolis could not support a Pastor, so priests would come from Pomeroy and neighboring parishes when they could. Some of these priests were Father B. Maria Gells, Father John Kallenberg, Father Jesseng, Father Loedig, Father Kramer, Father Quirk, Father Dorsey and Father Hartney. Rev. Kelly most likely served here as a missionary priest as well.

*Fr. John Albrinck*

St. Louis Parish was a part of the Diocese of Cincinnati from 1821 to 1868, when the Diocese of Columbus was formed. It remained in the Columbus Diocese until the Diocese of Steubenville was carved along the Ohio River from Steubenville to Ironton in 1945.

The first resident priest was Father Leonard Patrick McKiernan. He was appointed in 1872 and remained for about two years. During his tenure the Church acquired Mound Hill Cemetery. Unsuccessful in developing it as a Catholic Cemetery, called Mount Washington Cemetery, Father McKiernan sold it to the city for $2,900.00. When Father McKiernan left, the parish was without a pastor for about four years. Priests from Minerton, Athens and Jackson served during this time. Some of them were: Father W. T. D'Arcy, Father Cambell, Father M. M. A. Hartnedy, and Father Louis Grimmer.

Bishop Watterson of Columbus appointed Father John B. Gamber pastor on May 10, 1878. Since there was no Rectory, he built an addition 20 x 25 feet connected to the Church by a heavy door connected to his parlor. There were only about fourteen families in the parish in 1878. They agreed to pay him a salary of about $30 a month. This amount was to be raised by contributions, festivals, raffles, suppers, etc. The Penny Collections were to be used for gas, coal, candles, Mass wine, and other necessities. He loaned the parish $600 of his own money to pay off back debts and costs of the new addition. He hired a teacher and held school from June 1878 until June 1879 at a cost of $120. Despite their best efforts the parishioners could not raise enough money to support their priest and he had to move on. They were without a spiritual leader from 1882-1888.

In 1888, Bishop Watterson of Columbus sent Father J. B. Qeink to St. Louis Parish. Father Oeink built a small Rectory, gathered a few children and started a school.

He stayed about four years and when he departed the little school was abandoned. From 1892 -1902 the people were without a resident priest again. They were served by Father James M. McCann and Father D. Edward Meara who came from Minerton when they could. Minerton, a once flourishing mining town between Vinton and Wilkesville is abandoned today. The church of St. Mary located there, burned down about 1978, its cemetery overgrown and neglected. Father J. B. Mattingly, Athens, and Father Jon Schneider, Pomeroy also served during this period.

Father Lucius J. Kessler from Minerton was appointed by Bishop Moeller of Columbus to serve St. Louis in 1902. He made the church on Grape street do until 1907. The members of the church petitioned Bishop James H. Hartley of Columbus for permission to build a new church. Land was purchased at Fourth and State Streets in 1907. The church and rectory were built at the same time at a cost of $12,000. The church was dedicated May 16, 1908.

In 1915 Father Kessler was replaced by Father John J. Murphy. Under his watch Father Frederick W. Burkhart, a native son of Gallipolis was ordained into the priesthood. Father George F. Gressel followed Father Murphy in 1917. The walls of the church were frescoed at this time. He was transferred to Bridgeport

*Fr. Lucius Kessler*

in 1922 and was replaced by Father Nugent who stayed for one year. Father William F. Connolly was appointed in 1923.

During Connolly's stay a fire destroyed the Altar and Sanctuary on April 15, 1926.

Flames were leaping out of the Rose Window above the Altar when first discovered about 1:30 p.m. Walls and ceilings were damaged by smoke and heat. The fire was later discovered to have started in the basement beneath the Altar. Many people helped restore the church, which was ready for use by Christmas. The church was furnished with three new white altars, murals by J. F. Degering of Troy, N.Y., and new paint for the walls.

In 1928 Father William G. Dowd was appointed to St. Louis. During his service many improvements were made to the church foundation including sidewalks on Fourth and State Streets. He was followed by Father John Dunn in 1931 who retired within the year due to poor health. One Father Delaux and several other priests substituted during Father's illness. Then on May 21, 1932,

Father Charles B. Ryan came and remained for thirteen years. He made improvements to the church and rectory. The Sisters of Divine Providence came from Pomeroy each week to teach the children. Father Ryan went to Barnesville, Ohio and died in Steubenville, Ohio. Father V. G. Schiele was appointed pastor in August 1945. It was during his term that the Diocese of Steubenville was formed with Bishop John King Mussio at its Shepherd.

Father Adolph Golubiewski came to Gallipolis in 1950. His was a late vocation to the Priesthood. St. Louis was his first and only parish. He served here for thirty years. Under Father "G" a council of the Knights of Columbus was formed. They helped pay for his weekly radio program. At this time there were thirty families in the parish. He made many improvements in the church and rectory. In 1952 he bought the Roller Rink from Mr. Wilson Rusk, improved the building and opened it for skating.

On December 18, 1954, a second fire started in the basement of the church under the altar. The altar and sanctuary were destroyed, while the remainder of the church was badly damaged from smoke and water. Parishioners attended Mass at the Gallipolis State Institute until Easter while the church was being renovated. A seven-foot Crucifix, a replica of the famous bleeding Christ of Limpias Crucifix in Italy, was donated by the Knights of Columbus, for the wall above the main altar. Between 1956 and 1957, Father added a grammar school to the Roller Rink. The addition was built with help of parishioners at a cost of $43,000. But, because he could not obtain Sisters to teach, school was never held there. It was used for catechism classes and rented for a Head Start Program Also during his tenure twenty-four acres on Rt. 141 were given to the church by James and Harriet Davison to be used as a cemetery. The front acres became St. Louis Cemetery and the top of the hill was developed into a picnic and recreation area for the parish. In 1982 all but about three acres used for the cemetery were transferred back to the Davisons.

Father oversaw the construction of a Catholic High School at Cheshire in 1963. It functioned for about two years but was discontinued due to the small number of pupils who attended. The school was later sold, to be used as the Guiding Hand School. By 1968, Father remodeled the church for the fourth time. He had eight new windows designed and installed. Three black and white marble altars were purchased for the Sanctuary. An air conditioning unit, the gift of Mr. and Mrs. Vance Johnson was added for the comfort of the parishioners. Father Golubiewski retired in February 1980. Father moved to Sebastian, Florida where he died on January 6, 1991.

Father William R. Myers was appointed Pastor of St. Louis Church on March 7, 1980. The parishioners were reinvigorated by the new, young and enthusiastic priest. With the guidance of Father Myers, and following long and arduous meetings of the Parish Council, it was decided that the church should not be moved. Plans were initiated to renovate the church. Exterior work included a new roof, new gutters and downspouts. Brick surfaces were sandblasted and tuckpointed then waterproofed, metal and wood surfaces painted and caulked and the foundation coated with hydrocrite. The rectory was treated in the same manner. A new roof was placed on the Head Start Building (former roller rink). Parishioners cleaned and painted the interior of the rectory, adding new wiring, drapes and appliances for their new priest. In 1981 the pine trees in front of the rectory were removed. New landscaping was added with the placement of the Statue of Our Lady of Fatima, formerly located at the rear of the Head Start Building, as the centerpiece. Among many new programs at the church, a local chapter of Ohio Right to Life was established and organized in January 1981.

Bible Schools and Youth Retreats were begun with the assistance of the Franciscan Sisters of Christian Charity of Manitowac, WI who spent six weeks in our area each summer from 1981 through 1984. Soon, the Sisters moved here to serve the parishes of Meigs, Gallia and Mason. Their tenure lasted from 1981 until 1991. The sisters who served as pastoral ministers were: Sr. Judy Norwick (1984 -1991), Sr. Romana Klaubauf (84 -85), Sr. Lynne Marie Simonich (84-8 5), Sr. Mary Arnoldussen (85 - 87), Sr. Jean Kaiser (87-88) and Sr. June Smith (87 - 91).

Interior renovation of the church began in the fall of 1981. The Tabernacle was moved to the side altar and the statues of Mary and Joseph were grouped together over the left altar. The organ was moved to the choir loft where plexiglass and wood railings were added. The confessional was moved to the former infants room. Bronze and glass exterior doors replaced aluminum doors and new doors separating the church from the vestibule were added. The work was completed by Thanksgiving.

The Parish Diamond Jubilee was celebrated in August of 1983 with Mass and festivities concluded by the dedication of the renovated church by Bishop Albert Ottenweller and visiting clergy.

In 1985 a Verdin Alpha Bell System was installed in the Church Bell Tower.

Father Timothy Davison, native son of the parish was ordained a priest for the Diocese of Tulsa, OK. St. Louis Council #3335, Knights of Columbus was reactivated in July of 1989.

In 1990, for the celebration of the Bicentennial of the founding of the city of Gallipolis, and to celebrate 200 years of Catholic Heritage, the interior of the church was repainted. The church participated fully with the city during this celebration. Many events marked this special time in our history. A homecoming concert was presented using the new piano donated by Mr. and Mrs. Vance Johnson.

On October 3, 1990 Fr. William R. Myers was named Prelate of Honor with the title of "Very Reverend Monsignor' by His Holiness, Pope John Paul II. From August 1991 until August 1993, Brother John Vyszenski, Brother of the Immaculate Heart of the Diocese of Steubenville, served as Pastoral Minister at St. Louis.

In 1992, the church celebrated the Quincentennial of Christopher Columbus with a Feast of St. Louis Concert attended by Bishop Gilbert I. Sheldon 3rd Bishop of Steubenville. During this year, the parish signed a purchase agreement to buy the Eachus property at 85 State Street.

Between 1995 and 1998, a statue of St. Francis of Assisi, placed in the lawn behind the rectory, was dedicated in memory of Ken Boster, a van was purchased for use by the parish, a library was established in memory of Emil Janko, and the rectory was featured on the Holiday Home Tour of Gallipolis. A handicapped accessible ramp was constructed at the side of the church. An electronic pipe organ, purchased through the generosity of parish members, replaced the old organ. In 1996, the parish began celebrating the Feast of St. Louis with a spaghetti dinner and festivities, which take place on the last Saturday of the month of August each year.

The year 1999 saw the universal Catholic Church celebrated a Jubilee Year. One of our own young parishioners, Steven Cornett, published a "Millennium Moment" newsletter for the parish. The St. Louis women began a ministry of serving lunch to high school students on Thursdays, the program expanded with the Methodist church taking on another day of the week using our church facility as a base due to its close location to the school. The Presbyterians also offered lunch one day a week from their church, a real display of ecumenical spirit. The interior of the church was repainted, pews stained and refinished, and new carpet installed. The Tabernacle was placed on a new alter in the center under the crucifix.

The Jubilee of the Year 2000 was celebrated throughout the Catholic World with great joy as the Catholic Faithful responded to the request of the Holy Father, John Paul

The people of St. Louis Church began this special year with a dinner for the Parish on the Feast of St. Nicholas. For the entire year, official Jubilee celebration banners hung from the Church bell tower. The Marian stained glass windows of the church were cleaned and new memorial windows were installed in the windows of the sacristy and in other desired places in the church. Lenten fish fries were established and opened to the public. The parish held a mission as well as Forty Hours devotion and many parishioners attended Pilgrimage Visitations throughout the year. The Parish Homecoming Concert, held in September, was attended by the Most Reverend Gilbert Sheldon, Bishop of Steubenville. During this year, the Stebbins property, directly behind the church, was purchased. This addition to the property will allow for future expansion of church facilities.

The solemn closing of the Jubilee Year was celebrated with a Parish Epiphany Dinner in December of 2001. A memorial marker was installed at St. Louis Cemetery to honor the unknown buried there who were residents of the Ohio Home of the Epileptics, later known as the Gallipolis State Institute and Gallipolis Developmental Center. Msgr. Myers serves as Catholic Chaplin to the residents of this facility.

In March, 2002, the official Parish Sesquicentennial (1852 - 2002) Logo, to be displayed during the year, was unveiled. The logo was designed by parishioner Timothy Lynch. A Parish Mission was held. A new Parish Directory, which includes the new history including the years 1980 - 2002 was developed and published. The highlight of the Celebration was the Parish Festival for the Feast of St. Louis with Pontifical Vespers and reception on Sunday, August 25~. During this year, a safety and security system was installed in the parish facilities to provide first alert in case of fire or theft. Inspired by the year of celebration and recommitment of the church, the youth of the parish reorganized their numbers and named themselves the Y.A.C.H.T. Club. (Acronym meaning - Young Adult Catholics Hanging Together). They turned the garage attic behind the rectory into "Louie's Lighthouse" for their meetings.

# St. Louis Catholic Church History 1980-2002
## The Franciscan Sisters

Soon after arriving on March 7, 1980, Fr. Bill Myers met Fr. Mike Ellifritz, Pastor of Sts. Peter and Paul, Wellston. In the spring of that year, Fr. Mike offered the possibility of a Bible School and Petting Zoo for the students of St. Louis to take place in June that would be provided by the Franciscan Sisters of Christian Charity who were teaching at Sts. Peter and Paul Elementary School. The Bible School was a resounding success and the parishioners of St. Louis desired that it continue the following year. The summer of 1981 began a wonderful relationship with the Franciscan Sisters of Manitowac, Wisconsin. It was also the beginning of the 'infamous' "MGM Diocese -the Catholic parishes of Meigs, Gallia and Mason Counties working together to support the presence of Religious Sisters living in our area for a month during the Summer in order to have a Bible School in each parish. The students shared retreat experiences, trips to Kings Island and other parish events during those summers until 1984. Fr. Tony Giannamore, Pastor of Sacred Heart in Pomeroy, along with Sr. Janet Rectenwald who was working in Pastoral Ministry there, Fr. Bill Myers, Pastor of St. Louis in Gallia County and Fr. Raymond Jablinski, Pastor of Sacred Heart in Mason County in Point Pleasant, West Virginia were happy to combine their efforts, finances and resources to enable this project to succeed.

In the Fall of 1984, another phase of parish life would begin that was to have a lasting impact. An idea initiated by Fr. Raymond Jablinski and agreed upon by Fr. Bill Myers, the Franciscan Sisters were invited to establish a convent in the area and work throughout the year with youth, parish families and ecumenical endeavors. The convent was located in a house owned by Sacred Heart Church, Point Pleasant and opened in September of 1984 with many Sisters from area convents in Wellston, Woodsfield, Cambridge and Zanesville, all in Ohio, joining for Mass and dinner to celebrate this new beginning in our area. The three Sisters assigned to us were Sr. Romana Klaubauf, Sr. Judy Norwick and Sr. Lynne Marie Simonich. Our euphoria was short-lived and soon it was necessary for the Sisters to move. After searching for a short time, Mr. Kenneth Boster, a local landlord of many properties in Gallia County approached Fr. Bill about the possibility of the Sisters living in a garage apartment behind his home on Second Avenue in Gallipolis. The Sisters fell in love with the place and moved in early June of 1985. Both Sr. Romana and St. Lynne Marie were reassigned in the summer of 1985 and replaced by only Sr. Mary Arnoldussen. Sr Jean Kaiser arrived in 1987 and began the Franciscan Outreach Center, which would evolve into the Community Outreach Center operated by Sue Johnson and others. Also in 1987, Sr. June Smith would replace Sr. Mary and remain with us until the summer of 1991 when she and Sr. Judy Norwick would close the convent at 626 1/2 Second Avenue. The Sisters who served as pastoral ministers were: Sr. Judy Norwick (1984-1991); Sr. Romana Klaubauf(1984-1985); Sr. Lynne Marie Simonich (1984-1985); Sr. Mary Arnoldussen (1985-1987); Sr. Jean Kaiser (1987-1988); and Sr. June Smith (1987-1991).

From August 1991 until August of 1993, Brother John Vyszenski, Brother of the Immaculate Heart of Mary of the Diocese of Steubenville, served as Pastoral Minister at St. Louis Church. Brother John undertook many of the tasks as did the Sisters and also became good friends with Maym and Ken Boster, our Parish apartment landlord. Maym was a member of St. Peter's Episcopal Church and died on May 8, 1991. Ken became a Catholic before he died on September 28, 1994. A St. Francis Memorial honors Maym at the Episcopal Church and another St. Francis Memorial honors Ken at St. Louis Church. As an important footnote to the story, it was Virginia "Ginny" Gamroth, granddaughter of Maym and Ken Boster, who at the age of 18 on July 4~ of 1980 paid a visit to Fr. Bill at St. Louis Rectory, a simple gesture of a teenager visiting from California which resulted in a wonderful and lasting friendship for all concerned.

## Jubilees And Anniversaries
## 75th Diamond Jubilee

Our Parish Diamond Jubilee was celebrated Thursday, August 25th through Sunday August 28th 1983. Approximately 15 priests gathered for Mass at 6:30 p,m. on Thursday, August 25, Patronal Feast of St. Louis, followed by dinner in the Church Hall.

An Open House took place on Friday, August 26th for the community from 4-6 p.m.

Tours of the Church and the rectory, pictures, movies, refreshments and music by the French Chorale were featured. The Parish Dinner at the Holiday Inn took place on Saturday August 27th at 7:00 p.m. Dedication of the renovated Church took place on Sunday, August 28th at 5:00 p.m. with Bishop Albert Ottenweller and visiting clergy. It was a beautiful afternoon for the procession from the Gallipolis City Park to the Church.

A Dedication Ceremony and Benediction in Church was followed by a reception in the hall.

## Bicentennial Of Gallipolis (1790-1990) "Two Hundred Years Of Catholic Heritage"

The Community was bursting with pride on the occasion of the Bicentennial of Gallipolis (1790-1990), especially from July 4-October 21. Since the "French 500" consisted primarily of Roman Catholics, it was only fitting that St. Louis Church join in the festivities with great gusto. Our present Parish Flag was designed for the occasion. The tri-colors French Blue, White and Spanish Yellow were selected to replicate the colors and elements of the French Flag as it looked prior to the French Revolution. The Crown, Cross and Fleur-de-Leis are placed on a white panel to represent our Patron Saint Louis, the Catholic Faith and the Trinity. Special banners were made for the Church and displayed

Bicentennial Blessing of "La Premiere View"

on trumpets with the same symbols. The 4th of July Parish parade float featured students dressed as King Saint Louis IX, squires and pages; a flatbed band; Catholic Women's Club Officers; and the Knights of Columbus Color Guard. A Parish Concert was held on Sunday, August 19th at 3:00 p.m. in the Church with parishioners, young and old, sharing their vocal and musical talents. Bishop Ottenweller was guest for the 10:00 a.m. Mass and the Concert which included selections of sacred and secular music. St. Louis Church was also included on the Bicentennial Homes Tour, the weekend of September 15th -16. Father Bill was present for an explanation of Liturgical Art and other externals within the Church. On Saturday October 20th, a gala Costume Ball was enjoyed by nearly 800 people aboard the West Virginia Belle, which cruised the Ohio River from 8:00 p.m. to Midnight. Aboard were local Parish dignitaries in original 1790's costume as worn by priests and nuns of the time. Sr. Judy Norwick dressed as Sr. Elizabeth Ann Seton and Sr. June Smith dressed as Sr. Frances Cabrini wore original Religious Habits; Msgr. Bill Myers (Bishop Benedict Flaget); Fr. James Boehm, current Editor of the Steubenville Register (Fr. Junipero Serra); and Mr. John Edelmann (Fr. Peter Joseph Didier) likewise wore appropriate clerical attire for their roles.

The Bicentennial Parade of Saturday, October 20th featured many of the same students as were on the Parish Float for July 4th• The Parish Theme for the Bicentennial, "Celebrating Two Hundred Years of Catholic Heritage", was concluded with a Mass of Thanksgiving in the City Park on Sunday, October 21st, 1990 at 10:00 a.m. A procession of parishioners, altar servers, and Msgr Bill began from the St. Louis Church to the City Park where Mass was celebrated under a tent. Refreshments were served following the celebration and a small contingent proceeded to bless the Bicentennial Statue "La Premiere View" and privately rename it "The Holy Family."

## Quincentennial Of Christopher Columbus

The Quincentennial of Christopher Columbus was celebrated at St. Louis Church on Sunday, August 23rd at 4:00 p.m. with Bishop Albert Ottenweller, the Knights of Columbus Council p3335 and parishioners in attendance. A special Cross marking 500 years of Evangelization was presented by the Bishop to the Knights, this cross was taken to other Councils throughout the diocese to mark this 500th Anniversary of the discovery of America.

## Jubilee Of The Year 2000

```
St. Louis Church, Gallipolis, Ohio
Celebrates the Jubilee Year

Sunday, December 5, 1999              Saturday, August 26, 2000
Family St. Nicholas Banquet           Parish Festival and Spaghetti Dinner

Sunday, February 13, 2000             Sunday, September, 17, 2000
World Marriage Day - Anniversary Party Homecoming Music Concert

Saturday - Thursday, April 1 - 6, 2000 October 2000
Parish Mission                        Knights of Columbus Golf Tournament

Friday - Sunday, May 19 - 21, 2000    Sunday, October 29, 2000
Forty Hours Devotion                  All Saints Celebration Picnic

Sunday, June 25, 2000                 December 2000
Ecumenical Picnic                     Children's CCD Christmas Party

July 2000                             Sunday, January 7, 2001
Annual Kings Island Outing            Jubilee Year Concludes with Epiphany
                                      Celebration
```

The Jubilee of the Year 2000 was celebrated throughout the Catholic World with great joy as the Catholic Faithful responded to the request of the Holy Father, John Paul II, to more intently focus on the mystery of our redemption, a special "Season of Grace" during which we were invited to be converted and sanctified. The people of St. Louis Church began this special year with a festive dinner for the Parish on the Feast of St. Nicholas at the University of Rio Grande, a time devoted to the children's Christmas Party. The other events marking this Holy Year by the Parish included the blessing, anointing and decoration of our main entrance to the Church as the theme "Open Wide the Doors to Christ" was echoed throughout the world.

A Valentine's Day Dinner in honor of World Marriage Day, a Lenten Parish Mission, Forty Hours Eucharistic Devotions in May, the St. Louis Parish Festival in August and Pilgrimage Visitations throughout the year were all part of our Parish observance. A Holy Year Pilgrimage to Lourdes, Assisi, and Rome took place in October. The conclusion of the Jubilee 2000 Year was again celebrated with a special dinner at Rio Grande on the occasion of the Solemnity of the Epiphany on January 7th, 2001.

## Parish Sesquicentennial Celebration 1852-2002

The Parish Sesquicentennial Celebration began with a logo design contest in March of 2001. Mr. Timothy Lynch won the contest with adaptations made by Josette Baker, Saundra Koby and Msgr. Myers. A original ceramic replica of the Church built in 1908 was designed and made available for sale to the parishioners, a Parish Mission was held in March, a new Parish Photo Directory was published, a display of Catholic Art and History at the Gallia County Historical Society and items were gathered for placement of a time capsule.

The highlight of the Celebration was the Parish Festival on Saturday, August 24th and Pontifical Vespers and reception on Sunday, August 25th, the Parish Patronal Feast of St. Louis.

## Tributes And Anniversaries Of Our Pastor

Special Parish Celebrations included celebrations honoring Msgr. William R. Myers 20th Anniversary of Priesthood, May 17th, 1989; 10th Anniversary as Pastor of St. Louis Church on March 7, 1990; Appointment Vicar Forane or Dean of Immaculate Conception Deanery in 1989; Appointment Prelate of Honor with title of "Very Reverend Monsignor" on October 3rd, 1990; 25th Anniversary of Ordination to the Priesthood on May 17, 1994 and 20th Anniversary as Pastor of St. Louis Church on March 7, 2000.

## St. Louis Church Historical Milestones

**1980 March 7** Father William R. Myers arrives as new Pastor of St. Louis Church

**1985 January 6** Verdin Alpha Bell System installed in the Church Bell Tower

**May 31** Father Timothy Davison, native son of the parish is ordained a priest for the Diocese of Tulsa, Ok.

*Present Church Interior*

**October** Father Bill on pilgrimage to Europe

Rectory Interior Repainted

**1986 August** Parish Family expands with 15 new families joining the Parish

**1987 May 8** Pilgrim Virgin Statue of Our Lady of Fatima is brought on tour to St. Louis for Marian Devotions

*St. Louis IX Church*

**1989 July 17** St. Louis Council #3335, Knights of Columbus is reactivated

**1990 April 28** Church Parish participates in the Rally for Life in Washington, D.C., attended by over one million pro-life supporters

**February 19** Church Interior Repainted

**August 9** Parish Pilgrimage to Our Lady of Lebanon Shrine

**August 19** Bicentennial of Gallipolis St. Louis Parish Homecoming — Piano donated by Mr. and Mrs. Vance Johnson dedicated

**September 15** Official Bicentennial Historic Tour features St. Louis Church built 1908

**October 21** Celebration of Mass in the Historic City Park commemorating the landing and First Mass celebrated by the French 500 on October 17, 1790

**October 3** Fr. William R. Myers is named Prelate of Honor with the title of " Very Reverend Monsignor" by His Holiness, Pope John Paul II

**1991 January 6** Former Pastor Fr. Adolph Golubiewski dies at Sanibel Island, Florida. Father's body lies in state at St. Louis Church and Mass of Christian Burial is celebrated. Interment at Grand Rapids, Michigan.

**April 24** Unveiling of the Parish Historical Poster in honor of the Bicentennial of Gallipolis, designed by Paul A. Melia of Dayton artist of the Vatican Poster

**1992 March** Parish signs Purchase Agreement for 85 State Street, the Eachus Property Feast of St. Joseph.

**August 23** St. Louis Concert attended by Bishop Gilbert I. Sheldon, 3rd Bishop of Steubenville. Procession with the Cross of Evangelization honoring the Quincentennial of Christopher Columbus carried in procession to the Church.

*Msgr. William R. Myers*

**1993** August 10 St. Louis Youth travel to Denver, Colorado for World Youth Day with Pope John Paul II officiating. Attending were Michelle and Bo Davison, Michael Soles, Michael Bess, James Strait and Father Bill Myers.

**September 1** Parish Rectory move takes place to its new location of 85 State Street, (former Eachus Home ca. 1845). Former Rectory is named "Maison d'Ecole" and designated as a Parish Religious Education Facility.

**1994 May 6** 25th Anniversary Celebration of the Ordination of Msgr. William R. Myers, Pastor

**August 21** Exterior Renovations of Church and Rectory and interior renovations to the Maison d'ecole

**October 2** Celebration of the Golden Jubilee of the Diocese of Steubenville

**October 18** Parish Pilgrimage to St. Peter in Chains Cathedral in Cincinnati and Assumption Cathedral in Covington, Kentucky

**1995 February** St. Louis Parish Directory Published

**1996 June 9** Dedication of St. Francis of Assisi Outdoor Shrine in memory of Ken Boster

Purchase of Parish Van for Transportation

Begin parish Festival of St. Louis with spaghetti dinner, last Saturday of August

St. Louis Church is depicted in an Original "Cats Meow" and available for sale

**August** Began parish Festival of St. Louis with spaghetti dinner, last Saturday of August

**October 13** Parish Library is established in memory of Emil Janko

**September** St. Louis Church is depicted in an Original "Cats Meow" and available for sale

**1997** Miss "Missy Cosette", ghost writer from St. Louis Parish, responds to anti-catholic propaganda published in local newspaper much to the surprise of the perpetrator. August 23 Original "Cats Meow" of Maison d'Ecole Produced

**December 5-7** St. Louis Historic Rectory hosts the "Holiday Homes Tour" for the Christmas Season Special Event sponsored by the French Art Colony

**1998** February 18 Melkite Rite Mass celebrated at St. Louis by Msgr. Michael Campbell, Pastor of St. Gabriel Church in Minerva

*Cozette*

**August 6** Ramp constructed to provide Handicapped Accessibility to the Church

**August 16** St. Louis Parish Cookbook published for sale

**October 13** Millennium Pilgrimage to Fatima, Lourdes, Nice, Assisi, Loretto, Rome and Sorrento taken by parishioners Mr. and Mrs. Bruce Davison and Msgr. Myers.

**November 8** Purchase of Electronic Pipe Organ for the Church funded through the generosity of the Parish

**1999** Spring"Lunch Program" for High School students is provided by St. Louis Women on Thursdays in the Church Hall serving over 200 students.

**May30** Jubilee 2000 Official Celebration Banners are hung from the Church Bell Tower

**June** Major Church Interior Renovations

**August** New Church Kneelers are made and installed

**November** Millennium Moment Newsletter is published by Steven Cornett and distributed throughout the Jubilee Year

# 2000 2002 Jubilee Year Special Events

**Advent 1999** Parish Celebration of St. Nicholas Children's Christmas Party

Official Blessing and Anointing of the Church Entrance Portals for Jubilee Year

**February 13** World Marriage Day

**February 27** Marian Stained Glass Windows Cleaned and New Memorial Windows Installed

**March 10** Lenten Parish Fish Fries established and open to Parish and Public

**March 25** Jubilee World Day for Women

**April 2-6** Parish Mission

**May 19-21** Eucharistic 40 Hours Devotion

**July 9** Peace Pole installed in Rectory Garden and dedicated to Gregory Tap

**July 16** St. Louis Church hosts Pilgrimage for parishioners of St. Gabriel Church, Minerva, Ohio

**July 25** Pilgrimage to Our Lady of Consolation in Carey, Ohio

**September 9** Parishioner Josette Baker becomes a member of the Secular Franciscan Order, the Third Order founded by St. Francis of Assisi, making her profession at Concelebrated Mass and Ceremony in Charleston, West Virginia with Msgr. William R. Myers and Father Kieran Quinn, OFM, Cap. Presiding.

**September 17** Parish Homecoming Concert, Most Reverend Gilbert Sheldon, Bishop of Steubenville presiding, blesses new Memorial Stained Glass Windows.

**October 15** Purchase of former Stebbins Property

**December 3** Original Ceramic Replica of St. Louis Church designed and available for collectors.

**2001 January 7** Solemn Closing of the Jubilee Year: Parish Epiphany Dinner.

**June 24** Memorial Marker installed at St. Louis Cemetery honoring the unknown buried there who were residents of the Ohio Home of the Epileptics, later known as the Gallipolis State Institute and Gallipolis Developmental Center. Msgr. William R. Myers, serves as Catholic Chaplin to the residents of this facility.

**August 1** Parish Pilgrimage to Maria Stein, Ohio.

**August 26** Official Parish Sesquicentennial Logo announced, designed by Timothy Lynch.

**September 2** Safety and Security System installed in Parish Facilities by Lyntronics of Gallipolis.

New Display Case of Religious Articles available in the Church Hall.

**September 14** St. Louis Church participates in National Day of Mourning announced by President George W. Bush relating to the terrorist acts of September 11th in New York, Washington D.C. and Pennsylvania

**September 23** St. Louis Youth choose "The Y.a.c.h.t Club" as name or reorganized Youth Group. (Acronym meaning - Young Adult Catholics Hanging Together) Youth renovates Garage Attic for "Louie's Lighthouse", a meeting place for the new club ministry.

**2002** St. Louis Church celebrates its Parish Sesquicentennial with a parish directory; an historical display at The Gallia Co. Historical Society; parish festival & spaghetti dinner following a Pontifical Mass on Sunday, August 25, 2002, the date of our patronal Feast of St. Louis.

# Timeline Of Priests Who Came To Gallipolis

Father Peter Joseph Didier 1790-1791

Fathers Stephen T. Badin and M. Barrieres 1793 (Missionaries)

Father Stephen T. Badin 1808 (Passing through)

Father Edward Dominic Fenwick (Missionary and first Bishop of Ohio)

Father La Font 1818-1820

Father David J. Kelly 1854 (Occasionally — from Minerton)

Father John C. Albrinck 1854-1858 (Interim-from Minerton)

Fathers B. Marie Gells, D. B. Cull, John F. Kallenberg, Joseph Jessing, Loedig, Kramer, Quirk, and Hartney 1858-1872 (assigned to serve Mass at least once a month)

Father Leonard Patrick McKiernan 1872-1874

Fathers Louis D'Arcy, Charles Grimmer, M. Martin Alphonse Hartnedy, Francis J. Campbell 1874-1 878 (Interim priests from Minerton and Athens)

Father John B. Gamber 1878-1881

1882-1888 Priests from Pomeroy

Father J. B. Oeink 1888-1892

Fathers D. Edward Meara, Jerome B. Mattingly, John Schneider, James M. McCann 1888-1902 (Interim priests from Minerton, Pomeroy and Athens)

Father John J. Murphy 1915-1917

Father George F. Gressel 1917-1922

Father Nugent 1922-1923

Father William F. Connolly 1923-1928

Father William G. Dowd 1928-1931

Father John T. Dunn 1931-1932

Father Charles B. Ryan 1932-1945

Father V. C. Schiele 1945-1949

Father Adolph Golubiewski 1950-1980

Monsignor William R. Myers 1980

Father Fredrick W. Burkhart-First native son Priest-June, 1917

Father Tim Davison-Native son Priest, ordained for the Diocese of Oklahoma May 1985

# Pastoral Ministers
# Franciscan Sisters Of Manitowac, Wisconsin

Summer Bible School 1981 — 1984

Sister Romana Klaubauf 1984— 1985

Sister Judy Norwick 1984— 1991

Sister Lynne Marie Simonich 1984— 1985

Sister Mary Arnoldussen 1985 — 1987

Sister Jean Kaiser 1987— 88

Sister June Smith 1987 - 1991

# Brothers Of The Immaculate Heart Of Mary

Brother John Vyszenski, Pastoral Minister 1991-1993

# First Baptist Church

The First Baptist Church, now located at 1100 Fourth Avenue, is a beautiful, 32,000 square foot building on a 20-acre campus and was built at a cost of $2.7 million. Membership as of February 2002 is 962 and the church has an annual budget of $478,400. The members of this congregation have truly been blessed of the Lord in their faithful giving and works.

Those of the Baptist faith of Gallipolis have not always been so fortunate in their physical surroundings. A group of believers of the Baptist persuasion met on February 3, 1849, and elected James Mullineaux, John Morrison, Ruben Aleshire, Samuel T. Langley, Daniel Moore, Joseph Brown, Duncan McIntyre, David Wright, and August Wood as trustees with Langley as clerk. They took the name of the "Regular Baptist Church of Gallipolis". By 1852, they felt they were now strong enough to support a church and regular pastor. They began construction of their first church at approximately 416 Third Avenue between State and Locust Street. After a few years, the Baptists developed financial difficulties. The banks foreclosed on the church building and sold it to the German Lutherans.

Although they ceased to exist as an organization, they continued to meet in homes of various members. In 1878, Mrs. Richard Brading, a staunch Baptist, rallied the Baptist People in view of re-organizing the church. They made arrangements to use the Lutherans' building again, which they used for one year.

On January 3, 1879, the church was reorganized. Church services and Sunday School were now held in one room of the Gallia Academy building, with the pulpit being occupied by a different minister every two or three weeks. The group now accepted the name of the First Baptist Church of Gallipolis. All of this was the work of Rev. Gear, Rev. W. E. Powell (who later became pastor) and the thirteen members who were the congregation. These members were: Mr. and Mrs. W. Sterling, Mrs. M. M. Mossman, Mrs. Amelia McConnell, Mrs. Stephen Keller, Mr. W. D. Davis, Mrs. Rachel Hannan, Mr. and Mrs. Frank Cheney, Mrs. Mary Adkinson, Mrs. Richard Brading, Miss Frances Hannan and Mrs. Laura Keller. Mr. D. W. Davis was the first Sunday School superintendent and Mr. Frank Cheney was the assistant. The young people organized debating societies, singing schools, and later a young peoples' society for Christian work. On April 28, 1880, a recognition council officially recognized the Baptist group of believers as a duly organized New Testament Baptist church in the Gallia County Court House. There were 64 members at this time.

When the Rev. Charles Davis became pastor in February 1882, the congregation had decreased to 52, due to deaths and removals. They were still meeting in the old Gallia Academy building, but had a prosperous Sunday School connected with the church. Under the Rev. Davis' leadership, the group purchased the property on the corner of Third Avenue and Locust Street at a cost of $1,000. The church appointed D. W. Davis and the pastor as the committee for soliciting funds, assisted by Rev. R. W. Davis of Kanawha. By the summer, they had pledges of $2,500. Some donations were as little as a quarter. One of the 25-cent gifts was from Anna Cheney, then six years old; she married Alfred Davis and became the founder of the Ann Judson class. D. W. Davis passed away on July 19, 1884, and among his last words were: "Success to your building enterprise". Construction was started in 1885, but worked stopped until the fall of 1886, when the church received a $500 offer from John D. Rockefeller with the condition that the building be dedicated debt free. The building was completed at a cost of $6,000. Dedication and first services were held January 28, 1887. At this time, seven of the thirteen constituent members remained. Death had taken some of the most valuable members, leaving a membership of 72, consisting mostly of young people "with most of life in prospect".

Although the Baptist organization continued to expand, it was not until the twentieth century that the rapid stage of growth was reached. Long known as a missionary church, the members, in 1906, supported a mission on Mill Creek called the "Lone Oak Mission". In 1909, the church had a mission in Maple Shade (now Eastern Avenue), with Bible School being conducted each Sabbath afternoon by different members of the church. In 1912, with Rev. J. O. Newton as pastor, it was necessary to enlarge the building to accommodate the increasing congregation. In 1926, the Baptist parsonage (on Third Avenue next to the church) was purchased. During the depression, the

*Top & Bottom: through the years with changes and additions to the church at Third Avenue and Locust Street. Center: new church at 1100 Fourth Avenue, dedicated November 15, 1998.*

church continued to grow and in 1932, two new manual organs were purchased and the debt was settled with the help of the Social Stitchers. At this same time, the Mack home (a large residence located across Locust Street from the church, now razed) was rented as a temporary home for activities of the Bible school (Sunday School).

In 1938, the Baptist added a large, two-story educational wing containing 26 rooms. It was erected at the cost of approximately $30,000. Also included was a remodeling of the old church building. The exterior was made over to conform to the new and the interior was changed with new oak paneling, a chancel rail and new rugs.

Dedication week was December 25, 1938 to January 1, 1939 and included a week of nightly meetings.

From 1928 to 1940, under the leadership of Rev. George Sagan, the church had a major growth period. In 1940, there were 745 members in the congregation, making it one of the largest churches in the county. Enrollment of the Baptist Bible School, the largest Sunday School in the county, was 775. E. E. Caldwell was the general superintendent assisted by F. C. Halley. There were 28 classes, breaking the school into eight departments. In the Baptist Young Peoples' Union, there was an enrollment of 125.

Evangelistic and missionary endeavors of the church continued to grow. A radio ministry, "Echoes of Joy" was started in 1950 on the local station WJEH. In 1970, a group of 29 members, with Rev. Joseph Chapman, left the congregation to start a new branch now known as Faith Baptist Church. In 1971, First Baptist Church started the addition of another wing for Sunday School and classroom facilities. This was added on the Third Avenue side where the church parsonage once stood. The ProTeen program for teenagers was started in 1972. In the Fall, 1977, the Ohio Valley Christian School, sponsored by the First Baptist Church, was started. The adjoining property on Locust Street was purchased in 1981 and a new gymnasium was built for use by both church members and the Christian School. The AWANA program for youth was started March 10, 1982. Pastor Joseph Godwin resigned in 1987. Then a small group of members, with Pastor Godwin, started another church, the Fellowship Baptist Church.

Due to an increase in the congregation, the church was having difficulty seating all the members in the sanctuary. Therefore, on Easter Sunday in 1992, the church started having two morning worship services with Sunday School in between the services. Unable to expand in their current location, the property at the end of Fourth Avenue (known as the "old golf course") was acquired. The former Clendenin property was purchased for $150,000 without mortgage. Dedication service for the property was Sunday, May 8, 1994, with Rev Archie Conn leading the congregation in responsive reading and the doxology. A fund raising campaign was started in March 1995. All members were challenged to make anonymous commitments, according to their abilities, for a 3-year period, "Equal sacrifice, not equal gifts".

The new church is a one-story structure containing 20 classrooms, a fellowship hall, and church and school offices. The seating capacity in the auditorium is 700 (seating in the old church was 300). The new building houses grades K-6 of the Ohio Valley Christian School. Grades 7-12 continue in the old church at Third Avenue and Locust Street.

On August 30, 1998, the first services were held in the new church. Services were started at the old church at Third and Locust and concluded at the new church. Dedication services were held November 15, 1998. Dr. Paul Dixon, president of Cedarville College delivered the dedicatory message. Also present were former pastors Joseph E. Godwin, Wilson Wahl, Joseph C. Chapman, J. Edward Hakes and associate pastor, Harry Cole.

Church officers for 2002 include Deacons: Larry Marr, chairman; Woody Burnett, Bob Hood, Tim Carman, Ron Keenan. Matt Willis and Cliff Wilson. Trustees include: Kent Shawver, chairman; Joe Giles, Jeff Snedaker, Gene Spurlock, Chris Wood, Wendell Thomas and John VanMeter. Trustee Emeritus: Morris Haskins. OVCS Board includes: Jeff Smith, Charlie Stone, Polly Salisbury and Larry Miller. Deaconess include: Lottie Harvey, Barbara Wood, Cheryl Jarvis, Carol Rupe, Jean Wilson, Connie Bowman and Sue Murray. The Missionary Committee includes: Dave Clay, Odella Taylor, Eric Martin, Goldie Johnson, Phyllis Taylor and Rich Mahan, treasurer. The Choir Director is Cheryl Jarvis; Church Clerk, Carol Jean Hood; Financial Secretary, Bill Wamsley; Head Usher, Harold Taylor; Sunday School Superintendent, Roger Hood; Sunday School Treasurer, Sherri Jarvis; Church Treasurer, Lori Miller; and Educational Administrator, Dr. Fred Williams. The Pastor is Dr. Archie Conn and associate pastor and youth director is Rev. Alvis Pollard.

**Pastors who have served First Baptist Church include:**

1860 Rev. Bayliss Caid
1871 Rev. Richard W. Davis
1879 Rev. L. H. Gear; Rev. W. E. Powell; Rev. W. E. Lyons
1882 Rev. Charles Davis
1887 Rev. Charles Carroll
1889 Rev. C. A. McManis
1892 Rev. J. W. Mohler
1895 Rev. W. M. Tinker
1897 Rev. F. E. Brininstool
1899 Rev. J. L. Presser
1902 Rev. F. F. Brininstool
1904 Rev. Benjamin Stinson
1905 Rev. J. R. Reynolds
1907 Rev. T. F. Cary
1909 Rev. B. E. Dunn
1912 Rev. J. O. Newton
1918 Rev. W. Ross Yoaldey
1919 Rev. Robert W. Pierce
1927 Rev. W. H. Anderson
1928 Rev. George Sagan
1942 Rev. J. Edward Hakes
1949 Rev. William H Green
1951 Rev. Don Loomis (minister of youth and music)
1955 Rev. Tom D. Bunyan (associate pastor)
1958 Rev. Howard G. Young
1965 Rev. Joseph Chapman
1968 Rev. Harry E. Cole (associate pastor)
1972 E. Wilson Wahl
1974 Alvis G. Pollard (associate pastor and youth director)
1977 Joseph L. Godwin
1988 Archie Conn

# First Presbyterian Church

On March 15, 1815, several residents of our small river town formed The First Religious Society of the Township of Gallipolis. There were twenty-one subscribers to this organization. In April they elected three trustees: Jonas Safford, Nathaniel Cushing and Nathaniel Gates. The members, with pledges of $600, called a meeting of heads of families for the purpose of gathering a church. There were two Presbyterian ministers present The first pastor called was Rev. William R. Gould, a graduate of the University of Vermont He was also the first teacher of higher studies at Gallia Academy. He received a salary not to exceed $200 per year, and he was given the summer off for his enjoyment.

Early services were held either in the courthouse, located at the upper corner of the public square, or at the Academy at the corner of Second and State Streets. The object of the Society was "to maintain the preaching of the gospel in the town of Gallipolis".

The conduct of the members was subject to strict control Members could be dismissed or "churched" for being neglectful of prayer, being intemperate, using profane language or attending balls, horse races or the theater. Joanna Safford, who had attended a dance in Charleston, submitted her confession to be read in church. There are records of several church "trials", mostly resulting from intemperance. Often the guilty party was banned from services and Sacraments until there was a public repentance. One woman was cited on a charge of "willfully leaving her husband". In 1886 the Session expressed its displeasure at the choir's participation in a ceremony for the decoration of the graves of Soldiers on the Sabbath as a violation of the 4th Commandment

In early 1820 the Society split The splinter group became the First Methodist Episcopal Society. In 1828 the Articles of Organization were revised to conform to the constitution and customs of the Presbyterian Church.

The construction of a church building soon followed. Lot number 119 was purchased from Gallia Academy for $100. Pews were sold to raise the necessary $1650 estimated as the cost of the building. The cornerstone for the 40 x 60 foot brick building was laid on September 16, 1828. Information included in a bottle sealed in the cornerstone stated that J.P. Bureau was Mayor of Gallipolis and that John Quincy Adams was President of the United States. Gallipolis had a population of 700, and "in this village was one courthouse, 1 academy, 2 steam mills, 12 stores, and I meeting house." The building, located at 51 State Street, was dedicated on August 9, 1839.

Church services were canceled between 1850 and 1852 for 22 months due to an outbreak of cholera. The great influenza epidemic of 1918 closed the church during the month of October and the first two Sundays in November.

A typical collection for a Sunday in 1842 was between five and seven dollars. The minister's salary was $500 annually. In 1917 Rev. Berry had a salary of $1200, the organist was paid $104, and the total budget was $3100.

There was a split in the national Presbyterian Church which kept members in turmoil between 1837 and 1869. There were at least three issues which divided "Old School" from "New School". These were: 1) infiltration of a New England liberal interpretation of Calvinism; 2) dissatisfaction with the way the church conducted their frontier mission; and 3) slavery.

In 1855 twenty-two members seceded and formed an "Old School" branch.

One group actually "took possession" of the church building, leading to long suits in the courts. The schism ended in 1876 with the Article of Union, and both groups became associated with the Portsmouth Presbytery.

Women have long played prominent roles at First Presbyterian. In 1856 the ladies of the congregation met to establish a social circle. They raised funds through Christmas Eve suppers, quilting, and chicken suppers. In 1870 a resolution was passed which requested the Ladies Social Circle to appoint a committee of five to advise and assist the trustees in managing the affairs of the church. Women have served on various church committees since that time. Session minutes from 1911 request "two or more young ladies to secure subscriptions of members for the purpose of paying Pastor Williams". The Ladies were to be paid a commission of 5% of collections. In 1934 the first two women were elected to serve as elders of First Presbyterian: Dr. Ella Lupton, a physician, and Clara Worman, a teacher. The first woman to serve as pastor was Rev. Tura Hayes, who served as Associate Pastor from 1974-1984.

The congregation "calls" or selects the pastor, who has been recommended by the Pastoral Search Committee, elected from the members. Forty nine pastors have served First Presbyterian. Rev. Hugh Ivan Evans, who served from 1912-1917, later be

came national moderator of the General Assembly, the Presbyterians' highest governing body. During two wars our pastors left the church to serve as chaplains for the military. In 1861 during the Civil War Rev. R.D. Van Dusen resigned to become chaplain to the 12th Regiment of the Ohio Volunteers. During World War II Rev. Cecil Marley was granted a leave of absence to serve as a Chaplain in the U.S. Navy.

The current church structure has undergone many renovations: in 1881; in 1885 (an addition including parlor room, dining room and kitchen); in 1904, (Sunday school rooms were added); in 1923 (the exterior of the church was stuccoed); and in 1950 (stucco was removed and original exterior brick was repointed and repaired).

A new education wing was dedicated in 1940, and still another addition was built in 1956. The fifth and last building addition was in 1979, which included a second story, a new kitchen and office space. The church acquired several additional plots of land through the years to accommodate its additions and to include a parking lot. Minutes of September 30, 1869 reveal plans to build a tower in the front of the church, suitable for a bell. This bell was used as the community fire alarm for many years, but in 1897 the church trustees protested that use, and the city fathers heeded that protest. The stained glass windows were purchased in 1881 from William Coulter of Cincinnati at a cost of $207 and arrived on a steamboat.

The first church organ was purchased in 1839 from Nathanial Gates for the sum of $500. A second organ was bought in 1853. In June of 1887, a new pipe organ was purchased from Carl Barckhoff. In 1953, the organ was moved from the center of the choir loft to the right side and rebuilt. The current organ was purchased in 1991, when a new Moller organ was installed, leaving the old pipes in front of the new.

Music has always played a very important part in the services. Even the music did not always run smoothly. In 1886 the choir was reorganized, with four individuals being named as legitimate members. A proclamation stated that "no others will sing in the choir unless invited to do so by the organist".

The Presbyterian Church played a significant role in the American Revolution. The only clergyman to sign the Declaration of Independence was John Witherspoon, President of the College of New Jersey, now Princeton University.

Some British newspapers even referred to the revolution as the "Presbyterian Rebellion".

In addition to the Holy Bible the Presbyterian Church is guided by two key publications which form our constitution. They are The Book of Order and The Book of Confessions. The Book of Order states that "All power in heaven and earth is given to Jesus Christ by Almighty God..." It also defines the "Great Ends of the Church" which are: "the proclamation of the gospel for the salvation of human kind; the shelter, nurture, and spiritual fellowship of the children of God; the maintenance of divine worship; the preservation of the truth; the promotion of social righteousness; and the exhibition of the Kingdom of Heaven to the World."

From time to time, Presbyterians write down what they believe in a formal statement called a "confession". This does not replace Scripture; it is meant to interpret Scripture for a particular time. Scripture always remains primary. These statements of faith throughout the history of the church are gathered in The Book of Confessions.

First Presbyterian of Gallipolis is a congregation of the Presbyterian Church, U.S.A. The government of the church is a representative democracy. Elders, meeting as the Session, are the governing body of the local church. Each local church belongs to a presbytery. Gallipolis is part of the Scioto Valley Presbytery. Presbyteries are members of the General Assembly and are grouped into Synods. The General Assembly meets annually, in part to consider revisions to the constitution. Presbyteries elect delegates to the General Assembly.

First Presbyterian has a long history of commitment to the community and to mission. The church supports both national and international mission projects, while contributing locally to the Ministerial Association, the Outreach Center, Holzer Hospice, Serenity House, and countless other local missions.

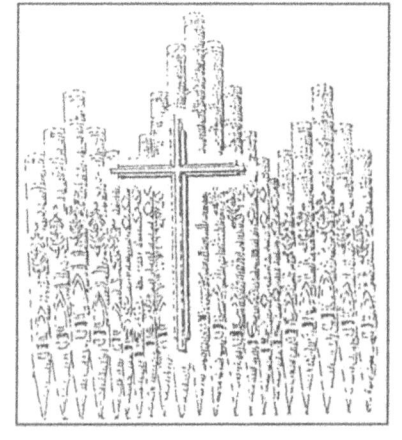

The church is currently served by a fifteen-member board of Elders, known as the Session, plus a twelve-member Board of Deacons. These officers are elected for three-year terms by the congregation.

First Presbyterian looks forward to celebrating its bicentennial in 2015 and remains a vital and committed presence in the community, still preaching the gospel and serving the Lord by serving others.

# Patriot United Methodist Church

The first Methodist Episcopal Parsonage for the Patriot Circuit for many years was Lot 68 in the Village of Patriot on Church Street. It was bought from George W. Eaches, on November 19, 1853, for $150.00. It was purchased by trustees including: Benjamin McDaniel, John Allison, Henry Wiseman, Henry Neal, and James Williams. Lot 68 is now owned by Juanita Cochran Tackett.

The second parsonage (Lot 20) was bought from J.C. Myers and wife Hannah on December 1, 1906 for $375.00. It was purchased by parsonage trustees of the Methodist Episcopal Church in the village of Patriot including: R.A. Howell, J.C. Minor, Fred Wenneyer, J.S. Queen, Ernest Zimmerman, and N.S. Calhoun. Lot 20 is now owned by Carol Davis.

The Lord Jesus saw the need of a church here in Patriot way back in 1845 when a man by the name of John Clark gave Glory to God. Mr. Clark bought 20 acres of land in 1828 from Henry Wiseman and sold it to Benjamin McDaniel in 1845. The deed for the land reserved 1/4 acres for church and burial grounds. This began the history of the church on the hill. Possibly it is the oldest institution in Patriot, being it was organized in 1827.

The first religious service in Perry township was held at the home of Andrew Friend by Elder Fueston, a Missionary Baptist, who was the first minister in the township. A society was formed among the first members of who are the following named persons and their wives: John Carter, E.E. Boggs, Abram Brewer, Joshia Rippley, Samuel Boggs, Robert Armstrong, Jacob Prose, and John Prose.

The second society formed at Patriot was called Sandfork Church. It was afterward moved to McDaniel settlement and is still known by the original name. The denomination was Baptist and their first minister was Elder Levi McDaniel.

The present church at Patriot was built in 1870 by David W. White and L.D. Koontz of Rodney, Ohio. On August 20, 1985, during remodeling of the church, Melburn C. Tackett, the Sunday School Superintendent, found a valuable piece of information concerning the history of the building of Patriot Church. This was probably the last board that was nailed under the side of the church seat. This message was written in pencil, and included are the exact words and spellings: Patriot Ohio Jan 10, 1871 David W. White was born Dec. 1st 1833. Built this house in 1870 and 71. Price nine hundred and 55 for the whole job. Carpenters D.W. White and L.D. Koontz of Rodney Ohio. Green bucks are very scarce about now. Times are hard weather is dry and has been ever since May no cold weather until Christmas and no rain. The wells are all dry in Patriot. Roads dusty.

The Patriot Church reported a good title on July 13, 1872 worth $1,000.00.

The tallest monument in Patriot Church Cemetery marks the grave of John Chich, who came to Patriot from England. He never married.

Mr. William Dixon Hall served as secretary of the Quarterly Conference for 50 years.

In 1862, Patriot Circuit was comprised of 15 churches. At a quarterly conference held at Patriot Church in 1880 a motion was made and carried to divide the circuit. There were 13 offical board members voting in favor and 3 opposed.

There were many elders who served for Patriot Circuit from 1862-1882, with a number of ministers and assistants to them. The circuit later changed to a charge. Jane Ann Miller now serves as the pastor.

There was a new addition built to the church 1955-1956 when Rev. Pearl Casto was the pastor.

The first trust fund to the church was received from the estate of Cecil Davis who was a Sunday School teacher in the church.

The church became Patriot United Methodist Church in 1968 when the merger took place with the United Brethern Church.

Miss Anna Simmerman needs to be remembered in this history because she is credited with searching for much of the history that is written on these pages. She is buried in the cemetery and left a trust fund at her death in 1958.

Two letters written by Mr. Everette E. Booten of Columbus, Ohio, for the Patriot Homecoming at the church October 7, 1934. He writes:

I have fond recollections of my childhood days when each Sunday my mother dressed me in my best Sunday go-to-meeting clothes, and escorted me to the old church on the hill. We all walked as we had no buggies in those days. People either walked or rode horses. The women used side saddles and wore long black riding skirts. I recall the dedication of the new church was turned over to the trustees by the contractor, David White, a local carpenter. Before it could be dedicated it had to be free of debt. I think $300.00 had to be raised at the afternoon services The Rev S. P. Vaughn was an eloquent beggar and the church was dedicated free of debit. Religious fever was manifest by almost the entire congre-

*Melburn Tackett found this board with a message of the year church was built & other details*

gation. Many visitors from surrounding churches were present. Many also became members of the church.

I remember the friends of an older generation the numerous branches of the Carter family, the Ripleys, the Paynes, the Simmermans, the Davises, the Roses, the Betzes, the Edlers, Mrs. Augusta Donohue and the Amos family. Added to these are a long list of children, many of whom came to school when I taught at Patriot.

In regard to the church building that preceded the present structure, I distinctively remember its appearance just prior to its wrecking and removal. It was about the same size of the present structure. It was a very dilapidated building which looked as if it had never been painted. It rested upon stone pillars with boards in between, and as I last saw it these had rotted away so that the building was very cold. On one occasion as I recall it, the men kept their overcoats on and the women kept on their heavy shawls, which by the way, have not been improved upon for warmth. Many of the men wore their sky-blue overcoats they brought back home with them from the war. The overcoats were made of heavy wool cloth that was almost rain-proof with brass buttons down the front.

I recall a protracted meeting that lasted two or three weeks by a minister whose name was Rev. J. M. Rife. It was quite a successful meeting and many members added to the church. He laid the ground works for the new church building but moved to another circuit. So ends Mr. Booten's letter.

From 1984-1987 the church was remodeled with new windows, double entrance doors, lowered ceiling, paneling, new lights, new padded pews, wall to wall carpet, white siding on the outside, new roof and awning over the steps.

The front of the church has been landscaped with many kinds of flowers and shrubs that have been given by or in memory of the dear ones that have attended the church. At the request of Emogene Mercer Edwards family, money was donated in her memory to erect a sign for times of church services.

April 6, 1986 dedication services for remodeling of the church was given by Athens District Superintent Ben Edwards, and pastor Pearl Casto. Trustees, Melburn Tackett (chairman), Lewis and Jane Ann Miller, Larry Fallon, Bobby Crews, Jerry Lambert and Juanita Tackett.

The complete parking lot was concreted 1992 and finished in 1995.

On October 22, 1995, the church celebrated 125 years with a homecoming. Rev. Pearl Casto was the oldest past pastor attending at the age of 90 years. Many friends and fellow-church goers shared the afternoon with a potluck lunch.

The church was granted incorporation papers from the state of Ohio on December 12, 2000.

Today the church has 16 active members and they are: Juanita Tackett, Hope Burnett, Mary Crews, Kristine Crews, Carolyn Lambert, Clyde and Hilda Hunt, Larry Fallon, Rashel Fallon, Raymond and Heather Cochran, Marvin and Wilma Saunders, Lewis and Jane Ann Miller, Dorothy Lu Miller.

The pastor from 1942, Rev. Wesley Fry has a son Paul,(and wife Pat) that still stop by the church for worship when they are in from Florida. Patriot United Methodist Church is located in Perry Township, in Gallia County, twelve miles west of Gallipolis. It is situated on a hill at the edge of the village of Patriot. Services are held each Sunday at 10:00 a.m. (Sunday School) and Worship 11:00. Evening worship at 6:30.

"WE STILL FEEL THE BENEDICTION OF THOSE STURDY SOULS AND TRUE WHO RAISED THIS TEMPLE OF GOD'S LOVE, BUILDING BETTER THAN THEY KNEW!

# Apostolic Faith Church

The Apostolic Faith Church of Bidwell was established under its present name in August of 1974. The founder and members of this established church were: Bro. and Sis. Lawrence and Dorothy Garnes, Robbie, Tish, Tammy, Andre, and Mike; Sis. Minnie Garnes all of Bidwell; Bro. and Sis. Richard and Linda Adams, Nici and Richard Jr.; Bro. and Sis. Sherman and Cheryl Johnson, Shelan and Sherman Jr. all of Chillicothe, Ohio; Bro. and Sis. Calvin and Bertha Freeman, Darlene and Timmy of Ironton, Ohio, the son and daughter-in-law of the late A. C. Freeman, one of the former pastors of the Union Baptist Church of Blackfork and a former Baptist Moderator in this area.

Our first meeting was to be held in the Gallipolis City Park. We came from our various cities prepared to "worship the Lord in the beauty of holiness". But, as can be expected, Satan tried to hinder the work God had called us to do. Through a myriad of tests God provided a place for us to hold our first meeting in a church in Pt. Pleasant, WV., pastored by Elder Wellman. Through him God blessed us with our first building for 18 yrs, on Fairview Rd. in the Fairview Cemetery.

We weathered the storm there through many obstacles, but continued to preach the gospel and worship God in spirit and in truth as God added souls to our congregation. One of our very first visitors was the late Bro. Randolph Fluellen. He was baptized in water in Jesus name (Acts 2:38) on April 19, 1975 and God filled him with the Holy Ghost soon thereafter.

We say God's spirit move in a mighty way in that little old church until he Blessed us to moved into His new Edifice on Easter Sunday April 19, 1992. He moved right along with us after eight seemingly long years in the building of His church, and he is still moving yet today.

Those who labored with us those eight years are still continuing on in the service of our Lord are: (Pastor) Elder Sherman and Sis. Cheryl Johnson, Min., Bill and Sis Sandra Mitchell, Deacon John and Sis. Kathy Garnes, Sis. Luella Henry, Sis Clara Jackson, Sis Dorothy Rippey, Sis. Patty Armstrong, Sis. Minnie Garnes, Sis. Ruth Smith, Sis. Connie Beach, Sis. Florice Boggs, and Sis. Virginia Garnes. Though we seem to be few in number with God we are a majority. We know he is in our midst because he declares in his word: For where two or three are gathered together in my name, there am I in the midst of them. Matthew 18:20. Come gather with us and help us lift up Jesus.

*Faith Apostolic Church*

# Bethesda United Methodist Church & Cemetery

Bethesda United Methodist Church - 1935

The church is located on State Route 775 at the junction of Hannan Trace Road. One half acre of land was deeded for a Meeting House by William, Lucinda and Mary Williams, 8 April 1844 for five dollars. The church building was erected in 1855. Additional church land was deeded by Wesley McDaniel, one quarter acre, 25 July 1900, for ten dollars, Salathial W. Williams deeded burial ground, 5 June 1878, ten dollars. Ann G. Williams deeded burial ground 28 December 1897 for two dollars. Albert and Gertrude Nance deeded burial ground 18 March 1956 of 0.268 acre.

First members of the church included John Armstrong, William Donaldson, Jr., Ann Thompson, Nathaniel Gilford, Sarah Gilford, Samual Gilford, Mary Gilford and Sarah McCombs. In August of 1861, when the structure was only six years old, the Sabbath School Union Celebration for the southern end of the county was held at Bethesda Methodist Episcopal Church. Much of the program was a patriotic rally to muster support for the Union at the beginning of the Civil War. The cemetery is located across the road from the church. The first burial that can be identified is that of William J. Williams in 1832, a Revolutionary War veteran. Most of the oldest burials are of the Williams family. There are 32 known veterans buried in the cemetery. Henry L. Myers places flags on the veterans graves every Decoration/Memorial Day. A cemetery association was organized in 1947 by trustees Robert A Howell, Elmer S. Niday, Otis Drummond, I.S. Vaught, A.K. Williams and chairman/treasurer John Allison. John served as chairman Treasurer through several decades in the late 1900s.

Until the year 2000 other trustees have included Margurite Carter, Lawrence Gates, Margaret Hall, Shennie Burnett, Walter Rose, Harold Provens and Henry L. Myers. Present Secretary-Treasurer Davis M. Carter has recently began to develop a master plan to record past and present burials and their locations. Church and cemetery is located in Walnut Township, Gallia County.

At one time a wooden bandstand stood on the church grounds. Yearly picnics, social gatherings, revivals, patriotic rallies, etc., were held there. Georgiana Clara Pope once told that on Decoration Day, Morgan Carter would line everyone up in a formation and marched them to the cemetery to place flags on the veterans' graves something she said the younger generation looked forward to every year.

Naming of the church may have derived from John 5, 2. Now there is at Jerusalem by the Sheep Market Pool, which is called in Hebrew tongue Bethesda. Moving five pouches. Jesus was said to have healed at the Pool of Bethesda. *Submitted by Henry L. Myers and David Carter*

from collection of Edwin Elliott and Bethesda United Methodist - 2002

# Centenary United Methodist Church

In the beginning God created... And, in the beginning November 20, 1866, a deed was written for land located in the village of Centenary, Green Township, Gallia County, Ohio, to be given by Henry and Rebecca Blazer to the trustees of Centenary Church and says in part "...shall. erect and build or cause to be erected and build thereon a good and substantial house or place of worship for the use of the members of The Methodist Episcopal Church in the United States of America and in further trust and confidence that they shall at all times forever hereafter permit such ministers and preachers belonging to the said church as shall from time to time be duly authorized by the General Conference of the said M.E. Church or by the Annual Conferences authorized by the said General Conference to preach and expound God's Holy Word..." Trustees receiving the deed were Rueben Graham, Henry Blazer, D.H. Rose, E.J. Russell, Thomas C. Stafford, Elijah A Stone, and Cyrus B. Rose.

Ansel Northup, assisted by the membership, built the church. A.C. Safford in a letter dated December,1944 to Harry Hulshorst says, "Money was scarce in those days and labor plentiful and the good people of the community donated generously with what they had, and it was erected and stands today in good condition as a monument to the vision and foresight of the good people of that vicinity."

Centenary United Methodist Church, named by Rev. John W McCormick, stands today 2002 with many additions and changes to the first structure. Need for more space resulted in the purchase of the old Welsh Congregational Siloam Church building for $350.00 on June 15, 1946. This church, located near Cora, was used for four Sunday School rooms, bathrooooms, and a furnace room at Centenary.

Extensive remodeling has been done on the building in the past 17 years—to name a few projects—shingled roof, carpet for the sanctuary, new heating systems, and windows. Ground broken in 1980 for yet another addition included a fellowship room, office and kitchen.

In 1945, electric lights were installed in the church. An addition to the church building was built in 1947. E. G. Mc Call was the Superintendent and Harry Hulshorst was the assistant. In 1948, a furnace was installed. In 1976, with Damon Stapelton as pastor, the restoration of the Centenary Church was begun. New windows and marble window sills were installed. The sanctuary was painted and wall-papered. New drapes were also hung. All of this work was done by the men of the church. Under the leadership and Rev. P.A. Casto and the expertise of Edwin Elliott, the church men completed the projects.

The Centenary Church building has stood now for nearly 136 years, not only because of the wood, the nails, the cement, but because of the people who have entered the door and of their willingness to learn, to give, and to endure.

Through the years Centenary congregations have been a part of the Gallipolis Circuit and now in the Athens district.

In 1969 Fairfield, another church in this district, closed its doors and merged with Centenary. Difficult times followed but due to good leadership and perseverence of members, Centenary survived.

Since 1866, 57 ministers have been assigned to Centenary with S. B. Matthews as the first. P.A. Casto, Orville White and Larry Lemley served longer than any other ministers. Seven years each. Ministers in the 90's have been Orville White, Harold Benson Sue Smith and Larry Lemley.

They have come to "preach and expound God's Holy Word."

# Elizabeth Chapel Church

*Pastor Alfred Holley wife Phyllis*

Elizabeth Chapel Church is located on the hill below the village of Thivener, an old settlement built around a mill which was established early in the 19th century by Nicholas Thevinen presumably one of the French 500. The village, officially named Thivener (a corrupted spelling of the name of the family Thevinen) acquired its unofficial name, Yellowtown, in a very peculiar manner. The legend tells of an eastern salesman who visited the old mill to presumably do business with one of the Thevinen's. It was a terrible rainy day that resulted in a muddy mess. Upon leaving the mill the salesman slipped in the yellow clay mud that is so prevalent in the area. The man got up, wiped his clothes the best as he could, and said, "This sure is a Yellow Town." The name stuck and although the Post Office's official name was Thivener, the quiet little village on the confluence of Bullskin and Raccoon creeks will always be known as Yellowtown.

The Church was organized about 1868 by the Bible Christian denomination and named after the Daughter of Hugh Plymale Sr., Elizabeth Plymale Berridge. Wife of Cornelius Berridge (the grandparents of John Berridge, John Bane, and Chester Leaper.) she was a sister to Hugh Plymale Jr. The Charter Members of Elizabeth Chapel were Abram Darst Sr., Nancy Darst, Frances Atkinson, Joseph Atkinson, Elza Brothers, Mary Ghrist, Nathan Earwood, Jacob Halley, Stewart Plymale, Sarah Plymale, Rebecca Strait, Joseph Angel, Annie Halley, and Claurinda Serriere.

The first sanctuary was built on land given by Hugh Plymale, Sr and dedicated on October 26, 1870. That first church building burned on a Sunday morning in 1900 from a defective flue as the congregation was on its way to worship. There was no insurance on the building and all was lost except the organ, which was saved by Morgan Plymale.

A committee comprised of Hugh Plymale Jr. (great grandfather of Judy Steger Walters), Frank Leaper (father of Chester Leaper, Police Chief of Gallipolis for many years), Tom Craft (grandfather of Carrol Smith), and Silman Cottrell was appointed to oversee the construction of a new building. During construction services were held in the one-room school building that was in the lot in front of the church (Yellowtown School). After much work and sacrifice the new building was dedicated on July 21, 1904. Bub Gilbert was the carpenter with free labor provided by local people. Mr. Gilbert's salary of $1.00 per day plus room and board was provided by Mary Gilbert Plymale the wife of Hugh Plymale Jr. Additional land was given in 1956 by Mrs. Myrtie Meal, in 1975 by Mr. and Mrs. Herman Brucker, and in 1999 additional property was given by the family of Myrtie Meal. The first addition was added to the building in 1956 and four have been added since.

The first ministers of the new church were Hiram Grover, John Porter, and Samuel Lewis. The first funeral was that of Lena Leaper, sister of Chester Leaper. The first wedding was that of Allen Romaine and Ann Melton. The first homecoming service was held the fourth Sunday of July in 1946. Charles Lusher was the pastor for the first homecoming.

The lectern that currently sits in the front of the church was hand made by George Wetherholt, a local funeral director who conducted many funerals at the church.

The largest revival was with Rev. Edgar Ewing, which lasted four weeks, and at the end of the meetings the "big baptizing" was held in Raccoon Creek just below the old milldam. Once during a revival, Raccoon Creek flooded, covering all roads leading to the Church. The waters did not dampen the congregation's spirit. They crossed the creek in boats and continued the meetings.

The current pastor, Alfred Holley, who has served the church longer than any other pastor (37 years), along with Associate Pastor Mark Beaver lead Elizabeth Chapel in its quest to serve the spiritual needs of its congregation. *Submitted by Tom Walters*

*Associate Pastor Mark Beaver wife Darlene*

# Fair Haven United Methodist Church

Fair Haven, Gallia County, Ohio is located on the Ohio River, at the mouth of the Kanawha River. It was laid out for the French 500 whose settlement was moved four miles downstream, where they settled Gallipolis in 1790. Much later (in 1908) because there were two Fair Haven settlements in Ohio, the postmaster, a Mr. Polsley, renamed the one in Gallia County Kanauga - - meaning "between the Kanawha River and Chicamauga Creek".

The census for 1840 lists four families living here: Alexander Rayburn (4 members), Andrew Allen (11 members), Calvin Shepard (8 members) and Cain Stewart (7 members). In 1890 there were only ten homes and two farms here. Since religious freedom was their reason for settling here, they began holding worship services in their homes. The John Deem home was one of the first used. Other families in Fair Haven at this time were; John and Susan Rothgeb, sons Evan and William, and daughter Eva; Bill Bryant, Frank Allen, Dave Edwards and daughter Meadie, and son Hoyt and Charlie; Mrs. Charles Jett and Hudson Maddy.

The nearest churches were in Addison and Gallipolis, and weather permitting, they would walk to services there. In 1896, the settlers organized the Fair haven Methodist Episcopal Church and on September 14, 1896, received a deed, which was signed by the trustees; Henry Sheppard, John Rothgeb and James Guthrie. Witnesses were Evan Rothgeb and M.L. Guthrie.

Mr. And Mrs. John L. Vance presented the church with a Bible, inscribed with their name and date, June 4, 1896. This Bible is displayed in the church today.

In 1896, they began construction of a church. Because they had little cash, they used the area's natural resources, such as lumber and stone. They were skilled carpenters and soon erected a clapboard building with colored glass windows, a hand-carved altar rail and a pulpit stand, a potbellied stove and oil or carbine lamps. This effort was started by William Deem who raised money by subscription, with the help of Ella Wagner, Gus Steele and others. The land was purchased (some sources say it was donated) by or from J.W or Charles and Lydia Stone.

The bell was gift from James Guthrie and had been used on the steamboat "Silver Cloud". The church entered the Ohio Methodist Conference that same year. Reverend T.F. Garrett was the first minister. The Willard Epworth League was also organized at this time.

In 1908 a land development company purchased land and divided it into lots for sale. Many new families moved into the area, increasing attendance and growth of the church.

In 1930, 18 small red chairs were purchased by the nursery class for their room for their room and are still in use today. Sometime prior to 1938 the first piano was purchased by the Ladies Aid. In December 1946 work started to move the church. A basement was dug and a 4' foundation constructed, thus accommodating a coal furnace and water system. In 1947 four classrooms were added to the back of the church and in 1950 a vestibule and new bell tower were built. Also a communion table was presented to the church by the Senior Ladies Class.

An electric organ was purchased through the efforts of the Young Women's Class, which collected donations from the community from 1958 to 1962.

In 1964, two silver flower vases were presented by the Young Adult Class and in 1982 brass altar ware was given in memory of the parents of Evelyn Rothgeb and Gladia Easter Sheets; and the parents and husband of Florence Russell Allen.

In 1979, a fund was started to add two restrooms and another classroom to the front of the church. This project was completed in 1983.

From 1991 to the present time many improvements have been made to the church, such as - - a ramp; air conditioners for the classrooms; central air; ceiling fans; vinyl siding on part of the church; windows replaced; padded pews; wall-to-wall carpeting; new concrete front steps; and a church sign has been erected.

This has all be accomplished through the dedication, hard work and tireless efforts of those people attending this church.

On Sunday, August 9, 1998, a picnic was held on the church lawn to celebrate the 100th year anniversary of the church. This was followed by a service in the sanctuary with former pastors, church members and congregation, local community and friends in attendance. *Submitted by Helen Burnett from notes compiled belonging to the late Evelyn Rothgeb, former church historian*

# Fellowship Baptist Church
## Little Is Much When God Is in It"

In the beginning God planted a seed in the hearts and minds of a group of fifty people who eagerly sought to serve the Lord. That tiny seed was nurtured by the Word of God and grew over the years to the present assembly known as Fellowship Baptist Church.

An organizational meeting was held on Sunday evening, February 28, 1988, in the basement of the home of Lowell (Buz) and Betty Call. One week later the first morning worship service was held at the Call's home with fifty people in attendance. On March 13, 1988, the congregation voted to call the assembly, Fellowship Baptist Church.

Three weeks later, a steering committee consisting of Buz Call, Dr. Ismael Jamora, and Doug Runyan led by Pastor Joseph Godwin, secured the basement of the French City Chiropractic building owned by Dr. David Thomas. Sunday and Wednesday services for all ages commenced under the appointment of Garland Lanier, the first Sunday School Superintendent of Fellowship Baptist Church. Over the next two years while the ministry of Jesus Christ was being preached. ideas flourished and a fellowship began which led to the decision to build a church.

In the Spring of 1988, fifty-six charter members pledged their faith to build a church to the honor and glory of God. Those included Pastor Joseph Godwin and Shirley Godwin; Mick and Minnie Agustin; Alan, Bev, and Adam Alberchinski; Eddie and Dibbie Vare; Genevieve Brown; Beau Bush; Lowell (Buz), Betty, and Barry Call; Ray, Wanda, and Twyllia Connelley; Leroy and Mildred Dailey; Jesse Davis; Fred and Becky Fournier; Tim and Rebecca Godwin; Johnie and Annabel Hagans; Sandra, Julie, and Jennifer Hardesty; Mary Ann Jamison; Dr. Ismael Jamora and Deanna Jamora; Garland, Susie, and Nancy Lanier; Lawrence, Helen, Jakim, and Micah Lanier; Jacqueline Miller; Paul and Madge Northup; William and Nelgene Pegg; Douglas and Jean Runyan; Wilson and Maxine Rusk; Russell and Pat Sessor; Cindy Thomas; and Mary Thomas.

Nearly fifty acres of prime land that overlooks the Spring Valley community at 600 McCormick Road in Gallipolis, Ohio, was acquired through Dan Evans, President and C.E.O. of Bob Evans Farms, Inc, and construction on the 11,350 square feet facility began in mid July, 1989.

Church laborers volunteered hours of work over the next several months. Finally, on March 4,1990, the second anniversary of Fellowship Baptist Church over one hundred twenty-five worshippers crossed the threshold into the new facility for the first morning worship services. Several weeks later, on Sunday, April 22,1990, the doors officially opened. and the public was cordially invited to the Dedication Service of Fellowship Baptist Church under the pastorate of Joseph Godwin.

Over two hundred twenty-five members and guests attended the activities throughout the day. Special recognition was extended to: Bill Pegg and Wayne Brown - general construction: Billy Daniel - masonry work; Edwin Elliott - electrical engineer; Dan Evans - major land contributor; and Ohio Valley Bank - loan facilitator.

Nearly six years later on the eighth anniversary on March 3,1996, another celebration was held as the $195,000 mortgage which had been purchased by Pastor Joseph Godwin, Bus Call and Dr. Ismael Jamora was burned.

Throughout the years a number of men have served as deacons. Those include: Buz Call, Bernard Crawford. John Godwin, Nolan Graham, Dr. Ismael Jamora, Garland Lanier, Bill Pegg, Jeff Porter, Douglas Runyan, Charles Sebert, Paul Stackhouse, Dennis Smith, and John Wilson.

In the Fall of 1999, Pastor Godwin announced his desire to retire as Founding Pastor of Fellowship Baptist Church The presiding Board of Deacons, spearheaded by Pastor Joseph Godwin, sought to interview several candidates seeking the pastorate. On June 17, 2001, Phillip Walker was selected by an outstanding vote of the congregation and assumed his duties as the second Pastor of Fellowship Baptist Church on July 30, 2001. Pastor Walker came to Gallipolis, Ohio, from Flint, Michigan, with his wife, Lorraine, and their four children, Andrew, Benjamin, Sarah and Abigail.

Fellowship Baptist Church is an Independent Baptist Church and believes that Jesus Christ is the virgin-born Son of the living God. and the Holy Bible is the source of power and strength for daily Christian living. The cornerstone is Romans 1:16 - "For I am not ashamed of the gospel of Christ: for it is the power of God unto salvation to every one that believeth..."

Sunday services begin at 9:30 A.M. where Bible instruction is offered to all ages. The morning worship service follows at 10:30 A.M., and the evening praise service begins at 6:00 P.M. An informal prayer meeting and youth program are held on Wednesday evenings at 7:00 P.M. *Submitted by Bev Alberchinski*

---

OUR INVITATION

To all who mourn and need comfort,

To all who are lonely and want friendship,

To all who are tired and want victory,

To all who sin and need a Savior,

To whosoever will,

This Church opens wide its doors

And in the name of Jesus Christ, the Lord, says,

WELCOME

# First Church Of God

pastors in the church's history. Pastors who served at the Third Avenue Church are as follows; 0. F. King 1914-1919, Neva Wilson, Luther Van Hoose, E. C. Venz, Stella Bane 1919-1916, H. M. Smith 1926-1953 and Stanley C. Hoelle 1953 - 1955.

The church grew and prospered. During Pastor Hoelle's term it was evident that more space was needed. A spacious new block building was erected on Garfield Avenue. Later, a bell tower, stained glass windows and a tan and brown stucco cover coat was added to the church building.

Pastors who followed Hoelle are H. McDonough 1955 - 1957, Cecil Mayle 1959 - 1964, L. B. Foudy 1964 - 1968, Paul Jones 1968 - 1972, W. Jenkins 1972, C.P. Conley 1973 - 1978, James Rainey 1978 - 1984. Paul Voss is the present pastor having come to the church in December 1984.

In 1995, the church acquired approximately 50 acres on route #141 within two miles from the city. Later, a pavilion, recreation area and pond was added. The church is now in the process of planning to construct a new facility in the near future.

Around the year 1910, Evangelist J. Gran Anderson, a pioneer evangelist of the Reformation Movement, came to Gallipolis and held a tent meeting on Second Avenue below Pine street. He stayed in the home of Charlie Kemp. Kemp was one of the first persons in this area to embrace the message of the Church of God.

0. F. King from West Virginia came to the Ohio Valley seeking employment. He heard Anderson's message on holiness, accepted it and stayed to become the first pastor of the work at Gallipolis, Pastor King began having services in his home as well as in the homes of others in 1914. Later a small building was rented on Third Avenue.

In 1919, a new building was erected at 156 Third Avenue where once the Auto Parts store was located now owned by Cremeans Funeral home. King pastured only 3 months after the church was completed. He died unrepentantly. His was the first funeral to be preached in the new edifice.

The first trustees of this new congregation were R. J. Collins, Joseph Danner and H. M. Smith. Later Smith became pastor. A position he held longer than any other

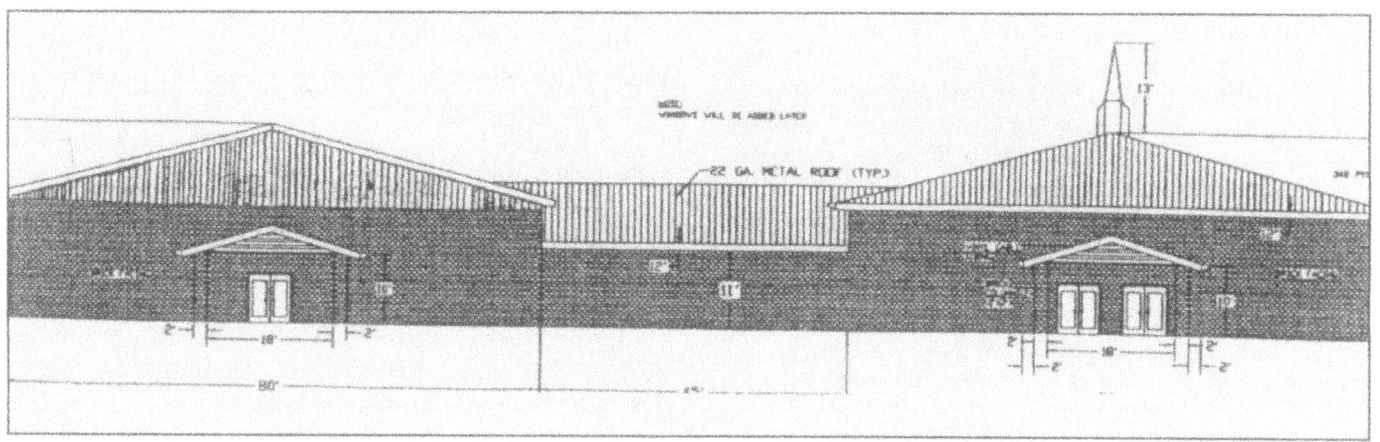

# French City Baptist Church

Our roots as a Southern Baptist Church goes back to 1958 when a spot survey by area missionary Robert E. Hall and Rev. J. L. Wade, pastor of Piketon Baptist Church was initiated.

In November of 1960, an Air Force recruiter named Sgt. Jesse L. Brown moved into Gallipolis. He contacted Robert E. Hall and Reverend Darrell Chapman, pastor of the Emmanuel Baptist Church in Jackson, OH regarding the development of a mission. On December 13, 1960 the first fellowship meeting took place in Sgt. Brown's home located at 401 Jackson Pike. Six people were present for the initial meeting. During January and February of 1961, three additional home fellowships were started.

On June 13, 1961, a lease was signed for the building in which regular worship services would begin. It was located at 158 Third Avenue, Gallipolis.

On February 3, 1963, the mission extended a call to Aggie Bently to serve as the first pastor. He accepted and moved onto the church field February 24th.

On January 26, 1964, the mission officially constituted to become French City Baptist Church. There were 42 official charter members on this day.

In November of 1964, Reverend Bently resigned and was succeeded by Reverend Raymond L. Pinson, who assumed the pastorate on February 7, 1965.

On April 7, 1965, the church building site committee recommended that the church purchase the Shahan property for the new site of the church. Property was located on State Route #160, three miles northwest of the city of Gallipolis. The price was $11,000.00. The church would place $4,500.00 down and pay the balance at the rate of $100 per month with no interest. On December 8, 1965, the plans for the new sanctuary were approved by the State Board. On Mach 27, 1966, the church applied for a loan of $22,000.00 from the Home Mission Board to build the sanctuary. The church set ground-breaking ceremonies for July 3, 1966, Mrs. Lona B. White (oldest church member) and Pamela Bryan (youngest church member) turned the first shovel full of dirt. On October 2, 1966, the first service was held in the new sanctuary. Eighty-four members were now on the roll (including eleven awaiting baptism.) The new building was officially dedicated on January 8, 1967.

Reverend Pinson resigned on may 8, 1968 as pastor. Under his ministry came the new building, as well as starting two new churches (Mason, WW and First Southern Baptist in Pomeroy, OH.)

On March 16, 1969 the church voted to call Reverend Robert Colvin, Jr. from Magnolia Springs, AL as pastor. He served until November 8, 1972. Under his ministry came a lot of numerical and spiritual growth.

On April 8, 1973, the church voted to call Reverend Jerry Lewis from the Clear Creek Baptist School to be the pastor. On April 11, 1973 Reverend Lewis accepted and became the new pastor. The most successful revival ever held came under this pastor's ministry. From October 29th to November 4th, 1973 a total of twenty-seven decisions for the Lord was recorded. On July 17, 1977. Ground-breaking services for the new educational building was held. The building was officially dedicated on June 24th, 1979. Reverend Lewis preached his final service for French City Baptist Church on July 29th, 1979.

Jerry Scott was called to serve in the capacity of interim pastor on January 6, 1980. He was officially called to the pastorate on July 13, 1980. Under his ministry came the building solid youth ministry. It set the standard for Associational Churches. He resigned as pastor on June 27th, 1982.

Danny Belcher preached his trial sermon for French City Baptist Church on June 2nd, 1983. He moved to Gallipolis from Kentucky in August of 1983. The Blood River Association was joined with the Scioto Valley Baptist Association to form and strengthen existing churches. Danny brought to French City enthusiasm and motivation. He continued to strengthen the youth and Sunday School ministry. He preached his last sermon on March 2, 1986.

*French City Baptist Church*

Reverend John Wood was called to French City Baptist Church during July of 1986. He developed a loving, supportive ministry for the elderly. He also set in motion the structured use of budgets, calendards and committees to guide and assist the church in doing it ministry. He served the longest of all previous pastors. Brother John retired from the ministry on March 1, 1995.

Charles Stansberry was called to French City Baptist Church on February 11, 1996. He was officially installed as pastor on March 1, 1996. A restructuring of the churches ministries occurred during his pastorate.

On June 1, 1997, Reverend Mark Michael was called to serve as the Minister of Youth. Reverent Michael resigned in December of 1997. Pat Miller served as Associate Pastor in 1998-1999. Reverend Stansberry resigned in July of 1999.

The church celebrated it's 35th anniversary with a note burning on July 17th and 18th of 1999.

Reverend John Adams served as Interim Pastor from January 1, 2001 through November 2001. The church is currently seeking a pastor. *Submitted by Sylvia Brown*

# Gallipolis Christian Church

## Celebrating Thirty Years Of God's Blessings

This year, 2002, the Gallipolis Christian Church celebrates thirty years of God's blessings. From the very beginning God has made it possible for the church to minister to those within the congregation and to those in the community and because of His goodness we know the next thirty years will be even sweeter.

It all began when the Gallipolis Christian Church assembled for the first time on February 20, 1972 in the home of John and Pat Elardo located at 509 Maple Drive, Gallipolis, OH. A group of twelve adults and five children were present for that first service. By April of the same year, Denny Coburn of Ironton, OH was called as the part-time interim minister. It was also on this day that the church began to meet in the "Old Warner Property" on Magnolia Drive; thus, in November the congregation moved into a remodeled two-car garage using it as its Sanctuary and holding Sunday School classes in the house. Denny Coburn was formally ordained and employed on December 31, 1972.

Due to the rapid growth of the congregation, the church purchased the Glen Powell property on State Route 588, May 31, 1974. In July, a groundbreaking ceremony was conducted for a new building with a Sanctuary, classrooms, and offices. The congregation entered the new building in March, 1975 and Denny Coburn became the full-time minister of the church. Dedication of the new building was held in June. In November, 1978, again due to rapid growth, a twelve pew extension of the sanctuary was made by taking part of the church's foyer and enclosing the front portico to provide additional space.

On October 29, 1988 a groundbreaking ceremony took place in order to build a new Sanctuary connecting it to the existing facilities. On May 19, 1991 the first services were conducted in the 500-seat Sanctuary and a formal dedication service was held in July of that year.

The Church was blessed to be able to call its first full-time Associate Minister, Derek Stump, in March of 1986. Subsequent Associate/Youth Ministers were Mic Bowen, Marty McCleary, Jeff Patrick and Russ Moore. The current Youth Minster is David Plumley of Lexington, KY.

In August of 2001, Michael Lynn of Virginia was called as the new Preaching Minister of the Gallipolis Christian Church when Denny retired in April, 2001 as Evangelist after 29 years of ministry to the congregation.

Today, the Gallipolis Christian Church continues to strive to meet the needs of the congregation and minister to its surrounding communities. The hope of the congregation is that the Lord will continue to give us opportunities and bless our endeavors as we strive to be a congregation of evangelism, worship, prayer, service and fellowship.

Gallipolis Christian Church
4486 State Route 588
Gallipolis, Ohio 45631
740-446-1863
Gcc@zoomnet.net
Michael Lynn, Senior Minister
David Plumley, Youth Minister

# Grace United Methodist Church

Methodism was introduced in Gallipolis as early as 1810; however, the first Methodist preaching is dated about 1817. In that year, the Reverend Henry Baker, a Methodist itinerant preacher, delivered the first Methodist sermon at the home of Ahaz S. Morehouse, a log house located at the mouth of Mill Creek. Many in the community were hostile and interfered with the services by cutting harnesses and saddles and molesting persons passing to or from the meetings. Therefore, the minister refused to come until another location was found. Calvin Shepard promptly offered his house on First Avenue as a place to worship. Mr. Shepard did many things to help establish Methodism in Gallipolis and because of his perseverance, faith, generosity and leadership; he may justly be called "the father of Gallipolis Methodism".

The first Trustees in 1821 were authorized to buy a lot for a church building on the 600 block of Second Avenue for the sum of $150.00. This first church building was a one story brick, which measured 44 by 50 feet and had a 12-foot ceiling. A storm damaged the church so seriously 28 years later that it was decided a new building was needed. The second one was a two-story building with a basement and contained four classrooms and a lecture room. Construction of a third church building was started in 1875 and the old church was razed and the parsonage was built in its place with the church being built beside it, which placed it on the corner of Second and Cedar Streets. The new building contained six classrooms, a vestibule below and a sanctuary above with a seating capacity of 700 and a gallery, which seated 150. The steeple was 150 feet above the pavement before it was removed and replaced with a bell tower.

From Trustees minutes dated June 17, 1898; Grace Methodist Episcopal Church was incorporated. Subscribers were: Homer C. Brown, Charles H. D. Summers, James W. Gardner, Edward W. Parker, Jenkin W. Jones, Anthony W. Kerns, Isaac F. Chapman, Edgar N. Deardorff, John H. Thomas, Notary Public, George W. Alexander, Clerk of Courts and Charles Kinney, Secretary of State of Ohio.

In 1909, the property immediately in the rear of the church on Cedar Street was purchased at a cost of $1500.00. The building was rearranged and used for social actives; a meeting place for church groups and was known as the Church Parlors. The church spire was removed in 1911 because of decay and in 1923 the church was wired for electricity. The "Church Parlors" were torn down in 1926 and the following were built to the church: a kitchen, dining room (seating 300), classrooms, gymnasium with stage, dressing rooms, restrooms and a choir room.

July 29, 1959, the cornerstone was laid for the new education wing of the church and the building comprises: 12 classrooms, a 2-room nursery, an office and two supply rooms. In the crypt of the cornerstone was placed a Holy Bible, a Directory of the church officials, local newspapers, coins of the period and selected Sunday school material. A dedication service for the Christian Education Building was held May 12, 1963.

In 1968, the Methodist Episcopal Church and the United Brethren Church became one and we took on the name United Methodist Church. Hence, our church became Grace United Methodist Church. During the 1970's, the church took care of many needs of the church, air conditioning was installed, parking lot with exit to Third Avenue completed, the Shaw property next to the church on Second Avenue was acquired, the dining room redecorated. In 1974-75 the sanctuary was completely restored, the elevator installed, offices for the associate minister completed, the choir room and church office remodeled and the electrical and plumbing modernized.

June 20, 1977, disaster struck in the form of a fire which devastated the sanctuary, the oldest part of the church's building complex. The dining and kitchen area suffered smoke and water damage while the education wing was unharmed. The first Sunday after the fire, church services were held in the parking lot facing the ruins of the church. The church was razed and August 27, 1978, during an impressive outdoor service a groundbreaking ceremony was held for the new sanctuary and office complex. From 1980-2001, we have seen changes in our church to become community friendly and inviting all to become a part of its ministry. The year 2000 saw the start of a contemporary service along with the traditional service. Because of this many young adults have become active in church life. Many things have changed over the years, many ministers, members and church programs have come and gone but Grace United Methodist Church will forever be a part of Gallia County History.

*Submitted by: Marjorie Gilliam Wood, Historian Grace United Methodist Church*

# John Gee A.M.E. Church

John Gee Church was organized in 1818 and was at that time called Bethel Church. In the beginning services were held in a small building across the street from the present edifice. It stood for many years as a church and also a refuge for soldiers during the Civil War and at the time of Leighton's Retreat, many refugees stayed in the church until they found a permanent place to go. It served as a safe harbor in the Underground Railroad connection.

In the spring of 1866, the building was in such bad condition, that Rev. Mortimer was sent from conference to investigate. Finding the building not worth repairing, he ordered it torn down.

In the fall of 1866 under the leadership of one of it's charter members the cornerstone of the present building was laid and dedicated in the fall of 1868. The other organizers of the church were Barbara Gee (John's wife), Henry Bell, William Napper, Thomas Scott, John Black, Alexander Woody, Leah Stewart, George Toney, and Jessie Devine. Because John Gee donated the land and led in the building of the structure, in 1886 the name was changed to John Gee A.M.E. Chapel.

Under the pastorate of Charles Newsome the bell was hung and still hangs in the bell tower. In 1888 the conference of the A.M.E. Church was held at John Gee. Present were prominent black figures in the black history, such as Bishop D.A. Payne, a writer, Bishop B.W. Arnett, a school teacher who became chaplain of the Ohio House of Representatives, and an elected member of the House from Greene County. Present also was Benjamin Lee who served as President of Wilberforce College.

Also Levi Coppin, remembered as Editor of the A.M.E.'s Church Review, a literary journalist and also his wife Fanny, noted in history for her great efforts in education.

The conference lasted four days. On the fourth several ministers who were present, preached at the local white churches.

Rev. Tolliver, who was pastor at that time (1887) planned the largest Emancipation Proclamation celebration in Gallia County History. It was one of several held at John Gee.

The last pastor who served at John Gee was Rev. James Harris of Huntington, West Virginia. In 1998 the membership was down to four people and the doors were closed in April 1998. John Gee still stands as a beacon in the community and is still serving God's people.

John Gee A.M.E. Church

# Mt. Carmel Baptist Church

In retrospect of by gone years, the Mt. Carmel Baptist Church turns not backward but to the future, and looking, we see a great cloud of witnesses from whom our beginning was born. In the year of 1901, some spiritual minded persons of the community felt the need of a Sunday Church School for the purpose of religiously educating the children.

Rev. James Calloway was elected the first Supt. of the Sunday School. The teachers were Sarah Belle Bryant, Katie Calloway, Margaret Ealy, and L. Nuby. The treasurer, Katie Calloway and the secretary, Joe Ford.

Soon after launching the Sunday School, Rev. and Mrs. B. R. Smith and many others from Porter, Ohio joined the group. By 1903, the Sunday School attendance had grown to such a large number and enthusiasm for spiritual guidance had so heightened that it was decided with the consent of the Board of Education that sermons and prayer service could be held in the school building. The schoolhouse was insufficient for the number of people who attended the morning worship. After prayerful and careful consideration, a small tract of land was purchased from Arch Dyer and a small building was erected. Sunday School and pray service and sermons were continued. Before the close of 1903, with the Spirit leading, a church was established. The charter members were Rev, and Mrs. Calloway, Mr. and Mrs. Turner Smith, Mr. and Mrs. Cephas Cooley, Mr. and Mrs. Geo. Ealy, Rev, and Mrs. I.V. Bryant, Rev, and Mrs. James Ferris, Mr. and Mrs. John Mayo, Mr. and Mrs. Joseph McDaniel, Mary Viney, and Ethel Bryant. The church was now ready for a name. A committee was appointed for this purpose. They selected the name Mt. Carmel, which means the Mt. of God. A bell was presented by John Powell. The first pastor was Rev. Cornelius Mundell. The first Deacon Board was: Turner Smith, Geo. Ealy, and Cephas Cooley. Mary Viney was elected church clerk Mrs. Lizzie Cooley was the first treasurer. Due to the shortage of laymen, ministers had to fill the officers for trustees. They were Rev. Ferris, Rev. Calloway and Rev. I. V. Bryant. An organ was purchased for the church. Although she was a small child, Edith Bryant was chosen pianist for Mt. Carmel. She served faithfully from that time until in 1942 when God called her from us.

After many years of hard work, Rev. Mundell accepted a call in Fostoria, Ohio and moved there. Rev. Calloway, who had served as Supt. for so many years, became the second pastor.

Other pastors who have served were: Rev. Riddle, Ferris, Mayo, Woodard, Gray, Bass, Epperson, C. M. Smith, B. R. Smith, O. P. Wright, Gillison, J. H. Rickman, Seth Winston, C. M. Payne, L. Hogan, Lee Williams, Vance Watson, E. Buffington, and Rev. H. Fletcher.

Twice the late Rev. C. M. Payne was called to the pastorate of the church. His first call was in 1919 and last in 1938. He served the church faithfully for 34 years until he resigned in June 1958. Rev. Payne was Pastor Emeritus of Mt. Carmel in 1958 and served in that capacity until his home going in 1962. Rev. Lacey W. Hogan succeeded Rev. Payne. His health did not permit him to serve long. The Rev. L. W. Williams of Columbus, Ohio was called and served well until his work compelled him to resign.

In May of 1969, Rev. Vance Watson was called to Mt. Carmel. Rev. Watson and wife Eloise served Mt. Carmel with love and faithfulness. Then in the March of 1989, on Easter Sunday, Rev Watson tendered his resignation. Rev. Watson continued his service until May 14, 1989. After 20 years of loving, faithful service, a special celebration was held, bringing to an end years of devotion to the church and community.

The church is a participating member of Providence Missionary Association, the Ohio Baptist General Convention and many national and foreign missions.

The organizations: The Sunday School, Bible Study, Prayer Service, Laymen League and others are very much alive in performing their Christian duty.

Though the building has changed through the years and her members and leaders come and go her course remains the same as it did in the days of old when the founding fathers said "We will name her Mt. Carmel." *Submitted by: Ethel Bryant Lee— Daughter of Rev. Bryant*

---

The present officers of our Church are:
Pastor: Rev. Gene A. Armstrong
Deacon: Glenn Miller
Trustees: Hollis Miller, Bobby Payne, Andy Gilmore, Richard Payne, James Williams, James Hogan
Church Treasurer: Ernestine Mundell
Church Clerk: Connie Evans
Financial Clerk: Mrs. Bernice P. Borden
Education: Corliss Miller
Dining: Mrs. Elaine Armstrong, First Lady
Pianists: Joanne Bass, Lori Lafferty

# Nazarene Church

In 1928, the church was organized by Rev. Perry Rude with the following charter members: Mrs. Laura Casto, Rev, and Mrs. Carl Clendenen, and Mrs. Mary Russell. The small store-front building was located on Eastern Avenue.

In 1935, the church was moved to a barn located on Fourth Avenue where the Holzer Clinic Sycamore Branch now stands. That same year the church moved to a small building on Olive Street, by the old train depot. Rev. Eddie Burnem was the Pastor. In 1936, the congregation moved into the little Methodist Chapel located at 1163 Second Ave. in 1939, Rev. Phineas Johnson became Pastor for a short period of time.

In April, 1941, the District Superintendent, feeling the future of the church was so uncertain, sent Rev. Vernon Shafer to Gallipolis to close the church. Rev. Shafer saw the possibilities of a great church and challenged the people to go forward for God. The congregation increased in number, and in 1944, a lot was purchased for a new sanctuary. On April 14, 1947, the Second Avenue sanctuary was dedicated. Rev. Shafer ministered at the Gallipolis church for twenty-two years, leaving in 1963.

Rev. Ronald Justice became the pastor in 1963. During the next nine years, attendance grew and the church purchased two properties on First Avenue and a parsonage at 121 Bastiani Drive.

In 1972, Rev. Ralph Scott came to us with a vision of building a new sanctuary. We purchased the remaining property on First Avenue, up to Mill Creek, over to and including the Old Mission Building. Rev. Scott left in 1974.

In September, 1974, Rev. John Utterback was called as our pastor. He helped in the building of our new sanctuary. He left in 1977.

Rev. Bob Madison came in October, 1977. While he was here, the community became aware of our church through his loving, compassionate outreach. The Madisons served our church for eleven years.

In August, 1988, God called Rev. Michael Bearden to our church. With his vision for a Family Life Center, plus starting the annual "Easter Pageant", the church grew. The land around the church was cleared for a new building; and the youth parsonage was moved to land that was donated to the church on Sunset Drive. The present parsonage located on State Route 218 was also purchased. The Beardens left in 1996.

In February, 1997 Rev. Cecil Jones came to minister. Pastor Jones was very compassionate and a great community leader. The Family Life Center was completed; and this building has become a tool for community outreach. Pastor Jones left in August, 2000.

January, 2001, saw the arrival of our present pastor, Dr. Robert Fulton. God has blessed with an increase in attendance. Additional staff members have been added to minister to our community: Pastor Daniel Campbell, Youth and Worship; Pastor Eugene Harmon, Visitation and Outreach; Pastor Ruth Ann Fellure, Children Ministries.

Gallipolis Church of the Nazarene opens wide its doors and welcomes everyone in the name of Jesus Christ our Lord.

*Nazarene Church*

# Paint Creek Regular Baptist Church

Paint Creek Regular Baptist Church stands as a religious institution whose inspirational influence has touched the lives of not only its own members, but persons of all denominations, regardless of race or color. It is a church whose very existence is a reminder to the forlorn and despairing that hope is never lost.

Imagine the 1800's— our forefathers under hardship and persecution, many unable to read or write, looking across the river at relatives, friends, and neighbors still under the bondage of slavery. In those times, with faith in Jesus Christ and feeling the need for a permanent establishment of free worship, a committee was formed consisting of Rev. James B. Steward, Gabriel Hurgo, Mr. and Mrs. Henry Howard, Susan Ward, Judith Ward, Mr. and Mrs. Isaac Lewis and Fielding Spears. This committee met in September 1833 in the home of Isaac Lewis which was located on the banks of a small stream called Paint Creek. This creek flows to this day through the lower end of Gallipolis emptying into Chicamauga Creek. Perhaps it was natural that the church was called Paint Creek Regular Baptist Church.

The Lewis home was used as the church until the early 1840's when the church had to relocate into a large barn on what is now 714 and 716 Third Avenue. At that time many of the people of color who had settled in the area were being forced to move elsewhere. Reasons were never stated but probably greed and prejudice were the factors. Thus the struggle for survival of this church and its congregation was taking place prior to the Emancipation Proclamation of 1863.

In 1870, the trustees purchased the lot at 833 Third Avenue from Mr. and Mrs. Viney. and it is the present home of Paint Creek. This purchase caused such a problem with surrounding white property owners that they started a squeeze, forcing the trustees to file a suit. After several years, a court order was rendered in favor of the church.

Paint Creek has served as a center of community activities throughout the years. The commencement exercises of Lincoln Colored School were held at the church prior to the desegregation of the city high school. Rev. C. C. Hart and other civic leaders brought suit upon all responsible persons who maintained that equal but separate rights in the schools should exist. A copy of this case is on file in Gallipolis and it states in part as of December 29, 1918, all high school students shall be enrolled at Gallia Academy High School and every effort toward segregation shall cease." This is accredited as being the first such suit filed east of the Mississippi River.

Paint Creek is also unique in that it is one year older than the oldest Chartered Negro Association within the United States.

Sunday School has always been a most important part of the church It provides the foundation for the spiritual education of our children. Enrollment in 1952 was 151 students. The Sunday School reached out with Vacation Bible School, which for years was combined with John Gee African Methodist Episcopal Church. The students attended classes at both churches for two weeks, and the teachers were from both churches. The Vacation Bible School is now held for one week and the teaching staff and students come from various churches in our community and Pt. Pleasant, West Virginia. We thank God that denomination has never been a dividing factor between the churches in our community.

During the 1950's, there were three choirs—Senior, Junior and Sunbeam Chorus. The Senior Choir continues today comprised of adult men and women. The Junior Choir was composed of high school students under the direction of a peer musician, singing mostly gospel. Toddlers and children through grade 8 made up the Sunbeam Chorus. This choir was very popular, and they sang at schools and on WJEH, our local radio station.

The church building has had renovations over the years but history was made in June 1998 when a tornado damaged the church destroying the original stained glass in the front windows. The glass was replaced matching as closely as possible to the original, and the repair of the bell tower and roof afforded the first change of color to the church structure. Also the property at 837 Third Avenue was acquired by the church and is the new shelter house area.

The church is now under the pastorate of Rev. Harry Scott, Jr., a native son of Gallipolis who began his walk with the Lord as a child at Paint Creek.

Abide in me, and I in you. As the branch cannot bear fruit of itself, except it abide in the vine, no more can you, except you abide in me." (John 15:4) Having faith in Jesus Christ, Our Lord, the membership continues to serve God in this community; and after 168 years, the doors of Paint Creek Regular Baptist Church remain open to all. *Written and submitted by Bobette Dexter Braxton*

# Providence Missionary Baptist Church

This is a picture of Providence Missionary Baptist Church in 1986 on Teens Run Road in Clay Twp.

The first Church was built in Harrison Twp. Gallia County, Ohio about 1821 on section # 7 near the junction of Rock Lick Creek and Big Bullskin Creek.

All records of the first several years have been lost. We only know that part of the history was handed down by the older generation to the present generation.

It is said that the building was built of logs, with an open fireplace for wood as fuel, with dog irons to secure the wood logs. Each log of the building was of buckeye timber.

This first building was furnished with seats made from split logs. Located eleven miles from the Gallia County Courthouse at Gallipolis, Ohio; in a near due south direction. It was the first Church built on the south side of Gallipolis, for more than twenty miles. The first building burned about 1826.

The second church was also built of logs and located one mile East of the first building, located on section 1 of Clay Twp. Gallia County, Ohio. It was completed in 1852. It also burned in 1887, but was replaced on the same site in 1888 with a frame structure which is still standing today. A cemetery is near the church it also is called Providence. The first church was on land donated by the Wm. Smith Family. The second and third was on land donated by the Geo. Clark Family.

In the year of 1821 two men by the name of John Lee and Joshua Rippley of the Sandfork Baptist Church came into the vicinity of Providence and begin preaching. Gaining a number of followers, a body was organized as an arm of the Sandfork Church. When they sought a name for the church, the name of Providence was mentioned and adopted.

They thought it an act of providence that a church was established in the sparsely inhabited neighborhood.

The first record book was destroyed. The second book shows in Sept. 1832 Hiram Dewitt joined the Church making the total of 31 members, Joshua Lewis was church clerk. In 1834 the Church membership started a subscription to build a meeting house. January 1836 Elder John Lee became Pastor. In 841 the Church obtained an act of incorporation from the general assembly, also at that time Wm. Wolfe was church clerk, and John Haskell was Pastor.

In 1848 John F.M. Hall was church clerk and James E. Caldwell was licensed to preach. September 1849 Levi Mc Daniel held a long revival, leading to a building a house of worship in 1851, Hamilton Day was the carpenter on the job being completed in 1852.

In May 1859 sixteen members asked to he dismissed to constitute a new Church. On Saturday before the second Sunday in June 1859 members James Henderson, A.J. Warren, James E. Caldwell, and John Houck formed a new church and named it Mt. Zion

In March 1860 thirty-three members presented a written request to be released to constitute a Church at Guyan Town House. It was constituted a Church on March 26, 1860 by James Henderson, A.J. Warren, and Issac Langdon. The name was called Providence Bethel Church, which was the beginning of the Mercerville Church.

Providence Church held its Centennial meeting beginning Friday night August 19, 1921 and continued until the afternoon of Sunday August 21, 1921.

After a century of worshiping in the present Lord's House, the Church in 1986 was involved in another building program where two classrooms, vestibule and restrooms were added to the present structure. In 1987 the church purchased additional land for the purpose of improving the parking lot and driveway. With the purchase of the additional land, in 1990 a building project nearly doubled the size of the present building with the addition of one more classroom, fellowship room and special restrooms to meet the needs of handicapped individuals.

In 2001 an additional 12 acres was purchased for a total of 14 acres. Presently the church is developing the land, with a fitness trail, ball field, play area, and in the future a church camp. All for the glory of GOD, calling it Providence for a church to survive in a sparsely populated area.

Providence Missionary Baptist Church

# Rodney United Methodist Church

Rodney United Methodist Church located in the village of Rodney at 6611 SR 588 approximately six miles west of Gallipolis, was established in 1851, its congregation meeting in Roscoe Fox's Store.

On October 4, 1856, George B. and Polly Smith sold Lot #13 for $20. to the trustees of Rodney Methodist Episcopal Church for the purpose of building a new church. Construction began in 1857, using bricks made of native clay baked in a kiln on the hill north of Rodney, now part of the Joe DeLille farm. It had an entrance on each side, one for women, one for the men, with seating on the inside separated also.

The pulpit stand, still being used today, was given to the church in memory of Rev. W. H. Gibbins, pastor in 1887, by his daughters.

In 1905, side doors were removed and one central entrance was built. Wood burning stoves were replaced with fuel oil stoves around 1948.

A front vestibule was built in 1950, and the entire church covered with stucco, grounds landscaped, concrete walk poured to the road in front of church, and horse hitching rails removed (realizing that the automobile was here to stay).

During the last year of Rev. C. E. Eyre's ministry in 1954, the sanctuary was remodeled with the chancel being raised extending the entire width of the room. In 1958, 1959, and 1960, under the direction of Rev. Charles W. Hill, four Sunday School rooms divided by sliding doors, a new gas furnace, and more concrete walks were added. During the June 1968 West Ohio Conference, the Methodist and United Brethern Churches merged forming the United Methodist Church.

In 1974, during the ministry of Rev. Daryl Fourman, the inside of the sanctuary was totally renovated including new carpeting and draperies. In the fall of 1976, three lots behind the church were purchased for the building of an educational wing. Early in the year of 1977, plans were drawn by Terry Vallance under the direction of Rev. Damon Stapleton and a building committee composed of Raymond DeLille, chairman; James Blevins, Jean Gillespie, and Elva Holbrook. The contractor was Bradley Harder.

On Sunday evening, July 10, 1977, ground—breaking ceremonies were held, and the footer was started August 17. Homecoming in September was held in the new building with a concrete floor but less a roof! Carpeting was installed in January 1978, making the new wing complete and ready to use.

The educational wing was consecrated in ceremonies on June 4, 1978, with noon dinner being followed by an open house reception. Rev. Hughey Jones, Assistant to the Bishop, West Ohio Conference of the United Methodist Church, and Rev. Wesley Clarke, Athens District Superintendent, were guest speakers morning and evening respectively.

At the Annual Homecoming, September 16, 1990, David Harris, Program Curriculum Chairman, Athens District, presided over the mortgage burning and dedication services along with Pastor Ed Mingus. A day-long praise service was held with special music furnished by the Builders Quartet of Ripley, WV.

On July 27, 1995, lightening struck the steeple of the church causing a fire which greatly damaged the sanctuary. Renovation after the fire included a new roof and wooden ceiling, new light fixtures, new oak trim and doors, and new carpeting. The antique pews were saved being stripped and refinished by members of the congregation with new velvet pads made for them. At this time new carpeting was also installed in the hallway and Fellowship Room.

A dedication of the sanctuary was held on March 10, 1996, with Rev. Arland King in charge of the service, Rev. James Waugh, Athens District Superintendent, guest speaker, and Joanne Wellington presenting special music.

The church acquired the old Rodney Grade School Building and property, and it is now the Rodney United Methodist Community Center for which a dedication was held on November 22, 1998. It is a center for weekly youth activities and many other events.

Down through the years, almost all of the many furnishings and appointments of the church were given in honor or memory of and by members and their families.

At this time, Rev. Arland and Martha King are the church's pastoral family. Services are: Sunday School at 10:00 a.m.: Worship at 11:00 a.m.: UMYF at 6:00 p.m.: Wednesday Bible Studies at 7:00 p.m. Many special services and events are held each year in this very active church including VBS each summer, a very large mission outreach, United Methodist Women meeting monthly, a Church-wide Retreat in the fall of each year at Camp Francis Asbury, monthly fellowship activities, an annual community St. Patrick's Day Dinner, and an annual Homecoming the third Sunday in September, just to name a few. *Submitted by Jean Gillespie on behalf of the congregation*

# St. Peter's Episcopal Church

The exact date that Episcopalians began organized worship in Gallipolis is not known but in December 1841 "the Rev. James B. Goodwin assembled a few professed friends of the Church, and proposed to them to organize a Parish of the Protestant Episcopal Church." The first vestry included Peter Menager, Senior Warden, Dr. Edward Naret, Junior Warden and members Charles Creuzet, Darius Maxon, Alonzo Cushing, A. C. Harrington, James Eaton, William Clendenin, Dr. Elisha Morgan, Augustus LeClercq, Joseph Drouillard and Robert Black. The vestry appointed Rev. Goodwin, a missionary priest from the Diocese of Virginia, as the first rector. Early services were held in the Court House on the Public Square and in a stucco building on the 200 block of Second Avenue.

The vestry negotiated to purchase a lot to build at 227 Second Avenue. Construction got underway about 1842/3 and services were held in an unfinished building. No deeds were ever recorded and the construction was abandoned. Sixteen years later in May 1858 another lot was purchased for $700.00 in the 500 block of Second Avenue from the Board of Education. A small two-story brick school building had to be torn down and within seven months a brick structure which cost $2,341.00 was ready and on December 19, 1858 St. Peter's was opened for religious services under Rev. A. B. Sturgess. On April 12, 1859 the building was consecrated by Bishop Charles P. McIlvaine.

The original structure is still the beautiful sanctuary of the church and remains essentially the same as it did in 1858.

The bell tower appears to have been added about 1868 after the anonymous gift of a bell. The bell weighs 960 pounds and must be rung only for religious services. It is never to be rung in celebration of any national, political or civil event or holiday unless religious services are also held. The bell from Marruley's, West Troy, NY has an inscription, "Presented to St. Peter's Church, Gallipolis, Ohio, July 1, 1868. In Memoriam. Come ye, and let us go up to the mountain of the Lord, to the house of the God of Jacob." Isaiah 2: 3. Bishop Onderdonk of New York was later discovered to have been the donor. He was likely related to Henry M. Onderdonk who served on the vestry in 1866.

By 1876 both morning and evening services were held on Sunday as well as Sunday School. In 1881 during Lent, Wednesday and Friday evening services were added.

In 1882 the vestry included A. Vance, William Cherrington, W. R. Morgan, S. A. Nash, E. S. Aleshire, A. L. Langley and Samuel Roberts.

The ladies in the 1880's were famous for their socials with supper, ice cream and cake for twenty-five cents, and a pancake festival with the operetta, Dairymaid's Festival, part of the benefit. A fall Sunday School picnic excursion was made on the K & O Railroad up the Kanawha Valley.

In 1883 "Seats were free" for the services. Extensive remodeling took place in 1884 and the pews were painted and grained to give the appearance of handsome oak. The walls were papered, a carpet and new furnace provided and a wide flagstone pavement replaced the old brick one with a wide step at the door. At one time there was a coal furnace with a register in the middle aisle.

It was 1888 before the first vestry minutes were kept. Women were not allowed to vote. It was agreed to try to get a free organist and a voluntary choir. A convention was held in Marietta.

In 1889 convention delegates were appointed by the rector.

In 1898 electric lights were added and in 1899 the vestry voted to get a new furnace. In 1900 a Parish House was built with water to be put in for the first time.

In 1901 those organizations giving reports were the Choir, Ladies Aid, Sunday School, Young Ladies' Guild, and I Serve. The vestry awarded a contract for a new pipe organ in 1903.

St. Peter's formed a corporation in 1911 to promote the cause of Christian faith and religion and to provide and maintain a place of worship. A rectory was also purchased at this time. In 1913 the parish picnic was held at the Fair Grounds at Cliffeside with about 300 in attendance with baseball and an orchestra part of the festivities.

In 1917 the annual meeting had only one male present, the rector, due to the war. In 1918 the flu epidemic caused the church to be closed. The bell rang in the morning and evening to remind people to worship at home.

In 1923 the first woman, Miss Maggie McClurg, was elected to the vestry. The Altar Guild was started in 1933. In 1949 a new front walk and steps were added.

In 1954 a new addition was finished and four rooms were later added for a church school. The pipe organ was replaced with a modern organ which was refurbished in the 1980's.

In 1974 the backlighted stained glass window depicting our patron Saint, Peter, and his brother Andrew attending their nets at the shore of the Sea of Galilee was added. It was designed by Rev. Albert H. Mackenzie.

In 1976 the vestry purchased the old Holzer Hospital and resold all except for a portion on which St. Peter's planned to expand. A building fund drive with matching funds from the Diocese allowed $300,000 for a new addition. Groundbreaking was in June 1978 and the building was completed in February 1979. The new building was consecrated August 10, 1980 by Bishop William G. Black.

Today St. Peter's continues to thrive with the present rector, Rev. Susan Rebecca Michelfelder. The vestry consists of Bill Davis, Senior Warden, Chris Murawski, Junior Warden, Tim Betz, Aline Clarke, Jim Doubleday, Bob France, Marlene Hoffman, Bobbie Holzer, Tish Hudson, Tammy Richards, and Carolyn Anderson, ex-officio. Christ has died. Christ is risen. Christ will come again. *Submitted by Vestry, St. Peter's Episcopal Church*

*St. Peter's Episcopal Church Sanctuary - Dates Back to 1858*

# New Life Lutheran Church

II Corinthians 5:17... Therefore, if anyone is in Christ, he is a new creation; the old has gone, the new has come!

John 10:10...I have come that they may have life, and have it to the full.

New Life Lutheran Church came into being and exists to live in and proclaim Christ's saving Gospel.

In the spring of 1971, a small number of Lutherans met to discuss the possibility of beginning a Lutheran congregation in the Southeastern Ohio River community of Gallipolis. A steering committee was formed and the local Episcopal congregation rented their facilities on a sharing basis for weekly worship. Worship services for the New Life congregation began on May 21, 1972.

On March 9, 1975, ground was broken and by the fall of that year, the congregation was located at 1210 State Route 160.

The membership of New Life professes a belief that Jesus Christ is the revelation of God's love for people as witnessed in His death and resurrection. Through that act, our sins are forgiven and we begin to live in a new life which goes on with God forever. This "new life" in Christ is nourished by God's Word and by the sacraments of Baptism and Holy Communion, and comes to its greatest fulfillment in this life as we live in the fellowship of all believers.

The Lutheran Church in general and New Life Lutheran specifically, strives to be a serving church. The congregation is determined to make its presence felt in the community, making it a better place to live as a result of serving Christ and proclaiming His Gospel.

Through the dedication of many lay persons this church desires to make an impact into the community, extending help to those in need. With the leadership of dedicated pastors and the Word of our Lord, this church will bring "New Life" to those who will accept it.

On May 20, 2001, the congregation held its first worship service in a beautiful new facility in the Spring Valley area. Dedication took place on June 24, 2001. We are most thankful and blessed, and certainly desire to use this facility and our entire God given resources in serving Him in our community.

# St. Martins German Evangelical Lutheran Church & Cemetery

Construction of the church began sometime in 1869 or 1870 and was completed in 1870. The church was built by Mr. Rutt near the center of the German settlement on the highest point of German Ridge, Walnut Township, Gallia County. On the 10th. day of May 1871, Frederick and Justine Klages, Klages, Ohio, donated land for the church and cemetery. The 3rd day of November 1916, Richard and Jane Tope deeded land for the hitching post lot. Additional burial ground was deeded by Todd and Teresa Baker, 29th day of July 1994. About 20 members dedicated the new church. Some of who attended the dedication and services were; Klages, Poppoe, Wedemeyer, Ropeter, Grube, Price, Muller, Rutt, Ahlborn, Cook, Wooda and Lear. The first recorded burial was in 1874, G. Wilamena Grube. Minutes were recorded in German from 1870 through 1906. Proceedings of the first recorded meeting the 20th day of November 1870 are as follows. "Meeting opened with song and prayer. One of the resolutions #3 was voted on and passed was any member who misses three meetings without good reason will be punished by paying $.25. First pastor was John P. Muller. Some of his duties included to preach the Gospel loud and clear according to Luther and confirm his teachings through a good and clean lifestyle. Signed by Frederick Klages, Secretary in 1859.

The Germans started migrating to what is now known as German Hollow/ Ridge, Patriotarea. Some time in the 1870's, they named the area Klages, Ohio. They came from Hanover Germany, Dorste County.

A memorial church was built in 1965 to honor the first German settlers. The church was paid for by estate money left by the late Fred H. Klages.

A tradition by the German people in dedicating a new home or church was for the carpenter to climb to the rooftop. A pine tree would be carried across the yard by men and taken to the carpenter. Two long ribbons were attached to the top of the tree and the other two ends were held by young girls.

The ribbons were usually ones that had been brought from German. Another girl bought a white plate with a glass of wine in the center, encircled with an ivy wreath. When the carpenter had the tree fastened to the gable end of the building, he spoke a few dedicatory words, drank the wine and threw the glass over the treetop. If the glass broke, bad luck would be expected to come to the occupants. If it did not break, it was a sign of good luck.

There are sixteen veterans buried in the cemetery. Henry L. Myers places flags on the graves every Decoration/Memorial Day. Members of the Veterans of Foreign Wars, Post #4464. Gallipolis erected and dedicated a flag pole in the year 2000. *Photo and article submitted by Henry L. Myers, President and caretaker of the church and cemetery. Some of the people identified in the picture are as follows: Fred and Ethel (Myers) Pope family, Earnest and Eda (Pope) Carter family, Erie and Elma (Pope) Rose family, August (Gus) Mae Miller family, Henry and Fred Klages and Pastor John Muller.*

## Walnut Ridge U.B. Church

The present Walnut Ridge U.B. Church was built in 1898. It was framed by James H.B. Lumas and his sons, Will and Clarence. The old church stood close to the Old Walnut Ridge Cemetery on Lincoln Pike, just off St. Rt. 790. Some of the charter members were Simion Blazer, Jim Caroll, Perry Clark, Monroe Fillinger, Nora Sanders, Pearlie Stewart, Settie Stewart, John and Carrie Notter.

Three of the older pastors were Ray Beegle, Stanley Hixon, and Floyd Bostick. A revival was held by Ray Beegle and Rev. Elias Wickline and there were over 100 souls saved. Floyd Bostick was the pastor in 1945 - the church entrance and bell tower were added in later years while he was still pastoring the church. Rev. Orville Carico came as pastor in 1950. He served two different times, with a total of 16 years.

In the year 1950, we had an attendance of 35 to 40. Hebert Notter was S.S. Superintendent. Hazel Myers and Mae Marr were the pianists. In 1953, Garland Williams was elected as the S.S. Superintendent, he served until his health failed in 1985. Rev. Richard Graham came as pastor in the early 60's. Rev. Jack Baldwin served in 1970, at which time we withdrew from the Evangelical Conference to become an Independent U.B. Church.

Rev. Ernest Baker served two different terms. He died in 1986. We had several fill-in pastors: Rev. Webb, Billy Payne, Ralph Riley, Jack Berry, Floyd and George Brumfield. Rev. Earl Hinkle served as pastor and fill-in pastor. He preached his last sermon July 12, 1988 at age 92. Rev. Keith Adkins served from June 1988 till July 8, 1990.

Our present pastor, Larry Hall, began ministering Sept. 23, 1990. Mrs. Flora Dailey serves as our pianist and Don Baker is presently serving as the S.S. Superintendent. Our oldest members are Glenn T. Marr, Sadie Notter, MaeBelle Pope, and Evelyn Williams. We have an attendance of around 30, with 15 active members.

St. Peter's Episcopal Church, Gallipolis, Ohio

Ewington Academy

# Gallia County Clubs & Organizations

*Downtown, Gallipolis, Ohio*

*Home of the French Art Colony*

# Daughters Of The American Revolution French Colony Chapter

Early in the year of 1926, fifteen organizing members met at the home of the organizing Regent, Mrs. Frank Bell. They arranged for the organization of a Chapter of the Daughters of the American Revolution, the first chapter of this society formed in Gallipolis, Ohio and 135 years after the French Five Hundred settled in Gallipolis. There were fifteen organizing members, a few former members of the Colonel Charles Lewis Chapter, Point Pleasant, West Virginia, the Return Jonathan Meigs Chapter, Pomeroy, Ohio and the others were members-at-large.

The application for a charter was sent to the National Society, Daughters of the American Revolution, in Washington, DC on April 11 and the charter was issued on either April 14 or 17, 1926. Its national number is 1727 and the name given by the NSDAR was "Esther Hull Chapter". This name was chosen because Esther Hull was the mother of two patriots of the Revolutionary War from Gallia County, Ohio, Joel Barlow and Eleazer Curtis. On October 20, 1926, the National Board changed the name of the chapter form "Esther Hull" to "French Colony", by a request from the newly formed chapter.

The organizing members were: Mrs. Frank (Fannie Holloway) Bell, Mrs. Hubert (Eleanor Neal) Carnes, Miss Lovell Condee, Mrs. J. E. (Maude Dunbar) Halliday, Mrs. W. N. (Helen) Gardner, Mrs. Charles D. (Minnie Shallcross) Kerr, Mrs. Anthony W. (Emma) Gatewood Kems, Mrs. Frank (Charlotte Hannan) Mills, Mrs. E. Lincoln (Mary Mullineaux) Neal, Mrs. William (Lady Halliday) O'Brien, Mrs. Louis B. (Helen Kerns) Shaw, Mrs. Carrie Bell Walker, Miss Jessie E. Walker, Miss Bessie B. Wetherholt and Mrs. George (Blanche Derry) Wetherholt.

This small group of historical, patriotic and educated women soon started many local projects that to this day stand as a record of their interests and achievements. The first of these was a bronze memorial tablet placed on the "Our House Museum" in 1927. This was the 170th. anniversary of the birth of General Marquis de Lafayette. The marker was placed to commemorate Lafayette's visit to Gallipolis and "Our House" in 1825. This new chapter decided to try and preserve, mark and save the historical points of interest in the city.

On October 19, 1933, which was the 152$^{nd}$ year since the surrender of Cornwallis, as well as the landing of the French settlers in Gallipolis, at two o'clock in the afternoon, the dedication of the new Memorial Gateway to Mound Hill Cemetery took place. This was a result of a five-year dream of chapter members. It was erected as a memorial to the soldiers of all wars but bears a tablet on which the names of thirty Revolutionary War soldiers whose graves in Gallia County have been marked. The gateway was designed by Downie Moore of Columbus and was built of native stone (rubble) and Bedford (In..) dressed stone. A bronze ornament on either column holds by day the heavy chains that close the gates at night. Urns of growing plants are on top of each column. Later, on October 19, 1969, another dedication took place, to rededicate a plaque on one side of the gateway that vandals had stolen.

During World War II, the chapter took as its main project the raising of money for blood plasma. In October of 1994, French Colony had a festive celebration at the French Art Colony honoring the men and women that served Gallia County and this nation during World War II. This was in conjunction with the 50th anniversary of the United States entering into the war. A national award for Commemorative Events was presented to the chapter during the annual NSDAR Continental Congress in Washington DC, April of 1995 for this event.

September 2001, French Colony honored the men and women of the Korean War at the French Art Colony with a Korean War POW veteran speaking and many items from this era were on display. Honoring the men and women of World War II and Korean War were year long celebrations of the sacrifices the men and women gave for the country. French Colony has always adhered to requirements and standards of both the NSDAR and the OSDAR by fulfilling the requests by both. Attendance at OSDAR Conference has been top priority and continues today with many chapter members in attendance. French Colony has had officers on both state and national levels. Members of French Colony are proud of their ancestors that helped to make it possible for all to live in freedom and continue to strive to preserve our rich history. *Submitted By: Marjorie Gilliam Wood, Historian French Colony Dar*

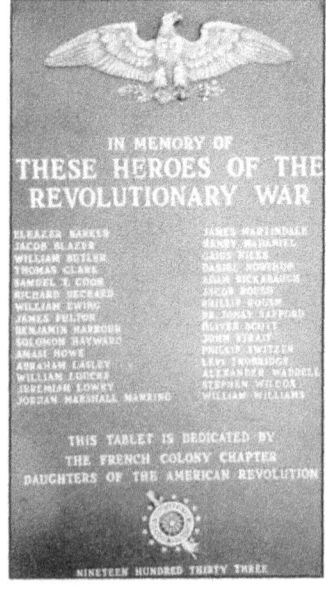

# Emancipation, Gallia County Style

September 22, 2001, one hundred and thirty-eight years ago, these word reach Gallia County, Ohio.

Whereas, on the twenty-second day of September, in the year of our Lord, 1862, a proclamation was issued by the President of the United States, containing, among other things, the following, to wit: That on the first day of January, in the year of our Lord 1863, all persons held as slaves within any state, or designated part of a state, the people whereof shall then be in rebellion against the limited States, shall be then, thence forward and forever free: and the Executive Government of the United States, including the military and naval authority thereof, will recognize and maintain the freedom of such persons, and will do no act or acts to repress such persons, or any of them in any effort they may make for their actual freedom.

The Emancipation Proclamation helped end slavery in the United States, but it didn't bring true freedom. It was a beginning.

The celebration of the freeing of the slaves began in Gallia County in 1863, and was held every year on September 22, no matter what day of the week. Now, the celebration is a two-day event and moved to the third weekend in September.

The Emancipation Celebration in our Gallia County history was always a mixture of religion and politics. The churches usually planned the event.

Every event began with music by a band, the reading of the Emancipation Proclamation, prayer, followed by speeches.

The first Emancipation on record (according to James Sands, a writer for the Gallia County Times Sentinel) was held in 1876 on a Friday. The colored citizens celebrated their Emancipation Proclamation with the reading of an explanatory letter from President Lincoln by Miss. Gee and speeches by Captains Reynolds and Phelps of Pt. Pleasant, W. Va. Over 1200 were present.

In 1887, the celebration was held in Vinton, where the crowd was reported at between 6,000 and 10,000. Both blacks and whites attended.

In 1889 the event was scheduled for the fairgrounds, but rain forced the celebrants to take refuge in the courthouse, where a reputable speaker named M. Langston held the assembly captivated for two programs, one in the afternoon and one in the evening.

Some of the noted speakers were Rev. Barnett and Rev. Biddle. Biddle's speech entitled "The History of Slavery", drew over 2000 people to a park located in Vinton. The Emancipation of 1892 was a real grand affair, being held at the fairgrounds on Eastern Avenue. The band played, and then Mr. J. H. Lewis called the crowd to order. A select choir says "America" after which Rev. P. A. Baker invoked God's Blessings on our nation and people in a very splendid manner. John P. Green, the first Colored State Senator in Ohio was introduced and delivered an interesting speech.

There was a parade in the morning including the following bands: the Gallipolis Cornet Band, the Treadways Band, the Barbers Band, and the Gallipolis Drum Corp. Also marching were prominent African American groups; the A. F. of L., Odd fellows, Galileans, The Order of Universal Brotherhood, Mutual Aid Society, and the Daughters of Zion. Many banners and mottoes, pictures of Abraham Lincoln, John Langston, Frederick Douglas and John Brown were on display.

In 1894, the Emancipation was held in Gallipolis again. A parade was led by the Dixon Goen's Band. The mayor of Gallipolis, Senator Hutsinpiller, and Professor Grey shared the limelight with the Grand Marshall.

In 1893, the celebration was held at Watson's Grove in Bidwell and at the Old Camp ground at Kerr in 1896. The speaker was Rev. J. M. Davis, of Rio Grande and Professor J. M. Riddle of Xenia, Ohio. Other notables included Rev. I V. Bryant, Dr. Jordan and Dr. J. J. Jackson of Bellefountaine, Charles Cottrell, Charles Doll of Columbus, Rev. W. J. Fulton of Rio Grande. Later years, Herman Bryant and the late Beulah Johnson, grandchildren of Rev. I. V. Bryant were speakers.

Other locations have been Quickles Grove, Bidwell, Bowman's Grove, Vinton, Glenn's Grove, Evergreen, and Bush's Park between Porter and Bidwell.

Some of the Gallia Countians who have served as president of the Emanciption are The late Merman Howell, Thurman Keels, Monroe Johnson Sr., Rev. C. M. Payne and his daughter, the late Dorothy Payne Lewis, who served 40 years. For many years, she was the only woman to hold the position. Her sister, Mrs. Bernice Borden, also served as an officer many years.

More recent leaders have been James D. Hogan, who served 21 year and under whose leadership the celebration became a two day event, James D. Keels, Ms. Sara Sow. the second woman to be president, Robert D. Gordon, and our current president Andrew (Andy) Gilmore.

All the leaders have added to the history of the Emancipation Celebration in Gallia County. In recent years, of guest speaker have included several nationally prominent persons such as, Barbara Ross Lee, Dean of Osteopathic Medicine, Ohio University, Athens; Ivin B. Lee, first black woman police chief in W. Va., Dr. William Anderson and the Rev. Jessie Jackson. In 1999 our speaker was J. Kenneth Blackwell, Secretary of State.

Recently our own hometown speakers have been Arthur Clark, Dr. Delbert (Frank) Garnes, Ralph Taylor, William Henry Jr., Hank Doss, and George Gilmore. This year we add Mrs. Elaine Armstrong, Dean of students at the University of Rio Grande.

Many changes have been made over the years. We now have a history committee that keeps an excellent record of the past and present of our people. We have several arts and crafts booths, a health fair and many other informational booths. We have better entertainment and bigger prizes for our children, a queen contest for our young ladies and food booths to satisfy all.

After the recent tragic terrorist's attack on our nation, freedom seems especially dear to every American. As a nation and as a people we must keep the faith in our God and in our country.

In closing, I want to leave you with these words from James Weldon Johnson. "God of our weary years, God of our silent tears, Thou who hast brought us thus far on the way. Thou who hast by thy might, led us into the light, Keep us forever in the path we pray. Lest our feet stray from the places our God, where we met Thee, Lest our hearts, drunk with the wine of the world, we forget thee. Shadowed beneath thy hand, may we forever stand, True to our God, True to our native land. God Bless the USA.

---

2001 Emancipation Celebration Historical Committee
Corliss Miller, Chairperson
Barbara Scott
Ernestine Mundell

# French Art Colony

The French Art Colony, now in its 35th year, was born in 1964 to fill a void in the community. It continues to be a major force in the arts. With education as its primary goal, school children are frequently targeted, however arts for all ages is the overall aim for this multi-arts center at 530 First Avenue.

The original organization began as an oil painting class. Mr. J. Raymond Hoy, a local furniture maker, studied art in Mexico and wanted adult art education available in Gallipolis. He located and equipped a small studio on the second floor of the K of P Hall, over a pizza parlor, at the corner of Second and Locust. He persuaded Sarah Moshier to teach oil painting and sought others who were interested in learning. Students in the first group included Louise Brink, Beth Cherrington, Elmer Daniels, Dr. Arthur Fleming, Bobbie Holzer, Richard North, Mr. Hoy, Nancy Bean Reed and Dr. Don Thaler. The class began in September, 1964.

By the following spring, another class began with several new students. As expenses began to accumulate, in spite of a modest rent of $20 per month and $7 electric bills, the need for a more formal organization became apparent. A club was formed, named the French Art Colony (FAC), a constitution written and the first officers were elected. Dr. Thaler was the first president, followed by Peggy Black Evans and Jan Thaler, Other early officers were Donna Nibert Goble, Carolyn Roth Grove, Reva Mullins, Marge Snedaker, Pat Martin Splete, Gordon Roth, Jack and Jenny Hudson and others.

Within two years the need to provide art instruction for school age children was obvious. Summer classes at various sites, often out doors, were scheduled and many new mediums were added to the curriculum. Additional teachers were added including Jack Slavin, David Lyons, Marjorie Rinehart and Tom Lacey. Art exhibits were held wherever and whenever possible—in the Park, the Lafayette Hotel lobby, Oscars on Sundays, the lobby of the First National Bank on Second.

The Ohio Arts Council, formed in 1965, became a part of the life and planning process of the FAC. The agency was small and locals were on a first name basis with Director, Don Streibig and his assistant, John Briley. It was not unusual for them to visit Gallipolis and stay overnight at the Thalers. Because of the work of the FAC, Gallipolis was selected as one of the first two sites in Ohio for the Artist in the Schools program. Gallipolis City Schools housed a weaver, Kati Meek, at Washington Elementary for the school year. The FAC organized other residencies including poets, writers, sculptors and dancers.

From 1968 onward, club members were looking for larger facilities and first floor space. More class rooms and better exhibit space was needed. About this same time, the Board discovered that we were using the registered trademark for French City Industries (the Hoy connection). A contest was held and Jack Hudson's pallette logo was chosen and used until the current French flag theme was adopted.

By 1970, members were traveling the alleys looking for a garage or old warehouse as a potential home for the growing agency. There were 65 members and even a little money in the bank. Hopes were high and in September, Dr. Thaler approached Dr. Charles Holzer, Jr., then on the Board of the Commercial and Savings Bank, "to see whether a bank like the C & S would agree to finance the French Art Colony." When questioned, Dr. Thaler explained the need for larger space. Dr. Holzer's Mother, Alma, had died in July and his first question was, "What about my Mother's house?" This was certainly a major step above a greasy garage and resulted in a lengthy discussion in the Thaler household that evening. It was finally decided to present the idea to the Board at a special meeting. Reactions varied from high enthusiasm to serious doubt that the amount of money needed could be raised.

After much deliberation, the Board decided to proceed and a strategy was defined. The first step was to convince the community that this was a proper site for an art center. Three experts were brought in from the State Architects office, the Dayton Art Institute and the OAC, all of whom concurred with our site and strategy. We determined expenses, planned a budget and ways to meet it and began working on a house we did not own. Simultaneously, incorporation and non-profit status was achieved. Having done our homework, the capital campaign began in the spring of 1971. Three year pledges were sought for a total of $77,500. Volunteers renovated the house and we were able to burn the mortgage two years later.

Over the years the FAC has remained a vital part of the community. The accomplishments are many including development of the Gallipolis City Flag, the 0.0. McIntyre County Park logo, the Festival Exhibit competition, Very Special Arts program for special needs children, the Holzer Medical Center collection and numerous arts programs. It has been a host site for the Governor, the Ohio Supreme Court, various other dignitaries, tourist groups and potential candidates for business and industry. The FAC is "one of those things that just can't happen" in such a small town and it remains one of the reasons why Gallia County is the brightest star on the Ohio River.

# Gallia County Garden Clubs

The garden clubs listed in this history have at one time or another been associated with The Ohio Association of Garden Clubs (O.A.G.C.). Active clubs in Gallia County as of January 31, 2002 are: Cheshire, Floral Friends, Gallipolis, Open Gate, Rio Grande, Vinton Friendship and Wayside.

Cheshire Garden Club was organized April 15, 1958 with the first meeting held in the home of Flora Long who became the first president. Members chose the rose as their flower, club song, "In the Garden," and club theme, "To beautify our lives as well as our community." Cheshire Garden Club has taken part in community projects such as plantings at Gallipolis City Park, Cheshire and Gallipolis Post Offices, and Gallia County Fairgrounds. Katie Shoemaker, current president and member for 42 years, has served as Gallia County Contact Chairperson several times and was secretary for Region 11 for two terms. Jackie Graham and Darlene Milam have served as secretary for the Gallia County Garden Club organization. Cheshire took part in the Gallipolis Developmental Garden Therapy Program. Charter members still in the club are Helen Preston, Mildred Scott, and Mildred Swisher, a lifetime member of O.A.G.C.

Floral Friends Garden Club: A few friends and neighbors met at the home of Anne Baker in September of 1994 to determine interest in forming a garden club. They selected the name, Floral Friends; the flower, iris; and the hummingbird. Later, an organizational meeting was held at the home of Dolores Baker with a Regional representative of the OAGC assisting. . The twenty-two members selected Anne Baker, president; Phyllis Ingles, vice president, Dolores Baker, secretary; and Pauline Myers, treasurer. The club has grown to include thirty members for 2001-2002.

The Gallipolis Garden Club: On September 25, 1947 twenty young women met at the home of Mrs. Carroll Swanson to organize a garden club. Two charter members still enjoy membership with the club, Elizabeth Phillips and Thelma Shaver. Benches were purchased for the Park, perennials planted around the Doughboy stature, at the old Holzer Medical Center emergency entrance, and at the Gallia County Junior Fairgrounds. Gardening books were donated to the Bossard Library, and yearly plantings are made at the flagpoles of Gallia Academy and Washington Elementary School. The late Mrs. Eugene Gloss headed the sale of hundreds of red Cherokee dogwood trees that can still be seen throughout the city.

Open Gate Garden Club: Open Gate Garden Club became affiliated with the O.A.G.C. in February 1950. Mrs. Georgianna Jenkins named the club. Club projects have included community beautification and contests, flower shows, arranging workshops, donations to Gallipolis Developmental Center, visits to nursing homes, flower judging, and speaking to other clubs. Financial support has been given to the Mohican Outdoor School, Wahkeena Nature Preserve projects, wildflower and birdseed funds, O.A.G.C. scholarship fund, the Victor Rees foundation, and Ameriflora. In 1996 Open Gate was recognized at State convention as the Victor H. Rees Outstanding Club.

Rio Grande Garden Club was first organized in 1926 and is probably the oldest garden club in Ohio. Under the direction of Mary Lewis, wife of President Dean Lewis, this club served primarily as a social club for Rio Grande College. They planted flower beds, decorated and lighted Christmas trees on the campus and several years ago, they were instrumental in helping plant thousands of bulbs on the campus walkways and beds that were donated by one of the college professors. They currently have three ladies who have been members for 30 plus years: Arlene Tracy, Sarah Blazer Holman, and Shirley Smith. Grandma Gatewood, famous for walking the trails of Gallia County until she was almost a hundred years old, was a member at one time.

Vinton Friendship Garden Club was organized in January 1955 and became affiliated with the O.A.G.C. Mary Ann McCarly and Thelma Barnes were two charter members. They grew to 22 members and current members are Pearl Burger, Ann Slaton, Thelma Barnes, Esta Downard, Betty Twyman, Betty and Mary George, and Opal Dunn. Honorary member is Verna Chamberlain. Beautification projects have included planting shrubs and flower beds in the town of Vinton, at the Post Office and the Vinton Elementary School.

Wayside Garden Club of Cheshire was organized in July, 1947, and was federated two months later. At the club's fiftieth anniversary in July, 1997, two charter members, Vivian Kirby and Beatrice White shared information about the club's beginning. A group of local ladies met at Vivian and Garnet Kirby's home with Marie Richards, County Contact Chairman, to organize the club. Other charter members were: Carrie Briggs, Nina Kail, Garnet Kirby, Lorena Reynolds, Ella Rothgeb, Louise Rouse, Marie Sheets, Alice Swisher, and Ruth Thompson. The club's objective was, "Living to create a better world in which to live." The rose was chosen as the club's flower. There were seventeen active members in the first year. Service projects have included publishing Garden Gimmicks and providing flowers for local organizations.

*Submitted by individual members of listed garden clubs and Maxie Oliver, Regional Director, Region 11 Ohio Association of Garden Clubs*

## FLORAL FRIENDS GARDEN CLUB

The first Garden Club met in Walnut Township, Gallia County, Ohio.

On September 1, 1994 an open meeting was held at the home of Anne Baker for the purpose of organizing a garden club. Floral Friends was chosen as the name of the club, the iris, the flower; and the hummingbird, the bird. Ten members were present. Officers elected were President, Anne Baker; Vice-President, Phyllis Ingles; Secretary, Dolores Baker; and Treasurer, Pauline Myers. Officers were installed by the Regional Director of Garden Clubs at a meeting at "Der Lowks House", the home of Dolores Baker.

Some of the annual projects have been donating gardening or plant books to The Bossard Memorial Library, sewing and donating teddy bears to the Pediatric Unit of the Holzer medical Center, donating lap robes to the Senior Resource Center, and providing gifts to the Serenity House.

*Submitted by Dolores Baker, News Reporter*

# Gallia County Historical Society

The Gallia County Historical Society, although virtually dormant for nearly four decades, has made remarkable strides since its formation in 1933.

The original incorporators, Charles E. Holzer Sr., noted physician, surgeon and founder of Holzer Hospital; Harry M. Miller, lawyer and utility executive; and Harold W. Wetherholt, editor and publisher of the Gallipolis Daily Tribune, were all very civic minded men and exercised great foresight in planning the historical society's future. The Society was and is still designed for:

"The promotion of historical study and research in the history of the State of Ohio and the County of Gallia; the collection, collation and preservation and publication, if possible, of historical facts pertaining to the State of Ohio and the County of Gallia; dissemination of historical information of the State of Ohio and County of Gallia by means of programs, special newspaper articles, cooperation with the schools in the county in the teaching of state and local history; cooperation with the library of the county with the compiling of separate Ohio and local history sections; purchase and rehabilitation of the Our House the City of Gallipolis as a historical museum; marking of historical places of interest throughout the county and such other further purposes as may be deemed advisable in the furtherance of one or more of the foregoing purposes."

With the above reason firmly in mind, Dr. Holzer Sr., along with his wife, Alma Vornholt Holzer, purchased in 1933 the Our House tavern, 432 First Avenue in Gallipolis.

Dr. Holzer had his personal secretary. Miss Alma McCormick, devote a considerable amount of time and effort to locate original French artifacts and furnishings to restore the Our House to as near its original condition as possible. He and Mrs. Holzer opened the museum to the public and staffed it with its own curator.

Wetherholt, through the Tribune and later the Gallia Times, had innumerable articles and photos published for all to see.

By far the most extensive historical research project carried out in the Old French City was the creation and publication of the Sesquicentennial Edition of the Gallipolis Tribune published August 27, 1940, in honor of the city's 150th anniversary of its founding.

The late J. Sherman Porter Jr. was brought to Gallipolis for the purpose of creating the special edition, and it remains unsurpassed in its completeness and accuracy of historic detail for the time frame involved.

The Society as a body remained essentially dormant from its founding until 1972.

In the early summer of 1972, at the home of Mrs. M. T. Epling Sr., 603 First Avenue, a re-organization meeting was called by Harold Wetherholt to get the historical society rejuvenated.

Among the actions taken at this meeting was the establishing of a committee to form a constitution and by-laws. Chairman of the committee was the late Manning E. Wetherholt. Others serving were Mrs. Charles (Mary) James and the late Mrs. O. Keith (Lola Mae) Suiter.

Following considerable work by the re-organization committee, an organizational meeting was held at Rio Grande College January 26, 1975, to elect officers and a board of 15 directors.

Officers elected were Manning Wetherholt, president; Albert Merriman, vice-president; Lola Mae Suiter, treasurer; and Mrs. Harry K. (Eva) Mills, secretary.

Members of the board of directors elected were: for a one year term: were Eva Mills, Dr. Charles Allison Weed, Gen. George Bush, Thomas Moulton, J. Sherman Porter; two year term: G. Randy Hand, M. D., Albert Merriman, Charles L. Dowler, Richard MacKenzie, and Prof. Robert Leith; three year terms, Mrs. Thelma Elliott, Mrs. Suiter, Mrs. Berc (Ruth) Tap, Manning Wetherholt and Mrs. Evan (Carolyn) Roderick.

Following the re-organizational meeting the Society began to hold regular monthly meetings with programs and speakers. The subjects covered a wide range of areas, but all pertained directly or indirectly to Gallia County and the state of Ohio.

Meetings were held in various places to accommodate the ever growing interest in local history. Among those locales were St. Peters Episcopal Church, Holzer Hospital and the Lafayette Hotel.

The Society finally purchased a permanent home in 2000 with the acquisition of the Business and Professional Building at 412 Second Avenue in downtown Gallipolis. This facility has a full time director and is open to the public during regular hours five and a half days per week. Except for the director, it is staffed by volunteers throughout the year.

The Gallia County Genealogical Society merged with the Historical Society in 1983. The combined societies have performed many activities since this merger. These activities include:

The erecting of historical markers for locations and events important to Gallia County has been an ongoing program.

Markers have been erected for:

Morning Dawn Lodge #7, F & A M., Pine Street Colored Cemetery, Bidwell, Silver Bridge, Water Towers, Waterloo Wonders, Samuel F. Vinton, John Hunt Morgan, John Gee

Publication of cemetery books for all townships in Gallia County.

Publishing of a variety of historical publications including an atlas, census books, marriage and death records, funeral home records, Railroad Reflector, and a variety of other data.

The Society offers for purchase a wide variety of items such as souvenirs, post cards, Christmas tree bulbs, various crocks and glasses and articles with the Bandstand on them, maps and brochures. Other Society activities include: History Day programs from the county high schools, First Family sponsorship, Jane McCafferty Awards program, Bicentennial activities

# Gallipolis Business & Professional Women's Club

The National Federation of Business and Professional Women's Club was chartered on July 15, 1919 in St. Louis, Missouri, at the Stetler Hotel. The Gallipolis Business and Professional Women's Club was chartered in April, 1935. Middleport Business and Professional Women's Club was the sponsor. Ethel Maud Young was the first club president. Lola Mae Suiter was one of the charter members, she died in September 1999.

The Gallipolis Business and Professional Women's Club is affiliated with The Ohio Federation of Business and Professional Women and the National Federation of Business and Professional Women. The state is divided into Districts, now Regions. The Gallipolis Club is in the Southern Hills Region. In the past the District Director was the leader of the District, in which she resided. Today we have a Regional President. Several members of the Gallipolis Business and Professional Women's Club has served as District Directors, officers and Chairpersons, in the District/Region and State. Marianne Campbell is a Past State President of Ohio/BPW. Madge Neal was a Past State Board Treasurer. Lucy Earwood is a Past State Board Secretary, Gladys Grant is a past State Nominating Chair. The Nike is our Emblem. The Goddess of Victory, fitting Emblem of successful women. In 1966 the Gallipolis Business and Professional Women's Club sponsored a " Follies" show done by club members, which was very successful. In 1974 the Gallipolis BPW Club started an Award— The "Women of the Year", Lola Mae Suiter was the first recipient of the award, presented by President Lucy Earwood. Our BPW Mission Statement: To achieve equity for all women in the workplace through advocacy, education and information. BPW Vision: To be the leading advocate for working women. BPW Objectives: To elevate the standards of women, in business and in professions. To promote the interest of business and professional women. To bring about a spirit of cooperation among the business and professional women in the United States. To extend opportunities to business and professional women through education and along lines of industrial, scientific, and vocational activities.

Past Presidents of the Gallipolis BPW Club: Ethel Maud Young, 1935-36, Margaret D. Carter, 1937-38, Bess Wetherholt,1939, Margaret McCormick, 1940, Zema Shaw, 1941-42, Anna Mae Evans, 1943, Thelma White, 1944, Anna G. White, 1945, Edith Hutsinpillar, 1946, Lola Mae Suiter, 1947, Hortense Epling, 1948, Margaret Pollock, 1949, Gail Russell, 1950, Mabel Tawney, 1951-52, Goldia J. Ward, 1953, Marguerite Hineman, 1954-55, Lola Mae Suiter, 1956, Marianne B. Campbell, 1957, Dorothy S. Sommer, 1958, Madge Neal, 1959, Lena Pleasants, 1960-61, Betty Ryal, 1962-63, Lola Mae Suiter, 1964, Irene Gilliam, 1965, Faye Thompson, 1966, Joan Wood, 1968-69, Bernice McMahon, 1970-71, Madge Neal, 1972, Mary Jane Neal, 1973, Lucy Earwood, 1974-75, Lola Mae Suiter, 1976, Gladys Grant, 1977-78, Joan Wood, 1979-80, Madge Boggs, 1981-82, Wilma Haycraft, 1983, Karen Burns, 1984, Connie Hemphill, 1985-86, Gail Belville, 1987-88, Denise Shockley, 1989-90, Mary Lou Tawney, 1991-92, Betsy Ball, 1993, Mary Lou Tawney, 1994, Lori Church, 1995-96, Joyce Davis, 1997-98, Gladys Grant, 1999-2000, Kathi Nagy, 2001-02.

In Memonam: Rachael Davis, 1943, Julia Conklin, 1947, Mabel Wise, 1947, Mrs. Byrd Rose, 1948, Anna Mae Evans, 1950, Margaret McCormick, 1951, Freda Wood, 1955, Edith Swisher, 1956, Margaret Carter, 1959, Ruth Richards, 1962, Arista Boggs, 1964, Irene Gilliam, 1966, Ethel Maud Young, 1969, Goldia Ware, 1973, Esta McKnight, 1975, Elizabeth Evans, 1975, Pearl Haffleld, 1976, Thelma White, 1976, Nell Gills, 1976, Flossie Trout, 1978, Zella Craft, 1980, Leona Trout, 1981, Edith Hutsinpillar, 1983, Elise Kimball, 1984, Edna Menshouse, 1984, Lena Pleasants, 1985, Audrey Hamrick, 1988, Ruth Avner, 1993, Madge Neal, 1997, Sandra Perkins, 1998, Lola Mae Suiter, 1999, Wilma Haycraft, 2000.

The Gallipolis Business and Professional Women sponsors "Girl of the Month" and "Girl of the Year", which are high school seniors. We hold a Tea to meet all applicants and a Tea for the nine girls of the month, to select the girl of the year. The nine girls of the month and their mothers are guests at a dinner meeting and the girls are given a plaque. The girl of the year receives a scholarship. Our fund raisers are selling nuts, candy and knives. We hold a raffle at Christmas. In the past the October meeting was "Bosses Night". In the past our club membership has been over a hundred, today our membership is twenty-three. Bernice McMahon is our oldest active member. Our meeting places have been Farmer's Hotel, Oscar's and presently the Down Under. Our meetings are held the third Monday of each month, 6:30 p.m., which are dinner meetings. We present programs and have guest speakers. Last sentence of the BPW Creed: To be true to myself, my fellow worker, and God.

*Lola Mae Suiter, last charter member*

# John Gee Black Historical Center, Inc.

On June 1, 1998, at the request of Dorothy Casey and Barbara Scott; the following persons met at the John Gee A.M.E. Chapel, 48 Pine Street, Gallipolis, Ohio; Bobby Casey, Edna Casey, Alice Bufford, (all Trustees of the Chapel), Wilbert Stoney, Promolia Smith, Rev. Gilbert Craig, James Dewey Keels, Bobette Braxton, and Josette Baker. The purpose of the meeting was to discuss the possibility of the building becoming a historical museum. This was because the remaining trustees and members were few and wanted to perpetuate the building by donating it and the property back to the black community.

The following issues were discussed in great detail; how to form such an institution, funding, purpose of center, necessary officers, and the name for this historical place.

It was decided that the name would be the John Gee Black Historical Center, Inc. The purpose of the center was defined as promoting education of the public in black historical events and their meaning as well as promoting the arts. The following officers were elected:

President - Dorothy Casey
Vice-President - Wilbert (Buck) Stoney
Secretary - Bobette Braxton
Treasurer - Barbara M. Scott
Incorporators - Promolia Smith, Dorothy Casey and Rev. Gilbert Craig
Chaplain - Wilbert Stoney
Advisors - Josette Baker and James Dewey Keels

Judge Tom Moulton was suggested as the Statutory Agent and he accepted on June 3, 1998. Our first donation to help in our venture was given by Dr. and Mrs. Isom Walker in the amount of $500.00. Also Alice Walker of Chicago gave in the amount of $1,000.00. The center has grown tremendously with many donations and much help. Gilbert M. Craig Jr. is the editor of our newsletter. Patty A. Craig is the news correspondent of our quarterly news letter. The center is a product of the community and is intent on giving back and enhancing the community.

*John Gee Black Historical Center*

# Knights Of Pythias, Naomi Lodge, No. 55

Dionysious, the ruler of Syracuse in ancient Greece, was a tyrant with a bad reputation and a troubled military record. There was a man named Pythias who had incurred the displeasure of Dionysious. Pythias was tried, found guilty and sentenced to death. Friends of Pythias intervened and Pythias was allowed to return to his home, arrange his business affairs, and see his wife and child before the execution. Pythias had a friend, Damon, who offered to stand good for the return of Pythias. Damon would be killed if Pythias failed to come back.

This friendship between Pythias and Damon touched the heart of Dionysious who eventually freed Pythias of all charges. It was this story of "true friendship" that provided the inspiration for the founding of what came to be called the Knights of Pythias or K of P for short.

It was near the close of the Civil War that a few men were inspired to use this ancient Greek legend to heal the wounds in America between the north and south.

The Naomi Lodge No. 55 of the K of P was organized in Gallipolis on June14, 1873 in the S.T. and R.. Langley building at the corner of State Street and Second Avenue, known later as the J. M. Kerr Hardware building and now the ground is occupied by a new building formerly known as Ohio Valley Bank property. It is probable that this area held the first Pythian building after a chapter had been issued by the Grand Lodge of the Knights of Pythias of Ohio on March 15, 1874, Naomi Lodge No. 56, and its charter members.

The charter members listed at that. time were: R.M. Cochran, W.T. Minturn, John C. Vanden, C.H. McCormick, John Vanden, J.L. Williass, F. Souverain, J.P. Hott, John T. Hampton, John Mullineauz, R.. Ceiphy, P.H. Pritchet, S.S. Pritchett, R. Safford, IW. Booton, James Gills, Ed Gills, George Alexander, Willaim Gatewood, E. Tippens, J.F. Jenkins, S. Goetz, Joseph Kinghorn, A.D. Summers, Henry Bolles, George W. Heaton, C. Phelps, S.A. Rathburn, Walter McFarland, Thomas King, A. E. Ward, J.J. Coffman, J.L. Guv, E.P. Ralph, A. C. Hughes, W.O. Martin, J.F. Gills, Thomas Hill, Lewis Billings, Jasper Hopkins, F.D. Young, George Shank, D. Callahan, and Jasper Alexander.

During the latter part of the 1880's the Naomi Lodge brothers, transferred their paraphernalia into the James C. Priestly property, occupying the third floor. Here, they remained nearly a decade. The Colony Theater now occupies the site at that building. They remained there nearly a decade.

The largest membership of the lodge was during the period from 1900 to 1920, at one time there were more than 300 members, but they later suffered heavy loss of membership due to the years of the depression.

In 1894 the lodge purchased the Henry W. Gilman three-story building at the corner of Locust Street and Second Avenue for $4,500, and it's home has been on the third floor of the building to the present time. The building was originally built by Gilman in 1884. He built it so that stores could be kept on the first floor. The second floor was designed for offices and the third floor was to be the home of the lodge called the Grand Army of the Republic (GAR). This fraternal organization was composed of veterans of the Civil War.

The most important item in it's history is the fact that the Federal Government was a tenant of the Gallipolis organization for nearly a quarter of a century. In 1903, it leased the ground floor of this building to the United States Government for ten years for use by the Gallipolis Post Office. in 1913, the lease was renewed for another decade and the post office remained there until it was moved to its present location on Second Avenue.

In 1928 the mortgage was paid off and it was burned at a banquet in its Castle Hall. This celebrating event had a record-breaking attendance.

At the time of the Gallipolis Sesquicentennial Celebration in 1940, the officers were Harry Cameron- Chancellor Commander, Charles Swanson-Vice Chancellor, H.W. Slaven-Prelate, French V. Trout-Master of Work, Gilbert Beard-Secretary, A.W. Riffle-Financial Secretary, Thomas E. Mills-Treasurer, Heber D. McClaskey-Master of Arms, Shelby Roberts-Inner Guard, Denis Sheets-Outer Guard, A.C.Safford, George T. Hamilton and Ed L. Mills-Trustees.

The lodge No. 55's main work in the 20th century, besides extolling the values of friendship, has been to support the K of P home in Springfield which provides all maintenance, clothing, medical, surgical and hospital needs for their retired members and wives who have no one to care for them. The true home atmosphere is a joy to all the residents. A member is expected to make some contribution but if he has none, none is required and a member who has much is not required to surrender all, but only make nominal contribution.

The Lodge also works closely with the various county Health Departments in providing assistance for those children under 15, regardless of race or creed, who need help for deficiencies of sight (except glasses) speech and hearing, who have no one able to provide these services for them.

The present officers are: Bobby C, Roach-Chancellor Commander, Glenn Johnson-Vice Chancellor, Matt O'Dell-Prelate, Edward Caudill-Master of Work, Tom Pasquale-Secretary, Raymond Delille-Treasurer, Jim O'Dell-Master Of Arms, Chris Frogale-Inner Guard, John Delille-Outer Guard. Current Trustees are Raymond Delille, John Delille, Bobby C. Roach.

*K of P Lodge #55 Building*

# The Gallipolis Lions Club

*Gallipolis Lions Membership 2002- Front row, LtoR, David Walker, Harold Thompson, Willis Leadingham, Norman Snyder, David Tawney, David Martin, Gene Wood, and Chris Homer. Back row, LtoR, Robert Hennesy, Robert Perkins, Ronald Noe, Ronald Canaday, Eugene Gloss, Willard "Buzz" Call, G. Richard Brown, James Clark, Jeff Snedaker, Francis "Odie" O'Donnell, Jeff Fowler, Max Tawney, Carl Woolum, James Ryan, and William Shondel. Members not shown: Hobart Wilson, Jr., Norman Tarr, Ronald Calhoun, Herman Dillon, Mark Dillon, Fred Wood, Albert Peterkowski, William Davis, Richard "Rick" Tipple, E.V. Clarke, Jay Caldwell, Steve McGhee, David Steele, Dan Thomas, and David Diddle.*

The Gallipolis Lions Club was chartered in October, 1956 in special ceremonies at the Grace United Methodist Church, with sponsorship by the Pomeroy and Point Pleasant Lions Clubs.

C. Mac McGraw, now deceased, was elected the first president of the new club, which held meetings the first and third Tuesday of each month in the Lafayette Hotel dining room. Other meeting sites later included the former Tyo's Restaurant on Eastern Ave., Oscar's Restaurant on Court St., and presently at the Holiday Inn.

The club has hosted two district conventions. The first in 1959 at the Lafayette Hotel and the Kyger Creek Power Plant, and the second in 1974 at the Holiday Inn and at Rio Grande College.

Elected officers of the club include a president, first vice president, second vice president, third vice president, treasurer, secretary, lion tamer, tail twister, and three additional members of the board of directors. This 10 member board is responsible for all decisions involving membership, finances, activities, and projects when it meets once each month.

Regular meetings are held on the first and third Tuesday of each month at 6:30 p.m. with dinner and an educational program or some form of entertainment.

When the club was chartered in 1956 it included four men who are still active in 2002. Max Tawney 88, Eugene Gloss 75, Francis "Odie" O'Donnell 72, and Hobart Wilson, Jr. 67.

O'Donnell was elected to the office of tail twister in 1956 and was re-elected to this post for 40 years until he stepped down in 1997. This is a state record and possibly a national and international record for the same person to hold this post for 40 years. He and fellow charter member Eugene Gloss, have both served on the board of directors for now 46 years. Gloss served as president in 1957 and Wilson held this office in 1965. Three members of the club have served as district governors of District 13-J. They are Willis Leadingham and William Shondel, both of whom are still active in the club, and Richard Turner.

Two members have been accorded the rare honor of Life Memberships, as voted by the board of directors. They are 88 year old Max Tawney and the late Everett McMahon.

Since the club's formation the primary goal has been fund raising for any visually impaired child in Gallia County, and more recently for senior citizens and other adults who require eye glasses. In 46 years the club has raised and spent over $180,000 on eye glasses, a braille wrist watch for a blind 13-year old girl, an Ortho-Rater machine for Gallia Academy High School, several expensive machines for the Visually Handicapped unit at the Rio Grande Elementary School, and other vision screening equipment for various schools.

The club has engaged in numerous fund raising projects in four decades, but the annual "light for sight" light bulb sale in the fall is the only one that survived, and is still considered a major source of income.

Club members have participated in fund raisers that included selling roses, smashing an old car, a booth at the Gallia County Junior Fair, directing traffic at the junior fair, selling ice cream at the Bob Evans Farm Festival, sponsoring three circus events, sponsoring a wheel chair basketball game, having a float in the 1990 bi-centennial parade; and currently a very popular and successful Lions Golf Tournament. From 1958 to the present the Lions have sponsored the Little Miss and Little Mister Gallia County contest at the Gallia County Junior Fair, and from 1959 until 1989 the club hosted the championship Pee Wee, Little League, and Pony League baseball teams at an annual banquet where trophies were presented to individual players and teams for their winning efforts. Over 1,000 youth baseball players and coaches were honored during this time, and over 2,500 young people have been contestants in the Little Miss and Little Mister contests at the fair in 44 years of Lion sponsorship.

In over four decades of fund raising the entire Gallia County community has always responded in an outstanding manner to all of the Lions' projects. The support has been somewhat incredible from the local businesses and individuals who contribute to the charity works of the club.

In its 46 years of existence several hundred men have been inducted into the Gallipolis Lions Club with many holding office or chairmen of committees. On Charter Night in 1956 membership included 40 men, and this number stands at 38 in 2002.

The makeup of the Lions is very diversified and has included men from all vocations and walks of life, but all of them were outstanding in upholding the Lions International motto of "We Serve."

# The Thursday Club

Gallipolis had already been in existence for one hundred years when, in June 1889, Miss Amy Nash and Miss Nellie Dages invited a select group of young women to join them in an experience of "literary enrichment." The purpose of the group was the study of books, the arts and the history and culture of foreign countries. The name of the club, "The Tourists," was soon changed to "The Thursday Club." The only time the club has failed to meet as scheduled in its 113 years of existence was during the terrible influenza epidemic of 1918/1919.

As early as 1895, the very enthusiastic young ladies were actively working toward the establishment of a public library for Gallipolis. To this end, they sponsored the publishing of a woman's issue of the Gallipolis Journal, printed on silk and auctioned off for $100 to the highest bidder. In addition to this sum, advertisements in the issue realized $1,500. Another fund raising event for the new library was a tea served at the home of Nellie Dages. The donation of a new book gained admission to the tea. In November 1898, the library was opened in two rooms located on the second floor of the Lupton building. The library boasted 1700 volumes and a treasury of $800. Miss Addie Vanden, a Thursday Club member, was the first librarian, a position she held until her death more than 30 years later. By 1904 Miss Vanden and Thursday Club proposed the city school board apply for a Carnegie Library for the community. This philanthropic grant by the Andrew Carnegie Foundation was repeated many times over throughout the United States, but is considered one of the Thursday Club's finest contributions to the county. The stained glass ceiling, original to the entry of the Carnegie Library, was moved to the new Bossard Memorial Library in 1978 with a $500 contribution from The Thursday Club. To this day, the club strives to improve children's book selections by an annual contribution to the Addie Vanden Fund at the library.

During WWI, The Thursday Club sent money to suffering Belgians and also adopted three Gallipolis area soldier boys who were stationed at the encampment in the city park for several months.

In 1927, The Thursday Club donated a heated bassinette to Holzer Hospital. The ladies acquired a portrait of George Washington in 1936 to present to the "Our House" Museum.

The Thursday Club helped to establish two other literary clubs in Gallipolis. "The Philomathean Club" was sponsored in 1896 and "The Pembrook Club" in 1929.

The ladies of The Thursday Club studied hard, but they also loved parties. Time and again the Gallipolis Journal reported the Thursday Club's very special social events including a "Napoleonic Tea," a "Colonial Tea," and many anniversary parties. The all day meetings and elaborate meals were modified by vote in 1949. Fancy dresses, gloves and hats of the past are gone. Today, following the program, coffee, tea and dessert are served.

*Members in 2002 Study Year*
Back Row, L to R: Mrs. James Orr, Mrs. Michael Dey, Mrs. Robert E. Jenkins, Mrs. Brent Johnson Middle row, L to R: Mrs. Herman Koby, Mrs. John Cornett, Jr., Mrs. Richard Mendieta, Mrs. R. William Jenkins, Mrs. John Cornett, Sr., Mrs. Randall Breech, V. P. Front Row, L to R: Mrs. Vance Johnson, Mrs. Sigismund Harder, Historian, *Mrs. Charles Holzer, Jr., Mrs. Resty Alonzo, President Not present: Mrs. Lenny Blosser, Treas., Mrs. Oscar Clarke, *Mrs. Arthur Darnborough, Mrs. Thomas McCormick *Indicates fifty year members

# Kiwanis Club Of Gallipolis

The Kiwanis Club of Gallipolis was presented its Charter on February 18, 1947, their sponsor was the Kiwanis Club of Point Pleasant, West Va.

The Charter was presented by the Lieutenant Governor of Division 5, to President Kenneth Welker. There were seventy-two Charter Members. Today the membership is thirty-one.

The Kiwanis Club of Gallipolis joins one of the world's largest, most respected service organizations: Kiwanis International. "Kiwanis" is taken from an American Indian term "Nunc Keewanis", which means "Self Expression".

The purpose of the organization is community and world-wide youth services, plus a humanitarian concept.

The official Kiwanis Motto is" We build".

The first meeting of the Kiwanis Club of Gallipolis was held in the Washington School Auditorium. In the past the Kiwanis meetings have been held at Molly's, Oscar's, Dale's and presentley held at the Down Under.

The Presidents, past and present are: 1947- Dr. Kenneth Welker*, 1948- Glenn Campbell, 1949- Dr. N. Foster*, 1950- D. Paul Davies, 1951- Paul E.Watson,* 1952- J. Sherman Porter,* 1953- Carroll K. Singer,* 1954 -   J. Howard Neal,* 1955- J. W. "Bill" Mills, * 1956- J. Dean Eisel, 1957- Emerson "Vic" Sherow,* 1958- Dr. T. J. Bradshaw, 1959- Dr. George Davis, 1960- John Heiskell,* 1961- John "Bud" Preston*, 1962- Dale C. Gilkey*, 1963- L. Claude Miller*, 1964- Kenneth D. Myers, 1965- Neil McMahon, 1966- Arthur Fletcher, 1967- William Northup*, 1968- Hollis E. Brown, 1969- Bruce Malcolm, 1970- Luther Tracy, 1971- Albert Durose*, 1972- Joseph Giles, 1973- John Taylor, 1974- Charles "Foxy" Grant, 1975- Ray Blowers, 1976- Kenneth Adkins, 1977- Carroll K. Snowden, 1978- Millard Cassidy*, 1979- William Milstead, 1980- Larry Boyer, 1981- D. R. Warehime, Jr., 1982- Thomas Moulton, Sr., 1983- Don Hodge, 1984- William Smeltzer, 1985- Kenneth Amsbary*, 1986-Elton Savage, 1987- Donald Howell, 1988- Larry Boyer. 1989- John Lester, 1990- William Standish, 1991- Jay Moore, 1992- Gail Belville, 1993- Claudette Huggins, 1994- Jay Cremeens, 1995- Henry Thrapp, 1996- Wayne King. 1997- Sam Wilson, 1998- Thomas Moulton, Sr., 1999- Charles "Foxy" Grant, 2000- Barbara Shelton, 2001- Herman Mayo, 2002- William Meek, Jr..

* denotes — deceased.

The Kiwanis Club of Gallipolis has had several Division 9 Lietutenant Governors during its years of service. They are: 1958- Carroll Singer,* 1961- John Heiskell,* 1969-70- William 0. Northup,* 1977-78- Albert R. Dursose,* 1986-87- William Smeltzer, 1996-97- Charles "Foxy" Grant.

The Kiwanis Club of Gallipolis has a Youth Foundation which was incorporated on April 7, 1954. The interest earned is used to sponsor youth projects. The Kiwanis Club of Gallipolis sponsors Key Clubs in Gallia Academy, River Valley and South Gallia High Schools.

Other fund raisers are the Annual Golf Tournament, Gallia County Junior Fair, Bob Evans Farm Festival and Frontier Entertainment Show. Majority of the funds is used for local and world-wide youth projects.

In July of 1987, the assembled delegates in Washington, District of Columbia at the 72nd. Annual International Convention voted to permit women to be sponsored for membership in Kiwanis Clubs.

It would be difficult to evaluate all the worth while work that has been done and continues to be done by the Kiwanis Club of Gallipolis.

The Kiwanis Club of Gallipolis is very proud to serve the community and also, help to serve world-wide for the improvement of humanity. The most recent world-wide project, $ 75,000,000 was raised to eradicate Iodine Deficiency. *Compiled by Gladys D. Grant, Club Secretary*

# Ole Car Club, Inc.

Individuals with an interest in antique and modified vehicles met September 11, 1978 at Bob Saunders Quaker State service station, on the corner of Second Avenue and Pine Street, to discuss forming a car club. At the next meeting on September 25, the following officers were elected:    President - David McCoy, Vice President - Ron Cornelius, Secretary - Charles Reynolds, Treasurer - Harold Thompson, Historian - Sidney R. Edwards. Also at that meeting the members selected "Ole Car Club" as the name of the newly formed club and the club logo shown above.

Charter members were; Harold Ault, Roger Carter, David Cunningham, Sidney B. Edwards, Thomas Gooch, Alvin Johnson, Larry Layne, Otis Layne, Elwood Lewis, Melvin Little, Kim Neal, Steve Owens, James Rothgeb, Chester Roush, Norman Snyder, and Michael Thompson.

The Club was incorporated as a nonprofit Ohio corporation June 14, 1 979. On August 12, 1979 the club conducted it's first car show at the Gallia County Fairground. Marion "Tex" Harrison and band provided music and 73 vehicles were on display. In 1981 the car show was relocated to Gallipolis around the City Park where it was held yearly on the second Saturday of August until 2001 when it was held at Wal-Mart due to the fire that destroyed a part of downtown Gallipolis. Over 200 vehicles have been registered and judged at car shows by club members. An average membership of 24 members enjoy discussing rebuilding and maintaining vehicles and the fellowship at bimonthly meetings. Club meetings have been held in David McCoy's living room and his garage at 49 Pine Street, as well as Rocchi's Restaurant on Eastern Avenue, and the Columbus & Southern Electric office on the corner of Second Avenue and Sycamore Street. In recent years the club has conducted car shows and cruise-ins, in addition to the August show, at numerous locations throughout Gallia County. Club members have participated in several parades and the club has made donations to many individuals and organizations as funds are available.

# Gallia County Schools

Downtown, Gallipolis, Ohio

Washington School, No. 2

# Gallipolis City School System

The city of Gallipolis has long enjoyed a rich heritage in the field of education. Its earliest beginnings were with the French emigrants, who included many persons of learning in the sciences and the arts. During the period of the French dominance of the colony, no attempt was made to establish formal education. In fact, formal public education was not formulated in Gallipolis until 1849. However, in those early years education was not neglected and private schools, along with tutors for the more wealthy families abounded.

Very little is known about education in Gallipolis before 1810. Francis Le Clercq, a man of fine educational attainments, as were many of the early French settlers, is thought to have been the first schoolmaster in the community. Needless to say, instruction must have been extremely limited while the colonists were engaged in the stern business of clearing a wilderness and adapting themselves to their strange environment. Sometime after the town and vicinity became more settled and following the arrival of immigrants from New England and Virginia, a special interest was taken in formal education. This interest resulted in the opening of temporary schools, and long range plans were made for the establishment of a permanent institution of learning.

A giant step was taken on February 8, 1810, when the citizens of Gallipolis and vicinity met to consider the expedience of erecting a building to be appropriated for the instruction of the youth and such other purposes as might be deemed of public utility for the purpose of establishing Gallia Academy. Colonel Robert Safford, distinguished for felling the first tree on the site of Gallipolis, was appointed chairman, with Nathaniel Gates serving as clerk.

The group formed a stockholders' company for the establishment of an academic institution in Gallipolis, with each shareholder having a vote for ten shares each of privately owned stock. This group of stockholders included: Edward W. Tupper, Francis Le Clercq, John P.R. Bureau, C.R. Menager, Henry Duc, Joseph Fletcher, Charles Clendenin, Matthew Buell, Lewis Thomas Rodgers, Lewis Newsom, Peter H Steenbergen, Rene Carel, Pereguine P. Foster, Luther Rees, John Kerr, Andrew Johnson, John B. Ferrard, Peter Ferrard, Christian Etienne, Lewis Vimont, John Atchinson, Charles Dinay, Andrew Lewis, David Irwin, Levi Mercer, Lewis V. Von Schrittz, John Bing, Orasha Strong, and James Wilson. These early stockholders made payment in carpenters and joiners work, beef, cattle, pork, hemp, flour, and other staple items.

A company was then organized, and by a special Act of the General Assembly of the State of Ohio, was on January 29, 1811, made a Corporation and Body Politic for Seminary benefits in the name and style of The Gallia Academy, with powers to remain and have perpetual succession forever.

A location opposite the Public Square and on the north side of Second Street was purchased. It included Lots 117, 118, and a part of 116, and extended as nearly as can be ascertained, from the Ohio Valley Bank corner to the Empire Furniture Company in the Adams building. Later Lot 119, occupied by the First Presbyterian Church and Lot 120, from the Public Library to the W.R. Tanner residence on Third Avenue were added. It is a note-worthy fact that the section made up of Lots 116-120 is today called the Academy Subdivision, being so designated on the plat at the Court House.

The school was quickly erected on the site of the Roedell and Fontana business establishments. It was a commodious two-story brick building, mounted by a cupola and having two large rooms downstairs with a hall between, and one large room on the second floor which was later divided into two rooms. Because of the exhaustion of funds it was not completed until 1818, but it was used in an unfinished state for religious services as early as 1812 and for Masonic meetings at a somewhat later date. Gallia Academy commenced its first formal session on May 24, 1819.

The drive for materials and funds continued for several years and the first Gallia Academy continued in its location at Second Avenue and State Street until it burned to the ground on July 15, 1847. Following the fire, Mr. J.C. Robinson opened on lower Second Street near the present Gallia Hotel, a school called the Collegiate Institute, which was attended by the older and more advanced pupils of the town. During this period the younger children attended a few private schools and the two district schools.

Gallia Academy occupied temporary quarters until 1853, when the new Gallia Academy was built on the site of the present Junior High. The two-story brick building was completed and opened for its first session on May 17, 1854. It was marked by a stone tablet placed in the front gable, on which was carved Gallia Academy, A.D. 1853. Twelve years later, in 1866, an addition was built. That building was torn down in 1916, and what now serves as the Gallia Academy Junior High School was erected.

From 1854-1867, the teachers in charge were Mr. and Mrs. Amos G. Sears. Beginning with their tenure, boys and girls were no longer segregated into different rooms as had been the custom, though they were seated apart in the same room and had their recess at different hours. The school was divided into two departments, the Preparatory and the Academic. Some of the subjects taught in the higher department were Chemistry, Natural Philosophy, Geology, Botany, Astronomy, Greek, Latin, and French, styled Ornamental, Music, Drawing and Painting and Book-keeping; also General History, Algebra, Geometry, Surveying, and English Grammar. Strange to say, young people were not formally graduated from the Academy at this time, though a number were prepared for Eastern colleges.

With the outbreak of the Civil War, a large number of Gallia Academy students answered the call to serve under the Northern and Southern flags. In 1863, the military authorities took over the building for hospital purposes. School was thus discontinued until reopening in 1864. The school now enrolled about three hundred pupils.

Gallia Academy was one of the first schools to be founded in the Old Northwest. Toward the close of the nineteenth century it was reestablished as Gallipolis High School in the old Union School building, and before the turn of the century the schools were combined to form what is today Gallia Academy High School, which is located on lands still owned by Gallia Academy trustees.

Public education in Gallipolis got its earliest start in 1849, when a meeting was held to promote public graded education. It was put to a vote of the people in 1857, and with a favorable vote plans were moved forward for the building of the first public school on the site of the present Washington Elementary School. By 1872, all of the sub-districts surrounding Gallipolis were brought into the City System, with those reaching grammar school to attend schools in the city of Gallipolis.

A leaflet in the form of a prospectus for the year 1869-1870, when Mr. S. T. Skidmore was principal, shows a reconstruction of the academic year into three terms, and a revision of the course of study. Beginning at this time, three distinct courses were offered in the higher department: English, Classical and College Preparatory. The first was a normal and scientific course fitting students for business or teaching, and requiring either two or three years for completion; the second, a liberal course of collegiate culture for ladies and gentlemen, requiring four years for completion; and the third, a course for young men desiring to enter college, demanding two years of earnest effort and application.

The Course of Study for 1872-73, shows that the time occupied by the Classical and College Preparatory courses was then three years, and that the essential difference between them was in the requirement of Greek in the latter, it being substituted for certain English branches.

The leaflet of 1869-70, announced also the awarding of diplomas for the completion of the higher courses and the giving of certificates to young men who satisfactorily passed the examinations for college entrance. It is not certain in what year the first class was graduated from Gallia Academy in the courses named above. The records of the Trustees, which from the first were imperfectly kept, show the granting of diplomas to a Commercial class in 1867, but contain no further mention of graduation until 1872. One of the diplomas awarded in 1872 was made of parchment. Mr. James E. Langley, said to have been a brilliant conversationalist and one of the finest young men ever produced by Gallipolis and Mr. James H. Clendenin, reported to have been

an exceptionally gifted student, were both admitted to Yale by certificates from Gallia Academy.

From 1870 to 1873, Gallia Academy instituted Physical Training. There were classes in gymnastics which furnished pleasant and healthful recreation for the young people. The instructor was Miss Amelia Dickinson. Mrs. S.F. Neal, formerly Miss Luella Hibbard, from Mt. Holyoke, holds the distinction of directing the first class in gymnastics at Gallia Academy and likely the first in any Gallipolis school. Miss Hibbard had Miss Dickinson's class in 1872-73, was composed of both boys and girls. There were by this time organized athletics at Gallia Academy and called into existence by the establishment of the Union High School. Each school had its champions.

In 1889, military training was introduced for the boys and a military company, the Nash Cadets was organized, but lasted for only one year. By 1891, the enrollment of Gallia Academy had dwindled to twenty-one and the school was closed. It was not to be opened again until 1895.

By way of one last effort to maintain Gallia Academy, the Trustees in 1895, invited Dr. H.W. Simpson, President of Marietta College, to come to Gallipolis to advise them concerning the reopening of the institution. At their request he outlined for the school a new course of study of high academic grade and recommended as teachers two young men soon to be graduated from Marietta. Accordingly, Gallia Academy was reopened in September 1895, with Mr. Robert Brown, principal and Mr. Charles W. Boetticher, assistant. It was operated on high academic standards with a small graduating class each year after 1897, but the number in attendance was not sufficiently large to justify the continuance of the school, and in 1900, it was closed for the last time.

For seminary benefits, the public high school had come to take the place of the academy. Full realizing this fact, the Trustees nobly took the only step whereby Gallia Academy might continue to fulfill the mission for which it had been founded. They leased to the Board of Education the building and grounds to become the home of the High School. They also arranged for the endowment of the Academy to be used for repairing and equipping the building and further providing that the scholastic standards of the High School, which at that time were not so high as those of the Academy, be raised to admit graduates to college without examination. In 1917, the Trustees formally deeded to the Board of Education the grounds and building; and with the consummation of that act, the Gallipolis High School entered into splendid heritage, being known thereafter by the name Gallia Academy High School.

Sometime around the turn of the century the schools in the district included Union, later changed to Washington, Garfield, Grant, Lincoln, and Douglas, and Gallia Academy. Later additions to the system included schools in East Gallipolis and Kanauga.

Although education had transitioned from a private school to a public system, the city schools retained a very high level of course offerings. In the early part of the century one finds that Gallia Academy under public sponsorship still believed in the classic education. The curriculum included Greek, German, and higher levels of mathematics and sciences. Gallia Academy has the distinction of being one of the first secondary schools in the United States to be accredited by the North Central Association of Secondary Schools and Colleges, and has continuously maintained that distinction since 1906.

One of the developments that took place in recent years is the centralization of the various city schools. Grant, Garfield, and Lincoln Schools, including the Lincoln High School, were absorbed into the Central System. East Gallipolis and the Kanauga School buildings were eliminated during this time.

With the growth of the suburban areas, townships surrounding the city of Gallipolis built new elementary schools. A vote was taken by the schools in Clay and Green Townships and their buildings became a part of the Gallipolis City School District on May 23, 1958 and August 19, 1958, respectively.

In 1956, one of the major additions to the Gallipolis City School District was the building of a new Gallia Academy High School at a cost of approximately $900,000.00. Prior to its construction and at the same site, a music, industrial arts and agriculture building was erected in 1952. With these expansions Gallia Academy High School now served grades 7-12.

In 1940, the individual building enrollment was Kanauga 33, Lincoln 91, Maple Shade, 32, Washington 754 and Gallia Academy 466, for a total of 1376. At the close of the 1964-65 school year the building enrollment was Washington 1059, Clay 143, Green 284, and Gallia Academy 1060, for a total enrollment of 2,546.

Today the Gallipolis City School District is a monument to the foresight and the efforts of those individuals who were committed to public education. The present school district includes Gallia Academy High School, the Alternative School at Clay, Green Elementary School, Rio Grande Elementary School, and Washington Elementary School.

Gallia Academy High School is located in downtown Gallipolis, Ohio, on a very constrained nine-acre campus where portions of the site are unusable due to erosion and steep terrain. The 99,160 square foot facility consists of three generations of buildings beginning in 1916 with additional construction projects in 1958 and 1976 resulting in three separate buildings located on the Fourth Avenue campus. Today the school houses 1,190 seventh through twelfth grade students.

Clay Elementary School is situated on an approximately 8-acre parcel of land on the southern edge of Gallipolis, Ohio. Clay Elementary School was constructed in 1955 as a one-story load bearing masonry, slab-on-grade and metal bar joist with metal deck roof structure. Two 1981 additions were made to the original facility; constructed in a similar fashion, providing three more classroom spaces and a library space. Today, the 16,463 square foot school building is currently serving as the Alternative School with both short and long-terzm units, Pre-kindergarten students, and the remainder of the facility being operated by the local Head Start program.

The 1957 Green Elementary School is a one-story load bearing masonry and metal bar joist and metal deck roof structure. The floor structure is slab-on-grade. A one-story 1961 one-classroom addition and a 1981 three-classroom addition, both of similar construction, have been added to the original. This nine-acre site contains adequate parking and separated play areas. The district bus garage is located to the rear of this school and the district has recently purchased 100 acres of land located directly adjacent to and across the tertiary road that accesses this school site. A soccer field has been constructed on this property enclosed with a chain length fence and having an electronic scoreboard. The school presently serves 374 students in Kindergarten through the Sixth Grade on its eastern Gallipolis campus.

Originally constructed in 1931, Rio Grande Elementary School is located in Rio Grande, Ohio just north of Gallipolis, Ohio. In both 1961 and in 1981, two-story additions and a 1961 one-story gymnasium were added to the existing three-story wood-frame, load bearing masonry structure. Today, the 33,507 square foot facility houses 287 students in Kindergarten through the sixth grade on this 1.9-acre site.

Washington Elementary School is a handsome Tudor English style masonry building that was originally constructed in 1930. The 1945 and 1965 additions have provided more classroom/cafeteria space and kitchen space respectively. Today, this 55,928 square foot facility houses 751 students in Kindergarten through the sixth grade. On October 8, 1948, Memorial Field, the district's sports complex adjacent to Washington, was dedicated to all veterans of World War l and World War II.

On June 10, 1968, the State of Ohio Department of Education granted a charter to the Gallipolis City School District to operate schools in accordance with the adopted policies and regulations of the State Board of Education. Mr. Jack W. Payton is the present superintendent in a long line of administrators that stretch back over a century and a half. The total Gallipolis City School District enrollment for the 2001-2002 school year stands at 2,442 students. Presently, 173 Certified Staff and 86 Classified Staff Members are employed by the district which covers 99 square miles. The present board of education is: Lynn Angell-Queen, President, David Walker, Vice President, Dannie Greene, Dr. Timothy Kyger, and Nancy Mullins. Ellen M. Marple has served as school district treasurer for the past 25 years.

The Gallipolis City School District, encompassing the city of Gallipolis, the village of Rio Grande and sections of rural Gallia County, serves a community rich in history. The instructional program in the Gallipolis City Schools is designed to provide a learning environment that will promote social, emotional, physical and intellectual development. The district's mission is "to create a nurturing environment that enables each student to develop to the best of his/her abilities, the lifelong learning skills necessary to communicate clearly, to solve problems, to use technology effectively, to appreciate the arts and to meet the obligations of a productive citizen in a democracy."

The Gallipolis City School District is working very diligently to raise the achievement of its students. From 1999-2000, the school district demonstrated a one hundred and fifty-five percent (155%) overall improvement on the 2001 Local Report Card. The 2002 Local Report Card indicates that the Gallipolis City Schools have moved up from "Academic Watch" to the "Continuous Improvement" category by meeting 14 of the 27 indicators currently used by the State of Ohio to measure performance excellence. This is an improvement of 3 indicators over the previous year. During the past five years the district has been increasing the number of indicators met on the Local Report Card by an average of two indicators per year.

Teachers in Gallipolis were from the first held in the highest esteem, and have learned from the pen of that distinguished teacher, Miss Hannah U. Maxon, that the early settlers and citizens spoke with pride and almost veneration of those who officially conducted the schools.

An institution may have all the other requisites, but until it has hoary years replete with honor behind it, the atmosphere will lack the bracing quality that makes young blood tingle. Dr. Guy Potter Benton: A Real College

"We earnestly hope that there will go forth each year from this school graduates with vision and high ideals, whose lives will add still more honor to the institution, which through the illustrious past possess in an eminent degree 'the bracing quality that makes young blood tingle.' *Submitted by James Craft*

*Central Office of Gallipolis City School District*

# University of Rio Grande
## A Timeline Of 125 Years

**The Beginning -** Through each stage of its history, the University of Rio Grande has marks of distinction. The evolving nature of a college moving toward university status over a century shows a constantly changing landscape of academic achievement and new buildings that in 2002 provide instructional space for a student body of 1950.

Rio Grande remains committed to meeting the educational needs of Southern Ohio and to assisting the people of the region to improve their lives. However, the institution now attracts 35 percent of its student body from a global market in contrast to its beginnings in 1876 when only local residents attended Rio Grande. This story could not he told today if it were not for the Reverend Ira Haning, a Freewill Baptist minister who persuaded Nehemiah Atwood, an affluent resident and entrepreneur, to use his wealth to establish a college. Following Nehemiah's death in 1869, the responsibility for making a dream become a reality transferred to his wife, Permelia.

In 1873. Permelia Ridgeway Atwood established an endowment and deeded 10 acres of land for Rio Grande College. The small college officially opened on September 13, 1876.

Years of Change

In its first years, Rio Grande provided leadership in preparing ministers and teachers. By 1915, Rio Grande's major focus had evolved into teacher training, which continued as almost a singular emphasis for approximately 60 years.

The affiliation with the Baptists formally ended in the early 1950s. During the same time, the farm adjacent to the campus and owned by the College (students worked there to produce dairy products) had to be sold to provide much needed operating funds for the institution. A young businessman, Bob Evans, became the farm's owner.

With the advent of the 1950s, a bold, new energy exploded on Rio Grande's landscape of history. Bevo Francis, a legendary basketball player, put Rio Grande on the map when he scored 113 points in a single game against Hillsdale College. The media attention given to Bevo and his legendary team helped to save a college that continued to have financial difficulty.

Momentum

In 1969, over 90 years after its founding, the North Central Association of Colleges and Schools approved Rio Grande's accreditation. The Jeanette Albiez Davis Library was constructed and dedicated three years before the first accreditation date; the library was crucial in winning accreditation.

President Alphus Christensen worked with area business and community leaders to establish a community college in partnership with the University. The Ohio Board of Regents provided state funding to Rio Grande Community College following passage of a permanent local tax levy among Gallia, Jackson, Meigs and Vinton Counties.

In 1974. Rio Grande Community College officially opened, adding a new partner to a well-established four year institution. Freshmen had new options in their academic choices. Two-year degree programs became possible as terminal degrees to gain em-

*Alumni Memorial Bell Tower*

ployment, or as preparation to complete four-year degrees from the University or other four-year institutions.

To this day, Rio Grande is unique among America's higher education institutions. It is the only comprehensive private institution in partnership with a public community college.

Expansion

In 1989, Rio Grande College was renamed the University of Rio Grande in recognition of its expanding facilities and curriculum. Some of the new degree programs added to the University's curriculum in the past ten years include a Master of Education program, Environmental Science, Bachelor of Science in Nursing, Information Technology, Music, Mass Communications, and a number of other programs that meet students' needs in southern Ohio and increasingly throughout the state and nation.

From 1996 to 1998, with tremendous community support and local assistance, Rio Grande established the Madog Center for Welsh Studies on campus (1996) and the Meigs Center in Middleport (1998). The institution also expanded its outreach to the public schools and became increasingly involved in all aspects of community development.

From approximately $9 million in 1991, the endowment has grown to $22 million today. Seventy-five percent of Rio Grande's students are commuters, many of whom are older adults; in fact, the average age for all students is approximately 25.

Although the University of 2002 includes a variety of new cyberspace options for learning, with distance-learning courses through the Internet and Instructional Television, the mission of the institution remains the same as Permelia Atwood envisioned. Personalized attention to students continues to be the heart and soul of Rio Grande.

Excerpted from "A Timeline of 125 Years: University of Rio Grande (2001); written by Kathleen Gierhart, Assistant to the President and designed by Jean Ann Vance, Director of Publications.

Contribution courtesy of Dr Barry M. Dorsey, 18th President of the University of Rio Grande and Rio Grande Community College.*Submitted by the Office of Alumni Relations, University of Rio Grande.*

*Atwood Hall*

# Ohio Valley Christian School

The Ohio Valley Christian School, located at 455 Avenue, Gallipolis, Ohio is a non-denominational educational ministry of the First Baptist Church. OVCS is recognized by the State of Ohio. It's mission is to develop Christian minds for Godly living through academic education consistent with Biblical truth for kindergarten through the 12"' grade. The school offers a full, traditional college prep program with extracurricular fine arts and athletics. Enrollment peaked in 1999 to 259 with students from 54 different churches of various denominations.

Pastor Wilson Wahl's and Pastor Alvis Pollard's ministries produced a vision for Christian education in the family at First Baptist Church. The Biblical foundation set by these leaders led the people to desire a Christian school.

In 1977 Pastor Joseph Godwin, working with the steering committee, opened the doors of Ohio Valley Christian School on September 7. That first year 39 students sat under the instruction of Debbie North, Sue Murray, Mary Felts and Ted Ball. The support staff included Carol Jean Hood and Kathy Keenan. Earlene Saunders, working as a volunteer, led the day-to-day operations as administrator.

A school governing board was established to develop policies and promote the vision of Christian education Original board members included Pastor Joe Godwin, Marie Edelblute, Dr. Ismael Jamora, Larry Marr, Estivaun Matthews, Ed Stewart, Earl Tope and Jeff Smith. These men and women were used by God to set a solid foundation for the ministry of OVCS.

In 1998, God blessed First Baptist Church with a beautiful new facility on Fourth Avenue in Gallipolis. That fall the overcrowded Locust Street building was relieved of pressure when the elementary classes moved to the new location.

Ohio Valley Christian School praises the Lord for the twenty-five years He has allowed this ministry of First Baptist Church to impact the lives of young people in the tri-county area. Over 220 alumni have graduated from this ministry with many serving God in their local churches here and throughout the United States.

The current staff consists of Sue Murray, Darlene Beaver, Debbie North, Sandra Mock, Carolyn Cox, Paul Queen, Cheryl Jarvis, Gina Tillis, Barbara Hood, Mike VanMatre, LuEllen Scouten, Jay Jarvis, Paul Terre-Blanche, Harold Taylor, Christy Perkins, Fred Willams, John Barlow, Roger Williams, Tammy Terre-Blanche, Kathy Keenan, Brenda Pollard, Steve Jenkins, Brenda McDaniel, Lori Miller, Bill Burleson, Tamela Weber, Greg Atkins, Kenny Coughenour, Penny Burleson, Lee Holcomb, Traci Sisson, Valerie Taylor, Donna Evans, Jean Zirille, Karen Barlow, Leah Rutherford, Bill Wood, Beth Carman and Lois Thomas.

The current board members are pastor Archie C. Conn, Mike Zirille, Rick McDaniel, Dr. Fred Williams, Jeff Smith, Larry Miller and Pastor Alvis Pollard. *Submitted by Dr. Fred Williams, Administrator (since 1982)*

*Dr. Frederick W. Williams, came to OVCS in 1979 and has been the Administrator Since 1982*

# Gallia County Memorials & Veterans

*Downtown, Gallipolis, Ohio*

*Dough Boy, Gallipolis City Park*

# A Loving Tribute To Our Mother and Father
# Bob and Jewel Evans

# With Love,
# Stan, Gwen, Robbie, Debbie, Steve and Bobby

# In Memory
# Carrol H. "Casey" McKenzie July 14, 1916 - June 16, 1995

Carrol H. McKenzie was born July 14, 1916, reared in Vinton County, and graduated from Pomeroy High School. Casey, as family, friends and his many business acquaintances knew him, came to Gallia County to become one of us in 1937. He accepted a position as bookkeeper for Evans Packing Company which was the beginning of a most productive life and career. Five years later, local businessman Emerson Evans sold him an interest in Evans Packing Company, and he became a key member of its ongoing success.

During the early summer of 1953, his expertise was again recognized and utilized when he became one of the founders and original directors of what was then the Bob Evans Sausage Company, now known as Bob Evans Farms, Inc. His leadership skills and insight, his capacity to understand all phases of running a business, plus his vision and sound judgment, natural ingenuity and initiative, were instrumental in the operation and achievements of both Evans Packing Company and Bob Evans Farms as they grew and prospered.

His interest and dedication to the agricultural community were also evident. He saw the need to improve the quality of livestock being produced in Gallia County and made a concerted effort to encourage farmers to adopt practices that would be beneficial and enhance their operations. These efforts included practices such as using genetically superior boars and bulls to improve livestock which enhanced the profitability of their operations. He developed programs that would provide local farmers with boars that would help them produce the quality animals that the livestock industry was promoting. This same type of desire led Casey to be involved with the 4-H and FFA youth programs. He was always supportive of the involvement of youth in these programs because how youth learning the skills in these programs would help them be successful adults. He became a member of the Gallia County Junior Fair's Board of Directors and was instrumental in the development of the Junior Fair Livestock sale, not only because it illustrated the need to produce better market animals, but it also helped young people provide for their future. In 1992, the Gallia County Agricultural Center, Inc. built and dedicated the C. H. McKenzie Agricultural Center in Casey's honor to serve the people of Gallia County. This facility houses the OSU Extension Office, the Farm Service Agency, and the Soil and Water Conservation Service and serves as a one -stop agriculture center for Gallia County.

Casey was an adept financier and was elected to the Board of Directors of the Ohio Valley Bank in 1980 and served actively on that board until 1986. In 1987, he was named Director Emeritus.

He served as a member of Gallipolis City Commission for four (4) years, a Trustee and Secretary of the Community Improvement Corporation and on the Board of the Gallia County Chamber of Commerce.

In 1984, he was selected as the Southeastern Ohio Regional Council's Man of the Year for Gallia County. This was done in recognition of his multiple contributions to Gallia County.

1984 was also important because Casey and his close friend Emerson E. Evans were able to have the Lifeline program established in Gallia County through their financial contribution. Their initial seed money in July of 1984 made it possible to purchase ten Lifeline units to place in homes of individuals in the area who wanted to remain independent, but still have the security of a direct connection to our local hospital's emergency department and responders who lived close by. That program is successfully in effect today.

In 1995, Casey was the recipient of The Bud and Donna McGhee Community Service Award. This award was presented to Casey who gave so much of himself to Gallia County. He was always encouraged and supported by his wife of almost sixty years, Eva Jo White, who he married September 30, 1935. He was an entrepreneur and philanthropist. In his quiet and unassuming way, he contributed immeasurably to the business, industry, banking, agriculture, elderly through Lifeline, and youth through the Gallia County Junior Fair Annual Livestock Sale.

# Memorial to Emerson E. and Evelyn Tope Evans

Emerson E. Evans - September 10, 1909 - June 26, 1990
Evelyn G. Tope Evans - September 21, 1912 - December 22, 1990.

Emerson E. Evans was born on a farm near Cadmus, Ohio in 1909 and by age fourteen he had lost both parents. He and his nine brothers and sisters survived by loving and caring for each other. This helped mold the philosophy which guided the rest of his life - to work hard and help others. He married Evelyn Tope and they had three sons - Merrill, Daniel and Larry. He devoted his life to his family, church and community. Many of his deeds were done in secret.

Many of Mr. Evans' contributions to society, both financially and motivating others for improvements, were made by him, fully realizing he would never personally participate in or benefit from them. In its early years, Mr. Evans contributed to the French Art Colony, a multi-arts cultural center. He made a generous financial contribution for the new Cliffside Golf Course, knowing he would not be playing golf again, but he said, "the community needs a golf course"

Hobart Wilson, Jr., Executive Editor of the Gallipolis Daily Tribune, in his Editorial at the time of Emerson E. Evans' death in 1990, describes one of Mr. Evans' talents and characteristics: "His ability to get individuals of all walks of life in one room to agree on various undertakings made impossible dreams a reality. Evans seldom took credit for the many successful projects he organized over the years."

Some of his best known business interests include helping organize Bob Evans Farms, Inc. and serving as Chairman of the Board from its beginning in 1953 till 1971. He gave 43 years of service to Ohio Valley Bank, having served as a Director, the President and Chairman of the Board. He established Evans Enterprises, Inc., a family business dealing in commercial real estate and other investments. In 1976, Mr. Evans was selected as Gallia County's "Man of the Year" by the Southeastern Ohio Regional Council.

Mr. Evans engaged for a number of years in breeding, researching promoting various breeds of cattle; breeding showing Grand Champions; and was an officer of local, state and national cattle associations. Wanting to help young people, he was a staunch supporter of Gallia County Junior Fair's steer, lamb and hog sales as well as working for the improvement of the fairgrounds and facilities. Mr. Evans was a recipient of The Ohi State University College of Agriculture and Home Economics Centennial Award for Distinguished Service.

Mr. Evans served on the Gallipolis City School Board from 1942 through 1949. Perhaps because he was unable to pursue a formal higher education, Mr. Evans always valued education. He was active in the establishment of Rio Grande Community College in 1972 and in 1980, the Board of Trustees of Rio Grande College conferred upon him the "Friends Degree" in grateful recognition of moral and financial support. In 1982 Rio Grand College established the Emerson E. Evans School of Business Management in tribute to his support of the business world and higher education.

Emerson was dedicated to improving the health care services and facilities in the area. He served on the Board of Trustees of the Gallipolis Clinic and was instrumental in the merging of Gallipolis Clinic and Holzer Hospital and also very actively involved in the financing and building of the Holzer Medical Center.

Concerning the Legacy and Leadership of his father, Emerson E. Evans, Dan Evans reminisces: "My father was able to see things far into the future of a company. In his time, it was unheard of that a company would have a three or five year business plan. As he talked about future goals to key people in companies, many became inspired. The effect on many Gallia County companies and organizations will be everlasting."

His wife of 59 years, Evelyn, graduated from Gallia Academy High School, a very active member of First Baptist Church, Gallipolis and served several terms on the deaconess board. Throughout her marriage Evelyn was devoted to Emerson and their three sons. Her support of his business endeavors was well-known.

# Memorial to Harland Martin

The following is taken from an article written by James S. Porter, known as J. Samuel Peeps, and published in the Gallipolis Daily Tribune following the death of Harland Martin on April 22, 1985:

Harland Martin did so many things in his lifetime that you can't list his achievements in toto, short of two or three columns in length. His birth date was Nov. 17, 1909, which of course was also the birth date of his twin brother, Herman M. Martin, Xenia.

He came to Gallipolis at not quite 30 years of age in 1939 as a Vocational Agriculture teacher at Gallia Academy High School. Prior to that he taught for six years:

One year in Ross County, and five years at Rome-Canaan in Athens County. After five years Martin resigned from the teaching profession and became associated with The Evans Packing Company. During the 28 years with that company he served as secretary, president and later chairman of the board of directors, until the company was sold in 1972.

For a number of years Martin owned and operated a farm on Lower River Road, farming and specializing in the breeding of Aberdeen-Angus cattle, and cattle feeding. He showed Aberdeen-Angus cattle at state fairs and at many county fairs and at the International Livestock Exposition in Chicago. He maintained a keen interest in youth organizations and worked in support of the Gallia County Junior Fair, Future Farmers of America, 4-H Clubs and Boy Scouts of America.

From the time the company was founded, Martin served on the board of directors of Bob Evans Farms, Inc. until his retirement in 1981, and he and his son, Roger, owned and operated Martin Ford and Mercury Sales Agency for 10 years in Gallipolis.

Harland Martin was a civic leader of great versatility and generosity, putting forward progressive ideas to advance his community. Years ago he proposed merger of the multiplicity of tiny township school districts into just one county local district; however, the people defeated it at a plebiscite modeled on the then-effective merger of Addison and Cheshire townships. His idea has now crystallized, his friends point out, so that there now exist only a local county and a city school district in Gallia County. The people elected him to the Gallipolis City Board of Education for eight years, and he served as president of it for two years.

Harland Martin served on the board of trustees of the Holzer Hospital Foundation elected in 1950, a busy 31 years that found him heading up the board itself and its executive committee, during the 1973 construction of the new $21,000,000 Medical Center on Jackson Pike. He resigned from the Holzer Hospital Foundation in 1981, and was made a Trustee Emeritus in 1985.

He also served for years on the board of the Ohio Valley Health Services. Martin was a member of the Southeastern Ohio Regional Council. He was president of the Gallipolis Chamber of Commerce for one year (1948), and he was one of the three persons who served as incorporators of the Chamber.

Since 1935, he was a Mason; he belonged to Aladdin Temple of the Shrine in Columbus, Ohio and the Gallipolis Shrine Club. He was a member of the Gallipolis Rotary Club, the French Art Colony, and was a Kentucky Colonel. A 1933 graduate, he was a life member of the Ohio State University Alumni Association and a member of the Presidents' Club at OSU, and he continually worked closely with the College of Agriculture because of his interest in the livestock industry and vocational education. He had served as a member of the OSU College Alumni Advisory Association and was given the Centennial Award for Distinguished Service to the university in 1979. He was graduated from Pennsville High School after attending public school in Monroe and Morgan Counties.

Martin served on the board of trustees of Rio Grande College since 1964, and was made a Fellow of the college in 1983.

Harland Martin was president of the Ohio Meat Packers Association for three years.

During that time, the association worked for stricter inspection laws. The Ohio General Assembly passed the first state meat packing plant inspection law, and Evans Packing Company became the first meat packing plant placed under the new law.

He was an active member of Grace United Methodist Church serving on various committees through the years.

With all of the time and effort that Harland Martin put into his work and the community, he could not have done it without the love and support of his wife, Freda, whom he married in 1938. Freda Anderson Martin (1912-2000) was from Pennsville, Ohio, a graduate of Ohio University and an elementary school teacher. After settling in Gallipolis, they raised their two children, Roger (1940-1996) and Ellen (1945- ). Freda was the sounding board and support system for Harland through their 47 years of marriage.

# John Timothy Evans (J. Tim)

A lifetime of farming, entrepreneurial successes, community involvement and generosity began in 1926 when J. Tim Evans was born to John Everette and Elma Reese Evans. He was their third child following Bertha Elizabeth and Elma Louise.

In 1942, while he was in high school, Tim's parents bought a Gallia County farm on Lower River Road near the dam. Here they began dairy farming with 70 head of Holstein and raised truck gardens. At one point they had more than 80,000 tomato plants. In addition to tending the garden, Tim was up at 3:30 each morning to milk the cattle before the milk truck came to pick up at 7 A.M. As the FFA president in high school, Tim was the first person from Gallia County to win the American Farmers Degree which was awarded to two honorees from Ohio. Six years later, they sold the dairy cow business and Tim bought into the Point Pleasant stockyards where be became a livestock dealer and began raising beef cattle.

In 1946, Tim married Betty Lou Rothgeb. Their children, David T. Evans (born in 1947) and Martha Evans Huestis (born in 1951) gave them seven grandchildren.

In 1953, Emerson Evans was ready to branch out and further develop Evans Packing Company so he allowed Tim to buy into the business where he worked in almost every department but primarily served as cattle buyer initially. He eventually became President of the business until 1974. During the same time, Tim was instrumental in the development of the business that would become Bob Evans Farms. Evans Packing Company bought a production plant in Xenia, Ohio, in 1953. In addition to processing beef, they also processed pork in conjunction with a new sausage production opportunity with Bob Evans. Three years later, the sausage venture reorganized into what is now known as Bob Evans Farms. The owners of Evans Packing Company joined with Bob Evans to establish the company.

Since its inception, Tim has been a member of the Board of Directors where he chaired the audit committee until 1996 and was Vice President of Bob Evans Farms at one point. With his children through college, Tim retired in 1974 at the age of 48.

Serving on Boards of Trustees, volunteering, fundraising and financial generosity quickly became priorities for Tim and Betty. In addition to supporting the American Cancer Society, Tim has served as fundraising chair for the Boy Scouts and 4-H's Canter's Cave project. Tim was a member of the Board of Trustees for Grace United Methodist Church; Holzer Hospital; Gallia Metropolitan Housing Authority and; the University of Rio Grande. During his more than 25 years with the University of Rio Grande, Tim and Betty contributed to new building efforts and established a scholarship fund.

John Everette Evans Jr., Emerson Evans, and Harlan Martin, his high school agriculture teacher, were strong mentors and helped mold him as a person.

After 54 years of marriage, Tim's biggest supporter, Betty, passed away in 2001.

Tim currently divides his time between his Sunset Valley Farm in Gallia County at Rodney and his residence in Palm Beach, Fla., with his wife, Deanie.

*J. Tim Evans*

# Morris E. Haskins

There are very few people in this world that can say they found success before the age of 30. Morris E. Haskins is one of those people.

Many Gallipolitans know him as a former Director and President of Ohio Valley Bank and benefactor to the restoration of the Ariel Theatre. A few less remember him as manager/owner of the Haskins-Tanner men's clothing store which, thanks to him and to the delight of his customers, was the first air-conditioned retail store in Gallipolis. Some know him as one of the founders of Bob Evans Farms. Very few know that he served as a second lieutenant in The Ohio State Guard or that he attended Marietta College for two years.

The Marietta High School grad married Dorothy Wallace in 1934. Soon after, his career began to flourish. He took on the position of Vice President and Director of the Retail Clothiers & Furnishers Association and Men's Apparel Club of Ohio. Under his management, the Haskins-Tanner Store sold more corduroy jackets than any other retailer in the country.

His business endeavors did not limit his love of community. At age 27, he was named the youngest Rotary Club president in Ohio. He also found the time to almost single-handedly raise $10,000 for a new municipal swimming pool.

In 1939, the 28-year-old Haskins began a relationship with Ohio Valley Bank that would span seven decades and continues today. He joined the Bank's Board of Directors in December of that year.

A few years later, his Ohio Valley Bank ties helped Haskins become part of a great American success story. The 1950s were a time of fresh opportunities. One such opportunity was seized by a handful of Gallia County visionaries and their entrepreneurial-spirited friend Bob Evans. Haskins was one of these leaders, who became a founding father of Bob Evans Farms, Inc. The company has grown from one restaurant with 12 stools to 488 restaurants with over $1 billion in annual sales.

In 1976, with 37 years of banking experience under his belt, Haskins became Ohio Valley Bank's seventh president. During his time in that office, Ohio Valley Bank opened the Jackson Pike Office, across from Holzer Medical Center, and installed Gallia County's first ATM. He served as Bank President until 1981. Then presided as Chairman of the Board of Directors until 1992. He remained on the Board until 1999.

Even though work at the Bank kept Haskins busy, he never lost his focus on community improvement. He served as President Associate of Cedarville College, served as a director of the Gallipolis Area Chamber of Commerce, was involved in the Gallipolis Retail Merchants Association and remained active in Rotary. Haskins teamed with his wife Dorothy to endow a scholarship at the University of Rio Grande.

In fact, the couple became well-known for their commitment to the community. In 1991 their commitment was noted in history. "One of the highlights of the past year [1991] was the renaming of the Ariel Theatre in honor of Morris and Dorothy Haskins. Their long time support and dedication to the downtown business district brings together two names synonymous with Gallipolis. A quarter of a million dollars was raised to honor Morris and Dorothy and to assist the Ariel as she prepares to serve our region into the next millennium," commented Ohio Valley Bank's President Jim Dailey.

After Dorothy passed away, he continued their support for the First Baptist Church by becoming a driving force behind the new building project which was completed in 1998.

To this day, Haskins resides in downtown Gallipolis. On December 23, 2001, he celebrated his 90th birthday by receiving over 300 cards and letters, including a giant birthday card signed by 189 Ohio Valley Bank, Loan Central, and Ohio Valley Financial Services employees.

*Morris and Dorothy Haskins*

*Trolley Car in Gallipolis, Ohio*

*February 1937*

# Gallia County's Civil War Bean Dinners

During the Great War of the Rebellion (the American Civil War 1861-1865) soldiers from Gallia County served in over forty combat units to help the north preserve the union. After the war a small number of these units held reunions in Gallia County. Meetings and reunions of Civil War soldiers became more common after the establishment of the Grand Army Posts in the county. The Grand Army of the Republic (the G.A. R.) was a union veteran's organization similar to today's American Legion organization. By the mid 1880s, many of the G.A. R. Posts in the county were holding annual reunions and inviting all honorably discharged union veterans to attend as opposed to men of a particular regiment, or company.

At many of the soldier's reunions, the soldiers prepared a campfire meal of pork, hard-tack, slap-jack- beans and hot coffee. By 1890 such reunions had become known as "bean dinners". In all, 14 or more G.A.R Posts existed in Gallia County, holding one or more reunions/bean dinners in the following towns: Gallipolis, Crown City, Patriot, Mercerville, Northup, Centerville/Thurman, Rio Grande, Bidwell/Porter, Vinton, Ewington, Chambersburg (near modern day Eureka), Gallia Furnace (near present day Gallia), Sandfork (formerly located in Walnut Township), and at Bethel School house in Ohio Township. The soldiers at Addison, Ohio in Addison Township also held reunions and bean dinners. The town of Rodney is known to have held bean dinners which may have been Civil War related.

Of the numerous Civil War bean dinners once held in the county, only two survive today. The villages of Vinton and Rio Grande have maintained their annual Civil War bean dinner. These two villages have helped preserve Ohio's unique Civil War Legacy, for instance, its unbroken link with the Civil War. By doing so, these villages have helped preserve what was in effect the Civil War soldier's "Veteran's Day". These annual dinners were sometimes attended by generals, colonels or even governors. The events consisted of marching soldiers, patriotic speeches, patriotic songs, dances, rifle drills, flag drills, tributes to fallen comrades concerning their sacrifices which the soldiers wanted remembered, war stories and etc. In later years the dinners became more festive in nature, but the Civil War soldier remained the dominant figure. Crowds of thousands attended these events. At Vinton and Bidwell, excursion trains brought hundreds of people to the dinners. People from Columbus, Fostoria, Marion, Lancaster, Logan and other points north were known to attend the Vinton Bean Dinner. This ws partly due to the home-coming aspect of the dinners as well.

An article written in 1957 by the late Harry R. Hurn, former editor of the Gallipolis Tribune, stated that the Bean Dinner at Vinton, Ohio (site of the Morgan Raid) originated in 1868. The oldest written record (found to date) of the Vinton Bean Dinner is the Soldier's Campfire of Corwin Post No. 259 G. A. R. held on October 13, 1883. The G. A. R. and its auxiliary unit, the Women's Relief Corps No. 280 sponsored the Vinton Bean Dinners for about three decades. The Vinton churches, H. K. Butler, the village of Vinton, the Vinton Grange and the V.F. W. also sponsored the Vinton Bean Dinners. For the last half century (since 1950) Vinton Post 161 of the American Legion and its auxiliary unity No. 161 has sponsored the Vinton Bean Dinners.

The consensus of knowledgeable people (one of whom was accomplished author J. Sherman Porter) is the Rio Grande Bean Dinner originated in 1870. The oldest written record (located to date) of the Rio Grande Bean Dinner is the Soldier's Bean Dinner held there on September 2, 1891. The I.Z. Haning Post No 332 G. A. R. of Rio Grande was organized on July 13, 1895 and began sponsoring bean dinners the same year. For a number of years now the Rio Grande Memorial Association and Bob Evans Farms Inc. have co-sponsored the Rio Grande Bean Dinners.

At today's bean dinners crowds of several hundred still enjoy the "soldier's meal" of white beans once called "army beans". Quantities of two to three hundred pounds of these beans are cleaned, soaked over night, then cooked for two and a half hours in iron kettles over open fires with jowl bacon, or ham for flavoring. Once cooked, the beans are carried in three gallon buckets to customers setting at picnic tables and served in Styrofoam bowls, or cups along with crackers or corn bread. In days of yore the customers ate their meals on army tin plates and drank coffee from tin cups. Additional refreshments, live music and the home-coming aspect of the dinners are still a part of these historic events.

*References Appendix*

List of 14 known G. A. R. Posts that once existed in Gallia County:

1. Blackaller Post No. 134, Gallipolis, organized 1867, (Gallipolis Journal, January 31, 1867 and October 24, 1867)

2. A. Blessing Post No. 126, Gallipolis, organized 1881, (The Bulletin, August 16, 1881)

B. Cadot Post No. 126, Gallipolis, new name for Blessing Post in use by 1889, (The Bulletin, June 18, 1889

3. Corwin Post No. 259, Vinton, org. 1882, Women's Relief Corps No. 280, (Auxiliary to Post 259) (The Bulletin, October 17, 1882 and The Bulletin, July 6, 1895)

4. Oliver P. Davis Post No. 363, Chambersburg, org. 1883, (The Bulletin, August 28, 1883)

5. George Crook Post No. 325, Crown City, in existence by 1884, (The Bulletin, July 29, 1884)

6. Amos Carter Post No. 388, Patriot, in existence by 1884, (the Bulletin, October 7, 1884)

7. Charles Lyon Post No. 447, Kyger, in existence by 1884 (The Bulletin, July 22, 1884)

8. John Leaper Post No. 397, Sandfork, in existence by 1885, (Gallipolis Jounal, July 29, 1885)

9. Ben Shuler Post No. 605, Cheshire, org. 1886, (Gallipolis Journal, September 8, 1886)

10. W.S. Hancock Post Nol 571, enterville, org. 1886, headquarters at Thurman, (The Bulletin, March 2, 1886 & December 24, 1889)

11. D. L. Morton Post No. 363,m in Mercerville, in existence by 1886

12. Harry Sisson Post No.____Bidwell/Porter, in existence by 1887, (The Bulletin, March 1, 1887)

13. D. W. Shenefield Post No. 734, Ewington, in existence by 1892, (The Bulletin, July 9, 1892)

14. I.Z. Haning Post No. 332, Rio Grande, org. 1895 (Gallipolis Journal, July 20, 1895)

Two other G A R. Posts that were mentioned frequently, but were not Gallia County Posts were Thomas Town Post No. 475

at Waterloo, and the Ben Terry Post at Millersport. The towns of Waterloo, and Millersport are located in Lawrence County, Ohio. (These towns are mentioned on pages 18 & 24 of Hardesty's 1882 History of Gallia County). The names of these posts are given here to show they have been eliminated as Gallia County Posts.

Notes on Gallia County's first G. A. R. Post. (Blackaller Post No. 134). This post likely named after post member Lieutenant Henry M. Blackaller, who left Gallipolis in June, 1867 to join his regiment in New Orleans only to die in Texas of Yellow Fever on July 12, 1867) seems to have had a short existence. Lt. Col. Lemuel Zenas Cadot was the Post's first (six month) commander (Gallipolis Journal February 21, 1867). This G. A. R. Post was still in existence the following year but it is not listed among the military units participating in the 1868 Memorial Day activities in Gallipolis. Col. Cadot, though, was involved being one of the commanders of the memorial battalion (The Bulletin June 3 1868). In 1881, Lt. Col. L. Z. Cadot became senior vice-commander of the newly organized Blessing Post No. 126 of Gallipolis (The Bulletin August 16, 1881). Obviously, Blackaller Post No. 134 was non-existant at this time. Within a few years the name of Blessing Post was changed to Cadot Post No. 126. (This likely occurred shortly after the death of Lt. Col. L. Z. Cadot on June 29, 1885). While Cadot Post was still called Blessing Post, Col. John L. Vance of Gallipolis, publisher of The Bulletin became a member of this post, though, not one of its first officers. He is listed as a member of Cadot Post No. 126 in 1888 (Gallipolis Journal August 15, 1888). In 1943 Mrs. Annie (Cherrington) Miller wrote that "comrade Vance of Blessing Post was mustering officer" when Corwin Post No. 259 of Vinton was organized in 1882. Colonel John L. Vance was a popular speaker at many of the Civil War bean dinners in Gallia County.

Information on Lt Henry M. Blackaller of the 9th, Reg. Calvary is given in the Gallipolis Journal June 13, 1867 and July 18, 1867. (This latter issue gives resolutions of respect for this late member of Post 134).

List of 40 combat units Gallia Countians served in during the Civil War. Starting with the Ohio Volunteer Infantry (O.V.I.) regiments we have the following:

The 13th, 18th, 23rd, 37th, 33rd, 36th, 53rd, 56th, 60th, 73rd, 92nd, 103rd, 107th, 116th, 117th, 133rd, 141st, 167th, 173rd, 179th, 185th, 192nd, 193rd, 194th and 195th. The 1st 2nd Ohio Volunteer Heavy Artillery, the 2nd Volunteer Calvary Regulars, the 7th Ohio Volunteer Cavalry, the 18th Ohio Cavalry, the 18th Ohio Battery (light Artillery), the 19th United States Regulars, the 141st Ohio National Guard (O.N.G.), the 142nd O.N.G., the Gallia Guards, and the Independent Company of Trumbull Guards. In addition some soldiers served in veteranized units such as the 18th O.V.V.I., 36th O.V.V.I., 53rd, O.V.V.I. and others; some Gallia Countians served in Virginia and Kentucky regiments. The 4th VA V.I. and 13th Va, V.I. Were two of these units.

The names of most of the above units were obtained from the "Personal History Section" and the section entitled "Gallia County in the War of the Rebellion" from Hardesty's 1882 History of Gallia County. Additional unit names were obtained from tombstone inscriptions listed in the Huntington Township Cemetery booklet prepared by the Gallia County Historical Society. The name of the 103rd O.V.I. unit was obtained from the June 8, 1868 edition of The Bulletin concerning Memorial Day activities in Gallipolis.

List of Campfires, reunions, or bean dinners.

Campfire at Vinton by Corwin Post No 259 G. A. R. October 13, 1883 (The Bulletin September 11, 1883)

Campfire and soldier's bean dinner at Chambersburg by Oliver P Davis Post No 363 G. A. R., October 31 1883 (The Bulletin October 23 1883)

Campfire at Crown City by George Crook Post No 32S4 G. A.R. (The Bulletin July 29, 1884)

Campfire at Patriot by Amos Carter Post No. 388 G. A. R. (The Bulletin October 7, 1884)

Reunion at Northup by John Leaper post No. 397 G. A. R. (The Bulletin June 12m 1888)

Campfire at Gallipolis Courthouse by Cadot Post No. 126 on august 12, 1892 (The Bulletin August 6 1892)

Soldier's bean dinner near Gallia Furnace at Shelton's School house, or Shelton's Grove by W. S. Handcock post No. 571 G. A. R. & Silas Boyer Camp No. 398 S. of V (sons of Veterans's), (Gallipolis Journal September 17, 1890 and the Bulletin August 26, 1890)

Campfire near Sandfork on August 21 & 22 1890 by John Leaper Post No. 397 G. A. R. & A. Gilbert Camp S of V. (The Bulletin August 5, 1890)

Bean dinner at Rio Grande by the soldiers of Rio Grande (Gallipolis Journal August 26, 1891)

Grand Bean dinner at Porter Station (Bidwell) on September 3, 1891 by Harry Sisson Post G. A. R. (Gallipolis Journal August 26, 1891)

Soldier's bean dinner and reunion at Ewington by D.W. Shenefield Post No. 734 G.A.R. (The Bulletin July 9, 1892)

Campfire & soldier's reunion held on W.H. Clark's farm at Lincoln on the 20, 21, & 22 of Sept. 1893, (Gallipolis Tribune Aug 23, 1893)

Grand campfire, and reunion at Mercerville by D.L. Morton Post No. 363 G.A.R. Sep. 10, 11, 12th, 1896 (The Bulletin Aug. 22, 1896)

Campfire & bean dinner at Bethel Schoolhouse in Ohio Township by D. L. Morton Post No. 363 August 14th & 15th, 1901 (The [Gallipolis] Weekly Tribune August 9, 1901)Soldier's bean dinner & reunion at Addison on September 16, 1905, Wm. Willis, Co. 153rd O.V.V.I. Chairman of committees (The Bulletin September 8, 1905)

There is a bean dinner at Rodney next Saturday" (Gallipolis Tribune September 12, 1913)

In reading the old newspaer articles concerning Gallia County's first G.A.R. Post (Blackaller Post No. 134). The word "encampment" is used several times in reference to this post. The question then arises, was this "encampment" a reunion? The answer appears to be no it was not a reunion, hence no bean dinner occurred. The word "encampment" appears to be an extension of the Post name, or title of the Post rather than a true encampment. Another example where the word "encampment" is used in a title position is the I.O.O.F. organization (Independent Order of Odd Fellows); "The Grand Encampment of the I.O.O.F. meets in Cincinnati on the first Tuesday of May", (The [Gallipolis] Journal April 22, 1869). Also, "The new Encampment of Odd Fellows in our town is to be institutive next Wednesday, August 12th. (1868) (The Vinton [county] Record McArthur Ohio August 6, 1868). And again, "the enormous sum of $1,170,390.38 remained in the treasuries of the different lodges and encampments of Ohio (Odd Fellows) at the close of 1873" (The Journal

May 14, 1874). The title of G.A.R. Post 134 as given in the Gallipolis Journal June 11 & 18, 1868 is as follows:

Head'rts Blackaller Encampment
Post 134 G.A.R.

The date (in the text of) the June 11th newspaper article is June 9, 1868. The date of the newspaper containing the 2nd title is June 18, 1868. The length of time involved here is nine days (perhaps longer since some newspapers are missing). What peacetime non-active military organization would hold an encampment for nine days? Even the national encampments of the G.AR. Usually lasted about three days. No, it appears the name "encampment" is just a title not a reunion of soldiers.

Mr. J.A. Metcalf, a former Vinton (area) resident had been an influential and persuasive gentleman in his day. Mr. Metcalf moved to Columbus, Ohio and opened The Capital Clothing Store. In 1910 Teddy Roosevelt was traveling through Ohio by train. Mr. Metcalf met the train, talked his way on board and persuaded T. Roosevelt to stop and make an unscheduled speech in Columbus, Ohio. By obliging Mr. Metcalf's wish, T. Roosevelt had to cancel a previously scheduled speech at Coshocton, Ohio much to the disappointment of the citizens of Coshocton. (The Vinton Leader September 1, 1910 & The Coshocton Daily Age August 26, 1910). It is in Coshocton County that another of Ohio's Civil War bean dinners (the Newcastle Bean Dinner) is held.

Trains bringing people to the Vinton Bean Dinner. J. A. Metcalf charters a special train for the Vinton Bean Dinner (The Vinton Leader July 12, 1912). "J. A. Metcalf of the Capital Clothing Company of Columbus has chartered a special Hocking Valley Train to run from Columbus to Vinton on Saturday August 3 on the occasion of the annual Gallia County G.A.R. Bean Dinner"…." The train is to make stops in Lancaster and Logan." The July 30, 1943 edition of the Gallipolis Daily Tribune stated "excursion trains ran from Fostoria, Marion, Columbus and other north-central places" bringing people to the Vinton Bean Dinner.

References which gives the location of the town of Lincoln, Ohio. The April 23, 1874 (Gallipolis) Journal gives a list of the Justices of the Peace and their Post Offices in Gallia County. On this list of J's of P. was Elkanah Cremeens of Harrison Township in the town of Lincoln. Also, in Hardesty's 1882 History of Gallia County the town of Lincoln is mentioned in the first paragraph of Harrison Township on Page 30.

Marching of soldiers at the bean dinners. "The soldiers marched but they were not so well-drilled as of yore when the bugle meant battle", Vinton Bean Dinner 1884. (Gallipolis Journal September 11, 1883). The soldiers marched at the 1883 G.A.R. Bean Dinner at Chambersburg too. "the comrades formed in company line and marched to the grounds." Battalion Drill and Parade at 1896 Rio Grande Bean Dinner (The Bulletin August 29, 1896).

Flag Drill was performed at the 1894 Vinton Bean Dinner by the young boys and girls of Vinton. (The Bulletin August 11, 1894).

Arms were kept by the G.A.R. When the Grand Army of the Republic was first organized, one of the political parties opposed the G.A.R. because it was armed. An article in the Cincinnati enquirer and reprinted by the Gallipolis Journal on April 4, 1867 stated "A secret Society in a free country, that keeps arms on hand, means mischief." This political opposition to the G.A.R. in the early days may have contributed to the short existence of Gallia County's first G.A.R. Post (Blackaller Post No. 134). A photograph taken of the Zaleski, Ohio G.A.R. Post (T.R.Stanley Post No. 223) in 1893 or 1894 was published in the McArthur, Ohio newspaper. "The McArthur Republican Tribune" on August 28, 1958. The photograph shows muskets belonging to the Zaleski Post stacked in two groups tripod fashion near the American Flag. Soldiers who were able to stack arms military fashion were able to do other military maneuvers with the weapons such as left shoulder arms, right shoulder arms, present arms, or in short "Rifle Drills."

Songs that were sung at the bean dinners included "Auld Lang Syne", "When Johnny comes Marching Home Again", "The Army Bean", "Tramp, Tramp, The Boys Are Marching", "My Country Tis of Thee", and "Marching to the War." At the 1912 Keystone bean dinner they played all the songs they sang, or played during the war, except the (new?) song "Casey Jones." The songs that were sung at the 1888 Soldier's Reunion in Gallipolis gives us an idea of some additional songs the soldiers likely sang at the bean dinners. "America" , "Battle Hymn of the Union", "Hail to the Chief", "Star Spangled Banner", and "Tenting on the Old Camp Grounds". (Vinton Leader August 11, 1894 and August 1, 1912. The Buletin November 6, 1883 & Gallipolis Journal August 8, 1888).

Dignitaries who spoke at the bean dinners. General Enochs, General Crook, General H A. Axline, Attorney General Tim Hogan, General S. H. Hurst, Governor Foraker, Governor McKinley (later president) Major Charles Townsend, Colonel Montgomery, Honorable J. W. Jones, Honorable R. J. Mauck, Honorable Stephen J. Morgan, Honorable J. W. McCormick, Reverend T. M. Ricketts, Reverend J. W. Dillion, Honorable O. H. Stewart, Judge John Morton Webster, Judge John G. Reeves, Dr. L. B. Turner, Dr. E. A. Hamilton, State Librarian Newman, Colonel John L. Vance, Honorable W. S. Matthews and many others. (The names of these dignitaries and others can be found in the booklet on bean dinners entitled "The Campfire" compiled by John Holcomb in 1997).

Interesting note concerning the bean dinner held near Gallia Furnace in Greenfield Township on September 4, 1890. The name, or term "Bean Dinner" was used for perhaps the first time in Gallia County in regard to this bean dinner. In fact one of the two articles about the dinner mentions"bean dinner" in quotation marks twice. "There was a 'bean dinner' at the Shelton Grove on the 4th inst." Then later "And everybody young and old enjoyed the 'bean dinner'".(Gallipolis Journal September 17, 1890). These quotation marks may imply the usage of new terminology. The other article on the dinner mentions bean dinner too, but not in quotation marks. The article stated briefly that a Grand Bean Dinner was to be held in John Sim's beautiful grove near Shelton's School house on September 4, 1890. No mention is made, however, that this grove was located near Gallia Furnace. But on page 191 in the book "Gallia County One-Room Schools: The cradle Years" published by the Gallia County Historical Society it states "Shelton School was located on the Gallia Centerpoint Road 3 1/2 miles from Gallia Furnace." Incidentally it was the Centerville G.A.R. Post that gave the dinner. General Enochs attended the dinner. *Submitted by John Holcomb*

# G.A.R. and Sons of Union Veterans

After the War of the Rebellion (a.k.a. Civil War), the Grand Army of the Republic (G.A.R.) formed in 1866 using the post system. The G.A.R. obtained federal militia status were issued federal military equipment. It was a fraternal lodge with password and ritualistic induction ceremonies. The organization disbanded in 1949 with only nine living members—the last one dying in 1956.

Posts were named for famous Union leaders, soldiers, and home towns and numbered in the order formed with numbers not re-issued. Gallia County had the following posts: Cadot Post #126, Gallipolis; Corwin Post #259, Vinton; George Crook Post #325, Crown City; D. L. Martin Post #363, Eureka; Amos Carter Post #285 Sprinkle's Mills/Cadmus; John Leaper Post #397, Moody/Sandy Fork; Charles Lyons Post #447, Kyger; W. S. Hancock Post #571, Thurman; Ben Shuler Post #605, Cheshire; Harry Sisson Post #626, Pine Grove; D. W. Shenefield Post #734, Ewington.

In 1881, the Sons of Veterans U.S.A. was organized nationally in Pittsburgh, Pennsylvania, as a male G.A.R. auxiliary composed of actual sons of Union veterans. Later, nephews, grandsons, great nephews, etc. were allowed to join. The organization was renamed Sons of Union Veterans of the Civil War (S.U.V.C.W.).

When G.A.R. members became too old, the S.U.V.C.W. took over its national militia activities. S.U.V.C.W. units fought in both the Spanish-American War and WWI. When the National Guard formed, the S.U.V.C.W. no longer acted in that capacity and returned to its roots donning replica Civil War uniforms. When the G.A.R. disbanded, it deeded all its property and national militia status to the S.U.V.C.W., which it still has today.

The following "camps" of the S.U.V.C.W. have existed in Gallia County. Unlike the G.A.R., S.U.V.C.W. re-issued camp numbers with different camp names so that a younger camp could have a re-issued low number. The list of Gallia County camps may be incomplete: Gallipolis Camp #23 (organized November 14, 1905; suspended June 30, 1906), Gallipolis; Shenandoah Camp #45 (organized June 20, 1910; disbanded June 30, 1911), Bladen; Zara Holcomb Post #174 (existed in 1888), Vinton; Louis Mauck Camp #230 (organized October 25, 1888; still exists 1898), Cheshire/Ewington; Dick Blazer Post #213 (organized August 9, 1887), Gallipolis; —?— Camp #285 (organized May 26, 1888), Sand Ford; Louis Cook Camp #285 (organized March 15, 1893; suspended July, 1899), Patriot.

Four other organizations plus the S.U.V.C.W. are called the "Allied Orders" of the

G.A.R.: Ladies of the G.A.R., Woman's Relief Corps, Daughters of Union Veterans of the Civil War, and Auxiliary to the Sons of Union Veterans of the Civil War. All are still active in Ohio but no longer in Gallia County.

Gallia County currently has no active S.U.V.C.W. Its residents belong to Brooks-Grant Camp No. 7; women belong to Maj. Daniel McCook Circle No. 104 Ladies of the G.A.R. both of Middleport.

On November 17, 2001, Crown City, Ohio, Sanford Dale Brumfield, the last REAL son of a Union soldier in the State of Ohio and life member of the S.U.V.C.W., died at age 92.
He was the son of Pvt. Sloan Brumfield, Company F, 1st Ohio Heavy Artillery.

Gallia Countians who currently belong include David North, Michael Trowbridge, William Plants, Myron Jones Jr., Donald Swisher, and Samuel Wilson. Work is being done to form a "camp" of the S.U.V.C.W. and a "circle" of the Ladies of the G.A.R. in Gallia County. Both permit direct, blood-related descendants of Union veterans or descendants of siblings of Union veterans to join. See <http://suvwc.org>. *Submitted by Keith D. Ashley*

# Gallia County Vietnam Veterans of America Chapter #709

On July 4, 1992, a group of Gallia County Vietnam Veterans assembled in Gallipolis, Ohio, to march for the first time in the annual Fourth of July parade. General Westmoreland, the guest speaker for the day, gave a very inspiring message to those assembled in the city park. A forming chapter of the Vietnam Veterans of America was initiated on July 2, 1993. Chapter Officers were chosen including: Larry Marr, president; Roger Fetterly, first vice-president; Alex Roese, second vice president; Bill Stansbury, secretary; Henry Myers, treasurer; and Bob Mitchell, membership chairman. The first directors chosen were: Clarence Hill, Bill Johnson, Rex Johnson, Rick Howell, Kennison Saunders, Rick Swain, and Jim Spaun.

In 1995, an Honor Guard was formed to march in local parades and other functions for the chapter and community. Over the years, chapter activities have included the sale of dog tags, participation in the Gallia County Junior Fair, sponsoring the exhibit of the Ohio Vietnam Memorial at the fairgrounds, operating a coffee break project at the Rt. 35 rest area for holiday travelers, and most recently, participating in local schools to educate students and faculty about Veterans Day.

The current Officers and Directors are: Larry Marr, president; Bill Guinther, first vice president; Bill Beaver, second vice president; Jim Cozza, secretary; Henry Myers, treasurer; Bob Mitchell, membership chairman; Flem Meade, director; Phil Weatherholt, director and Paul Myers, director.

Members of the Honor Guard are: Larry Marr, Bill Beaver, Bill Guinther, Jim Cozza, Steve Robinson, Betty Robinson, Phil Miller, Justin Williams, Richard Hinchman, Bob Mitchell, Flem Meade, Henry Myers, Roger Houck, Paul Myers, Pete Spencer, Bill Stansbury, Mike Williams, Phil Weatherholt, Roger Houck, and Dannie Wood.

Currently the chapter has 41 members and is an active organization for veterans and their families as they serve other veterans and the community. *Submitted by Larry Marr and Henry L. Myers*

*City Park October 17, 1965*

*Gallia County Court House 1937*

113

*Gallipolis City Park, 1913 flood*

*Aerial view of Gallipolis, Ohio*

# Gallia County Businesses

*Downtown Gallipolis, Ohio*

*Gallia County Produce, Third Avenue*

# Bossard Memorial Library

Located at 7 Spruce Street in Gallipolis, Ohio, the Dr. Samuel L. Bossard Memorial Library serves as the County District Public Library for Gallipolis and Gallia County. It is open 78 hours per week — M-F 8am to 9 pm, Saturday 9-5, Sunday 1-6 p.m. The library had 18,000 registered borrowers in 2001, and circulated more than 350,000 items to those borrowers.

Few other organizations have as rich a history of community involvement as the public library. Community support and involvement, as early as 1895, began, built, and supported library services through a variety of changes across three centuries.

After nearly one hundred years, the city of Gallipolis had no public lending library until the women in the community adopted the project. A variety of fund raisers were held to secure funds for a public library. The local newspaper reported the following in February 1898:

It has been several years since the ladies of the literary clubs in the city began the work of building up a fund for a public library. The fund of $648.85 now on hand has been secured through the following agencies: The Journal's "Woman's Edition," the concerts given by Miss Healey, Mrs. Dunbar, and by the Young Ladies Literary Club; the dramatical entertainment by the Young Ladies' Minstrels, and by numerous lectures and musical entertainments under the auspices of the Thursday Club. Recently a prominent lady interested in education and the welfare of the city, has contributed $50.00 to the above fund, an example worthy of imitation. The Library will be opened to the public at an early date in a convenient and pleasant location. The number of books at first must necessarily be limited, but valuable additions will be continually made, and a good librarian will be selected.

The "Woman's Edition" of the newspaper had been printed in silk taffeta and auctioned as a fundraiser. The newspaper was then donated back to the library for display — where it remains to this day.

The benefit in the city park, called a "Lawn Fete Social," in the summer of 1898 included an "impromptu circulating library, including at least twenty-five volumes of the rarest editions of the most interest works that have ever graced the shelves of a library, ancient or modern. While the collection caters entirely to the gentlemen taste strange to say these works might be classified as romance, with plenty of love in them, instead of science for which the sterner sex are supposed to have the weakness. A most efficient and agreeable librarian, in the person of Mrs. E. T. Halliday, has been secured. She will be very helpful to a gentleman in the choice of a book suited to his taste." There was no list of titles mentioned. A candy booth was provided for the children. The June 27, 1898 edition of the newspaper lists the books which comprised the Gallipolis Public Library, with the names of the donors. There were 285 items in the collection at that time — efforts to collect items continued until the library opened November 1, 1898.

Some of the early titles in the library included: Howe's Historical Collections of Ohio —donated by W. 0. Sibley; An American Girl in London, donated by Elise Henking; Garden and Farm Topics, donated by Lizzie Lasley; Twenty Thousand Leagues under the Sea, donated by Miss Dunbar; and Dr. Warrick's Daughters, donated by Birdie Cherrington.

In June of 1898, there was a business meeting of nearly all of the members of the Thursday Club at Mrs. J. W. Jones' for the purpose of incorporating a library association.

The paper reported "a recent law provides for a small levy on the general property of cities of the class of Gallipolis for the purpose of promoting public libraries. The company will be incorporated at once, and the library established in time to secure the benefits of the levy on the present duplicate. There are eighteen incorporators who will look after the general interests of the public in the organization and maintenance of the library."

The Gallipolis Public Library was incorporated June 16, 1898 by Francis E. Dunbar, Nell F. Johnson, Genevieve H. Maxon, Minnie C. Jones and others to maintain a public library on a $1000 capital, with Mrs. Johnson, President; Mrs. Jones Vice President, Miss Alice Cherrington, Secretary, and Mrs. Chas Stockhoff Treasurer.

The Gallipolis Public Library opened "for inspection" November 1, 1898. It was open from 2 to 5:30 p.m. and from 7 to 9 p.m The library opened with at least two thousand volumes on the shelves ready for circulation. Donations were continually solicited, with "good juvenile works" particularly acceptable. Parents were asked to contribute to the building of the Juvenile Department by giving books which their children had outgrown.

The first public library was open to residents of Gallipolis City. Non residents could draw from the library "on depositing... a sum equal to the value of the book, but required to pay two cents per day while the volume is retained" A fine of three cents per day was charged for the overdue books of city residents.

The public tax which provided for the funding of a public library was passed in June of 1898.

The tax referred to was described as "a good law, for the promotion of the moral and educational interests of our young men and young women. It is a law especially favorable to the poor boys and girls whose circumstances deprive them of the many benefits to be derived from reading good literature. It is a law so conservative in its provisions that the taxpayers will be fully and adequately protected." The tax in 1898 was 5-10 of a mill—or five cents in taxes on every $100.00 worth of property returned by the assessor. It provided about $1000.00 per year for the library association.

The first library was housed in two rooms of the Lupton Building, rented (by 1905) $108.00 per month. The first librarian was Addie Vanden.

On January 23, 1903, there was a re-organization of the Gallipolis Library — with a Board of Library Trustees appointed by the Board of Education. Minutes of that meeting read" Be it resolved that this Board of Library Trustees accept the generous offer of the Trustees of the Academy to donate their lot on the south east corner of Third Avenue and State St. as a site for the library." By May of 1903 the Trustees had selected Wilbur T. Mills as the Architect for the new library building. The architect was instructed to build a building within the limits of the appropriation of $12,500. Funding was provided by a grant by Andrew Carnegie, who was donating money to build libraries all over Ohio. Again, community support was needed for raising money to support the grant. The building was completed by November 30, 1904.

In 1909, the library was open 305 days and circulated 18,628 books per year (70% fiction) Over the next few years, the library maintained its popularity, although funds for the maintenance and operation of the library were limited. Addle Vanden continued her duties as librarian until her death January 28, 1929, when Mrs. Margaret Davis assumed the duties of librarian. At that time a memorial fund was established for Ms. Vanden, the interest of which would go to the library for the purchase of children's books.

In 1935, in order to receive the revenue from the Intangibles Tax, the following resolution was moved by Johnston and seconded by Halliday:

"Resolved that the Gallipolis Public Library open its doors to any county resident wishing to use it free of charge and on the same service basis as that for any city resident. This complies with section 5625.20 General Code of Ohio. Effective July 18, 1933."

Book circulation in May 1935 was 3,562. Two years later, library circulation was (March 1937) 2,196, plus a school circulation of 1,379.

Circulation was reported separately — 1,539 Adult by City, 42 Adult by County; 1,012 Juvenile by City, 2.654 Juvenile by County in October 1936. In 1938 the trustees moved to establish a library service in Holzer Hospital. In 1937 the librarian was instructed to spend enough money on books to supply "county stations". In 1941 the trustees moved to start a book station at O.H.E. (Ohio Hospital for Epileptics, currently Gallipolis Developmental Center) By 1939, the annual circulation of the public library had risen to 85,032.

In 1943 the Trustees began discussing the need for a "trained" librarian. Mrs. Davis resigned by September 1942. Several librarians were hired, with short durations, over the next few years.

In 1947 the Gallipolis Public Library was re-organized as the Gallia County District Library, to extend free library service to everyone in the county. Janet Gregg was employed in March 1948 as the first full time professionally trained Librarian. In November 1948 the county voted a half mill levy for auxiliary library support. In the summer of 1949, the library bought a used Bookmobile, and hired the first county librarian, Janet Gregg, to extend the library service to the 17,000 additional "clients" added by the restructuring of the library. The bookmobile visited 28 schools in the county and 45 small communities once a month, with a circulation of about 50,000 annually. Years later, Janet Gregg Polachek remembered the highlight of her years in Gallia County as extending the library service to the rural areas.

In 1968 Jonathan Louden became the Library Director. With his enthusiastic and energetic leadership, in conjunction with rapid changes in the community, the library grew quickly over the next ten years. Betty Lambert (Clarkson) was hired in 1976 as bookmobile librarian, and in 1977 Ed Rauh became the first full time professional children's librarian. Extensive children's programming was offered throughout the schools and communities, from bookmobile and library. Another type of children's programming - Dial-a-Story, (446-7666), a dial up story line which was so popular it continues at the library today.

In 1976 the library received its first Microfilm reader — and a collection of the newspaper on microfilm. This coincided with an interest in local history, as historian Henrietta Evans visited the library daily. A local historical (and genealogical) society was

formed, which began producing publications of interest — abstracts from the newspapers, cemetery records, abstracts of local court records — all of which made the library collection more popular with history buffs and genealogists from all over the country.

In 1978, with the help of money donated by a physician at the O.H.E., the library moved to a new location at 641 Second Avenue, and was renamed after its benefactor, Dr. Samuel L. Bossard (memorial library). The library remained a county district library with a mission to serve all of Gallia County.

In 1982 the library received a grant to purchase a new bookmobile and to implement "long distance" reference services throughout the county. The grant, written by Mrs. Clarkson, provided the library's first telefacsimile service (Fax). The bookmobile service became a full time community service, emphasizing family literacy, reaching children and parents in their homes, in the evenings and on Saturdays. Edith Stumbo became the primary bookmobile operator.

Library usage grew so dramatically in the 1980's that by 1991 an addition was funded for the library. Additional space for the bookmobile service, for customer parking, and for a dedicated children's area were added. Additionally, a larger meeting room was added to enhance the community use of the library.

The next major change in library service came with the Internet in 1996. Betty Clarkson, Director, helped to implement the State funded Ohio Public Library Information Network which placed computers in libraries and funded Internet access in all public libraries in Ohio. Technology usage and demand increased over the next five years. In 2001, with the help of a grant from the Bill and Melinda Gates Foundation, and another from Ameritech, the library expanded its public computers and services. In 2002 the library renewed its dedication to literacy by collaborating with the University of Rio Grande and RSVP to provide assistance in basic literacy — for all ages.

The Gallia County District Library has a strong history of involvement by the people, for the county-wide communities. Current funding for libraries comes from an array of resources, including donations from library patrons. A county-wide property tax continues to supplement a state-wide income tax, and grants and funding opportunities continue to be explored.

The Board of Trustees of the Gallia County District Library began a planning process in 2000 to research and plan the future of library services, ensuring free access county-wide through the next millennium.

Gallia County District Library Board of Trustees. 2002: Elaine Armstrong, Robert Jenkins, Claudia Lyon, Pamela Matura, James Morrison, James Orr, Larry Shong, President.

Bossard Library Employees in March 2002 are: Betty Clarkson, Director (MLS). Debbie Saunders, Treasurer (MLIS). Judy Wilcoxon, Deputy. Reference/Genealogy: Rebecca Carroll, Becky Slone, Suzan Chapman, Janie Smith, Barbara Ingram, Seleesa Rucker, Edith Stumbo, Thom Curnutte. Maintenance/ Housekeeping: Steve Moore, Tessie Johnson, Dinah Gunnoe.

Circulation! Reader's Advisory: Sharon Anderson, Susan Randolph, Kim Herdman, Kim Wilcoxon, Shannon Trewartha, Lisa Brumfield. Outreach/ Bookmobile: Jack Mowery, Rhonda McGuire, Peyton Materne, Lisa Henry, John Johnson. Youth Services: Marion Cochran (MLIS), Melody Shupe, Jae Trewartha (Teen Services) Technical/ Computer services: Carel Blank, Jeremy Wolfe, Randy Callihan. Library aides: John Allinder, Adam Carter, Andrea Bailey, Lois Martin, Maryanna Browning, Mekenzie France, Micah Eberhardt, and Sarah Booth

*Bossard Library can be reached at www.bossard.lib.oh.us or 446-READ, or email: Bossard@oplin.lib.ou.us*

*Betty Clarkson. March 2002.*

# Gallia County Junior Fair

It was in the summer of 1950 that the Gallia County Junior Fair had its actual beginning. That year the FFA and 4-H members was held a one day show on the lot of a local equipment dealer. In 1951 a two day fair was held on the park front in Gallipolis. Additional facilities were required and in 1952 the fair was moved to the Holzer Airport where it was increased in size and became a three day fair with rides, concessions, and a program.

Having outgrown that facility in 1955, the Evans Grocery Company donated land consisting of sixteen acres for a permanent fair grounds. In 1956 the fair was held on this new site and a restroom was the only building that year. In 1957, the first permanent building was erected on the fairgrounds for the housing and showing of livestock, and for the first time an Ohio governor was present to dedicate the building and visit the fair. In 1958 another new building, the Activities Building, was erected to permit the display of FFA and 4-H projects.

Two new buildings were added in 1960 with the first being a food stand for the use of 4-H clubs in preparing and serving food. This building has since been enlarged into a cafeteria-type concession stand with the addition of a dining room. Also, a building for sheep, swine and poultry was opened and with the donation of eight acres across the creek by the Evans Grocery Company, a huge new parking area was added at the rear of the fairgrounds.

In 1961 another building was erected for the display of commercial exhibits and designated as the Commercial Building. With 1962 came the Livestock Arena with a seating capacity of over 400 where Gallia County youth exhibit, show, and sell the animals grown as FFA or 4-H projects. In 1964, a modern building with restroom and shower facilities was completed. In 1965 the fairboard acquired seventeen additional acres for the development of a camping area. This serene and quiet campsite at the rear of the fairgrounds registered travelers and campers who in 1979 registered form 35 states.

In 1966 a new fair board office was built in the upstairs of the Commercial Building and in 1967 a roof was constructed over the fifty by fifty stage. Also in 1967 the Junior Fair was expanded into a five day fair for the first time with the addition of Tuesday night, a night with emphasis on religion and spiritual needs of the community. In 1968 new hard surface roads were built on the main fair grounds, flood control drainage was installed, and expansion of electrical wiring in all buildings took

*Gallia County Junior Fair*

place. In 1969, a new utility building which would house up to fifty horses was added to the grounds. In 1973 due to an increase of livestock entries, the horse barn was converted to a dairy barn and a new horse barn which would hold up to one hundred horses was constructed.

Before the 1974 fair, fans were installed in all barns. In 1975, new restrooms and shower facilities were added to the campgrounds and both the main fair grounds and camp grounds were connected to the Gallipolis City Northwest Sewer Project. Through twenty-five years the fair has grown and expanded to become officially recognized as the largest exclusive junior fair in the state of Ohio. The need for more land became a necessity, therefore in 1975, the board made a momentous decision and purchased an additional fifty-four acres adjacent to the present fair grounds. This brought the total acres now owned by the fair board to ninety-five acres.

In 1976, the first flea market was held. In 1977, the fair expanded to a six day event and a permanent fence was installed around the main fair grounds. Also, a new meeting room was added to the fair office and one half miles of roads was built in the parking areas. In 1978 lighting was added to the horse ring and other areas. In 1979, portable bleachers were purchased and permanent scales were installed.

In 1984 due to the large number of livestock project exhibits, the show arena was enlarged, the dairy barn was rearranged, and a milking parlor was installed. Also in 1 984, a new larger water main was installed to accommodate the large demand for water during the week of the fair.

In 1985 a ten year mortgage on the land purchased in 1975 was burned in a ceremony conducted at the fair grounds. A set of portable scales were purchased and a second set was added in 1986. Also in 1986 more portable bleachers were added to accommodate fair goers. In 1987, increased electricity needs demanded a new electrical service in the beef barn. In 1988, because of an increase in project numbers, the sheep/swine barn was remodeled by replacing all pens with smaller pens to house more sheep and swine projects in that barn. Also, two sets of ten-row bleachers were purchased to increase the seating capacity for events at the track.

In the fall of 1989, due to another large increase in project numbers in the sheep and swine barn, the Board realized that it was once again time to make necessary preparations for the construction of a new barn to house projects. In 1990 the dream became a reality as a new barn was constructed along side the sheep/swine building and dedicated ten days before the opening of the fair. The old sheep/swine barn was converted to a swine barn, electrical systems were completely overhauled and updated, parking areas were tiled and two more sets of ten-row bleachers were purchased.

During the 90's, many of the buildings were reroofed, camp sights were added, and restrooms were made more accessible to the handicapped. A wash rack for sheep and hogs was also constructed between the two barns.

In 1994-1996, the board of directors worked diligently to secure a lease arrangement with Producer's Livestock Association. Because of this arrangement, an auction facility became a reality and area farmers once again were able to sell their livestock at a local facility. Also in 1996, the midway was moved from the center of the fair grounds to the front of the grounds.

In 1997, the Bill Grey Pavilion was constructed to provide more space and time for the many fair activities. A new horse arena was also built in 1997. Due to deterioration, all hard surfaced roads on the main fair grounds were resurfaced to make them safer for fair goers.

As the twentieth century came to an end, the Junior Fair has continued to grow. In 1998 the Board acquired more than 150 acres of additional land which adjoined the current site on the east and south sides. This was done with the hopes of moving the fairgrounds and campgrounds out of the flood plain which has plagued the site with flash flooding as often as six times in one month. During late 2001 and early 2002 because of the concern for safety of campers in the campgrounds, the Board took measures to begin relocating the campgrounds to the new property above and to the east of the current location. These efforts are continuing into the 21$^{st}$ Century as the safety of visitors to all the various events on the fairgrounds is and has been a very important concern of past, current, and future Boards.

The Gallia County Junior Fair has provided and will continue to provide an opportunity for the youth of Gallia County to exhibit their talents and be recognized for their efforts. It is an exhibition of the year's hard work and of the cooperation and tireless effort on the part of both county and city residents. The Junior Fair has served as a means of inspiring youth to greater achievements while providing enjoyment and satisfaction for all who come to view the exhibits and program. This continues to be the goal of the Gallia County Agricultural Society.

# Gallipolis Developmental Center

The story of Gallipolis Developmental Center is best told by looking at the story of the people involved. This story would include the residents themselves, the employees and the impact it has had on the lives of the people of the local community, State of Ohio and even throughout the United States.

The medical roots of this area go back to Civil War times when the U. S. government established a 250-bed U. S. Army General Hospital here. Approximately 4,000 Union Soldiers were treated here as well as some Confederate Soldiers. Some of these soldiers paid the ultimate price while here and were buried in local cemeteries, including four Confederate soldiers, many in Pine Street Cemetery.

In 1889, in the home of Marie L. Shepard, a group of local citizens conceived the idea to build the first State maintained institution for epileptics in the United States. Through the efforts of these Gallipolitans, the Ohio General Assembly on April 11, 1890, passed an act creating a commission to provide accommodations for the epileptic and epileptic insane of the State.

Upon passage of the Bill, Governor James E. Campbell appointed a commission composed of John L. Vance, Gallipolis; C. C. White, Columbus; and George H. Bunning, Sidney; to make recommendations for a site for the proposed hospital.

After the commission had concluded its examinations of the many proposed sites, they requested and received written propositions from interested communities throughout the state. The commission met in Columbus on August 7, 1890, to select a building site. On August 8, 1890, Gallipolis was chosen as the city to receive the recommendation of the commission for the new hospital.

Some factors contributing to this decision were: local participation by the City of Gallipolis which proposed to give to the state clear title to about 100 acres of land; to construct waterworks and furnish water free of cost to the state for the use of the asylum; and to open all streets that were required by commission for access to the grounds.

The search committee hired architect J. W. Yost of Columbus. He identified many natural advantages for choosing the Gallipolis site to include: the availability of nearby stone from the hill behind the proposed grounds; the abundance of coal; reasonable rates for adjoining farm land which could afford favorable occupation for the, as then called, "inmates"; additionally the proposed land was naturally graded which would affect ease of building construction and by using inmate labor, the cost of construction could be reduced considerably.

The facility was designed to be totally self-supporting. This colonization concept would afford the Hospital the luxury of being practical, self-sufficient in respect to producing most food items to include dairy products, fruits, vegetables, meats and maintain its own boiler operation. This concept would also allow use of resident labor for maintenance, production and direct care of those "inmates" unable to perform self-help skills.

Upon acceptance of the commission and architect's report, the General Assembly on March 4, 1891, appropriated $40,000 for three stone residences. The first cornerstone was laid November 12, 1891. It weighed approximately 2,200 pounds and like the stone used for the erection of the buildings, was quarried from the hill at the rear of the grounds.

The original name given the hospital was the "Asylum for Epileptics and Epileptic Insane". But in1892, the General Assembly passed an act changing the name to the "Ohio Hospital for Epileptics" (O.H.E.).

The three buildings that were started in 1891, were opened for the reception of patients on November 30, 1893. By November 1894, nine stone residential buildings a kitchen, bakery and boiler house had been erected. At this time the O.H.E. housed 351 patients.

Between the years 1894 to 1907, the Hospital continued to grow. In 1907, the census of the Hospital was up to 1,300 with approximately 200 employees. The hospital estate was at 500 acres with over 36 buildings exclusive of barns, greenhouses and other buildings. Twenty-three of these buildings were occupied with patients. The total budget for the Hospital for the fiscal year ending November 15, 1907, was $246,391.

The Ohio Hospital for Epileptics continued to grow and follow the original colonization plan through the following four decades. In 1950, the name was changed from "The Ohio Hospital for Epileptics" to "The Gallipolis State Institute" (G.S.I.). In 1961, the G.S. I. served as the home for 2,358 patients suffering from epilepsy, retardation and mental health problems. It also employed a total of 710 citizens, with 443 of the total serving as direct care to the patients.

Although capital improvements were completed annually to the Institution between 1907 through 1957, most remember the Medical and Surgical Building as being a turning point in the history of the Gallipolis State Institute. The new Medical and Surgery Building was completed in 1959. It was designed to

accommodate the physically ill with complete medical facilities to include a surgical unit. The building is a five-story 48,565 square foot structure with 145 rooms. The building's original value was in excess of $800,000.

On September 7, 1979, the name of the center was changed again from "The Gallipolis State Institute" to the "Gallipolis Developmental Center" (G.D.C.).

In 1890 the facility became the site of the first and largest facility in the nation providing services to persons with epilepsy. By 2001 G. D. C. provided services to an average of 250 people with Mental Retardation. More than half of these people also had several multiple physically handicapping conditions or mental illness, and more than a third are over 60 years old.

Since 1977, more than $40 million in capital improvements have modernized this century old campus. Thirty-seven buildings have been razed and the new construction since that time includes eight 16-bed and four 31-bed residences, a new food service building, a new off-campus habilitation center, a new support services building, two buildings housing satellite gas boilers, a 35,000 square feet activity center which provides space for habilitation, recreation and therapeutic training, and a 7,000 square foot residence was constructed in 1995 and is home to 32 people.

Today, services at the Center are based on interdependent relationships that are characterized by human warmth, affection and mutual respect. Each person's choices, desires and preferences are respected. The focus of these interactions is to support each individual in performing and enjoying functional daily routines. Individual services are also provided which adapt the routine environment to ensure progress towards personal competence.

**SUPTERINTENDENTS**

H.C. RUTTER
1893 until 1901

W. K. COLEMAN, M.D.
1901 until 1902

A. P. OHLAMACHER, M.D.
1902 until 1905

W. H. PRICHARD, M.D.
1905 until 1911

G. G. KINEON, M.D.
1911 until 1943

J. G. SCHWARTZ, M.D.
1943 until 1944

G. R. ROBERTS, M.D.
1945 until 1965

FERDINAND E. FOURNIER
1966 until 1967

QUERICA D. DORONILA
1968 until 1968

ALEXANDER BIRKLE
1969 until 1970

BERNARD F. NIEHM
1970 until 1976

JOHN A. BEATTIE
1976 until 1980

ROBERT K. ZIMMERMAN
1980 until 1983

JEFFREY M. SPEISS
1984 until 1985

PAMELA K. MATURA
1985 until 1989

MICHAEL L. DEY
1990

AVERAGE NUMBER OF RESIDENTS, EMPLOYEES AND BUDGET

| FISCAL YEAR | RESIDENTS | EMPLOYEES | BUDGET |
|---|---|---|---|
| 1907 | 1,300 | 200 | $ 240,391 |
| 1940 | 1,800 | 330 | 566,810 |
| 1962 | 2,250 | 738 | 3,761,500 |
| 1977 | 1,253 | 876 | |
| 1978 | 1,125 | 955 | |
| 1979 | 995 | 1,042 | |
| 1980 | 948 | 1,040 | |
| 1981 | 657 | 934 | 14,353,588 |
| 1982 | 487 | 824 | 12,999,876 |
| 1983 | 366 | 666 | 9,736,941 |
| 1984 | 352 | 513 | 13,929,704 |
| 1985 | 301 | 500 | 13,419,500 |
| 1986 | 292 | 462 | 13,171,570 |
| 1987 | 301 | 464 | 13,553,350 |
| 1988 | 300 | 500 | 15,726,958 |
| 1989 | 320 | 540 | 15,809,040 |
| 1990 | 320 | 570 | 18,228,142 |
| 1991 | 320 | 585 | 19,428,091 |
| 1992 | 320 | 620 | 20,350,535 |
| 1998 | 247 | 514 | 22,240,081 |
| 1999 | 245 | 507 | 22,375,777 |
| 2000 | 242 | 515 | 24,187,214 |
| 2001 | 248 | 499 | 23,683,711 |
| 2002 | 249 | 465 | 24,539,660 |

*NOTE: Some resident figures have been estimated
Article written and submitted by Gene McGuire
This page provided by the generosity of past and present employees

# Holzer Medical Center

Journals of medicine in the Southeastern Ohio River Valley vividly reflect the history and development over the past nine-three (93) years of what is now the Holzer Medical Center. The surgical practice which culminated in the establishment of the original Holzer Hospital and Clinic in downtown Gallipolis, had its inception when Charles E. Holzer, Sr., M.D., came to Gallipolis in 1909 as resident surgeon at the Ohio Hospital for Epileptics (OHE), now the Gallipolis Developmental Center (GDC).

Following graduation from the Starling Loving School of Medicine, which later became the Ohio State University College of Medicine, Dr. Holzer Sr., as a protégé of two distinguished surgeons in Columbus, was sent to the State Hospital for a year of intensive surgical experience. It was not his intention to stay in Gallipolis, which at that time was isolated from other parts of the State of Ohio by poor roads and inadequate transportation, although Gallipolis was a busy river port.

Being the only surgeon in the locale, Dr. Holzer was called on during the year for emergency operations outside, in addition to his duties at the OHE. A man of unusual energy with a driving congenial personality, he soon made many friends. He sensed the need of the community for surgical care and hospital facilities, so when he was urged near the end of his resident year to remain in Gallipolis, he rose to the challenge and agreed to start a hospital.

Dr. Holzer was able to secure the money necessary to purchase a home in the 500 block on Second Avenue in downtown Gallipolis, and remodel it into an office and seven (7) bed hospital. This was truly the beginning of medical and hospital leadership in the area.

In 1917, Holzer Hospital moved from the house on Second Avenue to a new 25 bed facility on First Avenue at Cedar Street, expanding to 53 beds in 1926, followed by a series of additions until 1960, to achieve a 175 bed — 24 bassinet total. Charles E. Holzer, Jr. M.D., returned to Gallipolis in late 1945, with new visions to add to his father's dreams. Dr. Holzer Jr., formed the Holzer Clinic with six partners in 1950. Today it has evolved to over 100 multi-specialty physicians and is still growing.

Through the Holzer Hospital Foundation created in 1929, Dr. and Mrs. Holzer Sr., gave the Hospital to the community in January 1949, to be administered by a Board of Trustees representing the patient service area. This came from the urging of Dr. Holzer Jr., along with Miss Alma McCormick, who served the Holzer family and Hospital as family counselor, hospital administrator, executive secretary, record librarian, and most importantly, business and financial adviser for more than 60 years.

As the result of merging with another group of physicians known as the Gallipolis Clinic and their 25 bed Medical Center Hospital, it became possible to build what is now the Holzer Medical Center in its present location. In May, 1972, HMC opened with 265 beds and 30 bassinets.

Holzer Medical Center today, with ongoing renovation and expansion, culminates what Doctors Holzer Senior and Junior, with their unmatched foresight, envisioned and hoped for when it all began in 1909. Adding the latest medical services makes it possible for Holzer Medical Center to provide the most modern healthcare, diagnostics and treatment for area residents.

In 2002, total remodeling of the inpatient Rehabilitation unit, provision of dialysis services, and new therapy services facilities with a contemporary Fitness Center occurred. A new state-of-the-art Education and Conference Center opened in 2001, featuring a Holzer Heritage/Gallipolis mural along with lighted archive exhibits.

During 2000, a unique 14 bed Critical Care Unit was completed, with special space for Respiratory Therapy, along with total renovation of the Main Lobby and new Gift Shop. A 75,000 square foot structure on the South side of the Hospital, known as the Charles E. Holzer, Jr. M.D. Surgery Center opened in 1999, preceded by an exceptional Maternity and Family Center for obstetrics and pediatrics, occupying the entire third floor of the Hospital.

Holzer Medical Center is fully accredited by the Joint Commission on the Accreditation of Healthcare Organizations (JCAHO), and also designated by the Federal government as a Rural Referral Center.

Holzer Consolidated Health Systems is the parent of multiple Holzer entities: Holzer Senior Care Center, a 70 bed extended care facility close to the Hospital's Gallipolis campus; Holzer Medical Center-Jackson in Jackson County, the most futuristic hospital to open in Ohio, completed in December 2000, to meet health care needs of Jackson County residents and the surrounding area.

*Davis Hall, built through the generosity of the Davis Family of Oak Hill, Ohio, became the new home of the Holzer School of Nursing, with classrooms, library and dormitory for student nurses. This picture was taken on the day of its dedication in June, 1957.*

*A Winter view of the Cedar Street facility*

Looking toward the future, the challenge remains to motivate all who are a part of this great organization, to accomplish even greater advances. This is a vital aspect of the legacy passed on by Doctors Holzer Senior and Junior. The Holzer entities will move forward with determination and commitment, always guided by Dr. Holzer, Jr.'s sage words:

The Patient Is The Center Of All That We Do

**Remembering The Holzer School of Nursing 1920-1982**

In September 1920, the Holzer Training School for Nurses, which was to become the Holzer School of Nursing, began. In June 1982, the Holzer Medical Center School of Nursing ceased to operate as a Diploma School of Nursing. The story of its growth and accomplishments over a sixty-two (62) year period is significant, and important to the history of health care in the Southeastern Ohio River Valley.

Following establishment of the Holzer Hospital, and its move into the new Cedar Street facility in 1917, it soon became apparent that a sufficient number of experienced and qualified nurses were not available to staff the facility that would grow to become a vital medical center for Southeastern Ohio. It was not feasible to expect rural Gallia County, with a census of less than twenty-five thousand (25,000), to attract adequate numbers of trained nurses from hospital based schools in larger, more metropolitan areas, such as Columbus or Cincinnati.

However it was obvious, that with the Hospital and the medical leadership, along with the need for trained nurses, the community would have potential students. In 1918, requirements of the Nurses Examining Committee and the State Medical Board stated that Holzer Hospital met the eligibility criteria to have its own training school for nurses.

Observing all necessary requirements, Dr. Charles E. Holzer, Sr., and his wife, Alma Vornholt Holzer, a graduate and former Directress of Nursing at Grant Hospital in Columbus, founded the Holzer Training School. It was stated that the "earnest purpose of the school was to maintain a standard commensurate with the high ideals established by the hospital and to assist in meeting the demand of the public for a more complete and well rounded education for nurses

The school was duly registered and accredited by the Ohio State Board of Nurse Examiners. Lecturers for the School were Doctors Otto Vornholt, Leo Bean, J. S. Biddle, G. Barton, Milo Wilson, Mary Austin, D.O., and L. R. Hall, technician. Nursing supervisors were Emma Richards, Clara Vornholt, Mabel Howe and Mary Lauriseh. The school opened September 15, 1920.

The first uniform was a white and blue pin striped dress with long sleeves, detachable cuffs, collars and bibs. It had a separate, very stiffly starched, white apron that revealed very little of the students ankle. After the four month probation period, the students received the white bib, collar and cuffs. They wore black shoes and stockings. White shoes and white stockings were adopted in 1949. The uniforms were furnished and maintained by the Hospital until 1965.

When the school opened, no tuition was charged. Everything was furnished: meals, uniforms and books. A monthly allowance of $10 was provided for the first year, $12 the second year and $15 the third year. In 1927, that allowance was cut slightly. Then, in 1929, tuition of $35 was charged for three years, with a monthly allowance of $5.00 for all three years.

Nursing education at that time was a process of apprenticeship training, in which students were taught partly by classroom instruction, but largely by contact and participation. This remained the pattern until World War II.

The first dormitory for the Holzer Training School was known as Needham Flats, where Davis Hall is now located. The name was that of the former owner, Dr. W. F. Needham. The building had been used for apartments or "flats" prior to purchase by the Holzers in December 1918. For thirty-five years the "flats" were home to the young women enrolled in the school.

Construction of a new home for the School of Nursing, Davis Hall, began in 1955, to house both class and residence facilities under one roof. Davis Hall was completed in 1956 at a cost of $540,000, exclusive of furniture and non-fixed equipment. The project was financed with funds from the D. D. Davis Foundation of Oak Hill, Ohio. Mr. Davis served as trustee for the Holzer Hospital Foundation from 1938 — 1954.

The structure, a modified Georgian design of red brick and Indiana limestone, was built in a "U" shape to allow all student rooms to have a window and preserve a pin oak and cypress tree in the side yard. Forty-one student rooms, four lounges, three offices for instructors, six classrooms, plus offices for the director, the clerical staff and an apartment for the Housemother and Director of Nursing were included.

In 1952, tuition at the school was raised from $35 to $150 for the entire program. By 1962, it cost $935 for the three years, with that figure doubling by 1972. When the school closed in 1982, total cost to the student for the 33 month experience was in excess of $9000.

A decision was made in 1979 to phase out the Holzer Medical Center School of Nursing. The doors of Davis Hall closed in June 1982, when the last of over 800 nurses received their diplomas and joined the past graduates of the school.

The school gave more than nursing skills to its graduates, more than camaraderie from three years of living and sharing experiences, It is what each remembers it to be and pass along to those they serve.

*Needham Flats on First Avenue in Gallipolis*

# WJEH

*Original building for WJEH, 1950*

In a newspaper article by local historian, James Sands, dated August 8, 1990, radio was in Gallipolis as early as 1913 when the Gallipolis Wireless Association was formed. Members met on the second floor of the Ecker Building on Second Avenue where messages were sent and received. There was also a small amateur broadcast around town in 1930 as a teaching tool for young people.

But, it was not until 1949 that a commercial radio license was issued for Gallipolis, Ohio, by the Federal Communications Commission. This was due to the efforts of Truman Morris and E. W. Whipple of Huntington, WV and Gallipolis Attorney, John E. Halliday. Mr. Morris brought the idea to Mr. Halliday and the partnership began.

The original site chosen to build the radio station was the old fairgrounds (on Eastern Avenue), but, the Civil Aeronautics Association disapproved because of it's proximity to the already existing Holzer Airport. Consequently, a new suitable site on Portsmouth Road was chosen. Construction of a building began and necessary equipment was purchased.

On June 19, 1959, a few minutes after the FCC approval was received, WJEH, a 250 watt daytime station located at 990 on the AM dial, went on the air. John E. Halliday made the first announcement after the playing of 'Beautiful Ohio'. Formal ceremonies for the start of broadcasting were held in the Farmer's Hotel which was the location for the weekly Rotary Club Meeting. The program was delivered through The Ohio Bell Telephone Company switchboard and then through the radio station transmitter. At this time, WJEH became the only radio station in the tri-county area. The radio log (or schedule of programs) featured mostly talk related programs, including: "Chore Time", "Capitol Dome", "Top of the Morning", "On the Farm Front", "Meigs County Show", Musical Programs included: "Dance Band Review", "Harmony Shop", "The Old Time Gospel Singer", and "Organ Moods". Sports coverage, special events and news programs were added through the years and many different formats have been featured.

*John E. Halliday, founder WJEH*

Truman Morris was the first General Manager, Chuck Osterle; Chief Engineer, Marianne Boggs, Program Director; Bill Watterson, Jr., Director of Special Events; Sid Davis, Public Relations (Mr. Davis later became Chief Announcer for NBC in Washington, D. C.); Marjorie White, Women's Director; Adelaide Burnett, Musical Director; Joe Sailey, Disc Jockey. Art Waugh, Ray Kellogg, Bob Mager and Jack Morehouse made up the Engineering Department. Within the next few years, Mr. Halliday and Mr. Morris bought out Mr. Whipple's interest in the station after purchasing WBEX, Chillicothe, Ohio and Building WLMJ, Jackson, Ohio. In 1955, Mr. Morris moved to Chillicothe after selling his shares of WJEH and WLMJ to Mr. Halliday and purchasing his interest in WBEX. At that time, Marianne (Boggs) Campbell was named General Manager of WJEH.

In 1957, WJEH-FM, a 15,000 watt FM station at 101.5 was put on the air.

Paul E. Wagner, Cincinnati, Ohio, purchased the radio properties from Mr. Halliday in 1967. Mr. Wagner, a thirty year veteran of broadcasting, moved to Gallipolis with his wife, Dene, and daughter, Lynn. The Wagners both took an active role in the radio operations; Dene started a daily public affairs program, "The Chatterbox:, which continued for thirty years.

In 1977, a new 35,000 watt full-time stereo FM station was put on the air replacing WJEH-FM. New equipment including a transmitter was installed and a 250 foot tower and a transmitter building were constructed atop the hill overlooking the AM station on Portsmouth Road. The new station was assigned the call letters, WYPC.

*Present facilities for WJEH - WRYV*

*Paul E. Wagner, President/General Manager, Wagner Broadcasting Company, 1967-1998*

During the next couple of years, tragedy struck the stations again when the general manager was killed in a plan crash at the local airport. The chief engineer died suddenly, his son, the station engineer, was killed in an accident; the AM tower collapsed and in 1980, Mr. Wagner died.

Mrs. Wagner and daughter, Lynn, remained active in the station's day-to-day operation, including the supervision of a power increase for WYPC to 50,000 watts in 1985. In 1994, the construction of a "booster station" in south Point, Ohio, was completed following approval by the Federal Communications Commission and new call letters, WMGG, were assigned with the new 50,000 watt transmitter, the coverage area now included Huntington, WV, Ashland, KY and Ironton, OH.

Through the years, call letters from the FM station have changed in conjunction with different formats.

The year of 1998 marked an era of change for the radio stations. That year, Wagner Broadcasting was sold to Larry and Susan Patrick of Legend Communications of Ohio. Since that date, the building has been given a $100.00 renovation. All the broadcast and production studios are now totally digital and the stations now house twenty employees.

In 1998 WMGG-FM was changed to WRYV - 101.5, "The River". 990 WJEH-AM still proudly carries the same call letters that it did on its first day of broadcasting more than fifty years ago. *Submitted By: Dena Pellegrinon*

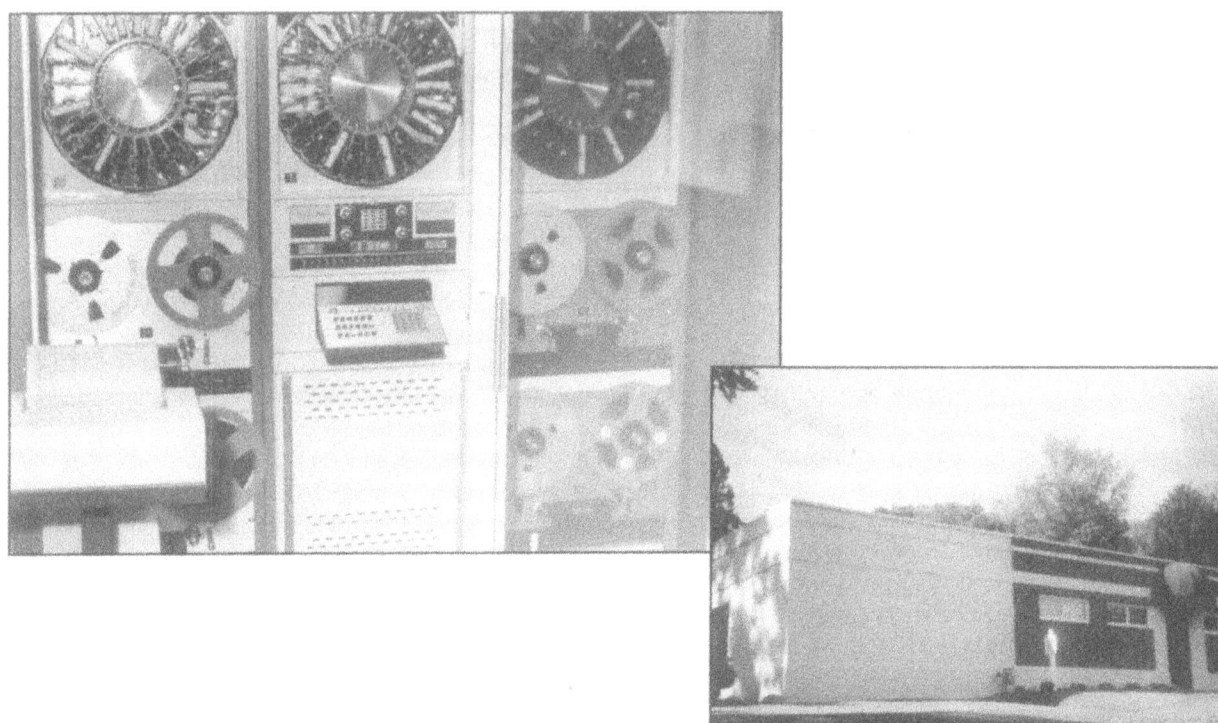

# AlanNET, Inc.

By Kris Dotson
Tribune News Staff

## Wired
### Local Youth Makes Strides With Business
### May 14, 2001

GALLIPOLIS-When parents think of the ultimate child, they pray he or she will be attractive, smart, successful and will hit the big time to take care of them in their old age-right?

Well, Lance and Judy Clifford have such a dream child in their son Alan.

This Gallia Academy High School 16-year-old has his own international computer company that he began at 14, but the story started much earlier.

The sophomore has been a "techie" since 12.

Clifford got his first computer when he was 11, on which he only occasionally played Sims (architect) games.

I first got the bug when we got the Internet," said Clifford.

He's always been inquisitive and very organized," said his father, Lance. "He soaked up everything he could-learning, networking and asking the right people the right questions on line."

Clifford volunteered as a community leader for GeoCities, the largest free home page provider in the world. From the family home computer in Northup, he helped the GeoCities MacIntosh Users Group grow to more than 2,000 members and more than 1 million hits in 1997.

He received first place recognition in February 1998 for his own personal web site, focusing on the Olympics, by being named a GeoCities Gold Metal Site.

Soon after, GeoCities issued publicly traded stock on Nasdaq and gave Clifford 10 shares. The company was then bought by Yahoo and Clifford sold his shares of stock to purchase his own personal computer.

Thus the seeds of entrepreneurship were planted.

At 13, he was hired by Market Source for Apple Computer as a sales and technical representative.

I sent in my application but put not applicable for the birth date and driver's license number," said Clifford.

They still hired me but when they found out I was under 18 the child labor laws came into play so they allowed me to use my father's personal information and to register us as a team," he added.

Dad would take him one weekend per month for about four months to Columbus, to work with customers at such businesses as Comp USA, MicroCenter and Best Buy.

He sold over $20,000 in one day at Comp USA," said Lance. "It was hysterical-the customers would approach me with these complicated questions and I would just smile and refer them to my son."

Clifford earned $17 per hour and used the money to reinvest in computer related equipment in the hope of beginning his own business.

Clifford's goal to own his own business became a reality in the fall of 1999 when AlanNET Inc. was launched.

Today, AlanNET provides internet service such as web site hosting and design, computer networking, equipment sales and consulting services for clients owning Apple or other PC computers.

The company has grown to include approximately 100 business clients in 15 states and Ontario, Canada. Hawaii and Vermont currently lead all states in purchasing services from him.

To meet the diverse needs of his business clients, Alan has subcontracted with Jon Mason, a senior at GAHS, and with others when necessary.

In fact, he owns computer servers in Raleigh, N.C., that are monitored around the clock by college students from North Carolina State University. When he's not attending high school, he controls the servers himself from his home.

Even though he just turned 16 last December, this young entrepreneur has a daily schedule that would rival any company CEO.

He takes college prep honors courses at GAHS and serves as an aide in the Guidance Department.

He's also the yearbook editior, in mock trial, student council, Knowledge Master Open, computer technician for Gallipolis City Schools, tennis and Key Club.

He recently was elected Key Club lieutenant governor for Division 9 East of the Ohio District. His after school hours are consumed by installing and networking computer equipment, wiring business offices and responding to cell and telephone calls or e-mail messages.

Want another shocker?

AlanNET Inc. grosses more money than the average family income in Gallia County-yet Alan takes home no salary.

Running his business effectively and efficiently and going to school full time prohibits monumental growth and requires full reinvestment.

This experience has always been about learning and nurturing his passion and innate ability," said Lance.

Clifford has had various offers to collaborate with potential investors in the hope of establishing a new software company.

*Footnote update - August 2002 :*

AlanNET, Inc. grew to approximately 200 clients in the summer 2001. Alan Clifford resides with his parents, Judy and Lance E. Clifford, in Northup. His mother is a teacher in the Mason County Schools (West Virginia) and his father is a administrator in the Gallipolis City School District. Alan's sister, Heather, graduated from Ohio University in November 2001. She currently is employed with Holzer Clinic as the Director of Marketing in Charleston, West Virginia.

Family History: Refer to Gallia County, Ohio-People in History to 1980, Vol. 1, p.83

# AEP's Gavin Plant:
## Producing Power Since 1974

The story of American Electric Power's General James M. Gavin Plant began on March 10, 1971 when AEP announced that it would build a 2,600.000-kilowatt generating plant near Cheshire in northern Gallia County. Ground was broken later the same month.

Gavin Plant's Unit 1 was placed in commercial operation on October 20, 1974 and Unit 2 followed on July 6, 1975. When completed in 1975, the plant cost approximately $660 million.

The plant's two identical units were the second and third of seven 1,300,000-kw units built by AEP in the 1970s, 1980s and 1990s. These are the largest coal-fired generating units in the world, and only two others of that size have ever been built. With its total generating capacity of 2,600.000 kilowatts, Gavin Plant ranks as the largest generating station in the state of Ohio.

General Gavin was a highly decorated military leader, best known for leading airborne troops behind enemy lines during World War II. Gavin, at that time assistant commanding general of the 82nd Airborne, led paratroopers on their historical drop behind German lines in Normandy on D-Day 1944. He later became chief of research and development for the Department of the Army. A 19-year director of AEP, Gavin served as U.S. ambassador to France during the Kennedy Administration and was the author of five books. He died in 1990 at the age of 82.

The plant's stacks measure 830 feet tall, while the cooling towers stand 492 feet high and are 420 feet in diameter at their bases. The plant burns approximately 7.5 million tons of coal each year.

In the years since 1975, significant additions have been made to the plant in order to comply with new U.S. Environmental Protection Agency regulations regarding air quality. Scrubber systems were completed on each unit in early 1995 in order to reduce emissions of sulfur dioxide from the plant. The scrubber systems were completed on each unit in early 1995 in order to reduce emissions of sulfur dioxide from the plant. The scrubber systems were completed at a cost of approximately $700 million — more than the original cost of the plant. In 2001, selective catalytic reduction (SCR) systems were installed on each unit in order to reduce emissions of nitrogen oxide.

During the plant's history, four men have served as its general managers: Bill Lizon, Andy Trawick, Duane Phlegar and Greg Massey. The plant is one of the largest employers in Gallia County, with approximately 300 employees as of January 2001, and an annual payroll of about $20 million.

Gavin employees are proud of their involvement in community activities. The plant serves as a partner in education with River Valley High School and Kyger Creek Middle School, and has been involved in OhioReads and Earth Day activities with Addaville Elementary School. Employees also assist with activities at Guiding Hand School and Buckeye Hills Joint Vocational School.

The plant supports area fairs and festivals, and purchases livestock raised by 4-H club members. As just one example, Gavin is one of the sponsors of the week-long Gallia County River Recreation Festival. The plant also supports a host of other local events, ranging from Special Olympics to the WalkAmerica for March of Dimes.

In addition, Gavin's 1,000-acre site has been certified as a national wildlife habitat by the Wildlife Habitat Council, a non-profit group based in Silver Spring, Md. Centerpiece of the Gavin wildlife habitat is its 20-acre wetlands area, which is home to more than 75 species of plants and where some 30 different types of birds have been observed.

*AEP's General James M. Gavin Plant*

# The Ariel Theatre

In 1895 local contractor W. H. Slaymaker erected a three-story building for the Ariel Lodge of Oddfellows at 426 Second Ave. in downtown Gallipolis. Occupying the ground floor rear portion was a theater called Ariel Opera House. Slaymaker broke ground on July 16 and the Ariel welcomed its first audience on Christmas Day.

The whole structure cost nearly $35,000 to build, a sum that had bankrupted the Oddfellows by 1899. A group of Pt. Pleasant businessmen owned it until 1919 and it was then bought by the Gallia Masonic Company, the current owner.

After the Oddfellows' demise, the name changed to Gallipolis Theatre until 1991 when it was renamed the Morris and Dorothy Haskins Ariel Theatre to honor Ohio Valley Bank's then most senior member and his wife. This account will utilize the name "Ariel" throughout.

From 1895 to 1963 leasing managers ran the Ariel. The first, Ikey Kaufman, was followed by Fred Wheeler and his son, Harry. In 1963 Harry dropped the lease to concentrate on the Colony Theatre and Kanauga Drive-In.

The Ariel immediately became a stop on a circuit that entertainers followed throughout Ohio and beyond. Thus Gallipolis audiences enjoyed the same fine entertainment seen elsewhere in the state, including, in part, headliners such as Will Rogers, Cecil B. De Mille, Ziegfelds Follies and Sarah Bernhardt.

An entertainer of enduring importance to the Ariel was Mt. Vernon, Ohio native Daniel Decatur Emmett, who at age 80 performed there with Al G. Field's Minstrels on April 8, 1896. Emmett was a composer and performer of Negro minstrel music and a self-taught fiddler. Much of his professional life was spent touring, first with circuses as a blackface banjoist and singer, and then with traveling minstrel shows as a singer and dancer. Emmett also wrote and acted in musical farces and gained a reputation for writing tunes and words for minstrel show finales, called "walk arounds." His most famous "walk around" written in 1859 as "I wish I was in Dixie's land," is a tune known simply as "Dixie." To commemorate the Ohio and Gallia County bicentennials in 2003, the Ariel will present a special public performance of "Dixie" and dedicate a seat there to Emmett.

Early on, live stage shows predominated, although silent movies could also be seen. Gradually the frequency of movies increased and live performances declined until the entertainment was almost exclusively moving pictures.

It was therefore unusual on Nov. 13, 1958 for country singer Hank Snow, his Rainbow Ranch Boys and comedian Sleepy McDaniel to appear in back-to-back shows at the Ariel. Hank had been scheduled to perform at Gallia Academy High School on Nov. 4, but arrived so late that the crowd had already been reimbursed and dispersed by the Gallipolis Downtown Coaches' Club, the sponsor. Make-up shows aside, the Club calculated a loss of $2,208.35 because of Hank's no-show on Nov. 4 and filed a suit for damages. Acting on it, then Sheriff Oscar Baird impounded Snow's pink Cadillac and went to the Ariel to break the news. An account in the Gallipolis Daily Tribune indicates Snow remained in Gallipolis an extra day to settle the matter.

After Harry Wheeler dropped the lease the Ariel gradually deteriorated. A leaky roof caused the plaster walls to crack and drop away in places, revealing rib-like laths. Pigeons entering through broken windows at the top of the fly gallery decided to stay. A state of flux ensued with the departure of some items and the arrival of others. Filth and cobwebs were everywhere. But, the fine acoustic quality that often characterizes old opera houses remained. It was Ariel's saving grace.

The decline vexed a community that values its history. In 1987 a plan to restore the Ariel as a performance hall for a symphony orchestra took hold, and spawned one of the finest stories of voluntarism that can be told anywhere. People came forward with equipment, materials, money, and their own hands to put the Ariel back in use.

The Ohio Valley Symphony, now in its 12th season, has been an energetic undertaking for the Ariel Board of Directors. An Ohio Historic Preservation Office Preservation Merit award earned in 1992 praised the many volunteers who had restored the theater. The second, an Ohio Governor's Award for Outreach, came in 1995.

By 1997 the Ariel Board identified a critical need to diversify programming and to increase the focus on youth. The board sees that now more than ever there is a need to provide young people good things to do and good places to go, to showcase their wonderful talents, give them an opportunity to explore and expand their talents and provide experiences that will help to build their self esteem. Just as the Ariel must assume this responsibility, so must the whole community.

*Ariel Theatre*

# Bob Evans Farm

The Bob Evans Farm in Rio Grande was home to Bob Evans, founder of Bob Evans Farms Inc.. and his wife Jewel for nearly 20 years. When they bought the farm in 1953, Bob and a group of eight family members and friends had been making sausage for local groceries and meat markets. They called it Bob Evans Farms Sausage — "made by a farmer on the farm" —and before long, the sausage was being delivered by a fleet of 14 trucks to nearly 1,800 locations.

Bob's television ads invited people to "come down and visit us" at the farm. Before long, so many people came that it was hard for Bob and Jewel to accommodate them. So in 1961 the company built a restaurant at the farm, with four stools and six tables, to better serve them. The Sausage Shop. which is now a Bob Evans Restaurant, was the company's first venture into the restaurant business. Visitors could sample sausage products and start farm tours from the shop.

Bob and Jewel Evans raised their six children in the large, brick farmhouse known as the Homestead. The Homestead is listed on the National Register of Historic Places. Built in 1825, it served as a stagecoach stop and an inn in its early years. The Homestead is currently undergoing a renovation into a museum with a planned opening in the spring of 2003.

Bob and Jewel lived in the Homestead and hosted sausage company customers, until a steadily increasing flow of visitors began to keep them too busy. Bob Evans Farms Inc. acquired the Rio Grande farm in 1973, to maintain as an active farm and as a recreation and local historical center.

Today, you can visit the original Bob Evans Restaurant and experience the traditions of an all-American farming community "down on the farm." hay, sorghum, corn and wheat are grown on the farm, which is also home to more than 40 horses and nearly 100 cattle.

A beautiful country setting of nearly 1,000 rolling acres awaits visitors to the Bob Evans Farm. The farm offers something for everyone - whether your interests are in taking a nostalgic journey to the past to sample simple pioneer living, shopping for unique specialty items, enjoying a day of family recreation or visiting the new Homestead museum - you're sure to come away with memories to share.

One of the most popular attractions at the Bob Evans Farm is the Craft Barn & Welcome Center. It is a reflection of the area's heritage and reputation for folk art and skilled crafts. A specialty store where shoppers can find one-of-a-kind items from 60 of the tri-state area's finest crafters and artists, the Craft Barn draws shoppers from throughout the region. Guests to this unique shop can find pottery, quilted items, wooden crafts, toys, handmade dolls, stained glass, tin ware, woven rugs, furniture, baskets, candles, jewelry and more.

The history of the farm and the southeast Ohio area is reflected in the farm's log cabin village, Adamsville Village. Originally settled in the early 1800s, it is today the site of four authentic log cabins and a log schoolhouse that have been reconstructed on the site at the Bob Evans Farm.

The farm is also an ideal site for family recreation, including horseback riding, canoeing, hay rides and camping. Horseback trails cover open areas and wooded hillsides for those seeking the adventure of hourly rides or even overnight trail rides, all led by experienced guides. Scenic Raccoon Creek, having retained its name even after being re-classified as an Ohio river, offers the opportunity for canoe trips as well as beautiful tent and RV campgrounds.

Special events at the farm take place in the spring, summer and fall. The Bob Evans Farm is the site for the annual Rio Grande Bean Dinner - a community dinner to honor the veterans of the Civil War. Now in its 132$^{nd}$ year, it is a traditional tribute to those who served their country. Other annual events include the Antique Car & Power Equipment Show now in its 26$^{th}$ year, the Down on the Farm Gospel Sing celebrating its ninth year, Lunch with the Easter Bunny, Bluegrass Festival, Youth Fishing Day, a Radio Control Fly-In, Volksmarch, National Barrel Horse Association Speed Show and others.

The biggest and most anticipated event at the farm is the Bob Evans Farm Festival a celebration of the harvest season, where tens of thousands of people gather to experience the rural America of yesteryear. Called a "weekend of fun for friends and family of all ages," it has been held annually since 1971. More than 150 crafters and artisans demonstrate their wares, many using tools and techniques nearly forgotten today. Musical entertainment, farm demonstrations, children's activities and farm contests are favorites at the festival, which is traditionally held the second full weekend of October.

*"The Homestead" Listed on The National Register of Historic Places, originally was A stagecoach stop and inn*

# Cherrington, Moulton & Evans Attorneys and Counselors at Law

*Staff: Front Row- Staci Campbell, Marilene Settle-Young, and Phyllis Russell. Back Row- David Evans and Thomas Moulton Jr.*

*K of P Building in the early 1900's*

In 1908 Henry William Cherrington opened a law practice in the old post office building, known today as the K of P Building. Henry was born in 1886 to Samuel and Rowena Cooke Cherrington. He graduated from GAHS in the class of 1902 and attended Marietta College for one year. He then read law under Judge Hunter of Columbus and a double cousin, Hollis Cherrington Johnston of Gallipolis. He passed the bar in 1908 and began the business as Henry W. Cherrington, Attorney at Law. In 1905 Henry had been appointed court stenographer and he used his shorthand skills throughout his life.

In 1911 Henry married Vivian Ayres and they became the parents of William Putnam (Bill) and Henrietta Cherrington. William was born in 1912, graduated from GAHS in 1930, Ohio University, Phi Beta Kappa, in 1933 and the University of Michigan School of Law in 1936. He passed the state bar and joined his father in practice in 1936 on the second floor of the K of P Building. Bill served as City Solicitor, Common Pleas Judge and Probate Court Judge.

Bill married Mary Lisbeth Lovell in 1941 and they had Suzanne (Sue), Henrietta (Henny) and Lisbeth.

In the fall of 1969 Henry stopped practicing due to ill health. By then he had practiced over 60 years, was known as Mr. Republican, was dean of the bar, and respectfully retained the title of judge. He had served as Prosecuting Attorney and Common Pleas Judge. He died May 2, 1971.

In 1970 Thomas S. Moulton, Sr. joined the firm with Bill. Tom married Sue Cherrington in 1969 when both were with the Attorney General's Office in Columbus. Both Tom and Sue were graduates of Ohio State University School of Law.

In August 1972 D. Dean Evans joined the firm. Dean married Henny Cherrington in 1966. He is a graduate of GAHS, Marshall University and Capital University School of Law. He served as City Solicitor of Gallipolis, Acting Judge of Gallipolis Municipal Court and Village Solicitor of Rio Grande.

As the firm expanded the offices were moved to the first floor of the building.

Sue Moulton joined the firm in 1979 and she was Gallia County's first woman attorney. Sue graduated from Staunton School for Girls and from Ohio State University.

Tom Moulton left the firm in 1979 to become Gallia County Probate Juvenile Judge, a position from which he will retire in 2003.

Sue opened her own office in January 1991 and was joined by her father in April of that year. Sue died June 2, 1995 and in 1997, her son, Thomas S. Moulton, Jr. a GAHS, Miami University and Ohio Northern University School of Law graduate joined Bill who continued to practice until 1998 when illness forced him to stop. Bill also practiced law in Gallia County over 60 years and was dean of the bar. He died August 28, 1998.

In 2001 David Cherrington Evans, son of Dean and Henny, joined his father in the practice of law. David graduated from GAHS, University of Cincinnati and the University of Cincinnati School of Law. David was sworn in in May 2001 and the very next day Dean was appointed Gallia County Common Pleas Judge by Governor Bob Taft to fill an unexpired term.

Dean left the law office in June 2001.

Shortly thereafter, Thomas, Jr. moved his offices to the K of P Building and became partners with David. Tom is Assistant Prosecuting Attorney and David is Magistrate for Municipal Court and Village Solicitor for Rio Grande.

At least one family member maintained a law office in the same location for 92 years. The firm continues a tradition of serving the Gallia County area with professionalism, integrity and respect.

The current office staff consists of Phyllis Russell who has worked for all four generations, Staci Campbell and Marilene Settle-Young and Mary Louise Hennesy.

*Submitted by Thomas Moulton, Jr. and David Cherrington Evans*

*Henry W. Cherrington, founder of firm*

# ElectroCraft
## A Rockwell Automation Business

### The 60's
Three men in Minnesota formed ElectroCraft Corporation in early 1960 and soon launched the Motomatic servo system, which quickly became successful. Unlike other companies, ElectroCraft took a "systems approach," producing both motors and amplifiers for industrial applications. In 1967, Robbins & Myers, a well-established company headquartered in Dayton OH built a motor manufacturing plant in Gallipolis OH, specializing in sub-fractional horsepower AC motors. This plant produced high-volume orders for manufacturers of office equipment, fans, heaters, and medical equipment.

### The 70's
ElectroCraft "wrote the book," literally, DC Motors, Speed Controls, Servo Systems, and has been respected as the principal authority on motion control by others in the industry, because of the proven track record of delivering superior quality and technology in motors and drives. The Robbins & Myers facility in Gallipolis grew rapidly in the 70's and built on two extensions to the plant, reaching its present size of 160,000 square feet. Motors produced in this facility served a variety of markets, including office automation, heating and cooling, medical, machine tool, pump, material handling, elevators, and food processing.

### The 80's
Robbins & Myers purchased ElectroCraft in 1980, and the two businesses combined resources to maximize the engineering and manufacturing processes for which both had earned strong reputations. In the mid- 80's brushless DC motors and digital controls were developed. As part of the consolidation of the two businesses, the Wisconsin facilities were closed, and manufacturing of DC brush-type servomotors moved to Gallipolis, where Robbins & Myers was successfully building AC motors for original equipment manufacturers. ElectroCraft Limited in Crewe, England, has worked closely with the Gallipolis plant over the years as both a sales office and a manufacturing and servicing facility.

### The 90's
In 1991 Reliance Electric purchased the Robbins & Myers Motor Group, which included ElectroCraft in Eden Prairie and Robbins & Myers in Gallipolis. Three years later, Rockwell International purchased Reliance Electric and its subsidiary companies, including ElectroCraft. In the 90's the Eden Prairie facility focused on providing complete automation systems for its industrial customers, and the Gallipolis facility developed close relationships with a number of medical equipment manufacturers and produced high volumes of motors for hospital beds and electric mobility scooters and wheelchairs.

In 2000 an important change was made by Rockwell Automation, combining the resources of Allen-Bradley, another strong subsidiary, and ElectroCraft, Eden Prairie. The Gallipolis OH business adopted a more contemporary trademark and logo in 2001 and now goes to market as ElectroCraft Engineered Solutions, a Rockwell Automation business, the "most valued global engineered solutions partner". In response to customer preference for single-source solutions for motors, gearheads, transaxles, and drives, ElectroCraft has adopted a new approach to marketing to target industries by developing closer customer relationships, understanding their industries, and designing products to meet their specific applications. ElectroCraft's core competency in 2002 is providing engineering expertise to the medical mobility industry. Other focus industries are floor care equipment, general mobility, and air/fluid movement.

The Gallipolis facility is ISO 9001 and 14001 certified and houses a UL-approved test lab. The Engineering team designs unique power solutions and builds prototypes for extensive testing, before releasing new products to Production. Gallipolis has an established work force in the factory, with many years' combined experience in production. The combination of innovation and experience provides our global partners the valuable total power transmission solutions they need to achieve success in their markets.

Among the first employees to work in the Gallipolis plant in 1967 were Clyde Day, Jim Kiskis, Mary Groves, Judy Garlic, Lowell Brown, Frances Belier, Norma Powell, Bob Rippey, Kay Spencer, Linda Jones, Wanda Blake, Sharon Barcus, Rosadeen Skeen, Pat Staley, and Carol Atha. Today, ElectroCraft is an important part of the community, with employment of about 400 people, who contribute time and resources to help the community in a variety of ways, including charities, food drives, educational opportunities, and community festivals.

Plant managers have included Mark Wright, Ray Ellis, Tim Hennessey, Paul Knotts, Don Richter, Ron Burton, Paul Schmidt, and Randy Finney.

---

250 McCormick Road
Gallipolis OH 45631-8597, 800.697.6715
Phone: 740.441.6200 Fax: 740.441.6303
Rockwell House, Gateway, Crewe, CW1 6XN UK
Phone: 44(0)1270 580142 Fax: 44(0)1270 580141
Visit us on the web: www.electrocraft.com

# Holzer Clinic

After graduation from the Ohio State University College of Medicine in 1909, Dr. Charles E. Holzer, Sr., became the protégé of two distinguished surgeons in Columbus and was sent to Gallipolis, Ohio for a year of intensive surgical training at the Ohio Hospital for Epileptics, now the Gallipolis Developmental Center. His contact with the area prompted him to remain here and, in 1909, he started his first hospital at 507 Second Avenue.

Shortly afterward, Dr. Holzer married Alma Vornholt, a nurse whom he had met while in training in Columbus. Together, in 1918, they opened the Holzer Hospital at First and Cedar. In 1922, the first addition to the hospital was begun; it was completed in 1926. Subsequently, Dr. Holzer found it necessary to acquire additional professional help, and he hired Dr. Vornholt, his brother-in-law, to assist him.

In 1939, another medical entity, the Gallipolis Clinic, was formed by Dr. Leo Bean, Dr. Homer Thomas and Dr. Norval Martin. The first location of the Gallipolis Clinic was at 52 State Street. In November, 1959, the Gallipolis Clinic relocated to the corner of Fourth and Sycamore Streets, added inpatient capabilities, and changed its name to the Gallipolis Medical Center Clinic. The medical staff at the Holzer Hospital continued to grow during this time. In 1946, Dr. Charles E. Holzer, Jr. returned to Gallipolis to practice medicine at the hospital.

The transfer of the hospital ownership from Dr. Holzer, Sr. to the people of this area occurred on January 1, 1949. He and Mrs. Holzer gave the hospital and equipment to the people of the five counties they most directly serve; Gallia, Jackson, Meigs, Vinton, and Mason. It was also during this period that the physicians practicing at the Holzer Hospital formed a separate partnership, the Holzer Clinic, which has steadily grown to its present stature as one of the largest group medical practices in Ohio and West Virginia.

During the early 1960's, there was continued growth of both clinic and hospital and, in 1965, it became apparent that future expansion of their independent facilities was necessary. It was decided that a joint effort was needed to insure the realization of a new medical center. In 1968, the physicians of the Holzer Clinic and the physicians of the Gallipolis Clinic merged into the Holzer Medical Center Clinic, and the Gallipolis Medical Center Hospital merged with the Holzer Hospital into the Holzer Medical Center.

On May 27, 1972, the Holzer Medical Center Hospital and Holzer Medical Center Clinic moved into new and expanded facilities at 90 Jackson Pike, Gallipolis.

*Charles E Holzer, Jr. M.D.*

In 1976, the Clinic opened its Jackson Branch in temporary facilities in Jackson, and several months later moved that operation to the Jenkins Memorial Clinic Building near Wellston. Three years later, in 1981, Holzer Clinic of Jackson County moved to its permanent location at 25 South Street in Jackson. In 1995, the Holzer Clinic Rehabilitation Center of Jackson County opened at 336 Main Street in Jackson, Ohio to locally offer specific rehabilitative care to Jackson County residents. In November 1997, Holzer Clinic of Jackson expanded and moved the Jackson Rehabilitation Center back on site.

In 1978, the Clinic changed its legal structure to a Limited Partnership Association and began doing business as Holzer Clinic Ltd.

In 1980, the Clinic opened the Sycamore Street Clinic in Gallipolis in the former Gallipolis Medical Clinic Building. Currently, our Occupational, Sports and Rehabilitative Medicine Department and Holzer Health Center function there.

In 1982, the Clinic opened the Meigs County Branch in Middleport. In 1995, Meigs Health Services of Holzer Clinic was affiliated with the Meigs County Clinic. In 1997, the two facilities were combined through a joint venture with Consolidated Health Systems (HMC) and Holzer Clinic. The Holzer Meigs Clinic is now located on the campus of Veterans Memorial Hospital.

On January 1, 1985, the Clinic changed its legal structure to a professional corporation and officially became Holzer Clinic Inc.

In 1986, the Main Clinic facility began a renovation and expansion project which added 33,000 square feet onto the professional building at 90 Jackson Pike in Gallipolis. An 1800 square foot expansion was completed in the Internal Medicine Department in 1994, and a two-floor, 9000 square foot addition along the north side of the Main Facility was completed in 1995. These latest projects bring the total Main Clinic square footage to approximately 91,000.

1988 marked the addition of two more facilities. The purchase of an existing medical office building in Point Pleasant, WV led to the opening of Holzer Clinic of West Virginia in May. A few months later the Clinic constructed and opened a fifth satellite facility-Holzer Clinic of Lawrence County in Proctorville, Ohio.

In 1993, Holzer Clinic acquired the Health and Rehabilitation Center in Charleston, WV. A new 16,000 square foot rehabilitation facility was constructed in South Charleston and dedicated in May, 1994.

The Clinic's growth in qualified medical staff, facilities, and medical care has been steady and continual as we maintain our mission to the people of Southeastern Ohio and Western West Virginia of being *"The Best Place To Come For Care And The Best Place To Work."* For more information on Holzer Clinic look for us on the web: www.holzerclinic.com

# InfoCision Management Corp.

In 1982, President and CEO Gary Taylor began InfoCision in his home. Now with 19 call centers in eight locations throughout Ohio and West Virginia, InfoCision is one of the country's leading providers of call center services.

From its very inception, InfoCision has been totally focused on utilizing information to help make the right decisions. In fact, Taylor derived the company name from the words "INFOrmation" and "deCISION." For the first three years, it operated as a consulting company, developing outbound telemarketing programs for its clients. In 1985, it began making the telephone calls internationally. Under Gary Taylor's leadership, InfoCision has been one of the fastest-growing private companies in America, expanding from its initial four Communicators to today more than 2,500 employees.

InfoCision specializes in nonprofit fundraising and recruitment, direct-to-consumer sales and business-to-business applications. It is a top-20 outbound, top-50 inbound company and a pioneer in Web-connected e-commerce. The company has grown through the successful implementation of a series of marketing plans. These plans have helped the company break into and become a leader in several highly defined niche markets. This has resulted in distinct, totally separate divisions that do a better job because of their vast depth of experience in handling similar types of phone calls. We have built our success on hiring dedicated Communicators for each of our five divisions: religious, nonprofit, political, volunteer recruitment and commercial.

InfoCision raises more money for nonprofit organizations than any other telephone marketing company in the world. It also has an unmatched reputation for quality, integrity and customer service. InfoCision has developed a proprietary inbound/outbound call blending solution, one of the most sophisticated applications in the industry.

Headquartered in Akron, the company operates call centers in Austintown, Boardman, Akron, Green, and Gallipolis, Ohio and in Clarksburg and Huntington, West Virginia. Our phone representatives, or "Communicators," are InfoCision's greatest asset and are compensated accordingly. This allows the company to keep good employees and build a family-oriented environment. In fact, many Communicators have been with InfoCision over 10 years. At the same time, employees get the chance to work with some of the largest and most prestigious nonprofit organizations in the world and a long list of Fortune 1000 companies. In short, InfoCision offers its employees more than just a job. It offers them a career.

In 2000, InfoCision – with the backing and support of the Gallia County Community Improvement Corporation – opened its Gallipolis facility in an unbelievable 10 days. Within its first seven months of being open, the center expanded three more times and currently employs nearly 300 people. InfoCision's Gallipolis call center offers employees a range of telephone marketing opportunities in its nonprofit, political and volunteer recruitment divisions. Employees of Gallipolis' newest call center, for example, place calls for conservative political organizations focusing specifically on protecting second-amendment rights. Others help recruit donors and volunteers for some of the nation's leading nonprofit organizations.

InfoCision has found a permanent home in Gallia County is proud to be a part of the renaissance taking place throughout the area. The company looks forward to continuing to develop strong relationships with the residents and businesses throughout the community.

# The Lafayette Hotel

The Lafayette Hotel opened May 3, 1928 with 58 rooms and the hope of becoming the hub of Gallipolis. It did.

The concrete and steel building, which was started in 1927 and constructed at a cost of $185,00 was owned and operated by George A. Tabit. Mr. Tabit bought the land, composed of lots 100 and 99, around 1921 for approximately $20,000. The lots originally belonged to Antoine Due and Charles Berthelot, but became a single property when the lots were purchased by Charles Creuzet.

The hotel is Georgian architecture and decorated in the French period. The art fresco in the lobby and dining room area is still intact and admired today. The three-story building housed a wide lobby, entered from Second Avenue, a dining room, ball room and large kitchen. The dining room seated 100 persons and featured dinner music Sunday, Tuesday and Thursday evenings plus dancing two nights a week. Its lobby boasted oriental chandeliers were the first of the pattern ever cast. The hotel was designed by John Q. Adams, who also designed the then new Columbus City Hall, the Majestic Theatre in Athens, Ohio and several Ohio University buildings.

The Lafayette's first guest was E. R. Jamison of Columbus. The hotel was the scene of many parties and balls and was involved in the celebration of dedication of the old Silver Bridge. On opening day, a dinner-dance entertained more than 200 people with music from the Pete Sullivan and the King Taste Orchestra.

It was first leased to Edward Sullivan, then in 1935, to Earl W. and Mary Smith and their daughter, Alice, until 1957. During the years in the hotel, Miss Smith reported there were many nights where there were so many guest that they had to have residents in the community help accommodate all the people.

During the Ohio River flood in 1937, the Lafayette was the only place in Gallipolis that served food, The Red Cross was quartered in the building. The water came just up to the doors and Miss Smith would have to board a boat outside the door in order to go across the park to the sheriff's office for news.

In 1957, William O'Brien and Jake Moore secured the operating lease of the Lafayette for nine years, The Tabit family sold the hotel to Eckford and Margaret Hodgson on October 27, 1960. On April 1, 1966, William O'Brien bought the hotel outright from the Hodgson. After a time, he closed the hotel and it remain empty until April of 1973 when the Hoyt Mullins family acquired ownership of the Lafayette Hotel Building.

After purchasing the building, Hoyt Mullins, his wife Lureva, and their tow sons, Victor and James began renovating and opening the downstairs space into a mini mall to accommodate their offices and businesses, Bernadine's, Mullins' Enterprises - My Sister's Closet and The Linen Cupboard. They leased the other rooms to the Alcove, The Shoe Café, The Hanson Family Bakery, Your Father's Mustache Barber and Beauty Shop.

The Mullins family started My Sister's Closet, but had acquired Bernadine's, a ladies' apparel shop, in 1967 from Margaret Jarvis, the widow of Paul Jarvis, who founded Bernadine's in 1947. James Mullins is the present owner of Bernadine's. In 1980, Hoyt Mullins added the full service restaurant, the Down Under.

Some of the businesses that have occupied space in the Lafayette are Commercial and Savings Bank, Credit Thrift, Wilcoxen's Barber Shop and more recently the Jody Kutts and the City Perk. Occupying the building at the present time are Bernadine's, Kipling's Shoes, The Purple Turtle, The Coach's Corner, The Empty Nest and Courtside Grill.

James Mullins and Robert Brenneman added thirteen apartments on the second and third floors.

The Lafayette Hotel Building is presently owned by James and Nancy Mullins and Steve and Linda Chapman

# The Libby Hotel

"The grand opening of the Hotel Libby was held Saturday evening (August 20, 1927) with hundreds of people from Gallipolis and other cities present at the celebration. It was estimated that more than 2000 people visited the hotel during the evening.

Everyone expressed themselves as delighted with the luxurious appointments and hospitable arrangements of the hotel. Flowers were banked behind the hotel desk and tastefully arranged in the lobby. An orchestra furnished music during the evening and from ten o'clock until midnight dancing was enjoyed in the hotel lobby. Visitors at the opening discovered that the hotel surpassed even the high expectations of it.

The above is how the Gallipolis Daily Tribune reported the opening of the Libby Hotel in Gallipolis in 1927. Work began on converting the old J. M. Kerr Hardware Company building into a hotel in April of 1927.

It was on April 1, 1927, that Charles Stevers and R. P. Thompson, owners of the store and the building, sold the building to John Clendenin. It was Mr. Clendenin who developed the hardware store into a hotel.

The J. M. Kerr Hardware Company had been located in the aforementioned structure since 1901 when J. M. Kerr & Company merged with E. W. Vanden & Company. Ironically both Kerr and Vanden had started independently in the same year, 1866.

In 1927 the Libby Hotel had 44 guest rooms. According to the April 12, 1927, Tribune, "The rooms will be furnished with metal furniture, steam heat, hot and cold water and telephones. All bedding and furniture will be new  There will be a reading light at the head of each bed, central lights on each ceiling and at each lavatory. Single rooms will be from $1.50 to $2 per night."

The Libby eventually would have a large restaurant and a coffee shop as well as rooms where salesmen could display their wares. In 1927 there were a lot of traveling salesmen who would come into town, set up a small display in the hotel and sell items out of their suitcases.

The Libby catered even to small conventions. For instance in 1935 some 300 members of the Jehovah's Witnesses from Ohio and West Virginia held a 2-day convention in Gallipolis.

In 1944 there was a rumor ciculating that a Nazi prisoner was holed up somewhere in the Libby Hotel. Nazi prisoners were sometimes transported through Gallipolis along Route 7 and Route 35. It appears that one of the Nazi prisoners had jumped out of the prisoner truck at First Avenue and Sycamore Street. He was later seen running down Second Avenue, running in between buildings. In 1944 the Libby Hotel had a rather large garage beside the hotel. The garage, as well as the hotel, were suspected as hiding places.

That garage at the Libby was called the Day and Night Garage and was run by H. P. Bradbury and later John Harrison. In the late 1930s and early 1940s new Studebaker cars were even sold out of the garage. In the early 1930s the Libby garage was often turned into the Libby Arena. Here professional boxing and wrestling matches were held.

It was about 1944 that the Greyhound Bus Line opened their Gallipolis station in the Libby Hotel. That year there were four daily bus runs from Gallipolis to Columbus. The Greyhound Bus Depot would be in the Libby for more than five decades. When Greyhound moved into the Libby, the barber shop of Harley Carman and the beauty shop of Mrs. Ward had to be relocated.

Presently the Libby Hotel is owned by Karen McGhee, the wife of Steve McGhee. Along with The American Red Cross, the law offices of local attorney Ron Calhoun and Bill Black Tax Advisory Services and Steve McGhee's Allstate Insurance business is located on the first floor.

# O.O. McIntyre Park District

The O.O. McIntyre Park District was created on March 10, 1975 by Probate and Juvenile Court Judge R. William Jenkins. The petition was filed by the Community Development Study Committee, a group comprised of local leadership who organized and conducted meetings with Ohio State University Extension Agent John Stitzlein and local Extension Agent Bryson "Bud" Carter to discuss improving the quality of life for the people of Gallia County. The Committee, under the leadership of Thomas E. Jones of Crown City, determined that creation of an Ohio 1545 Park District would provide public parks, outdoor recreation facilities and programs while protecting natural resources fur the benefit and enjoyment of the citizens and enhance the quality of life for all and future generations. The Committee petitioned Judge Jenkins to create the Park District. The Gallia County Commissioners Joe Stewart, C. E. Johnson and John L. Belville set aside .5 mills generated from Property Taxes to fund the Park District. Judge Jenkins then appointed the first Board of Park Commissioners Dr. William B. Thomas, Mr. Thomas E. Jones and Dr. Clyde Evans for three year staggering terms of office. Shortly after the creation of the Park District, Judge R. William Jenkins made a cash contribution to the new Park District that established the District's Capital Development Trust Fund for the purpose of receiving similar donations for development of the Park System in Gallia County. The Capital Development Trust Fund continues to be in existence for the purpose of continued development of Parks and Natural Areas in Gallia County.

One of the first actions of the new Park Board was engaging the Designer's Forum, a planning firm under the leadership of Richard Morse and Michael Strunk, to prepare a Comprehensive Plan for Parks and Recreation in Gallia County. This document published in 1977 provided the blueprint for land acquisition and development for the Park District and was recognized for Professional Achievement by the American Society of Landscape Architects. Concurrently, while the plan was being formulated, a scientific survey and needs assessment was conducted of Gallia County Residents and incorporated into the plan. Public Meetings were held throughout the County to receive input for the plan from citizens.

```
BOARD OF PARK COMMISSIONERS
LIST OF MEMBERS AND TERMS OF OFFICE

Dr. William B. Thomas    5/75 — 12/01
Dr. Clyde M. Evans       5/75 — 8/84
Mr. Thomas E. Jones      5/75 — 12/86, 7/96 to Present
Mr. George E. Pope       1/85 — 12/87
Judge Thomas S. Moulton  1/87 — 7/96
Mr. C. Ronald Halley     3/88 — 12/94
Dr. Allan Boster         7/96 — to Present
Mr. Tim Betz            10/01 — to Present

PROBATE & JUVENILE COURT JUDGES
Judge R. William Jenkins 2/73 — 2/79
Judge Thomas S. Moulton  2/79 — to Present
```

On January 24, 1976, the new Park District was formally named for 0. 0. McIntyre, pioneer syndicated columnist and favorite son of Gallia County. The public announcement was made at a Press Conference at the Holiday Inn. Mr. Emerson Evans, a member of the Community Development Study Committee played a leadership role in discussions with Maybelle McIntyre's decision to name the new Park District after her late husband. Mrs. McIntyre supported the Park District contributing assets of two properties and a final bequest of McIntyre's Memorabilia, library and a fine arts collection.

The Official Logo, registered with the Secretary of the State of Ohio, was designed by Miss Ellen Wetherholt who submitted the winning entry in a contest sponsored by the French Art Colony in November of 1976. The logo depicts the top hat, glove and cane, typical 1930's attire for 0. 0. McIntyre, superimposed over a Buckeye Tree Leaf, the official tree for the State of Ohio.

It was also in November that the Park Board adopted official By-Laws prepared by Assistant Prosecuting Attorney William Eachus.

In April of 1979, Josette Baker was appointed Director of the Park District by the Park Board and has served in this capacity for 23 years under the leadership of Judge Thomas S. Moulton, Probate and Juvenile Court Judge. Prior to her appointment, Joel Dennis served as Director from 1977-1978.

*O.O. McIntyre Park District*

# Ohio Valley Bank

On September 24, 1872, the organizational meeting of the bank was called. Rooms on Second Avenue in Gallipolis, Ohio were acquired by the organization and on the first of November, 1872, the bank was opened in those rooms. The Ohio Valley Bank had expanded its business to such a degree that it quickly outgrew these rooms. A new building was constructed in 1896 on the corner of Second Avenue and State Street in Gallipolis. At the time it was the tallest building in Gallipolis. This building was continually remodeled until the construction of the Bank's present Main Office in 1961. This modern banking facility boasted the first drive-thru windows and free customer parking in Gallia County.

Ohio Valley Bank's first branch opened in 1970 with the completion of an office in Rio Grande, Ohio, adjacent to the University of Rio Grande campus. During the bank's 100th anniversary in 1972, the Mini Bank was opened in Gallipolis, located opposite Fourth Avenue from Washington Elementary. In 1976, the Jackson Pike Office was opened across from Holzer Medical Center in Gallipolis, Ohio. Gallia County's very first ATM was installed at the Mini Bank in 1979.

The bank's first venture into banking outside the county line took place in 1991. Ohio Valley Bank acquired Civic Federal Savings Banks in Gallipolis, Jackson and Waverly, Ohio. Shortly after, the Ohio Valley Banc Corp. commenced operation as a one-bank holding company, with Ohio Valley Bank Company being a wholly-owned subsidiary. Ohio Valley Banc Corp. stock is still traded on NASDAQ under the symbol OVBC. Presently, Ohio Valley Banc Corp. owns two subsidiaries: Ohio Valley Bank and Loan Central.

A regional revolution in banking hours occurred with the opening of the OVB SuperBank in late 1996. This first SuperBank, located just inside Foodland, a downtown Gallipolis grocery, was the first to be open until eight each evening and stay open on Saturday and Sunday. Once again, Ohio Valley Bank brought a first to its community. Today, each full-service SuperBank is open a total of 62 hours a week. Banking laws changed in 1997, permitting the state-chartered bank to have full service banks in West Virginia. The Bank, which already operated a loan origination office in Point Pleasant, West Virginia was already in position to make yet another mark in history. Ohio Valley Bank established the first interstate bank between Ohio and West Virginia. Later that same year a branch office was opened in Columbus, Ohio, for the benefit of the Bank's long-standing relationship with Bob Evans Farms, Inc. 1998 brought the opening of three new SuperBanks. Two SuperBanks were opened in brand-new Wal-Mart SuperCenters in Cross Lanes, WV, and Gallipolis, Ohio.

Additionally, a SuperBank was opened within the Big Bend Save-a-Lot in Pomeroy, Ohio.

In May of 1999, Ohio Valley Bank announced its intentions to purchase two Huntington National Bank branches in Barboursville and Milton, West Virginia. The purchase would be completed by the end of September. The South Charleston SuperBank was opened in the Southridge Wal-Mart SuperCenter in August. Another SuperBank was opened inside the Wal-mart in South Point, Ohio in October.

In April of 2000 another SuperBank was opened. This SuperBank is located inside the 29th Street Wal-Mart in Huntington. Ohio Valley Bank went online on June 1, 2000, with it's community Web portal, www.ovbc.com. The portal offers internet banking, electronic bill payment, a community calendar, stock market information, news, weather and more. As of the end of January 2002, over a million visitors from several countries had visited www.ovbc.com.

The year of 2001 was a year of strategy and planning at the Bank. However, even the wisest, most experienced banker could not predict what was to come. The terrorist act of September 11, 2001, was felt by the entire nation and officially plunged the country into recession. Ohio Valley Bank CEO Jeff Smith led the company to be an example for the community by taking steps to improve the economy of the communities OVB serves. In October, a new SuperBank was opened inside the Kroger in Jackson, Ohio. Additionally, for the first time in the Bank's history, its directors approved a special "Freedom Dividend" to be given to shareholders. Through the "Freedom Dividend" over half a million dollars was reinvested in OVBC's shareholders.

Ohio Valley Bank has been a successful bank for over 129 years. During that time the Bank has endured two World Wars as well as the Great Depression and many other challenges.

# Ohio Valley Electric Corporation
## Kyger Creek Station

Ohio Valley Electric Corporation (OVEC) was formed on October 1, 1952, by 15 investor-owned utilities furnishing electric service in the Ohio River Valley area for the purpose of providing the large electric power requirements projected for the uranium enrichment facility being built by the then-Atomic Energy Commission. OVEC's power served this facility until September 2001 when OVEC generation was made available to its sponsoring companies. The parent companies of the sponsoring utilities are American Electric Power Company, Inc., Allegheny Energy, Inc., Cinergy Corp., DPL, Inc., FirstEnergy Corp., PowerGen PLC and Vectren Corp.

The Kyger Creek Plant was the first major industry to locate in Gallia County. At one point during construction, over 5,000 construction workers were employed. Construction projects and contract work through the years have employed thousands of workers from the Gallia County area. As one of the major employers in the community, Kyger Creek maintains a workforce of over 300 employees and has nearly 200 retirees.

When constructed, the Kyger Creek Station was among the largest power plants in the world. The plant operates five coal-fired generating units with a total generating capacity of 1,075 megawatts. Kyger Creek continues to rank among the most efficient coal-fired electric utilities in the United States.

Each of the plant's five boilers has 150 miles of tubing, which holds 52,000 gallons of water for the production of steam. Steam with pressure of 2,000 pounds per square inch and temperature of over 1,000 F is used to turn the turbine-generators for power production. Kyger's present stack was built in conjunction with a new ash collection system in the late 1970s and stands 1,000 feet tall. In 2001, construction began on a selective catalytic reduction (SCR) system for compliance with the nitrogen oxide reduction requirement of the Clean Air Act. The SCR system is scheduled to be in full operation by the summer of 2003. Bottom ash from the plant is recycled and sold as grit for roof shingles and for sandblasting material.

Kyger Creek Station strives to remain actively involved with area communities. Kyger Creek is proud to support local schools and takes part in student and school staff training and awareness programs.

*For more information regarding the Kyger Creek Station, visit the company's Web site at www.ovec.com.*

*Kyger Creek Power Plant*

# Our House Museum

*Our House Museum built 1819, located in Gallipolis, Ohio*

The Our House Museum, originally named The Cushing Tavern and Inn, was opened in 1819 by Henry Cushing and his sister, Elizabeth. The name of the tavern became known as Our House because Henry Cushing would go to the boat dock to greet travelers and would then invite them to come over to "Our House" and stay the night.

Elizabeth inherited the property which originally belonged to the Marquis DeHebercourt, the first postmaster in Gallipolis. She then sold half interest to her brother, Henry (for a dollar, it is said) and they built this fancy inn. They purchased the lot behind the inn and consequently owned all of the land to Second Avenue.

Our House is designed in the late Georgian or federal style of architecture with a southern influence and is constructed of bricks which, it is reported, had been used as ships' ballast. The long central hallway, high ceilings and Christian doors reflect that southern influence. The inn consists of a taproom, formal dining room, public dining room, with a drawing room, ladies' bedchamber, men's bedchamber, nanny's bedroom, ballroom, attic and kitchen (which is located in a separate building the courtyard).

Oriental rugs (made in the late 1700s and early 1800s) are used on the floors in the museum today. However, rush and canvas mats would have been used originally.

Although designed as a tavern and inn to house travelers, Our House became a meeting place for local citizens to gather, exchange news from around the country, talk politics and drink. Peach brandy was the popular drink since peaches were in abundance and the only way to preserve them was to mash the fruit and distill it.

The ballroom, with its original chandeliers, was the social center for the town. It was here that the Marquis de Lafayette was entertained in May, 1825, when he came to visit the colonies. A reception was given for him and, after a brief few hours, he departed, leaving behind his coat for reasons unknown to this day. It is now displayed in a glass case with the violin played at his reception. The ballroom was also the scene of a concert in 1852, given by Jenny Lind, known as The Swedish Nightingale, under the management of P. T. Barnum.

The museum also contains furnishings indigenous to that period. Many items, which have been donated by descendents of the original French Five Hundred. Examples are: A pre-1790 painting on wood brought to Gallipolis by a Mons. Gervais from France; a piano thought to be the first piano west of the Allegheny Mountains; a rosewood piano owned by the Menager Family, (one of the original settlers); a gold medallion given to Marie Bobien by Napoleon Bonaparte; a bronze statue of Napoleon (circa 1808), a gift to the Emperor which he took into exile on the Isle of Elba. He presented it to his personal physician, Dr. Meara, in 1818, and, later it came into the possession of Joshua Clark, a native of Gallia County. He presented it to the Our House Museum in 1936. Also of interest to visitors is the famous "convenient chair", an upholstered wingback chair serving as a convenience for the ladies instead of going to the "outdoor facilities" in the courtyard.

Because of the many stories of unusual sights and sounds experienced by visitors and staff at the museum, Our House is listed in "Haunted Houses of America" and "Haunted Ohio II". The tavern remained in the hands of the Cushing Family until 1865. Throughout its existence, the tavern has served as a Marine Hospital, Boarding house and rental property.

In 1933, the building was purchased and restored by Dr. and Mrs. Charles Holzer, Sr. In 1936, it was opened as a museum and in 1944, it became a state memorial, a gift of the Holzer family to the State of Ohio. It is currently administered by the Ohio Historical Society and operated by the Friends of Our House Board of Trustees, comprised of local residents. Tour buses bring hundreds of visitors to Our House each season, in addition to regular tourists; school children who are brought for educational tours; parties, weddings and receptions are scheduled throughout the year and concerts. Lectures and meetings are conducted in the ballroom. When the regular season is over, arrangements are made to open the museum for special events. These events are managed and served by a staff of volunteers under the direction of a Site Manager. At all times, when on duty, the volunteers are dressed in costumes appropriate to the attire worn by the French settlers in the early nineteenth century. This facility, known as Our House State Memorial, is located at 434 First Avenue in Gallipolis, Ohio. Phone - (740)446-0586. It is open May - 10 a.m. to 4:00 p.m. Saturday, 1 - 4 p.m. Sunday, June - August 10:00 a.m. to 4:00 p.m., Tuesday - Saturday; 1 - 4 p.m. Sunday; September 10:00 a.m. to 4:00 p.m. Saturday; 1:00 - 4:00 p.m. Sunday. *Submitted by Dene Pellegrinon, Vice-President Board of Friends of the Our House*

*Menager Rosewood Piano, (circa 1825), located in Our House Museum, Gallipolis, Ohio*

# Smith Buick- Pontiac, Inc.

*Smith Buick - Present location, 1911 Eastern Ave., Gallipolis Ohio*

*Judy Motor Sales - 1st Buick dealership owned by "Doc" Smith, 1954, located 215 Third Avenue, Gallipolis, Ohio*

Smith-Buick Pontiac, located at 1911 Eastern Avenue in Gallipolis, Ohio had its beginnings in the early 1950s.

The company was founded by Vaught "Doc" Smith. Doc was born August 25, 1924 in Huntington, West Virginia. He graduated from Huntington East High School and attended the University of Kentucky and Marshall University. He was a United States Army veteran who served in World War II.

In February of 1954, Doc purchased the local Buick franchise from Ed Judy. He started selling and servicing new Buicks at 215 Third Avenue in Gallipolis as Smith Buick Company. In 1959, the new car agency moved to 48 State Street in downtown Gallipolis. After seven years at this location, Doc built new sales and service facilities at its current location on Eastern Avenue.

In addition to the Buick line of automobiles, the agency sold German-built Opels until 1975 and Suzuki motorcycles for several years. However, the latest expansion of product line occurred in 1973 with the addition of Pontiac to the sales and service agreement following the passing of local Pontiac dealer, Bob Rees. That same year the dealership was incorporated as Smith Buick-Pontiac, Inc.

In the 1960s and 1970s, the agency performed the duties of deputy registrar by selling license tags and issuing driver's licenses for the State of Ohio; Doc's wife, Deanie, operated this department.

In 1988, a new 6000-square foot paint and body shop was added. This new body shop included eight work bays, two cleanup and prep bays, a manager's office, employee meeting and training rooms and a paint storage room.

*Picture of Vaught "Doc" Smith, founder of Smith Buick-Pontiac, Inc.*

In 1996, Doc passed the presidency to his son, Greg. However, Doc still continued working in the dealership in a less active, yet important, roll as chairman of the board and advisor. He worked until his death on October 16, 2001.

In 1997, the used car lot was expanded and filled in above the flood plain. This allowed the company to expand into a used car superstore in 1998.

The company currently employs 26 people. Of those, 16 have been employees there for 10 years or more. Former and current long-term employees from Gallia County include the following Body Shop personnel: Henry Gibbs, Ed Kirby, Glenn Lawson, Larry Griffin, Bill Lemley, Doug Fogelstrom, Rick Woerner; Service personnel: Vance Rees, Loren Beaver, Jr., Larry Casto, Kenny Williams, Jimmie Queen, Charles Goode, Henry Hensley, Randy Johnson, Vic Halley; Sales Personnel: Greg Smith, Bob Brickles, Harland "Woody" Wood, Don Carter, Brett Epling; and Office Personnel: Lou Long, E. Kay Evans, Evelyn North, Arlene Campbell and Cindy Epling.

Most of Doc's success was based on the fact that this is a family business with family values. Today the company's business philosophy, which has been successful for over 45 years, remains the same - - offer the customer the best service, competitive prices and quality products. With this philosophy, 45 years is only the beginning. *Submitted by Cindy Smith Epling*

*Smith Buick - 2nd location, 48 State Street, Gallipolis, Ohio*

# The U. S. Bank Of Gallipolis, Ohio

The bank in Gallipolis, Ohio currently known as The U. S. Bank, originally started as The Commercial and Savings Bank incorporated on September 9, 1908 in Gallipolis (see Commercial and Savings Bank history in this book). On August 1, 1979, The First National Bank of Cincinnati, Ohio purchased all of the capital stock of the Commercial and Saving Bank. The bank continued to operate under the name of the Commercial and Savings Bank until July 1, 1988 when it was renamed the Star Bank, along with all other affiliates of The First National Bank of Cincinnati.

In October 1988, a merger took place between the Gallia County and Lawrence County Star Banks. In 1990, there were nine offices of Star Bank, N. A., Tri-State, with 156 employees.

These in Ohio are: Main Office, 120 South Third Street, Ironton; Jones Street Office, 2301 South Third Street, Ironton; South Point Office, 702 Fourth Street East, South Point; K-Mart Office, K- Mart Plaza, Chesapeake; Chesapeake Office, 353 Third Avenue Chesapeake; Rome Office, State Route 7, Proctorville; Court Street Office, 25 Court Street, Gallipolis; Silver Bridge Plaza Office, 350 Upper River Road, and Spring Valley Office, 461 Jackson Pike, Gallipolis.

The directors of Star Bank, N. A., Tri-State in 1990 were: James L. Heald, Donald L. Crance, Robert L. Dalton, Daniel P. Davies, Jr., Bill W. Dingus, Bernard L. Edwards, D. Dean Evans, W. H. Ford, Charles E. Holzer, Jr., Charles C. Klein, Dean F. Massie, Philip L. Pope, J. Craig Strafford and Wayne F. White.

The building in which the U. S. Bank is located was built by the Commercial and Saving Bank in 1965. The drive-in facilities were expanded during the 1980's, after the bank acquired the old Sohio Service Station at the corner of Second Avenue and Court Street.

In the spring of 1998, the name was changed again from Star Bank to Firstar Bank. In the third quarter of 2002, Firstar Bank became the U. S. Bank, a branch of the eighth largest bank in the United States. As of March, 2002, the U. S. Bank assets are $171 billion. *Submitted by Alice Niday*

# B & E Shoe Service

The B (Bill) & E (Edith) Shoe Service is presently located at 427 Second Avenue in Gallipolis, Ohio. This shop was purchased by the Stapleton family December 19. 1969 by William F. Stapleton. Mr. Stapleton entered the First National Contest for repairing shoes in 1972. He won a Blue Ribbon and entered again in 1973 and won the Midwestern Silver Cup which covered twelve states including North and South Dakota, Nebraska, Kansas, Minnesota, Iowa, Mississippi, Wisconsin, Michigan, Indiana and Ohio. He won the Eastern Regional Award which covers twenty-five states. It includes everything this side of the Mississippi River.

Son, Steve Stapleton won the Midwestern Silver cup which above twelve states the only time he entered. William F. Stapleton was the sixth shoe repair man from Ohio to receive this award. William Steven Stapleton was the seventh since the contest started in 1938.

The contest consists of repairing one shoe out of three pair and judging is considered on how well contestants do. *Submitted by William F. Stapleton*

# Standard Plumbing & Heating

Harry W. Dexter founded the business in 1921. He was born 11/5/1898 in Liverpool, Nova Scotia, Canada. He learned pipe fitting in Nova Scotia He homesteaded in Helena, Montana in 1906 and later moved to Nitro, WV during World War I. He set up a shop in Catlettsburg, Ky selling acetylene light to plants in Kentucky, Ohio and West Virginia. He Elma Jewel Reese in Gallipolis and they married, had two children, John S. Dexter and Laura Mae (now Davis). He retired after 53 years passed away October 6, 1978.

Bobby C. Roach began working for Dexter in 1950. He learned the trade under the supervision of Shelby Roberts who also worked for Dexter. Bobby then purchased the business from Dexter in 1965.

It was originally located at 504 Second Avenue and then moved to 215 Third Avenue. It is now located on a large lot at 711 5th Avenue.

Many individuals worked for Bobby over the years. Some included Vernon Kuhn of the original Kuhn & Saunders Sheet Metal Service, Doe Davis after retiring from the City of Gallipolis, Gene Plants, who later started his own business of Plants Plumbing & Heating, Tim Lasseter, who owns Elite Mechanical Contractors and Roger Bennett.

At the time Bobby started the business, he was married to Nellie Overby and they had two children, Gary C. Roach and Vicky (now Browning). He later married Dorothy Criner and she had two children, Terri Criner and Chuck Derifield.

Bobby C. Roach has now been operating the business for 37 years serving many customers in the community of Gallipolis and surrounding areas. It still remains under the original name of Standard Plumbing & Heating and has been operating a total of 81 years.

# Video Connections

After retiring from teaching Adaptive Physical Education and coaching Special Olympics, I decided to turn one of my hobbies into a business. Video Connections was started on April 13, 2000. Weddings, graduations, birthday parties, family reunions, plays, transfers are some of the services available. Thank you Gallia County for your business! Video Connections by Patty Hays Memories can last forever! Transfer VHS to CD-R's.

Weddings
Graduations
School Plays
Class Reunions
740-446-3884
phays@eurekanet.corn

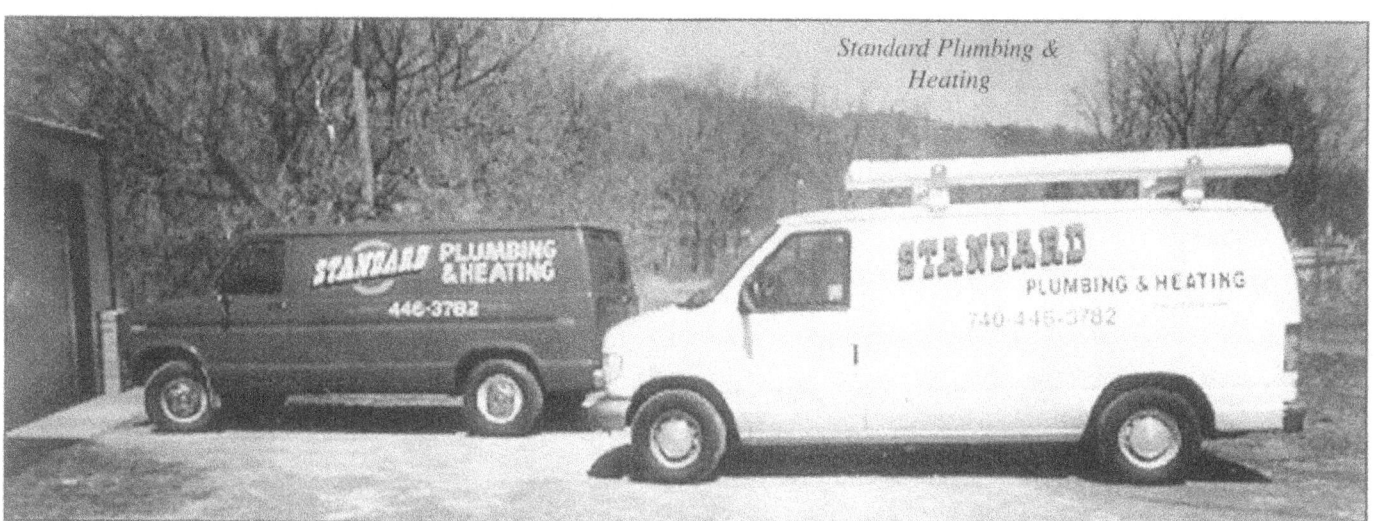

*Standard Plumbing & Heating*

*George A Tabit Broom Factory*

*Hutchinson Hardware Store*

# Gallia County Families

*Downtown Gallipolis, Ohio*

*George Massie home & family. A Jenny Lynn home was one built of unplanned rough lumber installed vertically & weather stripped with narrow strips of the same material. Many of the early homes were built like this in the interval between logs & weather boarding. This house was located on St. Rt. 141 on the site of the present Paul Stewart home (1977). Front Row: Doris, George, Armenta, Louise. Back Row: Artie, Herschel, Joan, Hollis, Homer Shaw, Gladys and Mildred*

**JOHN & ELIZABETH ADAMS** -John and Elizabeth had 2 sons John Quincy and George W.

I. George W. b9-18-1863 m. Jennie Thivenin 1-9-1896, Jennie died 11-16-1918 during the influenza outbreak. George d.2-27-1955 of old age.

*The Adams family - circa 1929
L: To r: Mike, Harry, Ray, Tom and Jesse Adams front: Jack Leroy, Nettie, Jack, Elizabeth, J.Q.(Pete), Quincy, and Annie Adams. Dog - Tiddlewinks*

II.John Quincy (Pete) b. 2-5-1853 in Rocksprings, Meigs Co., Oh. Pete was a moulder by trade. Pete married Mary (Elizabeth) Martin on 8-13-1881. Elizabeth was b.5-21-1863, d/o Henry & Mary Doyle Martin. Henry & Mary met on the ship coming from Ireland to America. Henry was from Wicklow Co. Ireland. Pete and Elizabeth moved to Gallia County in 1892 their youngest son was 4 mth. old. Pete d. 10-30-1935 and Elizabeth d.3-4-1950.

They had four sons.

A. Jesse Booth Adams b.1-24-1882, died 9-13-1938 m. Annie Pittard, they lived in Georgia. They had 5 children.

1. Lynn Elizabeth, 2. Jessie B., 3. S. Marian, 4. A. Janie, 5. J. Quincy.

B.Cleveland (Ray) Adams b.1-13-1885, d.5-22-1951, 1st Ethel Oliver in 1905. One child to this union, Thelma Lee Adams b.9-23-1905, d.4-28-1983.

Thelma m. Leroy Lester.

Ray's 2nd. m. Lillie Pearl Hudson. (the Georgia Peach) they had one son, Jack Leroy b. 12-20-1920,d. 1-25-1970. Jack m. Dorothy Ballard they had one son

Donald Ray (Moose) Adams b.1-6-1953, d.10-97.

Ray a WWI vet, Jack a WWII vet and Moose a Vietnam vet.

C.Theodore Thomas (Tom) Adams b.3-16-1889, d.2-28-1974 m. Nettie Frances Lawrence Dulaney. They celebrated their 50th". Wedding anniversary 12-02-1969. Tom was a WWI vet. They had 3 children.

1.Llada (Bonita) Dulaney b.6-14-1917, d.3-9-1978

2.John (Jack) Quincy Adams b.9-30-1920. Jack was a WWII vet.

3.Derry Eugene Adams b.12-12-1927. Deny was a WWII vet.

D.Harry Homer Adams, b. 8-28-1892,d.3-28-1957 He was a WWI vet. Harry m. Cleo Crabtree 3-1-1913, Cleo b.2-20-1897. A son Harold Claire (Mike)

Adams b. 5-19-1913, d.9-10-1978. Mike m. Grace Lucille Leport. They had two daughters Julia and Shirleyann Elizabeth Adams b. 10-13-1935. Shirley m. Glenn Harold Adkins 7-29-1953. Harold b.5-9-1932. They had 3 children.

1.Lissa Michelle b.9-3-1956 m. Jerry Hill, 1 child Sherry Lachelle b.7- 29-1972 to this union. Lissa is married to Mark Curnutte.

2.Stephanie Rachelle *b.12-14-1957*, d.7-21-1005, m. Jerry Fillinger. They had 1 son. Andrew Jerome (A.J.) Fillinger b.3-23-1985. A.J. lives with his grandparent Shirley and Harold Adkins.

Harry at the time of his death was married to Anna Kent.

*Submitted by Deny Adams.*

**PHILLIP AND SUZANNE (MARR) ADKINS** - Philip Anthony Adkins and Suzanne Leigh Marr were married March 23, 2002, in the Golden Valley Chapel, in Pigeon Forge Tennessee.

*Suzanne and Philip Adkins, March 23,2002*

Suzanne, born April 19, 1980, is the youngest daughter of Larry Glenn and Karen Beattie Marr of Gallipolis. She is the granddaughter of Glenn T. Marr of Patriot and the late Mae Notter Marr. Her maternal grandparents are the late J. Walton and Goldie Click Beattie of Mason County, West Virginia. Suzanne's older sister is Sarah Beth Marr, born June 24,1977, of Gallipolis. Suzanne is a 1998 graduate of River Valley High School and Buckeye Hills Career Center.

Philip was born September 4, 1975, the son of Anthony and Joan Maynard Adkins of Ewington. He has two brothers, Adam Adkins, who has a son, Austin and Joshua Adkins who is married to Shanna Arthur. They have a son, Ryland. Philip is the grandson of Lucy Maynard and the late Jesse Maynard and Ruth Adkins and the late Everett Adkins.

Philip is a 1995 graduate of Vinton County High School and Buckeye Hills Career Center. He is employed as a mechanic with All Power Equipment in Athens, Ohio.Philip and Suzanne reside in Vinton, Ohio.

*Article submitted by Mrs. Larry Marr*

**HENRY WILSON AND NOLA MIRIAM ELLIOTT ALLISON FAMILY** - The Allison family came from the MacAlister clan of Scotland, and they immigrated to the United States in the early 1700's eventually settling in Haverstraw, NY and, briefly, in Greenbrier County, WV then on to Green, Perry, and Walnut Townships in Gallia County. Benjamin Allison, a Revolutionary War Veteran, was the common ancestor of Henry's family.

*Henry and Miriam Elliott Allison—Easter Sunday 1967*

Henry Wilson Allison (May 12, 1907—September 3, 1971) was born in Ross County to Dom Pedro Allison (November 3, 1875—December 24, 1956) and Cora Gallaugher Allison (March 23, 1884—July 30, 1948). Dom's parents were Henry Wilson and Anna Provens Allison. Cora's parents were Henry and Malinda Cooper Gallaugher. His sisters were Agnes (Clarence) Williams and Viola (Loren) Straight. Henry was a fine athlete in many sports, and was a retail grocer, farmer, and wholesale egg dealer.

The Walnut Township, Gallia County, Elliotts came from England originally.

Nola Miriam Elliott Allison (September 12, 1916—November 27, 2001) was born in Walnut Township to Stephen Monroe (August 31, 1874—April 23, 1953) and Carrie Lee Martin Elliott (March 13, 1875—November 4, 1964). Stephen's parents were Warren G. and Mary Notter Elliott. Carrie's parents were John Quincy Adams and America Saunders Martin. Miriam's brothers were: Harold (Elizabeth), Garland (Jennie Russell), and Clyde (Zella Fulks) Elliott. Her sisters were Ruby (Bill) Stevers, Fern (Stanley) Davis, and Beatrice (Harris) Wellman. Miriam worked at some downtown retail stores and eventually retired from Gallipolis Developmental Center after 20 + plus years of service.

Henry and Miriam met while she was a Gallia Academy High School student riding the school bus which Henry drove. They married on June 3, 1933, and moved to Huntington, WV in 1934 where they owned a retail grocery store and wholesale egg business for approximately 8 years moving back to Walnut Township, Gallia County, in 1942. Three children were born in Huntington: Carolyn Jean—l936 (Carl) Gillespie, Ronald Lee—1938 (Ruth Barr) Allison, and Sandra Sue—1942 (Ralph) Hutchinson. A forth child—Judy Lynn—l946 (Russell) Fellure was born in Gallipolis.

Their grandchildren are: Carl Marty (Sharon) Gillespie, Randy Jay Gillespie, Travis Allison Gillespie, Ronald Mark (Amy) Allison, Scott Wilson Allison, Jill Paige Allison (Doug) Cox, Brett David Hutchinson, and Jacqueline Sue Hutchinson. Their great—grandchildren are: Powers Cobourne and Bruce Colin Gillespie, Caleb Patrick, Nathaniel Mark and Logan Wells Allison, and Josiah Alan and Benjamin Luke Cox.

Henry and Miriam lived most of their lives in Walnut Township, Gallia County, and Gallipolis. They were long time members of the First Church of the Nazarene where they were very active in working and sharing their faith. They were very loving, caring parents and

friends. They are buried in Mound Hill Cemetery.
*Submitted by: Jean Allison Gillespie*

## DR. THOMAS JUDSON & ANNA (GRIFFITH) ALLISON FAMILY

-Thomas Judson Allison was born 14 April 1870 at Centerpoint, Jackson County, Ohio.

His great-grandfather, Benjamin Allison, was born in New York state abt 1750. He served under Col. Wisner & Capt. Baly in the Revolutionary War. He married Rachel (?) and they had nine children, one of whom was Thomas. Benjamin died in Gallia County in 1807. His gravesite has never been located but his descendents have placed a headstone in Centenary Cemetery, Gallia County, Ohio.

Thomas Allison, grandfather of T.J., was born 24 March 1798. On 28 August 1817 he married Nancy Carter and they had twelve children, the last of whom was Henry David Allison, father of Thomas Judson. Thomas died 5 October 1868 in Gallia County, Ohio. He and Nancy were buried first in Chick Cemetery but later moved, at least their markers were, to M.E. Cemetery at Patriot, Ohio.

Henry David Allison was born 6 June 1841 in Gallia County, Ohio. He served in the 56th Regiment Ohio Volunteers during the Civil war. He was wounded, 11 July 1863 in the battle at Jackson, Mississippi. On 26 March 1868 he married Eleanor Jones Benglog. This union produced the following children: Anna Viola, Thomas Judson, Margaret Emma, Eldora, David C., William Matere, Benjamin Maron, John Edward, Jennie Edith, Ernest, Mary Elisabeth and Evan Harrison. Henry died 26 November 1899 and Eleanor 21 October 1915. Both are buried in Centerpoint Cemetery, Jackson County, Ohio.

Thomas J., son of Henry David and Eleanor (Jones) Allison, was born 14 April 1870 on the Allison homestead near Centerpoint, Ohio. He grew up on his father's farm at Centerpoint. After he left to attend college, he returned each summer to raise a crop of corn to help finance his medical education. He attended Rio Grande College, Lebanon College and received his M.D. degree from Baltimore University School of Medicine 14 April 1897. He practiced medicine in Centerpoint, Wellston, Centerville and Rio Grande, Ohio. Like all physicians in small communities a great deal of his practice was "making house calls". In the early years of his practice, this was done by horse and buggy. Many times when the weather was bad and Raccoon Creek was high, he had to be assisted on his rounds by the local farmers and their sturdy teams. When his wife and children talked him out of the buggy and into an automobile, his grandson at times rode in the rumble seat and opened gates for him. On 8 November 1899, at Nebo, Ohio he was united in marriage to Anna Griffiths and they had four children: Brinton J. married Hazel Carson, Margaret Eleanor married Francis Shane, Raymond T. married Evelyn Clark, Florence Mildred married William K. Welker.

Thomas J. practiced his profession for 39 years until his death on 3 august 1937. He and Anna are buried in the Baptist Cemetery, Rio Grande, Ohio.

*Submitted by: Wm. Allison Welker, grandson*

## DAVID MORGAN AND ETTA LORENE (WALKER) ALTIZER

- David was born June 26, 1925 near Northup, Ohio. He is a sixth generation Altizer of Emera Altizer who emigrated from Germany about 1750. Emera fought in the Revolutionary War. After the war he became a property owner in Montgomery County, Virginia. David's parents David Riley and Etta (Morgan) Altizer spent most of their lives on their dairy farm at Adamsville, Ohio. They had eight children, Sadie (Williams), Verne (deceased), Virgil died in infancy, Edna (Johnson), Garnet (Blazer), Orie, Hazel (Rice), and David.

All were members of the Calvary Baptist Church at Rio Grande.

*David M. & Etta l. Walker Altizer*

David's mother came from Wyoming County, West Virginia where her father operated a gristmill.

Etta (Walker) Altizer was born near Cora, Ohio November 25, 1928. Her parents were Jackson Tandy and Zelma (Phillips) Walker. Jack's father, Samuel Walker, came from Floyd County, Virginia to Gallia County in 1873. His mother, Elizabeth (Jones) Walker was born in Gallia County. Her father, David Griffith (Cardy) Jones, immigrated to this country from Wales in 1839 along with his father, Isaac, whose brother, John Jones, had immigrated earlier. David Griffith was a union soldier during the Civil War and is buried at Tyn Rhos Welch Cemetery.

Zelma was born at Swan Creek, Ohio daughter of Andrew and Etta (Trowbridge) Phillips. She was a descendant of Levi Trowbridge who fought in the Revolutionary War, and also lived at Swan Creek. The Trowbridge Family came to this country from Tauton, England as sea merchants about 1636 and lived near Boston, Massachusetts.

Jack and Zelma met while employed in Gallipolis and were married October 9, 1926.

Jack was a labor foreman for the State Highway Department. They raised their children on a small farm near Cora, they were Orva (Heissenbuttle), Etta (Altizer), Marcella (Harrison, Gilliam), Mary (Niday), Jackson Jr. (deceased) and Karen (McElyea). All were members of Cora Methodist Church, where Jack's mother was a charter member.

David and Etta met shortly after World War II. Etta was a senior at Rio Grande High School and he had just returned from serving in the Navy. They were married August 17, 1947. They lived at Adamsville and became the parents of David Rick, June 28, 1949 and Gary Lee, November 16, 1952. November 1955 they moved to their present home on State Route 325 South of Rio Grande. Shortly after they established their grade A dairy and had a very successful operation for 30 years.

Rick graduated from Rio Grande College, where he met and married Zee Dilley. He became a Jackson Production Credit Association employee. He worked in Ohio until 1990 when he accepted a job with Northwest Farm Credit Services in Spokane, Washington. Rick is Vice President of credit for five Northwest states.

Gary graduated from Morehead State University in Kentucky with a degree in Agriculture. He married Elizabeth Martin and soon established Altizer Farm Supply on Centerpoint Road just east of 325.

David and Etta have two grandchildren, Brian (who married Jessica Frank of Spokane, November 27, 1999) and Teresa. They have two great grandchildren, Bretton Lambert and Sydney Altizer. They are both 9th generation Altizer and Trowbridge Revolutionary War descendants.

## ORA HATTIE LEE AND ROBERT HUGH ANDERSON

- Ora Hattie Lee (November 14, 1894-November 14, 1994) was the daughter of Samuel Lee and Sylvinia Evaline "Eva" Harris Lee. She was one of ten siblings and all were raised in the Maple Shade area of Gallipolis, Gallia County, Ohio. She attended the Elijah Barnes School. She married Robert Hugh Anderson (1880-1957) on April 20, 1914, and they were the parents of six children. One died in infancy and was buried in the Pine Street Colored cemetery (the grave can no longer be found). The other living children are:

1. Arnetta (July 4, 1914) married Samuel Edward Dexter (1920-1983) of Nelsonville, Ohio, on June 22, 1942, in Gallipolis, OH.
2. Janet Mae (March 27, 1916) was a cook for Evans and Circle Restaurants on Second Avenue, Gallipolis.
3. Robert Christopher (June 30, 1926) served in the U. S. Army and married Helen Louise "Red" Armstrong (deceased) on November 22, 1948.
4. Ruth Elaine (July 17, 1929) married William Jackson (deceased) of Gallipolis, Ohio, and resides in Oklahoma City, OK.
5. Joyce Margaret (March 26, 1936) worked at Oscars Restaurant on Second Avenue, Gallipolis.

All attended the Lincoln Colored School and Gallia Academy High School, Gallipolis. Ora worked as a housekeeper for the Bovie and Thomas families. It was a good thing my grandmother could clean house because she hated cooking. If Grandma Lee had not lived with my grandparents when her husband died, the family would not know what a "home cooked meal' was. I remember when Grandma Ora put the water on to boil! She lived to be 100 so we had a lot of those water boiling experiences.

Robert was from Winchester, Kentucky. He was a jockey standing 4 feet 10 inches and raced horses throughout Gallia and Lawrence Counties. It was said that he was one of the best jockeys in the area. He worked for Holzer Hospital and the Ohio State Highway Department where he lost an eye and received a pension until his death. Robert's parents or siblings are not known.

One of my fondest memories of my grandfather was the day he taught me to tell time. He said "Bobette tell me what time it is." I said, "I can't tell time." In about 30 minutes, I could—thanks to my grandpa.

My grandparents moved from Chatham Avenue in Maple Shade to Fourth Avenue in Gallipolis. One of the greatest things about the house on Fourth was that it had no grass in the front yard. Why no grass? My grandparents allowed every child in the neighborhood to play in the front yard. My sisters and I went everyday to grandma's house to play and get some great food—from Grandma Lee, of course.

Family histories are under Benjamin Lee, Samuel Lee, Arnetta Anderson Dexter and Bobette Dexter Braxton.

*Submitted by Bobette Dexter Braxton*

**BRADY THOMAS ANGEL & BELVA MARTIN ANGEL FAMILY** - Brady was born June 18, 1898 in Gallia County, Ohio Twp., Bladen, Ohio. His great-grandfather, Joseph Angel was born 1818 in Ohio. Joseph was married to Elizabeth (Louisa) Gilmore June 12, 1840. Their children were: Matthew born 1841, William Henry born 1845, and Joseph born 1849. Joseph was a charter member of Elizabeth Chapel Church, Yellowtown, Ohio. His 50 acres of land was located at N4. T4, R15, Section #10 in Harrison twp.

*Brady & Belva Angel Wedding Picture July 7, 1920*

Brady's grandfather, William Henry Angel born 8-8-1845, Northup, Ohio, married Lucinda Chandler, December 19, 1871. He served in Co. K. 3rd WV Calvary during the Civil War. He was a messenger between General's Sherman and Sheridan troops. He was a very skilled horseman. The love and care for horses remained with him his entire life. Their children were: William Sheridan born 1870, John Sherman born 1874, Aneta (Nettie) Shaw born 1879, Louisa May Boyd born 1883.

Brady's father was William Sheridan Angel. He married Amanda Shull Larson from Glenwood, West Virginia. To this union were: J. Leafe Larson born 1891, Earl A. born 1894, Virgie Angel Caldwell born 1896, Edith Mae Angel Porter born 1906, Brady Thomas born 1898, Vertie Angel Mounts born 1902, Edith Mae Angel Porter born 1906, Lloyd C. born 1909. William was a river boatman for many years at Dam #26.

Brady married Belva Martin July 7, 1920. Daughter of James V. Martin and Myrtle Elliott Martin. Granddaughter of Jessie Martin and Rebecca McKinley Martin, also of William Elliott and Eliza McGuire Elliott from Swan Creek, Ohio twp.

Brady and Belva were the parents of sixteen children: Donald, James, Ralph E., Raymond R. (Bill), Betty L. Crouse, Josephine A. Gibson, M. Irene Holley, Earnest E., died in infancy, Dorothy L. Perkins, Barbara A. Chambers, Shirley L., Lucy J. Westover, Audrey M. Saunders, Brady F., Jr., Charles Roger, and Pauline Jeffers. Five of the boys served in the United States Military.

In the early years, Brady was employed by Hopson Railroad and the Nickel Plant of Huntington, WV. He was a lifetime farmer. He owned 96 acres of land on Cargo Road, Clay twp.

Belva Martin Angel, his wife, was an excellent seamstress, cook, and gardener. She was skilled at preserving vegetables and meats of all sorts. Canning 200 jars of each variety was her goal, until the family became smaller. She was never too busy to share with her fifty-three grandchildren.

The Angell Trail began on the Island of Guernsey, then to England in 1485, to Providence, RI 1631, Stokes and Surry County, North Carolina in 1758. Six Angell brothers: Mathias, Berry, Lawrence, Joshua, John L., Jr., and Henry, sons of the Rev John L. Angell and Mary Griner Angell of North Carolina, came to Gallia County, Ohio between 1812 and 1818. They settled in Clay, Harrison, and Ohio twps. According to Hardesty's History, B. Angel and Henry Angel were one of the first settlers in Clay twp. Their father, Rev. John L. Angell, was in the Revolutionary War. He served 11 months and 15 days. He was in the battle of Camden and in two battles at Wilmington, N.C. He was a private and First Sargent with north Carolina troops under Captains' Salatheel Martin, Bostic, Minor Smith, and Hill, also Colonials Hampton and Campbell. Their properties in Harrison twp., on State Route 218 became known as Angel or Angeltown. There are signs marking the location of Angel today. There was a grocery store at Angel, plus the Porter/Angel/Trotter, one room school.

Joshua Angell and his family left Gallia County in the late 1820's for Vanderburg County, Indiana. Lawrence Angell and his family moved to Mason County, (VA) WV. Berry, Henry and John L., Jr's descendants are still very much a part of Gallia County, Ohio.

*Submitted by: Reda K. Fowler*

**MARY ANNE TROTTER BAILEY** - "White Squaw of the Kanawha"

Mary Anne's story was part of a period when Virginia's peoples lived on the edge of a savage empire whose border had been pushed westward for over a century and a half. Settlers arrived and planted their roots in the new world, and later expanded their civilization beyond the Ohio and Mississippi rivers.

Born Mary Anne Hennis in Liverpool, England, probably in 1742. Her father served in the army under the Duke of Marlborough during the war under Queen Anne's rule. We are told she attended school from 1748 to 1760. She came from a family of some social standing because formal education among children of lower classes was denied.

*Ann Bailey, The Heroine Of Point Pleasant.*

Her parents were dead by 1761 and Anne indentured herself as a servant to pay her passage to America. The 19 year old came to the new world to join relatives, the Bells, who immigrated to the region around Staunton, Virginia. She probably served out her indenture by working and teaching the children in some other household in the immediate vicinity.

We believe that Anne and Richard Trotter were married in a church near Staunton. Richard was a veteran of Braddock's Defeat and a renowned fighter in border wars. Anne settled down to be a housewife and mother to their son, William.

*Bailey Chapel*

When Richard was killed on October 10, 1774, Anne's life took a drastic turn. She set out on a path of revenge against Indians.

She enlisted the aid of Mrs. Moses Mann in making a home for William. Her bravery astounded the Border War Veterans in the Garrison commanded by Colonel William Clendenin. She became a messenger and scout, galloping from one frontier post to another. She purposely let the Indians know that she "possessed supernatural powers" and true to their primitive ways they apparently believed her. This could explain why she was never taken prisoner by her red enemies.

One story goes that she was being chased by some Indians. An impassable thicket forced her to dismount and abandon her horse, Liverpool. Anne quickly scuttled into a hollow sycamore log on which the Indians took a breather without ever suspecting she was lying beneath them.

In 1785 Anne married John Bailey, a distinguished border leader from southwestern Virginia. He helped carry the mortally wounded Colonel Charles Lewis from the field of the Battle of Point Pleasant. The Reverend John McCue performed the ceremony which is recorded in Marriage Record I (Page 7) of the Lewis County, West Virginia, clerk's office.

In 1788 the couple went to Fort Lee, built by Clendenin on the present site of Charleston, West Virginia. John was a member of the garrison and Anne was the messenger between Fort Lee and Fort Randolph (Point Pleasant).

In the autumn of 1791, Fort Lee was under siege by a British-led horde of Indians. The War of the Revolution had ended, but there was continuing pressure in the border country by Indians and British, pressure that would end only with the War of 1812. Powder was used up at a dangerous rate and there was very little remaining. A hundred forty miles to the east was plenty at Fort Savannah along a wilderness road. She left in the night to avoid detection and raced along a mired packed trail to Fort Savannah at Lewisburg. She returned safe with the powder but exhausted to Fort Lee and the hurrahs of a grateful people. The powder supply was enough to save the Fort.

After the Treaty of Greenville (1795) Anne's warring years came to a close. Her son, William Trotter, and Mary Cooper were the first Virginians to be married in the old town of Gallipolis in 1800.

Two years later John Bailey died and was buried on a farm about 15 miles above Charleston. Anne went to live with William and Mary near Point Pleasant.

Unable to discard her wilderness ways, she rode back and forth from Point Pleasant to Lewisburg and Staunton as letter carrier and express messenger for several years.

In 1817 at age 75, she made her final trip to Charleston and spent the summer there in that region renewing old acquaintances and riding familiar trails. The next year she moved with her son to Harrison Township, Gallia County, Ohio. William had sold his Kanawha farm about three miles above Point Pleasant to William Sterett. In Gallia County, William was highly respected and served as Justice of the Peace for 21 years. There were 10 children born to this union, one was given the father's name of William. This William Trotter in turn had a son named Thomas. Thomas, when he married, had a son named, Virgil, who was my father.

Mary Anne Henness Trotter Bailey's worn, tired heart stopped in the autumn of 1825 age 83 years. She was buried in the Trotter Graveyard in Harrison Township, Gallia County, Ohio.

In 1901 the members of the Point Pleasant Battle Monument Commission learned the descendants were willing for her remains to be removed to the Tu Ende Wei Park in Point Pleasant, West Virginia, where it is today. The Colonel Charles Lewis Chapter of the Daughters of the American Revolution was responsible for this. The Mansion House Museum in the park displays a framed floral design made from Anne's hair, a general custom of the time.

Another memorial to her is about 8 miles from Covington, Virginia, on Highway U.S. 220, which leads through Falling Springs Valley. A large boulder beside the highway bears a metal tablet that says "Near this spot stood the rude hut in which Mad Anne Bailey spent the last years of her life. As a scout and Indian fighter she rendered valuable service to the first settlers of this section. Placed by the Rainbow Ridge Chapter of the DAR." This tablet is false because she lived her last years with her son.

A large boulder on Kanawha Boulevard in Charleston commemorates Anne Bailey's ride to bring powder to Fort Lee. Also there is a marker to her in Watoga State Park (on Route 63) near Workman's Ridge, which Anne is said to have used as a lookout point. There was a DAR Chapter in Charleston named the Anne Bailey Chapter.

There is an Anne Bailey Chapel on Route 218 Gallia County, Ohio, which holds services today. This Chapel was built in 1908 on the Trotter property where Anne Bailey died.

We can sing today "America the Beautiful" because the immigrants made their dreams come true. I like to think Anne Bailey has made "America the Beautiful" in her small way for all of us.

*Submitted by Mary Trotter and John and Effie Trotter.*

**BAIRD - CHENEY -** My Maternal Great Grandparents were Ora Baird (1890-1952) and Lola Gail Halfhill (1897-1966). They were married in 1916. They owned a farm in Addison Township and attended the Campaign Church. They had the following children: Wayne (1917-1978), Flossie (1919-1985), Francis (1921-1976), Twins: Dillie (1927) and Della (1927-1997), and Elmer (1931-1991). They also had two children that died in infancy.

*Ora & Gail Baird*

Wayne (my Maternal Grandfather) married Ella Bell Hershman (1917-1970) in 1937. Ella and Wayne started their married life farming in Addison Township. After World War II he moved his family to the city of Gallipolis where he went into business with Oscar, Glen, and Henry Baird and Roy Denney selling Plymouth and DeSoto automobiles and Case tractors. He later started the Ohio Valley Wrecking Company. He also owned a junkyard in South Bloomfield. Wayne and Ella had the following children: Sara (1938), Marvin (1940), John (1942), Ora (1944), Linda (1952), Louise (1953), and Regina (1953-1970). When Ella and Wayne divorced, he sold his business and moved to South Bloomfield and operated his junkyard there. He married Dorothy Day and they had the following children: Michael (1957), Phillip (1959), Charles (1961), Hope (1962), Patty (1963), and Gail (1965).

They lived in South Bloomfield until his last child was born. At which time he moved back to Gallipolis to operate the Gallipolis Auto Wrecking Company located right across the road from his first junkyard. He later became part owner with Roy Denney. They sold the junkyard to make room for Gallipolis' first shopping center. They moved their junkyard to Bunch Road. When Roy retired Wayne became the sole owner and operator of this business until his death. His children by the first wife attended school in the Gallipolis City District. They also attended the First Church of God then located on Third Avenue.

My Paternal Great Grandparents were Silas (1846-1928) and Elizabeth Cheney (1856-1923). They had the following children: John (1874-1951), Pearl (1876), Burton (1879), Guy (1881), Carrie (1884), Jennie (1887), Carl (1894-1930). Burton and Carl were stogie makers. They sold their stogies here and overseas.

John Leonard (my paternal grandfather) married Georgia Hylton (1900-1993). They had the following children: Lillie (1920-1996), John Junior (1922), Enabelle (1924), Jennie (Dot) (1927), Ray 1929-1997), Carl (1931). John was a painter. He painted houses and helped paint the Old Silver Bridge, which was dedicated in 1927.

Carl married Sara Baird in 1958 and they had the following children: Carl Leonard (1959), Timothy Ray (1961), twins Carla Denise (1963) and Richard Wayne (1963), and Delman Russell (1965).

Carl is a veteran of the Korean War, worked for North Produce and later the Gallipolis Developmental Center where he retired in 1994. He also drove a school bus for the Gallipolis City Schools for a number of years. Sara worked at the G. C. Murphy Co. for 36 years.

Carl Leonard joined the United States Navy in 1980 and retired in 2000. He now lives in Maryland.

Tim started to work for the Kroger Co. in 1977 and is now a manager for Kroger's located on Route 60 in Huntington, WV.

Carla married Paul Finnicum (1959) in 1988. She started to work in 1981 for State Farm Ins. Carroll Snowden Agency. She worked for State Farm until 1993 when their second child was born when she decided to quit to raise their two sons: John Paul (1989) and Joseph David (1993). Paul is a veteran of the United States Army where he served in the 75th Ranger Regiment from 1984-1988. He is now employed at M&G Polymers in Apple Grove. WV.

Richard married Brenda Lee Price (1962) in 1981. They have two children: Jessica Lee (1982) and Jennifer Renee (1988). Richard works at the Kyger Creek Power Plant and owns and operates a business at the flea market. Brenda is an employee at Wal-Mart. Jessica is a student at Marshall University and works part time at Wal-Mart.

Delman served in the United States Navy for four years. He was a car salesman at Turnpike in Gallipolis and also at Hamilton Chevrolet in Procterville. He is now the manager for Oakwood Homes in Gallipolis, OH.

My mother, Sara says that some of the best memories she has of her childhood began at her grandparent's farm. She talks about going upon the hill behind their house and chipping chunks of salt off the salt blocks and eating it. (Mom says no one can convince her that other farm kids didn't do the same thing). She also remembers catching the horses and leading them to an old saw mill so they could climb on them and ride them all over the hills. She also says that growing up in a junkyard was fun too. Their favorite games were jumping cars and finding a car with gas and driving it until the gas was gone, then they would get another car.

*Submitted by Carla Finnicum*

**LOLA GAIL (HALFHILL) AND ORA BAIRD -** Lola Gail Halfhill was born November 4, 1897 near Kyger (Cheshire Township, Gallia County, Ohio). Gail and Ora Baird (born February 5, 1890) met at Poplar Ridge Church and fell in love. When the young couple was courting, Ora and his brother Stacy (see The Bairds, Joseph & Esther) often walked Gail and her sister Nellie (see Frank & Dillie Halfhill) home after church. On January 15, 1916, Gail and Ora were married in Gallipolis, Ohio by Justice of the Peace Fred Millisor.

*Ora Baird with Jack and Jill*

A family man and hard worker, Ora worked for the railroad at Hobson yards in Meigs County. In 1922, they bought a large farm near Campaign Church (Addison Township Gallia County, Ohio). Ora mined coal to burn in the farmhouse fireplaces and carried it out of the hand dug shaft in a small cart on rails. In addition to farming several acres, Jack and Jill worked with Ora on the county roads and in the orchard he loved.

Ora and Gail were members of Bulaville Grange and good neighbors always helping others. The family attended Campaign Freewill Baptist Church where Gail took an active part in the Happy Homemakers Club and often spoke of her love for her family and friends. Always willing to do more than their share, Ora and Gail (see photo Baird! Cheney) worked together to provide a home for their children and grandchildren. Ora and Gail's large family often got together and their grandchildren's childhoods were filled with loving memories. Even though now grown many with grandchildren of their own, anytime they get together someone always says do you remember that time when...

On July 22, 1952, Ora died at his home in Addison Twp in the same small community where he spent most of his life. Even though ill more than 5 years, Ora bore his suffering with patience and found great pleasure in talking with his family and friends of his belief in the Divine Master.

After her husband's death, Gail and her son Elmer continued to operate the farm with help and encouragement from family and friends. Gail died unexpectedly on the Sunday (12/18/1966) before Christmas and was laid to rest next to her husband at Campagin only a few miles from where they lovingly raised their children and grandchildren: Marvin Wayne (2/19/1917-9/22/1978) see Baird-Cheney. Flossie Dale (8/19/1919-9/23/1985) married Ernest Boggess (9/16/1917) and lived in West Virginia— children: Donald (1938 - 1993), Robert (1942) & Dennis (1940). Frances Helen (11/24/1921-06/29/1976) married Wilmer Parsons (1913-1968) and lived in Vinton and Gallia Counties: children: Dorothy, Wilmer Jr., Elmer Ray, Esther, and Barbara (1954-1981). A daughter (1924) and son (12/9/1925 stillborn) died in infancy. Twin daughters Della Alena (see Baird-Casto) and Dillie Elinene (see Baird-Cormick) were born January 12, 1927. Lola Mae and Charles William grew up with their Mother (Dillie) in their Grandparents' home. Named for their beloved Uncle Elmer (see The Bairds), Elmer Franklin (3/8/1931 - 4/5/1991) married Bonnie Litchfield (10/18/1932) in 1954: children: John, Steve, and Debbie.

*Submitted by: Lola M. (McCormick) McCoy*

**MARVIN BAIRD FAMILY -** I am the second child of Wayne Baird and Ella Belle (Hersman) Baird. I have an older sister, Sara Lou Cheney. Look under Cheney for more about her. Next my brother John William Baird and wife Ellen of Reno, Nevada. Then Ora Franklin Baird, his wife Alice and daughter Terri of Eugene, Oregon. Sister Linda Sue (Richard) Macias of Fontana, California. Sister Ella Louise ( Joe) Woodall of Gallipolis. She has two children. A son Chris Somerville and daughter Tabby Somerville. My mother Ella and my 16 year old sister Regina, were both killed in a car accident in 1970.

*Marvin and Phyllis Baird Marvin Ray Baird Angie Baird Walters*

Mom and dad had divorced. Dad remarried. He married Dorothy Day and from this union came six children. Patty (Tom) Sims and three children, residing in Camden, Ohio, Hope (Mike) Armstrong and son live in Orlinda, Tennessee, Gail Baird of Gallipolis, Mike Baird and children of Gallipolis, Phil Baird and three children of Gallipolis, Charles (Cricket) Baird, wife Ellen and daughter of Gallipolis.

I was born and raised in Gallia Co. My Family were all farmers. Later dad went into the junkyard business, used auto parts and scrap. I grew up between dad's junkyard and my grandparent's farm, which was located on Possum Trot Road. I had always loved the farm, so when my grandpa died and my uncle Elmer got disabled from an accident, I moved to the farm full time to help my grandma and aunt keep the farm going. I remember this to be a time of hard work and long hours, but I also remember this as a very special time in my life. I had always helped do everything around the farm so I already knew what needed to be done.

My brothers John and Ora and I all joined the Marine Corps. We didn't join at the same time but we did serve at the same time.

While home on leave I met Phyllis Ann Butler. She had moved to Gallipolis from Ironton to attend Holzer Hospital School of Nursing. After graduating, she went to work at the hospital. Phyllis and I were married on December 20, 1964. We started our life together in California. But I got called to duty in Vietnam and Phyllis returned home. Later Ora got orders to Vietnam also. We served side by side for over six months.

While in Vietnam, Phyllis gave me a very nice Christmas present. Our son Marvin Ray was born on December 23,1965. I received the good news from the Red Cross on Christmas Day. Our daughter Angela Marie (Angie) was born on December 5, 1969. Angie is a nurse working at Cabell Huntington Hospital. She was also Homecoming Queen her senior year in high school. Marvin Ray (Bub) is the Manager of Tom's Auto Clinic of Gallipolis. And his wife Wendy live close by on Basil Road. We have two very special grandchildren, Cassandra Nicole (Cassie) and Elijah Adam.

As a family we have lived on Shoestring Ridge since 1969. After my discharge from the Marines, I went to work at Goodyear in Apple Grove, W. Va. My brother Ora and I had just gone to work on the afternoon shift when the Silver Bridge fell. After six years there, I moved to the Gavin Plant (AEP) in 1974. I worked there 27 years and retired February 1, 2001.

My family attends the First Church of God, 109 Garfield Ave. We have served on many boards and committees over the years. Phyllis teaches small children. Our children grew up there and went through the youth programs... And then.

**BAIRDS OF GALLIA CO. -** Our great-great grandfather, Richmond ( 1817- ____ ), married Catherine Thaxton in 1843. They lived in Virginia, where their first two children were born. They moved here from Prince Edwards Co., Va. They bought land in Addison Twp. The 1850 Census stated, they lived in Dwelling #861, family #871. His occupation was listed as a farmer. Richmond and Catherine had the following children: Mary (1849-1895), Alexander (1847——), and Joseph (1849-1917). They purchased more land in Addison Twp. in 1897. There was a log house along the road and a sandstone house on the hill, on this property. They helped quarry the rock and build the Campaign Church. They were buried in the White Oak Cemetery.

Their son Joseph our great grandfather married Esther Halfhill (1855-1907) in 1876.They had the following children: Minnie (1878-1878), Dollie (1881-1922), Elmer (1894-1936), Ira (1887-1966), Ora (1890-1952), Stacy (1891-1957), Ethel Baird (1893-1969) and one daughter, Lydia stillborn (?). All their children were born in Addison Twp. and buried in Campaign Cemetery. The land for the Cemetery was deeded to Campaign Cemetery trustees in two parts. First part by Joseph Baird and second part by Stacy Baird. Later the cemetery trustees deeded the cemetery to Addison Twp. trustees.

*Baird Family*

Three of Joseph Bairds' children married three of Frank and Dillie Lemley Halfhills' children. Ora Baird married Lola Gail Halfhill (1-15-1916). Stacy Baird married Nellie Halfhill (12-23-1922). Ethel Baird married Ora Halfhill (6-4-?). Dollie married John Swisher (1878-1960) in 1904. They made their home in West Virginia for a while and then moved to Bradbury, Ohio. Dollie loved children and some of the family looked to her as a mother. Dollie and John had five children: Ross (1904-1927), Muriel (1907-1985), George (1909-1910), Kitty (1912-1918), and John (1917-1988). Dollie died in Bradbury but was buried in Campaign Cemetery. After her death, John and son bought a farm in Gallia Co. and lived there until he died. His son's name was John. Elmer the oldest son of Joseph and Esther, gave up his schooling at an early age to help his parents with his brothers and sisters. Elmer never married. He and his brother Stacy bought their home place after the death of their parents. Elmer devoted his whole life to others. First to his brothers and sisters, then to his nieces and nephews. He passed away at the family home where he was born.

Ira married Alice Jones (1891-1971) in 1907. Ira and Alice moved to Middleport early in their married life. Ira was working at the Friendly Wells Furniture Store during the 1913 flood. Later he worked at the Hobson RR Yard Ira and Alice had the following children: Ada (1908- ), Garnet (1909-1909), Henry (1911-1972), Harry (1913-1941), Oscar (1915-1997), Raymond (1919-1922), Glenn (1919- ), twin boys (1919) stillborn. Ira divorced and came back to Gallia Co. and bought some land. He married Nannie Shriver. They had two sons: Roscoe (1930-1930) and Gerald (1931-1970). Aunt Nan was always good to Ira's children from his first marriage. As far as our family was concerned Aunt Nan was the best cook in Gallia County.

Oscar was Sheriff of Gallia Co. for two terms and finished out another term. Glenn helped build the American Legion hall and was Post Commander for three years. Ora married Gail Halfhill (1897-1966) in 1916. They moved to Middleport where he worked at the Hobson RR Yard. In 1921 they moved back to Gallia Co. and purchased a 78 acre farm from Joseph Rife. The price was one dollar plus other valuables. He purchased land two other times for the farm. Ora did his farming with two mules, named Jack and Jill. The mules were treated like pets. They had the following children: Wayne (1917-1978), Flossie (1919-1985), Francis (1921-1976), Dillie (1927- ) and her twin Della (1927-1997), and Elmer (1931-1991). A son (1925) and daughter (1929) died in infancy.

Ora and Gail started the Baird reunion. After they were both gone Wayne kept it going. It was later changed to the Baird - Halfhill reunion, bringing the two families together. After Wayne died Oscar kept it going for some time and then he put it in the hands of Wayne's son, Marvin.

Stacy served 15 months in England and France during World War I. When he returned home he and his brother Elmer farmed their land. After Elmer died, Stacy farmed the land until his health failed him. In 1952 he sold the land to the Coal Co. and moved to town.

From Stacy's marriage to Nellie Halfhill (1900-1954) came the following children: Sylvia (1923-1999), Charles ( 1927-1947), Grace (1929- ), Nora (1932- ), Stella (1934-1975), Mary (1936-1994), and Ann (1939- ).

Oscar bought the home place back and it is now in his family. All of our families have fond memories of the many Sundays spent on the home places. (Men pitching horseshoes, and the ladies cooking and visiting, and the children being children.)

Ethel married Ora Halfhill. They lived in Middleport where he worked in the Hobson RR yard. They later moved back to Gallia Co. where he worked in the coal mines. They had the following children: Lucille (1919-1971), Charles (1918-1918), Stacy Kenneth (1919-1977), Wilmer (Bee), Dana (1935 - 1985), and Georgia and Audrey died in infancy.

**STACY BAIRD FAMILY -** Our parents were Stacy Baird (1891-1957) and Nellie Dale Halfhill Baird (1900-1954). Stacy was the son of Joseph (1849-1917) and Esther Halfhill Baird (1855-1907). Nellie was the daughter of Francis Franklin Halfhill (1861-1946) and Dillie Rachel Lemley Halfhill (1874-1956). Our father Stacy Baird was raised on a farm in Addison Township and attended While Oak School and Campaign Church.

*Stacy & Nellie Baird*

When his mother and father passed away Stacy and his brother Elmer bought out the shares of the other brothers and sister. Stacy remained on the farm until he went to the Army on April 25, 1918. He served in France and England and was discharged from the Army on July 16, 1919. He returned to the farm and married Nellie Dale Halfhill on December 23, 1922. They became the parents of seven children: Sylvia Vail (1923-1999), Charles William (1927-1947), Grace Irene (1929), Nora Belle (1932), Stella Alene (1934-1975), Mary Ann (1936-1994) and Anna Mae (1939). Nellie Halfhill was raised on a farm in Cheshire Township and attended Africa and Jericho Schools and Poplar Ridge Church and later Champaign Church. Nellie and Stacy had a love for high school basketball games. The family also had a lot of picnics and gatherings in the summer. The women spent the afternoon visiting and the men and children played horseshoes and other games. Our parents stayed on the farm until our father had a stroke in 1952 and was then unable to work.

They sold the farm to a coal company and bought a home on Fourth Avenue in Gallipolis where they lived until they passed away. All family members except Sylvia and Wendell are buried at Campaign Cemetery. Nellie and Stacy's oldest child, Sylvia Baird, attended Oil Hollow, Bulaville Grade School, and graduated from Bidwell-Porter High School. She then attended an office training school in Columbus, Ohio. After graduation Sylvia worked at Pixley Electric in Columbus, Columbus and Southern Electric in Gallipolis, and then returned to Columbus to work at Columbus Coated Fabric until she was laid off. She returned to Gallipolis and married James Mayes in March 1946 and they have three sons: Harold Edward (1947), Harry Wendell (1949-1977) and Roscoe Stacy (1951). Sylvia worked at the glove factory in Gallipolis and after her children were born she moved to Athens, Ohio. She and James later divorced and she worked at Kimes Nursing Home in Athens and was a member of the Salvation Army Church. She resided in Athens until her death, whereupon she was buried in Columbus, Ohio. Sylvia's oldest son, Eddie, married Margaret Ann Hanna (1946) and they have two daughters, Gretchen Marie (1966) and Rhonda Pauline (1968). Gretchen has two sons, Christopher Michael (1989) and Joshua Duncan (1997). They all make their homes in Columbus. Wendell lived in Columbus until his death in 1977. Stacy married Bonnie Sexton and they later divorced. They had one son, Stacy. Nellie and Stacy's only son, Charles Baird, attended Oil Hollow, Bulaville, and graduated from Bidwell-Porter High School in 1944. He worked for Columbus Coated Fabrics until he joined the Army in 1945. He served in Italy. While home on terminal leave he was killed in a car accident in Cheshire, Ohio in January 1947. Grace Baird attended Bulaville Grade School and graduated from Bidwell-Porter High School in 1947. She worked at the glove factory and Baird Motor Sales. She married Ray Leonard Cheney (1929-1997) on April 15, 1955. Ray served in the Air Force from 1948-1968. During their marriage they lived in Maine, England, Indiana and North Carolina. Following Ray's retirement from the military they returned home to Gallipolis in 1968. He then went to work at Federal-Mogul in 1969 and retired from there on July 1, 1993. Grace worked at Kanauga Drive-In. While serving in the military they had five children: John Leonard (1956), Elizabeth Ann (1957), both born in England; Nancy Sue (1958-1959) and Gary Dale (1961), both born in Maine; and Donald Ray (1963) born in Indiana. John married Joyce Lynn Casto in 1979 and they have a daughter, Tracy Lynn (1984). Ann married Kelly Wayne Ager in 1995 and they have a daughter, Kaci Rae (1997). Gary married Susan Marie Swanson in 1984 and they have a daughter, Megan Rene (1987). Don married Rhonda Colleen Hughes in 1992. Don served in the U.S. Navy and they reside in Pensacola, Florida. Nora Baird attended Bulaville Grade School and graduated from Bidwell-Porter High School in 1950. She worked at Butler Drug Store and the telephone office.

In 1960 she married Oscar James Corbin (1916). She then worked at the Elder-Beerman warehouse in Dayton and upon returning to Gallipolis she worked at the Colony Theater. Oscar worked for the City of Gallipolis and after their marriage they moved to Dayton, Ohio where he worked construction and then at the state hospital until his retirement when they moved back home to Gallipolis. Nora and Oscar have three sons: Randall Lee (1961), Ronald Eugene (1962) and Richard Allen I (1964), all born in Dayton, Ohio. Randy married Lisa Fuller in 1984 and they have three children: Christina, Katie and Daniel Stephen. Ronnie married Terry Jo Steger (1964) in 1982.

They have two sons, Wesley and Casey. Richard married Loretta Jones (1967) in 1988. They have one son, Richard Allen II. Stella Baird attended Bulaville Grade School and graduated from Bidwell-Porter High School in 1952. After graduation she worked at the telephone company and in 1955 she married John Lane (1934).

She later worked at the Kanauga Drive-In and Gallipolis Developmental Center until her health forced her to retire. She passed away in 1975. Shella attended Campaign Church and the Church of God in Gallipolis. John worked at Evans Grocery, Thorofare, and Pennyfare Supermarket. Stella and John had two sons: Charles William (1959) and Mark Allen (1961). Both boys were very active in sports in high school and still enjoy bowling. Chuck married Tammy Hart in 1978 and they have one daughter, Jennifer Alene. He works at Holzer Hospital in Gallipolis, Ohio. Mark served in the U.S. Army and is now employed by Pepsi Cola in Athens, Ohio. Mary Baird went to Bulaville Grade School and started high school at Bidwell. She graduated from Gallia Academy High School in 1954. She worked at Evans Restaurant and Steak House in Gallipolis and at Tom Thumb in Columbus. She then worked at Crow's Steak House in Pomeroy, Ohio until her health required her to retire in 1994. Following her death in 1994, she was deeply missed by many of her former customers. Ann Baird attended Bulaville Grade School and graduated from Gallia Academy High School in 1957.

She then attended office training school in Columbus, Ohio. She worked for Crow, Crow & Porter from 1959-1984 and made her home in Pomeroy, Ohio. She then worked for Little, Sheets and Warner in Pomeroy and is now semi-retired. Ann married Frank Ryther (1929) in 1965. Frank worked for the State Highway Testing Lab and later retired from Philip Sporn in New Haven, WV. He and Ann still reside in Pomeroy, Ohio.

**BAIRD TWINS** - On January 12, 1927, Dillie (see Frank Halfhill) went to the home of her oldest daughter (see Gail and Ora Baird) on Possum Trot Road (Addison Township, Gallia County, Ohio) near Campaign Church to help Dr. Rife with the delivery of her new grandchild. Ironically, Grandma Dillie arrived just in time to name her new identical twin granddaughters, Della Alena (the oldest by 3 minutes) and Dillie Elinine, special gifts sent from God.

*Dillie E. and Della A. Baird*

Della and Dillie were often mistaken for each other and were known on occasion to have fooled teachers, boyfriends and even their own Dad. According to one story, Della (or was it Dillie) was asked by her father to take firewood to the house. She pretended not to hear and ran into the house. When Dad finally got to the house, Dillie was sitting at the kitchen table unwilling to tell on herself or her sister. When Della finally came out from under the table, both girls were in trouble. While the twins looked and dressed alike, they did have sisterly disagreements and Mom would make them sit in a chair together and hold hands until they kissed and made up.

In 1932, the twins started to a one room school (closed for consolidation in 1935) at Oil Hollow near where they lived. Due to a serious illness, Dillie was unable to finish that year. At Bulaville Grade School in 1937, Della's six grade teacher was Mr. George and Dillie's fifth grade teacher was Ms. Fulton. Della graduated from Addison Elementary Rural School District in 1940 and Dillie in 1941 and both girls went on to high school in Gallipolis. A wartime graduation, Della graduated from Gallia Academy High School on May 25, 1944. From her Gallia Script which sold for 15cents —"... eight boys ... in the armed services will not be present." Dillie graduated on May 23, 1945 from Gallia Academy High School. From her Gallia Script which sold for 10 cents "Another wartime graduation made it impossible for all the class of '45 to be here." Dad was very proud of his twin daughters and even though he hardly ever went to events in town, he attended both their graduations.

After high school, Della went to work in Columbus at a foundry. When Dillie graduated, Della returned home to work with her at the Ohio Valley Laundry, 841 Third Avenue, Gallipolis. Dillie's check stub from OVL reflected total wages for 1946 as $567.00. They rented a room together in town on Fourth Avenue where they could cook meals. Dillie and Della worked together at the laundry until early 1947.

The Baird Twins were always there for each other in both good and bad times. Dillie (see Baird/McCormick) and Della (see Baird-Casto) were very different in their own unique way but yet somehow the same.

*Submitted by Mary E. (Casto) Graham*

**BAKER-COMPTON-SCHOONOVER** - Twenty-two years have come and gone. It is now 2002 and time for additional facts on our family tree.

Our parents have passed away, most of our children have gray hair, and we have mourned the loss of several dear ones.

Thomas Richard Schoonover, April 1967. Walter Henry Schoonover, May 6, 1984. Marita Arlington Young Baker, February 8, 1989. Michelle Marie Compton Hantz, June 19, 1991. Bobby Lewis Schoonover, June 1992. Lester G. Lee, Feb 1993. Thelma Blanche Daugherty Schoonover, August 6, 1993. Wayne Anthony Baker, October 18, 1994. Francis Louise Saunders Schoonover, April 1995. James N. Compton, July 16, 1996.

Our parents, Wayne and Marita Baker, are buried at Clay Chapel Cemetery along with our grandparents, Charles W. and Addie M. Boster Baker; great grandparents Joseph P. and Mary Jane Lanthorne Baker; aunts and uncles Vance and Elaine Baker, Carl Baker, Lincoln and Mary Baker Call; as well as James N. Compton and Michelle Compton Hantz.

Marian (Ruth) was employed at Ohio Bell Telephone Company for almost five years, and was a Service Assistant/Instructor four of those years. She married Walter Freeman Schoonover August 6, 1955, at the Methodist Church in Clipper Mill, Ohio. They have three children: Walter Freeman, Jr., Wayne William, and Patricia Jean, as well as Thomas Richard Schoonover from a previous marriage.

Walter, son of Walter Henry Schoonover and Thelma Blanche Daugherty Schoonover, had two brothers, Bobby Lewis and William Henry, as well as a sister, Wanda Jean Schoonover Lee. Walter was employed by the Ohio River Company until he retired in 1986. During World War II, Walter served in the Merchant Marines. He received both his Steam and Diesel Engineers Licenses at Fort Trumbull, New London, Conn., where he graduated in the upper 10 percent of his class. While in the service, his ship stopped at ports in England, Holland, France, Germany, Italy, North Africa, and Australia.

Walter Freeman, Jr., married Jennifer Mann in Fort Wayne, Indiana. They have two daughters, Jordan Michelle and Madison Kathleen. Tanya Corrine Schoonover, from a previous marriage, attends Bowling Green State University. Walt graduated from OSU with a degree in Electrical Engineering; Jennifer from Purdue University also in Engineering.

Patricia graduated from Gallia Academy High School and has made her career in banking and finance.

Wayne William married Adeanna Lanham. They have three children: Telia Renee, Wayne William, Jr., and Carl Lewis. Wayne was in the U. S. Marine Corps and is now a civilian employee at Camp Lejuene, Jacksonville, NC.

Thomas Richard married Edy Mohler in Columbus. They had two children: Thomas Richard, Jr., and Tammy. Great grandchildren are TR, Josh, and Maggie.

Since Walter retired, he still works hard every day. He has a garden large enough to feed several families; Marian does a lot of canning. They have a cabin on the Muskingham River at Beverly, Ohio, where Walter fishes and Marian reads. They both like to "flea market" and Marian enjoys working on genealogy. She learned to "surf the net" in her 70's.

Patricia Baker Compton married James N. Compton. They had two daughters, Michelle Marie and Deborah Lynn. She retired from Probate and Juvenile Courts after 28 years in 1989. She enjoys working in her yard and flowers. She says she also washes a few dishes and the rest of the time she doesn't do anything! "After all, I'm retired!!!!"

Deborah graduated from Gallia Academy High School, where she sang in the Madrigals, and Gallipolis Business College. She and her cat, Holly, now reside with Pat in Gallipolis.

Michelle Marie married David Hantz in Florida. They had one son, John David, who lives in Greenville, NC. He currently attends Pitt Community College in Greenville and plans to enter East Carolina University in the fall.

Since the previous publication of Gallia County History 1980-page 25-26, we were admitted to the "First Families of Ohio" through William Loux lineage, who came to Gallia County around 1803.

We have some information to pass along which may help others:

Naturalization of Frederick Baker, formerly of the Empire of Germany— 'has taken an oath to support the Constitution of the United States—' Order Book A, Monroe County, VA, 27 January 1795.

Will of Frederick Baker, father of Joseph Baker m Sara Arnot Case No. 318, Monroe Co., VA., Died 1829, Will Volume 3, Page 9, Monroe Co., VA.

*Submitted by Pat Compton and Marian Schoonover.*

**BALDWIN FAMILY** - Brisco Hayes Baldwin (1897-1976) was married to Dora Belle Williams (1898-1987). He was a farmer who raised tobacco most of his life. Both Brisco and Belle were members of Elizabeth Chapel Church. Brisco's father, Dr. Isaac Hite Baldwin, was from Winchester, VA.

*Briscoe Hayes Baldwin and Dora Belle Williams Baldwin*

Dora Belle Williams' father was Alfred Hugh Williams (1869-1921) from Clay Township. His wife was Annie Elizabeth Boster (1873-1942) from Ohio Township. Their children were Dora Belle (Williams) Baldwin, Cora Francis (Williams) Wooten, and Noah Williams.

Noah Edgar Williams (1894-1979) was a veteran of WWI. He was notified to report for duty July 22, 1918, Pvt. Co B 364 Infantry then Co A 334 Infantry.

Cora Francis Williams (1926-1993) from Bladen, Gallia County, lived in Champaign County, Ohio, and married Joseph Emmet Wooten. Their children were Alfred, Talmage, Phillip, Phyllis, Elwood (who died at age 8 years) and Jackie who died before a year old.

Brisco and Belle Baldwin had two children in their marriage, Urban Hugh Baldwin (born 1923) Gallipolis, Ohio, and James Edgar Baldwin (born 1929) Leon, WV. Urban Baldwin married Mary Ann Clagg and had one daughter, Karen Sue Baldwin (born 1949). James Baldwin married Bette Jo Raike (born 1931) and had two children, Larry Thomas Baldwin (born 1950) and Melissa Ann Baldwin (born 1961).

Melissa (Baldwin) Evans married Larry Michael Evans of Nelsonville, Ohio, and they have three children: Suzanne Michelle Evans (born 1980), James Joshua Evans (born 1985), and Kari Ann Evans (born 1990). Larry Michael Evans retired from the Ohio State Highway Patrol in 1998.

*Submitted by Larry Baldwin.*

**ROBERT & JUDITH SHRIVER BALL FAMILY** - Judy was born in Gallia County on November 14, 1942, the daughter of Homer Floyd (1916-1974) and Helen Dunkle Shriver (1924-1972). Bob was born in Gallia County on May 10, 1941, the only child of Robert S (1918-1963) and Annabelle Bradbury Ball Fellure (1919-). Bob and Judy attended Rodney Grade School, a 3-room building where Bob's dad was a teacher, and graduated from Gaillia Academy High School. From 1963 to 1965, Bob served in the Army and was stationed in Okinawa & Vietnam. They were married on May 21, 1966. Bob went to work at Goodyear in Apple Grove, WV, in 1966; and he is still working there even though it is now M & G. Judy is a secretary for the First Presbyterian Church where they are active members. They have two daughters, Sue Ellen Bostic (1968) and Debra Kay Collins (1970). They also helped raise their nephew, Brian Dean Shriver Sue married David Allen Bostic, and they have two children - Amber Nicole and Kevin Isaac. Debbie married Robbie Ashton Collins and they have two children - Hannah Nickole and Karma Ashton.

*Homer & Helen Shriver*

Judy's family: In 1937 Homer was discharged from the CCC Camp, and in 1940 married Helen Dunkle. They had two other children, Gary Dean (1945-1998) and Linda Kay (1950-). Homer ran his own sawmill, farmed and was a supervisor in a lumberyard. Homer was the youngest son of John F. (1866-1928) and Chloe Saunders Shriver (1879-1938). They were married in 1897 and had three other sons, Alva (1898-1967), Arthur (1900-1965) and Curtis (1904-1957). John F. & Chloe moved from Swan Creek and made their home in Cora where they ran a farm. John F. was known for his ability to pick up a keg of nails with his teeth. John F.'s parents were John (1835-1913) and Amanda Glover Shriver (1849-1943). John was born in Germany and came to the USA when he was a young man. Chloe's parents were Jacob Riley Saunders (1854-1926) and Mahala Susan Beaver (1857-1943); and they were married in 1876 and had seven other children, Bessie, Verba, Henry, Viola, Charles, Calvin and Naomi.

*Bottom L: To R: Annabelle Fellure, Karma Collins, Bob Ball, Nicole & Kevin Bostic Sue Bostic, Judy Ball, Debbie & Robb Collins*

Helen was an only child of Charles Fredrick (1885-1948) & Margaret Yeager Dunkle (1899-1995), who were born and raised in WV. They were married in Huntington, WV, in 1923 and moved to a farm in Gallia County with Fred's dad in 1928. Fred's parents were John and Neva Eden Dunkle and Margaret's parents were Newman (1979-1967) and Elizabeth Pennington Yeager (1876-1948).

Bob's family: Robert & Annabelle married in 1940. Robert served in the Navy during WWII and continued his career as an elementary school teacher when he got out of the Navy. He was the first principal at Green Elementary School and held that position till his death. Annabelle helped to start Guiding Hand School and was the first teacher there. She is also responsible for where it is located today in Cheshire, Ohio.

Robert's parents, Jacob Ellis (1886-1970) & Ethel Wilson Ball (1890-1972), married in 1908 and had ten other children: Joseph, William, James, Charles, Mary, Walter, Paul, Kathryn, Eleanor and Jane Ann. Annabelle's parents, Horace Bion (1987-1944) and Luella Rupe Bradbury (1899-1992), married in 1917 and had six other children: Julia, Mary, Burdell, Naomi, Joe and Jim.

Bion was the superintendent of Gallia County Schools from 1933 till his death in 1944.

*Submitted by Judy Shriver Ball*

**JOHN AND NAVADA BARRY FAMILY** - John Devold Barry (son of James Barry and Grace Devold) was born April 25, 1865 in Noble Co., Ohio. He married Navada Moore (daughter of Lafayette Moore and Wilma Rossiter) September 22, 1887 in Gallia Co. Navada was born August 18, 1869 in Noble Co.

John raised tobacco, corn, cattle, and worked on the sawmill. Navada helped make ends meet by making the clothes for the large family. She grew flax, beat it into thread, and then wove it into a kind of linen. From this material, she made the clothing for the family.

*John & Navada Barry About 1920-1929*

In May of the early 1920's the Barry family moved from Gallia Co. to Lawrence Co. John, Navada, and three of the boys (Arnold, Clovis and Buck) loaded the furniture onto the wagons for the move. Since it was a hot May morning, the three boys tossed their jackets on the furniture wagon. Walking behind the wagons, the boys fell behind on the journey to the new home. As they walked to the new home, it started to get colder. Then, it started to snow. With no way to catch the wagons, the boys suffered in the cold and snow. According to the boys, they nearly froze to death.

John and Navada had the following children (those changing the spelling of their last name are noted): 1. Charley W. Berry was born June 22, 1888, Crown City; died November 6, 1967, Huntington, WV. Charley married Alta Theadoshie Myers. 2. Jesse Berry was born September 28, 1889, Guyan Township; died August 21, 1966, Brandenton, Florida. He married Hattie Carter. 3. Sylvia was born January 18, 1892, Guyan Township; died April 24, 1986, in Ironton. She married John Thornton. After their divorce, she married Charles Watson. 4. Chancy "Buck" was born May 19, 1894, Guyan Township; died March 16, 1983, Huntington, WV. Buck started chewing tobacco at the age of three. His mother disapproved of this habit and made his shirts without any pockets, depriving Buck of a place to put his wad. Not easily defeated, Buck just placed the wad under his hat. Despite his tobacco use, Buck lived to the age of 88 and chewed the entire time. He served in WWI and said the numerous leaches were the worst part of his military service. 5. James Lafayette was born November 15, 1896, Guyan Township. He died October 17, 1918, in Camp Taylor, Kentucky, of pneumonia while preparing to serve in WWI. 6. Lawrence was born October 27, 1898, Guyan Township; and died on August 6, 1998, in Ironton. He married Bessie Wilson and Edith Hart. 7. Clovis Berry was born September 17, 1902, Belville Creek; died January 22, 1970, Ironton. He married Lenna Lafon. 8. Arnold was born August 19, 1905, Guyan Township; and died August 8, 1990, Huntington, WV. He married Charlene Wilson and Stella Halleck.

John Devold Barry died April 9, 1929 in Gallipolis. Navada died January 1, 1960 in Willow Wood. They are buried at Good Hope Cemetery.

*Submitted by Vada Berry Mount.*

**BAYS** - Our names are Clara Ellen Bays Shaver, Margaret Marie Bays Reynolds and Homer Lusher Bays. Our parents were Andrew Daniel Bays (1896-1974) and Della Rose Barry Bays (1904-1977).

Dad came to Gallipolis in 1919 from St. Albans, West Virginia, looking for work in the days after World War I. His ancestors migrated to West Virginia from Virginia and North Carolina.

*Andrew and Della Barry Bays*

His parents were John William Bays (1864-?) and Susan Jane Roberts (1872-?). John William Bays' second wife was Sarah (1849-1936). His parents were James Madison Bays (1825-?), and Nancy Ann Veley (1833-?). James Madison Bays was born in Lena, Surly County, North Carolina and Nancy Ann Veley in Virginia.

Dad had several great aunts and uncles, all born in Virginia: Lewis H. Bays (1855-?), Thomas J. Bays (1857-?), James Madison Bays (1859-?), Patterson C. Bays (1861-1927), John William Bays (1864-?), Obediah Bays (1871-?), Ulysses Bays (1872-?) and Helen A. Bays (1875-?). The birthplace of the children born before 1864 is listed as Virginia; after 1864, West Virginia, as a result of the separation of the western counties of Virginia after the beginning of the CMI War.

Dad had five siblings:
- Martha Bays (1889-?)
- James Riley Bays (1890-1963)
  Oliver Estil Bays (1892-1979)
- Hattie Ann Bays (1897-1981) and
- Kate Ann Bays.

Our parents had the following children, grandchildren, and great-grandchildren:
• Kathleen Bays (1927-1985) married David Eau Claire Strait (1932-1969) in 1952. Their son is David Lee Strait (1956)
• Clara Ellen Bays Shaver (1930)
• Magdalene Bays (1931-1999) married Elmer Randolph (?-1998). Their daughter is Brenda Suzette Purvis (1959)
• Twins John William & William John Bays (1933-1933)
• Charles William Bays (1935-1996) married Virginia Faulkner in 1961. Their four children are Rocky Bays (1962); Christie Bays (1964-1993), whose son Timothy Halley married Vanessa Martin (?-2001) and has a son and daughter; Edna Helen Bays (1965) who married Chris Watson and their son is Drew Watson, and Daniel Bays (1967).

Charles later married Amy in 1970 and Esther Parsons (1952) in 1973.

Charles and Esther had three sons: Charles William Bays (1973) [whose son is Kyle Bays]; Stephen Winfred Bays (1974) [who, with Loretta Wagner, has three children, Stephen Bays, Stormy Bays, & Shane Douglas Bays]; and John Bays.

• James Andrew Bays (1939-2000) married Geneva Sue Birchfield (1942) in 1961. Their children are Michael Bays (1962) and Kimberly Sue Bays, who married John Blackburn. Their children are Amanda Blackburn (1989) and Andrew Blackburn (1991).

• Homer Lusher Bays (1942) married Mary Katherine Brown (1950) in 1966. Their children are Lisa Lynn Bays (1972) who married William Theiss in 1991. Their children are Kayla Lynn Theiss (1993) and Garrett Daniel Theiss (1995). Tammy Ann Bays (1977) married Benjamin Lewis in 2000.

Our parents were hard-working, God-fearing people who raised a large family in the difficult days of the Depression and the Second World War. We miss the guidance and companionship of our parents and our departed siblings, and cherish the memories of all of them.

**MICHAEL A. BEAVER AND TARISSA G. (HARLESS) BEAVER FAMILY -** Michael was born September 27, 1959 in Pomeroy, Ohio. His father is Jessie E. Beaver of Cheshire, Ohio and his mother was Myrna A. (Thomas) Beaver. Jessie was born January 5, 1930 in Yellowtown (Thivener), Ohio and was the son of Jesse A. Beaver and Garnet (Williams) Beaver of Gallia County. Jessie was born in a log cabin. Myrna was born in Los Angeles, California. She was the daughter of Harold Thomas of Cheshire, Ohio and Clarabelle (Bodkins) Thomas of Middleport, Ohio. Harold was originally from Gallia County but had moved to California for a short time. He and his brothers also ran a car repair shop in a building near the present Pepsi plant in Cheshire, Ohio. Harold's father was Floyd Thomas. Floyd was a carpenter and reportedly built several houses in the Cheshire area.

Michael's great, great, great, great grandparents were Louis Detalante (Detillion) and Mary Ann Louis (Langley) Detalante. Louis came to Gallia County from France in 1817 and bought land near present day Rodney, Ohio. Louis was reportedly born in France in 1778 and Mary was reportedly born near Paris (Seine, France) in 1789. Louis father was Jenue (John) of France. He was born in 1753 in France. Louis was an early farmer in Gallia County. He and his wife are buried near Rodney.

Augustus Detillion, son of Louis, was Michael's great, great, great grandfather. He was born in Gallia County in 1823. He married Rebecca Ewing. Rebecca was the daughter of Joseph Ewing and Elizabeth (Betsy) Gilbert. Joseph was born in Ireland about 1787. Elizabeth was reportedly born in Loudon, Virginia in 1819.

Michael spent his early years moving across Ohio as his father pursued work in road construction. He has lived in Gallia County most of his 42 years. Michael is a graduate of Kyger Creek High School (1978), Rio Grande College (B.S. Comprehensive Communications, Secondary Teaching Certification) and Ohio University (Executive Masters of Business Administration). He is currently employed as Assistant Program Director at the Gallipolis Developmental Center.

Michael's wife, Tarissa, was born in Huntington, West Virginia on April 29, 1960. She is the daughter of Danny Harless and Sally (Willis) Harless of South Point, Ohio. Danny was born in Huntington, WV on 8/24/35. Sally was born in South Point on 8/24/39. The Harless family was originally from Germany and Danny's family migrated into southern Ohio from Gilbert, West Virginia.

Tarissa was raised in South Point, Ohio. She is a graduate of Kyger Creek High School (1978) and of Rio Grande College (B.S. Business Education). She is currently employed as the Fiscal Director for the Gallia-Meigs Community Action Agency.

Michael and Tarissa have two daughters, Derecia Leigh, born 10/30/81, and Chera Michele, born 12/20/85. Derecia graduated from River Valley High School in 2000 and married Bastiaan Aarts of Uitgeest, The Netherlands on 7/21/01. Derecia now resides with her husband in The Netherlands. Chera is a freshman at Gallia Academy H.S.

**EDWARD BECK FAMILY** - On September 27, 1740, the good ship Lydia docked at Philadelphia,. PA. On board were Johann Heinrick Beck (1691-1766) and his family which included his eighteen year old son, Johann William Beck, immigrants from Germany to the English Colony.

*William Beck 1844-1925*

Johann Heinrich Beck was 49 years old when he brought his family to this country. With him were his wife, Anna. Maria, two sons, Johann William and George, as well as three daughters.
**JOHANN WILLIAM BECK (1721-1777) & ANNA BECK (1725-1777)** - From this union there were six children- Frederick, Susanne, George, Leonard, Eva and William. Both William and his wife, Anna Eva, passed away in the year 1777.
**LEONARD BECK (1759-1831) & SUSANNE (DEETER) BECK (1757-1844)** - Leonard Beck, fourth child of Johann William Beck, was born in Northampton County, PA in 1759. Leonard was in the Revolutionary War. He served his country from 1781 to the end of the war in 1783. During this service he was a drummer and a soldier, as was his brother, George. The children of Leonard and Susanne were Adam, William, John, Elizabeth, Jacob, Michael, Susanne, Daniel and Katharine.
**JACOB BECK (1790-1833) & MARY (CROFT) BECK (1795-1873)** - In 1815, they departed Westmoreland County, PA and settled in Gallia County near Gallipolis, OH. They were the parents of five children- Leonard, William, Jacob, Sarah and Susanna. Leonard (1810-1910) lacked only a few days living 100 years. Jacob and Mary Beck are buried in Centenary Cemetery Jacob was gored by a domestic animal, the effects of which caused his death at the age of 43. Jacob had acquired as much as 395 acres of land in Green Township. Mary added to the estate by wise management. Jacob's brother, Michael, settled in Beck's Mill, OH in Holmes County in 1822.

William Beck (1819-1900) was married to Jane Fletcher. They had one child, a son named William. William's parents separated and he was reared mostly by the Fletchers. His father remarried Elizabeth Rowson. They had several children.
**WILLIAM BECK (1844-1925) & SARA JANE (DENNEY) BECK (1841-1925)** - William served in the Civil War (1862-1865) and received an honorable discharge. In 1870, William married Sara Jane. They were the parents of seven children- Rose, Will, Ruben, Jane, John, Edward and Oscar.
**EDWARD BECK (1882-1971) & ETTA (ROTHGEB) BECK (1891-1920)** - Born to them were five children- Elsie, Marie, Edward, Ruby, and Francis. Elsie May married Charles N. Kuhn. Marie married Lee Hively. Edward died at age 10. Ruby married Vernon Holley. Francis married Debra Lear.
**CHARLES N. KUHN (1890-1979) & ELSIE MAY (BECK) KUHN (1909-1988)** - were the parents of four children- Donald, Francis, Helen and Nellie. Donald married Alice Keesee. Francis married Norma Jean Holston. Helen married Charles Plymale. Nellie married William Milstead.

Grandfather (Poppy) Edward was a farmer and a good man, always ready to help anyone in need.

*Submitted by Francis E. Kuhn*

**HAZEL EDITH BECK** - Hazel Edith Beck (December 30, 1914) married Clarence Hobart Wilcoxon (1896-1974) and had three children: Mary Elizabeth Wilcoxon Groves (June 11, 1930), Lawrence Arnett Wilcox on ( May 12, 1932) and Susie Iona Wilcoxon Lanier (December 8, 1934).

Hazel is the daughter of John Thomas Beck and Edith Elizabeth Jones Beck. Her mother's parents were Jonathan Rife Jones and Sarah Ann Rothgeb Jones.

Her Dad's parents were William "Bill" Beck and Sarah Denney Beck. William Beck was in the Civil War. I, Mary Groves, remember my great grandfather Jonathan Jones. He died in 1948. Clarence Wilcoxon's parents were Amos Wilcoxon and Emily Susan Sanders Wilcoxon. Amos's dad was in the Civil War. His name was Sutton Wilcoxon. He had four brothers in the Civil War also. They were Samuel, Richard, William, and Anthony. William, Anthony and Sutton are all buried at Mercerville, Ohio. Their parents were Henry H. and Nancy A. (Legget) Wilcoxon.

They came here to Gallia County from Carroll County, Ohio in 1842. Emily Susan (Sanders) Wilcoxon was the daughter of Joseph Sanders and Sarah Sheets Sanders. William Sanders, father of Joseph Sanders, served in the 1812 War. He came here from Fluvana County, Virginia, where he was born July 3, 1823. Joseph Sanders came here with his father and mother in 1835. His parents were William Sanders (1786-1861) and Sarah (Strong) Sanders (1798-1863).

Amos and Emily had nine children. They were Ollie Wilcoxon Saunders, Lottie Wilcoxon Thivener, Rodie Wilcoxon, Leaton Wilcoxon, Clarence Wilcoxon, Dewey Wilcoxon, Ersel Wilcoxon, Muriel Wilcoxon Mefford and Millie Wilcoxon Clagg.

Joseph and Sarah Sanders are in the Bicentennial Edition, May 1976 book.

Mary Wilcoxon Groves married Richard G. Groves in Bellefontaine, Ohio, August 15, 1958. Their children are Mark Richard Groves (July 27, 1959) and Janet Lyn Groves (May 26, 1961). They were both born in Bremerton, Washington.

Mary, Mark and Janet are all in the first families of Gallia County.

*Submitted by Mary Groves.*

**JOHN THOMAS BECK (1)** - John Thomas Beck (1879-1952) married Edith Elizabeth Jones (1892-1918) in 1909. They had four girls, Helen, Carrie, Esta, and Hazel. Hazel married Clarence Hobart Wilcoxen (1896-1974). They had Mary (Richard) Groves 1930, Lawrence (Reba Carroll) Wilcoxen 1932, and Susie (Garland L.) Lanier 1934.

Lawrence was in the army 1952-1954. He was on a troop-ship on his way to Japan when the Korean War stopped. He always said they knew he was on his way, that is why they quit fighting in Korea. After he came home from Japan, he returned to the farm to help Dad and Mom.

In 1955 Lawrence married Reba Carroll. Their first daughter, Jeannie was born in 1956. She is married to Keith Williams. They have Jeremy, Chris, Josh and Natalie. Barbara was born in 1957. She is married to Russell Ferguson. They have, Megan and Rusty. Carol Sue was born in 1959. She has Marc, Cara and Ryan. Tara was born in 1961. She married James Cunningham. He died in an accident at Wright Patterson Air Base. They had one son Matthew. Judy and Jody (twins) were born in 1969. Lawrence and Reba have four great grandchildren. Wade Williams, Hannah Williams, Shaylon Elbin and Marc Elbin Jr. Lawrence is retired from Goodyear and Shell of Apple Grove, WV. Reba still drives the school bus for Gallipolis City School. Reba makes the best ever cinnamon rolls. They live on a farm in Green Township. They like to go to antique sales.

*Submitted by Mary Groves*

**JOHN THOMAS BECK (2)** - John Thomas Beck (1879-1952) and Edith Elizabeth Jones (1892-1918) were united in marriage on November 11, 1909, in Gallia County. They became parents to four little girls. They were Helen Beck Walter (1910-1990), Carrie Beck Myers (1912-2001), Esta Beck Snodgrass (May 5, 1913), Hazel Beck Wilcoxon (December 30, 1914). Edith died at the young age of 26, leaving John to raise the four girls on their Gallia County farm.

Carrie Beck Myers went to the Safford School located at the corner of Route 141 and Safford Road. She also attended the Hawk

School for a short time. She graduated from Gallia Academy High School in 1929. Going on to college, she graduated from Rio Grande in 1931 in Education. Although she never taught in a formal school, she certainly taught her six children many wonderful things about life and how to treat our fellow man. Carrie married Hollis Myers February 6, 1932, in Point Pleasant, West Virginia. To this marriage, six children were born: Alton Myers, Carroll Myers, Phyllis Myers Hutcheson, Glenn Isaac Myers (who died at age 2 in 1941 and buried in Centenary Cemetery), Marilene Myers Culp and Darrell Myers.

Carrie and Hollis lived on a farm most of their life. They were grain and dairy farmers. They had one of the first pipe line milking parlors in Fairfield County, milking approximately 80 cows a day. They belonged to many farm groups, always supported their children in the school activities, whether it was 4-H, band, singing, or athletics; and always promoted the love of God. Three of their children were teachers (one leaving the teaching field to be a grain farmer of approximately 2,500 acres), one in building construction, and one in glass design with Anchor Hocking Glass.

Phyllis Myers married Robert Brown Hutcheson December 22, 1957. Two sons were born to Bob and Phyllis. Education was always very important, Phyllis, a teacher in Lancaster City Schools and Bob's father, a retired teacher of 51 years. So education was never a question. Our oldest son, Bryan, graduated from Ohio Northern with the College of Pharmacy and is a Pharmacist with Wal-Mart. He has three children, Samantha, Alex and Taylor. Keith, our youngest son, graduated from Marshall in accounting, is now a CPA and is a partner in a firm in Charleston, West Virginia. Keith and his wife, Scarlett, have two sons; Addison and Peyton.

Bob (1934-2001), a loving husband, father and grandfather passed away this past April 29, 2001. He loved building things. He built motels and apartments for Cardinal Industries, Inc.; built the first Cantina del Rio for Bob Evans and retired from Dominion Homes. He loved his family and built a wonderful home and life with understanding and love.

Carrie was and Phyllis and sister, Marilene, are members of the First Families of Gallia County dating back to the ancestor, James Martindale during the Revolutionary War period. Carrie, Phyllis and Marilene are also members of the Daughters of the American Revolution, French Colony Chapter. Our family is proud of its Gallia County heritage.

*Submitted by Phyllis Myers Hutcheson.*

**LESLIE AND DORIS JEAN BECK** - Leslie Beck was born on a farm on Graham School Road in Gallia County. He is the oldest son of Oscar and Marie (Hively) Beck. His siblings are Helena, Kathryn, Mary Lou (died at six months of age), and Bobby. Oscar was a farmer and as a boy, Leslie helped his father on the family farm. Marie was a homemaker.

Leslie married Doris Jean Cochran. Doris Jean was born in the village of Patriot, Ohio. She is the next to the youngest child of C.C. and Ethie Jane (Donahue) Cochran. Her siblings are Helen, Marie, Mildred, Charles, Raymond and Darlene (all deceased). Ruth, Juanita, and Hope reside in Gallia County. C.C. was retired from the C&O Railroad with 43 years of service. Ethie Jane was a switchboard operator and a homemaker.

*Leslie & Doris Jean Beck married 59 years*

Doris Jean was saved at Patriot United Methodist Church. She was baptized in Raccoon Creek. She later became a member and went on to hold various offices at Patriot United Methodist Church. She now attends church at the Church of Christ in Christian Union located on Eastern Avenue in Gallipolis.

*Beck Farm, Leslie and Doris Jean Beck Family Home For 45 Years*

Leslie was drafted in the Army in 1944. He served as a Motor Sgt. in France, Belgium and Germany. He was honorably discharged in May 1946. Leslie and Doris Jean then moved back to Gallia County. In 1947 they purchased the Oscar Beck farm located on Graham School Road. This farm had belonged to Leslie's parents. Leslie's father, Oscar, died the same year. The following year Leslie and Doris Jean sold the Oscar Beck Farm to purchase the 175 acre Henry Klicker Farm. This farm is located off Neighborhood Road. The Beck's operated this farm and a dairy for six years. Then they sold the Klicker Farm and purchased a farm on State Route 141. Leslie and Doris Jean have lived on this farm for 45 years. This farm is known as the Beck Farm.

Leslie and Doris Jean are the parents of six children Barbara Jean, who died at the age of 3 days, Linda of Columbus, Angela of Gallipolis, twin boys Tony and Tommy both of Gallipolis, and Lisa also of Gallipolis.

Leslie retired from the Gallipolis City Schools with 30 years of service. At the time he retired, he was the Maintenance Supervisor. He is a World War II veteran. Leslie has farmed all of his life and continues to maintain a working farm. Doris Jean is a homemaker and has also worked on the family farm.

Leslie and Doris Jean have been married for 59 years. They are thankful for God's many blessings.

*Submitted by Leslie and Doris Jean Beck*

**BECK CHILDREN** - Leslie and Doris Jean Beck are parents of Linda Jones, Angela Queen, Tony Beck, Tommy Beck and Lisa Beck. All five children were active in 4-H. Linda, Tony, and Lisa were in band. Tommy, Angie and Lisa were 4-H advisors. All five of the Beck children are graduates of Gallia Academy High School.

Linda (Beck) Jones played the piano for the Alexander United Methodist Church. She also played the piano at Patriot United Methodist Church where she was a member. Linda received her secretarial degree from Gallipolis Business College. She was a secretary at Nationwide Insurance in Columbus, Ohio. She is married to Ted Jones. They have two sons: Timothy and Kevin. After Linda's children were born, she left Nationwide to become a full-time mother. Timothy is a junior at Groveport High School where he is in the Tech Prep program. He works at Kroger as a cashier. Timothy plans to go to college after high school. Kevin attends Groveport Elementary School. Linda and Ted own a home in Columbus, Ohio, where they reside.

*Seated: Lisa Beck*
*Standing: Angela Beck, Queen, Tony Beck, Linda Beck Jones and Tommy Beck.*

Angela (Beck) Queen is married to Leon Queen. They own a home on Kraus-Beck Road. She is a gifted seamstress and is employed at the Gallipolis Developmental Center. They have three children: Dean, Jennifer and Jesse. They also have one grandchild, Levi. Dean is married to Crystal (DeVault) Queen. They have one son, Levi. They recently purchased a home on Daft Road near Cora where they reside. Dean is employed by Henkels McCoy Inc. as a foreman. Jennifer is a graduate of Gallia Academy High School. She is employed by the Gallipolis Developmental Center. She resides in Gallipolis. Jesse is employed by Henkels McCoy. He resides in Gallipolis.

Tony Beck attended Rio Grande College where he studied business. Tony is director and president of the Gallipolis Harley-Davison Owners Group. He is a Green Township Trustee. He owns a farm on State Route 141 in Centenary. He is also the owner of Tony's Tire which is also located in Centenary. Tony has two children:

Angel is attending college at Ohio Northern University, majoring in Pharmacology and Michael Anthony who attends Gallia Academy High School.

Tommy Beck is married to Jeanette (Lowery) Beck. Tommy is employed by American Electric Power. They have two sons: Jonathan and Joshua. Jonathan is a senior at Gallia Academy High School. After graduation he plans to join the U.S. Navy. Joshua is an honor student at Gallia Academy High School. After graduation he plans to attend college. Tommy built a home on State Route 775 where he and his family reside. Tommy and his family attend First Baptist Church on 3rd Avenue.

Lisa Beck has an Associate Degree in Business Administration. She is employed as a Licensed Practical Nurse. She is a homeowner and lifelong resident of Gallia County. She is a member of the Gallipolis Christian Church, Licensed Practical Nurses of Ohio, West Virginia Nurses Association, Ohio Nurses Association, Professional Business Women, Eastern Star, Humane Society, and Women of the Moose.

*Submitted by Leslie and Doris Jean Beck.*

## WILLIAM BECK AND SARA JANE DENNY FAMILY

- William Beck and Sara Jane Denny Family were parents of John Beck who married Edith Jones. Her parents were Jonathan and Sarah Jones. They had four daughters, Helen, Carrie, Esta, and Hazel. Edith died when Helen was seven and Hazel three. John raised the girls on a farm on Crouse Beck Road.

*1st row Leaton, Amos, Rodie*
*Back: Dewey, Ersel, Clarence Wilcoxon*

Joseph Sanders came to Gallia Co. with his parents in 1835. Both of his grandfathers were in the War of the Revolution and were both at the surrender of Lord Cornwallis. His maternal grandfather, John Strong, was taken prisoner by the British. Joseph was married in Gallia Co. to Sarah Sheets (who was a native of this county).

They were the parents of Emily Susan who married Amos Wilcoxon. She had nine children: Ollie, Lattie, Rodie, Leaton (World War I vetran), Clarence, Dewey, Ersel, Murid, and Millie. They bought a farm in Green Township in 1910 when my father, Clarence, was 13. Clarence married Hazel Beck. They had three children: Mary (Richard Groves), Lawrence (Korean War, Reba Carroll), and Susie (Garland Lanier). My parents moved on the family farm in 1943 when my sister Mary was 13.

Susie and Garland were married in Liberty, Indiana in 1953. They have three children: Lawrence (accounting/business administration, B.A. degree from Georgetown College, Georgetown, Ky.) married Helen Akers in 1974. They have three sons: Jakim, Micah, and Aaron. Kathie (social work, assoc. degree from Rio Grande College; dietetics B.S. degree from Marshall University) married Wayne Davis in 1978. They have two sons: Nathaniel and Alexander. Nathaniel married Lisa Turney in 2000. They have a daughter, Natalie Elise.

Nancy (education B.A., M.A. degrees from University of Rio Grande) married James Dell Baughman in 2000. Surnames from Gallia Co include Sanders, Strong, Sheets, Cothen, Beck, Denny, Rothgeb, Martindale, Flethcher, Shaver, Clark, and Rife.

## CHARLEY AND DOSHIE BERRY FAMILY

- Charley W. Berry (son of John Devold and Nevada Moore Barry) was born June 22, 1888 in Crown City. He married Alta Theadoshie Myers (the daughter of John Myers and Harriett Pyles, who was born September 12, 1888 in Gallia County) on December 23, 1912 in Gallipolis. Charley met his future wife while working for her parents in their lumber operation. As transportation was slow in those days, Charley stayed with the Myers family during the period he worked for them.

*Charley & Doshie Berry About 1962*

After their marriage, Charley worked in a sawmill, raised tobacco, corn and hay. He also raised cattle, chickens and hogs for butchering. Doshie helped with the farm work, and worked for a brief period as a switchboard operator (hello girl as she called it). It was after his marriage that Charley changed the spelling of his last name from Barry to Berry. The change took place at the prodding of his wife.

Charley joined Fox-Fairview Church on January 15, 1933 and was elected trustee of the church on May 7, 1934. Doshie had joined Fox-Fairview in 1902.

Charley and Doshie had nine children, of which eight lived to adulthood: 1. Genevivie Mae was born September 9, 1913, Guyan Township. She married George Newton (1909-1975) on July 15, 1933, Huntington, WV. She died May 3, 1995, Huntington, WV. 2. Stacy Irwin born on December 7, 1914, Guyan Township and died July 27, 1988, Athens, Ohio. He married Irene Kitter on August 2, 1945, in Ashland, Kentucky. They divorced in 1947. 3. John Emerson was born on February 19, 1916, Guyan Township and died December 30, 1989, Columbus, Ohio. Emerson married Zelma Cron (1914-1992) on January 15, 1938, in Ironton, Ohio. 4. Charles Ogal was born November 22, 1917, Walnut Township. Ogal married Ida Pearl Kingery (born 1919) on January 15, 1940, in Ironton, Ohio. Ogal died April 26, 1982, in Portsmouth, Ohio. 5. Anna Pauline was born on December 19, 1919, in Walnut Township. She married Sesco Adkins (1899-1975) on December 23, 1939 in Kentucky. Pauline died August 17, 1981, in Delaware, Ohio. 6. Nora Christine was born March 27, 1923, and died August 19, 1923, both events in Guyan Township. 7. Vada Darlene was born April 25, 1924, in Guyan Township. She married Sylvester Mount, Jr. (1923-1995) on February 16, 1943, in Catlettsburg, Kentucky. 8. James "Tom" Orlyn was born March 10, 1926, Guyan Township, and he married Hazel Thurman on July 25, 1943, in Russell, Kentucky. James died February 13, 1987, in Lancaster, Ohio. 9. Hattie "Teannie" Ernestine was born December 2, 1927, Guyan Township. She married Donald Hayes (1928) on July 15, 1950, in Huntington, WV.

Charley died November 6, 1967 in Huntington, WV. After Charley's death, Doshie alternated living with her daughters, Vada and Ernestine, until her death on December 30, 1972 in Huntington, WV. Charley and Doshie are buried in Fox-Fairview Cemetery.

*Submitted by Ernestine Berry Hayes*

**ANTHONY BICKEL** - Anthony Bickel was born 30 June 1790 in Pennsylvania. He was perhaps the son of Jacob and Margaret Bickel, although we've not obtained definitive evidence. He married Dinah (or Diana) Chappell say 1811, possibly in Wythe County, Virginia, where their first child was born.

Dinah was born 19 May 1796 in Wilkes County, North Carolina-the twin sister of Phillipina "Phoebe" Chappeli, wife of Francis S. Thompson. The name of their father is a matter of debate, but their mother's name was Julia as evidenced by her presence in the household of Francis and Phoebe in 1850 in Wythe County (aged 97 or 99 years).

The children of Anthony and Dinah: Rev. Aaron Bickel, born about 1813 in Wythe County, married 5 November 1840, Susanah C. Porter, Abraham, born 1817, married Agnes Jane Rickeft 6 April 1842, perhaps; Mary Bickel, born 1818 in Gallia County who married Atherton Fuller, 8 March 1838; Malinda, born 4 September 1821, married Henry Wise, 11 September 1840, died 8 November 1908 in Michigan, North Dakota; Robert Safford, born 9 January 1824, in Gallia County, died 18 July 1903 in Point Pleasant, West Virginia; Charles, born 1826; Nancy R., born about 1829, married David H. Taylor, 17 April 1855, Salmon R. (Pvt., Co. M, 7th OVC), born 1831 who married Susan A. Harrington, 7 August 1855, in Green Township, died 13 May 1864 at Andersonville prison, Andersonville, Georgia.

Anthony Bickel appears in the Gallia County records on the 1818 Chattels List in Green Township. He had removed to Perry Township by 1821, where he seems to have remained until his death on 24 May 1860, aged 69y- 10 m-24d. He was buried at Hulbert Cemetery in Green Township. Dinah died in Clay Township, 20 February 1874, aged 77y-9m-ld, and is buried beside her husband.

*Submitted by: Linda Gaylord-Kuhn*

**BICKEL FAMILY** - Anthony and Dianah Bickel were married in the summer of 1814 in Wythe County, Virginia, soon after Anthony was released from the army when the War of 1812 ended. Their first born son, Aaron, was born in Virginia in 1816, but before their second child, Abraham, was born in 1817, they had moved to Gallia County. They first settled in Green Township. On the 1820 census the adjacent entries from Green Township are Anthony Bickel, his brother Frederick Bickel, and Robert Safford. Within a few years Anthony had settled permanently on a farm in Perry Township and Frederick in Harrison Township.

Anthony and Dianah had nine children: Aaron (1816), Abraham (1817), Mary (1818), Melinda (1821), Robert (1824), Charles (1826), Nancy (1828), Salmon (1831), and George (1834). Anthony died in 1860. Dianah then lived with her daughter, Nancy Taylor, in Green Township until the Taylors moved to Nebraska in the early 1870's. She then lived with her daughter, Malinda Wise in Clay Township until her death in 1874.

Aaron Bickel became a minister. He married Susannah Porter in 1840, and Ruth Taylor in 1858. They were living in Illinois when Dianah died in 1874.

Abraham Bickel married Agnes Rickets in 1842. The family had moved to Texas by the 1870's.

Mary Bickel married Atherton Fuller in 1838. They lived out their lives in Gallia and Meigs Counties.

Malinda Bickel married Henry Wise in 1840. They lived on a farm in Clay Township. Malinda was widowed in 1863. She moved to North Dakota with several of her children in 1884.

Robert Safford Bickel married Lucinda Ann Toler in 1845 and Emma Chancelor in 1878. He was a merchant tailor in Point Pleasant, West Virginia. His autobiography and portrait are in the book, *History of the Great Kanawha Valley*, bicentennial edition, 1994.

Charles Bickel married Isabella Kelly in 1852. They were living in Nebraska City, Nebraska, by 1870. His life's occupation was brick mason.

Nancy Bickel married David Taylor and they lived in Green Township until moving to Nebraska City, Nebraska in the early 1870's.

Salmon Bickel married Susan Morgan in 1855. He served as a private in the 7th Ohio Cavalry in the Civil War and was captured at Rogerstown, Tennessee in November 1863. He died at Andersonville Prison in May, 1864.

George Bickel married Ann Dickey in 1862. He served in the Union Army in 1865.

Both Anthony and Dianah were descended from pre-Revolutionary American families.

Anthony's father, Jacob Bickel was born in Germany, but served in the Revolutionary War. He married Catharine Brown, in Pennsylvania, in 1766. Catharine's father, Michael Brown, was a Second Lieutenant in the Revolutionary army. Dianah's father, Stephen Chappell, was a third or fourth generation American from Virginia Beach. He was a Loyalist who fought and was captured in the Battle of Kings Mountain in South Carolina in 1780.

**CHARLES BINGLEY BICKEL** - Charles Bingley (C.B.) Bickel was born in Gallia County on May 26, 1826. He was the sixth of nine children of Anthony and Dianah Bickel, longtime residents of Gallia County. He was apparently named for the Charles Bingley character in Jane Austens book, Pride and Prejudice, which had been published in 1813. During his business career he identified himself by his initials, C.B.

Charles married Isabella Kelly in lronton, Lawrence County, Ohio, on December 30,1852. The ceremony was performed by Rev J.H. Creighton. Isabella Kelly was English, having been born in the Isle of Man. Her parents are believed to be Thomas Kelly and Catherine Kirk Kelly. In lronton, Charles and his older brother Aaron worked as brickmasons. Charles continued to work in the business of manufacturing and laying bricks and constructing buildings for the rest of his life.

Census records indicate that the first child of Charles and Isabella was a daughter, Mary Catherine Bickel, born about 1853 in Ohio. Their second child, John Kenneth Bickel, was born on September 5,1855 in either Ohio or Kentucky. By 1858, the family had moved to Missouri where their third child, Anthony A. Bickel, was born. Their fourth child, Charles Creighton ("CC.") Bickel, was born in Graham, Nodaway County, Missouri, on April 13, 1860. A daughter Rosa B. Bickel was born in Missouri in 1864, and a son George Bickel was born in Missouri in 1866.

By 1870, the family had moved to Nebraska City, Otoe County, Nebraska.

Mary Catherine Bickel married Jacob Shellenberger in Nebraska City on May 1,1872. Their son Marion C. Shellenberger was born in Nevada around 1873, and was living in Ely, White Pine County, Nevada in 1905.

In 1881, CB. Bickel & Sons manufactured 700,000 brick, which made it the largest of three such companies in Nebraska City. In 1890, he was also operating a grocery store under the name C.B. Bickel & Co. After 1874, C.B.'s sister Nancy Bickel Taylor and her husband David Taylor had also become residents of Nebraska City.

In 1885, C. C. Bickel was married to Mary Susan ("Molly") Hanks and John Kenneth Bickel was married to Minnie Elizabeth Burgert, both in Nebraska City. Anthony Bickel died in 1898, and Isabella died in 1899. George R. Bickel was living in Kansas City, Missouri in 1905 and died prior to 1938.

CB. Bickel died in Nebraska City on August 18,1907 at age 81. John Kenneth Bickel died two months later in the same city. CC. Bickel managed the Bickel Construction Company in Lincoln, Nebraska until 1926.

C.C. died in Lincoln, Nebraska in 1938. His sister Rosa Clev was living in Columbus, Nebraska at that time.

*Submitted by: Stephen Douglas Bickel*

**SAMUEL AND MARY (FULTON) BING** - Samuel C. Bing was born Sept. 5, 1755/6 in Chester County, PA or Cecil County, MD. He married Mary Fulton in Augusta County, VA on Aug. 3,1797 and died in Addison Township, Gallia County, Oh Dec. 27, 1827. Mary Fulton, the daughter of James and Jane (Matthews) Fulton, was born October 16,1776 in Augusta County, VA. and died August 26, 1856. They are both buried in Bing 1 Cemetery in Addison Township.

Samuel and Mary moved north to Gallia County in 1803 after the birth of their third child, Esther. They followed Samuel's brother John R. and William L. Bing as well as Mary's father and his family. In Augusta County they were blessed with a daughter Jane about 1798 and a son John III, born November 1, 1799. After they established their home in Addison Township, they welcomed Margaret, in 1804, James Carroll, January 25,1806, Samuel Russell, February 14,1808 and Mary in 1810.

Samuel was a Revolutionary Veteran, he enlisted July 25, 1778 in Capt. John Oglevees Company in the Middle Department. He, along with brothers William and Oliver, signed the Albermarle Declaration of Independence. He later served in Capt. Dickey's Company of Augusta County, VA, enlisting in April of 1779.

Mary and Samuel were married by Rev. John Montgomery, Pastor of Rocky Spring Presbyterian Church on the Great Calf Pasture River in Windy Cove, Augusta County, Va. The bond was posted by her father, James Fulton.

Jane, their eldest daughter, married Capt. Robert Guy December 4,1819, but they didn't live to raise their children: William A., Samuel B., Esther J., Mary C., and Amanda. That task fell to Mary Bing and these children are found in Mary's household on the October, 1840, Enumeration of Youth under twenty one.

John Bing the third, first son of Samuel and Mary, married Sarah Alice Entsminger January 11,1821. Their history is in a separate article.

Esther C. Bing married Charles Russell Dec. 7, 1820 in Gallia County and it seems Charles died before 1850. Esther Russell is shown on that census with a number of children but to date we have no proof that this is our Esther Bing Russell.

Margaret Bing married James Blake October 10, 1822 in Gallia County. She disappeared after the birth of their last child and once again Mary Fulton Bing moved into the void. She moved to James' home and helped raise Samuel Bing Blake, Eliza Ann, and James Melvin. Mary Fulton Bing died while still living in the home of James Blake in 1855.

James Carroll Bing married Sarah Rife, daughter of Joseph and Elizabeth Rife on February 1,1838. They had ten children, four sons and six daughters. I hope one of their line will write their history as my knowledge is too limited. James died November 4, 1876 and is buried in Rife Cemetery, Addison Township. Sarah died January 3, 1885 and is buried beside her husband.

Samuel Russell Bing married Lydia Sawyer, daughter of Thomas and Catherine Rees Sawyer, October 18,1831. Their four children were born in Gallia County. Francis Marion, September 19, 1832, died May 20, 1910; Sophia Jane, born August 19,1833, married Peter J. Roberts, September 10, 1850 and she died March 13, 1916; Mary Perthilla was born October 24, 1838 and married Silas Daniels, April 13, 1854. Samuel's will mentions only the three oldest children.

Some of the family believe Mary, born between 1810 and 1812, was the last child of Samuel and Mary Bing. I can't prove it either way but she did marry James C. Russell on February 18,1836 and died in Springfield Township, Gallia County, August 12,1885.

Samuel played a fiddle and was said to have played often for the dances in the area. He was a happy pleasant man. His grandchildren were part of the great migration west as he had been in this time.

*Submitted by: Virginia "Ginny" L. Kane*

**HAROLD AND CAROLINE BLACK FAMILY** - Harold Wilson Black was born in Knox County, near Mount Vernon, Ohio, on September 10, 1903. He was the fourth of five sons born to Earl Bismark Black and Nannie (Wright) Black. Caroline Louise Tulloss, the eighth of nine children of Benjamin Foster Tulloss and Emma Myers Tulloss, also residing in Knox County, was born on April 8, 1906.

*Harold & Caroline Black*

Both grew up on active family farms and had pioneer ancestors who moved to Ohio from either western Pennsylvania or Virginia to settle in the early 1800's Harolds family lineage includes the noted Ohio frontiersman and contemporary of Daniel Boone, Louis Wetzel, while Caroline's is dominated by her great grandfather, Rev. James A. Scott. Rev. Scott established the first Presbyterian churches in Knox County in 1809 and served as the pastor of the Mount Vernon church for most of his life. Both Harold and Caroline had grandfathers who served in the Union Army during the Civil War,

Harold graduated from Mount Vernon High School and studied agriculture at Ohio State University. He worked in the administration of CCC camps during the 1930's and as soil conservationist and soil scientist in numerous Soil Conservation Districts for the U S Department of Agriculture for the rest of his vocational career.

After graduating from Mount Vernon High School, Caroline attended both Kent State and Ohio Universities, and taught elementary school for five years prior to her marriage to Harold on September 10, 1931.

Harold, Caroline and their two daughters, Peggy (b. 1933) and Eleanor (b. 1937) moved to Gallipolis in 1950 where Harold served as the district soil conservationist until mid 1957. He and Caroline chose to return to Gallia County and the Ohio River in 1968 to be near family and enjoy their retirement years. Both were involved in renovating their older home at 6 Pine Street, and were active members and officers of the First Presbyterian Church. Harold served as "handyman on call" for the French Art Colony during Riverby's early years. Caroline died in 1976 at the age of 70, and Harold died in 1996 at the age of 92.

Their daughter, Peggy Anne (Black) Evans (m. Merrill Lee Evans 1952, div. 1971). after nineteen years as housewife and mother, was co-owner and operator of PJ's, a ladies clothing store in the Lupton Block building on Second Avenue in Gallipolis (1973-1986), and served as Secretary of the First Presbyterian Church from 1987 until her retirement in 2001. She continues to be an active member of the Gallipolis community. Eleanor Wright (Black) Heister and husband, Bruce, lived and worked through out the United States in California, Ohio, Missouri and Georgia, and internationally in Canada, Switzerland, Australia and Japan. In retirement, they now reside in Palo Alto, California and continue to enjoy traveling.

Grandchildren of Harold and Caroline Black: Jay Keith Evans (b. 1953; m. Teri Lee Woodward 1991; d.2000); Jodie Lynn (Evans) Davis (b. 1955; m. John Hollis Davis 1973); Alan Dean Evans (b. 1956; m. Carla Ann Willis 1978, Teresa Lynn Feustel 1984) and Megan Cara Heister (b.1976). Great Grandchildren: Clinton John Davis (b.1974). Seth Lee Davis (b.1979). Emily Ann Evans (b. 1980), Christopher Alan Evans (b. 1986) and Kelli Nicole Evans (b.1990).

**GARRED BLAKE FAMILY** - Our ancestors originated from Bridgewater and Somershire, England, the first ones came to America in about 1625. David Blake was the first to settle in Gallia County. David was the great great grandfather of Anslem J. Blake. Anslem married Harriett Fuller, March 1872. They were the parents of 11 children. My father, Garred Blake, being the youngest. Also the Fuller family came from England in about 1620 and settled in Lawrence County. Garred met his future wife, Ruby Craig, in 1915 at the old paw-paw church on Peterabranch Road. They were married in May 1918 and were parents of 6 children whom they reared on the old Blake farm on Hannan Trace Road. The children are: Leo, who married Lucy Galloway and they were parents of 7 children. Leo passed away at age 80 in March 1999; Lucy is still living in South Point, Ohio; Lester married Geneva Asbury. No Children. Lester passed away at 52 in 1973; and Geneva who is still living in Chillicothe, Ohio. Lillian married Russell Walford. They had 6 children. Russell passed on in 1984. Lillian lives in Gallipolis. Lloyd married Vivian Mason. They have one daughter. Lloyd passed away in 1992. Vivian still lives in Gallipolis.

Lulu Mae never married. She lives in Gallipolis with her black angora cat named Dominique who has been her family for 14 years. Louise married William Queen. They live in Canal Winchester, Ohio, and have 6 children, all living in that area. Our mother, Ruby, passed away at age 74 in 1970. Garred passed away in 1991 at age 100. They are resting in Mt. Zion Cemetery, Swan Creek, Ohio. Garred lived with their daughter, Lulu Mae, in Gallipolis after Ruby's death until the time of his passing. The old farm on Hannan Trace Road remains in our family.

Leo's children are Thomas, married 4 children: Donovan, married, 2 children; Patricia, married George Ward, 3 children; Jack, married, one daughter, Phyllis, married Fred Hite, three sons, Michael, deceased, three children, Rick, married, three children. Lillian's children: Ruby, married Virgil Halley, three children. Marlene married Dick Wills, no children. Jurrie married Aaron Reynolds, one son, Ronnal, never married. Emma married Charles Estep, two sons; Richard married, one daughter. Also, a granddaughter, Jennifer Wolford, was reared by Lillian. Lloyd's one daughter, Vera, divorced. Louise's children: William, married, one son; Pamela, single; Marcella, single, twins: David is married, Daniel is single. Terry, married, two children. There are 38 great, great grandchildren and one great, great, great grandchild.

*Garred Blake with Children - Leo, Lloyd, Louise Queen, Lillian Wolford and Lulu Blake*

Garred was a kind and gentle man. He farmed most of his life. He raised a vegetable garden when he was 98 years-old, and we had vegetables from it for his 98th birthday picnic. He lived according to the Golden Rule. His only vice was chewing tobacco. He started when he was 7-years-old, and continued until his death at 100 years.

One generation passeth away And another generation cometh, But the earth abideth forever.

*Submitted by Lulumae Blake*

**LULU BLAKE FAMILY** - I was born on the old Blake farm on Hannan Trace Road. It has been in our family for four generations. My parents were Garred and Ruby (Craig) Blake. My paternal grandparents were Anslem and Harriett (Fuller) Blake. They were of English descent. My maternal grandparents were Robert and Missouri Jane (Harbour) Craig. They were Scotch and Irish. I have three brothers and two sisters. They are Leo, Lester, Lillian, Lloyd and Louise. I am the fifth one of six children.

My brothers have all passed away now, just us three girls living. I had a happy childhood growing up on the farm until I was about 11 years old. I was a victim of polio. It took the next three or four years for me to learn to walk and try to care for myself But after a lot of struggling and determination, I finally got strong enough to walk on my own. It still is a struggle for me to walk but I make the most of it. I cared for my mother several years while she was ill until her death in 1970. Then Dad and I kept the home together for 20 years until his passing in 1991. He raised vegetable gardens and I canned them for our winter's eating. I have lived alone with my angora cat, "Dominique" for 9 years since my Dad's passing.

There have been many good times and pleasant memories despite the handicap. I love country music and I've been fortunate to attend many country concerts and meet the singers. One of the highlights of my life was my nieces, Pam and Marcella, surprised me with a trip to the Grand Ole Opry and a tour of Music City Nashville.

*Lulu & her cat Dominique*

My foster daughter, Brenda, and husband, Richard Sydenstricker, invited me for a trip to Pigeon Forge and Dollywood. enjoyed the time with them. My niece, Vera, has taken me to see the ocean a few times and through the Smokey Mountains. We have good times together. I have four foster grandchildren who are very dear to me. Joy married Sandy, two children; Dalton and Ceara, Bridgett, has Jimmie and three children; J.C., Shayla and Jacob.

Richell married Matt, no children yet. Rickie has Erica, no children yet.

We get together often and have many good times. It has been a tradition for many years for them to gather at my home for Christmas eve dinner. Dominique is a big part of my life. She is my constant companion. I have 20 nieces and nephews. Some of them visit me occasionally. My niece, Jurrie, and I have had many good times together.

My birthday is September 11. My 2001 birthday will always stand out in my memory because of the terrorist attacks on America.

*Submitted by Lulu Blake.*

**BLAZER-LOWERY (1)** - Cleopatra Lowery was born on June 16,1839 married in Gallia Co., to Harty (Cole) who was born in Rhode Island, and Melvin Lawery, who was born in Greenup Co., Ky. She died on September 9, 1878 of yellow fever and is buried in Centenary Cemetery in Green Twp. She was a victim of the epidemic that was brought to Gallipolis by the crew of the Steamboat John Porter, that originated from New Orleans, La. They were docked in Gallipolis due to a broken "rocker arm". Joseph Jefferson died at the home of his son, Jay L. Blazer in Ohio Twp. on Feb. 24, 1906, and was buried beside his wife, Cleopatra, in Centenary Cemetery. He was born on the same land that he was laid to rest on.

Joseph and Cleopatra had the following children: Inez Dewitt married John Wesley Archer; Hartie Anna E. married John William Wetherholt; Jay J. married Emma Arnette Trotter, Miriam Helen married Albert A. Halsted; Emaline "Emma" married Alden Jefferson Freeman; Peter Melvin married Mary Emma McKean.

They owned and lived for several years on the Harrington Place on the river road at the end of town. The first Blazer reunion of this large and prominent family was held at his home on May 25, 1878. There were 223 present, nearly all of whom were relatives and 56 absent; among them 53 nieces and nephews. There has been a Blazer reunion held in various places since the first one came into existence.

Joseph and Cleopatra 's daughter, Hartie Anna E., was the mother of my mother, Sarah Velvie (Wetherholt) Trotter.

*Submitted by: Hartie Trotter Sheets*

**BLAZER -LOWERY (2)** - Joseph Jefferson Blazer's grandfather, Jacob, his wife and family of twelve children: Adam, John, George, Christopher, Philip, Peter, Dorothy, Christina, Katherine, Phebe, Elizabeth and Margaret, left Holland in 1787 for America, landing in November, 1787. The voyage took about seven months. Joseph, son of Peter, remembers seeing some of their belongings which consisted of a large trunk or chest that would hold ten or twelve bushels. It had 200 pounds of iron on the outside and a key that would weigh two pounds; a meal sieve with a wooden bottom full of holes for the meal to pass through, and one Bible in the German language printed in 1740. It came into his possession in 1870.

The family settled first in the Shenandoah Valley, Va. and remained there until 1793, when they moved to Pennsylvania and remained there until 1803. The following members then moved to Ohio: Jacob Blazer and wife, Philip Blazer and wife, and Peter Blazer, Christina, Katherine, Phebe, Elizabeth and Margaret. The last two were married. They all settled in Green Twp., where Philip and Peter both bought farms and lived and died on the same. Christopher Blazer came to Ohio in 1832 and settled near Columbus.

Joseph's father, Peter, married Frances Atkinson on Feb 14, 1815 in Gallia Co.. Dorothy married David Bish and settled in Greenbrier Co, Va./W.Va. Christina married John Smeltzer; they owned and lived on a farm in Green Twp.; Katherine married John Long and moved on Paint Creek near Chillicothe, O.; Phebe married William Croe and went west; John Blazer lived and died in Pennsylvania; Adam Blazer went to Tennessee. His descendants live in Sevier County; George lived in Pittsburgh and was in the glass business and also steam boated.

Peter Blazer served in the War of 1812 under General Tupper. He died April 19, 1854 and is buried in Centenary Cemetery beside his wife Frances, who died in July, 1876. They were the parents of ten children. Their home was the home of the early itinerant Methodist preachers and was also used for divine worship.

Joseph Jefferson Blazer, was born in Centenary, Green Twp. on Christmas Day, Dec. 25, 1815. He was married four times: #1 Betsey Pritchett, Dec. 01,1836, no children; #2 Fmeline Cowden, March 22, 1838, 8 children; #3 Cleopatra R. Lowery, March 02, 1863, 6 Children, #4 Sarah U. Brothers, March 23, 1879, no children.

**BLAZER-WETHERHOLT** - Hattie Anna E. Blazer was born June 16,1865, near Gallipolis, the daughter of Cleopatra Lowery & Joseph Jefferson Blazer. She had the following siblings: Inez DeWitt-married John Wesley Archer; Jay J.- married Emma Arnette Trotter; Mirian Helen- married Albert A. Halsted; Emaline "Emma"- married Alderson Jefferson Freeman; Peter Melvin-married Mary Emma McKean.

*L: to R: Sarah Velvie (Wetherholt) Trotter, Child: Hartie Luella Trotter, Hartie Anna E. (Blazer) & John Wm. Wetherholt*

On June 26, 1887 in Gallia Co., Ohio, Hattie married John William Wetherholt, who was born on May 19, 1854 in Gallia Co., son of Jacob and Sarah (McKean) Wetherholt. Jacob was the son of Rebecca (Clark) and John Wetherholt. He was born c/a 1833 and died Dec. 27, 1864 and is interred in Providence Cemetery, Clay Twp. Sarah was born on January 16, 1832 in Westmoreland Co., Pa., daughter of William and Mary (Kerns) McKean. She died on April 9, 1915 in Gallia Co. and is buried beside her husband in Providence Cemetery.

Born to this union:#1-Goldie Wetherholt— Bn. June 3, 1889; Unnamed son (Died in infancy); Joseph Blazer B. Feb. 3, 1891; Sarah Velvie Bn. March 19, 1893; Viva Marie B. April 25, 1895; Jacob William-B. April 27, 1899; Hartie Winnie B. Feb. 26, 1902; Cleopatra B. Sept. 15, 1905.

Joseph Blazer married Mary Leaper and had Children: Beulah and Eleanor; He married #2 Emma Graham Wickman - no children; Sarah Velvie married on May 18, 1918, William Clemence Trotter, one child; Hartie Luella; Viva Marie married Corwin Ephriam Woofter on March 21, 1923-Children; Patricia Ann and Peggy Jo; Jacob William married Allene Adelaide Burnette — No children; Hartie Winnie married Virgil Clark, no children; Cleopatra married Harry C. Gilpin on May 23, 1953-no children.

Goldie passed away July 22, 1890 and is buried in Providence Cemetery, Clay Twp. next to her brother who died in infancy. Joseph Blazer taught school early in his life and later became a garage owner & operator. During WWI and II he served as a Chief Petty Officer in the Navy. He died in Boynton Beach, Fl. on May 10, 1968 and is buried in Providence Cemetery. Velvie taught school in the Gallia Co. Rural School System, retiring in 1958 after 31-1/2 yrs. She died in Huntington, W. VA. on Sept. 11, 1978 and is buried in Providence Cemetery. Viva Marie taught school in the Huntington, Wv. School System and after her retirement, moved to Boynton Beach, Fl., where she was a substitute teacher. She died December 15, 1989 in Madison, Alabama and is buried in Boynton Beach, Fla. beside her husband and daughter, Patricia. Jacob William was in the Navy in WWII. He lived in

Chester, PA. and was killed on June 30, 1958, in a trucking accident in Leesport, Pa. during a delivery for NuCar Carriers. He is buried in Glenwood Memorial Gardens in Broomall, Pennsylvania; Hartie Winnie taught school in Gallia Co. and later was employed as a bookkeeper. She died in Pt. Pleasant, W. Va. on August 9, 1986 and is buried in Providence Cemetery. Cleopatra also taught school when she was a young lady, but later changed professions and owned and operated a beauty salon in Huntington, W. Va. She died on June 29,1982 in Huntington and is buried there next to her husband in Spring Hill Cemetery.

During her lifetime, Hartie was very active in church work. In 1914, she was president of the Gallia Co. Sunday School Association and also president of the same association in 1915-16. She and John William were charter members of the Victory Baptist Church in Ohio Twp. They also were very active in the Providence Baptist Church in Clay Twp. which was near their home.

Hartie (Blazer) Wetherholt died at the home of her daughter, Marie Woofter in Huntington, W. VA. on December 22, 1924 and was laid to rest in Providence Cemetery, in Clay Twp., which was near her country home, on Christmas Day, Dec. 25, 1924. John William died on Oct. 15, 1937 at the home of his daughter, Velvie, on Clay Lick, who cared for him through his illness. He was laid to rest in Providence Cemetery, beside his wife. They are the parents of my maternal grandmother, Sarah Velvie.

*Submitted by: Carolyn Sheets Vallance*

**BOGGS- PETTUS FAMILY** - Madge Elizabeth Pettus Boggs was the first child born to Freeman Charles Pettus and Janet Elizabeth Kegan Pettus. She was born on July 22, 1934 in Powhatan, McDowell County, WV. Her family moved to Jenkins, Letcher County, KY; from there to Stirrat, Logan County, WV; then to a farm outside of Vinton, Gallia County, OH, and finally to 2981 Lincoln Pike, Gallia County, OH.

She attended Centenary Grade School and Gallia Academy High School where she received the Scholarship Key upon her graduation. She attended business school in Charleston, WV and then accepted employment in Columbus, OH.

In Columbus she met and married Warren Lincoln "Bob" Boggs on November 15, 1954. They had two children: Cynthia Lynn and Janet Cathleen. As sometimes happens, the marriage encountered some rocky situations and was destined not to last. Madge, Cindy and Cathy returned to Gallia County intending to reside with her parents until there was enough financial stability to permit their establishing a home of their own Freeman Pettus died on October 30, 1963 leaving a widow with no financial means. Madge needed a home for herself and two daughters as well as a baby-sitter. So Janet and Madge joined forces with Janet providing the baby sitting and Madge providing the funds to keep a roof over everyone's head and food on the table.

Madge was fortunate to obtain employment at the Ohio Valley Bank in May of 1961. She started there as a Note Teller in the Commercial and Real Estate Loan Department and retired almost 33 years later as Vice President and Controller.

Cindy and Cathy attended Green Elementary and Gallia Academy High School from which they graduated in 1973 and 1975 respectively. They attended college at Ohio University in Athens, OH both majoring in the field of Child Development-Early Childhood Education.

In July of 1977, Cindy married William Dean Thomas, son of John Richard "Dick" and Dorothea Miller Thomas. In October of 1981, Cindy and Bill became the parents of Alyssa Cathleen Thomas who welcomed a baby brother, Cody Miller Thomas, in October of 1985. The family resides in Lancaster, Fairfield County, OH. Bill is a registered nurse employed in the Trauma Center at Grant Hospital in Columbus and Cindy is a domestic engineer. Alyssa is currently attending Heidelberg College in Tiffin, OH and hopes to have a career in forensic medicine or medical research. Cody attends Lancaster High School and is an avid soccer player.

In August of 1980, Cathy married Mark Wailer, son of George Wailer and J. Wayne and Barbara Jones Wailer McAlpin. On December 5, 1986, Cathy and Mark became the parents of twin boys, Dane Kegan Waller and Thor McAlpin Wailer. Cathy is currently employed by Ohio University as the Administrator of their Child Development Center. Mark is a respiratory therapist at O'Blenness Hospital. Even though Cathy and Mark are no longer married they share the responsibilities of raising two teenage boys. Thor and Dane are also very enthusiastic soccer players.

**BOICE FAMILY** - Boice, originally Buys, Holland Dutch family of New York and New Jersey. Joseph and Keziah (Bowman) Boice came down the Ohio River to Gallia County, Ohio in the 1820's.

They formerly lived in Spring Hill Twp., Fayette County, Pennsylvania; both were born in Amwell, Hunterdon County, New Jersey. Joseph's father Johannis Buys, baptized July 1, 1711, Reformed Dutch Church of New York City was the son of Johannis Buys (1), born 1685 and Neeltje Claas De Graff. They were married September 10, 1710, in New York City. Elizabeth's sister was married to Isaac De Trieux (Truex-Traux). On Feb 9, 1690, all of these families were present at the Schenectady Massacre; a force of Canadians and Indians attacked them.

Johannis Buys parents were Jan Thyssen Buys and Jannetie Van Den Ham. Jannetie widowed in 1694 married Isaac Selover 1695; they lived on Manhattan Island, NY. Buys family second home was in Curacao, West Indies, they were involved in trade. The Stuyvesant, Bayard, Steenwyck, Schuyler and Van Courtland families were their social friends.

Joseph "Jersey Joe" Boice and wife Keziah came down the Ohio River by flat boat and settled at Jesse Creek, near Kyger, in Gallia County. They had the following children: John born January 10, 1795, died 1889, buried Kyger Cemetery; Martha (Patsy) born 1796 died 1877 married William Cooper, buried Kyger Cemetery; William born 1797 died 1858 married Susan Ables, buried on his farm; Sarah (Sally) born 1800 died 1882 married George W. Price, buried Miles Cemetery, Meigs County; George born 1802 died 1870 married Malinda Ables, buried in Gallia County; Thomas born 1806 married Elizabeth Shaver, moved to Illinois; Joseph, Jr. born 1808 died 1888 married (1st) Elizabeth Hill (2nd) James born 1810 died 1865 married (1st) Sarah Darst (divorced) (2nd) Cynthia West. Jacob born 1811 died 1894 married (1st) Mary Russell (2nd) Mary Bradbury.

Robert born 1812, Pennsylvania, died September 28, 1850, from typhoid fever, married Mary Ann Vance.

Robert and Mary had the following children: Newton (a deaf mute), Philinda married Gilbert Webster (Meigs Co.), Caroline married William Hubbell (Meigs Co.), Melvin married Caroline Mauck, Bartlett married Esther Rothgeb and Marcellus born May 3, 1847 died March 10, 1939 married Caroline Kent, 1920. Robert is buried VanZandt Cemetery with son, Newton and Mary is buried Kyger Cemetery with second husband, William Athey.

Marcellus, at age 15 enlisted in service in the Union Army and joining the $91^{st}$ regiment, Ohio Voluntary Infantry. Marcellus was the oldest male voter in precincts of Cheshire Township and the last Union solider in his township or any township of the county that bordered the Ohio River. Marcellus and Caroline had a daughter Emma Ethel, born January 6, 1875 and died March 3, 1949. Their son, Lester Milton, born April 8, 1881 and died November 1957 married Oleva Price of Rutland, Ohio, 1902. Lester and Oleva had the following children: Raymond Everett, Robert Roland and Delores Eloise. Marcellus C. Boice served as Justice of the Peace and known to friends as "Squire" Boice. Joseph, Keziah, Lester and Oleva are buried in Kyger Hill Cemetery. Many of the family members are buried in other cemeteries in the county.

*Submitted by: The Boice Sisters of Cape Cod, Elmore B. Johnson, Harriet B. Parks, Carol B. Dudik and Carolyn Grueser, Pomeroy, Ohio*

**BOSTER FAMILY** - All Boster families in Gallia County are descendants of Phillip Boster who arrived in Philadelphia, PA, aboard the English ship, Edinburgh, September 30, 1754.

*The Home Of John Floyd & Lutitia Ward Boster*

The family name was not originally "Boster". Like many other immigrants, the name has been given varied spellings. Those who migrated to Gallia County used the spelling "Boster"; however, on some county records, it is shown as "Boister".

There were many Boster relatives in Gallia County in the early 1800's living mostly in Harrison Township near Little Bullskin. Some ventured further west; but many chose to remain in Gallia County.

John Boster, a grandson of Philip, is the great,

great grandfather of our family. John was born December 26, 1789, in Pennsylvania and died in Gallia County about 1851.

Another Philip, the son of John, was our great grandfather. Philip was born December 4, 1813, in Virginia. His mother may have been Mary Nibert (or Nebert) who married John on March 3, 1808. Family lore says that Philip was married four times; but only three marriages have been substantiated. They are: Sally Adeline Boster, daughter of Jonathan Sr. and Mollie Huffman Boster, married December 3, 1835. Their children were Alexander born September 25, 1837; died November 8, 1902. Marion born c.1839, died November 8, 1902. Alderson born July 31, 1841; died July 29, 1889. Mary F. born c. 1843, died as infant.

Margaret Dewitt, daughter of John and Sarah Loucks Dewitt, married October 24, 1844. Children were John Floyd, born July 27 1845; died November 15, 1914. Isaac born 1847; died 1907. Margaret Ellen's birth and death is unknown, died as infant.

Eleanor Drummond, married March 14, 1953. Children were Viola born c. 1859; George born c. 1860, and Jesse born c. 1863.

John Floyd, the son of Philip and Margaret Dewitt, was our grandfather. On May 18, 1870, he married Lutitia Caroline Ward, daughter of William H. and Elizabeth Bickel Ward. They were the parents of four children: Hettie Anne born April 2, 1871; died 1914. Married to Addison Niday November 25, 1890. Parents of six children.

William Harvey (AKA Harvey R) born June 24, 1874; died March 27, 1940. Married August 11, 1911 to Caroline Samantha White, daughter of George and Liza Hill White, and parents of three children.

Huldah Elizabeth (AKA Hilda) born April 16 1884; died October 7, 1956. Married Rudolph Lusher June 7, 1905, and parents of eight children.

Florence Ethel born October 21, 1891; died December 15, 1945. Never married.

John Floyd and Lutitia were converted and joined the Mt. Carmel Methodist Church on March 4, 1883. Both are buried at Dickey Chapel, Mt. Pleasant Cemetery in Gallia County.

Philip Boster, the father of John Floyd, died April 22, 1874 and is buried at Macedonia Cemetery along with his last wife, Eleanor. Margaret Dewitt Boster, mother of John Floyd, died before 1850; place of burial unknown.

We three, Hilah Nelle (deceased), George Floyd and Mary Kathleen are the children of "Harve" and "Carrie" Boster. Our parents are buried at Mound Hill Cemetery in Gallipolis.

**DAVID AND SUE BALL BOSTIC** - David Allen was born in Xenia, Ohio, on April 28, 1964, the son of Charles and Cathy Gelder Bostic and the grandson of John and Gladys Donnally Bostic and Henry and Catherine Torrance Gelder. He has one sister, Charlene, who is married to Jack Wade and they have three children, Crystal, Wendy and Winston.

David graduated from Gallia Academy High School in 1983. He attended and graduated from Hocking Technical College in 1985. He spent several years as a mechanic and currently works for General Mills in Wellston, Ohio. He is also a member of the Gallipolis Bass Busters.

*Nicole, David, Sue & Kevin Bostic*

Sue Ellen was born in Gallipolis, Ohio, on April 1, 1968, the daughter of Robert S. Ball Jr. and Judith Carolyn Shriver. She has one sister, Debra Kay, who is married to Robb Collins and they have two children, Hannah and Karma. She is also the granddaughter of Robert S. Ball Sr. and Annabelle Bradbury Ball Fellure and Homer Floyd and Helen Elizabeth Dunkle Shriver.

She graduated from Gallia Academy High School. She spent several years working at Gallipolis Foodland, and is currently working at General Mills in Wellston, Ohio.

David and Sue married on February 20, 1987, and they have two children. The first is Amber Nicole, who goes by Nicole, was born June 21, 1987. Nicole attends Gallia Academy High School and is involved in the Key Club. Their son, Kevin Isaac, was born December 17, 1989. Kevin attends Green Elementary and is involved in many sports including, baseball, soccer and football. Both of their children were born at Holzer Hospital in Gallipolis, Ohio.

*Submitted by Sue Ball Bostic*

**H. BION BRADBURY** - The below picture shows 5 generations: Great, Great, Grandmother, Luella Rupe Bradbury, Great Grandmother, Annabelle Bradbury Ball Fellure, Grandfather, Robert Ball, holding Kevin Bostic, Nicole Bostic, and Mother, Sue Ball Bostic.

Luella Bradbury, wife of Bion Bradbury, lived to be 92. She died February 16, 1992.

Annabelle, the oldest of the family, married her second husband, Howard Fellure, in 1977. He died August 20, 1997 at age 88.

Mary Bradbury Breazeale died May 14, 1980.

Burdell Bradbury lives in Urbana with his wife, Virginia Fisher Bradbury. Both are retired school teachers.

Naomi Bradbury Mangum lives in Washington D.C. and is retired from the State Department.

Joe Bradbury lived in Pickerington, Ohio. He was also a retired school teacher. He died March 4, 2002 as I was writing this history.

James and Mary Berkley Bradbury live in Kyger, which was settled by Asa Bradbury in 1816.

My fondest memories are of the times we lived near Gallia, when I was in grade school and Dad was principal. It was during the great depression in the 30's. The house we lived in had six rooms with an open fireplace and coal cook stove for heat. There was no inside plumbing or electricity.

It was a time when neighbors helped neighbors. There was wheat threshing, sorghum making and harvesting hay.

Women were busy canning. In the fall we would gather nuts. At that time there were chestnuts, hazel nuts along with hickory and walnuts.

Dad kept a ledger of his salary and expenses. His salary was $216.00 a month; a haircut was 35 cents, a broom 65 cents, cornflakes 10 cents, wick for Aladdin lamp 35 cents, and artics 50 cents.

Mother, made most of our clothes and quilts from left over material. Comforts were made from woolen articles. Her quilting frames cost 85 cents, comfort batting was $1.18, and 10 yards of hope muslin was $1.00.

There was a garden and a cow. So we had vegetables, milk and butter.

*Five Generations Luella Rupe Bradbury, Annabelle Ball Fellure, Robert Ball Holding Kevin Bostic, & Nicole Bostic & Sue Ball Bostic*

During this time, Amos and Andy was a popular radio program. We didn't have a radio, but we went to a neighbor's to listen. We never ceased to marvel at how two men could do so many characters. There was Amos and Andy, Madam Queen, and Lightning.

It was a very happy time with hard work, few luxuries, and the simple things were truly enjoyed.

*Submitted by Annabelle Bradbury Ball Fellure*

**RICHARD WENDELL BRADBURY** - Asa Bradbury, one of ten children of Joseph and Elizabeth (Stevens) Bradbury, was born in Penobscot County, Maine on November 22, 1805. He came to Gallia County on the Ohio River by flatboat with his parents in 1816 and settled in Cheshire Township. On October 21, 1835, Asa married Electa B Harding, daughter of Perry and Mary (Smith) Harding. William Bradbury, born May 1, 1842, was one of six children of Asa and Electa. William served in the Civil War and was a member of the GAR. William married Louisa Belle Smith on June 2, 1869 and they had six children. The parents of Louisa Belle were Thomas Allison and Sarah (Draper) Smith. William was a merchant and farmer in Cheshire Township at Kyger.

Clyde Allison Bradbury, on of the six children of William and Louisa, was born at Kyger on Oct 31, 1873 and married his Cheshire Township neighbor, Flora Jenkins. Flora was born June 8, 1876, the daughter of Benjamin and Lucy (Evans) Jenkins and the granddaughter of William S and Cynthia (Scott) Jenkins and Oliver and Lydia (Armstrong) Evans. Charles Scott, the father of Cynthia Scott served in the War of 1812. Like his father, Clyde Allison (Allie) Bradbury was a merchant and farmer at Kyger, Ohio.

Wendell Bradbury was born November 20, 1911, one of twelve children of Allie and Flora Bradbury. Wendell married Audrey Rife, born September 30, 1912 on December 27, 1946 and they had one son, Richard Wendell Bradbury born November 1, 1947. Audrey had previously been married to Marvin Thaxton and had two sons William Darrell and Larry Marvin Thaxton. Audrey was the daughter of Hollis and Ethel (Thomas) Rife and the granddaughter of Sylvester and Louisa (Roush) Rife and Nathaniel and Rocena (Rumfield) Thomas.

Wendell was a graduate of Cheshire High School in 1929 and a farmer and lifelong resident of Cheshire Township. Wendell also served as trustee of Cheshire Township and was a member of Siloam Masonic Lodge #456 at Cheshire and Eno Grange. Audrey retired from the Gallipolis State Institute and was a member of the Cheshire chapter of the Eastern Star and Eno Grange. Wendell died Jan 17, 1988 and Audrey died April 24, 1999.

Richard Bradbury, son of Wendell and Audrey, married Linda Ann Sisson, the daughter of Wayne and Annabelle (Rupe) Sisson. They have two children Lan Ann and Brian Wendell. Lori married to Robert David Robinson on July 31, 1999. Lori attended Denison University in Granville, Ohio and is completing her Doctorate of Psychology at Xavier University in Cincinnati, Ohio. Brian has a daughter Mariah Ann born March 4, 1995.

Although Richard and Linda have lived in Columbus for several years, we continue to own the old Bradbuny Farm at Kyger, which has been continuously owned by the Bradbury family since it was first, purchased by Asa Bradbury in 1842. Although we currently spend many weekends and vacations at the farm, we look forward to returning to Gallia County on a permanent basis.

*Submitted by: Richard W Bradbury*

**BOBETTE OLIVIA DEXTER AND FRANK EDWARD BRAXTON, JR.** - Bobette Olivia Dexter was born in Gallipolis, Ohio, on December 22, 1943. She is the oldest of four daughters born to Arnetta Anderson and Samuel Edward Dexter. Her siblings are Janet Kay Dexter Davis (October 20, 1945- June 26, 1992); Rosann Dexter Hollinshed (October 16, 1947), and Marlene Sue Dexter (July 18, 1957).

Bobette attended Lincoln Colored School for her first two years of education and then went to Washington Elementary School after desegregation in 1951. She graduated from Gallia Academy High School in 1961. Upon graduation, she was hired by the Federal Bureau of Investigation, Washington, D.C., as the first Black American secretary, working there for the FBI for seven years. She transferred to the U. S. Department of Transportation and works for the Office of the Secretary; and the Federal Highway Administration, Office of Program Review and Investigations and Office of Civil Rights, attaining the position of Internal EEO Division Chief She retired in 1993. She worked as the secretary for her church, Clifton Park Baptist, for one year after retirement and then moved to Gallipolis where Frank and she had purchased their retirement home.

Frank Edward Braxton, Jr. (December 28, 1940) a native of Washington, D.C., as is his father, Frank Edward Braxton, Sr. (January 30, 1915). His mother was Geneva Althea Johnson Braxton (March 6, 1920 -June 6, 1988) of Richmond, VA. Frank was educated in the D.C. public schools, graduating from McKinley High School, obtaining a B.S. in mathematics and a B.S. in business administration from D.C. Teachers College (now the University of the District of Columbia), a masters in computers in education from Trinity College, Washington, D.C. He continues his studies at the University of Rio Grande. His work experience includes the Internal Revenue Service and George Washington University, teaching at Groveton High School in Virginia, teaching at Randolph and Newport Junior High Schools in Maryland, computer programming and technology at the Air Lines Pilots Association, Bradford Corporation, U. S. Department of Transportation, GEICO, and his own business, K"NARF The Web Doctor. He has returned to his passion— teaching—with Buckeye Hills Career Center, Rio Grande, OH, and is assigned to Vinton County High School, McArthur, OH.

Frank and Bobette are the parents of three sons. Shawn Christopher (February 8, 1965) married to Monica Marie Londo Green, residence Columbia, MD; Alfred Thomas Austin-Braxton (June 22, 1967) married to Gina Marie LeVine Callahan, residence Germantown, MD; and Joel Elliott (July 17, 1973) married to Nicole Dominique Robinson, residence Gaithersburg, MD. Bobette and Frank have seven grandchildren: Samantha Callahan, Nathaniel Jacob Green, Micheal Alexander Braxton, Olivia Marie Braxton, Nicholas Elliott Braxton, Thomas Edward Austin Braxton, and Geneva Dominique Braxton.

Bobette and Frank are members of the John Gee Black Historical Center, Inc. and the Gallia County Historical Society. Bobette is the secretary of the John Gee Center, and Frank is president of the GCHS.

(Family histories are under Benjamin Lee, Samuel Lee, Ora Le~ Anderson, and Arnetta Anderson.)

*Submitted by Bobette Dexter Braxton.*

**ROY D. BRIGGS FAMILY** - Roy Delbert and Ruby Elizabeth (Poulton) Briggs moved to Hanersville, in Gallia County, in early August 1954 with their two young sons, Gregory Vernon (born March 5, 1948 in Garrett, Ind.), and Terry Neil (born Dec. 16, 1950, in Zanesville, Ohio). Roy's move to Hanersville was as a member of the initial operations group for the Kyger Creek power station nearing completion at Cheshire, one of the two main power sources for the Atomic Energy Commission's uranium enrichment plant near Waverly, Ohio. The family had previously lived in Angola, Ind. (where Roy graduated from Tri-State College in December 1948), Duncan Falls, Ohio, and New York, N.Y., where Roy was employed with the Ohio Power Company.

Roy was born July 27, 1919, the youngest son of Elam Briggs (born May 11, 1880, in Greenbrier, Ohio) and Cora Belle Williams (born March 30, 1882 in Rinard Mills, Ohio). Roy's siblings were the late Everett Raymond Briggs and Edith Elsie (Briggs) Ring. Ruby was born July 9, 1922, the youngest daughter of Oscar Vernon Poulton (born Feb. 4, 1888, at Low Gap, Ohio), and Ada Mary Foraker (born March 9, 1890, in Greenbrier, Ohio). Her sisters are Ruth Beryl (Poulton) Salisbury, of Marietta, and the late Marjorie Ada (Poulton) Ullum. All were from the vicinity of Rinard Mills on the Little Muskingum River in Monroe County, Ohio. Roy and Ruby were married April 8, 1946, in Marietta, Ohio.

*The Briggs family Thanksgiving, 2001. From left to right: Doug, Ethan, Donna, Greg, Ruby, Bryce, Roy, guest (standing), Chad (standing), Ruth Salisbury, Melinda, Terry.*

Roy and Ruby's third son, Roy Douglas, was born in Holzer Hospital on First Avenue in Gallipolis on April 19, 1962. All the sons attended Washington Elementary and graduated from Gallia Academy — Greg and Terry in the 1960s and Doug in 1980. All three also attended college. Greg graduated from Rio Grande College, while Terry graduated from the University of Cincinnati, as did Doug, who initially attended Rio Grande College.

Roy worked at Kyger Creek as both operations and maintenance supervisor until his retirement in 1980, and he and Ruby still live in Hanersville in the house they moved into in 1954. They regularly attend First Presbyterian Church and they celebrated their 55th wedding anniversary in April 2001.

Greg retired in December 2001 after 30 years in media services at the Gallipolis Developmental Center, where Donna Ellen (High) Briggs, his wife, continues her work in the therapeutic program. They were married Dec. 3, 1971, and along with their son, Chad (born March 11, 1978 at Holzer Hospital), also live in Hanersville, just five houses from Roy and Ruby.

Terry lives in Cincinnati, as he has since 1974, and works as an architect.

Doug married Melinda Carol Powers, a former reporter for the Gallipolis Daily Tribune, on Oct. 1, 1994. They live near Morrow, Ohio. Doug, a civil engineer, is the Regional Projects Manager for right-of-way acquisition with the Ohio Department of Transportation's Lebanon, Ohio, office. Melinda is a part-time writer/editor and full-time mom. Their son Ethan Douglas, born Aug. 28, 1998, in Marietta, Ohio, and daughter Bryce Carolyn, born July 12, 2001 in Cincinnati, are the most recent and welcome additions to the Briggs family.

**EMERSON AND ANNA MARIE (KRAUS) BROWN** - Milton Brown was born in Pennsylvania in 1818 and died here in 1896. His father was born in Ireland and his mother in Pennsylvania. He and his first wife Anna Jane Ralston had the following children: John, Rufus, Orland, and Ann. With his second wife, Nancy Sigler, they had: Emerson, Richard Lee, Leander, Richard M., Obron, Lucius, George, and Bert.

*Emerson And Mary Brown With Their Children: Jacob Milton, Della, Lena, And Minnie*

Milton married Nancy, the daughter of Charles and Rhoda (Rosannah Slater) Sigler in 1853. The Siglers were living in Gallia Co. by 1818. Nancy was born in 1835 arid died in 1920. Milton and Nancy are buried in Mina Chapel Cemetery.

Emerson was the eldest son of Milton and Nancy. He was born in 1854 in Northup, Ohio. He and Anna Marie (Mary Kraus) were married on June 14, 1877.

Her parents were Jacob and Jane Kraus who immigrated from Hanover, Germany. Jacob was born in 1830 and died in 1902. Jane was born in 1831, but a record of her death has not been found. Mary was born in Green Twp. on Kraus-Beck Rd. in 1857. Her siblings were: Jacob, Catharine, Margaret, Phillip, Frank, John and Fred. Emerson and Mary had four children: Jacob Milton who married Bernice Esse Saunders, Della who married Matt Reid (they owned and operated The Gallipolis Dye Works), Lena who married Ben Pickens, and Minnie who married Theodore Hudson Walker.

Jake and Bernice were married in Gallipolis on April 21, 1909, and they had four children: Lucy Evelyn, Helen Margaret, Mary Gertrude, and Charles Jacob. (See biography of Jacob and Bernice Brown). Neither Della nor Lena had children, but Lena adopted a baby and named her Lena. Minnie had two children: Raymond and Erma.

Emerson and Mary lived on a farm on Portsmouth Rd. before moving to Fourth Ave. between Grape and Court Streets. Emerson owned horses and could be seen plowing gardens with them in the Springtime. He also planted melons on the island at the end of Sycamore St. There was a barge—type ferry there which was operated by turning a crank by hand. A horse and wagon could fit on the ferry to bring a load of melons to shore where he sold them to local grocery stores. The island was much larger then.

Emerson had two serious accidents. Once he lost control of his horse and buggy after being run off the road by a passing car. He lay in the ditch for several hours before being found and taken to the hospital. He and his son Jake were cutting hay on the levee when Emerson was cut severely on the leg by the sickle bar. He recovered after another hospitalization, but died later that year at the age of 79. That was August 20, 1935. Mary died in 1932 after suffering a stroke. They are both buried at Mound Hill Cemetery.

*Submitted by: Carol Robinson*

**HARVEY E. BROWN, JR. FAMILY** - Eulah Francis Miller married Harvey Eugene Brown, Jr. February 17, 1943 in Miami Beach, Florida. He was stationed in an army base there before he was to depart for South Africa during World War II. While he was abroad, Eulah and his parents worked at the Firestone Factory in Akron, Ohio.

*Harvey & Eulah Brown*

After the war, they returned to Gallipolis to their families. Harvey was the only surviving son of Lillie Mae Cox and Harvey L. Brown Sr. Eulah was the daughter of August Phillip Miller and Verna Mae Rice. Eulah had a brother Clayton Miller (married Kate Evans) and has a sister Mildred Odella Miller (married to Paul Kerns).

Eulah's great grandfather, John George Miller, was born July 31, 1826 in Kerchdorf, Bavaria. He arrived in Pittsburgh, Pennsylvania on the 12 of October of 1856. In 1862, they moved to Ohio. The family settled in a homestead on German Hollow Road. St. Martin Lutheran Church, which they attended, had many of its original services in German

Harvey's grandparents were Nancy Dewitt and Richard Milton Brown. Nine boys and one girl were survivors of this union. Only one great grandson, Toby Lee Brown, remains to carry on the name.

Harvey and Eulah had two children. They had one daughter Peggy Lou Brown (married to Charles E. Huber II) and a son Gary Lee Brown (married Jan Hudson) deceased.

Eulah worked for Kerr Drug store and was assistant manager of Gallagher's. She retired alter being a receptionist for Dr. T Jay Bradshaw. In fact Dr. Bradshaw drove Harvey to the Silver Bridge when it fell. Harvey's daughter Peggy called them from Point Pleasant to tell them that the bridge fell and she was at Wellman's Jewelry Store. They drove up and expected to see the sidewalk gone or only part of the bridge gone. Harvey walked the train bridge that crossed the river to get Peggy that night.

Harvey sold insurance for Western Southern Insurance Company when he first returned to Gallipolis. He then worked for Columbia Gas of Ohio where he retired after having a heart attack. He died January 31, 1996.

Eulah lives with her daughter in Gallipolis and enjoys her three grandchildren {Amy Huber, Abbey (Huber) Russell, and Toby Brown) and one great grand child (Alexis Russell)

*Submitted by: Eulah Brown*

**JACOB MILTON AND BERNICE (SAUNDERS) BROWN** - Jacob Brown was born on Aug. 5, 1877 in Gallia Co. to Emerson (1854— 1935) and Anna Marie (Mary Kraus) Brown(1857—1932). His grandparents were Milton (1818—1896) and Nancy (Sigler) Brown(1835—1920)and Jacob (1830—1902) and Jane Kraus (B. 1831) from Hanover, Germany. Jake died at his home at 549 Fourth Ave. on Jan. 11, 1958.

*Jacob Milton Brown And Bernice Saunders Brown Early 1900's*

Bernice was born near Cadmus in Walnut Township on Feb. 23, 1890 and died July 23, 1983 in Gallipolis. Her parents were Charles(1861—1945) and Maggie (Brammer) Saunders (D. 1893) who were married in 1889 in Gallia Co.. During a diphtheria epidemic, Bernice's mother and younger sister died and Bernice was reared by her grandparents Harvey(1831—1918) and Mary(Yates) (1832—1894) Saunders. Harvey's parents were John (1805—1870) and Sabra (Sturgill) Saunders from Fluvanna Co.,Va. settling here in 1834. John owned a drugstore in Waterloo, Ohio and made his own medicines, practiced dentistry, was an undertaker and watchmaker. John was born in Va. and Sabra was born in Ashe Co., North Carolina in 1811 of William and Sophie (King) Sturgill. Sabra's grandfather Dr. David King lived in Rhode Island and vaccinated the first person in that state about 1799.

When Bernice came to Gallipolis she lived with her uncle and aunt Rev. and Mrs. Tim Carey. Rev. Carey was pastor at the First Baptist Church. When she and Jake met, she was working at the state hospital. While they were courting, Jake gave her a pre—engagement ring which remains in the family. Without her knowledge, Jake rented a house on Court St. and furnished it. He took Bernice there, proposed to her and they were married in their home April 21, 1909.

They had four children: Lucy Evelyn who married James Taylor, Helen Margaret who married Thomas Welker, Mary Gertrude who married Henry Fowler, and Charles J. Brown who married Avonell Renshaw. Henry and Mary had two daughters: Carol Yvonne who married Charles Robinson and Nancy Anne who married Delbert Clark. Both girls are presently residents of this county.

Jake started out his life working as wharf master at the riverfront and later drove a delivery truck for the Ohio Valley laundry, was a watchman for construction of the city water reservoir, and was caretaker of the city park. He went back to driving a horse when in his retirement he had a job driving a horse—drawn ice cream wagon. His grandchildren enjoyed riding with him through Gallipolis selling the treats. Jake was accustomed to driving a horse and wagon

Jacob Milton and Bernice Saunders Brown: During W.W.II he tried to enlist in the army, but he did not meet the height requirement. He drove his horse and wagon to Camp Sherman and delivered supplies for the army until the end of the war. Bernice often cared for elderly people in her home and assisted with the home—deliveries of babies. She helped deliver several of her grandchildren. Jake loved to plant vegetable gardens and continued to be active until his death. The grandchildren all have very fond memories of both Jake and Bernice.

*Submitted: by Carol Robinson*

## WILLIAM E. AND WILMA R. BROWN -

William E. Brown was born on January 27, 1936 in Gallia County, Ohio and moved to Columbus, Ohio at the age of 7. He returned to Gallipolis in 1950 to live with his aunt and uncle, Myrtle and Cecil Mink of Northup, Ohio. He enrolled in Gallia Academy where he graduated in 1955 where he was a member of the Blue Devil Football team (No. 17). After graduation, he went back to Columbus and worked at the Columbus State Hospital as a painter until 1959 when he transferred to Gallipolis State Institute, paint crew.

*William E. and Wilma R. Brown*

Wilma was born on March 4, 1938, daughter of Ross and Ethel Roush. She attended Washington Grade School and Gallia Academy High School and graduated in 1956. She then attended Columbus Business University in Columbus, Ohio. She went to work for the Treasurer of the Ohio Conference of the United Methodist Church.

On April 20, 1957 she and Bill were married at the Grace United Methodist Church by Dr. Lester Roush, uncle of Wilma and Rev. Warren Wilson. minister of Grace Church. She and Bill lived in Columbus until his transfer to GSI. On February 21, 1958, their first child was born, Kimberley Anne; Jeffery Ross was born on December 20, 1959, and William Christopher was born on February 4, 1961. Wilma was a stay at home Mom until Chris started Community Kindergarten. At that time she went to work as secretary at The Grace United Methodist Church.

Bill was now working for the Goodyear Tire and Rubber Company. Wilma then went to work at the Gallia County Health Department as a secretary and worked until the children got too old for a baby sitter and too young to be left alone and was again a stay at home Mom. In 1971, the family moved from Evans Heights to 112 State Street across from Gallia Academy High School. In 1972 Wilma went to work for Bennett and King, a law firm in Gallipolis. She worked there until James Bennett was elected the Gallipolis Municipal Judge, in 1979, when she went to the Court as Clerk which took up the next 10 years of her life. All this time Bill was very active with independent slow pitch softball league and also the church league and had gone to work as supervisor at the Kaiser Aluminum Plant in Ravenswood, W. Va. and worked there until 1987 when the plant downsized. Kim graduated from Gallia Academy High School in 1976, Jeff graduated in 1978 and joined the United States Navy and Chris graduated in 1979. Kim is now living in Dublin, married to Thomas Duncan and the mother of two extended family children, Chelsea and Taylor Duncan. Jeff is living in Elkridge, Maryland, married to the former Cindy Crews also of Gallipolis and they have three children, William Ross (Willie), Joshua Brumfield, and Scarlett Olivia. Josh and Scarlett were born on the same day, one year and one hour apart. Chris is living near Rio Grande married to the former Anette Carter and is the father of four children, Kelsey Nicole, Shelby Lynn, Christopher Dylan, and Gregory Carter Smith.

Wilma worked for James Bennett for 28 years as a legal secretary and in 1990 was elected to the Gallipolis City Commission where she served as Vice President of the Commission for four years.

Bill retired from the Ohio Department of Transportation on June 1, 1999 and Wilma retired from the City of Gallipolis on July 31, 1999.

## JOHN ANDREW BRUMFIELD FAMILY -

John Andrew Brumfield (Jesse and Elizabeth Grove Brumfield) was born February 11, 1833. He married Abigail Massie (daughter of Jonathan Massie and Margaret Roach) on December 3, 1851 in Lawrence Co. She was born June 24, 1834.

John served in Company C of the 91st OVI during the Civil War. After the war, he worked his farm in Crown City. Abigail moved to Huntington after John's death. She was awarded a widow's pension of $8 per month.

John and Abigail had the following children: 1. Mahala was born September 25, 1852, and married John Gray. 2. Sarah was born November 14, 1854, and married Lonnie Bennett. 3. Louisa was born September 24, 1856, and married James L. Sims on October 28, 1884, Gallia Co. 4. Jesse was born March 9, 1859, in Lawrence Co. He married Sarah Ann Adkins in 1876 and Mary Frances Sheets in 1893. Jesse died on April 4, 1907. 5. Emma was born September 14, 1861, and married Bert Brumfield. 6. Abigale was born 1865 in Lawrence County. 7. Ellen was born 1868 in Lawrence Co. 8. Rebecca Ann was born September 4, 1870 in Gallia Co. She married George Chapman (1862-1954) on November 5, 1887 in Crown City. Rebecca died January 23, 1936 in Athalia, Ohio.

9. Mary A. was born November 20, 1874. She married Jesse M. Williams (1875-1954) on March 23, 1896 in Gallia Co. Mary died in 1945. 10. J. B. was born on July 1, 1877, and died before 1905. As J.B. is not listed on the military pension claim of his father, it is likely that J.B. died in childhood. 11. Rhoda M. was born October 12, 1878. She married Madore Everett on January 23, 1896 in Gallia Co.

*John & Abigail Brumfield About 1895*

John Andrew died on August 9, 1905 in Crown City. Abigail died February 16, 1916 in Huntington, West Virginia. They are both buried at Good Hope Cemetery near Crown City, along with John's brothers, James (1835-1903) and Sloan (1845-1920). James and Sloan also served the Union during the Civil War.

**BRUNICARDI FAMILY -** My grandfather, Antonio Brunicardi spent much of his early adolescence traveling back and forth between the United States and Italy establishing himself as a businessman. It was on a return trip from America that he met and fell in love with a young Italian woman. Laura, my grandmother was returning to Italy on break from school, she was helping my grandfather with the task of translation. The ship they were sailing on had lost his luggage and with that simple twist of fate, a marriage that would sustain the loss of three children, the birth of six and a world war had begun.

Antonio and Laura raised their six children: Gabriella (Rita), Giovanni (John), Louisa, Fortunate (Hope), Leticia (Lettie), and Oreste (Rusty) in Veteglia, a small town located in the Tuscan countryside. The family house was located along the Brenner Pass highway, a direct line utilized by all armies in World War II. This made the following years particularly cruel for a young family to endure and the memories heart wrenching.

The war had left my grandparents struggling like many of their friends and neighbors. The traveling my grandfather had done throughout the United States led him to believe he could start again in America and give his family a new life.

They arrived in New York and settled in Reading, PA, where they stayed with relatives for awhile. My grandfather, looking for a suitable place to raise a family, traveled south with my father, John, to a small town he had passed through earlier, Gallipolis, Ohio. A short time later my grandmother and the rest of the children arrived. The first Brunicardi family business was formed, a restaurant/bar called "Tony's", which enabled my grandfather to provide for his family. It was here that he instilled in each of his children the desire to have a dream.

This is apparent with my father, John. He graduated from Gallia Academy High School in 1954, where he excelled in music. After graduation, John joined the Air Force. His expertise with the trumpet opened many doors for him, including the Air Force Band and after that his own jazz group in New York. He went to Ohio University and graduated with his bachelor's and master's degrees in Music Education. His years as a music educator in southeastern Ohio showed him how important music education was in the development of young minds. This led to the start of Brunicardi Music in 1967, which would go on to help provide musical education for students throughout the area until its' closing at the end of 1999.

John and his wife Katie (McDaniel), a registered nurse, provided much for their three children: Laura Northup, Armanda Brunicardi, and Anita Brunicardi, but family pride and history far exceed the material aspect. What was once the driving force that brought my grandparents to America has since been passed on through generation to generation.

*Submitted by Anita Brunicardi*

**BURCHAM-BELVILLE** - I was the only child born to Helen Elizabeth (Dailey) and John E. Burcham. I was born April 08, 1937 at the family farm home on Indian Guyan Creek in southeastern Gallia County. I am the only child of two only children; therefore, I was the only grandchild of two loving sets of grandparents; James E. and Grace (Haskins) Dailey and John R. and Della (Ours) Burcham. I was the recipient of much love, guidance, and training from six loving people each day as the families lived only two miles apart. I attended Mercerville School for ten years and Gallia Academy High School for two years. During my schooling in Grades 1 thru 12, I missed only ten days of school; those being in the first year due to contacting all the diseases of childhood. I graduated from Gallia Academy High School in 1955 and entered Rio Grande College for two years. On December 25, 1955, I was married to John L. Belville, son of Eunice (Sheets) and Stanley Belville who were friends and neighbors of my family. John was in the USAF from 1952-1955. We became the parents of two children; Thomas Lee, born October 03, 1956, and Teresa Anne, born January 27, 1961, who married Robert G. Marchi on February 06, 1993. Both children graduated from Hannan Trace High School and attended Rio Grande College ; Teresa being the only one to graduate. As of this date, she is employed as the client-advocate director of the Gallipolis Developmental Center and lives in Gallipolis, OH.

John and I divorced in 1993 and I entered the work force at the Gallia County Department of Human Services and retired in 1999. On December 15, 1999, I married Lonnie W. Thompson and we reside in Gallipolis, OH.

We are both members of the Gallia County Historical Society, Gallia County Genealogical Society, and First Families of Gallia County. We usually spend the winter months in Florida with the "Thompson Clan".

**BURCHAM - DAILEY** - My progenitor, John "Scott" Sylvester Burcham was born in Frederick County, Virginia in 1769. He and his brother, Samuel were orphaned at a young age and were reared in a church orphanage. They received their family inheritance at the age of maturity and left Virginia to live in Clark County, Kentucky to be close to relatives. John met and married Nancy Anne Dowden, whose sister was married to Simon Kenton. During this time, he joined the army and served as a spy under the command of General Anthony Wayne and was discharged at Fort Washington, which is now Cincinnati, OH. After the war ended they decided to return to Virginia to live. When they began the journey, Nancy Anne was with child and went into labor as they approached beautiful downtown Guyandotte, WV. After the birth of her child, they decided to cross the Ohio River and build a home in Lawrence, County, Ohio. John purchased land and proceeded to build a home for the family. During this period, he moved his family into a cave where they lived until he had completed the cabin. One of their sons, William Fleming Burcham born June 29, 1820, married Rebecca Anne Harrison who was born in 1820 in Franklin County, Virginia. They became the parents of eleven children one being, John Henry Burcham who married Mary Jane Reed and they were the parents of my grandfather, John Reed Burcham who was born October 12, 1865. John R. Burcham married Della Ours and they became the parents of one son, John Everett, born December 09, 1912, who married Helen Elizabeth Dailey, daughter of James E. and Grace Haskins Dailey on August 22, 1934. To this union one child was born, Elizabeth Anne who has married twice; first to John L. Belville and then to Lonnie W. Thompson. During the marriage of Anne to John Belville, they became the parents of two children, Thomas and Teresa. Teresa is married to Robert G. Marchi.

**ANDREW BURKE** - Someone, somewhere, is a descendant of this couple.

This sketch is dedicated to that person.

Cynthia White was born 9 August 1816, a daughter of Gallia County First Family Alfred and Mary (Perry) White who settled in Perry Township along the Lawrence County line. Cynthia married (about 1835, perhaps in Illinois) Andrew Burke, son of William and Mary (Neal) of Lawrence County. Andrew was born about 1812 and taught at the first school in Symmes Township.

The couple must have lived in Illinois for a time, but Cynthia and a young son returned to Perry Township by 1840, being enumerated in her father's household that year. Cynthia's parents moved to Jones County, Iowa, about 1846. The 1850 Census finds them in Richland Township: Alfred White, 72, Mass; Mary White, 66, VT; William Burk, 13, IL; Mary White, 20y, OH. The fate of William Burk is unknown.

On 13 August 1855, Andrew and Cynthia purchased Town Lots 26 and 27 in Marion (Aid) from William Knowlton and sold them to Daniel Neal 7 January 1859.

Cynthia's sister, Sarah, married George Carter in 1858. The couple appears in Patriot in 1860: George Carter, 56, OH; Sarah Carter, *51*, PA; Mary White, 78, b. VT; Sarah Carter, 8, OH; Amanda James, 16, OH; Perry Berth [Burk], 11, OH. Who was Amanda James?

Cynthia Burk appears on the rolls of John's Creek Sabbath School in Lawrence County in 1861 and 1862. Andrew and his brother, John, are called "of Illinois" in the petition for division of the estate of their mother, dated 1 August 1865.

The will of Sarah Carter 23 October 1865 mentions "my Sister Cynthia residing in Gallipolis, and the widow of Andrew Burke deceased." Andrew was clearly not deceased at this time, as will be shown.

In a deposition dated 3 August 1867, Thomas Ramsey attests he loaned Cynthia $56 in June 1865, to repay a loan from her sister, Sarah. Stephen Keller, executor, pays in full Sarah's $100 bequest to Cynthia on 6 December 1867. On 26 February 1868, the Ironton Register gives notice of Cynthia Burk vs Andrew Burk non-suit.

Cynthia is enumerated in Gallipolis in 1870: Cynthia Burk, *45*, OH; Perry A. Burk, 21, OH; Thomas Ramsy, 41, Scotland.

Andrew Burk, 62, born Lawrence County, was admitted to the Lawrence County Infirmary 6 December 1876. That same date an 11-year-old Eliza Burk was also admitted. Eliza was "transferred" 8 February 1877; Andrew was "discharged" in April 1877. The nature of their illnesses is not preserved, nor is their relationship (if any). This is the last known record of Andrew Burk.

Cynthia is listed as "housekeeper" 1880 in Gallipolis: Thomas Ramsey, 49, England; Cynthia Burk, 61, OH; Mary Asher, 21, niece, OH, father born Ireland, mother born Ohio. Who was Mary Asher?

Thomas Ramsey's will, recorded 24 July 1880 Gallia County, leaves everything to his adopted son, Perry Alonzo Lyones [?Burk], then living in Columbus (no census found).

Thomas Ramsey's connection to the White family is intriguing. He seems to have been known by all; he was even executor of the estate of Cynthia's sister-in-law, Mary (Carson) White.

*Submitted by: Linda Gaylord-Kuhn*

**CLYDE D. AND FREEDA (DUNN) BURNETT FAMILY** - Clyde was born at Kanauga, February 6, 1926, to Truman Fulton and Stella (Smith) Burnett. He had six brothers, Morris, Woodrow, Vinton, Claude (his twin), Robert, and Truman Jr. and three sisters, Helen Strickland, Rachel Borton, and Mary Ann Bowman. His parents came to Kanauga from the Mercerville area. He served in the Korean Conflict and later owned and operated Burnett's Roofing and Heating Company until his retirement in 1987. He currently serves as Gallipolis Township Trustee and Central Committeeman for Kanauga precinct.

He married Freeda Dunn August 29, 1950, daughter of William James and Miriam Dunn Hudson. They were from the Pliny and Ambrosia, West Virginia areas. They have spent their married life in Kanauga and their four children were born and raised there. They are all graduates of Gallia Academy High School.

Jo Ellen Burnett was born April 1954. She married Robert Keith Garbesi. They are the parents of Jessica and Maria Garbesi. Their history is listed under Burnett-Garbesi in this book.

John Gordon Burnett was born in December 1955. After graduation he worked in the family business until 1987 when he became co-owner with his brother Tom. He is interested in hunting, camping, and outdoor sports. He also enjoys hunting for arrowheads and has an extensive collection.

*The Clyde Burnett Family*

He married Belinda Sue Burdette, daughter of Billy Joe and Phyllis Burdette Daniels. She is employed at Holzer Clinic. Their son Ryan Cliff graduated from Gallia Academy in 2001 and is employed by the family business. Joshua Clyde is in grade eight at Gallia Academy. Both like to hunt deer and squirrels and enjoy all outdoor sports. John and Belinda are now divorced.

Clyde Thomas Burnett was born May 1958. He married Tonia McCoy Caldwell, daughter of LeRoy McCoy and Sandra McCoy Garner. They lived in Kanauga with Jamie Caldwell, Tonia's son from a previous marriage. Jamie graduated from Gallia Academy in 1994 and married Amanda Thivener, daughter of Debbie and Garry Thivener. They have two daughters, Haleigh and Jalea. Jamie's father is Jack Caldwell.

Tom is co-owner of Burnett's Roofing and Heating Company. He is a fan of the Cincinnati Reds and the Ohio State Football team. Tonia is employed as a registered nurse at the Adena Hospital in Chillicothe, Ohio.

They are the parents of Thomas Aaron, a senior at Gallia Academy, member of Madrigals, captain of the football team, president of the National Honor Society, and plans to attend college after graduation. Brittany Lynn D is in grade five at Washington Elementary, a straight "A" student, involved in girls basketball, and other sports. They attend Fairhaven United Methodist Sunday School. They like skiing and vacationing at the beach.

Robin Leah Burnett was born September 1962. She married George Jackman Wharton in 1984. They are the parents of Daniel and Taylor Wharton. Their history is listed under Burnett-Wharton in this book.

We are the proud Grandparents of nine wonderful grandchildren and two great grandchildren.

**CLARENCE BURNS - GLADYS SIGLER FAMILY** - Clarence "Buzz" Burns was born October 5, 1901, at Mason, WV. He was one of 15 children born to Christopher Columbus Burns and Nettie May Roush Burns. He married Elma Gladys Sigler, born June 30, 1909, at Gallipolis Ferry, WV on June 30, 1925. To this union was born 12 children: Mildred, William, Robert, Clara, Thelma, Christina, Wilma, Clarence Jr., Carol, Loretta and James.

Clarence was nicknamed "Buzz" and was best known by this name, which he acquired because of his stature and speed at which he worked. He was a very hard worker and would do any menial job to support his family. He walked the streets during the depression begging for work. I especially remember one time when he was elated because someone had hired him to clean out ashes from their furnace. He made 50 cents and with it bought hamburger and we had hamburger gravy.

"Buzz" raised a garden, rabbits, chickens, and hunted game to help feed the hungry mouths. He had a huge strawberry patch and sold berries "baskets heaped up so people would get their Money's worth". How we hated picking those berries but the proceeds usually meant school clothes.

"Buzz" worked at the Marietta Plant, Gallipolis Locks and Dam, did carpentry work and painting. He called for square dances for years and taught many area people to dance: square, polka, Scottish, clog. He passed away November 5, 1989, at the age of 88.

Gladys was a sixth generation descendent of the French 500, having descended from Nicholas Questel (1765). Her grandmother was Aurora Burnett Berridge, fourth generation and her mother, Edna Berridge Sigler, fifth generation.

Gladys "Burnsey" worked at Holzer Hospital for 27 years in both housekeeping and central supply. She attended church regularly and instilled the importance of honest truth and integrity in each of us. She loved her flowers and I often heard her say that she could walk in her garden and feel God's hand in hers". She always wore an apron which served many purposes. She would gather eggs and vegetables. She would wipe tears. She always had a hanky in the pocket for runny noses and babies could always be kept from chilly air wrapped in her apron. She passed away December 2, 1994, at the age of 85.

Of the 12 children born to this couple, 10 are still living, almost all of them in the local area. We were blessed to have such good parents. We were never affluent but we made up for it in love. Can there be anything greater?

*Submitted by: Mildred Daft, daughter.*

**MILDRED BURNS-DAFT** - First Generation: Nicholas Questel was born in Chalindrey, France on June 4, 1765. He was the first born son of Jacques Questel and Marguerite Viardot. His father was a baker, but Nicholas became a coachman. He married Jeanne Claude LeMonte in October 1787 and they set sail for America with The French 500. Jeanne died aboard ship giving birth to their only child John Baptiste Questel. She was probably buried at sea since no record of her death has been found. Nicholas and his son John settled in Green Township. Nicholas died in 1832 at the age of 67 and is buried in the old Questel Cemetery located in a pasture on the Paul Niday Farm. Several of the old stones still remain standing.

Second Generation:
John Baptiste Questel was my third great grandfather. He became a farmer after inheriting his father's property. In 1816 he married Elizabeth Fuller in Gallia County and they had twelve children, seven who survived to adulthood. John died in 1849 at the age of 59, He too was buried in the old Questel Family Cemetery. Elizabeth died in 1853.

Third Generation:
Sarah Questel was my great, great-grandmother. She was the ninth child and fourth daughter of John and Elizabeth Questel. Born in Gallia County in 1837. In 1854 she married Richard B. Burnett in Gallipolis. They had four children. Richard is believed to have been a casualty of the Civil War between the states. Sarah married a second time to Henry McCorkle and had one child. Sarah died in 1911.

Fourth Generation:
Aurora Burnett was my great grandmother. She was the fourth child and second daughter of Sarah and Richard Burnett. Born in Illinois in 1859, she married Henry Sylvester Berridge in 1875. They had five children, Henry died in 1924 and Aurora died in 1944. They are both buried in Pine Street Cemetery in Gallipolis.

Fifth Generation:
Edna Iva Berridge was my grandmother. Born in 1876 to Aurora and Henry Berridge. She married Charles Ervin Sigler in 1894. I vividly remember my beloved grandmother. She had a disfigured hand and a player piano that we all loved to play. How I remember her big fluffy coconut cakes. Grandpa Sigler worked at the furniture factory and for several years at the old water works. They are both buried in Centenary Cemetery.

Sixth Generation
Elma Gladys Sigler was my mother. She was one of nine children born to Edna and Charles Sigler. She was born in 1909 at Gallipolis Ferry W. Va. She married Clarence "Buzz" Burns in 1925 and they had twelve children. I am the eldest. I am so blessed to have had two wonderful parents. Dad died in 1989. Mom died in 1994 after a bout with Hodgkin's Disease. They are both buried in Centenary Cemetery.

*Submitted by Mildred Burns Daft with some data supplied by Dr. Theodore Questrell and Nick Questrel.*

**BUSH FAMILY** - George Fletcher Bush, a blacksmith and a widower, who was born in 1858 in West Virginia, arrived in Bidwell with his two youngest children, Wayne Anderson Bush (born. in 1892) and George Leonard Bush (born in 1897) around 1910-1912. He set up a blacksmith business next to his home on State Route 554 directly opposite Bidwell Porter High School and Grade School.

His ancestors came to Norfolk, Virginia from Germany during the 1750's. In the years that followed, many of them moved westward into the region that later became West Virginia. George F. learned the blacksmith trade from his father. In 1884, he married Mary Oliver in New Haven, WVA. They had five children before Mary died at age 39 in 1902. The two older children, Ivan and Roddy, became blacksmiths and went to Westmoreland County, Pennsylvania, to work for coal companies. The middle child, Nellie became a housewife and mother. She and her two small children died in Columbus, Ohio, in 1919 during an epidemic outbreak of influenza. She was 30 years old.

Wayne and his brother George Leonard were still teenagers when they came to Bidwell with their father. George L. graduated from Bidwell Porter High School around 1915. He earned degrees from Ohio State University and Columbia University. He became a teacher and a high-school principal in the Cleveland area and was the author of several science textbooks and numerous articles for science journals. He was a Professor of Chemistry at Kent State University from 1947 to 1966. He had two sons, Richard Wayne (born in 1934) and Charles Arthur (born in 1941). Richard, a research chemist and the father of two sons, lives in Columbia, Maryland. Charles is a Professor of Medicine at Ohio State University and is also the father of two sons. George Leonard Bush died in 1974.

*The Bush Family Home and Blacksmith Shop Built In 1925 Under The Hickory Trees at Bidwell Porter Park*

Returning to the Bushes who remained in Bidwell, George Fletcher and his son Wayne continued in the blacksmith trade. George F. was also an inventor. The U.S. Patent Office granted him three patents from 1903 to 1915. Around 1915, Wayne worked for the railroad. He was also in the U.S. Infantry serving in Company L of the 69th Regiment. He was discharged in 1925.

In 1925, the Bushes purchased a 25-acre grove of trees halfway between Bidwell and Porter known as the Bidwell Porter Park from the Dustin family. In the 1880's the land had been used for political rallies, camp meetings, and Civil War reunions and was called Dustin Grove. In 1906, the Bidwell Porter Park Company leased the land to create an amusement park. They built a racetrack with a speakers platform and nearby stalls for horses, a grandstand, a baseball field, a dancehall and roller skating rink, and a lake. Many popular community events were held here including the Fourth of July celebration, the Bidwell Bean Dinner, and the Emancipation Celebration. Huge crowds came by train to the Bidwell Depot to attend these and other events held at the park. Here the Bushes built a small house and blacksmith shop under the hickory trees and the site then became known as the Bush Park. George F. and Wayne farmed a little on the side. George Fletcher Bush was a member of the Vinton Masonic Lodge No. 131. He died September 5, 1930.

Wayne lived the bachelor life until 1937 when he married Mildred Marie Westfall, the daughter of George and Elva Westfall of Rodney Road in Bidwell. Mr. and Mrs. Wayne Bush had five children, all raised in Bidwell in that little house under the hickory trees in what was once known as Dustin Grove. Doris Marie was born in 1938; Allen Leonard, in 1939; Ruby Lee, In 1942; Clara Suzanne (Suzy), in 1944; and Rosemary, in 1947.

Wayne became custodian of the Bidwell Porter School in the late 1930's. He remained in the position until 1958. Through the years he was popular with generations of students, teachers, and school bus drivers. He was always on hand to deal with problems at the school. He and his large family worked everyday after school to clean the classrooms in preparation for the next day's sessions.

Life in the little house was crowded so it was natural that the family spent much time out of doors. During the long summer months, Wayne and Mildred raised a large garden to feed their family. Cultivating, preserving, and storing the garden produce consumed hours and hours in which each family member made a contribution. Somehow there was ample time for fun, however. The children roamed the countryside picking blackberries in summer and paw-paws and hazelnuts in fall. Friends from school visited often and many joyous hours were spent playing in the surrounding woods and fields. Visits to the Westfall grandparents took the family through the village frequently.

Wayne Anderson Bush died in 1958 just five months after retiring from his custodial position at the school. Mildred Marie Westfall Bush continued to live in Bidwell until 1997. In the late 1970's she married Homer Painter, a retired Bidwell farmer and a widower. Homer died in 1994, and Mildred died in February 2000.

All of the Bush children graduated from local high schools, but future generations of the family were not destined to reside in Bidwell. Doris became a social worker in Akron, OH. She is retired and lives on the coast of Maine. Allen is a businessman and raised two sons and two daughters in Lockbourne, OH. His children all live in the Columbus area, and he has one grandchild. Ruby married Robert Preston of Vinton and moved to Tennessee. She has two daughters, a son and seven grandchildren and lives in Beersheba Springs, TN surrounded by her family. Suzanne moved to Norwalk, CT near New York City. She became an information specialist, and after a 27-year career in the Norwalk Public Library, she retired. She now works part-time for various Connecticut libraries when she is not visiting her summer home in Maine. She has one daughter, a free-lance stage manager who currently lives in Atlanta, GA. Rosemary married Jerry Neal and lived on a farm in Bidwell. She had a son and a daughter before she died tragically in 1974 from breast cancer. Her children were raised by their father in Grove City, OH. They each have one child.

Children's voices can no longer be heard among the trees in Bush Park and the school bell at the Bidwell Porter School on Rt. 554 has not called students to class for many years. But through cherished memories, the "Bush kids", who grew up in Bidwell in the 1940's and 1950's, can vividly recall exactly how it was way back when.

*Submitted by Suzanne Bush*

**HELEN AND GAYLAND BUSH** - Gayland was born in Putnam County, WV, on April 7, 1931 to Maggie Black Bush and William Everett Bush. He was from a family of eight children and is next to the youngest. His siblings are: Lambert, Clyde, James, Ofie, all deceased; Marie Pinschmidt of Palm Beach Gardens, FL; Elsie Gooch of Gallipolis and Geraldine Carter Benton of Bethel, OH. His family came to Gallia County when he was about five years old, and they lived on a farm at Bidwell, and later in the Campaign Creek area. His dad died June 7, 1939 and his mother died April 17, 1988.

In 1946 they moved to Gallipolis. Gayland graduated from GAHS in 1951. While in school, he started working part-time for the Gallipolis Tribune. In 1954 he joined the Navy and served on the USS Saratoga in the Mediterranean area. He married the former Aileen Blazer in 1955 and they had a son, David Keith, born May 24, 1956. David is married to the former Betty Rupe and they have two children, David Paul Bush (February 27, 1984) and Lindsey Dawn Bush (February 13, 1993).

*Thomas Scott, Helen, Gayland Bush Standing: Jamie, Tim, Bryan Bush, Mark & Nicholas Sheets*

After discharge from service in 1958, he again worked for the Tribune and retired in 1995, after working 40 plus years.

Gayland married Helen Folden Merrifield in 1964 and they have two children, Tim (August 11, 1965) and Vicky (July 13, 1973). Helen (May 22, 1933) is one of three daughters of Elta Hall Folden and Stanley Folden. Her sisters are Janice (Alan) Burnett of Reynoldsburg, Ohio, and Wanda Newport of Springfield, Ohio.

Helen was married in 1953 to James R. Merrifield, Jr. He was killed at the age of 25 in an auto accident in CA in 1959, which caused Helen to move back to Gallipolis, her hometown, from Morgantown, WV. They had a daughter, Cynthia Lee (September 19, 1954) who graduated from GAHS in 1972. She received her degree in elementary education from Miami University in 1976 and is presently teaching in Houston, TX.

Helen graduated from GAHS in 1951 and received a two-year degree in Secretarial Studies from Ohio University in 1953. She worked three years for the State ASCS office in Morgantown and transferred to Pt. Pleasant in 1959, working for the Department of Agriculture and the Western Soil Conservation District. After 29 years of working there, she retired in 1988.

Gayland enjoys gardening and woodworking. They are members of the Grace United Methodist Church.

Tim married Jamie Stewart of Logan, OH, and Vicky married Mark Allen Sheets of Gallipolis. Tim's family lives at Baltimore, OH, and Vicky and Mark live on Deenie Drive, Bidwell. Tim graduated from GAHS and Hocking Technical College in computer science. Vicky graduated from GAHS and the University of Rio Grande, with a degree in elementary education. She presently works as a substitute teacher and takes care of little Nicholas at home. She is active in church work and plays flute in the Symphonic Band at Rio Grande.

There are three grandchildren: Thomas Scott Bush (May 17, 1995), Bryan Scott Bush (November 21, 1999), and Nicholas Allen Sheets (December 11, 2000).

## JOHN SYLVESTER BUTCHER FAMILY -

John Sylvester Butcher, born February 22, 1846, died September 17, 1916. He was the son of Jacob and Sarah Caldwell Butcher, married Nancy Crowell, born in 1836, died 1907. They were married April 12, 1866 in Gallia County, Ohio. Their children are: Charles E. (1867-1894); James Austin; Melton (Melt) Melzer, born 1869, died January 3, 1943; Francis Elzinas, born 1870, died Dec 19, 1946; Jacob,( 1872-1901); Sarah Delia, born September 5,1873, died March 5, 1939; Clara Belle, (1879-1948); Thomas Heniger, born January 5, 1883, died April 30, 1957. John Sylvester Butcher's second wife, Nola Safford, was born October 21, 1875, died December 6, 1935. They had one daughter, Bertis Joanna, born May 26, 1915 and died May 28, 1982. Melton and Francis lived with Thomas and his second wife, Zoie Hecker Henry Butcher.

Austin married Emma Wright, children: Edna, Roy, Charles William, Ray, Helen and Willard Wright Butcher.

Sarah Delia married John Miller, children: Jacob Andrew, born May 4, 1898, died January 1967; Dayton, died April 9, 1923 in a motorcycle accident near Wellston, Ohio.

Harley died in a street car accident in Dallas, Texas.

*Butcher Family, 1950's In Front Of Old Dan Glassburn House, Bidwell Left To Right: Edna Goodall, Betty Goodall, Zoie Butcher SSeated: Thomas Butcher*

John and Sarah's daughter Lillie Mae was adopted by a family whose name was Wolfe. The Wolfes changed her name to Dorothy Mae. Sarah's other daughter, Edna Ethel, was adopted by Benjamin (Ben) and Virginia Siders Stewart. Ben worked at the Thompson-Francis Stove Foundry in Gallipolis, Ohio.

Clara Belle married Samuel (Sam) Smith. Their children; Nellie, Bessie,Frederick (Freddy), Bertha, and Gola Dean Smith.

Thomas Heniger Butcher married Alice Elizabeth Smith, Children: Gail Marie, Stella Leona, and Georgia Viola Butcher. Thomas' second wife was Zoie Hecker Henry, born November 4, 18 8 1, died December 19, 1972, Children; Richard Thomas, born 1918, and Merida Elmer, born 192 1. Both children died in infancy.

Bertis Joanna Butcher married Darius Virgil Halley, children; Linda Lee Halley Criner, Diana Kay, and John Darius Halley.

Edna Steward, Sarah's daughter, married Alonzo Cushing Goodall, children; John William, born 1935, Charles F, born 1936. Both boys died in infancy. Their daughter, Betty Jean was born January 3, 1934. She married Charles Monroe Cantrell, children; Edna Pearl, born April 5, 1960, and Mary Elizabeth, born August 7, 1962.

Thomas and Zoie Butcher were Betty Goodall Cantrell's great uncle and great Aunt. Edna and Betty lived with the Butchers after Alonzo's death.

Thomas and Zoie Butcher purchased the old Dan Glassburn home from William and Helen Phillips' children and grandchildren. The children and grandchildren were joint owners of the property. Ross and Nora, Joseph and Eliza Phillips being the principal owners (heirs of William and Helen Phillips). The house was the old Dan Glassburn Funeral Home.

Thomas Butcher worked as a section hand on the C&O Railroad (Old Hocking Valley Railroad). He worked the farm. after he retired from the railroad. The Butchers Lived on the farm until Thomas' death in 1957. Zoie sold half of the farm to John and Pearl Denney after Thomas death. She then sold the remaining acres and house to Virgil and Bertis Halley. Zoie lived there until her death in 1972.

The Cantrells moved a mobile home onto the property near the old house in 1967 Edna Goodall remarried in the old house and moved with the Cantrells to Ewington, January 28, 1974. Betty spent thirty-two years on that old farm, from February 28, 1942 until January 28, 1974.

John Halley, son of Bertis and Virgil, together with his sisters, Linda and Diana still own the land and buildings. They sold the old five room log cabin to Ed Moore of Addison, Ohio, in 2001. The cabin is being dismantled and will be moved and reassembled on Mr. Moore's property. See Charles and Betty Goodall Cantrell Family and Alonzo Goodall Family.

*Submitted By: Betty Cantrell*

## HENRY CALDWELL FAMILY -

Henry Caldwell, born May 27, 1781 in Giles County, Virginia, died January 16, 1859 in Guyan Twp., Gallia County married in 1763 Mary Ferrier, born May 14, 1785 in Ireland, died February 4, 1855, Guyan Twp., Gallia County. The Caldwell names has been spelled several different way on documents, Caldwell and Colwell are the most common. Henry's parents were Hugh and Ruth Holstein Caldwell. Henry's father Hugh came to America from Ireland. Hugh served in the Revolutionary War as a private from Virginia.

Henry and Mary had the following children: William, Hugh, Steve, James Preacher, Hasper, Robert, Mathew, Eunice, Margaret, Lucinda, Delilah, Polly and Avarel. William Caldwell, born November 19, 1817, West Virginia, died in Gallia County. He was married to Jane Sheets daughter of William and Elizabeth Henry Sheets. Jane was born May 17, 1817, (probably Gallia County as both the Sheets and Henry families were in Gallia County at the time) and died May 6, 1881 in Gallia County, Ohio. Documents of her granddaughter, Emma Caldwell Gatewood, Jane's name is shown as Becky Jane Sheets Caldwell.

William and Jane's children are: Hugh Wilson, Mary, Sarah Jane, Steve Monroe, Joe Thomas, Lewis Jackson, Edward Marion, James Robert, John Ferrier and William Henry.

*Hugh Wilson and Esther Trowbridge Caldwell and 15 children*

Hugh Wilson born June 17, 1848, Gallia County, died November 12, 1929, Santa Ana, California married Esther Trowbridge, December 10, 1872 in Gallia County, Ohio. Esther born February 27, 1853, Gallia County, died February 12, 1943, Santa Ana, California, was the daughter of Ferguson and Ruth Crawford Trowbridge. Hugh and Esther moved with several of there children to California and lived the remainder of their lives. Many of the fifteen children stayed in the Gallia County area. Hugh and Esther had the following children: John Wilson, Mary Etta, Thomas Jebulun, Alfred Granville, Myra Edith, David Avaril, Alma Ethel, Alta Esther, Asa Hubert (Bert), Emma Rowena, Ella Rojena, Effie May, Myrta Selena, Ida Estelie and Lucy Marie. Ella, Myrta, Etta, Estelle, Lucy and David lived in California near their parents.

Emma Caldwell, born October 25, 1887, Gallia County, died June 5, 1973 Gallipolis, Gallia Co., married Perry Clayton Gatewood May 5, 1907. Emma and Perry (P.C.) had the following children: Helen, Ruth, Monroe, William, Rowena, Esther, Robert, Elizabeth, Nelson, Louise and Lucy. More on the Gatewood family can be found in the history of James Monroe Gatewood.

Emma Caldwell Gatewood, age 67, was the first woman to hike the entire Appalachian Trail from Mt. Oglethorpe, Georgia to Mt. Katahdin, Maine. She began the trip on May 3, 1955 from Georgia and ended September 25, 1955 in Maine. It was a distance of 2050 miles and was accomplished in 145 days. She hiked the trail two more times and she hiked sections of the trail numerous times. In 1958, at the age of 70, Emma hiked the Adirondack in New York State and climbed six of the highest mountains. To help celebrate Oregon's Centennial, Emma walked 2000 miles on the highways from Independence, Missouri to Portland, Oregon in 95 days. She started blazing the Buckeye Trail across Gallia County a distant of 40 miles in 1964 at the age of 77. Emma hiked many trails over the years until her death in 1973.*Submitted by: Marjorie Gilliam Wood*

## CARL AND KATHRYN (KAY) CAMERON FAMILY -

Carl L. Cameron was born in Massilon, OH, May 7, 1931, the only child of Harry and Hazel Jenkins Cameron, Harry's family lived near Moundsville, WV. His great grandfather was thought to be German and had come from near Pittsburgh, PA, to Fairpoint, Oh. Carl S., Carl's grandfather, married Stella Kuhn in 1904. Of their four children, Harry was the oldest, born in 1905. He married Hazel Jenkins of Gallia Co. in 1926 while both were working in Massilon. Hazel's mother was Emma Criner and her father was Charles Jenkins who worked on the railroad and died of typhoid fever about 1910.

*Carl and Kay Cameron Scott, Marc, Jeff*

Carl graduated from Gallia Academy High School in 1950 and began working at Gallipolis State Institute (now Gallipolis Developmental Center), first as an EEG technician and later as an x-ray technician. It was during his x-ray training at Holzer Hospital that he met Kay, a medical technologist there. Kay was born in Circleville, Oh, January 10, 1931, to Neil and Luella Barr Morris. Neil's parents were Clifton and Anna Wagoner Morris of Pickaway Co. The Morris family had originally come to this country from Wales in 1765. Because Neil's father died where he was 5, he was raised by aunt and uncle. Luella's family lived in Fairfield Co. Her father, Clarence Barr, came from a family of eight children of Lyman and Sarah Kiger Barr. Luella's mother was Iva Harden. Iva's grandparents had come from Darbyshire, England, in 1835. Kathryn and her brother Paul were raised on the family farm in Pickaway Township, both graduating from Pickaway Township High School. Kathryn graduated from Ohio University in 1953 having been inducted into the national honorary society, Phi Beta Kappa, in her junior year. She came to Gallipolis to take a job at Holzer Hospital.

Carl and Kay were married Sept. 5, 1954, and always lived in Gallipolis continuing in their jobs until Carl retired in 1985 and Kay in 1993. Their three sons are Scot David born in 1957, Jeffrey Lee born in 1962, and Marc Alan born in 1967. Scott graduated from Ohio State University in 1979; later he earned a Master's in Education and taught school for one year. Leaving the teaching field, he began working for a computer company as an author. Finding he was able to do most of his work from home, he bought a home near Logan, OH, where he can enjoy the nearby state parks and do volunteer work for them.

After a busy four years in Gallia Academy playing basketball and participating in local little theater activities, Jeff was accepted into a six year medical school program at Youngstown State and Northeastern Ohio Universities College of Medicine. Upon graduation, he married Antonette Ferritto from Grafton, Oh. He did his Emergency Room residency in Akron before settling in Dover, OH, where he heads the group of ER physicians serving Union Hospital. He and Toni have two sons, Eric and Evan, and a daughter, Katie.

Marc was very active in band and vocal music in GAHS. He also chose to attend OSU where he met his future wife, Janet Larkins of Euclid, OH. After graduation in 1989, he began working in the field of residential property management. Marc and Janet now live in Cincinnati with their son Nick and twin daughters Rachel and MacKenzie.

Carl was actively involved with Boy Scout Troop 200 for many years. During this time Jeff and Marc both attained the rank of Eagle Scout. Carl was awarded the Silver Beaver Award by the National Council of Boy Scouts of America. Both Carl and Kay have been active in the Presbyterian Church, too.

The family enjoyed numerous camping trips visiting various areas of the country. Carl passed away suddenly on a trip to Colorado in 1996.

**WILLIAM CAMPBELL FAMILY** - When it was still part of the Northwest Territory, William and Sarah Campbell came to Gallia County with their newly married mother, Lucy Scotten Campbell Stillwell, and stepfather, Shadrach Stillwell. In 1800 Shadrach was included in the Gallipolis township census. He also took part in the registering of earmarking stock in 1802.

William and Sarah were born in Philadelphia, PA. Their father, James Campbell, died while living in Washington County, PA during the year 1784. Shadrach is known to have served in the Revolutionary War.

Sarah married Thomas Jones, 1813, in Wilkesville, OH. She died 1817 and is buried in Wilkesville Cemetery. They had one child named Levi Campbell Jones. William married Mary Daniel, daughter of James Daniel of Virginia, in Gallia County. They had three children, James, the eldest, died shortly before his marriage to Cordelia Strong. Juliet, who married Benjamin Boggs, had three children, Mary, Benjamin and Juliet. They moved to Mason County, WV. Harrison, born 1814 in Wilkesville, married Julia Ann Kent of Rupert, VT, in 1834 and settled on land in Gallia County. Julia was the granddaughter of Samuel Kent, who also served in the Revolutionary War, and in 1817, moved to Gallia County from Rupert, VT, with several members of his family. Her grandmother, Mary Noble Kent's family has been traced back to the 1650's in Southwick, Maine. Julia's mother and father, Amasa and Nancy Kent moved to Iowa shortly after her marriage to Harrison. Nancy Bushee Kent died not too long after they arrived and Amasa perished in an ice storm. Nine children were born to Harrison and Julia. They were Warren, Caroline, James, Mary, Agnes Martha, Juliett, Eliza E., William H. and Lucinda. After Mary died in 1844, William went to live with Harrison in Hamden, Oh. He died in 1870, living to be 88 years old.

*Submitted by Beatrice Arendall*

**CHARLES AND BETTY GOODALL CANTRELL FAMILY** - Betty Jean Goodall Cantrell was born January 3, 1934, on the old William Bray farm (later Tracy Casto farm) on Fairview Road near Bidwell, Ohio. She is the daughter of the late Alonzo Cushing Goodall and Edna Ethel Stewart Goodall.

After Alonzo's death, Betty and her mother went to Cincinnati, Ohio in the summer of 1941, Betty entered Webster Elementary School in Cincinnati that fall.

Betty and her mother returned to Gallia County to live with her great uncle and great aunt, Thomas and Zoie Hecker Butcher, on the old Dan Glassburn farm, one mile southwest of Bidwell at the junction of State Route 554, and Fairview Rd.

*Cantrell Family February 2000 Back Row: Pearl Cantrell, Mary Cantrell Nemeth Front Row: Betty Cantrell, Destiny Nemeth, Tabatha Nemeth*

Betty attended Bidwell-Porter Elementary School from March 1942 until she graduated from high school in 1953.

Betty married Charles Monroe Cantrell, October 31, 1956. Charles was born June 14, 1893, near Licking Texas County, Missouri. He is the son of David and Winnie Guice Cantrell. He died May 22, 1979, at Gallipolis, Ohio. Charles sold McNess products in Gallia County from 1957-1969. The Cantrells lived in the Butcher home. Their daughters, Edna Pearl, born April 5, 1960, and Mary Elizabeth, born August 7, 1962 were born while they lived with the Butchers. Both girls were born in Pleasant Valley Hospital, Pt. Pleasant, W.Va. Pearl and Mary attended Bidwell-Porter Elementary School. Both girls graduated from North Gallia High School, Pearl graduated in 1978, and Mary in 1980. The Cantrells moved to Alice Road in Ewington, Ohio, January 28, 1974. Mary finished the school year at Bidwell-Porter, then attended Vinton Elementary during her eighth grade year.

Betty graduated from Rio Grande College (now University of Rio Grande) in 1971, with a degree in elementary education. She graduated from Case Western University School of Library Science in 1973.

Betty was employed at the Gallia County District Library (now Bossard Memorial Library) from 1952-1969, and Davis Library, Rio Grande College (now University of Rio Grande) from September 1, 1966 until she retired June 30, 2000.

Pearl graduated from the University of Rio Grande in 1982, with a BS degree in history and in art (with emphasis in photography). She graduated from Ohio University, Athens, Ohio with a MA degree in history and archival science in 1987.

Mary graduated from Bowling Green State University, Bowling Green, Ohio in 1984 with a degree in Child and Family Development.

Pearl was the first professionally trained archivist for the Robert E. Lee Memorial Association, Strafford hall Plantation, Stratford , Virginia (Robert E. Lee's birthplace), from 1987-1989. She worked in Rugby Tennessee from 1989 until March 1996. She set up Historic Rugby's archives. She managed Newberry House (Rugby's Bed and Breakfast ) for one year. She returned to Rugby as lead interpreter, left Rugby in 1996, and returned to Ohio. She was employed as secretary for Bob Evan's Hidden Valley Ranch in 1997. She then worked at Infocision Management Corp., Gallipolis, Ohio fromNovember 6, 2000 until March 13, 2001. She was then employed as a care giver for Lois Hammond, from March 14, until August 18, 2001. Pearl was employed at Franklin Career Services, Fraziers Bottom, WV from August 31, through October 4, 2001.

Mary Cantrell was employed at the Learning Tree Day Care Center in Gallipolis, Ohio, then Miss Paula's Day Care Center. She was later employed at the Pillsbury Plant in Wellston, Ohio.

Mary married James Steven Nemeth of Chicago, Illinois. They were married at Gallipolis, Ohio, June 19, 1992, and resided in Denver Colorado from October, 1992 until May 1993. She is now employed at the Westerville Day Care Center.

The Nemeths have two daughters, Tabatha Faith, born July 22, 1995, and Destiny Charlene Nemeth, born March 18, 1997. Both girls were born in St. Ann's Hospital, Columbus, Ohio.

*Submitted by: Mary Cantrell Nemeth*
*NOTE: Also see Goodall and John Sylvester Butcher Family*

**BRYSON AND MARY KAY CARTER FAMILY** - Bryson Reed "Bud" Carter, a native of Guernsey County, was born to Samuel Boyd and Elizabeth Irene Reed Carter on December 21, 1939 near Quaker City, Ohio. He grew up on the family farm, participating in church, 4-H, FFA and band. He attended Oxford Grade School, and in 1958 graduated from Washington High School at Old Washington, Ohio, as Valedictorian of his class.

While attending Ohio State University, Bud married Mary Kathryn James, September 8, 1962, in Parkersburg, West Virginia. Mary Kay was the daughter of Archie Quentin and Hazel Corbitt James of the Parkersburg area. She was born September 7, 1940, attended Winding School and graduated from Parkersburg High School in 1958. When Bud asked Archie for her hand in marriage, he said, "yes." He went on to say that Bud would have a lot less trouble if he would just take the old '54 Plymouth he had sitting in the back yard instead of Mary Kay.

Bud and Mary Kay moved to Gallia County in the spring of 1963 immediately following Bud's graduation from Ohio State University with a B.S. degree in Agriculture. Neither Bud nor Mary Kay had relatives or ancestors in Gallia County. They chose to settle here in the 1960's, rear their family, and pursue their careers because they liked the county and the people.

They are both proud of their Appalachian background and heritage. Scotch-Irish and German ancestors of Bud migrated from Europe to America in the late 1600s and early 1700s. His great, great grandfather, John Carter, a miller by trade, helped build and operate the first steam flour mill on the Upper Ohio River in 1837at Clarington. Mary Kay's German— Irish ancestors also migrated to West Virginia from Virginia and Pennsylvania in the 1800s.

*Bryson (Bud), Mary Kay, Kevin S. & Stephanie K. Carter*

Bud began his career as a County Extension Agent in Gallia County, April 1, 1963, a position he held for more than 22 years. He earned his M.S. degree in Agriculture from the Ohio State University in 1973.

On January 1, 1986, Bud became District Extension Specialist, Farm Management for 16 counties in Southern Ohio. Although he worked out of the District Office at Jackson, Ohio, he and Mary Kay continued to live in Gallia County. He retired as an Associate Professor at Ohio State University on May 1, 1995 after completing 32 years of service to Ohio State University Extension and the citizens of Gallia County and Southern Ohio. Mary Kay continued her secretarial career at Holzer Hospital and the Evans Grocery Company shortly after arriving in Gallia County. She had previously attended Bliss College in Columbus and had worked at the Ohio Bureau of Employment and Ohio State University Hospital. While rearing their family she completed two years of college at the University of Rio Grande.

Their son Kevin Scott Carter, was born on February 28, 1966, and their daughter, Stephanie Kay Carter, was born on October 8, 1967. Kevin and Stephanie received their education in the Gallipolis City School System with Kevin graduating in 1984 and Stephanie in 1986.

Both Kevin and Stephanie graduated from Ohio State University (Kevin in Agriculture and Stephanie in Physical Therapy). Kevin obtained a M.S. degree in Marine Biology at Nova University, Ft. Lauderdale, Florida. He is currently a Natural Resource Specialist with the Broward County Department of Planning and Environmental Protection in Ft. Lauderdale, Florida. Kevin has one son, Derek Diaz Carter, born December 21, 1998.

Stephanie obtained her M.S. degree in Physical Therapy from the University of Miami, Miami, Florida. After practicing as a Physical Therapist for several years she returned to Ohio University in Athens where she earned her Ph.D. in Higher Education. She is currently an Assistant Professor at Mount St. Joseph College in Cincinnati.

Bud and Mary Kay are both active in the Grace United Methodist Church in Gallipolis. Bud is also a member of the Mid-Ohio Valley Amateur Radio Club.

**GEORGE EDWARD CARTER FAMILY** - George Edward and Dora Rosalie Wagoner Carter are Gallia County Natives. George was born at Swan Creek, Ohio, April 8, 1919, son of Clarence Lee and Ada Swain Carter. Rosalie was born at Cadmus, Ohio March 10, 1922, daughter of Daniel R. and Mary Slagle Wagoner. Both our parents were reared in Gallia County, Ohio. Farming and Trading was their occupation.

George and Rosalie graduated from Cadmus High School. George in 1939, Rosalie in 1940. They were married August 2, 1941 at Bladen, Ohio by Rev. Jennings Creameans, Uncle of George. We celebrated our 50th wedding anniversary August 2, 1991 with a trip to Niagra Falls, New York. They are the parents of Danile Lee (Tuck) Carter born August 20, 1942. Betty Jean Carter Scholl, born October 2, 1942, an Infant Daughter born January 26, 1944, deceased at birth.

*George Edward Carter and Rosalie Carter*

Daniel married Janet Elizabeth Hampton August 26, 1961. They are the parents of Doralene and Daniel Lee II. Daniel ( Tuck) worked for Carter and Evans Construction Company, served as a Deputy Sheriff of Gallia County, owned and operated a C. B. store in Gallipolis, and a grocery store in Waterloo, Ohio. He is presently employed as an equipment operator for a Construction Company. Janet is a home maker, has worked a a Deputy Sheriff, Secretary to a local Attorney, Nursing Home employee, and an employee of a small motors Plant.

Doralene is a Homemaker, talented artist, painting realistic pictures of Nature. Daniel Lee II is a registered Nurse having been employed by several Hospitals, presently employed at Pleasant Valley Hospital, Point Pleasant, Wva. He also writes poetry and does solo singing for recreation.

Betty Jean married Russell L. Scholl August 2, 1964, divorced 1984. They are the parents of Timothy Carter and Kelly Lynn Scholl. Jean is a Homemaker, a former Probation Officer for Licking, County, Ohio, Former Waitress at Mariott Inn, and presently employed as a Court Investigator for a Judge in Licking County, Ohio.

Timothy married Amy Savage August 26, 1997. He received a B. A. degree in Journalism at Ohio State University. He is currently employed by United Parcel Service. Kelly Lynn deceased 12 -27- 1996.

George began working as carpenter soon after graduation from high school. He has worked as a carpenter-contractor in Columbus, Ohio, Dayton, Ohio, Circleville, Ohio, Centerville, Ohio and Gallipolis, Ohio Areas, also Point Pleasant and Charleston, Wva. In 1956 George and Merrill Evans formed the Carter and Evans Construction Company. There were later joined by Forrest Mullins. Some of Carter and Evans handiwork still exists in Gallia County today. George retired May 1982.

George served in the United States Army from May 11, 1944 to November 11, 1945 under the command of General Mark Clark in the 10th Mountain Division, Fifth Army in Italy. He received the Purple Heart and Bronze Star Medals for out-standing service to his country. He received serious wounds while serving in the Italian Campaign in 1945.

Rosalie, Wife, Mother and Homemaker served as Clerk of Cadmus School Board during 1946 and 1947, employed by Gallaher Company, Gallipolis, Ohio. In 1960 began employment at Gallipolis State Institute where she retired May 2, 1982.

The Carters hobbies included boating, water skiing, flower gardening, camping and traveling. Just being Grandpa George and Granny Rosy to four Grandchildren was the greatest of all. They have had three special pets "Blizzard ( a horse), Fancy and Caddie their two Dogs.

George was deceased on November 3, 1997. Both George and Granddaughter Kelly are buried in Salem Cemetery, Gallia County, Ohio.

As small lad George and brother Ray walked several miles through deep snow to the Post Office to get a Christmas gift from an Aunt in Columbus, Ohio. Upon opening the gift at home, seeing a new sled, George exclaimed " Gee we could have rode it most of the way home.

From the barber chair small Timothy stated " Mommy I want a hair cut like Grandpa George, short on the side and shiny on top.

While riding in the truck with Grandpa four voices yelled in unison "Grandpa just pokes along when he drives and Granny goes "zoom".

Where ever the Carters roamed they always returned to Gallia County their "Home Sweet Home"

*Submitted by Rosalie-Carter*

**JOHN MERRILL CARTER FAMILY** - My name is David Merrill Carter (11-28-46) and I am the oldest son of John Merrill and Margaurite Pitchford Carter. I have been employed as District Administer with the Butler Soil and Water Conservation District in Hamilton (Butler County), Ohio for the past 25 years. Prior to moving to Butler County, I served as Vocational Agriculture Instructor at Hannan Trace High School from 1971-1976.

I graduated from Southwestern High School in 1964, and attended Rio Grande College two years and then transferred to Ohio State University where I earned a B.S. in Agronomy (Soils) in 1969 and an M. S. in Agriculture Education in 1975. I also worked for the United States Department of Agriculture's Soil Conservation Service in both Putnam and Gallia County.

*Merrill & Margauerite Carter with some of their Holstein dairy cattle. Main Carter homestead is pictured in the background.*

I have two children, LeAnne Marie Carter (11-3-82), a freshman in International Business at University of Cincinnati and Evan (11-9-85), a sophomore at Lakota West High School in Butler County. Their mother is Vicki L. Carter, a graduate in Nursing from both Ohio State and University of Cincinnati. She is currently employed as a Nursing Research Specialist at U. C. Both of our children have been blessed with musical talent. LeAnne, a member of University of Cincinnati Bearcat Marching Band (flute) and Jazz Band (piano) was a member of numerous musical groups while at Lakota West. She also served as a leader of their award winning Marching Firebird Band, elected by 250 other members: as Band Council President. Evan is playing snare drums in several musical groups in high school including the Marching, Jazz and Symphonic Bands. He also plays piano.

*Gregory L. & Braunlyn Carter celebrate their first place finish in the superstock class at the 2001 Huntington, WV soapbox derby.*

Gregory Leon Carter (11-14-40) continues to operate his own autobody shop in Rio Grande as he has for the past 30 years. He is a skilled autobody repairman and painter and I don't believe there is an part of a car he can't take apart and repair. He also constructed his modern body shop and residence using several innovative ideas with woodworking and mechanical skills.

Greg's daughter, Braunlyn (1-21-91) is also an accomplished musician. She plays piano and saxophone at Ohio Valley Christian School in Gallipolis. She has won awards at several talent contests with her piano and singing performance's. Their latest challenge has been participating in soapbox derby racing. In addition to helping construct her cars, her driving skills have earned her wins in both the stock and superstock classes at the Huntington, West Virginian Soap Box competition - - one of the youngest drivers to ever receive such high honors. As a result of her accomplishments, she has earned the right to participate in the world soapbox derby championships held at Akron, Ohio each summer. Although she has not won her division yet, her high placing in numerous races has earned her a 16th place in the world ranking.

My dad, John Merrill Carter, (8-4-20) sold his Century 21, Southern Hills Real Estate Business, in the mid 80s. My mother, Margaurite Pitchford Carter (10-16-22) retired from the Gallia County Treasurer's Office in 1980. *Editor's Note: During the course of my writing this information, my mother passed away suddenly (1-27-02) following a hard fought two year battle with A. L. S. disease. We made every effort to assist her including trips to the Cleveland Clinic and Ohio State University medical specialists. Mom had a deep love for her church, family and life in general. My dad was constantly at mother's side during her illness following their 58 year old marriage vow "to death do us part" to the very end. Mother will be greatly missed but her memory will be celebrated daily.

*David M. Carter enjoys a fall football game with his children, U. C. Marching Band member, LeAnne M. and Evan M. Carter*

Following mothers retirement, my parents continued to reside on their Walnut Township farm where Dad took care of his livestock (cats) and assisted mother with their Sandy Beaver Insurance Agency. We celebrated their 50th wedding anniversary in 1993.

Several farm acres in German Hollow were sold to the Amish in 1992 and the remainder is leased to a purebred Angus beef operation. We have been maintaining conservation practices on our land throughout the years and were recently named an official "Tree Farm" by the Ohio Forestry Association.

My parents have been members of the Bethesda United Methodist Church for over 50 years. Dad has served as Sunday School Superintendent and mother as church treasurer. I am currently serving as Secretary-Treasurer of the Bethesda Cemetery Association. Dad has exhibited his love for our country by proudly flying our American flag on his large flag pole high atop the farmstead hill for the past 30 years.

*Submitted by David Merrill Carter*

**SARAH L. WHITE CARTER** - Sarah L. White was born 15 March 1809 in Pennsylvania, the fourth child of Gallia County First Family, Alfred and Mary (Perry) White. We surmise, from family naming patterns, her middle name was Louise or Louisa.

Sarah married, as his second wife, John Richardson on 1 May 1833. John died 28 June 1850; the widow Sarah Richardson appeared, alone, on the Census in Gallipolis. John's will leaves Town Lot 97 in Gallipolis to his wife, Sarah, and her heirs; should Sarah not remarry and die without issue, the Town Lot would go to Elizabeth R. Calohan and Jared Baldwin and their heirs.

Sarah next married Jehu McDaniel, as his second wife, on 31 August 1851 in Gallipolis. Jehu was son of Henry and Hannah (Bryan) McDaniel, born 28 May 1792 in Greenbrier County, WV. He died on 7 August 1857 and was buried in Sandfork Cemetery in Walnut Township. His will included the following provisions: I wish my wife have two hundred and fifty dollars... one horse one cow and twelve Sheep and all that She Ever brought on the farm with her... if She accepts of this without any further Claims on my Estate.. .and my little Daughter Sarah Richardson to have one thousand dollars there is a note Executed by William C. Miller for property in the town of Gallipolis for the Sum of 2250$ Said note was Executed to me and by Me assigned two this Child I wish that assignment to Sand good but not to be considered as any part of my Estate.

Next Sarah married, as his third wife, George Carter on 14 February 1858. George was son of John and Mary (Lehr) Carter, born about 1802. The couple appears on the 1860 Census in Patriot: George Carter, 56y,OH; Sarah Carter, 51, PA; Mary White, 78, VT; Sarah Carter, 8, OH.... Receipts found in the estate papers of Jehu McDaniel show George and Sarah Carter received monies on behalf of Sarah Richardson McDaniel.

Sarah Carter's will, 23 October 1865, states: "I give and devise to my only beloved daughter Sarah Richardson McDaniel all my Estate real and personal with such exceptions as may be here in after mentioned... if my beloved and only daughter Sarah Richardson, Should not live to inherit the bequest of twenty two hundred & fifty dollars left to her by the last will and testament of her father Jehu McDaniel, and which money is now in the hands of Stephen G Keller... one half of the above sum of money Should be equally divided between Elizabeth Richardson the wife of Isaac R. Calohan of Gallipolis & Gerard Baldwin the only full brother of the said Elizabeth Richardson who is now the wife of Isaac R. Calohan".

Sarah died 15 November 1865 and was buried at Patriot Cemetery in Perry Township. Her gravestone reads, "Sarah R. McDaniel, wife of J., d. Nov. 15, 1865 age 57y". The younger Sarah sold her mother's property when she reached maturity and seems to have disappeared from Gallia County.

*Submitted by: Linda Gaylord-Kuhn*

## WILLIAM E CARTER'S ANCESTORS AND DECENDANTS

- John Carter was born 1774 in Shenandoah County Virginia and died Sept 18, 1866.

He married Mary Lehr on December 25, 1797 in Woodstock, Shenandoah County, Virginia. She was born in 1772 in Virginia and died on May 28, 1857. They came to Patriot, Gallia County, Ohio in 1810. John Carter was among the first pioneers that settled the Patriot area and a member of the first religious society in the Patriot area. John and Mary Carter are buried in Patriot Cemetery. Their children were George Carter, my direct ancestor, born 1802; Nancy Carter, Rebecca Carter, John Carter, Isaac Carter, William Allen Carter, Robert Carter, Thomas Carter, and Mary Carter.

*Carter Log Cabin*

George Carter married November 18, 1924 to Phebe Ripley. George died December 2, 1888. Phebe died in Iowa. George is buried in Patriot Cemetery. George and Phebe's children are Ammon J. Carter, my ancestor, born July 16, 1832 in Patriot Ohio; Frank Carter; Morgan David Carter; John Lee Carter;; Harriet Carter, Jane Elizabeth Carter, and Mary C. Carter.

*Carter Family*

Ammon J. Carter married Eliza Ann Waddell on April 19, 1854. She was a direct descendant Alexander Waddell, a revolutionary war soldier. Eliza was born on February 28, 1838 and died on October 20, 1883. Ammon and Eliza are buried in Salem Cemetery. Their children are Edward J. Carter, my ancestor, Harriet L. Carter, George F. Carter, Mary A. Carter, Albert Lee Carter, Margaret Carter, Etha Carter and Ina May Carter.

Edward J. Carter was born September 12, 1868 and died January 10, 1918. He married Elizabeth Rees on April 9, 1890. She was born October 17, 1873 and died June 23, 1903. Edward and Elizabeth are buried in Salem Cemetery. Their children were Clarence Carter, my dad; Nelle Grace Carter, Donna Carter, Addie Carter, Gladys Carter, and Everett Carter.

Clarence Carter was born March 27, 1890 and died in 1975. He married Ada May Swain in April of 1918, in Gallia County, Ohio. She was the daughter of George Swain and Emma Williams. She was born January 16, 1896 in Gallia County, Ohio and died in December of 1980. Clarence and Ada are buried in Salem Cemetery. Their children were George Carter, Emma Elizabeth Carter, Ray Carter, Charles Carter, Donald Lee Carter, Richard Carter and William E. Carter.

George Carter was born April 1919 and died November 1998. He married Rosalie Wagner. Their children were Betty Jean Carter and Daniel Lee Carter.

Elizabeth Carter married Charles Richards. Their children were Charles Burton Richards, Linda Richards, Anna Mae Richards, and Ruthie Richards.

Ray Carter was born November 1922 and died February 1984. He married Eleanor Trago. Their children were Jeff Carter and Rae Lynn Carter.

Charles Carter married Anna Lou Wood. Their children were Woody Carter and Gary Lee Carter.

Donald Lee Carter married Ruth Wood. Their children were Debra Lee Carter, Yvette Carter, and Robin Carter.

Richard Carter was born February 1932 and died march 1990. He married Bonnie Cook. Their children were Michael Carter, Rex Carter, and Charlene Carter.

William E. Carter was married to Gwendolyn Carter. Their children were Mark Allen Carter and Anette Lynn Carter. William W. Carter's wife is Carol Honey Irwin from Scioto County, Ohio.

William's son Mark married Mary Lisa Owen. Their children are Chris Carter and Cody Carter. Cody Carter competed in several Kiddie Tractor Pulls at the Gallia County Fair and Bob Evans Fall Festival. He has taken 1st. place in Kiddie Tractor Pulls. Cody also is known for his motorcycle riding ability and has ridden since age five. Cody won a Book Week Reading Award for reading the most books at Southwestern School when he was in the third grade.

Anette Carter was married to Greg Smith. Their son is G. Carter Smith. Carter also competed in Kiddie Tractor Pulls and took 1st place. His first love is the demolition derby and in 2001 as a young boy he was the announcer for the Mini Demolition Derby at the Gallia County Fair. Carter has won first place at the Gallia County Fair in Demonstration and Illustrated Talks on Health and Safety Issues three years. In 1999 Carter won first place at the Ohio State Fair in this category with a talk on Safety with Ohio Snakes.

Anette is married to Chris Brown. They have two children under school age, Shelby Lynn Brown and Christopher Dillon Brown. Shelby has been master of her own fate since the day she was born and frequently takes on herself to be the leader in groups that have much older children. Dillon had to learn at an early age to take his own part and has been calling his grandparents on the phone since age 2.

Daniel Allison originally purchased the land, 166 acres, on which the Carters now live in 1817 for $270. The house that stands to this day was built in 1818. Daniel Alison sold the property to Isaac Carter in 1830 for $570. Isaac sold the property to Augusta J. Carter in 1862 for $900. Augusta sold the property to Robert J. Carter in 1866 for $3500. Robert Carter sold the property to August Ahlborn in 1875 for $4,147. August sold the property in 1881 to Lewis Ahlborn for $1832. Lewis sold the property to Clarence Carter for $3000 in 1933. Clarence sold the property to its current owner, William E. Carter in 1955. The farm now consists of 270 acres.

Oberlin Carter who graduated first in his class from West Point in 1880 was raised in the Carter Log Cabin. William E. Carter and his son, Mark, restored the house back to a log cabin in 1986. Mark, his wife, Lisa and son Cody, currently reside there.

**CARTERS** - John Carter was born in Shenandoah County, Virginia n 1774. He married Mary Lehr, also born in Shenandoah County, in 1772. They were married on Christmas Day, 1797 in Woodstock Virginia. They were the recipients of a patent deed signed by President James Madison, August 3, 1816 for the southeast quarter of section 2, township 4, in range 16 for $1.25, per acre John Carter owned at least 1,600 to 1,700 acres of land in Ohio in various townships and his sons followed in his footsteps as far as purchasing as much property as possible once they were of age and had money.

John and Mary Lehr Carter had nine children. William Allen Carter was born February 13, 1807. He was the sixth child of John and Mary Lehr Carter. William married Caroline Halley February 26, 1829. They were the parents of eight children.

Charles Lee Carter was born September 1848. He married Sarah Catherine Clark February 5, 1871. They had four children and lived on Clay Lick (Carter Hollow) in Harrison Township, Gallia County, Ohio.

Oscar Lee Carter, son of Charles and Sarah Catherine (Clark) Carter was born November 4, 1871. Oscar was twice married. His first wife was Pearle Bessie Cooper. Oscar and Pearl had three children. A son died in infancy, daughter, Ivy, died of pneumonia at the age of eight years, and Nellie Justine.

*Seated: Charles Lee Carter, Bessie (Carter) Niday, Sarah (Clark) Carter. Standing: Oscar Lee Carter, Nettie (Carter) Lusher, William (Bill) Carter*

The infant Carter and Ivy are buried in Macedonia Cemetery.

Nellie Justine Carter married Jay Steivers and had one daughter, Norma Jean. Norma Jean married Loren Lloyd of Columbus, Ohio. Norma Jean Steivers Lloyd has three children, Loren, Brian, and Cherie.

Loren Lloyd is married to Rose McHaus and resides in Conshohocken, Pennsylvania.

Loren has three children, Jason, Chandra, and Charity. Chandra is a college student and Charity is married to Carl Yinger and has one daughter, Emily.

Brian Lloyd has two children, Brandy and Sandy. He is married to Sandra Lindsay. They live in Reynoldsburg, Ohio.

Cherie Justine Lloyd lives in Florida with her husband, Douglas Kitrell.

Nellie Justine (Carter) Steivers married Raymond Chennell. They had two daughters, Raymonda Julie and Raya Jane.

Raymonda Julie married William Law and has two children, Cherie and William. Julie and Bill live in Anaheim, California. They are proud to be members of "First Families of Gallia County" and visit the area whenever possible. Julie and Mary Lou (Carter) Saunders are working diligently to prove our connection to Robert "King" Carter of Carter's Grove near Williamsburg, Virginia.

Julie's daughter, Sherie married Mitch Hill and has two children, Mitchell, a college student, and Matthew, a high school student, all living in Bellevue, Washington. 'William Law' married Jean Schultz and live in Temoccula, California. William has two children, Kathryn and Jeanie, both students in the Temoccula School System.

Raya Jane married John Barker and has one child, Jon.

Jon Barker is married to Barbara McPherson. They have one child, a daughter, Mary Jo. The Jon Barker family live in Camarillo, California.

Oscar Lee Carter's second marriage was to Mattie MacGarlic in 1915. Oscar and Mattie had one son, Charles Dennis Carter born in 1916.

Charles Dennis Carter married Ruth Eleanor Smith in 1935. They had a daughter, Mary Lou. Mary Lou married Lewis Saunders. They live in Gahanna, Ohio. Their second home is a cabin, built in the 1800's near Mercerville. They have a daughter, Lee Ann. Lee Ann is married to Jerry Strait. Jerry and Lee Ann have two children, Kallie Marie Strait and Collin Saunders Strait. The Strait's home is in Gahanna, Ohio. They often visit "The Cabin on Bullskin Creek" in Gallia County, and are happy to be members of "First Families of Gallia County."

*Sumitted by Mary Lou Carter Saunders*

**RAYMOND S. AND HAZEL LEE (KINDER) CASEY FAMILY** - Raymond S. Casey was born October 9, 1916, in Gallipolis Ferry, Mason County, West Virginia. His great-grandparent, Sinclair and Jemima (Nibert) Casey came to Mason County some time before 1843 and owned farmland there. Raymond's parents were John Alexander and Sarah Jane (Lewis) Casey. They were living in Gallipolis shortly after Raymond was born. Sarah was a daughter of William M. "Fighting Billy" and Matilda (McDavid) Lewis; her great-grandparents were John "The Baptist" and Rebecca (Sowards) Lewis. Sarah died of influenza during the Spanish Flu epidemic of 1918 at age 40. John Casey died in 1939 at age 73. They are both buried in Pine Street Cemetery.

Raymond married Hazel Lee Kinder. Hazel's grandparents were Noah R. and Elizabeth (Lib) M. (Overall) Kinder. Noah was born about 1819 in Kanawha, Virginia, but lived most of his life in Gallia County. He and Lib lived on forty acres on Teens Run Creek near Chambersburg. Lib was born in 1832 in Tennessee; they married in 1849 in Gallia County.

Raymond and Hazel Kinder were married May 8, 1937, in Gallipolis. Their family included five children: James W. Casey of Powderly, Tx; Harold L. Casey of Columbus, Oh; Lewis E. Casey of San Angelo, Tx; Carol S. Varney of Colorado Springs, Co; Linda A. Lane of Gallipolis. Hazel died November 16, 1974 and buried in Pine Street Cemetery.

*Raymond S. Casey*

Raymond was a veteran of WWII and served in both the U.S. Navy and Army. During the Battle of Okinawa in 1945, he was a crewmember on a landing craft and was injured during this campaign. He later served in the Army as part of the U.S. Occupation Forces in Germany. He was an active member of the Veterans of Foreign Wars Post 4464, Disabled American Veterans Post 5.

Raymond worked hard all his life. He worked at various jobs and liked to refer to himself as a "jack of all trades." After WWII, he worked in the building construction, dirt work, and concrete. For several years he worked at the Gallipolis State Institute (GSI) as a patient attendant. Though he worked wherever assigned, his favorite worksite at GSI was called the "Farm Cottage". It was here that the less severely stricken patients resided and it was a more enjoyable duty than overseeing residents in other cottages. In later years, he was employed at Holzer Hospital and Ohio Valley Bank.

Raymond married Katherine Sims Boster on May 9, 1976. Raymond enjoyed his retirement years and loved living in Gallipolis. Their home on First Avenue was near downtown and the city park and allowed for daily contact with friends and family.

Raymond S. Casey died on May 2, 1993, and is buried in Pine Street Cemetery.

**BENJAMIN GRANT CASTO AND SARAH NAOMI BELLER CASTO** - Benjamin Grant Casto was born in Rockcastle, WV. On June 18, 1867 to Joseph and Mariah Morrison Casto. He was the youngest son of ten children. Twenty years later, on June 21, 1887 he married Sarah Naomi Beller. The newly weds lived with Joseph and Mariah until a few months after their first child, William Granville, was born on May 6, 1888. Benjamin and Sarah then bought a small farm on Shamblen Run about five miles from Kenna, WV.

Soon after the turn of the century, Benjamin became involved in a timber business in Greenbrier County, WV. He operated a steam powered sawmill that employed several dozen people and as many as a dozen yoke of oxen pulling logs from the forest. He had sold a large quantity of lumber to buyer from St. Louis, Mo. He shipped several rail cars of lumber to St. Louis and received no payment. He traveled to St. Louis to find there was no trace of the buyer or the lumber. As a result, the business failed and he returned to the farm. Soon afterwards, he moved his family to Cleveland, Oh where he worked as a street car conductor. He kept possession of the farm and again returned to it about 1913.

*Mr. & Mrs. B.h. Casto & Chin-woo*

In November 1916, Benjamin and Sarah bought a farm at the Western (upper) end of Bull Run in Vinton. OH. and moved his family to Ohio. By this time, he and Sarah had a growing family of ten children, three of whom were married. He farmed and worked as an agent for M.L. Trout Reality Co. of Vinton to maintain the rest of his family. In 1919, he rented the farm and bought a large frame house in the center of Vinton where he continued selling real estate. In 1928, he sold the farm on Bull Run to G.W. Wooldridge.

He and Sarah lived in the house at the center of Vinton until Sarah's death in 1945. Benjamin married Bertha Carper a year or so later and continued living in the same house. He died in 1958.

Benjamin served as mayor of Vinton for several years.

Benjamin and Sarah's children are : William Granville, born May 6, 1888 married Cora Alice Smith; John S. Born Nov. 3,1887 married Lucy Stone; Marie born Jan 3, 1892 married L.J. Bauer: Charles Victor born Mar 11, 1894 married Vinnie Clark; Clarence A. born Oct 19, 1896 married Florence Clark; Grace Elizabeth born Dec 13, 1897 married Clayte Edmiston; Ethel L. born Sept 15, 1900 married Findley Neuman; Edward Reynold Born Mar 15, 1903 died in infancy; Virginia Dare born Oct 5, 1907 married Bob Diggins; Mornia Irene born Jul 13, 1912 married Joe Daudelin.

Of the above family members, Granville, Charles and Grace lived out their lives in Vinton.

## DELLA ALENA (BAIRD) & KENNETH L. CASTO

Della A. Baird born 1/12/1927 (see Baird Twins) married Kenneth Loraine Casto (born 10/25/1922 in Madison, West Virginia, son of Amada Clonch Crandall & Henry B. Casto) on March 27, 1948 in Gallipolis, Ohio. An old fashion belling was held for the couple at the home of the bride's parents (see Ora & Gail Baird). Kenneth was a WWII veteran serving in the US Army Air Force (1943-1946) as a Carpenter General having spent nine months in the Pacific Theater receiving the American and Asiatic Ribbons.

Kenneth worked for many years in the Gallipolis area at several local garages (Baird Brothers Auto Co., Walter Wise Garage, Chevrolet and Ford Garage) as an auto mechanic. In the late 1940's, Della worked for Harley and Georgia Smith at their restaurant in the Kanauga area.

Five children were born in Gallipolis: Kenneth Larry (2/28/1949-2/8/199 1) married Linda Rose (12/511947 -1/4/1993) - Their children: Amada 4/28/1970 and Pennie 11/3/1975. Larry served in US Navy during the Vietnam era. Mary (Jane) Elizabeth born 7/15/1951 married Steven Graham (8/27/5 1) on 4/23/1971, their children: Charity (12/2/1971) and Candy (3/13/1976). Danny L. born 9/12/1954 was married to Kandy Blankenship, their children: Danny L. (10/29/1977) and Adam (7/25/1979).

*Della and Kenneth Casto Wedding Day March 27,1948*

The family moved to Chatham Avenue where Teresa (Teddy) Lynn was born 6/9/1957.

Teresa was married to Richard O'Dell on 8/14/1976, their children: Rebecaka S. born 9/18/1978 and Richard D. O'Dell II born 2/21/1980. Teresa then married Charles Yonis (11/9/1940-9/9/1992) in Circleville, Ohio on 2/11/1988.

Della & Kenneth's youngest son, Michael Keith was born on 3/16/1959. Mike is a Lieutenant with Scioto Township Fire Department.

In August 1963, the family moved to the Circleville, Ohio area where Kenneth worked construction and then as an auto mechanic for Ricart Ford and Don Thompson Lincoln Mercury. Born on 12/11/1968, their youngest daughter Candy died in infancy. In 1971, Della and Kenneth opened and operated a small garage and grocery store for several years.

The couple was best friends and partners in all that life had to offer, well and bad. You hardly ever saw one without the other and together they furnished their family with more than a house, it was a home filled with love, understanding and compassion. Della and Kenneth retired from their small family business in 1990 to spend more time with their grandchildren and great- grandchildren. Della and Kenneth's door was always open and they never turned anyone away. For over 48 years, Della and Kenneth faced life together with strength and dignity.

Della passed away unexpectedly at their home in Commercial Point on Sunday, June 22, 1997 and was buried in Beckett Cemetery. Kenneth was a life member of VFW Post 7941 South Bloomfield and Della belonged to the Ladies Auxiliary. Kenneth went to live with his youngest daughter, Teresa, until his death on 3/6/2000 and was laid to rest with his beloved wife.*Submitted by: Teresa L. (Casto) Yonis*

**HENRY L. CASTO** - Henry L. Casto was born 1841 in Jackson County, Virginia and died Aug 21, 1897 in Cheshire. On Dec 31, 1863 Henry enlisted in Company F 9th West Virginia on Nov 9, 1864 the Wva 9th and 5th Infantry's consolidated in the 1st West Virginia Vetern Infantry. Henry received the rank of Corpoaral he was discharged where his troop was mustered out on Jul 21, 1865 in Cumberland, Maryland. Between 1877 and 1880 Henry settled in Cheshire, and started his own coal business. On Feb 9, 1864 Henry married Adaline Ewing daughter of John and Elizabeth Ewing in Jackson County, WV. Adaline was born Apr 14, 1841 in New Lisbon, Oh and died Jan9, 1915 in Cheshire. Henry and Adaline had six children; Ellen born in 1864 and died Jul 8, 1896 in Cheshire. Her first husband was John Ewing and they had one child Catherine. On Nov 2, 1889 Ellen married John Thompson and they had two children Wilbur and Florence. Sarah Casto was born Sept 11, 1869 in Mason County, WV, her date of death in unknown. Roseta Casto was born Jan 30, 1871 in Mason County her date of death is unknown. William Casto was born Feb 8, 1874 In Mason Cunty and died Sept 7, 1946 in Cheshire, he married Ella Rife on Dec 23, 1897 in Cheshire. They had no children . Robert Carvosso Casto was born Apr 15, 1877 in Ripley, WV and died Jun 21, 1965 in Cheshire he married Mary Thomas and they had ten children Arthur Carvosso, Eva, Maggie, Floyd, Beulah, Paul, Donald, Freemont and Robert. Henry Casto was born Aug 11, 1880 in Meigs County and died Nov 25, 1950 in Middleport. On Jan 26, 1903 he married Lula Lewis in Middleport, they had six children Roy, George, Genevieve, Marie, Fred and Dora. Henry and Adaline and all their children except Sarah and Rosetta are buried in Gravel Hill Cemetery.

**PERRY CASTO** - The ancestors of Perry Casto were a family with Protestant ideals, resourcefulness and courage as part of their nature. His forbearers helped tame the wilderness and made a place for themselves in the New World.

Perry's ancestors were whalers and came into America at Rhode Island. They traveled downstream to the New Jersey Coast. David Casto Traveled to Cape May, New Jersey where he married Phoebe Gandy on August 17, 1752. After the births of their five children, they sought a better home site. They traveled through Pennsylvania to Hampshire, Virginia and then settled at Buffalo Creek, Virginia (later West Virginia). The couple's son William, was born before 1765. William married and established his home and farm near the Buchhannon River. He later moved to Jackson County, Virginia (later West Virginia) where died in 1841.

Benjamin Casto, William's son, was born in Randolph County, Virginia (later West Virginia) in 1800. And his wife, Sarah Shinn, raised several children on their farm in Jackson County. One of the children born to this couple was Moses Michael.

Moses Michael married Marriah Baker and established their home near Leon, West Virginia. Their log home was built from lumber obtained from Benjamin's farm. They were the parents of five children. Perry Casto, born November 18, 1880, in Jackson County, West Virginia was one of these children.

Perry, known to be an honest and upright individual, married Laura Keefer, daughter of Robert and Anna (Graham) Keefer in 1904. Perry and Laura were the parents of three children: Ray, who married Mary Russell, Anna, who married Walter Plantz and Ervin (Shorty), who married Lucy Casto. Perry farmed the land near his father's home until he decided to leave the area and seek a better life for his family in the city of Gallipolis, Ohio. The family moved to the Old French City in 1920's. Perry opened a grocery store on what is now Eastern Avenue and it proved to be a successful business venture.

Perry died August 3, 1934 from a heat related illness. Laura joined him in death in 1965. Their earthly remains reside in Bethel Cemetery, Leon, West Virginia.

**WILLIAM GRANVILLE CASTO AND CORA ALICE SMITH CASTO** - William Granville, the oldest son of Benjamin and Sarah Naomi Beller Casto, was born on May 6, 1888. He married Cora Alice Smith on April 25, 1910 at Point Pleasant, Wv. His parents, owned a small farm on Shamblen Run about five miles from Kenna, Wv. At that time, Benjamin and his family were in Cleveland, so Granville and Alice started housekeeping on the farm on Shamblen Run. In 1913, when Benjamin and Sarah came back to the farm from Cleveland, Granville and Alice with their first two children, moved to Kenna and took care of a boarding house and store belonging to Alice's father. Granville, with a team of horses and wagon, hauled freight and other supplies for the store at Kenna from the rail head at Ripley, a distance of about 12 miles.

In 1916, they moved to a small farm on Shamben Run however Granville wanted to move to Ohio to be near his family who had moved to Ohio that same year. In November 1917, they bought 104 acre farm just north of Ewington, Oh. The farm was one mile from Route 160 on Adney Road. In early December 1917, Granville and Alice and their four children moved to Ohio. Alice and the four children came on the train. Granville made the trip (three days) by horse and wagon with a few household belongings.

Granville and Alice lived on the farm for the next 32 years. Seven more children were born to them. During the depression years, they bought another 140 acres of adjoining land. The farm provided a livelihood for the family and all of the family members provided the labor. They had 25 acres of apple orchard, raised corn, wheat and hay and did a lot of truck farming but most of the cash income was from the dairy herd. Alice always said that when she and Granville were married, she had one cow and Granville had one cow. By 1950, she observed the Granville had 60 cows and she had none. She apparently felt short changed.

In 1948, they bought a vacant lot on North Clay Street in Vinton. In the summer of 1949.

*William Granville Casto & Cora Alice Smith Casto Taken April 25, 1960 On 50th. Wedding Anniversary*

They started building a two story brick house. In the summer of 1950, they turned the farm over to their son Jim and moved to Vinton. Alice was pleased to be in town with close neighbors and many friends and much church activity. Granville was still close enough to go to the farm each day. They finished out their lives in Vinton, Granville in 1975, and Alice in 1981.

In 1947 when their youngest child, Annalu, graduated from Vinton High School, Granville and Alice were special guests of the Alumni Banquet Association because all ten of their children who reached adulthood, graduated from the Vinton High School.

Their children are: William Victor born June 11, 1911 married Olive Shivley; Johnathon Grant born June 3, 1913 married Ruth Dodrill; Granville Leon born December 23,1915, married Marie Callahan; Raymond Smith born May 14, 1917 married Bernice Kuhn; Naomi Jane born March 10, 1919 married Bill Ewing; Edward Clayton born February 16, 1921 died in infancy; Stanley Eugene born June 28, 1922 married Betty Dunfee; (Stanley was killed in action in Germany on Apr 13 1945); Elizabeth Marie Born February 20, 1924 married David Birch; James Allen born August 5, 1926 married Verta Rece; William Harold born February 28, 1928 married Francyl Gragory; Annalu born August 17, 1929 married Joe Payne.

Of the above children, William Victor, Johnathon Grant, and James Allen have always lived in Vinton or Gallia County.

**CORNELIUS CHAMBERS AND MYRTA HARRINGTON FAMILY** - Cornelius Richard Chambers, Junior, and Myrta Alma Harrington were married in Gallia County on 9 November 1890 and continued to live in Gallia County until they moved to Logan County, Ohio, in 1919. They had nine children: Genevieve Lorraine (1892), Charles Marion (1894), Cornelius Howard (1896) Carl Evan (1898), Henry Lawrence (1900), Kathryn Louise (1903), Paul Aldis (1908), Claudia Beatrice (1910), and Richard Glenn (1912). Cornelius raised tobacco on a farm just north of Bladen, in Ohio Township on the Ohio River. The family worshipped at Bethel Church just west of Bladen and the children attended Bladen School.

Cornelius was the son of Cornelius Richard Chambers, Senior, and Mary Ann Evans. Cornelius, Senior, was born in Washington County, Ohio, in 1836. After the death of his father, William Chambers, in 1838, Cornelius lived with his guardian and uncle, John Chambers. John brought his family to Gallia County in about 1849 and founded Chambersburg, now Eureka, in Clay Township on the Ohio River. In 1862 Cornelius married Mary Ann, the daughter of Evan Evans and Eliza (Edwards) Evans of Ohio Township. Evan and Eliza came to Gallia County from Wales in about 1834. After their marriage Cornelius and Mary Ann moved to Vermillion County, Indiana, where they had a farm. Cornelius was drafted into the Union Army to serve in the Civil War. Their son Cornelius Richard, Junior, was born in Vermillion County in May 1865. Cornelius the father returned home from the Civil War in November 1865 and died in December 1865 from illness contracted during the war. In 1886 Mary Ann returned to Gallia County with her son, Cornelius. There she married William King. William Chambers, the father of Cornelius Richard Chambers, Senior was born in Dromara, County Down, Ireland. He came to America with his parents, William and Elizabeth (Hamilton) Chambers shortly after the beginning of the nineteenth century. They were among the early settlers of Washington County Ohio.

*The Cornelius & Myrta Chambers Family C. 1916 1. Cornelius Richard Chambers, Junior, 2. Genevieve Lorraine (Chambers) Rose, 3. Fred Rose, 4. Kathryn Louise Chambers, 5. Myrta Alma (Harrington) Chambers, 6. Charles Marion Chambers, 7. Henry Lawrence Chambers, 8. Cornelius Howard Chambers, 9. Claudia Beatrice Chambers, 10. Lena Rose, 11. Richard Glenn Chambers, 12. Carl Evan Chambers, 13. Paul Aldis Chambers.*

Myrta was the daughter of Marion Harrington and Katherine Howard, who were married in Gallia County in 1867. They resided in Green Township where they farmed. Marion was born in Gallia County 1844 and died in 1877. Catharine was born in Virginia 1846 and died in Gallia County in 1893. They are buried in Centenary Cemetery in Green Township. Marion was one of seven children of Aldis Harrington and Elizabeth Fowler. Aldis was born in Vermont in 1810 and came to Gallia County in 1818 with his parents, Giles and Anna (Murray) Harrington, both from Vermont. Aldis died in 1887; Elizabeth in 1892. They are buried in Centenary Cemetery, Green Township.

Surviving grandchildren of Cornelius and Myrta include Linda (Chambers) Brennan of

O'Fallon, Missouri; Dave Chambers of Irvine, California; Donald Chambers of Madison, Wisconsin; Faine Chambers of Decatur, Georgia; Anne (Chambers) Connors of Marietta, Georgia; Eileen (Chambers) Frisby of Columbus, Ohio; Suzanne (Crawford) Martin of Columbus, Ohio; and Barbara (Chambers) McBride of Urbana, Ohio.

*Submitted by: Donald Liggitt Chambers*

**FOSTER CHAMPER FAMILY** - Robert Foster Champer, (died 3-15-1984) son of George Walker and Mary H. Neal Champer, was married to Doris Irene Mayberry, who was born November 7, 1905, and died June 20, 1969. He retired from the Kyger Creek Power Company. Both are buried in the Mound Hill Cemetery. Robert and Doris had 5 children. They are:

1.Paul Edward, born Feb. 19, 1926. Died Feb. 6, 1989. Buried in Mound Hill Cemetery.

1ST wife was Maggie Buchonich, born April 14, 1919. Died Nov. 13, 1983. Buried in Mount Hill Cemetery. They had two sons:

1. Paul G. Champer, born July 12, 1953. Paul married Clarie Hangan of Chicago, on Nov. 8, 1980. They have three children: a. Valirie Champer, born April 6, 1984, b. Dylan Champer, born Jan. 17, 1990, c. Cory Champer, born Oct. 12, 1993.

2. Leon Champer, born Aug. 31, 1958. He married Jamey Heard from Elkgrove Village, IL on July 25, 1987. They have 3 children: a. Quinton Champer, born Nov. 22, 1989, b. Blake Champer, Feb. 25, 1992, c. Travis Champer born Aug. 21, 1994.

Paul and Leon have a dental practice in Naperville, IL.

Paul Edward married Blanche Filipek Statzer (second wife) on July 2, 1984 who resides in Gallipolis, OH. Blanche was born on March 16, 1928 in Raleigh, WV.

II John Robert, (Jack) born July 29, 1928. Died Nov. 14, 2001. Buried in Mound Hill Cemetery. III Mary Belie Champer Carder, born Feb. 14, 1933. IV Jane Ann Champer Phillips, born July 27, 1942. V Penny Lou Champer Simpson, born Sept. 19, 1946

**GEORGE AND REBECCA CHAPMAN** - George Marion Chapman (son of William Marshall Chapman and Amy Sowards) was born July 06, 1862 in Gallia Co., and died April 02, 1954 in Athalia, Ohio. He married Rebecca Ann Brumfield (daughter of John Brumfield and Abigail Massie) on November 05, 1887 in Crown City, Ohio. She was born September 04, 1870 in Gallia Co., and died January 23, 1936 in Athalia, Ohio.

George and Rebecca had the following children: 1. Stillborn (September 10, 1888. 2. Arilla Jane was born August 17, 1889. She died of pneumonia on March 23, 1909, Cabell Co., West Va., shortly before her wedding date and was buried in her wedding dress, on what would have been her wedding day. 3. George William was born on June 13, 1891 in West Virginia. He married Verna Clary, on February 24, 1918. George died on January 04, 1981, Huntington, WV. 4. John Marshall was born February 04, 1894 in Cabell Co. WV. He died June 20, 1895, in Cabell Co. 5. Nellie Maud was born August 25, 1896, Lesage, WV. She married Stanley Bowen on September 13, 1917. Nellie died on March 03, 1981, in Huntington. 6. Laura Goldie was born October 31, 1898, in Cabell Co. She married Ernie Clarne Bowen on September 03, 1919. She died on February 19. 1984, in Huntington. 7. Verna Fay was born September 07, 1902, Cabell Co.,West Virginia. She married Oren Schlegel on April 04, 1921, Cabell Co. Verna died on June 25, 1976. 8. Vergie was born September 07, 1902. She died May 05, 1909 in Cabell Co. 9. Infant (1904). 10. Sylvester was born March 22, 1905, Cabell Co. He married Iva Jones on January 15, 1927. Vester worked at INCO in Huntington and also operated a vegetable stand in Athalia. He died May 11, 1973, at his home. 11. Earnestine Chapman was born February 23, 1909, Cabell Co., and died April 14, 1983, Huntington, Wv. Earnestine married Iddo Allen Hayes on August 17, 1927, Ironton, Ohio. They first met at school in Athalia, Ohio, however, it was not love at first sight. Iddo didn't like Earnestine and she returned the favor and disliked Iddo.

*George & Rebecca Chapman About 1930*

They started dating as the result of a "box supper" at school. "Box suppers" were where boys would bid to purchase a supper made by one of the female classmates, the high bidder got to eat supper with the girl. Iddo recalled that some of the "box suppers" went as high as $20.00 for a popular girl. Some of the boys took great delight in outbidding a girl's boyfriend for the right to eat supper with the girl.

Iddo was not able to enter into any bidding wars, he only had sixty cents to his name. Using the money to buy a box of candy, he asked Earnestine to share it with him. As they hit it off, Iddo ended up taking Earnestine home to her sister's house later that day. Earnestine called it the "worst mistake he ever made.

**CHENEY - BECK-** We don't know much about our Great, Great, Grandparents Leonard (1-25-1810 —1-08-1910) and Mary (Swigert) Beck. Mary was born in Germany and they had at least one daughter, Eliza. Eliza (1856-1923) married Silas Cheney (1846-1928) in1874. Their children were John Leonard, Pearl, Burton, Guy, Carrie, Jennie, and Carl. Burton and Carl were Stogie makers. They sold their stogies locally and overseas.

My grandfather, John Leonard (1874-195 1) married Georgia Hylton (1900-1993) of Pikeville, Kentucky in 1918. They had six children: Lillian Mae (1920-1996), John Junior (1922), Enabelle (1924), Jennie (Dot) (1927), Ray (1929-1997) and Carl (1931).

Lillian had one daughter, Tammie Lyn Anderson. John Junior married Blanche Ashley of Augusta, Georgia. Enabelle (Ena) married Russell See of Point Pleasant, West Virginia and they had four children: Sharon Lyn, Russell (Rusty), Carl Leonard (Smokey) and Marshall Ray (Stormy). Jennie Eleene (Dot) married Freemon Paul Locke of Tyler, Texas. Ray Leonard married Grace Irene Baird (see Stacy Baird Family). Carl Safford married Sara Lou Baird of Gallipolis (see Baird/Cheney).

*John & Georgia Cheney May 9, 1943*

John L. was a painter by trade. He painted the Gallipolis Locks and Dam when it was constructed. He was also the contract painter on the old Silver Bridge which was dedicated in 1927. Grandfather rode a bicycle daily to both jobs from his residence on 1st hundred block on Fourth Avenue. His children anxiously awaited his arrival home each evening knowing that some little goodie had been kept from his lunch as a treat for them. This was done in a turn about fashion. My Dad, Aunts and Uncles spent Sunday afternoons with their Dad because there wasn't much time to spend with him during the week.

Many an afternoon, Grandma would load up the little red wagon with sandwiches, cookies, fruit, a freezer of homemade ice cream and the baby (which was my Dad Carl Safford) and went on a picnic. Mr. Safford who owned Empire Furniture at that time gave it to him and that is how Dad got his middle name.

Another fond memory they have is of the 1937 flood. They were only small children and knew little of the heartache and hard work that accompanies a tragedy of that nature. They lived on the second floor of the Gallia Hotel (tore down a few years ago). From the rear window, they could look out upon the Ohio River. They tell of seeing a two story house with a dog on the roof float down the river. There were many other strange sights but the puppy dog always stuck with them. It was like a vacation to the little ones because they were away from home. They did see the muddy mess left in their home from the six feet of water. None of them could ever forget the flood.

*Submitted by Delman Cheney*

**WILLIAM PUTNAM CHERRINGTON** - The Cherrington family has been in this area since 1805 when William Cherrington arrived from Virginia...one hundred ninety-seven years ago.

William Putnam Cherrington was the fourth generation of Cherringtons born in Gallia County on July 20, 1912, son of Henry William and Vivian Ayres Cherrington.

Henry, Bill's father, attended Marietta College one year and completed his requirement to practice law by studying under two attorneys as was the custom in those days. He achieved distinction as an attorney and was known as "Mr. Republican" of Gallia County. He died in 1971.

*Bill and Beth Cherrington*

William, or Bill, as he was known, attended local schools and lettered in five athletic sports at GAHS...football, baseball, basketball, golf and tennis and as of today still holds that record. He graduated from high school in 1930, from Ohio University in 1933 (taking only three years to do so) and was elected to Phi Beta kappa. He graduated from the University of Michigan Law School in 1936 and returned to Gallipolis to practice law with his father.

Henrietta Cherrington, Bill's only sister, married Frank Harmon O'Brien in October 1940. Harmon practiced law and was also Probate Judge in Meigs County until he retired and they moved to Florida. Harm died in 1986 and Henny moved to Hilton Head, SC in 1999 and died in January 2002.

Bill married Mary Lisbeth (Beth) Lovell in January 1941. She was the daughter of James Joseph and Ada Blanche Graham Lovell. Beth's claim to fame is that Betty Washington, sister of our first president, General George Washington, was her fourth great grandmother. Betty married Fielding Lewis of Revolutionary War fame and their granddaughter married Colonel Joseph Lovell, hence the Lovell lineage.

Three daughters were born to this union.. Suzanne, born November 2,1941, Henrietta, born August 4,1944 and Lisbeth Lovell, born April 23, 1948. Suzanne obtained a Doctor of Jurisprudence degree in 1966. While working for the Attorney General she met and eventually married Thomas Scott Moulton, Sr., an attorney from Lucasville, Ohio in 1969. They moved to Gallipolis to join the law firm of her grandfather and father. The firm name changed to Cherrington and Moulton. She was Gallia County's first woman attorney. She did not practice immediately as she was busy raising two children, Thomas Scott Moulton, Jr. born January 12, 1971 and Sarah Lisbeth, born July 28, 1972. Tom stayed with the firm until 1979 when he was elected Probate Judge, a position he is retiring from in 2003. Sue returned to practice in 1979 and served until she died in June 1995. Sue's daughter married Samuel Fitzwater in 1985 and they have a daughter, Molly Margaret, born February 14, 2001 and they live in Lillington, NC. Tom, Jr. passed the bar in 1997 and joined the firm.

Bill's second daughter, Henrietta, married D. Dean Evans in 1966. They taught school in Summit Station, Ohio and Dean attended Capital University where he obtained his law degree. They moved back to Gallipolis and Dean joined the law firm and the name of the firm became Cherrington, Moulton and Evans. Henny and Dean have two sons, William Claude, born September 14,1970 and David Cherrington, born September 30, 1974. William and wife Kirsten live in Denver, Colorado and David lives in Gallipolis where he and his cousin, Thomas Scott Moulton, Jr., have formed a law partnership. Dean left the practice to become Common Pleas Judge in 2001. Bill's grandsons are the fourth generation to practice law.

Lisbeth Lovell Cherrington was born April 23, 1948. She graduated from Marshall and Colorado State universities in communications and is now living in Bluffton, SC where she is a Certified Financial Planner for American Express.

Bill died in 1998 and Beth continues to live in the home she and Bill built in 1959 at 557 First Avenue.

*Submitted by Mary Lisbeth Cherrington*

**CHILDERS FAMILY** - Mosby Childers: Born in Virginia 1759, served in Revolutionary War, moved with wife Elizabeth Jeffries to Gallia County 1810, where they raised their 11 children: John, Abraham, William, Mosby Jr, Joseph, Mary Polly, Robert, Elizabeth, Martin, Andrew, Nancy, Hannah, and Henry. Mosby died 1843 Hancock County, Indiana.

Abraham Childers: Born Feb 1793, Virginia, died March 1871, Gallia County. He lived in Perry Township, became a farmer, married Rachael Rickabaugh, daughter of John Rickabaugh and Elizabeth Griffith, and raised a family: Levi, Lucinda, Andrew, Clarissa, Lewis, Perry, Mahala, Abraham Benton, John and William.

Abraham Benton Childers: Born 3 Aug 1835 Gallia County, and died 18 Aug Columbus, Ohio. 1880 Census-Gallia, showed an Abraham Benton Childers at Gallipolis, Raccoon Township, Ohio.

*Ola & Ben 1920*

Served in "H" Company 77 Ohio infantry during the war between the states. Enlisted as a private Sep 1861 to serve three years. However was discharged 17 Feb 1862 at Camp Dennison, Ohio on Surgeon's certificate of disability. Abraham married Rebecca Lewis, daughter of James A. Lewis and Rebecca McNerlin, Jan 1861, and raised a family of 7 children: Emily Josephine, John Lewis, Sara Jane, William Benton, Lucinda Clarissa, James Oscar, and Mary Margaret.

William Benton Childers: Born 3 Nov 1866 Raccoon Township, Gallia County, died 24 July 1954 Columbus, Ohio. Married Malissa Rothgeb, daughter of John Rothgeb and Alice Wilson of Gallia County, July 1895 in Franklin, County. William Benton Childers attended The Rio Grande College in Rio Grande. While attending Rio Grande he delivered mail on horseback. In the September 1882 yearbook, William Benton Childers is listed as a student in the English and Normal Department. Rio Grande is pronounced Rye-O because the local residents saw the name in a newspaper and weren't aware of the correct pronunciation. They tried to name it Adamsville after Adam Rickabaugh but the name was already taken.

When William Jennings Bryan ran for President at the turn of the century he mailed a handwritten letter to W.B. Childers(Franklin Co. Democratic Chairman) informing him when he would be in Columbus. W.B. accompanied Bryan on speaking engagements in the Columbus area. W.B. ran for the legislature in Ohio. At the time the McLeans Machine of Cincinnati controlled the Democratic party in Ohio. They informed W. B. he could have the nomination if he would "play ball with them." W.B. informed them he did not "play their kind of ball." Two-dollar bills were prolific around the polling places in Franklin County and W.B . didn't stand a chance.

James Benton Childers, Sr: Born Columbus 1897, died 1974, Miami, Florida married Clara McCorkle, daughter of Maston Clay McCorkle and Rhoda Cannaday.

James Benton Childers, Jr. Born 1926, Johnson City, Tennessee married Lucinda Gaskin, born 1946 Waco, Texas, daughter of James Gaskin and Ethelyn Crawford of Gaskin Texas.

Additional information is available on the Childers Family by contacting: Jack Childers

**BUELL WAUGH AND TRIXIE NEAL CLARK FAMILY** - Buell Waugh Clark, son of Isaac N. and Rachel Waugh Clark, and Trixie Neal, daughter of Thomas Jefferson Neal and Effie Boster Neal, were married in 1921 at Pomeroy, Ohio. Buell and Trixie were both born and reared in Harrison Township, Gallia County, Ohio. Buell attended Mt. Carmel grade school and Trixie attended Macedonia grade school, and Hilton (a 2 year high school). Both were members of the Grace United Methodist Church.

Shortly after their marriage, they made their home in Gallipolis, Ohio. Buell went to work in the grocery business for Wagner Brothers. At that time, Wagner Brothers was located on the corner of Second Avenue and Pine Street. He continued working with them until 1933, and during this time they started several other stores in Gallipolis, Pomeroy, Middleport, Pt. Pleasant, Crown City, Kanauga, Bidwell and Cheshire. The company dissolved in 1933. Buell went to work for the Evans Grocery Company in 1942, and left that job to work at the T.N.T. plant in Pt Pleasant, W. Va. during World War II. He worked at that job until the plant closed, after which he returned to the Evans Grocery Company, which was later changed to Thorough Markets. He retired from there in 1964. He died on October 15, 1985 at the age of 86.

During World War II, Trixie was employed by the Hixson Jewelry Store, 342 Second Avenue, Gallipolis, Ohio. She died on August 14,1989 at the age of 88.

To this union was born one son, Neal B. Clark. He attended Gallipolis Schools and graduated from Gallia Academy High School in 1940. Before enlisting in the Air Force in 1942, he was employed by the Hixson Jewelry Store. During World War II, he served in the Air Force 3 1/2 years, 1 year in the states and 2 1/2 years in England, Germany, France and was discharged in December, 1945. Returning to Gallipolis, he bought Hixson's Jewelry Store from Virgil and Vera Hixson and was owner and operator of that business for 45 years and retired from there in 1985 at age 62.

**NEAL B. AND JEAN E. BATES CLARK FAMILY** - Neal B. Clark was born to Buell W. and Trixie Neal Clark on September 23,1921, in Gallipolis, Ohio. He married Jean E. Bates, daughter of Merrill and Justina Bowman Bates, on February 22,1948, at the Oak hill Methodist Church in Oak Hill, Ohio. Jean was born February 25,1924, in Oak Hill.

After World War II, Neal purchased Hixson's Jewelry Store, 342 Second Avenue, Gallipolis This was a jewelry store for many years. Previous owners had been Charles Uhrig, in the late 1800's, A.K. Merriman, and Virgil Hixson. Neal is a certified master watchmaker. The store was incorporated as Clark's Jewelry Store, Inc., and the corporation also owned another store in Pomeroy, Ohio. It was formerly Goessler's Jewelry Store and has been in business for more than 100 years, and is the second oldest jewelry store in the state of Ohio.

Jean attended the Oak Hill Schools and graduated from high school in 1942. She pursued her career at the Holzer School of Nursing and graduated as a registered nurse from the first avenue address in February, 1948. There was a total of five students in her graduating class. In 1964 she became the school nurse for the Gallipolis City Schools until her retirement in 1988 at the age of 64.

To this union was born a daughter and a son, Nancy Jean Clark, born April 14, 1951, at Holzer Hospital, First Avenue, Gallipolis, Ohio. Nancy graduated from Gallia Academy High School in 1969, Morehead State University in 1973, and the University of Dayton in1985 with her Master's Degree in school counseling. Nancy was active in Grace United Methodist Church, Girl Scouts, and Morehead State University Band.

Joe Neal Clark was born April 18,1954, at Holzer Hospital, First Avenue, Gallipolis, Ohio. Joe graduated from Gallia Academy High School in the Class of 1972, Lees-McRae College in Banner Elk, North Carolina, and the Gem City College of Horology as a jewelry designer and diamond setter in 1976. During high school, he was active in drama and was a member of the All Ohio State Fair Youth Choir and toured Europe with the choir. He was active in the Grace United Methodist Church and Explorer Post 200. After graduating from Gem City College, Joe worked for his father in the jewelry business for 1 1/2 years and left to become manager of the Ford Jewelry Store in Athens, Ohio. On April 1,1980, Joe became part owner of Clark's Jewelry Store, Inc. and managed the Pomeroy store until June 10, 1985 when he became manager of both stores. Joe is a Mason, received the Knight of the York Cross of Honor, Alladin Shrine, Sons of the American Revolution, and a member of the Grace United Methodist Church.

On November 13, 1998, Joe married Linda Orcutt in Sevierville, Tennessee. Joe is the manager of the Whitehall Jewelry Store in Naples, Florida and Linda works in the Lundstrom Jewelry Store in Naples.

**PEARL IRENE BIGHAM & JAMES CLARK FAMILY** - Irene's great, great, great, great grandfather, Louis Victor Von Schriltz, and his wife Marie Courcelle, arrived in Gallipolis, with the French 500, in October 1790. Her great, great, great grandfather, Alexander Von Schriltz, was born in Gallia County on March 19, 1791. He served in the War of 1812.

Pearl Irene Bigham was born on June 19, 1938, in Hocking County, Ohio. Her parents were John Wesley Bigham and Nora Elizabeth Taylor, and her maternal grandmother was Tressa Von Schriltz.

Irene's childhood years were spent in Hocking County, where she graduated from Logan High School in 1956. She attended Ohio University that fall, and two years later was presented with a Cadet Certificate for teaching kindergarten through eighth grade. In the fall of 1958, her role as teacher replaced the position of student that Irene had held just six years prior in the same building!

*James & Pearl Irene Clark*

Irene met James Harrison Clark, from Athens County in January 1958, and they married on August 29, 1959. They both taught school in Hocking County their first year of marriage.

Their first child, Elizabeth Irene, was born on August 10, 1960, in Athens County, and temporarily, teaching was put on hold while Jim worked for a Savings and Loan Company, and Irene was a stay-at-home mom.

Jim's next job took them to Montgomery County, Ohio in 1963, where their son Kenneth James was born on April 9, 1964.

August 1965, found them heading west to Alpine, Texas. Jim had accepted a teaching position with Sul Ross State College. Rebecca Lynn was born on May 2, 1967 in Texas.

Due to the death of Jim's Mom, the Clarks came to Gallia County, Ohio, in 1971. (It was important to be closer to Jim's Dad since his parents just had one child.) They fell in love with the beautiful river town of Gallipolis. They had not been used to seeing much water in West Texas, and the river was a welcome beacon. Jim had been hired to teach at Rio Grande College. Irene was unaware that her ancestors had set up housekeeping here, over 180 years earlier. It was while doing genealogy research, many years later that this discovery was made. Her pursuit earned a First Families of Gallia County.

Their three children were educated in Gallia County, and two of them graduated from Ohio University, their parents' Alma Mater. Irene taught school in Gallia County for about fourteen years and Jim worked at Pleasant Valley Hospital as controller for over twenty years.

The Clarks are retired but have no problem keeping busy as they do volunteer work, church activities, genealogy, and travel.

It would appear that a river view home, in Gallia County, offers just what the doctor ordered for Jim and Irene Clark, transplants from Hocking, Athens, Montgomery Counties in Ohio, and Brewster County in Texas.

**EVERETT & JEWEL (LAYNE) CLARK FAMILY** - Everett Curtis Clark was born November 6, 1917 to Harry and Bessie (Shato) Clark in Bladen, Ohio. He was the second oldest of five children. He graduated from Gallia Academy High School in 1939.

In 1943, he married Jewel May Layne, who was the daughter of Charles and Emma (Montgomery) Layne from the Bladen area. She was from a family of six children.

He entered the U S Army February 9, 1942 at Ft. Hayes, Ohio. He was awarded a good conduct medal.He worked for Cameron-Allison Electric in the 50's, and then what is now Gallipolis Developmental Center for 21 years.

On January 19, 1945, a daughter was born, Wanda Lou who now resides in Guysville, Ohio. On August 24, 1950, a son Wayne Curtis was born. He now resides in Cary, North Carolina. On June 11, 1959, the second daughter was born, Waneta Mae. She still owns and lives near the land in Gallipolis where she was born and raised.

There are four grandchildren, Vincent Clark Beaver, Travis Michael Dennie, Dustin Curtis Dennie, and Veronica Yve' Clark.

**WILLIAM W. CLARK AND CHRISTENIA CALDWELL CLARK** - The first record I have of my ancestor William Clark was in 1818 when he was recorded in the records of Morgan Twp. of Gallia County. William was the son of Joseph Clark and Rachel Watkins of Gallia County. It was always told that his family came from England to Virginia and then to Marietta. When they came from England they hid their gold in the heels of their shoes so it would not be stolen.

They came from Marietta to Gallia County with other families named Weatherholt and Shepherd. William Clark settled in Morgan Twp. He was married to Christina Caldwell and to this marriage was born nine children. E. E. (Elmer), Alfred, Jake, Arthur, Joseph, Stella, Eva, Mary, and John, my grandfather. William Clark served for a while in the Civil War Co. C 194th. Ohio

Volunteer Inf., but returned home after an injury. He was a farmer in the Clark Chapel area. He helped build Clark Chapel Church and the Clark Chapel School. Two of his sons John and Alfred became medical doctors. They graduated from Starling Medical College; this became the Ohio State University Medical College. They graduated in 1893. Dr. Alf practiced medicine in Vinton, Ohio. Elmer moved to Oklahoma and Stella Swick Grimes became a teacher and remained in the county. Dr. John Clark practiced in a number of places, Oak Hill, Oklahoma, Ironton, Vinton, Wilksville, and served as chief physician at the Ohio Pen in Columbus. He was appointed for a five-year term by Governor Harmon. He served as an army doctor serving with the cavalry in Mexico in the pursuit of Poncho Villa. The other brothers and sisters were successful in their chosen fields.

*Submitted by: Mamie Clark Lloyd*

**ROBBIE AND DEBBIE BALL COLLINS FAMILY** - Robbie Ashton was born in Columbus, Ohio, on November 15, 1969, the son of Earl Joseph Collins and Nancy Ellen Weston from Jackson, Ohio. He is the third of seven children; the others are Earl Jr., Lori, Shawn, Chris, Carol, and Erin. Earl and Nancy took their family and left Columbus in 1974 for Livermore, California. They later moved to Yuma and Tucson, Arizona, before returning to Jackson, Ohio, in 1983. Earl and Nancy are members of the Church of Jesus Christ of Latter Day Saints in Jackson, Ohio.

Robbie graduated from Jackson High School in 1988. He worked for Big Bear for 12 years and currently works for Totes Isotoner in Cincinnati, Ohio, as a material control specialist.

*L: to R: Karma, Robb, Debbie & Hannah Collins*

Debra Kay was born in Holzer Hospital in Gallipolis, Ohio, on August 3, 1970. She is the daughter of Robert S. Ball Jr. and Judith Carolyn Shriven. She has one sister, Sue Ellen Bostic (April 1, 1968 -). While Sue and Debbie were growing up, their great grandmother, Margaret Yeager Dunkle, lived with them. In the same house lived their aunt Linda Shriver and her son Brian. Sue, Debbie, and Brian were raised practically as brother and sisters. They were and continue to be a close-knit family. When the two girls were young, The Ball Family attended Rodney Methodist Church. In the 1980's they began going to First Presbyterian Church in Gallipolis, Ohio, where they all still attend.

Debbie graduated from Gallia Academy High School in 1988. In 1993 she graduated from University of Rio Grande with a bachelor's degree in elementary education. Although she was a substitute teacher for Gallipolis City and Gallia County Schools for one year, she currently teaches eighth grade language arts at West Union High School. She moved to Adams County in 1995.

Robbie and Debbie married on May 18, 1996, at the First Presbyterian Church; and they have two children—Hanah Nickole Collins born June 22, 1993, from a previous marriage, and Karma Ashton Collins born January 25, 1997.

Hannah attends South Street Elementary in Jackson, Ohio. Karma attends Gingerbread House Daycare in Winchester, Ohio, and will begin kindergarten in the fall of 2002.

Debbie coaches the girls' soccer team at West Union High School. Robbie began a spring youth league in Adams County in 2001; he then started a girls and boys soccer team at Adams County Christian School in West Union, Ohio. Their daughter Hannah enjoys soccer and played in their spring youth league. They are hoping Karma will also enjoy this sport.

*Submitted by Debra Kay Ball Collins*

**JAMES WILLARD & JACQUELINE ANN AVERELL COONEN FAMILY** - James was born in Dundas Wisconsin August 23, 1920. His great grand parents, Arnold Verstegen and Anna Biemans came from the Netherlands in 1850. James grandfather, Martin Coenen served in the Union Army Co F fifth regiment, Wisconsin Volunteer infantry. The spelling of the name Coenen was changed to Coonen it's present spelling due to misspelled military records. James' father James Louis and his mother Petronella Biese Coonen owned a general store in Dundas Wisconsin. James is the eleventh of twelve children.

In 1942, James graduated from the Merchant Marine Academy at Kingspoint, New York. His first sea duty was aboard the Andrea F Luckenbach which was torpedoed and sank in the North Atlantic. After graduation from the academy, he joined the Navy as a Ensign and served as an engineering officer aboard various ships. He ended his Naval tour of duty as a Lieutenant (jg) with his last assignment bringing a ship to Bikini for the atomic bomb test.

*Jackie & Jim Coonen*

In 1950 James received a degree in mechanical engineering from the University of Wisconsin, and joined the Goodyear Tire and Rubber Co. In 1958 he became the Manager of Engineering for the Point Pleasant Plant. He retired in 1985.

Jacqueline Ann (Averell) Coonen born Akron, Ohio, March 9, 1928 the daughter of Max Wilson Averell and Ruth Marie (Milford) Averell. Max born in Brandon VT. 1905 and Ruth born in Akron 1908. Grandparents Dr E.L. Averell born 1866 and Annie (Auringer) Averell, Windsor Canada. The Averell name originated in England arriving in America spelled Avery. Wm. Avery settled in Ipswich, Mass 1637.

Maternal grandparents John Milford Born in Wales and Lillian (Sirdefield) Milford, England born 1880 arriving in USA 1881.

Jacqueline attended Kent State University graduating in 1979 from Rio Grande College majoring in Social Work. In 1979 she began work as a social worker at The Gallipolis Developmental Center retiring in 1990.

The Coonen Family includes three daughters, Carolyn (Coonen) Ford and husband Robert, Danville, California; Constance (Coonen) Morgan and husband John, Westerville, Ohio; Maureen (Coonen) Cox and husband Carl, Columbus, Ohio and son Michael Coonen and wife Sharon (Roberts) Coonen, Williamsburg, Ohio.

James and Jacqueline are members of St. Louis Catholic Church, Gallipolis, Ohio.

**COTTRILL FAMILY** - The first Edward Cottrill came from England. The next Edward Cottrill was born 4 April 1781 died 4 March 1848. He married Rhoda Langfold born 7 April 1780 died 19 March 1877. One of their sons was Joel born on 14 September 1826 died 25 August 1901 married Mary Patterson born 13 March 1831 died 1 April 1901. Both are buried in the Cottrill Cemetery in Gallia County, Ohio. One of their daughters was Isabell born 28 October 1850 died 14 August 1923. She married John Roadarmour born 22 August 1848 died 9 December 1913. Both are buried at Mound Hill Cemetery in Gallipolis, Ohio. One of their children was Emily Cordelia, my mother; born 5 June 1884 died 19 March 1973. She married Virgil A. Trotter born 9 October 1887 died 11 July 1968. Virgil is buried in St. Nick Cemetery, Gallia County, Ohio. Emily Trotter is buried in Mound Hill Cemetery. One of their children was Mary Rachel born 6 November 1924. Mary is now retired from teaching after 39 years of working. Their son John married Effie White and both are retired teachers.

Anna Isabel and Forest Ball had Don born 25 June 1941 that was a school psychologist in Columbus. He married Charlotte Ann Reed on December 27 1964. And they had Joan who married Tom Passen. Joan worked for the Ohio Chapter of the National Association of Social Workers. Tom worked for Techneglass. Donna June stayed at home.

Vivian and Millard Ankrom had Dick, Esther, Jerry, and Sue. Dick was a Columbus Policeman. He is retired and lives in Florida. Jerry was an electrician and died when he fell from a pole. Esther's husband was Eugene Grafmiller. Both have passed away. Sue's husband is Joseph Redmond.

Joan and Tom Passen had two Sons Craig, and Perry. Craig was born the 16th of March 1956, married Cindy Jo Goodyear the 2nd of September 1977. He is a project manager for Davis & Company. Their children are Brooke

Elizabeth born 36th September 1979 and Craig Michael Junior born January 1st, 1982.

*Bailey Chapel, Rt. 218, Gallia County,*

Perry Lee was born 23 August 1959. He married Joan Prilla Browning 28 June 1986. He owns an advertising firm in Canal Winchester. Perry and Joan's children are Casey Leigh born 23 September, 1988, Brett Thomas born 5 February 1981 and, Jessica Lynn born 3 December 1992.

Don Ball and Charlotte had two children, Donald Andrew born 7 July 1968 and Julie Kay born 13 March 1970.

The rest of the history of the Cottrill family can be found in the Trotter and Roadarmour history.

*Submitted by Joan Passen and Mary Trotter*

**ABRAHAM COX, JR.** - Abraham Cox, Jr. was born July 31,1823 in Monroe County, VA in area that now is West Virginia. His parents, Abraham Cox, Sr. and Nancy Mitchell were married November 27, 1818 in Monroe Co. Nancy's parents were Joshua & Nancy (Ross) Mitchell of Monroe Co., VA.

*Charles W. Cox    Jasper Newton Cox*

Abraham moved to Gallia County, Ohio about 1842 where he met & married Elizabeth G. Waugh on August 11, 1846. Elizabeth was born March 3, 1828 to John T. & Anna (Sloan) Waugh who were married in Gallia County April 8, 1824. Abraham had eleven children: Charles W., born June 6, 1847 who married Luella "Ellen" Bowen December 11, 1872: Jasper Newton, born September 13, 1850 who married Julia Ann Wooten January 28, 1874; Louella Frances, born March 17, 1852 who died March 18,1885; Milton Veora, born November 2, 1855; John Marion, born February 28, 1858 who married Eliza Ann Halley, December 21, 1881; Marshall Clint born February 18, 1860 who married #1-Ella Call,#2-Della Frances Harbour; Albert Galiton born May 13, 1862 who married Anna C. ? about 1886; Elizabeth Ann born November 24, 1864 and died April 4, 1865; Andrew Jackson born January 30, 1866, who married Mary Ellen Campbell; Freddie Lorian born August 2, 1868 and died April 11, 1890; and Miriam Jane born January 9, 1871 and died November 3, 1885.

Charles and Ellen Cox raised a family that included Vernie, Donie, Beonia and Minnie Mae in Gallia Co. After the death of daughter, Donie, little is known of Charles and his family.

*Front: Albert Galiton Cox John Marion Cox Marshall Clint Cox Andrew Jackson Cox*

Jasper and Julia Cox and his family of five children (Minnie, Melvin, Annie, Lottie & Addie) lived in Gallia County until 1888, when they moved to Montgomery County, Ohio.. A second son, William, was born there. Jasper then moved his family west to Marshall County, Kansas. Their last child, Flossie Lee was born there. When the land in Oklahoma Territory was opened for settlement, September 16, 1893, Jasper made the "Run". He staked a claim in what now is Noble County, Oklahoma. Many of his descendants live in Oklahoma. Milton Veora went west and the family lost tract of him.

John Marion & Eliza remained in Gallia County and had 7 children: Elizabeth, Stella Mae, James Earl, Clementine Frances, Verba Blanche, Clan Burmal and Sadie Marie. They all married and raised their families in Gallia Co. Descendants still live there.

Marshall Clint and Ella settled across the river in West Virginia. They had two children. Their son John Everett raised his family of eleven children in West Virginia.

Albert Galiton and Anna went to Kansas and later settled in Oklahoma Territory. They had three children: Edward L, Ira I. and Lula G..

Andrew Jackson and Mary Ellen settled in Noble Co, Oklahoma. They did not have children. Abraham Jr. died in Gallia Co., June 10, 1877 at 53 years of age and his wife Elizabeth died July 25, 1903 in Gallia Co., Ohio at 75 years of age.

*Submitted by: Dorothy J. Gum*

**DONALD LEE COX AND KATHRYN ANN COX** - Donald Lee Cox was born July 17, 1949 to Franklin Monroe (Pete) Cox and Mary Elizabeth Martin Cox at Bladen, Ohio. Donald attended Ethel School and Hannon Trace High School.

Donald has two brothers, Larry and Freddy and two sisters, Sandra and Nancy who all reside in Gallia County. One sister, Cindy, died in early childhood due to illness.

Donald's father, Pete, ran an auto body shop at their home in Bladen, Ohio. At an early age, Donald helped his father in the garage. This helped prepare him for his own business which he successfully runs and operates in Addison, Ohio which is a small engine shop.

*Donald, Kathy, Daniel, And David Cox*

On March 24, 1972, Donald married Kathryn Ann Carter at Elizabeth Chapel Church in Yellowtown, Ohio by Rev. Alfred Holley. They made their first home at Bladen, Ohio from 1972-1978.

Kathryn was born May 10, 1951 to Ellis Lloyd Carter and Annis Grace Glassburn Carter in Gallipolis, Ohio. Kathryn attended Green Elementary, Washington Elementary and Gallia Academy High School. Kathryn has one brother, Lloyd Joseph Carter.

Kathryn is a medical transcriptionist trained and employed at Holzer Hospital for several years until their children were born and stayed home to care for them. She is now employed by Holzer Clinic. She enjoys playing the piano and has shared her love of music with the boys.

Donald and Kathryn have two children, Daniel Lee Cox born August 21, 1974, and David Lee Cox born July 29, 1976. Both were born in Gallia County.

Daniel attended Addaville Elementary and Kyger Creek High School and the University of Rio Grande. He enlisted in the U.S. Army August 1993. He is making a career of the service and is currently stationed at Fort Polk, Louisiana, where he is Staff Sergeant and Crew Chief in Aviation working with helicopters. He follows in the footsteps of his maternal grandfather, Ellis Carter who served in World War II as a Staff Sergeant in the U.S. Army.

David attended Addaville Elementary, Kyger Creek High School, River Valley High School and the University of Rio Grande where he obtained an Associate Degree of Applied Science in Drafting and Designing. He is now employed by GKN Sinkter of Gallipolis, Ohio and lives at Addison, Ohio.

Both boys were very active in school sports, Band, 4-H and church activities. Donald shared his love of motors, hunting, fishing and motorcycles with the boys.

In February 1978, we moved to Addison, Ohio where we still reside. We attend church at Addison Free Will Baptist Church.

**GERALD AND WANDA COX** - Willard Gerald Con born 8th January 1943, in Columbus, Ohio to Willard Thomas and Geneva (McGuire) Cox. He was united in the Holy Hands of Matrimony with Wanda E. Cox, the 19th June 1965, Enterprise, Ohio by and in the home of Rev. Charles Jenkins. Gerald, being the oldest of seven children. He quit school in his grade school years to help his parents on Farms and provide for the younger siblings. He did so until his marriage at the age of twenty two. He began married life as a Truck Driver, starting on cheater-axle, to tri-axle, up to an 18 wheel Tractor Trailer. Driving across country, mainly on the East Coast. He did go to Anahiem, California to the West. He and Co-Driver, Leon Queen were hauling hazardous materials (dangerous cargo). Because of Snow they drove the Southern Route thru Texas, Arizona and New Mexico. His longest time on the road was two weeks hauling oxygen, back and for the from Romulus, Michigan to Sault St. Marie, Canada; along with Co-Driver Jim Swindler. At which time, they received a certificate stating how they gave above and beyond their call of duty.

Gerald taught himself to operate an inloader, loading cinders in the wee hours of the morning at the Kyger Creek Plant before the Operator arrived on the job. He now can operate most pieces of heavy equipment . Specializing in Coal Loading of Trucks with Peaker Run, Walter Stewart, LaMay and Waterloo Coal Company and has been the past seven years. Now operating a D-11 Caterpillar Dozer. He works hard to provide for his family and tries being a Good Role Model, for his Grandsons.

*The Gerald Cox Family*

Wanda Estelle born 27th May 1949 in Ranford Earl "Pete" and Ella Mae (Slone) Cox, in Gallipolis, Ohio. Wanda's goal in life is to be a good Wife, Mother and Grandmother. She's the oldest of six children. She's baby-sit and cared for Children, most of her life. Giving birth to Kimberly Edath 10th March 1966 and Denise Gaye 31st October 1968. Kimberly married Rickie Lee Cade 23rd February 1985. Son of Kenneth and Reba (Knipp) Cade. Denise married Terry Scott Phillips 16th April 1988, son of Edward "Ted" and Shirley Adele (Drake) Phillips.

Three grandsons have come to bless and brighten the Cox home. Gerald Lee Cade 13th July 1986. Aaron Scott Phillips 15th May 1989 and Terry Austin Phillips 21st July 1994. Sadly they lost their first and only Granddaughter at birth Angel Nichole Cade,7th June 1985.

Due to illness of the Cox's niece, Heather Cox. For ten months, they kept and shared their home with her two year old twins, Brianna and Tianna born 2nd July 1994. It was an experience and a blessing to have them. It was like caring for two year old triplets daily, having Austin and the two girls together. Wanda nicknamed them "The Brat Pack". Evenings and Weekends they were joined with Gerald Lee and Aaron while their parents worked .

Wanda quit school , finishing her sophomore year at Hannan Trace. Later, attended night school at Buckeye Hills receiving Certificates of Completion in Typing and Nurse Assistant Classes. She worked selling Avon and Tupperware. Was a Substitute Cook for Bidwell, North Gallia and Vinton Schools. Helping While Gerald worked, Wanda would drive their truck to Walton Coal to load the truck, so Gerald and his brother Richard could make evening/weekend coal deliveries to Gallia County Local Schools and other customers. She worked at Lorobi's Pizza in the Silver Bridge Plaza. Was one of the first hired to open French City Bakery, being Baker/Donut Fryer.

Volunteering time to be Rinky-Dink Cheerleader Advisor, Homeroom mother, 4-H Advisor, and Modern Woodsmen Youth Leader, Wanda loves writing, oil painting and photography. Some of her poetry "Driver of the Big Blue Truck". "If only we could see" and "My Husband" were published by World of Poetry and on their website. One of her photos " United in Memory" exhibited at Foothills Art Exhibit in Jackson, Ohio. Oil paintings exhibited at Art in the Park. Other hobbies, Cake Decorating brought First and Second place ribbons at Rio Grande Cake Show. Over the years, they lived in Pikeville, Kentucky; Bloomingrose, West Virginia (Boone Co.) Butler, Pennsylvania. In Ohio, Portsmouth; Waverly; Maumee; Clyde; Waterville; Vinton; Jackson; Wilksville and Gallipolis. Settling in Harrison Township at the junction of State Route 218 and Little Bullskin Road at their Hillside Haven. "Today, well lived, makes yesterday a dream of happiness, and tomorrow a vision of hope.

**JAMES (EARL) AND ALMIRA COX** - James Earl Cox, a lifetime native of Gallia County born 11th. February 1889 to John Marion and Eliza (Halley) Cox. He married Almira Layne, the 27th February 1911. Almira was born 17th. November 1894 at Bladen, Ohio to Ziba Monroe and Mary Jane (Johnson) Layne. Earl and Mide (her nickname) had eight children. (1) Thelma Gladys born 16th January 1912, married Truman Wolford. (2) Lenville Harley born 12th September 1915, married Estelle Jaquess, he died 17th , November 1963. (3) Denver Clifford born 5th September 1919, married Mary Fellure, he died 15th December 1990.(4) Carl Edward born 15th March 1921, married Elizabeth Sanders, he died 22nd March 1995. (5) Haskell Loren born 18th May 1922 and killed 27th January 1945 in Ardennes, Germany during World War II. (6) Violet Marie born 12th October 1923, married Harold Sowards, she died 18th December 2000. (7) Ranford Earl born 6th October 1928, married Ella Mae Slone. (8) Vivian Irene born 8th February 1933, married Leslie Kitchen. All of the Cox boys fought in World War II but Denver.

The Cox's farmed most of their lives, living off their land from their crops and animals. Earl worked with the building of the Raccoon Bridge on State Route 218 and other jobs. Owning farms (The Homeplace) on Hannan Trace Road in Harrison Township and a small farm on State Route 218 in Clay Township, where they last lived. Earl never got to live in the new house he built there. A seat on a hay-rake broke causing him to fall backwards, breaking his neck. Causing him to be paralyzed and confined to a circular bed for ten months, one week and two days at Holzer Hospital. Almira was at his side daily except to attend the funeral for Lenville, their oldest son Earl, never knowing of Lenville's death.

Earl was a kid at heart. He had nicknames for most of his children and 31 grandchildren. He loved telling riddles, rhymes, ghost stories and tales of past times. For those, who can remember Grandpa Amos on the Real McCoys, that was Earl. The old hat, the limp but most times, Earl used a cane. He was a character who made you smile and entertained the kids faithfully. Almira was quite, always busy working inside and out. She loved her cows and chickens. She cooked on a woodstove until Earl was hospitalized. She heated her home with wood and coal. Always tending to the chores herself, never complaining. She was content with what most call the old fashion way, never wanting the luxuries of modern times and life. Earl died 10th July 1964 in Holzer Hospital Almira died at home, 4th May 1979, leaving fond memories in the hearts of those who knew them.

**JASPER NEWTON COX** - Jasper Newton Cox was born in Chambersburg, Gallia County, Ohio on September 13, 1850. His parents were Abraham and Elizabeth (Waugh) Cox of Gallia County.. He was the second of eleven children. His siblings included: Charles W. who married Ellen Bowen in Gallia County; Louella Frances who died at age 23; Milton Veora Cox - little is known; John Marion who married Eliza Ann Halley and remained in Gallia Co, where many of his descendants still live. Marshall Clint who married #1-Ella Z.CalI; #2-Della F. Harbour settled across the river in West Virginia; Albert Galiton who married either Anna C. or Mary C. went west to Kansas and then to Oklahoma; Elizabeth Ann, who died at 4 months; Andrew Jackson who married Mary Ellen Campbell, went west and died in Noble County Oklahoma; Freddie Lorian who died at 22 years; and Miriam Jane, who died at 14 years of age.

Abraham Cox, the father of Jasper was born in Monroe County, VA and moved to Gallia County, Ohio about 1842 where he met and married Elizabeth Waugh, daughter of John T. and Anna (Sloan) Waugh. Abraham died in Gallia County at 53 years of age June 10, 1877 and Elizabeth died July 25, 1903 in Gallia County at 75 years of age.

Jasper Newton married Julia Ann Wooten on January 28, 1874. Julia Ann was born October 31, 1852. Her parents were Anderson and Eustatia (Martindale) Wooten of Gallia County. Jasper and Julia settled in Gallia County where six of their children were born. They were:

Minnie Edith; Melvin Wade; Virgil E. (lived 4 days); Annie Louise; Lottie Louise; and Addie Claud. About 1888 Jasper moved his family to Montgomery County, Ohio where a son, William Albert was born. In 1890 Jasper again moved his family, this time west, first settling in Kansas. When the strip of land known as

*Jasper Newton Cox Family
L to R: Addie, Julia Ann, Flosie and Jasper Newton Back Row L to R: William, Lottie, Annie, Minnie and Melvin "Wade"*

the Cherokee Strip was opened to settlement by white people, September 16, 1893, Jasper made the "Run". He was successful in staking his claim for 160 acres in what now is Noble County, Oklahoma. He dug a cave and built one room above it where his family could live while they built the home. Jasper and Julia lived there until they retired. Both are buried in McGuire Cemetery near Lucien, Noble Co., Oklahoma.

*Submitted by: Dorothy J. Gum*

**RANFORD "PETE" AND ELLA MAE COX** - The 6th October 1928 on Cox-Mercerville Road in Guyan Township, Ranford Earl "Pete" Cox was born to Almira (Layne) and James Earl Cox. He was the youngest son of five boys and three girls. When Pete was three weeks old, the family moved to the home place on Hannan Trace Road. In 1945 he left Gallia County at age seventeen, to serve in World War II. He served his time in Germany.

Irene (Pete's youngest Sister) gave his over sea address to Ella Mae Slone. Pete and Ella exchanged letters for a year. May 1947, Ella and Edith Queen paid 25 cents to mail carrier, Bill Buck Clark to ride into town. While walking down Second Avenue, they met Pete and George Swain at Fontana's unexpectedly. Pete had bought a 1930 Model A car and return home from the Army, a couple weeks earlier.

*Cox Family*

Ella Mae Slone born 13th. September 1931 in Cabell County, West Virginia to Shellio and Narie Ethel (Queen) Slone. Her family came from Bowens Creek, West Virginia to Brumfield Road in Harrison Township, Ohio when Ella was thirteen years old. Ella the third child, oldest daughter of two girls and eight boys.

Pete and Ella married 17th December 1947, in the home of Mr. & Mrs. John Lusher, in Mercerville, Ohio by Reverend Charles Lusher. They had six children; sixteen grandchildren; thirteen great-grandchildren and 1 gr.granddaughter deceased. Their children born and married are Wanda Estelle born May 27th 1949, Gallia County, Ohio married Willard Gerald Cox. Donna Jean born 30th December 1950, Gallia County, Ohio married Ronald Carrol Waugh. Linda Mae born 8th February 1952,Gallia County, Ohio married Daniel Lee Smith. Randy Lee born 21st January 1954, Gallia County, Ohio married twice (1) Delores Irene Martin (2) Francis Darlene Wells. Marsha Gaye born 23rd September 1955, Gallia County, Ohio married Marvin Lee Wickline Jr. Loren Dale born 8th April 1960 at the Point Clinic in Mason County, West Virginia married Jane Ann Clary.

Around 1956 Pete and Ella Mae began building their eight room, one bath home on the corner of Little Bullskin and Lewis Road, across from the 3 room Little Bullskin School House where Ella was janitor. All the Children were raised in the home they built.

Presently Grandson Nathan Smith and family resides there. Wanda and Linda lived there also through the years.

Several years Pete owned his own business as a TV Repairman in and around Little Bullskin and Yellowtown area. He began his career assembling TV's for Muntz TV in Columbus, Ohio. He served six years as Harrison Township Trustee. He retired 30th November 1987 from Gallipolis Developmental Center as a Therapeutic Worker.

Ella Mae, a working mother worked at Gallagers Drug Store; cook at Hannan Trace Elementary; Holzer Hospital Housekeeper; retiring as a Telephone Operator for Gallipolis Developmental Center 30th. April 1992. Pete and Ella now live at the Home place on Hannan Trace Road "Belly Ache Farm". They enjoy their cattle, being V.I.P. at Deercreek State Park and traveling every chance they get.

**WILLARD AND GENEVA COX** - Willard Thomas and Geneva (McGuire) Cox were married 8th September 1941 in Gallipolis, Ohio. Willard, born 12th July 1918 in Cabell County, West Virginia to Joseph and Mary (White) Cox. Having one brother; John Sanford and two sisters; Fay and Mary Francis. Geneva born 26th April 1924 in Gallia County, Ohio to George and Laura (Walls) McGuire. Geneva, the fifth of twelve children; Thurman, Sherman, Marvin, Mildred, Lester, Othie, Garnet, Rosalee, (twins) Lenvil & Glenvil and Corenna.

Willard and Geneva lived most of their married lives in Gallia County, Ohio. Living 32 of their 59 years of marriage, on the Farm of Paul Haskins, until Paul died and his family sold the farm. The farmhouse was located above the Harrison Townhouse on Little Bullskin Road. Most years it was a family job raising tobacco, caring for cattle and horses. The three oldest sons at various times rented and lived in Paul's lower farmhouse, below the Townhouse. After having to leave the farm, Willard and Geneva moved to Pattonsville Road on outskirts of Jackson, Ohio beside their daughter, Sharon. After Willard's death, 15th February 2001. Geneva rented a trailer, moving back to Harrison Township on State Route 218. Willard worked at the Barrell House in Columbus, Ohio when their first child was born. Also Buckeye Steel while there. His last employment was for the Gallia County Garage and Federal Mogul Plant. Geneva, a devoted mother, her children's welfare always came first, seeing they always had food on the table. She raised a garden and preserved food for winter and hard times, along with helping in the fields when needed. Geneva and Willard have seven children, five sons and two daughters.

Willard Gerald born 8th January 1943 married Wanda E. Cox. John Wesley born 24th December 1943 married Nancy Taylor. Shirley Ann born 10th February 1945 married twice: (1) James A. Bloomer (2) Thomas A. Stephens Richard Eugene born 1st October 1946 married twice: (1) Penelope Huling (2) Sandra (Blake) Knepper Stanford Othie born 11th March 1951 married three times: (1) Vallery Saunders (2) Deliah Darst (3) Wanda F. (Stiltner) Ward Dale born 4th March 1954 married three times: (1) Carol Swindler (2) Mary J. Hundley (3) Carol (Swindler) Cox Sharon Elain born 2nd March 1957 married James Wade Bishop.

*Cox Family*

The family has 13 grandchildren, 2 deceased granddaughters, 10 step-great-grandchildren, 1 deceased step-great-grandson.

Willard died at Holzer Hospital surrounded by his wife, all his children and mates, and most of the grandchildren, at the time of his death.

*Submitted by: Willard and Geneva Cox*

**REV. ARNOLD R. CROMLISH** - Rev. Arnold R. Cromlish was born January 25, 1913, in Gallia County. He died July 14, 2000.

His great-grandparents, John A. and Mary E. Cromlish, both born in Ausburg, Germany in 1827, came to this country and married in 1848. They came down the Ohio River from Pittsburg, PA on a boat. John was a glass blower by trade. Three children were born to them in Gallia County: Joseph Cromlish (born 1850); William Henry (1856-1939) and Mary L. (1859-1955). John A. and Mary E. both died in 1862.

William Henry Cromlish (Arnold's grandfather) married Mary Abelle Houck on October 7, 1882. Mary Belle (1860-1942) was the daughter of John Houck, a stone mason. William was a butcher and a merchant, operating a store on Shoestring Ridge Road and later at Clipper Mill. Six children were born to them: Harry Max (1883-1962), William A., (1887-1956), Elmer (1891-1893), Richard (1884-1918), Mamie (1884-1964), and Edith (1889-1923).

Arnold's parents, Harry Max and Ora Edna Lanthorn, were married in 1910. Ora was born in Huntington, WV on November 27, 1893, and died on August 26, 1971. Her parents, William Sheridan Lanthorn (1866-1957), and Emma Frances Clark (1866-1898), were married in 1885. William was a painter and a merchant. His store was located on Stanley Plymale Road.

*Rev. Arnold R. Cromlish*

Arnold was predeceased by his brothers Howard (1916-1968) in Springfield and Kenneth (1929-1990) in Columbus, and sisters Hilda (1921-1937), and Gertrude (1924-1939). An infant brother, Ernest, died on May 2, 1918. Arnold is fondly remembered today by his sisters Annabelle (Cromlish) Martin of Springfield (born September 15, 1918), and Fay (Cromlish) Manley of Middleport (born May, 1928), and his brother William (Bus) Cromlish (born November 5, 1910).

Arnold learned the trade of painting at a young age from his maternal grandfather, William Lanthorn. He graduated from Gallia Academy High School in 1934 and married Reva Marie Moore on June 2, 1934, in Gallipolis. Reva was born on June 19, 1910. She was the daughter of the late Augustus Moore (1881-1918) and Nevada (McKnight) Moore (1874-1918) of Bidwell. Arnold became a licensed ordained minister in the Church of God. His pastorates took them to Oklahoma, and various churches in Ohio, Michigan, and St. Paul, Minnesota — sometimes serving as interim pastor in later years. Arnold and Reva moved back to their hometown of Gallipolis in 1959 and bought a house on Shoestring Ridge Road. Reva Cromlish died on December 29, 1981.

Their family includes three children, Dotti and her husband, Howard Towle, of Los Angeles, CA, Linda and her husband, Rollin Yeakle, of Midland, MI, and David Cromlish and his wife, Suzanne, of Phoenix, AZ, nine grandchildren, and 10 great-grandchildren. Following Reva's death, Arnold married the former Eloise Taylor in Gallipolis on October 2, 1982. Arnold was active in the Church of God for 64 years and served as Pastor Emeritus at the Garfield Avenue Church of God in Gallipolis until his death.

**MILDRED BURNS DAFT FAMILY** - First of all, I am proud to be an American. I'm thankful to my forefathers who migrated from France to make it so.

Nicholas Questel (1765) and his son, John Baptiste, arrived here in 1790 with the French Five 500. John was the father of twelve children, one of them being my great-great grandmother Sarah. To her was born four children.

Aurora, my great-grandmother, was the 4th child. I remember Aurora very vividly. She was very small and petite, very feisty and very deaf. She would cup her ears to try to hear. She died in 1944 at the age of 84.

My grandmother, Edna Sigler, was the only daughter of Aurora. Edna had ten children, my mother Gladys Burns being one of them. That makes me a 7th generation descendant.

*Family of Mildred Daft*

I was born in Gallipolis on June 8, 1926 to Clarence "Buzz" and Gladys Burns. I was the first of 12 children. We lived in East Gallipolis and I attended the small two-room Maple Shade School for two years. I then went to Washington Elementary School through eighth grade. From there I went to Gallia Academy for almost four years. World War II occurred and three months before graduation I met Henry Franklin Daft. He was in the U. S. Navy and home on leave. I knew him only twenty-eight days but that was enough. We obtained our marriage license and was married by Earl Moore, Justice of the Peace. Frank returned to base in San Francisco and I followed three months later. He was discharged in 1945. He became a fireman at The Presidio of San Francisco. A few years later we moved to Lake Tahoe, California where Frank became a real estate broker. By this time, after eleven years, we had a daughter, Debra. We soon had another daughter Kimberly and then a 3rd, Theresa. One of the highlights of my life came while attending the 1960 Olympics at Squaw Valley, California and watching Peggy Fleming ice skate. We then moved back to San Francisco.

We decided in 1965 to move closer to family and moved to Columbus, Oh. I transferred with the telephone company and Frank became a car salesman. In 1974 he passed away. I moved back to Gallia County (Cora Mill) and worked at the Senior Citizen Center and Community Action Agency until my retirement in 1990.

My daughters Debra and Theresa are in Florida working with horses. They love it. Kim is a manager at AT & T Company in Columbus. Debra has one son Rudy, 22, who does construction and also lays carpet. Theresa has one son Joshua, 19, who is also a carpet layer. Kim has two daughters, Sara, 11 and Erin 10. Erin is in competitive gymnastics. Sara hasn't found her niche yet but seems interested in violin. I hope she pursues it

By the way I received my GED at the age of 52 and even took some college courses at Rio Grande College.

*Submitted by Mildred Daft*

**ABRAHAM DARST** - Abraham Darst (1710-1790) arrived in Philadelphia from Germany in 1743 or 1745. The Darsts were from the Palintinate Rhine River District part of Germany. The ordeal of getting out of Germany in those years was arduous. They had to pass through 36 custom checkpoints, and were fleeced unmercifully, and arrived in America in debt or broke. In addition, many had incurred the wrath of the Emperor through political upheavals, and their property was confiscated, and their lives were in jeopardy; most changed the spelling of their names, and for 100 years this fear persisted. In 1770 they purchased 250 acres of land south of Mt. Jackson, Virginia. He married Mary (1715-1777) of Mt. Jackson, Virginia. They had eight children.

Son, Abraham Darst 2nd (1745-1820), his wife, Nancy Shaver, (1715-1777) of Dunmore County, Virginia. There were five children.

Abraham brought his family to Ohio and purchased a tract of land at Eight-Mile Island, which is now Cheshire in Cheshire Township. He built the first cabin in Cheshire Township in 1794. The Darsts purchased the land from Phineas Matthews, land agent of The Ohio Company. The first marriage in Cheshire Township was Abraham Darst, Jr. to Kate Rife and the authority for this marriage were Abraham Darst and Joseph Rife.

Benjamin, (1793-1842), son of Abraham and Nancy Shaver, married Sarah Roush and they had five children, one son, Elijah.

Elijah (18 18-1876) married Maza Halfhill in 1838 and they had thirteen children. One son Harmon (23 December 1854-7 May 1913) married Appoline Werner, 17 December 1874, by W. J. Fulton. Appoline (15 July 1854-26 November 1940) was the daughter of George Werner and Appelonia Pfoloun. George and Appelonia (natives of Baden and Winehyne, Germany) were married in Germany. They came to America without members of both families around the 1800's. They had six children, one daughter; Susan Almira (Susie) Rife (31 October 1876-1948) married Horton H. Rife (13 December 1876-1958) 11 March 1893. Horton and Susie had five children: Floyd, Roy, Flossie, Walter, and Hazel. One son, Walter W. Rife (18 August1908- 27 June 1977) married Paulinc Athey (23 October 1910) 9 June 1931.

Please refer to the Walter W. Rife Family section for further family genealogy.

*Submitted by: Amanda Kay Maslen*

**DAVIS AND MORGAN FAMILIES** - Many of the early settlers of Gallia County were immigrants from Wales. Among them were David J. Morgan (born 8 September 1820) and his parents John Morgan "Tyrbach" (born 1785; died 1858) and Catherine Jane Lewis "Fran Goy". John and Catherine landed in New York in 1842 following the arrival in 1841 of their son David J. Morgan. He had moved on to Pittsburgh, later went down the Ohio River to Louisville and eventually back to Scioto Furnace were he found employment at $8.00 a month.

John K. Davis (Davies on the headstone in Tyn Rhos Cemetery) and Mary Francis Davis also came to the U.S. from Wales in 1842. They were the parents of Mary Davis who was born in Cardiganshire Wales (29 January 1834) and married David J. Morgan on her 19' birthday (29 January 1853).

*David J. And Mary Davis Morgan Home*

David & Mary lived near Nebo Church from 1853-1859 where their first four children were born. The family moved to the "David J. Morgan Farm" located on Dan Jones Road near Racoon Creek where eleven additional children were born. David J. died 2 February 1904 and Mary died 7 September 1915. Fourteen of the fifteen children reached adulthood, three becoming physicians, one a dentist and two of the daughters married doctors. The children were:
*Name - Location of residence - Born - Died:*
Magdalene - Green Township, Gallia County, Ohio - 1853 - 1932, John Francis - Colorado; Missouri - 1855 - 1938, Catherine - Columbus, Ohio - 1856 - 1941, Hannah - Washington C.H., Ohio - 1858 - 1904, James - Columbus, Ohio - 1860 - 1938, Fremont - Columbus, Ohio - 1862 - 1941, Mary Ann - Oak Hill, Ohio - 1863 - 1935, David - Gallia County, Ohio-1865-1878 Margaret-Gallipolis, Ohio-1867-1954, Deborah-Columbus, Ohio-1869-1943, Eunice-Columbus, Ohio-1871-1935, R. Theodore-Marion, Ohio-1873-1951 Gomer-Missouri-1874-1960 Everett-Marion, Ohio-1876-1957 Clara - Pomeroy, Ohio-1878-1970.

Only two of the children from this marriage remained in the county during their life times. The first born, Magdalene (born 31 October 1853; died 31 May 1932) married Henry Clay Priestley (born 12 March 1844; died 3 January 1926) a Green Township farmer. Their four children (three of whom remained in Gallipolis or Gallia County for their life times) were Hannah May (born 6 June 1875; died 28 November 1947) who married Clarence Rodgers, Bulaville Rd., Gallipolis Twp; John Morgan Priestley (born 26 February 1877; died 21 May 1938) who resided at 812 Second Avenue, Gallipolis; Mary Maud who married Charles Reynolds and lived in Columbus, Ohio; and David Clay Priestley (born 19 November 1891; died 2 July1964), Green Twp. The ninth child, Margaret (Maggie) (born 6 April 1867; died 11 November 1954) married Isaac Elmer Jones (died 1892) on 29 September 1886. From this marriage were Ethel Jane Jones (born 1890 died 1976) and Isaac Elmer Jones (born 1892; died 1949). Following the death of Isaac Sr., Margaret married Joseph Devacht Donnally (died 1957) in 1904. They had one child Julia Elizabeth (born 24 July 1906; died 30 April 1988) who remained in Gallipolis for her life time.

Three great-grandchildren were born in Gallia County and left when they reached adulthood: Clara Magdalene Rodgers (born 1915; died 1980), Archie Clay Priestley (born 4 November 1920) of Columbus, Ohio, and Esther Mary Priestley Collier (born 15 August 1924) of Chapel Hill, NC.
*Submitted by: Dr. Archie C. Priestley*

**DON DAVIS** - Don was born in Gallipolis, Ohio, on October 22, 1920. His parents were Cleveland W. Davis and Aletha Chick Davis. The other Davis children were Gerald, Tom, and Jean. His grandparents were William W. Davis and Rosanah Atwood Spence Davis. Grandfather Davis came from Cardinganshire, Wales. Grandmother Davis came from Virginia and the couple settled in the Centerville area. Grandfather Charles J. Chick was born in the Walnut, Perry Township area and married Amanda Woodruff. They settled in the same general area. Don's great grandparents also immigrated from Cardinganshire, Wales. David W. Davis and Ann W. Davis, also settled in the Centerville area. The maternal great grandfather, John Chick, immigrated from England. Great, great grandfather, Isaac Carter, was in Gallia County in 1812, and one of his daughters married John Chick. She was Lucinda Carter. Don graduated from GAHS in 1938 and from Ohio University in 1943. He served in World War II in Korea and upon his return, married Virginia Morris of Glouster, Ohio. His daughter, Karen Patterson, is a teacher in the Youngtown area and son, Jeff, of Pickerington, Ohio, works for State Auto Insurance Company. There are three granddaughters, Jeanette Dunlany, Teresa Yocum and Stephanie Paterson; two step-granddaughters, Katie and Libby Keener; three great grandsons, Aaron and Mathew Dunlany and Alex Patterson.

After the death of Virginia, Don married Bess Evans Grace. The insurance business was Don's livelihood for almost 40 years and he retired from Motorists Mutual Insurance Company in 1985. He served as Chairman of the Columbus Insurance Arbitration Committee for 6 years while working in Columbus. He is a member of First Families of Gallia County, Gallia County Historical and Genealogical Society, Grace United Methodist Church and VFW Post 4464.
*Submitted by Don Davis*

**JOHN BOYD AND ELIZABETH LOUISE JONES DAVIS** - J. Boyd and Elizabeth began their married life in secrecy. Being teachers and not permitted to be married, they kept their marriage secret for two years. They produced the following descendants: Margaret Boyd 1909, Hugh Merrill 1910, Mary Elizabeth 1913, and Jane Elliott 1914. J. Boyd and Elizabeth celebrated 64 years of married life together.

Elizabeth Louise Jones was born March 25, 1888 in Patriot, Ohio and died Oct. 24, 1976 in Columbus, Ohio. She married John Boyd Davis Dec. 28, 1907 in Kentucky. J. Boyd Davis was born August 17, 1885 in Rio Grande, Ohio and died October 1, 1971 in Columbus, Ohio. Both are buried at Calvary Baptist Church in Rio Grande.

John Boyd Davis and Elizabeth Jones Davis came from families of education, religious roots, civic responsibilities and independent, progressive dispositions. Both J. Boyd and Elizabeth graduated from Rio Grande College. J. Boyd taught at Rio Grande and worked as an assistant to his father, John Merrill Davis. Later, he taught in rural one-room schools in Gallia County and taught three additional years at the high school level in Ironton and Niles, Ohio. After moving to Columbus, Ohio, they continued their work in civic and religious organizations, assumed leadership roles in the community and church, and maintained connections to Rio Grande College. J. Boyd Davis served on the Rio Grande College Board of trustees and served as President of the Board from 1950 through at least 1969. Rio Grande College presented the Doctor of Public Service Degree to Elizabeth on October 25, 1953 and to J. Boyd on May 31, 1964. Boyd Hall at Rio Grande College was named in honor of J. Boyd Davis and dedicated January 31, 1970. J. Boyd and Elizabeth Jones Davis' connections to Rio Grande College continued until their death. The family connection to Rio Grande College was extended through their grandson, William Davis Grant ( class of 1967), his wife Gwendolyn ( class of 1969), their daughter, Catherine ( class of 1993) and their son Christopher (class of 2001).

*J. Boyd and Elizabeth Jones Davis*

Elizabeth Louise Jones' parents were Evan Nathaniel Jones (b.2/6/1837 in Wales d. 1/5/1918 in Patriot, Ohio and Mary Agnes Pillow ( b. 7/13/1848 in Lynchburg, Virginia d. 1/8/1918 in Patriot, Ohio). Nathaniel and Mary Agnes were married in Gallia County Jan, 9, 1884. Mary Pillow Carver was the second wife of Evan Nathaniel Jones and he was her second husband. His first wife was Elizabeth Bane 1848 - 1883 was born in Gallia County, Ohio.

John Boyd Davis was the son John Merrill Davis (President of Rio Grande College) b. 11/16/1845 in Harrisonville, Ohio d. 11/11/1920 Rio Grande and Jane Elliott Boyd Davis b. 6/11/1855 in Wilkesville, Ohio d. April 8,1930 in Columbus, Ohio.

**JOHN MERRILL AND JANE ELLIOTT ( ELLA ) BOYD DAVIS** - John Merrill and Ella Davis came from families of courageous, independent women having deep religious convictions and a high regard for education. John Merrill's father left Ohio and settled in the state of Washington while his mother remained in Ohio. Prior to Ella's birth, her mother became a widow. At age ten, Ella was orphaned thus reared by her grandmother ( Jane Elliott Boyd). Ella's great grandfather ( John Elliott) was a sea captain and lost his life at sea. Seven years later in 1816, Ella's great grandmother ( Frances Blaine Elliott) packed up, left Northern Ireland, and sailed ( for 15 weeks) to America with 9 of her

15 children. After landing in Baltimore, she and her children walked across the Alleghenies to settle in Ohio.

*Mr. and Mrs. John Merrill Davis*

John Merrill Davis was born November 16, 1846 in Harrisonville, Ohio and died November 11, 1920 in Rio Grande, Ohio. Having met at Ohio University, he and Ella were married on June 22, 1876 in Athens, Ohio. Ella, realizing the importance of education demonstrating her own determination and strong will, was the second woman to graduate from Ohio University. She was born on July 11, 1856 in Wilkesville, Ohio and died April 8, 1930 in Columbus, Ohio.

John Merrill and his 7 siblings Charles Madison, Hershel, Perry, Perrin, Emma, William Homer and, George C. were born in Meigs County, Ohio. John Merrill's parents were Samantha Chase (1827-1864) and William Davis (1821-1890). Samantha was related to Salmon P. Chase ( governor of Ohio and Secretary of Treasury under Abe Lincoln during the Civil War), to Samuel Chase (signer of the Declaration of Independence), and to Bishop Philander Chase (founder of Kenyan College).

John Merrill Davis served as a teacher at Rio Grande College from 1879-1919 (40 years) and was President of the College from 1887-1911 (25 years). Children born to John Merrill and Ella were Caroline Samantha 1877-1915, Charles Elliott 1878-1920 (married Carrie Mae Lawson), Bertha 1880 - 1880, John Boyd 1885-1971 ( married Elizabeth L. Jones), Ella 1887-1887, and William 1894-? (married Hazel Harbour). John Merrill and Ella's four children (who survived childhood) graduated from Rio Grande College. Caroline (Carrie), John Boyd, and William Davis taught at the college. William also coached football at Rio Grande. Charles served on the Rio Grande Board of Trustees for several years and taught Chemistry in Chillicothe. J. Boyd served on the Rio Grande Board for many years.

Ella's parents were Dr. John Elliott Boyd and Caroline S. Carr. Dr. Boyd (a physician) was born 1826 in Keene, Ohio and died in 1855. Caroline Carr was born 1830 and died 1866 in Wilkesville, Ohio. Caroline Carr gained fame while on duty in her brother's general store/post office. General Morgan of the notorious Morgan's Raiders, stopped in the general store/post office to mail a letter to his mother. Having an inquisitive nature, Caroline read the letter before sending it on its way.

**RALPH DAVIS 1901—1978** - Ralph Davis was one of the most influential farmers in the history of Gallia County agriculture. Born in 1901 to Reese and Rella Greenlee Davis. Ralph was born on the farm and lived there until his death in 1978. The farm was a Southeastern Ohio broom sedge farm of two hundred forty acres. The farm was badly run down and the cropland worn out and badly eroded. The family lived in the log house where Ralph was born. Ralph's father died in 1913 leaving Ralph and his mother with one hundred forty acres and a thousand dollar mortgage. Rella Davis was a shy and retiring in the extreme but was given great credit for the extraordinary success achieved in agriculture and stockraising by her son, Ralph. After Reese Davis's death she helped her young son with the farm work; and twain by dint of grinding toil, prudent living, careful and wise planning and progressive farm methods won in such measure as to attract attention and admiration far beyond the borders of this county. Ralph studied through correspondence at night and worked on the farm during the day.

*Ralph Davis*

Ralph studied with Ohio State University Agriculture Department. In 1918 Ralph and his mother built a new house replacing the log house Ralph was born in. The log house has been moved and restored to the Dr. Murray S. Willock Evergreen Farm. By 1925 Ralph knew they would have to make many changes to their land in order to survive. Beginning in 1925 Ralph worked with the Ohio State Agriculture Department and when Gallia County got a county agent he began with him. The county agent and Dr. Dodd of Ohio State University made many recommendations and Ralph followed them as best he could. During the 1930's and 1940's, Ralph applied lime and fertilizer to the worn out soil, set pine trees on eroding land and laid thousands of feet of tile. He started upgrading his livestock production, increased his flock of hens, added high quality sheep and added a purebred bull to his herd. Remembering the drought of 1930 he got the idea of building a pond for water. With the help of Ohio State Agriculture Department, he built several ponds over the years. By 1940 the farm was in full production. In 1943 Ralph married Anna Keller, a school teacher from Lawrence County. Ralph's mother passed away in 1944. In Anna Keller, Ralph found the perfect partner. Anna was dedicated to the life of a farmer.

Together they formed The Davis Egg Company. They also began buying Registered Hereford cattle. The egg company was a thriving business of six hundred laying hens. Ralph was known all over the State of Ohio for his prize winning herefords. Showing his bulls and heifers at fairs on the state and county levels. Ralph also won many awards for his accomplishments in agriculture. The Cleveland Farmers Club paid tribute to Ralph for the best experimental farm in the State of Ohio. Gallia County Agent Everett Royer made the announcement. He also won many awards in the county agriculture field. Ralph was known all over the State for his farming practices and his livestock production. Ralph was a dedicated keeper of the land and set a great example for one of the most important industries in Gallia County. Ralph maintained his high standards in farming until his death in 1978. Anna continued managing the farm until her death in 1996 at the age of ninety-three.

*Foot Note: Ralph and Anna Davis established a scholarship fund with the Ohio State University for students from Gallia County in the fields of Agriculture and nursing.*

**CHARLES & GENEVA BRUMFIELD DAY** - Charles Leslie Day b. 12/09/1880, d1/23/1972 in Gallia County, s/o Anthony and Louisa Barker Day, m. Florence Geneva Brumfield on 9/25/1916. Geneva d/o Thomas & Charlotte Johnson Brumfield. Geneva was b.10/19/1890, d1/23/1975. Charles and Geneva had 6 daughters:

1. Louise Memphis Day m. Roy Daniels, they had the following children: Jimmy, Joyce, Carl, Wayne and Shelba.

2. Luella M. Day m. Kenneth Raike.

3. Charlotte Leona Day, never married.

4. Hildreth C. Day m. Ralph Williams, they had the following children: David, Keith, Regina and Denise.

*Charles Leslie and Florence Geneva Brumfield Day taken around 1916*

5. Lillian Irene Day m. Vilas Unroe, they had 15 children: Billy, Bobby, Janet, Charles, Wendall, Charlotte, Jr., Fern, Vicky, Phil, Debbie, Terry, Pam, Greg and Anita. (not in birth order).

6. Delma Fern Day m. Marion Angel, they had 2 daughters: Tammy and Cathy. Delma is now married to Gene Brown.

*Submitted by: Hildreth Williams*

**(STONE) WHITE-DE BOARD** - We are the youngest daughters of Beulah and the late Orville F. Stone. Our mom, Beulah Wanda (Wood) Stone is 93 years old and her mother lived to be 97 years old. Like our parents we were born and raised in West Virginia, and proud to be the daughters of a coal miner. We have two sisters: Libby Mitchell and Jewel Eddy. We have four brothers living. Our brothers are: Ed, Ron, and Gary Stone. Larry passed away in 1998. Donald Lee passed away in 1944.

I, Gail White, am the seventh child and third daughter. And I, Naomi (Footsie) am the eighth child and the fourth daughter. I am also the baby of the daughters. Our brother Donald Lee was born April 6, 1931 and passed away March 2, 1944. Our brother Larry Ray, the baby of the family, was born July 9, 1950 and passed away January 28, 1998. Us younger children never grew to know Donald Lee but we sure miss Larry. He will forever be loved and missed deeply and dearly.

*Elva Gail (Stone) White*    *Naomi (Footsie) (Stone) Deboard*

Our fondest memories are of when we were children and in school. We remember the holidays and all of the food at the family get-togethers. We remember playing with all of our cousins. However, family get-togethers were never called Family Reunions because it was every weekend. It is sad, as we think about it how we had so many aunts and uncles and today we only have one uncle left, Uncle Eldion (Dude), which is Mom's baby brother. Mom and Dude are the only ones left in the Wood family. Everyone from Dad's family is deceased. We have lost many cousins too.

Our parents were hard working and honest people. But if necessary, Dad would take the strap to our behinds. We were made to get up and go to Sunday school every Sunday morning. We all have our own memories .

We both graduated from East Bank High School. I, Gail graduated in 1963 and came to Ohio soon after. I, Footsie graduated in 1967 and I also came to Ohio soon after. We were around Cheshire for a while living on Route 554, but later moved to Columbus.

I, Gail married Leonard A. White from Colcord, West Virginia in July of 1965. He is the son of the late Charlotte Douglas and Arch White. We are now divorced (1980). We have three children, Leonard and Larraine are twins. Our oldest daughter, Lenny Jo, married Dave Funk. We have one grandson.

I, Footsie married Charles (Sonny) DeBoard from Matawan, West Virginia. We are now divorced. We have two daughters: Sheila, whom is not yet married and Shefly, whom married Shawn Grey in November 2001. They have one daughter.

If any of the family members would like more information about their roots read *"The Family of Elijah and Lowe Wood"* and their daughter *"The Family of Beulah (Wood) Stone"*.

*Submitted by: Elva Gail White and Naomi Joyce (Footsie) DeBoard*

**DEER -VALLANCE** - In 1945, the Alfred Vallance, Sr. family moved from Monaville, (Logan Co.) W.Va. to Gallia Co, Ohio, to their farm on Shoestring Ridge, Lower River Rd., Gallipolis, which they had purchased from Charles Baker. Alfred worked for Island Creek Coal Co at Holden #1 Mine, retiring as a plumber. His wife ma, & their son Jack, lived on the farm & Alfred commuted on weekends from work until his retirement.

*Alfred, Sr. & Ina (Deer) Vallance*

Ina, the daughter of James & Henrietta (Sexton) Deer, was born along with her identical twin sister, Mina, on January 26, 1894 in Greenup Co., Ky. They & their siblings were orphaned at a young and ma, as a young woman, lived with Mitchell & Martha (Hilton) Stuart, parents of Jesse Stuart of "Whollow" in Greenup Co., Ky. Jesse became a famous writer & was made a poet laureate in Kentucky in 1954. Ma helped care for him & his other siblings & did other chores on the farm. Mina lived a short distance down the road from her, with another foster family. Every evening when all of the chores were finished, they walked a short distance from each of their homes & talked over the days happenings. They were inseparable until their deaths.

Ina met Alfred Vallance, Sr., & they were married on May 31, 1917 in Greenup Co., Ky. Alfred & his twin brother, Albert, were born at Argillite, in Greenup Co., Ky. on Sept. 24, 1886, the son of James Thomas & Susan (Abrams) Vallance.

To this union were born: Carl Wesley, Bn. March 18, 1918, #5&6 Holden, Logan Co., W. Va., Md. LaVerne Hall; Loretta May, Bn. January 5, 1920. Monaville, Logan Co., W. Va., Md. James A. Smith; Alfred, Jr., Bn. Dec. 2, 1921, Monaville, Logan Co.. W. Va., Md. Zelmalee Evans; Santford Clifford, Bn. August 19, 1924, Monaville, Logan, Co., W. Va. Md. Winifred Smith; Jack Franklin, Bn. January 16, 1933, Kitts Hill, Lawrence Co., Ohio ,Md. Carolyn Sheets. Two of the above are deceased, Loretta, January 9,2001 & Alfred, Jr., Dec. 17, 2001.

Carl became a minister in the Freewill Baptist Church. & still resides in Huntington, W. Va.; Loretta & James lived in Monaville, W. Va., where James worked for Island Creek Coal Co, retiring from 1-Iolden Mine #25 in Logan, Co..Loretta worked & retired as a cook in the grade school at Monaville. After their retirement, they moved to Inverness, Wa. When their health began to decline, they moved to Virginia to live with their daughter, Kay Frances Rosenquist. Alfred &Clifford served in the Army in WW II, & after their discharge ,made their home in Gallia Co. & retired from Kaiser Aluminum at Ravenswood, W. Va. Clifford now resides in inverness, Fla. Jack attended Clipper Mills Grade School & then Gallia Academy High School, graduating in 1953, & was drafted into the Army in 1953, serving in Korea, until April, 1955, when he was discharged & returned home; after his marriage, May 7, 1955, he resided & worked in Huntington, W. Va. In June of 1966, he became employed with The Goodyear Tire & Rubber Co., at Apple Grove, W.Va. & retired in 1991 with 25 years of service. He & his wife built a home in 1966 at Greenbottom, W. Va. on State Rte. 2 & resided there until 1995 when they purchased their present home in Huntington ,W.Va.

Ina passed away March 16, 1953 , & Alfred, Sr. passed away April21, 1968. Both are buried in Mound Hill Cemetery, at Gallipolis.

*Submitted by: Jack Franklin Vallance*

**AUGUSTUS DEFORE (1)** - A trip to Gallipolis with my husband Carroll R. McDaniel proved to be a very special event in my life. Since I've lost my parents and especially my father, Raymond Dufour, I've had a great feeling of loss not just because of their deaths but ,because I didn't talk to my father about his family while he was alive. His mother (Stella Dufour) never married, he had only one sister, Gladys , that was killed in a car accident in 1927. On a trip to Gallipolis with my husband to do research for his family, we first visited the Court House, trying to help him find his family. In one of the large books I came across my family name, Augustus Dufour. Never knowing I had any relatives living in Gallipolis, or Gallia Co. OH., I mentioned to my husband about seeing the name, but he was so preoccupied in his research that he ignored me. On the way home we discussed this, and he offered to help me find out on our next visit. On a second trip to Gallipolis, we visited the Historical Society, asked if there was any History on the Dufours, and all the wonderful people started bringing out all this information .

*Tombstone Of August De Fore*

A very nice lady by the name of Mary Lee Marchi, a very nice man, volunteer, do not know his name , brought out this Historical Book, and showed me a picture of the Dufour House. It was a Hotel, and he pointed out the window where I could get a glimpse of it. The house is located corner of 1st & State St. on the river, and chills came over me as I viewed the picture. This property has been known to have been a stop on the Underground Railroad. It makes me very proud to think that my ancestors helped many people gain their freedom. All the information they gave me and more research and census records, I've connected my G.Grandfather, Augustus Defore, (name spelling was changed for some reason) to the Dufour family in Gallipolis. William Dufour b. in France lived in Gallipolis, married Emily from France, together they had 2 sons, lived in Ohio Twp. Gallia Co. Oh. William had a brother, John Baptist Dufour, who built the Dufour House in honor of his Father's 100th. birthday, Jean B. C.Dufour lived to be 106 yrs. d. 1872 buried in Pine St. Cemetery in the city of Gallipolis,. William Dufour was killed in a Coal Mine accident on June, 11, 1868; he was a Mine Engineer, near Pittsburg Pa. William had 2 sons, Augustus & John Claudius Augustus is my G. Grandfather, and he m. Mary Ellen Urwin( his first wife) they had the following children:

Minnie b. 1867; William b. 1868; Frank b. 1870; Sarah b.1871; Annetta b.Jan.,25, 1873; Washington Windford b.,1877; Louise b. Aug.28,1878

Augustus, was in the Civil War (volunteer) serving 6 yrs 1861 to 1866.

He married his 2nd wife, Mary Ellen Rigney from Millersport Oh., (which is called Miller, OH) Rome Twp. Lawrence Co. Oh., they had the following children:

Nettie b.1878; Augustus Jr. (Gus) b. June 1882; Stella b. Sept. 1884, my Grandmother; Harry b.Sept.1887; Emma b. Nov. 1890; George b. Nov. 1891; 3 other children died in infancy, unnamed.

Augustus, b. Aug. 1, 1844, in Thane France, d. Oct. 19, 1916, and Mary Ellen b. Nov. 6, 1854 in Millersport, OH. They were married at Catlettsburg, Ky. Mar.8, 1915. They had all these children before they married. Augustus' mother, Emily, the wife of William, was committed to the mental institution at Athens, OH, in 1880, by Augustus' first wife, Mary Ellen Urwin. She possibly died there.

*Submitted by: Helen Marie (Dufour) McDaniel*

**AUGUSTUS DEFORE (2)** - b-Sept.30,1844 in Alleganey Co. Pa. d-Oct .19,1916, m-Mary Ellen Rigney b-Nov.06,1854, in Millers Port Ohio, buried Woodland Cem. (no headstone) Augustus is buried in the Soldiers plot at Woodland cem. He was a volunteer in the civil war for five yr,s, promoted to Corpl. Jan. 1862, Sergt,Jan.16,1865,He served from 1861 to 1866,His wife Mary Ellen is the daughter of Charles and Ella Rigney of Millersport Ohio(RomeTwp.) Census records for 1900 shows 9 children,6 living 1-Nettie b-1878, 2-Stella b-Sept.30,1884, 3-Gus b-June 30,1882, 4-Harry b-Sept11,1887, 5-Emma b-Nov.06,1890, 6-George b-May 22,1892, 7-Addie b-Sept 14,1895.

2-Grandchildren-Raymond Dufour b-June10,1903 d-Mar.02,1965, Gladys b- Sept. 1907 d-June01,1927, The family moved to Ironton in 1878 . He worked in the Iron Furnaces; The Dufour name is spelled so many different ways, Dufour, Defore, Dufoe, Dufoor, Dufoot, no one knows why the names are spelled so different. They are all related. Raymond is the father of Helen Marie Dufour ( Aldridge) McDaniel b-May 9, 1936 in Lawrence Co. Ohio, m-Carroll Ray McDaniel of Deering, Ironton, Ohio, 3 children from a previous marriage:

1-Janet Lee Aldridge Perkey, b-Aug.02,1952, 2-Penny Elaine Aldridge Lewis,b-Nov.28,1954, 3- Cindy Lou Aldridge Roach,b-Jan. 06,1956, 3 step children 1-Alden Eugene McDaniel b-April, 16 1948

Twins—2-Larry&Jerry McDaniel b- May 21,1952, 1-Daughter-Lisa Carol McDaniel, Collins b-May 24, 1965.

*Tombstone of Sergt. August Defore*

Raymond has 2 other daughters and a set of twins-Bernice Ilene Ratliff b-Aug, 06,1927, Mary Louise Aldridge b-Jan.17,1931, Jerry Ray & Judy Gay Dufour b-April16,1944, d-1944, His wife Delphia (Clark) Dufour b-Feb.02,1904,d-Oct.14,1990, They are buried at Zoar Cem. Coal Grove, Ohio, note. Agustus Defour is the Great Grandfather of Helen (Dufour) McDaniel.

*Submitted by Helen (Dufour) McDaniel*

**DE LILLE** - Rex Ernest Greenlee was born September 14, 1944, in Gallia County. He is the only child of Ernest Boyd Greenlee and Anise Swick Greenlee of Bidwell, Morgan Township. Rex attended Bidwell-Porter Elementary School and North Gallia High School. After graduation he served three years with the U.S. Army. He spent 30 months of that time in Worms, Germany. Rex retired from Buckeye Rural Electric after 32 years of service.

His wife, Mildred Louise DeLille Greenlee, was born on the family farm at Rodney on March 18, 1941. Louise was the youngest of nine children. Her parents were Joseph Elias DeLille and Tracie Marilyn Spencer DeLille. Louise attended Rodney Grade School and graduated from Gallia Academy. She continued her education at Rio Grande College, earning a B.S. degree in Elementary Education. She taught her first year at Johnstown, Ohio (Licking County). She then put in 30+ years of teaching for the Gallia County Local and Gallipolis City Schools.

Rex and Louise married August 26, 1967, at the Rodney United Methodist Church. They made their home on part of the DeLille family farm. They are the parents of three children. Phillip Rex Greenlee (September 20, 1969), married to Cheryl Taynor of Miami County. They have three sons: Logan Phillip, and twins Caleb Wyatt and Kyler Ezra. The second son is Gregory Greenlee (August 30, 1974), married to Erin Prose of Gallia County. He has one daughter, Kali Lynn Greenlee. The youngest child Suzanne Beth Greenlee (December 26, 1976) is married to Todd Hines of Athens County.

Phil is a graduate of Morehead University in Kentucky. His wife, Cheryl, graduated from Nationwide Beauty Academy in Columbus. Greg attended Hocking Tech in Nelsonville before his schooling with Ohio Operating Engineers Program. Erin is a graduate from Hocking Tech in the nursing program. Phil and Greg both work with the Ohio Operating Engineers. Suzy is a graduate of the University of Rio Grande. She is a teacher for the Gallipolis City Schools. Todd is a graduate of Ohio University with a chemistry degree. He is self-employed with a fencing business.

*Submitted by Louise Greenlee*

**MARTIN DE LILLE** - Martin's great, great grandfather, Antione DeLille, was born in France. He settled in the Wheeling, West Virginia, area, where he married Sarah Snyder in 1818. Their children were Isabella, Andrew, Joseph and John. Following Antione's death in 1829, his widow, Sarah, married George Martin who owned a 210 acre farm in Addison Township and also operated the tug boat "Condor" for the Pomeroy Coal Company on the Ohio River.

*Joseph De Lille 1827-1901*

Joseph DeLille (February 20, 1827-November 7, 1901) married Isabella Martin and they settled on a farm nearby in section 9 of Springfield Township. He was a successful farmer and was well known for wheat threshing in Southeast Ohio and across the river in West Virginia. He used the latest models of Huber steam tractors and threshers in this business. He served in the Civil War, as a wagoneer in the Ohio Volunteer Cavalry.

Martin's grandfather, Andrew DeLille (May 17, 1846-February 8, 1922) married Frances Wetherholt and they lived at Evergreen. Andrew continued the successful farming and threshing business. Their children were Joseph, Clarence, John, Ben, Hettie, and Andrew.

Joseph Elias DeLille (April 16, 1881-January 11, 1953) first married Minnie Mackinson in 1907. They had a son, William (May 19, 1908-November 17, 1933). Minnie died in 1912. Joseph married Tracie Marilyn Spencer (March 8, 1898-November 19, 1983) of Roane County, West Virginia, on September 8, 1917. Their children were Geneva, Ruth, Charles, Betty, John Martin, Raymond, Bruce, and Louise.

Joseph bought the 100 acre farm located just north of Rodney on the Bidwell Road in 1909. He worked with his father in the farming and threshing business. He also operated sawmills in the area.

The farm ownership remains with the family members who have nine dwellings on the Route 850 frontage.

Family members have long attended the Rodney Methodist Church.

The children of different times have attended schools at Rodney Elementary, Rio Grande High School, Bidwell High School, Gallipolis School System, and Rio Grande College.

Martin married Jo Phipps of Scioto County, Ohio, on June 8, 1950. They live in Columbus, Ohio. They have two children, Martin Jr. and

Pamela, five grand children, and three great grand children living in the Columbus area. Martin retired from the Ohio State University Physical Facilities Department with 30 years service. Following that, he has worked part time, doing engineering work for local consultants and enjoys traveling.

**MAURICE RAYMOND DELILLE** - Maurice Raymond DeLille was born October 14, 1933 on the DeLille family farm at Rodney, Ohio. He is the seventh child of Joseph Elias DeLille and Tracie Marilyn (Spencer) DeLille. Raymond attended Rodney Grade School and graduated in 1952 from Gallia Academy High School. He joined the armed services after graduation. He was stationed in Bamburg and Badoibling Germany, for two and half years. When he returned home he worked for A&P Grocery for 30 years and retired from the State Highway Dept. after 14 yrears of service.

Raymond married Rosalee Houck Jan. 12, 1954. She was the daughter of Roscoe S. Houck (died 1995 at age 87 yrs.) and Hazel Irene (Moore) Houck (died 1989 at age 78). Rosalee also graduated from Gallia Academy in 1953. She worked for Bill Wellman's Jewelry store and Paul Davies Jewelry. She also run the family owned DeLille Malt Shoppe.

Raymond and Rosalee had three children: Michael Raymond born 4-30-1958.

He has been married twice to Lisa Maynard and Brenda Davis. Robin Lynn was born 10-12-1959. She married Steve Barhorst in Sept. of 1977. He was killed in an airplane accident in October, six weeks after their wedding. She married Edward Caudill June 20, 1981. (Ed was born Quaker City, Ohio). They have two sons. Dustin and Bradley who are attending Gallia Academy High School.

The youngest daughter Kindra Jane was born 6-11-1962. She lives in Independence, Kentucky. She is married to Ronnie L. Robbins (who grew up in Mississippi). Kindra has two children Seth and Kierra and two step-children Kelsey and Tyler.

**PAUL STANFORD AND MARY MARJORIE MOORE DENNEY FAMILY** - Paul was born in 1909 to Samuel Witham and Mary Williams Denney. He married Mary Marjorie Moore (1913) and to this union was born Paul Franklin (1930), Francis Virginia (1931, died at age one of diptheria), Wyman Eugene (1932), Harold Edward (1934), Paul Richard (1935, died of whooping cough), Donald Lee (1936), Ruth Ann (1937) married Donald Shupe, Mildred Marie (1939) married Billie George. They were raised on Kerr-Harrisburg Road across the road from the Plymale Apple Orchard. Dad, his father Sam, and father-in-law Asa Moore cut the logs and then built the family home (pictured) which later two more rooms and a porch were added.

Paul was employed at the TNT Plant in Point Pleasant, WV. Mary had tuberculosis when Mildred, the youngest, was born and she was sent to a TB Hospital in Mt. Vernon, Ohio. Until she was well, the children's grandparents, aunts and uncles cared for them. Even though Mary's illness was tragic, it brought the family closer together, and remains that way still.

Paul and Mary divorced in the early 1950s and Paul remarried Margaret Sexton. From this union was born Pauline (McCoy), John Robert and Jimmy. Both Paul and Margaret have passed away.

*Family Home*

Mary remarried also, to Elmore Flowers from Point Pleasant. They currently live where Mary and Paul raised their family, but have built a new home and used the old log home for storage. Mary recently turned 89 in February (2002) and is in good health. They still belong to the Camper's Club, Senior Citizens and attend church in good weather.

*Submitted by Don and Mildred Denney*

**SAMUEL WITHAM DENNEY AND MARY WILLIAMS DENNEY** - Samuel was born June 26. 1885, to Dora Stevens Denney and Obediah Liston Denney. Mary, his wife, was born in Wales, December 5,1891, to Mary Jones Williams and Thomas J. Williams. Their children are as follows:

*Grandma & Grandpa on their 50th Wedding Anniversary. Chuckie says me too.*

Mrs. Ted A. McCulty (Dora Marie) was born August 24, 1907. Her children are Wayne, Gene, Mrs. J.C. Stout (Lois), and Bill.

Stanford Paul was born January 23, 1909. His first marriage was to Mary Moore. The following children were born to them: Paul Jr., Virginia (deceased), Wyman, Harold, Mrs. Don Shupe (Ruth Ann), Donald, Mrs. Billy George (Mildred) and a son died in infancy. His second marriage was to Margaret Saxton. The following children were born to them: Mrs. Lauchey McCoy (Pauline), John Robert and Jimmy.

Mrs. Edward Edwards (Anna Margaret), was born March 26, 1910. Her daughter Mrs. Gilmer Knotts (Katheryne Opal) October 28, 1911. They have a daughter, Mrs. Noel D. Heister (Sandra Kay).

Sam and Mary had a little boy born September 14, 1912. He died the same evening.

Oliver Wendell Holmes Denney was born September 9, 1913. He married Dorothy Deitrick. Their children are: Wendell Frances and John Robert, Denney, Oliver Wendell died of a heart attack October 1964.

Mrs. Bernard Kulrich (Mary Maybell Pauline) was born May 5, 1915. They have a son, John Edward Kurlich.

Thomas Obediah Denney was born November 1,1917. He married Nina Odell.

Mrs. Jennie Alice Irene Myers was born March 9, 1920. Her children are David Earl Myers. Mrs. Mary Langford, Patty Myers, Mrs. Ginger Dunn, and Mrs. Kathy Mandat.

John Everett Denney was born June 30,1922. Their children are: Mrs. Jack Corwin (Barbara Jean). Charles Samuel and John Michael. Barbara Jean died October 10, 1962.

Oscar Newton Denney was born November 23,1924. He died December 2,1924. He was 10 days old.

Mary and Sam lived on a farm all their lives complete with rail fences, no tractors, no cars, no indoor plumbing, electricity only in their later years, corn that was cut by hand and put in shocks and grain was cut with a cradle.

Mary Denney has these brothers and sisters: Anna Wilkinson, Sara Carpenter, Lizzie Evans. Jennie Shafer, John T. Williams and her twin sister, Hanna Broughman.

All are deceased.

Samuel Denney has these brothers and sisters: Mrs. Emmett Tope (Myrtle), Everett Denney and Mrs. James Walters (Rosa Odessa). All are deceased.

Mr. and Mrs. Sam Denney were proud of all their children. An interesting fact was that they had several teachers among them. They are Katheryne, her daughter, Sandra, and Sandra's husband Noel, Margaret her husband Edward Edwards, and their daughter Margeda, Thomas Denney, Maybell Kurlich's son, John Kurlich, John L. Denney's son, John Michael Denney. Mary and Samuel both attended Rio Grande College. He studied to be a teacher. He took the teachers' exam and passed it. Mary studied music and was an accomplished pianist. They met in college and later married.

**DONALD LUTHER DEWITT AND BETTY MAE (HILL) DEWITT FAMILY** - Donald was born on April 30, 1924 at Rodney, Ohio to Roy Delton and Lena Bell (Powell) DeWitt. His grandparents, Abraham Lincoln and Dora (Erwin) DeWitt came to Rodney, Ohio from Virginia in the early to mid-1800's. Abe and Dora had four other children besides Roy: Floyd (Marie) DeWitt; Esta (Hugh) Powell; Alma (Sam) Leppert; and Lottie (George) Woda. Abraham and Dora DeWitt lived on the property that is now known as the Holley Brothers Sand & Gravel in Rodney. Donald had one sister Ruth M. DeWitt (Richard) Stauss born on September 3, 1922 and deceased on January 18, 1970.

Donald married Betty Mae (Hill) DeWitt on August 14, 1946 in Pomeroy, Ohio, shortly after returning from Germany where he had been serving on active duty in the army during WWII. Betty was born on April 12, 1930 to Homer and Garnet (Martin) Hill, Sr. in Mason County, WV. Homer and Garnet had seven other children besides Betty; Edward (Thelma) Hill; Elmer (Reba) Hill; Homer, Jr. (Ethel) Hill; Marvin (Rose) Hill; Harold Hill; Juanita (Richard) Bane; and, Roy Hill.

*Family of Donald Luther Dewitt & Betty Mae Hill Dewitt L-R: Deborah, Louise, & Donna Dewitt in chair: Donald & Betty Dewitt*

Donald and Betty resided on Vinton Ave. in Gallipolis before buying property in Evergreen and locating there in 1958. They operated a plumbing, heating, and air conditioning business at their residence until they retired in June 1983. Their family includes: Louise DeWitt (David) Crist and children Tina, Tami, Devin, and Amanda living, and Dawn deceased on September 5, 1978; Deborah June (Bruce) Grant and children Dakota DeWitt and Cheyenne and Cree Stone; and Donna Lynn DeWitt (Flem Meade) and children Nicholas Anthony Mulholand, Rebecca Meade (Mike) Greene, and Tamara Meade (Robbie) Canady. Donald and Betty have seven great grandchildren and four step-great grandchildren. Daughter Louise resides in Zanesville, Ohio and is a Licensed Practical Nurse (LPN). Deborah resides in Evergreen and is also a LPN. Donna is a teacher at Washington Elementary in Gallipolis and resides in Vinton where she is the village mayor.

Donald passed away at his home in Evergreen on December 24, 1995. Betty still resides there.

*The following was written by Pauline (Woda) Farnsworth, Donald's cousin on December 29, 1995 in tribute to Donald after his death:*

Yesterday, my friend was laid to rest in the snow covered hills of southern Ohio, not a man of 71 but my childhood friend of 10 was gone. As I sat in the warm, little funeral parlor listening to the minister tell of Don's accomplishments, I was lost in my own thoughts of his childhood. After loosing his mother at an early age, and his father struggling with rearing his two children, and what must have been the breaking point for him, a disastrous second marriage, Don and his sister, Ruth, were thrust into an unlikely situation of being reared by two, rather sparse, grandparents.

I sat there reflecting about this man they were talking about, a man who cherished his family, and spent his life doing good for them. A man, who after spending time overseas with the army, found his way. He became a successful businessman, having owned and operated a heating and plumbing business, until he retired some 13 years ago.

I thought back to the funfilled days I had with Don and his sister, Ruth, on that little farm in the hills. I know I cherished each visit to Grandma and Grandpa's because of the companionship I had with my cousins. Don was gentle, even as a young boy. I don't remember him ever becoming angry or out-of-sorts (maybe he was on "good behavior" when the city cousin came to play). I only remember the times I had to be rescued from the top of the hills I had willingly climbed with Don and Ruth.

Yes, he was a "hero" as the song was sung at the service. He was truly a hero to his devoted wife, Betty, and to the three precious daughters he helped to mold into the beautiful women they are today.

I am glad to have known Don DeWitt and I will miss just knowing he's around.

**ARNETTA ANDERSON AND SAMUEL EDWARD DEXTER** - Arnetta (no middle name) was born on July 4, 1914, in Gallipolis, Ohio, to Robert and Ora Hattie Lee Anderson. She was the first of six children, one dying in infancy and buried in the Pine Street Colored Cemetery, Gallipolis, Ohio. Her siblings are Janet Anderson, Ruth Anderson Jackson, Robert Christopher Anderson, and Joyce Anderson. She was reared in the Maple Shade area of Gallipolis and attended the Lincoln Colored School where she cherishes the memories of the school plays and choir. She and her classmates performed at the now Ariel Theater on several occasions. She was a very good student, winning an essay contest sponsored by the Gallipolis Tribune and the business merchants on why people should patronize downtown businesses (newspaper article dated November 20, 1927).

She attended Gallia Academy High School but left to assist family members who lived in Point Pleasant, WV. When the flood of 1936 cut her off from her family in Gallipolis, she begged a ride from the postal carrier who got her safely back to Gallipolis. She obtained employment with Walgreen Drug Store as a dishwasher/cook. It was at this time that she met Samuel Edward Dexter (February 8, 1920-June 19, 1983) of Nelsonville, Ohio. His parents were Cash and Rose Calloway Dexter. It was said that Grandma Dexter was a relative of Cab Calloway. Sam was one of ten children. His brothers and sisters were William, Jack, Howard, Preston, Marcia, Nettie, Mildred, Roxie and Cash, Jr. All are deceased. Sam and Arnetta married on June 22, 1942, and moved to Butler, PA, but after only three months, they returned to Gallipolis where they made their home. They are the parents of four daughters: Bobette Olivia (married to Frank Edward Braxton, Jr.), Janet Kay Dexter Davis (October 20, 1945-June 26, 1992), Rosann Dexter Hollinshed (married to Charles "Snooky" Hollinshed), and Marlene Sue Dexter.

Arnetta was a housewife but later worked outside of the home at the laundry/dry cleaners in the 800 block of Third Avenue and later at French Colony Industries (we called it Hoys) where she was a machine operator making upholstery for custom-made furniture.

Sam graduated from Nelsonville High School, but he was required to quit school by his father who had his sons work in the coal mines to help the family. After working one day in the mines, my dad prayed that if God let him get out of there he would always provide for his family. He got a job at the local drugstore and was the first son to finish high school. Sam worked on different construction sites, hauled TNT during WWII where he encountered racial discrimination in Virginia, worked at the Gallipolis State Institute (now Gallipolis Developmental Center) and worked 20 years and retired from Kaiser Aluminum Corporation in Ravenswood, WV, because of health reasons.

Arnetta is an outstanding mother, cook, and homemaker and continues to be a care taker for her great grandchildren. (See histories of Benjamin Lee, Samuel Lee, Ora Lee Anderson, and Bobette Dexter Braxton.)

*Submitted by Bobette Dexter Braxton.*

**SILAS AND MARY E. FRANCES THIERRY DICKEY FAMILY** - Silas Dickey was born in Jefferson County, Ohio, January 30, 1836. He was the son of Richard and Rebecca Criss Dickey. They were both born in Washington County, Pennsylvania. Richard was born October 20, 1806, and Rebecca was born December 22, 1808. It is presumed that they married in Pennsylvania, after which they moved to Jefferson County, Ohio. Their first born was a daughter, Mary Dickey Hyland, who was born August 2, 1831, in Jefferson County, Ohio. Silas was the third of eleven children. The family moved to Gallia County sometime around 1838 as their sixth child Leroy was born November 15, 1839, in Harrison Township.

*Dickey Chapel & Cemetery Founded 1855 Harrison Township, Gallia County, Ohio May 2000*

Mary E. Frances Thierry Dickey was born May 3, 1841. She was born in Ohio. She was the daughter of Joseph Noble and Sarah Ann Dillman Thierry. Joseph was born March 20, 1816, at Marietta, Washington County, Ohio. He was the son of Francis Jean and Frances Fanny Blake Thierry. Francis Jean Thierry was born in France about 1765. He immigrated to Ohio in 1790. He was involved in many land purchases in the early 1800's.

Silas and Mary were married January 24, 1861, in Gallia County. They had six children all born in Harrison Township, Gallia County. Their first daughter was Isodora (Dora) C. Dickey Drummond born in 1862. She married Samuel T. Drummond November 12, 1884, in Gallia County.

The second daughter was Augusta Minnie Dickey Harbour. She was born December 20, 1865. She married James P. Harbour in Gallia County October 23, 1889. Augusta went to Lincoln School in Harrison Township as did her brothers and sisters. After marriage, she and her husband lived in Huntington, West Virginia. Because of her health in 1897, they moved to Pueblo, Colorado, where she died March 20, 1908.

A third daughter, Otta W. Dickey, was born 1868. She did not marry. She died February 11, 1892, in Gallia County, and is buried at Dickey Chapel Cemetery where her parents are also buried. A son, Ira W. Dickey, was born January 29, 1870. He died January 6, 1892, at San Diego, California. He is also buried at Dickey Chapel Cemetery.

Another daughter Etta Lenora (Nora) Dickey Wood was born August 8, 1875. She married Stephen Wood October 16, 1912. Their last child was son, Siro K. born 1878. No records has been found of a marriage for him.

The 1874 Atlas for Gallia County shows that Silas Dickey owned 120 acres adjoining 160 acres owned by his father-in-law, Joseph N. Thierry. Adjoining those parcels was 160 acres owned by Silas' father, Richard Dickey, all in section 25 and 26 of Harrison Township. The land for the Dickey Chapel and Cemetery was from one of these properties. The Dickey Chapel was founded in 1855.

Military records show Silas Dickey served in the Civil War. He enlisted May 2, 1864 and served until September 3, 1864, in the Army in Company E 141st Regiment OVI. He was a corporal. His brother, Leroy Dickey, from Harrison Township also served in the Army. He enlisted August 17, 1862, and served until June 24, 1865. He was a private in Company G 1st Ohio H.A.

Silas died in Harrison Township November 15, 1905. Executor of his will was Siro K. Dickey. Mary Thierry Dickey died July 1, 1911, in Harrison Township. They are both buried at Dickey Chapel Cemetery.

*Submitted by John Bertholf*

**DWIGHT HENDERSON DODRILL FAMILY** - Dwight Henderson Dodrill was born on October 19, 1918, in Huntington Township. He was the sixth child of John Herbert and Bertha Ellen Vance Dodrill. His brothers and sisters were: Lela, Delmer, Ethel, Donald, Pearl, Darrell, Evelyn and Wanda. They did not have a lot of material possessions, but they had an abundance of love for one another and a strong commitment to the Lord. This dedication and faith helped them through many hardships.

They lived on a farm on the corner of Dodrill Road and Shepherd Lane. Here they learned the value of hard work. The farm was their source of support. There were always chores to be done before and after school.

When Dwight's father died in 1932, he found himself in charge of the farm. These obligations forced him to drop out of school in the 10th grade. This was one of his lifetime regrets. So much so that at the age of 70, he took the GED test, and was awarded his high school diploma.

Dwight worked at the Railway Express Agency. Here he was very active in the union where he served as treasurer and chaplain. After he retired from there, he continued to work at the Lazarus Department Store. He was a member of the Ohio Defense Corp. and a very active member of the Maize Manor United Methodist Church. There he served on a number of committees and was President of the United Methodist Men. He was known for having a servant's heart. He was always looking for ways to help someone else. On a snowy day, he would set out, shovel in hand, and begin to clear driveways in his neighborhood and at the church. In the summer, he would take his lawn mower or pruning shears. He was very proud of his garden that flourished every year. His tomatoes were huge and he was always willing to share them and his tomato plants with relatives and neighbors.

*Dwight Dodrill Family
Dwight, Clyda, Dwight Bradley & Mona
1955*

On September 15, 1946, Dwight married Clyda Raynes, formerly of Buffalo, West Virginia. They had two children, a son, Dwight Bradley (1947) and a daughter, Mona Lynn (1953). Dwight Bradley married Monica Demko and they have two sons, Donovan and Dominic. Mona married James Emmett Tompkins and they have three children: James Jr. (March 6, 1979), Christina Lynn (July 13, 1981), and Elizabeth Ann (February 20,1983). After 48 years of marriage, Clyda was killed tragically in a car accident on September 16,1994.

Dwight continued serving his community and Lord until he suffered a stroke in May, 1999. He went home to his reward on January 29, 2002. There was never any doubt that he loved the Lord and his family very much. He left a legacy rich in Christian heritage.

He led by example and was proud to be a farm boy from Gallia County.

**JOHN HERBERT DODRILL FAMILY** - William Dodrill, a British soldier under Lord Cornwallis, stayed in the United States after England's defeat at Yorktown. He married Rebecca Lewis in Greenbrier County, Virginia in 1782. Their oldest son, George Dodrill, migrated to Gallia County, where he married Elizabeth Ewing of Ewington, Ohio. George and Elizabeth's youngest son was Andrew Dodrill, John Herbert Dodrill's grandfather.

Andrew Dodrill married Mary McCumber, and he worked at Keystone Furnace as an iron worker until he volunteered to the Union Army in 1862. He died in Tennessee in 1863. Their son, John Avery Dodrill, married Margery Tyler in 1870, and they had ten children. John Herbert was one son, along with the late Andy and Jim Dodrill of Vinton, Ohio.

John married Bertha Ellen Vance of Gallia County, in 1907. They had nine children: Effie "Lela" Strausbaugh (b.12-12-08, d. 05-20-96); John "Delmar" (b. 07-11- 10, d. 02-13-34); Ethel Gail (b. 05-18-12, d. 05-17-33); Donald Everett (b. 05-17-14, d. 08-09-89); Rebecca Pearl Twyman (b. 10-04-16, d. 01-07-94); Dwight Henderson (b. 10-19-18, d. 01-29-2002); Darrell George (b. 12-27-21, d. 5-20-96); Bertha "Eveyln" Humphrey (b. 3-30-24, d. 3-18-80); Wanda Belle Regan (resides in Columbus). John and Bertha lived on a hill farm in Huntington Township on the corner of Andy Dodrill Road and Shepherd Lane. All the children, except for Lela, were born on the farm with the help of a neighbor lady and a doctor who made house calls.

*John Herbert Dodrill Family seated: John Dodrill, Bertha Dodrill standing between parents: Wanda & Evelyn standing: Darrell, Ethel, Delmar, Lela, Donald, Pearl, and Dwight*

All of the Dodrill children attended a one room school house on Bunker Hill. They had to walk over a mile through mud and snow to get there. Their only source of heat was a pot-bellied stove. The school's water had to be carried from a spring. Only one teacher had all eight grades. But the teachers were good ones, such as Beatrice Clark, Wendell Love, Leah Ewing, Merle McCumber, and Mabel Jenkins. The Dodrill children attended Vinton High School for higher education. John's children learned to work hard and take on responsibilities early in life, with chores to be done before and after school. There was plenty to do as they raised almost everything that they ate: fruit, wheat, vegetables, cows, pigs, chickens, and sheep. They labored with everything from horses pulling a plow or wagon, to simple pitchforks and hoes.

The kids remembered picking wild blackberries, and their mother would can them in stone jars with sealing wax. At times their mother would spend hours stirring apple butter in a brass kettle over an open fire. Hogs were butchered to prepare a winter meat supply.

After chores were finished, homework was done by the light of kerosene lamps. Then in the winter, the children would warm themselves by the stove and then run to bed, where their mother covered them with blankets and rugs. Sometimes they would awaken to find snow on their bed covers.

Those were tough times, with little or no money, but the children were raised in the church and they were a close knit family that supported each other. The Dodrill children were, and are very proud of their heritage and the many loving lessons that they learned while growing up on the farm.

**BOB DRUMMOND** - Bob and Diana Elliott Drummond both grew up in Gallipolis, and attended GAHS. Bob joined the army soon after high school and during his three-year tour traveled around the world. They were married in June of 1967.

Bob's parents are Carl Drummond (deceased) and Leona Lucas Drummond. His siblings are Ellen Russell, Bonnie Schoonover, and Keith Drummond. They all live in this area and are still very close. His grandparents were Charles and Sarah Saunders Drummond, and Ora and Ida Porter Lucas (all deceased).

*Bob and Diana Drummond Family*

Diana's parents are Edwin and Louise Elliott. She has two brothers Mike and Steve. Around the time Edwin was finishing high school, electricity was coming to the area where he lived. He wanted to learn more about it and has not stopped yet. Now Steve and Mike, as well Bob, make their living in that same line of work. Her grand parents were Charles and Dorothy Steger and Oscar and Osa Elliott (all deceased).

Bob has now retired from AEP and enjoys devoting his time to working for the Lord and the church. Diana received degrees from Rio Grande College and Ohio University, and teaches at Rio Grande Elementary.

They have three children and two grandchildren. Their daughter, Chris, attended URG and Ohio University and obtained a B.S.N. in Nursing. She joined the U. S. Army and worked as a nurse for four years. She is now a stay-at-home mom with her two wonderful children. Her husband Captain Kermit Huebner is finishing his last year of residency in Emergency Medicine at Ft. Hood, Texas. They have two children. Andrew Joseph was born in Fort Knox, Kentucky in May of 1998. Sarah Elizabeth Huebner was born in Fort Hood, Texas in March of 2000. Chris and her family enjoy hiking and outdoor activities.

Bob and Diana's son Rob lives in Columbus, OH and works as a system operations coordinator in a bank. He enjoys writing and working out.

Their youngest daughter, Ellie enjoyed traveling during her college years and was fortunate to visit, Scotland, Wales, London, and France. She is now living in Columbus, OH and works for a pharmaceutical company. She enjoys mountain climbing and outdoor sports.

**CHARLES ALFRED (C.A.) & APRIL ELLEN (THOMPSON) DUNCAN FAMILY** - Charles Alfred (C.A.) Duncan was born March 1, 1943 in Ohio Township in Gallia County to Howard Jackson (Jack) and Mildred Jean (Millie) Lambert Duncan. Jack was the son of Floyd Francis and Margaret Ethel (Higgins) Duncan. He attended schools in the Portsmouth area and came to Gallia County in 1939 when he enrolled in secondary education at Rio Grande College. He was an excellent student and loved playing basketball for the "Redmen". He was a high scoring player in the college's history and was inducted to the Hall of Fame at its inception. He also served his country in World War II. While enrolled in college he met his wife Millie, who majored in elementary education. Millie's parents were Perry Phillip and Emma (Williams) Lambert. She attended Mooney School in grade school and graduated from Mercerville High School. Jack and Mildred earned their degrees at Rio Grande College and both taught in Gallia County schools for over thirty years. Their children include C.A., Phillip P., Alice M. and George Andrew (deceased).

*Charles Alfred and April Ellen Duncan*

April Ellen (Thompson) Duncan was born April 5, 1943 in Addison Township in Gallia County to George Frederick (Fred) and Marjorie Pauline (Polly) Kail Thompson. Fred's parents were George Clyde and Amelia Ruth (Frederick) Thompson. He attended Faneuil Hall in grade school and graduated from Cheshire High School. Fred worked for his father's farm and then purchased his own dairy farm. Later he worked at the Kyger Creek Power Plant for twenty-five years and retired as a foreman in 1980. Polly's parents were James Horace and Mabel Edith (Leonard) Kail. Polly attended Jerico grade school and graduated from Cheshire High School. Polly has always played an important role in the Little Kyger area; her life has been centered on homemaking, children, and church and community activities. Fred and Polly continue to be very involved in the Little Kyger community. Besides April they had the following children: Nan E., Pollyanna (deceased) and George H. Thompson.

Both C.A. and April graduated from Kyger Creek High School in 1961. They were married in 1962 and moved to Northup in Gallia County. They continued their education and earned B.S. degrees in elementary education from Rio Grande College (now the University of Rio Grande) in 1965. Later April graduated from the University of Dayton with a Master's Degree in Educational Administration. C.A. taught at Hannan Trace and Green Elementary Schools for three and seven years respectively. After ten years of teaching he decided to resign and pursue his first love, farming. Since 1975 we have managed a large herd of Simmental cattle and have averaged raising at least fifteen acres of burley tobacco a year. April taught at Hannan Trace and Clay Elementary Schools for five and twenty-three years respectively. Later she taught for two years at Rio Grande Elementary. She was also the principal of Clay Elementary for four years and assistant principal of Washington Elementary for six years. April retired from teaching and administrating with over thirty-five years of service.

When we moved to Northup, we moved into an old two-story brick house that dates back to the 1830's era. While living there we were blessed with three wonderful children: Paul Jackson Duncan, Edith Jean (Bostic) Duncan and Troy Alfred Duncan.

The experience of rearing a family in an antique house was quite a challenge. Since this is an old homestead, it is known by various names—some remember it as the Northup family land, others might call it the Harrington's, some as the Kerns Farm and others as the Amsbary and Lambert places. We have lived there for almost forty years and right now we call it Duncans's Running Springs Farm. We think Gallia County is a great place to live.

**EAGLE FAMILY** - George W. Eagle, born in 1821 to Henry Eagle and Eleanor Lewis in Raccoon Township, Gallia County, Ohio, was a prosperous farmer and livestock trader. He married Leantha Glenn, daughter of Hugh Tate Glenn and Samantha Pruitt. They lived in the home Leantha had inherited on Eagle Road, a.k.a. Mount Tabor Road. The home was intriguing and a copy of many Mount Vernon-Deep South homes, front pillars and all.

*The Restaurant that bankrolled Roselle's music education*

The author was privileged to explore the home in the early 1930's as a child, and later viewed from the road in the 1980's. It has now disappeared. The early visit revealed massive rooms with painted plaster walls trimmed with hand painted floral borders next to the 12-foot ceilings in the living quarters. The great room sported a huge walk-in fireplace with sliding panels inside each end, which hid a secret room behind the fireplace. Some say it was used as part of the Underground Railroad for fleeing slaves. Others say it was merely a place where George W. hid his money and treasures.

Once connected and adjacent to the great room was the cookhouse where the southern culture thought cooking was properly performed. George W. was a complex man, sometimes be-

*George W. Eagle and Family*

ing regarded as a tyrant. On the other hand, he insisted his children should have the opportunity for advanced education, daughters included. His eight children who survived infancy were as follows: Marietta, William Henry, Permella, John, Hortense, Sarah, Alda, Louella, Adelaide and George.

 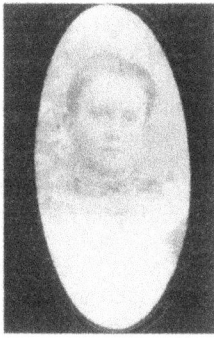

*Sarah Alda Eagle Shack with baby*   *Nellie Eagle Shack 1892-1904*

The author's grandmother, Sarah Alda Eagle, was a rebel. Chafing at her father's authoritarianism, she left home for Jackson, Ohio, and a career as a dressmaker's apprentice. In 1884 she met and married John D. Shack, a bookkeeper in his father's woolen mill in Vinton, Ohio. The wedding estranged daughter and father for the rest of his life. "The Shacks are good-for-nothing Methodists and Democrats to boot!" stated Baptist and Republican George W., citing cultural differences. However, George W.'s will in 1892 included Sarah along with her six remaining siblings to receive either a farm or something of equivalent value.

Sarah and John had two daughters, Nellie in 1892 who died of typhoid fever as a child, and the younger, Roselle, born in 1897. Roselle parlayed her musical talent into a lifetime of use as a radio entertainer and a private and public school music teacher. Sarah had opened a nice restaurant in Vinton to bankroll Roselle's education at St. Mary's of the Springs College in Bexley, and Normal School of Monroeville, Ohio.

It was in Monroeville she met and later married William Earl Burdue, prominent farmer and descendant of Patriot Nathaniel Burdue and other Huron County Western Reserve pioneers. Earl and Roselle produced three daughters: Marjorie, Betty and Dorothy Ann, all presently alive. Marjorie and Betty lived with their grandparents in Vinton, Ohio, in 1933-1935 to attend school.

Earl died in 1943 and Roselle in 1959.

The line continues with the three daughters and their three children each, plus many grandchildren. All are now scattered, in Ohio, Pennsylvania, Maryland, Colorado and California, and probably elsewhere as well.

The author and her daughter, Debbie Hodge, were inducted into the First Families of Gallia County in October 2001 as descendants of the Curry's and the Glenn's.

*Submitted by Betty L. Hodge.*

## GEORGE WASHINGTON EAGLE FAMILY

- The first Eagle's, George Eagle, his wife, Maria Elisabetha Henger, and their children came from Virginia to Gallia County, Ohio. They were in Gallia County by 1812. George Washington Eagle was their grandson.

*The Eagle family, Flora Ellen (left), Sarah Emeline (mother), Oral N., Myra Dell, George Washington and Elsie Lulu (far right).*

George Washington Eagle was the son of John L. Eagle and Racheal Fee. He was born in Ohio on October 17, 1850. He died on November 27, 1912, and was buried in the Valparaiso town cemetery in Valparaiso, Nebraska. He married Sarah Emeline Glassburn, daughter of Moses Glassburn and Margaret Russel in Saunders County, Nebraska, on November 28, 1878. She was born on April 7, 1856, in Gallia County, Ohio. She died on February 15, 1900, and was buried in the Valparaiso town cemetery. George knew her from Gallia County where they grew up together. He followed her to Saunders County, Nebraska, after her family moved there. He married her and they raised a family there.

Myra Dell, the oldest, was born on July 21, 1880. She choked on a chicken bone and died on April 7, 1901. She is buried in the same cemetery as her parents.

Flora Ellen was born on December 16, 1881. She married Alva Austin Nelson and died March 9, 1969. The couple was buried in the Valparaiso town cemetery. They had two sons. The first son, George, born about 1905, never saw the light of day and was buried in an unmarked grave the south side of his Nelson grandparents' plot in the Valparaiso town cemetery. Their son, Orville Roland Nelson, was born February 26, 1907, and died on August 21, 1993. Orville married Mable Florence Magnuson; they are buried in the Valparaiso town cemetery. The couple had three children.

Oral N. was born November 22, 1883. He married Bertha L. Sporer on September 1, 1915. He died August 24, 1963. They had one daughter, Opal. Opal was born on April 12, 1917; she died on May 11, 2001. She was married to George F. Ferry and they had three children.

Elsie Lulu was born November 2, 1887; she died on March 27, 1989. She married Roy Pautz and they had no children. She died on April 10, 1934.

*Submitted by Debbie Alley*

**ECKER FAMILY** - Great-Great Grandfather Conrad Ecker settled in Green Township in what was later called the village of Centenary. He came from Hanover, Germany in the mid-1800's trying to avoid the wars that raged through Europe at that time.

The Eckers were mostly farmers, businessmen and teachers. The last three generations appear as bank directors of Gallia County's three major banks.

*Johnny And Jeanie Ecker Sessions*

Great Grandfather Henry Ecker, son of Conrad is listed on the original board of directors of the Ohio Valley Bank. Grandfather Charles L. Ecker carried on the farm and business trade and was a director of the First National Bank until his death in 1928. My father, Horace B. Ecker served as a director of the Commercial and Savings Bank ( now First Star) for nearly twenty years. He was in the automobile business until the mid-1940's as the owner of the Gallipolis Motor Company. In 1945 he opened a real estate partnership with Carl Myers. The Ecker and Myers Real Estate Agency lasted until his death in 1958.

Horace B. Ecker was the third of five children born to Charles L. and Nora Stone Ecker in 1891. His elder brother, Charles L. Ecker, died in infancy. His eldest sister, Margaret Caroline Ecker was a high school Latin teacher in Pleasantville, N.Y., until her retirement when she returned to Gallipolis and lived until her death at the age of 97. His younger sisters, Hazel Ecker Hine and Pearl Ecker Hatfield also lived in Gallipolis until their deaths at age 94 and 89, respectively.

My mother, Florence Bott Ecker was born in Apollo, Pennsylvania and moved to Okmulgee, Oklahoma. She became a teacher but later decided in a nursing career and graduated from the University of Michigan's School of Nursing in 1928. She accepted a job as Nursing Instructor at the old Holzer Hospital of Nursing in 1930, met my father where she bought a car from him and they were married in January, 1931. I was born in October, 1931 and named for my father's sister, Margaret and my mother's sister, Jean. My brother was born in September, 1934 and was named Charles L. Ecker for both grandfather and uncle. However, with two living "Uncle John's" on both sides of the family and an older sister called Jeanie, he affectionately became known as just "Johnny".

Both my brother Johnny and I graduated from Gallia Academy High School. I went on to Denison University in Granville, OH and he to Ohio Wesleyan University in Delaware. After graduation and two years in the U.S. Army, my brother returned to Gallipolis and took over my father's real estate business. Later he switched to teaching and coaching at GAHS. In 1970 he coached the football team to an undefeated season and league championship. In 1978 he coached Rio Grande College to an Ohio Conference championship in baseball. Serious health problems compelled him to give up teaching and coaching, but a life long love of music and beautiful trained baritone voice enabled him to enjoy singing and entertaining until his death May 31, 2001. He along with our parents, grandparents and all aunts and uncles on the Ecker side of the family are buried in Mound Hill Cemetery.

After graduation from Denison University I lived and worked in Chicago for five years. I returned to Ohio State University for graduate work and met my husband, Kyle C. Sessions. We were married in Heidelberg, Germany in October, 1959. He is a retired history professor at Illinois State University and we have lived in Bloomington, IL for the past 35 years. We have three children and four grandchildren

*Submitted by Jeanie Ecker Sessions*

## HARRY (BUD) AND JEWEL (STONE) EDDY FAMILY

I was born and started life in those West Virginia hills in Red Warrior on June17, in the early 1930's. I am the first daughter and third child of Orville and Beulah (Wood) Stone. I was given the name Mearida Jewel by my grandmother and aunt Mattie Wood. I have only heard of my first name five times in my lifetime. I later made some changes to my name. Now it's Mearada Jewel. It was easy to change the spelling of my name because I have no birth date or name on record.

I have a total of three brothers and three sisters living. I have two brothers whom are deceased. My brothers are: Edward (Ed), Ronnie (Ron) and Gary Stone. My sisters are: Elizabeth (Libby) Mitchell, Gail White, and Naomi (Footsie) DeBoard. My deceased brothers are: Donald Lee and Larry Ray Stone.

*Jewel Eddy*

My husband, Bud, who has passed away, was born and raised in West Virginia also. He was the youngest child of Joshua F. and Mary Delphia (Seese) Eddy. His brother, James (Jim) and sisters Mary Estep and Ivy Holston are all deceased. Jim was the last to pass away on January 7, 2001. Today there are only four Eddy men left from Joshua and Delphia and three of those four are great grand children.

Bud and I shared many happy times and some sad times. But we also shared a short tine together. We were married 30 years, 4 months, and 3 days. He has been gone for almost 18 years now. I still love and miss him every day.

We had four wonderful children, two sons and two daughters. Steve, my oldest son passed away with cancer on February 6, 2001. Wayne, my youngest son is a disabled Veteran. He also has M.S., but he does well. He enjoys coon hunting and helping with the local school sports. His wife, Laura, is the mail carrier in Vinton, Ohio. They have two daughters. Terri whom married Cody Camden and Traci whom is still in high school. Their son Josh, the youngest is also still in high school. They have no grandchildren.

Carol, my oldest daughter has two children living and one daughter, Krystal Karol Wallace, is deceased. Her son James (J.L.) Wallace has one son, Matthew James Wallace. Her daughter Amber Whittington is still in high school. Her husband, Jim Whittington, has spent 18 years in the military and National Guard combined. Carol is going to college now to be a computer technician. She worked at nursing homes for a few years. Jim was an over-the-road Truck Driver for about eight years. They have one grandchild.

My youngest daughter, Dreama, married Donald Larry Taylor. Together they have one son, Marshall Taylor, who is in the second grade at Addaville Elem. Larry has a son Keith Taylor, who lives in North Carolina. Larry is a self-employed painter and Dreama works for the Buckeye Rural Electric Co. and have no grandchildren.

My heart was broken when we lost Steve; to loose a child at any age is such a loss. He left a widow, Sandra and two sons: Steve Eddy II and Robert J. Eddy. He also left a granddaughter, Mandy Eddy. He will always be missed and loved deeply and dearly. I am so thankful for the years that we had Steve and the grandsons he left behind for me.

As of today, March 16, 2002, I have eight grandchildren: five grandsons and three grand daughters, and one step grandson. I also have two great-grand children: one great-grandson and one great-granddaughter.

*Submitted by: Mearada Jewel Eddy*

## EDELBLUTE-MEADOWS

The year was 1938, I had just graduated from high school. Upon the urging of my pastor, O. M. Lasley, I came to Rio Grande College, a Baptist school, to enroll in the Summer Self-Help Program preparatory to enrolling in mid-September. Thus, began this chapter of my life because I never left these "hills" except for about five years—a few odd jobs and commitment to Uncle Sam.

I, Edwin Gibson Edelblute, was born October 22, 1920, eldest son of Ellsworth and Cora Gibson Edelblute. I was born in my parents' farmhouse on Burnt Pond Road in Ostrander, Ohio. Legend has it that it originally was swamp land and during a severe dry spell the swamp was burned—hence the "Burnt Pond Farm".

During my school days, I played basketball and baseball and was active in Future Farmers of America; and, in the summers, worked on my family's and neighbor's farms. The highest wage I received was 15 cent per hour. When I came to Rio Grande, I continued my farm work on the college farm which is now owned by Bob Evans Farms. R. R. Starbuck, a former Gallia County Agent, was the farm manager, and Ernest Blazer was the farm boss. It was at Rio Grande that I met Marie Meadows, but we never dated until the end of our second year. Prior to entering the service, I spent five months at UCLA in meteorology school.

I, Marie Elizabeth Meadows, was born February 7, 1920, in Gallipolis, Ohio. I was the last child born to Casby and Opell Wallace Meadows. My older sibling was Josephine, who later became Mrs. Ed Thompson. Sandwiched between my sister and I was my brother, Casby Jr. My parents as well as my brother and sister are all buried on the family plot in Mound Hill Cemetery.

At the time of my birth, my parents were living on the 1000 block of First Avenue in a double. We later moved to Chillicothe Road and a place called Branstetter Heights. Our property was just adjacent to that of my paternal grandparents, Joseph and Burdella Holley Meadows.

I attended grade school at Washington School and graduated from Gallia Academy High School in the class of 1938. That fall I entered Rio Grande College which was a two-year Baptist college. I graduated from there with a "cadet teaching certificate" and began teaching school in a two-room schoolhouse located in East Gallipolis.

While on furlough, Marie and I married July 7, 1944, in First Baptist Church, Gallipolis, by Dr. J. Edward Hakes. We then reported for duty at Dover Air Force Base in Dover, Delaware. After a couple of transfers, we ended up at the Goldsboro, North Carolina, Air Base when VE day occurred. I was discharged from the service at Wright Patterson Air Base in Dayton, Ohio, on February 5, 1946.

We moved back to Gallipolis that year and I went to work for Empire Furniture Company for eighteen years. During those years, our two daughters, Marsha Ann (1947) and Meda Sue (1950) were born. We lived at 33 Portsmouth Road, Gallipolis, for ten years and then moved in 1956 to our current home at 17 Edgemont Drive.

Once our daughters were in school, Marie began teaching at Washington Elementary. She started by filling in for a fifth grade teacher that was on maternity leave, and twenty some years later, she retired. During that time, she returned to Rio Grande College to finish her bachelor's degree.

In the Spring of 1964, Bill Matthews and I purchased a Gulf Oil Distributorship in Pt. Pleasant, West Virginia. We worked this job until 1980 when we sold out to Burliles. After retiring, we purchased a mobile home in a retirement park in Auburndale, Florida, and enjoy spending nearly six months of the year there.

God has indeed been good to Marie and me. We have had 57 years together without too many problems. We've been blessed with two daughters, two sons-in-law, and four grandchildren. The final blessings—all of our immediate family are born again Christians.

*Submitted by Edwin and Marie Edelblute*

**EDMISTON** - Philip Lee Edmiston and Mary Virginia Edmiston Lanier, descendants of Matthew Edmiston and Mary Lotz Edmiston. Matthew Edmiston and his sister Rebecca Edmiston came to Vinton, Ohio, in Gallia County from Virginia in the year of 1803. Matthew, a tax appraiser and farmer, was one of the 18 original voters at the time Huntington Township was formed in the year of 1810.

*Phillip Edmiston & Mary (Edmiston) Lanier December 2, 2001*

One of Matthew and Mary's sons, William, remained in Vinton, Ohio, and he married Margaret McGhee. One of their sons, Frances (Frank) Edmiston, a Civil War Veteran, remained in Vinton and he married Catherine Cherrington. One of their sons, Elbert (Bert) Edmiston, remained in Vinton and married Sarah Effie Patton. All four of their children, Kathryn, Clayte, Doris and Margaret, remained in Vinton and were educated in the Vinton Schools. Kathryn was one of the first students to graduate from the Vinton High School in 1916. Clayte, their only son, married Grace Elizabeth Casto and to this union were born three children—Harold, Philip and Mary—who were also educated in the Vinton Schools. Harold served four years in the Army doing World War II and then married Colleen Williams of Florida where they now reside. The other two children, Philip and Mary, have lived in Vinton, Ohio, their entire lives. Philip, after serving three years in the Army during World War II, graduated from Ohio State University and became a Doctor of Veterinary Medicine and has practiced this profession for forty-seven years in this community.

Mary attended Ohio University and graduated from the University of Rio Grande with a degree in Elementary Education and retired from the Gallia County Local School System. Philip married Ruby Russell and they are the parents of three children, Phyllis, Debbie and Pat, all educated in the Vinton Schools. Mary married Leo Lanier and they are the parents of two children, Elizabeth Lynn and Ronnie Lee, both educated in the Vinton Schools.

These children (Lynn Lanier Knoble, Phyllis Edmiston Brown, Ronnie Lanier, Debra Edmiston Grant, and Pat Edmiston), grandchildren (Adam Lanier, Wendy Brown Petrie, Misty Grant Backburn, Tisha Grant, Josh Brown, and Trevor Grant), and great grandchildren (Kelsey and Kendra Blackburn) make nine generations of Edmiston descendants in Vinton, Gallia County, Huntington Township, Ohio.

**JAMES AND DEBBIE NEAL EHMAN FAMILY** - James Henry Ehman (8-1-1956) was born at Holzer Hospital, Gallipolis, OH, a twin of Jenny Ehman Fraley. They were born to Albert Ray (5-31-1920 — 6-29-1987) and Virginia A. Baudy Ehman ( 3-27-1926—1-5-1997). He attended Centerville, Cadmus, and Southwestern schools.

*Settling an election bet Theodore Ehman wheels Noah Wood since he lost an election bet. They are at the old store building located at the intersection of state route 325 and at Gage in Perry Township.*

Jim married Debbra Lynn Neal (5-11-1960), who was born to John Richard (10-5-1938) and Joyce Lee Reapp Neal (9-13-1941) in Holzer Hospital, Gallipolis, OH. She attended Cadmus and Southwestern schools.

Jim works for AEP and Debbie worked for the Ohio Valley Bank. They were married May 28, 1983 at her home in Walnut Township near Mudsoc.

Their children are James Christopher (12-13-1985) born in Gallipolis, OH and Cory Neal (10-3-1987) born in Cabell Huntington Hospital, Huntington WV.

The Ehman family lives at Gage in Perry Township, Gallia County. Jamie attends River Valley High School; Cory attends Southwestern Elementary.

*Submitted By: Debbie Ehman*

**EDWIN AND LOUISE ELLIOTT FAMILY** - Edwin L. Elliott was born January 29, 1925, in Gallia County the son of Oscar and Osa Wickline Elliott. He had two sisters, Jennie and Ida, and brothers, Morris, Max, Carl and Lester. They are all deceased. Oscar was the son of Warren G. and Mary Notter Elliott and grandson of Jacob and Katherine Iron Elliott and Frances (from Germany) and Sophia Saunders Notter.

*The Edwin Elliott Family*

Osa was the daughter of Morris and MaryEllen Howell Wickline. She was the granddaughter of Samuel and Mary Irwin Wickline and Benjamin and Elizabeth Deering Howell. Her great grandparents were Jacob and Anna Barbara Wiseman Wickline and George and Jemima Russell Irwin. Osa and Oscar grew up in Waterloo and were both school teachers. He later became a funeral director/embalmer. He had a funeral home at Bethesda, Ohio, and later with Wetherholt, Elliott, Sanders Funeral Home on First Avenue in Gallipolis, Ohio.

Edwin graduated from Gallia Academy High School in 1943. He began installing wiring in residential homes in the 1940's when electricity was built into the rural areas of Gallia County. He was a heating and cooling contractor, worked at GDC and Buckeye Rural Electric before retiring in 1987. He now works part time in heating and cooling and service work.

He married Louise Steger May 16, 1945, in Greenup, KY. Louise is the daughter of Charles and Dorothy Harrison Steger. She graduated in 1945 from Cadmus High School. Louise has a brother, Kenneth Steger, Gallipolis, Ohio, and a sister, Naomi (Harold) Salisbury, Galloway, Ohio. Louise was born March 25, 1928, in Perry Township in Gallia County.

She and Edwin bought land just outside Gallipolis and built their first home. They have lived there 51 years. Dorothy Harrison Steger was the daughter of Isaac Delbert and Arminta Sheets Harrison. She was the granddaughter of John and Effamy Sowards Harrison and Brice and Sarah Saunders Sheets. Her great grandparents were Creed William and Elizabeth Neal Harrison. Her great, great grandparents were Solomon and Polly Dodd Harrison. Polly Dodd is said to have carried iris tubers in her apron when she walked from her home in Virginia to Lawrence County, Ohio.

Charles Steger was the son of John and Caroline Cline Steger. He was the grandson of William and Elizabeth Kerns Steger and John and Madeline Kerns Cline. His great grandfather was Frank Steger. Frank Steger was born in Germany.

Louise and Edwin Elliott have lived in Gallia County all their lives. Since 1958 they have been active members of Centenary United Methodist Church. Louise has had the honor of having her recipes published in local cookbooks, the "Reminisce" magazine and the national cookbook "The Best of Country Cooking", 1999, published by the Reimen Publication, Greendale, WI. She has also been a poll worker on election day in Gallia County for over 30 years. She and Edwin have three children, seven grandchildren and two great grandchildren. They are the parents of Diana (Bob) Drummond, Michael (Rebecca Lakin) Elliott and Stephen (Cathy Twyman) Elliott. Their grandchildren are Christina Drummond Huebner, Rob Drummond, Columbus, Ohio, and Ellie Drummond, Columbus, Ohio. Melissa and Joel Elliott and Bethany and Matthew Elliott. They have a grandson-in-law Captain Kermit Huebner and great grandchildren Andrew and Sarah Huebner. The Huebner's live in Killeen, TX.

*Submitted by Louise Elliott*

**EZRA ELLIOTT FAMILY** - During WWI, Ezra Elliott worked for Jeffery Manufacturing in Columbus, Ohio. Ezra married Fern Allison and they had the following children: Madge, Ralph and Dale. After a few years in Columbus, Ohio they moved back to the old home place at Mudsoc, Ohio, near Gallipolis. Ezra lived there until the time of his death in 1952.

Madge attended Mudsoc Grade School and graduated from Gallia Academy High School in 1934. Paul Northup and Carl Willis purchased a grocery store at 463 Second Avenue, Gallipolis in April 1937. May 2, 1937, Madge married Paul Northup and they worked together in the grocery store called the Gallipolis Food Market. The store closed in 1942 after the start of WWII. Paul and Madge had a son, Gary born in October 1942. For the rest of Paul and Madge's family history see the Northup Family.

Ralph Elliott, the second child of Ezra and Fern, married Clara Harbour about 1939 and to that union was born, Dottie, Janice, Wayne, Donnie, Dougie and Diane.

Ezra and Fern's third child Dale Elliott never married.

**MICHAEL EDWIN ELLIOTT FAMILY** - Michael Edwin Elliott was born July 7. 1950 in Gallia County to Edwin and Louise Steger Elliott. He and his parents have been life long residents of Gallia County. His maternal grandparents were Charles and Dorothy Harrison Steger from the Symmes Creek area near Cadmus. His paternal grandparents were Oscar and Osa Wickline Elliott from Mudsock. His grandfather Elliott was an owner of Wetherholt, Elliott, and McCoy Funeral Home in Gallipolis. Michael's siblings include a sister. Diana and a brother Steve. Diana is married to Bob Drummond. Steve is married to Cathy Twyman Elliott. Parents and siblings still reside in Gallia County.

Mike married Becky Lakin Elliott on December 31, 1972 at the Grace United Methodist Church. Becky was born October 5, 1950 and is the daughter of the late Richard (Dick) and Mary Rose Fisher Lakin. Her paternal grandparents were Charles Y. and Elsie McDaniel Lakin. In the 1930's the Lakins moved from Huntington, WV to a farm at Fairfield (near Rodney). Becky's maternal grandparents were Oakley and Mary Sheets Fisher of rhe Victory Ridge (near Mercerville) community.

*Elliott Family*

Michael graduated from Morestate State University. with a B.S. in Geology, in 1972 and the Masters in Business Administration program at Ohio University in 1994. Becky is a former cosmetologist and is now employed as a secretary at the University of Rio Grande.

Mike and Becky have two children. Melissa Michelle was born on January 14. 1980 and graduated from Ohio University in June, 2002. She is continuing her education toward a master's degree in Speech and Hearing Pathology. While enrolled at Ohio University. Melissa was active in intramural sports, the respite program and was inducted into several college honor societies including Golden Key and Mortar Board. Joel Richard Elliott was born November 8,1983. He graduated from Gallia Academy High School in June, 2002. He was a member of National Honor Society and the Blue Devil Football Team. He was named the Best Defensive Back in 2001 and an All SEOAL Academic for three years. He is continuing his education toward a degree in Computer Technology Engineering. His hobbies include fishing and hunting.

Mike and Becky's home is located on property formerly part of the Lakin farm. They have enjoyed growing up, raising their family, and continuing to live in a small rural community. It's been a wonderful environment to raise a family and to plan for a (hopefully) quiet retirement.

**STEPHEN LEE, CATHY TWYMAN, BETHANY RENEE & MATTHEW ELLIOTT FAMILY** - Stephen Lee Elliott was born January 4, 1958, in Gallipolis, to Edwin Leo and Dorothy "Louise" Steger Elliott, life-long residents of Gallia County. Steve is the youngest of three children. He was born one day after his sister Diana's tenth birthday. She said the last thing she wanted for her birthday was a baby brother. At least Steve was welcomed home by one sibling—his big brother, Michael Edwin.

Steve attended Green Elementary and Gallia Academy High School, graduating in 1976 from Buckeye Bills Career Center. He claims that while attending Gallia Academy his daily lunch consisted of two Remo Rocchi hot dogs.

Steve has been employed at Buckeye Rural Electric Co-Operative for the last 24 years. He began working in the appliance department which included heating and air conditioning services. Steve now works in the engineering department, and he and his father, Edwin, own and operate Elliott's Heating and Cooling.

On September 2, 1978, Steve married Cathy Lynn Twyman at the Ewington Church on Christ in Christian Union. The late Reverend Darrell Dodrill, uncle of the bride, performed the ceremony.

*The Elliotts Matthew, Steve, Bethany And Cathy.*

Cathy was born in Gallipolis, to Grady Lee and the late Rebecca "Pearl" Dodrill Twyman. Cathy's birthday is February 17, 1958, and her dad recalls, "It was the coldest day of the year."

Cathy's parents were both born and raised in Huntington Township. Grady was born on June 23, 1920, at his home in Ewington, the eldest of four children. Pearl's date of birth was October 4, 1916. She was the middle child in a family of nine. She left this world for her Heavenly home on January 7, 1994.

Cathy was welcomed home by her 16-year-old sister, Judy Caroline, and her 9-year-old brother, Ronald Lee. It is safe to say that Cathy was an "afterthought".

Cathy was valedictorian of both her Vinton Junior High class in 1972 and her 1976 North Gallia High School graduating class. She graduated from the Holzer School of Nursing in 1979 with a diploma in nursing, and from St. Joseph's College in 1988. She has been employed by the Gallipolis City School District since September 1982.

To this union, two children were given by God's blessing. Bethany Renee was born on December 22, 1983, in Gallipolis. Bethany's parents dedicated her life to God on April 1, 1984, with Reverend Thomas Rhoads officiating. She is a graduate of River Valley High School, and plans to attend the University of Rio Grande. She enjoys school, music and animals.

Matthew Stephen was born on April 22, 1987, at Holzer Medial Center, Gallipolis. Matthew was dedicated to our Lord on the fifth day of July, 1987, with Reverend Steve Cartwright. Matthew was able to wear the outfit that his dad had worn on his christening day, some 29 years before. Matthew will attend River Valley High School, and his interests include basketball, hunting, fishing and camping.

"The people of Gallia County have been a true blessing to our family, especially when Cathy was fighting leukemia in 1992 and 1993. We are proud to be part of this loving community."

*Submitted by Kathy Elliott*

**PLEASANT ARTHUR ELLIS** - Pleasant was born April 20, 1888 in Cheshire Township to James Ellis and Nevada Jacobs. Following in his father's footsteps, Pleasant worked as a coal miner for Marvin Thaxton and probably others. He spent part of his childhood living in the mining community of Henking in Cheshire township, where his father worked for C. A. Carl's coal company.

Pleasant married Vesta Mae Little on December 22, 1907 in Gallia county. Vesta., daughter of

Charles M. Little and Mary Ann George, was born February 8, 1890 in Cheshire township. Vesta's father was also a coal miner, working for C. A. Carl's coal company. The Little's resided in Henking. Pleasant and Vesta had the following children:

Sidney Arthur was born December 28, 1908 in Cheshire township. Sidney married Alma Etta Davison born January 3, 1911, daughter of Theodore Davidson and Idabelle Russell. Sidney and Alma had the following children: Roy, Betty Jo and Dale. Sidney was a laborer in the boat yards. He died June 26, 1945 of a brain tumor. Roy married Clara Anthony and had a son, Roy Jr. who was born December 11,1957. Dale Franklin was born January 14, 1934 in Cheshire township and married Grace Darst on May 12, 1953 in Gallia county. Grace was the daughter of Douglas Darst and Mary Gilmore. Children: Sidney Eugene and Oren Leo. Grace died January 20, 1991. Dale married second Margie Rae Morrow on September 11, 1991 in Portage County, daughter of Theodore and Evelyn (Ebie) Morrow. They have one son, Dale Franklin Jr. born March 29, 1992. He was born several weeks pre-mature and spent the first four months of his young life in the hospital.

Mary was born July 20, 1910 in Cheshire township. Eunice Marie was born April 11, 1912 in Cheshire township. Eunice married George Christy.

Maynard Hurst "Bemer" was born March 14, 1913/1914 in Cheshire township. Maynard married first Juanita Delaughter. He married second Jacqueline Mulford on November 1, 1960 in Gallia County. Jacqueline was born October 3, 1933 in Meigs County. Maynard worked as a truck driver.

Ruth Francis was born January 20, 1918 in Cheshire Township. Ruth married James Darst.

Mary Catharine "Kathleen" was born February 21, 1920 in Cheshire Township. Mary married Ernest Lowe on December 1, 1938.

Roma was born December 23, 1925. She married Egbert Litton.

Etta Mae was born October 18, 1927 and died April 23, 1985 in Pomeroy.

Lewis was born ca. 1930. He married Anna May. Children: Gary and Teresa.

Pleasant, Jr. was born December 13, 1932 in Cheshire township. He married Alice Vashti Harper on March 17, 1952 in Gallia County. Alice was born June14, 1934 in Meigs County. Pleasant worked as a coal miner.

Pleasant and Vesta lived their entire life in the Cheshire area. Pleasant died March 29, 1959 of heart complications. Vesta died March 17, 1972 in Pomeroy of circulatory failure. Pleasant and Vesta were laid to rest in Gravel Hill cemetery just outside of the hometown of Cheshire.

**JOHN E. & JANE (REES) ENTSMINGER FAMILY** - Some of the earliest non French settlers in Gallia County were the Entsmingers from Botetourt County VA. They arrived in 1797 and settled what is now Addison Township. The group was made up of John E. and Jane, his brother Joseph Ludwig and wife Mary Margaret Logue (daughter of Samuel Logue) and the boys' parents John H. Entsminger and his wife Mary Barbara Grandstaff. There were fourteen children in the two families making a new settlement all by themselves. Both John and Joseph were Revolutionary Vetrans and John had also served at Point Pleasant so they knew the country they were moving to first hand.

The story is told that as they traveled over very rough ground Jane would milk the cow first thing in the morning and put the cream in the churn. By the time the family made camp for the night the butter was ready to spread on their bread.

John and Jane's children were; Margaret born November 5, 1787 married Luther Shepard May 6, 1810 and died in May 1864: Mary born May 17,1789 married Joseph Grayum January 2, 1815 and died December 27, 1858; Elizabeth born March 11, 1791 married Daniel Grayum in about 1810; David G. born November 7, 1792 married Elizabeth Gross November 12, 1818 and died October 24, 1858; Jane born December 29, 1794 married Bela Latham July 17, 1825 and moved to Iowa where she died in 1869; Sarah Alice born March 23,1797 married John Bing III January 11, 1821 and died May 2, 1868 in Rutland, Meigs County OH; John Lewis born September 9, 1800 in Gallia County married Jane Kerr March 2, 1826 and second Sophia Sawyers December 22,1831 he died in April of 1847 in Meigs County. From these children we know Jane and John had at least twenty eight grandsons and twenty four granddaughters that lived. Many of this generation were among the pioneers who helped settle our great west, as their Grandparents had settled Ohio in their day.

These grandchildren were to fight the Civil War as the Grandfathers had fought the Revolution. However we find that children from one family were on both sides of that sad chapter in our History. Located as Gallia is on the border of the Ohio and Virginia there was no avoiding differences of opinion.

My second great grandmother, Sarah Alice Entsminger Bing, told of one son coming in the front door as another left by the back door. It did avoid a war in the house though.

**D. DEAN AND HENRIETTA EVANS** - D. Dean Evans was born in Gallipolis June 12, 1945 to H. Claude and Beatrice E. Fowler Evans. His father was a manager for Doxol Gas and his mother a homemaker. Claude's family came to Gallia County about 1915 and Bea's family has been in the county since 1815.

Dean graduated from Marshall University and Capital University School of Law. He taught school three years in Gallia and Licking counties. After attending law school he joined the law firm of William P. Cherrington and Thomas Moulton, Sr. in 1972. He has served as City Solicitor of Gallipolis, Acting Judge of Gallipolis Municipal Court and Village Solicitor for Rio Grande. In June 2001 he was appointed Gallia County Common Pleas Judge by Gov. Bob Taft to fill an unexpired term.

Dean's down time finds him at his farm on Rocky Fork Road where he brush hogs, works on old tractors, and keeps the place up.

Dean married Henrietta (Henny) Cherrington August 20, 1966. She was born August 4,1944 to William Putnam and Mary Lisbeth Lovell- Cherrington. She is a graduate of Denison University and taught school at Rio Grande College, BidwellPorter Elementary and Summit Station Elementary for a total of four years. Henny has been a professional genealogist since the 1970's and has researched hundreds of Gallia County families. She co-authored several books with Mary Ann Wood and in 1990, she, Mary Ann and John Lester compiled Gallipolis. Ohio. A Pictorial History. She has been an active participant in the Gallia County Historical/Genealogical Society since 1977. She was co-chair of Gallia County. Ohio People in History to 1980. She received an award for Individual Achievement from the Ohio Association of Historical Societies and Museums and in 1987 she received the Jane Roush McCafferty, C.G. Award of Excellence in Genealogy. She continues to volunteer on a daily basis and has been Corresponding Secretary of the group since 1979.

Members of St. Peter's Episcopal Church, Dean and Henny both served terms on the vestry and Henny is currently treasurer of the Episcopal Church Women and a member of the Altar Guild.

*Dean, Henny, Kirsten and Bill Evans*

Dean and Henny have two sons, William Claude Evans, born September 14, 1970 and David Cherrington Evans, born September 30, 1974. Bill graduated from the University of Cincinnati with a degree in marketing and from the

*Dean and David Evans*

University of South Carolina with a masters degree in Health Administration. He was employed by Cleveland Clinic for one year, worked for Excel, then for American Express in Cleveland and Hilton Head and Charleston, SC for about one and one-half years. In January 2000 he and his wife Kirsten Elizabeth Bayman moved to Denver. Bill and Kirsten married August 11, 1996 in Cleveland. Kirsten, daughter of Jim and Reita Bayman of Cleveland, is a graduate of University of Cincinnati and Case Western with a masters. Bill is employed with TIAA-CREF as a Certified Financial Planner and Kirsten is employed with Level 3 Communications. They live on Cherry Street in Denver and love the opportunity to ski and snowboard.

David graduated from University of Cincinnati undergraduate and University of Cincinnati School of Law. He was sworn in by the Supreme Court of Ohio in May 2001 and joined his father in the law firm. In June 2001 he and his cousin, Thomas Moulton, Jr. formed a law partnership. David is Magistrate for the Municipal Court and Village Solicitor for Rio Grande. David recently purchased a home on Belmont Drive and is glad to be part of the Gallia County community.

**ELEANOR KAY (RICHARDS) EVANS** - Eleanor Kay is the daughter of the late Robert Mills Richards of Gallia County and Ruth Arnold Richards of Meigs County. Kay, as she is known to her family and friends, grew up in Hanerville along with her brother Jack. She attended Gallipolis City schools and graduated from Gallia Academy High School.

Kay married Ralph Bennett of Gallia County in 1952. They had two daughters, Beverly Ann born May 2, 1953 and Jackie Kay born November 16, 1955. She and Ralph managed the Western Auto store on the corner of Third Avenue and Court Street.

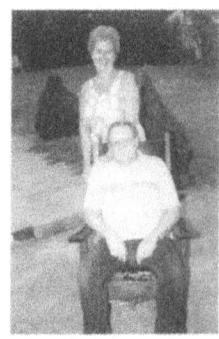

*Bill Joe & Eleanor Kay Evans*

On July 30, 1965 Kay married Bill Joe Evans of Gallipolis. Bill Joe was the son of Chauncey (Hank) and Ruby Evans of Gallipolis. While the girls were growing up, the family resided on Lariat Drive in Mills Village.

Bill Joe worked for Kaiser Aluminum in Ravenswood, West Virginia, as a long-distance driver. He died in 1989 from cancer.

Kay has worked for Smith Buick as title clerk and secretary for 30 years. She is an active member of Grace United Methodist Church as a Circle member and in United Methodist Women. Her leisure activities include reading and playing cards.

Daughter Beverly married Dan Dunkle from McConnelsville, Ohio on June 9, 1977 in Golden, Colorado. They have one son Drew D. Dunkle, who will graduate from Ohio University, Athens in 2002 with a degree in Finance. Their daughter Cara A. Dunkle will graduate from Gallia Academy High School in 2002. Bev is the secretary to the Gallipolis Chief of Police, Roger Brandeberry and Dan is the timekeeper for the Highway Garage.

Daughter Jackie married Tom F. Woodward III of Gallia County on June 21, 1975 in Waynesburg, Virginia. They have two children Robert F. (Robbie) and Morgan. Robbie is a graduate of Ohio Weslyan University in Delaware, Ohio with a degree in Earth Science. Daughter Morgan attends Otterbein College in Westerville and is pursuing a BS degree in Nursing. Jackie is RN Surgical nurse at Holzer Clinic and Tombo is farm manager for Sunset Farm.

In 1993 Kay moved to 739 First Avenue in the former Mildred Gilman home where she enjoys her beautiful view of the West Virginia hills and the Ohio River.

*Submitted by E. Kay Evans*

**JIMMIE ALLEN EVANS FAMILY** - John Edward Evans and Alma Kathleen Perkins were married on August 25, 1930. John was born October 4, 1902 and Kathleen on January 28, 1907. Kathleen was the daughter of Thomas Jefferson Perkins and Myrta Jones Perkins. They were lifetime residents of Gallia County. John and Kathleen set up housekeeping on Burnt Run Road. They had two sons, Jimmie Allen born August 9, 1931, and Edward Thomas on January 9, 1933. On June 8, 1936, they moved to a new house on John's father's farm on Raccoon Road. Kathleen died on January 1, 1960 and John on June 23, 1974.

Jimmie was active in FFA and Key Club while in high school. He graduated from Gallia Academy and later attended Gallipolis Business College. He operated a dairy farm for a short while, then became office manager for ASCS. In 1959 Jim met Nancy Jane McAllister, who came to Gallia County as Extension Agent in home economics. In the spring of 1960 they began dating and were married on April 2, 1961.

Nancy was a native of Jefferson County. She was born March 14, 1937, on a farm near Mt. Pleasant, Ohio. Her parents were Walter William McAllister (November 18, 1907) and Ruth Hannah Walker McAllister (May 4, 1904). Nancy graduated from Mt. Pleasant High School in 1955 and from Kent State University in 1959. She has a B.S. degree in Home Economics in Business. While at Kent State she was active in the Home Economics Club, Kappa Omicron Phi, the Home Economics Honorary, and United Christian Fellowship.

Nancy worked with the Extension Service until December 31, 1962, when she resigned to rear a family. Jim went to work for Mason County Motor company in 1963. They have four children: Allen Lewis (February 10, 1963), Janice Kathleen (September 2, 1964), Mark Andrew (May 21, 1969), and Barbara Ann (June 11, 1971).

Allen graduated from the University of Cincinnati in June of 1986 with an electrical engineering degree. Later that month he was hired by A.M.D. in Austin, Texas as an electrical engineer. He is now one of the top engineers in the company that employees 2500 people. In May of 1991 he married Sylvia Mendez. In 1995 Allen received a Master of Business Administration from St. Edwards University in Austin. Texas. On December 22, 1997, a son was born to Allen and Sylvia named Matthew David. Sylvia has two older sons from a previous marriage, Adrian age 27, and Anthony age 23.

Janice graduated from the Ohio State University with a Doctor of Veterinary Medicine in June 1990. In July of 1990 she was married to Barry Williams. In August of 1990, they moved to near Morristown, Tenn., where she worked for a veterinary clinic for ten years. In June of 2000 they moved back to the Evans farm on Raccoon Road. Janice is currently employed by an emergency night veterinary clinic in Ceredo, W. Va.

Mark after high school graduation went to work for the A.M.D. plant in Austin, Texas as an electrical technician. He has worked for two other companies, one of which sent him to Taiwan and Korea. Ashland Chemical Company presently employs him in Dublin, Ohio working on a new process for polishing computer chips.

Barbara graduated from Rio Grande University with a degree in elementary education in March of 1994. She worked as a substitute teacher for two years, while looking for a full-time teaching position.

In June of 1996 she was employed by Gallia County Children's Services where she is still employed.

After going to night classes for two years, she graduated from Ohio University with a Masters Degree in Human and Consumer Sciences.

Jim retired from Gene Johnson Chevrolet Olds as service manager in 1996. At the end of this school year, Nancy is retiring from the Gallipolis City Schools where she has worked with the school lunch program for fourteen years. Jim and Nancy have both been active at St. Peter's Episcopal Church where Nancy is an organist and Jim was treasurer for thirty-five years. They both are involved in many church activities.

**LEWIS EVANS FAMILY** - The Lewis Evans family came to the United States in 1839. He bought property in Greenfield Township which remained in the family until the 1940's.

His sons were John L. W., Owen L., and Lewis Jr. and one daughter, Anne.

John L. W. was my great grandfather. His son, Lewis Edward, my grandfather and John Everette who married Elnea Reese, my parents. I am Bertha E. Evans who married George L. Grace (1917-1975) on August 16, 1941. We have two daughters. Carse who married Frank McCain (1946-1980). They have four children, Elizabeth Ann, Amy Jean, Julia Grace and Timothy Warren. Elizabeth married John Fetherton; Amy married Mark Anderson and the others are single. I remarried in May 9, 1998 to a good friend Donald G. Davis. We are both past 80 years and enjoy doing just as we please.

*Submitted by Bess Davis*

**THOMAS EVERTON AND RELIEF HOWE EVERTON** - Thomas and Relief Howe Everton arrived in what would become Gallia County, OH, in 1796. They came following a brief stay in Whitestown Township, Oneida County, NY, where two of their children were born. Thomas son of Benjamin and Mary Duset was born in Milton, Norfolk County, MA 16 Feb. 1762. He served in the Revolution as a private from MA, he is found in the DAR Patriot Index. He died in Meigs County in 1848.

Relief Howe, daughter of Moses and Relief Howe, was born in Dover, Straford County, NH, October 10, 1763/1764 and christened October 23 of that year. She and Thomas married October 9, 1784, Bridgewater, Plymouth County, MA. Relief died in Meigs County in 1841.

Of their nine children the first two born in Kennebec, York County, ME. Betsy on August 31, 1785 and Relief on August 31, 1787. Betsy married Benjamin Richardson before 1815 and they had two known children. Betsy died in

Meigs County November 5, 1845. Relief married William Edwards December 8, 1814 in Gallia County OH. We believe they had at least four children.

The two born in Whitestown, NY were Jane, treated in a different article, and Ebenezer born May 7, 1794. He came with his parents to Gallia, and died in Meigs County OH, October 7, 1827.

Polly (Mary) was born in Gallia County, OH, November 25,1796, thus establishing their arrival in Gallia County before that date. Polly married James Stow August 26, 1819 in Meigs County, OH by whom she had one child. Second she married Thomas McAboy July 9, 1826. They had one daughter and three sons. She died in Meigs County, January 10,1839.

After Polly's birth the family decided to go to Upper Canada, now Ontario, to visit Thomas' brother who had been a Loyalist and moved before the Revolution. While there Thomas Everton Jr. was born on July 10, 1799. He married Deidamia Paulk in Troy, Athens County, OH on December 7, 1823. After three daughters and one son were born they moved to Adams County, IL. Thomas Jr. married a second time and had one son Arthur. That marriage was brief.

Nancy born August 30, 1801 in Gallia County married first Royal Phelps and had no issue. She married, second, on April 30, 1820 Jesse Stevens. In 1848, Nancy's father died, they were in KY on their way to Iowa. They returned and left again for Iowa after the estate was settled. Nancy died in Wilton, Muscatine County, Iowa, May 26, 1891.

Benjamin Everton was born December 6, 1804 in Gallia County and married Lucina Chasse 24 June 1829 in Meigs County. They had one son, Hiram B. Everton. Thomas and Relief deeded their land to Benjamin, in return for their care until death. Not a good idea, as Benjamin died April 17, 1837, ten years before his parents. Lucina settled with them for very little and they went to live with their daughter Betsy.

Sarah (Sally) Everton was born January 25, 1806 in Gallia County OH. She married Charles Richardson July 9, 1826 in Meigs County, OH. We don't know if he is related to Benjamin, her eldest sister's husband. She died June 16, 1834 in Rutland, Meigs County, Oh. Sadly we know very little about Sally's short life.

The Evertons were one of many families who settled in Washington County, became part of Gallia when it was formed and then became part of Meigs when it came into being. They never moved but the counties surely changed.

**EWING-GLENN FAMILY** - On April 29, 1888 in Huntington Township, Gallia County, OH, Anise Victoria Ewing (July 23, 1865-October 25, 1933) daughter of William Knox Ewing (August 24, 1828-July 11, 1876) and Polly Ann Viers (July 17, 1825-May 5, 1898) married Elza Armstrong Glenn (July 27, 1860-December 19, 1920) son of Franklin Jarvis Glenn (1835-September 6, 1906) and Samantha Howe Glenn (November 17, 1835-February 12, 1916). Anise Victoria's great grandparents were William Ewing and Mary McNeill. Elza's great grandparents were William Glenn and Ann Curry. The Ewings and the Glenns were among the early settlers of Huntington Township. Both of their families were from Scotland.

Elza and Victoria lived on a farm on Route 554 between Harrisburg and Bidwell in Springfield Township. Their two children were born there. Harry McKinley was born November 10, 1891, and died February 20, 1952, in Vinton, Ohio. Zelda Annenach was born Oct. 22, 1895 and died Nov. 5, 1990 in Columbus, OH. Zelda married James Earnest Hartley (1884-1953). They had two children: Glenn Ewing and Beatrice Ellen.

*Victoria Ewing Glenn 1865-1933 & Elza A. Glenn 1860-1920*

Harry married Anna May White (1900-1979), a school teacher, who was teaching in Harrisburg. They set up housekeeping in Vinton where Harry had a barbershop on South Main Street. They had five children.

1. Ewing Frederick (1935-1935) buried Fairview Cemetery, Springfield Township.
2. Arlene Marie married Buddy Charles Udrich. They had five children: Renee, Denis (1955-2000), Ronald, Gregory and Lynne.
3. Howard Eugene (1938-2001) married Judy Argabright. They had three children: Jeffery (1961-1988), Timothy and Susan.
4. Irene Victoria (May 11, 1940) married Daryl Leon Petrie (November 30, 1937) Gallia County. He is the son of Clyde Petrie and Nadine Kitts. Daryl retired September 30, 2001, from Ross Correctional Institute in Chillicothe, OH. They live in Jackson, OH. They have four children: Terry Christine (August 30, 1957) married Robert Edward Nicholson (June 15, 1957), son of Charles Ray Nicholson and Hester Rankin. They have a daughter, Natalie Victoria, born August 9, 1990. Robert owns Ron's Garage and Wrecker Service in Jackson, OH.
   James Russel (February 19, 1960) married Martha Hernandez. They have a son, Christopher James. Jim and Martha work at the V.A. Hospital in Chillicothe, OH.
   Robin Lynn (May 6, 1961) lives in Jackson, OH, and works at Mills Pride in Waverly, OH. She has three children: Rebekah, Travis and Haley.
   Steven Eugene (January 17, 1961) married Elena Gonzalez. They have two children: Tyler and Sara. Steve works for Xacta as a computer security consultant and Elena is a Spanish teacher for Northern Burlington Regional County High School in Pemberton, New Jersey, where they live.
5. Clara Belle (December 4, 1941) married Herbert Montgomery. They have two children: Lori and Brian.

*Submitted by Irene Glenn Petrie*

**WILLIAM KNOX EWING AND POLLY ANN VIERS FAMILY** - William Knox Ewing (1828-1876) was the oldest son of George Ewing (1807-1883) and Rosanna Knox (1806-1879) and grandson of William (Swago Bill) Ewing (1756-1822) and Mary McNeill (1771-1858). On October 1, 1849 William Knox Ewing married Polly Ann Viers (1825-1898) the daughter of John Viers (1787-1872) and Lydia Dillbone (1793-1840).

*William Knox Ewing 1828-1876 & Polly Ann Viers 1825-1898*

In 1874 William and Polly owned property in section 3 of Huntington Township. William was a carpenter. They had six children: Lucina, Semira, Anselm, Myrtle Belle, William Ellis and Anise Victoria. William and his first three daughters died of tuberculosis. William Ellis never married. Anselm married Rachel Wilcox, daughter of John Wilcox (1828-1888) and Elizabeth Gee (1829-unknown). On April 29, 1888, Anise Victoria (1865-1933) married Elza Armstrong Glenn (1860-1920) son of Franklin Jarvis Glenn (1835-1906) and Samantha Howe Glenn (1835-1916). Samantha's mother, Margaret Ann Viers Glenn (wife of Andrew Young Glenn) was a sister to Polly Ann Viers Ewing.

John and Lydia Viers were living in Huntington Township before 1820. They had ten children: Margaret married Andrew Young Glenn; Elizabeth Amelia married Jordan Ewing; Samuel married Anna Charlotte McCarley; James married Rebecca Ewing; Polly married William Knox Ewing; Andrew married Mahala McCarley; Sarah Anjelina married Samuel McCarley; William married Elizabeth Sherrit; John Allen married Mary Mahala Davis.

Anise Victoria and Elza Glenn had two children: Harry McKinley (1891-1952) and Zelda Annenah (1895-1990). On May 3, 1934, Harry married Anna May White (1900-1979) daughter of Job While and Rebecca Clary.

Harry and Anna had five children: Ewing Frederick, Arlene, Howard, Irene and Clara. Clara born December 5, 1941, married Herbert Montgomery, born August 3, 1943, in Brown County, Ohio, to Govie Montgomery and Grace Allen.

Clara graduated from Leesburg High School in Leesburg, Ohio, and Miami Jacobs Business College in Dayton, Ohio. She worked at Farmers and Traders Bank in Hillsboro, Ohio. Clara and Herb have two children: Lori Ann born April 3, 1971, and Brian Keith born November 16, 1973, in Highland County.

Lori married Danny Boyd May 4, 1996. They are divorced. Lori works for the Clinton County Children Services.

Herb, Clara and Brian run Montgomery Farms and Trucking Company in Highland County, Ohio. Herb also works at Airborne Express in Wilmington, Ohio. Herb and Clara live at 2346 Ruble Cemetery Road, Lynchburg, Ohio.

*Submitted by Clara Glenn Montgomery.*

**LARRY AUSTIN, SHERYL RAE (FRASER) AND RASHEL LYN FALLON FAMILY** - Larry Austin Fallon was born August 26, 1955, in the community of Gage, Ohio. He is the son of Vernard Fallon (deceased) and Ima Hope (Cochran) Burnett Fallon of Patriot, Ohio. Larry has one brother, Gary Lee Fallon of Patriot, Ohio, and one sister, Jane Ann Miller of Gallipolis, Ohio.

*James (Jimmy) Myers and son Alva Myers (early 1900's).*

Sheryl Rae (Fraser) Fallon was born in Gallipolis, Ohio, February 17, 1955. She is the daughter of Irwin Raymond Fraser of Silvercliff, Colorado, and Opal Faye (Neal) Fraser of Gallipolis, Ohio. Sheryl has one sister, Tami Fraser of Richmond, VA.

Larry and Sheryl were married April 15, 1978, at Centenary, Ohio. The minister was Rev. Pearl Casto.

Larry and Sheryl have one daughter, Rashel Lyn Fallon born May 25, 1981, in Gallipolis, Ohio. Rashel is a graduate of River Valley High School, Cheshire, Ohio, (1999), and Morehead State University (2001), Morehead, Kentucky. Her degree is in Agricultural Education.

Together, Larry, Sheryl, and Rashel are the owners and operators of Triple F Farm of Gage, Ohio.

Larry Fallon is a farmer and also a carpenter (Union Local 650). He is a graduate of Southwestern High School (1975), Patriot, Ohio.

Larry's father's family came to Ohio from Rush, Kentucky. His father, Vernard Fallon, was a veteran of World War II (Pacific Theatre) and a Laborer of Local 83. His mother's family is from Patriot, Ohio. She is a retired cook from the Gallipolis City Schools. She was a 4-H advisor for 30 years. She has been honored for her work with the youth of Gallia County.

Sheryl is a teacher for the Gallia County Local Schools. She graduated from Gallia Academy High School (1973), Morehead State University (1977), and University of Rio Grande, with a Masters in Education.

Sheryl's father came originally from Ontario, Canada, then Wyoming, to Tipp City, Ohio. He is a graduate of Tipp City High School. He is retired form the U.S. Army-a highly decorated veteran of the Korean and Vietnam Wars. He was a member of the Green Berets. Her mother, Opal Faye (Neal) Fraser was born near Lecta, Ohio. She is a graduate of Gallia Academy High School, Rio Grande College, and Ohio University with a Masters in Education. She is retired from Gallipolis City Schools.

*Picture of house*

The Fallon family is originally from Ireland. The Cochran family came from Germany. The Fraser family came originally from Scotland. The Neal family was from Germany.

A few interesting facts:

While living in Kentucky Larry's paternal grandfather, Justin Avery Fallon, traded horses with the legendary Jesse James.

Sheryl's maternal great grandfather, James (Jimmy) Myers was a long time undertaker in the Mudsoc, Ohio, and area.

**LAWRENCE EDWARD FELLURE** - Lawrence Edward Fellure was born on November 9, 1939 to Garrett Lesley and Nora Omelia (Noel) Fellure. When Lawrence was born the family lived on Turkey Run Road, Gallia County, Cheshire Township. Lawrence was the oldest of five children. Dotty Jean, John Robert, Betty Lou and Richard Fellure. Lawrence's dad Garrett Lesley Fellure passed away on March 12, 1988 at the age of 77. His mother Omelia Fellure passed away March 5, 1996 at the age 83.

*Larry, Carolyn and Chelsey Fellure November 2001*

Between the years of 1943 to 1946 Lawrence's family moved to Cheshire, then to Maple Shade in Gallipolis, and then to Mill Creek in Gallipolis. In 1946 the Fellure family moved from Mill Creek to a farm on Roush Road. Lawrence started to school in the fall of 1946 and attended at Addison, Ohio.

Lawrence went from the Addison school to Cheshire High School. Cheshire High School closed in 1957 and Lawrence then went to Kyger Creek High School. In his junior and senior years of school he played football and ran track. Lawrence graduated high school in 1958.

After High School Lawrence went to work doing strip mining. He worked in explosives, and drove a truck for the Co. Larry then went to work for Westinghouse in 1960 and worked there until 1962.

Lawrence married Judith Ann Warfuel on January 15, 1962. From this marriage two children were born. Barry Lee Fellure born March 31, 1963 and Pamela Sue Fellure born on December 28, 1964.

Lawrence worked for a short time in Ironworker Local, then he went to Columbus, Ohio and joined Carpenters Local 200 in September 1967, and worked for various contractors. They bought a house in Whitehall, Ohio and lived here until 1977 when Judy and he were divorced.

Lawrence met Carolyn (Plants) Rodgers in September 1978. They were married on July 6, 1979. Carolyn was born on March 6, 1952 and was the daughter of Gilbert Lawrence and Opal Irene Neal Plants. Carolyn had three sons from a previous marriage to George Samuel Rodgers. Paul Samuel Rodgers, born October 26, 1969 and twins, Jason Scott and Jeffrey Shane Rodgers, born August 2, 1973. They lived at Whitehall, Ohio until 1981 when they moved to a house on Taylor Station Road in Gahanna, Ohio. They lived in this house for ten years and the boys grew up there.

In February 1993 Larry, Carolyn and Chelsey moved from Columbus to Gallipolis on First Avenue. In April 1994 Lawrence went back to work in Columbus where he continued to work until December 2000.

Their children are all now grown. Pam Fellure married Scott Taylor on November 18, 1994. They have a daughter Shannon Leigh Taylor born May 29, 1995. Paul married Bobbie Hopkins on Feb 28, 1990 and they have two children Bridget Leigh born September 20, 1990 and Jaime Brooke born June 24, 1992. Their marriage ended in divorce in 2000.

Jason has three children Haley Orsbon born February 15, 1998, Jaron Scott Rodgers born November 23, 2000 and Jaci Gail Rodgers born September 28, 2001. Their mother is Brandy Russell.

Jeffrey's children are Allison Paige Rodgers born January 31, 1998 and Jeffrey Taylor Rodgers born December 11, 1999. Their mother is Tracy Six. Whitney Nicole Reitmire born March 20, 1993 lives with her mother Loretta Wallace. And Chelsey Marie Rodgers Fellure born August 15, 1992, whom his mother Carolyn and step father Larry adopted in November 1995.

In October 1996 Lawrence, Carolyn and Chelsey moved to Second Avenue in Gallipolis, where they still reside. Lawrence retired in the summer of 2001, and is now enjoying his free time, and working when he wants to.

*Submitted by: Lawrence E. and Carolyn G. Fellure*

**JOHN LEWIS FERRELL** - John Lewis Ferrell was born on April 12, 1827, in Monroe County, Ohio, died on December 24, 1916, in Richwood, Thompson Township, Delaware County, Ohio, and was buried on December 27, 1916, in Clairborne Cemetery, Richwood, Delaware County, Ohio. John married Mary E. Roush, daughter of John Roush and Elizabeth Jackson, on July 1, 1852, in Winfield, Putnam County, Virginia. Mary was born on November 16, 1833, in Frederick County, Virginia, died on November 24, 1921, in Lawrence County, Ohio, and was buried on November 27, 1921, in Richwood, Thompson Township, Clairborne County, Ohio. John and Mary moved to Perry Township, Gallia County, Ohio, sometime around 1860. They are in the 1860 and 1870 census for Perry Township, Gallia County, Ohio, and the 1880 census for Aid Township, Lawrence County, Ohio. John Served as a Corporal in the Civil War in Company F, 141st Ohio National Guard Infantry. He served from May 2, 1864, to September 3, 1864. He appears on the Company Muster and Descriptive Roll dated Gallipolis, Ohio, May 11, 1864. He enlisted May 2, 1864, in Perry Township, Gallia County, Ohio, for a period of 100 days. Eyes black, hair black, complexion dark, height 6 feet 1 inch. Mustered in on May 11, 1864, in Gallipolis. Appears on Company Muster-out Roll on September 3, 1864.

Their children are:

1. Mary M. Ferrell was born in 1853 in West Virginia. Mary married Archer about 1876.

2. Eveline Elizabeth Ferrell was born in 1855 in West Virginia and died on October 1, 1905, in Toledo, Lucas County, Ohio. Eveline married Robert Bailey McCarley, son of John McCarley and Agnes Nancy Boggs, on June 4, 1875, in Lawrence County, Ohio. Robert was born on February 21, 1849, in Gallia County, Ohio, died on February 6, 1914, in Toledo, Lucas County, Ohio, and was buried in Forrest Lawn Cemetery, Toledo, Lucas County, Ohio.

3. Margaret Ann Ferrell was born in 1856 and died about 1916.

4. Henry W. Ferrell was born in 1858.

5. John W. Ferrell was born in 1859.

6. Lucinda Ferrell was born in 1861.

7. Abraham Ferrell was born in 1864.

8. Isabell Ferrell was born in 1866.

9. Emma G. Ferrell was born in 1866.

10. Edward L. Ferrell was born in 1870 in Ohio. Edward married Mary J. Neal on February 14, 1893, in Lawrence County, Ohio.

11. Docia Ferrell was born on November 12, 1871, in Ohio. Docia married William A. Weberly, son of William Weberly and unknown wife.

12. Irena Ferrell was born on June 12, 1976, in Ohio.

13. Hattie M. Ferrell was born on November 12, 1876, in Ohio, died on September 22, 1960, and was buried in Woodland Cemetery.
*Submitted by Ruth E. Hall*

**JOHN K. FIFE** - John K. Fife was born at sea May 29, 1780, eight days before his family landed in America. In about 1800 he was living in Sweet Springs, Virginia, where he married Jane Walker December 20,, 1803. By 1810 John was in Gallia Co., Ohio where he married on December 7, 1810 Catherine Rupe (1791-1863). John was a carpenter, and built Cider Mills, and houses. It is believed that he helped to build the original Poplar Ridge Church. John died august 11, 1854. He and Catherine are buried in Poplar Ridge Cemetery.

They had eight children: (1) Mary Jane Fife, born in 1911, married Arthur Elwood Macoubrie who was murdered in Warren Co., Ohio. Mary Jane went to Missouri with her children and died in Carroll Co., Missouri, June 7, 1881. Mary Jane and Arthur had six children. (2) Melinda Fife, born November 11, 1815 married James C. Anderson and had one child. Melinda married second William Crawford and had three children. She married third George W. Rimmey and had one child. Melinda died September 17, 1884 and is buried in Poplar Ridge Cemetery. (3) Abraham W. Fife, born in 1818, married Emily Mayes (1823-1881). Abraham was a coal miner and lived in Middleport, Ohio. He died sometime after 1900. Buried in Middleport Hill Cemetery. They had five children. (4) Enoch R. Fife, born about 1820, also a coal miner, lived in Meigs Co., Ohio. He married Mary Ann Thomas and they had eight children. (5) George Adam Fife, born August 1, 1882, was a carpenter and built flat boats. He married Margaret Freelove Rowley (1826-1913) June 27, 1843. George Adam served in the Civil War, Co. C. 4th West Virginia Volunteer Infantry. George died August 9, 1895 and both are buried in Poplar Ridge Cemetery. They had ten children. (6) John Matthew Fife was born June 10, 1824. He was an architect, designing and building houses. John married Elizabeth Hester Russell (1824-1857) and they had two children. After Elizabeth died, John married Adriana Weldon (1824-1861). They had one child. Adriana died and John moved to Chillicothe, Ohio where he married Laura Parker. They had one child. John Matthew died June 13, 1892 in Chillicothe, Ohio and is buried in Grandview Cemetery. (7) Abel Sargent Fife, born September 1,1826 was a farmer, who lived in Crown City, Ohio and in Lesage, West Virginia. He married first to Harriet Noland (1832-1858) and they had one child. Harriet died in Abel. Married second to Mary Ann Rimmey (1827-?). Divorced. They had one child. Abel married third to Nancy M. Howard (1842-1929). Abel died March 9, 1896 and is buried in Oak Hill Cemetery at Lesage, W.Va. Nancy is buried in Green Bottom Cemetery at Lesage. They had 10 children. (8) Margaret Fife, born August 29, 1830, married Hezekiah Jones (1819-1900). He died November 11, 1900 and Margaret died November 24, 1901. Both are buried in Poplar Ridge Cemetery. They had eight children.

**WILLIAM LEWIS FOSTER III AND FAMILY** - William Lewis Foster III, born December 9, 1963 in Guthrie, OK, is the son of Ayrln (Lovelace) and the late William Lewis Foster II. The subject of this family sketch was reared in Meigs County, Ohio, along with his siblings, Eric Lee Foster and Terry Ray Foster. His father, who was born September 17, 1932, worked for several years as a truck driver, and his death occurred at Pt. Pleasant, WV on May 9, 1983. His mother, Ayrn, born June 18, 1944, later married Don Feugate and lives in Clifton, Colorado.

William L. Foster III, better known as "Bill" graduated from Southern High School in Meigs County, Ohio in 1982. On July 5, 1985, he married me, Terri Lynn Murray, the daughter of Charles A. and Donna (Palmer) Murray in Gallipolis, OH. I was born July 3, 1967 in Gallipolis, attended the Gallipolis City Schools and graduated from Gallia Academy High School in 1985. I have a brother, David, residing in Gallipolis, and a sister, Amanda Kay Murray, living in Columbus, OH.

*Bill, Terri And Keri Lynn Foster*

"Bill" is currently employed at Rent 2 Own in Gallipolis and also operates the business, EZ COMPUTERS from his home. I have been employed with Fruth Pharmacy for 11 years and am now a certified pharmacy technician. Our daughter, Keri Lynn Foster, was born February 26, 1998 in Gallipolis. We live on the property where Keri's great-grandparents, Anthony and Hallie (Rutan) Murray, resided for 51 years. On the day of Keri's birth, the Snowdrop flowers were in full bloom at the Murray homestead in Bidwell, and thereafter she became nicknamed, "Snowdrop" by her grandpa Murray. These blooming flowers are one of the first signs of new life each spring in Southeastern Ohio.

Keri's great-grandparents also include Donald and Ruth (Rathburn) Palmer of Bidwell, James and Almina (Reynolds) Lovelace of Colorado, and William and Daisy a.k.a. Doris (Wells) Foster of Parkersburg, WV. At the time, 2002, all of Keri's great-grandparents are deceased with the exception of Great-Grandma Ruth who is 90. More family history can be learned by reading family sketches published in the book GALLIA COUNTY, OHIO: PEOPLE IN HISTORY TO 1980, by the Gallia County Historical Society. Other related ancestors include the Rutan, Harman, Palmer, Darst, and Roush families in the same book.
*Submitted by Terri L. Foster*

**GEORGE EDWARD AND MOLLY ISLE WISE FOWLER** - Etna Fowler is in the 1840 census of Kanawha Co. Virginia. He married Mary (Polly) Fisher in Kanawha Co. 17 June 1833. Children of this marriage were: Amanda, (married Isaac C. Wolf in Jackson Co. Virginia, 5 May 1859); Susanna; James V. (married Ailcy Redman 9 Sept. 1861 in Jackson Co. Virginia and raised George Edward and Matilda after the death of Nancy Ellen Wallace and Edward Fowler); Henry Clay (married Martha Francis Casey 14 April 1870); Mary E.; and William Ambrose. George Edward Fowler was born 9 Sept. 1876 at Hogsett, W. Va. His father was Edward, born about 1843 died 18 June 1877, and his mother was Nancy Ellen Wallace born 16 Oct. 1846 died 29 Aug. 1885. They were married 26 Aug 1868 Gallia Co., Ohio. They are buried Buckle Cemetery, Apple Grove W.Va. Children of this marriage were: Joseph born 29 Sept 1869, James Isaac born 24 August 1873, and George Edward born 9 Sept. 1876. After Edward's death Nancy Ellen married Zadoc Hedge 20 Sept. 1880. A half-sister Matilda Hedge was born 24 June 1881 and married William Coleman.

Joseph married Elizabeth Martin. They had two sons, Carl and Eugene. They all lived in Nitro, W. Va.

*George Edward and Molly Isle Wise Fowler*

James married Rhoda Inez Wise a sister to Martha and Molly. Children of this marriage were: Thelma, Ruby, Charles (died young), and James Henry Fowler. They lived at Poca, W. Va.

George Edward married 25 Dec. 1901 1) Martha Francis Wise, born 1883, and died before 1903 no children were from their marriage; 2) Molly Isle Wise, (a sister to Martha) born 17 April 1886 married 2 Sept. 1904 Charleston W.Va. died 14 Dec. 1960 Holzer Hospital, Gallipolis. Rhoda Inez, Martha Francis, and Mollie Isle's parents were Henry Alexander Wise and Sarah Harriett Catron Wise. Children from Molly and George's marriage were: Clarence (died young); George Hamilton, married Mary Agnes Herrmann; James Henry, married Mary Ella Gertrude Brown; Rilla Francis, married 1) John Whealdon, 2) Elmer Rusk; Roscoe Lee, married Sarah Roush; and Paul, married Anna Susannah Steinbrink. George divorced Mollie and married 3) Minnie Brown Walker on 7 Oct. 1939. She was the daughter of Emerson and Anna Maria (Mary) Kraus Brown, (no children were from this marriage).

George Edward Fowler retired form the New York Central Railroad. Getting free passes, he traveled with his family to visit relatives throughout West Virginia. George's children all started out working at Mootz's Bakery here in town. James Henry and Mary's children were: Carol Yvonne born 15 Feb. 1935, 114 Fourth Avenue Gallipolis and Nancy Anne born 27 January 1944, 608 Fifth Avenue, Gallipolis. Henry didn't enter military service during W.W. II.; however, he went to work at the T.N.T. (munitions) plant in Point Pleasant. Here he earned an award for bravery: the T. N. T. got over heated and instead of leaving the building he turned on the sprinklers. He retired from the Ohio Valley Laundry, and worked for a while at building houses.

Carol Yvonne married Charles Emmett Robinson and moved to Columbus, returning to Gallia Co. in 1985. Their children were Janet Lynn and Rebecca Sue.

Nancy Anne married Delbert Franklin Clark their children were: Pamela Anne (died at birth), Anna Marie, Debra Jane, and Kyle Aaron, who all live locally.

*Submitted by: Nancy Clark*

**EMMOR AND SARAH BAKER FOX -** Emmor Fox was born June 1, 1807, in Pennsylvania. Emmor married Sarah Ellen Baker (daughter of Joshua and Catharine Rutzer Baker) on September 25, 1828, in Chester, Pennsylvania. Sarah was born on January 20, 1806, in Pennsylvania.

Emmor and Sarah had nine children:

1. Joseph Gardner was born on March 27, 1831, in Pennsylvania. He married Jane Drake (1837-1868) on January 3, 1856 in Gallia County. After Jane's death, he married Almyra Shuck (1846-1929) on October 10, 1869, in Gallipolis. Joseph died on April 16, 1917, in Geneva, Nebraska.

2. Evaline was born May 11, 1833. She married Joseph Null (1829-1907) on January 20, 1859, in Gallia County. She died on September 1, 1882.

3. Joshua Baker was born on November 9, 1834. He married Elizabeth Worthington (1835-1909) on October 19, 1854, in Gallia County. Joshua died January 23, 1893.

4. Philena Fox was born November 12, 1837, in Ohio. She married Christopher Columbus Myers (1835-1893) on November 8, 1855, in Gallia County. Philena died on July 14, 1914, in Lawrence County.

5. Rachel Ann was born December 9, 1839. She married Wilbur Shuck on September 13, 1866, Gallia County.

6. Rebecca was born June 29, 1843, Walnut Township. She married Stephen Massie (1840-1915) on February 28, 1863, in Gallia County. During the Civil War, Stephen served in the 173$^{rd}$ OVI in the Tennessee campaigns. Rebecca died in 1905 and is buried with her husband in Okey Cemetery in Lawrence County.

7. Sarah Elizabeth was born September 19, 1845, in Walnut Township. She married Henry Pyles (1844-1917) on August 25, 1864, in Gallia County. Henry served in the 193$^{rd}$ OVI and dislocated his ankle during a march in 1865. In 1890, Henry applied for a pension, stating he was unable to plow due to lameness in his left ankle. Sarah died on March 24, 1924, in Walnut Township and is buried beside her husband in Fox-Fairview Cemetery.

8. Emmor Jr. was born on January 10, 1851, Ohio. He married Sarah Ellen Lawrence (1852-1879) on January 9, 1872, Ohio. After her death, he married Harriet Morrison (1851-1933) on December 15, 1889. Emmor died June 1, 1910, in Geneva, Nebraska.

Emmor Sr. died on September 28, 1868, in Walnut Township, Gallia County, Ohio. Sarah died October 11, 1878, in Walnut Township, Gallia County, Ohio. Emmor donated the land for Fox-Fairview Church and Cemetery in Walnut Township where they are both buried.

*Submitted by Jerry Berry*

**EMMOR FOX -** Emmor Fox was born June 1, 1807, in Pennsylvania. He married Sarah Baker who was born January 19, 1806. They were the parents of Sarah, who married Wilson Pyles; Evaline, who married Nicholas Null, and possibly others.

Emmor and Sarah gave the land for the Fox Fairview Cemetery in Walnut Township and helped build the church. He died September 28, 1868, and she died October 5, 1879.

**ROBERT (BOBBY) ALLEN FRANKLIN & PAMELA KAY (NOLAN) FRANKLIN -** Married January 29, 1976. They have resided at the residence of 3116 Kriner Rd. for 25 years.

*Robert and Pamela Franklin*

Robert, born in Gallipolis, is the son of the late James L. Franklin & Nora Irene (Coon) Franklin. He had one son from a previous marriage to June Heard of Bainbrldge, Georgia. His name is Robbie Heard and he is married to Paula and they have a son by named Matthew. They live in Donalsonville, Georgia.

Pamela, born in Gallipolis, is the daughter of David & Doris (Roach) Nolan. She has one son by a previous marriage to John Ervin Franklin. His name is James Allen Franklin born 9/1/73 and he is married to Carrie L. (Hill) Franklin and they have a son named Cole Mitchell, born November 3, 2000.

Robert & Pamela have a daughter named Shannon Marie, born May 17, 1976. She married Brandon L. Pratt February 11, 1995. They have a son, Tyler Matthew, who was born 7/16/98. They are expecting another child on or about 7/10/02. Another daughter is Rachel Leigh Franklin who was born on December 9, 1983. They all still reside in Gallipolis.

**JAMES FULTON & JANE MATTHEWS' FAMILY -** James and his family came to Gallia between 1803 and 1806. He had married Jane Matthews, daughter of William and Mary Wright Matthews, in VA in about 1775. Their first child and my third great grandmother was Mary (perhaps Anne) born in Augusta Co. VA Oct. 16 1776. She married Samuel C. Bing August 3, 1797 and moved north to Gallia Co. in 1803. Her parents and siblings may well have come at the same time though we have no proof of that.

Jane died in 1819 in Gallia and though there are rumors James married again I can't seem to find any proof of a second marriage. The rest of their family of two daughters and four sons were William B. 1778 married Jane (Jinney) Lockridge, died in Gallia Co. 8 Apr 1871; Margaret born 1780 married Ferdinand Kinkead in Augusta Co. VA March 19, 1799 and died after 1839 probably in Gallia Co. OH; Thomas born 1785 married Margaret Hix January 8, 1811 in Gallia Co. and died November 20, 1858; John born 1790 in VA married Mary (Polly) Martindill April 23, 1818 in Gallia Co. John married second Nancy Shaver Adkins after 1830 and died April 8, 1857; and last James A. R. born 1795 in Virginia married Margaret Gross May 1,1823 in Gallia and died in 1857.

Some of the proof for this family comes from William Matthews will signed January 10 1799 in Augusta County, VA and additional information came from 'The Mathews Family: an anthology of Mathews Lineages" compiled by John R. Boots, Jr., c 1970.

James Fulton was a Revolutionary Veteran. He died at 89 years of age and is buried in Bing 1 Cemetery where he has a stone designating his War service. This couple had fifty six grandchildren that I have found to date, leaving a great heritage.

**STANFORD FULTON FAMILY** - Stanford J. Fulton, son of Henry Clay Fulton and Nancy Ellen Bowen, was born in Gallia County on March 3, 1888, the fifth of nine children. A farmer all his life, Stanford, is the great grandson of James Fulton, who settled in Gallia County in 1806. He married Emma M. White on December 3, 1913, and proceeded to raise a family of 4 boys and 6 girls on 50 acres in Morton's woods, acquired through his lifetime employers, the Morton sisters. Stanford died from cancer on August 30, 1949. He is buried at Prospect Cemetery, along with 2 sons and 2 daughters (Morton, Stanford Jr., Margaret and Donna). The five oldest children went to Yale School, a one-room school house located on Bulaville Road near the Shrine Club. Morton died at age 17 when he fell off the wagon he was riding in. Margaret and Donna died very young, age 3 and 1.

Eleanor, the oldest, had a son Robert (Jack). She made her home in the MacArthur, Ohio, area. She is buried near Albany, Ohio. Her boy, Jack, has 4 children and 4 grandchildren. He lives near Radcliff, Ohio.

Stanford's oldest boy, Charles Owen, served in WWII, married the former Marcella Bradley, and moved to the Dayton, Ohio, area. They had 3 children: Charlie, Judith and Charles. Charles Owen died in 1964 from an airplane accident. His youngest son, Charles Owen, Jr., died in 1968.

Florence Marie married Elmer Gothard on August 16, 1942, and raised five children, of whom 3 survive. Donna May and Russell Monroe are buried at Prospect while Elmer Eugene and Mary Ann now live in Texas. Florence lives with her youngest girl, Betty Jo Taylor, outside Gallipolis.

Edward A. Fulton served in the Korean War, married Ruth Ann Harlen, and had 7 children, one living in Florida and the rest around Ohio. They are Donald, Betty, Karen, Kenneth, Brenda, and Debra. Ed's wife passed away in 1995 from cancer. Ed lives in Bellevue, Ohio.

Next in line was Alberta Evelena. She married Robert Racer on May 15, 1947, bearing 3 children: Barbara, Robert and Mark. She made her home at the home place on Morton Woods Road. Alberta passed away on September 22, 1997. She is buried next to her husband at Rife Cemetery. All three children have their homes on the Morton Woods home site.

Della Faye was born December 28, 1932. She married Donald Winkel on April 30, 1951. They have 2 children: Dennis and Dianna, 5 grandchildren, and 1 great grandson. They make their home just outside Sandusky, Ohio. Della's husband is a retired electrician from General Motors.

Stanford Jr., the youngest, married Betty Venable on May 1, 1956. Stan lived in the Sandusky area after serving in the U.S. Army. He died in 1994 and is buried near his father at Prospect. They had 5 children, with Laurie, Dawn and Kelly, living in Indiana. Andrea died in 1962 and Jesse died in 1995.

*Submitted by Della (Fulton) Winkel*

**ROBERT KEITH AND JO ELLEN (BURNETT) GARBESI FAMILY** - Robert was born July 25, 1956, in Wheeling, WV, to Robert Eugene and Jean Kreachbaum Garbesi. He lived in Mt. Pleasant, OH, with his parents, brother Curtis Allen and sister Marilyn Denise until 1967 when the family relocated to the Pittsburgh, PA area of McMurray. Bob was active in football and cross country in high school and graduated from Peters Township High School in 1975. He attended WVU and worked for Fairmont Supply Company (CONSOL-DUPONT) in Washington, PA and Nashville, TN until 1989 when he and his family moved to Gallipolis. He now works for Burnett's Heating & Cooling, a family owned business since 1958.

Bob married Jo Ellen Burnett in 1981. (See Clyde Burnett family history.) Jo graduated from Gallia Academy High School in 1972 and from the Holzer School of Nursing in 1975. After marrying, they lived in Washington, PA. She worked at Magee Womens Hospital in the Neonatal Intensive Care Unit. Their first daughter, Jessica Nicole, was born at Magee Womens Hospital December 12, 1984. In 1985, Bob transferred to the Nashville, TN branch of Fairmont Supply. Their second daughter, Maria Gail, was born at Baptist Hospital July 30, 1986. Jo is employed by Holzer Medical Center in the Surgical Department.

Jessica is a junior at GAHS. She is a flutist with the marching and symphonic bands, active in tennis, gymnastics, and enjoys school activities. A member of the Rio Wranglers 4-H Club, she is active in 4-H and loves horse back riding. She loves her Arabian mare, SH Shenannigans.

Maria is a sophomore at GAHS. She plays the saxophone, participates in track and field as well as cross country, and enjoys many school sporting events. She is also a member of Rio Wranglers and loves horse back riding. She loves her Arabian gelding, Geyms Duke.

Bob's maternal grandparents trace to parts of Germany and paternal grandparents Northern Italy, hence the Italian name Garbesi. Bob and Jo own a 52 acre farm which originally belonged to Jo's maternal grandparents, John Gordon and Miriam Dunn Hudson.

They plan to remain in Gallia County raising their Arabian horses, and enjoying the comforts of home in Gallipolis.

**ALONZO BEEMER GARRETT** - Alonzo Beemer Garrett was born in Wayne Co., Va. on Jan. 21, 1847, son of Louis P. and Sarah E. (Hite) Garrett.

*Dr. Alonzo Beemer Garrett And Nancy Elizabeth Jones Garrett*

Loius P. Garrett was born in Wayne Co., Va. Oct. 8, 1821. He later moved to Catlettsburg, Ky. where he became a merchant. He died May 7, 1896. He married his wife at Burlington, Ohio on Oct. 12, 1844. She was born Oct. 10, 1826 and died at Catlettsburg April 19, 1922. She was the daughter of William Hite. His grandfather, Baron Von Yost Heidt emigrated from Germany to America in 1710 and after seeing the beautiful Shenandoah Valley, obtained a grant of several thousand acres of land in the valley from the King of England and founded a colony. He built a stone house in which there had been set a marble slab, stating that he was the first settler of the valley.

Alonzo Beemer Garrett, the subject of this sketch, received instructions from private tutors and was a student of Catlettsburg Academy and normal school and of the Eclectic Medical College of Cincinnati, Ohio 1866 to 1873. He became principle of a high school in 1867 and of the high school in Guyandote, W.Va. in 1868. He then practiced medicine in Gallipolis, Rutland, and Pomeroy, Ohio 1873 to 1885 and in Wayne Co. W.Va. 1885 to 1901. In 1896 he was elected to the State Senate from the Sixth Senatorial District of W.Va. He later was appointed American Consul to Nuevo Laredo, Mexico by President William McKinley and served in that capacity, 1901 to 1917 holding office during the administrations of Presidents Theodore Roosevelt, William Howard Taft, Woodrow Wilson, Warren G. Harding and Calvin Coolidge. He served as American Consul 1917 to 1924 at St. Stephen, New Brunswick, Canada. In 1925 he resumed the practice of medicine in Gallipolis where he continued until a short time prior to his death, which occurred Nov. 2, 1938. He is buried in Mound Hill Cemetery, Gallipolis.

When 14 years of age he enlisted as a drummer boy for service in the Civil War, selling his watch to buy the drum. He served in the 14th and 45th Ky. Mounted Infantry from July 1861 to Dec. 24, 1864 and was under the command of General James A Garfield (who later became president of the U.S.) during the Battle of Middlecreek, Ky. He was one of the first members of the G.A.R. and served as assistant inspector general in 1900, as national surgeon general, 1933/34, and in 1929 was medical director of the Department of Ohio. He was commander of Cadot Post No. 126 in Gallipolis and a member of several local lodges and the M.E. Church.

Doctor Garrett married Nancy Elizabeth (Libbie) Jones on March 14, 1878 in Gallipolis. She was the daughter of Levi Campbell Jones and Nancy Rife Jones, born July 21, 1862. Their children were Louis M. who was born July 23, 1879 and died June 30, 1886 and Francis Eugenie who was born Aug. 9, 1881 and died Sept. 14, 1881.

When I, Myron E. Jones, Jr. was 7 years old, we visited my great, great uncle and he had me shake his hand telling me that that hand had shaken the hands of President Lincoln and all of the presidents through President Roosevelt.

*Submitted by Myron E. Jones, Jr.*

**GATEWOOD FAMILY** - James Monroe Gatewood born Amherst Co., Va. January 17, 1817 and died Gallia County, Ohio February 5, 1901, was the first known Gatewood in Gallia County. At the age of 18 years, James engaged in the lumber business and learned the trade of a carpenter. The latter part of 1847, he bought land on Raccoon Island, Gallia Co. and went to farming and boating wood. He continued that business until August 1862 when James volunteered for the Union army and served 3 years, less 18 days. May 1868, James formed a company partnership with W. G. Fuller & Co., to manufacture furniture. December 1868, the first factory whistle blew in Gallipolis. In 1878, James sold his interest in the factory and 1880, built a sawmill known as Gatewood Lumber Company. Gatewood Lumber Company and Gatewood, Fuller & Co. merged in 1890 to become Gallipolis Furniture Factory. James married Virginia Lowry and had the following children: William married May Short, James Madison married Margaret Sheets, Emma married Anthony Kerns, (Emma Gatewood Kerns was a Charter member of French Colony Daughters of the American Revolution in Gallipolis), Kate married Charles Small and their daughter Maybelle Small journalist Oscar Odd McInytre, Sabrina married Stanley Brady, Laura married Charles Mullineaux, Charles Ringold married Laura Sims, Edgar married Jessie Bradbury, Nelle married George Bovie, Isadore and Louis died at a young age.

James Madison joined the army of the Civil War in Company G, Ohio Infantry in 1865 and was sent to camp near Charleston, WV. Soldiers were being discharged when he reached the Shenandoah Valley so he was placed on police duty until his discharge. In 1866, James went to Columbus, Ohio and enlisted in Co. C 31 Regulars. He was sent to New York then by boat to San Francisco, Portland and Fort Vancouver helping build Camp Hearuey. He was at the Battle of Caverus and was at the discovery of Goose Lake in California. He married Margaret Sheets on his return to Gallia County and had the following children: Olive married Ernest Housekeeper, Minnie married Trimble Jones, Arthur Paul married (1st) Irene and (2nd) Mary, Emma married Kenneth Leighton, Virginia and Ethel never married, Perry Clayton married Emma Caldwell (divorced), Melvin married Annabelle Owens, Major was killed in WWI and buried Meuse-Argonne American Cemetery, Romagne-sous-Montfaucon, (Meuse), France, Louise married Dwight Ghrist.

*James Madison and Margaret Sheets Gatewood family. Front Row: Ethel, Margaret, James, Virginia, Perry. Back Row: Melvin, Emma, Louise, Minnie, Olive, Paul.*

*Children of Perry Clayton and Emma Caldwell Gatewood Kneeling: Nelson, Monroe, William Standing: Robert, Ruth, Helen, Louise, Rowena, Esther, Louise, Elizabeth*

Perry Clayton Gatewood born October 21, 1889 died March 1, 1968 married Emma Caldwell. Perry graduated from Ohio Northern University with a teaching degree but spent many years in the same profession as his grandfather, a carpenter and also served as mayor of Crown City. His ex-wife, Emma Caldwell Gatewood at the age of 68, was famous in her own right becoming the first women to walk the Appalachian trail in its entirety in one season. She continued hiking until her death in 1973. PC and Emma's children were: Helen married Harold Moore, Ruth married (1st) Lewis Williams (divorced), (2nd) Carl Lemnitzer (divorced), Monroe married Marjorie Williams, William married (1st) Viola Caldwell (died), (2nd)Hazel Unroe, Rowena married Ernest Zenk, Esther married David Allen, Robert married Betty Seaver, Elizabeth married Anton Novak, (divorced), Nelson married (1st) Ella Hawkins (2nd) Phyllis Mesenbrink, Louise married (1st) Gilbert Milliron (divorced) (2nd) Neil LaMott, Lucy married Robert Seeds.

Ernest Monroe was born June 18, 1911, Crown City, Ohio died July 19, 1978 married Marjorie Williams. Monroe retired from the Ohio Bell Telephone Company serving as wire chief for many years. He with several others in Gallipolis helped to start the Little League Baseball Program now under the direction of Gallipolis Parks and Recreation. Monroe and Marjorie had the following children: Eleanor and Charles.

Eleanor born November 24, 1935 died June 29, 1979 married James Gilliam. Eleanor and Jim both attended Gallia Academy High School. During their senior year, her future husband and captain of the football team, Jim Gilliam, crowned Eleanor Homecoming Queen. Their children were: James Randall (Randy) married (1st) Karen Tabor (divorced) (2nd) Sue Adkins, Marjorie Lynn married Charles (Chuck) Wood, and Margaret Gwen married Dennis McGuire.

Randy and Karen had two daughters; Ginger Kay married Ronald Denney and Brandy Sue. Marjorie and Chuck's children are: Jessica Lynn married Michael Weber, Burton Charles and James Clayton. Gwen and Dennis have one son Joshua Neil.

Ginger and Ronnie have a daughter Krista Grace (Gracie). Jessica and Mike have a son Eric Michael Weber.

*Submitted by: Marjorie Gilliam Wood*

**BILLY RICHARD GEORGE** - Billy was the son of William Jasper and Nettie Mitchell George, born on April 6, 1933. He was raised on George Road about two miles west of Eno, attended Eno grade school and graduated from Bidwell-Porter High School in 1950. Bill spent three years in the army from 1953-1956 during the Korean Conflict. He married Mildred Marie Denney on September 9,1956, the daughter of Paul and Mary Moore Denney, born on April 17, 1939. In 1958, we moved to Chatham Avenue in Gallipolis. Bill was employed at Celenese Chemical Plant in Gallipolis Ferry, WV.

*The George Family*

We have a son, Gregory Richard, born in 1957, and four daughters: Nikki Marie, born in 1958, Vicki Von, born in 1960, Rita Kay, born in 1962, and Robin Ann, born in 1964.We moved to Kemper Hollow Road in 1963, where we lived until 1974, then moved to the Alex Thompson farm in Eno on State Route 554, which still remains our residence. Bill retired from the Akzo Chemical Plant ( Celenese, Stauffer) with 37+ years of service. Our five children graduated from North Gallia High School, Vinton, Ohio, and Buckeye Hills Vocational School of Rio Grande.

As of February 2002, we have 16 grandchildren, 3 great-grandchildren and are expecting three more great ones this spring.

## RICHARD "DICKIE" GEORGE FAMILY -
Richard was born in 1839 and married Mary Margaret Vance, who was from Vanceton, currently known as Morgan Center. They were married on March 16, 1864 in Gallia County and resided on Long Branch Road, one and half miles from Eno. They had ten children:

John Arnold - children: Monroe, Elsie and Wavel

Ben - children: Armendie ("Peach"), Bavena ("Dutch"), (Alvin), Russell, Benny, Leon Floyd, Martin and Ora Berry.

William Jasper - children: Fred Nance, Earl George, Opal - m Ray Hughes, Myrtle - m Charlie Logue and Goldie - m #1, Ivan Mitchell, #2, Charlie Mitchell and #3, Billy George Jacob V - children: Ray, Victory (Tuck), Ralph, Waley and Charles Wade

Elmer ("Mel") - children: Ewing, Wendell, Roy, Turley, Don, Ruby, - m Ern Russell, Fern, Glenna, m - Dewey Cockran and Larlyn ("Cluster") Russell.

Floena ("Lenie") - children: Harvey, Clarence, Gerald, Walter, Turley, Paul, Goldie, Hazel, - m Robert Grate, Earl and Dariel.

Margaret Roush ("Maggie") - children: Lola, m - Worthy Bright, Von and Burl Roush Tish Amy - married Lewis Throckmorton and had one daughter. Lived in Marion

*Submitted by J. C. Mitchell and Billy George*

## GETTLES FAMILY -
Beverly and Clare Gettles reside at 602 First Avenue, the former home of Elias Wetherholt, in Gallipolis. They were married on August 20, 1966, at the First Presbyterian Church.

*Clare & Beverly Gettles*

Clare is the son of Coleman Clare and Edna Arnold Gettles. Clare Gettles hailed from Frankfort, Ohio, and Edna Arnold's family was from Meigs County. Philip Roush, a Revolutionary War soldier, was an Arnold ancestor. Clare and Edna Gettles were married on March 3, 1933, in Gallipolis. Clare was the first president of the Gallipolis Chamber of Commerce, worked as an engineer on the construction of bridges and dams, and died of pneumoma after aiding victims of the 1937 flood. Dr. Edna Gettles graduated from Kirksville School of Osteopathic Medicine in Missouri in 1942. She practiced in Mason Country for many years with Dr. Roy Eshenaur at Point Clinic and died in 1985 in Gallipolis.

Beverly, the daughter of William Walter and Lorena Dunlap Webb, came to Gallia County from Harrison County, Ohio, in 1951 when Ohio River Collieries at Cheshire employed her father as master mechanic. Walt and Lorena were married on August 1, 1936, at Freeport, Ohio. Walt attended the University of Akron, and Lorena attended Ohio University and taught for five years in one-room schools in Harrison County. The Webbs ran Webbs' Grocery in Centenary from 1961 to 1983. Walt died in 1973. One of Walt's relatives was John Fitch, unaccredited inventor of the steamboat. Both the Webbs and Dunlaps settled in Harrison County prior to 1820.

Clare graduated from Greenbrier Military Academy, attended Georgia Institute of Technology, and served in the U.S. Air Force from 1958 to 1962. He retired from Babcock & Wilcox Construction Co. Beverly is a Gallia Academy, Rio Grande College, and Western Reserve graduate. She was librarian at Rio Grande College from 1961 to 1972. She retired in 1999 after 27 years at Hannan Trace, River Valley, and South Gallia.

Clare and Beverly are the parents of three children. Vicki McBrayer, formerly married to Charles McBrayer of Corbin, Kentucky, has three sons, Charles, William, and Joseph. Kathryn Gettles-Atwa graduated from New York University's College of Arts and Science, Institute of Fine Arts, and School of Law. She married Sami Atwa on July 12, 1996, in Brooklyn, New York, and is an attorney in New York City. Sam is from Cairo, Egypt, and attended Ain Shamps University in Heliopolis. James Gettles graduated from DeVry Institute of Technology in Electronics Engineering Technology and works for AdL Technology. He married Kendra Phillips of Athens on June 9, 2001, at the French Art Colony. Kendra graduated from the University of Rio Grande in 1999.

The Gettles are members of the First Presbyterian Church of Gallipolis where Beverly has served as deacon, trustee, elder and clerk of session. Beverly is a member of the Philomatheon, Riverside, and Books and Friends book clubs. Clare works at O'Dell Lumber, does woodworking as a hobby, and constructed a fourteen-foot rowboat christened the Dogham Queen.

## JONATHAN AND MARY GILBERT -
Information on this family has been very difficult to gather, due to the time period and lack of complete courthouse records. Even after extensive research, much information about this family remains a mystery. However, this story is submitted to honor their memory and encourage further research by their other descendants.

Jonathan Gilbert was born in New York 11 Sep 1780 and died 26 Nov 1861 in Green Township, Gallia County. He married Mary (IGS #F5 179996 indicates that Mary's surname was Lacy) probably in New York, although no proof of this has yet been found. My calculations from tombstone dates indicate that Mary was born 12 Nov 1786. Census records indicate either New York, New Jersey, or Massachusetts was her birthplace. Jonathan and Mary are both buried in Rose Cemetery in Green Township.

Mary "Polly" Gilbert, was born to them in 1810 either on Long Island or in Genesse County, New York. Many families by the name of Gilbert existed in New York in that time period. It would be a daunting task to sort through all of the J., John, and Jonathan Gilberts in the 1810 New York census index for this family.

Family tradition indicates that when Polly was ten years old, the family came to Gallia County by taking a flatboat down the Ohio River from Pittsburgh, Pennsylvania. How they got from New York to Pittsburgh was not included in the family story, unfortunately.

Jonathan Gilbert and a large family are found in Gallipolis Township in 1820 on page 42 of the federal census. In the household are: 3 males (to 10 years), 2 (10-16), 1 (16-26) and 1 *(26-45)*. There are 2 females (10-16), 1 (16-26), 1 *(26-45),* and 1 *(45+)*. Three family members were in agriculture.

A partial reconstruction of the family was made by consulting the records for Rose Cemetery, Gallia County marriage records, and obituaries. It is believed that some of the children are: Mary, who married Henry Kerns; Theodore, born c 1815, married Marietta (?), Mary Ellen Martin, and Samantha (?); Abraham, who married Mary Kerns, sister of Henry in Aug 1848; Harriet Eliza who married Stephen Northup on 21 Dec 1843; and Rebecca, born c1826. More information on Mary Gilbert and Henry Kerns is elsewhere in this book.

*Submitted by: Sunda Anderson Peters*

## JOSEPH GERALD GILES FAMILY -
Joseph Gerald Giles was born June 22, 1935 at his grandparents' home, in South Point, Ohio. His parents were Clarence Giles and Mabel Hazlett, the daughter of George W. and Mary O. (Webb) Hazlett. Joe was raised in his grandparents' home amongst his many aunts and uncles. His mother was one of the oldest of twelve children and although Joe was an only child, he was raised with a lot of "brothers and sisters". This probably accounts for his love of competition and sports.

*Alice and Joe Giles*

After graduating from South Point High School in 1954, Joe entered the Army, serving in Alaska while testing cold-weather gear and in Korea. After discharge from the army, Joe worked for Carolina Lumber Company in Point Pleasant, WV. He worked there for approximately three years before coming to the French City Lumber Company in Gallipolis, Ohio. James H. Staats of Point Pleasant, WV. and Joe left the lumber company after a few years, to start their own business in the mobile housing industry. August 1968, was the grand opening of the French City Home Center, Inc., with "Big Jim" as general manager and Joe as manager of the Mobile Home division. Joe worked there until his retirement in 1994, when he sold his half of the business to Jim's family.

Joe is a lifetime member of Kiwanis and served as president in 1972. He also has coached Little League baseball in the summer.

Shortly after coming to Gallipolis in 1957, Joe met Wanda Jeanette Thomas, daughter of Walter Benson and Evelyn M. (Wilcox) Thomas of Gallipolis, Ohio. Although Wanda attended schools in Gallipolis, she graduated from Rutland High School in Meigs County where she was caring for her grandparents at the time. Joe and Wanda were married March 25, 1961. Wanda worked as a telephone operator for 28 years at Ohio Bell Telephone in Gallipolis until the local switchboard closed in 1981. Although Joe and Wanda had no children of their own, they greatly enjoyed their nephews and their great-nephews and nieces. Wanda passed away on August 30, 1995.

On April 12, 1997, Joe and Alice Beard Pasquale (see Pasquale-Beard in this book) were married. Joe has attended First Baptist Church since 1959, and Alice has attended since 1942, but they never met until 1996 when they were in the same Sunday school class. Alice retired from nursing in 1998, and Joe was already retired. They both are active in the church and enjoy traveling with friends. Joe is on the Board of Trustees of the church and serves as an usher. One of Joe's passions is golfing wherever and whenever possible. He is an avid sports fan and both he and Alice enjoy going to sporting events and supporting the high school teams. When Joe and Alice married, Joe automatically became a grandpa, a role that he dearly loves. Both Alice and Joe greatly enjoy their grandchildren, Tessa and Levi Thompson and Alex and Mikayla Pasquale.

*Submitted by Joe Giles*

**WADE HAMPTON GILLISON** - Son of John R. Gillison and Ella Bessie Tinlsey was born May 17, 1897, Thurmond WV, Fayette County. He was one of four sibling.

1. Carrie Louise, birth date unknown, married Ephraim Mundell, August 28, 1916 by R. E. Dunn, Justice of the peace in Gallipolis, Gallia County

*H. Gillison*

2. Lillie Mae, born May 21, 1895 in Fayette County, married Henry Scruggs, son of Charles and Roma Smedley Scruggs, December 27, 1915. She died and is buried in North Lewisburg, Ohio.

3. Bessie Ella, born April 12, 1899, married Alexander "Cap" Smith, May 28, 1927. She died August 24, 1949.

Wade, Carrie, Bessie, his father and mother are buried in Providence Church Cemetery, Kerr, Oh. His father's brother, William E. Gillison is buried there also. William E. was pastor of this church in the 1920s.

The Gillison family roots are in Madison and Culpepper counties of Virginia where they were well known and still are. Wade and his sisters attended school in WV and Evergreen one-room school in Springfield Township, OH.

Wade's mother, Ella Bessie Tinsley Gillison was the daughter of Moses and Ellen Richardson Tinsley of East Virginia, born August 28, 1872. Died July 19, 1929 at age 56yrs, 10m 22d.

Wade had two aunts who lived in Virginia. 1. Everline Frances Gillison, who married King Haywood Arrington at Ettan, Madison Co., Va. They had one son, Wyatt Franklin and two grandsons - Wyatt Edgar and Leroy Arrington, Batimore, Md. 2. Annie Louise Gillison, married Harry Holden and they had four sons, James Wesley, Freddie, William Augustus and Melvin - three daughters, Lillie, Tillie and Maggie.

3. Alice Gillison married here first cousin William Gillison. Two sons, Gabe and Armstead, one daughter - Anna Louise Lindsay. She lives in Caledonia, N. Y.

Wade H. Gillison never married. His only descendants in this area are Hazel Marie Smith, deceased and Barbara Mae Smith Scott, daughters of Bessie and a grand nephew, Harreld Christian Scott.

Wade served his country as a soldier in World War I and World War II. He was an active member of the American Legion. He was a member of CCC (Civilian Conservation Corp) serving at Cadiz, Ohio. He was a well-known farmer in this area. He was a member of the Providence Baptist Church and is buried in that cemetery.

His family were coal miners in West Virginia in the early 1900s, but due to the health of his father and uncle, they bought 80 acres of land at Kerr, Oh to farm, later sold 15 acres to C. W. Pendleton. Wade lived on the remaining acreage until he became ill and moved to Gallipolis where he spent his last days with niece Barbars and her husband Harry Scott.

The Gillison land was given to the Providence Missionary Baptist Association by Hazel Smith and Barbara Scott in 1984.

**CARL WILMER AND CAROLYN JEAN (ALLISON) GILLESPIE FAMILY** - Carl's family of Gillespie descended from the MacPherson clan of Scotland. They immigrated to the United States in the early 1700's. The name Gillespie means the "keeper of the Kirk" (church), and they are Protestants.

Carl was born at home on April 10, 1934, in Gallia County, Green Township, Rodney community, to Troy Coe (son of James Thomas and Henrietta Little— Page Gillespie) and Clementine (Clemmie) Fuller (daughter of William Henderson and Pollianna Jones Fuller) Gillespie. They came to a farm on Cora Mill Road, Green Township, in the early 1900s from Greenbrier~ County, White Sulpher Springs, WV. They reared eleven children——with Clemmie becoming a widow and single mother after the death of Troy in September 1933. Carl's brothers and sisters are: Ismael, James, Henderson, Myrtle, Jean, Mary, Lola, Frank, Troy, and Ruth, all deceased except Myrtle, Jean and Mary. Carl attended Rodney Grade School, graduated from Gallia Academy High School in 1953, served in the U. S. Army from 1955 through 1957, retired from Kaiser/Ravenswood Aluminum Company in January 1997, after 39_ years of employment. He enjoys gardening, raising cattle, and was, at one time, an auctioneer.

The Allisons were of the MacAlister clan of Scotland and immigrated to the United States in the 1700s eventually settling in Haverstraw, NY and briefly in Greenbrier County, WV then in Green, Walnut, and Perry Townships, Gallia County.

*The Carl Wilmer and Carolyn Jean Allison Gillespie Family*

Jean was born in Saint Marys Hospital, Huntington, WV, on May 3, 1936, to Henry Wilson (son of Dom Pedro and Cora Gallaugher Allison) and Nola Miriam Elliott (daughter of Stephen Monroe and Carrie Lee Martin Elliott) Allison. Both Henry and Miriam were reared in Walnut Township and lived most of their lives in Gallia County with the exception of about eight years spent in the grocery business in Huntington, WV. Jean's brother and sisters are: Ronald Lee (Ruth Barr) Allison, Sandra Sue (Ralph) Hutchinson, and Judy Lynn (Russell) Fellure. Jean attended Mudsoc and Washington Grade Schools, graduated from Gallia Academy High School in 1954, worked as a secretary, bank teller, in home caregiver, homemaker and does volunteer work.

Carl and Jean met in high school and were married on April 10, 1955, Easter Sunday (also Carl's twenty-first birthday) at the First Church of the Nazarene, Second Avenue, Gallipolis. With the exception of six months, or so, of Carl's time in the army and spending their first Christmas away from home at Junction City, KS, they have lived in Gallia County-first in a small mobile home at 544 Second Avenue, then in their present home at 3930 SR 588, Gallipolis, since October 1957. Their Sons: Carl Marty, born January 19, 1958; Randy Jay, born April 2, 1959; and Travis Allison, born January 16, 1973; were reared here. Marty (Sharon) with sons Powers and Bruce Gillespie and Caleb Patrick live at Mt. Sterling, KY. Randy lives at the home place on 588. Travis lives in Nashville, TN. All three also graduated from Gallia Academy High School.

Carl and Jean are very .active members of Rodney United Methodist Church. The entire family enjoys playing various musical instruments and singing. Even their grandsons now are learning to play guitars and can sing well. This love of music seems to have been passed down through the generations of both sides of the family.

*Submitted by Jean Allison Gillespie*

**GILLIAM** - This is a continuation of the history of Marcella Ann Walker Harrison Gilliam from 1980. Marcella was married to Marion (Jack) Harrison, an employee of AEP as an Investigator and Collector and she worked at GDC as an LPN. In 1986 Jack contacted the virus Guillian Berre. He was paralyzed from his neck down and it took several months of therapy before he was able to walk. After their retirement Marcella and Jack took a trip to Europe and began camping and spending winters in Florida. On February 2, 1995 they were in Melbourne Florida at Long Point Campgrounds where Jack suffered a massive heart attack and died. He was 64 years old.

Marcella became reacquainted with John Gilliam who lived in the area where she had grown up. His wife Susan had died of cancer. Marcella and John were married May 25th, 1996. John had retired after 40 years from Heidelberg Printing Company as a Service Representative.

*John & Marcella Ann Walker Gilliam*

John and Susan had two sons, John Sherman and David. John is an M.D. in Oklahoma and Dave owns Gilliam Machinery Company at Wilmington. John has eight grandchildren. Marcella and Jack's son Mark now lives in Gallipolis and works at Kyger Creek Power Plant. Mark's wife Cindy is a Nurse Manager for Pediatrics and Obstetrics Department at Holzers. Mark and Cindy have three children, Emily a junior at Rio University, Beau a senior and Ory a freshman at Gallia Academy.

Marcella and Jack's daughter Marlene is married to Fred Childers and they live in Mills Village. Marlene is a Nurse Trainer in Department of Surgery at Holzer Clinic. She has a daughter Chelsi in fifth grade and son Joshua in first grade at Washington Elementary.

Fred is a supervisor of Department of Human Services for Gallia County.

Marcella and John live on a farm south of Rio Grande. They spend time traveling and camping with friends. They spend winters in Florida where John enjoys surf fishing and Marcella is content to shop for antiques and read. Marcella is president of the Cora WSCW, member of the DAR, Gallipolis Eastern Star, Women's Circle at Grace Church and treasurer of Rio Grande Garden Club. John belongs to VFW, Post 4464 Thurman Masonic Lodge and serves as an usher and trustee at Grace Methodist where they are both members.

Marcella and John enjoy their thirteen grandchildren and spend as much time as possible with their four children. She feels her parents instilled in each of their children the importance of family. John was an only child and his parents Jesse and Sylvia are both deceased. He is "Brother John" to Marcella's sisters and enjoys being a part of the Walker family. Both Marcella and John enjoy good health and are thankful for all they have, living in a great country and most of all enjoy their friends and relatives in Gallia County. They feel it is nice to travel and see other parts of the world but always nice to come home.

**GILLUM/GILLIAM FAMILY** - Hugh Gillum/Gilliam born July 13, 1909 in Elliott County, Kentucky came to Gallia County with his wife and children during the 1940's. Hugh was married April 1, 1931 in Elliott County, Kentucky to Irene Lura Fraley. At a young age, Hugh went to the coal mines with his father, John Gillum. Hugh and Irene lived in Stirrat, Logan County, West Virginia where Hugh worked in the coal mines until an injury caused him to leave mining. They brought their family to Green Township, Gallia County, Ohio and bought a farm and began farming. Irene changed the spelling of the name Gillum to Gilliam when they came to Ohio. Irene worked at Holzer Hospital as a telephone operator. They had the following children: June Marie married Clifford Scott, James Randall married Eleanor Gertrude Gatewood and Juanita Jeanette married (1'st) Glen Crabtee (deceased) (2111) Joel Atha (deceased).

*Hugh and Irene Fraley Gilliam at 25th Anniversary*

James Randall Gillum born March 2, 1934, Stirrat, Logan County, West Virginia married Eleanor Gertrude Gatewood. Jim played football in school and was one of the smallest people on the field but was one of the toughest. Captain of the team his senior year, he had the pleasure of crowning his future wife, Eleanor, homecoming queen. Jim owned West Side Transfer Moving Company in Marietta, Ohio at the time of his death, March 9, 1975. He planned to move his family to Marietta but because of his death the company was sold and Eleanor and the children stayed in Gallipolis. Jim and Eleanor had the following children: James Randall (Randy) married (lst.) Karen Tabor (divorced), (2nd.) Sue Adkins, Marjorie Lynn married Charles David Wood, Margaret Gwen married Dennis McGuire.

Randy and Karen had the following children and grandchild: Ginger Kay married Ronnie Denney and they have a daughter Krista Grace (Gracie). Gwen and Dennis have one son Joshua Neil.

*First Row: Juanita Gilliam Crabtree, June Gilliam Scott, Eleanor Gatewood Gilliam. Row two: Glenn Crabtree, Clifford Scott, James (Jim) Gilliam*

Marjorie and Chuck married March 27, 1976 at Grace United Methodist Church, Gallipolis, Ohio. Marjorie is a secretary at Carter's Plumbing, Inc. Gallipolis and Chuck works for AEP as a transmission lineman. Marjorie is currently president of the Gallia County Genealogy Society, historian for French Colony DAR and Grace United Methodist Church. Marjorie and Chuck have the following children: Jessica Lynn, Burton Charles and James Clayton.

Jessica is married to Michael Weber and they have a son Eric Michael Weber. Jessica was active in choir and worked on the school yearbook while in high school. She attended University of Rio Grande and is now a stay at home mother. Burt while in high school set many Ohio high school records in track as a thrower of shot put and discus. He attended the University of Tennessee, Knoxville, TN and University of Rio Grande, Rio Grande, Ohio and has helped coach many high school and college athletes in these sports. Clayton is currently at West Liberty State College, West Liberty, West Virginia studying graphic design. Clayton has decided to attend college in Ohio next fall and may change his major. While in high school Burt and Clayton participated in football and wrestled. While Burt excelled in track, Clayton excelled in wrestling and both in football.

*Submitted by: Marjorie Gilliam Wood*

**GLASSBURN FAMILY** - My Great, Great, Great, Great Grandfather came here in 1774.

David Glassburn, born 1730-1832 came here during the Battle of Point Pleasant, Oct. 10, 1774 or Lord Dunmore War now considered The First Battle of Revolutionary War. He was wounded hereabouts and recovered at the spring where we now get our water.

John Glassburn, the oldest son of David, born 1779 died 1856, married Mary Richardson in 1802. In 1804 they moved to Gallia County.

David Glassburn, second son of John & Mary Glassburn, was the first white child born in Springfield township 1805 died 1895, he married Mary Sawyers and was a supervisor of Gailia County for 28 yrs.

Nathaniel, their fourth child born 1839 died 1913, married Sarah M Vaughn, Sept. 1857. Clem Glassburn was their seventh child born 1884-1954. He married Rose Cloud in 1908.

Their first child, Vaughn Cloud Glassburn was born July 1909 died Nov. 1990, married Thena Jane Moore, Oct. 24, 1931.

Their first and only child, James Vaughn Glassburn was born Aug. 29, 1941. His first child was James C. Glassburn, of Bidwell, born Dec. 15, 1966. He has two sons, James R. Glassburn and Joshua L. Glassburn. His second child, Jane A. (Glassburn) Brandeberry, born May 20, 1972, of Bidwell, married Michael L. Brandeberry of Rio Grande on June 26,1993. They have two sons, Levi K. and Jacobi W. Brandeberry. His third child, Aimee E. (Glassburn) Smittle, of Rio Grande, was born April 11, 1973. She has three children, Shelby V. Smittle, Chelsea A. Brown and Ty I. Smittle.

James V. Glassburn married JoAnne Switzer, (born June 20, 1951) on Dec. 8, 1989. Her first child was Anthony W. Switzer, born Dec 6,1968 of Newport News, VA. he married, Michelle Arrington on May 23, 1998. They have one daughter, Serena Arrington. Her second born were twins, Thomas L. Switzer of Vinton, and Timothy A. Switzer of Huntington, WV. Born Nov. 12, 1976. Thomas has one daughter Lindsay N. Switzer. *Submitted by: James V. Glassburn*

**GOODALL FAMILY** - Alonzo Cushing Goodall was born December 22, 1873 at Henderson, WV., one of eight children; Melinda (Lynn), Benjamin (Ben), William, Sarah, Florence, Mary and John, to William Townshend and Virginia Ann Teays Goodall.

*Goodall Family
Alma Goodall, Alonzo Cushing Goodall Holding Elsie Goodall Ca. 1902*

Alonzo was a coal miner, carpenter and farmer. He worked in the West Virginia coal fields in his early days. Alonzo married Georgia Ann Monroe, who was born in 1882, and died July 15,1903. They were married in July 1898. They had two daughters, Alma Cushing Goodall, born July 12, 1899, and Elsie Myrl, born July 2, 1901.

Alma married Alfred Waugh, who was born January 28, 1892, and died March 10, 1971. They had two daughters, Opal and Fern. Elsie married Elmo Adkins. Their children were Elmo (Moe) and Pearlie Mae. Alma, Elsie and their husbands are deceased.

Alonzo Goodall married, his second wife, Elizabeth Ann Porter. She had three sons from a former marriage, Gordon, Fred and Benjamin Lincoln Franklin.

Gordon was a pile driver, helping to build the Silver Bridge.

Alonzo and Elizabeth Porter Franklin had two sons, James Lester, born October 16, 1904, died August 7, 1981; and Alonzo Cushing (Cush) Goodall, Jr. born January 12, 1907, died March 9, 1955.

James Lester Goodall married Stella Leona Butcher, Daughter of Thomas and Alice Elizabeth Smith Butcher, children; Alice Elizabeth (died in infancy), and James McCullough Goodall, born December 28, 1929. Stella died in 1995. Lester's second wife was Georgia Viola Butcher, (1912-1997),daughter of Thomas and Alice Elizabeth Smith Butcher. Their children Delores Faye, born August 24, 1933; Warren Ralph born July 9, 1938; Rita Sue, born October 6, 1946; and Dr. Thomas Goodall, born July 19, 1948.

Alonzo Cushing Goodall Jr. married Flo Waugh. Their children were Harry and Florene Goodall.

Alonzo Cushing Goodall Sr. married Edna Ethel Stewart, adopted daughter of Benjamin (Ben) and Virginia Siders Stewart. They had three children; Betty Jean, born January 3, 1934; John William, born 1935 and Charles Jr. born 1936. Both boys died in infancy

Alonzo worked in the coal mines in Ohio. He farmed the old William Bray farm (later known as the Tracy Casto farm) on Fairview Road. in Springfield Township, Gallia County, not far from Bidwell, Ohio. All of Alonzo and Edna's children were born there.

The Goodalls moved from the Bray farm to a farm in Gravel Valley, near Vinton, Ohio, then they moved to the Chauncey Porter farm near Yellowtown; going from there to a farm near Bladen, Ohio. They moved to Storys Run, Cheshire, Ohio, where Alonzo again worked in the coal mines. From there, the family moved to the Coughenour Hollow, then to Ripley Hollow, where Alonzo died March 3, 1941.

After Alonzo's death, Edna and Betty went to Luella and Lincoln (Live) Butcher's home on Little Kyger Road. They then went to Cincinnati, in August 1941, where Edna was employed as a domestic by Carrie and Paul DesBennett.

Edna and Betty returned to Gallia County, February 28, 1942 to live with Edna's uncle and aunt ,Thomas and Zoie Butcher. Thomas was Edna's mother, Sarah brother.

Betty grew up in her great uncle and great aunt's home from age 8. Edna lived there until 1974, except for the years 1948-1952, when she worked in Huntington, WV for Anna and Adelbert James. She returned to Ohio and worked as a care giver for Eliza Swick in Vinton, Ohio. She returned to the Butcher home in the summer of 1952 to care for her aunt Zoie. She, her daughter, Betty, Betty's husband Charles Cantrell and their daughter, Pearl and Mary lived with Zoie until her death in 1972. Thomas died in 1957.

*Submitted by James M. Goodall
See also Charles and Betty Goodall Cantrell Family and John Sylvester Butcher Family*

**DAVID AND CYNTHIA (CINDY) ROUSH GRAHAM FAMILY** - Both Cindy and David were born in Gallipolis, Oh. David's parents are E. Glenn and Jacqueline (Grubb) Graham. He was born March 25, 1956, attended grade school at Green Elementary and graduated with Gallia Academy Class of 1975. While in school he was very active in 4-H, FFA activities and varsity football. Presently he works the family farm and is employed at Kaiser Aluminum, Ravenswood, WV. Cindy's parents are Jim and Roberta (Bertie) Johnson Roush. Cindy was born February 18, 1957, attended Washington Elementary Grade School and graduated from Gallia Academy High School, Class of 1975. While attending school, she was involved with Girl Scouting for over ten years and attained the rank of Senior Girl Scout, was crowned Miss Gallia County, 1973, and graduated in the top 10% of her graduating class. She graduated from the University of Rio Grande, magna cum laude, with a degree in Communications and returned to college within a few years and received her certificate to teach high school. Presently she teaches honors classes in English and speech at River Valley High School, Cheshire, OH. Her hobbies include her family and their activities and working with young people.

David and Cindy have three children. David James (Jamie) was born September 7, 1976 in Gallipolis, Ohio, attended Green Elementary School where he was very active in all sports and upon attending River Valley High School continued playing sports (football and basketball) and graduated from River Valley High School with the Class of 1996. Presently he helps his father and grandfather with the family farm in Northup, Oh and works for the State of Ohio as a meat inspector. He attended college in Wyoming. Martha Cathryn (Cassie) Graham was born December 11,1982 in Gallipolis, OH, attended Green Elementary School and graduated in the top 10% of her class from Gallia Academy High School, 2001. While attending high school, Cassie was very involved with sports (volleyball and softball) and during her senior year was named to the S.E.O.A.L. First team for volleyball. She also represented the Gallia Academy High School Key Club in world competition for public speaking twice and won second place in the world in Atlanta, GA and first place in the world in Chicago, Il. She was president of the Key Club. Cassie was very involved in 4-H for over ten years. Presently she is attending Ohio State University and was accepted into the John Glenn Institute on campus. At OSU, Cassie actively participates in Campus Crusades.

Joseph (Joey) Cole Graham, the third child, was born November 5, 1985 in Gallipolis, Oh. Joey attended Green Elementary School and presently attends River Valley High School. Like his siblings, he is very involved with sports (football, wrestling and baseball). Also, Joe has been a 4-H-er since becoming old enough to be a member. He shows cattle and hogs at the Gallia County Junior Fair, is active with Phoenix, the singing group at River Valley High School and FFA. He attends 4-H camp regularly and is a camp counselor.

Cindy and Cassie are members of French Colony Chapter Daughters of the American Revolution. Cindy and the three children can trace their ancestry to Revolutionary War soldier, Levi Trowbridge. All three children have previously been active members of Fleur-de-lis Society, C.A.R. (Children of the American Revolution).

This entire family currently attends and participates actively in Elizabeth Chapel Church.

*Submitted by Cynthia Graham*

**HIRAM T. GROSECLOSE** - Hiram T. Groseclose, son of William Petrus and Sarah (Tobler) Groseclose, was born 23/26 July 1830 in Wythe County, Virginia. He married Frances Jane, daughter of Francis S. and Phillipina "Phoebe" (Chappell) Thompson 15 November 1854 in Wythe County. Frances Jane Thompson was born April 1837, probably in Wytheville, Virginia. Hiram was a farmer and served in the Civil War (Pvt., Co. G, 195th " Regiment Ohio Vol. Inf.). He enlisted at Gallia County on 20 February 1865 and was discharged at Alexandria, Virginia on 18 December of that year.

Hiram and Frances removed from Wythe County shortly after their marriage. Based on the birth places of their children as given in census and other records, the family stopped in West Virginia from at least September of 1855 through March of 1858. They then removed to Gallia County between March 1858 and August 1862.

The couple had ten children, some of whom shortened their surname to Grose. All but the first two children were born in Gallia County.

Phoebe Ellen (or Phoebe Elizabeth) was born 3 September 1855 in West Virginia and married James R. Wolf 6 February 1873.

Mary Luvica Alice was born 26 March 1858 in Seven-Mile, Cabell County, West Virginia. She may have married James P. Lambert 20 April 1877, but certainly married James Harvey Sheets son of Henry Wilson and Mary Jane (Bailey) 14 July 1878.

James H. Grose, born 26 August 1862, married Mary Saunders 17 May 1883.

Agnes V. Grose, born 30 November 1864, married Jeremiah P. Gothard son of John R. and Rachel A. (Clark or White) 31 October 1884.

Lucy A., born 11 June 1867, married William Harbour son of Richard P. and Clarinda (Stover) 16 December 1888.

Elmon Elmer Grose, born 10 March 1870, married Eliza Jane about 1893.

Earnest E. Grose, born 16 December 1872, married Anis Wray 29 January 1895.

Robert F., born 18 December 1874, probably died young and was buried at Stewart Cemetery in Guyan Township.

Minnie E., born 2 August 1877 in Yoho, married Jonas B. Starkey son of Edward and Catherine (Barnett) 13 October 1904.

Daniel W., born 30 August 1881 Crown City, married Nellie E. (or Nettie E.) Sims daughter of Dallas and Izola (Truesdell) 18 June 1901.

Hiram Groseclose died 17 November 1903 in Creuzet and was buried at Stewart Cemetery in Guyan Township. Frances Jane died 7 April 1905 and was buried beside her husband. 1403 Words]

*Submitted by Linda Gaylord-Kuhn*

**MARILYN BROOKS GROSSI** - Marilyn was born in Rodney, Ohio, and is a granddaughter of Joseph and Tracie DeLille. She is also a great granddaughter of Reverend George W. Brooks and Dorothy E. Brooks, both long time residents of Rio Grande. Both sets of grandparents are buried at Calvary Cemetery in Rio Grande.

Marilyn's parents were George Randall Brooks and Geneva DeLille Brooks, who were both born in Rodney. They both also graduated from high school in Rio Grande. Marilyn has a sister named Carolyn McClain, who lives in Redlands, California and a brother named George Brooks. He resides in Mission, Texas.

After high school, Marilyn lived in California for many years, including, San Bernardino, Lancaster and Santa Barbara. But now she has returned home and lives in Columbus (Dublin). Her maternal family have been long time residents of Gallia County, since 1818 and she is proud to be the niece of several aunts and uncles in the area.

In the summer of 2001, Marilyn planned a reunion of the Brooks family and had sixteen members attend for activities such as, taking a tour of family cemeteries, grabbing a snack at an ice cream shop where many generations before had been and visiting the old home in Rio Grande. It was the highlight of the reunion. Amongst the family members present was Marilyn's aunt, Anne Brooks Benjamin. She is originally from Ohio and has written for the County Historical Society.

Marilyn's daughter, Rachel Brooks-Rather, has also relocated to her mother's home of Ohio. She is currently attending Ohio University and is working towards her Ph.D. degree in English. She plans to one day be a college professor.

They are proud to be descendents of some of the founders of Gallia County, including Antoine DeLille, whom Marilyn is the great, great, great granddaughter of.

**MARY AND RICHARD GROVES** - Richard G. Groves came to Gallipolis, Ohio in the fall of 1966, after retiring from the Navy. He was born and raised in Bellefontaine, Ohio. He went to the Navy 2-3-1945 at the age of 17 and spent 21 years in the Navy. After 13 years of service, he married Mary E. Wilcoxon, she was born and raised in Gallipolis, Ohio, and graduated from Gallia Academy H.S. in 1948. Mary went to live in West Liberty Ohio in 1951 and met Richard in 1957. They married in August 15, 1958, and went to Bremerton, Wash., where Richard served about three yrs. While there, Mark Richard Groves was born July 27th 1959 and Janet Lynn Groves was born May 26, 1961. Then we moved to Long Beach, Calif. and Richard was on the USS Hornet No. 9 and we spent about 2 yrs. there.

Richard was on the Honor Guard when Pres. Harry S. Truman was elected and marched in the inaugural parade (1948).

We went to the Philippines the day after President Kennedy was killed. We stayed in the Philippines for almost three yrs. Mary went to work for Robbins Myers the first day of June 1967, the day the plant opened. She worked there for 25 years and 3 mos. and retired in 1992. Mary is an avid quilter.

Mark and Janet both graduated from Gallia Academy. Mark graduated from Marshall University in 1982. Janet graduated from Rio Grande College in 1986.

Mark is married to Lois Peters Bosley, and they live in Pt. Pleasant, WV, with Zach Bosley, Lois's son.

Janet lives in Barboursville and works at M.G. This used to be Goodyear.

Mark works at the City National Banks.

Direct surname from Gallia County include: Beck, Denney, Fletcher, Chapman, Jones, Rothgeb, Rife, Martindale, Wilcoxon, Sheets and Sanders.

Mary, Mark and Janet are members of the first families of Gallia Co.

**LEOTA ANN WALKER GUINTHER** - Leota Ann Walker was born December 19, 1924 in Gallipolis, OH. to Lee Walker (1902-1988) and Grace Ellen Roush (1909-1982).

Lee was born in Gallipolis, OH. to Vinton Walker and Ella N. Robbins. Vinton and Ella moved to Gallipolis from Mason County, WV. The siblings of Lee were: Hugh, Lona, Ruth, Nancy, and Vivian. All of the children left Gallia County except Hugh and Nancy. After Lee and Grace divorced Lee left Gallia County for California to pursue a career in horse racing. Having been raised next to the old Fair Grounds in Maple Shade, Lee had racing in his blood from a very early age, in his mid to late years he was a trainer. He died in Florida in 1988.

Grace Ellen Roush was born March 10, 1909 in Addison Township to Susan Warner and Orrin Roush. Other children by this marriage were; Faye Merle Roush Reese and Ray Roush. After Susan & Orrin divorced, she purchased a house in Maple Shade, next to the old Fair Grounds. Susie married a second time to James Monroe Smith, and they had one daughter, Mary Jane Smith. The house on Chatham Avenue saw five generations come and go.

Grace's entire life revolved around hard work (which is a trait she thankfully passed on to her grandchildren). She went to work at the O.H.E. / G.S.I. when she was 16 years old. She retired after completing 52 years of service. When not working at the G.S.I., Grace spent her time taking care of her mother, sister, niece, daughter, grandchildren, and great grandchildren.

Leota married Denver Leo Davis June 10, 1941 in Maryland when he was serving in the Navy there. Leo was the son of Hazel Stella Smith and Denver Leo Davis, Sr. He was born in Addison Township. To this union were born two children, Mary Lee Davis (Marchi) born July 30, 1942 and William (Bill) Denver Davis born June 25, 1945. Leota and Leo divorced in 1946.

In 1948 Leota married Bernard Malcolm Guinther of Syracuse, OH. They were the parents of one son, L.A. Guinther. Although Mary Lee and Bill were the step-children of Bernard, he never failed to show them anything but the love of a natural father, they inturn loved him as their father. Bernard passed away in 1981, Leota lived until 1987, after battling cancer for 10 years. Although she was in terrible pain for a long time, she never complained. If you should ask her how she was feeling, she always gave you a smile and the same answer every time, "Okay Honey".

Leota and Bernard worked at the Gallipolis State Institute retiring after 32 years of service. Both loved to spend their weekends camping with their youngest son L.A., and frequently their grandchildren would also go with them. Both Leota and Bernard had a special bond with their grandchildren; Brian K. McDade, Melissa (Missy) Dawn McDade Whaley, Colby Davis, and Carmah L. Davis Setzer.

*Submitted by their daughter, Mary Lee (Davis) Marchi*

**FRANCIS FRANKLIN & DILLIE RACHEL (LEMLEY) HALFHILL** - In 1882, Francis Franklin born in 1861 son of Jacob and Abigail

Halfhill (see Halfhill- Livingood) married Zelpha Thomas (1866-1886) buried at Poplar Ridge. Their daughter, Nora, married Wilmer B. Adams and lived in California returning to visit her family bringing a groundhog she called her baby and carried in a basket.

*Dillie and Frank Halfhill*

Frank married Dillie Rachel (born in Cheshire Twp January 9, 1872, the daughter of Andrew and Mary Shoemaker Lemley) on June 4, 1891 and they lived in the Kyger area of Cheshire Township only 1/2 a mile from where he was born. In addition to farming, Frank worked for the railroad at Hobson Yards. The family attended Poplar Ridge Freewill Baptist Church in Cheshire Twp and their children: Ora Edwin (1894-1974), Lola Gail (1897-1966), Nellie Dale (1900-1954), Bud Lawrence (1901-1934), Thelma (1902-1958), Vail (1906-1973) and Phyllis (1907-1996) all went to Africa and Jericho Schools in the Kyger area. Their first child, a son Harrison born Aug 10, 1892 died on Oct. 31, 1892 only two months old.

When three of Frank and Dillie's children (Gail, Nellie and Ora) married Jacob & Esther Baird's children (Ora, Stacy and Ethel) generations of close family ties were formed. (See Children of Frank and Dillie Halfhill and The Bairds).

At his death in 1946, Frank was buried at Gravel Hill in Cheshire Twp. While Dillie spent most of her life in the Cheshire community, she went to live with her youngest daughter (Phyllis Burns) in Evergreen, Ohio in 1951. At her death in 1956, Dillie, the last of her family, left a legacy of memories for her 24 grandchildren and 52 great-grandchildren and was laid to rest in Gravel Hill with her husband Frank.

Family and friends enjoyed sitting around listing to Dillie tell stories from the past. Her parents, Andrew (2/25/1826-4/13/1918) and Mary Shoemaker (1833-1925) Lemley, were married on February 2, 1854 by William S. Jenkins. Memories from Civil War history were passed down from Andrew and Mary to their children and grandchildren. In one of the most turbulent times in our nation's history, Andrew served his country during the Civil War as a Private in Unit Co. B, 91 Reg., Ohio VI from 1862-65. In the summer of 1863, word was spreading like wild fire that the famous John Morgan and his raiders were headed for Meigs and Gallia County. With rumors of all kinds striking fear into the hearts of local residents, the women left behind had to take charge of protecting their homes and families. Mary hid their horse and items critical to their survival in the hills behind the house until Morgan's Raiders was no longer a threat to her family. Andrew returned home to his wife and family and Dillie Rachel was born in 1872. Dillie held membership in the Daughters of America Chapter No 277 at Kyger. In 1918, Andrew died at the age of 92 and was buried in Lemley Cemetery (near Popular Ridge Church).

*Submitted by: Dillie E. (Baird) McCormick*

**FRANK AND DILLIE HALFHILL CHILDREN** - Ora Edwin Halfhill (2/7/1894- 1/7/74) born in Cheshire Township married Ethel Marie Baird on 6/23/1916. They lived in Meigs and Gallia County and moved in 1934 from Addison Twp. to the Roush farm near Kyger in Cheshire Twp. Ora worked in the coal mines and at Hobson. Ora died in Pomeroy and Ethel (see Bairds) in CheshireTwp. and both are buried at Campaign. Children: Lucille Marie (1917-1971) (Ray Clark) — son died in infancy. Charles E. (5/5/1918 - 9/13/1918). Stacy Kenneth (1919-1977) (Dorothy Walters) children: Kenneth, Lawrence, Larry, Patty, Patsy, Florence, Golda, Sharon and Denver. Wilmer B. (1922 - 2002) (Alzada Cart) - children: Wilmer Edwin, Lowell E., Judy L, Douglas, Joseph Frank and Tommy. Dana Ray (1935-1985) (Etta Jo Fitch) — children: Hershel, Eddie, Rankin, Margie and Rhonda. Georgia and Audrey died in infancy.

As the oldest daughter, Lola Gail (1897-1966) often helped at home with her younger brothers and sisters. Gail married Ora Baird (1890-1952) - see Gail and Ora Baird.

*The Halfhill-Lemley Family*

Nellie Dale (4/11/1900-1954) married Stacy Baird (1891-1957) — see Stacy Baird

Bud L. (1901-1934) married Georgia V. Hill (1869-1933) and lived in Meigs County. Bud worked as a crane operator at Hobson Shops.

Thelma (11/29/1902-1958) born in Cheshire Twp married Fonzo Taylor (1901-1984) May 4, 1921 and lived at Poplar Ridge on his family farm. Fonzo worked at Hobson. There were always exotic and unusual birds and at least one set of twin baby lambs to admire. Fondly remembered as Uncle Fonzo, he was always willing to help— "Fetch it in the machine" (car). Thelma, a correspondent for the newspaper, was a member of the Daughters of America, Little Kyger Grange and Poplar Ridge Church.

They are buried at Gravel Hill. Children: Fonzo Jr. died in infancy. Florence (Fess Rose-deceased) children: Grace and Fess Jr. and then Fletcher. Dorothy (1924-2000) (James Hawley) - Children: Steve, and Bob, Roger (PFC killed in Vietnam) and Thomas Arrington - Children: Juanita and Clara Ellen (1964-1966). Virginia (Dee Thomas) children: Al, John and Sally. Carl (Anna Hodge) children: Gary, Larry, and Sandy. Leroy (11/22/32 -1/2/56 car wreck). Louise (Jack Brown) - children: Jackie, Mike, Charles and Janice. Juanita (Mike Balnoschan) children: Mike, Greg and Denise, one died in infancy.

Vail (1906-1973) married Walter Paulins and lived in Cheshire Township and later Jackson County. Children: Walter Jr. (Mary White) children: Walter Jr., Pam, Penny, Patsy and Kim. Lewis (Dorothy Roush) children: Steve, Allen, and Howard. Affectionately remembered as the kissing Aunt, Vail greeted you with a peck on the cheek.

Phyllis (1907-1996) married Matthew Burns (1907-1992). The couple lived various places in Gallia County and many years in Evergreen. Mack was a housepainter and Aunt Phyllis worked for Holzer Hospital in the kitchen and laundry, at a glove factory and as a housekeeper. Aunt Phyllis grew beautiful African violets and Uncle Mack always had a new car even before it was popular to trade every few years. The last of her family, Phyllis and Mack were buried at Gravel Hill.

*Submitted by Danny L. Casto & Sara (Baird) Cheney*

**MATTHIAS AND ELIZABETH (LIVINGOOD) HALFHILL** - Matthias and Elizabeth (Livingood) Halfhill lived in Pennsylvania where their son, Samuel (1790-1884) was born in Fayette County. Samuel, a veteran of the War of 1812, and his wife Anna (1794-1867) lived in Pennsylvania in the early years of their married life. At least two children were born before the couple moved to Gallia County, Ohio where many of their descendents still live. Samuel was buried in Kyger Cemetery in Cheshire Township with his wife Anna.

*Jacob Amd Abigail (Berrit) Halfhill Are Buried In The Cemetery At Poplar Ridge Church.*

Samuel & Anna's children: John (1817-1889) married Nancy Darst in 1834; he died in Jay County, Indiana. Margaret (1828-?) married Samuel Haynes in 1850. Sarah (1835-1908) married Lorenzo Dow Taylor in 1854. Peter (5/15/1833-10/2/1896) married Susannah (1825-1868 daughter of Thomas and Ann Manring Athey) on 9/5/1850 and lived in Addison Twp on a farm near Campaign Church. Samuel and Susannah were buried at Campaign in the little cemetery near where they lived and raised their six children: Thomas (1849— 1876) married Lucinda Hix in 1876; he died at 26 and is buried at Campaign,

Samuel (1854 -?), in 1885, Mary E. (1858-1940) first married William H., Scott who died. Mary was married on 9/15/1904 to Andrew Peck (1842-1920) who had served in W. Va. Cavalry. Still known with affection as Aunt Mary Peck (doesn't everyone have an Aunt Mary), she was buried with Andrew at Campaign Cemetery near her home inherited at their father's death. Cora A. (?) married Oral Price 1897, Homer (?) married Elta N. Lambert in 1892 and Esther A. Halfhill born (1855-1907) in Addison Township married Joseph Baird (1849-1917) on 12/7/1876. At her death on Nov 15, 1907 in Addison Twp from typhoid fever, Esther was buried in a small cemetery on land her husband's family later deeded to Campaign Church. Esther & Joseph had 7 children - See The Baird family history.

Jacob Halfhill (12/27/1832 -?) married Abigail Berrit (4/10/1824 — 11/23/1895) on 7/31/1853 and lived in Cheshire Twp. Jacob and Abigail were buried at Poplar Ridge Cemetery. They were the parents of eight children: Cynthia Ann (1854-?) married Frank Dennison; Sarah (1857-?) married Bill Rupe. Fondly remembered as Aunt Cal and Uncle Bill Rupe, they had apples or some little homemade toy for the children when they came to visit. Samuel A. (1859-?) married Laura Mary Thomas in 1881 and after her death Fannie Thomas in 1890. John W (1864-?) married Augusta Darst in 1899. Charles F (1865-10/9/1891), Jacob (12/13/1868-?), Lewis (1869 -1871) and our great-grandfather Francis Franklin Halfhill, who was born in 1861 in Cheshire Twp, married Dillie Rachel Lemley (see Frank Halfhill).

*Submitted by: Ella Louise (Baird) Woodall and Sara L. (Baird) Cheney*

**BILL HALL FAMILY** - John Thomas Hall moved his family from Kentucky to Crown City in early 1890s. His son, Albert Hall was born 1875 and married Maggie Kits Hall, born 1877 and had a son Manuel. Manuel married Lola Holston.

Manuel and Lola Holston had five children, William (Bill), Gerald, Carl, Ruth and Faye. William (Bill) born October 20, 1919 in Crown City, Ohio. He married Juanita, May 31, 1947. They will celebrate their 55th anniversary in 2002. Bill and Juanita's son, Bill Jr., graduated from Rio Grande College in 1973 and the family moved to Florida. Bill, Jr. worked for the International Mining Company for twenty-nine years in Florida. Bill, Jr. married Virginia Chrichfield and has a son Charlie and daughter Laura. Laura is married to Bill Winters and they have a daughter, Reed. Gerald married Helen Metz (both deceased). Their children were Dick and Steve. Steve married Joella Dailey. Carl married Elizabeth Caraway. They had one son, J.C. and he married Cindy Williams; JC and Cindy's daughter Ruthie married George Johnson (Sheriff of Mason County, WV) and they have one son. Faye married Gene Tucker and have a son, Scott. Faye and Gene divorced and Faye married Chick Whelchel and adopted a son, Scott. He married Sherrie. Faye was a real estate broker in Washington DC for several years.

Bill and his siblings, Gerald, Carl, Ruth and Faye, all finished elementary school at Crown City. Bill and Gerald graduated from Mercerville High School. Carl attended high school in Rome, Ruth in Point Pleasant and Faye in East Huntington, WV. Bill was a great high school athlete receiving honors in basketball, football and track and field. He attended Marshall University and played basketball and football for Coach Cam Henderson. He quit school when his father died in 1940 to take his father's job and support the family during the depression. During World War II, Bill was inducted into the army in 1942 and served three years as First Sergeant in the South Pacific.

*Bill Hall Family*
*Top Row, L: to R: #1Ruthie, #2 Laura, Reed & Bill Winter, #3 Bill Hall, & #4 Sharie, Scott & Faye Whelchel. Middle Row, left to right, Carl, Bill, Elisabeth & Juanita Hall (sister Joe Rowe), Laura, Jeff, Faye, Chick Ginger, J.C, Cindy, Charlie & Bill, Jr. Third row, left to right, #1 Grandma, Grandpa Hall, #2 Carl, Bill, Mom, Ruth, Faye & #3 Steve, Dick, Bill Jr., & Dan*

After the war, Bill purchased the Kool-Vent Aluminum Awning company in Huntington, WV. Bill and Carl purchased a farm on the Rodney Road and operated it for several years, selling the last tract fifty years later in 1991 to the Corner Stone Church. Bill laid out the Green Acres Subdivision on State Route 141. Bill owned and operated a men's clothing store on Court Street and Third Avenue in Gallipolis for several years. He supervised the installation of the sanitary sewer system in Gallipolis in the late 1950s and early 1960's. Bill was personnel director at the Gallipolis State Institute for many years. Bill served as personnel manager for M. Ward for a few years and then worked for the Florida Department of Transportation retiring in 1991. Bill returned to college and received a degree in real estate, selling and appraising real estate until 2000.

**DARIUS VIRGIL AND BERTIS JOANNA BUTCHER HALLEY** - Virgil was born in Gallia County August 8, 1911. He died December 31, 1986. He married Bertis December 21, 1938 in Greenup, Kentucky. Bertis was born in Gallia County May 26, 1915.

Virgil's paternal great-grandfather was Henry Halley (1821-1853). He married Clarinda Cottrell (1830-1905). They had two children Shannon and Silas. Henry died when Shannon was three years old. Clarinda married George Serrier.

Virgil's grandparents were Shannon Halley (1850-1912) and Emma Northup (1856-1918). They were married in 1879. Their children were Darius, Clay, George and Clarence.

*Darius Virgil And Bertis Joanna Butcher Halley*

Darius Irvin Halley (1880-1/31/1911)on November 24, 1904 married Omega Ethel White (2/7/1880-5/27/1963). They had three sons Harold Chester (2/28/1906-2/2 8/1908), Victor Edwin (11/16/1908-5/16/1985), Darius Virgil (8/08/1911). Darius died six months before Virgil was born. They had been living in Delaware, Ohio and Omega returned to Clay township when her husband died. She later married John Roman Harrison (1876-1954) in 1919. They had one son, Alfred Vance (6/22/1920-1963) and they adopted Robert Harrison (1928-1944).

Virgil's maternal great, great, great, great grandfather was William White. His son Nicholas S. married Mary McDaniel. Their son Absolom (1773-1871) who came to Gallia County from England married Phoebe Adcock. Their son Nicholas (1806-1893) November 9, 1826 married Mary Angel (1806-1879). Their son John (1832-1922) on October 18, 1868 married Hannah Jane Davis (1842-1932) They were the parents of Virgil's mother Omega Ethel White (2/7/1880-5/27/1963). Her sisters were Clemma, Thelma and Mrytie and her brothers, Wesley, Jasper, and William E.

Many of the Whites and Halleys are buried at St. Nicholas Cemetery on Friendly Ridge in Gallia County. The cemetery was named after Absolom White's son Nicholas.

Bertis', paternal great grandfather John Butcher Sr. was born February 14, 1781 in Virginia and moved to what is now West Virginia. He married Elizabeth Rohr (1785-1822) on December 9, 1807. They had three children Sara(1809), Elizabeth(1811) and Mary Jane(1812). The family moved to Gallia County by 1812 where they had Samuel(1812), George(1814), Jacob(1815), Jonas(1816), John Jr.(1817), June(1817). After his first wife died, he married Mary (Polly) Vance in 1825. He died September 26, 1864.

Bertis' grandfather Jacob married Sarah Colwell(1816-1906) in Meigs County. They had John Sylvester February 22,1844. The other children were George, Delila, Hiram, Christina, and Sarah. John served nearly four years as a member of Company B 36th O.V.I. during the Civil War. He married Nancy Crowell and their children were Charles, Jacob, Austin, Milton, Francis, Thomas, Sarah, and Clara. Nancy died in 1907.

John married Nola Settla Safford September 21, 1909. They had one daughter Bertis Joanna on May 26, 1915. He died September 17, 1916.

Bertis' maternal great, great grandfather was Colonel Robert Safford. Robert, son of Challis and Lydia Warner Safford, was born July 7, 1768 in Hardwick, Mass. He arrived in what is now Gallipolis June 8, 1790 with Major Burnham's party ahead of the French settlers to clear the land to build cabins. He was said to have cut down the first tree. In 1793, he married Catherine Cameron, one of the French 500. She was born in France in 1768 and died in Gallipolis in 1852. They had seven children. He held many leadership jobs and was very active in the community. He died at the age of 95. He and Catherine are buried at Centenary Cemetery. Their son Robert Jr.(11/20/1865) married Almira Cubbage. They had eight children. Their son Lewis M. (8/22/1830) married Joanna Jane Spicer in Gallipolis December 31, 1856, daughter of David and Elizabeth (Rial) Spicer. Their eleven children were Flizabeth( 10/12/1857), Charles E.(2/16/1859), Lydia C.(10/12/1860), Natalie L. (11/22/1862), Alice L.(9/19/1864), David R.(9/29/1866), Lena M.(1/17/1868), Thomas C.(1/26/1871), Emma D.(9/26/1872), Nola S.(10/21/1875), and Edna P.(12/19/1878).

Nola married John Sylvester Butcher. They had one daughter, Bertis Joanna. Nola died December 6,1935.

Virgil graduated from Mercerville High School in 1928, attended Rio Grande College and played football there in 1928-29. He was a World War II Navy Veteran.

He was associated from 1935 until his death in 1986 with the Wheeler family theater business and helped build the Colony Theater and Kanagua Drive-In. He also worked for the Miller Construction Company in the 1930's, helped build the Gallipolis Golf Course, and was head greenskeeper of the course retiring after 45 years in 1979.

Bertis graduated from Bidwell-Porter High School in 1932. She was a homemaker. They had three children Linda Lee (5/09/1943), Diana Kay (6/23/1946), John Darius (4 13/1952).

Linda married Ervin Criner (8 18/1937) in Gallipolis on November 26, 1965. They have two children Leanna Marie (6/13/1967) and Daniel Curtis(5/27/1970). Leanna on December 23, 1993 married William Jack Bowen (8/25/1959). They have two sons William Lee (1/30/96) and Nicholas James Patrick (2/14/1999).

Diana married Charles Raming (8/2/1949) on November 25, 2000.

John married Brenda Sue Stover (10/11/1953) December 24, 1973. They have three children, John Darius Jr. (8/11/1976), Jessica Sue (8/28/1981), Megan Joanna (7/24/1984).

**BENJAMIN AND ELIZABETH REYNOLDS HARBOUR FAMILY** - In the year 1811, young 18 year old Benjamin Harbour came to Gallia County, Ohio, from Patrick County, Virginia. Why he chose Ohio and how he made the trip are unknown. This is a trip of some 300 miles which could be driven in about 6 hours today. You could wonder how long it took in 1811. The trip entails crossing the Allegheny Mountain Range and the hills of West Virginia. When he arrived in Gallia County, he found a wild undeveloped state without roads, mills or other conveniences. Ohio was just beginning its development.

Benjamin Harbour was born in 1793 in Henry County, Virginia. He was the son of David and Esther Cronk Harbour. They were both natives of the area around Henry County, Virginia. David was second generation descendant of Thomas Harbour who came from Wales to Virginia being of record in 1728 with land ownership in Hanover County, Virginia. Benjamin married Elizabeth Reynolds April 11, 1809, in Patrick County, Virginia. Elizabeth Reynolds was born 1791 or 1792 in Virginia. There are 11 children born to this marriage. The first two children Dorcie Harbour Morgan born about 1810 and Madison Harbour born about 1811 were born in Virginia. Esther Harbour Richardson was born about 1813 in Gallia County. The trip from Virginia becomes even more interesting when you think that young Benjamin had a new young wife and two very small children with him.

*Harbour Cemetery Guyan Township, Gallia Couty, Ohio May 2001*

After arriving in Ohio, Benjamin was drafted into the Ohio Militia to serve in the War of 1812. He was a sergeant under Lt. Jordan Manrling, Detachment of Col. John McDonald's Regiment. He served from November 28, 1814, to April 10, 1815, at Upper Sandusky. During this time, he acquired a bronchial condition which continued the rest of his life. He was granted a pension in 1855 when he was 62 years of age. He also was awarded a land grant for 40 acres in Ohio, believed to be in Gallia County. The first election for the new Perry Township of Gallia County organized March 4, 1816, was held at the house of Steven Gales April 1, 1816. Benjamin was elected as one of the two constables. There were twenty four votes cast at that election. He was known to be still serving in that capacity in 1829.

Other children of Benjamin and Elizabeth were David Harbour born 1815; Caroline M. Harbour Perkins born 1817; Elizabeth Harbour Holston born 1817; Richard Henry Harbour born February 25, 1824; William Harbour born 1826; Ruth Harbour Wetherholt born 1830; Joney Harbour Allen born 1828; and Thomas Harbour born December 17, 1840 all believed born in Gallia County. Benjamin was a landowner in Gallia County and probably was a farmer most of his life. Four of his sons; Madison, David, Richard Henry, and Thomas, all married in Gallia County and raised their families in the county. Son, William, did not marry and is thought to have lived with his father and mother.

Elizabeth died March 26, 1859, in Gallia County. Benjamin died 1874 in Gallia County. They are buried in the Harbour Cemetery under a large oak tree. This site is along the Cox-Mercerville Road in Guyan Township. There is one other burial there, John L., son of D-S Harbour. It is believed this is the son of David and Sarah Harbour, David was the son of Benjamin. The graves are very close to the road under the oak tree. The site is on the south side of the road about 3/4 mile east of the junction with State Road 218. There is a bronze marker for Benjamin with stone marker for Elizabeth and John. This site is a quiet reminder of one of the real pioneers of Gallia County.

*Submitted by John Bertholf*

**THOMAS AND NANCY ANNA DAVENPORT HARBOUR FAMILY -** Thomas Harbour was a farmer. He lived most of his life in Gallia County, having been born there December 17, 1840, to parents Benjamin and Elizabeth Reynolds Harbour. He was their youngest child of a total of 11 children. There is no record of what education he might have received, but any he had was in Gallia County Schools. He did not marry until he was 25 years old. He married Nancy Anna Davenport January 4, 1866, in Gallia County. Anna was a native of Gallia County, the daughter of Chapel R. and Keziah Thorp Davenport. She was born January 4, 1845. Thomas and Anna had seven children, all born in Gallia County.

Della Frances Harbour Cox was born November 21, 1866. When he was nineteen years old, she married Marshall Cox. Their marriage in Gallia County was April 25, 1866. They moved to Huntington, West Virginia, where they raised their family.

*Thomas & Nancy Annna Harbour with daughters & son. Gallia County, Ohio Ca. 1887*

James Preston Harbour was born March 2, 1868. He was twenty-one years old when he married Augusta Minnie Dickey October 23, 1889. She was a native of Gallia County, the daughter of Silas and Mary E. Frances Thierry Dickey Harbour. She was born December 20, 1865. Before their marriage, James had gone to Huntington, West Virginia, to get employment with the railroad. He came back for their marriage in Gallia County, after which they settled in Huntington for a few years. They had a daughter, Lenora Estelle Harbour Vaughn, born July 29, 1894, in Huntington. They discovered Augusta had consumption and were advised to move to a drier climate. In 1897 they moved to Pueblo County, Colorado. They had two more daughters there, Mary Ernestine Harbour Swope born August 27, 1898, and Erma Wylmuth Harbour Bertholf born October 19, 1902. Augusta died in Pueblo March 20, 1908. James remarried and had three additional children. He died in Pueblo August 23, 1956.

Records show a son, Thomas, born August 1872 in Perry Township, Gallia County. There is no further record of this Thomas. It is possible he died as an infant. A son, John R. Harbour, was born July 1, 1870. He married Margaret or Maggie Rodgers July 27, 1893, in Gallia County. They settled in Huntington, West Virginia, where John was a hotel keeper. They both died and were buried at Huntington. A daughter, Myrta H. Harbour Masterson, was born August 7, 1872. She married Homer G. Masterson July 17, 1893, in Gallia County. They also settled in Huntington, West Virginia. He was a carriage maker there, probably for the railroad company.

A third daughter was born January 21, 1875, named Minnie J. Harbour. She married young to Harry A. Day on February 26, 1893. She died the following year on May 22, 1894. She is buried next to her parents at Bethel Church Cemetery, Ohio Township, Gallia County. The last child was son, Luther E. Harbour, born November 19, 1880. He married Vesta Mae Swindler in Gallia County. She was the daughter of John M. and Adaline Henthorn Swindler, a pioneer family in Gallia County. Vesta Mae was born January 12, 1880, in Guyan Township, Gallia County. They lived in Gallia County for several years. They moved to Pueblo, Colorado, in 1915 and later to Olney Springs, Colorado, where they died and were buried. They had a large family.

In 1878, Thomas purchased forty acres of land in Ohio Township south of the road from Blandensburg to Mercerville. He and Anna lived there until she died November 19, 1911. Her address was shown as Leeper, Ohio, at her death. In 1913 Thomas was found to no longer be able to handle his affairs and his son, Luther, was made guardian. On August 30, 1915, he was sent to the State Hospital in Athens to be cared for. He died there October 14, 1915. In February 1916 his estate was settled by sale of his land which paid his outstanding bills. Thomas did not have any living descendants in Gallia County at the time of his death.

*Submitted by John Bertholf*

**KARL & DORIS HARDER** - On the 19th day of June 1906, Karl Manard Harder was born the fourth child of Herbert and Emma Fitzpatrick Harder, in the small town of Wilkesville, Ohio. Karl attended Wilkesville Elementary and high school until he graduated in April of 1923. Soon after graduation, Karl moved to Iowa and attended Graceland College until 1924. He achieved a certificate with which to teach, and taught in a one-room school building, often teaching children older than he was.

He continued to teach until 1929 when he married Doris Arletha Snyder, the third daughter of Nina and Milton Bunch Snyder. At this time Karl left the teaching profession and started his career in building; a trade passed down to him from his father and grandfather. This career took him many places, including Columbus, West Virginia, and many more. During this time Doris worked as a substitute mail carrier, unloading heavy mail sacks from the train running through Vinton, Ohio.

After their marriage, Karl and Doris lived with Nina and Milton Snyder in Ewington. The couple had 5 children: Theodore Ray, Bradley Eugene, Cletus Leroy, Phyllis Marlene, and Terry Lee. Just prior to the arrival of their third child, Karl and Doris moved into a small home in Ewington, where they lived their entire lives. Karl continued to work at a career in building and trucking, while Doris carried the mail and cared for her husband and children. Later in life, when the boys reached their teenage years, Karl started a business called "Harder and Sons Construction". He worked along side his sons building schools, houses, businesses, and any other jobs offered to them. This family tradition is being kept alive through Karl's second son Bradley, and his grandson Steve Harder.

*Karl and Doris Harder*

Karl and Doris spent a lifetime in the Gallia County area. After Karl's retirement, he and Doris spent countless hours driving around and enjoying the scenery that they loved so much. They enjoyed collecting antiques and restoring old furniture, but most of all they enjoyed spending time with their five children, 14 grandchildren, and 22 great-grandchildren.

Karl passed from this earth in April of 1987 and Doris followed later in August of 1994. They both lived long, prosperous lives and were highly respected by their friends, family, and community.

*Submitted by: Daughter Phyllis Mulholand & Great Granddaughter Amber Shepherd*

**SIGISMUND L. HARDER FAMILY** - Sigismund(Sig) Harder, born 1925;grew up in a small town at the shores of the Baltic sea in East Prussia. His father was an architect and builder, his forefathers craftsmen and teachers who had lived for centuries in the northern part of Germany. His parents were among the 13 Million Germans who were expelled from their home country in 1945 when the Red Army overran eastern Europe. Sig was a German soldier during the last two years of WWII and an American POW for 2 1/2 more years thereafter. Attending to hundreds of sick and wounded in the camps would become an invaluable foundation for his later work in medicine. He went to medical school in Goettingen, Germany, from 1947 — 53 and immigrated to the United States in 1955, crossing the Atlantic Ocean on a small freighter through a horrifyng winter hurricane. Alix, his wife is of Austro—German ancestry. She was born in Prague, Czechoslovakia. In May 1945 she and her mother fled from the Russian troops to the American occupied sector of Bohemia. In November of that year she and all the other 3 1/2 million Germans from Czechoslovakia were expelled from the country where her ancestors had lived for more than 500 years. For two days she walked across snow—covered mountains carrying very few possessions which seemed to become heavier with every step. On a sunny Sunday winter morning —the church bells were just ringing—peace and freedom came to her when she set foot on Bavarian soil.

At one lucky moment she met Sig Harder at a railroad station in Hamburg. Ten years later they started a new life together in the United States. Sig trained in internal medicine for five years at the the Cleveland Clinic. In 1962 Sig and Alix looked for the best possible place to practice medicine and raise their three children, Elisabeth,Bert and Tom.

*The Harder Family*

When they came to Gallipolis it was love at first sight: the charm of the small town by the Ohio river, the excellence of the Holzer staff and most of all the humanitarian spirit of its leader, Dr.Charles E.Holzer, made the decision easy. Sig would become the 16th member of the Clinic and its first foreign graduate. In 1997 he retired after 35 years of practice.

Their children moved on and have families of their own. Liz married Skip Christensen whose late father, Dr. A. Christensen, founded Rio Grande Community College. They live in Tucson,Arizona. Skip practices law and Liz, with a master in psychology, supervises a church sponsored counseling agency. They have two children, Jessica and Mark who are students at Arizona University. Tom and his family live in Philadelphia.

He practices Internal medicine and Rheumatology, while Debra, a doctor of medicine and music, teaches piano, gives concerts and watches over their two girls, Alysa,15, and Lexi,7. In 1984, Hubert who had just graduated from OSU in Biochemistry, died in an airplane crash over the Ohio river. Alix's son Wolfgang is married in Germany. Today Sig and Alix still live in the old Beilstein home on Garfield above the Ohio river which is as beautiful as it was when they came.

**CHESTER FRANKLIN HARDESTY** - Chester Franklin Hardesty was born in Lawrence County, Ohio, on April 18, 1921, son of Chauncey Theodore and Lyda Ellen Shockley Hardesty. He married Jeanne Maridell Houck on March 13, 1944. She was born in Guyan Township, daughter of Pleasant Richard and Jesta Clementine Saunders Houck on December 30, 1923.

Chester was inducted into the Army on August 10, 1942. He achieved the rank of Sergeant of Company E, 378th Infantry and was an expert marksman. While serving in the European Theatre during World War II, Chester was wounded in action near Ft. Bassee Yutz, France, on November 13, 1944. He was awarded the Purple Heart, the Bronze Star, EAME Theatre Medal, two Battle Stars, and a Good Conduct Medal.

*Chester & Maridell Hardesty Christmas 1980*

After his discharge from the Army, Chester and Maridell bought a farm in Guyan Township. Their son, Larry Gene, was born on March 5, 1945, and their daughter, Barbara Ann, was born on January 26, 1947. Larry and Barbara started their schooling at Mercerville.

The Hardesty family moved from the farm to Green Township in 1956. Larry and Barbara finished their schooling in Gallipolis City Schools.

Larry was married to Sandra Sue Langdon. Sandra was born on November 20, 1945, to James E. and Betty J. Wiseman Langdon. Larry and Sandra had two daughters. Julie Ann was born January 18, 1974. She is currently teaching science at Gallia Academy High School. Jennifer Sue was born January 16, 1976. Jennifer and her husband, Jason, have three children: Nicole, Katie and Zachary. Jennifer and Jason are stationed in Misawa, Japan with the Air Force. Larry and Sandra were divorced in 1984.

Barbara was married to Edwin Eugene Harbour. Gene was born October 8, 1945, to Dale and Betty DeWitt Harbour. Barbara and Gene are the parents of three sons. Davis Mark was born December 14, 1966. He and his wife, Joann, have three children: Brendon, Mallorie and Rebecca. Daniel Michael was born October 28, 1968. He and his wife, Debbie, have two children, Matthew and Jessica. Brent Matthew was born December 15, 1969. He and his wife, Christy, have one son, Dillon. All three grandsons are currently living in Florida. Chester passed away on October 15, 2000. He was a wonderful husband, father and grandfather. Maridell continues to live at their home on State Route 141.

*Submitted by Maridell Hardesty*

**SANDRA LANGDON HARDESTY** - On November 20, 1945, Sandra Sue Langdon was born to James and Betty Wiseman Langdon in Gallipolis, Ohio. She had two brothers, James Michael born October 19, 1946, and Charles Ernest (Jack) born August 22, 1949.

James was born November 24, 1911, in Gallia County, the son of Ernest and Edith Swisher Langdon, Ernest was born February 25, 1883, in Springfield Township, Ohio, the son of Arnon J. and Serepta Kincaid Langdon. Edith was born June 24, 1886, in Gallia County, the daughter of James Ralza (Dick) and Lecta Thomas Swisher.

*Nicole Sue, Katie Elizabeth, and Zachary Ryan Grimm July 2001 grandchildren of Sandra Hardesty*

Betty was born March 15, 1923, at Cadmus, Ohio, the daughter of Ernest and Alice Clyse Wiseman. Ernest was born March 21, 1897, near Cadmus, Ohio, the son of John and Bertha Pyles Wiseman. Alice was born May 4, 1902, near Cadmus, Ohio, the daughter of Clifford and Nellie Barger Clyse.

In 1952 Sandra's parents were divorced and she moved with her mother and brothers to Jackson, Ohio. On August 15, 1954, her mother married Elwood Brown, born April 8, 1929, near Minford, Ohio. The family moved to Minford and four more children were added to the family: Ruth Ellen born June 17, 1955; Joseph born February 17, 1957; Rex born April 4, 1958; and John born July 16, 1961.

Sandra graduated from Minford High School in 1963. She moved to Gallipolis in 1964 where she worked at the Wiseman Agency while she attended Gallipolis Business College. In January 1965 she began working as a secretary for Bob Evans Farms. She has worked in several different divisions of the company for a total of 33 years now.

On April 2, 1966, Sandra married Larry Hardesty, who was born on March 5, 1945, the son of Chester and Maridel Hardesty. They had two daughters: Julie Ann born January 18, 1974, and Jennifer Sue born on January 16, 1976. Sandra and Larry were divorced in 1984.

Julie graduated from Gallia Academy High School in 1992 and from the University of Rio Grande with a BS degree in math, science and secondary education in 1998. She taught math for three years at River Valley High School and is presently teaching science at Gallia Academy High School.

Jennifer graduated from Gallia Academy High School in 1994. On September 2, 1995, she married Jason Grimm, who was born December 25, 1975, and is the son of Roger and Cathy Grimm. Jason and Jennifer moved to Offut Air Force Base in Omaha, NE, where Jason was stationed in the Air Force. Twin daughters, Nicole Sue and Katie Elizabeth, were born on March 27, 1998. In November 1998 Jason and Jennifer were transferred to Misawa Air Force Base in Misawa, Japan. Then on March 5, 2000, Zachary Ryan was born.

Sandra now lives in Rio Grande and is an active member of Faith Baptist Church at Rodney, Ohio. She plans to spend the rest of her life in Gallia County where many of her ancestors were early settlers in Cheshire, Addison, Walnut and Springfield Townships.

**MARTIN GLENN HASH AND JEWELL LENORE (FISH) HASH FAMILY** - Martin was born June 19, 1938 at Bidwell, Ohio. His parents were William Glenn Hash and Levina (Surber) Hash. Glenn and Vina along with his Grandfather Robert Lee Hash, were descendants of pioneer settlers. The Hash's, Surber's, Landreth's, and Shupes were from Grayson and Smythe County Virginia and Ashe County North Carolina.

Martin's father Glenn and his father Robert (Bob) Hash were farmers and timber and sawmill workers along with Gene Sheets and Hannah (Surber) Sheets.

Glenn and Vina bought the Isacc Miller farm, section 11 of Morgan Township which included the old Miller Cemetery, and at that time, 1921, the old one room Miller School.

*Jewel and Martin Hash*

Glenn and Vina moved their family from Princeton, McDowell County, West Virginia to Gallia County Ohio in 1921, by way of a team of horses and wagon. They were parents of nine children; Ruth Hersman, Dorcas Dodrill, Frank, Virginia, Maggie Morgan, Robert Neal (a Korean War Vet.), James Leonard (Phyllis McCarley), Clarence (Ruth Franklin), and Martin (Jewell Fish).

Martin and Jewell reside on the old Hash Farm on Hash Lane and George Road in Morgan Township. We have many loyal friends and neighbors and are proud of the Hash family tradition in Gallia County and Morgan Township.

His wife Jewell Lenore Fish Hash was born in Putnam County, West Virginia on April 6, 1938, the daughter of E. Lowell Fish and Mildred Waters Fish. Lowell was born in Putnam County, W. Va., on June 23, 1907 and Mildred Waters Fish was born Feb. 3, 1917 in Morganton, N. C. Her parents were John C. Waters and Cordelia Smith Waters. John was a construction worker and worked his way north building Locks and Dams. He and Cordelia lived in Gallipolis during the thirties while he was working on the Gallipolis Locks and Dam.

Jewell and her parents and brother Howard moved to Gallia County in Nov. 1953.

Martin and Jewell are the parents of 3 daughters and 1 son. Judith Gwen (Rob) Phillips of Bidwell, Mary Amy of Rio Grande, Rebecca Ann

(Greg) Gardner of Circleville and Martin Lowell (Pam) Hash of South Point. They have 10 Grandchildren and 2 Great Grandsons.

**JOHN HENRY, SR.** - One son, John Henry, Jr., born Virginia 1769, died July 1842, Gallia County, Ohio. John Jr.'s son, Brice, born 1805 Virginia, died ca. 1861, Guyan Township, Gallia County, Ohio; married Rachel Stover September 26, 1833, Gallia County, daughter of Elijah Stover and Mary Scarberry. Rachel born March 7, 1813, Giles County, Virginia, died ca. 1880, Guyan Township, Gallia County.

Brice and Rachel's son, Libni, born April 1840, Lawrence County, Ohio, died May 4, 1902, Scioto County, Ohio; married Nancy Jane Norris November 21, 1854, Lawrence County, Ohio, daughter of John Norris and second wife, Eleanor Woods. Nancy Jane born August 9, 1843, Gallia County, and died June 9, 1907, Scioto County.

Only child of Libri and Nancy Jane, Louvinda Jane Henry born August 20, 1865, Gallia County, died September 9, 1949, Scioto County, Ohio. Louvinda married Jonathan Pollard October 21, 1885, Idaho, Pike County, Ohio, son of Andrew Pollard and third wife Susannah Ashbaugh. Jonathan Pollard born June 2, 1866, Pike County, died March 7, 1962, Scioto County, Ohio.

One son, Samuel Curtis Pollard, born December 19, 1892, Upper Nile Township, Scioto County, and died May 20, 1980, Scioto County, Ohio, married Minnie Ethel Mason May 29, 1917, Ironton, Lawrence County, daughter of James William Mason and Martha Mariah Cox. Ethel born September 2, 1893, Upper Nile Township, Scioto County, died March 28, 1985, Scioto County.

Daughter Erma Ethel Pollard born May 27, 1925, Scioto County, married Wallace Dale McClurg May 28, 1946, Greenup County, Kentucky, son of William Isaac McClurg and Mae Beatrice Webster. Dale born April 22, 1924, Scioto County, died November 12, 2001, Pike County Ohio.

Daughter Lois Ann McClurg married Jack Ronald Walker a descendant of John Henry Sr.'s daughter. Elizabeth born December 25, 1767, Botetourt County, Virginia, died November 7, 1832, Mason County, Virginia; married Thomas Hannan December 28, 1781, Botetourt County, Virginia. Thomas born 1757, Frederick County, Virginia; died April 18, 1837, Mason County, Virginia.

Son, Esom Hannan, born May 29, 1784, Betotourt County, died January 26, 1866, Mason County, West Virginia; married second Sarah Switzer April 14, 1831, Gallia County, daughter of Philip Switzer and Nancy Bridger.

One daughter, Miriam Hannan, born 1835 Mason County, died April 6, 1869, Gallia County; married Rev. Brooke Gwathmey Hereford October 30, 1851, Mason County, Virginia; son of Robert Hereford and Virginia Lewis. Brooke born December 16, 1829, Mason County, and died April 13, 1899, Lawrence County, Ohio.

Son Robert Esom Hereford born June 8, 1856, Henry County, Missouri; died November 18, 1934, Mason County, West Virginia; married Grace Truman Withers April 29, 1880, Mason County, daughter of John Morton Holliday Withers and Sarah Ann George. Grace born June 26, 1861, Mason County, West Virginia; died September 20, 1923, Chendein District, Mason County.

Son Virgil Edwin Hereford born December 10, 1882, Mason County, died February 22, 1963, Mason County, West Virginia; married Rose Mary Dabney November 8, 1903, Arlee, West Virginia; daughter of Clark C. Dabney and Christina Gard. Rose born July 16, 1882, Mason County, died May 1972, Cabell County, West Virginia.

Daughter Marguerite Hereford born April 2, 1918, Mason County, West Virginia, died October 3, 2001, Gallipolis, Gallia County, Ohio; married Denver Archibald Walker September 15, 1940, Ashland, Kentucky. Denver, son of William Henry Walker and Corda Edith Skidmore, born December 24, 1912, Kanawha County West Virginia; died March 14, 1962, Gallipolis, Gallia County, Ohio.

Son, Jack Ronald Walker, married Lois Ann McClurg, June 8, 1968, McDermott, Ohio. The only grandsons of Wallace Dale McClurg-Erma Pollard and Denver A. Walker-Marguerite Hereford, Jonathan Roland and Jeffrey Ryan Walker descendants of John Henry, Sr., through both their grandmothers.

*Submitted by Erma Pollard McClurg.*

**HIVELY** - The first Hivelys to come to America were brothers Christopher and Jacob Haible who arrived at Philadelphia, Pa. in 1749 on the ship Jacob. They had come from the village of Mehrstetten, Germany. Hively cousins still live there in Germany. Sometime after Christopher and Jacob arrived in Pennsylvania, they changed their name from the German Haible to Hively.

Christopher Hively was born 1728 in Mehrstetten, Germany. He married Sophia Catharine Schupp 1753 in Pennsylvania. Their eldest child was Jacob who was born ca. 1755 in Pa. He married Veronica Heydt B. 1751-D. 1816. They moved from Pa. to Botetort Co. Virginia.

*Jacob and Martha Ann Dewitt Hively*

They had several children there including a son named James who was born 1793 in Virginia. James was married in Botetort, Va. in 1818 to Frances Huffman ca.1790 died before 1848 in Gallia Co. Ohio.

Children: John F. b 1820 in Va.; d. 1860 at Gallia Co. OH.; m Oct. 8 1840 at Gallia Co. Oh. to Elizabeth Catherine T. Watts (b. 1818 in VA. d. after 1870); OH. Mary Frances, Metilda A., David James, Andrew, William J., Martha J., Winfield Scott, Lucinda E., John McIntyre and Paul.

Jonathan b. 1822 at Giles Co..,VA; d. Jan. 21, 1865 at Nashville, TN. m. Oct. 13,1842 at Gallia Co. OH. to Mary Watts (b. July 26, 1811 at Greenbrier, VA; d. Feb. 3, 1891 at Gallipolis, OH. Ch. William James.

Jacob C. b 1824 at Giles Co. VA.; d Jan. 26 1897 at Harrison Twp. Gallia Co., OH. to Martha Ann DeWitt (b. June 3, 1825 in OH; d. June 11, 1906 at Harrison Twp., Gallia Co., OH); Oh: John, James, Angeline, Sarah, Arkansas, Charles M., Caroline, Jacob F., Romaine, Jennie M. and Lilly.

Martha Ann b. c.1826 at Giles Co., VA; m. May 5, 1850 at Gallia Co. OH. to Andrew A. Grant (b. 1822 in VA.)

Lucinda Jane b. Ca. 1828 at Giles Co. VA.

Caleb b. at Giles Co., VA.1831 d. July 1, 1906 at Ainsworth, NE; m. Oct. 10, 1850 at Gallia Co., OH to Mary Harriet Allison (b. 1829 in OH; d. Aug. 26, 1887 at Manhattan, KS) ch. Lucinda E., John J., Rebecca Angeline, David M, Martha, Napoleon, Latitia, and at least one other unknown daughter.

Arminta b. 1834 at Giles Co., VA; m. May 24, 1854 at Gallia Co., OH. to Moses Bostick.

James and Frances second son Jacob was a teenager when he came with his parents, brothers and sisters from Virginia to Gallia Co. Ohio in the 1830's. James and Frances and family settled on a farm in Harrison Township in the Lincoln Ridge area.

When Jacob was twenty years old he married in 1844 Martha Ann DeWitt b. 1825 d.1906 who was a daughter of John and Sarah Loucks DeWitt.

Although Jacob and Martha had several children when the Civil War started, he enlisted in 1862 and served until 1865. While in the service he sustained a gunshot wound to his left thigh, which left him with a disability for the rest of his life. Jacob and Martha's son Charles Matheny, b.1857, d.1903 was married in 1884 to Louisa Elvira Houck b. 1862 d.1937. She was a daughter of Abraham Houck and Rachel Green Houck b.1836 d.1897.

Charles and Elvira's children were:

Lola, b.1885 d.1962, m.1906 Harvey Notter b. 1870. They had two son's, Ray, b.1909 d.1984 and Charles b.1911 d.1914. Ray m. Virginia Chenowith d.1984. No children. After Harveys death in 1916, Lola m. 1919 Tracy Johnson b.1878 d.1931. They had one daughter, Irene b.1925 d.1989. Irene m. 1943, Harold Neal b.1920 d.1991

James Elbin, b.1886 d. 1951. He married 1918, Roxie Tipton b.1900 d.1997. Their children were: Richard, Robert b.1923 d. 2001, and Beatrice b.1925 d.1983. Waldo Leslie, b. 1887 d.1995, never married.

Eva Marie b. 1889 d.1963. Married 1917 Oscar Beck b. 1885 d.1947. Their children were: Martha Helena, m. Garland Lear, Leslie, m. Doris Jean Cochran, Kathryn m. Bradford Massey, Bob, m. Hermine (Mini) Bigl, Mary Lou b. 1928, d.1929.

Edwin, b. 1892- d. 1893

Wallen, b. 1893 d.1947 m. 1921 Louise Rood, b.1900 d.1965. Their children were: Ray, m. Helen Williams, Martha m. Ed Fillinger b.1918 d.1998, Jaunita m. Wayne Price. Lillie Emogene b.1928 d.1929.

Mae b.1895 d.1980 m. 1914 William Kerns, their daughter Marcella, b.1916 d. 2001.

Joseph Lee, b. 1897 d. 1961 m. 1930 Marie Beck b.1911 d. 1990, their children were: Marietta, m. Homer Burger, Charles Lee, m. Wanda Shaver, Edward m. Shelah Reynolds. Maurice, m. Florida Maynard, Joe, m. Jea.nie Morrison, Danny, m. Ruth Casto, Walter, m. Margaret Kirby, Marlin.

Stanley, b,1899 d.1966 m. Margie Irion, b.1906 d.1996. No children.

Roma, b. 1901 d.1901.

Charles was only forty-six years old when he died, leaving his eight children fatherless. His two oldest sons were James who was sixteen and Waldo who was fifteen. It became their job to provide a living for their mother and five younger brothers and sisters. An older sister was helping a neighbor with her work. James and Waldo raised tobacco to sell. They had a garden for summer vegetables and for their mother to can for winter use. They had farm animals for meat, milk and eggs. They all survived and grew to adults. Lee and Wallen served in World War 1. Waldo never married but stayed at home with his mother who died in 1937. He died in 1955.

*Submitted by: Martha Helena Lear and Jean Beach*

**ELVA F. ROBERTS HOLBROOK FAMILY** - Elva born May 31 1916, died June 7, 2001, married June 9, 1938. George Lee Holbrook born December 3, 1915, died October 20, 1950. They had four children. Pat (Ray, died) Galyen 6 children and 11 grandchildren, Dallas (Bethany) Holbrook, Katherine Eloise Holbrook, died, and Sharon (Morgan, died) Holbrook Howard.

George Lee Holbrook's parents were Avery Holbrook and Ora Estel Hillman. Grandparents were Thomas Hillman and Eliza Robinson. They came to Ohio in 1921 from Kentucky.

Elva's descendants have lived in Rodney, Ohio since the Bings and Alexander Waddell families came to Ohio from Augusta Co. VA. In 1805.

*Elva F. Roberts Holbrook Family*

Elva Roberts Holbrook's parents were Robert Earl Roberts, Sr. and Callie Catherine Mitchell, married November 18, 1913.

Earl Roberts' parents were Thomas Marlow Roberts and Francis Elizabeth Waddell married March 3, 1876. Grandparents were Peter JL Maxey Roberts and Sophia Jane Bing married ) October 10, 1850. Great-grandparents were Franklin Waddell and Mary Scott married April 28, 1853. His great, great-grandparents were Rev. William Waddell born June 20, 1806 and died January 10, 1889 and Elizabeth Hughes born 1804 and died August 27, 1879. He was elected 1863 to be sheriff of Gallia Co. 1864 and 1865.

Callie Catherine Mitchell's parents were John Mitchell and Zibba Jane Jeviett and came to Gallia County in 1911. They owned a grocery store on the corner of Third and Grape Street in Gallipolis. The building burned in recent years

Earl and Callie Roberts had ten children: John, died (Dorothy, died) Roberts, one child; Elva, died (George, died) Holbrook, four children; Thelma Rees McClure, died, two children; Irene, died (Neal, died) Wise, seven children; Robert Earl (Ruth) Roberts, Jr., two children; Orin Roberts, died; Loren Roberts, died; Glenn (Glenna Mae) Roberts, one child; Mary (Eugene) Moore, seven children; and Sophia (Gordon) Swisher, one child.

Sophia Jane Bing Roberts' father was Samuel Russell Bing. Her brother was Thomas Marlow Bing. He was a Union soldier CO. F., 141, O.V.I. Her nephew was Simeon H. Bing and he with legislation decided how many school days.

Mary Scott Waddell's brother John W. Scott organized CO. H. 141 Ohio Volunteers. Her sons George E Waddell was in the Spanish-American War and Charles Waddell was in the Navy in 1812.

Maxey Roberts was Corporal of Ben Rutherford's CO. G. 195th regiment of infantry of Ohio Volunteers.

Peter J L Roberts served under Captain Ramsey's 1st U.S. Rifles Reg.6. He also was valet ,1813, for General McArthur for a while. He was born in Washington Co, NY.

The Roberts family tree goes back to 1660. Peter Roberts I married Sarah Baker, April 27, 1685. The Roberts are: Peter, Peter, Philip, Peter Thomas, Zopher, Peter J L, Peter Johnathan Maxey Roberts born 1826 April 13 and died December 21, 1895.

*Submitted by: Sharon Holbrook Howard*

**HOLCOMB FAMILY HISTORY** - The Holcombs came to this country during The Great Migration (1620-1633). Thomas Holcomb was born in Devonshire, England about 1600, and about 1630, embarked for Massachusetts, on the ship "Mary and John", and landed at Dorchester, near Boston Massachusetts, where he lived till 1636. In that year, in company with Rev. John Warsham, he moved to Windsor, Connecticut, where he died in 1657. He was married before leaving England to Elizabeth Ferguson, who bore him several children.

Son Joshua Holcomb was born 1640 in Windsor, Connecticut; died 1690. He married Ruth Sherwood. Joshua Holcomb was elected Deputy of the General Court to represent Simsbury at Hartford, Conn.; re-elected 1671 and 1690; received Royal patent for lands at Simsbury in 1670, 1671, and 1690; was granted original tracts of land in Conn. By King Charles II, 23 April 1687; signed as selectman of Simsbury petition to Court in 1687; joined in signing 27 June 1687 agreement with pastor for church there.

Son Thomas Holcomb II, Simsbury, Connecticut, was born in 30 March 1666-died 5 March 1730. He had two wives; his second wife being Rebecca Pettibone (9 March 1675-c14 April 1731). They married 5 December 1700.

Son Return Holcomb was baptized 31 May, 1713 at Simsbury, Conn. He married Jerusha Addams 10 January 1733/4 at Simsbury, Conn. He died at Spencertown, Columbia Co. N.Y.

Son Zephaniah Holcomb was born in Hartford, Connecticut 19 August 1750 and died at Otsego Co. New York 16 March 1822. He served in the Revolutionary War under George Washington. He had two wives; first being Taphena Niles.

Son Samuel Robert Holcomb, Columbia County, New York was born 28 February 1777 and died 24 January 1864 in Vinton, Gallia County, Ohio. He was a Colonel in the War of 1812. He married Indian John Ewing's daughter, Sarah, in 1802. They moved to Mason County, West Virginia, then to Gallia County in 1805. Samuel Holcomb laid out the town of Vinton in 1832 for Samuel Vinton, for whom the town Vinton was named. Holcomb served in Congress for twenty-two years, was Gallia County sheriff and tax collector 18 years, and was a member of the state legislature.

Daughter Taphena Holcomb was born 8 January 1811-died 23 July 1883 in Gallia County. She married Charles Whipple Matthews ) 1803-1889) and had 12 children.

Daughter Lydia Lillian Matthews (6 September 1856-20 November 1936) married Dr. Charles A. Rife (26 November 1858-29 October 1933) on 24 March 1880.

Daughter Taphena Abigail Rife (31 January 1883-1 February 1956) married Harlan Athey (9 January 1887-4 June 1967) on 1 January 1910. To this union were born Pauline (23 October 1910) and Clair (25 April 1913-1986).

Daughter Pauline married Walter W. Rife (18 August 1908-27 June 1977) 9 June 1931. Please refer to the Walter W. Rife family for the remaining genealogy of the family.

*Submitted by Pauline Rife*

**HOLZER DESCENDENTS** - Genealogical research can be historically worthwhile, scientifically useful, and often confusing as Dr. Holzer, Sr. discovered. Each search he commissioned proved different. His favorite was done in 1916 by Dr. Seeger, Ex-Regent College of Heraldry that produced a coat-of-arms dating back to the first Crusade in A.D. 1096 first borne by a Sir Knight Crusader Johann von Holzer. We know the word Holzer means "wood-cutter" in German and were happy to find another Johann Holzer on a trip to the Bavarian Alps. He was an artist and painted the domed ceiling of St. Anton's Church in the 18th. century. We would be happy to claim him.

By request there follows a short summary of Alma and Charles Holzer descendents: Three of their five children are deceased—Charles, Jr., Richard and Louise—as is Frederick Holzer, son of Virginia and Richard.

Christine, born on Charles' first birthday, married a successfully writer, Frank Harvey. Their children: Michael, business executive, Texas; Mimi, N.J., whose art hangs in Pediatrics at Holzer Medical Center and Henry, another successful artist, Bucks County, Pa. Christine, a well-known concert pianist is now gaining acclaim with her sculpting.

Elizabeth Reynolds, former model and dancing instructor, married a lawyer. Their children: Frederick Reynolds, who leaves his work in a library to make "in demand" drawings of 19th century British salmon flies and Jeffrey, a master electrician in Colorado, whose wife Kathy, and children, Andrew and Kelly, all like visiting Gallia County.

*Mrs Holzer and daughters by Statue of Dr. Holzer Jr.*

Louise Brink (deceased) who lived many years in Gallipolis historic Gates House was knowledgeable of antiques, outstanding at decorating and well-trained in art. Her children are practicing lawyers:

Michael (whose young athletic son is Jon) has a law firm in Princeton and a farm in Virginia. Lisa, (SC) married Theodore Williams (lawyer) and they are parents of Audrey, Anna and Ted. Richard Holzer married Virginia Beasley (both deceased) and they are parents of Jenny Holzer, internationally acclaimed artist, married to Michel Glier, head of Williams College Art Department. They are the parents of Lili, talented in art and with an inherited love of horses. Richard's second daughter, Julie, a graduate of Ohio University, is a horse breeder and equestrian.

The children of Charles (deceased) and Bobbie Holzer are: Karin, married to Dennis O'Neil (retired teacher, now enjoying the stock market). Karin, after many years at Williston Northampton School, in Massachusetts (where an instructorship has been established in her name) is now head of the Association of Independent Schools in the State of Ohio. They now live in Galena. Their son David is at Nationwide (computers) and his wife, Carol Lynne is a Public Health Nurse. Two talented children, Erin and Ryan, keep them busy.... Charles E. Holzer, III, an Epidemiologist, University of Texas Medical Branch, Galveston and his wife, Jean (John Bradford descendent) who works at Boeing on the space program. Robin and husband, Bill Blackwell, are working on MBA's at Rice and Christopher is in child development and loves art. John Holzer and wife Ann live in Richmond, Indiana. John is with Mosey Manufacturing and Ann is an MSW at St. Vincent's Hospital. They have 3 daughters: Allison, recipient of academic scholarship, talented in science and art and a Carleton College graduate is teaching at Scattergood School, Iowa. Meredith, majors in Spanish at Indiana University, plays basketball, and writes fascinating letters, and has already made several trips to Spain. Emily, an eighth grader, has been awarded a scholarship at Westtown (PA) Preparatory School and excels at needlework. Christiana Holzer Gallant (teacher) met her husband, Tom, (radiologist) at Colby College, ME. Their oldest son, Nathan (UW) left for Portland, Oregon to write the great American novel, instead works at a television station and directs weekend news. Andrew is a promising drama major at the University of Wisconsin. Lara, has recently received a Merit Scholarship Commendation and enters college this fall. Amy Holzer met her husband, Dudley Irvin (Senior Vice President Bank One) at Kenyon College. She is a graduate of Capitol School of Nursing, an avid school volunteer, leader of Junior Achievement and Junior Great Books in Westerville. Two sons: Alexander, a 5$^{th}$, grader likes soccer and bowling and Eric, also a 5$^{th}$ grader, who excels in soccer, good grades and art.

**HOLZER, JR.** - Charles Holzer. Jr. joined his father in the practice of surgery (1946) and a scant two years later, the Holzer Clinic was formed. Three fine physicians were then in practice with his father, Drs. Vornholt, Foster and Richards. Charles turned down the offer to own the hospital. Many specialties, such as pediatrics, had not yet reached Gallipolis and it was his dream to expand services and to entice as many specialists as possible to the region. He was convinced that the very best would come only if they had an equal share in planning and remuneration. He was impressed by the skill of his father, the doctors and nurses and other personnel who were here, but he knew more was needed. He had attended Mercersburg Academy, Haverford College, Cornell University Medical School (where he finished second in his class and won one of the two academic prizes) and The School of Surgery at the University of Cincinnati.

*Holzer, Jr. Family 1962*

In 1940, he married Roberta (Bobbie) Wilhelm, whose father was an official at the Marietta Manufacturing Co. (He was a member of the Mayflower Society and it was the great-granddaughter of Miles Standish and John Alden who married Jacob Wilhelm (a German, whose name then descended to many Welch, Scotch, English and Irish). His parents had met at Denison University, his father in the class of 1869. His mother was honored in 1933 (age 90) as its oldest living alumna. Bobbie's mother was the daughter of the owner of Heslop's Machine Works (boat repair). She had roots in England and Virginia, was active in the Episcopal Church and D.A.R. Bobbie loved her first year of marriage in Manhattan, except for the four flights of stairs to the 72$^{nd}$ Street Apartment and the "morning sickness" that appeared in April. Their first three (of five) children were born in Cincinnati, where there were only three flights of stairs, a zoo within walking distance and a husband rarely home. Back in Gallipolis, she often entertained visiting physicians and was amazed when any accepted. (She served filets wrapped in bacon to an orthodox Jewish couple. She also forgot it was Friday when she served a Catholic doctor sirloin steak and he (nicely) asked if he could fry himself an egg.

Charles was especially active at the Clinic and Hospital where he made daily "rounds" and knew and respected every person who worked there. He also served on the Boards of Ohio University and Stuart Hall; received Haverford's Alumni of the Year Award, was Professor Emeritus at the University of Cincinnati, helped pass the Guiding Hand School levy and gave his share of his parents' home to the French Art Colony. He was very active in the Episcopal Church, an avid reader, loved being with the children, loved climbing mountains (especially Alps) and began running again at age 60, completing 13 marathons. He returned to Cincinnati every Wednesday for surgical rounds that began at 8 a.m. for many months after moving to Gallipolis. It was necessary in those days to leave by 5 a.m. to arrive on time. Since Bobbie knew a baby sitter in Cincinnati, she often went along with the three children in tow. He was responsible for arranging the Residency Program with the Department of Surgery in Cincinnati. Physicians who have finished medical school and their internship and several years of their approximately five years of surgical training come to work at Holzer for a period of time. They bring many positive ideas with them and learn what it is like to work with private patients. The program is now over 40 years old. His family often thought he should have more time at home; but they were proud that he always answered each telephone call, was always ready to go to work at a moment's notice even if some stranger was in trouble during a vacation and envious that he could operate all night, come home, take a shower and go back for a full day's work—often.

**HOLZER** - Carl and Elizabeth Holzer left Cologne, Germany in 1848 with Carl Schurz. They migrated to America, and once there they settled in Indiana. Their son, William Henry Frederick Holzer (teacher and railroad foreman) married Susan Frances Kinter of Defiance County, Ohio. Kinter's father invented a clover-seed huller, a hay loader and was an early developer of bee culture.

William and Susan's son, Charles Elmer was born in Van Wert, Ohio in 1887. Charles left home to work his way through college. In 1909, at the age of 22, he graduated from Ohio State's Starling Loving School of Medicine. He later furthered that education by studying in New York, London and Vienna. After graduating in 1909, he came to Gallipolis, Ohio, for a year's intensive surgical experience at the Ohio Home for Epileptics (then the second largest in the world) with every intention of returning to Columbus.

However, friends who were unhappy with only a visiting surgeon or with driving over bad roads to get to Columbus urged the young surgeon to practice in Gallipolis. One such friend offered Charles a loan of $4500 (repayment to be $500 every six months) for the purchase of a house to be used as a hospital. He accepted the offer and opened a seven-bed hospital (Alcorn

House, 507 Second Ave.). The marble floor of the operating room was acquired by purchasing excess dresser tops at twenty cents each. Four years later, a move to the Hanson house (535 Second Ave.) provided thirteen beds.

*Dr. Charles E. Holzer's 60th. Birthday party seated is Mrs. Alma Holzer*

Many of Dr. Holzer's days were to be spent on horseback or in buggy, rowboat or red Hupmobile in order to reach the ill who lived in remote areas on both sides of the Ohio River. Those difficult travels made him an early leader in providing better roads, an airport and the ill-fated Silver Bridge. The Silver Bridge collapsed in 1967 after 37 years of operation.

Not only did Gallipolis, Ohio, become Dr. Charles Holzer's home; he became its great benefactor. Quite by accident, in 1914, he met the lovely, young Superintendent of Nurses at Columbus' Grant Hospital. She consented to move to Gallipolis to work for him and in a short while, Alma Vornholt would become his wife. She was the daughter of Frederick and Sopbia (Berner) Vornholt of New Bremen, Ohio, with roots in Schleswig Holstein, Germany.

Before Dr. Holzer enlisted in the U.S. Army, the two had begun a new hospital and a family that would grow to five: Charles Jr., Christine, Richard, Louise and Elizabeth. Young, talented and tireless Alma McCormick would become business manager and join the Holzers in their efforts. Together, they improved health care, established a School of Nursing (1920), restored the historic Our House and improved education. They also supported various conservative projects, flood control and Rio Grande College.

In 1949, a 47-bed hospital was given to the Holzer Hospital Foundation (representing the people of Ohio counties: Gallia, Meigs, Jackson, Lawrence and Vinton and West Virginia county: Mason.). The hospital began operation during World War I and was expanded several times. It was vacated in 1972 for the move to the $21,000,000 complex on Jackson Pike.

Dr. Charles Holzer was President of the Board of Education for ten years, members of the Community Association and the Tri-State Medical Society (Ohio, West Virginia and Kentucky), in addition to serving on the Boards of Rio Grande College and Ohio University. Not only did the Holzers leave legacies which included the hospital, the School of Nursing, the restoration of the Our House Museum, the first Gallipolis airport and the original Silver Bridge, they also left many devoted patients who had been served through the years.

They would be pleased to know that among their progeny are artists (one internationally known and one whose delightful prints hang in Pediatrics); a sculptress (originally a concert pianist); the Head of Independent Schools in the state of Ohio; an epidemiologist at the University of Texas (Galveston) who has been the recipient of prestigious awards for work in racial tolerance; outstanding teachers and nurses; and most importantly, loving, caring parents who hope to inspire new generations to also care about providing better lives for all.

**LARRY AND NANCY MYERS HOOD FAMILY** - The Myers / Hood family goes back eight generations to a common ancestor.

*Five Generations: Mary Louella Amos/Myers, Nancy Elizabeth Myers Hood, Mary Elizabeth Hood Rumley, Hannah Elizabeth Rumley, Jenna Elizabeth Halley*

Mary Shoemaker m. Andrew Lemley:Andrew Lemley m. Mary Louella Allen, James Theodore Lemley m. Cora Ralph, Neva Lemley m. Pearl Amos, Bessie Lemley m. Henry Hood Mary Louella Amos m. James Columbus Myers, Harold Hood m. Ida Mae Thompson Nancy Elizabeth Myers m. Harold Larry Hood Mary Elizabeth Hood m. Richard Rumley Hannah Elizabeth Rumley and Jason E. Halley, parents of Jenna Elizabeth Halley.

In 1928, two brothers, Abraham, age 21 and John, age 18, sons of John and Catherine Niday Myers came to Gallia County. Family history claims they were born in Giles County, VA. Abraham married Jane Fralicks, dau. of George and Peggy Yates Fralicks of Pittsylvania County, VA. in Gallipolis, OH., in 1834. The marriage was without issue.

Both brothers settled in Walnut Twp. and Meyers Hollow was named from John.

On the second Sunday of August the Myers Family Reunion is held. The first gathering of the family was in 1918.

John, Nancy's great-great-great-grandfather, married Mary Polly Fralix (Fralicks), Jane's sister, in Gallipolis in 1833. Their eldest son, Christopher who was a Civil War veteran, farmer, and schoolteacher married Philena Fox and was the father of James William Myers.

The Myers family became eligible for First Families going back to James C. Myers' side of the family to Jacob and Catherine Iron Elliott. Catherine was born January 6, 1818 in Gallia County, Ohio. She died May 1, 1894 and is buried at Fairview. Their daughter Laura Elliott (born April 14, 1859 died February 22, 1941) married James William Myers (born April 28, 1857 died March 12, 1939) who was a storekeeper, carpenter and undertaker at Mudsoc. They became the parents of fourteen children, seven boys and seven girls. One boy and one girl died at an early age. Their children and their spouses were: Jacob Columbus and Hannah Elizabeth Shafer Myers (grandparents of Nancy Myers Hood); Warren Delman and Artie Gothard Myers; Eliza Jane Myers and Albert Tope; Ira Edward and Ora Odessa Ball Myers; Nancy Catherine Myers (born June 1, 1884-died May 14, 1891); Jesse Arnold Myers (born May 12, 1886-died October 8, 1887); James Curtis and Anna Pearl Massie Myers; Daisy Maud Myers and Elmer Drummond; Alva Clarence and Lena Echelmyer Myers; Nellie Pearl Myers and Claude Dailey and also John Knox Wiliams; Ora Ethyl Myers and Fred Pope; Lottie Marie Myers and Omar Russell Henry; Shirley Garnet Myers and Levi Watson Neal; Morris Edgbert and Laura Edith Woods Myers and also Gladys Swisher Myers.

Nancy's grandparents, Jacob Columbus who was a produce dealer and Hannah Elizabeth Shafer Myers had four children. Carl Clarence married Willie Martin and had a daughter Tharon Hannahbelle who died in an automobile accident in 1937. Elmer Willard born March 4, 1898 died July 23, 1913. Geneva Esta married William Earl Monteith. Their marriage was without issue. Nancy's father, James Columbus married Mary Louella Amos and had six children. Richard Aaron married Polly Ann Miller and they had four children. Nancy Elizabeth married Harold Larry Hood and had three children; Mary Elizabeth married Harold Richard Rumley and had two children, Hannah Elizabeth mother of Jenna Elizabeth Halley and Jacob Richard; Larry Joseph married Barbara Jean (Bobbi) Stewart and had two children, Larry James (L.J.) and Amy Christine; Bill Harold married Brenda Kay Fife and had two children, Adam Lewis and Emily Anne. William Amos married Sharon Kay Russell and had three children. James Allen married Evelyn Tyo and had a daughter; he married Vicki Lynn Miller and had two daughters. Michael Albert married Cynthia Creviston and had two sons, Helen Patrice married Dale Simpkins and had a daughter.

Nancy's parents, James and Mary Myers, moved to Marion County, Ohio in the late 1950's. Larry's parents, Harold and Ida Hood, lived in Gallia County until their deaths. Although all of Nancy and Larry's siblings moved away from Gallia County and reared their families elsewhere, Nancy and Larry continued to live in Gallia County and reared their family in Addison. Nancy is a retired teacher from the Gallia County Local Schools, Larry is retired from Carter's Plumbing. Their children chose to remain in Gallia County and reared their families in Addison also. Elizabeth works at Firstar Bank, Joe works at Kyger Creek Plant, and Bill works at Gavin Plant. Their families have always been active in school and community events.

**BETTE NULL HORAN** - Bette is the daughter of the late Ernest E Null and Clarice Howard Null both of Gallia County. She was born July 7,1932 in Gallia County. and resided with her parents and brother Merrill, sisters Marianna (Dille) and Barbara (Richards) at 50 Vine Street. She attended Gallipolis City Schools and graduated from Gallia Academy High School.

Upon graduation, Bette went to work for Dr. Donald Warehime at Warehime Clinic, 530 Second Avenue. She attended Jefferson Business College and later graduated from LPN school and worked for Holzer Hospital.

*Bette Null Horan*

In 1975 she and her sister Marianna Dille purchased Knight's Department Store on Court Street from the Jack Knight family who had operated the store for many years. Upon the death of her sister, Bette became the owner and still operates Knight's Department store on Court Street in Gallipolis.

On March 15,1975, Bette married Donald Horan from Cincinnati, Ohio and they resided at 48 Vine Street. Don retired from construction work in 1993. He died May 28, 1998 from a heart attack.

Bette is an active member of Grace United Methodist Church and enjoys gardening, visiting with friends and her poodle Riley. Submitted by Bette Null Horan

**ROSCOE HOUCK** - Roscoe Stanton Houck of the Crown City community was the son of Noah and Mary (Danner) Houck. He married Hezel Irene (Moore) Houck whose parents were Robert and Amanta (Deenphy) Moore.

Roscoe was a dairy farmer, county commissioner and later worked at the G.D.C.

They had two children Ray Richard Houck, who married Diana Fife. (Diana died from injuries when a car hit her while riding a bicycle).

Ray was a barber in Gallipolis for several years before moving to Toledo, then to Fort Recovery where he worked for Fort Recovery Industries.

Ray and Diana had three children: Allen Ray (Carol) of Franklin, Tenn.

Brent (Cindy) of Findlay, Ohio and Teresa (Dean) Hunt of Salem, N.C.

Ray and wife Ruth ,now both retired live in Fort Recovery and spend winters in Florida.

Roscoe and Hazel also had a daughter Rosealee. She married Raymond DeLille. See: Raymond DeLille.

**ARTHUR M. HOYT FAMILY** - Arthur Mann Hoyt, was born September 17, 1911, and Virginia Rebecca Evans was born May 11, 1916, in Gallipolis, Ohio. Our parents were both farmers so we each grew up on the farm.

Arthur's parents were Albert Maurice and Mary Margaret Stone Hoyt, his grandparents were Mahlon M. and Barbara Ann Martin Hoyt George and Emily Liddy Stone.

Virginia's parents were Robert Lee and Annie Dove Plymale Evans, her grandparents were Edward R. and Rebecca McCoy Evans and John Taylor and Emma Byer Plymale.

Her parents and grandparents lived in the area of Covington, Virginia. They moved with their family, including a nephew Estus Plymale, whom they considered as their own, to Gallia County in 1915. Virginia was the only child born in Ohio, and never knew her grandparents, because at that time, Covington was a very long distance to travel.

Arthur was the oldest of the three children: a sister Ruth Hoyt Pitchford and brother, Harold Stone Hoyt. Virginia was the youngest of eight children; brothers, John, Basil, Leslie (Tim), Wilford and Claude, and two sisters; Ruby Evans Houck, and Erma Evans Evans.

Arthur and Virginia were married in Catlettsburg, Kentucky in 1933 and were blessed with three wonderful children; Mary Ann, Ansel Martin and Judith Kay.

Arthur spent many of his working years with Standard Oil Company. He was transferred from Gallipolis to the Pomeroy Sohio Station on East Main St. in 1951 and so began their life in Meigs County. A few years later, he had his own Sohio Service Station on West Main St.

Mary Ann graduated from Gallia Academy High School, Gallipolis and was married just before we moved to Pomeroy in 1951. So, with Ansel and Judy we moved to 102 Union Ave. in November 1951. They both graduated from Pomeroy High School.

As life long Methodists, one of the first things was to locate the United Methodist Church on Second St.. The family has been affiliated there ever since.

Mary Ann married Dr. Thomas Crawford and they live in Baltimore, Maryland. They have three children: Dr. Mary Cacia (Ryan) Masser, Kristin Ann (Neil) Trueblood and Thomas Gregan (Donna) Crawford. Seven grandchildren: Olivia, Rosemary and Mitchell Masser, Kelsey and Elisa Trueblood, and Cameron and Lindsey Crawford.

Ansel married Barbara Joan Norton of Wellston and they live in New Richmond, Ohio. They have two children: Andrew Mark (Jennifer) Hoyt, and Debra Gwyn (Calvin) Hughes, and five grandchildren: Kelly and Lauren Hoyt and Candice, Ashley and Andrew Hughes. They all live in the Cincinnati area.

Their daughter, Judith Hoyt Morris, returned to Meigs County several years ago. She was a secretary and retired last year from American Electric Power.

Arthur was working with Wackenhut Security at the Gavin Power Plant when he retired in 1976. Virginia worked at Philip Sporn Power Plant for twenty five years and retired in 1980.

They enjoyed traveling and going to antique shops. One of their favorite sports was bowling in leagues for many years until Arthur's health no longer permitted it.

They celebrated their golden wedding anniversary shortly before his death in 1983. He is buried in the family plot on Mound Hill Cemetery in Gallipolis, Ohio.

Their children and grandchildren have inherited their love for antiques, family togetherness and family history. Virginia still lives on Union Avenue in Pomeroy, and enjoys family, friends, crochet and needlepoint work, traveling and church activities

*Submitted by Virginia Evans Hoyt*

**CHARLES E. HUBER FAMILY** - Charles E. Huber II and Peggy Lou Brown were married March 22, 1969, at the First Presbyterian Church in Gallipolis. They met at the church when he was in the Air Force and visited his grandparents on the weekends.

*Peggy And Charles Huber*

They have two daughters. Amy Brooke Huber is a legislative service manager for the Committee For Education Funding in Washington, D.C. She is engaged to Tim Sechler, who is a senior application developer for Lockheed Martin in Gaithesburg, MD. They are planning a wedding on May 19, 2002, in Washington, D.C. Abbey Beth Huber married David T. Russell on November 19, 1999, and they have one daughter, Alexis Brooke. They reside in Gallipolis.

Charlie has had a few jobs while in Gallipolis, but his favorite was the owner of Charlie's and Company, a snack shop, on Court Street. He is now employed by Wilcoxen Funeral Home of Pt. Pleasant as an embalmer and director.

Peggy is a teacher and has taught at many schools in the city and county. Her first position was in Henderson, WV. She was at the traffic light when the Silver Bridge fell. Her father walked the railroad bridge that night to get to her in Pt. Pleasant.

Charlie's family was from the Middleport-Pomeroy area and were originally from Germany. Charlie's grandfather, Charlie "Duco" Huber, had Eddie's on Second Avenue before the Davis-Shuler fire. He and his wife, Dora, always had a good food and flower garden at 35 Grape Street. Many people would stop for seeds and plants. Charlie's parents are Betty Jo Camp and Charles E. Huber. He has twin sisters, Deidre and Diane, that live in Maryland.

Peggy's parents are Eulah Francis Miller and Harvey E. Brown, Jr. She had one brother, Gary Lee Brown, deceased. Some of Peggy's family was from the German Ridge area in Gallia County and were originally from Germany. Her great grandfather, John George Miller, was born in Kirchdorf, Bavaria, in 1826. He came to America in 1856 and to Ohio in 1862. A homestead was built on German Hollow Road where her grandparents, August Phillip Miller and Mae Rice Miller , also lived. Many enjoyable times were spent there with cousins, aunts and uncles. It was a wonderful place to spend a childhood.

Peggy and Charlie's families met before the couple was married. Charlie's grandfather,

Charlie, found Peggy's great grandfather, Richard Milton Brown, along side his wrecked buggy at State Route 141. The newspaper stated that it was lucky that someone found him because traffic was so sparse on that route.

Peggy and Charlie still attend the First Presbyterian Church and enjoy the members and activities. Abbey was also married at the church and attends as well. They like living in a smaller community and hope that some of their family will remain in the area and Gallia County will continue to grow and be a great place to raise a family.

*Submitted by Peggy L. Huber*

**WILLIAM K. HURLOW & E. GARNETT (BROYLES/MCPHERSON) HURLOW FAMILY** - William Kenneth Hurlow was born July 19, 1944 in Pt. Pleasant, WV to Leemon Joseph and Nora Chloe (Robinson) Hurlow. Bill is a 1966 graduate of Pt. Pleasant High School. From 1966 to 1968 he served in the United States Army in Vietnam. In 1968 he entered in the Boilermakers Union Local 667 Apprenticeship program and completed it in 1972. He presently works for the union with 30 years of service and will soon be retiring.

On October 5, 1980 in Gallia County he married Ethel Garnett (Broyles) McPherson. She was born October 5, 1944 in Gallia County to John Luther "Red" and Adeldia Marie (Stover) Broyles. Garnett is a 1963 graduate of Kyger Creek High School. From 1977 to 1990 she was employed as a teacher for Head Start where she received her Early Childhood Development Associate Degree. From 1990 to 1995 she provided child care in her home.

Bill brought 1 child and Garnett brought 2 children into the marriage which were all raised in their home on State Route 218.

Garnett's first child, Angela Hope McPherson was born on September 21, 1967 in Gallia County. Angie is a 1986 graduate of Hannan Trace High School and she attended Rio Grande College. From 1988 to 1990 she was employed with the Gallia County Health Department and from 1990 to 1999 she was employed with CIGNA Health Care as an Administrative Assistant.

Angie married Ronald Andrew Saunders, son of Russell L. and Patricia (Cain) Saunders on July 28, 1990 in Gallia County and moved to Columbus. Ron is a 1985 graduate of Hannan Trace High School and a 1990 graduate of the University of Rio Grande with a bachelors degree in Accounting. He is employed by the Bureau of Alcohol, Tobacco, and Firearms as a Forensic Auditor and has 12 years of service, 10 of which were with the Office of Inspector General for the Department of Housing and Urban Development as a Senior Auditor. In 1996 he received his Certified Government Financial Manager credentials, in 1999 his Certified Internal Auditor credentials and in 2001 his Certified Fraud Specialist credentials. On July 12, 1999 in Columbus they were blessed with triplets. A daughter, Carsyn Malyn, a son, Clayton Andrew, and a daughter, Camryn Paige.

Garnett's second child, Ross Hugh McPherson was born September 30, 1969 in Texas.

He is a 1989 graduate of Hannan Trace High School. In 1989, he completed an Advanced Welding program at Buckeye Hills Career Center. In 1990 Ross started employment with the Laborers Union Local 543 where he presently works. He resides in Gallia County and enjoys hunting and wildlife on the family farm.

Bill's child, Robert Joseph Hurlow was born March 23, 1975 in Gallia County. Bob is a 1993 graduate of River Valley High School. He served in the United States Navy from 1993 to 1996. In 1999 he started attending the University of Rio Grande where he will soon receive a degree in Business/Information Technology. He resides in Gallia County.

*Submitted by: Garnett Hurlow and Angie Saunders*

**HUTCHINSON, WHEATON AND PRIESTLEY FAMILIES** - William Henry Hutchinson (born 7 March 1838) is pictured with great grand-daughter Mary Ellen Wheaton on 10 April 1924.

*William H. Hutchinson And Mary Ellen Wheaton Priestly*

He was the son of Benjamin and Martha King Hutchinson of Tynsboro, MA and came to Gallipolis in 1866 after being discharged from the Union Army following the Civil War He served as a private in Co. H 137th OVI and was a member of Cadot Post, G.A.R. of Gallipolis. After establishing the Hutchinson Hardware Store at 50 Court St., with which he was associated for 45 years, he married Sarah Tracie Peirce of Tynsboro, 15 November 1866. Their only child, Alicia Octavia Hutchinson was born 19 November 1867 at 214 First Avenue. Mr. Lemuel Perry, who resided at the northwest corner of Locust and Third Avenue, built a home for the family one door north of his on Third Avenue where the Hutchinsons resided from August 1888 to November 1904.

On 22 August 1888 Alicia became the wife of Walter George Wheaton (born Kalamazoo, MI 30 March 1866) who had come to southern Ohio with his mother, Dr. Laura Marion Wheeler Wheaton, following her marriage 19 December 1876 to Judge Tobias Plantz of Pomeroy, Ohio. Walter served as bookkeeper, assistant cashier and cashier of the First National Bank organized in 1861 by National Charter #136 and located on Second Ave. in Gallipolis. He built their family home at 534 Second Ave. in 1894; the elder Hutchinsons joining them November 1904. Their home was the scene of many happy and gala social events. Their two children Laura Tracie (born 4 March 1891) and William Walter (Buzz) (born 28 April 1894) enjoyed the school and activities of the area. Laura performed in her class play "The College Widow" which was presented at the Opera House on May 25, 1909. William carried the cross at St. Peter's Episcopal Church, participated in the elaborate production of "The Mikado" given 9 May 1911 under the auspices of St. Peter's Parish Guild, and gave a memorable speech titled "Cheerfulness" at his 1911 high school graduation.

As both children planned to attend college, the family including Mr. Hutchinson (Mrs. Hutchinson had died 23 February 1910) moved to Columbus and resided at 311 West 10th Avenue, directly across from The Ohio State University. Mr Hutchinson, known widely for always wearing a high silk hat, died 11 December 1924 and along with his wife Sarah, Walter George and Alicia (Alice) Wheaton and their daughter Laura Tracie Hull are buried at Mound Hill Cemetery (Lot #30, Section #8).

William (Buzz) Wheaton, a prominent businessman, married Columbus native Sarah Elizabeth Stuber (born 26 December 1897, died 7 August 1960). To this union were born two daughters Mary Ellen (born 22 December 1922) and Sarah Alicia (born 8 May 1928, died 28 October 1930). In 1951 the 1911 Gallia Academy High School class had their only reunion. Mr. Wheaton saw 11 of his 13 classmates for the first time in 40 years. Among them was Dr. David Clay Priestley (see Priestley Family) of nearby Green Township. As a result of this chance reacquaintance, the Priestley's son Archie, who graduated from Centenary School, Gallia Academy High School (Class of 1937) and The Ohio State University College of Veterinary Medicine (Class of March 1943) met and married Mary Ellen Wheaton on 19 June 1953. They have resided in Columbus, OH and are the parents of Mary Alicia Priestley (born 16 June 1954, married Lawrence James Walker, Jr. 16 October 1994) of Columbus, OH and David Wheaton Priestley (born 19 May 1956), married Susan Janet Osterhout 3 September 1978 of Birmingham, MI. Their grandchildren are Sarah Angeline Walker (born 24 August 1997), Daniel Wheaton Priestley (born 21 January 1987), and Morgan Elliott Priestley (born 12 May 1990). Through the years the Hutchinson, Wheaton and Priestley families have always been very proud of their Gallipolis and Gallia County heritage.

**HUTSINPILLER FAMILY** - Abraham Hutsinpiller (1772-1854), needing more land for his growing family, came to Gallia Co. from Greenbrier Co., VA/WV, in 1808 with his wife Mollie (Wax), daughter of Revolutionary War soldier Henry Wax, and their seven children. They settled in Green Township. Here they added four more children. He subscribed to the building of Gallia Academy.

He was the son of Jacob Hotzenpiller (1714-1813) and Elizabeth Hoover. Jacob farmed in Hampshire Co. VA at "Hotzenbeler's Mill", then later moved to Greenbrier Co. VA. Abraham's grandfather was Staffen Hatzenbuhler, born near Hatzenbuhl in the Palatine of Germany, who arrived in Philadelphia in 1728 on the ship "Mortenhouse". Stephen married Elizabeth Brumback, daughter of immigrant Melchior Brumback, in Virginia. They purchased land from Jost HITE in the Shenandoah Valley. Stephen was a farmer, blacksmith, freeholder, constable, overseer of roads, and fought in the Virginia militia against the Indians. He and Elizabeth had 12 children, and a number of his descendants moved to Ohio.

Abraham and Mollie's children were: i. Hannah (1799-1850+) married James Rea, moved to Illinois, then Red Oak IA; ii. Jacob (1801-bef. 1847) iii. William (1802-1847+), married Mary Hawver, went west after the death of his wife and first child, leaving a surviving child, Augustus, with his brother David); iv. Elizabeth (1804-1847), had one child, Andrew Hutsinpiller who married into the Rader family of Ohio; v. Mary (1806-1840), married Charles C. Wood; vi. Polly (1806—1806) ; vii. Nancy (1808-aft 1840) married Reuben Graham; viii. John H. (1810-1877) , a steamboat captain, married Sarah Ann Shephard, 3 children; ix. Rebecca (1812-1840), married John Graham, 3 children; x. Henry (1815-1872) , married Jane Dodge, ill health all his life, lived in Jackson Co, then returned to Gallia Co; xi. David (1817-1881), a prosperous farmer and stock raiser, served on the County School Board and Mt. Zion Methodist Church.

David Hutsinpiller, the 9th child of Abraham and Mollie, married Mariah Winsor, a descendant of Roger Williams, founder of Rhode Island, and of Govs. Bradstreet and Dudley of Massachusetts Bay Colony. They lived near Rodney in Green Twp. They had eleven children: i. Reuben (1842-1864) , died in Andersonville prison in the Civil War; ii. Lydia (1843-1905), married John Mills, 4 children; iii. Ina Maria (1845-1932), married Rev. Wm. H. Gibbons, 2 children; iv. Ada (1847-1937), married Robt. Johnson, reared her niece Clio Nichols; v. Charles (1849-1937) married Frances Kerr, 3 children; vi. Simeon David (c1851-1924) a Methodist minister, died in Glendale CA, married Frances Aston, Alice Martin and Stella Wheelock in turn; vii. Jesse Winsor (1853-1924 ND) , married Adda Williams; viii. Anna (1856-1929), married John Kerr Powell, 6 children, (see Powell Family); ix William Mills (1858-1943 CA), served School Board, retired to California ; x. Rose (1860-1897), teacher, married Harrison Nichols, 3 children; xi. Jessie Fremont (1867-1923 IA), married Charles Nichols, 1 child, Clio. Jesse and Adda, William, Rose & Harrison, and Jessie and Charles all homesteaded in Dakota Territory.

Submitted by Margaret Powell Hetrick (Mrs. Richard A.)

**JOHN E. AND CAROL JACKSON** - The John E. Jackson family moved from Lawrenceburg, Indiana, to Gallipolis on August 11, 1983, with children Annette, John J., Amy and David. Carol's mother, Garnet Blum, also moved to Gallipolis, living at Pinecrest Care Center until her death on December 24, 1983.

John and Carol (Blum) Jackson were married April 19, 1968, in Columbus, Ohio. John is currently pastor of New Life Lutheran Church. He served as an Army Chaplain in the Ohio National Guard and the US Army Reserves, including nine months in Bosnia as a NATO Chaplain, until his retirement from the army in November 1998.

John has been active in many community activities and on many civic committees. He was instrumental in organizing Keep Gallia Beautiful, a group dedicated to the beautification of Gallipolis and Gallia County.

Carol is a physical therapist working in the schools from 1983-1993, then joining the Holzer Medical Center staff in Therapy Services.

Annette, John J., Amy and David graduated from Gallia Academy High School in 1985, 1987, 1991, and 1992 respectively.

**CARL JAMES FAMILY** - My father Carl Eugene was born Sept. 14, 1933, to Frank and Norma Barcus James. He married Jo Ann Call on Jan. 30, 1954 in Gallipolis. Jo Ann was born March 18, 1938 to Joe Donald and Leota Mae Cobb Call.

Carl went to work for Union Barge Line Corp., Pittsburgh, Pa., when he was 18, as a deckhand. After 48 years on the river Carl retired as a river boat Captain on Jan. 3 1,1999.

*The James Family*

Jo Ann was a wife, mother and homemaker. She enjoyed her church, her home, garden and the farm animals; but most of all she enjoyed her children and grandchildren.

They had five children. Their oldest son Bruce was born April 28, 1956 and died March 9, 1975.

Brent M., born June 10, 1960, married Tamyra L. Pope, born March 12 1960. She is the daughter of Walter J. and Phyllis Wooten Pope. Brent and Tami were married May 2, 1982, at Providence Church by Rev. Earnest Baker. To this union was born two children:

*Carl and Jo Ann Jones*

Gavin M., born April 9, 1985, and Kari B., July 7, 1987. Brent has retired from Gallipolis Development Center as a mason. Tami is a clerk at B.M.V. Gavin is a junior and Kari a freshmen at G.A.H.S. They also run the family farm with registered Black Angus cattle at Leaper, Ohio.

Brice D. James was born January 31, 1965. On July 24, 1987, he was married to Teddi Ann Wooten at Elizabeth Chapel by Rev. Alfred Holley. Teddi was born December 12, 1963 to Ted and Mary Davis Wooten of Bidwell, Ohio. Brice and Teddi have one daughter, Lydia Brooke born Nov. 15 1998 and are expecting their second child in August. Brice, a Manager at Wal-Mart and Teddi, a Lab Technician, have just moved to Parkersburg, WV. They enjoy raising Cocker Spaniel dogs.

Carla J., born September 1, 1968, married William K. Swisher, born June 23, 1963, son of Gordon and Sophia Roberts Swisher. Rev. Ralph Workman married Carla and William on May 29, 1987, at Providence Church. They have a daughter Lauren A., born February 10, 1991, and a son, Jordan K., born May 10, 1996. Carla is a childcare provider at Wee Care Day Care, and Bill is a mechanic at Pechiney Rolled Products and also a sergeant in the W.Va. National Guard. The children enjoy working with their 4-H projects which are lambs, pigs and dogs.

Kristy J. was born July 31, 1970. She married Timothy Huffman on June 30, 1997, at Gatlinburg, Tennessee. Tim was born September 24, 1959, to Bob and Jewell Jeri Adkins Huffman of Homosassa, Florida. Tim and Kristy reside on the family farm at Sweetland, W.V. where they raise registered Black Angus cattle on their 250 acres. Kristy is a Quality Control Technician at Skilton Contracting, and Tim is a vehicle operator for the West Virginia Department of Highways.

Jo Ann passed away on March 1, 2002, and Carl resides at the family home on Teens Run Road.

*Submitted by Brent M. James*

**JAMES/JACOBI** - When the first history book came out, in 1980, we were still trying to learn when the first of our James's came to America and where they were from. We now know the name was originally Jacobin and they came from Ober Kostenz in Palatinate, now Germany.

Mathias Jacobi and his brothers, Adam, Peter, and Jacob, are listed as passengers on the ship, Patience, landing at Philadelphia on August 11, 1750. They came by way of Rotterdam and Cowes, England. The Eighteenth Century Register of Emigrants lists them as leaving Obr Kostenz for America.

Church records for Ober Kostenzin in the archives at Boppard, Germany, gives our line as far back as Meinhard Jacobi born 1638 married Agnes Catharina. The earlier records are missing so we don't have her last name of date of marriage. But we do find Agnes Catharina, wife of Meinhard Jacobi, buried on January 21, 1695. Meinhard was buried April 30, 1710, and he was 72 years old.

Meinhard's son, Franz Nicolas, born 1668 is our line. He married Anna Catharina Persch daughter of Joannes Persch on May 15, 1691. We find the baptismal records for six of their children, including our next grandfather, Johannes Jakob Jacobi. Jakob (Jacob) was born August 16, 1693. He married Anna Catharina (last name not give in records) on January 23, 1711. Their son, Johannes, Mathias Mathias Jacobi, born August 10, 1730, is our Mathias James who died in Gallia County in 1817.

Mathias and his brothers settled in Berk-Lebanon-Lancaster area of Pennsylvania. We find the marriage of Mathias Jacobi son of Jacob Jacobi, deceased, to Elizabeth Herchelroth daughter of Johann Herchelroth, deceased, on May 13, 1755. Elizabeth was born March 25, 1737. Her baptism is listed as May 17, 1737, at the Muddy Creek Church in East Cocalico Township, Lancaster County. These same records give us the birth of their first son Johannes (John) Jacobi on March 17, 1756. John died in Gallia County in 1845.

By 1772 Mathias and two of his brothers, Peter and Jacob, are in Loudoun County, Virginia. Tax and land records show them there until 1790, when Mathais and his family moved to Bedford County, Virginia. From 1790 to 1803 we find Mathias and his sons, John, Henry, Adam and Lawrence, on either tax records or deeds, also a daughter, Eve, who married Samuel Hibbs. It was her marriage record, that first lets us connect the James name to the Jacobi name. In her marriage record is a note from Mathias Jacobi giving permission for his daughter, Eve James, to marry Samuel Hibbs, signed Mathais Jacobi in German letters. After this, we found several documents with both names on them.

It is hard to know when they first started using the English version of James. We do know that in Pennsylvania, when Germans entered their land or applied for naturalization, their German names were often translated into English by the English Clerks. Also, in order to own land, you had to be naturalized; and the name may have been changed then. About 1756, schools were formed to teach the German children in Pennsylvania, but only in English. The timing was just right for Mathias's children, born in Pennsylvania to be taught English. So the name was probably changed over a period of years as the children born there grew up.

Mathias Jacobi/James and all of his children moved one at a time to Ohio shortly after 1800. Mathias and his wife, Elizabeth, first moved from Bedford County to Greenbrier County, VA. about 1801. There they lived near a daughter, Catherine, who had married Adam Butcher, until 1808, when they moved to Ross County, Ohio. Mathias and Elizabeth stayed in Ross County where their sons, Henry and Adam, had located until about 1815. Then they moved to Gallia County and lived with their son, John James, until they died; Mathias in 1817, and Elizabeth in 1819. They are buried in Mt. Zion Cemetery in Green Township.

John James and his wife, Julia Ann, had moved from Bedford County, VA, to Gallia County about 1803. They lived in Green Township between Centenary and Fairfield until they died; John, March 17, 1845, and Julia Ann, October 3, 1851. They are buried in Centenary Cemetery.

John's seventh child, William, born April 11, 1798 in Bedford, VA, is our line. He married Elizabeth McKean, daughter of Robert and Mary McKean. Elizabeth was born in Pennsylvania, probably Westmoreland County where her grandfather John McKean lived.

Our line continues with William's son, Lewis, born March 8, 1847, married Mariah Jane daughter of George and Catherine Proctor Allman. Lewis's son, William George, married Cora, daughter of Charles and Amanda Thompson Pritchard.

George and Cora James had four children: Walter, born 1901, never married; Rush, born 1903, married Martha McLaughlin; Ola born 1905 married Elmer VanSickle; and Frank, born 1907, married Norma Barcus. Cora died in 1909, and Lewis and Mariah helped George raise these children. Ola and Elmer VanSickle moved to Coshocton County, Ohio; but Frank and Rush lived and raised their families in Eureka, (Chambersburg) in Gallia County.

Rush and Martha were my husband Richard's parents. They are buried at Bethel Cemetery in Ohio Township. Rush died in, 1987, and Martha died in 1975.

Since the 1980 history Richard and I have not found new ancestors to add to the family. We have added three new grandchildren; our son Dale has one son. Ryan has two: Joshua and Roy.

*Sources: Church records, deed, tax records, census, cemetery records, marriage records and personal knowledge.*

*Submitted by: Richard and Mary James of Gallipolis, Ohio and Richard James, Jr., of Fairland, Ok.*

**JEFFERS-PARKINS CONNECTION** - On June 13, 1953, a new family unit was established when Leon Jeffers and Marinelle Parkins were united in marriage. Leon is the second son of Lloyd and Erma Fraley Jeffers. Leon has two brothers and one sister. Marinelle is the daughter of Edward and Bonnie Taylor Parkins. Marinelle has two sisters and one brother.

The Lloyd Jeffers family lived in Gallia County, moved to Meigs County, and then back to Gallia County, settling permanently on a farm near Cadmus where they operated a dairy. Their children, Lowell(Eddy), Leon, Ray, and Betty all attended Cadmus High School. Lloyd, Erma, and Ray are now deceased.

*Leon & Marinelle Jeffers and their children: Beth, Steve, Donnie and Jimmy in 1976*

The Edward Parkins family lived in Gallia County, moved to Muskingum County, and then back to Gallia County, settling permanently on a farm along Symmes Creek in Perry Township.

Edward taught school in various Gallia County elementary schools and then enjoyed twenty-five years of retirement before his death in 1987. Bonnie died in 1998. Edward and Bonnie's four children, Earl, Mildred, JoAnn, and Marinelle all attended Cadmus High School, as did their parents.

Immediately after their marriage in 1953 Leon and Marinelle established their first home in Alexandria, Virginia. Their first three children were born there, Steven Brent (1954), Bethany Leigh (1956), and Don Clinton (1960). Leon learned the masonry trade, and Marinelle taught school. In 1965, they returned to Gallia County to a secluded farm home near Cadmus which they had purchased while living in Virginia. Leon established his own masonry business, laying brick, block, and stone, combined with farming on a small scale. Marinelle resumed her teaching career. In 1967 their fourth child, James Eric, was born. His siblings were always reminding him that he was the only Buckeye among them; and that the dictionary defined a buckeye as: a worthless nut.

The next twenty or so years brought laughter and joy mixed with tears and grief: happiness and joy with the accomplishments of each child as they graduated from college, married and established their own homes and families; tears and grief when one son, Don Clinton, lost his life in an automobile accident in 1977.

Leon and Marinelle now enjoy seven grandchildren and one great granddaughter.

Steven Brent graduated from Ohio University and married Joy Grover. They have one son, Jeremy Don, and one daughter, Amy Marie. Jeremy married Christina Snodgrass and they have one daughter, Selina. They all reside in Cincinnati.

Beth graduated from Ohio University and married Robert Ruff. They have two daughters, Annah Elizabeth and Molly Morgan. They reside on the farm along Symmes Creek where Beth's grandparents had lived.

James Eric graduated from The University of Rio Grande and married Lori Lyons. They have three sons: Tyler James, Justin Eric, and Jonathan Bradley. They reside in Jackson, Ohio.

Leon and Marinelle now enjoy gardening, traveling, horses, and stay busy with a new venture as proprietors of a bed and breakfast, Cedar Knoll Cabin.

*Submitted by Marinelle Jeffers*

**JENKINS FAMILY** - Heath Allen Jenkins was born June 16, 1971, at Holzer Hospital in Gallipolis, Ohio, to John and Brenda (Barker) Jenkins. Heath is a seventh generation resident of Gallia County through the Jenkins, Jones, and Scott Families. Ancestors from both of these family lines arrived in Gallia County during the first quarter of the nineteenth century.

Heath remained in Gallia County until 1984 when his father's job took the family to Steubenville, Ohio. The family remained there through 1989, allowing Heath to graduate from Edison South High School. Heath went on to pursue his bachelor's degree at Youngstown State University and Malone College. It was at Malone College that he met his future wife, Lora Lee Mills, of Lancaster Ohio.

The couple married on June 12, 1993, and took up residence in Gallia County.

Lora graduated from the University of Rio Grande in 1995 with a degree in Elementary Education. She began her teaching career that fall at Vinton Elementary in the Kindergarten class.

Three children have been born to Heath and Lora. The first, Matthew Tyler, was born April 21, 1996, then came Morgan on August 13, 1997, and Noah, on October 11, 1998.

Heath remained self-employed in the antique business from 1993 till 2001, with the exception of two years of employment at Letart Corporation Sand & Gravel of Gallipolis Ferry,

W.V. from September '97, till October '99. Heath is currently employed as the pastor of the Calvary Baptist Church of Rio Grande, Ohio.

Lora is currently a stay-at-home mom. She is also active in BSF (Bible Study Fellowship) and in the activities of her church.

Heath's parents, John and Brenda (Barker) Jenkins, are both graduates of Kyger Creek High School class of 1969. John was born July 19, 1951, to Walter A. and Helen (Bias) Jenkins of State Route 7 South, Cheshire. After High School, John began working at Karr and Van Zandt Motors of Pomeroy. He went on to work at Meigs Mine #3 and then hired on with American Electric Power Company. He remained with AEP for 24 years until he left to work for Midwest ISO in Carmel, Indiana, in September 2001.

Brenda was born December 3,1951, to Jack and Peggy (Gray) Barker of Huntington, West Virginia. Her family moved to the Addison area in 1959. Brenda and John were wed Feb. 6', 1970, by the Rev. Jack Barker, the bride's Father. Brenda worked at Holzer Hospital, as secretary at Kyger Creek High School, and taught at Gallia Christian School.

She currently is active in Ladies Christian Ministries.

Heath has one brother, Seth, born August 15, 1974. He graduated from Perry High School in Massillon, Ohio, in 1992. He was wed to Ginger White in Canton, Ohio, May 10, 1997. They have one daughter, London, born July 28, 2000. Seth and Ginger now reside in Salt Lake City where Seth is the Associate Pastor of First Church of the Nazarene of Salt Lake City.

**ROBERT WILLIAM AND ANNE ELIZABETH HALLIDAY JENKINS** - Bill and Anne Jenkins were both born in 1937. He was born January 27th in Nitro, West Virginia, the son of Robert Earl and Ruby Tawney Jenkins. She was born in Holzer Hospital, the first daughter of John Ernest and Marjorie Biddle Halliday.

The Halliday lineage evolved from the French Five Hundred. Ann's father, John Ernest Halliday, son of John Earnest Halliday Sr. and Maude Dunbar Halliday, daughter of Samuel and Caroline Miller Dunbar, daughter of William C. and Caroline Newsom Miller, daughter of Lewis and Gabrielle Menager Newsom, daughter of Claudius and Mary Bobine Menager - who were members of the French Five Hundred and the first couple married in Gallipolis.

Anne lived in Gallipolis in her family home on Cedar Street with her brother, Tom and her sister, Mary B., attending Washington School and graduating from Gallia Academy in 1955. Bill traveled to several cities while his father served in the U.S. Navy during World War II and lived in Pensacola, Florida, Arlington and Williamsburg, Virginia, and Pleasanton, Kernville and Invokern, California. Returning to Gallipolis, he graduated from Gallia Academy in 1954.

Furthering his education, Bill received his B.A. degree from Vanderbilt University and his J.D. degree from Ohio State University. Anne followed the Halliday family tradition and was a 3rd generation graduate of Ohio Wesleyan University. Anne then taught school in San Diego, California, and, after marrying Bill in 1960, taught in the Columbus City School System.

Bill Jenkins opened his law office in October, 1961, at 19 Locust Street. He served as Gallipolis City Solicitor from January 1962, until February, 1973. From February 1973, until 1979, he served as Gallia County Common Pleas Judge in the Probate and Juvenile Divisions of the Court. Bill followed his father in the ready-mixed concrete business. He operated Jenkins Concrete until selling it to Arrow Industries in 1991. He also managed the O'Dell Lumber Company which his family purchased in 1976 until son, Robert, took over in 1995.

Anne kept busy raising their two children, Robert Earl II, born May 24, 1961, and Jodi Halliday, born March 21, 1963. She served on the Samuel Bossard Memorial Library Board continuing a family tradition of service initiated by the grandmother, Maude Dunbar Halliday, continued by her mother, Marjorie Halliday, and now by her son, Robert. Anne was a board member during the construction of the present library building. Anne was a member of the Board of Trustees of the University of Rio Grande.

She also served on the Gallipolis City Recreation Board during the period when the present swimming pool was built.

Son, Rob, graduated from Gallia Academy and the University of New Mexico. He married Michelle Leffingwell in 1984, and they have three children: Robert William II, Caitlin Tawney, and Joseph Edward. Daughter Jodi, graduated from Gallia Academy and Vanderbilt University. She married Brian Bair in 1988, and they have two children: Halliday Biddle and Benton Alexander.

**WALTER A. JENKINS** - Walter A. Jenkins, was born in Cheshire Twp., Gallia Co., Cheshire, Ohio, on March 21, 1910. He is the son of James A. and Mintie Van Kirk Jenkins, grandson of George W. and Caroline Shuler Jenkins, and great-grandson of William S. and Cynthia Scott Jenkins, who are mentioned in Hardesty's *Gallia County's History of 1882*.

Walter was the tenth child born into a family of thirteen children. As Walter was growing up, he attended several one-room school houses: Africa, Eno, and White Oak Schools. He would walk a mile or two to school with his brothers and sisters, cutting across the hills to take a shorter route to school.

When Walter was 22, he married Helen Irene Byas, born September 30, 1915. They were married August 24, 1932, at Addison, Ohio. After their marriage, they resided for a short time on Ward Road, near where he currently resides. This is the place where he relates a humorous story of an event which occurred early in their marriage:

As young newlyweds, they enjoyed passing their spare time playing a competitive game of dominoes. Prior to this one particular game, Helen had started a large pot of beans cooking over the fireplace, which was to be their dinner meal. During the game, the beans were forgotten, and not until Walter began to smell something burning, did they realize the beans had boiled dry and caught on fire, as a result of their love for a good game of dominoes.

In the years that followed, a daughter, Grace Darlene, was born into their family. They later moved to Cheshire, Ohio, where he owned and operated an automotive repair shop. Within the next year or so, Walter and Helen bought land below Cheshire, and Walter built their home where they resided for nearly thirty years.

As time passed, four more children were added to their family. A daughter, Shirley Anne, a son, James Allen, who died at 15 months of age from double pneumonia; another son, John Arlen, and another daughter, Linda Lee.

During this time, Walter owned and operated another automotive repair garage where he also sold gasoline. He later worked for the State Highway, and Gallia County Highway Departments. In the late 1940's and early 1950's, he owned and operated a logging and sawmill business, which was a source of lumber that provided building materials for the local community and surrounding area. In the mid 1950's, he went back to work at the Ford Garage in Middleport, Ohio, where he had worked prior to having his own automotive garage business.

Because of the building boom, in the late 1950's and early 1960's, he worked in the building trades and highway construction. He finally retired from the Chris Craft Corporation, in Gallipolis, Ohio, in 1972, after taking a short intermission to build his home where he now resides.

On August 24, 1982, Walter and Helen celebrated their 50th wedding anniversary with a family outing at the home of their son, John, which was attended by their children and grandchildren.

Helen went to be with the Lord, February 1992, due to an illness complicated by a stroke.

Walter has continued to live in the local community, and on March 21, 2002, he celebrated his 92nd. birthday at his home with his family. He has 11 grandchildren, 23 great-grandchildren, and 10 great-great grandchildren.

**JOHN FRANCIS (JOHNNIE) AND HELEN P. NEWMAN JOHNSON FAMILY** - John (Johnnie) Johnson was born April 4, 1899 in Gallipolis. His parents were Alden Luther Johnson and Oma L. Criner. Oma is proven to be a blood relative to Sarah Angel and, known to be here by1810 and thus all her blood relatives are eligible for First Families of Gallia County. Johnnie had one sister, Aileen and four brothers, Herman Luther, Donovan Theodore (Ted), James Austin (Fat) and Paul. Johnnie attended Gallia Academy High School and played football. His sister and brothers are deceased except for Paul. He lives in Las Vegas. Johnnie married Helen P. Newman of Hamden, Ohio February 25, 1933 in Ironton, Oh. He was a businessman, owning the B & B Pool Room and B & B Hotel. These were named for daughters Becky and Bertie. He also worked for Kemper-Thomas as a salesman and became a realtor and had his own real estate business for ten years before his death June 14, 1962. His wife, Helen, was born in Hamden, Ohio to John and Martha Alice Salmons Newman. Helen had one brother, Tom, and four sisters, Autye, Margaret, Audrey and Eleanor (Nell). She graduated from Hamden High and began nursing training in Gallipolis at The Holzer School of Nursing in 1929. She graduated in 1932 and first became a private duty nurse helping with many home deliveries working with the late Dr. George Barton. She worked as an industrial nurse at Kyger Creek Power Plant when it was under construction during the mid 50's. She finished her nursing career after twenty years as medical floor supervisor of the Gallipolis State Institute Hospital in 1978. Helen died November 5, 1982.

*Submitted by Roberta Roush*

**JONES FAMILY** - On the 7th of June 1839, Isaac Jones, his wife Gwen, their five children, and Isaac's twenty-year-old son, David Griffith Jones, left Cilicinen, Wales for America. They joined Isaac's brother, John, who had settled in the Tyn Rhos area of Gallia County, Ohio. David Griffith Jones was born 15 August 1819. On his baptismal record his mother's name was given as Rachel Griffith but no other information is known about her.

*Elizabeth Jones Walker*

David Griffith (Cardy) Jones found employment in southeastern Ohio in the iron furnaces of the region. He met and married Mary Ann McCrary Marcum, a widow with two sons. They met while he was employed at Vernon Furnace, Lawrence County, Ohio. David Griffith returned to Gallia County where he purchased land in Perry Township. He worked at Gallia Furnace, Greenfield Township both before and after his Civil War service. While at Gallia Furnace, Dave "Cardy" molded a mortar and pestle which was in the possession of the Davis family of Oak Hill for many years before being placed in the museum at Tyn Rhos. David and Mary Ann were the parents of eighth children. Mary Ann delivered the eight child the month after David "Cardy" enlisted in the Civil War. She took care of their eight children while he served three years in the army. David Griffith became a United States citizen 26 October 1862 at the courthouse in Gallipolis, Ohio.

The oldest son of David and Mary Ann was David Birchard (1847-1908). He followed his father into the Civil War as a seventeen-year-old. After returning from the war, he married Catherine Jones and they had six children. After Catherine's death, David married Sarah Walp and they had one son. The second child, Isaac Newton (1848-1927), married Sarah Isabel Canterbury. They had two daughters. Not to be outdone by his father and older brother, Ike joined the Ohio National Guard before his sixteenth birthday. As an adult, Ike was a stonemason who helped carve the stones for the public library in Huntington, West Virginia. Ike was also a schoolteacher in Lawrence County, Ohio.

Isaac's birth was followed by the loss of two sons, both named John. This loss was followed by the birth of a daughter, Elizabeth 1855-1929). Elizabeth married Samuel Jackson Walker; they had nine children. Elizabeth was a charter member of the Cora Methodist Church in Perry Township. The sixth child was Samuel Houston (1857-1932). Sam married Mary Elizabeth Kabish from Jackson, Ohio. They were the parents of six children. Sam was a carpenter and a stonemason. He helped build the Cambrian Hotel in Jackson. Sam moved to Colorado later in life and died there. A second daughter, Rachel, (1861-1918), followed Samuel. Rachel married James Bennette Hutchinson. Rachel and James were the parents of ten children, living near Jackson, Ohio.

The last child of David and Mary Ann, born as a father entered the war, was Thomas Edward (1862-1924). Tom married Lena Weiderman, and they had three children. He worked in construction including the Arcade in downtown Dayton, Ohio. They later moved to South Point, Ohio and began farming. More information on the Jones family and their descendants can be found in the book "Keeping up with the Jones", by Mary Walker Niday.

*Submitted by Cynthia Niday Menzer*

**EVAN NATHANIEL JONES AND MARY AGNES PILLOW** - Easily recognized from a distance, Evan N. Jones was known for wearing a silk hat and broadcloth suit. Evan Nathaniel's dream to improve his station in life was probably not realized as he continued to wear his silk hat and broadcloth suit until they were threadbare. Nevertheless, he was always the gentleman. Others found his speaking voice pleasant to hear and they enjoyed listening to his accent.

*Evan Nathaniel And Mary Agnes Jones*

Evan Nathaniel Jones was the son of Nathaniel (1814-1879) and Mary Elizabeth Davis (1814-1890). Evan was born February 6, 1837 in Wales and died on January 5, 1918 in Patriot, Ohio. He married Elizabeth Bane on March 1859 in Gallia County, Ohio. Elizabeth Bane was born September 6, 1859 in Gallia County, Ohio and died September 25, 1883 in Gallia County. Evan Nathaniel and Elizabeth Bane Jones had the following children: Nathaniel, Evan, Mary and Margaret Ann (married Thomas E. Davis).

Following Elizabeth's death, Evan N. Jones married Mary Agnes Pillow Carver on January 9, 1884 in Gallia County, Ohio. The marriage was a second marriage for Mary Agnes as well as for Evan. Mary Agnes was born July 13, 1848 in Lynchburg, Virginia and died January 8, 1918 in Patriot, Ohio, (three days after the death of her husband). Evan Nathaniel and Mary Jones had the following children: Everett 1887-1915, Elizabeth Louise 1888-1976 (married J. Boyd Davis), Eva 1889-1898, and Leila 1891-1901. During the Civil War, Evan N. Jones served in Co. H, 60 Regiment, OH Infantry from March 12, 1862, 1862-Nov. 10, 1862.

Mary Agnes Pillow's parents were Edwin Pillow (born 1812 in Halifax, Virginia and died 1865 in Mason County, West Virginia) and Mariah Vernon (born 1812 in Charlotte County, Virginia and died 1862 in Mason County, West Virginia). The Pillow family ancestors have been traced back to Jasper Pillow born 1710 in Virginia. The parents of Mariah Vernon were Jonathan and Elizabeth Mathews Vernon. Elizabeth Mathews and Jonathan Vernon were born in England.

*Submitted By: Gwen Grant*

**GLEN AMMON JONES AND HELEN HARRIS JONES FAMILY** - Glen was born on March 17, 1913 in Patriot, Gallia County to David Bert and May Carter Jones. He was the youngest of three children. David Ray was his older brother and Mary Jane "Peggy" was his sister. He died December 25, 1972 in Gallipolis, Ohio.

*Glen Ammon and Helen Harris Jones Family*

Glen's great-great grandfather, Alexander Waddell was born in 1732 in Glasgow, Scotland. He was a weaver by trade. He came to America in 1755. In 1770 he married Eleanor Rausch. She was born in 1751 or 1752 at Mill Creek Valley near Mt. Jackson, Virginia. Her parents were John Adam and Susannah Schlern Rausch.

Alexander and Eleanor had twelve children; one of which was Glen's great grandfather, John Waddell. John was born December 19, 1776. He moved to Gallia County in 1814. His first wife was Margaret McColm. His second wife, Mary "Polly" Wigner was Glen's great grandmother. John and Polly were married March 23, 1820. In 1817 Alexander and Eleanor moved to Gallia County to be close to some of their children there. Alexander Church in Green Township was named for him. Eleanor died October 9, 1827 and Alexander died September 6, 1834 at the age of 102 years.

John and Polly had nine children. Their daughter Eliza Ann, who married Ammon J. Carter, were Glen's grandparents. Ammon was a well known carpenter in Patriot. His parents were George and Phebe Ripley Carter Ammon and Eliza's daughter, Ina May, married David Bert Jones on November 16, 1904. David was the son of David N. and Jane Davies Jones and the grandson of Nathaniel and Mary Elizabeth Davies Jones.

Bert and Ina raised their children in the Patriot area. Glen attended Patriot School. He married Helen Harris on June 4, 1936, at Rodney,

Gallia County. Helen was born June 4, 1917 at Emma, Floyd County Kentucky and died March 14, 1999 at Gaillipolis, Ohio. Helen was the daughter of David Banner and Gypsy Lee Burchett Harris of Floyd County, Kentucky. She was a sister to David Banner, Jr. and Albert Claude Harris.

Glen begin his married life as a farmer. He worked at various jobs in Gallia County and also at TNT in the Point Pleasant W.Va. area. For a short while the Jones family lived in Wooster, Ohio. After returning to the Gallia County area Glen began working for Buckeye Rural Electric, which he retired from. Helen worked for and retired from Bob Evans Drive In, later known as Kentucky Fried Chicken. They had two children. Robert Glendon born July 8, 1937 at Cora, Perry Township and Judith Claudette born May 26, 1943. Bob married Linda Lou Kelton Stillwell of Gallipolis, Ohio. Judy married John Mack Fuller of Gallia County.

Glen and Helen had three grandchildren, Kathy and Randy Jones and JoEllen Fuller. Prior to her death Helen also enjoyed four great grandchildren. Kathy's children, Kaela and Glendon and Jo Ellen's children, Dustin and Chelsea.

**HEZEKIAH JONES** - My 2nd great grandfather was Thomas Jones, born 1770/74 in Virginia. He shows up first in 1812 in Wilksville, Ohio when he joined Capt. Roadnour's Mounted Co. He then married Sarah Campbell in 1813, who died in childbirth. His second marriage was to Elizabeth "Betsey" Burns on December 17, 1817 in Jackson, Ohio. They had 3 children: Hezekiah, born September 29, 1819, James and Harriet. Hezekiah married Margaret Fife, d/o John K. and Catherine Rupe Fife, on March 16, 1851 in Gallia County, Ohio. He served in the Civil War in Co.I 4th Regiment W.Va. Infantry with the Union Army.

He died November 11, 1900 and they are buried in Poplar Ridge Cemetery, Cheshire Twp., Ohio.

*Larry Jones & Sue Jones Summer 2000*

They had 8 children: Jacob m. Rosanna Yeager, George m. Mary ?, Sarah Jane m. William Van Kirk and William Willis, Asa died in infancy, Ellsworth m. Sarah Flint, Mary m. Samuel Flint, Ulysses Grant, and Edward William, born April 11, 1870, died November 3, 1955, m. Effie Belle Shoemaker, d/o Jacob and Matilda Siders Shoemaker, on October 28, 1896 in Gallia Co., Oh. Both are buried in the Poplar Ridge Cemetery. Jacob was a private in the 13th. Reg. Co. H, OVI. Jacob was the s/o George and Malinda Wilt Shoemaker, all buried in Lemley Cemetery, Cheshire Twp. Edward and Effie Belle had 9 children. They were Clinton Edward m. Anna Viers, Pearlie died in infancy, Maggie Alice m. Cecil Blaine Topping and Charles Hill, William m. Dorothy ?, Ferdie Guy, born May 15, 1905, died July 6, 1981, m. Rosa Eblin, December 17, 1938, Gallia Co., Oh. She was born March 21, 1916 and died July 31, 1992. They are both buried in Poplar Ridge Cemetery, Cheshire Twp., Gallia Co. She was the d/o Jesse and Erie Adkins Eblin. Carl and Harlan were twins both dying in infancy, and Jessie Viola m. Ralph Lemley. Fredie and Rosa had 5 children. They were: Betty born October 8, 1939 m. Charles Crouch and Roger Hollingsworth, Rosa Mary born May 7, 1942 m. Gerald Newsome, died August 31, 1982, buried Dayton, Ohio.

Yvonna Sue born March 29, 1944, James born March 17, 1946 died May 3, 1971, buried in Poplar Ridge Cemetery, Robert born October 12, 1948 died December 8, 1948, buried in Poplar Ridge Cemetery. Yvonna Sue Jones had Lawrence Junior Jones born November 8, 1966, Gallia Co., Ohio and he died February 24, 2001 in Gallipolis, Ohio and is buried in Poplar Ridge Cemetery. Yvonna Sue's mother, Rosa Eblin Jones' brothers and sisters were: Willie Harlan, Maggie Ellen m. Demps Lanthorn, Iva Rolena m. James Harold Barcus, John Jefferson, Clyde Edward, Naomi Marie m. Earl Saunders and Everett McGuire, and Oliver Russell m. Thelma Day.

Yvonna Sue Jones still lives in Gallipolis, Ohio.

*Submitted by Yvonna Sue Jones*

**NATHANIEL AND MARY ELIZABETH DAVIES JONES FAMILY** - A ddarlenno, ysteried. A ystyno, cofied. Let him who reads, reflect. Let him who reflects, remember.

*Nathaniel and Mary Elizabeth Davies Jones.*

Nathaniel was born February 13, 1814 in Tregaron, Cardiganshire, Wales. He died August 9, 1879 in Perry Township, Gallia County. He was a brother to Evan, Hugh, John, James, David, Margaret, Charlotte, and Elizabeth. He married Mary Elizabeth Davies on May 23, 1834 in Cilcennin, Wales. She was born July 11, 1814 in Cilcennin, Cardiganshire, Wales and died August 25, 1890 in Perry Township, Gallia County. She was the daughter of Jenkin Davies.

Nathaniel was a tinner by trade. His brothers Hugh and John had a tin factory in Neath, Wales.

Nathaniel also had a certificate to practice as a cattle and horse doctor and this is what he did prior to coming to America.

Elizabeth was a very pretty little lady who had the nickname Betty bach, which means little Betty in Welsh. She loved to fox hunt and to attend fox hunting parties.

*Cora Mill*

They had three children while living in Wales. Mary, Elizabeth and Evan N. who was born February 6, 1837. In 1838 they left Wales and came to America. A trip that took seven weeks across the stormy Atlantic. They settled in Pittsburgh, Pennsylvania where Nathaniel was an iron and steel worker. David N. was born in Allegheny County, Pennsylvania on December 29, 1840. In 1841 they moved to the Tyn Rhos area of Gallia County. There they had four more children, John N. (Jack), Jenkin N., Katherine (Kate) and Anne.

In 1855 they moved to Gage, Perry Township, Gallia County and bought the Henry Bane farm. They accumulated 700 acres in this area. It was only a stone's throw away from their house that Nathaniel gave the Welsh community the tract of land to build the first Siloam Church. Adjoining this church was the Siloam (Jones) Cemetery which is Nathaniel and Elizabeth's and several of their descendents final resting place.

A cherished memory of the grandchildren was the immense orchard on this farm. Another memory that is told is one of Nathaniel's house. This home had a built-in hiding place for valuables and money. It was so cleverly hidden that the family that purchased the house from Nathaniel had lived there twelve years and never discovered it until one of Nathaniel's descendents told them about it.

Nathaniel fought for three years during the Civil War alongside his brothers and sons. He was a private in the 18th Regimental Infantry.

The children of Nathaniel and Elizabeth Jones and their spouses were-Evan N., married first to Elizabeth Bane and second to Mary Pillow Carver; Mary, John Johnson; David N., Jane Davies; Elizabeth, John Callahan; Anne, Joseph Looney; Katherine, Dave Jones, Jr.; Jenkin N., Mary Davies; and John (Jack) N., Agnes Jones Harkness. The boys in Nathaniel's family all took the middle initial N., for their fathers name Nathaniel, which was the Welsh custom.

**ROBERT GLENDON AND LINDA LOU KELTON STILLWELL JONES FAMILY** - Bob was born July 8, 1937 at Cora, Perry Township, Gallia County to Glen Ammon and Helen Harris Jones. His great-great grandparents, Nathaniel and Mary Elizabeth Davies Jones left Wales in 1838 and in lived in Pittsburgh, Pennsylvania before settling in Gallia County in 1841.

Nathaniel and Elizabeth had eight children; one of which was Bob's great-grandfather, David N. Jones. David married Jane Davies on January 30, 1868 in Gallia County. To this union was born four sons, Thomas H., Jenkin A., John E., and Bob's grandfather David Bert Jones.

*Robert Glendon And Linda Lou Kelton Stillwell Jones*

David Bert married Ina May Carter on November 16, 1904 in Gallia County. Bert and Ina raised three children (all deceased) David Ray, Mary Jane "Peggy" and Bob's father Glen Ammon Jones. Glen married Helen Harris on June 4, 1936 at Rodney, Gallia County. Bob has one sister Judith Claudette born May 26, 1943 in Gallia County.

Bob has lived in the Gallia County all of his life except for the short period when his parents lived in Wooster, Ohio. He attended Gallia Academy High School and graduated from there in 1955.

He married Linda Lou Kelton Stillwell on July 22, 1957 in Richmond, Union County, Indiana. Linda was born March 26, 1940 in Gallipolis, Ohio and is the daughter of Franklin Harold and and Mary Alice Reapp Kelton. Franklin was born July 25, 1918 and Mary was born February 22, 1920. Linda's adoptive father was Leo Stillwell. Linda attended Gallia Academy High School and graduated from there in 1958. She has one brother, Franklin Harold Kelton, Jr.

Bob began his married life working at Firestone. He later went to work for Goodyear Tire and Rubber in Applegrove W.V.. In 1968 he began his own business, General Tire Sales in Middleport, Ohio. He retired and sold his store after working 25 years in the tire business. Linda went to work for Robbins and Myers, now Rockwell, in 1967. She retired from there in March, 2002 after 34 years service.

They raised two children. Kathy Lynn was born January 25, 1961 and Robert Randall "Randy" born March 21, 1963. They were both born in Gallipolis.

Kathy married Russell T. Hodges of Mt. Airy, N.C. on July 4, 1987. They have two children, Kaela Lynette born November 10, 1987 and Russell Glendon born January 27, 1989. Kathy and her family reside in Mt. Airy, N.C.. Randy married Belinda Lee Broyles on September, 11, 2001. She is the daughter of Benny and Donna Broyles. Randy and Belinda live in Gallipolis.

Bob, Kathy, Randy, Kaela and Glendon are members of First Families of Gallia County. Bob is a sixth generation and Kathy and Randy are seventh generation Gallia Countians through Bob's great-great-great grandfather Alexander Waddell who settled in Gallia County in the early 1800's.

**THOMAS JONES** - My third great grandfather was Thomas Jones. According to the 1850 census he was born ca. 1770 in Va. He came to Wilksville, Ohio and enlisted in Capt. Roadenour's Mounted Infantry and served in the War of 1812. On May 10, 1813 he married Sarah Campbell in Wilksville. She died April 5, 1817 giving birth to my 2nd Great grandfather Levi Campbell Jones. Thomas remarried twice more, having 3 more children. He died sometime after October, 1853 in Cheshire, Ohio and is buried in Poplar Ridge Cemetery.

*Jonathan Rife Jones & Sarah Ann Rothgeb Jones*

Sarah is buried in Wilksville Cemetery. Levi Campbell Jones married Nancy Rife July 2, 1837 and they had 12 children. She was the daughter of Henry Rife and Tabitha Martindale Rife, Tabitha's father was James Martindale who fought as a Lt. To Col. Broadom in the South Carolina Malita, American Revolution. Levi had serious cancer and died December 12, 1880. Nancy lived until October 12, 1898. Both are buried in the Rife Cemetery, Addison, Ohio. Two sons of Levi and Nancy served in the Civil War and died. Henry was in the 53rd OVI and died of measles at Camp Diamond in Jackson, Ohio. He's buried at Jamestown Cemetery there. Thomas enlisted in the 91st. OVI and died in the battle of Opequan Creek, Va. and is buried at Winchester, VA. The youngest son of Levi and Nancy was my great grandfather Jonathan Rife Jones who was born November 27, 1859, married Sarah Ann Rothgeb May 30, 1878 and they had 10 children. She was the daughter of Jacob and Susan Shaver Rothgeb. Her gg grandfather John George Rothgeb fought in the American Revolution in VA. My grandfather Charles Ellsworth Jones was the second of their children, born August 18, 1883. He and two of his brothers moved up north to Wyandot Co. where he met and married Leefee Belle Kollar on March 1, 1908. They had 6 children, two sons of which died in infancy. My father Myron was born November 27, 1909, married Lucy Ann Chapman, from Wood County, Oh. That's where they lived, had 3 children, died and are buried. My brother Daniel and my father were killed in an airplane crash in 1958. My sister Janet Eileen McCordock still lives in Michigan. My second wife Barbara and I moved from Wood County in 1990. Both of our former spouses having died, we married here in Gallia County in 1990. I was born July 27, 1931 and graduated from Bowling Green High School in 1949. During high school I joined the 4th Infantry Ohio State Guards, Co. H and the Ohio National Guards Co. C 148th Infantry, 37th. Division.

I joined the U.S. Air Force on March 8th. 1950, attended Weather School and was later sent over to serve in the 15th. Weather Squadron at Kadena and Naha air bases at Okinawa, Japan. From there I was placed in Weather Intelligence in the 2143rd Air Weather Wing, Tokyo, Japan. Served there and in Korea for about 30 months as a S/Sgt. While there I met and married my first wife Nobuko Miyazaki. We returned to the states after my discharge and we had 4 daughters namely, Lauren, Mariann, Mimi and Ginger.

*Submitted by Myron E. Jones, Jr.*

**GORDON K. KENT WITH DAUGHTERS SHARON DAUER AND KATHIE EVANS -** Myrle Adney Kent, born in Porter, married Edrie Avanelle Morehouse, born in Bidwell. They were the parents of: Kenneth H. and Gordon K. Kent. Gordon was born in Columbus, Ohio, in 1930. He and his wife, Garnette Faulkner, are the parents of three children: Sharon L. (Kent) Dauer of Westerville, OH; Kathie C. (Kent) Evans of Johnstown, OH, and Gordon K. Kent II of Winkelman, AZ.

*Gordon K. Kent with Daughters Sharon Dauer and Kathie Evans*

Gordon was a member of the U.S. Navy Reserve and is a retiree from Columbus Auto Parts. He is the fourteenth generation of Richard and Elizabeth Kent of Nether Wallop, Hampshire, England (about 1520). He is the fifth generation of Samuel Kent who after the Revolutionary War migrated from Connecticut to Vermont where he married Mary Polly Noble. They, with their son, Samuel, and his wife, Mary Stebbins, and families moved to Gallia County in 1815. Samuel and Mary Stebbins were the parents of Milton Kent.

John Adney had one of the county's first sawmills at Vinton on Big Raccoon Creek in 1819. John and his wife, Barbara Lesene, were the parents of Johnathan Adney. Jonathan and wife, Electa Glenn, were the parents of Wealtha Janette Adney, wife of Milton Kent. Here the timbering/saw milling tradition continued from Milton to his son, John William Kent (wife Augusta Maria Howe) to their son, Kenneth Howe Kent, to his nephew Gordon Kent. At seventeen, Gordon was working with his uncle in southern Ohio and West Virginia cutting lumber with a portable saw mill.

Sharon (Kent) and David Dauer have three children and four grandchildren: Annette Dauer, Donna (Tony Newell) parents of Christopher, Daniel and Mandolyn Newell; David M. Dauer II (Brandie Miller) parents of Paige Elizabeth Dauer.

Kathie (Kent) and Gary Evans are the parents of two children and one grandson: Katherine (Gary Woods) parents of Cole Woods and Gary (April Jacobs) parents to be July of 2002.

Gordon, Sharon and Kathie became members of First Families of Gallia County in 1999. They proved: 1815-Samuel Kent and wife, Mary Noble, on Samuel Kent and Mary Stebbins; 1817- John Adney and son, Jonathan Adney. They also connected to previously proven families of: Ahas S. Morehouse, Lucinda Sisson and Rebecca Cobb. In 2001, they proved Electa Glenn and connected to her previously proven parents, William Glenn and Ann Curry.

Sharon and Kathie wish to express their sincere appreciation to Dr. and Mrs. Lawrence Morehouse for his entry in the 1980's publication of Gallia County, Ohio History. Through this entry they were able to make contact and exchange much information. They also wish to thank Estivaun Matthews for extensive materials she made available to these "Kent" cousins.

*Submitted by Sharon Dauer*

**FREDERIC KERNS AND SUSANNAH SYLER** - On 22 March 1807 Frederic Kerns and Susannah Syler married in Gallia County. Frederic was the son of Henry Kerns and Catherine Hotzenbella of Greenbrier County, Virginia. Susannah was the daughter of Christian Siler and Margaret (Groover?) of Gallia County. Susannah never saw her parents again after they moved to Preble County, where Christian and Margaret are buried in Mound Hill Cemetery, Eton. Their illegible tombstones are some of the earliest in the cemetery.

The children of Frederic and Susannah are: Henry Kerns who married Mary Gilbert; Margaret Kerns married John Smelter; John Kerns married Elvira Blazer, Hannah M. Tyler, and Jane Lawson; Adam Kerns married Susan Perkins; Catherine Kerns married Emanuel Bisch; Elizabeth Kerns married William Steiger; George Kerns married Julia Ann Loucks; Jacob Kerns married Elizabeth Roadamour; Susannah, died in infancy. Sarah Kerns never married; Mary Kerns married Abraham Gilbert and Lewis Howell; Mariah and Madelain Kerns died in infancy.

Frederic volunteered and was promoted to 2nd Sergeant in Major Womeldorff's Regiment of Capt. John Roadamour's Mounted Company in the War of 1812. The company served from 1 Aug to 4 Sept. 1813. The company marched to the aid of Gen. William H. Harrison, but did not have "the pleasure of meeting the enemy; neither British or Indian yet they were applauded for obedience to orders, and correct deportment," according to Frederic in his application for bounty land dated 11 Oct.1850. He was discharged at Upper Sandusky. Frederic's pay was $12.83 for the one month and four days, but he received an additional $14.00 for the hire of his horse and $6.50 for forage and rations. He did receive bounty land of 40 acres—NE 1/4 of NE 1/4 of Sec. 8 Twp. 4 Range 16 in Gallia County. He also owned other properties in Gallia County.

Henry Kerns married Mary "Polly" Gilbert on 14 Apr, 1829 in Gallia County. On 2 Dec, 1835 the school examiners for Gallia County wrote that they had "examined Henry Kerns as and for a teacher, and approbate him to teach the following branches, viz. reading, writing and arithmetic; and further that he sustains a good moral character."

On 2 April, 1838 Henry was elected treasurer for Green Township. According to his obituary, "he was a good natured kind man, and probably without an enemy in the world. He was always a resident of this county, and the good name he leaves behind makes his loss keenly felt by all."

Mary's death was caused by injuries received from a 14 foot fall from a window at age 88. Her obituary noted, "She was dutiful to her God, a member of the M.E.Church and highly regarded by her friends."

Frederic Kerns, 30 Nov.,1775— 6 Apr, 1867, Susannah, 12 Oct., 1787— 6 Nov., 1874, Henry, 4 Mar.. 1808— 30 Mar., 1881, and Mary, May 1810— 24 Aug 1898 are all buried in Centenary Cemetery surrounded by family and friends.

*Submitted by: Sunda Anderson Peters*

**KERR FAMILY** - John Kerr, Jr. (1772-1858) came to Gallipolis at the age of 20 on his way west. Here J.P.R. Bureau persuaded him to stay as a helper. John Jr. was born on his father's farm in Chambersburg, PA, son of John Kerr Sr. and Mary Dougherty, and brother of Joseph Kerr ("Ohio's Lost Senator "), Jean (McKinley), Sarah (DeCamp), James Kerr, Mary (Patterson) and Samuel Kerr.

John Jr. married 21 April 1804 Christiana Nisewanger (1804 VA-1841 OH) (see Nisewanger). They located on a farm near Rodney in Green Township. To build his log cabin he cut the first trees in the township. He served as Sheriff Magistrate, Prosecuting Attorney, Associate Judge, and Gallia Co. Commissioner. Two of his nephews died at the Alamo.

Children were John Nisewanger, Richard Speer, Maria Daugherty 1809-1833 unmarried; William Sprague, Sarah Mills, Joseph Hamilton., Harriet, Susan, James Charles, Samuel, and Jacob Sprague Kerr.

John Nisewanger Kerr 1804-1885 married (1) Isabella Morrison, nine children: Mary Ann, married A.J. Powell (see Powell family); Augustus P.; John Richard; Maria C. (Walker); James M..; Susan C. (Blake); William M.; Samuel J.; infant, d. inf.. He married (2) Caroline Cherrington, seven children: Charles Wesley, died young; Harriet (Mills); Charles Warren; Frances (Hutsinpillar); Edward; Cassius; Aleri, died young. He was a wealthy farmer in Springfield Twp., and served as County Commissioner 1842-1848. He was instrumental in having the Hocking Valley Railroad come to Gallia Co. with Kerr Station on his farm.

Richard Speer Kerr 1807-1848, married Nancy Wood, had four children; lived and died in Raccoon Twp.

William Sprague Kerr 18 10-1854 wife Mary Ann Vanden, six children, Justice of Peace and store owner in Gallipolis.

Sarah Mills Kerr 1812-1835 married Augustus Williams, moved to Lucas County, Ohio, where she died, no children.

Joseph H. Kerr 1814-1893, wife Elizabeth Cubbage, five children, lived in Huntington Twp., later in Vinton Co., OH, and ran an underground station before the Civil War, receiving escaped slaves from his brother-in-law George Payne, and sending them north to Wilkesville, OH.

Harriet Newell Kerr 1816-1898 married Daniel Womeldorf, eight children, moved to Tazewell Co. IL, and after her husband's death came back to Gallia Co., returning later to Tazewell.

Susan Mills Kerr 1818-1840 married George Payne, died aged 22 of a fever, leaving one child; her husband was an ardent Abolitionist, ran an underground station in Gallipolis.

James Charles Kerr 1821-1847, wife Margaret Rodgers; died a month after his marriage near upper Sandusky, no children.

Samuel Kerr 1824-1898, wives (1) Mary Gardner (2) Mary Hayward, (3) Charlotte Hayward, (4) Lucy McNeally (Samuel was a veterinarian who took care of the sick during the cholera epidemic. He married these women, his nurses, in order to protect their reputations as they tended the sick with him during the nights). He served in the Civil War as a veterinary surgeon, was a magistrate for 30 years, and died in Gallipolis.

Jacob Kerr 1826-1909, wife Catherine Powell, seven children. He served as a Justice of Peace lived in Green Twp., Gallia Co, then moved to Knox Co. IL, then to Marshall Co. Iowa where he died.

*Submitted by Margaret Powell Hetrick (Mrs. Richard A,)*

**FREDERICH AND AUGUSTA (WEDEMEYER) KLAGES FAMILY** - Frederich was born 1 April 1846, died, 29 April 1935. Son of Frederich, born 1811, died 1886 and Justine (Wese) Klages, born, 1818, died 1894. Augusta (Wedemeyer) Klages, born 12 September 1846, died 2 July 1927, daughter of Edward, born 1820, died 1903 and Elizabeth (Schriber)

*Top Picture Sitting: father: Frederich Klages. Top Row L-R. son-Albert F., (August Pope) son-Fred H., and son Henry J. Bottom PictureBottom L: to R: son Fred H. (mother) Augusta (Wedemeyer) Klages. Frederich and Augusta daughter: Lena-husband-August Pope.*

Wedemeyer, born 1825, died 1902. They were married 3 September 1868 (Frederich and Augusta). Klages came from Hanover, Germany, Dorste County.

They came to America in the 1800's, settled in Walnut Township, Gallia County, German Hollow/Ridge, Patriot area. They attended the one room school located on German Ridge. English was taught for three months and German was taught for three monhs. It took a special act of the State legislature to enable it to use tax money to conduct school in German. It was the only public school in the history of Gallia County to be bilingual. Frederich was a civil war veteran, Co. B, 173 OVI-Rank-Do. 2 September 1864 thru 26 June 1865. Son Henry J. was a Spanish War veteran, Rank, Private, Company I, First Regiment of Infantry Ohio Volunteers, 1 August 1898 thru 25 October 1898.

Children: Fred H., born 14 March 1871, died 7 October 1957 Albert F., born 14 April 1881, died in Peru, Indiana 1953. Buried in Romulus, Michigan.

Lena W., born 10 May 1869, died 11 December 1927. Henry J., born 10 May 1869, died 2 July 1947. Henry J. and Lena W. were twins.

**CURTIS KNIGHT** - My third great-grandfather, Curtis Knight was born in 1783 in Maryland and his wife, Hannah Davis, my third great-grandmother in 1789 in Virginia. They were married in Grandview Township, Washington County, Ohio in 1809 where they were living before they married. Grandview Township later became part of Monroe County where they continued to live except for a few years in Tyler County, Virginia. They first came to Gallia County about 1836 and lived in Clay and Green Townships.

Nine children were born to Curtis and Hannah before they came to Gallia County. The children were born in either Ohio or Virginia. They are William in 1810, David about 1812, Curtis W. about 1814, Sarah about 1817, Nancy in 1819, Susan about 1821, Fanny about 1826, Friend in 1827 and Isaac about 1828. Four of the children were married in Gallia County: Sarah Knight to Davis Trotter in 1836, David Knight to Evaline B. Gilmore in 1836, Nancy Knight to Jesse Wallace in 1840 and Susan Knight to William H. Grow in 1842. Curtis W. Knight married Martha Ann Hufford in Lee Co. Ia, in1849 and Fanny Knight to Frances Rogers in 1849. Friend A. Knight and Martha Ann Benson were married in Wapello County, Iowa in 1850. It is not known if William and Nancy were married about 1835, or if Isaac ever married.

Death came early to some of their children. David died about 1852 leaving six children and his widow remarried Jonathan Boyce (husband of David's sister, Sarah) in 1859 in Wapello County, Iowa. Sara Knight Trotter lost her husband in 1842 and was left with four children. In 1849, she married Jonathan Boyce in Wapello County and they had four known children before she died about 1858. William died in 1877 in Wapello County as did Nancy Knight Wallace in 1889.

Curtis was a farmer but apparently did not own land in Gallia County as no land records have been found. The family stayed in Gallia County for eight years. In 1842, the newly purchased Indian Lands were being sold by the Federal Government in Iowa where my second great-grandfather Jesse and his wife Nancy, the daughter of Curtis and Hannah, had previously gone in 1843. Curtis and his family followed their daughter moving to Iowa in 1844 where they purchased land in Green Township in Wapello County. He was a first settler and served on the first election board. Curtis died in 1861 and his wife Hanna in 1875 both in Wapello County and are buried in the McIntire Cemetery. Their grandson, Curtis F. Knight was in the Civil War and served in Company C, 47th Iowa Infantry. He married Nancy C. Clehouse in 1889 in Clinton County, Missouri. He was a hostler and died of war injuries in 1900 in Henry County, Missouri.

I am Donald W. Koepp born in 1939 in Los Angeles, California and married Kathleen Rose Vacchetta in Ventura, California in 1968. We live in Thousand Oaks, California.

*Submitted By: Donald W. and Kathleen Rose Vacchetta Koepp*

**HERMAN L. KOBY** - The family of Herman L. Koby moved to Gallia County and resided in Rio Grande, Ohio, in 1966. Dr. Koby joined the administration of Rio Grande College as Dean of Students and served the institution as Academic Dean as well. He retired in 2000 after 33 years at Rio Grande, including 23 years as Vice President and Secretary-Treasurer of Rio Grande Community College, which he was instrumental in creating.

The Kobys moved to Spring Valley in 1969 and then to the corner of State Street and Third Avenue in 1986.

*Herman L. Koby Family*
*Back Row: Gordie Humbert, Kirsten Koby Humbert, Keith Koby, Kathryn Koby, Todd Morando. Front: Jeremy Humbert, Herman Koby, Saundra Koby, Lindsay Humbert, Kim and Noah Morando*

Dr. Koby, the eldest of four siblings, was born in 1933, in Tiffin, Ohio, to Louis and Mildred Koby. He was educated at Bowling Green State University and received his Ph. D. from Ohio State University. He married Saundra E. Avery, a native of Bowling Green, Ohio, in 1963. She was the only child of Gerald and Doris Avery. Both Herman and Saundra have been active members of the Gallipolis community. Herman served in leadership positions in the Gallipolis Rotary Club, Gallia County Housing Association, Gallia County Mental Health Board, The Benevolent Society of Elks, Gallipolis City Commission (1996-1999), Saint Louis Catholic Church and the Knights of Columbus. Saundra served leadership positions in The French Art Colony, St. Louis Catholic Church and Women's Club, and Rio Grande College Women's Club and the Atwood Heritage Club.

All Koby children were born and raised in Gallia County, graduating from Gallia Academy High School. Kirsten Elaine (Gordie Humbert), 1966; Kim Marie (Todd Morando), 1969; Keith Allen, 1974; and Kathryn Leigh, 1978. Kirsten, a graduate of Ohio University, resides in Delaware County, Ohio, is a homemaker and has two children, Jeremy and Lindsay Humbert. Kim, a graduate of the University of Kentucky and Ohio State University, resides in Butler, Pennsylvania, is a speech therapist in Butler County Schools, and has one son, Noah. Keith, a graduate of Ohio State University, moved to New York City in 1999 and is an executive for Time-Warner Pay Per View Television, "In Demand". Kathryn will graduate with a degree in elementary education from the University of Rio Grande/Rio Grande Community College in May 2002.

**FRANCIS E. KUHN FAMILY** - Francis E. Kuhn was born January 9, 1936 in Centenary, Green Township, just west of Gallipolis, Ohio. Centenary has really changed since he was a young boy, gone from muddy roads and a one room grade school that his mother attended to blacktop roads and plans for building the city high school in this community. The old one room grade school still stands. His grandfather, Edward Beck, referred to this community as "the garden spot of the world" due to several well kept farms, good livestock and good neighbors. Francis is the son of Charles N. and Elsie May (Beck) Kuhn.

*Francis E. Kuhn Family*
*Seated: Francis, Norma, Colton, Caleb, Janet, Karla Standing: Courtney, Carlos (Carter Not Pictured)*

He has a brother, Donald Kuhn, and two sisters, Helen J. Plymale and Nellie M. Milstead. He had two half brothers, Vernon and William Kuhn. Several of his ancestors on his mother's side, surnames of Beck, Fletcher, Denney and Rothgeb, were early settlers of Gallia County. Francis' ancestors on his father's side came to Gallia County from Marietta in 1854 and located in Clay Township. Francis attended grade school in Centenary and graduated from Gallia Academy High School in 1954. He served two years in the U.S. Army, taking basic training at Fort Carson, Colorado, then on to Germany, and was discharged on December 17, 1957. He was employed in the aluminum industry for 36 years in Ravenswood, West Virginia. He has now retired to a small farm in Fredericktown, Ohio, where he and his wife manage a flock of registered Targhees sheep.

Francis married Norma Jean Holston on November 22, 1958. She was born on November 22, 1937 in Crown City, Ohio, the daughter of Leonard and Clara (Sheets) Holston. She has one half brother, Jerry Holston, living in San Antonio, Texas. Three half brothers are deceased Wayne Holston, Tom Holston and Dale Sheets. Norma's ancestors were also early settlers in southern Gallia County. The Sheets' were some of the first to settle in that part of the county. Norma attended grade school in Crown City and graduated from Fairland High School in 1955. Francis and Norma have two daughters. Karla Jean Kuhn was born October 8, *1959* and Janet Sue Kuhn was born October 4, 1963. They both graduated from Gallia Academy High School. Karla continued her education to become a nurse and Janet an elementary teacher. Janet is married to Carlos Campbell. They have four children Courtney, Caleb, Colton and Carter.

Francis and Norma attend the Nazarene Church in Fredericktown, Ohio, and enjoy traveling. "We have had a good life with many blessings and have many fond memories of the years we lived in Gallia County."

*Submitted by Francis and Norma Kuhn*

**LAMBERT FAMILY** - Phillip Lambert was born in Wythe County, Virginia, around 1770. The records I have been able to find do not make this a fact. Phillip had eight or ten children. Pearsol, his second son, was my great, great, great grandfather. Phillip's property sold in Ohio on February, 1846 after his death in 1845.

*Charles & Alta Scott Lambert*

Pearsol Lambert, their son, was born in Wythe County, Virginia, in 1805. Pearsol was married two times. His first wife was Jinny Harper. They were married on March 16, 1826. She was born in Logan County, Virginia. To this union, four children were born. His third born was Henderson Lambert. Pearsol later married Isabell Rose and they had four more children. Pearsol died in 1845 in Gallia County, Ohio.

Henderson Lambert was born in Greenfield Township, Gallia County, Ohio. He married Catherine McCoy on April 20, 1848. They had three children between them. He married Mary Janetta Spencer McCoy in 1856. My grandfather, the second Henderson Lambert, was born September 1, 1861, to their marriage. The first Henderson died on August 25, 1876, in Hamilton County, McLeansboro, Illinois. He is buried in the McCoy cemetery in Hamilton County, McLeansboro, Illinois.

Henderson Lambert, my grandfather, was born in Knights Prairie Township, Hamilton County, McLeansboro, Illinois, on September 1, 1861. He married Ina Brock on January 6, 1889, in Hamilton County. My father was their first child. They had eight children altogether. He died on June 20, 1946, in DeWitt County, Clinton, Illinois. He was buried in Mount Nebo Cemetery in Hamilton County, McLeansboro, Illinois.

Jesse Walter Lambert, my father, was born in Hamilton County on March 18, 1890. He married my mother, Annie Laura Tucker, on December 25, 1922, in Macon County, Illinois. They had six children, one dying in infancy. I, Alta Ruth Lambert, being the fourth child. Jesse Walter Lambert died on January 17, 1972, in Hamilton County, McLeansboro, Illinois. He is buried in Mount Nebo Cemetery in Hamilton County, McLeansboro, Illinois.

Alta Ruth Lambert was born on November 29, 1928, in DeWitt County, Clinton, Illinois. She married Charles B. Scott on July 15, 1960, in Rockford, Illinois, in Winnebago County. We have one child born, October 14, 1962, in DeWitt County in Clinton, Illinois. Her name is Deborah Gail Scott.

Deborah (Debbie) Gail Scott was born October 14, 1962, in Clinton, Illinois. She married Dick Merriken on September 28, 1985, in Clinton, Illinois. They have three children, Kurt, Amanda, and Charles.

*Submitted by Alta Scott*

**GEORGE F. LAWLESS (LOLLIS)** - George Lawless, the second son of John Lollis and Elizabeth McNeil was born in Gallia County, Ohio. He grew up on the Lollis family farm in Springfield Township. He married Harriet Caroline Humphrey on March 13, 1869, in Gallipolis. "Hattie" was born in Virginia on March 15, 1846, to William Humphrey and Elizabeth Gordon. George and Hattie were blessed with five children including William Albertus (February 12, 1870) and two sets of twins, Frances E. and Samuel (January 17, 1877) and Pearl and Earl (February 24, 1884). George worked the family farm in Springfield Township through at least 1887. In October of that year, his wife sold Lot 4 in Porter to George's sister, Mary Lollis Brant. By 1899, George had moved his family to Kyger in Cheshire Township. Shortly after 1900, they moved again to Columbus. George died in Columbus on May 1, 1906, as the result of a fall from a window. Hattie died of pulmonary tuberculosis on January 26, 1917. George and Hattie are interred in Green Lawn Cemetery, Columbus, Ohio.

William Albertus known as "Bert" was born in Porter, Ohio, and died October 30, 1933, at his Mill Creek Road residence in Gallipolis. Bert listed his occupation as a miner prior to his three-year enlistment (June 10, 1896-June 9, 1899) in the U.S. Army for the Spanish American War. Bert rose to the rank of Sergeant in the 8th Regiment, U.S. Infantry. He was assigned initially to F Company and later M Company with service in Ft. Russell, Wyoming; Chickamauga Park, Georgia; Rio Piedras Island, Puerto Rico; and Havana, Cuba. After an honorable discharge, he returned to Cheshire Township where he took up farming with short stints as a miller and on the railroad. Bert, long suffered from malaria and other medical afflictions as a result of his military service in the tropics. He eventually was awarded a disability pension. He married Eva May Thomas on November 29, 1901, in Gallipolis. "May" was born November 15, 1881, in Wyoma, West Virginia, to Reuben Thomas and Rachel Ellen Fife. She died on July 15, 1966, in Columbus. Bert and May had two daughters, Lenora (1902-1987) and Ruth (1904-1992). Lenora Lawless married Donovan Frasier on December 23, 1919, and ultimately moved with him to Fayette County, West Virginia, for work in the coal industry. They had three children (Virginia May, Frances Ann, and Billy Donovan). All married and propagated the family with many descendants. Ruth Lawless married James Thomas Forsythe on June 28, 1924, in Urbana, Champaign County. Ruth had a daughter, Dorothy Marie (Lawless) Cox, prior to three children with James Forsythe (William Robert, Lillian Mae, and Mary Jayne). All married and have provided many Lawless descendants. Bert and May Lawless and Don and Lenora Frasier are interred in Gravel Hill Cemetery.

*Sergeant Bert Lawless (Marked With X) M Company, 8th. US Infantry In Havana, Cuba In 1898*

Less is known of the other children. "Fannie" (Frances) Lawless married Emory Gore and resided in Columbus, Ohio. She passed away on March 9, 1965, and is interred with her husband in Green Lawn Cemetery. Fannie had a daughter, Thelma, from a previous marriage. Thelma may have died as a child. Her siblings, Samuel and Pearl, died as children prior to 1900. Her brother, Earl, died at age 21 on March 26, 1905, from typhoid fever in Columbus, Ohio, and was buried near his parents in Green Lawn Cemetery.

*Submitted by David Monroe Lollis, Jr., grand nephew of George Lawless*

**LAWRENCE FAMILY** - Michael Lawrence b.12/18/1858, d. 11/11/1915, s/o John and Susan Rodgers Lawrence of Griffithsville, Lincoln Co., W.V. m. Eveline Webb, d/o Leonard and Elizabeth Cook Webb. Michael and Eveline had 12 children, two died in infancy. The Lawrence's moved to Gallia Co. around 1904.

I. Wm. Frank b. 3/20/1880, d. 11/18/1902 killed in a hunting accident. II. J. Leonard b. 12/17/1883 d. 7/03/1964 m. Ora Spurlock b. 8/16/1888 d. 10/1967. Children: 1. Macel b.11/18/1909 d. 08/1973. 2. Helen b. 09/11/1907 d. 02/03/1994. 3. J. L. Jr. b. 12/17/

1913 d. 08/28/1978. 4. Ray III. D. Catherine b. 1887 d. 1965. m. Delbery Huffman b. 1888, d. 1960 Children: 1. Mabel C. b. 09/25/1920 d. 08/22/1976. 2. Robert B. b. 06/12/1915 d. 11/18/1995. 3. Lowell D. b. 08/20/1918 d. 02/24/1999. 4. Helen. IV. Ferd E. b. 12/14/1889 d. 03/25/1962 m. 03/30/1918 to A. Mae Mink . b. 05/30/1898 d. 02/22/1995, their daughter I. Jean b. 1924 d.1946. V. Elva M. b.05/15/1897 d. 1947, m. Clarence "Pud" Mulford. b. 11/19/1896 d. 02/26/1968, one son Clarence Jr. "Jay" b. 02/17/1922 d. 03/16/1986.

The three of them ran the family service station in Cheshire.

*Michael & Eveline Lawrence c. 1905*

VII. E. V. "Larry" "Dago" b. 12/01/1893 d. 11/28/1966, m. Genevieve Doster.

Dago played football and baseball at Marshall University, and pro football for a Detroit team. In 1920 he played pro baseball, on the farm team the "Gassers" down in Shreveport, Louisana.

VIII. Nettie b. 02/17/1895 d. 11/25/1976, Thanksgiving Day. She married Fred Dulaney, they had one daughter Llade " Bonita".

When Bonita was 11mt old 5/27/1918 Fred drowned while working on the boat the Enterprize.

Nettie's 2nd marriage was to Tom Adams b. 03/16/1889 d. 02/28/1974. They celebrated their 50th wedding anniversary on 12/02/1969. They raised three children. #1. Bonita b.06/14/1917 d. 03/09/1978. Bonita married Annis Erwin b. 12/13,1914 d. 1964. Bonita 's 2nd m. to Charles Gilfilen b. 2/28/1911 still reside in Gallipolis, very talented remarkable guy.

Annis and Bonita had two children: Freddie b. 08/02/1936; Joann b. 07/23/1934 m. Joseph Ross b. 4/11/1930 d. 10/25/1997, s/o Raymond and Ruth Frye Ross.

Joann & Joe had three children:

A. Mark b. 01/12/1956 m. Nancy Horner They have two children: A. Joey b.11/14/1986 b. Lauren. b. 12/28/1990 B. Terry b. 6/27/1957 m. Peter Mitchell

They have one child:

Melissa b. 2/7/1974 married Todd Graf They have two daughters Kaylee and Dallys

Terry is married to Bob Hageman C. Jan b. 09/25/1958 m. Tom Clark. They had two children: Zackary b. 3/10/1982 Emily b. 12/10/1984.

Nettie and Tom had two sons: #2. Jack b. 09/30/1920 m. Charolette Herron on 6/17/1950.

They have two daughters:

Linda b. 04/04/1951
Kathleen b. 02/19/1956
#3. Derry, b. 12/12/1927 m. Dortha Estes on 10/16/1954. Dottie b. 5/14/1935. They raised three children: a. Llada b. 6/17/1953 m. Jimmy Holstein

They had one son Adamwayne Adams b. 6/11/1985 B. Ted b. 12/30/1961 m. Mary Hoffman

They have two daughters: Brooke 7/14/1988 and Rachel 8/18/1992.

Terry b. 03/02/1963 m. Beth Taylor Hudson, they have three children:

1. Lauren Hudson, b. 09/19/1986, is also the daughter of Conard Hudson Jr. and the grandaughter of Lyda Farley and the late Conard Hudson Sr. 2.Beau b. 11/19/1992, 3.Taylor 09/06/1994

IX. Lula b. 04/24/1899, d. 04/16/1988, never married but took care of her mother until she passed away and was always there to help the rest of her family.

X. Glada b. 11/22/1903, d. 12/13/1943, m. H. Waldo Davidson in 1927.

One daughter Sarah E. "Patty" b. 06/15/1928
XI. Ash b. 06/03/1901, d. 02/1978, m. Sarah Breedlove b. 08/02/1926, d. 05/1983.

Children: Howard and Andy Breedlove, Mike, Derry, Llade, and Marilyn.

*Submitted by Llada Adams*

**LEAR FAMILY** - The history of the Lear's began with the arrival in Gallia County of Frederick Yohan Lear from Hanover, Germany. He married Elizabeth Cardwell and had several children, including a son named Fredrick (1854-1915). Frederick married Rosina Niday (1861-1952).

*The Lear Family, Front L: to R: Virgil, Eustace, Lizzie, Mary, Hoadly, Ogle, Back L: to R: John, Crony, Ed*

They were married 3-13-1881. Rosina was the daughter of Henry(1827-1909) and Elizabeth (1826-1890) White Niday. Their children were: Crony, (1882-1955) married Minnie Sheets (1888-1974). Their children were, Haskell, Mildred, and Sylvia. Hoadley,(1884-1968) married Edna Fellure, Their children were, Gordon, Henrietta, and Veva. Eustus, (1885-1968) married Alice Hively. Their children were, Irvin, Delora, Garland and Kathleen. Edman (1887-1959) married Effie Elkins. No children. Elizabeth, (1889-1982) married Calvin Sanders (1889-1981) their children were, Garnet, Merritt, Calvin, Dale, Celestine, Nadine, Fred. John (1893-1967) married Mary Hineman, their children were, Eugene, Dixie, Doris, Curtis, Frederick. Virgil (1895-1975) married Pearl Wells (1910-1995).Their children were, Otis, Richard, Wilbur, Russell, Maxine, and Bernice. Ogle (1899-1969) married 1929 Hazel Wells their children were: Beatrice, Rose Lee, Virginia, and Tom. Mary (1901) married Herschel Brumfield (1899-1999). Their children Frank, Winona Forrest, Elizabeth, and Robert Francis. Verta , b,1904, d. 1923.

*Submitted by: Dale & Garland Lear*

**LE CLERC, SIMONIN AND FAMILY** - Peter Louis LeClerc and wife Louisa Constance were part of the French 500 settlement. They had the following daughters Adele, Athalia, Felicitie, Clarissa, and Sophia. Peter and Louisa are buried in the Pine Street Cemetery. Adele and Athalia were born in France before the family traveled to America. Some sources say Athalia was born in Gallia County, but her daughters in the census of 1880 say she was born in France. There is a story about two LeClerc girls being captured by Indians and then released. An Indian beaded bag was given to them, which is now housed at the Our House Museum in Gallipolis.

Athalia LeClerc married Anthony Francis Simonin b. France in Gallia County on October 9, 1809. Their children were Elila, Virginia who married a Brierly, Clarissa married a Pickens and moved to Meigs county, Romain who moved to Mason County, Ky, Peter who settled in Lawrence County, Ohio and Rosina/Rosana born November 12, 1820. The family is mentioned in a court case in chancery court from May 1839-Ch. 1, pages 225-232 concerning Garden Lot 22. The family traveled some between Gallia County and Mason County, KY.

Rosana married Joseph Circle (1811-?) on April 2, 1835. His parents are unknown but believed to be related to the Circle family of Meigs County, Ohio). Joseph appears in Gallia County in the 1830 census in Gallipolis. They were the parents of the following children: Charles Edgar, Minerva, Clarinda, Frances J., Susannah, Wesley, Anna, Maggie, Letitia, and Emma. The family appears in the 1840 census as having one male under the age five, one male 20 < 30, 3 females under 5 and 1 female 15<20. In the 1850 Gallia census lists Joseph, Rosana, Charles, Minerva, Clarinda, Francis and Susannah.

Joseph and Rosana lived in Gallia County until the mid-1850's when the family moved across the Ohio River to Mason County, VA/WV . Joseph's occupation was engineer and he had an accident that left him disabled according to the 1870 and 1880 census. Rosana died on July 15, 1888 and was buried in the West Columbia Hill Cemetery. According to her obituary "she was the mother of 14 children six survive and she was a constant member of the M.E. Church for 43 years." Joseph's death and his burial place are unknown.

Charles (1837-1921) was a Civil War Vet. He enlisted in the 4th W.Va. Company A Infantry as many men from Gallia did. He used his blacksmithing talents throughout the war and was at Vicksburg. During the war he married Mariah E. Harless, a native of Boone County, VA/WV in Gallia County October, 1862.

They had the following children William Sherman, Rosa Catherine, Linnie May, Ella Uretta, Eva Gertrude (1875-1947), and Charles Edgar Jr.

In 1895 Charles and Mariah moved to Cabell County, WV. His daughter Linnie had married Edward Diffenbach. He was an educator and newspaper owner and he had moved to the

Huntington and Ceredo area. All the children, except Ella who married Robert Fogelsong, moved to Cabell County.

Eva Gertrude married Stephen Jerome Ellette in 1899 Cabell County and had 4 children:

Stephen Clayton (1901-1969), Arthur Charles, Eva Marie and Roy Edgar. Sylvia Carolyn 1934-1965 was born to Stephen C. and Mabel Pettit Ellette in Charleston, WV. She moved to New Orleans, LA. with Jacob J. Willem. Their only child Sheri Kim was born May 1958. She married Richard A. Pettit in 1987 in Perry County, Oh. but, they have mostly lived in WV to be close to her grandmother Mabel who is 96. She works as a genealogy specialist at the Boyd County Public Library in Ashland, KY. She also lectures on genealogy and history and is proud to have been a First Families speaker as well as a member. She had always loved the city of Gallipolis long before she knew she had roots going back to the beginning of Gallia County. She did not start doing genealogy until 1990, but remembers the summer of 1982 going through Pine St. Cemetery and exploring not knowing she was related to anyone in the cemetery.

*Submitted by Sheri K. Pettit*

**BENJAMIN LEE AND FRANCIS PAYNE LEE** - Benjamin Lee, my great, great grandfather, married Francis Payne. Their parents' names are not known, but the 1900 census indicated that their families came from West Virginia (then Virginia).

He and Francis had twelve children. One son died of pneumonia six days after his birth in 1911.

Their other children are:

1. Frank Lee (1870-1952) married his first wife, Lena Briggs (1874-1939) of West Virginia on December 22, 1915, and later married Carrie Rippey (September 7, 1896-March 13, 1986).

2. Samuel Lee, my great grandfather (1871-1937), married Sylvinia Evaline "Eva" Harris (1874-1958) on July 23, 1892. She was from Kanawha County, WV. They were the parents of eleven children

3. Fred Lee married Myrtle Long on December 26, 1901.

4. Benjamin's only daughter, Mary Lee, married Daniel King on January 17, 1889.

5. Henry Lee, only recorded in the 1900 census at the age of 18, was known to have married and reared four children in Gallipolis.

6. Robert Lee died May 7, 1901 at 17 years and said to be buried in Mound Hill, Gallipolis..

7. Prestley Lee married his first wife, Mary Waver, on October 10, 1921, and his second wife was Mabel NeaL

8. Ernest Lee recorded in the 1900 census at the age of 12.

9. Harvey Mack Lee moved to Arizona after serving in the 10th.Cavalry, U. S. Army. He was one of the 23 soldiers captured at Carrizal and sent to Chihuahua City, Mexico, where they were marched through the streets in their underwear.

10. Floyd Lee married Frances Banks on June 9, 1924.

11. James 'Dick' Lee was known to our family and he moved to Pittsburgh, PA.

Benjamin served in Company C, 5th U.S.C. Inf. This is the only information on his tombstone which is in Pine Street Cemetery, Gallipolis. Benjamin Lee and his children were residents of the Maple Shade area of Gallipolis where they owned their homes and gardens.

(See family histories of Samuel Lee, Ora Lee and Robert Hugh Anderson, Arnetta Anderson and Samuel Edward Dexter, and Bobette Dexter and Frank Edward Braxton, Jr.)

*Submitted by Bobette Dexter Braxton*

**SAMUEL LEE AND SYLVINIA EVALINE "EVA" HARRIS LEE** - Great grandfather, Samuel Lee (1871-1937) married Sylvinia Evaline "Eva" Lee (1874-1958) on July 23, 1892. They came from Kanawha County, WV to Gallipolis, OH. His parents were Benjamin and Francis Payne Lee of Gallipolis, and her parents were from Pt. Pleasant, WV. Sam and Eva were the parents of eleven children. One son died on January 18, 1911, 5 days old and was buried in the Pine Street Colored Cemetery, Gallipolis, Ohio, that grave site can no longer be found. The first three children were born in West Virginia and the rest in Gallipolis, Ohio.

1. Ora Hattie, my grandmother (November 14, 1894-November 14, 1994) married Robert Hugh Anderson (1880-1957) of Winchester, Kentucky, on April 20, 1914.

2. Mae married Alfred Burton on October 1, 1917.

3. Christopher was a laborer working at the Ohio Hospital for Epileptics (now the Gallipolis Departmental Center). He married and moved to Flint, MI; and his daughter, Elaine Lee, is a lawyer, judge and author in California.

4. Fremont was a laborer; he married and moved from Gallipolis.

5. Melissa married Sherman Eagle Gordon on July 22, 1922.

6. Edna married Charles Grant on June 27, 1924 and her second husband was William Casey.

7. Helen married H J. Spencer of Columbus, Ohio, on June 25, 1924.

8. Thomas "Bus", unmarried, was the chauffeur for 0. 0. McIntyre and his wife. He died on the Silver Bridge when it collapsed.

9. Susie married William "Joe Dink" Jackson of Gallipolis, Ohio.

10. Robert "Bill" married Mary Scott of Gallipolis.

My great grandfather died before I was born, but one of my best memories of my Grandma Lee is that I taught her how to make my favorite breakfast—poached eggs on toast—when I was five. All of us have one great memory of Grandma Lee. She smoked a pipe. When she needed tobacco for it, we all wanted to go to Ilene's Store to get the Kool cigarettes she used in it—a modern day pipe smoker she was. The effect? None of us smoke!

The story continues under the histories of Benjamin and Francis Payne Lee, Ora Lee and Robert Anderson, Arnetta Anderson and Samuel Dexter, and Bobette Dexter and Frank Braxton, Jr. Submitted by Bobette Dexter Braxton.

**JUNIOR LESLIE AND BETTY JANE (Welch) LEMLEY FAMILY** - Junior Leslie Lemley was born June 15, 1926 in Gallia County, Ohio to Perry Leslie (Pade) Lemley and Pearl Inez (Cremeans) Lemley. His great grandfather, Anthony Lemley, was the first Lemley to arrive in Gallia County. At the age of 24,he worked his way down the Ohio River on a boat. He disembarked at Cheshire, Ohio and went to work cutting timber and clearing the land where Cheshire Village now stands. In 1851 he married Mary Shoemaker, and in 1861 he fought in the Civil War where he was wounded in the battle of the Shenandoah Valley.

Another of Junior's ancestors, his great grandfather Perry Ralph also served in the War between the States and made a prisoner of the war in May of 1864 at the battle of Cloyd Mountain, Virginia. He was released from Andersonville Prison in April of 1865.

*Poplar Ridge Vagabonds L: toR: Luther Lemley, Junior Lemley and cousin Harold Hood.*

Junior's family resided at Poplar Ridge in Cheshire Township. His father, Pade, was a farmer and a miner and Pearl was a homemaker know for her quilting abilities. Junior also has one brother Luther Brian (Grace) Lemley.

*Betty Jane Lemley,Junior Leslie Lemley, Theresa Jane Price and Leslie Albert Lemley*

In 1944 Junior graduated from Cheshire High School in a class of six boys and six girls. He served in the Army from January 11, 1945 to December 21, 1946 during World War II. On June 30, 1949 he married Betty Jane Welch, who was born November 15, 1931 in Mercer County, West Virginia. Betty was employed by Sylvania Plant and Holzer Hospital. She was also recognized for her professional seamstress and quilting abilities. Her parents, Rev. Albert Welch Sr., a dairy farmer who routed milk from Winfield to Charleston, West Virginia, and Elizabeth (Scott) Welch, a homemaker, came to Gallia County in

1946 from Putnam County, West Virginia. Betty Jane is a descendant of General Winfield Scott, of the Civil War; and her maternal grandmother, Lucreia (Hubbard) Scott, was of the Cherokee Indian Tribe.

Junior was employed by Gallipolis State Institute as a store keeper from 1949 until 1977 when he retired. He is well-known for his vocalist and instrumental faculty. One of first vocal groups he performed with was in 1938 with the Poplar Ridge Vagabonds. He later sang with family members as the Lemley Quartet and as a trio with his children. He and Betty have two children: a son Leslie Albert (Kathie) Lemley, and a daughter Theresa Jane Price, both of whom still reside in Gallia County. They have four grandchildren, Wendie Sue (Bill) Holley and Michael Norris Lemley born to the family of Leslie; and Rebecca Elaine (Frank) Overstreet and Franklin Lee (Marcia) Price to Theresa. They are also the proud great-grandparents of seven great grandchildren: Jared Allen, Cody Michael and Kaitlyn Elaine Holley, Dyln Michael Lemley, Hannah Nicole and Gage Michael Overstreet, and Gracie Lynn Pirce.

**REX ANDREW LEMLEY AND CARRIE CHRISTINE WARD LEMLEY** - Carrie Christine Ward and Rex Andrew Lemley were born in Cheshire Township, Gallia County, Ohio in 1909. They attended elementary school together at the Africa Rural School, a one room schoolhouse in Cheshire Township. Carrie pursued her education and eventually taught in the same school that she and Rex attended. On November 29, 1930 they eloped to Greenup Kentucky where they were married. They had to keep their marriage a secret until the end of the school year.

*L: To R: 1st Row: Brian, Andrew, Kathryn Jean, Jim Shaw, Christine, Clark Harrison Back Row: Tricia, Steven Shaw; Dan, Stephanie, Beth Harrison*

Rex Lemley was the 8th child of James Theodore Lemley (11/1/1870- 3/12/1952) and Cora Ellen Ralph, (9/01/1870-9/09/1959) who was the daughter of Perry Ralph. Perry Ralph served in the Union Army, with Company C, Ohio Volunteers. He enlisted at the age of 16, and was captured by the Confederates at the Battle of Cloyds Mountain. He eventually was incarcerated in the Andersonville Prison; He was imprisoned nearly a year, miraculously survived the ordeal of Andersonville Prison. Perry returned to Ohio and married Mary Jane Fife, thus being the father of Cora Ellen Ralph.

Andrew Lemley, who came down the Ohio River from Pennsylvania, was one of the first settlers in the area of Cheshire. He was 24 years old when he arrived in the vicinity of Cheshire in 1850. Mary Shoemaker and Andrew Lemley were united in marriage in 1851. Andrew was in the Union Army from August 8,1862 to June 24, 1865. He was in the 91st Ohio Volunteer Infantry Co. B. James Theodore Lemley and Cora Ellen Ralph were married on April 10, 1890. They were the parents of 9 children. They were: Bertha m. Wayne Shaver; Bessie m. Henry Hood; Belva m. Robert Harrison; Leland m. Manila Darst; Leslie m. Pearl Cremeans; Alberta m Corbie James; Ralph m. Jessie Jones; Rex m. Carrie Ward; Ray m. Alice Thompson.

*Carrie & Rex Lemley*

Carrie Christine Ward Lemley was the youngest child of John Ned Ward (12/30/1864-12/24/1932 and Christina A. Arnold, (7/11/1870-5/29/1946). They had three children: Mildred m. Henry Luellen; James N. Ward, m. Thelma Rose; and Carrie m. Rex Lemley.

Carrie attended Rio Grande University and received a 2 year degree to teach in 1938; and a B.S. in Elementary Education in 1957. She taught school for a total of 38 years at Kyger, Kyger Creek, in Gallia County and Walnut Twp. in Pickaway County.

Rex was a farmer; Highway worker, bus driver and store keeper. He and Carrie owned both of the stores in the village of Kyger at different times. These country general stores sold everything a family needed; from groceries, feed for animals, gasoline and oil. At Christmas holiday time the store was stocked with bulk candy, nuts, oranges and even salt fish. Rex and Carrie did not keep the store open on Sunday. But if someone needed an item he would accommodate them.

They had one child, Kathryn Jean Lemley (8/23/1931) who married James W. Shaw, (11/03/1931) at the Kyger Methodist church on September 20, 1952. Both Kathryn J. And James were graduates of Rio Grande University and both had careers in education. Kathryn taught elementary and retired as a Media Specialist. Jim received his M.Ed. From Ohio University and was a Teacher, Coach, Guidance Counselor, and Administrator. He retired from the State Department of Education, Division of School Finance. They now divide their residences between Ohio and Florida.

Their children are James Steven Shaw, who was born in Gallipolis, Ohio on October 12, 1954. He is a graduate of Rio Grande University and received his M.Ed. from Ohio State University. A daughter, Stephanie Jean Shaw Harrison, was born on May 21, 1959 at Circleville, Ohio. She is a graduate of the State University of New York, majoring in Communications.

James Steven married Patricia Sue Wilkinson in 1981. They have two sons, Andrew Paul, who was born in Delaware, October 12, 1987. Brian James Shaw was born on May 28, 1990 in Delaware, Ohio. Steve is a consultant for the Ohio Department of Education. The J. Steven Shaw family reside in Delaware Ohio.

Stephanie Jean married Daniel Robert Harrison in 1980. Daniel is a Computer Programmer with the International Business Machines Corporation. The Harrison family presently live in Milford , Ohio. They have three children; Christine Ann, (September 19,1985) Elizabeth Helen, (June 30,1989) who were born in Vestal New York. One child, Mary Kathryn was born in Cincinnati on September 18,1995; lived 55 days and died November 14, 1995. Clark Daniel, who was born on April 21,1997 in Cincinnati. Ohio.

Rex Andrew Lemley and Carrie Christine Ward Lemley descendants consist of one daughter, and son-in-law; two grand children, and spouses, and a total of 6 great grandchildren, One great grandchild deceased.

Rex passed away on January 8, 1990 at his home in Circleville, Ohio. Carrie Lemley passed away at Willow-Brook Christian Village in Delaware, Ohio on May 16,1995. Both are interred at Poplar Ridge Cemetery, in Cheshire Township, in Gallia County.

*Submitted by daughter Kathryn Jean Lemley Shaw*

**JOHN G. LEWIS AND FAMILY** - John G. Lewis was born August 13, 1854 in Greenbrier County (West) Virginia.

John was a big man 6ft. 3 in and 230 lbs. He worked as a coal miner, deputy sheriff and owned a restaurant.

He married Julia A. Yeaguer on July 3, 1879 in Meigs Co., Ohio. She was the daughter of John Benjamin Yeaguer and Mary Polly Jones. They had ten children: John Archibald, Julia Lula, William Robert, Harry L, Charles, Susan A., Lawrence (b. March 1897 d Sept. 1906), Mattie and Roxie.

John Archibald was born Sept. 10, 1880 in Meigs Co. He married Ina Isabelle Little on May 6, 1904 in Meigs Co, Ohio. They had three children: Wesley, Leona and Helen.

Julia Lula was born Apr. 4, 1882 in Cheshire Township. She married Henry Casto on Jan 26, 1903 in Meigs Co. Oh. They had six children: Roy, George, Genevieve, Julia Marie, Virgil Frederick and Dora Marie. Julia died May 5, 1959. Henry was born Aug. 11, 1880 in Carlton, Meigs Co. Ohio and died Nov. 25, 1950 in Middleport, Ohio.

Julia and Henry are buried in Gravel Hill Cemetery, Cheshire.

William Robert was born May 21, 1885 in Cheshire Township and died Mar. 16, 1951 in Middleport, Ohio. He is buried in Gravel Hill Cemetery.

George Harry was born Aug. 13, 1887 in Camden, WV. He married Susan May Warner on Mar. 28, 1909 in Meigs Co. Oh. They had nine children: Betty, Dorothy, Harold, Katherine, Lawrence, Margaret, Norma Jean, Art "Pappy" and Edward W.W..

Charles was born May 1891 in Cheshire Township and died in 1961. He married Jenny

Mae Wise. She was born 1892 and died in 1958, Charles and Jenny had five children: Richard, Charles, Julia, Robert and James. They are buried Gravel Hill Cemetery.

Susan Lewis was born Oct. 27, 1894 in Cheshire Township and died in June 1979. She married George Veith, born in 1884 and died in 1973. They had five children: John, Georgia, Ann, Frank and Hetty. They are buried in Gravel Hill Cemetery.

Mattie Lewis was born Sept. 1, 1889 in Cheshire Township. About 1919 she married Virgil Albert Byers, b. Aug. 22, 1890 in Middleport, Ohio. Virgil and Mattie had four children: Clarence, Helen, Myrtle and Dorothy. Virgil and Mattie died unexpectedly at their home on Storys Run on August 8, 1927 and are buried in Gravel Hill Cemetery.

Roxie Lewis, the last child of John G. and Julia was born Dec. 18, 1893 in Cheshire Township and died July 31, 1982 in Columbus, Ohio. She married David

Oiler,b. 1898, d. 1958. They had one child Violet. They are buried in Gravel Hill Cemetery.

**CHARLES M. LITTLE** - Charles M. "Charley" Little was born April 21, 1866, in Jackson County, West Virginia , to Robert C. Little and Elizabeth Hysell. A second generation coal miner, Charley moved with his family in the 1880's to the coal mining community of Carlsburg in northern Cheshire Township, Gallia County.

*Back Row L: To R: Foster, Alma and Howard Little Front Seated - Morris "Mouse" Little*

In January 1889, Charley married Mary Ann George. Mary was born July 31, 1871, in Mason County, WV, to William George and Rhoda Fanny Hoffman. The George family, originally from Davis Creek, Kanawha County, West Virginia, also settled in the coal mining community of Carlsburg and like many mining families moved back and forth depending on the volume of work available.

Settling in Cheshire Township, Charley helped organize a Sabbath School in Carlsburg and was appointed Secretary. Like his father, Charley was a Republican and occasionally participated in local politics, having his hat thrown in the ring for constable and serving as a polling place clerk in Cheshire Township. Charley was a subscriber and regular reader of the "Meigs County Republican" and later in life was known to walk a mile or more to catch a Joe Lewis fight on the radio.

Charles and Mary had the following children:

Vesta Mae Little was born February 8, 1890, in Cheshire Township and died March 17, 1972, in Pomeroy, Meigs County, Ohio. She married Pleasant Arthur Ellis on December 22, 1907, in Gallia County, Ohio.

Clarence McKinley Little was born September 26, 1891, in Meigs County and died May 24, 1950, in Gallipolis, Ohio. He married first, Edna Josie Collins on July 28, 1909, in Meigs County. He married second, Ida Schlecht on May 2, 1938, in Gallia County. He married third, Stella Willis on July 18, 1942.

Alma Esther Little was born February 10, 1894, in Kanawha County, WV, and died January 26, 1977, in Pike County, Ohio. She married Stanley Vernon "Jack" Swisher on September 16, 1916, in Gallia County.

Clara B. Little was born February 18, 1899, in Cheshire Township and died of pneumonia on September 13, 1900, in Gallia County.

Howard Benjamin Little was born July 8, 1901, in Cheshire and died March 16, 1960, in Hillsdale County, Michigan. He married first Bertha Carmen on December 23, 1922, in Gallia County. He married second, Adrian Little on March 7, 1927, in Meigs County.

Millard Little was born January 17, 1903, in Cheshire Township and died of measles June 2, 1903, in Cheshire Township.

Clinton Little was born May 10, 1904, in Cheshire Township and died of measles September 25, 1904, in Cheshire Township.

Foster Alden Little was born June 29, 1905, in Cheshire Township and died February 17, 1967, in Lorain County, Ohio. He married first Effie Gertrude Gandee on January 1, 1925, in Meigs County. He married second Agnes Elizabeth Simpson ca. 1945 probably in Summit County, Ohio.

Morris Hanley Little was born December 15, 1907, in Cheshire Township and died of tuberculosis March 9, 1936, in Cheshire. He married Francis Manley October 19, 1929, in Gallia County.

Charles William Little was born January 31, 1910, in Cheshire Township and died of pneumonia July 8, 1910, in Cheshire.

Robert Bernard Little was born October 1, 1911, in Cheshire Township and died of pneumonia May 10, 1912, in Cheshire.

Francis Elizabeth Little was born May 10, 1915, in Cheshire and died of tuberculosis April 14, 1947, in Cheshire. She married first Orville Smith. She married second Glen Arlen Kiser.

*Submitted by Shari L. (Little) Creech*

**FOSTER LITTLE** - Foster Alden Little was born June 29, 1905, in Cheshire Township to Charles M. Little and Mary Ann George. One of at least twelve children born to a poor coal mining family, he spent all of his happy childhood in Cheshire.

Foster first attended school at Cheshire Academy but graduated from the new Cheshire High in 1923. He watched the new Cheshire School being built and became involved in many of its activities. He and his brother Howard participated in a school play at the K of P Hall entitled "Al Martin's Country Store" where Foster played the part of Ned, a loafer. He also played the lead in a school play "Deacon Dubbs", playing the part of Deacon. He became the first "cheerleader", faithfully following Cheshire's illustrious new football team, befriended a new student from Columbus named Harold Long, and recited "The Christmas Story" at the Little Kyger Grange. Later, stories will be told of his trips with Otto Rothgeb to all of the area baseball games.

*Foster and Agnes Little ca. 1945*

Foster married his first wife, Effie, on January 1, 1925, in Meigs County, Ohio. It is believed that they worked at the old OHE together and that is where they met. They settled into married life in Cheshire Township and Foster, following in his father's and grandfather's footsteps, became a coal miner. He worked in the mines out toward Carlton for the Rothgeb family.

Foster and Effie had the following children:

Hilah Florence Little born November 15, 1925, and died August 11, 1973, in a tractor accident in Columbus, Ohio. She married Ovid Glandon May 6, 1950, in Columbus and had three children: Scott, Nikki, and Mark.

Eugenia Pearl "Jean" Little was born July 14, 1928, and died February 24, 1929, of tubercular meningitis.

Robert William Little was born November 4, 1929. He married first Jeanette Golini June 14, 1952, in Lorain, Ohio. He married Gayle Gandee September 17, 1962, in LaFollette, Campbell County, Tennessee, and had two children: Robert Jr. and Shari.

Shirley Little was born June 13, 1931, and died October 18, 1934, of congenital heart disease and rickets. *Submitted by: Robert Little Sr.*

**FOSTER LITTLE, JR** - Foster Little, Jr. was born August 28, 1936 in Cheshire, the youngest of five children born to Foster and Effie Little. Foster attended Cheshire High, loved sports and is fondly remembered by classmates as "Junior". After high school, Foster enlisted in the United States Marine Corp. Foster married Brenda Gail Robbins, August 24, 1958 in Nash County, North Carolina. Brenda was born, December 13, 1940 in Nash County, North Carolina to Lynwood and Edith (Denson) Robbins. Foster and Brenda had four children: Marci, Kandi, Mark and Andrea.

Marci JoDean born, June 6, 1960, Balboa, Ancon Canal Zone, Panama. Marci married Edward Allen White, Jr., August 18, 1979, in Nash County, North Carolina. Edward was born February 28, 1958 in Nash County, son of Edward and Melba (Hyde) White. Marci is an Information Security Specialist at RBC Centura Bank. Edward is the Director of Water Services for Edgecombe County, North Carolina. Children of Marci and Ed are Stephen, born April, 1984,

David, born August 8, 1985. The White's live in Nashville, North Carolina.

Kandice Kay born September 25, 1961, Balboa, Ancon Canal Zone, Panama, married first Vince Lawson; one child, Taryn Lawson born August 15, 1982. Taryn is expecting her first child, a little girl on March 4, 2002. Kandi married second John Stacy Ondejko, January 21, 1991; they have one son, Andrew Travis Ondejko, born April 15, 1992. The Ondejko's live in Mission Viejo, California.

*L:to R: (First Wife) Brenda, daughter Marci, and Foster Little Jr. Christmas 1960*

Mark Travis born September 13, 1962 in Balboa, Ancon Canal Zone, Panama. Mark married first Leane Costello, August 21, 1987 in Nash County, North Carolina. He married second, Lisa Sieg from Ramsey, Indiana. Her family owns and operates the Cousin Willie Popcorn Factory. Mark works in Hollywood as a set designer and has worked on many movies and television shows including: Speed, The Nutty Professor, Ellen and The Hughley's. Mark currently lives in Northridge, California.

Andrea Michelle was born May 17, 1968 in Columbus, Ohio. Andrea married Martin Streicher on September 15, 1990. Martin was born June 1, 1964 in Pennsylvania to Jack and Helen (Cohen) Streicher. Children of Andrea and Martin: Madeline Foster born July 27, 1991 in Dallas, Texas and Ethan Samuel, born October 26, 1993 in Berkeley, California. Andrea was a jewelry designer and is now a "stay at home" mom. Martin works for Berkeley Software and produced the "You Don't Know Jack" computer games.

Foster Jr. married second, Janet Ruth Davis July 4, 1976 in Barlow, Kentucky. He married third, Anita Jean Hughes, October 18, 1986 in Dallas, Texas. He married fourth, Maria "Mary" Esperanza Luis, April 11, 1998 in Harlingen, Cameron County, Texas. Mary was born December 21, 1953 in Chapman Ranch, Texas and is the daughter of Macario and Gaudelupe (Garcia) Luis. Mary is a plant manager for Bonworth International in Matamoros, Mexico. Foster is currently a real estate broker with Century 21. They reside in Harlingen, Texas.

Foster Jr. retired from the Marines after a distinguished career. He served the military in many capacities and attended specialized training which included: jump school, personnel administration, FBI school at Quantico and the FAA Air Security Guard School. He served in the Panama Canal Zone, Korea, Iwabuni, Japan and Vietnam. Through the military, he also was a part of the first group of "Sky Marshals" flying the friendly skies, protecting passenger flights and profiling hijackers. In the United States he has lived in Ohio, North Carolina, South Carolina, Kansas, Texas and California. Foster also spent one year living in Torcross, Devon County, England on the English Channel and one year living in Katoomba, New South Wales, Australia, touring the respective countries. Among his many adventures, he has backpacked the Inca Trail in Peru. He enjoys fishing, hunting, watching sports and of course, traveling.

*Submitted by Marci J. (Little) White*

**HILAH F. LITTLE** - Hilah Forence Little was born November 15, 1925 in Cheshire Twp.

Hilah was the oldest child of Foster and Effie Little. Hilah loved her hometown of Cheshire and had many friends there. She graduated from Cheshire High School in 1943. For her futures in the year book her nickname was "Bozobonerack" because she was so thin and she aspired to work in journalism. Hilah was an average student, dated in school and enjoyed bumming rides with her girlfriends and going into town to the movies or bowling.

*Children of Ovid and Hilah (Little) Glandon L: to R: Scott, Nikki and Mark Sept. 1989*

After graduating from high school, Hilah moved to Columbus and worked as a waitress while she put herself through beauty school. After graduating from beauty school, she worked as a hairdresser for Lazarus. She married Ovid Leland Glandon on May 6, 1950 in Columbus. Ovid was born February 17, 1927 to John Glandon and Hazel Burt. After her marriage, Hilah worked for Columbus Public Schools driving school bus and mowing. She was a also a Girl Scout Leader for several years.

Ovid was a Navy veteran and worked for Borden Milk Company, from which he eventually retired. Ovid was very outgoing and loved drawing and painting. He also enjoyed riding and tinkering with new and vintage motorcycles. Ovid was a 32nd degree Mason member of Humboldt Lodge in Gahanna and VFW Post 4153. The Glandon's were members of the Oakland Park UMC. Hilah and Ovid had three children: Scott, Nikki and Mark.

Scott Ovid was born April 21, 1953 in Columbus. He met and married Shirley and helped raise her three boys. Scott has an AAS in Electronic Engineering and works for IBM in Web hosting design and implementation in Chicago.

He is currently installing infrastructure for IBM in Montreal and Calgary. On July 26, 2001, Scott married Lena while on vacation at his Uncle Foster's in Texas. He currently resides outside Chicago.

Nikki Lynn was born July 9, 1954 in Columbus. Nikki favors her mother in appearance and grace. Nikki married Jim Scott Sept. 1, 1973 in Columbus. Jim was born February 6, 1952 in Independence, Mo. to Dane Scott and Marjorie Burgess. Nikki enjoys crafts, bicycling and camping. Nikki and Jim have two children: Kristopher Michael was born December 1, 1978 in Columbus. Kelly Nicole was born May 29, 1981 in Columbus. They have a beautiful home on the edge of Dublin, Ohio.

Mark Glandon was born August 7, 1957 in Columbus. Mark married Adele Sborgia and had two children: Matthew Mark Glandon was born April 14, 1981 in Columbus. Holly Glandon was born April 8, 1983. Mark and Adele divorced. Mark works for Ohio Vision group making prescription eye glasses. He shares Ovid's love of motorcycles. Mark purchased the family home and lives in Columbus. Hilah died August 11, 1973 of injuries sustained in a tractor accident. Ovid died October 3, 1995. They are buried in Friends Cemetery, Londonderry, Ohio. *Submitted by: Mark Glandon*

**LEVERT JAMES LITTLE** - Levert was born February 10, 1890, in Henking, Cheshire Township, the eldest of six children born to Samuel D. Little and Flora Frazier. Levert married Lottie Mae Bennett on August 25, 1909, in Mason County, WV. Folklore handed down through generations indicates Lottie placed a note in a bottle and threw it in the river; Levert found the bottle and then Lottie.

Levert and Lottie had the following children: Adrian born December 25, 1910, in Cheshire Township married Howard Benjamin Little on March 27, 1927, in Meigs County. They died in Hudson, Hillsdale County, Michigan. Children: Roger Keith and Raymond.

*Levert Little about 1938 with children, Flora "Sis" Earnesteen "Teen", Celia and Dorsel*

Bernice was born April 1, 1914, and died in Hudson, Michigan, July 21, 1992. She married Everett Treat. Child: Alice Marie.

William Samuel Little born about 1915, died ca. 1975 in Clayton, Michigan. William probably first married Mary Brickle and had one child, Jimmie Franklin Little. William married Maureen Atkinson around 1936, children: Grace and William. Around 1948, William married Maxine Shaffer, children: Barbara and Norma. William last married Viola. He worked in the CCC camps during WWII.

Dorsel, born June 26, 1918, in Meigs County and died of injuries sustained in an automobile accident. Dorsel married Naomi Cuer. Children: Herm, Virginia and Dan. Dorsel was a WWII veteran.

Flora "Sis", was born around 1920. She married Francis Cuer (brother to Naomi). She also married Bill Mason and had five children including Linda, Carolyn and Patricia.

Worley, born August 26, 1922, in Meigs County, moved to Adrian, Michigan, and managed a Western Union. He was a communications specialist in WWII. Worley married and had children: David and Julie. Worley died young of a heart attack.

Earnesteen was born May 26, 1922, in Meigs County and died about 1987 in Wauseon, Ohio. He married Fern Marshall. Children: Donny and Marsha. Earnesteen was a WWII veteran.

Laura Belle skipped off to the grocery store around the age of nine, for a loaf of bread. On the way back she was hit by a motorist and died of those injuries. Her mother, Lottie, kept the loaf and showed it to her granddaughter, Grace Anne, many times, relating the sad story.

Dorothy Mae died young of pneumonia.

Celia Ann Little was born January 24, 1937, in Pomeroy, married Bill Kelley June 22, 1953, in Hudson, Michigan. Children: Bill, Mark and Delea. They still reside in the Clayton, Lenawee County, Michigan, area.

Levert, like his father, was a coal miner. He moved back and forth between Gallia and Meigs counties, as work dictated, once living in a two-story home in Pomeroy. By the time of the great depression and WWII, Levert was suffering from diabetes, a disease to which he would eventually loose both legs. Their children were moving north following the promise of work. It was with heavy hearts that Levert and Lottie, along with the youngest children, left their home and started north around 1942.

The family still returns to visit and enjoys the beautiful motorcycle rides, back to Gallia County, Ohio.

*Submitted by David Charles Little*

**ROBERT W. LITTLE, SR.** - Robert W. Little, Sr., was the third child born to Foster and Effie Little on November 4, 1929, in Cheshire, Ohio. Robert or "Bob" relays stories of the depression and the start of World War II. While both the war and the depression had deeply affected the community in which he lived, he shares many happy memories of his childhood in Cheshire, Ohio.

Leaving Cheshire as a teen, Bob moved to Lorain to live with his father and to find work. Finding it difficult to find a good steady job, he enlisted in the United States Army on October 1, 1946, serving three years. After leaving the service, he returned to his hometown for a short time before moving back to Lorain and working on the B&O Railroad and eventually the Lorain City Police Department. He married first Jeanette Golini on June 14, 1952. Bob and Jeanette divorced and on September 17, 1962, he married Gayle Gandee.

Bob and Gayle settled briefly in Cincinnati, Ohio, where their first child, Robert W. Little, Jr., was born September 11, 1963. The Little family then moved outside of Eaton, Preble County, Ohio, following Bob's job with Avco. After reductions in Avco, Bob went to work for Johns-Manville in Richmond, Indiana, where he worked for several years. They purchased a house in West Manchester, Preble County, Ohio, and on June 22, 1965, their daughter, Shari Lyn Little, was born.

*Bob & Gayle Little
September 2000*

Bob and Gayle got involved in the new community in which they lived, pushing for a new high school to be built and serving the West Manchester United Methodist Church. Bob went to school part-time and obtained a real estate license and dabbled in real estate. Bob was a UAW member and was active in the union. They were members of the Moose Lodge in Richmond, Indiana, and Bob became a member of the local Lions Club and eventually the American Legion where he served as post commander. He has been a lifelong Republican as was his grandfather and great grandfather.

After retiring, Bob went back to work as a consultant at Envirotech. Gayle works as a registered nursing supervisor at Wayne Hospital in Greenville, Ohio. Bob is currently a West Manchester Village Council Member and has served on the rescue squad board for several years as president. Bob and Gayle still reside in West Manchester.

Bob Jr. is an EMT and lives in Cincinnati. He is engaged to marry Diane Jacob. The wedding is planned for September 2002. Bob Jr. was an active volunteer for fire and rescue in his hometown and also volunteers for political campaigns.

Shari lives at Cowan Lake State Park outside of Wilmington. Shari married Paul E. Creech on October 13, 1990, in Preble County, Ohio. They have one son, Ryan. Shari has been very active in the Democratic Party and enjoys working on genealogy.

With great fondness for their ancestor's old hometown, the Little's still visit Cheshire as often as possible.

*Submitted by Robert W. Little, Jr.*

**WILLIAM SAMUEL LITTLE** - William Samuel Little, born about 1915 to Levert James Little and Lottie Mae Bennett Little, was raised in Cheshire, Gallia County, Ohio.

With William's "knack" for precision and interest in tools, he was among the best machine operators and mechanics in his field. William worked with setup (dies), operation and breakdown of all machines until the project was complete. Work of this nature often required travel to Hardie Pump and Sprayer (Mfg.) in Hudson, Michigan, and M&S Company in Morenci. William retired from American Chain and Cable in Adrian, Michigan.

*William Samuel Little With Maureen Adair Atkinson "Bill & Adair" About 1936*

Disappointed to learn he was medically disqualified from serving his country during WWII, William sought out the CCC camps where he made his contribution.

William probably first married Mary Ellen Brickle; son, Jimmie Franklin Little, was born in 1934. Jimmie married Betty Jo Mulford. Children: Yvonda, Ricky and Scott. Jimmie worked with the railroad, transferring to Columbus in the 1960's.

William next married Maureen Adair "Molly" Atkinson around 1936; children: Grace and William.

Grace Anne, born 1937, married Clarence Hammel September 13, 1954; children: Samuel, Randy, Cynthia and Jennifer. Grace Anne married Ron Winroth December 14, 2000; they live in Las Vegas, NV. Sam first married Jodie Hartley; children: Tenijha and Joshua. He second married Kim; son is Joseph. Sam, a chiropractor, lives in Michigan with wife, Melisha. Randolph J. "Randy" first married Sherri Segrist, children: Lara Jean and Jacob J. He and current wife, Ramona, live in Michigan. Cynthia Gay first married Douglas Miller August 10, 1974; children: Steven Douglas, Julie Anne, Alicia Renee Adair, and Ashley Lynn Miller. Cynthia married second Roger Miller in 1996. She is a lab technician in central Ohio. Jennifer Lynn, an MRI tech in Columbus, Ohio, is single.

William Charles Little born March 13, 1938, married Sharon Anita Hartley in Detroit, Michigan, March 2, 1957. William served in the USAF SAC for nine years, tried retail grocery and formed his own Home Remodeling Company around 1974. He was Assistant Boy Scout Leader for several years. The family made a number of trips back home to visit brother, Jimmie, in Gallia and Meigs Counties; enjoying the beautiful countryside and warm hospitality of the people. William died in Fairfield County, Ohio, October 14, 1996.

William Charles and Sharon Little children: Robert Anthony, David Charles, Wayne Eugene, Carma Sue, Joseph Roy, William James, Gertrude Elizabeth, and John Paul.

Robert first married Rita Stahr June 4, 1989; daughter, Makaylah Rose. He next married Sherry Root June 18, 2001; they enjoy golf and Robert pursued electrical sales/management.

David studied electronics, enlisted in the Army, and was medically retired from gas and oil management. He married Val Jean Barrett July 11, 1981, and adopted her son, Mike.

Wayne, a master mechanic, owns Wayne's Marathon in Columbus, Ohio. He married Margaret Butcher December 19, 1981; daughters: Amy Beth and Melissa Ann. Wayne is now single.

Carma, a hair stylist who enjoys bowling, first married David Morgan April 23, 1983, and Donald Ray Hallman, Jr., July 7, 1994. Children: April Marie Little, Joseph William and Amber Sue Morgan.

Joseph, a manager (lumber industry), enjoys fishing, hunting and playing cards. He married Stephanie Lee Sparks October 27, 1990; their son is Joseph Samuel "Sam". Joe has been instrumental in paving the way for brother, Will, to achieve independent living.

William "Will" enlisted in the Marine Corps and served in Japan. He studied heating and cooling, though preferred working outdoors until an accident left him a quad in 1999. He has great determination as he participates in physical and occupational rehabilitation. William and Suzy Horn have three children: Tanya Mae, William CJ, and Nathan Scott. He now shares a life with friend, Beth Vest, and her daughter, Brittany.

Gertrude "Trudy" studied accounting; is in business management and enjoys camping, Euchre and antiques. She married Brian Starcher October 20, 1989; children: Zachary Tyler and Olivia Hope.

John, the youngest, is in management and sales (lumber industry). He was with the Army on foreign soil during the Gulf War "Desert Storm" and is single.

William Samuel married third Maxine Morris Shaffer. Children: Barbara and Norma. Barbara Lee married John Jenkins, children: Jenna and Jason. Barbara died very young. Norma Jean married Dean Marks, children: Scott, Todd and Carrie. They live near Adrian, Michigan.

Many members of this family work in education.

William married last, Viola.

William Samuel Little inspired a great work ethic and love for fishing and card games, particularly Euchre and Poker, in many of his children and grandchildren. Those, whose lives he touched recall how much William enjoyed returning to Cheshire to visit friends and family. He fondly dubbed Cheshire, Gallia County, Ohio, his "old stomping grounds".

*Submitted by William J. Little*

**WILLIAM HAYDEN (BILL) LLOYD AND OPAL ELIZABETH MILLER FAMILY -** As the clock chimed six o'clock—Christmas evening—December 25, 1954, one could hear the melodious refrains of the Estey Concert Organ pealing forth the strains of music relating to the Holy Season, with selections echoing that a wedding was at hand. Seated at the organ was Mrs. Steve (Peg) Thomas and at her side was brother Roger Williams rending beautiful words intertwined with the season and the ceremony which was at hand. The Rev. John Daniel Davis, minister of the Thurman Methodist Church (a light amid the hills), performed the exchange of the wedding vows between Opal Elizabeth Miller and William Hayden Lloyd.

*Opal And Bill Lloyd*

Opal is the great, great granddaughter of Lewis Wickline—noted gun smith and grand daughter of Charles (Jennie Patterson) Wickline—Cadmus village blacksmith. Her parents were J. C. & Parnie (daughter of Charles Wickline) Miller. Her paternal lineage was Daniel (Elizabeth Frye) Miller born in Germany, served in the Civil War, prisoner in Andersonville Prison, and served as Gallia County Commissioner in the late 1890's. Her parents were both—at one time—teachers in the one-room schools in the area of Gallia and Lawrence Counties. Her father taught 40 _ years and retired from the Rio Grande School system. Her mother gave up teaching to become a wonderful homemaker. Opal's 37-year tenure included Perry Township Elementary, Centerville Junior and Secondary, Cadmus and Southwestern High Schools from where she retired in 1975 with precious memories of wonderful students and friends. William is the great grandson of Rev. Daniel J. (Ann Jones) Lloyd who came from Wales in the early 1800's. He was a Baptist minister and also noted blacksmith in the Charcoal Iron Industry in the Jackson and Lawrence County areas. His son, William (Alice Cherrington) Lloyd, was the grandfather, and their son, Howard Payne (Maridoris Williams) Lloyd, was Bill's father. Two brothers, John D. and Howard Paul, with twin sisters, Jean and Janet, comprise the family. Janet died after only 20 days. Though the Lloyd's were engaged in agriculture, music remained paramount in their lives. Grandfather William road horseback from Centerville to Jackson to participate in the famous Jackson Male Chorus. Many of his nieces and nephews were instructors in the field of music at Ohio State and Princeton Universities. A nephew was a tenor in the Metropolitan Opera. His maternal lineage is also Welsh with his great, great grandfather William (Mary) Williams who come to America in the early 1800'S. Mary became ill and was buried at sea. Their son, David W. (Mary Griffiths) Williams made their home in the Sardis community in the Oak Hill area. In 1869 our great grandfather David and his brother, Jonathan, built the present Sardis Church building and the Ty Capel (Tea House) which were dedicated in 1870. Both stand proudly and serve currently as a part of the Oak Hill Presbyterian Parish. David W.'s son, John D. (Cora Rainer) Williams, was the father of his mother, Maridoris Williams Lloyd. The Williams' families were also involved in music and made lasting contributions to the Welsh Gymanfa's. Bill was associated with the Refractories Industry which produced heat resistant materials for the steel, glass and iron industries. He retired after 37 years, with fond and lasting memories of his active years in this field, and the many loyal and special friendships developed which followed him into retirement.

Since retirement, both have enjoyed the great opportunity to serve as volunteers in many varied ways—serving in the Chaplainry program at Holzer Hospital, presenting programs for those confined in nursing homes and serving as a volunteer organist where needed. "Time cannot steal the treasured moments we claim our own."

*Submitted by Opal and Bill Lloyd*

**JOHN LOLLIS -** John Lollis was born in Rockbridge County, Virginia, in March 1819 or 1820. Census records suggest that his parents came from Maryland. John married Elizabeth Margaret McNeil, the daughter of George McNeil, near the small town of Cedar Grove in Rockbridge County on September 26, 1844. Their first child, John William Lollis, was born in Virginia on February 20, 1846. The family migrated to Gallia County in the fall of that same year. John and Elizabeth were blessed with four more children, George F. Lollis (November 1, 1848), David Henry Lollis (September 5, 1851) Samuel Wesley Lollis (October 7, 1854), and Mary Elizabeth Lollis (June 3, 1858). The location of the family farm can be pinpointed in January 12, 1854, when deed records document John's purchase from Dewitt Clinton Burage of 100 acres in section 12 of Springfield Township along Campaign Creek. By 1860, the family holdings had increased to 330 acres in Springfield Township.

*John Lollis*
*1819-1901*

John's luck seemed to change thereafter. His wife, Elizabeth, died October 7, 1863, and was buried in the Lawless (Lollis) Cemetery in Springfield Township. His son, John William, enlisted in the 23rd Ohio Infantry Regiment (Volunteers) in Gallipolis on February 15, 1864. After muster into Company D in Ironton the following week, he subsequently caught the measles and died in the U.S. Army Field Hospital in Gallipolis. John William was interred alongside his mother. John married Lucretia Eno on March 15, 1869, and was divorced by September of that same year. By 1874, John owned 230 acres in Springfield Township and none by the time he relocated to Addison Township in 1885.

John married Matilda Rife on June 20, 1888, in Flanegin's ice cream parlor in Meigs County. Matilda was born on November 15, 1856, to Anderson Rife and Sophia Scott. She was previously married to Andrew Ryther (1870) and

Calvin R. Mapes (July 9, 1879). Matilda had one daughter from prior marriage, Lenora Mapes, born January 15, 1880. On April 2, 1889, Margaret Ann Lollis was born to John and Matilda. Later that year, John, a virile but arthritic 69, filed a claim application for a dependency pension. His property at the time was limited to a horse, a wagon, and a small house on a two-acre lot in Addison. Five years later, on October 6, 1894, Edwill Foster Lollis was born to John, now age 74, and Matilda. John died on December 23, 1901, in Addison, Ohio. His final resting place is unknown. Matilda died February 9, 1910, and is interred in the Old Thygar Cemetery in Middleport, Ohio. Lenora Mapes raised her orphaned half-brother in the greater Cincinnati area. Foster Lollis was a businessman having served honorably in World War I. He passed away in 1985. His sister "Maggie" married Millard Hathcock and had three children (Mildred, Millard and Jack). Maggie died in 1970.

*Submitted by Steven Lollis, great, great grandson of John Lollis.*

**SAMUEL WESLEY LOLLIS** - Samuel Wesley Lollis, fourth son of John Lollis and Elizabeth Margaret McNeil, was born in Addison Township, Gallia County, on October 7, 1854. He married Charlotte Christina Lutz on October 10, 1882. Charlotte, nicknamed "Chatty" by her husband, was born January 18, 1864, the third child of Martin Lutz (1820-1896) and Mary Roush (1840-1921).

*Mollie Lollis December 3, 1889*

Her mother, Mary, was the great granddaughter of Jacob Roush, the Indian fighter and Gallia County Revolutionary War veteran. Samuel and Chatty farmed in Springfield and Cheshire Townships but moved to Gallipolis by 1910 where Samuel was employed in a furniture factory. The Lollis couple was blessed with six children. They include Millie Elizabeth (May 25, 1883-March 4, 1947), Morris Edward (December 3, 1884-July 26, 1936), Martin Henry (March 1886-January 20, 1959), John Samuel (October 26, 1887-October 12, 1968), Mollie Maude (December 3, 1889-May 12, 2001), and David Monroe (July 3, 1893-May 8, 1973). Samuel died on October 28, 1930, while Chatty died September 4, 1974, at the astonishing age of 110. The family is buried in Forest Rose Cemetery, Lancaster, Ohio, except David who rests in Riverside Cemetery, Troy, Ohio.

Millie Lollis was employed as a saleswoman in Gallipolis, and later served as a clerk and the head of housekeeping for the Lollis family hotel business in Lancaster, Ohio. She was a member of the M. Z. Kreider Chapter of the Order of Eastern Star of Lancaster and the Royal Neighbors Lodge of Gallipolis. Morris was employed as a local clerk and later worked in hotel management for his brother. Neither Millie nor Morris ever married. Martin Lollis was an accomplished musician and later a sales representative for a brewery distributor. Martin played percussion in several local bands and musical combos providing performances for showboats, civic groups, and radio stations. He married twice but never had children. John Samuel Lollis was a businessman with a cigar shop and other business interests. "Sam" also served with his brother Martin as a sales representative for a brewery distributor. Mollie Lollis was the most educated family member from her generation. Mollie graduated from Gallia Academy and Gallipolis High School in May 1910 and later graduated from Ohio University in Athens with a Bachelor of Science in Education. She was a teacher in Gallia (1920's) and Fairfield (1930's-1970's) Counties. Mollie played and taught the piano, was an advocate for literacy, a student athlete, a history buff, a champion for women's right, a patron of the arts, and a member of numerous civic organizations to include the DAR and the Order of Eastern Star. She recently passed away at the age of 111, just surpassing her mother's longevity. David Lollis was a successful businessman owning and managing a chain of hotels. He was married twice, first to Bertha N. Cushman (1882-1950) in May 1917 and then to Vira Olas Brown (1906-1939) in May 1930. Monroe and Vira had four children including Sherman Wesley, David Monroe Junior, Edward Burton, and Loretta Sue. All four children married ensuring numerous descendants.

*Submitted by Mrs. Debra Lollis Lobdell, great granddaughter of Samuel Lollis*

**DR. SOLOMON S. LONG** - Three generations of my ancestors (maternal) were laid to rest in the Centerpoint Baptist Cemetery. Solomon S. Long, M.D. (my great.grandfather), his wife and family. Doctor Long and his family migrated to Centerpoint from North Carolina shortly after the Civil War, evidently due to the economic situation immediately following the war in 1865. At this t.ime he owned large plantations at Grassy Creek and Jefferson, North Carolina and approximately forty slaves that were freed; many of whom wept and begged to stay with him, and he did bring one or two to Centerpoint with him.

Of course, moving was by covered wagons which the men folk rode through from North Carolina. He soon purchased land and had a house built. This house was razed a few years ago. He also had an office building erected consisting of two rooms, which still stands.

I remember hearing about a skeleton that he had standing in a corner of his office. He had some kind of a device fixed up enabling him, while sitting at his desk, to cause the arms and legs of the skeleton to move.

My grandmother, the late Nancy Virginia Jones, told me about how she and her sister, who later became Candace Edwards Stamper and their mother rode horseback (sidesaddle) from North Carolina and how they stopped at inns to rest as many days as they cared to, seemingly enjoying their journey.

*Office Building in Centerpoint Ohio where Dr. Solomon Long practiced medicine*

Not once realizing the sorrow that was awaiting them at Centerpoint, they learned of the drowning of their 16 year old brother, Rowan Long, who was swimming in Symmes Creek near Chimney Rock. He had dived and his head must have hit a rock.

I remember hearing how that after my future grandmother came to Centerpoint that a former suitor from North Carolina came to Centerpoint to visit the family. I understand that Dr. Long thought that his daughter should marry the son of a Senator of North Carolina. So Grandmother, being a lady, abided by his wishes and married John Andrew Madison Jones, a fifth generation descendant of Daniel Boone.

Dr. Long died a wealthy man in his generation. Besides his Centerpoint estate, he owned property in Huntington, W. VA., Ironton and Columbus, Ohio.

Tragedy struck in 1923 when my mother suddenly passed away leaving us eight children. Grandmother brought us all to Centerpoint to live with her and she was in her 70's. I loved to sit in their "General Merchandise Store" and I vividly remember those tive big glass candy jars on a high shelf, namely, cinnamon drops, Peppermint lozenges, Winter-green lozenges, bon bons, and stick candy.

Grandmother passed away six months later. I don't remember the minister but I remember his text, 'She Hath Done What She Could".

My father, Paul Prior Overturf, passed away five months after my mother.

I graduated from Rio Grande High School in 1927 along with my brother John E. Overturf.

My late husband, Elisha Vitatoe, is buried in Cheshire Gravel Hill cemetery.

Refer to Jones-Overturf-VitatOe elsewhere in book.

*Submitted by Virginia O. Vitatoe Hartley*

**LOUCKS/LAUX FAMILY** - My father's family name of Loucks Laux can be traced back over a thousand years to early medieval Europe in the Pyrenees-Bay of Biscay area of France and Spain before there even was either a France or a Spain. As du Laux, the name appears prominently during the many feudal conflicts preceding and accompanying the rise of the major kingdoms. Even as these were becoming established, they still had little control over my ancestors, who were more closely allied to England, presumably because of continuing Norman hereditary claims.

After their area had been brought fully within the domain of the French kings, most of my forebears became Huguenots under the evangelistic mission work of Jeanne d'Albert. Her son, born about this time, was later crowned King of France as Henri IV. Although he nominally repudiated his Huguenot beliefs and swore he would uphold the faith of the Church of Rome and root out all "heretics" from French soil, he proved to be the Huguenots' friend and protector—so much so that he was eventually assassinated.

Subsequent French kings, step by step, dismantled all of Henri's protective measures, until there were massacres and widespread government-conducted persecution. About half of the Huguenots, including many of my ancestors, fled to the Palatinate region of Germany, but the French then conquered that area, and many fled to Holland, free but destitute. Queen Anne of England took pity on them and invited them to London, though even there they still begged for a living.

Then a very unlikely thing happened. They chanced to be observed on the city streets by a group of American Indians, present in England as guests of the Queen. The Indians were moved with compassion and offered them sizeable portions of their own land in New York if they could find a way across the ocean. The Queen financed their passage, with their commitment to repay her by working on jobs promised by the Royal Governor of New York. However, his jobs proved impractical, and they could not even make a living, much less repay. Nevertheless, Gov. Hunter would not release them.

A number left anyhow and reached the Mohawk Valley, where, with the help of the Indians, they were able to adapt to their new life. But the Governor overtook them, returning most to New York and hounding the rest until they fled to western Pennsylvania, some of them moving on to Ohio.

Having fought on the side of the English in the French and Indian War, they fought even more loyally on the side of the colonists in the American Revolution. One such Revolutionary War fighter was W. E. Loucks of Gallipolis. His descendant, also W.E. Loucks of Gallipolis, fought in the Civil War.

From medieval petty kings and barons, counts, and chevaliers, as well as ecclesiasts, in Western Europe, to paupers and beggars there and in England and at first in America, the Louckses have taken their place as full-fledged contributors to our modern American democracy.

*Submitted by: Joann Loucks Walker*

**LOWERY - COLE FAMILY** - Melvin Lowery born February 24, 1800 in Greenup County, Kentucky, his parents died when he was 10 years old. It is believed that Melvin's father's name was Patrick Lowery from Ireland. He married Harty Cole, February 22, 1822 in Belpre, Washington County, Ohio moving to Gallia County in 1828. According to information from Harty's granddaughter Emma Gatewood Kern's application paper for the Daughters of the American Revolution, her father was Asa Cole from Washington County, Ohio. Her grandfather, John Cole was a private solider in Captain James Hill's Company, Colonel John Daggett's regiment from Bristol, Rhode Island. John Cole is buried in Washington County, Ohio near Marietta. Melvin was known as a faithful and zealous class-leader nearly his entire live after joining the Methodist Episcopal Church at a camp meeting held at Rome, Lawrence Co., Ohio in 1836. He was beloved by all that knew him and was known as a good, kind, confiding husband and an affectionate father. In Harty's obituary it says: "As a mother, she was a wise and prudent counselor, ever anxious for the spiritual and eternal welfare of her children." She was also considered a very kind person always ready to assist the wants of suffering humanity. Melvin and Harty had the following children: Louise married Mathais Sheets, Virginia Elizabeth married James Monroe Gatewood, Amanda married Thomas Cole, Oscar, Sophronia married Joseph Spaulding Dyer, America married Henry Morton, Cleopatra married Joseph Jefferson Blazer, Alonzo married Maria Jane Ray, William. Melvin died April 16, 1868 and Harty died August 12, 1866 and are buried in Pine Street Cemetery, Gallipolis, Ohio.

*Virginia Lowrey Gatewood and James Monroe Gatewood*

Virginia was born February 26, 1825 married James Monroe Gatewood October 12,1845 the same day that her sister Amanda married Thomas Cole. Virginia and James were married in a church that stood years ago near or on the lot of Clay Chapel. James Gatewood was engaged in the lumber business in Louisiana where they remained until 1847 upon returning to Gallia County, Ohio. They moved to Ohio Township and bought a farm on Raccoon Island and James took up farming. In 1869, they emigrated to Gallipolis and took up their home at 76 State Street. Later they would sell this house to their granddaughter's husband Oscar Odd McIntrye as an anniversary present for his wife, Maybelle Small McIntyre. They then moved to Fourth Avenue and later to Second Avenue where they lived the rest of their days.

Virginia and James had the following children: William Lowery married Mary Mixer Short, James Madison married Margaret Ann Sheets, Isadore died young, Emma married Anthony Kerns, Kate Harty married Charles Small, Sabina married Stanley Brading, Louis died young, Laura married Charles Mullineux, Charles married Lura B. Sims, Edgar married Jessie B. (last name unknown), Nellie Virginia married George Bovie. James Madison and Margaret Sheets descendants are shown in the family history, Gatewood Family.

*Submitted by: Marjorie Gilliam Wood*

**CLARENCE COLSON, JR. AND KATHRYN FOSTER LUMAN** - Clarence Colson Luman, Jr. (1-22-1922) was born to Clarence Colson and Dora Frances Null Luman in Walnut Township, Gallia County. He attended Cadmus Hill and Cadmus schools. Clarence enlisted in the Army during World War II and served in Northern Africa and Europe. He married Laura Kathryn Foster (5-17-1925) on February 22, 1949. Her parents were Thomas Jones and Malinda Dixie McGlone Foster who resided in Fort Gay, West Virginia.

After serving in the Army, Clarence (Junior) worked on riverboats, for Buckeye Rural Electric, and on dam and bridge construction for Dravo Corporation in several States. After retirement, they reside on a farm in Walnut Township near Cadmus.

Their children are Sharon Rebecca (2-24-1950) and Debbi Jean (3-24-1953). Sharon married William Ailiff in 1970. Later they divorced. Debbi married Eddie Thompson on September 3, 1982. Their children are John Coulson (12-30-1989) and Joseph Neil (8-2-1991).

**JAMES HARRISON BARTHOLOMEW LUMAN CLARENCE COLSON LUMAN** - James Harrison Bartholomew Luman was born June 10, 1842, most likely in Muskingum County, Ohio, to William Thomas and Tabitha Dorcas Harrison Luman. He married Sarah Lois Worthington, March 19, 1864. She was born to Mahlon (July 7, 1794-August 6, 1856) and Elizabeth Ware Worthington (January 25, 1797-November 1866), February 19, 1842. Her death was May 17, 1912. Mahlon's parents were Thomas and Amy Worthington. Elizabeth's parents were Thomas and Catharine Ware. James and Lois resided in Walnut Township near his parents. He was a farmer and a carpenter who helped build the Fox Fairview Church and the Mudsoc store.

The children of James and Lois were as follows: Nola (unmarried); Mariah married Joe Allbright, January 6, 1884, by Joseph Fox. Elizabeth married Perry Myers, May 27, 1888. Cora married John Williams. Lida married Will Myers. William married Nancy White. Clarence Colson married Dora Frances Null.

Clarence Colson Luman (January 26, 1881-September 21, 1941), who was a son of James and Lois Worthington Luman, was born in Walnut Township and married Dora Frances Null (April 1, 1885-September 23, 1978) on September 10, 1903. Dora was the daughter of Nicholas and Elizabeth (Massie) (Thornton) Null. They resided in the Mudsoc and the Cadmus communities. He taught in several one room schools until retirement in 1940. Their children were as follows:

Harry Carlisle (June 11, 1904-September 2, 1991) married Mary Stewart (March 31, 1902-August 13, 1995).

Roland Edgar (October 21, 1906-August 8, 1991) married Esther Rebecca Neal.

James Hayward (November 27, 1908-August 29, 1972) married Lydia Glenna Wood on January 23, 1918.

Edith Belle (April 1, 1911) married Everett Massie (April 11, 1902-February 12, 1977).

Fred Bruce (July 25, 1914-January 18, 1988) married Louise Shemik.

Charles Woodrow (November 23, 1916) married Mary Rhem.

Kenneth Wayne (May 30, 1919) married Marjorie Blake (November 20, 1920).

Clarence Colson (January 22, 1922) married Kathryn Foster (May 17, 1925).

Edna Lois (March 17, 1924) married James Mills Rodgers (June 17, 1923-March 12, 2000).

Daniel Emerson, who was born in 1927, was dead at birth.

## JAMES HAYWARD AND LYDIA GLENNA WOOD LUMAN
James Hayward Luman (11-27-1908—07-29-1972) married Lydia Glenna Wood (b. 01-23-1918). (M. Nov. 12, 1938), Hayward was born in Walnut Township, Gallia Co. to Clarence Colson and Dora Frances Null Luman. He attended Pine Grove and Cadmus Schools. He served in the U.S. Navy during World War II. He worked for a time for his brother and at the OHE. He worked several years a the McKnight-Davies Hardware retiring in 1972.

Lydia was born to Charles Luther and Ruth Eleanor Jones Wood. She worked at the Gallipolis Developmental Center retiring in 1984.

Their children are Ruth Ann (12-02-1943) who married Sam Hamilton (Div.) and Andy Sattler Jan.21, 2000. Her children are Lori Ann (10-10-1965) who married Greg Russell. Lori and Greg's children Greg (7-31-1988), Samantha Ann (6-16-1990), Mary Beth (12-09-1998) and Nathan Scott (3-18-00). Sammy Hamilton married Beth Elliott: Their child is Cory (6-6-1992).

Stephen Wood Luman, born May 5, 1948 and died April 25, 1988.

Charles Norman Luman (8-11-1949) married Joan Fox (8-16-1952). Their children are Charles Robert (12-9-1976) who married Kara Powelson on June 19, 1999 and Carrie Ann Luman (01-02-1981).

## ROLAND EDGAR AND ESTHER REBECCA NEAL LUMAN FAMILY
Roland Edgar Luman (October 12, 1906-August 5, 1991) married Esther Rebecca Neal (October 2, 1909) on March 14, 1939. Roland's parents were Clarence and Dora Null Luman. Esther's parents were John Fletcher and Rebecca Ellen Pyles Neal. Roland worked for a wholesale furniture company in Huntington in the late 1920's and 1930's. He and his father purchased a farm in Section 6 of Walnut Township, and he began farming after his marriage. Their children were Donald Edwin (March 12, 1940) and Carolyn Sue (June 1, 1942).

Donald continues to farm, purchasing with his sister three adjoining farms and raising grain, hay, tobacco, and cattle. She graduated from Rio Grande College and Marshall University and taught in the county schools for thirty years.

## WILLIAM THOMAS LUMAN (LOOMAN)
William Thomas Luman (Looman) was born July 9, 1800 in Virginia and died June 4, 1887 in Walnut Township, Gallia County, Ohio. He married Tabitha Dorcas Harrison who was born May 11, 1810 in Virginia. They were married January 15, 1831 in Jefferson County, Ohio ( courthouse record). She died December 26, 1864 and was buried in Clark Cemetery; in Walnut Township. William's second wife was Sarepta Fralix ,whom he married October 19, 1867. She died December 5, 1890.

Their children were: Emily, born Dec. 17, 1831. She married Andrew Canterbury, April 29, 1854.

Rebecca, born 1833 and married William Stewart, April 19, 1854.

Sarah was born 1835 and married William White Sep. 19, 1856.

Tabitha Jane was born Sept. 7, 1837, and married Levi Canterbury in 1859. She died April 25, 1919.

Thomas, born 1841. He married Edith Tipton in Gallia County, Ohio and moved to Iowa.

James Harrison Bartholomew, was born in 1843. He married Sarah Lois Worthington, March 9, 1864, and died in 1916.

Rachel, born April 13, 1845. She married James Worthington, Aug. 16, 1860.

Eliza, born Dec. 16, 1847, died oct. 19, 1859.

Nancy, born in 1848.

James Luman and James Worthington served in the Civil War together. Each married the others sister.

William Luman purchased 240 acres in Walnut Township, Gallia County, Section 34 during 1846 according to the record of the sale of public lands. He had lived in Blue Rock Township in Muskingum County previous to this time.

## CLYMENIA (CALDWELL) LYKINS
Grandmother Clymenia was born April 18, 1897. She was the daughter of William "Will" H. Caldwell and Clara A.( Williams) Caldwell. Her sister, Rebecca was born June 1898 and died at a young age. Her paternal grandparents were Stephen M. and Sarah A. (Sheets) Caldwell. Her Maternal grandparents were William Preston and Rebecca (Tagg) Williams.

Grandmother lost her father, Dec. 11 1898. She, her mother, and sister were living in the household of her Grandfather Williams, when the 1900 Gallia County, Ohio Census was taken.

When Grandmother Clymenia was four years old, her mother married Jess Woodyard. She later became a "big sister" to several more siblings.

When she was sixteen, she took employment as a domestic helper in the home of David and Tennessee Lykins in Huntington, West Virginia. Soon she met David's half brother, John Jackson "Jack" Lykins, also of Huntington.

On November 24, 1913 my future grandparents were united in marriage in Huntington (Cabell County).

My grandparents started their family early in their marriage. Their first child, Anvis Lanelle was born Sept. 2, 1914. On September. 13, 1915 Anna Masterson was born. John Jackson, Jr. was born March 9, 1918.

Grandmother Clymenia died Jan. 17, 1919, shortly before her twenty second birthday. Her funeral was held at the Crossroads Methodist Church. She was buried at the Highland Cemetery, Saltwell Road, Huntington in the Lykins Family Plot.

After her death, the children were reared by their father and his parents, "Tom" and Minnie Lykins.

Although the children would be reared by the paternal side of the family, Grandmother Clymenia's family was not forgotten. Both sides stayed in touch with the other . All three children visited their Grandmother Clara, Jesse, and their family after they moved to Columbus, Ohio.

If Grandmother Clymenia had lived, she would have also enjoyed her six grandchildren and many other new additions. Anvis married Alva Hagtley, Anna married Paul Byrd, and John married Thelma Waugh.

## MAJOR OLIVER G. LYLE FAMILY
Oliver Guy Lyle was born at Kyger, Cheshire Township, on January 1, 1886, only child of Emmett and Esther Virginia (Jennie) Coughenour Lyle. He attended the Kyger Schools and was a graduate of Gallia Academy. In his early years he taught school at Kyger and in Kenton, Ohio, home of his aunt Mary Lyle Stevenson. He married Bessie G. Bell on December 31, 1908 in Gallipolis, Ohio. Bessie, a descendant of "Mad" Ann Bailey, was born October 14, 1882, at Raccoon Island, Clay Township, to William W. and Effie Irion Bell. The Lyles made their home in Gallipolis where Oliver was a city mail carrier for 36 yrs. And Bessie a store clerk. Their daughters were Virginia Bell (Mrs. James E. McClintock) of Cleveland, North Olmsted and New Mexico and Pansy Grace (Mrs. Wayne Darnell), better known as Pat, of Columbus.

*Oliver Lyle with daughters Pat and Virginia and Wife Bessie about 1918*

Oliver had a long and distinguished career as a soldier. Prior to World War I he was an officer and drill master of Company F, Ohio National Guard. He began the war as a First Lieutenant and serving stateside, rose to the rank of Captain. In the intervening years he was an active reserve officer reaching the rank of Major. During World War II he drilled and trained cadet nurses at Holzer Hospital School of Nursing. A true soldier, he was probably as well versed in military maters as any one who ever lived in Gallipolis. Though he attained the rank of Major, his national Guard contemporaries called him "Cap'n Lyle".

He began work in the Gallipolis post office Sept. 30, 1907 and in the first twenty years estimated he had carried 250 tons of mail. Later in life he lost both legs to complications of diabetes, but quipped that he had walked them off carrying the mail and estimated 13 times around the globe. He was an avid stamp collector and voracious reader. Before the dams changed the Gallipolis waterfront, the family enjoyed swimming, boating and picnicking on the river. During floods Oliver always participated in American Legion relief efforts. Major Lyle was a member of Grace Methodist Church, Modern Woodmen of America, Naomi Lodge, Knights of Pythias and Lafayette Post, American Legion. Oliver died July 24, 1957, at VA hospital in Huntington, West Virginia, and was buried in Gravel Hill Cemetery.

Oliver's ancestors include seven proven early Gallia County residents. His great grandfather James Reynolds, a veteran of the War of 1812, served the U.S. Army as a spy out of Fort Gratiot (Port Huron, Michigan) in 1814. James returned to Gallia County and married Elizabeth Guy, daughter of John Guy of Addison Township, on November 2, 1815, moving to Cheshire Township. Elizabeth died March 28, 1869, James on November 30, 1881 at age 93; both are buried in Van Zant Cemetery. Their daughter Elizabeth Jane Reynolds, born August 2, 1835, married Isaac Lyle on January 26, 1857. They had three daughters and one son, Oliver's father Emmett Lyle, born April 24, 1860, in Salem Township, Meigs County.

**MACK FAMILY** - The immigrant ancestors of the Mack family originally settled in Meigs County, Ohio in the late 1850's. Their descendants have been prominent citizens and business owners there and also in Cheshire Township, Gallia County for more than 100 years.

Martin Mack and Barbara Schmeisser married November 2, 1859 in Meigs County, Ohio. Martin b. ca. 1826. immigrated from Germany. Barbara, was the daughter of General John Schmeisser and Margaret Meinhar(d)t, was born ca. March 16, 1837 in Treinz Germany. Barbara's mother, Margaret, was originally from Oppau, Germany.

After marrying, Martin and Barbara Mack moved to St. Louis, MO for a short time before moving back and settling permanently in Meigs County. Martin Mack was a cigar maker by trade and had a factory in Rutland, Ohio. He drowned in the Ohio River April 30, 1875. Barbara died February 24, 1917. Martin and Barbara had the following children: Katharine, Karl, Augusta, Charles, George, Mary and Sophia.

Katharine Mack was born February 23, 1861 in St. Louis, MO and died July 11, 1948 in Los Angeles, CA. Katherine married Clayton Weese, April 30, 1882. Clayton was born March 10, 1856 and died February 25, 1904. Clayton and Katharine had two children: Orah L. and Mack. Orah L. was born in 1888 and died December 31, 1890. Mack was born April 8, 1892 and died October 30, 1973 in Los Angeles, CA.

Karl Mack was born ca. 1861 and died in 1862.

Augusta was born ca. 1864, married Peter Sutcliffe June 22, 1892. They moved to Chicago, IL.

Charles Mack b. March 1867, married Harriet E. Tate October 28, 1891 and they eventually settled in Kyger, Cheshire Twp. (See Gallia County History, Volume I; Charles C. Mack Family by Harold Mack.) Charles owned a store and millinery in Middleport and a branch store and hotel in Kyger. On June 24, 1891, the Charles Mack & Co. Store in Kyger was destroyed by fire. The goods worth $1500 were insured for $1200. By 1893, the Kyger store was back in operation and advertising to buy 1000 bushels of dried apples from the local fruit farmers. In 1893, Charles was working in the Carlton store and was also appointed co-clerk of the Carl's Coal Works Company store after their reorganization. The mine and apparently some of the surrounding property was seized and sold to settle debts but soon reopened. Charles stayed in Canton for awhile before returning to the Kyger store to be close to his family. Charles and Harriet had three children: Ivan, Fred C. and Grace. Fred and Ruth (Roush) Mack had one son, Harold Mack, who still resides in Cheshire, Gallia County, with his lovely wife Odella. Harold is one of Cheshire's eldest and most respected residents. In 1921, Harold was featured in a large newspaper article with photograph at the fine age of three, having the distinct pleasure of boasting nine "living" grandparents: Mr. and Mrs. Charles Mack of Kyger, Mr. and Mrs. Alex Scott of Old Kyger, Mr. and Mrs. H. H. Roush and Mr. and Mrs. Joseph Roush, both of Cheshire and his great-great grandmother, Mrs. James Tate, formerly of Kyger but in 1921 lived in Florida.

George b. June 1868, died March 24, 1870.

Mary b. May 1874 and Sophia b. 1875 never married and both assisted their sister, Kate Weese, in running the family businesses.

*Submitted by: Mark Meinhart and Shari Creech*

**WILLIAM MALABY DESCENDANTS** - This biographical sketch is dedicated to the honor and memory of great-grandfather, William Malaby, to his many descendants (whoever you may be) throughout our great land, and to the open-hearted, friendly people of Gallia County.

*Pictured are Top left - William Malaby 1831-1907) Top right - Mary Ann Jones Leonard (1848-1928) Lower photo - Urma Vella Malaby, husband, Junnie H. George, Peg, Lillian, Daryl, Bill*

William Malaby was born June 27, 1831 in Cheshire Township, Gallia County. He was the son of John Malaby (1793-1843) and Mary Shaver (1805-1879). Known siblings include Elizabeth (d. 1850) m. Earl Miles Fulton, Nancy (1824-1906) m. Samuel Fulton, Eleanor (1828-1873) m. Caleb M. Caldwell, Catherine (1837-1871) m. John Coughenour and John (b. 1841) m. Mary Coughenour.

William was a farmer and on September 20 1855 he married Mary Kincaid (1834-1866), daughter of Nimrod Kincaid and Katherine Yeager. Their children were Theodosia (1856-1918) m. Francis Marlow Fulton, Randall Perry (1858-1929) m. Elnora Catherine Leonard, twins - Lovias (1860-1861) and Lovina (1860-1912) m. Noah Frederick, Mary Catherine (1862-1944) m. John V. Leonard, Samuel (1865-1937) m. Viola Johnson and Cora E. (1866-1942) m. Elmer Coughenour. Their mother, Mary Kincaid Malaby, died when Cora was just three weeks old.

Around 1871 William married Mary Ann Jones Leonard (1848-1928) daughter of Levi Campbell Jones and Nancy Rife, the widow of Marion Leonard, and brought her and her two children, Elnora Catherine (1867-1962) m. Randall Perry Malaby and Frederick Henry (1868-1962) m. 1. - Clara Chaflen and 2. - Connie Bussie, back from the west to Gallia County.

To the children above a new family was added: William Frederick (1872-1962) m. Annis Elizabeth Adkins, Laura E. (1874-1892) died in childbirth m. William Edward Welker, Nancy Lodice (1875-1961) m. William Edward Welker, Ross Oliver (1877-1897) died in a hunting accident, Roma May (1879-1960) m. Chauncey Vaughn Russell and Bessie (1881-) m. James H. Carmichel.

Number "16" of the William Malaby heirs, Grandma Urma Vella, was born September 21, 1886 in White Oak, Gallia County. She died April 17, 1968 and is buried in Milford Center, Ohio. On December 9, 1908, she married Junnie Herbert George (1885-1951) in the Methodist Episcopal Church, Gallipolis. Their children include Mom - Rella Margaret "Peg" (1909-1999) born in Bulaville, elementary school in Pleasant Valley. She loved to ride her horse "Barney" and play her harmonica in those Gallia County hills. Married Loree L. Coe, son of Emery Miles Coe and Lotta Mae Marsh, on April 28, 1930 in Marysville, Ohio. She is buried there. Bessie Lillian (B. 1913) m. Lawrence A. Fadely, Daryl Herbert (b. 1915) m. Helen Francis Means. Both Aunt Lily and Uncle Daryl were born in Uncle Doc and Aunt Libby Garrett's big red brick home on the Ohio River near Athalia. Billy James (1922-1980) m. Evelyn Gene Wilson and is buried in Marysville, Ohio.

William Malaby died May 5, 1907 and he and his wives, as well as several of his children, are buried in Campaign Cemetery, near the church where Grandma Urma Vella played the organ and sang for weddings and funerals.

The family is proud of its Gallia County roots and heritage - and of the thousands of you who also claim a share of the William Malaby legacy.

*Submitted by Elinor Coe Adams*

**ISSAC T. MANLEY** - Isaac T. Manley was born August 12, 1848, on Silver Run in Meigs County, OH, son of Samuel Manley and Mary Ann Barton. On May 31, 1867, he married Sarah Dodson, daughter of John and Melinda Wines Dodson. Sarah was born August 1850 in Meigs County. On November 6, 1863, Isaac enrolled in Company G, 45th. Regiment, Kentucky Infantry Volunteers. He was discharged for medical reasons. On March 7, 1865, he enlisted in Company G, 195th. Regiment Ohio Volunteers. He served a short time before being discharged. After being discharged Isaac worked on the river boat, The Fleetwood. He also worked at a flour mill in Cheshire, on the river as a fireman for Tipling Coal Co. in Hartford, WV, and for H. L. Casto's coal bank. Isaac and Sarah had ten children: Allena born November 5, 1869, in Middleport and died February 15, 1967 in Bidwell, married William Edgar Little on June 22, 1885, in Cheshire. They had 11 children Franklin, Edith, Abbie, Eva, Jesse, Bennett, Roy, Ezra, Georgia, Effie and Cuba. Orlando Manley was born May 8, 1872, in Cheshire and died January 14, 1903, in Gallia County. On August 17, 1895, he married Millie Stewart in Cheshire. They had two children: Edward and Elsie. Myrtle Manley was born December 15, 1875, in Middleport and died September 6, 1962 at Secoal, WV. She married Ernest Aleshire on April 16, 1894, in Cheshire. They had six children: Glenna, Verna, Rosa, Sara, Albert and Basil. Nan Manley was born March 16, 1876, in Middleport and died March 1, 1962, in Pomeroy. She married Al Frazier September 14, 1894, in Cheshire. They had six children: Eileen, Sparkle, Glenna, Richard, Georgia and Clifford. Georgetta Manley was born October 27, 1878, in Cheshire and died July 30, 1906, in Gallia County. She married Moses Frazier on November 20, 1897, in Cheshire. They had two children: Lewis and Edgar. Lewis Manley was born May 15, 1883, in Middleport and died April 4, 1952, in Middleport. He married Eva Frazier on February 14, 1903, in Cheshire. They had one child: Finley. Lewis's second wife was Ida Russell Willis married on January 25, 1907, in Middleport.

They had four children: Lewis, Leon, Ira and Rosalee. Carl Manley was born October 27, 1885, in Cheshire and died February 20, 1966, in Pomeroy. He married Ella Russell on November 2, 1906, in Middleport. They had eight children: William, Maggie, Lawrence, Charles, Lucille, Ruth, O'Dell and Emogene. Emmett Manley was born March 11, 1888, in Cheshire and died March 31, 1969, in Pomeroy. He married September 16, 1909, in Middleport. They had one child: Minnie "Midgi". Emmett married Bertha Frazier. They had five children: Audrey, Barney, Clifford, Ancil and Corrine. Maudie Manley was born April 10, 1891, in Cheshire and died October 11, 1915, in Meigs County. She married Eddie Little on September 10, 1907, in Meigs County. They had three children: Dowl, Letha and Violet. Corbett Manley was born August 1, 1893, in Cheshire and died August 18, 1977, in Gallipolis, OH. He married Gaye Rice on October 27, 1913, in Meigs County. They had four children: Walton, Charles, Teresa and Evelyn.

*Submitted by Kevin Manley*

**MARCHI FAMILY** - Louis Gino Marchi, was born June 12, 1897 in Rio Preto, Brazil. His father, mother and two sisters had traveled to Brazil from Bagni di Lucca, Italy to run a coffee plantation. When Louis was three years old there was an uprising and his father was murdered. Mrs. Catharina Marchi took her three children back to Italy. Louis remained in Italy until coming to America in 1914 at the age of 17. He was processed through Ellis Island and settled in Philadelphia, Pa. with family. Louis fought in WW I for the United States and gained his citizenship. In 1923 he went back to Italy, and married Ines Buonamici, born May 26, 1905, in Bagni di Lucca, Italy. Mr. Marchi returned to America in 1924 at the request of his father-in-law Roberto Buonamici to exhume and ship the body of Agnera Buonamici from Gallipolis, OH. back to Italy. Agnera was the brother of Ines and had died in Gallipolis.

Louis and Ines had one child born in Gallipolis, Lillian Catherine (Mimi) July 21, 1924. They moved and settled in Marietta, OH. Louis Gino Marchi, Jr. was born December 14, 1929, and Robert Lino Marchi was born February 26, 1931. The family moved to Parkersburg, WV, where the children attended St. Xavier Catholic School. In 1941 they moved to Gallipolis. They owned and operated the Pretzel Bell Bar & Restaurant on Court Street.

The children attended school in Gallipolis and graduated from Gallia Academy High School. Mimi graduated in 1943 and Holzer Hospital School of Nursing in 1945. The day she received notice that she passed her state boards and was a registered nurse, she was killed in an automobile accident just below Cheshire, OH.

Louis G. (Gee) graduated from high school in 1949 where he excelled in football, and then attended Ohio University on a football scholarship. Gee enlisted in the Navy and served 4 years. Gee married Jody Blair of Athens, OH. They had the following children; Michael, who owns Marchi's Carry-Out in Gallipolis, Marissa, and Mary Ann, both living in Zanesville, OH. He and Jody divorced. He then married Wanda Glover and they had one son Scott. Gee developed A.L.S. (Lou Gericks Disease). He passed away in 1990. All of the family was appreciative of the wonderful care Wanda gave Gee during his illness. Wanda and Scott Marchi live in Gallipolis.

Robert Lino (Bob) also excelled in football at Gallia Academy High School, Bob & Gee were known as "The Marchi Boys". Bob won a scholarship to Ohio University, in Athens, OH. After graduating in 1953, he immediately joined the U.S. Army, and was sent to Korea. He was discharged as a 1st. Lieutenant. After being discharged, he enrolled in law school at Ohio State. In 1957 he married Betty Lou Baker. They had one son, Robert G. He married Terri Belville and they reside on Cedar Street in Gallipolis.

Betty passed away in 1988.

Bob owned and operated Marchi Distributing from 1959 until his retirement in 1992.

Bob was elected to the Gallipolis City School Board in 1978 and served until 1986. He was elected as a commissioner on the Gallipolis City Commission in 1998 and serves to present.

In June of 1993 Bob married Mary Lee Davis McDade. They reside at 620 Fourth Avenue. Three children come to this marriage, Robert G. Marchi, Brian K. McDade and Melissa D. McDade Whaley.

*Submitted by Mary Lee Davis Marchi*

**ROBERT L. MARCHI & MARY LEE DAVIS MARCHI** - Robert (Bob) Lino & Mary Lee Davis Marchi live at 620 Fourth Avenue, Gallipolis, Ohio. They were married June 1993.

Bob was born in Marietta, Ohio, February 26, 1931 to Louis Gino Marchi, Sr. and Ines Buonamici. Louis was born in Rio Preto, Brazil in June 12, 1897, where he lived the first two years of his life. He then moved to Bagni di Lucca, Italy. He died in Gallia County in 1980. Ines was born in Bagni di Lucca, Italy and died August 1989 in Gallia County (See Louis G. & Ines Buonamici Marchi Story for more details on this line). Bob had two siblings, Louis G. (Gee) and Lillian Catherine (Mimi) Marchi, both deceased.

Bob spent his early childhood in Parkersburg, WV. The family moved to Gallipolis in 1941, where they owned and operated the Pretzel Bell Bar and Restaurant on Court Street for many years. He graduated from Gallia Academy High School in 1949. While in high school he played many sports but excelled in football receiving many trophies and honors. Some of these include: All South Eastern, 1947; All Southeastern & Best All Around Player in the league in 1948; All State & United Press Player Of The Week, 1948.

Bob attended Ohio University on a football scholarship and graduated in 1953. He spent two years in the U.S. Army in Korea, and was discharged as a 1st. Lieutenant. After attending law school at the Ohio State University, for one year, Bob decided to open his own business. He returned to Gallipolis and started Marchi Distrubiting which he operated from 1959 to 1992. He sold the business in 1992 and retired.

Bob is very concerned about the community and active in public affairs. He was elected to the Gallipolis City School Board of Education in 1978 and served until 1986. He is currently a commissioner on the Gallipolis City Commission having been elected in 1998 and again in 2000.

Bob married Betty Lou Baker (born 1931, died 1988) in 1957. They became the parents of Robert G. (February 20, 1963) who is married to Terri Belville. Bobbie and Terri reside in Gallipolis.

Mary Lee Davis Marchi was born July 1942 in Gallipolis to Leota Ann Walker and Denver Leo Davis. She has one brother from this marriage, William (Bill) Davis (1945) who is a building contractor in Gallia County. Leota and Leo divorced in 1946. In 1948, Leota married Bernard Malcolm Guinther of Syracuse, OH. Mary Lee and Bill were raised by Leota, Bernard and maternal grandmother Grace E. Roush Fadeley. In 1960, another brother was born, L.A. Guinther. (For more information on this family see Leota Ann Walker Guinther story).

Mary Lee attended Gallipolis City Schools from 1948 to 1959 and graduated from Kyger Creek High School in 1960. She attended Southerton School of Cosmetology and Rio Grande College. Mary Lee and Donald Ray McDade of Letart Falls, OH. were married August of 1961. Two children were born to this marriage. The first child, Brian Kelly McDade (November 23, 1962) married Teresa Meaige (Mason Co., WV) in 1982. They are the parents of Brittany L. and Brett L. McDade. Brian and Teresa were divorced, and both have since remarried. Brian's second marriage is to Karen Davis of Kanauga, OH. Karen is the mother of 3 children: Jeremy, Chase and Zack Davis. They reside in Cheshire Township.

The second child of Mary Lee and Don is Melissa (Missy) Dawn McDade (December 7, 1965). Missy married Jeffery Thomas Whaley (See Whaley story) in 1987. They are the parents of one child, Beau Jacob Whaley. They reside in Green Township.

Mary Lee has been employed by the Gallipolis Developmental Center, Marchi Distributing, and Ohio Valley Bank. From 1992 to 1999 she owned and operated Mary Lee's Fabric & Quilting, 322 Second Avenue, Gallipolis. She is presently employed as Director of the Gallia County Historical & Genealogical Society. She is a member of the Friends of the Our House Board, past board member of the G.C.H.& G. S., and a life member of G.C.H.& G.S.

Mary Lee Marchi, Brian, Brittany & Brett McDade, Missy & Beau Whaley, Robert G. &

Terri Marchi are all members of First Families of Gallia County.

Being an eighth generation Gallia Countian Mary Lee's direct ancestral lines in Gallia County include: Beard, Bunce, Curry, Cramer, Davis, Edwards, Fox, Glenn, Harrison, Kelcher, Pflum, Roush, Smith, Salser, Tharp, Williamson, Wise, Warner, Walker, Ward.

*Submitted by Mary Lee Davis Marchi*

**GLENN THOW MARR FAMILY** - Glenn Thow Marr born in Cleveland, Ohio, the son of Scottish immigrants, married Carrie Mae Notter Marr, (born July 21, 1914), at the home of her parents on October 2, 1938. Mae was the daughter of Ansel Isaiah Notter (1866-1952) and Susanna Wells (1887-1939).

After their marriage they built a home in Walnut township. They became the parents of five children, Joycelyn, Larry, Beverly, Edward and Kathy Lynn (stillborn May 3, 1952).

*Glenn and Mae Marr, 1972*

Joy, born December 3, 1939, died August 5, 1991, as a result of cancer. She was a bank officer for The Ohio Valley Bank. She married Donald Barlow, June 30, 1957.

Larry, born May 3, 1943, married Karen Beattie, Leon, WV on May 31, 1969. He attended Rio Grande College, and graduated from The Ohio State University with a B.S. Degree in Animal Science and a Master's Degree in Agriculture Education. He is an U.S. Army Vietnam Veteran and retired from Buckeye Hills Career Center in 2001, where he was a vocational supervisor for 27 years. Karen, B.A. Marshall University, taught at Southwestern H.S. for 12 years. Their children are Sarah Beth born June 24, 1977, is a 2001 graduate of the University of Rio Grande, Bachelor of Social Work. She's employed with Woodland Centers, Gallipolis as a case manager; and Suzanne Leigh, born April 19, 1980, married Philip Adkins, on 03-23-02, who is employed with All Power Equipment, Athens. They live in Vinton.

Beverly, born August 8, 1944, married Neil Daniel Watson. Their marriage ended after 18 years. Beverly is Customer Service Coordinator at Ohio Valley Bank. Their children are Neil Ashley, born 4-23-73, employed at Luigeno's, Jackson, and Kathy Lynn, born 5-22-75, a graduate of the University of Rio Grande, Associate Degree in nursing. She married to Joe Bill Bond, on 11-02-97, and the parents of Josephine Mae Bond born 1-3-00. Kathy is a registered nurse Holzer Medical Center, Jackson, and her husband is employed by the State of Ohio as a corrections officer. They reside in Centerpoint.

Ed, born July 16, 1950, married Paula Perroud, Rio Grande, Ohio, 5-16-69. He is employed as an application engineer with Emko Meir, Columbus, Ohio. Paula is a graduate of Hocking College, Associate Degree in nursing, employed by the State of Ohio as a health nurse. They reside in Canal Winchester, Ohio. Their children are: Christopher, an engineer born 9-29-71, graduate of Portland State University, B.S. Mechanical Engineering and he's employed as a Engineering Manager, Consolidated Metco. Chris married Eileen Scheiber, St. Louis, Missouri, 10-30-99, She is a graduate of the University of Missouri, B.S. and M.S. in Industrial Engineering and is an engineer with Freightliner. They reside in Lynn, Oregon; Heather born 2-28-76, graduate Bachelor of Fine Arts, Ohio University, is a graphic artist designer, Victoria's Secret Corporation, Columbus; and Natalie born 3-12-82, is employed with Oasis Corporation, Columbus, Ohio.

Glenn born 4-23-16, attended Cleveland School of Technology. An excellent machinist he still spends hours in his shop at home. He was a bridge superintendent 19 years with Engle Construction, retiring in 1976. Mae was a homemaker, known as a wonderful cook, talented musically, and a dedicated wife and mother. Mae and Glenn enjoyed traveling visiting forty states. They celebrated 50 years of marriage before her death in 1989.

*Submitted by Larry and Karen Marr*

**LARRY MARR FAMILY** - On May 31, 1969, Larry Marr and Karen Beattie were married at the Creston United Methodist Church, Mason County, W.Va. Larry Glenn Marr was born May 3, 1943. son of Glenn and Mae Notter Marr of Peter Cave Road in Gallia County. He is the grandson of the late Isaiah and Susanna Wells Notter of Gallia County and William and Mary Marr of Cleveland, Ohio. Larry who attended Mudsoc Elementary School, is a 1961 graduate of Southwestern High School. He attended Rio Grande College and received a Bachelor of Science Degree in Animal Science from Ohio State University in 1966. At that time, he was commissioned a second lieutenant in the United States Army, and in February 1967, began his tour of duty which included Ft. Knox, Ky., Ft. Bliss, Texas. and a tour of Vietnam in 1968, serving as an infantry platoon leader and a MACV Advisor to the South Vietnamese troops. With his tour of duty completed in December 1968, he returned to Ohio State University to become certified as a vocational agriculture teacher. In 1974 he completed the vocational supervisor internship program from Kent State University. In 1976, he received a Masters Degree from Ohio State, in vocational agriculture education.

Shortly after his return from the military, he married Karen Rose Beattie. They had met in 1966 when she was serving on the faculty of Southwestern high School. Karen, born February 20, 1943 is the only child of the late Joseph Walton and Goldie Click Beattie. She is the granddaughter of the late Orville and Rose Sommer Click and Andrew and Osa Ray Beattie, all from Mason County, WV. She graduated from Point Pleasant High School in 1960, and received a Bachelor of Arts Degree in home economics from Marshall University in 1964. She taught home economics from 1964-1976, at Southwestern High School.

After their marriage the Marrs made their home at 1819 Chestnut Street, in Gallipolis, and in 1972, moved to their present home at 39 Hilda Drive, Gallipolis.

*L: to R: Sarah Marr, Suzanne Marr Adkins, Karen Marr, Larry Marr*

In 1969, Larry began teaching vocational agriculture at Hannan Trace High School, followed by teaching Vo-Ag at Gallia Academy, (1971-1974), and in 1974 assumed the position of vocational supervisor at Buckeye Hills Career Center, Rio Grande. In August 2001, he retired from Buckeye Hills Career Center after being employed there twenty-seven years. Currently he is a part time instructor at the University of Rio Grande. He is the president and one of the founding members of Gallia County Vietnam Veterans of America, Chapter #709, and participates frequently with their Honor Guard in local parades.

The Marrs became members of the First Baptist Church in January of 1970. Larry is currently chairman of the Deacon Board there as well as being an usher.

The Marrs' are the parents of two daughters, Sarah Beth Marr, born June 24, 1977, a 1995 graduate of Ohio Valley Christian School, and a 2001 graduate University of Rio Grande, Bachelor of Social Work, and a licensed social worker. She is employed as a case manager with Woodland Centers of Gallipolis. Suzanne Leigh Marr Adkins was born April 19, 1980, is a 1998 graduate of River Valley High School and Buckeye Hills Career Center. She married Philip Adkins, born 09-04-75, on 03-23-02, and they live in Vinton, Ohio.

*Submitted by: Larry and Karen Marr.*

**NOEL FRANKLIN AND NORMA KATHRYN (ELLIOTT) MASSIE FAMILY** - Noel Franklin Massie was born January 21, 1931, in Lecta, Ohio, to Linus P. and Anna Woolum Massie. He graduated from Waterloo High School in 1948. Noel had one brother, Bobby, who died at the age of two years. Noel attended Rio Grande College for a short time in 1948. He enlisted in the U.S. Marine Corps in 1951 and served for two years.

He retired from Atlantic & Pacific Tea Company (A&P) after thirty years of service. He helped his dad on the farm and has since been farming. He served on the Gallia County Soil & Water Board 1984-1986 and is now presently on the board. He is a trustee of the Gallia County

*Noel Franklin And Norma Kathryn (Elliott) Massie*

Farm Bureau and a member of the Gabby Gang Farm Bureau Council. He is also a fifty-year member of Waterloo Mason #532 and a Past Worthy Patron of the Order of Eastern Star of Waterloo Chapter #447. Noel's father, Linus, was the son of Perry and Elzenia (Myers) Massie. Noel's mother, Anna, was the daughter of George and Cordellia (Miller) Woolum. Noel and Kathryn were married on July 12, 1953, in Gallia County, Ohio. Norma Kathryn (Elliott) was born June 6, 1934, to Walter F. and Beatrice "Bea" Ruth (Rose) Elliott. She had one sister, Frances Ruth, who married Robert K. Brown. Ruth passed away March 16, 1984. There were no children. Kathryn graduated from Gallia Academy High School with the class of 1952. She was employed by the Evans, Thorofare and Pennyfare Grocery Companies. She also worked for the Ohio Valley Bank Company for over thirty-one years. Kathryn is a Past Worthy Matron of Waterloo #447 Order of the Eastern Stars. She has been the Assistant Treasurer for the Gallia County Agricultural Society for the past twenty-two years. She is a member of the Gabby Gang Farm Bureau Council. Noel and Kathryn have two sons, Timothy Stephen, wife Pamela (Kautz), and Robert Eric, wife Connie (Burleson). They have six grandchildren, Timothy Jason, Jeffrey Stephen, Erica Sue, Robert Heath, Travis Kail and Adam Franklin Massie. Kathryn's father, Walter, was a son of Ira F. and Myrtie S. (Walter) Elliott. Kathryn's mother, Bea, was the daughter of Charles R. and Faye B. (Smeltzer) Rose. Ancestors on Kathryn's side go back to the Alexander Waddell family who came from Scotland 1755 and moved to Gallia County, Ohio, in 1817. His brother, Matthew, was the first school teacher in Green Township, Gallia County, Ohio.

*Submitted by Kathyn Massie*

**TIMOTHY STEPHEN AND PAMELA SUE (KAUTZ) MASSIE FAMILY** - Timothy Stephen Massie was born July 26, 1956, in Gallipolis, Ohio, to Noel F. and Kathryn Elliott Massie. He graduated from Gallia Academy High School in 1974. Tim graduated from the Ohio State University in 1978 with a Bachelor of Science in Agriculture. He received his Master of Science in Education degree from the University of Dayton in 1986, and has completed other course work at Ohio University and University of Rio Grande. Tim is currently employed by the Gallipolis City Schools at Gallia Academy High School where he taught Vocational Agricultural for 13 years, was a guidance counselor for three years, and the Assistant Principal for the last eight years. He has been a director of the Gallia County Agricultural Society for twenty-two years and has served as President five years, treasurer for three years, and secretary for fourteen years. He has also served on the Ohio Fair Managers Association Board of Directors for eight years, a member of the Waterloo Masons #532 and Pomeroy #186 Order of the Eastern Star, a member of the Gallipolis Area Jaycees for eighteen years. Tim married Pamela Sue Kautz (formerly of Meigs County, Ohio) September 3, 1978, in Meigs County. Pam was born July 22, 1958, to Dale Malcom and JoAnn Battrell Kautz of Chester, Ohio. Pam received her Associate Degree in Medical Records at Hocking Technical Institute in 1978. Pam was employed by Woodland Centers for eight years and by the Wiseman Insurance Agency for fifteen years. Pam is a member of the Pomeroy #186 Order of the Eastern Star of which she was past Matron in 1983.

*Timothy Stephen, Pamela Sue, Timothy Jason and Jeffrey Stephen Massie*

She has been a Longaberger consultant for thirteen years and a Branch Advisor since 1999. Tim and Pam have two sons, Timothy Jason Massie and Jeffrey Stephen Massie. They live on Alexander Church Road, Gallipolis, Ohio (Green Township). Jason graduated from Gallia Academy High School in 1999 and is currently enrolled in the John Deere School at Owens Community College in Toledo, Ohio. He is interested in agriculture and was a 4-H member for 10 years and an FFA member for six years. He earned his State FFA degree and his American FFA Degree while in the FFA. Jason was also interested in sports and played baseball and basketball at Green Elementary and Gallia Academy. Jeffrey is currently a junior at Gallia Academy High School. He played baseball and basketball at Green Elementary and basketball at Gallia Academy where this year he is on the junior varsity team. Jeff has been a 4-H member for nine years and an FFA member for one year. Tim has one brother, Robert Eric Massie of Bidwell, Ohio, who is married to Connie Burleson Massie. They have four children, Erica Sue, Robert Heath, Travis Kail, and Adam Franklin. Pam has one brother, William Dale Kautz of Pomeroy, Ohio. He is married to Crystal Whitlach and they have twins, William Jacob and Jenna Morgan. Tim's family lines date back to the early 1800's in Gallia County through his mother, Norma Kathyn Elliott Massie.

*Submitted by Tim Massie*

**AARON MATTHEWS FAMILY** - The Minute Men of Capt. Jonathan Barnes Company (49 in number) marched from Brookfleld, Massachusetts, on 19 April 1775, on receipt of the news of the Battle of Lexington, which was received on the afternoon of the same day. The general alarm was given, the company assembled and started immediately, and reached Cambridge early the next morning.

Sgt. Aaron Matthews was one of the minutemen. Aaron was the great grandson of John and Margaret V. (Hunt) Matthews, who were married in Charlestown, Massachusetts, 7 December 1658, by Richard Russell, Esquire, Royal Commissioner for the Colony, and the grandson of John Jr. and Mary (Johnson) Matthews, and the son of Daniel and Eunice (Morse) Matthews of Massachusetts. Aaron and Mary (Hubbard) Matthews were the parents of Phineas Matthews of Gallia County, Ohio. Aaron Matthews died in 1778.

Phineas Matthews was born 27 July 1770 in New Braintree, Massachusetts. Phineas was eight years old when his father, Aaron, died. Phineas was taken by his Uncle Daniel Matthews, who was a brother-in-law of Gen. Rufus Putnam.

In the spring of 1793 Phineas came to Marietta with the Ohio Company. The country was at war with the Indians so Gen. Putnam sent Phineas back to Massachusetts until the war closed. In 1795, Phineas drove a wagon with two yoke oxen for Col. Israel Putnam. It took eight weeks to travel about 800 miles. They arrived in Marietta 1 September 1795.

Phineas was made tax collector for Washington County, which at that time included Athens, Meigs, and Gallia County.

On 13 January 1803, Phineas married Mary Russell (4 August 1783-4 June 1815) Daughter of Moses Russell Sr. (a soldier of the Revolution of the Virginia Continental Line). There were seven children of this union, one Charles Whipple Matthews born 7 December 1803-died 20 November 1936.

Charles married Taphena Holcomb Matthews (8 January 1811-1883).They were the parents of Lydia Lillian Matthews (6 September 1856-20 November 1936).

Lydia Lillian Matthews married Dr. Charles Augustus Rife (26 November 1858-29 October 1933) on 24 March 1880 at Cheshire, Ohio by W. J. Fulton. Five children were born to this union, one being Phena Abigail Rife (31 January 1883-1 February 1956). Phena married Harlan Athey, son of William Lewis Athey and Lillie Tate. Harlan was born 9 January 1887 and died 4 June 1967. To this union were born Pauline (23 October 1910) and Clair (25 April 1913-1986).

Pauline Athey married Walter W. Rife. Please refer to the Walter W. Rife Family History for further family references.

*Submitted by Melissa Chasteen*

**MAUCK FAMILY** - The Maucks are originally from Switzerland. Rudolph Mauck born about 1700 Bern, Switzerland, came to America about 1740. Received a patent January 17, 1749, from Lord Fairfax for 400 acres at Hamburg Hamlet, now in Page County, Virginia. He and his wife (unknown) had 5 children: Elizabeth, Rudolph (married Catherine Ulrick), Henry, Richard and Daniel.

Daniel was born in Switzerland about 1742 and died 1803 Hamburg, Shenandoah County,

Virginia. He was married twice, first in 1762 to Barbara Harnsberger and had 7 children: Catherine, Abraham, Elizabeth, Marie, Barbara, Susan, and Molly. By his second wife, Rebecca Baker, whom he married in 1777, he had David, Joseph, Daniel, Robert P., Jacob and Elizabeth Ann.

*Mary Catherinre Mauck, taken 1890 Gallia County, Ohio*

Daniel served in the colonial militia in 1753. In 1761 he had 200 acres in Culpepper County, Virginia, by patent from Lord Fairfax in 1765. He received 283 acres at Hamburg and settled there with his wife and two children about 1767. He was a farmer and did custom milling. Altogether he owned nearly 1500 acres of land. He was connected at different times with the Reformed, Lutheran, Mennonite, and Dunkard sects. In or before 1801 he donated a tract on the principal highway, near the center of his Fairfax farm, for a church building which he, and others of varying faiths, erected with a stipulation that it should not be owned by any particular church organization but belong to the community and be available for the services of all faiths. It was known as the Mauck Meeting House and still stands today in 2002.

Robert P. Mauck was born May 8, 1782, Hamburg, Shenandoah County, Virginia, died Addison Township, Gallia County, Ohio, 1834. On January 7, 1811, at Shenandoah County, Virginia, he married Esther Ruffner, daughter of Peter Ruffner and Elizabeth Burner. Esther was born August 1786 Shenandoah County, Virginia, and died October 1860 Cheshire Township, Gallia County, Ohio. Robert first married Christina Ruffner, but she died in childbirth 8 months after marriage. Three years later he married her sister, Esther. Family moved from Virginia to Addison Township, Gallia County, Ohio, in 1826.

The children of Robert P. Mauck and Esther Ruffner are: Celinea Baker (married John Rogers), Rebeckaah Ann, Newton Eglon (married Anna Rothgeb) (see Rothgeb family history), John Joseph (married Elizabeth Sigler), Joseph Mandslaw, Mary Catherine (see Rothgeb family history), Nancy Jane (married Guy), Melissa Liddy (married Valentine Switzer), and William Stage.

*Submitted by Jack Childers*

**MAYO "EMPTY NEST"** - The children are grown and have lives or families of their own. That leaves us to our golden-retirement years together.

We were both born and grew up in Gallia County. Earl Franklin Mayo, Sr. was born at Kerr, Ohio, the son of the late Edwin and Catherine (Guthrie) Mayo. He is the youngest of six children—Robert and Lawrence (deceased); Ivan of Waverly, Ohio; Juanit Howard of Cincinnati, Ohio; Pauline Smith of Spokane, Washington. Earl attended school in Bidwell, Ohio and Bidwell-Porter High School and Rio Grande College. He is presently employed at Ohio Valley Electric Co.

*Mayo Family*

Vada was born in Bidwell, Ohio to the late Lusher A. and Mildred (Clark) Evans, a family of seven Children—James, Marjorie, Richard, Charles, and Clara (deceased) and Luella Henry of Bidwell, Ohio. She attended Bidwell-Porter schools and Rio Grande College. She recently retired from the Gallipolis Developmental Center after thirty four years of service as a Licensed Practical Nurse and Residential Care Supervisor.

We have enjoyed our lives together, and raising our children to be substantial citizens of the community and county. Our oldest son, Herman is the County Coordinator for JTPA. He has a lovely wife Venita (Smith) Mayo from Pt. Pleasant, West Virginia, two daughters whom we enjoy very much -Whitley Ann and Dannielle.

Our next son Earl, Jr. is affiliated with the Foodland Grocery Chain.

Carman (Mayo) Mitchell is our daughter. She is married to Dennis Mitchell of Gallipolis, Ohio, They have one child Jamil, a delightful, lovable boy. Carman is employed in the teaching profession with The Gallipolis City and Gallia County School Systems.

Lusher, our youngest son is employed at Bob Evans Sausage Shop. He prefers to be youngest child instead of "baby in the family".

Our Christian faith has sustained us through the years.

We do gardening, enjoy sports, fishing, sewing and crafts, and travel many places within the U.S.A and Canada.

We like to help others, whenever we find anyone in need.

**HERMAN ALEXANDER AND VENITTA MARIE (SMITH) MAYO FAMILY** - Herman was born February 2, 1957, in Gallipolis, Ohio. He is the oldest child of Earl F. Mayo, Sr., and Vada E. Evans Mayo. Both of his parents graduated from Bidwell-Porter High School. Earl Sr. is a maintenance mechanic at Ohio Valley Electric Corp. Vada is retired, after 34 years of service, from the Gallipolis Development Center. Herman's maternal grandparents were Lusher Alexander Evans and Mildred Warrenteen Clark Evans. Grandpa Evans worked for the WPA and did farm work. Grandma Evans was a homemaker and a practical nurse. They spent their entire lives in the Bidwell community.

Paternal grandparents were Edwin "Peter" Mayo and Sarah Catherine Guthrie Mayo. Grandpa Mayo worked on area farms. Grandma Mayo was a homemaker and very active in Providence Baptist Church. They made their home on Buckridge Road, Kerr.

Herman graduated from North Gallia High School and the University of Rio Grande. Herman is a member of and past president of the Gallipolis Kiwanis Club. He is also a member of Ancient York Lodge #33 Prince Hall Grand Lodge of Ohio F. and A.M. Herman is employed by Gallia-Meigs Community Action Agency.

Venitta was born May 28, 1957, in Gallipolis, Ohio. Her parents are Wallace A. Smith, Jr., and Inez M. Heidelburg Smith of Pt. Pleasant, West Virginia. Wallace was raised in Pt. Pleasant and graduated from Lincoln School in Gallipolis, Ohio. He is a U.S. Navy Vet. He is retired from the Goodyear Plant, Apple Grove, West Virginia. Inez grew up in Chicago, IL, and graduated from Englewood High School. Inez is a life-long homemaker.

Venitta's paternal grandparents were Wallace A. Smith, Sr., and Florence Virginia Moore Smith. They made their home in Pt. Pleasant, West Virginia. Grandpa Smith was employed at Rossi's Barber Shop in Pt. Pleasant. Grandma Smith was a life-long homemaker.

Maternal grandmother was Theresa Heidelburg Grey of Chicago, IL. Grandma T, as her grandchildren knew her, operated a catering business in Phoenix, Arizona.

Venitta grew up in Pt. Pleasant, West Virginia, and graduated from Pt. Pleasant High School. Venitta was active in sports as she grew up. Venitta is a maintenance mechanic employed by Ohio Valley Electric Corp.

Herman and Venitta met on June 1, 1987. They were married on January 1, 1988, at Trinity United Methodist Church in Pt. Pleasant, West Virginia. Herman and Venitta make their home in Gallipolis Township. They are the parents of two daughters, Whitley Ann and Danielle Alexandra.

Whitley Ann was born on June 1, 1989. She is in the seventh grade at Gallia Academy Junior High School. Whitley is a junior Girl Scout, plays on her school's junior high volleyball team. She also plays youth softball. She is a good student and takes pride in her work. Whitley enjoys the latest music and is a good dancer.

Danielle Alexandra was born on May 30, 1991. Danielle is a fifth grade student at Washington Elementary. Danielle is involved in various activities such as Girl Scouts, and the fifth grade school band. She also plays youth softball and basketball. Danielle does well in school and enjoys art, reading and writing.

Venitta loves to sew and to make clothing for her and the girls, plus home decorations such as window curtains. Venitta is involved in all of the girl's activities.

We are very much home oriented and enjoy doing things that the entire family can enjoy. The family enjoys outdoor activities such as fishing, camping and bicycle riding. We are members of Trinity United Methodist Church, Pt. Pleasant, West Virginia.

Herman's siblings are Earl Mayo, Jr., Carman (Dennis) Mitchell, and Lusher Edwin Mayo. All make their homes in Bidwell, Ohio. Venitta's brothers and sister are—Wallace Smith III, Paul (Neesha) Smith, William (Zennie) Smith, Theresa (Arthur) Silva, Walter (Gretta) Smith, and Christopher Dean Smith. All presently live in Pt. Pleasant.

*Submitted by Herman Mayo*

**ARTHUR MC CALL FAMILY** - The McCall family was among the first settlers in Gallia County. James C. McCall was born in Virginia but migrated to Gallia County in the late 1870's. Much of the history has been documented in a previous edition of Gallia County History. The direct descendants with whom this profile is associated is a great, great, great, grandson of James C. McCall.

Arthur McCaslin McCall was born March 12, 1879, in Gallia County, the son of James Henry McCall and Lucinda Clementine Folden. He had two brothers: Emmett and Oscar; and two sisters: Rosa and Esta. Oscar died at the age of 3. Emmett married Lillian Tope. Rosa married Clem Tope. Esta married Virgil Carter.

*The Mc Call Sisters in 1949*
*Front L: to R: Alice, Ann, Edith Rear L: to R: Bessie, Daisy, Edna*

In 1901, Arthur married Ruey Baker, the daughter of John Baker and Barbara Hay, in Gallia County. About 1908, Arthur and Ruey moved to Troy, Ohio. The reason for their relocation is not known. Ruey Baker McCall died in childbirth on February 17, 1917, leaving Arthur to raise six young daughters. Arthur was unable to cope alone, so the daughters were sent to live in various locations with relatives. Although Arthur would have four other marriages, there were no other children. Arthur McCall died September 22, 1954, and was laid to rest in Maple Hill Cemetery, Tipp City, Ohio.

The daughters of Arthur McCall: Alice Sabra born December 30, 1902, in Gallipolis; died September 29, 1974, in Dayton, Ohio. Alice married Floyd Pauley with whom she had five children: Kenneth, Mildred, Harold, Gordon, and Joyce Ann.

Edna Mae born in Gallipolis on June 20, 1905; died January 28, 1987, buried at Centenary Cemetery, Gallia County, Ohio. In 1932, Edna married Harry Hulshorst with whom she had one daughter, Barbara.

Ann Myrl born February 15, 1907, in Gallipolis; died May 8, 1996, in Dayton, Ohio. She is buried in Mound Hill Cemetery, Gallipolis. Ann married Joseph O'Dell in 1953.

Bessie Lucinda born December 4, 1908, in Shelby, Ohio, died April 30, 1998, in Fort Myers, Florida. She is buried in Mound Hill Cemetery, Gallipolis. Bessie married J. Merrill White on June 5, 1929, in Rodney, Ohio, and had one daughter, Marjorie.

Edith Faye born January 2, 1911, in Houston, Ohio; died June 1979 in Pt. Pleasant, West Virginia. She is buried in Mound Hill Cemetery, Gallipolis, Ohio. Edith, a long-time elementary school teacher in Gallia County, never married.

Daisy Leona born June 12, 1912, at Lockington, Ohio, died March 18, 1972, in Oxford, Ohio. She is buried beside her sister, Edith, at Mound Hill Cemetery, Gallipolis, Ohio. In Oxford, Ohio, Daisy married Kapp Dunn with whom she had one son, David.

*Submitted by Lisa Gigante D'Amico*

**CLEAO MC CALL FAMILY** - Cleao McCall was born December 31, 1909, in Harrison Township; the son of Emmett and Lillian Tope McCall. Cleao had one brother, Loren McCall (deceased) and one sister, Audrey Johnson, who resides in Gallia County. After attending the Martin and Safford Schools, he graduated from Gallia Academy High School in 1926 and received a teaching certificate from Rio Grande College in 1932. He taught at the Blessing, Northup, Rodney and Graham Schools and later operated a grocery store at Second and Olive Streets. Cleao and Hilah Nelle Boster were married January 15, 1936. She was born July 1, 1912, in Harrison Township and was employed as a telephone operator for Ohio Bell. Her parents were Harvey and Carrie White Boster. Hilah Nelle had one brother, George Boster, and one sister, Kathleen Dowell; both now living in Florida. Cleao and Hilah had one child, Phillip, born in 1937. The family moved to Columbus in 1942, where Cleao and Hilah worked at the Curtis Wright Aircraft Factory. Cleao passed away in 1956 and Hilah Nelle in 1994.

The following are excerpts from a letter written by Adda McCall prior to 1931. Adda was a sister of James Henry McCall, Cleao's grandfather:

*Alexander and Lucinda Howell Mc Call*

James McCall son of James C. McCall and Elizabeth Northup was my grandfather. He was born on a farm in Gallia County August 12, 1806. He like his father operated a large farm, but his time was not completely given over to farming as he taught school for several years in a school building made of logs for you understand they were pioneers of that part of Gallia County. January 17, 1818 he married Martha Phelps who was born June 4, 1807.

My father, Alexander McCaslin McCall was born May 18, 1829, in Gallia County on Claylick, the son of James and Martha Phelps McCall. He was a farmer and stock raiser and had large holdings of land in Gallia and Lawrence Counties. December 5, 1850, he married Lucinda Howell who was born May 25, 1834. She was the daughter of Elizah and Rebecca Roadarmour Howell."

The children of Alexander and Lucinda McCall were: Sarah McCall 1851-1931 who married George H. Northup; Martha R. McCall 1853-1878 who married James Houck; James Henry McCall 1855-1939 who married Lucinda Folden; Alexander McCall 1858-1858; Mary F. McCall 1859-1901 who married James Buckle; Lafayette Lincoln McCall 1862-1957 who married Emma Hummerich; Elmer McCall 1866-1933 who married Irene Soupene; Carrie McCall 1869-1966 who married George Smith; Adda McCall 1872-1951; Rosa McCall 1877-1878.

*Submitted by Phillip McCall*

**JOHN MC CARLEY** - John McCarley was born in 1754 in Poss, York County, PA, and died on May 17, 1814, in Gallia County, Ohio. John came to Gallia County, Ohio, in 1806, with his children, probably from York County, Pennsylvania. We think John came from Scotland, but no proof has been found as yet. He took patent deed to the west half of section 13, Raccoon Township in February, 1806, later adding the northeast quarter section 23, Raccoon Township. John died May 17, 1814, at age 60. Among his chattels were three Bibles and a pot-still. The Gallia County Genealogical Society has accepted John, his son, William, and wife, Rachel Totten, and his grandson, John, as First Families of Gallia County, Ohio. No proof of whom John's wife was has been found as yet, and she was not mentioned in his will. We suspect his wife died in Pennsylvania before John moved to Gallia County.

John's children were:

1. William McCarley was born in 1783 and died on August 20, 1869, in Morgan Township, Gallia County, Ohio.

2. John McCarley was born about 1784, died on December 31, 1827, in Gallia County, Ohio, and was buried in McCarley Private Cemetery. John married Ann Glenn on June 9, 1813. Ann Glenn died before 1815. John next married Martha Carr in 1815. Martha was born November 29, 1793, died on September 7, 1851, in Gallia County, Ohio, and was buried in McCarley Private Cemetery.

3. Moses McCarley was born in 1799 and died on June 17, 1851.

4. Elizabeth McCarley was born about 1785. Elizabeth married Noah Walp on August 16, 1847, in Gallia County, Ohio. Noah was born in 1820 in Pennsylvania.

5. Margaret McCarley was born about 1786.

6. Zebiah McCarley was born about 1789 in Gallia County, Ohio, died on February 3, 1860, in Calhoun, Harrison County, Iowa, and was buried in Calhoun, Harrison, Iowa.

7. Samuel McCarley was born in 1798.

*Submitted by Ruth E. Hall*

**ROBERT BAILEY MC CARLEY** - Robert Bailey McCarley, son of John McCarley and Agnes Nancy Boggs, was born on February 21, 1849, in Gallia County, Ohio, died on February

6, 1914, in Toledo, Lucas County, Ohio. He was buried in Forest Cemetery, Toledo, Lucas County, Ohio. Robert first married Elizabeth Dare. Elizabeth was born about 1851. There was one child from this marriage, Sarah A. McCarley.

Robert next married Elizabeth Wright on August 17, 1871, in Gallia County, Ohio. Elizabeth was born on March 7, 1848, and died on August 12, 1874, in Walnut Township, Gallia County, Ohio.

Children from this marriage were:

1. John Franklin McCarley was born June 27, 1872.

2. Mary Alice McCarley was born on August 5, 1874, and died 1930.

Robert next married Eveline Elizabeth Ferrell, daughter of John Lewis Ferrell and Mary E. Roush, on June 4, 1875, in Lawrence County, Ohio. Eveline was born in 1855 in West Virginia and died on October 1, 1905, in Toledo, Lucas County, Ohio.

Children from this marriage were:

1. Jessie Love McCarley born September 2, 1876, in Gallia County, Ohio, died January 26, 1954, in Columbus, Franklin County, Ohio (hospital) and was buried in Mifflin Cemetery, Gahanna, Franklin County, Ohio. Jessie married Stuard Savage, son of Filmore M. Savage and Unknown, on November 23, 1892, in Marion, Ohio. Stuard was born on March 30, 1873 in Carey, Wyandotte, Ohio, died January 28, 1955, in Gahanna, Franklin County, Ohio, and was buried in Mifflin Cemetery, Gahanna, Franklin County, Ohio.

2. Oba Walford McCarley was born on June 13, 1878, and died on July 2, 1945, in Toledo, Lucas County, Ohio.

3. Charles McCarley was born on May 19, 1879.

4. Robert Luther McCarley was born on March 17, 1881, in Lawrence County, Ohio, and died on August 6, 1882.

5. Mary Elizabeth McCarley was born December 13, 1882, in Pedro, Ohio, and died September 23, 1933, in Newberry, Michigan. Mary married Lewis Elmer Lemming, son of Levi Lemming and Mary Margaret Gallimore, on October 7, 1899, in Portage, Ohio. Lewis was born on August 22, 1878, in Jackson Township, Shelby County, Ohio, and died on December 20, 1941, in Gibbs City, Michigan.

6. Nancy Lillian McCarley was born on February 8, 1885. Nancy married Henry Trefc, son of Jacob Trefc and Elizabeth Wagoneer, on December 13, 1901, in North Baltimore, Wood County, Ohio. Henry was born on August 20, 1875.

7. Myrtle May McCarley was born on March 18, 1887, in Lawrence County, Ohio, died on August 14, 1962, in Toledo, Lucas County, Ohio, and was buried in Forest Cemetery, Toledo, Lucas County. Myrtle married Gilbert Alexander Lemming, son of Levi Lemming and Mary Margaret Gallimore, on March 22, 1905. Gilbert was born on February 18, 1876, in Jackson Township, Shelby County, Ohio, died on October 12, 1937, in Toledo, Lucas County, Ohio, and was buried in Forest Cemetery, Toledo, Lucas County, Ohio.

8. Daniel Wilson McCarley was born on April 5, 1889. *Submitted by Ruth E. Hall*

**WILLIAM MC CARLEY -** William McCarley (John 1) was born in 1783 and died on August 20, 1869, in Morgan Township, Gallia County, Ohio. He is buried in Ewington Cemetery in Morgan Township, Gallia County, Ohio. William was married four times and had children by two of his wives that we know of. William was married to his first wife, Susan Denny in Virginia. He was married to his second wife, Rachel Totten, on September 13, 1810, in Gallia County, Ohio, by David Ridgeway. She was the daughter of John Totten and Drusilla. Rachel was born about 1775 in Tazewell, Virginia, and died before 1816.

He married his third wife Sally (Sarah) Boggs on July 18, 1816, by David Boggs. She was the daughter of Andrew Elliot Boggs and Susannah Bowen. Sarah (Sally) was born about 1794 in Greenbrier County, Virginia (West Virginia) and died about 1829 in Jackson County, Ohio.

He married his fourth wife Anna Wallace on October 11, 1829, by Samuel R. Holcomb.

William sold the inheritance from his father, John, to David Ridgeway in 1819.

His children with Rachel Totten were:

1. John McCarley was born in October, 1811 and died on December 25, 1885, in Walnut Township, Gallia County, Ohio. John married Agnes Nancy Boggs, daughter of Alexander Boggs and Agnes Nancy Boggs, on April 28, 1833, in Gallia County, Ohio. Agnes was born about 1811 in Greenbrier County, Virginia (West Virginia) and died after 1884.

2. Rachel McCarley was born about 1812. Children with Sarah Boggs are:

1. William Gerley McCarley was born on July 16, 1819, and died on November 12, 1895, in Ewington, Ohio. William married Sarah Woods.

2. Andrew Franklin McCarley was born in 1821 and died on November 4, 1895. Andrew married Mary Dodrill on February 2, 1843. Mary was born in 1822.

3. Andrew Jackson McCarley was born on February 17, 1823, in Jackson County, Ohio, and died in 1908 in Jackson City. Andrew married Susanna C. Woods, daughter of William Woods and Rebecca Edminston, on April 18, 1851, in Gallia County, Ohio. Susanna was born on February 28, 1822.

4. Samuel Jackson McCarley was born on June 7, 1825, died on July 16, 1893, and was buried in Old Vinton Cemetery, Vinton, Huntington Township, Gallia County, Ohio. Samuel married Sarah A. Viers on February 2, 1848. Sarah was born on December 29, 1817, and died on April 5, 1891.

5. Moses McCarley was born on February 23, 1827, and died on November 15, 1867, and was buried in Old Vinton Cemetery, Vinton, Huntington Township, Gallia County, Ohio. Moses married Clarissa Rhodes.

*Submitted by Ruth E. Hall*

**JONAS MC CARTY -** Jonas McCarty and his wife, Catherine Zirkle, came to the Cheshire, Gallia County, OH, area in 1794. Jonas was the son of James McCarty. Catherine's parents were George Adam Zirkle (born 1738, PA) and Elizabeth Ridenour (born 1745, PA).

According to Deed Record, Vol. 20, page 586, Jonas and Catherine McCarty deeded land for a school that became known as the Turkey Run or Liberty Hall School. The McCarty's were paid $20 for the land and the deed was recorded on July 24, 1847. They also established a church which first met in their home.

According to the Hardestry History of Gallia Co, OH 1882, the first religious services were held at the residence of Jonas McCarty and Paul Darst and the first church society, Free Will Baptist, was organized at the house of the latter December 15, 1805, Rev. Eli Stedman, Pastor. Members listed were: Joseph and Margaret Rife, Daniel and Anna Romine, Paul and Sarah Darst, William and Tacey Butler, Esquire Bullock, Sarah Bullock, Henry Jones, David McCarty, Jessie and Rachel Fleshman, Anthony VanSickle, Joseph Higgins, William McDowell, Jesse Carpenter, Timothy Smith, Sabret Scott, Jonas McCarty, Charles Shepard, George W. Putnam, Phineas Mathews, Elizabeth Aleshire, Catherine McCarty, Alsie Gray, Mrs. Eblin, Elizabeth Wright, Nancy Scott, Esther McCarty, Polly Smith, Rebecca Vanmeeter and Polly Mathews.

Children of Jonas and Catherine were George Adam (February 10, 1788-December 6, 1877) married Nancy Rife and Elizabeth Taylor; Jonas (October 7, 1791-June 20, 1851) married Esther Rife; Mary (1795-1886) married William McDowell; Eve (died before 1850) married Ephraim Smith; David (died November 12, 1828) married Sally Far; John (1798 September 22 1825) married Sarah Slater; Benjamin F. (February 5, 1800-April 1887) married Elizabeth Rowley; Rebecca (born 1801) married Daniel Cogswell and Phineas Rowley; James (January 19, 1803-July 18, 1887) married Caroline Kirkpatrick; Silas (about 1810); Elizabeth (January 1800-March 12, 1899) married W. P. Jones and Equilla Cossler and Sophia (born 1813). Jonas and George Adam were born in Shenandoah County, VA, while the rest of the children were born in Gallia County, OH. Jonas and Catherine McCarty were buried in McCarty Cemetery near Cheshire, Gallia County, OH.

*Submitted by Betty Robinson*

**JONAS MC CARTY -** Jones McCarty, born October 7, 1791, in Shenandoah County, VA, was the son of Jonas and Catherine (Zirkle) McCarty who migrated to the Cheshire area in Gallia County, OH, in about 1794.

In Gallia County in 1811, Jonas married Esther S. Rife (born March 23, 1791, Greenbrier County, VA) daughter of Joseph and Margaret (Carpenter) Rife.

Children of Jonas and Esther were: Nancy who married Solomon Swisher; Eliza who married Basil Hacket; Esther Jane who married John Lindley; Moses who married Mary Darst and Elizabeth Cummins; Rachel who married David Coughenour; and Jonas who married Sophronia Jones.

Jonas died June 20, 1851 (see wills dated November 12, 1849, and June 12, 1851-Gallia County Courthouse). Esther died September 4, 1884, at the residence of her son, Jonas McCarty, near Cheshire, Gallia County, OH. At the time of her death, Esther had 61 grandchildren, 104 great grandchildren and 22 great, great grandchildren. Esther belonged to Freewill Baptist Church in 1811.

Both Jonas and Esther McCarty are buried in the McCarty Cemetery near Cheshire, OH.

*Submitted by Erica Klooz*

**MOSES MC CARTY** - Moses McCarty was born to Jonas and Esther (Rife) McCarty in Cheshire Township, Gallia County, OH, January 30, 1820.

Moses' first wife was Mary Darst, daughter of Joseph and Mary Darst. Mary was born December 26, 1822. Moses and Mary had 9 children, seven of whom died in childhood:

*Moses Mc Carty, Son Of Jonas and Esther Mc Carty and Elizabeth Ann (Cummjns) Mc Carty, Second Wife Of Moses Mc Carty*

Ester Eveline (died November 16, 1855, age 5), Jonas W. (died November 24, 1859, age 3); Fastsa R. (died November 25, 1859, age 12); Moses Wilson (died November 27, 1859); Sarah Jane (died November 28, 1859); John (died December 26, 1859, age 3) and Missouri (died 1859, age 1). These children and their mother, Mary (died June 3, 1901) are buried in Pleasant Hill Cemetery, located in Randolph County, Jackson Township, Indiana. Daughters Josephine (born May 1853) and Mary Ellen (born 1846) lived to adulthood. Josephine married Simon Raines.

Prior to the death of the children, Moses had left his first wife and married Elizabeth Ann Cummins (born August 23, 1837) on November 17, 1865, at Joseph Teaberry, IN.

In 1872, Moses left Salmon, IN, and staked out a homestead 6 1/2 miles southeast of Beaver City, NE, where he farmed. This homestead, located on the Sapp Creek, has been in the family since that time and is owned by Betty Robinson, Ervin Volga and Karen Coffey. At one time, Josephine and Simon moved to Beaver City also.

Six children were born to Moses and Elizabeth: U.S. Grant (1864-1866); infant daughter (1867-1867); Laura Matilda (September 16, 1868-August 2, 1910) married Lewis Thomas; Eva Elvira (September 2, 1872-January 7, 1958) married John Wentling; James Adam (June 27, 1876-June 27, 1964) married Elvira Alice Vining; Elizabeth Ann (June 27, 1876-July 16, 1897-twin of James) married William Schenk. All of these children settled in the Beaver City area. After Elizabeth Ann's death, her husband and children moved to Canada.

Moses died June 6, 1911, at the age of 91 and Elizabeth died October 6, 1911, at the age of 74. Both are buried in the Mount Hope Cemetery near Beaver City, NE.

*Submitted by Kathy Wilmot*

**DILLIE ELININE (BAIRD) MC CORMICK** - Born January 12, 1927, Dillie and Della (see Baird Twins) grew up on a farm in the Great Depression. During World War II, War Ration Books were needed to purchase goods. The rule was "if you don't need it, DON'T BUY IT." The fruits, vegetables and meat they raised were canned on a wood cook stove or outside in a large kettle over an open fire. They churned milk to make butter and cottage cheese and collected eggs. Dad drove a new Model T (later held together with bailing wire) into town and they sold produce and eggs to buy things they needed.

*Dillie E. Mc Cormick*

Dillie was married to Charles Richard McCormick born 2/3/1927 (recently discharged from the US Navy having served in the Pacific in WW II). Named for maternal Grandmother Lola Gail (see Gail and Ora Baird) and paternal Grandmother Gracie Mae (Hatfield) McCormick, their daughter, Lola Mae was born October 31, 1947 (Holzer Hospital, 1st Avenue, Gallipolis, Ohio) and delivered by Dr. Lewis Brown. Born 01/15/1949, Mark S. Mc Coy (US Navy 1967-1970) radioman aboard the Aircraft Carrier Franklin D. Roosevelt and Lola were married on 12/29/1968 at Campaign Freewill Baptist Church by Reverend Andrew Parsons. After retirement from GDC Human Resources in 1996 with 30 years of service, Lola joined Mark, a Certified Legal Video Specialist, in his business Legal Video Services.

Charles William was born February 14, 1949 at Holzer on 1st Avenue and delivered by Dr. Brown. Bill was a member of US Army & West Virginia National Guard from 1968-1976. On 1/22/1969, Bill and Diana Jean Long (born 0 1/22/1949) were married at Grace United Methodist Church in Gallipolis. They have one son, Charles William McCormick Jr. (1/23/197 1) also born at Holzer on First Avenue. With more than 32 years service, Bill is currently the Columbus, Ohio Terminal Manager for CSX railroad.

Dillie and the children went to live in the country with her parents on a large farm in Addison Township and they attended Campaign Church. In the early 1950s, Dillie worked at Holzer for over ten years as a nurse aide and later as an assistant in the X-ray department. In 1962, Dillie went to work at Gallipolis State Institute (later Gallipolis Developmental Center) as an Attendant and graduated from Psychiatric Aide 1 class on November 8, 1966. After the death of her mother, the family moved on February 14, 1967 back to Gallipolis. With help and encouragement from family and friends, Dillie obtained her LPN license and retired from GDC in 1986 as a Licensed Practical Nurse.

Over a 100 family and friends gathered at the First Church of God Fellowship Hall on January 12, 2002 to help celebrate Dillie's 75th. birthday. Dillie's Grandson (Charles William and Shannon R. (Gast) McCormick Jr.) and great-granddaughter Julie Ann (born 10/26/1998) came all the way from Jacksonville, Florida for this very special occasion. Grandma Dillie loves her family very much and is looking forward to the arrival of new great granddaughter later this year.

*Submitted by Charles William McCormick, Sr.*

**MCCOY - DENNEY FAMILY** - Lauchey was born (November 5, 1949) in Kimper, KY to parents of Earnie and Myrtle Stiltner McCoy. He is the fifth generation of famous Hatfield - McCoy feud of 1860.

He has two sisters; Loretta and Don Keeton of Ewington, Ohio. Loraine and Ken Kiser of Racine, Ohio. One brother, Lawson McCoy of Vinton, Ohio.

*Lauchey and Margaret Pauline McCoy*

His family moved here from Kentucky in 1954 and he attended Vinton Elementary and North Gallia High School.

Margaret Pauline Denney was born March 23, 1951 in Gallia County to Paul S. and Margaret Saxton Denney.

She has two brothers; John R. and Ruth Davis Denney, Bidwell, Ohio. James (PeeWee) and Charlotte Smith Denney of Letart, WV. Pauline attended Bidwell-Porter elementary and North Gallia High School, where the two met and remember the only dates they were allowed was to church on Wednesdays and Sundays. Upon graduation in May 1970; the two were married on July 19, 1970 and still reside on Alice Road, Ewington, Ohio.

Lauchey is a mechanic and electrician for Southern Ohio coal Company (Meigs Mine #2 Mine) for the past 28 years now.

Pauline is EMT-P for Gallia County Emergency Medical Services for the past 16 years now and is a CPR instructor for American Heart Association.

Together they run a small business called Country Boutique.

Pauline enjoys flea markets and craft shows.

Lauchey's full-time hobby, shared with his brother, includes drag racing and collecting a few old cars.

*Submitted by Lauchey and Margaret Pauline McCoy*

**MC COY - WARREN** - Rev. Andrew Jackson, better known as "A.J.", Warren was born on Feb. 4, 1820 in Allegheny Co., Virginia. About 1826 when he was six years of age, his family moved to Greenbrier Co., Va. In the 21st. year of his age, he united with the Methodist Protestant Church; was licensed to preach in 1842 and ordained in 1843; he traveled for the regular work of the church for eight years and after much deliberation and study of the scriptures, he concluded to join the Baptist Church, and remained one of the most earnest and faithful advocates of its doctrines during his long and useful life.

*Rev. Andrew Jackson & Mary Ann (Mc Coy) Warren*

He was ordained as a Baptist preacher in 1851, & came to Ohio in 1863, from Va./W.Va. during the "Great Rebellion", (Civil War). He served pastorates in Mason Co., Va/W.VA, Gallia, Lawrence and Pike Co., Ohio. He served at Providence Baptist Church in Clay Twp., Gallia Co., for about 30 years in succession. He traveled a great deal as a regular missionary and established several permanent Baptist Churches. He was Moderator of the Ohio Association, eight years, and Clerk for many years. He was chosen Moderator of the Gallia Association when it was organized and served for six years. It is said that he was one of the best text preachers of his day.

He was married to Mary Ann McCoy, on January 31, 1844 in Greenbrier Co., Va/W.Va..

Mary Ann was born June 16, 1820 and died at her granddaughter, Vesta Alice (Warren) Sheets' home on John's Creek Road, Guyan Twp., on Dec. 23, 1898. To this union the following children were born: Marion L. (1845-1892) Bn. Greenbner Co., Va./W.Va., Spouse Emily Frances Clark; Clark Brown (1846- 1925)Bn. in Greenbrier Co., Va./W.Va., Spouse Nancy Ellen Long; John L. (1848-1906) Bn.Cabell Co., Va./W.Va; Sp. Levenia Angeline Clark Augustus N. (1849-1909) Bn.Cabell Co. Va/W.Va., Sp.Nancy A. "Nannie" Brown; Andrew Jackson, Jr. (1851-1920) Bn. Cabell Co., Va./W.Va., Spouse Rachel Russell; Virginia Elizabeth "Ginny" (1855-1932) Bn. Glenwood, Mason Co, Va./W.Va., Spouse Rev. Edward Lewis Sheets; Jennette A. "Nettie" (1857-1890), Bn. Glenwood, Mason Co., Va./W.Va., Never married. Hezekiah Chilton (1860-1934) Bn Glenwood, Mason Co., Va/W.Va., Sp. Elizabeth Della "Dellie" Farren; Mary Frances "Fanny A." (1861-1895) Bn. Glenwood, Mason Co., Va/ W. Va., Spouse James Justice Hatfield.

Marion L.'s children: Newton, Mary E., Oscar Burton "Bert", Lela Ellen & Willie E. Warren.;

Clark Brown 's children: John E., Leota "Ota" Pearl, Leotie "Otis", Goldie & Katie B. Warren;

John L's children: Virgil Jackson, Vests Alice, Victor, Verta May, Veva, Vernard, Vance E. Warren; Augustus N.'s Children: Irvin L. Warren; Andrew Jackson, Jr's children: Calvin A., Clyde T., Otho, Mollie, Chloe, Charles Loren, Josie, Edward James, Myrtle "Myrtie", Emmitt, Warren; Virginia E's. children: Adoniram Judson, Fanny A., Andrew Herschell, Emmett Eugene, Provy W., Mary, Sheets; Hezekiah Chilton's children: Ollie (Daughter). Hezekiah moved to Linwood, Lafayette Twp., Ind. where he served as Justice Of The Peace. He is buried in Wesley Chapel Cemetery, Richland Twp., Ind.,Mary Frances "Fanny A.'s" children: Fred E., Elmer E. and Walter Hatfield.

Rev. Andrew Jackson "A. J.", died on May 27, 1896, aged 76 years, and 8 months and 23 days. and is buried in Fairview Cemetery ,Wilgus, Lawrence Co., Ohio, beside his wife, Mary Ann. The cemetery is located behind the Fairview Baptist Church.

They were charter members of the Long Creek Missionary Station Church, before it was later called Fairview Baptist Church., as it is known today. His funeral (memorial service) was in Sept., 1896 at Mercerville. It was largely attended and the house was filled to capacity. Rev. John M. Kelley, of Ironton, Ohio, delivered the funeral sermon. He was 80 years old & a co-worker in the ministry with him.

I am a descendant of his son, John L. Warren, through my mother, Vesta Alice (Warren) Sheets. The Warren's were very active in church work and had very melodious singing voices, for which they were noted.

*Submitted by: Robert Franklin Sheets*

**BUEFORD FRANCIS MC DANIEL, FOURTH GENERATION** - Bueford McDaniel was born August 11, 1836, in Walnut Township, Gallia County, Ohio, died May 30, 1907. He was the sixth child of Ephriam and Elizabeth (Shumate) McDaniel. He married Cynthia Catherine Powell, daughter of Rezin and Delana (Nance) Powell, born May 20, 1837, Mason Township, Lawrence County, Ohio, died January 20, 1925, Walnut Township Gallia County, Ohio, buried in McDaniel Cemetery McDaniel Crossroads. They had the following children: Charles W. (Uriah) born October 24, 1860, Walnut Township, Gallia County, died January 7, 1940, buried in Olive Cemetery, married Margaret Ridge March 19, 1887, in Lawrence County, Ohio.

Rezin Ephriam born April 2, 1863, married Mildred Almeda Lasley in Lancaster, MO, November 28, 1886, died September 28, 1939.

John Wesley born November 4, 1865, died April 2, 1901, in Davis City, Iowa, married Elmie Francis Prose, December 31, 1886.

Simeon Paul born August 10, 1869, married Viola Donnely March 29, 1894, Portsmouth, Ohio, died about 1945 in Seattle, Washington, taught school in Washington Court House, OH, Pueblo, CO.,Oregon and Seattle, Washington.

Perry Lansing born 1871, died before October 18, 1877, in Ohio.

Ida Mae born June 20, 1874, in Gallia County, Ohio, married three times: 1. Charles Slagle. 2. M. W. Vincell. 3. Sherman. Ida Mae taught school in Lawrence and Gallia Counties and Pueblo, CO. and was a postmaster 1907 at Waterloo, Ohio.

*Submitted by Larry McDaniel: Great, great grandson of Francis McDaniel*

**CARROLL RAY McDANIEL, SEVEN GENERATION** - Carroll Ray McDaniel b Jan. 31, 1925 m Gladys Pemberton b April 13, 1930 d 1988.

Three children m June 23, 1947. 1) Alden Eugen b April 16, 1948, Twins Larry Jay and Jerry Ray b May 21, 1952.

Alden Cheryl Kelsey Morehead, KY. Three children: SheIly Lynn b Sept. 15, 1972, William Ray b Sept. 28, 1975, CbristopherRayb Feb. 15, 1979.

Jerry Ray m. Peggy Belcher, four children. David Bryan b Nov. 9, 1977, Sarah Beth b Aug. 11, 1980, Michael Ryan b Sept. 5, 1985, Matthew Tyler b July 19, 1994.

*Jerry, Alden, Larry, Carroll and Lisa Mc Daniel*

Larry Jay m. Vicki McKnight two children. Larry Shawn b April 15, 1974. Jeromy De July 11, 1978 Second m Helen Marie Aldridge (Dufour) b May 9, 1936 m Nov. 19, 1964. One daughter Lisa Carol b May 24, 1965 m Rick Collins, 2 children Alicia Marie b Feb. 5, 1986, Eric Allen b Aug 7, 1989. One child by Ada Ainsworth, Brandon Lee b July 9, 1992.

Three step children: Janet Lee Aldridge b Aug. 2, 1952, Penny Elaine Aldridge Lewis b Nov. 28, 1954, Cindy Lou Aldridge Roach b Jan. 6, 1956.

Carroll worked for the C. & O. Railroad in Huntington, .W.VA. Oct. 14, 1944 started in the signal dept. then as an assistant Signalman, signal maintainer, traveling Mechanic finally Signal Inspector 1982, retired July 5, 1989.

*Submitted by Lisa McDaniel Collins, daughter of Carroll*

**CECIL HERBERT MCDANIEL SIXTH GENERATION** - Cecil H. McDaniel born March 25, 1895, died June 9, 1962, married Erycle Lexie Neal October 27, 1915, Gallipolis, Gallia County, OH, died February 13, 1942, second wife, Artie (Delaney) Caldwell, married May 25, 1942. He was the son of Charles and Margaret (Ridge) McDaniel. Erycle is the daughter of Thomas Watson Neal and Ida Mae (Diggens) Neal.

Twins: Nile Charles and Neal William born July 4, 1916; Rader Cecil born October 3, 1919, died January 22, 1996; Walter Emerson born December 2, 1921, died November 13, 1973.

Twins: Carroll Ray and Carl Stewart born January 31, 1925. Carl Stewart died October 15, 1990.

Twins: Otis Francis and Orville born September 18, 1927. Otis Francis died March 9, 2001. Orville died August 10, 1928. Mary Ida Belle born October 26, 1929, John Wesley born May 27, 1932, died April 15, 1993.

Nile Charles, M. Ruth Woolem, Columbus, Ohio. Neal William married Ethel Call, Scioto County, Ohio, second wife, Linda Spears, Springfield, MO. Rader Cecil married Bertha Smith, Gallipolis, Ohio. Walter Emerson married Claira Bradley, New Orleans, LA. Carroll R. married Gladys Pemberton, Ironton, Ohio, second wife, Helen Marie (Dufour) Aldridge, Ironton, Ohio, Lawrence County. Carl Stewart married Virginia Ruppert, Fairborn, Ohio. Otis Francis married Margarite Perovish, Waterloo, Ohio.

Mary Ida Belle married Carl Clarence Martin, Bowling Green, OH.

John Wesley married Donna Jean Grate, Waterloo, Ohio. Cecil and his first wife, Eyrcle, operated the McDaniel Grocery at McDaniel Crossroads which went bankrupt during the depression of 1929, also had a mail route from Wilgus to Rock Camp about 1915. He was a carpenter and a dairy farm operator in 1946. He bought another grocery business from Cecil and Thelma Cotton, his sister and husband. The grocery was located between Waterloo and Cadmus on State Route 141. He operated the grocery business until his death.

*Submitted by Jerry McDaniel, grandson of Cecil*

**CHARLES W. MCDANIEL, FIFTH GENERATION** - Charles W. born Oct. 24, 1860 died Jan. 7, 1940, married in March 19, 1887 to Margaret Isbelle Ridge born Dec. 13, 1871, died Aug. 10, 1938. She had 8 children:

1. Clarence Alden born Jan 5, 1888 died Aug. 5, 1951, married Dottie Boggess on March 29, 1909 she was born Sept. 12, 1886 died Oct. 20, 1972.

2. Bertha Carrie born Feb. 23 1889, died March 7, 1961, married John Henry Heidorn born July 24, 1881 died Dec. 6, 1957,

3. Leslie Rosetta, born July 8, 1892, died Feb. 8, 1983 married Leroy Merrow March 9, 1910.

4. Cecil Herbart born March 25, 1895 died June 7, 1962 married Ercyle Lexie Neal on Oct. 27, 1915,

5. Thelma Clarice born Sept. 23, 1900 died Feb 1, 2001. She lived 100 years 4 mos. 8 days married Cecil Cotton on Aug. 14, 1916 born Jan. 15, 1900 and died Aug. 12, 1987,

6. Ralph Emerson born Dec. 17, 1902 died Aug. 15, 1980 married Nov. 13, 1924 to Cora Blanche Taylor Feb. 27, 1907 died Jan. 25, 1995.,

7. Roy Clyde born Oct. 28, 1906 died July 27, 1959 married Lola Miller Oct 1934 b Aug. 21, 1915 died April 7,1971).

8. Emil Ray born Aug.10, 1915 died March 27, 1977 married to Inez Spears on March 14,1938 born Jan. 25,1919 died Sept. 17, 2001.

Charles W. McDaniel lived on Long Creek in Wilgus, Ohio. He taught school at Wilgus, Arabia, Greasey Ridge and Gallia in Greenfield, Township, Gallia Co. He married Margaret Ridge when she was one of his students, he was 26 and she was 15 at the time, he was a well known carpenter and built a barn in Wilgus in 1905 ,that still stands today. He operated a funeral business at Wilgus in the early 1900 and built his own coffin. He sold the funeral business to W.W. Phillips, after agreeing to not open another funeral business in that area. He was Postmaster at the Post Office in Arabia year 1905.

*Tombstone of Charles & Margaret McDaniel*

*Submitted by Davied McDaniel 2nd Great Grandson*

**EPHRAIM MC DANIEL & ELIZABETH BETSY SHUMATE, THIRD GENERATION** - Ephriam McDaniel was born in Monroe Co., VA. March 21, 1806. He moved to Walnut Twp., Gallia Co., Ohio when he was four years old married Elizabeth Betsy Shumate June 4, 1827 in Gallia Co. She is the daughter of Silias and Sarah (Cornwell) Shumate. Ephriam died Jan. 8, 1885 both are buried at Olive Cemetery, Walnut Twp., Gallia Co., Ohio.

*Ephraim McDaniel Tombstone*

They had 15 children: Henry born Feb 1, 1828 d in infancy. 2) Ursula born May 29, 1829 died Oct. 5, 1906, married Alfred L. Loucks. 3) Perry born Feb 18, 1831 died May 27, 1896 married Catherine Roush. 4) Minerva born Nov. 19, 1832 date of death unknown, married Robert J. Scott . 5) Marion born Sept. 18, 1834 died June 27, 1914 married Phoebe Bird. 6) Beuford Francis born Aug. 11, 1836 died May 30, 1907 married Feb. 12, 1860 Cynthia O. Powell born on Buck Creek Mason Twp., Lawrence Co., Ohio May 20, 1837 died Jan. 20, 1925 in Gallia Co., Ohio. 7) Mary born Oct. 13, 1838 died April 14, 1913 married Lorenzo B. Prose. 8) Hiram died in infancy May 6, 1839. 9) John born Nov. 17, 1840 died May 16, 1861 never married. 10) Margaret Elizabeth born Sept. 22, 1842 died 1931 married first to Joshua Hall and second to Rev. William Wiseman. 11) Benjamin Franklin born Jan 1845 died in Davis City Iowa married Cynthia June Patterson. 12) Sara born Dec 13, 1847 died April 3, 1910 in Washington C. H. , Ohio Fayette Co. She married John Lambert born Jan. 11, 1848 Aid Twp., Lawrence Co., Ohio died July 26, 1921 in Dayton, Ohio. 13) Wesley born Aug. 29, 1848 died 1928 in Chesapeake, Ohio married Mary Wiseman 14) Abigal born three mo. in 1850 census not in 1860 census 15) Diannah born July 1,1851 died in infancy.

*Submitted by Alden E. McDaniel: Great, Great, Great Grandson*

**EPHRAIM MC DANIEL** - Ephraim McDaniel was born March 2, 1806, in Monroe County, (West) Virginia. He was the son of Henry McDaniel, Jr., and Hannah Bryan. He was their ninth known child. He married Elizabeth Betsey Shumate June 4, 1827, in Gallia County, Ohio. She was the daughter of Silas Shumate and Sarah (Sally) Cornwell.

Many books incorrectly refer to Ephraim McDaniel as the first white male born in Walnut Township, Gallia County, Ohio, including Hardesty's "History of Gallia County". The truth is Ephraim was actually born in Monroe County, Virginia, (now West Virginia) on March 2, 1806. His parents did not move to Gallia County, Ohio, until 1812.

The 1850 Census of Walnut Township, Gallia County, Ohio, listed Ephraim McDaniel as a 45 year old male farmer who was born in Virginia with $500 worth of real estate. He and his wife had 12 children living with them at this time. The children were listed as Ersula-21, Perry-19, Minerva-18, Marion-16, Francis-14, Mary-13, John M.-10, Margaret-8, Benjamin L.-5, Sarah-4, Wesley-3, Abigail-3 months.

Ephraim McDaniel and his family were also recorded on the 1830, 1840, 1870 and 1880 census of Walnut Township, Gallia County, Ohio. He and his family were apparently missed by the census taker in 1860 as no record of him can be found on that particular census. Ephraim McDaniel lived in this area of Gallia County, Ohio, for over 70 years. He was a farmer in Gallia County, Ohio, throughout the entire course of his life.

Ephraim McDaniel died in Walnut Township, Gallia County, Ohio, on January 8, 1885, and his wife died on July 20, 1891. They were buried in the Olive Cemetery, in Walnut Township, Gallia County, Ohio.

Ephraim McDaniel and his wife had at least fifteen known children, namely Henry, Ursula, Perry, Minerva E., Marion J., Beuford Francis, Mary, Hiram, John M., Margaret E., Benjamin F., Sarah, Wesley, Abigail and Diannah. Ephraim McDaniel was a second cousin once removed of the President of the United States Abraham Lincoln.

Henry died as an infant. Ursula married Alfred L. Louks, Perry married Catherine Roush, Minerva Elizabeth never married and we have no record of her after 1850. Marion J. McDaniel married Phoebe Elizabeth Bird. Beuford Francis McDaniel married Cynthia Catherine Powell. Mary McDaniel married Lorenzo Barthenius Prose. Hiram McDaniel died as an infant. John

M. McDaniel died at the age of 23 from tuberculosis on his way home after being discharged from service in the Civil War. Margaret Elizabeth McDaniel married Joshua Hall and Andrew Wiseman. Benjamin Franklin McDaniel was married to Cynthia June Patterson. Sarah McDaniel was married to John Lambert. Wesley McDaniel was married to Mary Augusta Wiseman. Abigail and Diannah appear to have died as infants.

*Submitted by Kelly R. Greer*

**HENRY MC DANIEL, SR., FIRST GENERATION** - Henry McDaniel, Sr., born 1730, Ireland, moving from Scotland to Northern Ireland. He and his father, Alexander, immigrated to the new world on the ship "Bachelor" arriving in New York in 1740. His brothers, Caleb and Sylvester, came at a later date. Henry Sr. served as captain in the French and Indian War. He later settled in Halifax, Pittsylvania, Greenbrier and Monroe Counties in Virginia. He was an appraiser and surveyor, surveying land for President George Washington on January 27, 1777. An appraiser for the Court of Bedford County, VA, he helped lay out the town of Peterson, VA. He was on the Board of Trustees in 1799 when Monroe County was formed from Greenbrier County, VA. Henry Sr.'s first wife was Mary Ann Porter, died between 1785 and 1793. She had eight children: James, John, Henry Jr., William, David, Nancy, Patsy and Ann. He married his second wife, Ann Catherine Keller. She was a Gore before her first marriage December 25, 1793, died in 1840. Henry Sr. died 1819. They had two children: Isacc and Peggy.

*Submitted by Jeromy Dee McDaniel*

**HENRY MC DANIEL, JR., SECOND GENERATION** - Henry Jr. was born October 7, 1763, Pittsylvania County, VA, in the spring of 1779.

At age 15, he enlisted in the Revolutionary Army at Bedford County, VA. He was part of Lynches Rangers. After obtaining his discharge at the end of the Revolutionary War, he returned home to Greenbrier County, VA, and worked at farming and took up the copper trade.

On May 15, 1788, he married Hannah Bryan, born September 9, 1770. Legend has it that Hannah was an aunt to Abraham Lincoln. Sources say Henry Jr. came on a hunting expedition with Daniel Boone in 1799. He liked this part of the country, and he returned in 1808 to claim his property. He went to Chillicothe, Ohio, to pay for his section of land, 648 acres in fertile Symmes Creek Bottom, which is now Walnut Township, Gallia County. It was required to buy a section of land which is 648 acres because he was in the Revolutionary War. Henry Jr. was the first settler in Walnut Township, Gallia County, in 1810. While building his cabin on this land, he lived in a hollow sycamore tree which measured approximately eight feet in diameter. Upon completion of his cabin, he moved his family here in 1810 from Monroe County, VA. In 1799 his personal property tax in Monroe County, VA, was $2.60 but in Walnut Township in 1810 it was 12 cents. Henry Jr. was a constable, auctioneer and Justice of the Peace of Walnut Township. He married several couples in his capacity as Justice of the Peace. Henry Jr. and Hannah had 10 children:

1. John born May 1, 1789, died December 21, 1854, married Mary (Polly) Shumate August 8, 1812.
2. Caleb born September 2, 1790, died October 19, 1874, married Martha (Patsy Williams on September 4, 1811.
3. Jehu born May 28, 1792, died August 7, 1857, married October 14, 1813, to Elizabeth Boggs, born September 2, 1792, died July 20, 1841.
4. Sarah McDaniel born 1796, married Andrew Boggs.
5. Bryan born 1797, married January 3, 1819, to Elizabeth Prose, born April 7, 1800, died February 13, 1888. Bryan accidentally shot himself with a gun while cleaning it in 1822.
6. Alexander born 1802, died November 21, 1875, married January 25, 1825, to Margaret Shumate, born September 30, 1810, died January 14, 1896.
7. Benjamin born March 21, 1804, died March 22, 1883, married Mary Smith 1828, born in 1796.
8. Ephriam born March 2, 1806, died January 8, 1885, married June 4, 1827, to Elizabeth (Betsy) Shumate, born May 12, 1813, in Lawrence County, Mason Township, died July 20, 1891, Walnut Township, Gallia County, OH.
9. Celia born 1810 died 1864, married February 16, 1826, to Elizah Shumate born 1803, died August 4, 1880.
10. Hiram died as an infant. He was the first child born in Walnut Township, Gallia County, OH.

Note: Children of Alexander are Ephriam and Celia. All had the same set of grandparents, Silas and Sarah Shumate as well as Henry Jr. and Hannah McDaniel. Silas is a brother to (Polly) Mary, John's wife.

*Submitted by Mary McDaniel Martin, third great grandfather*

**HENRY MC DANIEL, JR.** - Henry McDaniel, Jr., was born on November 7, 1763, in Halifax County, Virginia, to Henry McDaniel, Sr., and his first wife, Mary Ann. Some believe that his mother's maiden name was Porter, and that she was the daughter of Ambrose Porter. The parents of Henry McDaniel, Sr., are unknown at this time.

Nothing is known about Henry McDaniel, Jr.'s, early childhood, until he enlisted to fight in the Revolutionary War. However, we do know that he grew up in Halifax, Pittsylvania and Bedford Counties in Virginia. He enlisted in the Revolutionary Army from Bedford County, Virginia, when he was only 15 years old in the spring of 1779. He fought in the Battle of Stoney Point, and at a skirmish at Hawfield's on the Yadkin River in the "Carolina", and he was wounded in the Battle of King's Mountain. Some historians consider this battle to have been the turning point of the Revolutionary War.

After his military service in the Revolutionary War, Henry McDaniel, Jr., settled in Greenbrier County, VA, in an area that later became Monroe County, VA, and is now a part of West Virginia; i.e., the Peterstown area. His parents and siblings had moved to this area while he was serving in the Revolutionary War. He is recorded on Tax and Census lists on Monroe County through 1811.

Henry McDaniel, Jr., received a land grant for 648 acres (one section) in the fertile area of Symmes Creek bottom, which is today known as Walnut Township in Gallia County, Ohio.

Family legend says that Henry McDaniel first came to Ohio in 1808 and that he built his log cabin before he brought his family to the area. While he was building this log cabin, he slept in a hollow tree in order to protect himself from wild animals.

The 1812 Gallia County, Ohio Chattels (Tax) List shows Henry McDaniel as a resident of Green Township (this area later became Perry and finally Walnut Township). Henry is shown here in 1812 as the owner of six horses and four cows.

As a Justice of the Peace, Henry McDaniel married many of the young couples in this area. He also conducted many of the various lawsuits that developed. Because of a shortage of lawyers, a class of men called Pettifoggers were employed in the various courts. According to an article in the *Hanging Rock Iron Region*, Henry McDaniel was one of the most noted Pettifoggers in the area. Henry McDaniel also acted as the auctioneer at many sales in the area as well.

Henry died on September 28, 1838, and his wife, Hannah, died on May 5, 1841. They were buried on their farm in a private cemetery. The grave plot is fenced with an iron fence and was once marked by the French Colony Chapter of the DAR.

Henry McDaniel and his wife, Hannah, had at least nine children, namely: John, Caleb, Jehu, Sarah, Bryan, Alexander, Benjamin, Ephraim, and Celia.

Henry's wife, Hannah Bryan, was the daughter of Lydia Lincoln and her first husband. Hannah was a first cousin once removed of a man who would become President of the United States after her death; i.e., Abraham Lincoln.

*Submitted by Kelly R. Greer*

**DAVID WILLIAM (BILL) MC KENZIE AND WILMA CHARLENE (LEEDY) MC KENZIE FAMILY** - Wilma Charlene (Leedy) McKenzie was born March 17, 1934, in Jackson, Ohio. She resided at the family farm located on Jisco Road until she entered nurse's training in 1952. Her parents came to Jackson, Ohio, from Wytheville, Virginia, and their move to this area was influenced by Mrs. Gertrude Allie Copenhaver Leedy, her grandmother.

Gertrude Allie Copenhaver Leedy came to Jackson, Ohio, from Wytheville, Virginia, in 1920 and purchased a farm on Pleasant Grove Road. Allie's husband was William Josiah Leedy. To this union were born: Rupert Roosevelt, Edward Vance, Lucy (Leedy) Tudor, Lillian Gertrude (Leedy) Miller, Isaac Rufus Leedy, and William Neal Leedy.

Rupert and Avis Layne Walters Leedy, Charlene's parents had six children: Rupert Dean Leedy, Ennis Hope (Leedy) Keller, Wilma Charlene (Leedy), McKenzie, Vivian Janette (Leedy) Roe Bevins, Donald Walters Leedy and Mary Avis (Leedy) Evans.

Charlene's first introduction to Gallia County was when she visited her Aunt Katherine Elizabeth Walker who resided in Kanauga, Ohio. Charlene came to Gallipolis, Ohio, in 1952 after graduating from Jackson High School and entered nurse's training at Holzer School of Nursing. Charlene graduated in 1955, then passed the state board exam and became a registered nurse. She was employed at Holzer Medical Center from 1955 to 1977.

*David Mc Kenzie, Charlene Mc Kenzie Phillp, Jeffrey and Jozie*

David William (Bill) McKenzie was born January 2, 1935, in Racine, Ohio, the son of James William McKenzie and Laura Ellen (Shain) McKenzie. James W. McKenzie was born in 1905 in Beaver Falls, Pennsylvania, and Laura E. McKenzie was born 1907 in Antiquity, Ohio. James' parents were David Newton McKenzie and Adda Mitilida (Morrison) McKenzie. Laura's parents were Samuel B. Shain and Susan L. (Watson) Shain.

Charlene met David in 1952 when he was a patient in Holzer Hospital. They were married October 14, 1956, in Oak Hill, Ohio. He served two years (1954-1956) in the U.S. Army in Germany and holds a life membership with the 14th Armored Cavalry. He worked at Kyger Creek (OVEC) for two years and entered the University of Rio Grande in 1958. After graduating with a B.S. in secondary education, he taught at Southwestern and Gallia Academy. In 1964 David was employed by the U.S. Department of Agriculture (USDA) and retired in 1992.

To this union, three children were born—James Phillip McKenzie, July 27, 1958; Jeffrey David McKenzie, December 14, 1960, and Jozie Patrize (McKenzie) Roberts, March 17, 1962. All three children were born at Holzer Medical Center and graduated from Gallia Academy High School. James Phillip graduated from the Ohio State University with a B.S. in Dairy Science and Agriculture Education. Jeffrey David graduated from the University of Rio Grande and is a medical technologist at Veterans Hospital in Durham, North Carolina. Jozie Patrize is a graduate from the University of Rio Grande and teaches school at New Haven Elementary in West Virginia.

*Submitted by Wilma Charlene McKenzie*

**THOMAS MC KINNEY FAMILY** - In 1918 or 1919, Annie Crowe McKinney and her son, Thomas Clinton McKinney, came to Addison Township from Fayette County, WV. Thomas's father, William W. McKinney, died November 30, 1915, in a mine explosion at Boomer, WV. On December 24, 1928, Annie married Jacob Vance Baker. Jacob died in 1947 and is buried in the Baker Cemetery, Addison, Township. Annie died January 28, 1968, in Holzer Hospital, Gallipolis, and is buried in Reynolds Cemetery, Addison, Ohio. Thomas was born August 25, 1909, in Mount Carbon, WV; on November 23, 1932, he married Darlene Louise Kingery, daughter of William Henry and Nancy Katherine Callicoat Kingery in Catlettsburg, KY. Thomas worked at various power plants from 1953-1971 as an electrician. He was a member of the Solom Masonic Lodge 456 of Cheshire, Grand Chapter of Royal Arch Masons Chapter 80 of Pomeroy, Grand Council Royal and Select Masons Bosworth Council 46 of Pomeroy, Ohio Valley Commandry No. 24 Knights Templar of Middleport, and he was a Master Mason for 37 years. Thomas and Darlene had five children: Audrey Ellen born August 19, 1934, in Cheshire; in 1952 she married Arnold Ray Mitchell in Cheshire. They had three children: Pamela Rae born June 26, 1954; Robert Clinton born January 19, 1956; and Teresa Ellen born August 7, 1961. Audrey died unexpectedly April 14, 1980, at her home in Cheshire; she is buried in Reynolds Cemetery, Addison, Ohio. Thomas and Darlene's second child was Owen Clinton McKinney who was born November 26, 1935, at the home of his parents. His first wife was Charlotte Priddy. They had four children Ronald Eugene born March 21, 1957; Peggy Sue born September 17, 1958; Randall Eugene born February 11, 1960; and Patricia Ann born January 20, 1961. Owen died November 11, 1996, at his home in Addison from cancer and is buried in Poplar Ridge Cemetery, Cheshire Township. Thomas and Darlene's third child is Selby Ann born May 9, 1937, at Holzer Hospital, Gallipolis. On June 24, 1956, she married Raymond Eugene Manley at her parent's home. They had three children: Cathy Jo born November 18, 1958; Joseph Ray born July 6, 1966; and Kevin Eugene born February 15, 1970. Raymond died August 20, 1996, at his home in Middleport, Ohio, from a heart attack. He is buried in the Middleport Hill Cemetery. Thomas and Darlene's fourth child is William Richard born April 8, 1940, at his parent's home on December 28, 1963. He married Virginia Rose James at Eureka, Ohio. They had two children: William Matthew born February 21, 1967, and Valerie Rose born January 8, 1970. Thomas and Darlene's fifth child is Evelyn Juanita, born May 16, 1946, in Pt. Pleasant, WV. On February 28, 1965, she married Lloyd James Sears. They have two children Evelyn Darlene born July 3, 1965, and Lloyd James, Jr., born November 3, 1972. Thomas died December 9, 1991, at his home in Cheshire from heart failure. Darlene died June 13, 1999, at Holzer Medical Center from a heart attack. Both are buried in Reynolds Cemetery, Addison, Ohio.

*Submitted by Shelby Manley*

**MC MULLEN, MC MILLEN, MC MULLIN** - Edward McMullen was born in Botetourt County, Virginia, in 1735. He married Catherine Morelock in Augusta County, Virginia, in 1760. Their four children were John, Elizabeth, Margot, and Agnes. Edward served as a Sergeant in the Revolutionary War. He died in 1788.

Edward's second marriage was to Sarah Robinson and resulted in twelve children. One of their sons, Edward Tate McMullen, born in 1767, in Greenbrier County, Virginia, married Sarah Reed (Reid) in Botetourt County, Virginia, in 1787. Their marriage produced twelve children. The third child, Joseph McMullen, was born in 1793 in Augusta County, Virginia, married Jane Gay (Guy) in Gallia County, Ohio, September 15, 1815. They had six children. Joseph later married Lydia Cromwell and his third wife was Polly Steel. Joseph died in Morgan Township, Gallia County, Ohio.

Joseph and Jane Gay (Guy)' s daughter, Amanda, born 1816, married James McGhee, Jr. Their daughter Jane McGhee was born in 1840. She married John S. Wallace in 1857. They were my great grandparents.

John and Jane had four children: Altona (Koontz), Hattie (Volborn), Ellen (Glenn), and James Franklin. Their son known as "Frank" married Catherine "Kitty" Grate. Their children were: Leah (Wilcox) Walter, Theadore, and Cecile.

Cecile married Von C. Thompson who were the parents of Bess (Wilson), Joe, Lonnie, Leah (Wion) and Tommy.

*Submitted by Leah Thompson Wion*

**NIDAY-MENZER FAMILY** - Cynthia Melaine Niday was born May 18, 1968 to Victor Joe and Mary Elizabeth Walker Niday. Her parents brought her home to the same house where her father was born and grew up. The Niday farm, Fairmount Jersey Farm, is located on Lincoln Pike near Northup, Green Township, Gallia County. Her grandparents, Victor Paul and Margaret Donnally Niday lived across the road, and she had cousins living a few miles away. Cynthia's maternal grandparents, Samuel Jackson Tandy "Jack" and Zelma Phillips Walker lived at Cora, Perry Township, Gallia County. They had lived in Cora almost all of their married lives and raised their children in that community. In 1969, they moved to Thurman, Ohio.

*The Menzers
Cynthia & Mike in back & sons Zac & Drew*

Cynthia has one brother, Victor Richard Niday, who was born on August 1, 1969. Growing up, they attended Green Elementary School and Gallia Academy High School. Both children were active in 4-H. Cynthia played the trombone in the high school band. After graduating from Gallia Academy High School in 1986, Cynthia attended Rio Grande Community College and Ohio State University. Cynthia met and married Michael James Menzer, a graduate of Bucknell University. Mike is the son of Paul Johnson and Barbara Ann Lee Menzer. He was born May 30, 1963 in Syracuse, NY; he is the youngest of four boys.

Mike and Cynthia's oldest son, Zachary Paul Menzer, was born February 1, 1990 at Holzer Medical Center in Gallipolis, Ohio. When Zac was seven weeks old, the Menzer family relocated to Granville, Licking County, Ohio. A second son, Drew Donnally Menzer, joined Zac on June 7, 1991. Drew was born at Riverside Methodist Hospital in Columbus, Ohio. Currently, Zac plays the saxophone and has aspirations of becoming an architect. Drew plays the violin and plans to become an attorney. Both boys love tennis and golf. Cynthia has been a stay-at-home mom since Zac was born. She has also been active at the boys' school and in community activities. Mike works for Paramount Financial Group, the company he started in 1987. He is active on several boards and loves to golf in his spare time.

Their Gallia County roots are the Niday, Donnally, Walker, Phillips, Graham, Engel, Jones, Trowbridge, McCall, Cherrington, Lang, Blake, Phelps, James, Martin, and Elliott families. Only one of Cynthia's greatgrandparents was not born in Gallia County. Even though they have not grown up in Gallia County, Zac and Drew have deep roots in this area. They love to visit their grandparents and all of their aunts, uncles, and cousins that still live in Gallia County. The Menzer family will always have affection for Gallia County and our Gallia County families.

*Submitted by: Cynthia Niday Menzer*

**CYNTHIA JEAN MIDDLETON** - Cynthia Jean (Waugh) Middleton was born on 24 February 1974 in Gallipolis, Ohio. She is the daughter of Ronald Carrol and Donna Jean (Cox) Waugh and has an older sister Carrie Rene' (18 Aug. 1971) and a younger brother Jeremiah Ronald (29 Jan. 1977).

*Clayton & Cynthia Middleton*

*Kyra Elizabeth Middleton*

She is the 12th generation to live on American soil. She went to school at Hannan Trace School. She was one of the first to start college in High School through Secondary Education at the University of Rio Grande, going during her junior and senior years. She graduated with Honors in 1992 and went on to get a scholarship at Mary Baldwin College in Staunton, Virginia. She went to school there in the Fall of 1992 playing Volleyball. Due to the rising costs of the private school, she returned to the University of Rio Grande in 1993. There she majored in Psychology and minored in Political Science, graduating in 1996, with a Bachelor's Degree in Science. While at school, she met and fell in love with Clayton Middleton. He graduated in 1995 with a Business Administration degree and became a Real Estate Appraiser. After three year of dating, they were married on September 21, 1996 at St. Louis Catholic Church in Gallipolis, Ohio. They moved back to Clayton's hometown of Sidney, Ohio and have been there ever since.

Since that time Cynthia has worked at New Choices, a domestic violence shelter, where she worked as a house monitor and administrative assistant, while training to become a Victim's Advocate. Then in late 1997, she became a Legal Advocate helping women and men through the court system, ensuring that their voices were heard. In 1998, she started a weekly support group for battered women while advocating for them in court. Also that year, she became involved with the Leukemia Society of America and walked in the Inaugural Rock 'n' Roll Marathon, 26.2 miles in San Diego, California. In 1999, she started a child advocacy program for the shelter and became a child advocate. She was a mentor at Central Elementary and became a Big Sister through Shelby County Big Brothers and Big Sisters. In the spring of 2000, she began volunteering for the Shelby County Juvenile Court system as a court appointed Guardian Ad Litem (GAL). On November 3, Clay and Cynthia were blessed with their first child, a daughter named Kyra (keer-rah) Elizabeth Middleton. She was the first grandchild on both sides. After the birth of their daughter Cynthia went back to work part-time and quit New Choices in June of 2001. She helped to organize and start the Shelby County CASA/GAL Organization, which officially opened its doors in March of 2002. She is the director of this program, which trains volunteer Court Appointed Special Advocates (CASA) to help children that are in abusive and neglected homes through Juvenile Court. Her husband, Clayton, became a Sidney Police Officer in 1998, where he has been a road officer, school resource officer and is now a detective.

**JAMES MILLER & AMANDA WHITE** - James was born in October 1796 in Rockingham County, Virginia. It seems likely he was related to one of the Miller families in the area, but no evidence has been discovered. We know only that his mother's name was Nancy. James married Amanda White in Gallia County on 1 November 1825. Her obituary calls James a resident of Gallia County at the time of their marriage.

Shortly after James and Amanda married, the couple removed first to Marion County, and then to Fairfield County, Ohio. Following a brief stay in Cedar County, Iowa, James purchased 86 acres in Jones County, Iowa on 3 February 1848. There the couple remained. The area was known as Bowen's Prairie, located in Richland Township. Unfortunately, the couple was not found there on the 1850 Census, however they do appear at Bowen's Prairie in 1860: James Miller, 60, VA; Amanda, 52, NY; Alexander, 20, OH; Hana, 17, OH; John R., 14, IA; Alex, 17, farm hand, OH. The 17-year-old "Alex" Miller is not believed to be a son of James and Amanda, though he may certainly have been a relation.

According to Amanda's obituary, the couple had ten children, "six of whom live to mourn her death". Only six children are known. Mary, born 14 April 1830 in Gallia County, married first John Moore about 1849 and second, Luther McVey 23 May 1861. "Perry", whose full name may have been Oliver Perry Winslow, was born 3 April 1833 in Gallia County. He married first, Elizabeth J. Murphy 28 December 1856 and second, Elizabeth Catherine Cook 14 October 1862. Alfred Samuel (or Samuel Alfred) was born about 1837 in Marion County and married Martha Jane Rolston 11 April 1859. Isaac "Alexander", born 10 May 1839 in Marion County, married Corneia "Nell" Mundinger 13 August 1864. Moriah, seen as "Hana" in 1860, was born about 1843 in Marion County. John R., born about 1846 at Bowen's Prairie, married Sarah (aka Maria) Kellum of Warrensburg, Kentucky, daughter of Ben and Maria (Farley) Kellum on 5 May 1867.

Amanda White, second daughter of Gallia County First Family Alfred and Mary (Perry) White, was born 25 June 1807, probably in Pennsylvania. Descendants of Amanda had been doubtful of her parentage, but the recent discovery of an article in the Gallipolis Journal 18 March 1875 seems to put the debate to rest. Sixty years ago Alfred White and Mary, his wife, both long since dead, settled in Gallia County... They were the parents of quite a family of children, all remarkable for their longevity. The children now living are Mrs. Armennie Scurlock, aged seventy years, Mrs. Amanda Miller, aged sixty-eight, Rufus White, aged sixty-four, Mrs. Cynthia Burke, aged sixty, George White, aged fifty-six, and Mrs. Rachel Thompson, aged fifty-two. These parties had not been together for thirty-two years,' until the other day, when they met at Rufus,' in Perry township.

James Miller died 25 Jul 1876 in Jones County, Iowa and is buried at Bowen's Prairie Cemetery beside his mother, Nancy. Anianda (White) Miller died 11 April 1896 and was laid to rest beside her husband.

*Submitted By: Linda Gaylord-kuhn*

**JOSEPH MILLER, INDIAN AGENT** - Joseph Miller, b. 1762, son of John Miller, came from Wheeling, Virginia (WV) to Gallipolis, Ohio about the year 1790. He lived in the stockades and was employed by the government as an Indian Agent from about 1790 to 1795. He carried the mail by canoe from Gallipolis, Ohio to Mayesville, Ky. under hostile conditions. At one time the Indians attacked and killed a helper and wounded the other. This occurred near Sciotiville on the Kentucky side. Joseph jumped into the river calling to the wounded man to do the same. They kept the canoe between them and the Indians and swam to the shore. After binding up the broken arm of the wounded man and taking the mail they walked to Gallipolis, following a trail back of the river.

Joseph married Elizabeth Diggins June 20, 1797 at Gallipolis, Ohio. She was Irish, a Roman Catholic, and spoke French. He was a man of great physical endurance. He could run all day without any great amount of fatigue. He was five feet ten inches in height, having dark hair and blue eyes. He always wore buckskin clothes.

At one time he commanded the settlers in a fight with some Indians in Ohio, some distance from the river.

In 1800 Joseph was a Justice at Gallipolis. About the year 1796 he settled with his family at the mouth of Federal Creek in Lawrence County. Being a strong Federalist, when some people passing in a boat inquired the name of the creek he replied "Federal Creek" This gave the name to the creek. His home stood just above the mouth of the creek a few rods from the river. He owned 56 acres. Nineteen acres where he lived remains in the family today and is owned by his great, great, great grandson, James T. Knight and his wife Clara.

Joseph and his brother Isaac enlisted in the war of 1812. The war ended before they saw action.

Joseph hunted with the great pioneers, Daniel Boone, Lewis Wetzel and his first cousin Simon Kenton.

Soon after 1800 the old pioneer John Miller came to make his home with his son Joseph, bringing his wife and widowed daughter Mrs. Susan Druilliard with her children.

Joseph Miller spent his closing years in the quiet of a farmer's life, highly respected by the community. He was quite a reader in his old age and kept posted on the political movements of his time. He would lie for hours under a shade tree reading history and current events.

Joseph and Elizabeth had ten children, Elizabeth, Nancy, Lydia, Hetzie, Mary, Jacob, James, Isaac, Abraham and Robert. Joseph died in 1845 and was buried in the Millersport cemetery with his wife beside him. They had no tombstone but the tombstone of their son Jacob was wrongly placed on Josephs grave. We recently found his grave.

When the last of the Indians passed down the river on their way West, Joseph spoke to them in their native tongue and invited them to come ashore and eat apples in the orchard. They enjoyed his hospitality. No Indians were ever again seen upon that river. They have gone and so have the pioneers.

*Submitted by Clara Knight*

**LEWIS AND JANE ANN (FALLON) MILLER FAMILY** - At the time of the last Gallia History Book, we were expecting our second child. We were blessed with a little girl. We named her Dorothy Lu. Dorothy, after my Aunt Dorothy Juanita Tackett who was a great influence on my spiritual life, and Lu after Lewis, my husband. I was born at Gage, Ohio, to Vernard Fallon who passed away in 1982 and Hope Cochran Fallon who now lives at Patriot, Ohio, which is her birth place. On her father's side was the Rev. John A. Davies from Wales. Augusta, her grandmother on her mother's side traveled here from Hanover, Germany. She was the daughter of Christopher and Hannah Raulf who settled outside of Patriot in 1863.

My father's name was rooted in Ireland, O'Fallon; but, in the sixteenth century, the Gaelic prefix was dropped. He grew up in Rush, KY. He came to Gallia County in 1938. He served in the army from February 9, 1942 till January 1946. He received Decorations and Citations for the Asiatic-Pacific Theater Ribbon with three Bronze Stars, Philippine Liberation Ribbon with one star. There is a town in Illinois called O'Fallon and some day I plan to go there. I have two brothers Gary and Larry. Lewis's father was Vergil Ray Miller who was born June 27, 1914, in Addison, Ohio, to James and Cario (Betz) Miller. James was born in Sebasties, Kansas, November 13, 1881. Neal Cario was born March 26, 1888, to Colonel D. and Helen (Reed) Betz of Addison Township.

*Lewis Miller Family*

Lewis' mother, Mary Elizabeth (Roush) Miller was born December 13, 1918, at Cheshire, Ohio. She was born to Orren Roush who was born November 4, 1872, and Martha Viola (Folden) Roush. Viola, was the daughter of Tom and Mary (Saxton) Folden. Vergil and Mary have both passed away. Lewis has two living brothers, James Orren and Hoyt. He has three sisters: Kay, Joyce and Kathy. His oldest brother, Dean, lost his life when the Silver Bridge went down. Carrie Elizabeth, our oldest daughter, was named after her grandmother and great grandmother. She and her husband, Joel Justice, both graduated from Ohio State University and live in Columbus, Ohio. Dorothy will graduate this fall from Columbus State College. Lewis and I were married May 5, 1974, in the Patriot United Methodist Church. After a dear friend and mentor, Rev. P. A. Casto retired from this church, he suggested I pastor it. I am now the Lay Pastor of the church where I grew up and was married. What a blessing to serve in the same church that my great grandmother attended. We feel blessed to have been raised in Gallia County. We look forward to taking our grandchildren to the little church on the hill, walk them on the trails of Raccoon Park that was a corn field when I road the bus to Perry School,and take them to the city park where we have spent many 4$^{th}$ of July events. I hope one day to set them on the counter of my little art shop in Patriot and tell them about their ancestors from Germany, Wales and Ireland, who came to find a peaceful land to worship God and raise their families. Something I have learned in writing this, "We do not realize how much we don't know, till those that really knew are gone."

*Submitted by Jane Ann Miller*

**JAMES MILLS AND EDNA LOIS LUMAN RODGERS** - Edna Lois Luman (March 17, 1924) married James Mills Rodgers (June 17, 1923-March 12, 2000) on September 13, 1945, at the Grace Methodist Church in Gallipolis. Edna was born in Walnut Township, Gallia County, to Clarence Colson and Dora Frances Null Luman. She graduated from Cadmus High School. Edna worked for Keller's Grocery, Evans Grocery, and retired from the Gallipolis Developmental Center. Jim was the son of James Mills and Guineth Eggleton Rodgers. He graduated from Gallia Academy. Jim served in the U. S. Navy, worked for the Evans Grocery Company, and retired from the Ohio Valley Electric Corporation's Kyger Creek Plant. They have five children born in Gallia County:

James Mills III (December 11, 1946) married Frances Bible.

Frederick Colson (January 25, 1949) married Cathy Aston on September 19, 1993. They have one daughter, Jordan Elizabeth (July 4, 1998).

Lois Marlene (September 29, 1959) married Larry Snyder (divorced). They have two children, Melissa (June 14, 1970) who married Chadwick Wooten in 1989; they have two sons Derek Allen and Tyler Colson Wooten. Son John David (March 18, 1976) who has three children: Kanessa Davielle (mother Courtney Watson), Jacob David (mother Patricia DeWoody) and Ryan James (mother Kathy Vandusen).

Marsha Ann (October 7, 1951) married Edward Pauley (divorced) and Rob Rohrs. Their children are Elizabeth Marie Pauley Smith (January 9, 1976) and James Edward Pauley (June 17, 1977).

Nancy Ellen (July 23, 1954) married Mark Denney (divorced) and Bob Crowell. Her daughter is Kara Nicole Denney (June 24, 1978).

*Submitted by Edna Rodgers*

**(STONE) EDDY-MITCHELL** - We are the oldest daughters of Beulah (Wood) Stone and the late Orville F. Stone. Beulah is still living at the age of 93; we are so lucky to still have her. Our father, Orville and his twin sister, Marvel, were born on August 10, 1907. Marvel married William (Bill) Bass. Dad was given the name Arvel but later changed it to Orville and changed his Social Security number to Orville. Marvel passed away in May of 1994 and Dad passed on November 8, 1994. He was 87 years, 2 months, and 8 days old when he died.

We are the daughters of a coal miner and very proud of it. We were born and raised in West Virginia. We grew up in Kanawha County's Cabin Creek, Boone County's Wharton and Raleigh County's Dorothy, West Virginia.

*Elizabeth (Libby) Mitchell*

I, Jewel (Sis) married Harry (Bud) Eddy and left West Virginia for Ohio in Sept. of 1961. I am now living in Gallipolis, Ohio, where I look after my mother. And I, Elizabeth (Libby) married James (Jim) Mitchell and left West Virginia for Ohio in l958. I am now living in Columbus, Ohio where I am a homemaker and look after my grand children and great grand children.

We often get together to laugh and talk about the good times of our childhood. We remember the deep snows, running to the outhouse to get in and out quickly, and the holidays, especially Christmas and Independence Day. Dad would help clean the house and go on a hunt for the "perfect" tree. Once he brought a tree home, he would trim it and decorate the house for hours. He would make a large dish of Fruit Salad. Everyone enjoyed and loved his "famous" Fruit Salad. No one can make Fruit Salad like our Daddy did.

*Jewell Eddy*

I, Jewel remember the Christmas that Dad hid my necklace and bracelet set that I wanted so badly. He let me hunt for it for a while. We would listen to Cap Andy and Flip and Gangbusters on the radio while he made a big pan of fudge. On Independence Day, Dad would order ice cream from the company store. It came in 5 gallon buckets packed in dry ice. We would have the flavors Vanilla Chocolate, and Strawberry. Needless to say it never melted.

I, Elizabeth lost Jim, who was my best friend, on December 21, 1995. Our son, Dewayne, married Sharon Gibson. They have 2 daughters and 1 son. Our 2 daughters, Elizabeth Gail (Princess) and Marlene both married. Princess married William (Bill) Edison. She has one son. She later changed the spelling of her name to Gayle. Marlene, my youngest, married Kenny Bailey. She has one son.

I, Jewel have 3 children living. I lost Steve, my oldest, on February 6, 2001. My son, Wayne married Laura Wellington and has 2 daughters and 1 son. Carol, my oldest daughter, married Jim Whittington and has 1 daughter together and a son of Carol's. They have 1 grandson. Dreama, the baby, married Larry Taylor and have 1 son together and one of Larry's.

We want all of the future generations to know a little about their roots so, we wrote a little about our childhood. We hope they all will someday enjoy some of the memories they have with us and with their families.

As of today, March 16, 2002, I, Libby have 3 grand children, 2 step grand children, 6 great grand children, and 3 step great grand children. I, Jewel, have 8 grand children, 1 step grandson, and 2 great grand children.
*Submitted by: Jewel Eddy & Libby Mitchell*

**ASA WASHINGTON MOORE** - Asa was born to Silas and Millie Moore on December 11, 1880. He had a brother, William Franklin, born in 1878. The boys were admitted to the Gallia County Children's Home at the ages of seven and nine years old on October 5, 1887, after their mother passed away and father being incapable to care for them. Chris and Belle Getting of Rodney, having no children, took the boys into their home to help care for their large farm. At the age of 15, Uncle Willie left the farm in search of his father.

He later settled in Coalton, Ohio, married Louise Friend and had two daughters, Clara (Chloe), and Jeanette. My father, Ma, went north in the fall to husk corn on the larger farms. He met and married Flora May McNeir in Union County, Ohio. To this union was born Ruth (Harry) Lowry, Edna (Marion) Wood, Eva (whom died in infancy), Helen (Frank) Hill, Harold (Helen Gatewood), Charles (Alice Wood), Mary (Paul Denney), Blanche (Joe Carr) and Walter. The whole family moved back to Gallia County in 1919 onto the property of Chris and Belle Getting, which they gave to my dad for returning home. This property was located on Rodney Harrisburg Road, about two miles from Rodney. We were raised here among the fruit trees, cattle, sheep, tobacco, and the best "applejack", so they say.

In later years we learned Grandpa Silas had remarried and had a son, Elmer, in Jackson County then remarried once more to Sarah Jones in Vinton County, where they had four children, Everett, Millard, Wayne, and Vona Penney. Grandpa Silas was a Methodist Minister that traveled by horse from church to church holding revivals.
*Submitted by: Mary Moore Flowers*

**CALEB MOORE** - Caleb Moore, son of Caleb and Rebecca (Walters) Moore, was born in Gallia County, Ohio, October 29, 1847. He was one of eleven children. His siblings were Samuel, Elizabeth, Mary Ann, James, Jacob, Joseph, Rebecca, Timothy, Tabitha and Sophia. The father of these eleven children was a cabinet maker. Several of his woodworking creations are still in the possession of the family today.

Caleb, like his father, also built items from wood. He was also a farmer. He was a healthy man who tended to friends and relatives placed under quarantine and would escape catching the illness from those he tried to help. He would skate barefoot on Raccoon Creek when it was frozen. He would also cut ice blocks eighteen inches square, pack them in sawdust and use them in his icehouse to keep meat and other food items cool. Caleb liked to work in his flower beds and his garden. He was well versed in the knowledge of herbs. Early in life, he united with the Harrisburg Freewill Baptist Church and he lived a consistent Christian life.

Caleb married Barbara Fee, daughter of Henry and Rachel (Denny) Fee on October 23, 1866. They were the parents of seven children: Maggie, Frank, Augustus, Rose Emma, Edna, Mary Blanche and Dora Maud.

*Caleb Moore*

Caleb and Barbara's daughter, Mary Blanche, married Bert Russell on August 12, 1900. They had the following children: Anna, who married John Gilfilen; Carl, who married Kathryn Watson; Nellie, who died in infancy; and Mary, who married Ray Casto.

Barbara died April 8, 1900, as a result of an asthma attack. After her death, Caleb lived with Mary Blanche and her family in Porter, Ohio. Caleb spent his entire life in Gallia County, living at Harrisburg until he moved in with his daughter. He enjoyed tending to his daughter's roses. His Grandchildren remember that he played mumbly peg with them and he liked to rock in this rocking chair and sing. One song they remember him singing was "Will There Be Any Stars in My Crown?"

Caleb, in his ninetieth year, joined his wife in the Great Beyond on July 17, 1936. His earthly remains were laid to rest beside his wife in Fairview Cemetery, Bidwell, Ohio.

Today, his descendants are scattered throughout the United States and Canada.
*Submitted by Mrs. Mary Casto*

**HERBERT HARRY "HERB" AND JEAN ADAIR McCOY MOORE FAMILY** - Herbert was born June 20, 1935 in Haydenville, OH. His great-great grandparents, George and Martha Bagley Moore came to Hocking County, OH., from the central Pennsylvania farming area in the early 1850's via the canal system. During the War between the States, George Moore served in Washington D.C. as a special security agent to the Capitol. They had seven children which included Herb's great grandfather, Charles and wife Elizabeth Williams Moore. Elizabeth's parents were Obadiah and Margaret Mitchell Williams from central Tennessee. Their children (all deceased) were: Gertrude Achauer, Mildred Decker, Lillian (Pete) Matheney and Herb's father Porter P. Moore. Herb's mother was Kathryn Chesher and her parents were Charles and Lula Maude Evans Chesher. Besides Herb, they had the following children: Paul P. Moore and James J. Moore (deceased). Many of Herb's family were involved in the manufacturing of clay products and farming.

Herb's first introduction to Gallia County was in 1956 when he enrolled in elementary education at Rio Grande College (now the University of Rio Grande). While enrolled in college he met his wife, Jean Adair McCoy. She majored in secondary education. They were married following their June graduation August 14, 1960. In 1964, they earned their Master of Education Degrees from Ohio University and Herb later received his A.A.S. from Cincinnati College of Mortuary Science in 1969.

*Herbert Harry "Herb" and Jean Adair (McCoy) Moore*

His wife, Jean Adair McCoy was born in Vinton, Ohio on October 9, 1938, the daughter of the late Vernon H. and Elsie Pickens McCoy. Vernon was born April 5, 1910 and Elsie Pickens was born in Buffalo, WV November 8, 1918. Vernon was a funeral director/embalmer with the family business, McCoy Funeral Home of Vinton, OH, and Elsie is a licensed funeral director/cosmetologist. Vernon's parents were Rev. Gideon Francis McCoy and Elizabeth Stevens McCoy. Reverend McCoy came to Mason Co., WV from Illinois. Elizabeth was a native of Mason Co., WV. Her parents were Andrew and Minnie Bailes Pickens. The Pickens family has its origins in Ireland.

Herb began his professional life as an elementary teacher and principal in the Fairborn City Schools from 1960-1968. Jean also taught and was a guidance counselor on the junior high school level. Both returned to Gallia County permanently in June of 1968, when they became a part of the family business, McCoy-Moore Funeral Homes, Inc., of Vinton and Gallipolis. These firms have more than a century of continuous years of operation.

Their family includes three sons, Jay Herbert Moore and wife Melissa Armstrong. Melissa is from Jackson, OH. The second son is Joe Aaron Moore and wife Sarah Evans from Rio Grande, OH and youngest son, Jared Adair Moore.

**LAFAYETTE MOORE FAMILY** - Layafette Moore, (son of Deighton Moore and Anna Bates), was born March 16, 1842, in Noble County, Ohio. He married Willma W. Rossiter, (daughter of Jesse Rossiter and Elizabeth Bennett), on October 27, 1867, in Caldwell, Ohio. She was born October 28, 1848, in Noble County.

On August 22, 1862, Lafayette enlisted in the 116th Regiment OVI, earning a bonus of $23. On January 1863, while on a march to raid St. George, Virginia, Lafayette fell ill with "cold and hot" spells. Lafayette's military doctor treated him by bleeding Lafe "largely from the arm".

Lafayette was taken prisoner at Winchester, Virginia, on June 15, 1863, and held prisoner for three months. On July 8, 1863, he was paroled as a prisoner of war at City Point, Virginia. Lafayette was mustered out of service in Richmond, Virginia, on June 4, 1865, and was paid a bounty of $25 and was owed $75.

*Moore Family 1895
Standing L: to R:Ida, Monzona, Minnie, Alpatha, Willma, Nevada, and Milma. Seated: Willie, Ollie, Jessie, Seldon, Stanley, and Lafayette*

In 1865, Lafayette was diagnosed with chronic pericarditis, which related to his January,1863, illness. His 1881 examination detected hypertrophy of the heart with a labored irregular pulse, but failed to confirm pericarditis. Lafayette's physician did not link this condition to military service. By 1887, Lafayette received a disability pension of $4 per month. His heart disease was deemed the equivalent to the loss of a hand or foot. In 1891, the disability pension was increased to $10 per month.

In 1913, Lafayette sought an increase in his pension. His letter to the Pension Commissioner stated he "paid atturney 2 dollars...to rite aplication for age and servis pension. I supposed he nowed all about wrighton applications". Lafayette's letter had no impact, his pension stayed at $10 per month.

Lafayette and Wilma had the following 12 children:

1. Monzona (April 11, 1868-January 13, 1949) married Louisa Watson. He operated a sawmill in the lower section of the county.
2. Nevada (August 18, 1869-January 1, 1960) married John Devold Barry (1865-1929).
3. Alpatha (September 23, 1871-December 8, 1943) married Crawford Walters.
4. Mialma (July 1, 1872-January 17, 1951) married (1) Adam Kessner Friel (1863-1916) and (2) Harvey Dillon.
5. Oley (July 27, 1875-June 25, 1876).
6. Ida (December 4, 1878-February 15, 1914) married Lafayette Barry (1874-1965) on December 24, 1896, in Gallia County.
7. Minnie (February 11, 1880-December 16, 1915) married Charles Edward Watson (1878-1954).
8. Willie Ann (May 20, 1882-April 19, 1968) married Redmond Lake Rose (1874-1946).
9. Ollie (November 8, 1884-April 8, 1956) married (1) Wiley Wallace, (2) Lafayette Barry (1874-1965).
10. Jessie (February 3, 1889-July 11, 1970) married Lafayette Harrison (1884-1967) in 1915.
11. Seldon (April 19, 1891-January 1969).
12. Stanley (September 24, 1893-July 22, 1960) married Clara Emma Johnson (1886-1961) on March 11, 1922.

Lafayette died January 4, 1914, in Guyan Township. Willma died May 21, 1938, in Linnville, Lawrence County. They are buried at Good Hope Cemetery in Guyan Township.

*Submitted by Nathan Hatcher Hayes*

**T. J. MOORE FAMILY** - Of English, Irish and German descent, the Moores, Whites and Livesays came from northern Ohio and Greenbrier County, West Virginia, respectively, settling in the fertile valleys and wooded hills of Gallia County. Thomas J. Moore and Margaret Livesay married and had 7 children described in the family history written in 1980 Gallia County History, pages 240-241.

*Members of Moore Family attending April 26, 1939 Golden Wedding Anniversary of T.J. and Margaret Livesay Moore*

This continuation of the T. J. Moore family is written in 2002 after a 21-year pause that witnessed life events and developments in the family course. The 7 children born to T. J. Moore and Margaret Livesay Moore were Earl, Jake, Ted, Bess, Florence, Leona and Marguerite whose lineage this paper follows. Earl, the oldest and Jake started from scratch, first in the grocery business then taxi cabs until finally buying an automobile agency (Moore Motor Sales) that succeeded more than 3 decades (1930's-1960's) selling Dodge and Plymouth at the Moore building (built 1935) in downtown Gallipolis.

They also sold automobiles out of buildings they built on State Street; and their sister, Leona and her husband, Rupert Trout, carried the business on as Trout Dodge until 1974 at the State Street location. The buildings on State Street still stand as business venues, while the Moore building on Second Avenue is also a vital link in business activity of Second Avenue, Gallipolis. Earl died in 1954 leaving 4 girls and 1 son (Halma Smith, Eve Griffin, Marge Smith, Dorothy Ebersbach and Gordon Earl) all of whom have married and passed on, except Gordon, and left numerous children. Of particular interest is the union of Eve (Griffin) Moore and John "Jack" Griffin which brought 14 children, the first 10 being boys before 3 girls and 1 more boy were born. Earl's 4 girls went forth multiplying and Gordon is childless. Bess and Marguerite married Charles Jeffers and Lawrence Hineman in unions producing no children; however, Marguerite, a teacher and principal of 40 years plus at Bidwell and Hannan Trace elementary schools, has legitimate claim to thousands of admiring and loving students fortunate to have had her as an adult role model.

To this day at the very young age of 89 years, Marguerite lives at 427 Third Avenue, Gallipolis, and maintains her own residence keeping in touch with numerous nieces, nephews, their families and neighbors, teachers and other friends. Leona (Moore) Trout had one child, Teddie Anne, who met with a tragic automobile accident and death at age 19 years. Florence married Chauncey Sprague and they had 2 boys and 2 girls. The boys, Buster and Tommy Sprague, were successful long-term automobile salesmen. Florence and Chauncey's girls, Virginia Mae and Lucille, married and had many children, nieces, nephews and great nieces and nephews through the Kenneth (Virginia Mae) Adams and Paul (Lucille) Skidmore unions. Jake T. Moore, Earl's brother in the car business, married Jewell Arrington and their union brought forth one boy, Robert A. (Bob) Moore and Judith Kay (Pat Moore) Grant. Bob married Penny Fish (Moore) and had one child, Christine Moore (Sass) who has 3 children, all girls. Bob is a psychologist in Gallipolis and has devoted 30 years plus in the service of the good people at GDC. Penny carries on the tradition of her family at HMC where she has served the health community more than 30 years. Christine lives in Bainbridge, Georgia, and works as a physical therapist director at Bainbridge Hospital. Judith (Pat Moore) Grant lives in Delaware, Ohio, with her husband, Bob Grant. They have 3 girls, Lisa, Shannon and Heather.

Last, but not least, is Ted Moore, brother of Earl and Jake, also in the automobile business. Ted married Fairie (Fraley) Moore and their union brought one son, Richard Allen Moore, who married Jenny (O'Neal) Moore, a union resulting in 3 sons, 2 grandsons and a granddaughter. It is from this marriage that the Moore name will flow through future generations. Richard Allen is a former and current city commissioner who has served the city and community well over three terms, and it is his legacy and that of this Moore generation that the light and the hope will pass on to future generations of Moores, Sass's, Grants, Adams, Spragues, Skidmores, Griffins, Smiths and Ebersbachs as well as the many good people they have helped and touched.

*Submitted by Robert Moore*

**MOREHOUSE FAMILY** - The first Morehouses to appear in Gallia County were Ann Morehouse Barlow, wife of Elnathan Barlow, her brother Thaddius Morehouse, and their nephew, Ahas S. Morehouse. Ann, Thaddius and Sarah(mother of Ahas or Ahaz) were children of David Morehouse and Ann Squire(s), residents of Fairfield, Connecticut.

Ahas' parentage has long eluded this researcher. A recent request for Fairfield church records yielded the answer. The Reverend Philo Shelton, Rector of Trinity (Episcopal) Church, Fairfield, Connecticut, between 1785-1825, kept a record "of those Christians, Baptized, Confirmed, Admitted to the Communion, Married, and Buried by him…" In that record, on June 20th 1801, he baptized 13 children, all of whom were listed by name, followed by a father's name, except "Ahaz Silleck" whose name was followed by his mother, Sarah Morehouse. Sarah married William Pearce at Weston, Connecticut, on April 20, 1806. This researcher's grandfather always said that his great-grandfather, Ahas' father's name was "Selick" or "Selic" Morehouse. It looks as if he was partly correct. Ahas' father's last name was probably Silleck or Selleck.

It is not clear when Ahas first shows up in Gallia County, but Elnathan Barlow and Ann Morehouse Barlow, were married in Connecticut on March 23, 1802 and were in Gallipolis by 1806. It is possible that Ahas was sent to Ohio with his aunt and uncle. Elnathan Barlow served in the War of 1812 and died at, or near, Detroit, Michigan.

A muster list of volunteers from Gallipolis, found at Our House Museum, lists two names of interest to members of this family – Stephen Sisson and, immediately below him, "Selic" Morehouse. Since this list seems to predate the actual outbreak of the declaration of war against Great Britain, it does not prove that either man actually participated in the War, but is interesting because it proves that Stephen Sisson was in Gallia earlier than previously believed. Ahas married Stephen Sisson's sister Lucinda. Ahas would have been about 16 years old at the time of the muster roll. It is entirely possible that the "Selic" on that list was a young Ahas using his middle name. The name carved on his tombstone in Fairview Cemetery is Ahas S. Morehouse.

Ahas married Lucinda Sisson in Gallipolis on June 23, 1818, in a service performed by Samuel Barlow, Justice of the Peace, a brother of the late Elnathan Barlow. She was a daughter of Wilson Sisson and Rebecca Cobb. Wilson died in Otsego County, New York, before the family moved to Gallia. Rebecca Cobb Sisson married for a second time to Rufus Hill, and is buried in a grave in Pine Street Cemetery once marked with a stone identifying her as Rebecca, "consort of Rufus Hill, daughter of Stephenson Cob." She was a child of Stephen Cobb and Olive Amsbury or Armsby.

Ahas and Lucinda were parents of seven: Sarah (named for his mother), wife of Keiser Sawyers; Mary, wife of Robert Guinn; Rachel, wife of Sherman Parker; Edward, died in 1850 was unmarried; Daniel, died at age three years; Elnathan Barlow, husband of Margaret Ward; and Daniel W., husband of Letitia Eleanor Owen.

**ELNATHAN BARLOW MOREHOUSE DESCENDANT** - Eldest surviving son of Ahas and Lucinda, Elnathan Barlow Morehouse married Margaret Ward on March 22, 1855. Margaret was a daughter of Benjamin Ward and Nancy Burns. As a 62 year old widow, Margaret married Adam A. Worthington. She and Elnathan Barlow Morehouse were parents of three children , Emma, wife of George Frederick; Elnathan Barlow Morehouse, Jr., husband of Florence Myers; and Perrin Gardner Morehouse, husband of Lucy Ellen Scott. They were married on April 30, 1887. Perrin Gardner Morehouse was named for his father's first cousin, Dr. Perrin Gardner. Perrin G. Morehouse and Lucy Scott were the parents of six children, Raymond Harrison Morehouse, husband of Esta Smith; Elnathan Perrin , husband of Addye Jane Davis; Edith, wife of Clyde Settlemire; William McKinley , husband of Beulah Whiteacre; Ivor Wagner , husband of Jennie Brothers; and Inez, wife of Ferdinand Reynolds and then James Leslie Rutan. Lucy Scott was the daughter of Margaret Scott and Jordan Mannering, and the granddaughter of Martin Scott and Susan Beard.

Elnathan Perrin Morehouse(1890-1969) and Addye Jane Davis(1892-1973) were married on December 20, 1911. They were parents of four, Essie Pearl, wife of Hollie Russell Allen; Elnathan Paul , Sr., husband of Amy Bernice Dye; Jessie Pauline, died on June 23, 1920, at ten days; and Mable Wanda Morehouse. Addye Jane Davis was one of eight children of Orrin Franklin Davis and Jennie Boatman. Orrin's parents were Joseph Davis and Eunice York McCarley. Eunice was a daughter of Samuel McCarley and Elizabeth Boggs. Samuel was a son of John McCarley, an early miller in Raccoon Township. Jennie Boatman was one of two daughters of Aaron Boatman and Rebecca Jane Smith. Aaron's parents were Barney Boatman and Eliza Ward. Both Aaron and Barney served in the Civil War. Rebecca Jane Smith's parents were James H. Smith and Elizabeth Caroline Vance.

Elnathan Paul Morehouse, Sr., married Amy B. Dye on February 22, 1941 in Akron, Ohio. Amy was a daughter of Thomas Ferrell Dye and Elma Etta Hetzer of Reedsville, Meigs County, Ohio. Elnathan Paul "Buster" (1917-1985) was a graduate of Bidwell-Porter High School, Ohio Northern University and was employed in management by Goodyear Tire and Rubber Company for over 40 years. He was an elected member of the Akron City Board of Education for more than 27 years, retiring because of poor health. Amy(1919- ) a graduated from the Holzer Hospital School of Nursing in 1940 and was a registered nurse at Akron City Hospital for about 35 years. She is retired and living in Florida. They were parents of three children , Elnathan Paul Morehouse, Jr., Alyce Louise and Elizabeth Anne. Alyce has a son and a daughter and one grandchild. Beth has one son.

This researcher, Elnathan Paul Morehouse, Jr., is a retired public school teacher in Akron, a former member of the U. S. Peace Corps in Nigeria, West Africa, former president of the Akron Education Association, former elected member of the Board of State Teachers Retirement System of Ohio. A resident of Akron, Paul was elected in April, 2002 to serve as treasurer of the Ohio Genealogical Society in Mansfield, where he has served as a board member for the past three years. He is also president of the Ohio Society of the War of 1812, a member of the Sons of the American Revolution and a member of First Families of Gallia County and First Families of Ohio.

**LAWRENCE GLEN "LARRY" MOREHOUSE FAMILY** - Larry Morehouse was born on July 21, 1925 on a ranch near Abilene, Kansas. On October 6, 1956 he married Georgia Lewis of Lafayette, Indiana. A son, Timothy, is Chair of the religion department at Trinity School in New York City, New York. Their daughter, Glenn Morehouse-Olson, lives in St. Francis, Minnesota where she freelances as a communications and marketing director for theaters in the St. Paul-Minneapolis area and raises three daughters: Zoey, Abilene, and Jolie.

Larry and Georgia reside in Columbia, Missouri, where Larry retired from his job as Professor of Pathology at the School of Veterinary Medicine, University of Missouri, and Georgia retired as a Research Associate in MU's dairy department. Larry is a member of First Families of Gallia County and owes his discovery of his Gallia county "roots" to the lady shown in the accompanying picture. Although she died at the turn of the last century long before Larry was born, she is his grandmother. Her name is Anna Marie Kent. It is through her records and stories that Larry traced his ancestors to Gallipolis. Larry is a descendant of Ahaz S. Morehouse and Lucinda Sisson who were married in Gallipolis in June of 1816. Larry's lineage follows to Daniel Morehouse, to Edward Ahaz Morehouse, and to Edward Morehouse, his father in the Morehouse line. In the Kent line, his history traces to Milton and Wealthy Janetta (Adney) Kent, parents of Anna Marie, and, along those parental lines, to Samuel Kent II, and Samuel Kent, a patriot of the War of the American Revolution. It is through this line that Larry is now a member of his local chapter of the Sons of the American Revolution (SAR).

*Anna Marie Kent*

Ahaz S. Morehouse and Lucinda (Sisson) Morehouse lived in a log house at the mouth of Mill Creek in 1817. An intriguing story of early religious persecution associated with their attempts to hold the first Methodist Church services in Gallipolis is related on page XV of the History of Gallia County (1882). In that same source, Larry's great grandfather Daniel is listed as an assessor for Springfield township in Gallia county and was a farmer with a Pine Grove address. He married Letitia Eleanor Owen in Gallia County on June 28, 1859. Edward Ahaz and Ida were their children, and Larry is a grandson from Edward Ahaz's marriage to Anna Marie Kent. Daniel's sister Rachel married Sherman Parker and their sons, Ed and Charlie, were physicians in the Gallipolis area.

It is not surprising to find many close knit (and closely related) families in Gallia County in those days of the early 19th century. From a humble start 35 years ago with Anna Marie Kent and her family, Larry has followed many generations of Sissons, Kents, Adneys, Glenns and Morehouses. He credits whatever success he has had to the assistance of others. Cousins, aunts, and people he never knew before furnished most of the information. Larry feels it is a humbling experience in genealogic work to realize how little one actually did by oneself. It's simply a matter of knowing who to talk with at the right time.

**THOMAS SCOTT MOULTON, SR.** - Thomas Scott Moulton, Sr. was born in Portsmouth, Ohio, August 11,1932, the son of Earl Chandler and Lucile Moore Moulton. He was reared on the family farm in Lucasville, Ohio, which had been in the family since 1887.

Two brothers, David and Earl Chandler, and two sisters, Nancy and Martha (Mrs. Frank Cunningham) are deceased. His remaining sister, Mrs. Robert (Sarah) Minkler lives in Des Moines, Iowa.

*Judge Thomas S. Moulton, Sr. and Granddaughter Molly*

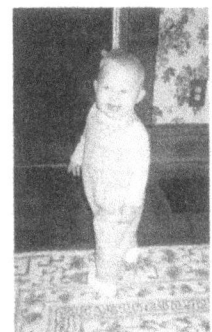

*Molly Margaret Fitzwater, 1 Year Old*

Tom served in the U.S. Army as a commissioned officer, being stationed in Germany with the 66th Tank Battalion of the Second Armored Division of the 7th Army.

His Doctor of Jurisprudence Degree was obtained at Ohio State University in 1959. He met Suzanne Cherrington, Gallipolis, Ohio, who had just obtained her law degree in 1967, while both were working for Attorney General William Saxbe. They married in 1969, and moved to Gallipolis in 1970, to join the the law firm of her grandfather, Henry W. Cherrington, and father, William P. Cherrington; and the firm name became Cherrington and Moulton. Sue's brother-in-law, D. Dean Evans, husband of Henrietta Cherrington. received his law degree from Capital University in 1972. He joined the group; and the firm name became Cherrington, Moulton and Evans. Tom was elected Probate Judge in 1979, and has served in that capacity ever since. He will retire in 2003. Sue continued to practice until her untimely demise in 1995.

Sue and Tom had two children: Thomas Scott, Jr., born January 12, 1971, and Sarah Lisbeth born July 28, 1972. Tom. Jr. received his law degree in 1997, from Ohio Northern University and became the fourth generation of the family to join the firm. He and his cousin, David Cherrington Evans, a graduate of University of Cincinnati Law School in 2000, and son of Dean and Henrietta Evans, have formed a partnership and are practicing together at 462 Second Avenue.

The newest member of the Moulton family arrived February 14, 2001. She is Molly Margaret Fitzwater, daughter of Sarah Lisbeth and Timothy Samuel Fitzwater who were married in 1997. They live in Lillington, NC. Tom and Tom, Jr. love her visits to Gallipolis where they are eagerly awaited.

Tom and Tom, Jr. and their three cats, Bear and Casper. both Himalayans, and Jumper, a Maine Coon breed, occupy their beautiful two-story colonial residence.

*Submitted by Thomas Scott Moulton*

**JAMES & PHYLLIS MULHOLAND** - On the 30TH. day of Dec in 1955, Phyllis Marlene Harder McClaskey traveled to Columbus, Ohio where she met James Clifton Mulholand. They continued their journey on to Indiana, where they married. They were married 32 years and 11 months.

James was born in Wilkesville, Ohio on January 21, 1931, the son of James Clarence and Maie Fletcher Mulholand. James had eight sisters and one brother. Phyllis was born November 27, 1935, in Ewington, Ohio, to Karl Manard and Doris Arletha Snyder Harder. Phyllis had four brothers.

*The Mulholand's*

Phyllis attended the Ewington one-room schoolhouse for the first six years of her education, at which time she transferred to the Vinton School to complete grades 7 through 12. Here, she earned her High School Diploma. After graduation, Phyllis obtained a job at the Gallia County Courthouse as a clerk in the auditors office. Phyllis remained in this position until the birth of her first child, Rick McClaskey. Rick is the son of Robert McClaskey, whom Phyllis married in April of 1954. Phyllis left her position at the courthouse to be a fulltime wife, mother, and housekeeper. Robert was killed tragically soon after their marriage in July of 1955, while working as a linesman for the Columbus & Southern Ohio Electric Company.

James attended the Wilkesville School. Here he received his High School Diploma after returning from the Navy, where he had spent four years serving his country. James then continued his career as a sprinkler fitter with the Local 669 union, at which he worked for 40 years. In December of 1955, James married Phyllis; and three additional children were born: James Anthony, Eric Manard, and Penelope Dawn.

James' career as a sprinkler fitter often took him out of town, so Phyllis then cared for the children. Phyllis worked as a full-time mother until her children were in school. Then, in 1967, she began her career as a school bus driver for the Gallia County Local School System. That same year, she began working as the clerk of the Village of Vinton. James and Phyllis built a new house and moved back to James' home place at Wilkesville in 1979. At this time, she became the Clerk for Wilkesville Township and still maintains this position today.

In July of 1986 James was diagnosed with cancer forcing him to retire from his job. He was blessed with two years and four months with his wife, children, and grandchildren before he passed away on November 17, 1988. James was liked by all who knew him.

*Submitted by: Daughter Penny Shepherd & Granddaughter Amber Shepherd*

**CHARLES AND DONNA SUE MURRAY FAMILY -** At this time, six generations of our Murray family have lived in Gallia County. Our first-known Murray ancestor, Peter Murray, settled in Morgan Township in 1845. He was born in Ireland. His great, great grandson, Charles, is the son of Anthony and Hallie Rutan Murray. Most of our family's history has been recorded in the book, *Gallia County Ohio People in History to 1980*.

*Standing L: To R: Terri Murray Foster, William "Bill" Foster, Amanda Murray, David Murray, Charles Murray Seated: Donna Sue Palmer Murray and Keri Lynn Foster*

Charles became an elementary school teacher after attending Rio Grande College. He began his teaching career in Ross County, Ohio, in 1960 and taught in public schools of Ohio for 31 years. In 1991, he retired from the Gallipolis City Schools and worked 18 months full-time at the University of Rio Grande as an assistant to the Director of Multi-Ethnic Affairs. In 1994, he changed his employment to the Brunicardi Music Store in Gallipolis and taught piano there until the business closed. He continues piano instruction at his private studio.

Music has always been a prominent part of the Murray household. Charles met his future wife, Donna Sue Palmer, during high school music activities. Charles graduated from the Bidwell-Porter High School in 1957. Sue graduated from North Gallia High School in 1959. After both started their teaching careers, they were married at the Eno Methodist Church on August 11, 1963. Sue, the daughter of Donald and Ruth Rathburn Palmer, attended Ohio University and taught her initial years as a music teacher at Amanda-Clearcreek High School in Fairfield County. She continued her education and became an elementary teacher, teaching at Hamilton South in Franklin County and Washington Elementary in Gallipolis. In 1977, the Ohio Valley Christian School was organized, and she has remained there as the kindergarten teacher since its founding. Charles received his Masters Degree in School Administration from the University of Dayton in 1984.

The family of Charles and Sue Murray consists of three children: Terri (Mrs. William Foster), born July 3, 1967; David, born May 7, 1969, and Amanda, born July 23, 1974. They lived at 119 Lariat Drive during their childhood days and were graduated from Gallia Academy High School in Gallipolis. Terri attended URG part-time and has worked as a certified pharmacy technician. David attended diesel mechanic school and works as a mechanic. Amanda graduated from the University of Cedarville and works at the Northwest Bible Church in Hilliard, Ohio. Charles' and Sue's grandchild, Keri Lynn Foster, born February 26, 1998, lives with her mom and dad in Bidwell, Ohio.

Charles enjoys local history. For fifteen years, he wrote and edited the "Gallia County Glade", the quarterly newsletter of the Gallia County Historical/Genealogical Society. One of his most cherished achievements was to co-*write The History of Gallia County's One-Room Schools: The Cradle Years,* published in 1993. Also, he was instrumental with locating and recording the census of Gallia County's cemeteries, a major project of the society in the 1970's.

*Submitted by Charles A. Murray, December 2001*

**BENJAMIN FRANKLIN AND MARY ETTA (CLARK) MYERS FAMILY -** Benjamin, born, 22 March 1873 died, 17 September 1932, Son of Noah Franklin, born, 9 December 1845 died, 6 December 1902, and Mary (Allbright) Myers, born, 30 December 1850 died, 25 June 1937. Mary (Clark) Myers, born, 31 May 1879, died 23 August 1922, daughter of Perry, born in 1845, died, 1917, and Eliza Clark born, 1853, died, 1918. Perry Clark, Veteran, Co, K, 3, W.Va. Cav.

*Back row L-R: Murrell, (Mary and Benjamin) James. Second Row L-R: Chester, Perry, Althea. Front Row L-R: George and Vernon.*

Myers' came from Germany to Philadelphia, Pennsylvania, settled in Locust Bottom, near Glen Walton Virginia and Giles county, Pembroke, Township, Allegheny mountain (mountain lake) Virginia. From there they migrated to Walnut township, Gallia county, Lecta Ohio, area, Myers Hollow. They attended one rooms schools, Low-Gap, Thornton road, Myers school: Myers Hollow, and Pine Grove School, Mt. Zion Road, Walnut township, Gallia County. In August 1918, the Myers gathered at the home of Enoch Bethel Myers, Myers Hollow, for a family reunion. This gathering was originated by James W. Myers. The group decided to meet the following year. They have continued this tradition every year since then. The reunion was moved to Fox Fair-View Church, Mt. Zion Road, Walnut Township. The 83rd. Reunion was held 12 August 2001. The reunion is set for the 2nd Sunday of August. Many of the Elder Myers' are buried in the Fox Fair-View Cemetery. James C. Myers stated that various spelling of the name caused the family name to be recorded in so many ways, such as Myers, Meirers, Meyers, Maher, Mahor, Mowyer, Moyer, Meir, Mire, Mires, Moirs, Myres, Miers, Moyers, Myer, Mires, Marrs, Meirs, Mayer, etc... He said he found the name in Virginia as early as 1662, and in New York, 1709.

CHILDREN

Chester Arthur born 23 March 1911 died 28 April 1966.

James Monroe born 14 April 1899 date of death-unk. died in Akron Ohio Area.

Vernon Vaughn born 24 April 1903 died 14 February 1985.

Murrell Clark born 28 June 1904 died 8 May 1975.

George Manchester born 7 June 1905 died 1978.

Perry Franklin born 8 April 1907 died, 31 December 1936.

Althea Mae born, 21 April 1909 died, 8 May 1967.

Benjamin Franklin and Mary Etta (Clark) Myers were married 7 December 1897.

*Submitted by Henry L. Myers*

**CHESTER ARTHUR AND GEORGIANA CLARA (POPE) MYERS -** Chester was born 23 March 1911, died 28 April 1966, born and raised in the Lecta Ohio area, Walnut Township-Gallia County. Son of Benjamin Franklin-born 22 March 1873, died 17 September 1932 and Mary Etta (Clark) Myers-born 31 May 1879, died 23 August 1922. Georgian -born 14 November 1908, died 17 May 1999, born and raised in the German Hollow (Patriot) area, Walnut Township, Gallia County. Daughter of August J .born 19 November 1860, died I December 1935 and Lena (Klages) Pope, born- 10 May 1869, died 11 December 1927. Chester and Georgiana were married at Kitt's Hill, Ohio, 21 December 1932.

Children: Chester Eugene, born 22 October 1933, died 25 May 1992. Floyd Donal, born 25 December 1934 - children - Luana and Aneda-(mother) Brenda Rigsby. Henry Lee, born 15 April 1936 (Pauline Trubee) children-Christine Lynn and Gregory Lee. Gregory died - 16 September 1997 (mother) Virginia D. Owens.

Lloyd Leo, born 7 April 1941 -children-Christopher and Shelby (mother) Lynda Fraley.

Monna June (Edwin Cheatham) born, 9 June 1938. Charlotte Jane_(Ronald Patrick) born, 23 October 1942-children-Jeff and Randy.

Children were born and raised (Patriot) German Hollow/Ridge-Gallia County, Walnut Township, attended Cadmus Grade/High School and Southwestern High School.

*Back row L: to R:. Floyd D., Chester E., Henry L. front row L: to R: Monna J., Charlotte J., Lloyd L.*

*Chester and Gorgiana wedding picture.*

Grandparents: Benjamin Franklin and Mary Etta (Clark) Myers and August Jr. and Lena (Klages) Pope.

History : Henry placed his name in the record books of Gallia County Basketball League, Cadmus High School, 1955, when he set a new all-time high scoring record for an individual by dumping in an amazing 56 points against Mercerville. He also scored 48 points against the Cheshire Bobcats, 1955. He ended up as top scorer in the 1955 Tourney as he scored 60 markers in three games. Other team players who assisted in making these high scores possible were: Ray Jeffers. Joe Willis, Donald Smith, Buck Farney, Bob Ruff and Tim Stumbo. Cheer Leaders-Sue Wiseman, Virginia Spenser, Eudora Spenser, Rosalie Meadows and Janet Meadows. Coach: Glen Wiseman. Managers: Harold Daniels and Ray Davis. Henry, his daughter's and son-in-law's military career spans 60 years. Henry: 20 years-U.S. Air Force-MSgt.; daughter-Christine-13 years, U.S. Air Force-Major; son-in-law (Christine's husband) Jim-27 years, U.S. Air Force-Colonel. Henry and Jim served tours of duty in the Vietnam War.
*Submitted by Henry L. Myers*

## CHRISTOPHER COLUMBUS MYERS FAMILY

Christopher Columbus Myers (son of John William Myers and Mary Polly Fralix) was born May 29, 1835. He married Philena Fox (daughter of Emmor Fox and Sarah Baker) on November 8, 1855, in Gallia County. She was born November 12, 1837, in Ohio.

Christopher and his wife had a family farm in Walnut Township. While several of his brothers served the Union during the Civil War, there is no record of military service for Christopher. While he did attend the 1888 Reunion of the 141 OVI, he likely just attended with his brothers.

*Christopher And Philena Myers, About 1880*

Christopher and Philena had the following children:

1. James William was born April 28, 1857, Yarico, Lawrence County. He married Laura Elliott on November 11, 1875, near Lecta, Ohio. They were the parents of Jacob, Warren, Eliza, Ira, Nancy, Jessie James, Daisy, Alva, Clarence, Nellie, Ora, Lottie, Shirley, and Morris. James William died on March 12, 1939, in Gallipolis.

2. Oliver Anderson was born January 28, 1860; he died December 1, 1945. Oliver married Margaret Susan Baker.

3. John Lafayette was born July 19, 1862. He married Harriett Amanda Pyles (daughter of Samuel Piles and Martha Jane Cox) on April 24, 1886. She was born May 14, 1865, in Walnut Township. Their children were Samuel, Alta Theadoshie, Archie, Allen, Anna Susan, Martha, Amer, Ora, and Meda. John died on July 29, 1914, and Harriett died on June 29, 1945. They are both buried at Fox-Fairview Cemetery.

4. Mary Elzena was born October 3, 1865. She married Perry Massie. Mary died October 26, 1939, Lecta, Ohio.

5. Sullivan A. was born July 28, 1867, and died 1885.

6. Joseph Lewis was born 1869 and died 1960. He married Zonie Thornton. After Zonie's death, he married Nancy Ada.

7. Sarah Augusta was born June 30, 1871. She married Thomas Allen Pyles (brother of Harriett Pyles) on August 27, 1893. Sarah died January 8, 1936.

8. Perry C. was born August 1, 1873, and died July 10, 1874.

9. Rebecca Anne was born 1875, and died in 1929. She married John Colwell.

10. George B. was born October 19, 1878, and died June 1, 1967. He married Myrtie Fillinger.

11. Stephan Dallas was born August 5, 1880, Walnut Township, Gallia County. He died on June 16, 1963, near Lecta, Ohio. Stephan married Stella Jane Brumfield.

12. Charles Denver was born June 1, 1884, Gallia County, and died April 16, 1954, Huntington, West Virginia. On December 4, 1902, he married Cora S. Bostic in Gallia County. He moved to Huntington, WV, and started the Myers Transfer and Storage. Many of his descendants still live in the Huntington area.

Christopher died on April 7, 1893, and Philena died on July 14, 1914. They are both buried in Fox -Fairview Cemetery, in Walnut Township. Philena's parents donated the land for Fox-Fairview Church and Cemetery, where many members of the Myers and related families are buried.
*Submitted by Rhonda Day*

## JERRY ALLEN AND MARGARET MONTGOMERY MYERS

Jerry was born in Guyan Township, Gallia County, on April 9, 1939, to Clarence Columbus and Grace Eileen (Houck) Myers.

*Jerry Allen And Margaret Montgomery Myers*

Jerry's paternal grandparents were Stephen and Stella (Brumfield) Myers. His great grandparents were Christopher Columbus and Philena Fox Myers. His great, great grandparents were John William and Mary Polly (Fralix) Myers. John William Myers came to Gallia County in 1828 and purchased 40 acres through the U.S. land grant. The land could be purchased for $1.25 per acre with the stipulation that a cabin be built, crops be planted and the land improved in a 10-year period. A certificate was first issued showing intent; and after the 10 years, a patent would be issued for ownership to the property.

Jerry's maternal grandparents were Jasper Adam and Lizzie Edna (Clary) Houck. Jasper's parents were Noah and Mary (Danner) Houck. Noah and Mary were the parents of 14 children.

Lizzie Edna (Clary) Houck was the daughter of Marion James and Eva (Caldwell) Clary.

Jerry has been a life-long resident of Gallia County. He has one sister, Carolyn Fay Myers Fenice, Columbus, Ohio, and one brother, Raymond Earl Myers, now deceased (October 27, 1986).

Jerry attended Mercerville school and participated in sports such as football, basketball and track. Jerry is now an avid golfer and hunter. He is now retired from O.V.E.C.

Margaret is the daughter of John Monroe and Bonnie Irene (Phillips) Montgomery. She was born July 26, 1939, in Eblin Hollow, Ohio Township, Gallia County, Ohio.

Her father, John, was the youngest of 12 children born to James Preston (Pete) and Sarah Jane Caldwell Montgomery.

Her paternal great grandparents were Thomas Jefferson Lafayette and Lucretia (Haskins) Montgomery, and g-g-grandparents were Tom and Tacy (Swindler ) Montgomery , who were early settlers of Guyan Township coming to the area between 1810 and 1820.

Her maternal grandparents were Willie and Iva Mae (Lewis) Phillips. Willie was the son of Andrew and Etta (Trowbridge) Phillips of Ohio Township. Iva Mae was the daughter of Elza and Sarah F. (Blake) Lewis.

Margaret had three sisters and three brothers, Alice Frances, Janet Faye, Barbara Jean, Robert Lewis, Jerry Monroe (deceased) and

Howard Wayne. Margaret too has been a life-long resident of Gallia County and retired from Gallia County Human Services after 25 years of service.

They are the parents of three children: John Allen, who is married to the former Julia McComb, and they have two children, Kristopher Allen and Jodi Lee Myers. Donna Louise is married to James Weaver Kessel, and she has two daughters, Whitney Anne and Elizabeth Reid Parsons. Ronald Dean is married to the former Patti Ellen Hoof, and they have a son, Logan John.

Margaret and Jerry make their home on Neighborhood Road, Gallipolis, Ohio.

**ALDEN AND HELEN NEAL FAMILY** - Harry Alden Neal (August 22, 1911-May 4,1980) was the son of John Fletcher and Rebecca Ellen Pyles Neal. He was born in Walnut Township near Mudsoc. He married Helen Marie Thornton (August 21, 1915) on April 25, 1936. They attended Pine Grove School. She attended high school at Gallia Academy; he attended Waterloo High School. After their marriage they lived in the same area of the township and farmed raising turkeys, cattle, pigs, and tobacco. Alden also worked as a carpenter in the area building houses and barns.

Their children were: John Richard (October 5, 1938) who married Joyce Lee Reapp (9-13-1941). Richard's and Joyce's children are Debbra Lynn (May 11, 1960) who married James Ehman, Teresa Ann (October 14, 1962) who married Gene Layton, and Melissa Dawn (April 7, 1976) who married Thomas Lambert. Their grandchildren are: Derrick Layton (December 31, 1984), James Ehman (December 13, 1985), Cory Ehman (October 2, 1987), Chelsea Layton (January 10, 1989), and Kaylee Lambert (December 9, 1999).

Earl Edward (March 12, 1940) married Karen Alene Parks on June 20, 1960. Their children are: Cara Dawn (April 2, 1962) who married Jack Bambenek; Christian Shawn (February 14, 1965) who married Charlene Letchford, and Theodore Paul (February 28, 1966) who married Lisa Hauldren.

Earl and Karen's grandchildren are Elise Rebecca, Christian Alexander, and Trevor Alden, Mary Elizabeth, Jessica Lee, Rachel Neal, and Jacob Michael.

**JOHN FLETCHER NEAL** - John Fletcher Neal (Sept. 14,1868 -April 20,1945) was born in Harrison Township to Watson Marion and Elizabeth White Neal. John was married to Rinda Hall (June 24, 1868-August 16, 1905) on June 24, 1891. Their children were Bertha Ellen (March 2, 1893-February 2, 1948) married Carl Grimes on August 7, 1920. They had one son Carl C. Grimes (June 1, 1922); John Marcus (August 1, 1897-April 1946) married Gladys Faye Cox in Indiana; Ruth Elizabeth (November 26, 1899-June 22, 1959) married George Edward Sherman.

John's second marriage was to Rebecca Ellen Pyles (January 1, 1873-March 13, 1964), daughter of Henry Wilson and Sarah Fox Pyles on August 7, 1906. Their children were Elmer Glen (September 24, 1907-August 4, 1974) married Frankie Evelyn Noel daughter of Calvin and Martha Wiseman Noel; Esther Rebecca (October 2, 1909) married Roland Edgar Luman, son of Clarence and Dora Frances Null Luman. Their children were Donald Edwin and Carolyn Sue. Harry Alden (August 22, 1911-May 4, 1980). Alden married Helen Thornton (August 21, 1917), daughter of Clark and Lalla White Thornton. Their children were John Richard and Earl Edward.

John attended college at Lebanon, Ohio and taught for a time. He farmed in Section 33 of Walnut Township raising sheep, cattle, hay, corn, and fruit which he sold at the iron furnace area in Lawrence County.

**RICHARD AND JOYCE NEAL FAMILY** - John Richard Neal (October 5, 1938), who was born in Walnut Township, is the son of Harry Alden and Helen Marie Thornton Neal. He married Joyce Lee Reapp (September 13,1941) in Marion, OH, September 21, 1959. She was born in Gallipolis, OH, to Harry Edwin (September 18, 1917-March 15, 2000) and Martha Leon Smith (June 8,1919-June 14,1992). He worked for Pennyfare Markets and farmed in Walnut Township. She was a homemaker and sold Tupperware for several years. In recent years they have operated a greenhouse business at their home.

Their children are: Debra Lynn (May 11, 1960) married Jim Ehman (August 1, 1956) on May 28, 1983. Debbie's and Jim's children are: James Christopher (December 13, 1985) and Cory Neal (October 3, 1987). Teresa's Ann (October 14, 1962) married Gene Alan Layton (September 6, 1961) in August,1984. Teresa and Gene's children are Derrick Ryan (December 31, 1984) and Chelsea Nicole (January 10, 1989). Melissa Dawn (April 7, 1976) married Thomas Lambert (February 9, 1975) on December 10, 1994. Their daughter is Kaylee Ashlynn (December 9, 1999).

**WALTER NEAL, JR..** - Walter Neal, Jr. was born November 17, 1786 to Walter Neal and Winifred Wood Neal in Bedford Co., Virginia. He married Deborah Arnot, daughter of Henry and Elizabeth Truesdale Arnot, on April 10, 1804. Her sister had married his brother Charles. Walter and Deborah were the parents of eleven children: Margaret, Anna Maria, John, Winifred, William, Henry, Thomas, Anderson, Watson, Martha, Rachel Jane. Several of the children were born in Virginia and some after he moved to Ohio. At the 1820 Census, he was living on Symmes Creek in Walnut Twp. He lived also in Warren Co., Indiana. He lived in several places in Ohio; but at the time of his death in 1873, he lived in Harrison Twp and is buried on the hill in back of his house. Deborah died in 1843 and is buried in Neal Cemetery at Mudsoc.

He remarried after Deborah's death to Elizabeth Lanthorn in 1844. They had three more children.

Walter was a farmer, which was a necessity at this time, but also was a hunter, a Justice of the Peace for Walnut Twp., and built a mill, a loom, and constructed houses.

**WALTER NEAL JR.** - Walter Neal Jr, born November 16, 1786, came to Ohio in 1812 settled at Stormes Creek called Bottles Place, approximately 4 miles north of Ironton. He went to Portsmouth and enlisted in the War of 1812. In the year of 1820, he moved to Flag Springs, north of Waterloo. Walter Neal, Jr, son of Walter Neal Sr. and Winifred (Wood) Neal, died February 23, 1873 in Harrison Township, Gallia County. He was a private in the War of 1812, a farmer, handyman, salesman, Justice of the Peace, married two times. His first wife was Deborah Arnot, daughter of Henry & Elizabeth (Truesdale) Arnot, was born May 24, 1787 in New Jersey. They were married April 10, 1804 in WV and Deborah died December 1843. There were eleven children; Margaret, born June 14, 1805 died June 4, 1888, Getaway, Lawrence County; Anna Mariah Neal, married John Miller in 1822, was born 1806 and died 1880; buried in Miller Cemetery, Waterloo, OH; John Neal, born January 10, 1808, died March 14, 1895; Winifred Neal, born Mary 1, 1810, died December 3, 1897, married William Rose, November 5, 1830; William Neal, born 1812, Monroe County, WV, died 1847; Henry Neal, born April 5, 1815, died July 15, 1890, married four times at Storms Creek, Lawrence County, Thomas Neal, born March 29, 1817, died, March 24, 1918, married January 6, 1837, he lived to be 101 years; Anderson Neal, born, October 11, 1821, Gallia County, lived on county line near McDaniel Crossroads. The living room was in Lawrence County and the kitchen in Gallia County. In 1826 bought land, later sold it to his brother; Watson Neal, (G.G. Grandfather). The tale is, he was kicked in the head by a horse, (this was in Walnut Township, Gallia County, buried at Neal Cemetery at Mudsoc, State Route 775) She was pregnant with second child and after his birth she named him Marian Watson Neal; Martha Neal, born, 1831, died 1917, married August C. Boster, July 24, 1854; Rachel Jane Neal.

Second wife - Elizabeth Landthorne, widow of David Landthorne had three children, Clarinda, Francis Marion and Susan. Watson Marion Neal's children: John F. born September 14, 1868, died July 16, 1905; Thomas Watson, born October 24, 1870, died April 15, 1933; Celesta, born November 15, 1872, died November 1883; Frank, born April 9, 1875, died May 31, 1942; Mary M. born September 8, 1877, died June 24, 1963; Fanny, born December 17, 1879, died September 13, 1931 and Myrtie, born March 1882 and died 1945.

*Submitted by Carroll R. McDaniel*

**WATSON MARION NEAL** - Watson Marion Neal (April 23, 1848-April 4, 19 10) was born in Gallia County, the son of Watson and Rebecca Caroline Allison Neal. He was married to Elizabeth White (March 23, 1849-March 8,192 1) on January 24, 1867. She was born in Baltimore, MD to Levi and Catherine Hunt White. They both are buried in Mt. Zion Cemetery in Walnut Twp.

Their children were John Fletcher, who married Rebecca Ellen Pyles; Thomas, who married Ida M. Deegans; Celeste, who died November 1, 1883; Frank, who married Emma F. Bostick; Mary, who married Eura E. Saunders; Fannie, who married Simeon N. Queen, and Myrtie, who married Llewelyn Phillips.

**WATSON NEAL** - Watson Neal, who was born in Walnut Township 12-20-1825 was the sixth son of Walter Neal, Jr. and Deborah Arnot

Neal. He married Rebecca Caroline Allison 12-20-1845.

They were the parents of two sons: Thomas (11-4-1846—4-14-1910) and Watson Marion (4-23-1848) who was born after his father's accidental death caused by a horse.

Watson Neal was a farmer and a Methodist. Rebecca married George Ripley December 1, 1849.

**NIDAY FAMILY** - The book, *The Family vonNida,* tells the story of the immigrants from Germany who brought this name to the New World. The Nidas settled in Virginia. Later, one of their descendants, Peter Nida and his wife Elizabeth Shuck Nida, with their twelve children, left Virginia sometime between 1828-1831, coming to Gallia County, Ohio. They settled in the Lincoln Ridge area of Walnut Township. Peter and Elizabeth both died in a cholera epidemic in 1849. Peter and Elizabeth's youngest son, Lewis, was born 01 June 1816 in Virginia. He married Jane Blankenship 03 December 1835 in Lawrence County, Ohio. Peter and Elizabeth had fourteen children: unnamed twins, Comfort, Jane, William, Franklin, Dempsey, Hannah, Hester, Elizabeth, John, Chapman, Asel, Sarah, Oliver, and Aracancis. They lived on the farm that Peter and Elizabeth had owned. After Jane's death in 1860, Lewis married Martha Perkins Kerr, a widow with several children. Lewis and Martha had three children, Addison, Emory, and Ezra. Later in life Lewis took the Niday spelling of the name; he died 28 June 1888.

*Victor J. Niday & Mary Graham Niday Wedding Picture*

Franklin Dempsey Nida, son of Lewis and Jane Blankenship Niday, was born 19 December 1840 in Walnut Township, Gallia County. He married Martha Catherine McCall 08 June 1865. Martha was the daughter of James and Martha Phelps McCall. The McCall history can be found in the 1980 Gallia County history book. She was born 07 December 1845 in Harrison Township. Dempsey served in the Union Army. They had nine children: Eugene, Emory, James Franklin, Victor Jerome, William Lewis, Blanche, Chauncey Glanville, Pearl, and Tressie.

Victor Jerome Niday, the fifth child born to Dempsey and Martha, married Mary Graham 07 October 1894 at the home of her parents, Ezra and Magdelene Lang Graham. Victor was born 09 May 1872, and Mary was born 27 February 1871. Victor and Mary met at a "singing school" on Lincoln Ridge. Victor was the teacher. They had four sons. In 1904, Victor and Mary bought the Blessing Farm on Lincoln Pike, which was henceforth known as the Fairmont Jersey Farm. He built most of the barns still standing on the farm today, and they built the house that their descendants still occupy. Victor was an Ohio State Representative, elected in 1932 and 1934. After Mary's death Victor married Pearl Ingalls Gillingham.

The oldest son, James Franklin, married Wilma Smeltzer; they had eight children. After Wilma's death, Frank married Kathleen Rager Meade. Frank owned a farm in the Canal Winchester area and later ran a feed store in Columbus. The second son was Victor Paul; he was in the navy at the end of World War I. He married Margaret Donnally, daughter of Edward and Kathryn Engel Donnally. An Engel family biography appears in the 1980 Gallia County book. Margaret taught school at Hawk and Safford Schools before her marriage. Paul and Margaret were the parents of two daughters and two sons. Paul and Frank began to run a dairy on the family farm, which retailed milk in Gallipolis. Milk bottles can still be found embossed with the words: Niday Bros. Jersey Milk Registered. Later Paul served as Gallia County Treasurer for two terms.

William Raymond was the third son born to Victor and Mary. Raymond married Alice Dorothy Brammer in Columbus. Raymond moved to Columbus, Ohio where he was a teacher and a principal for the Ohio State School for the Blind. Raymond and A. D. were the parents of one daughter. The youngest son, Carlos Graham married Margena Stillings; they had two children. Carlos ran the Gallipolis Dairy.

*Submitted by Cynthia Niday Menzer*

**VICTOR JOE & MARY ELIZABETH WALKER NIDAY FAMILY** - Our story up to 1980 is printed in the 1980 Gallia County History Book. Since that time both Vic and Mary have retired. Mary retired in 1996 from Washington Elementary School in Gallipolis where she had served for sixteen years as the school librarian. Vic had been a dairyman all his life and for a few years drove a school bus for the Gallipolis City Schools. In 1992 Vic discontinued the Niday Dairy that had been in operation since his father returned from World War I. The dairy barn on Lincoln Pike still bears the name "V.J. Niday and Sons" which stands for Victor Jerome Niday, Vic's grandfather. Since discontinuing the dairy Vic has continued with his beef herd on the family farm that was purchased by the Niday family in 1904.

*Vic & Mary Niday*

Since 1980 Mary has participated in the following activities: served as President of the Pembroke Club in Gallipolis, served as secretary for the Gallia County Historical Society and served on the board at the Our House. For more than ten years she served as Historian for Grace United Methodist Church in Gallipolis. During the years Mary served as church historian she compiled and helped write a history of Grace Church covering the years 1821 to 1990. It is now waiting to be printed. Mary served on the committee for the countywide event of school children to celebrate the bicentennial of the United States Constitution, sponsored by the DAR and the Gallia County Historical Society. Mary also helped with the DAR one room school project. Vic serves as usher at Grace Church. Vic and Mary were pleased to accept the invitation to put their home on tour for the bicentennial in 1990 for the 200th Anniversary of the founding of Gallipolis.

As stated in the 1980 History, Vic and Mary have two children. Victor Richard and Cynthia Melaine now married to Michael James Menzer. The Menzers have two sons, Zachary Paul and Drew Donnally. Vic and Mary take great delight in their two grandsons and with their son Richard enjoy holidays, birthdays, programs and special events with the Menzers. The Nidays have enjoyed trips to Hawaii and Alaska since their retirement and enjoy vacations with their children and grandchildren.

In 1997 Vic and Mary started a hobby that continues to interest them. They take pictures of barns. They document the owner's names, location of the barns, different types of barns, and other detailed information. They have attended barn tours throughout Ohio and attended the Ohio Barn Conference in Wooser in 2001.

Vic and daughter Cynthia Melaine are charter members of First Families of Ohio. They along with Mary are also lifetime members of the Gallia County Historical Society. Vic and Mary feel God has blessed their lives and thank God for all the many wonderful gifts He has given them such as their wonderful parents, their children, their grandchildren and their home together.

**VICTOR RICHARD NIDAY** - Victor Richard Niday is the son of Victor and Mary Niday of Gallipolis. At present Richard is living in the Columbus area. He was a member of the Triangle 4-H Club during the ages 9-19, where he enjoyed showing beef and dairy cattle, model rocketry and various other projects. Richard won trophies in FFA for his interest in computers and various other FFA projects. He served as acolyte at Grace United Methodist Church in Gallipolis several years. Richard served one year as president of the Methodist Youth Fellowship at Grace Church where he also helped with the sound system. Richard received three MVP trophies and athletic key when he graduated. He was a member of the track and cross-county teams during his four years at Gallia Academy. Richard attended Hocking Technical College. At his present job he is employed as a "Lead" and spends most of his time using a computer to program items coming in and out of the warehouse where he works at Bath And Body Works.

Richard enjoys vacations with his parents and family events with his sister and her family and is a fun uncle to his two nephews. He spends

*Victor Richard Niday*

*Nolan Family*

much of his free time with one of the four computers he has set up at his home. Richard was married in 1994 at Marysville, Ohio and three years later divorced. He continues to take computer classes sponsored by his employer. He also enjoys playing Magic cards with friends and entering tournaments.

**JOHN NISEWANGER FAMILY** - Col. John Nisewanger (1742-1821) came to Ohio in 1790 when it was still in the Northwest Territory. He is named in the 1806 and 1810 tax lists of Gallia Co. He lived in Salisbury Twp., which later became part of Meigs Co. He served as Justice of Peace, Overseer of the Poor and Supervisor of Roads in 1806.

He was born in Frederick Co., VA, where he married Margaret (GUT?) and had 6 children. He fought in the Revolutionary War in the Virginia militia. He took part in the battle of Point Pleasant against Cornstalk in 1774 and other battles, rising to Lt. Col. He arrived in Marietta in 1790, serving at the fort. He purchased land from the Ohio Company. He died at the home of his daughter Susannah in 1821, aged 78, and is buried in Middleport.

He was the son of Jacob Neuschwanger (1716 - 1754 Frederick Co. VA). According to the latest research, Jacob was born 1716 in Germany and came to Virginia with his father and brother John before 1738. He married in Germanna VA Maria Gertraudt Brumback, daughter of Melchior Brumback and Mary Elizabeth Fischback and they settled in Jost Hite's colony in the Shenandoah Valley. Jacob was the son of Christian Neuschwanger(1673 Eggiwil, Bern, SWI-about 1737 VA) and Anna Magdalena Steffan. Christian helped to build Fort Neiswanger and the church at Opequon.

John and Margaret's children were: I. Jacob (1767 VA- 1834 TN), married Susannah Wright, 6 children: married (2) Caroline Crockett, 1 child, moved to South Carolina, wealthy landowner; II. Susannah (1770 VA- 1845 Wyandot Co. OH) married Hamilton Kerr /Karr, 9 children; III. Sarah (1772 VA- 1831 Gallia Co., OH), married Charles Mills, 6 children: IV. John Jr. (1775 VA-1806 Gallia Co), married Peggy Coleman, Winifred Buck, 1 child; V. Christiana (1783-1873), married John Kerr Jr.; 10 children (see Kerr family); VI. Rachel (1785 VA-l826 Gallia Co.), married James McCormick; 8 children.
*Submitted by Margaret Powell Hetrick*

**DAVID ALLEN NOLAN III & DORIS LORENE (ROACH) NOLAN** - Married October 3, 1953, David is the son of David Allen Nolan II and Hattie Gertrude (Swain) Nolan.

Doris is the daughter of Chancey Hollis Roach and Ola Ellen (Miller) Roach.

They have (4) children. Pamela Kay (Nolan) Franklin is married to Robert Allen Franklin and they have (3) children- James Allen Franklin (married to Carrie (Hill) Franklin with a child, Cole Mitchell) Shannon Marie (Franklin) Pratt(married to Brandon L. Pratt with a child, Tyler Matthew), and Rachel Leigh Franklin. David Allen Nolan IV has a daughter Cindy (Nolan) Roberts (married to John Paul Roberts and children Seann and Kaitlyn).

Timothy Dale Nolan with (3) children by his second wife Christina White. The children are Christie (Nolan) Johnson (married to Mark Johnson with a daughter, Destiny), Timothy Scott (Scottie) Nolan, and Mark Nolan. He also has (2) children with Tara Pennington whose names are Aundria and Aurora.

Anthony (Tony) Wayne Nolan is married to Paula (Watson) Nolan and have (2) children named Brandon and Brady.

**NORTHUP FAMILY** - The Northup's came to Gallia County from England. They settled in Green Township at Northup, and that is how Northup got its name.

My great-grandfather was George Northup. He married Sarah McCall. They lived on a farm on Northup-Yellowtown Road. They had six children: Fred, Charles, Laura and three that died in their early teens from the measles.

Charles married Anna Cottrill. They had four sons: Cecil, Stanley, George and Ross. Fred married Ella O'Dell and they had five children: O'Dell, Mildred (Mervin) Harrison, Paul, Pearl Burnette, and Ruthie who died in infancy.

O'Dell married Estelle Frances Denney and they had two children: William O'Dell (Bill) and Estelle Mae.

Bill married Maxine Powell and had two children: Debra (Kurt) Smith and Jeffery. Estelle married Richard Layne, born to this union were four children: Steven, Bethany (Mike) Sheets, Shawn and Belynda.

At the time Bill was born there were four generations who lived in the home place. Northup's lived in the home place until 1952, since that time there have been four different families that have owned the family home.

My grandfather Fred was a mail carrier, co-owner of the Gallia Produce and a very strong Republican leader.

My father O'Dell, at the time of his death in 1951 was also a mail carrier, on the Gallia County School Board and also on the first Gallia County Fair Board.

I have many happy memories of my childhood: going with my father to deliver milk to the Springhill Dairy, going to the woods with my great-grandfather John Isaac O'Dell to get certain branches of trees for him to make Bill and I whistles and cow whips.

My grandparents Cecil and Estelle Denney had a store across from the depot in Bidwell. We would visit them by taking the train from Gallipolis to Bidwell. When we were ready to come home we would take the train from Bidwell back to Gallipolis.

We now have the fourth generation attending Gallia Academy High School, my father, O'Dell, graduated in 1927, three of my children: Steven in 1975, Belynda in 1975 and Belynda in 1982 and myself, Estelle, in 1951. My mother Frances graduated from Bidwell-Porter High School in 1927 and my son, Shawn, from North Gallia High School in 1980. Gallia County is home to me and my family.
*Submitted by: Estelle Northup Layne*

**PAUL NORTHUP FAMILY** - George H. Northup was Paul's grandfather. In the early 1500's the Northup family migrated to America on one of the first boatloads of immigrants from England. They came to Gallia County by way of Marietta, Washington County, Ohio. Daniel Northup first settled in Northup, Ohio then was captured by the Indians and lived part of the time with the Indians and part of the time with his family in Northup.

George H. Northup, a descendant of Daniel Northup, married Sarah McCall. (Note: The McCall family at one time owned the ground between Lincoln Pike and Bethsadia Road.) To the union of George and Sarah were born Willie, who died around 3 years old and two other children who died in their teens, the other children were Charlie, Fred and Laura. The Northup Homestead or Farm was approximately two miles on Northup-Yellowtown Road.

Charlie Northup married Annie Cottrell and to that union was born Cecil who married Virginia Kems and lived in Cleveland, Ohio where Cecil worked in the automobile business. They had two daughters and three boys, Charlie, Stanley and Ross. Charlie married Pearl Waddell and had two children. Stanley married Katherine Stollings and they had a son Charles who lived in Columbus, Ohio and Stanley who works at Columbia Gas Company. Ross married Edith Elliott and they had two daughters, Jean and Kathleen.

Fred Northup married Ella O'Dell and to that union was born. O'Dell, Mildred, Paul, Pearl and Ruthie. O'Dell married Francis Denney and they had two children, William and Estella, nicknamed Susie. William became a school teacher and Estelle Mae (Susie) became a secretary. Mildred married Mervin Harrison and had three children, Stanley, Elmer and Jeanie. Paul married Madge Elliott and had a son, Gary. Pearl married Buell Burnett and had four children. Ronnie, Kathy, Karen and Roger. Ruthie was the fifth child of Fred and Ella's and she died in infancy.

**ERNEST E. AND CLARICE HOWARD NULL** - Ernest Edwin "Ernie" Null was born at Waterloo in Lawrence County to John Franklin and Harriett Eakman Null on January 14, 1908. He had one sister Lillian Rushie, born December

15, 1892; two brothers William Fredrick Null, born on January 11, 1904 and Carlton Emerson Null, born January 27, 1911. His early years were spent in Cadmus and Waterloo attending school and working for his father at the Null General Store. He attended Rio Grande College and later taught in a one-room school.

*Pictured below is the immediate family of Clarice and Ernest Null. Front row L: to R: Todd Fowler, Lori Richards Fowler, Bill Richards, Mike Null. Second row Barbara Null Richards, Bette Null Horan, Merrill Null, Holly Michigan. Third row: Susan Null Calhoun, Jack Richards, Bethany Dille Oder, Ronnie Dille, Jo Ellen Dille Kueck, Mark*

*Ernest E. & Clarice H. Null*

Ernie married Clarice Estella Howard December 15,1926 in Gallipolis, Ohio. She was the daughter of Chester Finley and Sadie Coleman Howard of Gallia County. The Howard family operated a rolling general store in the McDaniel Cross Roads area. Clarice's siblings included Leland, Robert, Emerson, Merrill, Phyllis, Ruth, Aldeth, Gertrude, and Marcella. In 1932 the family moved to Gallipolis where Ernie worked for Western & Southern Life Insurance Company as Superintendent for thirteen years. In 1946 he became a partner in Ball Furniture Company with his brother Carlton and sister Lillian. He worked there until 1995 when the business closed.

The Nulls had a small "farm" in Gallia County where they enjoyed spending their free time. Ernie was an avid deer and turkey hunter.

Clarice and Ernest had four children: Merrill, Bette Horan and Barbara Richards — all who live in Gallipolis and Marianna Null Dille, who is deceased.

Clarice Howard Null died on September 13,1990 at age 83 in Gallipolis, Ohio after a brief illness. Ernest Null died May 18, 1999 at age 91.

(For more detailed information, refer to the Null family history at The Historical Society, First Families of Gallia County membership applications, and People in History to 1980, Gallia County Ohio .)

*Submitted by Barbara Null Richards*

**NICHOLAS NULL** - Nicholas Null was born October 10, 1829 and died February 10, 1906. In 1883 he sold forty acres in Section of Walnut Twp. According to Duane Null's Waterloo, Nicholas was a teacher in Lawrence Co., Oh in August 1870. He married three times. His first marriage was to Mahala Rankins on January 21, 1852 in Lawrence County. She was born October 10, 1834. Their children were Vinton Armstrong Null (June 6, 1853) m. Sarah A. Brown July 10, 1871 in Gallia County, Diana Adeline Null (November 21, 1854) married Robert Massie March 5, 1874, and Mary M. Null (February 17, 1858).

Nichols's second marriage was to Evaline Fox (May 11, 1833) who was born in Pittsburgh , PA. She and Nicholas were married January 20, 1859. She died September, 1882 of consumption. Their children were Sarah Ellen (February 6, 1869) married ...Corn, Rebecca Evaline (March 28, 1861) married Jake Dempsey, Elizabeth Ann, (October 10,1862-October 26,1866), Mariah Alice (April 23, 1864), Arclissa Jane (January 26, 1866) married Jim Massie, Rees Monroe (July 13, 1868), Stephen Columbus (November 27, 1870), and Cynthia Emmaline (March 21, 1875) married ... Williamson.

Nicholas's third marriage was to Elizabeth Massie who had also been married twice before. Elizabeth Massie (November 24, 1844) first married George Massie April 11, 1863 in Lawrence Co., OH. Their only child was Calvin (1865). Her second marriage was to Ambrose Thornton January 24, 1868. Their children were Harmon, George, and Nancy. Elizabeth and Nicholas were married December 8, 1882 in Lawrence County. Children born to them were Tallitha Catherine (October 13, 1883) who married Isaac Myers and Dora Frances (April 1, 1885-September 23, 1978) who married Clarence Luman.

**O'DONNELL FAMILY** - Francis B. "Odie" O'Donnell was born December 5 1929, in Shawnee, Ohio (Perry County). The son of Thomas J. O'Donnell and Florence Kelly O'Donnell. Other children in the family were Joseph, Irene, and John.

Florence died in 1949, Thomas J. in 1962, Joseph in 1944, and Irene in 1985. All except Thomas are buried in New Lexington. He is buried in Logan. He graduated from Logan HS in 1947. He served two years in the US Army, 1951-1953, including 19 months in Germany.

Odie came to Gallipolis in September, 1954 and lived in the home of Clyde and Emma Ingles at the corner of Third and Locust Street until he married. On January 12, 1958, he married Anita Genene Tope, the daughter of Wendell V. and Marianna Irwin Tope at the St. John Catholic Church in Logan, Ohio. The Tope family operated a dairy farm on old Route 35 between Rio Grande and Rodney. Her brothers and sisters include Leland "Bud" Tope, Karen Hamrick, and Gaynelle Lynch.

Francis and Anita had two children; Patrick Andrew born December13, 1961 and Matthew Tope born April 17, 1964. Patrick O'Donnell is single and lives in Grand Rapids, Michigan. Matthew O'Donnell married Theresa Ann Sobjack of Perrysburg, Ohio in October, 1992 in Columbus. They have two children, Sean born 1994, and Timothy born in 1997. Their residence is Westerville.

Thomas was a distributor of petroleum products and gasoline for the Standard Oil Co. (SOHIO) for 38 years in Shawnee, New Lexington, and Logan.

Odie came to Gallipolis as a sports director and disc jockey at the radio station WJEH from 1954 until 1957. His "Odie's Roundup" program in the afternoon became widely known and led to his selection as Mister Deejay USA in 1956. O'Donnell also worked for the Radio Station WMOV in Ravenswood, W Va. for three years, The City Loan and Savings Co. in Gallipolis for two years, and as Sports Editor, and later as a correspondent for the Gallipolis Daily Tribune from 1957 until 2002. From 1963 until his retirement in January 1996, Odie was an outside salesman for the G & J Auto Parts and Parts Plus Auto Store, operated by U. A. and John Cornett, Sr.

Odie served as the public address announcer for all of the GAHS home football games from 1960 until 2000. As of this writing, he has been the official scorebook keeper for all of the GAHS home and away boys varsity basketball games for 39 years.

He is a member of Post 27 American Legion, VFW Post 4464, a Life member of DAV Post 53 in Meigs Co., Knights of Columbus Council 3335, St. Louis Catholic Church, and served from 1960 until 1969 as a Board of Director of the Gallia County Agricultural Society. He is a charter member of the Gallipolis Lions club in 1956, and held the post of Tailtwister for 40 years, a state record for this office.

Odie was inducted into the Ohio Prep Sportswriters Hall of Fame in Columbus in 1998 and is a Kentucky Colonel.

**OILERS FAMILIES** - Most all of the Oilers in Gallia and the surrounding counties are descendents of one Samuel Oiler (Oyler) born 1781 in Pennsylvania and migrated through Virginia and later to Gallia County, Ohio. Samuel had two families (maybe three) marrying Polly Caldwell in Rockbridge County,Virginia December 24, 1811. This union produced eight children some of whom stayed in the Virginia area and some came to Ohio. The children were: Henry Oiler, Sarah (Sally) Oiler, Rhoda Oiler, Susannah Oiler, Samuel Oiler, Rebecca Oiler, John Oiler,Sr. and James D. Oiler. These eight children each had families and as they migrated, some ended up in Gallia, Jackson and Vinton Counties. Polly died in 1832 and is buried in Ewington Cemetery. Samuel married again in 1832 , this time to Elizabeth Bass born in Virginia, but they were married in Gallia County, October 13, 1832. This marriage produced six more children and the author of this article is descended from this union. The children were:

Frederick Franklin Oiler, Jacob Oiler, Peter Pearl Oiler, Andrew Jackson Oiler and George W. Oiler. Fredrick Franklin was my 2nd Great Grandfather and he served with his four brothers in the Civil War. The five brothers all served in

Company A: 27th Ohio Volunteer Regiment. They all returned home after the war. Andrew was wounded in the thigh at Kennesaw Mountain, Georgia in 1864 being part of Sherman's Army.

*Jim, Margaret, Set, Deidra, Emily*

Frederick Franklin (2nd G. Grandfather) married Miranda Ervin March 18, 1860 in Gallia County. This union produced thirteen children: Hannah, Nancy, Mary M., Martha A., Andrew Jack (1st G. Grandfather) Eliza E., John Henry, Corn, Melissa, Lemuel Perry, Frederick Sanford, Sarah L., and James. Many of the present day Oilers in this area are from Frederick.

Frederick Franklin is buried in the Ewing Cemetery in Huntington TWP.

Jacob Oiler had three children: Thomas B, Samuel D., and Orletha J. Jacob is buried in McGhee Cemetery in the village of Vinton.

George W. Oiler had four children: Mary E., Frederick, George H., and Elsey.

Samuel Oiler, the progenitor of this line died about 1850 and he and Elizabeth his wife are buried in Sheppard Cemetery in Huntington Twp.

Frederick Franklin Oiler had as one of his children Andrew Jack Oiler which was my 1st. G. Grandfather and his wife Mary Alice Hutchinson. They lived in the Siver Run area and later in Syracuse of Meigs county. They are both buried in the Gravel Hill Cemetery in Cheshire.

The children of Andrew Jack Oiler and Mary Hutchinson of Horse, Ky. were: George Oiler, Marion Oiler, James Lewis Oiler (grandfather) David Oiler, Clara Oiler, Lenora Oiler, Sara Oiler, Jerry Oiler, Clarence Oiler, and Martha Jean Oiler.

James Lewis Oiler (my grandfather) and wife Margaret Wall of West Hanilin, WV. had the following children consisting of 5 boys and one girl. Harry Richard, William Andrew, Robert Douglas, Charles Lewis, Kenneth Leroy (father) and Gail Lorraine.

Kenneth Leroy married Anna Grace Diddle of Syracuse in Meigs County and had Mary Margaret Oiler and James William Oiler now a resident of Gallia county and a retired science teacher for the Gallia County Local Schools. James married the former Janis Diane Philhis of Beverly, Ohio and had one son, Seth William Oiler now of Troy, Ohio. Seth married the former Christine Siebert of Tipp City, Ohio and has one daughter Isabelle Grace Oiler. James married again, this time to Margaret Elizabeth (Boggess) Hall who has two children, Emily Anne and Deidra Lynn. James and Margaret live with their family in the Rio Grande area of Gallia County. *Submitted by: James W. Oiler*

**JAMES L. & MAXIE A. OLIVER** - James Loren (Jim) and Maxie Ann Maddox-Oliver have lived in Gallipolis, Ohio since August 1973 when Jim was transferred to the Gavin Power Plant in Cheshire, Ohio from the John Amos Power Plant in Winfield, West Virginia. Jim and Maxie were born on Cabin Creek, West Virginia — both at home, in coal mine communities — Kayford and United, West Virginia. Jim's father, Douglas Franklin Oliver, was born in Syracuse (Meigs County), Ohio and graduated from Syracuse High School. Doug's father, John Oliver, was a stonemason who laid stone for the foundation of the railroad bridge that crosses the river between Gallipolis and Point Pleasant, West Virginia which still stands. "Doug served in the Army in Hawaii and ended up in the coal mines on Cabin Creek where he met and married Arbutus Love Selbe. They had three children, Jim, Metzel (Mickey) and Johnny.

Jim and Maxie graduated from East Bank High School, East Bank, West Virginia and married in 1953. He worked for the State Road Drafting Department in Charleston, West Virginia until he was recruited to the Milwaukee Braves baseball training camp and sent to a triple A baseball team in Florida. Jim then joined the Marine Corp. for a two-year stint at Camp Le Jeune, North Carolina in the 2nd Marine Division, Topographic Section.

Upon his return to civilian life, he began working for the AEP Kanawha River Plant in Glasgow, West Virginia. Jim retired from the Gavin Power Plant in Cheshire, Ohio in January 1995. Maxie worked as a secretary for 11 years, took 10 years off when their children were born and returned to work as a medical transcriptionist for Woodland Centers Mental Health Center for 18 years.

Jim and Maxie have two daughters, Keith Anne, and Jo Ellen who graduated from Gallia Academy and Ohio State University. Keith Anne is married to Jeffrey Scott Ream, and they have two daughters, Kristen Margaret and Carty Lynn. Jo Ellen is married to Dr. Albert K. Bartko and they have three children, Allison, Bret, and Kathryn.

Although Jim knew he was moving back to his father's "stomping grounds," Maxie did not discover until researching genealogy that her grandparents were married August 31, 1904 at the Gallia County Courthouse in Gallipolis. She later discovered that her great great grandparents were married in Vinton County, Ohio in 1812. Maxie's research has uncovered Welch ancestry under her maiden name of Maddox with a rich history of varied occupations such as preaching, store owners, bookkeeping, teaching, etc. Some of the history of the Maddox family can be found in a book written by James Corbin Kessel in 1986 called "The Corbins and Their Kin — a Record of the Oliver Perry Corbin Family.

**DR. DONALD AND CAROL P. O'ROURKE FAMILY** - Donald Eugene O'Rourke, was born 16 Jan 1932, Buford, Georgia, the son of Willard Grady O'Rourke and Farris Gratis Poole. He married Carol Margaret Pierson on 26 Jun 1965, the daughter of Allan Helge Pierson and Margaret Elizabeth Moline, in Marietta, Georgia. Donald graduated from Emory University, Atlanta, Georgia, 1953, and from the Medical College of Georgia School of Medicine, Augusta, Georgia, 1957.

After an internship in Macon, Georgia, he served in the United States Air Force, for two years as a Flight Surgeon. He returned to the Medical College of Georgia, Department of Obstetrics and Gynecology in 1960 for a three year residency. From 1963 until 1967 he was on the full-time faculty in the Department of Obstetrics and Gynecology, teaching medical students, and residents, achieving the rank of Assistant Professor. While there, he developed a teaching program for obstetrical patients using television for one of the first times in the nation. This program, funded by a Federal Grant, assured consistency and clarity in patient education, with enhanced use of the patients instructor's time. In 1967, he joined the Holzer Multispecialty Medical Clinic in Gallipolis, Ohio, in the Department of Obstetrics and Gynecology, practicing there until retirement in 1997. At Holzer, from 1975, he also held an appointment as Clinical Instructor, on the Ohio State University College of Medicine, Department of Obstetrics and Gynecology Faculty, Columbus, Ohio. Donald, a long time member of the Gallia County Historical and Genealogical Society, serving on the Board for a number of years, has volunteered more time there since his retirement. In April 2000, Donald received the Genealogical Society's annual. Jane Roush McCafferty, C. G. Award of Excellence in Genealogy, in recognition of his contributions.

*Donald And Carol P. O'Rourke Family L: to R: Mike, Molly, Don, Carol, Gene, Bruce O'rourke*

Carol Margaret Pierson, was born 11 Nov 1942, Montclair, New Jersey, the birthplace of her parents. All four of her grandparents had been born in Sweden. Using the Swedish National Archives, some of her ancestors have been traced back to the mid-1600's there. Her maternal grandfather had his own tailor shop, and her paternal grandfather, built estate-size residential homes in New Jersey. Carol graduated from the Medical College of Georgia School of Nursing 1964, Augusta, Georgia. She taught full-time on the Medical College of Georgia faculty in the School of Nursing. After the family was established, she returned to full-time nursing. In 2000, she received her masters degree in nursing from the University of Cincinnati, Cincinnati, Ohio. In Gallipolis, Ohio, she was one of the first women to serve as City Commissioner, serving eight years. Carol was the first woman to serve as President of the City Commissioners. One of her major projects as City Commissioner was to start a perpetual Tree Committee for the city.

Hundreds of new trees have already been planted in the ongoing project. One of her favorite Ariel volunteer activities has been with the Theatre and the Ohio Valley Symphony Orchestra.

Their children: (1) Donald Eugene, Jr., born 27 Feb 1967, Augusta, Georgia, married on 07 Oct 1995, to Lisa Marie Vorhees, born 13 Nov 1963, Wheeling, West Virginia, daughter of Gareth Francy Vorhees and Dorothy Rose Marie Smith. Lisa graduated from West Liberty State College, Wheeling, West Virginia. Donald, Jr., "Gene" graduated from Bates College, Lewiston, Maine, and the University of Cincinnati, Cincinnati, Ohio, and works as a computer consultant for Accenture. Lisa is a retail manager. Living in Cincinnati, their children are (a) Abigail Sydney, born, 05 Dec 1997, (b) twin, Emily Marie, born 11 Feb 2000, and (c) twin, Garrett Pierson, born 11 Feb 2000.

(2) Bruce Allan, born 28 May 1968, Gallipolis, Ohio, married on 01 May 1999, Lee Winfield Bowers, daughter of Dr.Glenn Wilson Bowers, Jr. and Frances Anne Winfield. Lee, born 08 Dec 1968, Winston-Salem, North Carolina, graduated from Miami University, Oxford, Ohio.

Bruce graduated from Wake Forest University, Winston-Salem, North Carolina. Living in Atlanta, Georgia, Bruce is a financial consultant, and Lee is a retail manager for Rich's and Federated Department Stores. Their son, Brady Allan, was born 12 Feb 2002, Atlanta, Georgia.

(3) Michael Patrick, born 22 Mar 1970, Gallipolis, Ohio, graduated from Appalachian State University, Boone, North Carolina. He now lives and works in St. Paul, Minnesota, at U. S. Bank, in the Investment Department. He attends St. Thomas University, St. Paul, Minnesota, pursuing a Masters Degree in Business. He married Audrey Anne Dahl, 09 Jun 2001, in Oak Park Heights, Washington County, MN. Audrey was born 25 Aug 1979, in San Diego, CA, daughter of John David Dahl and Evangeline Diaz Alvarez. Their son, Chase Ashby, was born, 09 Nov 2001, St. Paul, Ramsey County, MN. Audrey will resume her studies at the College of St. Catherine, St. Paul, MN.

(4) Molly Kathleen, born 21 Mar 1972, Gallipolis, Ohio, graduated from Hope College, Holland, Michigan. Molly received her masters degree in education from Rio Grande University, Rio Grande, Ohio. An elementary school teacher, she planned to travel to many parts of the world before marriage. She taught several years in Michigan, two years in Peru, and currently in the second of three years in Kuwait. She has visited many countries, both enroute and adjacent to those where she teaches. For instance, she spent one month crossing Costa Rica, with an Outward Bound Group.

*Submitted by: Donald E. O'Rourke*

**OVERTURF-DURST** - Our first known Durst was David, supposed to have died on his way home from the War of 1812 in Black Swamp, Ohio. His wife was Christine Roush. Records show that they purchased land in Kyger Township from Abraham Durst. Thomas Dillman Durst, son of David and Elizabeth Blackburn Durst, was born October 9, 1859. He married Mary Shirley, daughter of Joseph and Orilla Sayre Shirley, who was born May 16, 1864. She was a school teacher.

One of their eleven children was Sidney Durst, born April 25, 1900. He married Iva See, daughter of George and Mary Beattie See. George Ludwig See married Margaret Tachundi and came to America from Silesia, Germany. Mary's parents were Moses and Margaret Wilson Beattie who came from Ireland about 1858. Their son Fredrick settled near the present town of Arbuckle in Mason County. At that time it was Greenbrier County, Virginia. He was killed in his home by Shawnee Indians during a raid in 1763. His son, Michael See was killed by Indians on May 17, 1792, near Fort Randolph. The same day Michael was killed, his son William was born. William See married Sarah Pruitt. William See Jr. married Margaret Sayre and were the parents of George, who became father of Iva.

Sidney (1900-1968) and Iva Durst (1898-1979) were the parents of two children. Paul Curtis Durst was born February 13, 1931. He married Diana Vittone from Masontown, Penn. They have a daughter, Paula Lynn, born February 24, 1966 and reside in Charleston, W. Va.

Ralph Clinton Durst was born October 2, 1929 in Leon, West Virginia. He attended Yeager and Grant Elementary School and graduated from Point Pleasant High School. He served in the Korean War in an observation batallion. Upon his return from Korea, he entered a Pharmacy training course at Holzer Hospital and became a Pharmacy Technician. He has remained in this position at Holzer for twenty-five years.

He married Naomi Overturf, who was born September 24, 1932 in Middleport, Ohio. She is a graduate of Middleport High School and Holzer School of Nursing. She worked on the staff at Holzer until 1965 when she became Director of Nursing at Gallipolis Clinic and Medical Center Hospital. At the present time she is a night supervisor at the Gallipolis State Institute.

They are the parents of three children. Mary Ann was born May 16, 1965 and attends Gallia Academy High School. Their twins Judy Ann and Julie Ann were born July 6, 1968 and attend Washington Elementary School.

Naomi is the daughter of Virginia Vititoe Overturf and the late Francis Overturf. There were three other children born to this union. Dorothy Louise (1937-1974) was married to William Harman and their children are Lisa Thompson, Mitchell, and Janice Hill. Paul Edward Overturf, born in 1939, married Marjorie Henneke (1942-1975) and their children are Paul Edward, Jr. (1959-1974) and Melodie. Judith Ann, born 1945, married James Dowling and their children are Joseph and James.

Naomi is the only descendant of Dr. Solomon Long that presently resides in Gallia County. Refer to Vititoe — Jones — Long —Overturf.

*Submitted by Ralph/Naomi Durst*

**OVERTURF-DURST FAMILY** - The Durst-Overturf family has seen many changes since our history was written for the 1980 Gallia County Family History Book.

Mary Ann Durst graduated from Gallia Academy in1984 and continues to live in Gallipolis.

Judy Durst graduated from Gallia Academy in 1986. She attended L.P.N. School at Buckeye Hills Career Center and is presently employed at Holzer Medical Center. She married Kevin Halley June 29, 1991 with the wedding taking place at the Ariel Theater. Kevin is the son of Roger and Doris Halley of Crown City, Oh, and is employed at Pleasant Valley Hospital.

*Durst -Overturf Family*

Julie Durst graduated from Gallia Academy in 1986. She attended L.P.N. School at Buckeye Hills Career Center. She then attended Hocking Technical College for a R. N. degree and is presently employed at Holzer Medical Center. She married Max Ours, May 14, 1994. Max is the son of Barbara Ours of Crown City, OH, and Max Ours of Washington Court House, OH. and is employed at Carmichael's Farm and Lawn. Julie and Max have one daughter, Amy June Ours. Amy was born October 4, 1995 and attends kindergarten at Ohio Valley Christian School.

Ralph retired from the Holzer Medical Center Pharmacy in 1993. He remains active in various veterans' organizations, the Conservation Club, Animal Welfare League and Friends of the Library.

Naomi retired from Gallipolis Developmental Center in 1996. She held the position of R. N. on night shift for 25 years.

Mary Ann, Judy and Julie were adopted when they were infants. Judy and Julie were reunited with their birth family in 1999. Mary Ann was reunited with her birth family in 2001. Birthdays and holidays now have a large number of family members in attendance.

More reference to the Durst-Overturf family can be found in the 1980 Gallia County Family History Book under the names of Jones-Long-Overturf-Vititoe. Submitted by Mary Ann Durst.

**PASQUALE –BEARD FAMILY** - Louis Michael Pasquale was born April 11, 1937 in Kenova, WV. to Julius (Lapelli) and Margaret (Gustin) Pasquale. Louis was raised in Kenova until the early 1950's, when his family moved to Gallipolis, where his father, Julius, was working construction on the Kyger Creek Plant. Louis had three siblings: Thomas E. born September 8, 1938, John born March 1, 1940 and Sharon (Sherry) born June 14, 1944. He attended Gallia Academy High School until his senior year when he quit to join the navy. He later finished high school in the service.

On December 14, 1959, he married Alice Kay Beard, at High Point, NC. They had three children, a son, Louis Michael Pasquale, Jr. (see Pasquale—Stinson Family) and twin daughters, Julia Lynn Pasquale and Donna Gwynn (Pasquale) Thompson (see Pasquale-Thompson

Family). Julia is a registered nurse having received an associate degree in nursing from Rio Grande College in 1986. Since graduation, she has worked in critical care and emergency nursing until the summer of 2000, when she entered the School of Medicine at Marshall University, Huntington, WV. Louis and Alice also have four wonderful grandchildren: Levi and Tessa Thompson, and Mikayla and Alex Pasquale.

Louis worked as a deckhand for the Union Barge Line for a short while, then began working construction as a pipefitter. He belonged to the Plumbers and Steamfitters Local of Portsmouth. Louis was an electrician and also did refrigeration while working for his father at Gallia Refrigeration. He later took over the refrigeration business for his father. In addition, he started and managed Pasquale Electric until his death.

Louis was very active in the community having been a member of the Gallipolis Volunteer Fire Department and served on the Gallipolis City Commission. He also belonged to the Masonic Lodge, Shriners, Lions Club, Elks, and Cliffside Golf Club. Louis was a member of the First Baptist Church.

Alice Kay Beard, daughter of Gilbert and Irene Beard was born in Gallipolis, Ohio on May 20, 1937. She is a member of the First Families of Gallia County (see related history—Gilbert Beard, Rothgebs of Fairhaven, Fife-Vance, and Martin Rup families in "Gallia County Ohio People in History to 1980", by the Gallia County Historical Society). Alice went to school in Gallipolis, graduated from Gallia Academy in 1955 and entered the Holzer Hospital School of Nursing. After graduating in 1958, she worked at the Holzer Hospital in the operating room as a staff nurse and later as supervisor, until she started working at the School of Nursing. While working, she also attended Ohio University, obtaining her B. S. degree in 1977 and a year later getting her Master's degree in Nursing from the Ohio State University. After teaching at Ohio University for approximately two years, Alice returned to the Holzer School of Nursing until it closed in 1982. She then worked in the Emergency Department of the Holzer Medical Center and later as a case manager on the nursing units. After over forty years in nursing, Alice retired in 1998.

Louis passed away on April 15, 1991. Alice was remarried in April 1997 to Joseph Gerald Giles. (see Giles history in this book)

*Submitted by Alice Beard Giles*

**PASQUALE – STINSON FAMILY** - Louis Michael Pasquale, Jr. was born October 5, 1960 in Gallipolis, Ohio. He is the son of Louis and Alice Beard Pasquale (see Pasquale-Beard history in this book). Michael attended schools in Gallipolis, graduating from Gallia Academy in 1978. He then entered the army, serving in Germany, Hawaii and the States. He was honorably discharged in July 1985, having served six years, ten months and thirteen days. Michael is currently serving in the West Virginia National Guard.

After the service, Michael worked for Pasquale Electric and also attended Rio Grande College. He graduated in 1987 with an Associate Degree in Electronics Technology. He continued working at Pasquale Electric until going to the Phillip Sporn Plant at New Haven, VW in 1989. Although, Michael is an experienced electrician, his passion is working with computers. Therefore, in January 2002, after nearly thirteen years of service, Michael left the Phillip Sporn Plant and re-enrolled in Rio Grande University to pursue his bachelor's degree in computer science.

*L: to R: Mikayla, Michael, Robin and Alex Pasquale.*

On October 4, 1986, Michael married Robin Lynn Stinson, daughter of Fred and Phyllis Joy (Dingess) Stinson of Gallia County. Robin was born January 13, 1964 at Logan W.V. Robin's parents are from Chapmanville, W.V. and moved to Gallia County. She attended North Gallia and Buckeye Hills schools and graduated from North Gallia High School. She graduated from Rio Grande College with an associate degree in nursing in 1986. Robin is a registered nurse and worked for thirteen years on the Obstetrical Unit at Holzer Medical Center. For the past three years, she has worked in Urgent Care at the Holzer Clinic, where she is currently employed. Robin attends the Ash Street Church in Middleport, Ohio and teaches an adult Sunday school class.

Michael and Robin have two children, a daughter, Mikayla Lynn, born August 11, 1988 and a son, Alexander Julius (named for his great-grandfather, Julius Pasquale) born July 18, 1990. Both attend the Ohio Valley Christian School in Gallipolis. Mikayla is in the eighth grade and enjoys designing and decorating her bedroom. Alex is in the fifth grade and likes computer games.

*Submitted by: Mike Pasquale*

**PASQUALE – THOMPSON FAMILY** - Donna Gwynn Pasquale was born January 26, 1962 in Holzer Hospital, Gallipolis, Ohio. She is the daughter of the late Louis Pasquale and Alice Giles, and the stepdaughter of Joe Giles. Donna has a twin sister, Julia Lynn, who is four minutes older. Julia is a registered nurse (see Pasquale—Beard Family in this book), but her favorite role is that of "special aunt" to her nephews and nieces.

Donna attended schools in Gallipolis and graduated from Gallia Academy High School in 1980. She graduated from Rio Grande College with a bachelor's degree in elementary education in 1984. She taught school at Mason, WV. for six years, until going to Washington Elementary, Gallipolis, Ohio in 1990 where she is currently teaching. In 1991, Donna obtained her master's degree in Special Education from Marshall University in Huntington, WV. She became Nationally Board Certified in Education in 1999. Donna puts a lot of work into her classroom, and loves to see the students grow and change throughout the year.

On May 30, 1984, Donna married Dwight David Thompson, son of Emmett and Pauline (Herrmann) Thompson of Cheshire, Ohio (see Emmett Eugene Thompson Family in Gallia County Ohio People in History to 1980 by Gallia County Historical Society) Dwight worked at E. T. & S. (Emmett Thompson & Sons) Sand and Gravel at Gallipolis Ferry, WV. The name is now changed to Letart Corporation, where he is still working. He and his brothers, Roy and Jon own the business. Dwight and Donna were later divorced in May 2001. Both still live in the Cheshire area.

Donna and Dwight have two children, Levi Emmett Thompson, born May 10, 1986 and Tessa Lynn Thompson, born October 3, 1988. Levi attends River Valley High School and is a sophomore. He is an avid reader and enjoys four-wheeling on his ATV. Tessa is in the seventh grade at Kyger Creek Middle School. She also is an avid reader and loves animals and birds. Right now, she is considering being a veterinarian or an ornithologist, but that could all easily change tomorrow.

*Submitted by Donna Thompson*

**THOMAS E. AND MARY BELLE PASQUALE FAMILY** - Thomas E. Pasquale was born in Kenova, WV September 8 1938 to Julius and Margaret (Gustin) Pasquale. Julius was born October 12, 1908 and died March 2 1983. Julius was born to Louis Lapille and Vincenza Conzolina, both natives of Italy. Margaret was born May 15, 1913 and died January 3, 1998. Margaret was born to George Gustin and Birdie Tibbs both of Superior, Ohio

Thomas has 3 siblings: Louis born April 11, 1937 and died April 15, 1991; John born March 1, 1940; Sherry born June 14, 1944. Julius and Margaret along with their 4 children came to Gallipolis in 1953. Thomas graduated from Gallia Academy High School in 1957. Thomas met Mary Belle Cook and married on June 14, 1959.

Mary Belle Cook was born August 2, 1935 and is the daughter of John and Mamie Walker Cook. John Cook born June 5, 1900 in True Summers, WV and died March 12, 1988 and Mamie (Walker) was born July 10, 1902 in Gallipolis Ferry, WV and died February 1993. Mary Belle has 13 siblings: Charles, Virginia, (Gibson), Walter, Cecil, John Jr., Ruth (Northup), Lucy (Mitchell), Faye (Pierce), Donna (Sheline), Larry, Dale and Eleanor.

Thomas and Mary Belle owned and operated Belle Contracting Company. They had three children: Pamela, born May 14, 1960; Patricia, born November 16, 1962; and Thomas J. (T.J.) born April 10, 1966.

Pamela married Keith Wiseman August 13, 1983. Pamela is attending Rio Grande College and Keith is an employee of the Kyger Creek Plant. They have three children: Britt, born May 11, 1986; Andrea, born May 30, 1991; Nathan, born October 18, 1994. Britt attends Gallia Academy High School and is an honor roll student. Britt has participated in the soccer team and is the President of the Gallia Academy Key Club.

Britt also has participated in History Day for five years and won Best of State at National Level in 2001. Andrea and Nathan both attend Green Elementary School. Andrea is a student at the French Art Colony and Nathan participates in soccer and baseball

Patricia and Mark Gay married February 4, 1994 have a unique family. Mark and Patricia adopted each other children. They have 6 children: Brian, December 31, 1979; Jeremy, January 28, 1979; Amy, June 26, 1982; Jessica, October 13, 1982; Laura, December 14, 1984 and Shayne, August 5, 1985. Laura and Shayne attend Gallia Academy High School. Brian is employed as a construction worker. Jeremy works for a barge company and is married to Kami Holcomb and they have a son, Logan, born October 25, 2001. Jessica and Rob Means have a son named Ethan born April 10, 2001. Amy and Boone Farmer have a son Josh born August 24, 2001. Patricia and Mark both are employed at Rockwell. Patricia attends Gallipolis Career College and has been on the honor roll for the year.

Thomas J. married Kelli Brownell May 27, 1989 and they have two children. Kelsi, born April 30, 1994 and Brooke, born November 20, 1998. Thomas J. has been employed with the Ohio Lottery since 1988 and Kelli is a Registered Nurse and employed at Holzer.

**RONALD C. PATRICK AND CHARLOTTE JANE (MYERS) PATRICK FAMILY** - Ronald was born January 25, 1939 in Hardy, Kentucky, the son of Charlie J. and the late Grethel (Mounts) Patrick. He has two brothers, Kenneth R. and Danny C. Patrick, and two sisters, Garnet B. (Patrick) McNeal and Nina G. (Patrick) Palk.

*Warren, Grace, and Henry Patrick.*

Ronald attended school in Hardy, Kentucky and is a graduate of American School. He has been employed by the Gallia County Highway Department since 1986 and is currently a Bridge Superintendent.

His wife Charlotte Jane (Myers) Patrick was born at home on October 23, 1942 at Patriot, Ohio the daughter of the late Chester A. Myers and the late Georgianna C. (Pope) Myers. She has three brothers living in Gallia County, Floyd Donald Myers, Henry Lee Myers, and Lloyd Leon Myers, and one sister, Monna June (Myers) Cheatham living in Rustburg, Virginia. She also has one brother who is deceased, Chester Eugene "Gene" Myers.

Charlotte is a graduate of Southwestern High School and has spent most of her life in Gallia County. She is and has been employed at H & R Block in Gallipolis since 1970. Ronald and Charlotte were married on October 24, 1960 in South Carolina. They have two Sons, Ronald Jeffrey "Jeff" Patrick born on August 29, 1961 in Chicago, Illinois and Randall "Randy" Jay Patrick born on May 25, 1964 in Columbus, Ohio.

Jeff graduated from Gallia Academy High School in 1979 and then graduated from Summit Theological Seminary in Peru, Indiana. He is presently the minister of Rio Grande Christian Church in Rio Grande, Ohio. He is married to the former Barbara Alice Stevenson from Point Pleasant who was born on April 12, 1962. She is a Branch Manager for Ohio Valley Bank Corp.

They have one son Henry Leon Patrick who was born on February 11, 1991 in Gallipolis, Ohio.

He is an honor student at Ohio Valley Christian School in Gallipolis, Ohio and involved in many sports programs.

Randy graduated from Gallia Academy High School in 1982 and then graduated from Toledo University, School of Pharmacy, in Toledo, Ohio in 1989. He is a registered pharmacist with K-Mart Corporation in Gallipolis, Ohio. He is married to the former Kelly Jo Browning from Zanesville, Ohio who was born June 28, 1968 in Zanesville, Ohio. She presently works for the Gallia County Schools System as a teachers aide. They have two children, Victoria Grace Patrick who was born on January 30, 1990 and Warren Browning Patrick who was born on March 6, 1993. Both were born in Gallipolis, Ohio and presently attend Southwestern Elementary School in Gallia County. They are both honor students and participate in "On the Right Track". Grace is a member of the Girl Scouts and Warren participates in soccer.

The Patrick's are members of the Gallipolis Christian Church and Rio Grande Christian Church.

Charlotte's family lines extend back to the 1800's with the surnames of Myers, Pope and Klages.

Our family is truly proud to be Gallia Countians and we strive to make it a better place to live.

**JOHN AARON AND OPAL (STEWART) PAYNE FAMILY** - I'm from a family of Gallia County from way back. My great grandparents were born and raised in the county. Also my grandparents who were James and Tacy (Sanders) Stewart and Charlie and Cora (Barlow) Donnally.

I was born in Gallia County at Mercerville, Ohio. My parents were Oty and Sabra (Donnally) Stewart. I have one brother, Norman Stewart.

John came from a family of four older sisters and two younger brothers. John was born in Roane County, W.VA. His parents were Clinton and Ella (Halbert) Payne.

Their family moved to Gallia County in 1937 from Roane County to the farm at Vinton when John was 9 years old. John and I are parents of twin daughters, Jerri (Payne) Samples and Kathy (Payne) Alderman, and a son Johnny Payne. Grandparents of ten grandchildren (Chris, Ryan, Kari, Alison, Michael, John, Jill, Craig, Scott and Beth.) and one great-grandchild, Talyn Alderman.

My family lived in Huntington, W.VA and Springfield, Ohio before moving back to Gallia County, when I was a freshman in high school.

John and I first met when we were freshman at Vinton High School. Graduated in the same class four years later.

*John & Opal Payne*

I found employment in Columbus with Farm Bureau Ins. Co. where I worked for five months following graduation. At this time an opening became available in the Probate Court office in Gallipolis which I graciously accepted. I worked there three years.

After dating for three years, John and I were married at Vinton Baptist Church by Rev. Earl Cremeans in 1950. We celebrated our 50th anniversary with a reception at the same church, May 14th, 2000.

John remained on the farm doing farming with his dad. We purchased the farm from John's parents in 1960. In 1957 we purchased 11 dairy cows from James Jacobs. We milked those cows at Jacobs' for three months while John's brother-in-law, Bob Thompson, built us a milking parlor on the family farm. We continued milking cows for 35 years along with John driving the school bus for 12 1/2 yrs. At this time we sold the cows and machinery to our son Johnny and daughter-in-law Denise and family.

John and I are supposed to be retired, but we try to keep busy with whatever is going on, on the farm, at the church, school, and with the grandchildren.

We are active members of Vinton Baptist Church which we pray will continue to grow. I also do mentoring at the school when needed.

Submitted by Opal Payne

**ROBERT MORTON AND DEBORA MAY DOUGHTY PEGG FAMILY** - Robert Morton Pegg was born July 13, 1954 at Holzer Hospital in Gallipolis, Ohio to Elias William Pegg and Nelgene McKean Pegg. Robert is the younger brother of his twin brother William McKean Pegg.

Robert graduated from Gallia Academy High School in 1972. After attending Morehead State University at Morehead, Kentucky, for pre-pharmacy studies, he went to Atlanta, Georgia and graduated from Mercer Southern School of Pharmacy in 1977. He did his pharmacy internship at Price & Son's Pharmacy, a local pharmacy which was located at the corner of State Street and Second Avenue. Robert started his practice at Rite Aid Pharmacy in the Silver Bridge Plaza in Gallipolis, Ohio. He then went to work for Fruth Pharmacy at Gallipolis, Ohio, where he became the pharmacy director of the 22 store chain. He was the President of the Gallipolis Area Jaycees in 1983. An avid flyer, Robert got his private pilot's license in 1992 and is presently a member of the Mason County Flying Club.

Robert married Debora May Doughty on October 27, 2001 in Charleston, West Virginia.

Debora graduated from Winfield High School in 1974. After graduation she worked at Bobbie Brooks Textile Company and the Rite Aid Pharmacy Warehouse of Nitro, West Virginia. She is presently a chemical operator at Dow-Union Carbide of Charleston, West Virginia.

*Bob & Debora Pegg*

Their family includes one son, James William Doughty, a computer programmer of Cross Lanes, West Virginia.

Their residence is in the Meadows Subdivision in Green Township.

## FREEMAN C. AND JANET ELIZABETH KEGAN PETTUS -
Freeman Charles Pettus was born on March 15, 1909 in Pageton, West Virginia to Charles William (Chap) and Bessie Miles Pettus. He was one of five children of this couple.

At the age of three Freeman's family moved to Powhatan, McDowell Co., WV here his father became a coal miner. At the age of 12, Freeman also became a miner because his father had died at a very young age and this left the boys to provide for the family.

Freeman developed a love for baseball and played for a company team which travelled to different mining towns. One of these was Jenkins, KY and it was there he met Janet Elizabeth Kegan who was one of seven children born to Bernard (NMN) Kegan and Mary Jane Hand Kegan. "Pet" played for the Detroit Tigers farm club at Wheeling in the Middle Atlantic League and at Charlotte, NC as a team mate of the late Hank Greenberg who later became a star for the Tigers.

Freeman and Janet were married on June 10, 1933 in Jenkins, KY by Rev. J. S. Hale. They set up housekeeping in Powhatan, WV and on July 22, 1934 welcomed their first child, Madge Elizabeth. When she was three, Janet and Pet moved to Jenkins, KY. On January 8, 1938, their second child, Joan Marie was born. They remained in Letcher Co. until 1942 when they moved to Stirrat, Logan Co., WV. While there they added two more children to the family, Ina Claire Jane and Freeman Charles, Jr.

In 1944 the family moved to a farm in Gallia County, Ohio just outside of Vinton. Janet had to quickly adapt to doing without amenities she had become accustomed to in the mining towns—no running water, no inside plumbing, no company store, no walking to wherever you wanted to go.

In December, 1945 the family moved to a residence at 2981 Lincoln Pike. Having learned that it was impossible to hold down a full-time job and farm, too, Pet accepted employment with Houdaille-Hershey Manufacturing in Huntington, WV. He was very active in the Local 3739 of the United Steelworkers and served several terms as president. He was also an avid Mason and maintained a membership in the Kenova Lodge 110, A.F. & A.M. as well as the Kenova Chapter 46 Royal Arch Masons. He was a 32nd degree Mason. He died in Cabell-Huntington hospital on October 30, 1963 at the age of 54.

In addition to raising her four children, Janet served as a 4-H Advisor for 30-plus years. She continues to live on Lincoln Pike and attends the little country church at Northup. She reached the age of 89 on November 27, 2001 and enjoys a reasonable measure of good health even though she must depend on assistance to walk. She continues to try to read all of the large print books in the Bossard Library and to solve current crossword puzzles.

## WILLIAM H. PHILLIPS FAMILY -
William Harvey Phillips - born, November 20, 1931, Porter, Ohio, Parents: William Paul Philips an Dorothy M. (Smith) Phillips, graduated Bidwell/Porter High School, 1949. Military service, 4 yrs. U. S. Navy, U. S. S. (CL 145), married Sopha G. Stout, 12 Dec. 1953. Occupation: 4 years Evans Super Market, 8 years Valley Bell Dairy, 23 years owner Cottrell's Grocery, Porter, Ohio.

*William H. Philllips Family*

Children - 1. William Wayne, born 11 September 1955, graduated 1973, N.G.H.S. married Monna Lynn Houck, 19 August 1978, born, 23 January 1957. Parents, Farrell Allen Houck and Marlene (Evans) Houck. Children - 1 - Willliam Allen, born 11 September 1980 and 2 - Gregory Wayne, born October 9, 1986.

2. Charles F., born March 6, 1960, graduated 1978, N.G.H.S., married, Carol Ann Reynolds, October 9, 1982, born September 1962. Parents - David L. Reynolds and Mary Lou (Krump) Reynolds. Children, 1. Charles F. Jr., born June 3, 1983 and 2. - Lindsay Nicole, born April 2, 1985.

Sopha G. Stout, born January 13, 1934, Cabin Creek, WV, Parents, Jahue Christian Burkit Stout and Danford F. (Dunn) Stout.

William Paul Phillips, born June 21, 1910, Gallia Co., Ohio, died September 30, 1972, married Dorothy M. Smith, April 14, 1931, Greenup, KY, parents, William Andrew Phillips and Marinda Caroline Pierce. Occupation - Rolling Store for E. L. Cottrell General Merchandise in 1930's. After Edward L. Cottrell's retirement in 1967, William Paul and Son William H. became owners, changed name to Cottrell's Grocery. After William Paul's death in 1972, William H. and wife Sopha G. became owners.

Dorothy M. Smith, born October 30, 1909, Putnam County, WV, died July 14, 1972, parents, James Henry Smith and Isadora B. Rowsey. Children of William Paul and Dorothy Marie Smith, 1. - William Harvey, married Sopha G. Stout, 2. - Robert Lee, born December 30, 1932, died June 21, 1961, car accident, married Mildred E. Myers, 3. - Gerald E., born December 17, 1934, married Janet Joyce Scott.

William Andrew Phillips, born June 17, 1874, Lawrence Co., Ohio, died July 25 1948, Gallia County, OH, parents, William Henry Phillips and Helen DeLille, married Marinda Caroline Pierce, April 16, 1902, born, June 7, 1883, died February 12, 1962, parents, David Pierce and Emily Glassburn. Children, 1.- Georgia Elizabeth, born August 21, 1903, married Fay Coder, 2 Dorothea Marie, born March 7, 1906, married Richard Thomas Cole, 3. William Paul, born June 21, 1910, married Dorothy Marie Smith and 4. Robert E., born July 10, 1922, died July 16, 1922.

William Henry Phillips, born October 3, Vinton Co., Ohio, died December 12, 1924, Gallia Co., Ohio. Parents, Henry Phillips and Elizabeth Skirvin, married Helen DeLille, March 21, 1869.

Helen DeLille, born February 3, 1851, Gallia Co., Died December 12, 1925, Gallia Co., Oh, parents, Joseph DeLille and Isabella Martin. Children, 1 - Lillie Belle, born May 21, 1870. Died December 12, 1925, Gallia Co., parents, Joseph DeLille and Isabella Martin. Children, 1 - Lillie Belle, born May 21, 1870, married Fredric Hesse, 2 - Joseph Henry, born November 16, 1871, died January 22, 1945, married Eliza Ann Pierce, 3 - William Andrew, born June 17, 1874, died July 25, 1948, married Marinda Caroline Pierce, 4. - Charles Roscoe, born July 30, 1883, married Nora Ward.

Henry Phillips, born February 20,1810, Gallia Co., Ohio, died May 18, 1899, Decatur Township, Lawrence County, Oh, parents, William Phillips and Mary (Polly) Hartman, married 1. Elizabeth Skirvin, December 30, 1846, 2. - Rebecca (Warren) Rankin, May 3, 1855.

Elizabeth Skirvin, born October 6, 1830, died July 29, 1883, Lawrence Co, Ohio, parents, Nathaniel Skirvin and Maria Bumgardner, Children, 1.- William Henry, born October 3, 1847, married Helen DeLille, 2.- Mary Jane, born August 9, 1850, never married, 3 - Francis Marion, (Frank M.), born February 14, 1852, married Louise Delaney. 2nd wife, Rebecca (Warren) Rankin, widow of Bartlett Rankin, children of Barlett and Rebecca,, William, Rhoda, Joanna, James Perry and Hiram. Married Henry Phillips, May 3, 1855, Children of Henry and Rebecca, 1. - Abraham, married Mary Ellen Bloebraum, 2. - Andrew Jackson, married Harriet Delaney and 3. - Henry, married Alice Thompson.

William Phillips, born October 22, 1792, August Co., Va., died December 28, 1874, Gallia Co., in War of 1812, 5th Regiment, VA Militia, Alexander Givens Co., under command of colonel James McDowell. Came to Gallia County in 1817, met Mary (Polly) Hartman, married in Raccoon Township, April 19, 1818 by William Blagg Justice of the Peace.

Mary (Polly Hartman, born October 31, 1785, Maryland or Pennsylvania, died February 25, 1881, Gallia County, Spring field Township,

Gallia County, Ohio. Children, 1. - Henry B., September 20, 1819, died May 18, 1899, 2. - Rachel, born September 18, 1821, died October 11, 1868, Phillipsburg, Missouri, married John A. Stanley, 3. - Abraham B., November, 1822, died, 1903, married Mary Jane Carr, 4. - Susannah, born December 30, 1824, died, June 24, 1877, married Lewis Dyas, 5. - Elizabeth, born 1827, died Kansas, married David Dyas.
*Submitted by William H. Phillips Family*

**DAVID A. PICKENS FAMILY** - David A. Pickens, born January 6, 1883 in Columbus, Ohio, was the son of Edward and Catherine Barnes Pickens. Edward's parents were Patrick and Ann Shea Pickens, both born in Ireland although the Pickens family was not Irish, per se, but French. David married Margaret Jane Turner, February 18, 1919, at Logan, Ohio. Margaret, born September 13, 1894, near Bethany Church, Perry Township, Hocking County, Ohio, was the daughter of Albert and Rosetta Hood Turner.

*David and Margaret Turner Pickens and children*

David and Margaret came to Gallia County in 1919, with the Keener Sand and Clay Company. They always lived near Kerr and all their children were born there. David was an active, friendly man, and was quickly right at home in his new place. Always interested in his adopted community, he built baseball diamonds, tennis courts, football fields, rebuilt the road to Mound Hill Cemetery and planted the row of sycamore trees on the park front. A devout Catholic, he or Urban Cornett traveled to Pomeroy, Ohio, (Meigs County) every Friday for years, to bring the Sisters to Gallipolis to teach Catechism. David's most lasting monument may well turn out to be the old organ at St Louis Catholic Church in Gallipolis. He engineered it up to the choir loft and no one has been able to get it down to this day. Fishing and hunting were his favorite pastimes and he was not above building the ponds to fish. David loved all sports but his first love was baseball and he together with Stanley Evans and Ed Myers fielded their own team, the "Gallipolis Gauls".

Margaret quiet, industrious, family and home loving, was perhaps an embodiment of her Pennsylvania Dutch ancestors with enough of the old Virginians (the Turners) thrown in for fun. To no one or to no living thing was she ever unkind.

David and Margaret had five children: Margaret C. married and divorced George Margoles, Eugene was twice married, first to Venitta Thabet (deceased) and second to Otlie Dauber, Julia married Earl Prose, Louise married Vance Johnson, Mary Ann was married twice, first to Charles Y. Lakin (deceased) and second to Charles F. Wood.

Their grandchildren are: Margaret's; Christina, John and George, Julia's; Susan, Thomas and Martha, Louise's: David, Mark, Julianna, Brent, Caroline and Elizabeth, Mary Ann's; Charles, Michael, Ann and William.

David's legacy for the love of sports has been passed down through his son, grandchildren and his great-grandchildren. Eugene played baseball on the semi-pro team in Gallipolis. Tom Prose, David, Mark and Brent Johnson, Chuck, Mike, Ann (Carter) and Willie Wood, continued the sports tradition. Burt and Clayton Wood, Shannon and Markie Carter. Brianne and Hayley Johnson in Gallia County are continuing this Pickens's tradition.

David died April 10, 1966 and Margaret died November 3, 1979 and both are buried at Mound Hill Cemetery. Three of David and Margaret's children are also buried near their parents, Eugene, Margaret and Mary Ann.
*Submitted By Chuck & Marjorie Gilliam Wood*

**JOSEPH AND JOSEPHINE (DEL CARLO) PIEROTTI FAMILY** - Joseph Pierotti, born in Italy in 1882, left his home in Bagni Di Lucca, Italy at the age of twelve years. He traveled alone throughout many of the European countries, selling watches and other articles to make his living, and to send money back home to his mother and three sisters.

*The Joseph and Josephine Pierotti Family 1942-1943. First Row: Josephine (Del Carlo) Pierotti, Joseph Pierotti. Second Row: Eva Josephine Pierotti, Frank Pierotti, Vince Pierotti, And Hugo Pierotti.*

He eventually came to America from LeHavre, France on or about the twentieth day of April, 1903. He arrived at the port of New York on the vessel Aquitania and settled in Buffalo, New York. This is where he met his future wife Josephine Del Carlo. Joe worked as a boiler maker until they left Buffalo. After leaving Buffalo they lived in several different states while raising their family of three sons, Vincent, the eldest, Hugo, and Frank.

In 1914, his middle son, Hugo, was stricken with what was then known as the "the white swelling" of his left leg (possibly polio). They took Hugo to a hospital in France. This was during World War I; and, after being there for only three days, the hospital was bombed.

*Joseph Pierotti and son, Vince at 312 Second Ave. Taken about 1921*

The family was then taken to the mountain home of Joe's mother in Italy. Joe made his way back to America, shoveling coal on a tramp steamer to avoid fighting in a war against his adopted country.

He came to Gallipolis in March of 1917 and worked for Attillio "Boss" Fontana at his fruit stand on Second Avenue. He eventually opened his own fruit stand at 312 Second Ave.

After being in Italy four years, the family came back to the U.S. by boat, and then on to Gallipolis Ferry, W.V. by train. They were then driven by Jimmy Call's Hack to John Lane's ferry boat, crossing the Ohio River to Gallipolis where they were welcomed by "Papa Joe".

Hugo was later sent to a Crippled Children's Hospital in St. Louis, Missouri, where he stayed during the summer months. He returned home by train as far as Logan, Ohio, where he was met by his family. He attended school in Gallipolis, wearing leg braces, and was carried to classes by a janitor, Mr. Jeeters. He had to learn to speak English while attending school, because only Italian was spoken in the home. He graduated from Gallia Academy High School in 1933, having to walk with a cane the rest of his life. Even with leg braces, he served as altar boy at St. Louis Catholic Church. He married Esther Burris, and they had one daughter. Upon Vince's death in 1944 Hugo and Esther took over Vince's, his brother's bar on Court Street. They later went into the shoe repair business at H&E Shoe Shop at 427 Second Avenue, until retiring to Florida where Hugo died in 1993 at the age of 82.

After prohibition, Joe, like most other Italians in Gallipolis, had converted his fruit stand into a family run restaurant and bar, Joe's Place. Joe and Josephine had one more child, a daughter Eva Josephine. The whole family made Gallipolis their home the rest of their lives, except for Hugo. Joe died in 1945 and Josephine in 1961.

**SAMUEL PILES FAMILY** - Samuel Piles (son of Francis Piles) was born September 15, 1839 in Lawrence Co. He married Martha Jane Cox (daughter of William Cocke and Ann Dalton) on August 17, 1864 in Lawrence Co. Martha was born July 24, 1841 in Virginia.

Samuel enlisted in Company I of the 18$^{th}$ OVI. While loading timbers in Tennessee in April 1862, he suffered a hernia. On May 1, 1862, he was taken prisoner, stripped of his clothing and blankets. In the prison camp, Samuel was exposed to measles and developed lung and Typhoid fever. The treating physician for the lung disease did not think Samuel would survive the condition. On the evening of October 18, 1865, two doctors performed emergency nighttime surgery to reduce the strangulated inguinal hernia. Because of his medical problems, Samuel received a pension of $6.00 per month; eventually this increased to $25 per month.

*Samuel Piles Abt 1888*

While Samuel spelled his last name Piles, his wife and most of the children changed the spelling to Pyles. They had the following children: 1. Harriet Amanda was born May 14, 1865 in Walnut Township. She married John Lafayette Myers (July 19, 1862-July 29, 1914) on April 24, 1886. Harriett died on July 29, 1945 in Lawrence. 2. John William was born December 01, 1866, and died January 14, 1896. He married Ada Darling. 3. Mary Susan was born May 04, 1868 in Gallia Co. She married Louis Wilson Coleman on October 3, 1888. Mary died February 15, 1934 in Lincoln, Nebraska. 4. Thomas Allen was born April 04, 1870 in Lawrence Co. He married Sarah Augusta Myers (June 30, 1871-January 08 1936.) on August 27, 1893. Thomas died on February 24, 1937. 5. Julia Ann was born February 14, 1872 in Lawrence County and died November 08, 1917 in Haverhill, Ohio. Julia was married to David Vance. 6. Lewis Wilson Piles (March 14, 1874-April 26, 1881). 7. Ada Ellen was born December 17, 1875 in Lawrence County. She married Sylvester Estep (June 4, 1876-March 5,1961). Ada died on September 6, 1946. 8. Floyd Washington was born October 05, 1877 in Lawrence County. He died on May 08, 1940 in Springfield, Ohio. He married Hattie Della Carroll (September 07, 1879-August 22, 1963). 9. George Roscoe was born February 21, 1880 and died April 12, 1971. He married Carrie Lewis (February 21, 1884-September 11, 1975). 10. Kimber Samuel was born May 07, 1882 in Lawrence County, he died July 7, 1965. Kimber married Lenna Massie (April 19, 1884-August 17, 1944). 11. Sadie Melissa was born May 16, 1885 near Lecta. She married Orval Lester Hall (March 15, 1883-February 1977) on March 20, 1904. Orval was one of the last Circuit Riders for the Methodist Church in Ohio. Sadie died March 26, 1945.

Samuel died September 2, 1894. Martha died November 23, 1919 in Ohio. They are both buried in Fox-Fairview Cemetery in Walnut Township.

*Submitted by: Jeffrey Lee Hayes*

**DARLENE & JACOB PILLOW FAMILY -** Jacob J. Pillow was born on Christmas morning, 1992 in Columbus, Ohio to Darlene M. Pillow. Darlene M. Pillow was born on September 1,

*Darlene And Jacob Pillow, December 1994*

*Melvin and Norma Pillow, December 1995*

*William And Hattie Pillow, Gallipolis 1910*

1961 in Lancaster, Ohio. She is one of 2 children (Darla) born to Melvin Pillow and Norma Clay. Melvin R. (Brownie) Pillow was born on January 18, 1927 in Johnstown, Ohio. He is one of 13 children born to William Thomas Pillow and Hattie Boardman. Melvin married Norma Clay on December 17, 1955. He retired from the Ohio Department of Natural Resources - Division of Parks & Recreation after 32 years of service, and is a Veteran of WW II. William Thomas Pillow was born on February 6, 1883 in Mason County, West Virginia. He was one of 12 children born to William Johnathon Pillow and Lucile Gardner. He was raised in the Mason County, West Virginia area along the Kanawha River and later resided in Gallia County. William married Hattie Boardman May 3, 1906 near Point Pleasant, West Virginia. Family records state he worked in the FullerHutsinpiller furniture factory in Gallipolis, as a cabinet maker and was a farmer. William died December 21, 1956. He is buried next to his wife Hattie in Glenrest Cemetery, Reynoldsburg, Ohio. William Johnathon Pillow was born September 22, 1845 in Lynchburg, Virginia. He was

*The William T. Pillow Family, 1939*

*William J. And Lucille Pillow, Gallipolis 1910*

*Edwin And Mariah Pillow, Virginia 1841*

*Mary Agnis Pillow-Jones, Patriot, Oh. Early 1900's*

one of 12 children born to Edwin Pillow and Mariah Vernon. He lived in Mason County, West Virginia and Gallia County, Ohio. His occupation was a farmer. William married Lucile Caroline Gardner on November 12, 1868 in Point Pleasant, West Virginia. William served in the Civil War in Company B, 13th West Virginia Infantry. He served from enlistment date of October 8, 1862 until honorably discharged at Wheeling, West Virginia June 22, 1865. He served as a private. William died December 7, 1928. He is buried at Mound Hill Cemetery, Gallipolis, Ohio next to his wife Lucile. Edwin Pillow was born May 20, 1812 to Jasper Pillow and Sary Willson. He married Mariah Vernon from Cubs Creek Virginia in 1841. Edwin and family first appear on the Mason County, West Virginia Census in 1860 where he is listed as a farmer. Edwin died December 28, 1865. He is buried next to his wife, Mariah at Concord Cemetery, Mason County, West Virginia. Jasper Pillow was born February 11, 1760 in Amelia County, Virginia. He was a Corporal and served several enlistments in the 4th Virginia Regiment Continental Establishment. His name first appears on the payroll of Captain John Morton, April 1776 - US Pension Office and was paid 2 lb. He was present at the surrender of Yorktown and was discharged February 1/4, 1778. Jasper's second marriage was to Sary Willson in 1791 (3 known children). A note in the Pillow family bible states he served in the war of 1812 as an Indian Scout and was killed in the war. Place of death is not known at this time. Sary is recorded as being buried in North Halifax County, Virginia. .

Darlene & Jacob Pillow reside in Gallia County. Darlene currently works for the O.O. McIntyre Park District as their Park Naturalist. Jacob is a student at Washington Elementary. The Pillows are proud to be Gallia Countians and are delighted to be part of the Gallia County, Ohio History Book.

**CHARLES PLYMALE AND FAMILY** - Charles was born in clay township on May 15, 1933. He is the son of Estus (deceased 1970) and Elise (Brucker) (deceased 1963).

*The Plymales - Charles, Helen, Bonnie, Tina And Rodney*

Charles was raised on Raccoon Road. He has five sisters: Mary Anna Tye, Louella Plymale, Adell (Carroll) Caldwell, Ruby (George) Kinder and Louise Grover. Charles was a graduate of Gallia Academy in 1952. He went into the Air Force after he graduated and served his time. He has retired from Wright-Patterson Air Force Base, as an aircraft mechanic.

Charles married Helen Jean (Kuhn) on February 3, 1958. Helen's parents are Charles N. Kuhn and Elise May (Beck) Kuhn. Both are deceased, 1979 and 1988. Helen was born May 5, 1938. She was raised on Centenary Road. Charles and Helen still have the home places.

Charles and Helen were blessed with three children. Bonnie Lynn (James) Jones. They have two children Levi and Carrie. The Jones reside in Floyds Knobs, Indiana. Rodney Charles (Mandy Chamberlin) Plymale have two children: Miranda and Zachary and reside in Reesvillle, Ohio.

Charles' wife, Helen has one sister Nellie (William) Milstead and two brothers, Donald (Alice) Kuhn and Francis (Norma Jean) Kuhn. Helen has three nieces and three nephews: Dwayne, Dean, Debbie Kuhn ,Karla Kuhn, Janet Campbell and Roger Milstead.

Helen had two half-brothers: Vernon and William Kuhn. They are both deceased.

Helen attended school at Centenary, where there were three rooms which housed grades 1 through 8. Those days were happy ones. Helen graduated from Gallia Academy in 1956.

Helen is employed by Airborn Express at Wilmington, Ohio. She plans on retiring soon. The Plymales plan on coming back to Gallia County and Gallipolis and living life to its fullest.

*Submitted by Helen J. Plymale*

**AUGUST JR. AND LENA (KLAGES) POPPE** - August Jr., was born, 19 November 1860, died 1 December 1935, son of August, born 11 January 1819, died 27 February 1893, and Louisa (Rettberg) Poppe, born 3 September 1818, died 26 October 1896. Lena (Klages) Pope, born 10 May 1869, died 11 December 1927, daughter of

*Bottom-L-R. Georgiana and Woodrow. Top-L-R. Elma Eda, Anna (Parents: Lena and August) Frederick*

Frederick, born 1 April 1846, died 29 April 1935 and Augusta (Wedemeyer) Klages, born 12 September 1846, died 2 July 1927. Augusta and Lena (Klages) were married 29 March 1888. The Pope (Poppe) came from Hanover Germany, Dorste County in the 1800's and settled in Walnut Township, Gallia County, German Hollow/Ridge, Patriot area. They attended a one room school on German Ridge. German was taught for three months, and English for three months. It was the only public school in the history of Gallia county to be bilingual. Then the State legislature, partly through the influence of Gallia County's Representative Dr. Jehu Eakins, granted the District this privilege. The school burnt down in September, 1930.

Children
Frederick George Henry, born 14 March 1889, died 1 March 1962, Georgiana Clara, born 14 November 1909, died 17 May 1999, Anna Loria, born 17 November 1897, died 25 December 1914, Eda Augusta, born 24 December 1890, died 23 November 1970, Elma Amolia, born 28 August 1894, died 1 February 1990, Woodrow Luther, born 9 September 1912

*Submitted by Henry L. Myers*

**HIBERT HOLBROOK (H.H.) PORTER** - Hibert (Hib) was born in Harrison Township, Gallia County, Ohio on September 10, 1873. He was the son of Vinton and Mary Ann Porter. He had six brothers: Thomas, Clinton, Rev. John, Elza, Charlie, Edward and one sister, Laura. His father Vinton was born in 1832, married Mary Ann Leaper in 1858 and died in 1908. Vinton and Mary Ann are buried in the Porter plot in the Mercerville Cemetery.

The Porter's were imigrants from England. Hib's great-great grandfather, Thomas Flint Porter, served seven years in the British Army during the Revolutionary War. After the war, he came to America as a stow-away aboard ship. He was the second documented settler in Harrison Township. This was documented in 1810. He lived on Bullskin Creek and was killed by a falling tree and buried on the Porter farm in 1836. Thomas Porter II, the son of Thomas Flint Porter, was born in England and immigrated to America about 1780. He married Nancy Hall in New York. He was a shipbuilder, came to Marietta, Ohio where he built a ship that he later took to New Orleans, selling it. On his journey, he contracted yellow fever and died in Louisville, Kentucky. He is buried in Louisville.

*The Cabin on Bullskin Creek"*

Thomas Jefferson Porter, son of Thomas Porter II, was born in Marietta, Ohio in 1807. He came with his grandfather, Thomas Flint Porter, to Gallia County in 1810. He resided in section fourteen in Harrison Township. His neighbors were the Trotters, descendents of Ann Bailey. He died in 1877 and is buried in the Mercerville Cemetery. He was the grandfather of Hibert Holbrook Porter.

Hib was twice married. His first wife was Stella Boster. They had one daughter Mary. Mary married Clyde Smith. They had one daughter, Ruth Eleanor. Stella and Mary passed away within a few years of each other leaving Hib to raise his granddaughter, Ruth.

They lived in his home near Mercerville.

Ruth married Charles (Charlie) D. Carter and Hib married Charlie's mother, Mattie Mae (Garlic) Carter in a double marriage ceremony in Catlettsburg, Kentucky in 1935. On January 30, 1936, Ruth gave birth to a daughter, Mary Lou. Ruth died eight days later. Hib and Mattie raised Mary Lou in the same home where her mother Ruth was raised. Mary Lou married Lewis Keith Saunders on August 1, 1954. They reside in Gahanna, Ohio and have one daughter, Lee Ann. Lee Ann married Jerry Lee Strait, Jr on May 9, 1987. They have a daughter, Kallie Marie, born January 24, 1994 and a son, Cohn Saunders Strait born November 24, 1999. They reside in Gahanna, Ohio.

Mary Lou was twelve years old when Hib Porter, her great-grandfather, deeded her 100 acres of the Porter Homestead. In 1959, Lewis and Mary Lou purchased an additional forty acres of the Homestead on which was a log cabin. Hib's brother, Rev. John and Rosetta Porter began their married life in this cabin located near the junction of Burnt Run Road and Mercerville Road, now known as State Route 218. Two of their children were born in this cabin, Chauncey Porter and Nora Belle (Porter) McKean. Mary Lou was very close to her great-grandfather Hib and considered him a wonderful friend. Hib passed away in 1957 leaving her a heritage that she continues to cherish. Mattie passed away in March of 1976.

Mary Lou, Lewis, Lee Ann and Jerry have completed restoration of "The Cabin on Bullskin Creek". Many happy days are spent there.

*Submitted by Mary Lou Carter Saunders*

**POWELL FAMILY** - Andrew Jackson Powell arrived in Gallia County in 1831, aged 21, descended (Thomas II, Moses II, Nicholas) from Thomas Powell, born 1641 in Wales; to Long Island, NY, in 1653; purchased from the Indians the Bethpage area. Andrew, a carpenter, brought his father and brothers to Ohio and settled near Bidwell, building barns, bridges and churches, including the Bidwell Methodist Church dedicated just after his death in 1892. His home and John's still stand south of this church for which John donated land.

Andrew Jackson Powell married March 9, 1849, Mary Ann Kerr, eldest child of John Nisewanger and Isabella Morrison Kerr. Children: Elmer, Cassius, John and Isabelle "Belle" Powell.

John was born September 26, 1854, graduated from Gallia Academy; married September 26, 1877, Eugenie Langley, who died the following year; married (2nd) September 27, 1882, Anna Deborah Hutsinpiller, daughter of David and Mariah (Winsor) Hutsinpiller. Children: Edith Belle, Earle Jackson, Adah Mariah, Raymond Hutsinpiller, Mary Eugenie and Carleton David.

John established a post office; express office; school and store to found Bidwell; later bought the tile works. He served as County Treasurer 1908-1913, (all of his children except Earle served as Deputy Treasurer), and as State Representative 1915-1918. He was a trustee of Rio Grande College for fifteen years. He moved, August 1909, to Gallipolis to a home on First Avenue for which he and Levi White planed all of the lumber. This home, moved by barge, now stands on Airport Road.

*The Powell Family 1921 Powell Family Reunion In Gallipolis, Ohio L: To R: Simeon Hutsinpiller, Earle, Callie, Carleton, Edith, Raymond, Doris, Lucile, Ed Neal, Ina Hutsinpiller Gibbons, John Kerr Powell, Anna Hutsinpiller Powell, Adah, Richard, Mary, Thurman Fletcher, Jeanne. Seated On The Steps: Mary Elizabeth, Alice, Margaret, John, Don.*

Edith graduated from Rio Grande; taught in Ohio and Oregon where she married Shadrach Powell (no relation). She settled (teaching) in Washington, DC, with daughter, Alice Winsor (carpenter). Earle and wife, Callie (Russell), with daughter Mary Elizabeth (Anderson), went to Philadelphia, PA, where Earle owned a Buick dealership. After Callie's death, he married Blanche Robinson, a Gallia County schoolmate. Adah taught school before marrying Edward Raymond Neal, a banker, (his ancestors are buried at Mt. Zion Cemetery); moved to Columbus. Children: John Edward and Richard Carleton. Raymond left for Oregon after graduating from Rio Grande; taught in one-room and two-room schools where he met Lucile Raider, whom he married in 1917. Children: Don Carleton; Doris (Schultz); Anne (Matthias). Raymond taught at two private schools in Washington, DC, and went to France during World War I. Mary married, 1914, Thurman Fletcher, a Columbus physician. Children: Margaret (Fox); Jeanne (Howe); Martha (Binder). Carleton, born 1894, worked with his father in Gallia Treasurers office and the Ohio Legislature; graduated from Ohio State University; served in the Field Artillery in World War I; a major in the Reserves. He moved to Cleveland, then Akron; employed at Goodrich Rubber Company. He married Esther (Weygandt) Harris, who published genealogical books and *Ohio Records and Pioneer Families*. Children: Margaret Ann (Hetrick); Robert Carleton; William Weygandt.

John Kerr Powell died August 29th, 1935, in the home of daughter Mary in Columbus. Anna died December 7th, 1929, in their home on First Avenue. They are buried at Mound Hill.

(Interesting Fact: John and Anna Powell did not know that they were distant cousins. They were both descended from Melchior Brumbach who came from Germany to Virginia in 1714. His daughter, Elizabeth, married Stephen Hutsinpiller, from whom Anna descended; daughter Maria Gertraudt married Jacob Nisewanger, from whom John descended. The Nisewanger family from Virginia settled in Ohio several years before the Hutsinpillers from West Virginia.)

*(Note: John Kerr Powell's autobiography, "Eighty Years of Life," and books about the Powell, Kerr, Hutsinpiller, Nisewanger and Winsor Families are in the GCHGS library.)*

*Submitted by: Doris Powell Schultz (Mrs. Ruby Albert)*

**REVEREND WILLIAM POWELL** - My Gallia County connection starts with my grandfather, Rev. William Powell, from Northern Wales. He was born May 11, 1826 in Llanelly, Breconshire, South Wales and for a time was a miner. Later he became part of a revival movement in the churches of Southern Wales. He started preaching in Bethania Congregational Church in Llanelly, and in the fall of 1859 took pastoral charge of the Congregational churches of Nebo, Hebron and Aberdaron in Carnarvonshire, North Wales, and in May 1862 he accepted a call to the Congregational churches of Rhiw, Nautglyyn and Llansanan, and there at Rhiw he was ordained in May 1863. He served these churches for four years. He then went to Denbigh where he met and married Anne Williams in 1863. The Independent Churches of Wales were also called Congregational. The name Independent and Congregational were used interchangeably in Wales at that time.

Around 1871 the Rev. William Powell family consisting of Rev. Powell, his wife Anne Powell and two children, William Rees and Martha Anne came to the USA to the Trumbull County area of Ohio. Their third child, Mary Catherine, was born in Trumbull County. Later, the family came to Gallia County as they are in the 1880 Census of Gallia County. In the Census, they have five children. My father, Thomas Everett, was born in Raccoon Township, Gallia County in 1878. Rev. Powell served the Congregational churches of Centerville and Carmel for four years. There was a need for ministers who could speak Welsh as many of the people there were from Wales and preferred to have the sermons in Welsh. The Welsh people, many of whom spoke both English and Welsh, had a preference for the Welsh language as they wanted to keep their native language. Later the family moved to Minnestoa where Rev. Powell continued his preaching in Welsh to the many churches in the Mankato area that preferred the Welsh language. My grandmother Powell died in childbirth in 1882 and in 1899 my grandfather returned to Wales to do more preaching. He had an asthma attack December 16, 1899 and died in Rhyl, North Wales is buried there.

I was born April 23, 1916 near Valentine, Nebraska on Easter Sunday. We left the Valentine area when my father died from the 1918 influenza epidemic. Millions of people died from the influenza all around the world.

My only other contact with Ohio came in 1927 when we lived in Elyria, Ohio and I went to school there for one year.

*Submitted by: Thomas Edison Powell*

**ROBERT (BOB) POWELL AND VICKIE LUETTA THOMAS POWELL FAMILY** - Bob was born in Cleveland, Oh., on April 19, 1936. His grand-parents, Rees and Emily Powell spent most of their lives in Cleveland. Rees was born in Wales and came to Cleveland at the age of five. Bob's other grandparents were

Blair and Verda Koon who came to Cleveland from central Pennsylvania. Bob's parents were Arthur and Evelyn Powell.

Bob came to Rio Grande College in 1956 and studied elementary education, graduating with a Bachelor of Arts degree.

Vickie is a life-long resident of Gallia County who still lives on the farm where she was born on December 1, 1938. Her parents were Harley G. and Vada M. Thomas. Harley's parents, Max and Lula Gooch Thomas were also born in Gallia County and lived most of their lives on a farm near Tycoon Lake in Raccoon Township. Vada's parents were Felix and Etta Hamrick They came to Ohio from Webster Springs, West Virginia. Felix was from a well-known family in that part of West Virginia.

Vickie attended school in Rio Grande and graduated from Raccoon Twp. High School in 1956. The following September, she enrolled in Rio Grande College to study in the field of education. It was during this time that Bob and Vickie met and later married.

Bob is retired from a career in public school teaching and administration, most of it in Gallia County. Vickie is also retired after a thirty year career at Washington Elementary School in Gallipolis. Both attended Marshall university and received Master's degrees. Currently, Vickie is a substitute in the Gallipolis City School District, is active in several organizations, is a Trustee of the Ohio Farm Bureau Federation, and teaches Sunday School at Grace United Methodist Church. Bob is on the staff of the church and does some of the visitation of its members. They raised cattle for 34 years, plus tobacco and hay. Currently, some hay is still on the farm.

Their family includes two daughters, Jane Ann who lives in Hamden, Oh, and Virginia, better known as Ginny, who lives in Pennsylvania and supervises 4-H agents in the northern half of New Jersey. She is married to Don Rickards.

**JOHN PRIESTLY FAMILY -** John Priestly (1805-1878), spinner in woolen factory in Warley, England m. Feb 23, 1826 Hannah Crabtree ( 1802-1896) Midgley, England.

In 1840, they came to Zanesville, OH where Hannah's brother, William Crabtree, was living. They were 52 days crossing the ocean. They had nine children and the two youngest, Richard and Henry Clay, was born in Zanesville.

The family came to Gallipolis in 1849 and John become foreman at the Woolen Mill. They lived at the corner of 2nd and Vine but John also bought in 1852 a 262-acre farm located on Lincoln Pike in Green Twp. The farm remained in the family nearly 150 years.

Four of the nine children lived in Gallia Co. James (1825-1897) m. Mary Sterrett from Pt. Pleasant, Susan (1830-1889) m. Henry Beall, Richard (1848-1923) m.Hattie Beardsley (later lived at Winfield, W. Va.) and Henry Clay (1844-1926) who m. Magdalene Morgan (1853-1932) whose parents were David J. Morgan and Mary Davis who had a farm in Perry Twp. They were the parents of 15 children. The oldest was Magdalene who m. Henry Clay Priestley in 1874. They lived on the farm bought by his parents in the original house that had served as an overnight stop for people going to Gallipolis on business or to shop. That house was torn down and a new house was built in 1896.

Henry and Magdalene had four children: Hannah (1875-1947) m. Clarence Rodgers, John (1877-1938) m. Susan Bomberger, Maud ( 1882-1974) m. Charles Reynolds and David Clay (1891-1964) m. Esther Martha Platt. David Clay (known as Clate or "Doc") graduated from O.S.U.in1914 from the College of Veterinary Medicine. He started his practice on horseback and served the community for 50 years. He married Esther Martha Platt (1892-1968) Sept. 16, 1919 in Toledo, Oh. Their children are Archie Clay Priestley (1920) and Esther Priestley Collier (1924).

Archie m. June 19, 1953 Mary Ellen Wheaton and they live in Columbus, Oh. Their children are David and Alicia and there are three grandchildren. Mary Ellen's father and his parents lived in Gallipolis. Her grandfather, Mr. W. G. Wheaton became the cashier at the First National Bank in 1892. Mr. Wheaton m. Alice Hutchinson whose parents were W. H. and Sarah T. Hutchinson. Mr. Hutchinson was a leading hardware merchant in Gallipolis.

Esther Mary m. November 23, 1947 Francis Nash Collier, Jr. (Feb. 11, 1917) from Birmingham, Ala. They live in Chapel Hill, N. C. and have three children—Martha, Cathy, and David— and five grandchildren and one great-grandchild.

Archie and Esther Mary attended Centenary School, Gallia Academy High School and were members of The First Presbyterian Church.

They are both graduates of O.S.U.- Archie from College of Veterinary Medicine and Esther Mary from the College of Education.

**MARVIN PULLINS FAMILY -** Marvin Paxton Pullins was born January 2, 1939 in Meigs County at Summer, Ohio near Chester, Ohio. He was the seventh child of seventeen born to Okey R. and Mattie Louise Gillian Pullins. After moving several times in and around Meigs and Athens Counties, his parents settled on a farm in Athens County near the Meigs line and there, at a country store, Marvin met and re-newed a friendship to Rachel Darlene Hawk, daughter of Ross and Zura Eldora Swartz Hawk of Shade, Ohio. The two had previously attended Shade School together. Rachel has two older sisters and two older brothers. They are Betty Kathleen Hawk, (Eugene O.) Williams and Caryl Mae Hawk (John H.) Ruth, Merle Albert (Willa Jean Van Dyke) Hawk (deceased) and Lloyd Edwin (Mary Kathryn Smith) Hawk. Marvins's brothers and sisters are Theodore Okey Pullins, William Joseph Pullins, Inez Claire Pullins (Wilbur) Windland, Bernice Pullins (Ray) Midkiff, Mary Lou Pullins, Rankin, (LeRoy) Fryar, James Edgar (Kay) Pullins, Eliza Junior (Cricket) Pullins (deceased), Freda Louise Pullins (Ben) Carsey, Judy Ann Pullins (William) Leach, Wilma Kay Pullins, (Marvin) Buckley, Robert Valentine (Janice) Pullins, June Elaine Pullins (James) Ridenour, Donnie Creed Pullins, Wilbur Earl (Lisa) Pullins, Donna Sue (Leslie) Ummensetter and Roger Thomas Pullins.

Marvin married Rachel on September 1, 1962. He has worked on Ford tractors and farm equipment for several different dealers coming to Gallia County to work at Carter Tractor Sales on Eastern Avenue on March 1, 1968. He moved his wife and family here on May 1 of that year. There are three children. Kelly Darlene, Kevin Duane and Marvin Lloyd. They all graduated Gallia Academy; Kelly in 1981, Kevin in 1983 and Marvin in 1987.

Kelly went on to Hocking Technical College receiving her Medical Assisting Degree in 1983 and marrying Joseph Richard Gleason of Point Pleasant, WV. They now live in Grove City, Ohio and have two children; Miranda Brooke, born June 29, 1987 and Tyler Joseph, born December 1, 1988.

Kevin works at Kyger Creek Power Plant and lives at Rodney, Ohio. He married Mindy Jane Kite of Plas Road, Vinton, Ohio and they have three sons. Levi Duane, born March 23, 1993, Kevin Lucas (Luke) born May 19, 1995 and Lane Matthew, born September 14, 2000.

Marvin married Star Elaine Tackett of 648 Fourth Avenue, Gallipolis, Oho. They have two sons. Stephen Ross, born June 29, 1986 and Cody Ray, born July 3, 1991. Marvin has worked at Carter Tractor Sales for fifteen years and is now entering the Ohio Highway Patrol April 10, 2002.

Marvin, who is now retired and working at home, and Rachel, who has worked at Rockwell automation for twenty-five years, are members of Grace United Methodist Church have made Gallia County their home settling on their farm at 1779 Adamsville Road, Bidwell, Ohio.

*Submitted by Marvin and Rachel Pullins*

**HENRY WILSON PYLES -** Henry Wilson Pyles (11-18-1844—06-15-1917) was born in Lawrence County, Ohio to Francis and Susanna Wiseman Pyles. He married Sarah (Sally) Fox (9-19-1845—03-25-1924), the daughter of Emmor and Sarah Baker Fox, on August 25, 1864. Wilson and Sally were the parents of nine children: Jerusha Susan (5-29-1865—02-13-1936) Eugene Baker( 03 -21-1867—6-6-1937) Sarah A. (02-13-1869—09-20-1924) married Thomas Herrell; Martha L. (1-01-1871—02-06-1936) married William Plybon; Rebecca Ellen (1-6-1873—03-14-1964) married John Fletcher Neal; John Thomas (7-16-1875—07-22-1939), Lester, Emma, Austin (5-21-1882—10-6-1912). Both Wilson and Sally as well as six of their children are buried in Fox-Fairview Cemetery in Walnut Township.

The Pyles family lived in Section 32 of Walnut Twp. They had a large orchard area and raised sheep from which they spun yarn and wove material for clothing, etc.

*Submitted by: Sue Luman*

**SALLY JO PETERSON QUAMME -** My roots to Gallia County.

I come from good stock. My father, Waldo Peterson, always told me that and as I learn more about my genealogy, I discover how true his words were. He was born in a tar paper shack on the prairies of South Dakota in a blizzard in 1911; his 13 month old brother asleep in a crib nearby.

My grandmother, Mary Stevens Peterson, had moved to SD to homestead with her parents. Her mother had visited a fortune teller who told her that great fortunes were to be found in a far-away place. After meeting in Midland, SD, my grandparents set up meager housekeeping on the land they agreed to "prove up". In her later years, grandma wrote stories about her homesteading experiences and thereby allowed me a glimpse of her youthful strength and courage. She endured many hardships and yet in all of her 103 years, she was always cheerful and gentle.

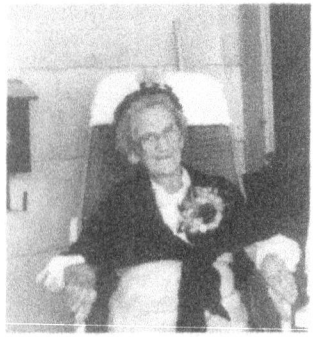

*Mary Stevens Peterson*

Grandma was born in Hedrick, Iowa in October of 1890, the fifth child of Mary Margaret Phelps and Benjamin Stevens. Benjamin was a homeopathic doctor and grandma often talked about how he would gather plants to make liquids and powders and pastes for her family and others in the area when they were ill. Mary Margaret, her mother, was also born in Hedrick, the 14th of the very large family of 16 children of Benjamin Blake Phelps and Jane McCall.

*Sally (Sarah) Blake*

Jane and Benjamin were both probably born in Marietta, Gallia County. They lived on a farm in Gallia County near Kanauga until the spring of 1852 when they moved to Iowa.

Benjamin, born in 1811, was the son of John Phelps and Sally (Sarah) Blake. Sally was born in the stockade of Fort Harmar whose site is now within the city of Marietta, Ohio. She is said to be the first white child born in what is now Marietta and the third white child born in the state of Ohio. After John died in about 1812, Sally married Rev. John Strait, a Revolutionary War soldier, who had been granted land in Gallia County. Sally died in 1878 and is buried in a cemetery near Thiviner in Clay township. Since joining the Gallia County Historical Society, I met a relative who sent me a picture of Sally. I was shocked to see the resemblance between Sally and her great granddaughter, who was my grandmother, Mary Margaret Stevens Peterson.

Jane McCall, born in 1815, was the 8th child of 12 born to James C. McCall and Elizabeth Jane Northup. They lived in Section 13 of Green Township, adjoining the homestead of Elizabeth's parents, Daniel Northup and Ann Hampton Collins. Daniel was a good businessman and owned large tracts of land in and around Gallipolis, including an area in Green Township now called "Northup."

**JAMES A. QUEEN FAMILY** - James A. Queen was born August 18, 1865 at Queens Ridge, Wayne County, and WV. He met and married (1) Nancy Ellen Counts, daughter of Isaac Fullen and Polly (Queen) Counts, born October 14, 1869 and died July 28, 1900. . To this union 7 children were born: Nettie, Nora, Nan, Jay, William "Bill", Owen and Perry. James A. met Nancy "Nannie" Melissa Duty, daughter of Andrew Jackson and Martha "Hay" Duty. And they were married February 12, 1905 on the Lincoln-Wayne County Line at Cove Gap, WV. They were the parents of 12 children - Nannie, born May 3, 1907; Charles born June 6, 1908; Cecil born April 21, 1909; Nona born June 28, 1910; Jesse born June 19, 1912; Albert born January 24, 1914; Frank born February 20, 1916; Arden born December 2!, 1918; James born January 10, 1920; Jack born December 19, 1921; Nila Mae born May 12, 1924; Nola Edith born December 18, 1928. Jim, as he was called by everyone who knew him, and his wife Nannie moved several times in and around Lincoln and Cabell Counties in WV before moving to Harrison Township, Gallia County, OH in the summer of 1939. To a 395-acre farm at the old Burdette Orchard on Brumfield Road near Mercerville, Ohio... They were living there when Arden, James and Jack were drafted into WWII. All three boys served in the South Pacific. James was killed in the Palau Islands on October 26, 1944. Perry, and Narie, who married Shelly O. Slone, moved with their families to Gallia County, OH on the Petty Martin farm in Harrison Township. Jesse, and Albert, with their families, followed their parents to this 395 acre farm and helped with the 100 acres of apple orchard. Frank, Arden, Jack, Nila Mae and Nola Edith all met their future mate and were married while living on this 395-acre farm. Frank married Clara Cremeans;

*James A. And Nannie (Duty) Queen*

Arden married (1) Delores Pinkerman and (2) Eva Mooney; Jack met and married Garnett McGuire; and Nila Mae married Haskell Lear of Little Bullskin, Northup Route; . Nola Edith finished grade school at Phillips Elementary, Harrison Township and went on to graduate from Mercerville High School, Mercerville, OH in 1948. She met and married in 1949 Charles Edwin Jenkins, son of Charles and Hazel (McGhee) Jenkins of Jackson, Jackson County, OH. Charles and Edith were the parents of three boys: Danny Allan born January 3, 1951 Gallipolis, Gallia County, OH; Kenny Lee born October 23, 1952 Huntington, Cabell County, WV; and Jay Edwin, born June 14, 1960, Columbus, Franklin County, OH.

**SEVENTH GENERATION OF QUESTEL FAMILY** - Burns-Harrington.

Gladys (Sigler) Burns (1909-1994) married in 1925 to Clarence "Buzz" Burns (1901-1989). Their daughter, Thelma (Burns) Harrington, (1933- ) married (1955) "Tubby" Harrington Jr. (1935- ). Herbert Harrington Sr. (1904-1987) married (1924) Ethel (Dray) Harrington (1909-) Herb and Thelma Harrington had four children: Billy Joe (1952- ) resides in Gallipolis, Ohio. Married first to Brucella Chadwick, had two daughters: Serena and Vivian. Later married Cheryl Merrick, had two sons: Adam and Josh. Billy has five grandchildren, he receives disability from working at Robbins and Myers.

Edward Lee (1956- ) resides in Gallipolis, Ohio. Married Jody Kidwell in 1995, he works as a farmer and mechanic.

Brenda Kay (1957- ) resides in Grove City, Ohio married Allan Wheeler in 1974 and divorced in 1982.

They had one son, Chad, who married Jenna Felty (2002) and had one son, C.J. Later married Harry "J.R." Graham Jr. in 1994, raised two stepchildren, Brandie and Josh. Syna Lynn (1960-1992) married Hitoshi Yokokawa in 1981 and had one daughter, Yumiko, who married Ray Cox (2001) and had one daughter, Mykaila. Syna is buried at Centenary Cemetery.

Herb and Thelma raised Yuniiko along with many other children. They began foster care in 1974 and received an award in 1981 from Gov. James Rhodes. They had children of all ages, races, and backgrounds; many were abused physically, mentally, and emotionally. They continued foster care until 1984 when they moved from Gallipolis to Columbus. Thelma then took care of children in her home and later went to work at Big Lots during the evening. Herb worked at the Gallipolis Terminal from 1957 until 1983. For those 26 years he delivered fuel oil to homes. After they moved to Columbus, Herb became a carpenter and worked for Bill George and Associates. He retired in 1997 and they returned to Gallipolis to reside. It was not until March 2001 that they lived alone for the first time in their marriage. Just as they began to grow accustomed to their peaceful lifestyle, they had to take Herb's mother, Ethel, into their home and care for her. In addition, Thelma also baby-sits for her great-granddaughter, Mykaila, while Yumiko attends college.

Herb and Thelma have been members of the Gallipolis Church of Christ in Christian Union on Eastern Avenue for several years. Their children and foster children were raised in church. Brenda, followed her Christian upbringing and is now a member of Brown Road Community Church in Columbus. Thelma and Herb set an excellent example not only for their own children, but the community. They may not have had wealth, but they gave those around them love and kindness. They give all their thanks and praise to God.

**RAIKE FAMILY** - Abram and Susan Raike came from Germany to Greenup, KY, with one girl and five boys. Their son Jacob was born in 1809, Jacob married Louisa Barnhart September 25, 1828. Their son Frederick married Lucy Jane (maiden name unknown). They had three sons, William Peyton, Frank and John. Frederick's second wife was Mary Phillips. They had seven children, Benjamin, Alice, Wilhelmina, Ida, Goldie, Mary and Albert. Frederick's son Wiliam Peyton married Mary Jane Fetters, a Dutch girl from Pennsylvania. They owned a dish boat, the "America" in which they made their living. They traveled from Pittsburgh to New Orleans selling queensware. The "America" had no motor and was steered with a pole when going down river. They would wait for a towboat and trade scrap iron, rope and furs to compensate for a tow back upriver.

*Captain John Raike's boat and home, junction of Routes 7 & 35, Kanauga, Ohio during the 1937 flood*

William Peyton and Mary had eight children, William, Frederick, John, Ethel, Douglas, Mae and stillborn twins. William Peyton was robbed and murdered on his boat, the "Mountain Queen" in 1909. His son William was robbed and murdered under the railroad bridge in Kanauga in 1929. Frederick was accidentally shot in the leg while duck hunting and bled to death before they could row to shore. Ethel was struck and killed by a car in Addison, Ohio April 30, 1976. Mae was cook on a towboat and Douglas worked for M. T. Epling in Gallipolis, Ohio and died in 1991. John died May 30, 1976 in Greenup, KY while cleaning his father's grave.

John McKinley Raike married Lena Mae Witham July 16, 1919. Lena died June, 1989. Her grandparents, Oliver and Louise Canaday Betz, farmed in Gallia County. John and Lena owned many towboats including the "Junior, Dana Mack, Ida Mae and Edward Boggs". They had three children, John Bradfield born October 1, 1920. He married Phyllis Sopp in 1946. They have two children, Heather and John and all reside in Columbus. Norma Jean born August 2, 1927 died in 1941 of cancer. Dana McKinley was born June 3, 1925 on their houseboat the "Star" which was tied up on the Kanawha River near Henderson, WV and died May 29, 2000.

John and Lena moved to Kanauga in 1927. The Silver Bridge was built beside their home in 1929. In 1937 the flood brought water to the bottom of the second story of their home. John tied his sternwheeler towboat, "Edward Boggs" to their house so the family wasn't left homeless during the flood.

Dana was raised and worked on the river as a pilot until 1954. Dana also worked at the Gallipolis Daily Tribune and the First National Bank and retired from the Central Trust company. Dana married Artie Rupe December 26, 1953 and they had a daughter, Terry Jean, born January 5, 1960. Terry works for The Shelly Company. Terry is the fourth generation to live in the Raike home located next to where the Silver Bridge collapsed in 1967. According to family members and various occupants over the years, the house is still visited by the ghost of William Peyton Raike and descendants.

*Submitted by Terry Jean Raike, Kanauga, Ohio*

**CARL MELVIN AND WANDA BELLE DODRILL REGAN FAMILY** - Wanda Belle Dodrill Regan was the youngest child of John Herbert and Bertha Ellen Vance Dodrill. She was born on August 13,1926, at the family's farm on Andy Dodrill Road in Gallia County. Wanda had four brothers: Delmer, Donald, Dwight, and Darrell; and four sisters: Lela, Ethel, Pearl and Evelyn.

Wanda walked to Bunker Hill School, with some of her brothers and sisters, for the first and second grades. Verna Welker was Wanda's teacher for those early years. Then for the third grade, the Dodrill kids walked to Bunker Hill School, or sometimes Dwight or Pearl took them in the buggy, to meet the bus. The third grade class was in the Vinton Academy (now the Town Hall). The fourth through 12th grades were held in the High School (old Vinton Elementary). Wanda graduated in 1945, and went to Columbus to work for the State of Ohio.

On March 27, 1948, Wanda married Carl Melvin Regan. Melvin was born February 27, 1918, in Columbus. He was a decorated World War II veteran, with over five years of service to his Country.

Wanda and Melvin had two children. Danny Lee was born on September 26, 1950, and Beverly Sue was born on May 5,1953. They both grew up in Columbus, and attended Circleville Bible College.

Danny married Roxanne Wilson on June 24, 1972. They had two children, Justin Matthew, born August 28, 1973, and Andrea Elizabeth, born May 16, 1976 Danny builds and remodels homes in and around Columbus. On June 23, 1995, he married Karen Landrum, and became step-father to her two children, Alex and Nick, Beverly married Bryan Feathers on June 7,1974. Bryan is a minister, and Beverly works for Fifth Third Bank. They had two sons, Jeffery Bryan, born July 10,1977, and Nathen Allen, born June 24, 1980. Jeffery married Heidi Clarey on July 7, 2001.

Nathen married Sonya Jarred on May 5, 2001.Wanda retired from the State of Ohio on February 27, 1985. She is enjoying retirement and loves serving the Lord by singing in her church choir. She enjoys quilting and has made several quilts for her adoring family.

Melvin Regan passed away on December 25, 2000, shortly after moving into their newly constructed home in Westerville.

Wanda has joined a local health club, where she walks and visits with friends. She is still quilting and singing, and plans to do just that, until her heavenly homecoming.

Wanda is the last surviving child of John and Bertha Vance Dodrill.

Submitted by Wanda Dodrill Regan, and rewritten by niece, Cathy Elliott.

**HENRY AND JEANETTE REYNOLDS** - Henry Allen Reynolds born August 26, 1866 Nicholas County, WV and died June 6, 1928 Gallia County was the son of Archibald VanBuren Reynolds and Elizabeth Frances Odell. Henry married Jeanette Almeda Haynes 1890 WV. Jeanette was born August 3, 1872 Fayette County, WV died April 5, 1944 Gallia County, daughter of Newton and Margaret Bays Haynes. Their children were Margaret Isabell born 1891 WV died 1980 WV spouse George Walter Dooley; Mary Elizabeth born 1893 WV died 1981 Gallia County spouse John Floyd Leonard; Edward Newton born 1895 WV died 1978 Gallia County, spouse #1 Helen Dyer, #2 Irene McCormick; John Joseph born 1897 WV died 1941 Wayne Co, Ohio spouse Gladys Brown; George Homer born 1899 WV died 1979 Wayne Co, Ohio, spouse #1 Mary Smith #2 Edna Hofsetter, *Levi Wilbert born January 31, 1901 Nicholas County, WV died November 24, 1953 Hamilton County, Ohio spouse Reva Reah Reynolds married 1921; Esther Ruth born 1902 WV died 1902 WV; Ida Grace born 1903 WV died 1912 WV; Charles Carter born 1906 WV died 1978 Gallia County spouse Audrey Collins married 1959; Nellie Vieva born 1909 WV died 1948 Gallia County spouse Benjamin Lincoln Franklin; James Viro born 1910 WV died 1979 Gallia County, spouse Marietta Atkinson. Henry moved his family to Gallia County about 1914, coming from Nicholas County, WV. Henry and Jeanette are buried in Fairview Cemetery near Bidwell, Ohio.

*Henry And Jeanette Reynolds*

*Levi And Reva Reynolds,*

Levi Reynolds and Reva Reah Rupe born January 9, 1903 Eno and died February 11, 1974 Gallipolis daughter of Oscar and Stella Rupe, lived in Logan, Ohio and Levi worked for the railroad for a short time. They returned to the Rupe family farm and Levi became a farmer. Their children were Esther Alice spouse Wendell James; Florence Olive spouse #1 Ralph Dexter, #2 Jack Layfield, #3 Bobby Erwin; Elza Ralph born June 23, 1925 Eno died October 19, 1982 Gallia County; Margaret Lucille spouse Edwin Thaxton: Helen Elizabeth born May 8, 1930 died September 11, 1999 Jackson County, Ohio spouse George Ferrell; Reva Frances, spouse #1 Rom Rhoses, #2 Delbert Hanna; Mildred Louise, spouse #1 Charles Bush, #2 Dexter White. After the death of Levi, Reva moved to Gallipolis and worked at Haskins and Tanner also Gallipolis State Hospital. Grandchildren were Martha and Gerry James, Audris Layfield, Wilma Thaxton, Chuck, Debbie and David Ferrell, Jeff Rhodes, Susan and Ed Bush. Levi and Reva are buried in Gravel Hill Cemetery near Cheshire.

**JOHN R. (JACK) AND BARBARA N. RICHARDS** - Jack's parents were the late Robert Mills Richards (Gallia County) and Ruth Arnold (Meigs County). Both he and his sister Eleanor Kay were born in Pt. Pleasant, West Virginia. In 1941 the family moved to Gallipolis. Jack attended the Gallipolis City schools and graduated from Michigan State University with a Bachelor's degree in Business Administration and later from the University of Dayton with a Master's degree in Educational Administration. He received his teaching certification from The Ohio State University.

*Jack & Barbara Richards*

Barbara is the daughter of the late Ernest Null and Clarice Howard (both of Gallia County). She was born in Huntington, West Virginia. Her family which consisted of her parents, her brother, Merrill, sisters Marianna (Dille) and Bette (Horan) soon moved back to Gallia County. Barbara attended the Gallipolis City schools and graduated from Ohio University with a Bachelor's degree in Comprehensive Business Education and later from the University of Dayton with a Masters degree in Educational Administration.

Jack and Barbara were married at Grace United Methodist Church in Gallipolis. They moved to Germany where Jack was serving with the US Army. Their son Bill was born in Buren, Germany—the first American child born in the County of Buren. In 1964 the Richards family moved to Knoxville, Tennessee where Jack was employed by the Kroger Company as store manager. In 1967 they moved to Des Moines, Iowa where Jack was employed by Super Value Food Stores as a field representative. Daughter Lori was born while the family lived in Des Moines.

In 1972 the Richards family moved back to Gallipolis where Jack was employed as manager of the Jones Boys Department/food store on Pine Street. When Buckeye Hills Career Center opened in 1975, Jack became their first Marketing instructor and taught for 22 years before retiring. In 1974 Barbara returned to teaching business/computer classes at Gallia Academy High School, retiring in 1997.

They are the parents of two children, Bill who is employed by the Ohio Valley Bank as Marketing Coordinator and lives in Gallipolis, and Lori who is employed by Nationwide Insurance Company as subrogation claims representative. Lori is married to Todd Fowler of Worthington and she and Todd currently live in Westerville.

Jack and Barbara are members of Grace United Methodist Church, Gallia County Retired Teachers Association, First Families of Gallia County, and the French Art Colony. Barbara is the Editor of the Gallia County Retired Teachers newsletter, the GAHS Alumni newsletter and the Gallia County Historical Society newsletter, The Glade. She also works with the Gallia County Convention and Visitors Bureau. Jack is active in the Gallipolis Shrine Club, the Elks Club, and various Masonic organizations.

Jack and Barbara try to spend as much time as possible at their cabin on Norris Lake in Tennessee—their home away from home. It is a vacation spot for family and friends, relaxing, boating, fishing, and enjoying life.

Family genealogies may be found at the Gallia County Historical/Genealogical Society.

*Submitted by Jack Richards*

**ROBERT MILLS AND RUTH ARNOLD RICHARDS** - Robert Mills Richards was born November 24, 1909 in Rio Grande to John Elias (Jack) and Ruth Mills Richards. His brother John Earl was born in 1911 and sister Mary Margaret was born in 1913. The family moved to Gallipolis where John F. Richards became deputy auditor. The Richards family traces their ancestors back to Thomas and Eleanor Jones Richards of Cardiganshire, Wales who came to this country in the early 1800's. (For additional genealogical information, refer to First Family Applications and Gallia County Ohio People in History to 1980.)

*Bob and Ruth Richards*

Ruth Mills Richards was the daughter of James McCormick Mills and Mary Jane Halliday. Upon the death of her husband John E. in 1917, she worked for the Gallipolis Daily Tribune for 33 years.

*Pictured below are the immediate family of Bob and Diz Richards. Front row left to right: Bill Richards, Barbara Null Richards, Todd Fowler, Lori Richards Fowler; middle row: Robbie Woodward, Cara Dunkle, Morgan Woodward, Drew Dunkle; back row: Jack Richards, Eleanor Kay Richards Evans, Dan Dunkle, Beverly Bennett Dunkle, Jackie Bennett Woodward, Tombo Woodward.*

Bob married Ruth "Diz" Arnold of Pomeroy, Ohio on September 2, 1932. Diz was a graduate of the Holzer School of Nursing. She was the daughter of Clarmont and Edna Ashworth Arnold of Meigs County. Bob and Diz were the parents of John Robert (Jack) and Eleanor Kay Richards Evans. The family lived in Pt. Pleasant, WV until 1941 when they moved back to Gallipolis. Bob was employed with the Evans Grocery Company until he retired in 1962.

Bob and Diz were very active members of Grace Methodist Church. They enjoyed golf, bridge and travel with their many friends. Diz died September 23, 1981 and Robbie died September 8, 1991.

**THOMAS KEITH AND LISA ANN ROUSH RICHIE FAMILY** - Both Thomas (Tom) and Lisa were born in Gallipolis, Oh. Tom's parents are Bobby Lee Richie and Rosalee Pierotti Richie. Tom was born June 15, 1961, attended grade school at Green Elementary and graduated from Buckeye Hill Vocational Schools, Class of 1979. After graduation he worked for Bob Roach of Standard Plumbing and Heating. He then owned his own plumbing business (Elite Plumbing) for a few years and currently works on the line crew for Buckeye Rural Electric Company. He has been involved in helping coach softball and baseball for his children. His wife, Lisa, was born May 13, 1964, attended Washington Grade School and graduated with Gallia Academy Class of 1982. While in school, she was quite active in band and vocal groups. A member of Madrigals, a singing group at Gallia Academy and a member of Gallia Academy High School Band Flag Corps. After graduation from high school, she attended the University of Rio Grande and graduated from the Southeastern Business College. She has worked as a secretary for Credit Thrift and Grace United Methodist Church and now works as a library aide at Kyger Creek Middle School for the Gallia County School System.

Their oldest child, Thomas Jacob (Jake) Richie was born May 11, 1983 in Gallipolis, OH. Jake attended Green Elementary School and while there was very involved in softball, basketball, Midget League Football and baseball. He began his high school career at Gallia Academy and, beginning his junior year of high school, transferred to River Valley High School. While there he continued playing football and wrestled. He was also involved with singing in their vocal choir "Phoenix" and participated in their annual school musical. Presently, Jake attends the University of Rio Grande and plans to transfer to Marshall University in Huntington, WV and become a teacher.

Valerie Lianne Richie was born December 9, 1989 in Gallipolis, Ohio. She is presently attending Green Elementary School and is in the sixth grade. Valerie is a very good student and has always participated in all sports offered for her age group. She began with T-Ball and has continued playing softball every year. Besides softball, Valerie has been involved with basketball. For the past few years, she has been on a cheerleading squad that has taken many district, regional and national honors. Valerie and her brother, Jake, have both been members of the Fleur-de-lis Society C.AR., "Children of the American Revolution". They can both trace their ancestry to Revolutionary War soldier, Levi Trowbridge. Both children have been involved with 4-H and shown pigs at the county fair.

The Richie's attend Christ United Methodist Church on lower Route #7 in Gallia County.

*Submitted by: Lisa Richie*

**RICKABAUGH FAMILY** - List of Swiss Emigrants in the Eighteenth Century to the American Colonies shows Heini Riggenbacher of Zelingen Switzerland (44 years of age), Barbara Thommen his wife (39 years of age) and children: Elsbeth 7/30/1724, Hans Adam 11/28/1726, Johannes 10/24/1728, Jacob 6/25/1730, Margreth 3/18/1732, Henrich (Henry) 5/22/1735, Barbara 10/20/1737, and Anna 11/28/1739, left for America. Heini's two youngest children died on the voyage and his wife died at Philadelphia. His son, Hans Adam, returned to Europe 1749-1750 to collect inheritance from the estate of his grandfather, Adam Thommen who had died in 1743.

*Adamsville Log Cabin Village*

Henry was born 5/22/1735 Basel Switzerland and died August, 1780, Shenandoah County, Virginia. His children include John, Adam, Henry, Barbara (married Bernard Wirhbarger), Margaret, Peter, and Mary.

John Rickabaugh, reported to be among the earliest settlers of Gallia County, Ohio, came here from Shenandoah County, Virginia in 1800 with his brothers Henry and Adam.

In 1803 Adam built a grist mill on Big Raccoon Creek in Raccoon Township. This is now the present site of Adamsville, Ohio, (where the Bob Evans Farm is located), named after Adam Rickabaugh. Adam was first married in May 1785 to Catherine Koontz in Rockingham County, Virginia. Issue were: Christena, Lydia, John, Elizabeth, Peter, Ann and Mary. Upon Catherine's death in 1806, Gallia County, Ohio he married her sister Mary Koontz in 1807 in Gallia County, Ohio. They had the following children: Rachel, Adam, William, Mahlay, & Joseph. This Adam was born 3 Jan 1761 Shenandoah County, Virginia and died 23 July 1836 Adamsville, Gallia county, Ohio.

John, born 1760 Shenandoah County, died 1836 Raccoon Township was the son of Henry Rickabaugh of Switzerland and Mangdalina Lionberger of Shenandoah County, Virginia. John was a farmer who married Elizabeth Griffith, daughter of John Griffith, in 1784 Shenandoah County, Virginia. They had five children: Henry (married Mary Polly Danner), John (married Tabitha Shelton), Rachael (born 10 August 1797, Gallia County, Ohio died 31 October 1867, Rio Grande, Gallia County, Ohio, married Abraham Childers) (See the Childers Family of Gallia County, Ohio), Sarah (married Joseph Childers), & Adam (who married Catherine McCoy). Both Abraham Childers and Rachael Rickabaugh Childers are buried at Old Pine Cemetery, Rio Grande, Gallia County, Ohio. Additional info. is available on the Rickabaugh Family by contacting: Jack Childers, RD3 Box 480, Fenwick Island, DE 19944

**WILLIAM RIDGE** - William Ridge was born in Greenfield Twp., Gallia Co. on March 1, 1851. His father was William Ridge b the in State of Penn. His wife was Sarah Coply from Elizabeth Twp., Lawrence Co., Ohio. They married on 25th of Nov. 1849 in Lawrence Co., Ohio. William Ridge Jr. married around Jan. of 1871 to Sarah Lambert from Gallia Co., Ohio. She was the daughter of William H. Lambert & Permeila Roberts from Vinton Co., Ohio. William & Sarah Ridge had the following children: Margaret Isabelle, she married Charles W. McDaniel on March 19, 1887 b Dec. 13, 1871 d Aug. 7, 1938.

*William & Sarah Ridge Tombstone*

Laura M. b March 9, 1873 d June 11, 1873 (lived 3 mo. 2 days), David William Ridge Sr. b March 7, 1878 d Dec. 7, *1953*. First Marriage (Margaret Callahan) they had the following children: Charles, John Edwin, Mrs. Reese Thomas, Mrs. Roy Workman, his second wife (Jennie Williams) they had the following children David H. Jr., Nara Luther, Margaret Norman, and Rena. NOTE: John Edwin was killed in a coal mine accident on July 16, 1931 at Jisco coal mine in Jackson, Ohio. Charles E. was b Jan 28, 1881 d April 18, 1955. First m to Winifred Coffee. She was b Aug. 8, 1883 d Sept. 8, 1923 m second time to Gettie Graham, he had the following children: Everett, Clinton, Stanley, Walter, Jack, Mrs. Howard Hoffman, Mrs. James McCall, Mrs. Clyde Scott, Mrs. Donald Powers, Mrs. Danny Hoftetter, Louisa A (Ridge) Phillips b May 15, 1884 d Jan. 15, 1967. She m Henry H. Phillips May 15, 1901. Children: Edward, Mrs. Faye Swick, Mrs. Edith Kinker, Mrs. Avonelle Frankhammer, Mrs. Goldie Leffier, Mrs. Phyllis Evans, Mrs. Louise Donley, Anna B. (Ridge) Miller b March 31, 1886 d July 18, 1971 m George Felte Miller, they had 6 children: Homer, Perle, Raymond, Donald, Mrs. Gretchen Gardner, Mrs. David Lillian Fisher, Mrs. William Margaret Flemington, Mrs. Essie Morris. Ollie D. (Ridge) Riley b June 23, 1891 d Sept. 14, 1958 m to Edward H. Riley July 28, 1905. Children: Mrs. A. H. Derr, Mrs. Myrtle Yonts, Mrs. Taylor Pavey and Mrs. Carroll Hayes, one son Richard. Permelia Ridge, b 1890 lived in Colo., and d out there. John Stanley Ridge killed in coal mine accident July 31, 1929, Jacksonville, Ohio. Hayehetta Ridge, b May 16, 1896 d Nov. 16, 1898, 2 yrs. 6 mos. Fredrick b March 21, 1903 d July 1, 1903, 3 mos. 10 days.

*Submitted by: Larry Shawn McDaniel, 3rd Great Grandson*

**DR. C. A. RIFE** - Joseph Rife 1758-1827 came to Gallia County from Greenbrier County, Virginia. Joseph Rife was the son of Jacob and Catherine ? Rife and grandson of John Jacob Reiff who died in 1756 in Lancaster, Pa. He married Margaret Carpenter in Greenbrier Co. Va. and they and their 5 children came here to start a new life. When they settled along Campaign Creek he built the first water powered gristmill in 1808.

Son, Jonathan Rife (10 October 1814-16 July 1882), married Rozetta Abigail Rowley Shuler (2 June 1825-4 January 1892).

Grandson, Charles Augustus Rife, was born 26 November 1858, Campaign Creek, Addison Township in Gallia County. At the age of six, he lost his left forearm in the gears of a cane mill. He was holding a stock of cane when his arm was drawn into the gears. In the accident, he lost his left forearm and the ligaments and tendons were pulled in his upper arm and chest. He carried the scars of the accident the rest of his life.

After Charles completed his grammar school, he took a teacher's exam and began teaching school. He taught at the Turkey Run school, Cheshire Township. One of his pupils was his future wife, Lydia Lillian Matthews.

Charles was ambitious, saved his money, and with the help of his family attended Rio Grande College. He walked about twenty miles from his home to Rio Grande.

Charles studied medicine and graduated from the Starling Medical College, which is today known as Ohio State Medical College. He did his internship in Cincinnati, Ohio.

Charles and Lydia Lillian Matthews (6 September 1856-20 November 1936) were married 24 March 1880, at Cheshire, Ohio by W.J. Fulton.

Dr. Charles began practicing medicine at Kyger in 1882. He practiced medicine in Addison, Cheshire, Morgan, Huntington, and Rutland townships. He traveled throughout the area by horse and buggy.

Dr. Rife was instrumental through his letters to the American Medical Association about epileptics, in getting the Ohio Hospital for Epileptics located in Gallipolis. This was the first hospital solely for the epileptics and treatment of epileptics.

Dr. Rife assisted Dr. Holzer, Sr. to perform his first operation in Gallia County. This operation took place on the patient's kitchen table, and it was for stomach cancer. Dr. Rife believed in the establishment of the early hospital. He recommended and accompanied his patients to Holzer Hospital.

Three young men, Dr. Wallace Tate, Dr. Charles Ely, and Dr. Lucky, of the community studied and did their internship under Dr. Rife.

Dr. Rife and his wife Lydia were the proud parents of five children: Clara Virginia, Taphena Abigail, Stanley Marvin, Cora Rowley, and Charles Beecher. His eldest daughter was known all her life as Charlie Rife's girl, since she was born before her father was a doctor. The other four children were distinguished by the title Dr. Rife's children. This created some sibling rivalry in his children.

On 9 March 1932, the Gallia County Medical Society held a dinner commemorating Dr. Rife's 50 years of practice in the medical profession in Gallia County.

Dr. Charles Rife's daughter, Taphena Abigail, married Harlan Athey and had two children, Pauline and Harlan Clair.

Please refer to the Walter Rife Family History for further family references as daughter, Pauline, married Walter Rife.

*Submitted by: Kevin T. Napier, M.D.*

**HOLLIS W. RIFE** - Among the early Rifes who migrated to Gallia County was Jacob Rife born May 16, 1789 in Greenbrier County, Virginia. He left Greenbrier and settled in the Old Kyger vicinity of Cheshire Township in the early 1800's. He was married to Mary Darst, brother of Martin Darst on April 20, 1809 in Gallia County by Eli Stedman. Jacob and Mary had three children, Anna born 1811, Alvin born June 29 1813, and Anderson born in Cheshire Township on April 22, 1822.

Anderson Rife married (1) Sophia Scott on Dec 1, 1842 and (2) Mary E Roush on October 4, 1868. Anderson may have had 10 children with Sophia and 3 children with Mary.

Sylvester Rife, son of Anderson and Sophia (Scott) Rife was born in Cheshire Township on May 28, 1848. Sylvester married Louisa Roush daughter of George and Elizabeth (Darst) Roush. Louisa was born September 22, 1852 and died December 11, 1912. Louisa and Sylvester were married April 11, 1870. The children of this union were Mina born Nov 15, 1871 died August 18, 1934, Horton born Dec 13, 1873 died July 13, 1958, Howard born Oct 16, 1877 died May 26, 1914, Amy born Dec 15, 1879 died July 31, 1915 and Hollis born August 17, 1882 died July 2, 1943.

Hollis W Rife married Ethel Mary Thomas daughter of Nathanial and Rocena (Rumfleld) Thomas. The children of this marriage were Ada C born July 25, 1907, died December 5, 1998, Audrey A born September 30, 1912, died April 24, 1999, Evelyn F born October 6, 1915 and Ermal J born June 29, 1922 died November 15, 2000. Ada married Wilber Earl Ward who for many years carried the mail on the Cheshire rural route. They had one son, Wilber Ward Jr. Audrey Rife married (1) Marvin Thaxton and had two Sons: William (Bill) and Larry Thaxton. Audrey's second husband was William Wendell Bradbury and they had one son Richard Wendell Bradbury. Evelyn married Raymond Roush and they had one daughter Carol. Ermal married George Grover Cremeans and they had three sons, Thomas, Fred, and Frank.

*Submitted by Lori Bradbury-Robinson*

**JOSEPH RIFE, SR.** - The millstone in the picture was one of two that was used in the Joseph Rife mill on Campaign Creek, Addison Township, Gallia Co, Ohio. Joseph Rife came to Gallia Co. after migrating from what was then Greenbrier Co., Va. and built the mill in 1808. It was donated by Earl Shaver in 1991 and dedicated in 1995. It sits at the Addison Township Building, Bulaville, Ohio.

*Myron Jones With The Millstone From His 4th Great Grandfather (Joseph Rife).*

Joseph Rife was the son of Jacob and Catherine ? Rife and grandson of John Jacob Reiff who died in 1756 in Lancaster, Pa. He married Margaret Carpenter in Greenbrier Co., Va. and they and their 5 children came here to start a new life. Their children were Joseph, Jr. who married Betsy Howard, Catherine who married Abraham Darst, Jacob who married Mary Darst, Henry who married Tabitha Martindale and Esther who married Jonas McCarty. Joseph Sr. was born in 1758 in Greenbriar Co, Va. and died in 1827 in Gallia Co., Ohio.

The line we're going to follow is through Henry Rife and Tabitha Martindale Rife. Henry was born in 1790 in Greenbrier Co., Va. And married Nov. 28, 1811 in Gallia Co. They had 7 children and he died in April 1833 and is buried in Rife Cemetery, Addison Township, Gallia Co., Oh. along with his wife. Their children were Jonathan who married 1- Eliza Cottrell, 2- Rosetta Rowley Shuler, Nancy who married Levi Campbell Jones, James who married Mary Erwin, Mary who married Rev. James Lasley, Nathan who married Elizabeth Darst, Catherine who married Calvin Hughes, and Joseph who married Fanny Darst, twin of Elizabeth Darst.

Nancy married Levi Campbell Jones on July 2, 1837. Their children were: Elijah, who died young, Lovina Margaret who married William Butcher, Henry who died in the Civil War, Warren died in infancy, Thomas died in the Civil War, Mary Ann who married, 1- Marion Leonard, 2- William Malaby, Levi died in infancy, James married 1- Alma Rosanna McCarty, 2- Alice Augusta Fulton Rife, Eli Elijah married Anna Cotterill, Sarah Ellen married Zenas Logue, Jonathan Rife married Sarah Ann Rothgeb, Nancy Elizabeth (always went by Libbie) married Dr. Alonzo Beemer Garrett. Levi and Nancy were my great great grandparents through their son Jonathan Rife Jones, to Charles Ellsworth Jones, to Myron E. Jones, and to me, Myron Ellis Jones, Jr. The Jones family is also written in this book.

*Submitted by Myron Ellis Jones, Jr.*

**WALTER RIFE FAMILY** - The Rife's came from Greenbriar County, Virginia in the fall of 1800. Many members of the family died young. Two brothers Jake and Joseph came to Ohio. Jake located at Old Kyger, the first homestead probably on the land now owned by Ronald Jividen—this farm was known as the Jake Rife place.

Jake Rife married Mary Darst 20 April 1809 sister of Martin Darst and they had three children. Son Anderson (4 January, 1817-10 January 1867) had three wives, the first being Sarah Scott. They had seven children. One son Sylvester (28 May 1848-24 March 1919) married Louisa Roush (22 September 1852-11 December 1912) on 11 April 1870. They had three children. Son Horton Hayes (13 December 1873-13 July 1958) married Susan Almira (Susie) Darst (31 October 1876-1948) on 11 March 1893. To this union were five children, Floyd, Roy, Flossie, Walter, and Hazel.

Our Daddy, Walter (18 August 1908-27 June 1977), graduated from Cheshire High School in 1928. Two of the things he talked most about during his high school days were playing football and keeping in touch with what was happening at Rutland High School. Daddy married Mother, Pauline Athey (23 October 1910) 9 June 1931. Mother, incidentally, was what was interesting at Rutland High School.

Daddy and Mother had two daughters; Janet Lorene (9 October 1938) and Lois Christine (28 June 1942).

Janet Lorene married David Huber Fulton (2 December 1938) 25 May 1957. They are the parents of Kathleen Sue, Melissa Jayne, and Stephen David.

Kathleen Sue (26 December 1957) married William Charles Maslen (24 August 1954) 23 June 1978 at Griffin, Ga. They are the parents of Cara Lyn born 8 February 1980, Douglas James born 11 April 1983, and Amanda Kaye born 18 April 1984. They divorced in 1986. Kathleen remarried to Daniel Fendel (19 March 1952) on 23 June 1996.

Melissa Jayne (19 March 1960) married Cary Dewitt Chasteen (9 October 1965) on 7 September 1991. They have one child Colter Davis Chasteen (18 June 1998).

Stephen David (22 February 1963) married Tama Lynne Swander (13 July, 1967) on 28 April 1990. To this union was born Lauren Elizabeth 5 January 1993 and Benjamin Stephen 21 December 1996.

Lois Christine married Lark Napier, Jr. (22 February 1943) 23 March 1963. They are the parents of Lark Napier, Jr. and Kevin Tawn Napier. They divorced 7 May 1979.

Lark Napier, Jr. (25 March 1964) is the father of Leigh Ann (25 September 1985), Lark Napier III (18 December 1993), and Travis (30 May 1996).

Kevin Tawn (21 January 1967) married Alison Faye Heape (22 June 1968) on 23 June 1990. They are the parents of Jordan Walter (9 October 1994), David Charles (2 May 1995), and Abigail Christine (14 February 1999).

Daddy and Mother were graduates of Rio Grande College in 1937 and 1950 earning a degree in Elementary Education. Both graduated from Marshall University with a Master's Degree in School Administration in 1958.

Daddy was a teacher in the Cheshire Township schools for 37 years, 35 of which he served as principal. He began his career at the old Kyger one room school in 1929 and ended it as Principal of Cheshire-Kyger and Addaville Elementary School in 1973.

Mother began her teaching career in a one room school, Storys Run, Cheshire Township and ended it as Elementary Supervisor of Gallia County in 1973. She retired with 32 years of service to the education profession.

Janet and David Fulton and Christine Napier are all graduates of Ohio University. Janet taught school until she decided to quit that and devote herself to the children and horses. David went on to have a career with Delta Airlines retiring as Captain of the L1011. Christine retired from a teaching career with the Gallia County Schools in 1999.

Melissa Chasteen graduated from the Veterinary School of Medicine at the University of Georgia. Today she has a large animal practice in Griffin, GA. specializing in Equine.

Stephen David graduated from Georgia Tech with a degree in aeronautical engineering. Presently he is pilot with Alaskan Airlines based at Seattle, Washington.

Kevin Tawn Napier graduated from University of Georgia and the Medical College of Georgia with a degree in medicine. Today he is practicing internal medicine in Griffin, GA.

Our Mother lived in Cheshire Township for 88 years. In 1999 we sold the family farm and almost all of the family today lives in Griffin, Georgia.

*Submitted by: Janet Fulton, Christine Napier*

**ROADARMOUR FAMILY** - John William Roadarmour married Isabelle Cottrell on 9 December 1869. John was a farmer and he sold lumber. My mother said they could give their father any kind of math problem and he could figure it out in his head.

Willie Willis, their first child, was a farmer until he moved to Gallipolis, and then he worked in Spears Meat Market. He married Myrtie Buckle and they had one daughter Dorothy Faye. She taught school in Gallipolis and in Reading in Cincinnati.

Mary Rhoda, a seamstress, did not marry. She visited people's homes and sewed for them. Then she worked for Nan Deardorff who owned a store.

Pluma Edith married Thomas Wetherholt. They had a store at Angeltown. After several years they moved to Columbus. Pluma and Tom had three children: Delle, Anna Isabel and Vivian. Delle died of the flu in 1918. Anna Isabel, "Babe" married a Columbus bus driver Forest Ball. Their children were Donna June, Joan, and Don. "Babe" worked at a Defense Construction Supply Center. Vivian married Columbus policeman, Millard Ankrom. They are both deceased.

Ethel and Fred Boggs, a blacksmith, had one daughter, Mary Isabel.

*Emily Roadarmour Trotter*

Mary Isabel Boggs graduated from Rio Grande College with a BS in education in 1950. She has a Masters Degree that she received in 1964 from Peabody College in Nashville Tennessee. She taught school in Gallipolis and retired from Sharonville Schools in Cincinnati, Ohio.

Emily Cordelia married Virgil Albert Trotter in Point Pleasant on August 28, 1913.

Virgil was a fanner and raised sheep. Later Emily worked in a school cafeteria. Emily loved music and played the organ at Bailey Chapel. Their first child was John Thomas. John Trotter served in World War II. He graduated from Ohio University and is now a retired teacher from Gallipolis. Their second child was Mary Rachel. Mary Rachel Trotter graduated from Gallia Academy High School in 1942. She attended Ohio University and Rio Grande College, receiving a BS in Education May 26, 1948. She specialized in reading at Xavier University, Cincinnati, Ohio and received a Masters Degree in August 1977. She retired from teaching from Chillicothe City Schools in 1983. She lives at 154 Hirn Street, Chillicothe Ohio.

John and Effie Trotter had two children. Ted is a teacher in South Carolina. He married Brenda Kay Carroll. They have two children, Melanie Amber born 9 November 1976 and Christopher Matthew born 1 September 1978. He is in construction work. Melanie married Trent Teal, and had a boy Cody.

Julia lives in San Clemente, California. She is a chiropractor that works for an insurance company. She married Phillip Taylor. Her son Bundy lives in Hawaii.

There is more of the Roadarmour story in the Cottrill Family Story. Since there is no more of the family carrying the Roadannour name, my mother Emily was the last one in our branch of the Roadarmour family.

*Submitted by: John & Mary Trotter*

**ALDEN ROADARMOUR** - Alden Lothrop Roadarmour was born 22 July 1846 in Gallia County. He married Mary Harney. He taught school for a while, but then he became a lawyer and settled in Gallipolis.

Alden also would write a report for the newspaper and one told that his wife had entertained the Art Needle Club at the Roadarmour home, according to James Sands as published in the Tribune. The only requirement said that was needed was to be old and at least once a year be able to drag a man to the annual dinner. Six young girls who volunteered their services to be waitresses livened up the party. It seemed all loved to eat though.

The games that were played at the party were word games and sent most of them to the dictionary.

The following week, after the Tribune came out, Roadarmour received each day that week an anonymous note attached to wooden switches. Except on the seventh day "someone" had placed on the porch a pot of tar, a bag of feathers, a bundle of switches and several envelopes with verses inside.

"The shades of night are falling fast
When through a buckeye village passed?
Nine women armed with a pot of tar
Feathers and switches and all of them for
A man who by them had been kindly fed
Sheltered and a few good things said.
Until the faces of six young girls
With airs and graces, and smiles and curls
Not unlike the serpent of old
Lured him away from the elder fold
He called them old women with scraggy necks
Which wrings the hearts of the gentler sex;
And they felt with indignation and hate
Too good for him was the trader's fate"

The poem goes on to tell how the ladies intended to tar and feather Roadarmour and for him to repent and call the ladies young.

"Apologize ! Apologize ! at any cost,
On bended knee let words be wrung
Goddess of Youth and Beauty, be with us yet-
Lest he forget, Lest he forget
That we are young, that we are young.

Roadarmour probably decided not to be so truthful after this for there is no report of anyone that was tarred and feathered in 1804. He was able to get along with the womenfolk without any trouble.

*Submitted by: Mary Trotter*

**DWITT LEONARD (BUCK) AND MILDRED LOUELLA (MC CARLEY) ROBERTS FAMILY** - Dwitt was born November 19, 1917, in Hamlin, West Virginia, the son of Eustace and Carrie (Black) Roberts. He was about three years old when his parents came to Gallia County in 1920. They settled in the small community of Ewington, Ohio. Dwitt graduated from Vinton High School in 1936. After graduation, he tried his hand at farming. He enlisted in the U.S. Army in 1941 and served until 1945. After WWII he came back to Gallia County, where he met Mildred McCarley whom he married on November 22, 1946. Dwitt had two brothers and a sister. His brother, Albert, was killed in WWII. His younger brother, James Earl (Pete) and his sister, Virginia (Pearl) McClaskey, also lived in the Ewington community.

His wife, Mildred (McCarley) Roberts, was born February 3, 1915, in Alice, Ohio, to John Harry and Lola May (Sprouse) McCarley. Her siblings were: Dorothy (Sam) Oiler, Clair (Ann) McCarley, Fern (Charles) Moore, Lowell (Mary Ann) McCarley, Walter (Marian) McCarley, Phyllis (Leonard) Hash, and Joe Cline McCarley.

In 1953, Dwitt and his family moved to Gallilpolis, Ohio, where he began working for

French City Meats. The children born to Dwitt and Mildred Roberts were twin daughters: Sheryl Lynn Roberts of Pickerington, Ohio, and Sharon Ann (Louie) Bush of Gallipolis, Ohio, and a son, Gregory Brent (Cyndra) Roberts of Ewington, Ohio. Dwitt and Mildred both found great pleasure in their grandchildren. They had a wish that all of them would receive a college education. Mildred died December 4, 1990, and was not able to see her dreams met. Dwitt died May 2, 2000 and was able to see part of his dreams met. They had give granddaughters:

Amy Davis - A 1995 graduate of the University of Rio Grande with a Bachelors Degree in Education. She received her Masters Degree in Education from Marshall University in 2001.) Amy is married to William (Coby) Davis and teaches the second grade at Green Elementary in the Gallipolis City School District.

Rebecca Wilkins - A 1996 graduate of Ohio University with a Bachelors Degree in Education. She also received her Masters Degree in the Talented and Gifted Program from Ohio University in 1997. Rebecca is married to Douglas Frederick Wilkins of Rio Grande, Ohio, and teaches the first grade at Olde Sawmill Elementary in the Dublin city School District.

Jessica Crouse - A 1997 graduate of River Valley High School and a part-time student at the University of Rio Grande. Jessica is married to Brian Crouse and is the mother of Dwitt and Mildred's only great grandchild, Tristen Scott Crouse.

Ashley Roberts - A 1999 graduate of River Valley High School and presently a junior at the University of Rio Grande.

Kaitlyn Roberts - A third grader at Rio Grande Elementary.

Dwitt and Mildred would have been very proud of all the accomplishments of their children and grandchildren. Perhaps the greatest legacy the Roberts family has left Gallia County is the accomplishments of Ashly Ann Roberts, a junior at the University of Rio Grande. Ashly excels in track and field. She began her success in track and field at River Valley High School. In 1999 she placed third in the discus at the State track and field meet. In 2000 at the University of Rio Grande, she was runner-up at the NAIA Outdoor Track and Field Nationals held in British Columbia, Canada. Also as a freshman at the University of Rio Grande, Ashly was named an NAIA All American in the discus as well as being named the University of Rio Grande Female Athlete of the Year at the Bevo Francis Tournament. As a sophomore at the University of Rio Grande in 2001, she finished third at the NAIA Outdoor Track and Field Nationals in the discus which was again held in British Columbia, Canada.

"The family of Dwitt and Mildred Roberts are proud to be from Gallia County and hope to make Gallia County proud of them."

**RICHARD B. AND SALLY J. ROBERTS** - Richard Berridge Roberts was born on December 6, 1938 at Holzer Hospital in Gallipolis, Ohio to Nellie Mae (Reese) and Shelby Franklin Roberts. He has an older sister Mary Margaret (Roberts) Jenkins who was born on July 13, 1933. While growing up in Gallipolis he attended Washington Elementary and Gallia Academy High School and graduated from Gallia Academy in May 1956. Sally Jean (Botts) Roberts was born on May 21, 1940 in Columbus, Ohio to Helen Melissa (Wisecarver) and Eugene Henry Botts. Sally attended elementary schools in different parts of Columbus and graduated from Linden McKinley High School in Columbus in 1957. After graduating Sally worked at Nationwide Insurance on High Street until her marriage to Richard on December 27, 1958 at Hansberger Methodist Church in Columbus, Ohio. Richard after graduating from high school enlisted in the United States Air Force and attended several language schools during his career. He was trained in the Russian, Czech and French languages and also self taught in German and some Greek. To their marriage was born on September 10, 1960 Richard Allen Roberts at the US ARMY Hospital in Lanstuhl, West Germany. They resided at the time in Otterberg, W. Germany and a year later moved to Darmstadt, W. Germany where Richard was assigned to an Air Force Intelligence Unit. In 1962 they returned to the states while Richard was studying French at the State Department Language School in Arlington, Virginia and it was on October 30, 1962 that their youngest son Larry Jay was born at Fort Belvoir, Virginia Military Hospital. In early 1963 they moved to the island of Crete in the Mediterranean Sea just south of Athens, Greece, while Richard was stationed there with the Air Force. After living on Crete for four years they were reassigned to Goodfellow AFB, Texas and in 1968 moved to Offutt AFB, Nebraska where they lived in LaPlatte, Nebraska while Richard worked at the base and flew on air recon aircraft. In 1969 they once again returned to Germany to Rhein Main AFB and resided in the city of Langen near the base. Richard flew on RC130 aircraft from this base for the next four years. Sally became employed with Central Soya of Germany while they were stationed there and ran the office for this international company. In summer of 1973 they returned to the states and were stationed at Fort George G. Meade, Md. While Richard was assigned to the National Security Agency, Sally worked for the Arbitron Radio and Research in Beltsville, Md while they lived here. Also Richard graduated from University College, University of Maryland while in Maryland. His major was Public Administration with minor in Russia and Slavic Languages.

After retiring from the service the Roberts' returned to Gallipolis, Ohio where they still reside to this date. Richard worked for The Vernon Company in promotional advertising sales for 25 years retiring just this past year. Sally worked for the SEOEMS SYSTEM and then later for Marchi Distributing. Presently she has a small antique and collectible business out of the house. The boys both graduated from college with Richard graduating fro University of Rio Grande and Larry from Morehead State University in Morehead, Kentucky. Richard married Jozie Patrize McKenzie and they have one child, a son Christopher Allen and live in Gallipolis. Larry is a Major in the Army and is married to the former Rosa Ortega of El Paso, Texas. They are currently living in Manassas, Virginia. Thus the Roberts family goes on into eternity.

**ROBERTS' SISTERS** - Jessica Lynn Crouse, Ashley Ann Roberts, and Kaitlyn Marie Roberts are the daughters of Gregory Brent and Cyndra Lynn (Wiseman) Roberts of Vinton, Ohio. They are the grandchildren of the late Dwitt Leonard and Mildred (McCarley) Roberts of Ewington, Ohio, and John C. Wiseman of Point Pleasant, West Virginia, and the last Evelyn L. (Riser) Gooch of Vinton, Ohio. Their great grandparents were Eustace and Carrie L. (Black) Roberts of Ewington, Ohio; John H. and May (Sprouse) McCarley of Alice, Ohio; Earnest and Alice (Clyse) Wiseman of Gallipolis, Ohio; and Eli and Emma Riser of Point Pleasant, West Virginia.

Jessica, as a student at River Valley High School, ran cross country for two years, played varsity basketball for two years, and participated on the track and field team for four years. Jessica also ran cross country for the Cincinnati Express Women's Cross Country Team. In cross country at River Valley High School, Jessica closed out her high school career with Top 10 finishes in 6 of her last 9 races. She set the Lady Raider Cross Country record at 21:06 in 1996 which still stands. In the Junior Olympics, Jessica was named USATF All American at the Nationals in cross country which was held in Lexington, Kentucky. Jessica won many accolades for herself and her high school in track and field. She participated in district and regional meets. Jessica was awarded the Raider Award in track and field and the Top Gun Award in cross county. Upon graduation from high school, Jessica continued her running talents at the University of Rio Grande. She was a member of the URG Redwomen Cross Country Squad which won the Mid-Ohio Conference Championship in 1997 and finished 16 th in the Nation at the NAIA Cross Country Nationals held at Kenosha, Wisconsin. In 1998, Rio's cross county team earned an at-large bid to the NAIA Women's Cross Country National Championships again held in Kenosha, Wisconsin. The Redwomen cross country team finished second in the Nation academically in the 1998 season. In 1999, Jessica ran cross country for the Redwomen while injured. Jessica has married Brian Crouse and is the mother of their 18-month-old son, Tristen Scott Crouse. She is also the 1994 and 1995 winner of the Gill Dodd Rotary Mile in the girls age 15 and over category.

Ashly began her great athletic career at River Valley High School. She played two years of JV basketball; but, her forte was in track and field. As a freshman, Ashley set a new school record in the discus at 99'1". She participated in the Division 11 District Meet in the discus and the shot put. She then went on to the Division 11 Regional Meet in the discus. As a sophomore, Ashly received the 1997 Raider Award in track and field. She participated in the Division I District and the Division I Regional track meets in both the discus and the shot put. Ashly qualified for the State in the discus and took 15th in the State. As a junior, Ashly won more accolades for River Valley High School. She competed in the Division 11 District and the Division 11 Regional meets in both the discus and shot put. She qualified for the State track and field meet in both the discus and shot put. As a senior in 1999, Ashly again participated in the Division 11 District track meet in both the discus and shot put. Ashly went on to the Division 11 Regional meet where she was runner-up in the discus and also qualified for the State in the shot put. At the OHSAA Track Meet, Ashly placed 13th in the shot put and third in the discus with a throw of 138'11". Ashly is the first 3-time State Competitor for River Valley High School. In 1996, Ashly and Jessica became the first siblings in River Valley history to advance to the Division II Regional track and field meet.

After graduation, Ashly then joined her sister, Jessica, as a member of the University of Rio Grande Track and Field Team. Ashly has performed in both the Indoor and Outdoor Track and Field Programs at the URG. As a freshman, Ashly qualified for the NAIA Indoor National Track and Field Meet at Lincoln, Nebraska, in the 20 lb. weight throw. She won the All Conference Award at the American Mid-East Conference in the shot put at 3 8' 11 1/2" Also as a freshman, Ashly qualified for the NAIA Outdoor National Track and field meet held at Abbottsford, British Columbia, Canada, in the discus. Ashly was named an NAIA All American in the discus when she finished second in the Nation with a throw of 145'3". As a sophomore at the URG in 2000, Ashly was chosen the Rio Grande Female Athlete of the Year at the Bevo Francis Basketball Tournament. Ashly qualified for the NAIA Indoor Track and Field Nationals held at Johnson City, Tennessee, in the shot put and the 20 lb. weight. Ashly again qualified for the NAIA Outdoor National Track and Field Meet held at Simon Fraser University at Abbottsford, British Columbia, Canada. Ashly participated in the hammer throw and the discus. She placed third in the Nation with a throw of 148'10". Thus she was named NAIA All American in the discus. As a junior at the URG, Ashly continues her athletic accomplishments. She has already qualified for the NAIA Indoor Track and Field Meet in the 20 lb. weight which again will be held in Johnson City, Tennessee.

This saga continues because the Roberts' sisters have a younger sister, Kaitlyn Marie, who is in grade school at Rio Grande Elementary. Kaitie has played tee ball for the Vinton Tigers. In 2001 she was a member of the Rio Express Junior Olympic Track and Field Team. Kaitie participated in the sub-Bantam girls shot put, 100-meter dash, and sub-Bantam girls 1500 meters. Kaitie advanced from the District Championship in Washington Court House, Ohio, to the Ohio Junior Olympics State Meet held at Baldwin Wallace College in Cleveland, Ohio, in the girls 1500 meters. Kaitie presently plays girls basketball for Southwestern in the O. O. McIntyre Park District teams. As you can see, Gallia County should be especially proud of these three young ladies.

**CHARLES EMMETT AND CAROL (FOWLER) ROBINSON** - Charles (Chuck) Robinson was born at Bidwell, Ohio on Feb. 3, 1932 to Charles Bradford (Bobbie) and Janie (Welker) Robinson. He and Carol were married Aug. 5, 1955 at Brookville, Indiana. Her parents were James Henry and Mary (Brown) Fowler of Gallipolis. She was born Feb. 15, 1935. Chuck grew up in the Bidwell community and graduated from Bidwell-Porter High School in 1949. He served in the U.S. Army in Germany and returned home a short time before he and Carol were married and they moved to Columbus, Ohio. He was employed at University Hospital and held the position of plant engineer when he retired in 1984. They returned to Gallia Co. in 1985.

Carol grew up in Gallipolis and graduated from Gallia Academy High School in 1953, entering Holzer School of Nursing that fall. She worked at various nursing positions in Columbus. In 1992 she helped organize and became the coordinator for the Gallia Co. Adult Daycare. She held that position until retirement.

*Charles E. And Carol (Fowler) Robinson*

Chuck and Carol have two daughters: Janet Lynn who was born in 1956 and Rebecca (Beckie) Sue born in 1962. Both girls graduated from Whetstone High School in Columbus. Janet is the mother of two boys: Timothy Jacob Eshelman who is a student at Logan High School and Daniel Charles Eshelman who graduated from Logan High School. Daniel and his wife Lauren are serving in the U.S. Marine Corps and are the parents of Tyler Charles who was born Aug. 3, 2001. Janet is married to John Lent and they live in the Hocking Hills near Logan. They operate their own business. Beckie is the mother of two girls: Lisa Nicole Rader who is a student at Ashland High School in Ashland, Ohio, and Cierra Rae Campbell who is enrolled in kindergarten.

Beckie is employed in a cardiologist's office in Mansfield. Chuck's father Bobbie sang and played the piano, entertaining in such places as the Ariel Theater where he played the piano during silent movies. Bobbie's ancestors included Seasholes, Miller, and Dillon. Bobbie's parents were Charles and Mary (Seashole) Robinson of Gallipolis. Charles owned a wallpaper and paint store. Chuck's maternal grandparents were Wilson Emmett and Cora (Glassburn) Welker. Mr. Welker retired from the railroad.

Surnames of Chuck's mother's family are: Glassburn, Sawyers, Lasley, Fee, Might, Richardson, Bass, McMillin, Guy, Lockridge, Reed, Welker, and Harding.

They were pioneer settlers in Springfield, Addison, Cheshire, Morgan, and Huntington townships. Chuck's fourth great-grand father David Glassburn and a great-uncle John McMillin fought in the Battle of Point Pleasant.

Carol's father worked at the munitions plant during W.W.II and also drove a truck. Her mother enjoyed ceramics and doll-making. Her grandparents were George and Molly (Wise) Fowler of Meigs and Gallia Co. George retired from the New York Central Railroad, and Jacob Milton and Bernice (Saunders) Brown of Gallipolis.

Jake's maternal grandparents were the Krauses from Hanover, Germany. Bernice's family lived in Walnut Township. She was knowledgeable about nursing and assisted in the deliveries of several of her grandchildren. Her ancestors include Brammer, Yates, and Sturgills.

Carol and Chuck enjoy spending time with their family and hobbies include spending time in the out-of-doors, hiking, and bird-watching. They are interested in genealogy and Carol does oil painting.

*Submitted: by Carol Robinson*

**JASON SCOTT RODGERS FAMILY** - Jason Scott Rodgers was born on August 2, 1973, at Holzer Hospital in Gallipolis, Ohio, Gallia County. He was the first born of a set of twin boys born to George Samuel and Carolyn Gail (Plants) Rodgers from Point Pleasant, WV. His twin is Jeffrey Shane Rodgers. Another brother, Paul Samuel Rodgers was born October 26, 1969

*Jason Rodgers, Brandy Russell, Haley Micah Orsbon, Jaron Scott Rodgers, And Jaci Gail Rodgers*

Jason's grandparents on his dad's side were Paul Sylvester Rodgers and Virginia Lee Glover Rodgers from Point Pleasant, WV. Paul Rodgers used to have a plumbing company in Point Pleasant that went by the name of R & R Plumbing Company on Lincoln Avenue. Virginia, his grandmother, worked at Somerville Dry Cleaning Shop in Point Pleasant as a seamstress.

Jason's great grandfather on his mother's side was Christopher Columbus Plants born near Point Pleasant, WV, on March 7, 1858. He died September 7, 1925. Christopher was married to Adra Ella Plants. She was born June 19, 1878, and died March 8, 1942. To this marriage there was born eleven children of which Jason's grandfather Gilbert Lawrence Plants was the fifth.

Gilbert Lawrence Plants was born on April 2, 1908, at Henderson, WV, and on February 28, 1935, he married Opal Irene Neal who was the daughter of Joseph Daniel and Mary Elizabeth Taylor Neal from West Columbia, WV. Opal was born on October 15, 1916. To this marriage was born fourteen children of which Jason's mother, Carolyn Gail Plants Fellure, was the tenth. Gilbert Plants died on May 8, 1986, and Opal died August 31, 1991.

Jason's first few years were spent in Gallia County where he attended school at Bidwell-Porter Elementary School in Bidwell, Ohio. Jason's parents were divorced in February 1975. Jason's mother then moved to Columbus, Ohio, where she met Larry Fellure and they were married on July 6, 1979, in Whitehall, Ohio.

When Jason was eight years, the family moved to a farm in Gahanna, Ohio, where they lived for ten years. Jason attended school at Lincoln Elementary School and Gahanna-Lincoln High School where he was active in sports such as cross country racing and football. Jason continued to live in Columbus until spring of 1997 when he returned to the Gallia County area.

Jason always liked coming back to the country when he was younger and did so all his life. He had returned on the weekends with his stepfather, Larry Fellure, and enjoyed hunting, fishing, swimming and other activities where they had a camper in the Cheshire, Ohio, area.

Jason got a job working for Ponderosa in Gallipolis. He met a girl there named Brandy Russell whom he is still with now. They have been together about two years now. Brandy has a little blonde-haired daughter that Jason considers his own. Her name is Haley Mika born February 15, 1998. Jason and Brandy have a son born on November 23, 2000, on Thanksgiving Day, named Jaron Scott Rodgers; and they have a daughter born September 28, 2001, named Jaci Gail, named after Jason's mom, Carolyn Gail Fellure.

At this time, Jason and his family live on Route 218 in Mercerville, Ohio, below Gallipolis and Jason and Brandy both work in the Crown City, Mercerville, area.

*Submitted by Jason Scott Rodgers*

**ROSE - ADKINS - DAILEY -** Edward Rose born in Montgomery County, Virginia, married Winifred Neal. One of their sons, William married Mary Adkins in Gallia County in 1811 Their daughter Burthana married Vincent Dailey who was born in Monroe County, Ohio in 1828. He was the son of John H. and Catherine Sutherland Dailey. Vincent became a minister at an early age and was a farmer and preacher in Gallia County. He and Hiram Rankin laid out the village of Crown City. He was a soldier in the Civil War, attaining the rank of corporal and fought in Morgan's Raid. Vincent and Burthana Rose became the parents of ten children, one of whom. James Lewis. married Elizabeth Memphis Garlic in 1852 and became the parents of ten children. one of whom, James Eustace Dailey born June 08. 1881, married Grace Maude Haskins. who was born on May 22, 1887 to Henry G. and Elizabeth Crawford Haskins. They were married February 28, 1908 in Maysville, Kentucky . They became the parents of one child, Helen Elizabeth who was born August 18, 1909. Elizabeth married John Everett Burcham on August 25, 1935 and they had one child, Elizabeth Anne, born April 08, 1937. She married John L. Belville on December 25, 1955 In Crown City Methodist Church and became the parents of two children: Thomas Lee and Teresa Anne who married Robert G. Marchi and reside in Gallipolis, OH where both are employed.

**ROTHGEB FAMILY -** The Rothgebs can trace their history back to Jacob Radigab born about 1578 in Schwameningen, Zurick, Switzerland. We pick up their story with Hans Jacob Rothgeb born 1708 in Wallisellen, Zurick, Switzerland, and died 1752 in Mill Creek, Shenandoah County, Virginia.

On May 29, 1735, the ship, Mercury, with William Wilson as master, left from Rotterdam, Holland, arrived at Philadelphia, Pennsylvania, with 186 passengers. Among them were Hans Jacob and his wife, Barbara Haller, whom he married on the trip up the Rhine River from Switzerland to Holland. If anyone wants more information about the trip, contact Jack Childers, email childers@dca.net, and I will send you the complete history. Hans had a son, John George, born 1741, Fredrick County, Virginia, died 1817 Mill Creek, Shenandoah County, Virginia. He, with three wives (at different times), had a total of 19 children. With his second wife, Barbara Bear, he had a son named John (Sr.).

*John Newton Rothgeb 1910*

John Sr. was born December 29, 1781, Mill Creek, Shenandoah County, Virginia, and died December 2, 1869, Addison Township, Gallia County, Ohio. He married Anna Strickler, daughter of Abraham Strickler and Ann Brubaker of Shenandoah County, Virginia. Their children were Noah, Ann (married to Newton Mauck), Reuben, John Jr., Levi, Mary Polly (married to Daniel L. Mauck), Barbara (married to William Rathburn), George, and Captain Samuel (married to Francis Leonard).

John Rothgeb born April 16, 1818, Luray, Shenandoah County, Virginia, died February 9, 1849, Addison, Gallia County, Ohio. Married July 11, 1843, to Mary Catherine Mauck at Addison, Gallia County, Ohio. Their children were Ester Ann (married Barlett Boyce), Mary Catherine (married to Robert Fulton), James, and John Newton who was born April 18 1849, Addison Township, Gallia County, Ohio, and died January 25, 1931, Merchantville, New Jersey, at his daughter's home. Notes for John: Born and reared in Gallia County, Ohio, was a member of a very prominent family. He was superintendent of the Columbia Bridge Shops. He was married to Alice M. Wilson on January 27, 1876, Cheshire, Gallia County, Ohio. They had the following children: Malissa Ola (see Childers Family History), Arna B. (who married William H. T. Needham, son of Alfred Needham). Notes for William: William was born in 1874, Gallipolis, Gallia County, Ohio, and died 1951, Columbus, Ohio. He was a printer by occupation and editor of Gallipolis Times. Mr. O. O. McIntyre applied for a job at the Times and Needham told him that he would never make it in the newspaper business. He fired him and O. O. went to New York and became a world famous Broadway reporter, but they remained good friends until the end. Additional information is available on the Rothgeb Family by contacting Jack Childers.

*Submitted by Jack Childers*

**JACOB AND BARBARA WIDECK ROTHGEB -** Jacob and Barbara Rothgeb arrived in Gallia County about 1811 from Page County, Virginia. I suspect John and Samuel Rothgeb, half-brothers of Jacob, arrived at the same time. Another half-brother, Joseph, did not arrive until later. Jacob, John and Samuel are listed on the 1812 Gallia County Chattels. Jacob born September 25, 1768, Page County, Virginia, died March 31, 1851, Gallia County, Ohio, son of John George and Madelene Biedler Rothgeb. Barbara born 1770 Germany died about 1826 Gallia County, Ohio, daughter of Henry and Christina Offenbacker Wideck. They married April 26, 1792, Page County, Virginia. Their children were Henry, born February 1794, Virginia, died January 15, 1873, Gallia County, spouse Sarah Burcher, married 1832; Rudolph born 1800 Virginia, died 1865, Gallia County, spouse Caroline Vance, married 1833; George born 1804, Virginia, spouse Milly Slaugher married 1827; Jacob, Jr. born July 25, 1806, Virginia, died 1833(?), Gallia County; Madelene born 1808, Virginia; David born April 11, 1809, Virginia, died June 24, 1878, Gallia County, spouse Elizabeth Scott married 1836; Christine born 1810, Virginia, died February 1891, Gallia County, spouse Joseph Darst married 1842; Joseph born 1812, Gallia County, spouse Catherine Shaver married 1834; Elizabeth (Betsy) born December 6, 1817, Gallia County, died March 2, 1898, Gallia County, spouse George Washington Rupe born June 1, 1809, Shenandoah County, Virginia, died October 18, 1888, Gallia County, married 1837. My source for Jacob and Barbara's children is Gallia County, Ohio, Journal of Wills, Inventory and Sale Bills Vols. 3-C and 4-D, Estate Settlement of Jacob Rothgeb, Jr., Page 281, dated October 21, 1837, lists Henry, George, Rudy, Christina, Molly, David, Joseph and Betsy as heirs. It also states that Betsy was underage and did not receive her share until she reached majority in 1837. After Barbara's death, Jacob married Madeline Nye April 12, 1831, Gallia County. Their children were Tobias (1832-1901) spouse EstherRandall; Julia (1833-1860) spouse William Gordon; John (1835-1895) spouse Margaret A. Swisher; Benjamin (1836-1901) spouse Margaret Swisher.

Jacob and two of his children Jacob, Jr., and Mollie are buried in the Rothgeb Cemetery in Cheshire Township. They have monuments. I suspect Jacob's spouses are there also but no marker.

I am a descendant of Jacob, Sr., Betsy Rothgeb Rupe, Joseph Rupe, Oscar, Reva Rupe Reynolds and Louise.

*Submitted by Louise R. White*

**AUGUSTUS ROTT-RUTT FAMILY** - August "Gus" Rott was the son of Christian and Caroline Rott. Christian Rott and his family left Europe from the port of Breman, Germany and came to America aboard the Bark, "Stella." They arrived in New York on December 6, 1867.

August was born near Hannover, Germany on March 7, 1844. He had two sisters; Christina b. 1851 and Caroline b. 1855, both born in Germany. When he was eighteen he was required to serve two years in Kaiser Wilhelm's German Army. In one battle, he reached for his canteen to get a drink. It was empty. A bullet had gone completely through it. He said he made up his mind right then to go to America. So when his two years was up, with a little money in his pocket and a few clothes he left for America.

*Front Row-August Rutt & Rachel Rutt. Back Row-William, Emma, August (Gus), Otto, Lena, Herman*

After reaching New York he began inquiring about German Ridge in Walnut Township, Ohio. Some of his friends had already come over and were living in that area. He arrived in Thurman, Ohio completely destitute. After inquiring about Cadmus, he was told to catch the mail wagon. Not being able to speak English he couldn't explain that he didn't have any money. Upon arriving at Patriot, Ohio the driver demanded payment. Without any success at communication August pulled out his empty wallet and handed it to the irate driver and walked away.

August stayed with his friend Fred Klages, who was also from Hanover, Germany. As he was a good carpenter, August soon had enough money to buy his own farm. At his death he owned three large, fully equipped farms.

He married Rachael Alborn Reimsnyder Aug. 29, 1869 in Gallia County, Ohio. Rachael was born November 21, 1849 in Germany. Their children were William Gustave Rott (1872-1940) a watchmaker m. Mary Stella Lloyd; Emma (1872-1940) m. William R. Wood; Lena Christiana (1875-1929) who never married; Otto (1880-1938) a farmer m. Nora E. Canturbury; August E. (1882-1942) a carpenter m. Clora Mayme Webster; and Herman August (1877-1946) a carpenter m. Elva Effie Drummond daughter of William A. Drummond and Lovina Lowks Drummond.

Herman and Elva Rott-Rutt had four children; Laylin Drummond Rutt born June 18, 1904, who taught school over forty years, m. Mary Lou Haynes; Willa Alma Rutt Saunders born June 22, 1906, a teacher and later clerk at the Gallia County Court House, m. Stanley Albert Saunders; Dale A. Rutt born July 30, 1911, a machinist who lived in Columbus m. Reta Deckard; and Laura Margaret Rutt Queen born November 1, 1913, a beautician with a parlor in Gallipolis, and later in Columbus m. Earl Queen.

According to stories Christian came to live with his son August in Walnut Twp. for a number of years. After having an argument over using August's trees to build furniture for friends Christian left and went to New York. While he was in Gallia County Christian became an American Citizen March 14, 1873 in the Gallia Probate Court. Augustus became an American Citizen later in the year on October 13, 1873.

**JAMES W. AND ROBERTA F. JOHNSON ROUSH FAMILY** - James W. Roush was born in New Haven, WV, on May 1, 1938, to Ralph Waldon and Iva Florence London Roush. His father, Ralph, was born in Mason County, WV, May 11, 1913, and mother, Iva Florence London, was born August 4, 1916, in Meigs County, OH. She died November 12, 1973, in Mason County, WV.

*Roberta and James Roush*

James Waldon Roush married Roberta Frances Johnson, born October 18, 1939, Gallipolis, OH., on November 8, 1959, in Gallipolis, OH. Roberta is the daughter of the late John Francis and Helen Purle Newman Johnson. They have another daughter, Rebecca Ann. Rebecca "Becky" married Clarence Harley Archer on August 1 and currently they live in Rogers, AR. John Francis Johnson was born April 4, 1899, in Gallipolis, OH,.and died June 14, 1962, in Gallipolis, OH. He was the son of the late Alden Luther and Oma L. Criner Johnson. John "Johnnie" Johnson was a realtor at the time of his death. During the 1940's and 1950's, he operated the B & B Pool Room, The B & B Hotel, Schartz Restaurant and was a salesman for the Kemper-Thomas Company. Helen Newman Johnson was born September 30, 1908, in Hamden, OH. Her parents were the late John and Martha Salmons Newman. Helen entered Holzer Hospital School of Nursing in 1928 and graduated as a registered nurse in 1931. She retired as a medical floor supervisor for the Gallipolis Developmental Center Hospital in 1978.

James and Roberta have two daughters and five grandchildren. The oldest daughter, Cynthia "Cindy", was born February 18, 1957, in Gallipolis, OH., and married Glenn David Graham, son of Glenn and Jacqueline Grubb Graham, September 5, 1976. They are the parents of three children, David James Graham, born September 7, 1977; Martha Kathryn "Cassie" Graham, born December 11, 1982, and Joseph Cole Graham, born November 5, 1985. All three were born in Gallipolis, OH. Their youngest daughter, Lisa Ann, was born May 13, 1964, in Gallipolis, OH., and married Thomas Keith Richie, the son of Bob and Rosalie Pierotti Richie, November 20, 1982. They have two children, the oldest, Thomas Jacob "Jake" Richie, born May 11, 1983, and Valerie Lianne Richie, born December 9, 1989. Both were born in Gallipolis, OH.

James Roush retired after working 43 years for the Ohio Valley Electric Corporation, and Roberta Roush retired after working over thirty years as a pre-school aide at the Community Nursery School located at First Presbyterian Church in Gallipolis.

James was an active member of Local 430, UWA, while working in the maintenance department. He also served two years active duty in the United States Army 1961-1963. Roberta is a member of French Colony Chapter Daughters of the American Revolution and currently serves The Ohio Society DAR as their State Historian, is a charter member and serves as secretary of Gallia Academy High School Alumni Association, served as a board member of Our House and Gallia County Historical Society. While serving the board of GCHS, four years were served as President from January 1998 through January 2002. Both James and Roberta are members of Grace United Methodist Church and Wesley Weds Sunday School Class, Gallipolis, OH.

Presently, both are enjoying retirement. James loves fishing, working in his yard and boating. Roberta "Bertie" enjoys volunteer work, especially with DAR and the Historical Society.
*Submitted by Roberta Roush*

**ROSS RAYMOND ROUSH FAMILY** - Ross Raymond Roush was born on a farm in Meigs County on April 27, 1895 son of Ephriam and Jesse Darst Roush. He married Clara Holter on June 1914 and she died on September 14, 1921. To this union was born two sons, Ralph Raymond Roush, May 27, 1915 and Howard Maxwell born July 29, 1917. For many years Ross was a teacher in the Meigs County School and later in the employment of the New York Central Rail Road Company. He then came to Gallia County where he was employed with the Ohio Hospital for Epileptic (Gallipolis State Institute, Gallipolis Developmental Center) and remained an employee until his retirement in 1961 after 37 years of employment. While working there he met and married Ruby Ethel Shato, daughter of Ira and Addie Rose Shato on August 18, 1923.

*Ross & Ethel Roush*

They lived on the grounds of the OHE until they could afford a home and at that time Ross brought the boys from Meigs County to live with him. They had been living with their grandparents after the death of their mother. To the union was born two daughters, Opal Imogene, August 27, 1926 and Wilma J. on March 4, 1938. Opal (Gene) graduated from Gallia Academy in 1944 and entered Christ Hospital School of Nursing under the Cadet Program. On May 22, 1948 she married Louis G. Cheek of Aurora Indiana and they have one daughter, Sandra Lu born on June 25, 1961. Sandy married Steven Morris on May

26, 1986 in Westport, Connecticut. They live in Burlington, Vermont and have two sons, Alexander Steven born on July 13, 1996 and Shaun Louis born on June 3, 1998.

Ralph married Faye Kincaide on January 14, 1938 and to this union was born two Children, DorisAnn on May 22, 1942 and Darrell Alden on June 9, 1947. DorisAnn married Charles Rearick on April 19, 1968 and they have no children.

Darrell married Janice Brofft on October 31, 1987. They had two children, Darren born on August 21, 1967. They had one son together, Christopher Adam born on July 3, 1987. Darrell passed away on August 21, 1996 and Ralph passed away on June 3, 1987.

Darren married Sarah Sneed on June 28, 1997 and has one son, Shawn Race born in October of 1986.

Howard lived in Phoenix, Arizona all his adult life. He served in the United States Army in occupied Japan. He returned to the States after serving two hitches in the Army and married Maxine Sieffiert and she died on July 3, 1998 and Howard died on his father's birthday, April 27, 2000 just a couple of months before his stepmother. Wilma married William E. Brown on April 20, 1957 and they have three children, Kimberley Anne (Tom) Duncan with two children, Chelsea and Taylor Duncan Jeffery Ross (Cindy Crews) with three children, William Ross (Willie), Joshua Brumfield and Scarlett Olivia; and William Christopher (Anette Carter) with 4 children Kelsey Nicole, Shelby Lynn, Christopher Dylan and Gregory Carter Smith.

Ross was a gentle man, an avid reader and lover of his six grandchildren.

He was a member of the Grace United Methodist Church where he was a member of St. John's Bible Class and next to the last member of this class. Ross passed away on April 26, 1983 at the age of 87 years and 364 days. Ethel retired from GDC in 1963 and spent time with the grandchildren and great grandchildren and working in the kitchen of Grace United Methodist Church cooking dinners and making noodles as long as her age permitted, past 80 years of age, when she hung up her apron. Ethel was a member of the Grace Guild Bible Class.

Ethel sold their home at 19 Neil Avenue the following year after Ross passed away and lived with daughter and son-in-law Wilma and Bill Brown until her death on July 3, 2000 at the age of 98 years.

**PELEG M. RUMFIELD** - On April 28, 1839, Peleg M. Rumfield was united in marriage to Rachel Pettit by Samuel Moody in Morgan County, Ohio. To this marriage were born twelve children as follows:

Francis M., born March 31, 1840; Ozias born June 17, 1842; Hiram, Aug. 1, 1844 in Athens County; Mary Jane born about 1846, Rocena Dec. 26, 1848; Lucinda, Aug. 29, 1850; Thomas Phillip, born Jan. 17, 1852 at Fry's Mill, Perry County. The following were born in Green Township, Hocking County, Ohio: Josiah, July 30, 1853; Lyman, Dec. 10, 1854, Jonas Henry, Sept. 20, 1857; and Minerva, July 30, 1859. Irena was born in Meigs County on August 5, 1861.

Peleg served as a private in Company H of the 53rd. Ohio Volunteer Infantry during the Civil War. He died at home in Meigs County on May 29, 1862 while on furlough. For his service, his widow, Rachel, was awarded a $12.00 monthly pension until her death on June 15, 1886. It was probably her only source of income. Peleg and Rachel are buried in the Wright Cemetery in Salem Township, Meigs County. According to their monument, at the time of their death, Peleg was aged 42 years 2 months 2 days, and Rachel was 66 years 8 months and 29 days old.

Hiram Rumfield's biography is listed on page 36 of the Salem Township section of Hardesty's 1883 Meigs County History. Lucinda married William Taylor on June 2, 1872. Josiah married Kate Mays on Sept. 2, 1880. Lyman married Sarah Burrage on Nov. 11, 1882. Jonas Henry married Sara Jane Ritz on April 24, 1884. Irena married Jacob Taylor on June 5, 1880. Minerva married Taylor Mays on Nov. 18, 1877. On Dec. 23, 1866, Rocena Rumfield married her Salem Township neighbor, Nathanial Thomas, born Mar. 16, 1831 died in Cheshire Township April 6, 1909. Nathanial was the son of James and Mary (Halfhill) Thomas. Nathanial served as a Private in Company H on the 18th Regiment of the Ohio Light Artillery. Rocena and Nathanial are also buried in the Wright Cemetery. The children of Rocena and Nathanial were Emma, born Aug.14, 1874; Charles, born Sept. 30, 1878; Rachel, born June 13, 1883; Ethel, born June 25, 1886 died August 9, 1970, and Mabel, born June 27, 1891. Emma married John Roush.

Rachel married Cornelius Rife. Charles married Millie Lemley. Mabel married Roy Thaxton.

On Aug. 25, 1906 Ethel Thomas married Hollis Rife, born in Cheshire Township on Aug. 17, 1882; died July 2, 1943. Their children were Ada, Audrey, Ermal, and Evelyn.

*Submitted by Brian*

**GEORGE WASHINGTON AND ELIZABETH ROTHGEB RUPE FAMILY** - George Washington Rupe was born June 1, 1809 in East Virginia and died October 18, 1888 in Gallia County. He came to Ohio with his parents Henry and Elizabeth Price Rupe in 1812. He married Elizabeth Rothgeb May 12, 1837. She was born December 6, 1817 and died March 2, 1898. They had eleven children. Caroline married Washington Arnold, Jonathan married Caroline Swisher, Joseph married Mary Ralph, Adaline married Frances Butcher, Jacob married Mary Richie, Washington married Fedalia Butcher, William married Sarah Halfhill, Perry married Laura Lyle, Frances married Mary Might.

Frank was born January 10, 1864 and died January 23, 1938. He married Mary Might, daughter of Jonas and Mary Schuler Might. She was born August 22, 1873 and died March 25, 1963. They had five children, Arthur, Homer, Raymond, Marion and Leo.

Arthur was born June 19, 1893 and died November 6, 1970. He served in World War I and taught school at Storys Run. Arthur married Violet Langford Grover. Violet had three sons by previous marriage to Ura Charles Grover. Son, Urn was born June 20, 1914 and died April 21, 1999. He married Raymah Rothgeb. They had three children; Edwin born March 30, 1941, John born September 6, 1944 and Gretchen born February 10, 1946. She died at birth. Emory was born November 4, 1915, died May 27, 1935. Robert was born October 11, 1922, died June 8, 1987. He married Norma Roush. They had three children. Geoffrey was born March 17, 1949, Marsha born July 9, 1951 and David was born June 17, 1954. He died at birth. They live in Albuquerque, N. M.

*Arthur Rupe's General Store, Kyger, Ohio - 1930s*

Arthur and Violet lived and owned a General Store in Kyger, Ohio. They had four children. Wanda Jean born January 25, 1930 Ina Louise born March 16, 1931. She married James Johnson November 16, 1952. They had four children. James was born October 10, 1953. He married Katherine Judd. Debra was born November 23, 1955 and died June 28, 1986. Craig born October 28, 1959, Linda born October 9, 1961. She married Greg White and they have one daughter, Erin Leigh born July 26, 1990. Linda married Michael Brown May 17, 1999. Ina and family live in Sarasota, Fla. Artie (twin) was born January 22, 1935. She married Dana Raike December 26, 1953. Dana was born June 3, 1925 and died May 29, 2000. They have one daughter, Terry Jean, born January 5, 1960. They live in Kanauga, Ohio. Arthur (twin) was born January 22, 1935. He married Carol Greene March 25, 1956. Carol was born October 7, 1936. They had three children. Stephan Arthur born December 26, 1956, died at birth. Rebecca born November 28, 1958 married Mark Streitmatter June 28, 1980. They have two daughters. Bethany born August 19, 1983, Amy born July 19, 1987. Cynthia born may 18, 1962 married Dallas Love December 20, 1981. They have three children. Katie born June 30, 1986, Adam born August 20, 1987 and Andrew born December 19, 1994.

*Submitted by Ina Louise (Rupe) Johnson, Sarasota, Florida*

**HENRY AND ELIZABETH RUPE** - Henry and Elizabeth Rupe arrived in Gallia County 1812 from Shenandoah County, Virginia. Henry, born 1770, died May 20, 1836, Gallia County, son of Martin and Margaret Rupe. Elizabeth was the daughter of David and Hannah Price. Their children were David Price, born 1807, died 1873; George Washington, born June 1, 1809, Shenandoah County, Virginia, died October 18, 1888, Gallia County, spouse Elizabeth Rothgeb, married 1837; Andrew, born 1810; George Isaac, born 1816, died 1884; Ransom Henry, born 1822, died 1890; Elizabeth Emily, born 1823. After Henry's death, Elizabeth married Horatio Nunnery in 1841; this marriage ended in divorce.

Washington and Betsy Rothgeb Rupe lived back of Kyger near where they both grew up. Washington was a farmer. They are buried in the Poplar Ridge Cemetery. Their children were Henry, born 1838, died 1840; Caroline, born 1840, died 1924; Jonathan, born 1842, died 1920; Joseph born January 18, 1845, died May 15, 1908, spouse Mary Conor (Polly) Ralph married 1869; Adaline, born 1847, died 1869; Jacob Henry, born 1849, died 1936; Baby, born and died 1851; George Washington, born 1853; William, born 1856, died 1943; David Perry, born 1860, died 1836; Franklin Sherman, born 1864, died 1938.

Joseph and Polly Rupe lived at Eno. Polly was born December 5, 1846, at Eno and died January 8, 1929, at Eno. She was the daughter of Obadiah and Sarah Smith Ralph. Joseph was a farmer. Both are buried in Robinson Cemetery at Eno. Their children were Elza Mills, born 1870, died 1940, spouse, Alwilda Roush, married 1899. Asa Oscar, born May 7, 1875, died October 8, 1956, spouse, Estella Maud (Stella) Miller, born May 30, 1881, Meigs County, Ohio, died February 5, 1960, Athens County, Ohio, daughter of Reuben and Margaret Ellen Minor, married 1902; Bernice Ora, born 1880, died 1966, spouse George Washington Searles, married 1900; Chester Clarence, born 1887, died 1925, spouse Garnet Roush married 1911.

Oscar and Stella Rupe lived near Eno. Oscar was a merchant and later became a farmer. Their daughter, Reva Reah, was born January 9, 1903, at Eno, and died February 11, 1974, at Gallipolis, spouse Levi Wilbert Reynolds, son of Henry and Jeannette Reynolds. Their grandchildren were Esther, Florence, Ralph, Lucille, Helen, Frances and Louise Reynolds. Oscar and Stella are buried in Gravel Hill Cemetery.

*Submitted by Esther James*

## ISAAC WAYNE RUPE AND BERNICE E. THOMPSON FAMILY

Wayne Rupe was born June 28, 1918, in Cheshire, OH. He attended school there and graduated in 1935. After graduation he bought a truck and hauled coal for the mines. Later he joined the CCC as a truck driver for $30 a month and hauled trees for reforestation of some of Ohio's forest. Wayne married Bernice Thompson July 2, 1937. Bernice was born April 26, 1921, in Cheshire. They had four children: Donald Benton, Betty Alice, Barbara Jo and Charlene. The family moved to Delaware, Ohio, in 1942 where he worked for Humphries Ford as a mechanic and service manager. In 1955 they moved to New Philadelphia, OH, where he worked for the Humphries new Ford dealership. In 1958 they moved to Lakeland, FL. He worked for Lakeland Ford Company for a couple of years before acquiring a teaching position at Polk County Vocational and Technical College. He taught auto mechanics for a couple of years before being promoted to Assistant Administrator of the college. He held this position until his retirement in 1983.

Wayne was the great, great, great grandson of Martin Rupe II and Christina Zircle who came to Gallia County in 1801 from the Shenandoah Valley in Virginia. Martin and his descendants farmed the fertile soils of Gallia and Meigs counties for over the next 100 years. Wayne's parents were Isaac Newton Rupe and Alice Mae Rupe, Alice being the daughter of Juel Enid Rupe. Wayne's brothers and sister were Kathyrn who married Bruce Yeauger; Alva who married Viota Abbot; and Raymond who married Betty Ralph. Isaac Newton worked for the New York Central Railroad for 30 years. He was the eighth child of 13 born to James Newton Rupe and Alice Jane Barret. James was the sixth child of 12 born to Matthasis Cory Rupe and Emily Searles. During the Civil War, Matthasis was a First Sgt. With Co. I, Fourth Reg. of the WVA Volunteers Infantry.

*Isaac Wayne Rupe And Bernice E. Thompson On The Steps Of Old Kyger Store.*

He served in many campaigns form the Kanawha Valley WVA to Vicksburg, MS. Matthasis was the oldest of six children born to Martin Rupe III and Hannah Halfhill. Bernice's parents were Charles Benton Thompson and Blanche Hazel Rupe. Charles was born June 16, 1894, in Cheshire. He was a baker and operated a small business form his home in Cheshire. About 1938 they moved to Delaware, OH, where he worked for Gorgeous Bakery as a baker and bread truck driver. Charles and Hazel's other children were Cassius who married Virginia Kinard; Myrta Belle married Charles McCarty; Vivian married Robert Jollif; Gloria married Harvey Dunlop and Lester married Virginia Stratton. Charles' parents were William E. Thompson and Amy Belle Halley. They lived exclusively in Cheshire and William worked for the Postal Service. He was the first rural mail carrier for Cheshire from 1903 to 1923. He and Amy had six children: Charles, William, Elsie, Nell, Lenora and Goldie. William's parents were Thomas Benton Thompson and Milissa King. Thomas' parents were Jesse T. Thompson and Matilda Laurence. Jesse was born in PA and moved to Brown County, Ohio, from PA, circa 1820 then to Gallia County, circa 1850. Blanche Hazel Rupe was born April 21, 1898, in Addison, Ohio to Cassius A. Rupe and Myrta Ellen Simms. Hazel had two brothers, Roy and Ray Rupe, who served overseas during WWI. Roy married Huldah Millron and their daughter, Wileen, married Howell Edwards. Cassius worked for the Hocking Valley Railroad and after retirement spent many a day fishing the mighty Ohio River and working his garden along its bank in Addison. Cassius' parents were Ransom Henry Rupe and Barbara Halfhill. Ransom was a stone mason by trade. Other children were Mary Jane married Martin Rutherford; Faithful married Peter Darst and Juel Enid married Edyth Adaline Evans. Ransom's parents were Henry Rupe and Elizabeth Price. Henry was a brother to the above-mentioned Martin Rupe II and followed his brother to Ohio from the Shenandoah Valley, Virginia, in 1812.

*Submitted by Barbara J. Rupe Smith*

## CHARLES RUSSELL

The Russell family is of Norman origin. In early England, the Red Fox was known as the russell, therefore, the English name, Russell, carried the meaning of "The Red Fox". The motto of the family is "Che Sara Sara" (What will be, will be.)

Through the centuries, the family acquired large land holdings in England. The head of the family in 1538 was Baron Russell, who later held the title of Duke of Bedford. The first Russell's in the New World settled on the present site of Newport News, Virginia, in 1621. After 1700 more Russells came and settled in New England and Virginia.

Charles Russell was born in what is now Huntington, New Jersey, in 1759. He was the youngest of five children. His siblings were Mary, William, Thomas, and Moses. In 1774 the family moved to Berkeley County, Virginia. During the Revolutionary War, he adhered to the Patroit cause and was present at the Battle of Yorktown, Virginia.

He married Mary Elizabeth Noland on May 4, 1791, in Berkeley County, Virginia. They were the parents of the following children: Sarah, James C., Thomas, Moses, Mahlon, John, Samuel B., William and Charles. Charles, a carpenter, and his brother, Moses, who married Mary Noland's sister, Esther, moved their families to Gallia County in the early 1800s. Moses settled in Salem Township and Charles settled in Springfield Township. Charles built the first house in Pine Grove, now called Porter, Ohio, for Barlow Morehouse. In 1830 when Joseph Fletcher surveyed the village of Pine Grove, Charles Russell, as proprietor, received sixteen cents for each lot sold. Charles died March 11, 1839, and is buried in Fairview Cemetery.

Charles' son, Samuel B. Russell, who was a blacksmith and stone mason, married Francis Lawless in Gallia County on March 20, 1826. They were the parents of the following children: Harvey, Charles, Sylvester, Betty, Mary, Nancy, Ann, Sara, Lucinda, and Felista. Sylvester Russell was born July 18, 1835, and married Angeline Bowman, daughter of David and Susan (Walters) Bowman, on August 9, 1860. In 1864 Sylvester came to Gallipolis and enlisted with the 173rd Regiment of the Ohio Volunteer Infantry. He served with Company I of that regiment until the end of the Civil War. Sylvester and Angeline were the parents of ten children: Burt, Edward, Charles, Warren, Harvey, Mattie, Mary, Maggie, Eva and Fanny. Like his father, Sylvester was a blacksmith and stone mason. He died December 15, 1912, and is buried at Clark's Chapel.

Burt Russell, a blacksmith, married Mary Blanche Moore, daughter of Caleb and Barbara (Fee) Moore on August 12, 1900. They were the parents of the following children: Anna, who married John Gilfilen; Carl, who married Kathryn Watson; Mary, who wed Ray Casto, and Nellie, who died in infancy.

Through the generations, the family has been known by their good deeds and expert craftsmanship. The main attribute of the Russell family is that they sought to live by the Golden Rule. *Submitted by William E. Plants*

**DAVID AND ABBEY BETH HUBER RUSSELL FAMILY** - The only time David has left Gallia County was after graduating from North Gallia High School, when he joined the Army and was stationed in Hawaii. During those years in the army he went to Japan, Malaysia, Singapore, Korea, and also completed many special training courses. As his service years were done he returned to Gallia County and has been happy to be settled here.

*David & Abbey Russell*

He was born on March 11, 1971 to Dale Thomas and Susan Elaine (Willis) Russell. David has a younger brother Jeremy Adam who also lives in Gallia County along with his parents. Most of his family has stayed in Gallia County. His grandfathers were both very successful businessmen. Dale Edward Russell owned and operated Dale's grocery store on Third Avenue. Dale was also responsible for the building of the Vietnam Memorial in the Park when his son, Tom was in the service. His wife Margaret Jones Russell was a nurse. David's other grandfather Raymond Leon Willis started Willis Tire Company, which is still in operation today, where his mother and brother work.

Tom Russell started Tom's auto Clinic on Eastern Avenue on September 1, 1975 and years later bought General Tire Sales in Middleport, Ohio David works at the store on Eastern Avenue.

On November 19, 1999 David married Abbey Beth Huber, who is the daughter of Charles and Peggy Huber. David and Abbey have one daughter Alexis Brooke.

Abbey has, also lived in Gallia County her entire life, except when she attended the University of Toledo, after graduating from Gallia Academy High School. She graduated from Toledo in 2000 with a Bachelors of Education in Public Affairs and Community Service.

Her father had Charlie's and Company Snack Shop on Court Street for many years. Her mother is a schoolteacher. Abbey is the younger of two children. Her sister Amy lives in Washington D.C.

David and Abbey plan on staying in Gallia County to raise their family.
*Submitted by Abbey Huber Russell*

**JOHN SAMUAL SANDERS** - John Sam was born in 1851 at Gallia County, Ohio. He was the son of Samuel H. and Rebecca Cook Sanders.

Samual H. Sanders was born June 27, 1816 at Fluvanna County Virginia to William and Sarah Strong Sanders. William served in the war of 1812. Some of his sons served in the Civil War, or the War of the Rebellion, as it was first named. The family came to Guyan Township, Gallia County, Ohio in 1835.

John Sanders Jr, the great grandfather of John Sam, was born in 1764 at Janets Creek, Goochland County Virginia. He was a soldier in the Revolutionary War. His pension number from the war was S 7454.

*Lewis And Mary Lou Saunders*

John Sam was a farmer, mail carrier and at one time had a store. He was twice married.

His first wife was Laura McComas. They were married in 1872 and had twelve children. He married Mary Sheets in 1899.

Joseph Milton (Joe) Sanders was born in 1879 to John Sam and Laura Sanders. He married Celestia Brumfield in 1908. Joe was a teacher. He taught in several one room schools in Gallia County. He is listed in "Gallia County One Room Schools: The Cradle Years" published in 1993 by the Gallia County Historical Society.

Joe told his grandson, Lewis Saunders, that he preferred the name "Saunders" and changed his name from Sanders to Saunders. He died in 1947 and is buried at the Mercerville Cemetery.

Otto Bryon Saunders was born to Joe and Celestia Saunders in 1912 at Gallia County, Ohio. Otto married Frances Beaver. Otto and Frances lived on State Route 218 near Mercerville in the home built by his dad, Joe Saunders. Frances died in 1974. Otto died in 1987. They are buried in the Mercerville Cemetery.

Lewis Keith Saunders was born to Otto and Frances Saunders, February 25, 1934. Lewis married Mary Lou Carter, August 1, 1954 at the Mercerville Baptist Church by the Rev. Earl Cremeens. Lewis and Mary Lou are graduates of Mercerville High School. Lewis served from 1956 to 1958 in the United States Army. They live in Gahanna, Ohio and spend a lot of time in Gallia County at their 1800's restored log cabin.

Lee Ann Saunders was born to Lewis and Mary Lou (Carter) Saunders, July 6, 1962 at Wooster, Ohio. She married Jerry Lee Strait, Jr., May 9, 1987. They have a daughter Kallie Marie Strait, born January 24, 1994 and a son, Cohn Saunders Strait, born November 24, 1999. They reside in Gahanna, Ohio. Lee Ann "Saunders" Strait and her family are honored to be members of "First Families of Gallia County".
*Submitted by Lewis K. Saunders*

**JAMES SANDS** - James Sands was born in 1947 in Ironton, Ohio. He is a graduate of Ironton High School where he lettered three years in both baseball and football, being named co-captain of the football team in 1964. He graduated from Ohio State with a B.A. degree in history and from the Methodist Theological School in Ohio with a Masters of Divinity degree. For the past 32 years he has been a pastor of the West Ohio Conference of the United Methodist Church. He has been the senior pastor of the Community United Methodist Church in Circleville, Ohio, for the past four years.

Patty Brackenridge Sands was born in 1949 in Marietta, Ohio. She is a graduate of Warren Local High School and has attended Washington Technical College. She is planning to complete her degree in the near future. She is currently a children's librarian with the Pickaway County Public Library but has spent most of her working years as an accounting clerk for Doctors Curtis and Bays, Youth for Christ and the Midwest Seafood Company. Patty's parents are Andrew and Caroline Ullman Brackenridge of Vincent, Ohio. The Brackenridges came to the Marietta area in the early 1800's from Argyleshire, Scotland at the behest of Nahum Ward. The Brackenridges were known for their sheep and the sheep barn at the Washington County fair is named after their family. The Ullmans came to America in 1830 from Alsace-Lorraine, settling in Noble, Monroe and Washington counties.

*Jim And Patty Sands*

James Sands' parents are Donald and Mary Lou Norris Sands of South Point, Ohio. The Sands family came to New York from England. A part of the clan migrated to Louisville, Kentucky, in the 19th century before settling in Ironton in the 1880'S. Some of them married into Gallia County families later. The Norris clan left Gloucester, England in 1806 for Nova Scotia. They also lived in Ontario and Harrison County, Ohio, before becoming some of the earliest settlers in Union County, Ohio.

James and Patty were married in 1977. Born to James and Patty were three daughters: Jennifer, born in 1978; Joy, born in 1980; and Shellie, born in 1982. Jennifer is married to Jason Prall and they have two children, Anthony and Alyssa. They live near Hamilton, Ohio, where Jennifer is a teacher and Jason is a machinist. Joy was killed in an auto accident in 1995 and is greatly missed by her many friends and family. Shellie is a student at the Virginia Marti School of Fashion and Art in Cleveland. All three girls were involved in band and athletics in school. They also were a part of several church mission trips and church ski trips.

For the past 27 years James has written a weekly column on Gallia history for the Sunday Times-Sentinel. He has also lectured on Ohio sports history in several places. His talk on the Waterloo Wonders has been given numerous times.

*Submitted by James Sands*

**RUSSELL L. SAUNDERS FAMILY** - Russell Lee Saunders was born on May 2, 1944 to Saul and Bessie Emogene (Arbaugh) Saunders. While attending Southwestern High School, Russell met his future wife, Paticia Cain. Pat was born April 8, 1944 to Oscar and Edith (Scherer) Cain. Russell and Pat were married on June 6,1964 in Gallipolis, Ohio. They then moved to Columbus, Ohio to set up housekeeping.

*The Russell L. Saunders Family, 2001 Row 1: Christi, Clayton, Camryn, And Carsyn Row 2: Russell Lee And Pat Row 3: Debbie, Russell Allen, Rob, Ronald, And Angie*

In the early I 970s, they relocated back to Gallia County to live at the Saunders homestead situated on 73 1/2 acres and located on scenic route 790.

Three children were raised in their home: Russell Allen, born October 13,1965; Ronald Andrew, born December 25, 1966, and Robert Anderson, born November 4, 1978. Russell Lee worked as a barber for 15 years (both in Columbus and Lawrence County) before going to work for AKZO Chemical, where he is still employed as a maintenance mechanic. In 1997, Pat began employment as a seamstress with Graham's Upholstery.

Russell and Pat's eldest son, Russell Allen, graduated from Rio Grande Community College in 1986 with an Associate's degree in manufacturing technology. He began employment with the Point Pleasant Polyester Plant in 1987 where he continues to be employed as a chemical operator.

Russell has a daughter from a previous marriage, Christian Rushelle (Christi), born September 16,1991. Christi enjoys playing many sports. On January 23, 2000, Russell Allen married Deborah Lynn Mingus. Debbie was born February 24,1973 to Joseph Mingus and Suzan (Farmer) Mingus Chapman. Debbie obtained a bachelor of science degree in accounting from the University of Rio Grande in 1995. In 2001, she obtained a Masters Degree in Library and Information Science from Kent State University. She is employed as the Clerk-Treasurer of the Gallia County District Library.

Russell and Pat's second son, Ronald Andrew, obtained a bachelor of science degree in accounting in 1990 from the University of Rio Grande. On July 28,1990 he married Angela HopeMcpherson. Angie was born to Roger H. McPherson and E. Gamett (Broyles) McPherson Hurlow on September 21, 1967. Angie attended Rio Grande Community College. In 1990, Ronald and Angie moved to Columbus, Ohio, where Ronald was employed by HUD as a Senior Auditor. Angie was employed by Cigna Health Care as an Administrative Assistant.. On July 12,1999, they were blessed with triplets: Carsyn Malyn, Camryn Paige, and Clayton Andrew.

In 2001, Ronald began employment with Alcohol, Tobacco, and Firearms as a Forensic Auditor.

The youngest of Russell and Pat's children is Robert Anderson. Rob was born November 4, 1978. He graduated from Symmes Valley High School in 1997. After high school, he enlisted in the Army Reserves and attended the University of Rio Grande. Rob is now employed at the Big Lots Warehouse in Columbus, Ohio.

The Saunders Family believes in the importance of family and in living the Christian life. We want to live by the words found in Joshua 24:15, 'As for me and my house, we will serve the Lord'.

*Written by: Debbie Saunders and Pat Saunders*

**STANLEY SAUNDERS FAMILY** - Stanley Albert Saunders (1906-1981) was born in Gallia County March 12, 1906, the son of Henry Anderson Sanders/Saunders (1882-1951) and Nancy Jane Myers (1878-1971). Brothers and sisters of Stanley were Hollis Woodrow, Roy Thomas, Hazel Fay, Ina Ruth, Nellie, Alfred Earl, Clara Fern, Saul Myers and Vance Judson. Stanley married Willa Alma Rott/Rutt, the daughter of Herman Rott/Rutt and Elva Effie Drummond, March 9, 1931. Stanley worked for his uncle Herbert Saunders, owner of Saunders Monuments. He later bought his own monument shop in February 1943. Saunders Monument Company was located on Third Avenue in Gallipolis. Willa taught school and later worked as a clerk in the Gallia County Court House. They had one son, Arlen Emerson Saunders born September 12, 1931. Arlen married Anna Mae Betz, daughter of Basil W. Betz and Betty Marie McCallster, October 1. 1949. Both Arlen and Ann graduated from Gallia Academy and had a Masters Degrees from Morehead State University. Arlen taught industrial Arts at Ripley Union Lewis High School in Ripley, Ohio, Montclair College in New Jersey and Ohio University in Athens, Ohio. Ann taught 2nd grade in Higginsport, Ohio, New Jersey, and Athens, Ohio. Arlen and Anna had four children, Pamela Sue m. John Rudy Rodgers, Stanley William, Stephen Arlen m. Carlita Wickline, and Andrew Jay m. Susan Culp.

Grandparents of Stanley were John Alfred Sanders (1862-1927) and Samilda Neal (1863-1935), daughter of Henry Neal and Mary Mossbarger. They were married June 9, 1881 in Gallia County. Children of John Alfred and Samilda were Henry Anderson, Arthur Sylvester, Emmett Neal, Loren McGee, Robert L., Herbert Lonzo, and Chole.

Great Grandparents were John Anderson Sanders (1834-1889) and Elizabeth Frances Martt (1841-1911). John and Elizabeth were married December 17, 1859 in Gallia County. John ran a stagecoach near Lecta, Ohio. Children of John and Elizabeth were John Alfred, Mary Ann, William Riley m. Evelyn Lewis, Luella Casander m. McClellan Estell Roach, Emma Frances m. John Brumfield, Electa Lyndonia m Marchel Cron, Ida May m. Lewis Gothard, Victoria Romain m. John Kreger, Sarah Ester m. Fonnie Robinson, Eura Otabeinb m. Ruby Meyers, Bertha Lizabeth, Augusta Manchester m. Deskin Stewart, Savannah Almeda m. James Roger and Ada.

*L-R: Stanley Albert Saunders, Nellie, Alfred Earl, Henry Anderson Saunders; back: Ina Ruth, Nancy Jane Meyers*

Stanley's great great grandparents were Jesse Sanders (1804-1865), and Nancy Anna Strong (1800-1856), daughter of John Strong. Jesse married Nancy Anna Strong February 1, 1825 in Fluvanna Co., Virginia. Jesse's father John Sanders/Saunders b. November 13, 1764 married Elizabeth Ann Cawthorn. John was in the Revolutionary War as was John Strong, Nancy Anna Strong's father. They were both at the surrender of Lord Cornwallis. John's pension papers are S-7454 at the National Archives. He was sixteen years old when he enlisted. John's parents were John Saunders and Elizabeth Hancock who were married October 23, 1758 in Virginia. Jesse and his two brothers Jacob and William came over the Blue Ridge Mountains from Virginia to settle on the Lawrence and Gallia County line. All three brothers married daughters of John Strong. William married Sara Strong and Jacob married Elizabeth Strong.

Jesse and Nancy had the following children, John Anderson, George D., Sophia m. Francis Knotter, Susan Margaret m. Edward Sheets, Louisa m. James Elliott, Frances C. m. John H. Sheets #2, Anna, Sarah Strong m. Brice Sheets #1, and Mary Elizabeth m. Ancil Elliott.

**SCOTT FAMILY** - These are the ten generations of my Scott line who have lived in or are still living in Cheshire Township, Gallia County, Ohio.

1. Sabret Scott (c1760/70-1838) was the first Scott to settle in Cheshire Township. He came to Gallia County after the 1800 Ohio census but before the end of 1805. He was listed as a member of the first church society on December 15, 1805, along with a Nancy Scott (presumably his wife). This church society later became the Old Kyger Freewill Baptist Church which Scott descendants still attend today. He farmed land on what used to be Stingy Creek Road where he raised two sons and eight daughters.

*Elisha And Elizabeth (Fraser) Scott*

2. Charles Scott (c1786-1854) was born in Virginia. He married Mary Darst (1782-1831), daughter of Abraham and Mary Darst, in 1807. They had four sons and four daughters. Charles served in the War of 1812. His second marriage was to Barbara Darst (1794-1875) in 1832. They had one son.

3. Elisha Scott (1818-1892) married Elizabeth Fraser (1822-1895) in 1841. She was born in Inverness, Scotland, to Alexander and Catharine (Ross) Fraser. Elizabeth was almost one year old when she arrived in New York on May 10, 1823, with her parents on the ship "Friends" from the port of Greenock, Scotland. They had six daughters and five sons.

4. Benjamin Franklin Scott (1851-1912) married Sarah Margaret Swisher (1851-1873), daughter of William and Irena (Wheaton) Swisher in 1872. They had one son who was raised by his grandparents, Elisha and Elizabeth Scott, after the death of his mother. His second marriage was to Sarah Druzilla Athey in 1876.

5. Chauncey Franklin Scott (1873-1926) married Augusta Gordon (1877-1919) daughter of Alexander and Sarah (Ralph) Gordon in 1894. They had one son and one daughter.

6. John Benjamin Scott (1894-1936) married Florence Lydia Rupe (1905-1991) daughter of James and Lydia (Searls) Rupe in 1921. He served in France during World War I and after his return resided in Columbus, Ohio, where he was considered one of the best bricklayers in Columbus. They had two daughters. Garnett Daisy Scott (1896-1988) married Benjamin Rupe (1894-1980) in 1916. They had one son.

7. Edith Lucille Scott (1922) married George Leo Gardner (1921-1997) son of George and Florence (Ralph) Gardner in 1945. He served 4 1/2 years in the Army during World War II. They had one daughter. Betty Geneva Scott (1926) married Carroll Snider (1921-1982) in 1947. They had two sons and one daughter.

8. Linda Lou Gardner (1946) married Larry Michael Cox (1948) son of Franklin and Mary (Martin) Cox in 1972. They had one daughter and one son.

9. Amanda Diane Cox (1973) married Daniel Joseph Polcyn II (1973) son of Daniel and Debra (Neal) Polcyn in 1994. They had two daughters. Her second marriage was to Bradley Allen Perry (1957) son of Donald and Lona Perry in 2002. Stephen Michael Cox (1976) is unmarried.

10. Stephanie Noelle Polcyn (1997) and Madeleine Scott Polcyn (2000).

*Submitted by Edith Scott Gardner*

**JEFFERSON SCOTT** - In 1844, Jefferson Scott was a slave of John Hockaday, Halifaz County, North Carolina. His master, being a kind person, didn't want to see his slaves sold or mistreated in any way by his relatives after his death. He decided to set them free.

In May 1844, He gave Jefferson Scott, Randall Carter, and William Mumford a certificate of freedom, which they were to carry on their person at all times. This prevented them from being caught and returned to slavery.

*Christian and Stephanie Scott*

Hockaday had three daughters by a slave woman, name unknown, which he gave to these three men as their wives. Caroline Hockaday was given to Jefferson Scott. When the Scotts started north for Ohio they already had six children.

Jefferson Scott's father was a full-blooded Cherokee Indian and his mother a mulatto. He was born in 1794. He and Caroline were parents of Cornelia, John, Mary, Delilah, Frances, James Edward, Albert, and six other children who were born in Ohio.

Jefferson and Caroline Scott; their children, the Mumfords, and the Carters traveled for about five months with all their earthly goods and treasures in a one-horse cart. They traveled through dangers along the New River, Kanawha River, through Charleston until they reached Point Pleasant. There they viewed the "promised land" across the Ohio River. They settled in what is known today as Adamsville, Ohio.

Later, great, great, grandfather and his wife moved to Fostoria. There, Jefferson died at the remarkable age of 113 years. Jeff and Caroline had two sons named James, James Edward and James Monroe. James Edward is my great grandfather. He was born in Halifax County, North Carolina in 1843. During the Civil War he was a member of the first colored Regiment recruited in Ohio.

James Edward married Mary Bunch, daughter of Andrew and Frances Bunch. They were the proud parents of nine children, one of which was my grandfather, Eugene Lester Scott. He was born April 17, 1870. He was a miner. He was a foreman of a mine for thirty years and a teacher. He received his education at the academy at Centerville.

Grandfather Eugene married Bessie May Smith on March 12, 1900, in Gallia County. They were the parents of four children, one of which was Harry Dolphis Scott, born January 15, 1909. Harry attended Bidwell Porter Schools and Nelsonville Schools. Harry married Barbara Mae Smith on January 6, 1965 in Chillicothe. Unto this union was born Harreld Christian Scott on December 5, 1972.

Christian attended Washington Elementary as a child and graduated from Gallia Academy High School in June of 1991. After high school, he attended the University of Rio Grande from 1991 until 1996. He majored in Education with concentrations in music and history. The university is located near the sites of Jefferson Scott's first settlement after arriving in Ohio from North Carolina. Centerville, the place where Eugene received his schooling, is less than 3 miles from Rio Grande. In 1998, seeking to further his education, Christian went back to Rio Grande to obtain a masters degree in education.

On July 21, 2001, he married a beautiful young lady named Stephanie Nichole Long. She is also a teacher. To this date they have no children. Yet are hoping that one-day they will continue the rich history one generation further.

As Christian looks back at his ancestors, he thanks God for the path they paved for him. He also thanks God for Christian parents, who trained him to love God, love your family, and to love history. "A nation or group of people which forgets its history is destined to repeat it."

*Submitted by: Christian Scott*

**SCOTT-TAWNEY** - My husband and I are natives of Gallia County, as were our parents and grandparents. I am the daughter of L. Max and Mabel (McBride) Tawney. My mother's parents were Willis Carlton and Lottie Jane (White) McBride. Max's parents were Floyd Milton and Luella Sinnett Tawney. Lewis's parents were Bert Albert and Cora (Yeauger) Scott. Alan's father was Lewis Scott. Alan's mother was Geneva Roush.

*Row 1, Tandy Flint, Julie Smith
Row 2: Back Row, Alan Scott, Dianne Scott, James Scott and Becky Scott.*

Geneva's parents were Lester Dale and Mazie Letty Darst Roush. The Roush family is a descendant of Jacob Roush, who came to Cheshire in 1797 from the Shenandoah Valley. Both the Scotts and Roushes trace their line through Jacob's son Adam.

Alan was born September 28, 1940 in Cheshire and spent his childhood on Stingy Creek close to farms of both his grandparents. His cousin, Paul Bradbury, and brother, Allison can talk for hours about the things they got into. Alan's parents moved to Gallipolis to enroll him in kindergarten. He lived at 1129 Second Ave. with his three brother: Allison, Richard, and Randy.

I was born March 15, 1943 and spent my childhood at 154 First Ave. in a lovely home overlooking the Ohio River. My fondest memories were spent at the B. Lewis Jones farm in Thurman. His wife, Agnes, was my mother's oldest sister. I would take the Greyhound bus from the Libby Hotel to get there. I spent hours combing their creek bed for petrified wood. My flower beds are lined with them.

Alan and I were married on December 2, 1962 at the Grace United Methodist Church. This is the same church in which my parents were married and where our children were confirmed and baptized. Both our daughters were married there.

In October 1963, we bought a lovely home overlooking the Ohio River on McCarleyville Rd. just below Gallipolis. It was here we raised three children: Tandy Elizabeth, born November 1, 1963, Julie Ann, born May 21, 1966, and James Alan Carlton McBride, born February 17, 1970.

Alan recently retired after working 43 yrs. on the railroad. He now devotes his time to gardening and woodworking. I have a greenhouse and plant business. We both enjoy the outdoors and crafts.

We are grateful to have so many relatives in the area. Our richest blessing is to have our four grandchildren; Andrea and Derek Flint, children of Steve and Tandy and Shannon and Chad Smith, children of Julie and Greg living in the area. We hope they will cherish the memories of their childhood in Gallia County too.

**SCOTT - WILLOCK FAMILY** - The earliest Scott family of Gallia County appears to have arrived with Sabret Scott shortly before 1805 and settled on Stingy Run, 3 miles NW of Cheshire. Sabret was probably born about 1760. In 1782, Sebret (sic) Scott was listed as head of household, Fairfax County, VA. In 1805, Sabert (sic) Scott was a member of the FW Baptist Church of Cheshire. His first wife, Nancy, died before 1820, and then married Margaret Fitzpatrick in 1824. His children were Charles born about 1786, Isabell born about 1787, Margaret "Peggy", Nancy, Elizabeth born 1792, Sarah "Sally" born 1794, Mary "Polly" and Thomas born 1799.

Elder son, Charles Scott, was in the War of 1812 and was elected trustee of Cheshire Township September 4, 1814. His first wife was Mary Darst; and in 1832, he remarried Barbara Darst. By Mary, he had John (?) born 1808, Elizabeth born 1810, Cynthia born 1812, Benjamin born 1815, Sophia "Sarah" born 1817, Elisha born September 3, 1818, Lydia born 1821, Charles C. born 1823; and by his second wife he had Vinton born 1834. He last appears in the 1850 census, a 64-year-old farmer worth $2,500.

Younger son, Thomas Scott, married Anna (1801-1899) and had Lucretia born 1819, Hester, Clarissa "Clara", Sarah "Sally" born 1823, and Rosella born 1843. He died in 1862. Up until this time, burials were made in the family graveyard on Stingy Run. Around 1960, Ohio Power Company removed the entire graveyard to a site behind the new part of Gravel Hill Cemetery and turned Stingy Run into a lake.

Elisha Scott was born 1819, presumably in the "Kygerville" vicinity of the Homestead, and married Elizabeth Fraser on September 16, 1841. She had immigrated with her parents, Alexander (1778-1857) and Catharine Ross (1788-1870) at the age of one, from Inverness, Scotland, and never lost her Scottish brogue. Elisha purchased a 70-acre tract on Stingy Run March 17, 1847, and was a relatively prosperous farmer, owning the first steam thrasher in the area, and had a large family including: Alexander born 1842, Charles born 1845, Kathryn born 1848, Benjamin Franklin born 1850, Mary E. born 1852, Barbara E. born 1856, Elisha V. born 1857, Anna L. born 1859, Sarah A. born 1862, and Nida W. born 1864. Elisha Scott died October 14, 1892, and was buried in the Gravel Hill Cemetery, west of Cheshire.

Benjamin Franklin Scott, unlike his father, had a family of mostly daughters, "so he worked us like boys", but still had a hardscrabble existence, never owning property, but moving repeatedly around Gallia, Meigs, and Mason Counties as a tenant-farmer. He married Sarah Druzella Athey September 20, 1876, and had a large family: Rosella May born April 2, 1878, Iva Edna born February 22, 1880, Ella Elizabeth born September 17, 1882, Atwood Haning "Bud" born January 15, 1885, Mary Drucilla born January 17, 1886, Cora Alma born June 15, 1890, and Eigan Merle born August 15, 1897. Ben Scott died in Pomeroy January 5, 1912.

Rose Scott, his eldest daughter, worked as a seamstress in Pomeroy's Red Anchor Department Store, where she met and later married Eber Clarence Willock, July 1, 1905, and lived near his parents home on Beech Street, Middleport. A year later, son Eber Scott was born July 6, 1906, and Frances Kathryn July 17, 1911. E.C. Willock worked for NYC railroad at Hobson and provided employment for many Scott in-laws. E. Scott Willock met Clara Belle Murray, teacher at Pomeroy High School, and married July 1, 1942, and had two sons, Murray Scott born September 21, 1943, and Stanley Dexter born January 18, 1946.

*Submitted by Murray S. Willock*

**JAMES SCURLOCK** - Little is known by this researcher about Lt. James Scurlock and his wife, Lydia Poore, prior to their arrival in Ohio except that they came to Bloomfield Township (now Jackson County) from North Carolina where at least some of their children were born. The name of Lydia's brother, Hugh Poore, appears on the Listers and Appraisers roster for "Raccoon" Township in 1807. The earliest appearance of the Scurlock surname in Gallia County seems to be the marriage record of their daughter, Martha, on 6 December 1810. After Jackson County claimed Milton, Bloomfield and Madison Townships on 1 March 1816, the Scurlock and Poore surnames all but disappear from the Gallia records for several decades.

James and Lydia had eight known children: William Scurlock, born 1781-90, married Mrs. Sally (Humphreys) Long 21 April 1816 in Gallia County. She was a daughter of Morris Humphreys, and married (first) Gabriel Long.

Hugh Scurlock, born about 1787 in NC, married Jane Friend on 20 April 1820 in Gallia County.

Joshua Scurlock, born about 1789 in NC, married Martha Long of VA by 1824. Martha "Patsy" Scurlock, born say 1792, married Robert Erwin 6 December 1810 in Gallia County-Patsy's uncle, Hugh "Poor", performed the ceremony.

John Scurlock, born 27 April 1794 in Stokes County, NC, served in the War of 1812 (Pvt., OH Militia, Capt. Woods Co.). John's marriage fails to appear in the county records, however George and Joseph Scurlock attest to the marriage of their brother, John, and Armenia White, performed by Patrick Knapper, J.P., on 26 February 1824 in Gallia County. Armenia, born 30 August 1805 in Pennsylvania, was the eldest daughter of Gallia County First Family Alfred and Mary (Perry) White. The couple resided at Keystone Furnace in Bloomfield Township, and had seven known children (all apparently born there). Mary Ann Scurlock, born 27 Feb 1825/26, married James Henry "Nicholas" Bishop 5 September 1851. James, born 10 August 1826, married Nancy Davis 24 July 1848. Alfred, born about 1830, married Mary Graham. Almond Lansford (probably "Almon", after his mother's brother), born about 1833/34, married Susannah Oyler. After Almond's death, Susannah married John Dickerson on 3 Mar 1873 in Gallia County. Martha Scurlock, born about 1836, married first David Crawford and second Gilbert M. Huntley. Amanda, born 1839, married Stephen Aldridge 27 October 1859. Isaac, born about 1843, married Harriet Aldridge 21 September 1865. John Scurlock died 1 August 1864 and was buried at Perkins Cemetery in Bloomfield Township. Armenia (White) Scurlock died 28 May 1895 and was buried beside her husband.

Thomas Scurlock, twin brother of John, is believed to have died young.

Thomas James Scurlock, born about 1796 in NC, married Margaret Jenkins.

Joseph Scurlock was born about 1799 and married Eleanor Stephenson. He was of Jackson County on 5 April 1878, aged 79.

George Scurlock, born about 1801, married Elizabeth Hanna and was living in Rocky Hill. Jackson County, on 3 April 1878, aged 77.

Following the death of her husband, Lydia (Poore) Scurlock married George Campbell in this county on 2 February 1812. James Hanna performed the ceremony.

*Submitted by: Linda Gaylord-kuhn*

**GEORGE W. SHACK** - The saga of George W. Shack and his kin, the McGhees began locally in Columbiana County, Ohio. In 1783 James McGhee, son of George McGhee from County Westneathe, Ireland, was born in Johnstown, Pennsylvania. By 1806 he was married to Margaret Hazlett, originally from Belfast, Ireland. By 1820 James and Margaret had settled in New Lisbon, Columbiana, Ohio, where he plied his trade as a miller. The McGhees were a very musical, avant-garde kind of people who likely offended the conservative groups of Columbiana County. When the opportunity to settle in Gallia County was realized, they relocated to Vinton. James' daughter, Mary Ann, married John D. Shack, son of Jacob Shack, in New Lisbon in 1829. They produced a family of four children—Margaret, George W., Romaine, and Susanna.

George W. married Hannah Shively, daughter of Jacob Shively and Matilda Gibson in 1856. Their children were Virginia, George Edward, and John Dieter. Virginia married John Adams Matthews. George Edward married Eliza Shurtz. John D. married Sarah Alda Eagle (great grandparents of the author). In 1849 George's sister, Margaret, married Matthew Grate and moved west. By 1870, after Matthew's death, Margaret and her children, Ellen, James, Margaret, and William, moved back to Vinton and lived with her mother, Mary Ann. Margaret's other children, Romaine and Kittie, stayed with their uncle, George, who was a very kind and generous person. Kittie later married James Frank Wallace, son of John Wallace and Jane McGhee, in 1892, and they had Leah, Walter, Theodore, and Cecile.

*The Shack-McGhee-Hamilton Woolen Mill*

In 1852 James purchased a mill from John Adney and was in partnership with his grandsons, George W. Shack and Asher Hamilton, until his death in 1858. The mill was very profitable from onset until George became ill and was unable to meet the challenges of progress. The mill was strictly water powered and the cost to convert the mill to steam power would have been prohibitive. By the time George W. died in 1908, the mill was no longer profitable.

Cecile married Von Thompson and they had Bess, Joe, Lonnie, Leah, and Tommy. Cecile was a teacher. Von was postmaster in Alice and also owned and operated an early "shopping mall" or general store (source: Lonnie Thompson).

Virginia Shack Matthews' children were Lavinia, Max, George, Madge, Lucille, Floyd, and Helen. George Edward Shack's children were Helen, George, Sylvia, Jennie, and Gerald. John D. Shack's children were Nellie, who died of typhoid fever at age 12, and Roselle who followed the McGhee musical legacy by becoming a music teacher. She was a teacher until the day she died. Roselle married one-time school teacher and prosperous potato farmer, William Earl Burdue, and they had three gifted daughters—Marjorie, Betty, and Dorothy Ann. Marjorie married Kenneth Burris and they had three children—Barrie, Paul, and Valerie. Betty married Edward C. Hodge, Jr., and had two daughters—Debbie and Becky and son, Jonathan, from her first marriage. Dorothy Ann married Edward Alloway and had three children—Mike, Tom, and Cheryl. Becky Hodge married Robert Frasure and had three children—Jennifer, Jeff, and Jaime. Jennifer Frasure married Kris Burgett. She is continuing the McGhee passion for music through her music teaching career. My mother, Betty Burdue Hodge, was the source of many Vinton stories and at age 66 became a college graduate with a degree in journalism cum laude.

The author, Debbie Hodge, and her mother, Betty, were inducted into the First Families of Gallia County on October 13, 2001, as descendents of the Currys and the Glenns.

*Submitted by Debbie Hodge*

**SHAVER FAMILY** - Thomas Shaver came to Gallia County by boat with his wife, Susan Clark Shaver, in October 1816. His mother, Nancy; sister, Comfort, and brother-in-law, Thomas Armstrong; two other sisters, Nancy and Mary, and brother, John, came in 1819. They were all sick and Dr. Safford cared for them. They then moved out to the farm about three miles west of Addison on the Campaign River. Thomas farmed there and later worked for J.P.R. Bureau for years walking back and forth the nine miles to work every day. Because of this, his endurance and agility were greatly enhanced and he was well known for it. It was said that he could outrun deer and foxes on foot and even outran a stagecoach both coming from Chillicothe to Gallipolis. He was of the Millerite Religion and believed that the world was going to end in 1882. His did as he died on January 12, 1883. His parents were David Shaver who was born c1755/65 and died August 28, 1818, in Kent County, Delaware, and his mother was Nancy born September 28, 1775, in Virginia and died May 24, 1864, Gallia County. She is buried in the Campaign Cemetery, Addison Township, Gallia County, Ohio. A new tombstone was placed for her in July 2001 by members of the Jones Reunion as she was their fourth great grandmother.

*New marker at Campaign Cemetery, Gallia County, Ohio*

Thomas Shaver was born July 22, 1794, in Delaware, married Susan Clark on August 9, 1814, in Kent County, Delaware, and he died January 12, 1883, in Gallia County, Ohio. Susan was born September 2, 1792, in Kent County, Delaware, and died August 11, 1874, in Gallia County. Both are buried in the Shaver Cemetery, Addison Township, Gallia County, Ohio.

Susan Clark's parents were Abraham Clark born c1765/74 and died April 24, 1824, in Kent County, Delaware. Her mother was Ann born c1770/72. Susan had two brothers, Abraham and Thomas.

Thomas and Susan had 8 children and the seventh was Susannah who married Jacob Rothgeb. The Jones' come out of his marriage. Many of the descendants of Nancy and David Shaver live in Gallia County to this day.

*Submitted by Myron Ellis Jones, Jr.*

**SHEETS FAMILY** - The George Sheets family in Gallia County is not an easy family to prove. According to the book "Revolutionary War Soldiers who lived in Gallia County, Ohio", George was drafted in the Virginia Militia from Augusta County, Virginia in 1777. He served under Captain Arbuckle at Point Pleasant on the defense of the frontier; he served nine and one-half months. He applied for pension November 7, 1834 in Gallia County, Ohio and it was granted. George was born 1759 in Bucks County, Pennsylvania and moved to Augusta County, Virginia when he was very young. George came to Ohio about 1806 and is found on the 1820 and 1830 Gallia County census. Some think he died in Gallia County while others believe he moved to Indiana with his son Joseph and died there.

*Margaret Sheets Gatewood and James Madison Gatewood*

No will has been found for George or no trace of any wives but in family papers it has been found that George was married at least twice. He had the following children that are known: Joseph. John H. married Susannah Henry in 1820, William married Elizabeth Henry, Anna married Richard Powell in 1817, Leonard and George married Anna Henry. According to Emma Caldwell Gatewood's family history, she shows that her great-grandparents were William F. and Elizabeth Henry Sheets and her husband; Perry Clayton Gatewood's great-grandparents were George and Anna Henry Sheets. She also writes that William and George were half brothers stating they had different mothers but no names for their mothers. So far no records can be found to document this information.

Emma Caldwell Gatewood's great-grandparents, William born 1795, Augusta County, Va. died March 7, 1871, Gallia County, Ohio and Elizabeth Henry Sheets were married July 21, 1814 in Cabell County Virginia. William and Elizabeth had the following children: Jane married William Caldwell, Nancy married Louis Garlic, Susan married James Sanders, John H., Mary (Polly), Elizabeth married Brice Henry, George Washington married Susan Sanders, Lewis Jackson married Levina Johnson, Brice Hannan married Samantha Wilcoxen, Sarah and Minerva.

Jane Sheets, born May 17, 1817 died May 6, 1881 in Gallia County, married William Caldwell, son of Henry and Mary Ferrier Caldwell, November 28, 1833 in Gallia County.

Jane and William had the following children: Hugh married Esther Trowbridge (parents of Emma Rowena Caldwell Gatewood), Mary Elizabeth, Sarah Jane, Steve Monroe, Joe Thomas, Lewis Jackson, Edward Marion, James Robert, John Ferrier and William Henry. Perry Clayton Gatewood's great-grandparents, George born September 30, 1806, Virginia died September 20, 1870, Guyan Twp., Gallia County married Anna Henry August 31, 1830 in Gallia County, Ohio. George and Anna had the following children: Henry Wilson married Mary Bailey, Harve, Libni, Samuel and Susan.

Henry Wilson and Mary Bailey had daughter Margaret Ann Sheets, born May 19, 1860 and died April 8, 1947. Margaret Ann (Maggie) married James Madison Gatewood (parents of Perry Clayton Gatewood).

More on the family of Perry Clayton and Emma Caldwell Gatewood can be found in the Gatewood Family history.

*Submitted by: Marjorie Gilliam Wood*

**SHEETS - TROTTER -** I was born on May 15, 1916 in Guyan Twp. on the farm that my grandfather, Brice Hannan Sheets #2 owned and was later owned and operated by my parents, Alphonso Curtis and Vesta Alice (Warren) Sheets.

*Robert Franklin & Hartie (Trotter) Sheets*

I was the youngest of twelve children, which consisted of six boys and six girls. The farm is located where John's Creek flows into Indian Guyan Creek, which made it a good and fertile location. I helped raise tobacco, hay, corn, etc., working along beside my father and some of my siblings until I was grown and married.

I attended Campbell Grade School, as did my father and all of my siblings. It was a one-room school and was located two miles south of Mercerville, on what is now Ohio Rte. 218. It was one and one-half miles from home, which I walked to and from each day. I attended from the first grade on, until Campbell School was closed, and my classmates and I were transferred to Mercerville to complete our grade school years. I then attended Mercerville High School and graduated in 1935. While in high school, I was a member of the basketball and football teams.

My parents, myself and all of my siblings attended Mercerville Baptist Church, which dad helped rebuild in 1927. We were all active and the Warren family was noted for their fine singing voices.

After graduation, I married my high school sweetheart, Hartie Luella Trotter, on May 04, 1935 at the courthouse in Pomeroy, Meigs Co., Ohio. Hartie is the daughter of the late Sarah Velvie (Wetherholt) and William Clemence Trotter and was born on March 3, 1919 in Harrison Twp. Gallia Co. Velvie's parents were Hartie Anna E. (Blazer) and John William Wetherholt. William's parents were Thomas and Luella "Sid" (Hazlett) Trotter. All were Gallia Co. natives. Her third gr-grandmother was the famous Anne Bailey of Revolutionary War fame.

Hartie also graduated from Mercerville High School in 1935 at the age of 16, due to two double promotions. She was a cheerleader for the varsity and we were both active in school functions. She was musically inclined and excelled in playing three musical instruments. She was a member of Providence Baptist Church in Clay Twp., where she taught Sunday School and was church pianist.

After our marriage, I ran her mother's farm on Claylick, and in 1937, we moved to Huntington, W. Va. where I was employed at Spring Hill Dairy Co., which was sold to (Guyan Creamery and later to Valley Bell Dairy, from which I retired in 1981. Hattie worked as a beautician in her Aunt Cleo Wetherholt's beauty salon for a short while, but later stayed home as a homemaker. We have one child, Carolyn Cleo, who was born on May 10, 1936 on Claylick in Harrison Tp., Gallia Co. On May 7, 1955. she married Jack Franklin Vallance, youngest child of the late Alfred Sr. and Ina (Deer) Vallance of Gallia Co.

We are both members of 26th. Street Baptist Church in Huntington. I am a former usher and Hartie taught in the Jr. Dept., where she later became Supt. of that Dept.

On May 04, 2000, we celebrated our 65*th* anniversary, receiving many cards, gifts & flowers from our family and friends. We are thankful for the many acquaintances we have made over the years.

My daughter and I have compiled two histories of the Sheets Family, one of which includes some of Hartie's family ties.

We are still residing in Huntington, W. Va. and enjoying our retirement years. Submitted by Robert Franklin Sheets

**SHEETS-VALLANCE -** I was born in Harrison Twp., on Claylick, at the home of my maternal grandmother, Sarah Velvie (Wetherholt)Trotter., on Mother's Day, May 10, 1936, an only child of Robert Franklin and Hartie (Trotter) Sheets. We moved to Huntington, W. Va. in 1937 due to my mothers's employment. I attended, Gallaher Elem. Lincoln Jr. High, and graduated in 1954 from Huntington East High School. I worked from 1954-1977 at Connecticut Mutual Life Insurance Co., Island Creek Coal Sales Co., and the main office of the former B and B Food Market.

*Jack Franklin & Carolyn (Sheets) Vallance*

On May 7,1955, I married Jack Franklin Vallance at the Thomas Memorial Freewill Baptist Church, in Huntington. His brother, Carl, pastor of the church, performed the ceremony. He is the son of the late Alfred, Sr. and Ina (Deer) Vallance of Gallia Co., Ohio, who originated from Greenup Co., Ky. He was born in Kitts Hill, Lawrence Co., Ohio on January 16, 1933; attended schools in Gallia Co., graduating from Gallia Academy High School in 1953. Served in the army from 1953-1955, part of which was in Korea. Retired in 1991 from the former Goodyear Tire and Rubber Co. in Apple Grove (Mason Co.), W.Va. Since retiring he spends some of his leisure time doing his favorite hobby of woodcarving and woodworking, with projects such as clocks, rocking horses, etc.

We are members of the 26thStreet Baptist Church in Huntington. Jack is a former teacher in the Primary Dept. and of the Men's Bible Class. At present, he serves as church usher & teaches in various Sunday School classes in the absence of the teacher.

My maternal grandparents were the late Sarah Velvie (Wetherholt) and William Clemence Trotter. Velvie's parents were Hartie Anna E. (Blazer) and John William Wetherholt. William's parents were Thomas Morgan and Louella "Sid" (Hazlett) Trotter. My paternal grandparents were Alphonso Curtis and Vesta Alice (Warren) Sheets. His parents were Brice Hannan #2 and Samantha (Wilcoxen) Sheets. Vesta's parents were John L. and Levenia (Clark) Warren.

I have many memories of my childhood, which are too numerous to mention, but some special ones are when I visited my grandmother, Velvie, who was a teacher in the Gallia Co. rural schools. Before I became of age to attend school, I occasionally attended school with her.

I remember trying to skate on the creek, next to the school grounds. I fell through the ice and found that I didn't have the capabilities of the older children. I also remember one of the older boys misbehaving in class, and inserting one of his school books into the seat of his pants before taking his punishment. After the first blow with the paddle, my grandmother knew just what action to take next.

I remember the "Pie Suppers", (whomever bought the pie, would have to eat it with the one who baked it., who was generally the one they were sweet on.) Then there were the "Treat Bags", that my grandmother prepared each Christmas for her pupils, which contained goodies, such as candy, popcorn balls, oranges, apples, etc. I was delighted when she would let me help with these.

Also, when I was small, I remember the fun times at the family reunions of my father's family that took place at my Grandpa Sheets' home on John's Creek in Guyan Twp. His brothers & sisters and their families would come and I can still hear the laughter and reminiscing of their childhood days and the "tall tales" that were told. I remember the "labor of love" that my father & his brothers had when they took turns cranking the ice-cream freezer until it was done & then sometimes they would make one or two more freezers, so that the crowd would have plenty.

I am proud of my Gallia County roots & family ties; they cannot be replaced.

*Submitted by Carolyn Sheets Vallance*

**SHEETS - WARREN -** Alphonso Curtis Sheets was born in Guyan Twp. on Nov. 25, 1874, the youngest in the family of ten children of Brice Hannan #2 (1834-1912) and Samantha (Wilcoxen) Sheets (1834-1919).

He was born on his father's farm, which he later owned and operated with his wife, the former Vesta Alice Warren, whom he married on Sept. 6, 1893. It is located where John's Creek flows into the Indian Guyan Creek. He spent his life there. During his boyhood days, he helped his father raise cane to make molasses, which was shipped by riverboat to markets downriver. It was used as a sweetening and in most homes, it was a necessity. In later years, tobacco replaced cane as a money crop.

*Alphonso C. Sheets Family Ca. 1919 Row 1: Eva May, Robert Franklin, Alphonso, Vivian Ilene, Vesta, Mary Maudelle, Roscoe Curtis Row 2: Garland Amor, Haschal Lewis, Millie Fay, Harold Hannon, Grace Pauline, Merrill Warren*

He attended Campbell School, as did all of his children. It was a one room school located two miles south of Mercerville on what is now Ohio Route 218 and was one and one-half miles from his home. He walked to and from school everyday during the school term, which was much shorter then than now, as it gave the boys more time for farm work.

Alphonsa's father, Brice #2, served as a Union soldier in the Civil War and fought in the "Battle Above The Clouds", Lookout Mountain, Chattanooga, Tenn. He also fought in various other areas in the Shenandoah Valley.

Vesta Alice was the daughter of John L. and Levenia "Venie"(Clark) Warren. Her grandfather was Rev. Andrew Jackson Warren, Sr. who preached in Gallia, Lawrence and Pike Co., Ohio and in Mason, County Va./W.Va. He & his family moved from Mason Co. to Gallia Co. during the "Great Rebellion" in 1863. As a young lady, before her marriage, Vesta taught school & was very active in church.

There were twelve children, 6 boys and 6 girls, born to this union, of which I was the youngest of the group. The children and their spouses and children are as follows: Garland Amor (1894-l965) Mabel Early, No. children; Millie Goldie Faye (1896-1973) Earl Unroe (Virgil, Lucille, Maxwell, Rachel, Elzie); Mary Maudelle (1897-1926) Charles Hughes (Edna Louise, Ruth Alice); Eva May (1899-1949) Never married; Genevieve (1902-1902) Died in infancy ; Harold Hannan (1903-1952) Tressie Stevers (Louis Arden, Mary Alyce); Haschal Lewis (1903-1986) Norma Stevers( Haschal David, Sydney Alan) (Harold and Haschal were twins); Merrill Warren (1906-1947) Reta McKean (Ferrell Warren, Roberta Suzanne); Grace Pauline (1908-1937) Lawrence Horn (Merrill Dewey, James Lee); Roscoe Curtis (1912 - ) Vehna Hager (Larry Eugene, Ronald Curtis); Vivian Ilena (1915-1996) Charles Stenton (Donna Louise); Robert Franklin(1916- ) Hartie Trotter (Carolyn Cleo).

Two of the sons were in WWII, Merrill W. "Shiner", served in the navy and was in the invasion of southern France. Roscoe Curtis was in the army and stationed at Ft. Lewis, Washington.

Alphonso , Vesta and family attended ,and were active in the Mercerville Baptist Church, which he helped rebuild in 1927.

He died on March 30, 1959 in Huntington, W. Va. and she died January 28, 1935 at her home on John's Creek. Both are buried along with several members of their family in Old Mercerville Cemetery in Guyan Twp.
*Submitted by: Robert Franklin Sheets*

**SHEETS - WILCOXEN -** Brice Hannan Sheets #2 was the son of William F. and Elizabeth (Henry) Sheets, who was one of the first settlers in Guyan Twp., emigrating from Virginia in 1806- he was born on February 28. 1834, on their farm that was located at the intersection of Johns Creek and Rocky Fork Rd.( In re the number following his name, Brice had a cousin with the same identical name. To distinguish them when they were referred to and also to sort & deliver their mail , numbers1 and 2 were added to their name.)

*Brice Hannan & Samantha (Wilcoxen) Sheets*

On April 29, 1855, in Gallia Co., he was married to Samantha Wilcoxen, daughter of Henry H. and Nancy A. (Leggett) Wilcoxen. Samantha was born in Carroll County, Ohio on May 21, 1834.

To this union the following children were born: #1 Sarah F-bn. May 1, 1855— D. January 5, 1877, Md. Daniel W. Smith; #2 Rev. Ira Jackson-bn. February 22, 1857— D. May 2, 1938-Md. Martha Ann Fil!inger;#3 Silas Henry-bn. March7, 1859- D.July 19, 1950— Md. Bertha Missouri Morrow;#4 Elza Sylvester-Bn. February 25, 1861—D. February 10, 1932- Md. Elizabeth Charlotte Houck; #5 Nancy Elizabeth- Bn. February 18, 1863—D. August 20, 1957— Md. John Hill Hineman; #6 Emma Roseltha —Bn. January 16, 1865—D. November 16,1959-Md. CharlesBevan;#7 Paulina Indiana—Bn. May 2, 1867 - D. January 28, 1919— Md. Bennett Ellsworth Hineman; #8 Celestial A. — Bn. September 6, 1869— D. August 7, 1870; #9Etta May — Bn. May 25, 1872-D. March 20, 1949— Md. I) Edward McIntire—2)Claude McCall; #10 Alphonso Curtis — Bn. November 25, 1874—D. March 30, 1959—Md. Vesta Alice Warren.

Brice built a home on Johns Creek Rd., in Guyan Twp., where he & Samantha farmed and raised their family. When their health began to decline, their son, Alphonso and his wife Vesta cared for them through their illness & respective deaths. Alphonso inherited the home & a portion of the farm. He also bought and paid for some of the shares of land of his siblings.

Brice and Samantha were Baptists by faith. She was a devoted member of Siloam Baptist Church since early in her life and at her death, she was the last of the charter members of that organization.

Brice enlisted in the Civil War on February 14, 1865, in the 195th Ohio Volunteer Infantry and rec'd his discharge on July 6, 1865, at Cumberland, Md. he fought in the "Battle Above The Clouds", on Lookout Mountain in Chattanooga, Tenn. He died on April 4, 1912 and was interred in Old Mercerville Cem. in Guyan Twp. Samantha died on July 19, 1919 and is buried beside her husband.

They are the parents of my paternal grandfather, Alphonso Curtis Sheets.
*Submitted by: Carolyn Sheets Vallance*

**LUTHER ENOCH SHEPARD -** Luther Enoch Shepard was born 1 August 1812 in Marietta, Ohio. He was the son of Calvin Dewey Shepard and Mahala Oliver; grandson of Enoch Shepard and Esther Dewey of Westfield, Massachusetts; great-grandson of John Shepard and Elizabeth Noble. John Shepard was the son of John Shepard and Elizabeth Woodruff; and grandson of William Shepard and Experience Hart. Luther's occupation in 1850 was brick mason, in 1860 he was a farmer and by 1870 he was listed as druggist. Equally remarkable, Luther had three wives and fifteen children.

Luther's first wife was Elizabeth M. Maddy whom he married 4 March 1841 in Gallia County. She was born 17 March 1819 and died 19 September 1853 in Louisa, Kentucky, and buried at Maddy Cemetery in Addison Township, Gallia County.

Children of Luther and Elizabeth Maddy (five)-James Oliver, born 22 June 1842, Franklin Dewey, born 7 October 1844 in Gallia County, Ohio; died of cholera on board the "Annie Laurie" 15 August 1866; buried at Maddy Cemetery, Ray, born about 1846, Elmon Luther, born 10 September 1848 in Gallia County, Ohio; married Rebecca C. Jones, Wilbur Fish, born 25 October 1850.

Luther's second wife was Elizabeth Johnson, whom he married 3 April 1855. Elizabeth was born 7 October 1821 in Kanawha County, West Virginia and died 16 August 1861 in Gallipolis Township. She was buried at Maddy Cemetery.

Children of Luther and Elizabeth Johnson (two)-Mattie F., born 21 August 1856 in Kentucky; died 29 January 1867 in Ashland, Mary Agnes M., born 3 February 1859 in Ohio; married Walter F. Smith 26 December 1882; died 16 April 1889.

His third wife was Agnes Mann Thompson, daughter of Francis S. and Phillipina "Phoebe" (Chappell) Thompson, born 24 Jun 1839 in Burkes Garden, Tazewell County,Virginia. Her mother and four of her siblings (Alexander, Thomas, Frances Jane, and James C.) came to Gallia County. The first we learn of the arrival of Agnes in Gallia County is at the time of her marriage to Luther on New Year's Eve, 1861.

Children of Luther and Agnes Thompson (eight)- John Chapelle, born 5 Jan 1863 in Gallia County; died 1869, Annavi, born 5 Jan 1864 in Kentucky; married Lewis Sieweke 28 Sep 1887, Lucy Jane, born 19 June 1866 in

Ashland, Kentucky; married Ralph Asa Andrews, 10 May 1887; died 15 August 1961; buried at Ashland, Kentucky, Grace Artie, born 9 May 1868 in Kentucky; married Charles D. Boggess 26 December 1899; died 16 December 1 906, Earl Alexander, born 18 December 1870 in Kentucky; married Nellie M.Swope 10 July 1907. Roxie Emma, born 25 March 1874, Nellie Aurelia, born 7 March 1876 in Kentucky; married Thomas A. Shoemaker 8 June 1902, Cora Hutsinpiller, born 23 Jan 1879 in Ashland, Kentucky; died unmarried.

Luther died in Ashland, Kentucky, 23 July 1885 at the age of 73, leaving four minor children. Agnes survived him by nearly a quarter of a century and died in Ashland, Kentucky, 15 June 1908-shortly before her sixty ninth birthday.

*Submitted by Linda Gaylord-kuhn*

**BRIG. GEN. WILLIAM J. SHONDEL, USAF** - Married to Mary Frances Notter, daughter of Elwin E. and Vesta M. (Wray) Notter of Northup, General Shondel became a resident of Gallia County in 1972. His parents were John Robert and Helen A. (Bidinger) Shondel of Clinton, Ohio. General Shondel was born on October 18, 1943, in Barberton, Ohio, and married on October 18, 1966, in Chillicothe in a civil ceremony.

*Brig. Gen. William J. Shondel, USAF, 1966*

Genealogists have traced the general's lineage to Mathieu Schandel of Schirrhoffen, Alsace, France. Mathieu's son, Jean, served with Napoleon and was mayor of the town from 1812-1816. Jean's son, Christian, was said to be a bodyguard of Napoleon and served with him in the Moscow and Waterloo campaigns. Jean, Christian, and their families immigrated to Canton, Ohio, in 1830 via LeHavre, France, later moving to Wayne County, Ohio. Christian's son, John, changed the family name to Shondel and was a merchant in Doylestown, Ohio. The general was named for his grandfather, William J. Shondel. (A complete family history is on file in the Gallia, Wayne, and Summit County genealogical libraries.)

General Shondel served in the Air Force for 40 years, beginning as an AFROTC cadet at Ohio State University. While there, he served as commander of a wing of over 2,000 cadets. In 1965 he was commissioned as a lieutenant with an MA degree in history and progressed through subsequent ranks, culminating with his promotion to general in 1966. While on active duty, he was selected as an Outstanding Air Force Supply Officer of the Year. During his career, General Shondel served with the Air Force Reserves and Air National Guard in various positions including Flight and Squadron commander, Director of Logistics, and finally Chief of Staff of the West Virginia Air National Guard. He was the first non-rated officer to hold that position and also that of Assistant Adjutant General for Air in the State. In March 2001 General Shondel retired from the Air Force and was awarded the Legion of Merit.

Now associated with Marshall University as Director of Purchasing and holding an MBA degree, the general has been active in many community and professional organizations. He has been President of the Gallipolis Lions Club and District Governor of Lions Clubs International. He re-chartered the Ohio State University Alumni Association's local chapter in 1981 and served as its President. He was President of the National Guard Association of West Virginia and the first President of the WV Association of Higher Education Purchasing Officers. General Shondel has remained active in the President's Club of Ohio State University, its Alumni Association and that of Marshall University, the Air Force Association, and the National Guard Associations of the United States and West Virginia.

General Shondel and his wife have made their home on her family farm on Lincoln Pike for the past quarter century. With no children, they have devoted their lives to horses and their farm, endeared of the land and the people of Gallia County.

*Submitted by Brig. Gen. Shondel (retired)*

**DOYLE AND HENRIETTA SHULER FAMILY** - Doyle Titus Shuler was born on the Shuler family homestead on 9-6-1914. Doyle attended Cheshire High School until having to drop out his senior year to support his family during an extended illness of his father. During this time, Doyle worked in the family store and coal mine. In October of 1942, he enlisted in the army. He served as a Photographer and Laboratory Technician until his discharge in January of 1946.

After the service, Doyle started Shuler Construction Company with his brother Emmett. In 1963, he founded the Doyle T. Shuler Co., which he owned until his death on 8-7-1977. Doyle was a very civic minded man and was a blood donor, a member of the Masonic Lodge and the Rotary club. He was an active member of the Cheshire Baptist Church and was very involved in the building of the Sunday School addition built in 1963. A metal cross built by Doyle still graces the church steeple today, and the church chimes were purchased in his memory.

On 11-16-1948, Doyle married Henrietta Skaggs, the daughter of Charles Lee and Della Ann Skaggs. Henrietta was born in Red Jacket in Mingo Co.,W.Va. on 1-8-1924. The family moved to Cheshire in 1927. Henrietta graduated from Cheshire High School in 1942 and worked at the Imperial Ice Cream factory for a while. She worked in a factory in Middleport, Ohio during W.W.II making uniforms for the army. While her children were at home, Henrietta worked at home keeping books for the family business. She was also very active at her children's school in PTO, Band and athletic boosters, and other volunteer duties. Henrietta has been an active member of the Cheshire Baptist Church for many years. She has served on various committees and has been a Deaconess, Christian Board member and a Church Trustee. After Doyle's death, Henrietta worked as an Account Clerk III for the Department of Human Services from 1979 to 1986.

Doyle and Henrieta had three children: George Michael (1-8-1950), Penny Lynn (4-4-1952), and Mary Ann (4-8-1961). Michael is the father of two sons, David Michael (8-13-1968) and Caleb Titus (10-24-1978). Michael married Brenda Amos on 2-20-93. David married Mary Cunningham Wolfe on 5-21-93. They are the parents of two sons, Jeremy Wolfe (5-29-1987) and Nathaniel Doyle (3-2-94).

Penny married Mark Jeffery Roush on 6-7-1980. They are the parents of two children, Daniel Thomas born on 11-28-1984 and Hannah Lee born on 8-2-1990. Mark and Penny were divorced in 1994.

Mary Ann married Gregory Dean Mulford on 4-19-1980. Mary Ann and Greg have two children, Megan Renee born on 9-11-1981, and Matthew Dean born on 11-4-1990.

Henrietta Shuler still lives on the river front property in Cheshire, Ohio that she and Doyle purchased in 1952.

**HOWARD SHULER FAMILY** - Howard Shuler was born on 4-8-1878 in Old Kyger, Ohio. He was the son of William and Mary (Scott) Shuler and the grandson of Christopher and Anna (Rife) Shuler. His great grand father, George, first came to Gallia County from Virginia in around 1817 and settled in the Kyger area.

*Front L: to R: Hilah, Howard,Lilith, Helen, Doris Back: Doyle, Emmet, George*

Howard was born on the family homestead on what is now Rt. 554 and lived their until his death on 12-26-1958. In 1905, he married Liith Thompson, the daughter of Emmet Pierce and Molly Thompson, and they had nine children. Two of their children,Homer and Mary, died in infancy and another Deane died at age 13. Their surviving children were Emmet, Doris, Doyle, George, Helen and Hilah.

Howard and Lilith had a store on Rt. 554. Howard was a 50 year member of the Order of Knights of Phthias while Lilith belonged to the DAR. Both attended church at the Old Kyger Freewill Baptist Church. Lilith died on 2-8-1957.

Emmet William was born on 4-13-1908. He served in the army during World War II. Emmet married Helen Hess and they raised Helen's nephew Charles Hess. He later married Barbara Stout. Emmet died on 4-4-1971.

Doris Shuler was born a twin on 11-19-1912. Her brother, Deane, died in his teens. Doris married Hortie Roush and they had three children, Howard Horton, Carolyn Joy, and Joseph Dean.

Doris and Hortie raised their children on Roush Lane in Cheshire and later built a home on part of the original homestead of Doris's grandfather Christopher. Both Doris and Hortie were active members of the Old Kyger Freewill Baptist Church. Doris died on 9-18-1976 and Hortie on 12-25-1986.

Doyle Titus was born born on 9-16-1914. He served as a sergeant during WW II. Doyle married Henrietta Skaggs on 11-16-1948. They had three children, George Michael, Penny Lynn, and MaryAnn. Doyle died on 8-27-1977. Henrietta continues to live in their home in Cheshire, Ohio.

George Franklin Shuler was born on 2-9-1918 and was a Veteran of WW II and was missing in action for a time in the South Pacific. He died on 11-30-1947.

Helen Alberta was born on 9-5-1922. She graduated from Cheshire High School and married Edward Spears on 7-3-1942. Helen and Ed had two children, Donald Deane, who died at age 4 and Leah Cameron. Ed died on 3-14-79 and Helen remarried Reverend Miles Trout on 2-14-1982. Helen has been an active member of the Old Kyger Freewill Baptist Church for many years.

Hilah Kathleen was born on 5-15-1924. She graduated from Cheshire High School and married John P. Herrman on 10-1-1942. She and Jack had 2 children, Mary Jacklyn and John Michael. Hilah and Jack moved to Belpre, Ohio. They now spend their winters in Florida.

**WILLIAM AND MARY (SCOTT) SHULER FAMILY** - George Shuler was born on 6-15-1784 in Bucks Co., Pennsylvania. His parents are unknown but many of the early Shulers in PA had immigrated from Germany in the early 1700's and it is possible he was descended from that line. He moved to Virginia and married Mary Long in Rock bridge VA in 1800. George and Mary had 9 sons and 2 daughters, sons John, William, George, Christopher, and Levi were born in Rock Bridge VA. In about 1817, the family moved to Gallia County and settled in the Kyger area. Four more sons were born in Ohio, Jeremiah, Hanson, Daniel and Eli. One daughter, Elizabeth was probably born in VA. A second daughter, Tinca, was born in 1822. George died in 1864 at the age of eighty.

One of George's sons, Christopher married Anna Rife, the daughter of Jacob Rife on 5-11-1837. Christopher was listed in the census records as a farmer but he also performed many of the local weddings. He and Anna had eight children: Mary, Amanda, Jacob, Alexander, Bartlett, Margaret, William and Christopher. In 1854, Christopher purchased land on what is now St. Rt. 554 near Old Kyger. Christopher's son William was born in 1851 on the family farm. Christopher died in 1857 leaving Anna to raise the family. In 1863, at the time of Morgan's raid, two men were found in the Shuler barn. One of these men died several hour later from a gun shot wound . He is buried in Gravel Hill Cemetery. The story handed down by the family is that he was a "Southern Soldier" but this has not been confirmed. Nothing is known of the other soldier. Bullet holes from the raid can still be seen in the old barn. Members of the Shuler family still place flowers on the killed soldier's grave.

In 12-118-1877, William married Mary F. Scott, the daughter of Elisha and Elizabeth Scott. Elizabeth's place of birth was listed as Scotland. William bought the homestead from the estate of his mother in 1874. He and Mary had 4 children: Howard (4-8-1878), Elma (11-14-1880), Iva (9-15-1884), and Ernest (3-22-1888).

William died in 1918. His wife Mary lived to the old age of 96, dying in 1950. William and Mary's descendant still own most of the original land purchased in 1854.

**DR. AND MRS. MEL P. SIMON AND FAMILY** - Dr. Mel P. Simon was born on October 29,1935 in San Pablo, Isabela, and northern Philippines. His father, Melecio G. Simon was a District Supervisor of the Public School System, married Lucrecia Palattao Simon and had 12 children, 6 boys and 6 girls.

Mel was the 8th. child in the family. Two of the older brothers died before Mel was born.

*Dr. & Mrs. Mel P. Simon's Family Back Row, Standing, L: to R: Sherwyn , Tess, Lydia, Mel, Agnes And Paul Second Row, Standing: Ross (Between Sherwyn and Tess) Sitting, L: to R: Lauren with the dog, Hazel Malu And David*

Two sisters, Filipinas and Isabela, and one brother, Joe became school teachers, while one older sister Lu and a younger sister Trini became nurses. Mel completed medical school in 1959 from the University Santo Tomas that was founded in 1711 by the Dominican Order in the Philippines. Older brother, Fred, completed Civil Engineering and got employed in Akron, OH. Younger sister Remy became a pharmacist and later on a Medical Technologist at Holzer Medical Center in 1977. Younger brother Lib became a Radiological Technologist, married Carrie Simon, younger sister of Lydia, then moved to Oxnard, California with their children, P-Jay, Francis and Bernadette, all born in Gallipolis, now all nurses in California.

Mel and Lydia came to the United States on June 30, 1959 with port of entry in Anchorage, and interned on July 1, 1959 at Cook County Hospital in Chicago while Lydia was appointed a Staff Nurse at Mayo Clinic in Rochester, Minnesota. They were married on October 24, 1959 at St. John's Cathedral in Rochester, Minnesota. Two of the children, Malu , now a Pediatric Dentist in Evanston and Sherwyn, a medical doctor in Cincinnati, were born in Chicago during their first 7 years of married life. The youngest son, Paul Robert was born at the old Holzer Hospital in downtown Gallipolis on April 14, 1967.

After Completing residency training in surgery and Urology on June 30, 1966, Mel was appointed Assistant Chief of the Department of Urology at Cook County Hospital in Chicago. In October 1966, the late Dr. Charles E. Holzer, Jr. invited Mel to come to visit the Holzer Clinic and Hospital Douglas Wetherholt who was an Assistant Administrator of Holzer Clinic in 1966 met Mel and Lydia at Charleston Airport. After the interview, Dr. Holzer and Dr. Leonard Harris who was Chairman of the Executive Committee of Holzer Clinic convinced Mel to be a Clinic Urologist. After 5 years of working for Holzer Clinic as a partner, Mel decided to build his own Clinic, the Hillcrest Urological Clinic, Inc. and opened on January 1, 1972. Since then, it has continued to operate as a Clinic up to the present time serving Gallipolis, Gallia County and the surrounding counties in Southeast Ohio, Kentucky and West Virginia.

In 1974, along with four other local physicians, Mel formed and built a 120-bed nursing home, formerly known as Pinecrest now called the Arbors Skilled Facility located on Pinecrest Drive, serving the local and surrounding communities.

A board certified Urologist, Mel is also a pilot and Aviation Medical Examiner designated by the Federal Aviation Administration to examine private pilots. A full Colonel of the United States Air Force Reserve, he serves his duties with the 74th Medical Group of Wright Patterson Air Force Base in Fairborn, OH.

He was also past presidents of Mason County Medical Society, Central Ohio Urological Society, Society of Philippine Surgeons in America, and Tri-State Fil Am of KY, WV and OH. Mel & Lydia heads the medical mission to the Philippines for the past 19 years operating on indigent patients, help build fresh water wells and nutrition projects, and spearheaded a construction of a Community Hospital.

A member of the Board of Trustees of the University of Rio Grande, Mel seats in Board Meetings at the University. A member of Rotary Club of Gallipolis, he was President of the Gallipolis Rotary Club in 1987-88 and the first one from Gallipolis to be elected as District Governor of Rotary International in 1998-99 for District 6690 with 54 Rotary Clubs and 4,200 Rotarians in central and southeastern Ohio. On May 13-16, 1999, Mel held the first historic Rotary District Conference at University of Rio Grande and Downtown Gallipolis with 54 Rotary Clubs and 4,200 Rotarians from southeastern and central Ohio.

Their family includes Main, a Pediatric Dentist, who is married to David and have two children, Lauren and Ross, both figure skaters and they reside in Evanston, IL; Sherwyn who is a doctor in Cincinnati, OH is going to be married to Dr. Tess Sola of Elgin, IL and Paul, a businessman, is married to Dr. Agnes Enrico of Charlestown, WV. Mel and Lydia resides at 155 First Avenue, Gallipolis, OH.

**SIMS FAMILY** - Burrell Sims (1st) born ca. 1816 in North Carolina, died December 7, 1893, Guyan Twp., Gallia County married Jane Harmon born October 25, 1822 believed in Meigs County, Ohio and died March 24, 1904 in Guyan Twp., Gallia County. Burrell and Jane are buried in the Sims

Cemetery, Guyan Twp., Gallia County. The name Sims has been spelled many different ways, Sims, Simms, Syms, Symms, etc that makes searching records a long hard task. It is believed that Burrell's father was John Sims also being in Gallia County at the same time but has not been documented, except from stories passed down to family members. It is also believed that Jane's father was Conrad Harmon from Meigs County and he is buried near Jane and Burrell in the Sims Cemetery.

Burrell and Jane had the following children according to Burrell's will: Burrell, Clara LaJulia, James L., Richard, Dallas A., Carlton, Rhoda, William Sherman, Charles F. and Mary.

Burrell Sims (2nd. Burrell) born March 1849 died March 12, 1930, Guyan Twp., Gallia County was twice married. He first married Eliza Williams and had the following children: Jesse Gilbert, Janie Anna, Burrell Bert (this is the rd Burrell we find), James Wilburt, Lewis Harve, Ella F., Eliza R. (Lyde), George, Emma, Effie Viola. Burrell's wife Eliza died when Effie was two years old and he married Bertha Gatewood after all his children were grown.

Effie was born January 5, 1894, Crown City, Guyan Twp, Gallia County and died May 15, 1976, Gallipolis, Gallipolis Twp. Effie married Elijah Michael Williams, June 1911 in Crown City, Ohio. Effie and Lige made their home in Gallipolis and lived for many years at 517 Fourth Avenue. Effie was a homemaker and Lige retired from the Gallipolis State Institute. They had the following children: Marjorie Agnes, Mildred, Clarence, Alva and Dwight. Effie and Lige are buried at Crown City Cemetery.

Marjorie Agnes born December 8, 1912, Crown City, died December 7, 1990, Gallipolis, married Ernest Monroe Gatewood on January 11, 1934. Marjorie was a homemaker and was very active at Grace United Methodist Church. She worked with the Women's organization of the church, the Grace Guild Sunday School class and was a communion steward for many years. Marjorie and Monroe had two children: Eleanor Gertrude and Charles Edward. Marjorie and Monroe are buried at Memorial Gardens Cemetery, Gallipolis.

Eleanor born November 24, 1935 Crown City, died June 29, 1979, Gallipolis married James Randall Gilliam, September 5, 1954. Eleanor and Jim had the following children:

James Randall II, Marjorie Lynn and Margaret Gwen. Eleanor died in a boating accident on the Ohio River and Jim died March 9, 1975 from a heart attack.

James Randall (Randy) (1st.) married Karen Tabor and had two daughters: Ginger Kay and Brandy Sue. He married (2) Sue Adkins. Marjorie Lynn married Charles (Chuck) Wood and has the following children: Jessica Lynn, Burton Charles (Burt) and James Clayton (Clayton). Margaret Gwen (Gwen) married Dennis McGuire and they have one son: Joshua Neil.

Ginger Gilliam married Ronnie Denney and they have one daughter: Krista Grace (Gracie). Jessica Wood married Michael Weber and they have one son: Eric Michael (Eric).

*Submitted by: Marjorie Gilliam Wood*

**WAYNE FRANKLIN SISSON** - John Franklin Sisson was born September 12, 1881 in Cheshire Township, (Gallia County, Ohio. He was one of eight children of James Oscar and Elizabeth (Mulford) Sisson. He married Nettie Halfhill born May 11, 1885, daughter of Samuel and Laura (Thomas) Halfhill; granddaughter of Jacob and Abigail (Barrett) Halfhill and Washington and Virginia (Armstrong) Thomas.

John died November 4, 1930 and Nettie died February 7, 1933.

John and Nettie had seven children, all born in Cheshire Township, Gallia County:

(1) Edgar Dale Sisson was born August 15, 1905. On January 9, 1945, he married Mary B. (Bradbury) Rupe, who had one son, Wade and two daughters Margie Jean and Gertrude Rupe by a previous marriage to Earl Rupe. Dale and Mary had no children. Dale was a World War II veteran and a coal miner and together, Dale and Mary operated a general store in Kyger for many years. Dale died April 21, 1985 and Mary died January 5, 1996.

(2) John Carl Sisson was born January 7, 1907. He married Ruth Davis Evans. Carl and Ruth had no children. Ruth died April 21, 1970; Carl died July 19, 1976.

(3) Fred Clair Sisson was born August 10, 1908. On November 22, 1930 at Pomeroy, Ohio, he married Neva Gail Mulford, daughter of Elza and Lona (Darst) Mulford. Gail was born February 3, 1912 in Cheshire Twp. Fred and Gail had two children: Philip F., married 1) Carolyn Kreuger, had four children, 2) Carol Ros; and Frances Ann Sisson, married Michael Schukert, had two children, Dane and Jill. Fred, a schoolteacher and farmer, died November 20, 1996. Gail died July 24, 2001.

(4) Helen Elizabeth Sisson was born June 28, 1910. She married Bamzel "Bud" Fife on Oct 30, 1934 in Marion Ohio. They had no children. Helen died January 26,1981. Bud died November 21, 1993.

(5) Hazel Frances Sisson was born March 13, 1914. In January 1932 she married Perry Ralph. Hazel and Perry had four children: Carol Irene, married Curtis Althouse; John Edward, married Shirley Porter; Donald Perry, married Mary Jury; and Sandra Kay, married Tyrus Cramer, died 1969.

(6) Wayne Franklin Sisson was born September 13, 1919. On November 1, 1941, he married Annabelle Rupe born Sept 20, 1924 daughter of Raymond Rupe and Birda Kennedy Sadler. She is the granddaughter of Frank and Mary (Might) Rupe and Lewis and Ellen (Shoemaker) Sadler. Wayne and Annabelle had four children: Richard, married Evelyn Swisher Blazer, had a daughter Annette; Robert Wayne, married Iva Stewart, had three children: Robert, John, and Melisa; Carolyn, married (1) Robert Hart and (2) Richard Cooley; Linda, married Richard W Bradbury, had two children: Lori and Brian.

Wayne was a World War II veteran, coal miner, Gallipolis State Institute employee and retired from the Ohio Valley Electric Company - Kyger Creek plant. Annabelle retired as a cook from the Kyger Creek Local School District. Wayne and Annabelle are lifelong residents of Cheshire Township.

(7) Grace Sisson was born August 20, 1921. On December 20, 1940 she married Marvin Thomas. Grace and Marvin had two children: Judy Ann, married Merrill Wilcoxen; and David Lee.

*Submitted by Linda Sisson Bradbury*

**ASAHEL SKINNER AND HIS TWO BRIDES** - Asahel Skinner was born August 22, 1771 in Norton, Bristol County, MA to Daniel Skinner and his wife Abigale Briggs. After the Revolution Daniel and his family which then included six children, moved to what is now Penobscott County, ME near Corinth where he established Skinner Settlement. half-way between Bangor and Corinth. The settlement included a church an inn and several houses. On February 22, 1798 Asahel married Phebe Gould, daughter of Nathaniel Gould Jr., and his wife Ruthanna Bickford.

Not long after their twelfth child Asahel, Jr. was born May 18, 1814 Asahel decided it was time to move south to the Northwest Territory. From a letter he wrote we know he took a milk cow and twenty one pair of shoes. Apparently he didn't expect to find a shoemaker in the wilderness. The original plan was to go at least as far as far western PA. We don't know for certain how they traveled but assume it was overland by wagon. When they were near Erie PA their money had run out. So they spent a year or two in the area to replenish their funds and as often happens two of their daughters Abigale and Hannah decided to marry and stay in PA. Hannah married Warrner Waid and Abigale stayed too, as she had set her cap for Warner's brother William.

So in 1816 or 1817 Asahel, Phebe and eleven children left Meadsville headed south. For this leg of the journey they used a flatboat probably with a small shelter in the middle. David had been born in PA on April 24, 1816. When they came to the mouth of Leading Creek they found friends and decided to stay. There in a temporary home Lucinda was born on Aug 12, 1817. Neither mother or baby lasted long. The children, not mentioned, that made up the family that arrived in Gallia were Daniel born March 28, 1801. Alona born August 19, 1802 married William McKee; Joseph born November 15, 1803 married Mary (Polly) Gaston and second Jane MacFarlin; Joel born July 31, 1805 married Diadamia Richardson and second Eleanor Whitted; William born November 4, 1806 married Mary Ann Carver; Olive born March 12. 1808 m John Henry Chase and second Richard Reeves; Isaac born April 12. 1809 died unmarried; Edna born September 12, 1810 married Hiram Chase.; Pheobe Rhoda born August 12, 1812 married William B. Hartinger; Asahel Jr.. married Lurancy D. Rathburn and second Jane Hogue; and David born Apr 24, 1816 married Mary Elizabeth Burwell.

After Phebe's death Asahel married Jane Everton daughter of Thomas and Relief (Howe) Everton on March 19, 1818 in Gallia County. Their first child Lucinda, named for babe Asahel lost, was born December 28, 1818 in Gallia County. She married Daniel Clark Rathburn MD.

After Meigs County was separated from Gallia the Skinners were part of Rutland, Meigs Co. They had eight children born in Meigs. Elizabeth (Betsy), John Osborn MD, Samantha, Darius Calvin, Thomas Everton, Isaac and an unnamed babe that died at birth.

Since this big family won't fit close to five hundred words I will say Thomas E. was my great grandfather and I do have histories on all of the children if anyone wants them.

*Submitted by: Virginia L. Kane*

**CLARENCE EDWARD SKINNER AND ELIZABETH ELLEN JENKINS** - In 1883 Owen and Eliza Morgans Jenkins, and their children: Elizabeth Ellen, born 31 May 1876; Mary Jane, born March 1878; Owen Thomas, born 31 March 1880; and Catherine C., born 7 July 1882; immigrated to Gallia County from Aberystwyth, Cardiganshire, Wales. Owen, born 3 Jan 1849 in Aberystwyth, was the son of Thomas Jenkins and Elinor Evans. Eliza, born in 1856, was the daughter of Morgan and Elizabeth Morgans of Aberystwyth.

*Back Row: John Thompson, Clarence Skinner, David Jenkins, Brady Graham, Emory Wetherholt Center Row: Mary Thompson, Hazel Jenkins, Katie Graham Front Row: Elizabeth Jenkins Skinner, Maggie Wetherholt*

Family tradition indicates that they stayed with Eliza's uncle, John C. Morgan, and his wife, Catherine C. Morris when they first arrived. John and Catherine's children were: Elizabeth, Catherine, Ann, David, Margaret, Lewis Charles, John James, and Mary Jane. Catherine, aka "Kit," and Mary Jane, aka "Sis," were well-known shoemakers in the Gallia and Jackson County area. Many members of this family unit are buried in Bethel Cemetery in Perry Township.

Three more children were born to Eliza in Gallia County: David Morgan Jenkins on 7 July 1884, Margaret "Maggie" on 3 Oct 1886, and Minnie "Betty" on 7 July 1889. Mary Jane married John Thompson, Owen Thomas. married Hester Fink; Catherine "Katie" married Brady Graham, David married Hazel Lynch; Maggie married Emory Wetherholt; and Minnie married William H. Francis.

Family tradition says that Owen Jenkins was murdered somewhere along the Ohio River and that Eliza went to the Cincinnati area to identity the body and arrange burial Twenty years of research for proof of this event have yielded no results. The search continues.

Owen's death may have occurred around July 1886, when most of the children were placed in the Gallia County Children's Home, where they remained until adopted or placed with a foster family. Three of the Jenkins children stayed in Ohio, three were transplanted to West Virginia, and one moved to Connecticut, but they continued to stay in touch through correspondence, visits, and annual family reunions.

Elizabeth Ellen, also known as "Nellie," remained at the home until she married Clarence Edward Skinner in front of the fireplace in the right front room of the Children's Home on 12 Apr 1897. They were married sixty years before Clarence passed away on 19 Sep 1957 at the age of 86. He was the son of John Wesley Skinner and Madeline Kerns. Nellie passed away 10 Oct 1966. Both are buried in Walnut Grove Cemetery in Columbus.

They were the parents of: John Owen, my grandfather, 21 Aug 1899 - 17 Mar 1977, married Verna Eulela Weekley; Edith Mabel, 10 Feb 1908 - 22 Nov 1995, married Frank Perry Hudnall; Anna Loretta, living in Oklahoma, married Robert Arthur Decker, plus two or three unnamed infants, all born in Gallia County.

They lived in Green Township until the 1913 flood convinced them to move to Licking County, where they resumed farming. In their retirement years they lived in the Worthington area.

*Submitted by: Sunda Anderson Peters*

**DANIEL SKINNER** - Daniel Skinner, son of Asahel and Phoebe Gould Skinner was born in Corinth, Maine, March 18, 1801 and died in Rutland, Meigs Co., OH, September 13, 1844. He is buried in Miles Cemetery beside his father.

*Daniel Webster And Margaret Northup Skinner*

Daniel moved with his family to Rutland, Gallia County, OH in 1817. According to a letter written by Asahel Skinner to his own father, Phoebe died shortly after their arrival in Rutland. Asahel then married Jane Everton.

Daniel married Nancy Wynn November 10,1825. After her death, he married Hannah M. Tyler, October 10, 1836 in Gallia County, Ohio. Hannah was born in 1818 in Maine and died October 10, 1878 in Gallia County, Ohio. Hannah died in the Yellow Fever epidemic that also took the life of her son, John Wesley. Yellow fever was brought to the area on the steamer John S. Porter from New Orleans. It was tied up and deserted by its crew because of the epidemic.

Daniel and Hannah had four sons, Daniel Webster, George Washington, Henry Clay, and John Wesley. Daniel was a miller in the southeast portion of Rutland. He was also the constable one-year and a township trustee for seven years.

Daniel and Hannah's son, Daniel Webster was born July 15, 1837 in Rutland. He married Margaret Northup on August 18, 1861 in Green Township, OH. Their son, George Emory was born in 1862 in Gallia County, OH. They settled on the Skinner farm in Pliny, Mason County, WV. Their son, Cyrus Melvin was born in 1868 in Ohio. According to a granddaughter of Daniel, Margaret was struck by lightning. Although it did not kill her, it caused brain damage. She lived with the family and they took care of her until her death, June 22,1918. Daniel also died in Pliny, November 6, 1910. Margaret and Daniel Webster are buried in Mt. Union Cemetery, Pliny, Mason County, WV. George Emory Skinner married Augusta Ellen Poston, daughter of William Granville Poston and Mary Louise Oberholzer on January 1, 1885 in Mason County, WV. Augusta was born in 1865 and died in 1938. George died in 1927. Both died near Pliny and are buried in Mt. Union Cemetery. George and Augusta had six children: Ernest Egbert, Grace Gertrude, Minta Maude, Helen Hester, Roy Russell, and Virginia Pearl.

My grandmother was Minta Maude. Maude was born June 15, 1888 in Mason County, WV and died March 7, 1937 of liver cancer in Belle, Kanawha County, WV. She married Clarence Luther Brown at the Skinner farm on October 18, 1916. Clarence was born September 9, 1896 in Belle, and died November 6, 1969 in Charleston, Kanawha County, WV. Minta is buried in Witcher Cemetery and Clarence is buried in Spring Hill Cemetery. They had five children.

Gladys lived —one day.

Clarence Lester was born August 16, 1918, in Kanawha County, WV. He was killed in action at the Anzio Beachhead and declared dead on May 25,1945. He was a member of the Armored Tank Division. His memorial is at the U. S. Overseas Cemetery, Netuno, Italy.

Laura Ellen was born April 21, 1920, Opal Mae was born September 17, 1923 and died October 4, 1999, and Florence Alma was born October 18, 1927 and died November 5, 1991, both in Kanawha County, WV.

*Submitted by: Katherine M. Thomas*

**JOHN WESLEY SKINNER AND MADELINE KERNS** - John Wesley Skinner was born 17 Apr 1844 in Rutland Township, Meigs County, to Daniel Skinner and Hannah M. Tyler, who married 6 Oct 1836. Daniel was the son of Asahel Skinner, b. 1771 Norton, Bristol County, Massachusetts, d. 1851, and Phebe Gould, 7 Oct 1774 -13 Aug 1817, pioneers, who settled in Meigs County in 1817.

*John Wesley Skinner*

Asahel and Phebe left Maine in 1816 because of "the year without a summer, caused by the explosion of a volcano named Mt. Tambora on an island in Indonesia from April to July 1815. The resultant ash cloud reportedly caused snow on July 4 and severe crop failures throughout New England and Europe in the summer of 1816.

On their way to Ohio, the family stayed briefly in Randolph Township, Crawford County, Pennsylvania. It was long enough for the two oldest Skinner daughters, Abi and Hannah, to meet and marry the Waid brothers, William and Warner. They remained in Pennsylvania.

Hannah was the daughter of Dean Tyler, b. 3 Mar 1776 in Scarboro, Cumberland County, Maine, d. Meigs County,1828, and Hannah Dyer b. Maine, d. probably in Meigs County.

When John was six months old, his father passed away. Daniel may have been a shoemaker, as well as a farmer, since the inventory of his items sold at auction included shoemaker's tools and two pounds of sole leather. Hannah bought one bay horse at the auction and probably got to keep the one bay mare that was listed as "not sold." Daniel is buried in Miles Cemetery, Meigs County.

Hannah became the second wife of John Kerns, son of Frederick Kerns and Susannah Syler and brother of Henry. Hannah then moved to Gallia County with her children, Daniel Webster (1837-1910), Henry Clay (1841-1921), and John Wesley Skinner. Hannah and John Kerns had one son, Charles G. Kerns.

John W. married Madeline Kerns, daughter of Henry Kerns and Mary "Polly" Gilbert, on 17 Apr 1867. To John W. and Madeline were born the following children: Viola Belie, 10 Feb 1869 - 24 Jun 1910, married James Martin Watts; Clarence Edward, 3 Sep 1871 - 19 Sep 1957, married Elizabeth Ellen "Nellie" Jenkins (my great grandparents); Mary E., 15 Jul 1875 - 16 Aug 1875; and Cora Augusta, 3 Dec 1877 - ?, married Lewis Hawk and Thomas Evans.

In August 1878, when Clarence Skinner was seven years old, a tragic event occurred in his life. The story is well-known in Gallia County history. A boat named the John Porter, aka Bronze John, pushing a chain of barges from New Orleans to Pittsburgh, brought yellow fever to Gallipolis. A unique monument to the yellow fever victims stands at the center of the southern side of Central Park in Gallipolis. At one time it contained the rocker arm from the John Porter. Among the names listed are those of Clarence's father, John W. Skinner, and his grandmother, Hannah Tyler Skinner Kerns.

*Submitted by: Sunda Anderson Peters*

**SLONE FAMILY** - Shellio and Narie Ethel (Queen) Slone moved to Ohio on Brumfield Road in Harrison Township around 1943, coming from Cabell County, West Virginia. Shellio and Narie were married 5th September 1925 in Catlettsburg, Kentucky (Boyd Co), Shelly born 9th February 1905 was the only child born to Ora Mae (Nida) and Frank Morrell Slone. Narie born 3rd May 1907 in Lincoln Co., W.Va. to James A. and Nancy Melissa (Duty) Queen. Shellio and Narie were the parents of ten children, two sets of twin sons. (1.)James Morrell born 12th October, 1926 Cabell Co., W.Va. married Violia Elizabeth Fillinger, having three children. (2) Jessie Richard born 7th November 1928 Salt Rock, W.Va. married Thelma Saunders, having five children. Their oldest son, Richard Michael injured (broken neck) 8th July 1970 in a swimming accident at Bakers Landing. He passed away 2nd December 1970 at Holzer Hospital. (3) Ella Mae born 13th September 1931 Cabell Co. W.Va. married Ranford "Pete" Cox, having six children. (4) & (5) Twins: Herbert Gale and Shelly Dale born 1st July 1933, Salt Rock, W.Va. Herbert Gale married twice; 1. Charlene Beaver having three sons. 2. Zeffie Loveday. Shelly Dale married Zenia Sanders having one daughter, born four months after his death. He was killed in a two car accident 12th September 1953 in Columbus, Ohio. (6) Pauline Gaye born 16th June 1937 Branchland, W. Va. married Rex H. Unroe having three daughters and adopting one daughter. (7) William Lee born 7th December 1941 Branchland, W. Va. married Faith Ann Hope having one son. Bill was killed in a two car accident 5th December 1975 in Point Pleasant, West Virginia. (8) Jack Wilson born 22nd January 1945 Salt Rock, W. Va. married Mimi Sharon Tarbett having three sons. The youngest, Christopher Wade was killed in a single car accident on Ohio State Route 218, Gallia Co.

*The Slone Family, Shellio and Narie Slone*

August 1988. (9) & (10) Twins; Donald Ray and Ronald Jay born 8th December 1949 in Gallia County, Ohio. Donald Ray married Sheila Kay Forth having two sons. Ronald Jay married twice: 1. Sandra Sue Montgomery having one son. 2. Sheryl (Staton) Fitch. The Slone's had five living generations with the first being Shellio Slone, Ella Mae Cox, Wanda E. Cox, Kimberly Edath and Gearld Lee Cade.

Shellio farmed, worked for the State and County Garages, Harrison Township Trustee, owned and operated Slone's Sunoco Gas Stations in Kanauga and Gallipolis, Ohio. Narie was always a mother and homemaker. caring for and feeding her family. Always children and grandchildren with her, trying to teach them the right way of life. She passed away at home 16th May 1979 on Rocklick Road (Gallia County). Shellio died at Holzer Hospital the 11th October 1988.

**ALEXANDER SMITH, JR.** - Alexander Smith, Jr. is the son of Alexander Smith, Sr. and Isabel Steenbergen Smith. He was born April 1, 1889, one of nine siblings in Gallia County. His parents were farmers, so he grew up with that knowledge. He worked for the Chesapeake and Ohio Railroad as a laborer in the Parson's Yard, Columbus. He worked as a deckhand on the river boats, Gordon C. Green and others. He worked for the Joe Miller Rock Quarry business in Rodney and Keener's Sand and Clay Company, Kerr, Oh.

He served his country as a soldier in world War I in France. He talked about crossing the Atlantic ocean on a boat loaded with soldiers committed to keeping their country safe.

He worked as a laborer in building the Gallipolis Dam. During the depression he worked as a laborer for the WPA and would walk five to six miles to work.

*Alexander "Cap" Smith and Joe Smith*

He built a home for his bride Bessie Ella Gillison (b. 4-12-1899), Fayette County, WV at Kerr, Ohio. This land was once owned by Dave McDaniel.

Seven years after their marriage, the first child was born, February 8, 1931. Her name was Barbara Mae. On February 14, 1934, their second child was born, Hazel Marie.

He was a great story-teller, one that could hold one's attention for hours; which he did often, especially on Sunday afternoons in the summer and around the Warm Morning Heating stove in the winter. He talked of family members and their relationships. He loved people and had many, many friends, both black and white.

His beloved Bessie died at the age of 50 leaving him to raise his two daughters.

In the late 60s, his health failing, he moved to Gallipolis (828 Fourth Avenue) where he lived until he died suddenly July 31, 1969.

His daughter, Hazel never married. Daughter Barbara married Harry Dolphis Scott, January 6, 1965 in Chillicothe, Ohio at the home of their pastor, Reverend L. V. Gause and on December 5, 1972, Alexander Smith's only-grandson ws born - Harreld Christian Scott.

"Uncle Cap" as he was lovingly called left a rich legacy.

*Submitted by Barbara M. Smith Scott*

**SMITH-EDELBLUTE** - In the spring of 1965, two young high school students were working after school at Ruth's Floral on Cedar Street in Gallipolis, Ohio. It was at this location that the two of them arranged their first date. Those two students just happened to be Jeffrey Earl Smith and I.

*L: to R: Jeff and Marsha Smith, Meredith and Nathan Smith, Marie and Eddie Edelblute. Seated Sarah Nicole Smith*

Jeff is the oldest child born to Earl (1929-1983) and Bette Gibson (1930-1993) Smith. He, along with his four siblings, grew up in the

Fairfield community on the "back forty" of his grandparents' farm. This property had been purchased by his grandfather in 1947 from the McCormick family. Earl was born to George Pleas (1894-1973) and Martha McGuire (1900-1963) Smith in Big Creek, West Virginia. He was one of the 17 children born to this union, and he was one of the "Smith brothers" who relocated to Ohio from Kentucky with his parents in 1947. Bette was born in Gallia County to Dallas Roy (1886-1962) and Mollye Hodge (1894-1938) Gibson. She was one of nine children born to this union, and their family home was on the ridge overlooking the Carmichael farm in Green Township. Today, Jeff's three brothers, Gregory George, Ronald Eugene, and Mark Dallas, all live in Gallia County. His only sister, Tameron Lee Smith Hawk, lives in Beavercreek, Ohio. Earl and Bette Smith and Dallas and Mollye Gibson are buried in Mound Hill Cemetery; George and Martha Smith are buried in the Newman Cemetery, Hi-Hat, Kentucky.

I, Marsha Ann Edelblute, was the older of two daughters born to Edwin Gibson (10/11/20) and Marie Elizabeth Meadows (2/7/20) Edelblute. Until the age of 8, my family lived at 33 Portsmouth Road, Gallipolis. At that time we moved to my parents' current residence at 17 Edgemont Drive, Gallipolis. Edwin was born in Ostrander, Ohio, to parents of German heritage, Ellsworth Arthur (1879-1968) and Cora Ann Gibson (1887-1980) Edelblute. They are both buried in Radnor, Ohio. Edwin came to Rio Grande College and there he met a pretty, young cheerleader, Marie Elizabeth Meadows Edelblute—my mother. She was born in Gallipolis, Ohio to Casby (1894-1962) and Opell Wallace (1894-1973) Meadows. Casby and Opell were both born and raised in Ashton, West Virginia. They moved to Ohio in about 1915 and owned and operated Empire Furniture. Casby and Opell are buried in Mound Hill Cemetery. My father worked for Empire until he joined his friend, Bill Matthews, to form the corporation of Matthews and Edelblute, a Gulf Oil distributorship. Mother's teaching career began in the two-room school house which is located just behind Gene Johnson's Chevy dealership. She retired from Washington School after 29 years of teaching. My only sister, Meda Sue Edelblute Harris, currently lives in San Antonio, Texas.

Jeff and I both were born in the old Holzer Hospital and both graduated from Gallia Academy. I graduated from airline training school in Kansas City, Missouri, and pursued a career with the federal government in Cincinnati. While I was there, Jeff began his college career pursuing a bachelor's in business from Ohio University. During spring break of his junior year in college, we were married. The ceremony was held March 21, 1970, in First Baptist Church, Gallipolis. Jeff completed his degree and went on for his master's degree in education, and I worked for the College of Arts and Sciences. After a short stint in the Army, Jeff accepted an invitation for employment at The Ohio Valley Bank Company, and we moved back to the beloved hills of Gallia County. He has been with the bank for thirty years and presently holds the title of President.

Our lives have been doubly blessed with the addition of a son, Jeffrey Nathan Smith, on November 17, 1978, and a daughter, Sarah Nicole Smith, on October 14, 1985. Nathan is a graduate of Ohio Valley Christian School, Gallipolis, and Cedarville University with a bachelor of nursing degree. He married Meredith Ann Gombis (7/21/79), daughter of Dr. Leon and Kathy Gombis of Palos Heights, Illinois, on June 17, 2000. They currently reside in Yellow Springs, Ohio. Sarah is currently a high school student at Ohio Valley Christian School.

Once the children were in school, I returned to school and obtained a degree in Early Childhood at the University of Rio Grande. Today, I am a stay-at-home wife and mother and volunteer as a mentor at Vinton Elementary.

Our family are active members of First Baptist Church, Gallipolis, where Jeff and I both teach Sunday School. In addition, Jeff is a charter member of the board of Ohio Valley Christian School and serves on the University of Rio Grande Board of Trustees.

Today, Jeff and I feel as if we have come full-circle because in 1998 we purchased the Vornholt home on Cedar Street—just next door to the place that we arranged our first date and just across the street from the place of our births. How fortunate we feel that we can be a part of this fine community, and it is our prayer that we can be found faithful to our family, community, church and our Savior—the Lord Jesus Christ!

*Submitted by Marsha E. Smith*

**SMITH-GIBSON** - On September 9, 1948 in Prestonsburg, Kentucky, Earl Smith and Bette Lee Gibson were married. They set up housekeeping on the Smith family farm (formerly the McCormick farm) in the Fairfield Community. The house in which they lived was located on Fairfield Centenary Road.

Earl was born on March 25, 1929, in Big Creek, West Virginia, to George Pleas and Martha McGuire Smith. His family later moved to Hi-Hat, Kentucky, where his dad worked in the mines. There were 17 children born to this union, but only ten lived to adulthood. These included: Hannah Calhoun, Bluford, Earl, Henry J., Delmond, Dorothy Hayes, Frank, Nell Rose Caudill, Harry (Burt), and Bob. On April 4, 1946, the Smiths moved to Gallia County, bought the family farm, and operated the Smith Market and Sunset Inn on old Route 35.

Bette was born on March 21, 1930, in Gallia County, Ohio, to Dallas Roy and Mollye Hodge Gibson. The family lived on the ridge which overlooked the Carmichael Farm in Green Township. There were nine children born to this union, and they are: Jewell Vanco (12/15/09), James Evan (2/24/11-3/7/58), Beulah Mills (10/24/13-2/24/77), Donald (1915-1971), David Ronald (8/12/17-8/93), Emma Lorene (8/22/19), Harold Wayne (5/23/22), Archie Eugene (9/4/26), and Bette. Bette was only eight years of age when her mother died so she lived the majority of her childhood in the home of her oldest sister, Jewell. Dallas was a tobacco and cattle farmer.

While living in the old farmhouse on Fairfield Centenary Road, Earl and Bette's oldest son, Jeffrey Earl (11/13/49) was born. Shortly afterwards, they moved to the back of the Smith Farm and into a house on Fairfield Church Road. They lived at this address for the reminder of their lives. The other children born to them while residing here were: Gregory George (12/6/51), Ronald Eugene (11/23/54), Tameron Lee Smith Hawk (12/18/59), and Mark Dallas (3/9/61). Earl was a truck driver both in this area and in Huntington, West Virginia. He was selling and leasing used trucks at the time of his death on June 23, 1983. He is buried in Mound Hill Cemetery.

Bette was a stay-at-home mother until her youngest left home. At this time, she began working at Holzer Medical Center as a receptionist at the Front Desk. She also worked in the hospital gift shop, and at the time of her death was the secretary for the radiation oncology department at Holzer. She died on August 23, 1993 and is buried in Mound Hill Cemetery.

Today, Bette and Earl have seven grandchildren and one great grandchild. Another grandchild, Amy Noelle, is buried in Memory Gardens, Gallipolis.

*Submitted by Marsha E. Smith*

**GLENN ARCHIE SMITH AND BARBARA GAIL SMITH FAMILY** - Glenn was born November 22, 1935 in Pikeville, Kentucky to Ira and Roma Gladeus Burnett Smith, who were also natives of Pike County, Kentucky. Ira's parents were Charles and Zetta Stratton Smith. His mother's parents were Corbett and Linda Blackburn Burnett. Ira's father, Charles Smith, was born in Cabell County, West Virginia on Twelve Pole Creek. Ira's mother's parents were the Richard Strattons. Charles Smith was orphaned at an early age and was raised by a Smith family. He took the name of Smith.

*Glenn & Gail Smith*

Glenn was educated in Pike County schools, graduating from Pikeville High School in 1953. He attended Indiana Tech in Fort Wayne, Indiana and Pikeville Junior College before earning his Bachelor of Science degree from the University of Kentucky in 1962. He began his engineering career in Gallia County, Ohio with the Ohio Department of Transportation. From 1963 to 1966 he was with the U. S. Army Corps of Engineers at Cape Canaveral, Florida, at Fort Jackson, S. C., and at Fort Stewart, Georgia as Resident Engineer. He returned to Gallia County to the Ohio Dept. Of Transportation and worked in Athens and Hocking Counties. In 1969 he was elected as Gallia County Engineer and served until 1975 when he was appointed by Governor James Rhodes as District Deputy Director of District 10, ODOT, in Marietta, OH.

He served as District Engineer until 1980 when be became Assistant Manager of Buckeye Rural Electric Cooperative. In 1981 he became Manager and served in that capacity until 1991 at which time he was appointed City Manager for the City of Gallipolis. In 1994 Glenn was appointed to fill the unexpired term of the Guernsey County Engineer in Cambridge, OH., returning to Gallia County in 1996 to seek the office of Gallia County Engineer, which he continues to hold.

Gail was born February 12, 1935 in Oak Hill, WV, the daughter of William Ross Burgess and Beatrice Virginia Smith Burgess. Both parents were natives of Oak Hill. Her paternal grandparents were Jacob Patrick Burgess and Ada Mae Brooks Burgess. They came to West Virginia from Bedford, Virginia. Her maternal grandparents were Henry Edward Smith and Emma Katherine Beasley Smith. Henry also came from Bedford, VA.

Gail was educated in Fayette County, WV schools, graduating from Collins High School in Oak Hill in 1953. Her father was with the U.S. Dept. Of Interior, Bureau of Mines, and was transferred to the Pikeville, KY office. Gail attended Pikeville Junior College from 1953 to 1955 where she met Glenn. They were married November 24, 1956. Gail worked at the University of Kentucky Medical Center as a medical secretary while Glenn was an engineering student. She took time out to raise her three children and returned to work in 1977 as secretary to the Superintendent of the Gallipolis City Schools. In 1982 she returned to college to pursue a Bachelor of Science degree in Education. She taught the medical secretarial program at Buckeye Hills Career Center and retired in 1995.

Glenn and Gail are the parents of three children: Glenn David of Dublin, OH; Lisa Michelle of Portsmouth, OH; and Michael Douglas of Gallipolis. Grandchildren are Brittany Nicole Smith, Brianna Marie Smith, Brandon Michael Smith, Lauren Elizabeth Coriell and Evan Francis Coriell.

**GAIL AND GARREN SNYDER FAMILY -** Gail Clinton Snyder and Garren Lianne Luster were both born in Zanesville, Ohio, Muskingum County. Gail was born to Clinton and Hazel (Garrett) Snyder on March 27, 1945. Garren was born on September 20, 1945 to Teddy and Garnet (Ihinger) Luster. The Snyders were Maysville High School sweethearts and were married in the South Zanesville Methodist Church on June 6, 1965. Their first child Gina Lynn Snyder was born August 18, 1967.

*Gail Snyder Family*

Her brother Graydon Clinton Snyder was also born in Zanesville, on September 22, 1974.

Little sister Gwenda Leann Snyder, was born May 17, 1984 at Holzer Hospital here in Gallia County. All three children were graduates of Gallia County high schools. Grady, like his mother, is a graduate of Ohio University, Athens, Ohio. Red hair is a family trait and grandson, Carson Gail Hodge, born September 15, 2000 has his share of red curls.

Gail worked for the AEP Power Plant in Philo, Ohio. After it closed, the family relocated to Gallia County in 1976 where Gail was employed by Southern Ohio Coal Company for twenty-five years until the Meigs Mines closed. Both Gail and Garren had grandfathers who mined coal in the early 1900's. Garren began teaching elementary school at age nineteen in Zanesville, and continued in Gallia County at Bidwell-Porter and Addaville Elementaries. She retired after thirty-two years but continued as a substitute teacher for several more years.

Gail and Garren both enjoy golfing at Cliffside. The family attends Grace United Methodist Church where Garren sings in the choir.

**ROBERT SPENCER FAMILY -** Robert (Bob), the third of nine children born to Lee and Nannie Spencer, moved from Johnson County, Kentucky, to Gallia County in 1949. Shortly thereafter, he was drafted into the Army and served in the Korean Conflict from 1950-1952. Bob had just been discharged when he met Joy Saunders. The sixth of eight children born to Heber and Ruby Saunders. Joy was born and raised in Gallia County. During their courtship, Bob began attending Mayo State Vocational School in Paintsville, Kentucky, studying to be an electrician, while Joy continued working as a bookkeeper at the Gallia County Farm Bureau. They married in 1954. About a year later, they moved to Van Lear, Kentucky, just a short distance from Paintsville. After Bob received his diploma in 1956, they moved back to Gallipolis. Bob worked at Gallipolis State Institute (now the Gallipolis Developmental Center—"GDC," for short) as an attendant until an opening became available in the Electrical Department in 1968. He retired as the Electrician Foreman in 1991 after 34 years at GDC. Joy has been employed by the Gallipolis City Schools for the past 21 years. She started at Washington Elementary School, moved to Clay Elementary School, and currently works as a teacher's aide at Green Elementary School.

*The Robert & Joy Spencer Family*

Bob and Joy have four children. Carla, the oldest child, is a teacher in the Gallia County School System. She is married to Robert (Bob) Willey, a professor and the Track and Cross-Country Coach at University of Rio Grande. They reside in Gallipolis with their daughters Kelsey, Kali, and Kacie. Melinda, the second-oldest child, received her PhD from University of Michigan in 1997. She has been employed by Northwestern University for almost six years; however, she recently accepted a position as the Senior Advisor for Planning and Policy Development for the University System of New Hampshire. Joel, the third-oldest child, lives in Columbus, Ohio, where he is employed by DSCC as an Inventory Management Specialist. Jeremy, the youngest child, resides in Gallipolis and is employed by Gavin Power Plant, where he works in the Operations Department.

When Bob and Joy returned to Gallipolis from Kentucky, they lived in a two-room apartment on Second Avenue. A short time later, they bought a small house on State Route 7, where they lived for almost 12 years. In 1968, they moved into a new house on State Route 218, where they lived for nearly 33 years. They recently moved to 661 Second Avenue, just across the street from the two-room apartment that they lived in over 45 years ago. Bob and Joy attend Faith Baptist Church. They feel that God has richly blessed them and their family.

**HERMAN SPRAGUE FAMILY -** Herman is the fourth generation of the Sprague Family in Gallia County. James Sprague was born in Sydney, Maine in 1806. He moved to Gallia County with his family in 1812 and was one of the earliest settlers in Gallipolis Township. James married Jane Mossman in October, 1826. They had one son John E. in 1838. Jane died in March, 1839. In 1859, James married Elizabeth Denney. The marriage produced eight children. One of these children was Charley, who was Herman's grandfather Charley Sprague was born in 1849, near Evergreen in Springfield Township. He married Catherine Levisay in 1888. They had six children. Their son Harry was born March 29, 1890. Harry married Alice Reiter in June, 1933. She was born in White Sulpher Springs, WV. Alice and Harry had two children. Herman was born on May 15, 1938 and Roy was born on May 8, 1941.

*Herman and Allena Sprague, June 2001*

Herman married Allena Hoffman in June, 1967. From this union Stephanie, Matthew and Heather were born into the fifth generation of Spragues in Gallia County. Herman and Allena live on the same farm Harry Sprague, Herman's father, bought in 1930. Herman graduated 1956 from Bidwell-Porter High School and retired from Bidwell-Porter after teaching thirty-four years. He was a graduate of Rio Grande College in 1960.

Allena Sprague was born in Charleston, WV to Carney and Louise (Rollins) Hoffman. She moved to Gallia County in 1956. She graduated from Gallia Academy High School in 1967, from Rio Grande College in 1983 and from Dayton University with a Master's degree in 1986. Allena is presently teaching at Gallia Academy.

Matthew Sprague, having been raised on the farm, continues the Sprague Family tradition of farming. He has taken over operation of the farm since his father retired. Matthew married Mona Steele of Spencer, WV in April, 2001. Matthew is a supervisor/dispatcher of Roadway Trucking and Mona is a child psychologist in the Jackson County School System in West Virginia as a therapist. They look forward to building a home on the farm.

Stephanie married Shawn Howard in September, 1996. They live in Dickson, TN. Both of them work at Vanderbilt Hospital in Nashville. She is a nurse supervisor while Shawn is in management.

Heather married Jerry Priddy on May 29, 1993. Jerry was born in Racine, Oh. Heather teaches in the Gallia County Local School System. Jerry works presently at the Gavin Power Plant, Cheshire, OH, in construction. They are planning on building a home as well on part of the Sprague Farm.

Herman and Allena look forward to their future in Gallia County and the joy of being parents and grandparents.

*Submitted by Herman and Allena Sprague*

**MARIAH STEENBERGEN** - Mariah Steenbergen was the wife of Miles Steenbergen. She and her husband's last names are not certain, because they were slaves on the John William Steenbergen Plantation, Gallipolis Ferry, WV. It was also known as the Poplar Grove Farm in Mason Co., VA in the mid 1800s.

*Mariah Steenbergen*

Miles, Mariah and their children were set free and were told to cross the Ohio River and go as far away from its banks as possible. They settled in an area known today as Buck Ridge on the Springfield - Green Township line.

They brought their seven children along also. 1. Matthew, b. May 8, 1869, 2. Henry, b. August 5, 1849, 3. Elizabeth (Lizzie), b. May 29, 1850, 4. William, b. October 9, 1851, 5. George, b. April 23, 1853, 6. Isabel (Belle), b. August 27, 1856 and 7. Abraham, b. April 29, 1862.

Mariah and family were among the slaves who lived on this plantation and later her husband and sons went back in the summer months to work for the Steenbergens.

Matthew Steenbergen died September 8, 1924, age 53 years. He is buried in Springfield, Ohio. George W. Steenbergen married Minnie Garner and they were the parents of three children, Arthur, Henrietta and Lillian. George died November 8, 1922 at age 53 in Gallipolis. Abraham died June 17, 1923 at age 56 in Gallipolis Township, cause of death, - chronic parenchymatons. William married Fanny Wilson, January 31, 1887 by John J. Thomas, Probate Judge. Date of death unknown. Elizabeth (Lizzie) married Willis Williams October 10, 1867 by Justice of Peace William Waddell. Her second marriage was to George Garner. Isabel married Alexander Smith, son of Joseph and Mary Agnes Wilson Smith. They were parents of George Wilbur, married Florence Lewis, Mary Elizabeth, married Ben Coyer 1st husband and 2nd husband David Tink McDaniel. She had two daughters - Iona, who married Miles Hackley and Edna who married Zeb Howard. Their daughter Pearl married Lewis Green, St. They had William who married Ruby Keels, Louis married Marcella Harris; Alfred married_____, Charles married Maxine Smith; Franklin married Esther King Morgan; Louise married William Penick, Mildred married Howard Lee and several children died as infants. Robert (Bob) married Clara Ann Johnson - no children.

Mariah married Reverend Edward Howell. They had four children - Thomas (Tommy) married Frances and had one daughter Diane, Edward married Mildred Smith and had a son Tommy, Ella and Martha Catherine never married.

Gordon married Bessie Viney Figgins - no children.

Joseph (Joe B.) and Barbara Ellen never married.

Alexander Jr. married Bessie Gillison and had two daughters, Hazel b. February 14, 1934 and Barbara Mae, born February 8, 1931. She married Harry D. Scott. They had one son - Harreld Christian, born December 5, 1972.

*Submitted by Barbara M. Smith Scott*

**BEULAH (WOOD) STONE FAMILY -** My husband, Orville Stone and I moved from Kanawha County, West Virginia to Gallia County, Ohio in the summer of 1971. We have lived in Kanauga, for 31 years.

Orville is now deceased and I am at the age of 93, still living in the home we had built in 1988. Orville passed away on November 8, 1994, after 64 years together. We enjoyed many holidays, birthdays, and anniversaries together.

Orville worked for the railroad on section, which was laying, and checking the tracks. Sometimes there would be a trolley car he could ride. If not he would walk from Kayford, West Virginia to Cabin Creek, West Virginia, which was a total of 15 miles, more or less. He then quit the railroad work and became a coal miner, in 1936, After working in the mines for 32 years he took an early retirement in 1968, because of a sequence of accidents.

We had nine children but only seven are living today. Edward (Ed) married Iona Miller. They have five daughters and two sons of Iona's. Jewel (Sissy) married Harry (Bud) Eddy. Bud now deceased. They had two sons and two daughters.

Her son Steve is now passed away. Elizabeth (Libby) married James (Jim) Mitchell. Jim has now passed away. They had two daughters and one son. Ronnie (Ron) married Marilyn (Knight) (Dear). They have two girls of Marilyn's. Gary married Maxine (Meade) (Howard). They have two sons and one daughter together and three daughters of Maxine's. Gail married Leonard White, but are now divorced. They have two daughters and one son. One of the girls and the boy are twins. Naomi (Footsie) married Charles (Sonny) DeBoard, but are now divorced. They have two daughters. Larry married Darlene Lott and left one daughter behind when they both passed away. Donald Lee passed away at the ripe age of 13 in 1944 and never married.

*Beulah Stone*

I have never worked outside the home. Nor have I ever driven a car or ever lived alone. I traveled by air for the first time at the age of 92, going from Columbus, Ohio to Orlando, Florida on July 1, 2000. In August of 2000 I flew from Columbus, Ohio to El Paso Texas. I enjoyed flying. I also enjoy watching my family work with the computers and have put my old photographs on the Internet. I enjoy looking at them.

I was born June 23, 1908 and have outlived all of my family members, except a younger brother Eldion (Dude) Wood. I have lived a nice, enjoyable life and I thank God everyday for all the blessings in my life and my good health at the age of 93.

I hope this information and History Book will some day bring merriment to the future generations. I am trying to make as many happy memories for the family as I can so, I can leave them with the best gift possible. Hopefully they will all enjoy reading this book as much as I enjoyed living and writing this brief summary.

As of today, March 16, 2002, I have lost other than Orville, who was my best friend, 2 sons, 1 grandson, and 1 great granddaughter. I have 15 grand children, 12 step grand children, 13 great grand children, 8 step great grand children, 8 great great grand children, and 8 step great great grandchildren.

Any more information the family wants can be found in the Elijah and Louie Wood family in this book.

*Submitted by: Beulah W. Stone*

**ED, RON, AND GARY STONE -** We are the sons of Beulah and the late Orville Stone. Our mom lives in Gallipolis, Ohio in Gallia County. Two of us have moved from Gallia County to Columbus, Ohio, in Franklin County and the other one to Orlando, Florida. We were born and raised in Ohley, Eskdate, Wharton, and Dorothy in West Virginia.

We had a nice childhood. There were nine children. We have two brothers deceased: Donald Lee, the oldest, and Larry Ray, the youngest. We never knew Donald because he died so young, but Larry sure left his mark in our lives. We have four sisters: Jewel Eddy, Libby Mitchell, Gail White, and Naomi DeBoard.

Our dad was the only son of Charles Lewis and Elizabeth (Cressy) Stone. Dad's sisters were Myrtle Jackson, Marvel Bass, which was his twin, and Bea Nole. There were three half sisters: Clara (Stevens) Martin, Ruth (Stone), Wadell Nunley, and Kathleen (Stone) Willis Estep. There were also two half brothers: Ed Stevens and Philip Stone. Dad's family has all passed away. Myrtle, the oldest, was the last to pass away. She died 2 days after dad. Dad passed away on November 8, 1994. Myrtle passed away on the 10th., which was the day of dad's viewing.

Our mom's maiden name is Wood. She is the daughter of the late Elijah and Louie (Ellison) Wood. Her sisters were: Virgie Rogers, Thelma Kirkpatrick, and Garnet Wood, who never married. Her brothers: Dana, Carmel, and Eldion (Dude) Wood.

Mom will be 94 years old on June 23, 2002. She has out lived all of her family except her younger brother Dude. Mom also has a story in this book and she put a tape and letter of her life in the time capsule in January of 2000, which is to be opened in the year of 2050. She was 92 years old at the time. The time capsule was buried on January 15, 2000 at Krodel Park in Point Pleasant, West Virginia. We hope some family members will be around at that time, to get her letter and tape, so many of mom's grand children will be gone or so old at that time. There were five families who also put letters and tapes in the capsule.

We each have our own memories of being the sons of a coal miner, living in coalfield camps. The coal burning heat, someone would bank the fires to burn at night, usually dad. No one wanted the fire to burn out especially on those cold, winter nights. And like our sisters, we're proud to have had a coal miner as a father. We sort of hope that one day there will be a song written about a coal miner's son (excuse the pun.)

Our memories of the company store, the money was called script. We could use script for the movies or anything else at the company store. Instead of our parents giving us money, we would go to the store and draw script. If there was a great deal of script used mom would have to write a note. All script was drawn from dad's paycheck. The miner's paychecks looked somewhat different than other paychecks. We don't know why it was called script. We're not sure that any coal miners have to use script today. Only the children of a coal miner know what we mean.

The coal miners would go on strike and the whole coal camp would eat pinto beans and potatoes because that was the cheapest food. Sometimes we had no meat, however, if we were lucky, we would have cornbread. All of us children to this day like our beans; we call it a coal miner's meal.

Some families were lucky and got a new TV when they first came out. Most of the time there would be from 30 to 50 families in a camp. The families who didn't have a TV would gather at the homes of those whom did. In the summer their homes would be so crowed they would open the windows so everyone outside could see the black and white TV. Those were the days.

We remember our first TV, in the middle of the 1950's. The antenna was taken to the top of the mountain and put up. There was always someone walking the mountain to check for fallen trees or tree limbs. There were so many things that could've fallen on top of the antenna wire. We always knew when something went wrong on the mountain because sometimes we would only get to see half of the movies or game shows. When that happened it was usually snow or something of that nature. We were so thankful when dad decided to put the antenna in the yard, it was so much easier just to step outside and turn it.

The smallest children in the family would get to eat what was left out of dad's dinner bucket from work. They always thought it was a treat to get dad's extra food. Mom would always put extras in his dinner bucket just for that reason.

Dad was a smart man considering he was uneducated. We can remember children in the town would pay him 50 cents to cut their hair. And some men would bring their children and grandchildren to the house to let dad give them their first hair cut. He never had any schooling in barbering. By and by, he was an all around good person and a great dad, even though he was rough and tough on our behinds.

I, Ed served in the Korean War and lived a long, single life until I married Iona Miller from Point Pleasant, West Virginia on April 7, 2001. I am the stepfather of her seven children.

We are now both retired and living in Columbus, Ohio.

I, Ron married Marilyn Amys from Michigan. We do a great deal of traveling. I am a self-employed contractor but I am thinking of retiring soon. We too live in Columbus, Ohio.

I, Gary married Maxine (Mead) Howard from Tennessee. We have three children together: one daughter and two sons. We also have three daughters of Maxine's. I was an over-the-road truck driver for years. I am now a supervisor at the Orange County trash dump. I have a great deal of paper work to do. I will be retiring in a few years.

We hope the family will learn and enjoy reading about their family roots. We also hope the future generations enjoy reading our memories.

*Submitted by: Edward (Ed), Ronnie (Ron), and Gary Stone*

**LELA DODRILL STRAUSBAUGH FAMILY** - Lela Dodrill was born on December 12, 1908, the oldest child born to John and Bertha Dodrill. She grew up on the family farm on Dodrill Road in Gallia County, graduating from Vinton High School in 1926.

Lela attended Rio Grande College to study elementary education. The first year after graduating, she taught at Willow Grove, and the next year at Coal Valley. Both schools were one-room schools with all eight grades.

Lela married Donald Strausbaugh, who was also a graduate of Vinton High School. Donald was the son of Issac and Myrtle Guy Strausbaugh. They moved to a farm near Danville in Meigs County, where they raised their two children: Paul and Donna Ruth.

During World War II, in the forties, teachers were needed and Lela taught the first four grades at Salem Center for three years. The following year, she taught the seventh grade at Rutland.

In 1952, the Strausbaughs moved to Columbus, Ohio, where they spent the remainder of their lives. Lela taught the first grade for eighteen years at South Miffin School in Columbus.

Paul's children are Paul Jr. and Darlene. Paul was married to Dorothy Ramey, who passed away October 4, 1997. Paul Jr. married Grace Neff and they had four daughters: Michelle, Selena, Heather, and Scarlett. Presently, Paul has three granddaughters: Maelin, Lexus, and Hunter, all living in Columbus.

Darlene had one daughter, Robin Thompson. Darlene is married to Jim Miller, and they reside in Delaware, Ohio.

Donna had one daughter, Diana. Donna is married to Robert Meredith. Diana is married to Johnny Joyce, and they have two children, Lyndsay and Nicholas. All reside in Columbus, Ohio.

*Submitted by Donna Strausbaugh Meredith*

**GORDON H. SWISHER FAMILY** - Gordon Handley Swisher was born May 27, 1927, son of the late Erman E. and Vesta (Schaffer) Swisher. He is the youngest of three sons, Daniel was born in 1923 and Ura was born in 1914. He was raised on the family farm near Cheshire, Ohio.

On February 18, 1951, he married Sophia Maxine Roberts of Rodney, Ohio. She was the youngest of ten children born to Robert Earl and Callie (Mitchell) Roberts, Jr.

In October of 1951, Gordon had a farming accident and lost his left hand at the wrist. He continued faming until February, 1969, when he and his brother Daniel bought out the John Deere dealership from William Vanco. The Ohio Power Electric Co. had bought their farms to build the Gavin Power Plant at Cheshire. They bought three acres of land on Upper Route 7, above Kanauga and built a new building. They moved the business to this location in February, 1970, where it stayed until 1987, when Gordon and Sophia sold the business to retire and move to Homassasa Springs, Florida. In July, 1958 Gordon and Sophia built a new brick home on Little Kyger Road, just one half mile from where Gordon was raised.

On June 23, 1963, William Keith Swisher was born after twelve years of marriage. Growing up Bill was involved in sports, 4-H, and graduated from Kyger Creek High School in 1981. He went on to attend Rio Grande College and graduated with a Diesel Mechanics Degree in 1984. After graduating high school he enlisted with the Army National Guard, completing his basic training at Fort Benning, Georgia. He served with the Ohio National Guard for 10 years, and has been serving with the West Virginia National Guard for the last 8 years. Bill has achieved the rank of E6. He is employed at Pechiney Rolled Products Ravenswood, West Virginia.

On May 29, 1987, Bill married Carla Jean James of Crown City, Ohio. She was the fourth of five children born to Carl Eugene and Jo Ann (Call) James. Bill and Carla have two children,

Lauren Ashley born February 10, 1991 and Jordan Keith born May 10, 1996. Lauren is a fifth grade student at Kyger Creek Middle School and is active in 4-H, basketball, baton, and flag corp. Jordan is in Preschool at Wee Care Day Care and is active in 4-H and T-ball. They reside in the family home on Little Kyger Road in Cheshire, Ohio.

*Submitted by William Swisher*

**STANLEY VERNON "JACK" SWISHER -** Stanley Vernon "Jack" Swisher was born September 22, 1893 to Vernon Swisher (1855-1939) and Adrian McCarty (1858-1920) in Cheshire, Ohio. Stanley was married to Alma Esther Little on September 16, 1916 in Gallia County, Ohio by Rev. J. Otto Newton.

*Alma (Little) Swisher Ca. 1965*

Alma Esther Little was born February 10, 1894 in Kanawha County, WV to Charles M. Little (1866-1942) and Mary Ann George (1871-1953).

Stanley and Alma had one son, Marvin B. Swisher born November 2, 1919 in Cheshire, Gallia County, Ohio. Marvin died August 21, 1936 from spinal meningitis. Family folklore indicates that Marvin was attending a party and accidentally fell through the porch, believing that the injuries caused the development of the disease. Losing her only child, Alma continued to mother and grandmother the neighbor children, nieces and nephews and eventually great nieces and nephews. Alma was especially close to her nephew, Forrest "Sonny" Elwood Smith, born 10 July, 1933 in Cheshire Twp. Gallia County, Ohio. Sonny was the son of Francis Little, Alma's little sister. Francis became very ill with tuberculosis and eventually died from that terrible disease on April 14, 1947. Sonny and his wife Pat, looked after Alma later in life.

Stanley worked as a machinist helper for the New York Central Railroad. During their marriage, they lived on the main street of Cheshire in two different houses for as long as anyone can remember and both homes still exist. Stanley was a very kind man who liked to smoke a pipe and hunt squirrels. He once cut a hole in the backyard fence so the neighbor's child could visit with them without going near traffic. They were very social people and enjoyed getting the machine out of the garage for a Sunday drive.

Alma kept a beautiful home and was loved by everyone. She was a fantastic cook and everyone remembers her homemade egg noodles. Alma had a beautiful yard that offered much imaginative play. The big back yard behind the Swisher home offered the added adventure of a working "outhouse" for those great nieces and nephews already spoiled by indoor plumbing. Alma's hobbies included growing gladiolas and other beautiful flowers to take to the cemetery. Alma attended the Methodist Church in Cheshire.

Stanley died in 1957 as a result of throat cancer. Alma died January 26, 1977 in Pike County, Ohio of a stroke. Stanley, Alma and their son Marvin all rest now at Gravel Hill Cemetery overlooking their hometown of Cheshire, Ohio.

*Submittd by: Foster Little, Jr.*

**DAVID TAWNEY FAMILY -** My name is David M. Tawney, I was born on September 16, 1944, at 154 First Avenue, Gallipolis, Ohio, to Luther Maxwell Tawney, son of Floyd M. Tawney and Luella Sinnett Tawney, and Mabel McBride Tawney, daughter of Willis Carlton McBride and Lottie Jane White McBride. I have three sisters, Betsy of Henderson, W.Va., Becky of Gallipolis, and Nancy of Gallipolis.

*David Tawney and Grandchildren*

I have spent my entire life in Gallia County. I attended Washington Elementary School, graduated from Gallia Academy High School in 1962, and graduated from Rio Grande College with a Bachelor of Science in Elementary Education in 1967.

I attended Winona School of Professional Photography, Winona, Indiana in 1967.

I taught in the Hannan Trace Elementary School from 1966-1969 and in the Mason County School System from 1969-1971, I became a business partner with my father in 1971.

Some of my achievements are Eagle Scout (Troop 200) two palms — 1960. I attended the 1957 Jamboree in Valley Forge, Pennsylvania, where we camped out for one week and spent another week in Washington, D.C. I attended the 1960 Boy Scout Jamboree in Colorado Springs, Colorado.

I was very fortunate to have visited 10 European countries with my father, Max, in 1958. We attended the 1958 World's Fair in Brussels, Belgium. We visited England, Holland, Ireland, France, Spain, Italy, Switzerland, Austria and Canada.

While in Gallia Academy High School, I participated in four years of track, three years of basketball and two years of football.

At Rio Grande College I was a member of the Archon Fraternity and am now a charter member of the Rio Grande College "R" Booster Club.

On July 19, 1964, I married the former Sharon Grose who was born and raised in Charleston, W.Va. Sharon's father was Robert E. Grose (deceased), and her mother is Nancy Hawkins Grose Stewart. Nancy is married to Troy Gene Stewart. They live in Gallipolis. Sharon's paternal grandparents are Anna Grose Hern and Paul E. Grose. Her maternal grandparents are Goldie and Homer Harkins. We divorced in 1986.

We have two sons Tim, born January 26, 1965 and Chris, born October 2, 1969.

Both attended Washington Elementary Grade School. Tim graduated from Gallia Academy High School in 1983 and the Ohio State University with a BS in Social Work in 1990 and is currently employed at the Gallipolis Developmental Center.

Tim married the former Lisa Whaley in 1990. They have two sons Cory David, born December 14, 1990 and Coby Aaron, born October 13, 1993. They both attend Washington Elementary School. Chris graduated from Gallia Academy High School in 1988 and from the Ohio State University in 1992 with a BA degree in Criminology and Criminal Justice. He received a paralegal certificate from Capital University Law School's Paralegal program in 1995 and is now currently attending Capital University Law School. Chris is employed by Compensation Consultants in Dublin, Ohio. Chris married the former Jill Goddard in 1998. They have two children Ashley Nicole, born July 26, 1997 and Chase Austin, born January 14, 2001. Jill works at Riverside Hospital in Columbus, Ohio and is attending Columbus State University pursuing a Nursing Degree. Chris and his family live in Powell, Ohio. Some organizations I belong to are Gallipolis Masonic Lodge, Scottish Rite, Elks, Moose, Ohio Gun Collectors Association, Chamber of Commerce, Member of B.S.A., The-State Area Council, Executive Board of Retail Merchants, Professional Photographers of America and Ohio, Gallia County Gun Club, Point Pleasant Gun Club, National Rifle Association, Gallia County Conservation Club, Gallipolis Lions Club and I am a Kentucky Colonel.

In 1971, I became a partner in Tawney's Studio and Jewelers, which my father has owned and operated since 1933.

I am a great lover of the out doors and sport hunting. My hunting expeditions have taken me to Ohio, Pennsylvania, South Dakota, Idaho, Oregon, Wyoming, Colorado, Georgia, New Mexico and Alaska. I have been very fortunate to have visited the vast wilderness of Alaska on three different occasions. Some of my beautiful hunting trophies can be seen in my place of business in Gallipolis.

I played industrial Softball from 1966 to 1990 for Bob Saunders Quaker State Team and the Grace United Methodist Softball Team from 1966 to 1996.

I presently own and operate Tawney Jewelers and Studio in downtown Gallipolis and reside at 77 State Street in Gallipolis.

**FLOYD M. TAWNEY FAMILY -** In September, 1916, as autumn started showing her signs of approaching winter, Floyd Tawney donned his Sunday clothes and walked two miles from his home on Thoroughfare to Clendenin, West Virginia, where he boarded the train for Charleston. From where he took another train to Gallipolis, Ohio.

At that time he was 55 years of age and had fathered eleven children, six of whom were still at home. He said the reason he was moving was to "get out of West Virginia politics", and to enable his children to have a good education. Floyd had been a Deputy Sheriff in Clendenin,

He knew Charles Drake, a West Virginian transplanted to Ohio, who had bought a farm in the Fairfield Community and had endless praise for the "level land" in Ohio. Therefore upon his arrival in Gallipolis, Floyd went to a realtor who took him in his fine buggy to look at various farms for sale.

One property which he considered was the farm bought later by another West Virginian, Troy Gillespie. The farm is beyond Fairfield and on the way back to town, Floyd stopped with the Drakes and spent the night.

As Mr. Drake was taking him back to town the next day, a rain came up and since they were in a wagon, they drove in for shelter at the Charles Kerns farm. Here Floyd learned that the Kerns farm was for sale. He and Mr. Kerns started talking and immediately Floyd knew that this was the place he wanted to live.

The price was $10,000 for the 160 acres of "good laying" land, which cost included the farm machinery, which wasn't too good but better than Floyd had. Also, Mr. Kearns had 19 head of cattle which he offered for an additional $500.

Floyd took an option on the farm and paid $100 down, He had one big problem—he didn't have $10,500, but he had a hill farm in West Virginia. So the day after his return, he sold his farm for $5,000 and was on his way to Ohio.

Floyd was born July 30, 1861 in Giles County, Virginia and was married to Annie Taylor. Mrs. Floyd Tawney died at the birth of her youngest child. To Floyd and Annie were born: Artie, who married Herman Cart; Robert who married Grace Jones; Elmer who married Ollie Summers; Addie Lee who died at age 16; Mary, who married Edwin McCormick; and Annie who married Fleet Summers.

Later, Floyd married Luella Sinnett and to them were born: Alma, who married Asa Milhoan; Earl who married Lucille Powell; William who married Nellie Pell; Ruby who married Robert Jenkins; and Max who married Mabel McBride.

On October 16, 1916, Floyd and Luella, with Artie, Mary, Alma, Earl, Ruby and Max arrived in Gallipolis, at their new home. Willie age 12, had been left back home to take care of the livestock.

After Floyd and his family settled, he returned to West Virginia and he and Willie drove 5 cows, 1 horse, and 1 dog to Charleston to board the Chris Greene which brought them down the Kanawha into the Ohio and Gallipolis.

Two interesting happenings on board the boat—the cows had to be milked morning and night and the milk was given to the deck hands. One of the fellows wanted some extra milk so he just slipped in and milked one of the cows. As the Tawneys were leaving the boat, everyone wanted to shake hands with old Jim (dog). He respected their wishes, except when he reached the one who had done the milking, he refused to give his paw to the guilty one.

Also, as they neared Gallipolis, the captain told Floyd that he'd have to pay fifty cents for every head of livestock unloaded at the city wharf but he said he knew where he could pull in and unload with no cost. So they pulled in at the slip of Bush's Mill at First and Spruce, and Floyd, Willie, and their animals debarked, walked through town and out Chillicothe Pike to their new home.

Floyd Tawney loved the land! And he gave his children an intense love for nature and all growing things. The farm was paid in full in 3 years—one year they raised 525 bushels of wheat, which at that time, during World War 1, was selling for $2.10 a bushel—enough to make a big payment on the farm.

Floyd came down with scarlet fever five years after we moved to Gallipolis. we thought he was going to die. The doctor had given up on him, When you had scarlet fever back then you were not suppose to drink water at all, according to the doctor. Our neighbor George Powell came to see Floyd while he was sick. Floyd told George to draw him a pitcher of water from the well outside. Floyd drank all of the pitcher of water and it saved his life. Floyd recovered and went back to farming.

The Tawneys soon found out that by moving into the Fairfield community they had found as perfect a place could ever be— Fairfield Church was the center and the Christian spirit lived by the people was indeed unusual.

The Tawneys came down with small pox and the neighbors felt that those West Virginians had indeed contaminated their area. As they passed by in their buggies and wagons, they stayed as far on the other side as possible. But one neighbor, Edwin McCormick, brought groceries and ice and left them in the barnyard. There must have been a method in his madness, because he later married Mary, who died at the birth of their daughter, Emma Lou.

On a hot summer day June 23, 1944, as Floyd, almost 83 years old, was hauling in a load of wheat (in the sheaf), one wheel of the wagon dropped into a ditch, threw Floyd off and his horses didn't stop. His neck was broken and he died several hour later, but not until he had given his final instructions as to what was to be done. A mighty oak had fallen—there would never be another Floyd Tawney.

Luella lived on with William and his family at the home until December 7, 1967, when she died of a massive heart attack and died, almost 95 years old. She was a wonderful woman, always kind and thoughtful to others, who managed a big household, found time to do not only the huge demands upon her, but also to make beautiful quilts treasured by her family. She was "the main spoke of the wheel."

After Floyd had sold his farm in Clendenin to a big West Virginia company, and they struck oil. There were 54 oil wells drilled on the land and it was said if Floyd would have kept the land, he would have become the richest man in West Virginia instead he ended up a poor farmer in Ohio.

**MAX TAWNEY** - I started to work at Watt's Studio the day after I graduated from Gallipolis in 1933. My dad wanted me to stay on the Farm and if I did he would give me a ten acre field. I told him I would rather work in a business, I think I could make more money. It hurt me to see my dad having tears running down his cheek, I know he wanted me to stay on the farm. But I had enough of getting up at 5 am milking 4 or 5 cows by hand, taking care of the cattle, horses etc. After the chores were finished I then walked a mile to school. But I am glad my dad taught me to work and make something out of myself and I still get up at 5 a.m. and do something. I can always find something to do.

*Max Tawney*

But I went into the photo business and did very good. One year after I worked and learned how to do photography, Mr. Watts had a heart attack and said to me, I want to sell you the business for $5,000." I had nothing like that. My dad mortgaged his farm and set me up in business at 33 Court Street. I worked day and night taking photos and some days I would take in 70 to 80 rolls of film and work till 12 or 1 o'clock in the morning developing and printing. I had to hire a photographer and I made good money and that was in the 1930's when a dollar was a dollar. I paid my dad off in less than one year.

Then I got married to Mabel McBride and she liked jewelry so much we opened a jewelry store in with the photo store and it did good. I talked her into traveling to foreign countries but she did not like to travel. But I wanted to see the world and I sure did by myself. I have been in 72 foreign countries and what an education it has been to me. I am now 88 and I am thinking about retiring and taking it easy, but I don't think I can. I have to be busy doing something and I always can find something to do. it makes you live longer. My mother lived to be 95 and one of my brothers lived to be 93. I hope I can make it to 96.

**DONALD (DON) MURRAY THALER AND JANICE (JAN) M. FOSTER THALER FAMILY** - Dr. Don and Jan moved to Gallipolis from Buffalo, New York, July 1, 1963, with their son, David John, born August 2, 1961 in Buffalo. Dr. Thaler was born in Niagara Falls, New York in 1930, son of Ida Merklinger Thaler and Clarence David Thaler. He came to Gallia County to join the Holzer Clinic as orthopedic surgeon at Holzer Hospital, located at the corner of First and Cedar Streets. Jan was born in Fremont, Ohio in 1934, daughter of Lola M. Cypher Foster and John William Foster. She met Don at Ohio State University, where they were both students. Jan, a former Professor of Nursing at the University of Buffalo, was recruited immediately by the Holzer School of Nursing as instructor in all nursing subjects to help seniors pass their Boards. Later, she served as curriculum consultant to enable the school to obtain accreditation for the program.

*Donald & Janice Thaler*

Their second child, Kathleen Lynn, was born November 9, 1964. Kathleen resides in New Orleans, LA with husband, Kevin Thompson and daughter Kelsey, born July 4, 1992. They own and operate Evidence Management, LLC. Jennifer Lee Thaler was born September 19, 1967. She is married to Nathaniel S. McCormick, an architect, and they have one child, Madeleine, born March 16, 2000, Jennifer is Executive Director of F.O.R. Kids, Inc., in Norfolk, VA. Son, David, is a general contractor in Gallia County, with expertise in preservation. All three children graduated from Gallia Academy. In April, 1966, the Thalers moved to their current home at 2253 Neighborhood Road. Dr. Thaler's mother moved from Painesville, Ohio in 1970, living next door in the log house they restored. In 1974, Dr. Thaler became partners with his brother Jim, in Thaler Ford Sales, Inc.

Dr. Thaler chaired the Building Committee for the new hospital and clinic on Jackson Pike from 1968-72. Following the move of Holzer Hospital and Holzer Clinic in 1972, Dr. Thaler continued to be active on many of the administrative committees. He chaired the Clinic Executive Committee for several years, was Vice President of the medical staff, President and Treasurer of the Gallia County medical Society and Co-chairman of the Gallipolis Bicentennial Commission in 1990. In 1982, Dr. Thaler left the Clinic to open a private practice at 2881 Jackson Pike. Shortly after the Thalers arrived in Gallipolis, they became active in helping to form an arts group, which became the French Art Colony. They continue to serve the FAC as trustees, patrons and volunteers.

Mrs. Thaler was co-owner and operator, with Peggy Evans, of PJ's, a women's clothing store at 330 Second Avenue, from 1973 to 1987, serving as president and other offices in the Gallipolis Retail Merchants Asso. for eleven years. She was office manager for Dr. Thaler until he retired in 1996. Following this, she became active in historic preservation and chaired the Historic Preservation Review Board for the City of Gallipolis. The Thalers were responsible for saving the Oscars Building on Court Street and the Gillingham Building at Pine and Second. They are currently involved in preserving and upgrading the Lupton Block Building on Second, damaged by fire in August, 2001. Jan has served on the board of the Gallia County Convention and Visitors Bureau since it was established. Mrs. Thaler is Chairperson of the Gallia County Bicentennial Commission. Both Thalers have been active in the Presbyterian Church, (USA) and many other community and state-wide activities.

**D. KEITH THOMAS FAMILY** - David Keith Thomas was born August 18, 1932 in Gallipolis, Ohio to Thomas Albert and Elizabeth Mildred (Jones) Thomas. Keith was raised in Gallipois and graduated from Gallia Academy (1950). He met Phyllis Ann Waters at Ohio Wesleyan University. They both graduated from O.W.U. (1954) and were married September 5, 1954 at the LeRoy Methodist Church in Westfield Center, Ohio.

*Phyllis And D. Keith Thomas*

Phyllis was born November 30, 1931 in Wadsworth, Ohio to William and Dorothy (Chase) Waters. She was raised in Columbus, Ohio and graduated from North High School. Her father was born in Medina County, Ohio. The Waters ancestors came from Yorkshire, England and include surnames of Waters, Woodward, Swigart, Broderick, Calvert and Hartman. Dorothy Chase Waters was born in Meigs County, Ohio. Surnames from this side of the family include Chase, Bing, Skinner, Noble, Burwell and Entsrninger.

The Thomas family lines go back to Cardiganshire, Wales. Keith's great-great grandparents, David J. and Jessdinah (Crane) Thomas immigrated to America in 1837. They settled in Racoon Township, Gallia County with their four children, one of whom was Daniel Thomas. Daniel Thomas married Hannah Roderick. They established their home in Gallia County and called it "Brushy Point." There was a school house by that name nearby. Here they raised their family of ten children, providing for them by farming. Their ninth child, Abraham Luther Thomas was Keith's grandfather. He married Ethel Coral McMillin and they made their home at Cora, Ohio in Gallia County. To this union was born six children, with Thomas Albert being the fourth child.

Keith's grandmother was the daughter of Charles and Elizabeth (Koontz) McMillin. At age fourteen Charles had enlisted as a soldier in the Civil War. His parents were Edward and Laura Holcomb McMillin. Laura's father was Samuel Robert Holcomb, who served as a Colonel in The War of 1812 and was Gallia County sheriff His wife was Sarah Ewing. Samuel Holcomb's parents were Zephaniah (a Revolutionary War soldier) and Tryphene Niles Holcomb. The Holcomb's go back to 1630 in America. Sarah's parents were John and Ann Smith Ewing.

Keith's mother's parents were John E. and Sarah (Jones) Jones of Cora, Gallia County. Both of their grandparents came to Gallia County from Tyn Rhos, Wales in 1838 and 1846. The John E. Jones family is included in the Gallia County Ohio - People in History to 1980 on pages 197 and 198.

After his graduation from college, Keith served as an officer in the United States Air Force. Upon completing his tour of duty, he returned to Gallipolis to enter into business with his father. In 1933 Thomas A. Thomas and Clarence Brumfield opened a clothing store on Second Avenue known as "Brumfield-Thomas." Clarence died in 1946, and in 1958 the store name was changed to "Thomas Clothiers." The business expanded to include "The Hub" in Gallipolis, "Carter's Menswear" in Point Pleasant, West Virginia, and "New York Clothing House" in Pomeroy, Ohio. T. A. Thomas died in 1964 and Keith and his mother remained partners until his retirement in 1995. Mildred is a life-long resident of Gallia County and still lives in the family home on Second Avenue.

Keith and Phyllis live on Halliday Heights in Gallipolis where they raised their three children. David Mark was born November 16, 1955 (in Honolulu, Hawaii), graduated from Gallia Academy and Hocking Tech College, and resides in Gallia County. Kari Lynn was born January 30, 1958 in Gallia County, graduated from Gallia Academy and The Ohio State University. She is married to Eric L. Saunders and they reside in Gallia County with their five sons: Thomas Eric, Justin Keith, William Clint, Benjamin Harold and David Andrew. Stephen Keith Thomas was born in Gallia County on November 9,1960. He graduated from Gallia Academy and Ohio University. He and his wife, Mia, live in Logan, Ohio with their two children Bethany Rebecca Elaine and Nathaniel Stephen Keith.

Keith and Phyllis have always taken an active part in the community and Grace United Methodist Church, and are proud to be Gallia Countians.

**ALEXANDER THOMPSON** - Alexander Thompson, son of Francis S. and Phillipina "Phoebe" (Chappell) was born 22 February 1828 in [Wytheville], Wythe County, Virginia. He married Barbara Lambert daughter of Samuel and Nancy (Johnson) 22 April 1849 at the Evangelical Lutheran Church in Wythe County. Barbara was born 25 December 1835 in Wytheville. Barbara's brother, Andrew Lambert, also came to Gallia County where he died 29 November 1924.

Shortly after the birth of their first child, the couple moved to Gallia County and settled in Green Township (1860 Census). They removed to Guyan Township prior to 1870, settling on a farm near Crown City.

Alexander served in the Civil War (Pvt., Co. A., Reg't OVI, Capt. Cadot's Company), enlisted 15 August 1862 in Gallia County and discharged 10 June 1863 at Camp Dennison.

The couple had nine known children, all but the eldest born in this county:

Mary, born about January 1850 in Wythe County; married John Bright 11 December 1871, died 14 August 1910, buried Campbell Cemetery in Guyan Township, living 1880 Mason County, WV ("John Q. A. Bright").

Lucinda Jane, born September 1853, married Thomas Porter, 5 July 1874 in Crown City; died November 1877, buried Campbell Cemetery.

James M., born 12 October 1855, died 20 January 1867, buried Campbell Cemetery.

Stephen Edward, born about 1856, married Margaret E. Ward, 25 December 1881.

John C., born 12 July 1859, died 20 January 1867, buried Campbell Cemetery.

Phebe Ann, born February 1864, married Lorenzo D. Brumfield, son of B. Franklin and Malinda (Massie), 11 August 1888.

Emma Alice, born 1865, married 1) Albert H. Corbitt, son of Hiram and Rosa (Langford) 2 July 1884; m. 2) as his third wife, Lewis P. Halley, son of James Timothy and Margaret Jane (Wood) 12 January 1900, died 1934, buried Halley-Haskins Cemetery in Guyan Township.

William Thomas, born April 1867, married Minnie Belle Greer, daughter of John W. and Sarah Jane (Peters), 5 May 1889, died 1935; buried Centenary Cemetery in Centenary.

Charles E., born 26 May 1872 in Guyan Township, married May E. Unroe daughter of Jacob A. and Francis Matilda (Thompson), 25 June 1894.

Alexander died of consumption at his home in Guyan Township, 5 July 1894, age 66y-4m-1d and buried at Campbell Cemetery. Barbara (Lambert) Thompson, died 28 February 1925 in Guyan Township and is buried beside her husband.

*Submitted by: Linda Gaylord-Kuhn*

## HAROLD E. AND HANNELORE (LORI) THOMPSON FAMILY

Harold was born October 3, 1936 on the family farm at Eno, Morgan Township, Gallia County, Ohio. He attended the Eno grade school the first four years, then transferred to Bidwell Porter High School where he was graduated in 1954. He had one brother Paul E. who was born February 23, 1926. Their father Alec M. was the only child of Albert Curtis and Alice Arnold Thompson. The parents of Albert were Thomas B. and Melissa King Thompson. Thomas served in two Ohio Units during the Civil War, Co A, 16th. Reg. Ohio National Guard and Co D, 141st Reg. Ohio National Guard. Thomas' parents were Robert and Susan S. who came to Gallia County from Westmoreland County, PA around 1840. They settled in Cheshire Township in what is now known as Thompson Hollow Road.

Harold's Mother, Laura Keeler Thompson was one of five children of Asbury and Genevieve Rife Keller who lived on a farm on Keeler Road in Addison Township, Gallia County, Ohio. Laura's siblings were Emmett Vernon, Gladys, and Sylvia. Asbury's parents were David and Emma Wright Keeler. David served in the Civil War, was wounded, and was a prisioner in Andersonville Prison in Georgia for approximately 14 months.

Harold enlisted in the US Army in October, 1958 and after basic training at Ft Knox, KY, and Military Police training at Ft Gordon, GA, was sent to Heidelberg, Germany where he served until February, 1962. During this time he met his wife Hannelore (Lori) Mackamul who was born in Mannheim, Germany, December 10, 1939, to August and Hildegard Mackamul. Lori came to the United States in September 1961 and worked in Scarsdale, New York, as a nanny. They were married in the Porter Methodist Church June 2, 1962.

Harold began his career in banking in 1962 as a bookkeeper at the Commercial & Savings Bank in Gallipolis. He and his wife Lori moved to Ironton, Ohio in June, 1963, where he served as a loan and collection officer for City Loan & Savings Company. While living in Ironton, two children were born; Michael E. born March 11, 1964 and Sherri D. born June 22, 1966. In June, 1968, the family moved back to Gallipolis, Ohio where Harold was employed by the First National Bank of Gallipolis as a teller and Loan Officer. He advanced to Vice President and after the bank was sold to The Central Trust Company, N.A., he was made President in 1984, a position he held until he retired in September, 1991.

He is a charter member of the Ole Car Club of Gallipolis, a board member of the Gallia County Historical Society, a board member of the Gallia County Council on Aging, and a member of the Gallipolis Lions Club.

Their children Michael E. and Sherri D. reside in Gallia County, with Michael being employed as a communications technician at the University of Rio Grande and Sherri also employed at the University as a secretary.

## JAMES C. THOMPSON

James C. Thompson was the youngest son of Francis S. Thompson and Phillipina "Phoebe" Chappeli of Wythe County, Virginia. Francis was born about 1783 to Andrew and Ann (Nancy) Thompson. An Irish immigrant, Andrew served his new country during the Revolution and by 1810 settled in Wythe County.

Phoebe Chappeli was born 19 May 1796 in Wilkes County, North Carolina. Her twin sister, Dinah, married Anthony Bickel and came to Gallia County by 1818.

Francis Thompson had as many as 14 children (four by his first wife, Anna Catharina Kegley); seven have been identified as children of Phoebe: Johannes, born 3 June 1822 and baptized 4 August at Zion Church in Wytheville; Thomas, born 11 February 1826, who married Rachel White; Alexander, born 22 February 1828, who married Barbara Lambert; Mary, born 1830, who married John M. Wilson; Frances Jane, born April 1837, who married Hiram T. Groseclose; Agnes Mann, born 24 June 1839, who married Luther Enoch Shepard; and James C., the subject of this sketch.

It's not known whether Francis Thompson ever made it to Gallia County. No trace of him has been found after he sold his last parcel of land in Wythe County on 15 August 1855. Phoebe was not seen again until she appeared in the household of her son, James, in 1880 in Green Township.

James Thompson, a blacksmith by trade, was born in Wytheville 26 February 1843 and served his country during the War of the Rebellion (Pvt., Co. A, 91st Regiment O.V.I.). He enlisted 15 August 1862 in Gallia County and was discharged 24 June 1865 in Cumberland, Maryland.

The first wife of James Thompson was Marium Topping, daughter of William Topping, whom he married 28 March 1866 in Gallia County. Marium was born 28 October 1840, died 30 January 1898 and was buried at Calvary Baptist Cemetery in Raccoon Township. She was the mother of James' only two children, Jesse and Walter.

Jesse E. Thompson, born January 1868, married Rosa Z. Watts 10 November 1889. The couple resided in Bidwell, then in Gallipolis until at least 1920. Jesse died 16 May 1952 in Tiffin, Seneca County, Ohio.

Walter W., born 22 June 1874 in Rodney, married Alta Roma Howard daughter of William A. and Martha A. (Tipton) 5 August 1900. They resided in Bidwell in 1910 but removed to Columbus, Ohio, by 1920.

Mary (Stringfellow) Ecker became the second wife of James Thompson on 24 September 1902. She was the daughter of John Stringfellow and Hanna [Speeds] and the widow of Frederick D. Ecker. Mary was born 24 May 1838 in Jackson County, and died 11 August 1921.

James again married on 29 November 1923. His third wife was Mrs. Mary E. (Simpson) Hufford, daughter of Joseph Simpson and Barbra Fysner or Frezeuer, born 7 February 1851 in Bremen, Ohio.

James died 19 March 1924 in Lancaster, Ohio, and was buried at Calvary Baptist Cemetery in Raccoon Township, Gallia County.

*Submitted by: Linda Gaylord-Kuhn*

## THOMAS THOMPSON

Thomas Thompson was a son of Francis S. and Phillipina "Phoebe" (Chappell) Thompson, born 11 February 1826 in Wytheville, Wythe County, Virginia. He married Rachel White, youngest daughter of Gallia County First Family Alfred and Mary (Perry) White, 15 September 1845 in Gallia County. Rachel was born 10 Jul 1823 in Perry Township.

*Rachel (White) Thompson*

Census records indicate the couple had nine children, six of whom have been identified- John R., born 22 February 1850, married Curnelia Jane daughter of John Francis and Sarah Elizabeth (Sowards) Burcham 17 December 1876 in Lawrence County; Charles Simon, born March 1857, married 1) Luella E. _____ (born about 1859 Ohio) say 1877, and 2) Emeline _____ (born 1867 Ohio) between 1883 and 1890; William M., born October 1857, married Missouri Ann _____ (born April 1867 Kentucky) about 1887;

Thomas Abraham, born January 1863, described as divorced in 1910 (wife unknown); Wilson R., born circa 1860, married Mary M. J. Raredon 3 August 1886 in Gallia County; Mary R., born October 1866, married (was his second wife) Robert S. Stout 10 July 1884 in Gallia County.

Thomas was the first of his siblings to arrive in Gallia County but was soon followed by others. Alexander Thompson and wife Barbara Lambert settled in Yoho. Agnes Mann Thompson met and married Luther Enoch Shepard in this county, but removed to Greenup County, Kentucky shortly thereafter. Frances Jane Thompson and husband Hiram T. Groseclose came from Wythe County to Guyan Township by 1865. James C. Thompson and wife Mary E. Simpson settled in Green Township. It's not clear whether their father made it to Gallia County, but their mother certainly did: Phoebe was living in the 1880 household of her youngest son, James, in Green Township.

Thomas Thompson served in the Civil War (Pvt., Co. C, 194th Regiment OH Vol. Inf). He enlisted 14 February 1865 in this county and was discharged 24 October 1 865 in Washington, DC. Although Thomas and Rachel never owned property in Gallia County, he and Rachel lived there many years. Enumerated in Rodney in 1860, they removed to Perry Township before 1 870. By 1 880, they removed to Ironton (Lawrence County).

The southward hound passenger train at Etna station on 30 August 1882 killed Thomas, a laborer on the Iron Railroad. The widow Rachel never remarried but moved from place to place throughout the remainder of her life. She appeared on the 1890 Veteran's Census in Labelle, Lawrence County, but moved to Proctorville later that year. She lived in West Chester, Iowa from 1892 to 1893; with her son, William, in 1900 in Hunnewell, Greenup County, Kentucky; and with her grandson, Oscar L. Thompson, in 1910 in Columbus, Franklin County, Ohio. Rachel died 19 May the following year in Toledo, Lucas County, Ohio. Her death certificate erroneously states she was born in Williamsburg, Pennsylvania, the daughter of Alfred Hoyt and mother unknown. Funeral and other records contained in the widow's pension verify her true identity.

*Submitted by: Linda Gaylord-Kuhn*

**THOMPSON-FORBUS FAMILY** - In 1927, the Von C. Thompson family, consisting of a daughter, Margaret Bess, two sons, Joe Frank and Lonnie Wallace, moved to Alice, Ohio. Von purchased and operated a general store, post office, gasoline pumps and was station master for the B&O railroad. My sister Leah Kathryn was born in 1931 and I came along three years later in 1934.

*Judge Tommy L. and E. Lavona (Forbus) Thompson*

In 1941, Dad sold the store and moved the family to Gallipois. During the war Dad worked at the TNT plant in Point Pleasant. In 1939 Bess married William H. Wilson of Gallipolis. Joe and Lonnie served in the Navy, after which Joe married Eloise Hall of Gallipolis and Lonnie to Jerry Williams of Crown City. Leah married Robert (Smokey) Wion of Dayton in 1951.

I graduated from Gallia Academy HS in 1952, entered the Navy during the Korean Conflict and was honorably discharged in 1955. I attended Rio Grand College for one year. I married E. Lavon Forbus of Point Pleasant in 1956.

Lavon and I moved to Columbus and I entered OSU undergraduate school, receiving a B.A. degree in History in 1959. I immediately entered OSU College of Law and graduated in 1961 with the Juris Doctor degree. My best friend and faithful companion, Lavon, kept the family financially afloat.

I clerked for the Franklin County Prosecutor during law school and become a prosecutor upon graduation. I remained professionally employed in that office for thirteen years, the last five as First Assistant Prosecutor.

Lavon and I birthed four children, Leah Kathryn in 1957, Margaret Lynn in 1958, Mark Vonley in 1963 and Matthew Scott in 1964.

In 1975, I was elected Common Pleas Judge and was re-elected four consecutive six-year terms. During these years, I lectured at symposiums, legal education courses and civic organizations.

I retired from elective office in 1996, but return to the Court several months of the year as a visiting judge. During the winter months, Lavon and I winter in Stuart, FL where my sisters Bess and Leah have residences and Lonnie visits for several weeks.

Our daughter Kathy married Terry Walls of Proctorville, Ohio, who teaches school in southern Ohio. They have two children, Chelsea, a freshman in college and Corey.

Our daughter Lynn married Rusty Bookman of Crooksville. Rusty is Principal of the Meigs schools, where Lynn teaches first grade. Lynn and Rusty both attained MA, plus degrees. They have two boys, Benjamin and Daniel.

Mark V. has been employed since high school in research facilities of Chemlawn/True Green and lives in Layfette, Ga. He married a Georgia peach, Jennifer Matlock, a speech theorist with Layfette Schools. They have two children, Mason and Jenna. Mark has a son, Kaileb Legg.

Matthew S. graduated from Ohio University in communications and married Tina Richards of Urbana, Ohio. Both are employed as supervisors at Honda Motor Company in Marysville, where they live with two children, Morgan and Ethan.

*Submitted by Judge Tommy L. Thompson and E. Lavona (Forbus) Thompson*

**THOMPSON-WILLIAMS -** I, Lonnie Thompson, was born at Vinton, Ohio, July 06,1927 to Cecile (Wallace) and Vonley C. Thompson.

When I was three years of age, we moved to Alice, Ohio, where my parents purchased a grocery store, gasoline station, dry goods store, feed store, railroad depot, and the post office. Our family consisted of three sons and two daughters; Joe, Tommy, Lonnie, Bess, and Leah. The family lived there until I was thirteen and during this period, I attended Vinton Elementary School. My parents sold the store and we moved to Gallipolis, OH where my father went into the insurance business. I attended Gallia Academy High School where I played football, basketball, and baseball. At the age of seventeen, I enlisted in the US Navy for two years; was discharged in 1946 and returned to high school and graduated.

I enrolled at Rio Grande College and attended for one year and was active in all sports. I met and married Virginia Geraldine (Jerry) Williams in 1947. We became the parents of Larry, born in 1948, Lonna Jo, born in 1949, and three years later, 1952, we became the parents of twins, a daughter Theresa and a son Timothy, who died at birth. The three children have made me a grandfather six times and a great-grandfather two times; all boys! I also have two stepchildren, four step-grandchildren, and two step-great grandchildren. I was manager of the Fort Pitt Shoe Store for three years. I then went into the insurance business in 1952 until 1965. 1 went into the construction business as a boilermaker where I remained until retirement in 1989.

My wife died in 1996 of cancer. Three years later I met and married Anne Burcham Belville and became a stepfather to Thomas Lee Belville and Teresa Anne Belville-Marchi.

My hobbies are golfing, fishing and traveling. I built a home in Gallipolis, OH, in 1963, and still live here.

Anne and I have been going to FL every winter for three months, which allows me to play golf twelve months per year. My health is above average for my age; maybe a "tad bit" overweight.

I have been a member of the Elks Club for forty-three years, a life member of the Gallipolis Gun Club, the American Legion, and Veterans of Foreign War. I am a charter member of the Cliffside Golf Club and a member of the Grace Methodist Church.

**THOMPSON/WION FAMILY -** The Von C. Thompson family, two sons and a daughter, Joe, Lonnie, and Bess moved to Alice, Ohio in 1927. I was born in 1931. Our father had a General Store, Post Office, gasoline pumps, and was a station agent for the B&O RR. Tommy was born in 1934.

*Bob "Smokey" & Leah Thompson Wion*

In 1941, Dad sold the store and the family moved to Gallipolis, Oh. Dad started to work at the TNT plant in W.Va. Bess married in 1939. The other children entered school in Gallipolis. Our Mother started teaching school in Gallipolis in 1943.

I graduated from GAHS in 1949 and entered Rio Grande College. After earning a cadet teaching certificate I started teaching second grade at Reynoldsburg, Ohio. I had met the "love of my life", Bob Wion at Rio Grande and April 4, at 4:00, on the 4 yard line of Reynoldsburg football field, we were engaged. Four months later, August 4, at 4:30 we were married at the Presbyterian Church in Gallipolis.

Bob and I moved to Dayton, Ohio. He transferred to The University of Dayton and I taught second grade at Fairborn for two years while Bob earned his BS Degree in ED.

After graduation in 1953, Bob started his coaching career. He was head football, basketball, and baseball coach at Covington HS, a town north of Dayton. I started teaching first grade there. We moved to Barnesville, Ohio in 1958, after five happy years in Covington, Oh.

Our daughter, Kristal was born at Barnesville in 1959, the same summer that I graduated from Rio Grande College. We foster homed a 16 year old boy, Jim Doty, from the Belmont Childrens Home. He became family! After two successful football coaching seasons, we moved to Martins Ferry, Oh.

Bob's Martin Ferry football teams won 33 games in a row. They were featured in LIFE magazine in 1962. Our foster son, Jim, went to Vietnam in 1963. I taught first grade in Martins Ferry and cheered for the teams.

The next move was to West Lafayette, IN. where Bob coached at Howe HS. I taught first grade and went to graduate school at Indiana U. finished my courses and received my MA in 1970.

In 1968, Bob was offered the HS coaching job at Worthington, OH. Bob coached until 1975. Kristal finally went to school in the same place for nine years. She graduated in 1977. I taught first grade. Bob was inducted into the Ohio High School Hall Of Fame in 1983 and has received many coaching awards in his career. We both retired from Worthington Schools in 1984. Kristal graduated from OSU in 1983.

Kristal married Peter Eckhardt in 1990 and our grandchild, Kathryn Leah, was born in 1993. Kristal and Peter are both teachers in Martin Co., Stuart, FL.

Bob and I built a home in Gallipolis in 1990 where we spend our summers and we winter in Stuart, Fl. Near our "kids". Bob enjoys golf in Ohio and Fl. Leah enjoys her flower garden in Ohio and Fl. On August 4, 2001 we celebrated our 50th wedding anniversary.

*Submitted by: Leah Kathryn Thompson Wion*

**JOHN AND EFFIE TROTTER FAMILY -** My name is Ted R. Trotter. My mother and dad are Effie and John Trotter. They reside at Holzer Senior Care Center, Room 126 in Gallipolis, Ohio.

*The Trotters*

John and Effie were born in Gallia County where they spent most of their lives. They grew up in Gallia County, went to school in Gallia County, and lived there the biggest bulk of their lives. After they were married on November 13, 1941, they stayed in Gallia County.

John and Effie attended Rio Grande College where they earned the right to teach school. John taught at Phillips School, Dungannon School and Fink School all one room schools.

John's career as a teacher was interrupted by the Army. In 1942 he entered the Army as a medic. During his stay in the Army, he worked on those soldiers who had been injured and sent to the hospital where John was assigned. He was discharged in 1945. Effie lived with him during most of his Army tenure. During this time, their first child was born in 1944. Her name was Julia. A year after he got out of the Army, their second child was born. Ted was born in 1946.

After John finished college at Ohio University, they both went to Rutland to teach. Shortly after their move to Rutland, they found their way to Gallipolis. Effie taught mostly third grade at Washington Grade School. John taught primarily English at Gallia Academy Junior High School.

When John and Effie left Rutland to come to Gallipolis, they lived at 520 Fourth Avenue. The year was 1950. In 1959, they moved to 645 Fourth Avenue where John and Effie lived until August, 2001. That is when they moved to Holzer Senior Care Center.

John and Effie retired from teaching in 1974 with a combined total of seventy years of teaching. John had thirty-seven years as a teacher and Effie had thirty-three years of experience as a teacher. During their retirement, they traveled to California, Texas, Florida, South Carolina and other places of interest. They enjoyed the time to visit with their grandchildren. Now they enjoy the time they get to be with their great-grandson, Cody.

John and Effie's first child was Julia (Julie) Taylor. She lives in San Clemente, California. She works as an insurance advisor. She has one son, Bundy, who is a skydiver in Hawaii.

Ted lives in Rock Hill, South Carolina. He teaches fifth grade at a private school in Rock Hill. He has twenty-seven years of experience in the teaching field. His wife, Brenda, is a payroll clerk at a temporary hiring agency in Rock Hill.

Ted and Brenda have two children, Melanie Teal and Chris. Melanie is a customer service representative working in Rock Hill. Chris is a contractor building houses in Rock Hill and Charlotte, North Carolina.

Melanie has one child, a son named Cody Teal who is 3 1/2years old.

The Trotter family has rich history beginning with Anne Bailey, Ted's great-great-great-grandmother. She was a heroine during the Revolutionary War. She is buried at Point Pleasant, WV

**MARY TROTTER AND FAMILY -** On November 6, 1924, a little girl was delivered to Virgil and Emily Cordelia Roadarmour Trotter. They named her after her grandmothers and called her Mary Rachel. We lived on Rt. 218 in a white house on a hill behind Bailey Chapel.

My history starts with Richard and Mary Anne Trotter. I find them first close to Staunton, Virginia. At the Augusta Presbyterian Church which is north of Staunton, there is a Trotter buried in the cemetery. Across the road in an older cemetery holds the Bell family, their relativess.

*Mary Trotter*

William married Mary Cooper and had ten children:
1. Phillip, 2. Elizabeth, 3. John, 4. William, 5. Mary, 6. Davis, 7. Sarah, 8. Phebe, 9. Jane Ann, 10. Nancy

Their son William married Rosannah Houck. They had 11 children:
1. Infant Frances, 2. Elizabeth Jane, 3. Mary Ann, 4. Armenia, 5. John, 6. Marion, 7. Nancy, 8. Sarah, 9. Phebe, 10. William, 11. Thomas Morgan

Thomas Morgan Trotter, my grandfather married Luella Elizabeth Hazlett and had three boys.

1. William Clemence, 2. Virgil Albert, 3. Luther Morgan

I started going to the Porter School which was a one room schoolhouse. My cousin Carl (Luther's son) and I started as first-graders. My teachers were Lottie Hively, Elmer Caldwell, and Kermit Price. I attended there until the third grade when we moved to Gallipolis. I graduated from Gallia Academy High School in 1942. The second world war had started and what was the largest class going through, we turned out to be one of the smallest.

In the fall of that year I started in Rio Grande College. Because money was in short supply, I would work 2 or 3 hours a day to earn my way beside carrying a full load of classes. I went winter and summer from 1942, 1943, and 1944. Then I started teaching. I was 19 years old. Also I went the summers of 1946 and 1947 and received my degree B.S. in Elementary Education on May 26, 1948. Mr. Gower, Superintendent of Ross County Schools gave me a job at Londonderry and I taught there three years.

One of my professors at Rio Grande, Mr. A.A. Medved, wrote to me wanting to know some information about Anne Bailey. I had to look up the answers which began my interest in genealogy. I still correspond with him at Christmas-time.

Then I moved to Chillicothe and taught at Mt. Logan, Hopewell, McArthur, Massieville, and Tiffin Schools. From 1974 to 1976 I attended Xavier University and received my Masters Degree in 1977. I retired July 1, 1983 after teaching 39 years.

Through the years I have enjoyed traveling through Maine and the New England States, Boston, New York City, and Philadelphia. When Isabel Boggs, my cousin, lived, we spent together one Christmas in Florida and one in California.

I have been on one cruise through the Caribbean which was very enjoyable. I also took a short trip to Mexico.

Today I spend some of my time volunteering at the Adena Medical Center, doing art work at Senior Center, and singing in the Walnut Street Methodist Church Choir. I have sung in this choir for 55 years, and sang in the Grace Methodist Church Choir in Gallipolis for four years in high school. I have always enjoyed music.

I am also active in the Ross County Retired Teacher's Association where I am Special Advisor to the President, one of my former third grade students Roger Oney.

My mother passed away in 1973, but I still reside at 154 Hirn Street, Chillicothe, Ohio. I am active in the Ross County YMCA. I like to sew, knit, read, and am learning to run a computer.

*Submitted by: Mary Trotter and John Trotter*

## TED AND BRENDA CARROLL TROTTER

**FAMILY** - My name is Ted R. Trotter, My present address is 1206 Christopher Circle, Rock Hill, South Carolina, 29730.

My parents are John and Effie Trotter. John and Effie grew up in Gallia County, where they both lived. John lived off of Route 218 and Effie lived on Macedonia Road in Northup.

John taught school (predominately junior high English) in Gallipolis retiring after 37 years of teaching. Effie taught (predominately 3rd grade) An interesting note about John and Effie: both taught in one-room schools at the beginning of their careers.

Effie's mother and father were Pearl and John White. She had two brothers (Lawrence and Warren) and two sister (Mary and Bertha).

John's mother and father were Emily and Virgil Trotter. He has one sister Mary, a retired school teacher. She lives in Chillicothe, Ohio.

John and Effie attended church at the Chapel Hill Church of Christ in Gallipolis. They attended the Church of Christ in Gallipolis for many years being very active members.

John and Effie Trotter have two children, Julie Taylor and me (Ted Trotter). Julie lives in San Clemente, California. She has one son, Bundy Taylor, who lives in Hawaii.

I married Brenda Carroll from Beech Bottom, WV December 23, 1971. Her dad and mother were Shirley and Lawrence Carroll. Brenda has two sisters (Darlene Colgrove and Lynn Smith). She has two brothers (L. B. and Paul).

Brenda and I have two children (Melanie Teal and Chris). Melanie has a boy named Cody Teal who enjoys talking with his great-grandparents Effie and John Trotter.

*Submitted by Ted Trotter*

## WILLIAM CLEMENCE TROTTER - Anne

Hennis was born in Liverpool, England in 1742. At the age of 19, in 1761, after the death of her parents, she came to America and lived with relatives in Staunton, Va. by the name of Bell. In 1765, she married Richard Trotter, a distinguished frontiersman and a survivor of Braddock's defeat. In 1767, a son William was born. In the year 1774 Dunmore's War began and Richard Trotter enlisted in General Lewis' army and at the battle of Point Pleasant (Va.-W.Va.), which is said to be the first battle of the American Revolution, he was killed on Oct. 10,1774. When Anne heard of her husband's death, she wanted to avenge it. She left her son, Wm. with a neighbor, Mrs. Moses Mann and went to recruiting stations and urged enlistments, etc. She married John Bailey at Lewisburg, in Greenbrier Co., Va./W.Va. on Nov. 3, 1785. He was a frontiersman from the Roanoke River. They went to Fort Lee which was erected in 1788-89 by the Clendenin's, and was on the present site of Charleston, W.Va.

*William Clemence Trotter*

In 1791 a large number of Indians attacked the fort and it was soon discovered that the supply of powder in the magazine at the fort was almost gone. General George Clendenin asked for volunteers to go to Lewisburg, which was 100 miles away, the only place that a much needed supply of powder could be secured. There were no volunteers among the soldiers. Anne yielded to the call and rode her horse "Liverpool". and returned with two horses laden with the powder. She is known as "Mad Anne Bailey". John Bailey died in 1802 & was buried near Charleston. After her husband's death, she went to live with her son William, who married Mary Ann Cooper in 1800 & lived on a Kanawha River Farm above Pt. Pleasant. In 1817, he moved his family and mother to Gallia Co. in Harrison Twp. Later, Anne had a cabin on the Trotter Farm on Big Bullskin Rd. It stood near where Bailey Chapel now stands. She lived there until she died in 1825. Her burial was in the Trotter Cemetery which is located on the hill overlooking the farm where her cabin stood. In 1901 her remains were taken to Tu-Endi-Wei Park in Pt. Pleasant, W.Va. and reinterred.

William and Mary were the parents of ten children, one of which was also named William, William married Rosannah Houck & one of their Sons was Thomas Morgan Trotter, a well known farmer and stock grower in Harrison Twp. On August 26, 1885, he married Luella "Sid" Hazlett. Luella was the daughter of John Lowen "Lone" and Rachel (Lunsford) Hazlett. They had three sons, William Clemence, Virgil and Luther. William Clemence, born in Harrison Twp. on June 02, 1886, was my maternal grandfather.

On May 18, 1918, in Gallia Co., he married Sarah Velvie Wetherholt. To this union one daughter was born on March 03, 1919, in Harrison Twp., Hartie Luella Trotter (named for both of her grandmothers.) On May 04, 1935, In Pomeroy, Ohio, she married Robert Franklin Sheets, youngest child of Alphonso C. and Vesta (Warren) Sheets. To this union one child was born, also in Harrison Twp., on May 10, 1936, Carolyn Cleo Sheets. On May 07, 1955, in Huntington, W. Va., Carolyn married Jack Franklin Valiance, son of Alfred, Sr. and ma (Deer) Valiance.

A few years after his father's death,, William moved from the family farm in Harrison Twp, which had been sold, to Gallipolis where he was employed and later retired from the GSI.

He passed away on December 11, 1965, in Burlington, Lawrence Co., Ohio and is buried in St. Nicholas Cemetery on Friendly Ridge in Clay Twp.

*Submitted by: Carolyn Sheets Valiance*

**TROTTER - WETHERHOLT -** Sarah Velvie (Wetherholt) Trotter was born March 19, 1893 in Ohio Twp., the eldest daughter of the late John William and Hartie Anna E. (Blazer) Wetherholt. Hartie Anna E. is the daughter of Cleopatra (Lowery) and Joseph Jefferson Blazer. John William is the son of Jacob and Sarah (McKean) Wetherholt.

*Sarah Velvie (Wetherholt) Trotter*

Velvie as she was known, worked as clerk in a grocery store at Leaper, Ohio when she was a young lady, after her parents moved from Ohio Twp. to Harrison Twp. She later attended Rio Grande College and stopped for a while to teach school in 1914-15 through 1917-1918 at Pine Grove, Angel, and Friendly Ridge. She later resumed her education at Rio Grande College, graduating with the class of 1928, receiving her diploma in teaching. She resumed her teaching, full time, from 1927-1958 at the following schools: Lincoln, Fairview, Smoky Row, Phillips, Carmel, Smith, Pine Grove, Harrison Rural, Harrison Local, Claylick and Little Bull Skin, from which she retired, teaching a total of thirty-one and one-half years (When she was teaching full time in the yr. of 1927. she took evening and weekend classes to get her credits so that she could graduate with the 1928 class.)

All of her pupils, over the years, had a special place in her heart; some kept in contact via telephone, some young, some after they were grown and married. She looked forward to these calls with great delight. At the funeral home viewing after her death, one of her former students made a comment that "If it hadn't been for her as her teacher, she wouldn't have had the start that she had." She bonded with each pupil, making for happy memories and a close relationship, during school and after her retirement.

She was married on May 18. 1918 to William Clemence Trotter son of Thomas and Luella "Sid" (Hazlett) Trotter. To this union, one daughter, Hartie LueIla, (named after both grandmothers), was born on March 3, 1919 in Harrison Twp. On May 4. 1935, Hartie married Robert Franklin

Sheets, youngest child of Alphonso C. & Vesta (Warren) Sheets. She & Robert had one daughter, Carolyn Cleo, born May 10, 1936 in Harrison Tp. On May 7, 1955, Carolyn married Jack Franklin Vallance, youngest child of Alfred Sr. , & Ina (Deer) Vallance.

She was a member of Providence Baptist Church, where she served as Church Clerk, pianist & Sunday School teacher. During summer vacation from school, she taught piano lessons.

In 1936, she purchased the Claudie McCall farm on Claylick Road at Northup, Ohio. She taught & also farmed, raising cattle & selling milk, etc. She resided here until the mid 1940's, when she sold the farm & moved to Gallipolis, Ohio, where she resided in the Mack Apts. on Third Ave., until she purchased her home at 535 Third Avenue. She resided there until Sept, 1971, when she sold the property to Claude Miller., & moved to Huntington, W. Va. to be near her daughter & family, due to declining health. She resided in Huntington until her death on September 11, 1978. She is buried next to her parents in Providence Cemetery in Clay Twp.

She was a member of the National Retired Teacher's Association & the Ohio Retired Teachers Association. When she moved to Gallipolis, she moved her church membership from Providence Baptist Church to First Baptist Church, where she was active in the Ann Judson Bible Class & other organizations of the church.

She was preceded in death by her parents, an infant brother (Unnamed), brothers, Joseph "Joe" or better known as "Blazer", J. William "Bill",Wetherholt. An infant sister, Goldie. She was survived by three sisters, now deceased at this writing, Winnie Wetherholt, of Gallipolis; Marie (Mrs. Corwin Woofter), who resided & is buried in Boynton Beach, Fla.; & the youngest of the family, Cleopatra "Cleo" (Mrs. Hany Gilpin) of Huntington, W. Va.

*Submitted by: Hartie Trotter Sheets*

**TROWBRIDGE FAMILY** - Enlisting at the outbreak of the Revolutionary War in Captain Thomas Clark's Derby Company, Levi Trowbridge marched to relieve Boston at Lexington alarm and was on duty two days. Family tradition credits him with a later enlistment and says he was taken prisoner with his brother by the British and confined in a prison ship, where both had the smallpox, of which his brother died.

*Esther Evelyn Trowbridge Caldwell at home in California*

After his marriage to Hannah Smith, he settled on a farm in Oxford, Conn. until the spring of 1810 when he immigrated to Washington County, Ohio moving to Athens County, in 1820 and came to Gallia County in 1836 where he remained the rest of his life. He was a prosperous farmer and pursued an active life until shortly before his death. Levi and Hannah had the following children: Jacob, David, Philo, Chauncey, Archibald, Anna, Sarah and Hannah.

Jacob Trowbridge born Dec. 12, 1790, Fairhaven, Vermont, died April 19, 1867, Swan Creek, Gallia County, Ohio was married (1st) Sarah Shepard and (2nd) Mary Boomer. Jacob was a carpenter by trade; came in 1806 to Ohio building a flourmill in Marietta with a Mr. Carver then going to Cincinnati where it is believed he helped build the first mill. He also helped to erect and start the running of the first steam engine used west of the Allegheny Mountains. According to his descendants he enlisted in the War of 1812, angered when taken prisoner at General Hull's surrender of Detroit, Jacob ran his sword into the ground breaking it off at the hilt. He also participated in the battles of Chippewa, Lundy's Lane and New Orleans. After his marriage he settled on a farm in Washington County and engaged in farming until the spring of 1836 when he moved to Swan Creek, Gallia Co where he spent the remainder of his years. Jacob and Sarah Shepard had four children and he had nine children with Mary Boomer.

Ferguson Trowbridge born September 9, 1821 and died December 1, 1862, served in the Black Hawk Indian War, settling in Crown City, Ohio after his marriage to Ruth Crawford. He farmed and was a boatman on the Kanawha, Ohio and Mississippi rivers. During the Civil War, he enlisted in the Army for three years. He served in Company G, 117th Ohio Infantry, which became Company G, 1st Ohio Heavy Artillery under Captain James Monroe Gatewood. During the war, he contacted a fever and trying to reach home died at the home of his uncle, Anselm T. Blake, near Crown City, Ohio. Ferguson and Ruth had the following children: Esther Evelyn, Adelaide, Asa Hiland, Samantha Adella, Zebulon Henry, Imogene, Jefferson Davis, and Alice Selina. During the Civil War there was a fear of Morgan's Raiders passing through the area, Ruth took her children and everything they could get on a wagon and hid in a cave. They stayed there several days until the scare of Morgan's Raiders past.

Ferguson and Ruth's eight child, Esther Evelyn Trowbridge born February 27, 1853 died February 12, 1943, Santa Ana, Ca. married Hugh Wilson Caldwell, All fifteen: John, Etta, Thomas, Alfred, Edith, David, Emma, Ethel, Alta, Bert, Ella, Effie, Myrta, Estelle, Lucy, were born in Gallia County. Etta, Lucy, Myrta, Ella and David moved to California with their parents.

Esther and Hugh's daughter, Emma Rowena born October 25, 1887 died June 5, 1973, Gallia County, Ohio married Perry Clayton Gatewood. Emma and PC had eleven children, Ruth, Helen, Monroe, William, Esther, Rowena, twins Robert and Elizabeth, Nelson, Louise and Lucy.

*Submitted By: Marjorie Gilliam Wood*

**GRADY LEE TWYMAN FAMILY** - Grady Lee Twyman was born June 23, 1920 in Ewington, Ohio to Vesta Versulla Plummer Twyman and Creed Collins Twyman. Grady was the oldest of four children.

His siblings are Beatrice Elizabeth Cremeens, Lloyd Gordon and George Washington.

Grady had one older sister, Dorothy, that died at the age of two.

Grady's grandfather, George W.D. Twyman, came to Gallia County in 1915 to teach school at the Ewington Academy. He later moved to Pike County, where he became a justice of the peace.

On November 30, 1940, Grady married Rebecca Pearl Dodrill in a private ceremony at Russell, Kentucky. They kept their marriage a secret for a few months before they were ready to tell their families that they were wed.

Rebecca "Pearl" was born October 4,1916, at her home on Shepherd's Lane in Gallia County, to John Herbert Dodrill and Bertha Ellen Vance Dodrill. She was welcomed by older siblings, Lela, Delmar, Ethel, and Donald. Pearl's younger siblings, Dwight, Darrell, Evelyn and Wanda Belle soon followed.

Grady and Pearl began their lives together on a farm in Gallia County, moving several times before completing their family. Their children and grandchildren are as follows:

Judy Carolyn, born November 17, 1941, married to Clarence Thompson on October 31, 1959. Their children are: John Edward "Butch", married to Debbie Adams, with two children, Jennifer Danielle and Jody Lee; Rebecca Louise "Becky", married to Charles Reece, with one child, Bristol Charles; and Grady Brett, who likes to work with his hands and collect "things", just like his namesake. They all now reside in central Ohio.

Ronald Lee, born October 5,1948, married Joyce Marie Burger on July 24,1965.

To this union was born, Rodney Lee, who resides with Jesus; Brandon Heath, married to Trenia Minton, with two children, Tyler Heath and Rory Lee, residing in Baton Rouge, Louisiana, and Dama Nichole, married to Brent Schultz, with one child, Kaylee Nichole, residing in Cincinnati, Ohio.

Cathy Lynn, born February 17, 1958, married Stephen Elliott on September 2, 1978. Their children are Bethany Renee and Matthew Stephen, and they all reside in Gallia County.

Grady, along with his sister and brothers, attended grade school at the Ewington Academy building, and then spent their high school years at Vinton High School.

Grady served in the army during World War II, and he traveled to nearly every state in the Union, but he always loved coming home to Gallia County. He served with CCC in Ohio, Oregon, Nevada, and Utah, and helped to develop the Hoover Dam beach area.

The following years found Grady operating a sawmill, running a gas station, farming, and operating a bulldozer, while Pearl was raising the family and working as postmaster for the Ewington Post Office.

Pearl retired in March 1982 after many years of faithful service. She enjoyed serving the Lord and attended the Ewington Church of Christ in Christian Union her entire life. She went to be with her Lord on January 7,1994, after a long illness.

Grady retired from Kokosing in 1982. He cared for Pearl until her death and he later married the former Nancy Slone. For many years she had been a neighbor in the Ewington community.

Grady continues to be a member of the Ewington Church, the American Legion Post 161, the Huntington Grange, and he's a 42-year member of Ohio's Operating Engineer's.

**RONALD LEE TWYMAN AND JOYCE MARIE (BURGER) TWYMAN FAMILY -** Ronald was born October 5,1948 in Gallipolis, Ohio to Grady and Rebecca (Pearl) Dodrill Twyman. Ron was one of three children from this union. He has two sisters, Judy Thompson, married to Clarence, of Pataskala, OH and Cathy Elliott, married to Steve, of Rio Grande, OH. Ron received his Bachelors degree in Education from Rio Grande College (now University of Rio Grande) in June 1972. He earned his Master's Degree in Counseling from the University of Dayton in 1985. After teaching for 13 years, he became a Guidance Counselor at North Gallia High School in 1985. The Gallia County Local Schools became consolidated and North Gallia High School was closed in 1992. Kyger Creek High School was renamed River Valley High School where Ron continues to serve as a Guidance Counselor.

*Ron and Joyce Twyman*

Ron married his high school sweetheart, Joyce Marie Burger on July 24,1965 in Londonderry, Ohio. Joyce Marie (Burger) Twyman was born to Roy Donald Burger and Mary Fern (Rife) Burger on March 12, 1948 in Gallipolis, Ohio. She was one of six children born to Roy and Mary Fern. Her siblings, three sisters and two brothers are:

Carole (Ray) Kemper of Mt. Sterling, OH; Linda (Roger) Deel, Vinton, OH; Patricia (Patrick) Stout, Bidwell, OH; Donald Kris (Amy Hines) Burger, Bidwell, OH and a brother Roger Donald who died at the age of 17 months. Joyce has been employed in the Gallia County Local School District since 1967. She has worked as an educational aide and secretary at the North Gallia High School, and has served as secretary to the superintendent of the Gallia County Local School District since 1980.

Ron and Joyce have two children, Brandon Heath Twyman, born June 27, 1973, and Dama Nichole born January 22, 1976 in Gallipolis, Ohio. They had one son, Rodney Lee, who was taken to heaven two days after his birth on September 7, 1968. Brandon married Trenia Lee Minton on July 2, 1994. They are helping to carry on the Twyman name with the birth of two sons, Tyler Heath, born August 25, 1998, and Rory Lee, born April 23, 2001, both born in Baton Rouge, LA. , where Brandon's family still resides. Brandon earned his Bachelor of Science Degree from Louisiana State University in 1996, majoring in Kinesiology. Their daughter, Dama, married Brent Schultz on August 10, 1996. She obtained her Bachelor of Science Degree in Elementary Education from the University of Rio Grande in 1998. Dama and Brent have a daughter, Kaylee Nichole, born February 3, 2000, in Killeen, TX. Dama and her family now reside in Batavia, OH.

Ron and Joyce have lived in Gallia County most of their lives, except for a few months when Ron attended a technical school in Akron, Ohio. They returned and lived in a mobile home, and later built their home at the same location which is 322 Ewington Road. They are active members of the Ewington Church of Christ in Christian Union which is located next to their home.

*Submitted by: Joyce Twyman*

**KEITH KENT AND HELEN MAE LEVIS TYLER FAMILY -** Keith K. Tyler is the direct descendant of George Tyler, the first settler of Huntington Township, Gallia County, Ohio. George Tyler came from England and migrated to Ohio from Bluefield, Virginia settling on a farm on Big Raccoon Creek.

Keith Tyler married Helen Levis. Their children are Francis Eugene, Jane Ann, Lee Elmer and Janice Faye.

Keith was born near Ewington, Ohio and Helen Mae Levis was born at Wilkesville, Ohio, Vinton County. Keith was a farmer and mechanic. He worked for City of Gallipolis and North Gallia Local School District as a mechanic. For the Gallia County Highway Department until his retirement. Helen was a housewife and retired from the North Gallia High School as a cook.

Francis Tyler married Opal Geer of Wilkesville. They have one child, George Timothy. Francis married Wilma Pearl Martin Mays of Ewington. They have one child, John Henry. Francis is married to Mary Fitch Claypool. They reside in Vinton, Ohio. He worked for the Porter Texaco Filling Station, Porter, Ohio and Central Hardware Store in Gallipolis, Ohio, until retirement.

Jane Ann Tyler married Wyman Denney of Harrisburg, (deceased). She married Everette Shank, of Wilkesville, (deceased). She is married to Don Leo Burns, of Radcliff, Ohio. They reside in Wilkesville, Ohio. Jane Ann worked for the State of Ohio, at the Gallipolis Developmental Center for twenty years with the last eight years as Director of Volunteer Services & Foster Grandparent Program; and for Vinton County, five years as Auditor's Deputy and ten years as Engineer's Deputy.

Lee Tyler married Cora Marie Thorn of Prattville, Alabama. They have two children, Keith Lee H and Miriam Renee. Entered the Air Force following graduation. Then worked for G&J Auto Parts. Moved to Prattville, Alabama. Now resides in Gastonia, NC with his wife Virginia Windon Baylor, formerly of Gallipolis, Ohio. He works for Bowman & Hollis Mfg., Charlotte, NC, as Manager of Purchasing and Machine Shop.

Janice Tyler married Earl Basil Harris, Jr., of Ewington, Ohio. They have two children, Elizabeth Jane and Alan Eugene. Janice lived in St. Albans, WV and worked for an Optometrist. She is married to Walter Ray Wedemeyer, formerly of Gallipolis. They reside in Bidwell, Ohio. She is a Receptionist, employed by Western-Southern Insurance Company, Gallipolis, Ohio. George Timothy Tyler married Anne Langham of Columbus, Ohio. They have two children, Claire Alcie and Sarah Elizabeth. They reside in Granville, Ohio. Tyler graduated from Columbus College of Arts & Design and Ohio State University. He is the Ohio District Representative for United States Cycling Federation.

John Henry Tyler resides in New Albany, Ohio. He graduated from Ohio State University. He works for Tym. Keith Lee Tyler married Catherine Corinne Kenley of Gastonia, NC. They have two children, Justin Keith and Kenley Corinne. They reside in Gastonia, NC. Keith works for Freightliner Company at Mt. Holley, NC, as Off-line Supervisor.

Miriam Renee Tyler married Thomas Freeman of Prattville, Alabama. They have two children, Blake Tyler and Hampton Glenn. Renee works for the State of Alabama, as Social Services Supervisor. They reside in Prattville, Alabama.

Elizabeth Jane Hams married Mike Lawson of Vinton, Ohio. They have two children, Amanda Mae and Emily Michelle. Janey, Amanda and Emily reside in Bidwell, Ohio. Janey works as a Lab Technician for Holzer Medical Center, Gallipolis, Ohio.

Alan Eugene Hams married Debbie Reiser of Gallipolis, Ohio. They have three children, Zachary Todd, Chadwick Alan, and Kayla Renee. They reside in Thomasville, NC. Alan works as a Plant Supervisor for Borden Chemical Company.

**ULDERICH - ULDRICH FAMILY -** On 22 March 1922, Luther Grant Ulderich (1876-1957) and Estella Montgomery (1876-1934) daughter of William Riley Montgomery (1849-1902) and Elizabeth Light (1858-1929) purchased 72 acres in Section 25 of Huntington Township, Gallia County, OH.

*Luther Grant Ulderich and Estella Montgomery*

It took the family one week to travel by horse and wagon from Braxton County, West Virginia to Huntington Township. The family included: Luther; Estella; three of their six children: Ralph (19), Icie Mae (17), Gladys (6); Luther's parents: Henry Mortimer Ulderich (1853-1924) and Catharine Brady Ulderich (1850-1931) daughter of John Brady and Elizabeth Barker.

Luther's sister and brother-in-law, Jane and Roscoe Blaine Poling were in Huntington Township prior to their arrival. Their children were Herman (who was killed in France during WWII), Oleta and Wanda.

Henry, Catharine, Luther, Estella and Gladys are buried at Mt. Tabor Cemetery in Huntington Twp, Gallia County, Ohio.

Henry's parents were Heinrich M. Ulderich (born 1808 Germany - died 19 July 1889 Braxton County, West Virginia and Mary Louisa Sadler (born 1830 Germany - died 1 Jan. 1916 Braxton County, WV) buried: Fairview Cemetery, Braxton County, West Virginia.

Luther and Estella's daughter, Icie had three children born in Huntington Township: Darrell (1926-1976) married Clarice White. Three children: William, June, Larry. Wilda (1929) married Clarence Bickers (1924 - 1986) Four children: Carolyn, Michael, Linda, Terry Lynn (1957-1973).

Buddy Charles (1932) married Arlene Marie Glenn (1936) daughter of Harry and Anna (White) Glenn. Five children: Diane, Renee, Dennis Alan (27 July 1955 Gallia County - 21 December 2000 New Jersey), Ronald Eugene, Gregory Charles, Lynne Kristine.

In September of 1955 Buddy, Arlene, Renee and Dennis moved from Vinton, Ohio to Kettering, Ohio. Buddy was a foreman for Stewart Builders in Dayton, Ohio In 1960 he bought Belmont Marathon Service. He and Arlene sold the business in 1991.

Their son, Dennis married Trudy Griffin, daughter of Warren and Donna (Penrod) Griffin. They had three children: Emily, Dennis Jr, John. Dennis graduated from Wright State School of Medicine, Fairborn, Ohio. He was a resident at Cleveland Clinic. He practiced medicine in New Mexico and Texas. He was married for the second time to Deidre Ann Clarke of Philadelphia, Pennsylvania on 4 January 1998.

Renee graduated from Fairmont East High School in Kettering, Ohio. She attended Miami Jacobs Business College and Dayton Art Institute. She worked as a secretary for York Electric and Frigidaire. In 1979, she started working for General Motors where she is a buyer. During this time, Renee married Nikolas Pullano, son of Peter and Esther (Hansen) Pullano of Sandusky, Ohio. They have two children: Angela Corinne, and Vincent Niklolas. Renee and Nick divorced in 1994. She married John Lamont of Xenia, Ohio in Maui, Hawaii on 11 January 2000.

*Submitted by: Renee Uldrich Lamont*

**DONNA UNDERWOOD FAMILY** - Presently Donna Underwood lives at 1775 Northup Road in the Northup, Ohio area. She has two children. Her son, Gabriel Underwood Stewart was born in Gallipolis and graduated Gallia Academy High School, Class of 1992 and the University of Rio Grande, Class of 1997. While in school, he attained the rank of Eagle Scout with the Boy Scouts and presently works for Oak Hill Banks of Jackson, Ohio. His wife, Tera, is the daughter of Brenda Hobbs Hanson of Patriot and the late Richard Hanson. Tera currently works for the Gallipolis City Schools as a teacher.

Donna's daughter, Hannah Marie Stewart, was born in Gallipolis, graduated from Gallia Academy High School with the Class of 1996. While attending school in the Gallipolis City Schools, she was a cheerleader from grade 5 through 12 and currently works for the firm of Citi Financial in the Columbus area.

**UNDERWOOD FAMILY** - Augustus Campbell (A. C.) Underwood and his wife Merle left the coalfields of Logan County, West Virginia in 1958 in search for a place to settle with his family. After looking at several farms throughout Ohio, they chose Gallia County, Ohio to make their home.

They purchased farmland on Floyd Clark Road, known today as Homewood Drive, in Bidwell. With Merle and A.C. were their two youngest daughters, Betty and Sharon. Their oldest daughter, Virginia (Jenny) her husband Charles Riedel and their two children, followed her parents and moved to Gallia County to start a partnership and run the family farm. Their other daughter, Jacqueline, her husband Russell Greene and two sons, and their only son; Robert (Bobby), his wife Orlena and son choose to stay in Logan County at this time.

Their first business venture was purchasing milking cows and operating a Grade B Dairy. A.C. felt that this was not enough and then decided to purchase a local gas station in the small village called Porter. The gas station was first known as "Porter Texaco Corner". Then before it is closing it became "Porter Exxon". It was a wonderful business venture for the family that made many good and life-long friendships. While the gas station was a full-time business that A.C. and Charles Riedel managed, Robert and his family decided to move to Gallia County and help in the running of the family dairy business.

The gas station, "Porter Texaco Corner" was a gathering place for people of all sorts, from politicians to preachers, sometimes called "The Crossroads of America" because of the variety of daily discussions that took place between the patrons. The old building still stands at the intersection of State Route 554 and Old State Route 160. I am sure if you stood outside and listened you could still hear conversations, laughter, and popping of the pop bottle tops that went on in this building for years and years.

A.C. and Merle's daughter, Betty attended North Gallia High, graduated and married a local young man, Paul Hollingshead. Sharon attended Bidwell-Porter Elementary and then graduated from North Gallia High and married a local young man, Doyle Saunders. They both stayed and raised their children in Gallia County. The family decided after the two younger daughters had married and gone to raise their own families to sell off the dairy business but kept the gas station. In May 1993, "Porter Exxon" finally closed after 35 years of service. A.C., Merle, and Virginia are deceased now but the majority of the family have stayed and made Gallia County their home.

UNDERWOOD FAMILY TREE

Augustus Campbell Underwood (Deceased) - Merle Centers Underwood (Deceased) - Virginia Underwood Riedel (Deceased) - Jacqueline Underwood Greene - Robert Underwood - Betty Underwood Hollingshead - Sharon Underwood Saunders – Virginia - Charles Riedel – Mary - Charles II – Michael – Jacqueline - Russell Greene - Russell II (Deceased) – Ralph - Russell III - Robert Underwood – Orlena – James – Betty - Paul Hollingshead – Sheri - Paul II Sharon - Doyle Saunders - Doyle II (D.J.) - Bobbi Jo.

**HOWARD CURTIS AND IVA MAE (WOODS) VANCE FAMILY -** Howard Curtis Vance was born 25 June 1885 in Morgan Township, Gallia County, Ohio near an area once known as Vancetown. His great grandparents Thomas and Sarah (Colwell?) Vance were among the first settlers of Morgan Township. Thomas and Sarah had at least 10 children, which included Howard's grandfather, George W. and wife Mary Ann (Rowland) Vance. Mary Ann's parents were Samuel and Frances (Thaney) Rowland of Maryland and Pennsylvania respectively. George W. and Mary Ann Vance had at least 8 children among them was Henderson V. Vance, the father of Howard. Henderson V. Vance was married to Rebecca Denney. She was the daughter of Franklin and Demarious (McClaskey) Denney. Howard moved with his parents from Morgan Township, Gallia County to Rutland Township Meigs, County and then returning to Huntington Township, Gallia County where he met and married, Iva Mae Woods.

Iva Mae Woods was born 20 Aug 1897 in Vinton, Huntington Township, Gallia County, Ohio. Her great grandparents William Woods and Rebecca Edminston were among the first settlers of Huntington Township. They came from Greenbrier Virginia. They had at least 9 children including: William Woods Jr., the grandfather of Iva. William Woods Jr.'s wife was Jane Henry. Jane's parents were David and Prudence Henry who came from Pennsylvania. William Woods Jr. and Jane had at least 5 children one of whom was William T. Sherman Woods the father of Iva Mae. William T. Sherman Woods wife and the mother of Iva was Mary Elizabeth Long. Mary Elizabeth was the daughter of Horace and Fanny Jane Prevo (Long).

Howard Curtis Vance and Iva Mae Woods were married 7 June 1919 in Huntington Township they had the following children. Sylvia Lorena born 25 March 1920, Hazel Marie born 22 September 1922, Everett Leo born 19 July 1923 and Verna Grace born 18 March 1929; all born in Huntington Township. Howard and his family moved to Hamden, Ohio in Vinton County sometime around 1937and he died there on the 21st. Of August 1939. He was brought back to Gallia County and was buried next to his parents at the Franklin Cemetery in Huntington Township.

Iva Mae later married Dwight L. Brown the 27 of June 1948. They were married until his death in 1960. Iva Mae went on to live until 19 Feb 1980. After her death she was laid to rest next to her second husband Dwight L. Brown at the Greenlawn Cemetery in Columbus, Ohio.

## JOHN AND SUSANNA VARNEY

John Varney was born April 1, 1819 near Winchester, Ohio. His parents were Jedediah Varney and Hannah Hinds. In 1840 John headed West in a covered wagon to Illinois. When he returned he built a wharf boat at Gallipolis and opened a store in Patriot. In 1843 he married Susanna Rawson. She was the daughter of Captain William Rawson and Mary Ross. She was born December 25, 1823 and died March 9, 1904.

*Sarah Varney Broughman*

John and Susanna moved to Waterloo and built a home there. Their children were Emma, Sarah, Lydia, Charles, Julia, Eleanor, Johnnie and Romie. Later the family moved to Des Moines, Iowa where he bought land and opened a country store.

During the Civil War the family lived in Adamsville. John kept a large country store, farmed, operated a mill on Raccoon Creek, and ran stage coaches to Point Pleasant. His coaches saw heavy use and sometimes he hid his horses in a cave so the soldiers didn't steal them.

Their farm on Raccoon Creek was the site of many get-togethers for swimming and baptizing. John was a jovial and good natured man. Gallipolis was the nearest town and he opened a hotel there. In 1876 shortly after Rio Grande was founded, he had his own brick burned and built a 14-room home in Rio Grande where he lived until his death in 1906 at age 87. This home was then owned by Rio Grande College and called Varney Hall. He would be pleased to know that at this date, it is still standing and is used as a museum.

John was a red-hot Republican and Susanna was just as ardent a Democrat. Their political arguments were friendly but often heated. John wore a big silk hat and carried a gold-headed cane. Susanna was said to be meek and gentle.

Their daughter, Sarah, was born March 8, 1850. In 1871 she married Jacob Broughman, a young farmer from Botetourt County, VA. They lived in Adamsville and Jake worked the Varney farm. Sarah was a cheerful, optimistic and sensible woman. Their children were Frank, Rawson, Susie, Nelle, Charlie, John and Arch. Nelle Broughman married Robert Campbell of Thurman. Their children were Pauline, Ruth, Robin, and Robert Jr. Pauline and Oscar Horstman's daughter is Susan. She and Tom Morgan have three children, Perry, Pete and Kristen. They also have a granddaughter Kelly. Robin's son is Wynn Rollert.

During her older years Sarah spent winters at Dayton Ohio with her daughter, Nelle Broughman Campbell, but she always returned to her own home in Rio Grande in the spring. Sarah died at the age of 95 at the home of her son, Frank and Nina Broughman, in Sistersville, WV. She and Jacob are buried at the cemetery at Calvary Baptist Church near her parents who were two of the first members of the church..

The family all believed Gallia County was "God's Country" and looked forward to visiting often.

*Submitted by: Grace Wilson, John and Susanna's granddaughter. Edited by Susan Morgan, John and Susanna's great great granddaughter*

## NANCY CLARK AND TOMMIE VAUGHN FAMILY

Nancy J. Clark was born to Neal B. and Jean Bates Clark on April 14,1951, in Gallipolis, Ohio. She married Tommie D. Vaughn, son of Tommie T. and Della Vaughn. on June 16, 1974, at the Presbyterian Church, State Street, Gallipolis, Ohio. The marriage was performed at the Presbyterian Church due to the renovation of Grace United Methodist Church brought on by a fire that destroyed the church.

Nancy graduated from Gallia Academy High School with the class of 1969, from Morehead State University in 1973 with a Bachelor of Arts Degree and the University of Dayton in 1985 with a Master's Degree in School Counseling. When Nancy returned to Gallipolis in 1979, she was employed as a teacher in the Gallia County Local Schools and in 1981 she got a position teaching English in the Gallipolis City Schools. She later became one of the guidance counselors at Gallia Academy. She is active in the Grace United Methodist Church chancel and bell choirs and Daughters of the American Revolution. During college at Morehead Nancy marched in the band and was fortunate to march in the Inaugural Parade for President Nixon in Washington D.C. in 1972.

Tommie was born in Martinez, California on May 1,1952, and graduated from Rowan County High School, Morehead, Kentucky with the class of 1970. He enlisted in the United States Air Force in 1972 and was discharged in July, 1979. His tour of duty took him to Texas, North Carolina, Hawaii, and Las Vegas. He graduated from Wayne Community College, Goldsboro, North Carolina and is a Certified Watchmaker, Jeweler, and Gemologist When he returned to Gallipolis he went to work for Neal Clark at Clark's Jewelry Store, Second Avenue until 1991 since that time He has been with Paul Davies Jewelers . He is an active member in all bodies of the Masonic lodge, active in the Grace United Methodist Church chancel choir and the Retail Merchants Association of downtown Gallipolis.

To this union was born one daughter, Christine Elizabeth Vaughn, May 5,1982, at The Ohio State University Hospital in Columbus, Ohio. Christine is an active member of the Grace United Methodist Church, Daughters of the American Revolution and she has one love which is music. In high school, she took piano lessons and loved to play her trumpet. During high school she participated in many musical opportunities, Dance Show Choir, All Ohio State Fair Band in Columbus, Ohio for two years and a trip to Europe with the American Musical Ambassadors. She graduated from Gallia Academy High School in 2000 and attends The Ohio State University in Columbus, Ohio. As a freshman at Ohio State Christine had the honor of being a member of The Ohio State University Marching Band, the music sorority (Tau Beta Sigma) and The University Band She is pursuing her career in the College Nursing.

## VON SCHRILTZ

In 1789 many citizens left their native France. During this event, Louis Victor Von Schriltz and his relatives Jean Louis, and Mathurin, joined a group of French people and prepared to leave for America to escape the reign of terror in France.

*1st Row Children: Von C. Thompson, Carney Thompson, Hopey Thompson. Back Row: Leonidas Thompson, Glenwood Thompson, Lydia Lenore Edmundson Thompson (decendent of Louis Victor Von Schriltz)*

The emigrants had purchased deeds from the Scioto Co. of the Northwest Territory in the United States. They set sail February, 1790 from Harve de Grace, France. The Von Schriltz who came with the French to America obviously had a close relationship, as all their given names were French.

My progenitor, Louis Victor VonSchriltz arrived in Alexandria, Virginia with the French and the widow Margueritte (Palia) Courcelle. On July 5, 1790 they were married. The marriage contract can be found in the Cincinnati Historical Society, "Gallipolis Papers".

Louis Victor interested himself in real estate, as evidenced by deeds found in the recorder's courts of Washington, Adams, and Meigs counties, Ohio. In 1798, Louis Victor VonSchriltz sold his lot #14, "adjacent to the publik place", to Francis Le Clereg for $15.00. In 1800, Louis Victor brought considerable land, "all contiguous to the town of Gallipolis" from P.A. Pithoud for $200.00 and 262 acres in section 28, adjoining the Ministerial Mile Squae from Edward Tupper for $524.00. In 1814, Louis Victor purchased 106 acres lying in Salem Township, then Gallia County, for $119.00 from William Parker.

In 1815, Louis Victor VonSchriltz became one of the founders of "The First Religious Society" in the Township of Gallipolis. The Presbyterian Church was founded as an outgrowth of this Society.

In 1816, L.V. VonSchriltz paid taxes on property in Salem Township, part of Gallia County. It became part of Meigs County in 1819. L.V. and Marie Margueritte and their son, Alexander, with his wife Elizabeth and two daughters settled in Salem Township permanently. Louis Victor gave 3 acres of land there for a schoolhouse and a place of worship as recorded in 1836, Meigs County, Ohio.

Marie Margueritte preceded her husband in death. She is buried in the VonSchriltz Cemetery, Meigs County. Louis Victor died in Salem Township October 26, 1837. He is buried beside his wife in the VonSchriltz Cemetery.

Alexander Lewis Joseph VonSchriltz, the only child of L.V. and Marie Marguerette, was born in Gallipolis March 19, 1791. On February 12, 1811, Gallia County, he was married to Elizabeth Long by J.P.R. Bureau. Alexander volunteered for the War of 1812 and received 40 acres of bounty land for his service.

Alexander and Elizabeth had 9 children, 5 girls and 4 boys. Their daughter, Frances VonSchriltz, born 1817, was my great, great, grandmother. She married William Halliday in 1935.

Their daughter, Elizabeth Halliday, married Matthew Edmundson in 1860. They were my great grandparents. Their daughter, Lydia Lenore Edmundson, born 1866, was my grandmother. She married Leonidas (Lon) Thompson in 1885.

Lon and Lydia's sixth child, Von C. Thompson, born 1900, was my father who spent most of his life in Gallia County.

*Submitted by Leah Thompson Wion*

### VON SCHRILTZ AND TAYLOR FAMILIES

- Flatboats, carrying French 500 passengers, docked at the Gallipolis shores in October 1790. Louis Victor Von Schriltz, my great, great, great, great grandfather was among those weary people who stepped ashore on Gallipolis soil over 210 years ago.

*Flatboats*

The promised "Paradise" was quite different from the picture Playfair had painted while they were still living in France. A fort of crude blockhouses greeted these newcomers along with Indians who were occupying the surrounding wilderness. The Indians were not unfriendly since they assumed the settlers had come from Canada, where the French and Indians were friendly.

During his stay in Gallipolis, Louis Victor Von Schriltz, was listed as one of the founding fathers of the First Religious Society of the township of Gallipolis formed on March 15, 1815.

Daniel Boone would have been a familiar face passing through the area during the 1790's. A mirror hanging in the Our House Museum bad a label on it that said, "Presented to Louis Victor Von Schiltz" by Daniel Boone. The mirror bears a different label today, but during the Founder Days of 1998, the inscription honored my ancestor.

The French 500 left an impressive mark on the village of Gallipolis over two centuries ago, but their influence remains strong today. I am proud to be a resident of the town that my forefathers helped to establish many years ago.

*Submitted by: Pearl Irene Clark*

**PHILLIP WAGONER** - Phillip Wagoner came to Beaver Falls, Pennsylvania from the Rhine River in Germany at the age of 15, where he worked on a Dairy Farm a few years. He married Ellen Caleher. She had worked her way from Ireland on a ship. Her duty was to milk and tend goats that the ship was carrying on the top deck; she was blown overboard three times.

*Phillip and Anne Reynolds Wagoner*

They came from Beaver Falls down the Ohio River on a Flat Boat with their family, household goods, team of horses and a cow, where they purchased a farm on one thousand acres in Greenfield Township, Gallia County. They spent the remainder of their lives in Greenfield Township.

Phillip was around 85 years when he died. He was married twice, and raised the following children by his first wife: Jacob, Phillip, Catherine, James, Adam, and Dan. These children were born in Beaver Falls. His first wife died, then he married Anne Reynolds. Five children were born to them, all in (Greenfield Township, Mary, Anne, John, and twins Franklin and Joseph were drowned in Symnes Creek at the age of ten years.

Marriages: Jacob married Harriet Norman and is buried in the Wagoner Cemetery which is located on the home farm. Phillip married Gusta Neal; both are buried in Chillicothe, Ohio. James was not married; He is buried in Oregon, Catherine married Sam Norman and is buried in Staunton, Va. Adam is buried in Oregon. Dan married Rosalie McDaniel; both are buried in Gallia Baptist Cemetery, Greenfleld Township.

Children: Jacob had the following children, Charles, Fletcher, Anna and Ross. Phillip had Ella and Herchel. Catherine had Gertrude. Dan had Lula, Rose, Lester, Nora Mae, Cozie, Earl, Franklin, Floyd, Fred, Roy and Dan.

Daniel R.Wagoner was the last survivor of Dan Wagoner's family. He was born January 24, 1898, deceased March 26,1992. His wife Mary was born August 10,1899, deceased December 19,1983, was the daughter of John and Dora McGiffen Slagle.

They lived on a farm where they set up housekeeping, in Walnut Township, Gallia County, Ohio. They were typical farmers, raising farm crops, farm animals, gardening and rearing six children: Rosalie Carter, Vernon and John Daniel Wagoner, Marylene Irion, Carolyn Jeffers, and Carma Briggs. They had nine grandchildren and six great grandchildren, one great great grandchild.

Marylene Irion was deceased March 14, 1996. Dan, Mary and Marylene were buried in Gallia Baptist Cemetery, (Greenfield Township, Gallia County, Ohio.

*Submitted originally by Daniel Wagoner Revised by Rosalie Carter*

**WALKER FAMILY** - Samuel Jackson Walker was born February 14, 1850, in Floyd County, Virginia, to Tandy and Catherine Greer Walker. A second son, James Pleasant, followed him on December 5, 1852. Catherine Greer Walker died in childbirth with third son. Tandy later married Octavia Richards who raised Samuel and James along with the children that followed. Tandy joined the Confederate Army and shortly afterwards died at Chimberazoo Hospital in Richmond, Virginia. Civil War records obtained from the National Archives state that he died of lumbago. His family never knew why he did not return from the war.

*Samuel and Elizabeth Walker*

In the spring of 1873 Samuel Jackson left Floyd County with a friend to search for better opportunities. His brother, James Pleasant, also left Floyd County in the early 1870's and raised a family in Indianapolis, Indiana. Samuel and his friend obtained employment for a period of time at Gavley Bridge, West Virginia, where they made barrel staves. During the economic crisis known as the Panic of 1873, they were dismissed and they traveled westward. A stop in Gallipolis told them of employment at Gallia Furnace. On their journey there, they sought shelter at a stagecoach stop at Gage, Gallia County, Ohio, where Sam found employment as a farm hand. Here he met Elizabeth Jones, also employed in the household. Sam and Elizabeth were married May 19, 1875. Sam farmed in Perry Township, Gallia County, on the road now known as Pioneer Trail. He served as a director of Cora School Davis Mill District. Elizabeth was a charter member of Cora Methodist Church. Elizabeth taught Sam to read, and he became an avid reader.

Sam and Elizabeth had nine children. Mary Victoria (1875-1931) married Jonathan Francis Work; they had no children. James Birchard (1877-1965) married Cecilia Evans who died in childbirth. He later married Helen Clark. Jim and Helen had one son, Clyde Birchard Walker. Clyde and his wife, Dawn Dye, and their children lived in Thurman, Ohio.

The third child of Sam and Elizabeth was David Jones Walker (1879-1964). He married Mary Catherine Martin. They lived on Mud Creek near Rodney; they had no children. Rachel Ellen "Nell" (1881-1935) married Luther Lot Phillips. They had two children, Rolla Alton and Elizabeth. The Phillips family lived near Thurman, Ohio.

The fifth child, Virginia Catherine "Kate" (1884-1961) married Harry Claibourne Kent. They had two daughters, Wonga Walker and Mary Bess. Kate and Harry lived at Kerr, Gallia County, Ohio, and later followed their daughters to the state of Oregon. The sixth child was a daughter, Jessie Lee "Jess" (1886-1961). Jess never married. Sam and Elizabeth's seventh child was an infant daughter who died at birth June 26, 1889. A son, Samuel Jackson Tandy "Jack" (1890-1972), followed this loss. Jack married Zelma Phillips and they had six children, Orva Blanche, Etta Lorene, Marcella Ann, Mary Elizabeth, Jackson Tandy, and Karen Linn. Jack and Zelma lived near Cora, Ohio, on present day Pioneer Trail Road. They later moved to Thurman, Raccoon Township, Gallia County. The last child of Sam and Elizabeth was Charles Leonard (1897-1981). He married Margaret Akin Jones, and after her death he married Vivian Canatsay. Leonard had no children. Detailed information about the Walkers can be found in the book *Keeping Up With the Joneses* by Mary Walker Niday available at Bossard Memorial Library.

*Submitted by Cynthia Niday Menzer*

**DENVER A. WALKER AND MARGUERITE (HEREFORD) WALKER FAMILY -** Denver A. Walker was born December 24, 1912, Kanawha County, West Virginia, to William Henry Walker (son of John Walker and Mary Jane Fowler) and Corda Edith Skidmore (daughter of Archibald Solon Skidmore and Louisa Ellen Rayburn). Bill and Corda were married April 20, 1906, in Red House Shoals, Putnam County, West Virginia. Other children born to Bill and Corda were Mercades (died infancy), Alma (married Melvin Hull), Ralph (married Vivian House), Darryl (first married, Esta Steinmetz, second Mary Wojack), Vada Marie (first married Harold Blackhurst, second Charles Kinemond), Francis (married Paul D. Halley), Maxine (first married a Mr. McAtee, second Michael Fudwick), Doris (married James Uebing) and Corda Virginia (never married). Mother Corda Skidmore Walker died in Meigs County, Ohio, from complications of childbirth when daughter Virginia was born. At that time the children were placed in foster homes in the area. Denver and Francis were placed together in Porter, Gallia County, Ohio, with Era and Mamie Denney on their farm State Route 554. It was to this farm that Denver brought his bride in 1940.

Marguerite Hereford was born April 2, 1918, Southside, Mason County, West Virginia, to Virgil Edwin Hereford (son of Robert Eson Hereford and Grace Truman Withers) and Rose Mary Dabney (daughter of Clark C. Dabney and Christina Gard). Virgil and Rose were married November 8, 1903, in Arlee, Mason County, West Virginia. Other children born to them were Dymple Maude (married Marvin Snyder), George Worthy (married Ruth Pratt), Robert William (married Mary Gardt), and Virgil E. (married Pearl Bletner). Marge was a graduate of Holzer Hospital School of Nursing in 1939 and was privileged to work closely with Dr. Charles Holzer, Sr.

Denver and Marge were married September 15, 1940, at Ashland, Kentucky. He continued to farm raising Hereford cattle, was a construction contractor, active in the Republican Party, served as county committeeman, Bidwell-Porter Local School Board, Gallia County Board of Education, County Commissioner, Gallia County Sheriff from 1964 until 1972, and as superintendent of the Gallia County Highway Department until his retirement. Marge made wedding cakes professionally for several years. Their family includes four children, Jack Ronald Walker and wife Lois McClurg, Mary Carol and husband Hank Thompson, Roselee Walker, and Roger Walker and grandsons Jonathan Roland and Jeffrey Ryan Walker (sons of Jack and Lois).

*Denver A. Walker, Marguerite (Hereford) Walker Celebrating Their 50th Wedding Anniversary*

Denver A. Walker died March 14, 1992, in Gallia County, Ohio. Marguerite Hereford Walker died October 3, 2001, in Gallia County, Ohio. There were buried together at Vinton Memorial Park, Vinton, Gallia County, Ohio.

*Submitted in loving memory by Jon and Ryan Walker*

**HAROLD LLOYD AND BETTY (ROUSH) WALKER FAMILY -** Harold was born September 2, 1931 in Kanauga, Ohio. His grandparents, William and Anise Tucker Walker, moved to Ohio from Red House, WV in 1919. Their children were Stella, Lottie, Walter, Ernestine, Lawrence, Oscar, Ralph, twin brothers who died in infancy, Charlotte, and Harold's father, Lloyd Walker.

*Betty Roush and Harold Walker*

Helen Hix was Harold's mother, and her parents were Eli and Rebecca Mayes Hix. Besides Helen, they had Mae and Garnet. After Helen's mother died, her father married Myrtle Farley; and they had Fred Hix. Lloyd and Helen had the following children: Virginia, Myrtle, Ervin, Harold, the youngest.

Harold enlisted in United States Naval Reserve, graduated from Gallia Academy High School (1950), and worked at Gallipolis Terminal until December 1951, when he was called to active duty in the Korean Conflict. He served as cook on an LST taking troops to Vieques, Martinique, Granada, and Greenland until 1953; he then resumed working at Gallipolis Terminal.

Betty Evelyn Roush, youngest daughter of Lester and Mazie Darst Roush, was born December 5, 1930 west of Cheshire (on Stingy Creek). Betty has two sisters, Ethel and Geneva. Their grandparents were Orestes Newton and Lottie Vance Roush. Their children were Lester, Freddie, Goldie, Irene, James, Lloyd, Florence, Leona, and Alva. Mazie's parents were Newton Lincoln and Mary Rupe Darst. Their children were Ira, Stella, Ross, Harlow, Clarence, twins Mazie Lettie and Mary Etta, Bud, and Walden.

After graduating from Cheshire High School (1947), Betty was employed as secretary at Evans Packing. Through their employment, Harold and Betty met and were married November 15, 1953 in Gallipolis by Reverend Paul Niswander. In 1964, Harold accepted employment at the Ford agency in Gallipolis where he did Ford accounting for sixteen years. In 1980, he began employment at Rio Grande College (now University of Rio Grande), from which he retired December 1996 as Director of Finance. Betty's business association with the Evans family included employment with Evans Packing, Bob Evans Farms, Triple EEE Ranch, and Evans Enterprises, Inc., from which she retired December 1996 for a total of forty-four years.

Harold and Betty's family includes two daughters Paula Sue (Polly), born September 29, 1958 and Letty Jo, born September 21, 1960. Both Polly (1976) and Letty (1978) graduated from Gallia Academy High School. Polly has two children Kelsey Denise Salisbury (born July 5, 1985), a junior at Ohio Valley Christian School, and Garrison Wade Salisbury (born June 2, 1989), a seventh grader at Ohio Valley Christian School. Polly has been employed at Ohio Valley Bank twenty-seven years and is currently Assistant Secretary of the corporation. Letty graduated from Cedarville College (now Cedarville University) in 1982 with a Bachelor of Arts Degree and a Master of Science in School Counseling from University of Dayton in 1986. She began her teaching career with Gallipolis City Schools in 1984, and is currently English Department Chairman, teaching Senior English and Honors Language Arts at GAHS.

On May 21, 1983, Letty married Matthew R. Willis, a licensed funeral director/embalmer with Willis Funeral Home of Gallipolis. They are the parents of Brianne Rae Willis (born June 10, 1986), a sophomore at Gallia Academy, and Brooke Joelle Willis (born July 2, 1991), a fifth grader at Washington Elementary.

All of the family are active members of First Baptist Church and have held various offices of the church. They are proud to be Americans and thank God for His many blessings.

**WALLACE (WALLIS) FAMILY -** My Wallace family was born in Virginia. The father, my third great-grandfather, named either John or David, believed to be from Scotland, was a millwright and while not documented it is thought that he performed his trade at the numerous mills located along the Staunton River. No land records have been found for him but the families into which his children married were often located in areas to this river.

Eight known children were born to John or David Wallace and his wife Nancy (possibly a Mills), my third great-grandparents. Their first child was David, born in Lynchburg, Campbell County in 1800 as was Jane about 1809. Jesse was born in Halifax County in 1811. Woodson was born about 1823 in Pittsylvania County. The remaining children according to census records, Elizabeth born about 1803, William Harrison "Buck" born 1807, James born about 1813, and Nancy year unknown were also born in Virginia and probably in Halifax, Campbell or Pittsylvania Counties. Evidence exits for this as David Wallace married Juda Eads in 1822 in Pittsylvania County as did Jane Wallace to Thomas Eads (brother of Juda) in 1828. It is thought that Nancy Wallace married Woodson Overby in Halifax County in 1838.

David Wallace and Juda, my second great-uncle and aunt, were my first relatives to come to Gallia County. In 1831, they lived in Cabell County, Virginia for about three years. He was a millwright and it is likely he was employed at one of the mills in Green Township in Gallia County. After several years, he moved to Gallia County in August 1835, along with his wife Judah. He then purchased 160 acres of land in Green Township (southwest quarter, section 1, township 15, range 15) along with his brothers: William, Jess and James. They later sectioned the land into four parcels, each receiving 40 acres, and by 1843 they had all sold their shares.

After the land was sold David moved to Apple Grove, Mason County, Virginia where he was a successful farmer as did Jane and husband Thomas Eads. David and Nancy both died in Mason County, West Virginia and are buried in the Winston B. King Cemetery. Jesse who married Nancy Knight in 1840 (my second great-grandparents) and Woodson Wallace who married Rachel Humphreys in 1831 in Greenbrier County, Virginia all eventually moved to Wapello County, Iowa where they farmed. It is not known what happened to James but it is believed that he married Susannah Bright in 1840 in Gallia County. The last known relatives of my family to live in Gallia County were descendants of Elizabeth Wallace and Meady Martin who married in Halifax County, Virginia in 1822. Elizabeth died about 1869 in Gallia County.

I am Donald W. Koepp born in 1939, in Los Angeles, California married to Kathleen Rose Vacchetta in 1968, in Ventura County. We lived in Thousand Oaks, California.

*Submitted by: Donald W. and Kathleen Rose Vacchetta Koepp*

**JESSE WALLACE** - My second great-grandfather, Jesse Wallace, was born in 1811, in Halifax County, Virginia. He purchased land in Green Township, Gallia County, Ohio in 1835. While living there he was married in 1840 to Nancy Knight who was born in Virginia in 1819. In 1842, so the story goes, Jesse walked to what is now Wapello County, Iowa to establish a Preemption Land Claim. He staked our land in Keokuk Township by night and then hid in the brush in the daytime until he was allowed to file a claim at the Government Land Office in 1843. He built a log cabin and then walked back to Gallia County with a jug of whiskey taking a drink every so many miles. When he got back to Ohio he sold his Gallia County land and then moved his wife and family to Iowa. Nancy's parents, Curtis Knight and Hannah Davis who were living in Clay Township, Gallia County, Ohio also moved to Wapello County, Iowa in 1844. Jesse was later joined by his brother, William and Woodson. Jesse died in 1892 and Nancy in 1889 both in Wapello County, Iowa where they are buried in the McIntire Cemetery. Jesse is considered one of the first settlers of Wapello County, Iowa.

*Jesse Wallace & Nancy Knight about 1870 Ottumwa Iowa*

Jesse and Nancy had seven children. Curtis was the first and only child born in Gallia County in 1841. The rest of the children were born in Wapello County, Iowa: David M. in 1843, Louisa in 1850, William K. in 1852, Isaac in 1854, Nancy Jane in 1860 and Lucinda in 1865. All the children were married in Wapello County, Iowa: Curtis to Louisa Nash in 1864, Louisa to James Branson Brewer in 1867, William K. to Sarah Jane Shadley in 1875, Isaac to Martha Frances Eslinger in 1876 and Lucinda to James E. Lee in 1889. One son, David M. served as a Union soldier during the Civil War and was killed in 1864 at Marks' Mills in Arkansas.

Their daughter Nancy Jane, my great-grandmother, married Gershom Hull Nash in Wapello County, Iowa in 1883 and they moved to Benton County, Oregon in 1903. They had four children born in Wapello County: Ella Adella in 1884, Jesse Hull in 1886, Ruth Ann in 1892 and Iva Beulah in 1899. My grandmother know as Elva married Charles W. Wright in Benton County, Oregon about 1905. He died at age 47 in Portland, Oregon in 1919 leaving Elva with five children to raise. After his death Elva stayed in Oregon until she moved in 1931 to Los Angeles, California with her children where she died in 1958. Her youngest child, my mother, Ruth Edith Wright married my father, Walter Louis Koepp, in Los Angeles in 1932. Walter died in 1965 in Los Angeles, California and Ruth died in 1989 in Albert Lea, Minnesota.

I am Donald W. Koepp born in 1939 in Los Angeles, California and married to Kathleen Rose Vacchetta in 1968 in Ventura, California. We live in Thousand Oaks, California.

*Submitted by: Donald W. and Kathleen Rose Vacchetta Koepp*

**WALLACE - MCGHEE -** Ishum Wallace met Sarah/Sally Eagle in Greenbrier, Va. (W.Va). They were married in Gallia Co. 1824. Their son John S. Wallace, born 1832, married Jane McGhee, daughter of James A. McGhee Jr. and Amanda McMillen. John served in the Civil War from Gallia. Co

*John & Jane McGhee Wallace*

John and Jane had four children Altona, (married William Koontz) two children (Karl and Nola), Hattie, (married Kris Volborn,) no children, Ellen, (married William Glenn) two children (Wallace and Hazel), and James Franklin Wallace. The latter was my grandfather. He married Catherine "Kitty" Grate in 1892. Their four children were: Leah, (married Harry M. Wilcox) no children, Walter, (married Lera Waters) three children (Helen Virginia, Robert "Bob" and Joann),Theadore "Ted", (married Helen Trout) two children (Theadore "Ted and Marjorie), and Cecile, who married Von C. Thompson, five children Bess, married William H Wilson, one child (Jack A Wilson) Joe, married Eloisse Hall, five children (Robert "Bob", Penny, Thomas Joe, John Bradley, and Luanne), Lonnie, married Geraldine "Jerry" Williams, three children (Larry, Lonna Jo, Theresa), second marriage to Anne Burcham Belville, Leah, married Robert "Smokey" Wion, one child (Kristal), and Tommy, married Lavon Forbes, four children (Leah Kathryn "Kathy", Margaret Lynn, Mark, and Matthew.

*Submitted by: Leah Thompson Wion*

**TOM AND JUDY WALTERS -** Tom and Judy Walters are both natives of Gallia County. Oakley and Erna Walters adopted Tom as a toddler. Judy is the daughter of Harold and Frances Steger. Both of them grew up on their family farms near Thivener. As children they were both active in Thivener Pioneers 4-H club and Elizabeth Chapel youth activities. The Gallia County Junior Fair was the highlight of the year for them. Tom and Judy both attended the one-room school at Yellowtown, and then went on to Clay Elementary and Gallia Academy high school, then to the University of Maryland together.

Tom is retired from the U.S. Air Force after twenty years of service. His tours of duty took him to Texas, Mississippi, Alabama, Maryland, Libya, Italy, and Japan. Since his retirement in 1983, he has been driving a school bus for Gallipolis City Schools. Judy works for ElectroCraft, a Rockwell Automation business, in the Marketing Department. She also volunteers her time to help the community through the United Way. Tom and Judy are both still active in their home church, Elizabeth Chapel.

*Tom And Judy Walters*

They have two sons. Wayne is married to Julie Harrison and now lives in Watkinsville, GA. They have four children. Courtney is sixteen, and Cameron, Hannah, and Wesley (the triplets) are six. Wayne designs America's Cup lifejackets and has a part-time screen-printing business. Julie is very dedicated to serving her community through volunteer work, such as Make-a-Wish Foundation. David is married to Tammy Mannon and lives on the family farm at Thivener. They have two children. Monique Leming is eleven and attends school at Washington. Colton is two and is a delight to his family as he learns new skills daily. David works for the City of Gallipolis and has a part-time plumbing business, and Tammy works for Gallipolis Developmental Center. Their special interest is in raising horses.

Tom's family has had roots in Gallia County for more than 100 years (Walters and Bowman), and Judy's family can be traced back to the First Families in Gallia County (Kerns, Plymale, Cottrell, Langford, Syler). Even though they enjoyed living in other places during Tom's Air Force career, there's no place like home, and they are glad to be back home on the family farm in Gallia County to live.

**WARREN FAMILY** - John Warren and Jane McCallister married on March 10, 1807, in Monroe County, Virginia. To this union Andrew Jackson Warren was born on February 4, 1820, in Alleghany County, Virginia. When A. J. was six years of age, his father moved the family to Greenbrier County, Virginia. Mary Ann McCallister, A. J.'s grandmother and James's mother died 1838 in Greenbrier County. In her last will and testament dated December 12, 1835, she was desirous to dispose of all her worldly estate as it hath pleased God to bless her with. She bequeathed to her son-in-law, John Warren: one large kettle, one oven, one checkrein, and one large chest.

A. J. professed a hope in Christ in the 21st year of his life and united with the Methodist Protestant Church. A.J. was licensed to preach in 1842. He was ordained and set apart to the full gospel ministry in 1843. He than traveled the next eight years in the regular work of the church. It was during this time that he met his future wife, Mary Ann McCoy. Mary Ann McCoy was born June 16, 1819, and her father was Lewis McCoy of Tazewell, Virginia. A.J. and Mary Ann married on January 31, 1844, at Lewisburg, Virginia. When after much deliberation and faithful study of the scriptures, A.J. concluded to join the Baptist Church. Reverend Andrew Jackson Warren was ordained as a Baptist preacher in 1851.

*Reverend Andrew Jackson Warren*

The Early Years In Gallia County

The Warren family has enjoyed life in the lower part of Gallia County for six generations. It all started during the Civil War when the Reverend Andrew Jackson Warren and his wife, Mary Ann McCoy Warren, along with their nine children (Marion, Clark Brown, John Lewis, August, Andrew Jackson Jr., Virginia, Jeanette "Nettie", Hezekiah Chilton, and Mary Frances) moved to the area from Virginia. Reverend A. J. ministered for many of the local Baptist churches affiliated with the American Baptist Association. He was a prominent member of the Association, being chosen as moderator of the Gallia Baptist Association and serving for six years. He was Ohio State moderator for eight years and clerk for many more years. He was a charter member of many Missionary Baptist Churches in this community and others, too. Rev. A.J. died on May 27, 1896, in Lawrence County, Ohio. His beloved Mary Ann died on December 23, 1898, while visiting her granddaughter, Mrs. Vesta Warren Sheets, at Mercerville.

Clark Brown Warren was born November 6, 1846, in Greenbrier County, Virginia, and married Nancy Ellen Long on December 4, 1867, in Clay Township. Ellen was born on May 10, 1851, in Gallia County to Anderson and Nancy McGath Long. The Long family was early arrivals to this county. Clark and Ellen's home was a log cabin on their farm on Davis Road in Ohio Township. They had six children: John, Maggie, Leota Pearl (twin), Leola Muriel (twin), Golda Belle, and Katie W. Besides a farmer (known for his orchards), Clark was a Justice of the Peace and also delivered mail via horse and buggy. Clark died on June 12, 1925, at his farm. Ellen was the third oldest resident of the county at the time of her death on March 6, 1948, at Eureka.

Leota Pearl "Ota" Warren was born on June 30, 1877, in Ohio Township. Ota and Luther Harbour begot twins: Wye Wakefield and Dollie Leota born on September 11, 1901. Luther was the son of Thomas and Nancy Ann Davenport Wye. Ota married Otis Winfield Taylor, and they raised Dollie and their children: Hilda, Rachel and John Warren Taylor. Luther married Vesta Swindler and they had a family. In 1916 Luther moved his family to Ordway, Colorado, where other children were born to this union. Luther died on April 20, 1949, at Ordway. Leota died in 1963 at Eureka.

*Submitted by Jerry Allen Warren*

**THE WARREN FAMILY, LATER GENERATIONS** - Wye Wakefield Warren married Garnet Lucy Waugh on September 23, 1924, at Gallipolis, Ohio. Garnet was born December 29, 1905, in Ohio Township to Alfred Wilson and Mary Jane Smeltzer Waugh. The Waugh family arrived in Gallia County in the late 1700's. Wye and Garnet had four children: Mabel Leota, Alfred Lee, Robert Sheldon, and James Lorten, named for his Uncle Lort Waugh. Wye was a farmer, coal miner, worked for WPA during the Great Depression, and worked on the original building of the Gallipolis Locks and Dam at Eureka. Garnet worked at Holzer Hospital for 23 years. They divorced and later Garnet married Erie Phillips. Erie died in 1985. Garnet passed on October 30, 1988. Wye died on May 12, 1994, at Gallipolis. Wye lived his life in Ohio Township and Clay Township.

*Jerry Warren*

James Lorten Warren was born on September 21, 1933, in Ohio Township. Nancy Frances Drummond was born on April 15, 1935, in Harrison Township to Harry Clifford and Murlie Celeste Johnson Drummond. At the time of Nancy's birth there had been a sudden winter storm. A doctor had to be summoned to the house on a sled by her brother, Marshall Paul "Pete" Drummond. Nancy's grandparents were Samuel and Nancy Susan Ferrell Drummond, and William "Wild Bill" and Missouri Frances Mart Johnson. William had been in some of the fiercest battles of the Civil War and his father, Joshua, had been in the War of 1812. The Johnson family home was a farm in Guyan Township. There is a family cemetery on this farm. Nancy was named for her grandmothers. Both the Drummond and Johnson families arrived in Gallia County in the early 1800's. The Drummond family had been some of the very earliest settlers of Kanawha County before making the trek to Ohio. James and Nancy married one year after being introduced to each other, by Charles Lee Barcus, on the sidewalk in front of the shops in downtown Gallipolis one evening in 1955. July 28, 2002, marks forty-six years of marriage. For as many years, James has worked in the road construction business, and Nancy has been a homemaker. Together they've worked the farm. Today, they enjoy giving wise counsel to their three sons: James Calvin, David Eugene, and Jerry Allen; and their four grandchildren; and one great grandchild. James and Nancy make their home in Clay Township.

Jerry Allen Warren, the youngest of the sixth generation of the Warren family to make lower Gallia County home, was born August 31, 1963, at Gallipolis. He was educated in the Gallipolis City Schools and graduated in 1982 from Gallia Academy. Jerry earned his undergraduate degree in education in 1987 from the University of Rio

Grande. He has taught at the secondary level since 1989 in the Mason County Public Schools. Jerry earned his graduate degree, also in education, from Marshall University in the spring of 2002. Jerry resides in a home he built on three acres, next door to his parents in Clay Township, overlooking the mighty Ohio River.

The Warren family is proud of the rich heritage of the area. We hope that our family has in some way enriched this heritage and can be some source of pride for the community in the future as well.

*Submitted by Jerry Allen Warren*

**CARRIE RENE' WAUGH -** Carrie Rene' Waugh (August 18, 1971 born in Gallipolis) is one of the 12th generation to live on American soil. (Refer to Ronald and Donna J. Waugh for more info on family background). She has a sister, Cynthia Jean (Waugh) Middleton and a brother, Jeremiah Ronald Waugh. All were raised in Gallia County, but due to employment Carrie is living in West Chester, Ohio.

*Carrie Rene' Waugh*

Carrie graduated from Hannan Trace High School on June 2, 1989. She completed her Bachelor of Science in Education, March 1995 with a major in Early Childhood-Elementary Education from Ohio University. She began her career subbing for Gallia County Local Schools in the fall of 1995. Received a five-month long-term subbing position at Bidwell-Porter Elementary as a third grade teacher. She loved working there and accepted a summer position as a day camp teacher for the Title I Camp Discovery. No full-time teaching positions were available the following year so she accepted a position with Adams County-Ohio Valley Educational Service Center. August 1996, she moved to West Union, Ohio and became the Head Teacher for Tiffin Preschool. She was a facilitator for children ages three-five. She worked in Adams County from August 1996 to June 1998. In the summer of 1997, she received the position of Junior Girls Division at Camp Lohikan in Lake Como, Pennsylvania. She said the three months stay in the Pocono Mountains was amazing and rewarding. Spending six days off during the summer traveling throughout Pennsylvania and New York as a tourist. One of her highlights was to have her picture taken with Katie Couric of the today show. Her last year at Adams county, she trained and raised $2,500 for the Lukemia Society of America, on behalf of a four year old named Jessica who attended Bentonville Preschool. She became her inspiration for strength and endurance as she completed the Inaugural Rock 'n' Roll Marathon of 26.2 miles, on June 21, 1998 in San Diego, California. Following the marathon, she moved to Cincinnati, Ohio to begin graduate school at the University of Cincinnati in Curriculum and Instruction through the Education Department. While attending full time, she accepted a primary teaching position with Cincinnati Public Schools. In July of 1999, she received a Master of Education Degree with focus on Instructional Design and Technology. She completed her degree in thirteen months at the top of her class. Although she could easily move into the business with this degree, she chose to remain in public education. Carrie taught at the neighborhood school, James N. Gamble Elementary for three years. She gained invaluable experience but chose to turn down the continuing contract. Instead she ended her contract and began subbing for three suburban districts; Sycamore Community, Mason City and Lakota Local Schools. From this experience, she decided to move to West Chester and accepted a teaching position with Lakota Local Schools. In the Fall of 2002, she shall receive the National Board of Professional Teaching Standards Certification as an Early Childhood Generalist.

**JEREMIAH RONALD WAUGH -** Jeremiah Ronald Waugh was born on 29 January 1977 in Point Pleasant, West Virginia. He is the son of Ronald Carrol and Donna (Cox) Waugh and has two sisters Carrie Rene'(18 August 1971) and Cynthia Jean (24 February 1974). He is the 12th

*Jeremiah Ronald Waugh*

generation to live on American soil. His ancestors have lived in Gallia County since 1800, and he is the eighth generation to live there. During his life thus far, he has lived on Teens Run Road, Waugh Road in his ancestral home, and since 1978 on Rock Lick Road where his parents purchased property from his grandfather Shellio Slone and built their home, where they still reside. He attended Hannan Trace schools until completing his freshman year when the high school was closed through consolidation (1991-92). Along with Southwestern, North Gallia, and Kyger Creek that became River Valley High School, located in Cheshire, Ohio... At that time, he changed from the county school to city, attending and graduating from Gallia Academy in 1995. He was involved in many school activities but his favorite sport was football, which he played through his senior year. After graduation, he went to the University of Rio Grande for one year and to Ohio University living in Athens for two years. In November 2001 he moved to Cincinnati, Ohio for employment at Cost Plus World Market as Head of the Beverage Department. He is also continuing his education in Computer Networking at ITT technical school.

**JOHN WILSON AND GOLDIE JANE WAUGH -** Mary (Waugh) Hendrix, daughter of John and Goldie Mary was born January 9,1941 to John Wilson Waugh and Goldie Jane (Swain)Waugh on a small farm near Cadmus, Ohio. According to her late brother, Carrol E. Waugh and the research that he did prior to his death, "we are the 10th generation of this Waugh family to live on American soil." "The Reverend John Waugh, born 1630 in Tyrone, Ireland, died 1706 in Virginia; John Jr., William, Tyler, and George followed." Others were to settle in Ohio Township, Gallia County; John Tyler, Powhatton, Alfred, John Wilson and Mary Emma Waugh-Hendrix. Mary was the fourth child of John and Goldie. She had four brothers, Clifford Roland, Ivan Lowell, Carrot Everett and John Foster. The death of John occured August 1973, Goldie. December1976, Clifford, January 2000 and Carrol, September 1986.

*John & Goldie Waugh*

September1961. Mary married Roger Crump who worked for (GC. Murphy Co. in Gallipolis. Mary was working as a personal secretary to Emerson Evans at the Ohio Valley Bank at that time. Mary and Roger had two children; Brian Eric born August 1966 and Angela Diane born April 1969. Mary is now married to Billy Hendrix who is from Portland, Arkansas.

John and Goldie's relationship started at a "pie social" early 1920's. John said, "she was the prettiest girl there and her pie was the best." Lie was the lucky winner of both. John and Goldie were tennet farmers on the Homer and Lulu Waugh farm prior to their purchasing the farm October 25, 1945. The farm consists of 100 acres and is located in Ohio Township, section 21, Gallia County.

Mary remembers her early childhood days on the farm as being filled with love, sacrifice and parents who wanted to instill the love of God in their children's lives. She attended Swan Creek Elementary School, was a member of the Swan Creek Cygnets 4-H Club. The leader was Ms. Joe Donald (Margaret) Pollitt. Ms. Pollitt was also the first and second grade teacher. After attending eight years at Swan Creek, Mary attended 4 years at Gallia Academy High School. She then spent the next 20 years raising her children. At the age of 34, Mary decided to fullfill a lifetime dream and attended the University of Louisiana in Monroe, Louisiana in 1974. After four years at the University, she received her Bachelor of Science Degree in Nursing. The following years were spent working in the hospital setting and teaching nursing at the Delta Ouachita Community College.

Breast cancer cut her teaching career short, so she took early retirement and she and her husband Billy moved back to Crown City and the family farm. Years of dreams started to materialize when ground was broken for the new farmhouse. The purchase of the farm took place in 1968 with the intention of someday returning to the family roots. Grandfather, Alfred Waugh, built a barn in the late 1800s on the property. The barn was built of oak, hard pine and poplar. It had mortice and tennon construction and was all hand hewn. This barn was in need of much repair so it was decided that it would be feasable to use some of these timbers in the new farmhouse. After much preperation and planning, and a builder named Roy Bickle, the farmhouse was completed and our furniture arrived from Louisiana on October 25, 2001, This was 56 years to the day when John and Goldie originally purchased the farm.

Billy has adapted to the rigors of farm life without complaint. His days are long and spent checking the internet for e-mail messages, sending letters to friends in the South, reading, working on fence lines with friends and family, tilling the ground with his new John Deere, and just working to be a good steward of the land.

Mary's days are spent reading, gardening and waiting to visit Blake Edward Kidner who was born May 6, 2001. Blake has the Waugh blood in his veins and his parents Ed and Angela, who live in Baltimore, MD. will be encouraged to keep the Waugh family name here at Waugh's River Hill Farm, Waugh Road, Crown City, OH.

*Submitted by Mary Waugh Hendrix*

**RONALD (RONNIE) CARROL WAUGH -** Ronald (Ronnie) Carrol Waugh is the 11th. generation to live on American soil.

*Ronnie and Donna J. Waugh*

Members of his family have lived in Gallia County since 1800. 1st Rev. John Waugh, born 1630 Tyrone, Ireland, died in 1706 in Virginia. His descendants were John Jr., William, Tyler, and George. George was one of the first Waugh's in Gallia County, Ohio Township, Range 14, Lot 560, John Tyler, Powhatton, Alfred, John Wilson, Clifford Rolland, and Ronnie born 29 December 1949 in Gallipolis, Ohio. He is the eldest son of Clifford (26 August 1925-27 January 2000) and Mildred Juanita "Cox" Waugh-Crum-Jordon (27 December 1929-25 August 1992) and the only child born to this union. He has an older brother Earl Eugene Cox (24 March 1947) and siblings of Clifford and Letha "Beaver" Waugh (20 March 1934-30 October 1994) of Port Clinton, Ohio. They are Alfred Mansfield (21 June 1952, Anthony Wayne (5 February 1954), Patricia Ann (18, December 1968), Clifford Allen (26 November 1962), William Gwynn (20 March 1962), three deceased Cathy and twins Timothy and Jeffrey.

Ronnie and Donna Jean "Cox" Waugh both graduated from Hannan Trace High School, and were married 9th October 1970. He was in the Navy stationed in Long Beach, California on the U.S.S. Bronstin. They were blessed with their first daughter Carrie Rene' (18 August 1971- Gallipolis). In 1972 they moved to Norfolk, Virginia where he was stationed on the U.S.S. Alywind and was on a Mediterranean Cruise when they were blessed with there second daughter Cynthia Jean (24 February 1974-Gallipolis) On June 15, 1974 they returned home to Gallia County. His first job was for Gallipolis Developmental Center as a hospital aide/nurses aide, attended two years at the Gallipolis Business College and enlisted in the Army National Guards 3664th. Maintenance Co. as Sergeant in Point Pleasant, W.Va. On 29 January 1977 they were blessed with a third child, Jeremiah Ronald, born in Point Pleasant, West Virginia. In 1981, Ronnie became full time with the Army National Guard until October 19, 1997 when he retired. During this time, he was a little league coach; 4-H Advisor (with his wife), Guyan Volunteer Fireman 1984-88, Asst. Chief 1989-90, Chief 1991-97. Worked at Reliance Automation 1997-2000. In March1998, he helped form the Harrison Township Volunteer Fire Department and is Fire Chief there. He is now employed by Crown Excavating since 2000 and enjoys fishing and hunting in his spare time.

Donna is Democratic Central Committeeman for Harrison Township. Her most valued profession was being a wife and mother, she said it was the breath of life itself and nothing could ever replace the memories, love, laughter, joys and pain. She is a poet and self-taught artist, published in many anthologies and was recognized in 1995 and 1998 with an "Editors Choice Award" by the National Library of Poetry, her poem "Mankind's Transformation" published in Voices by Illiad Press received "Honorable Mention" and in 1996 The Presidents Award for Literary Excellence". She also gave permission for her poem to be published in "Poetry's Elite: The Best of 2000". Her art has been exhibited in Art in the Park, at the Riverby and she has painted a slate, which was included on the art structure that stood in the yard there for some years, two of her children Cynthia and Jeremiah were involved in completing this structure as well. While exhibiting her art at the Foothills Art Festival in Jackson County, our State Representative John Carey and his wife Lynley purchased her painting called "Deer Meadow" in 1999. She and her husband still live in Gallia County on Rock Lick Road and were blessed with their first grandchild Kyra Elizabeth Middleton on November 3, 2000.

**MICHAEL ARTHUR, JESSICA LYNN WOOD AND ERIC MICHAEL WEBER FAMILY -** Michael Arthur Weber was born June 3, 1971 at Camden-Clark Memorial Hospital in Parkersburg, West Virginia to Keith Weber and Brenda Spencer Weber Johnson of Pomeroy, Ohio. Michael graduated from Eastern High School in Reedsville, Ohio in 1989, attended Ohio University in Athens, Ohio for two years then transferring to Hocking College in Nelsonville, Ohio where he graduated in 1994 with an Associates of Applied Business degree in Computer Science. Michael moved to Gallia County in 1996 to work at Rockwell Automation (formerly Robbins-Myers) as an I. T. Technician. Michael volunteered as a camp counselor while in school at the United Methodist Church Camp Francis Asbury in Rio Grande, Ohio where he met another camp counselor, Jessica Wood. Michael married Jessica Lynn Wood on July 17, 1999.

*Michael & Jessica Wood Weber with Eric Micheal Weber*

Jessica Lynn Wood was born October 31, 1976 at Holzer Hospital in Gallia County to Charles and Marjorie Gilliam Wood of Gallipolis, Ohio. Jessica graduated from Gallia Academy High School in Gallipolis in 1995 and attended University of Rio Grande, Rio Grande, Ohio for two years. Jessica is a stay at home mother of one. She is active in the Esther Circle of the women's group at Grace United Methodist Church. She is also very active in French Colony Daughters of the American Revolution and has served as a personal page at the Ohio State DAR conference for several years. During the March 1999 conference she served as a personal page to the State Regent from Tennessee, Linda Tinker Watkins who is currently the National Daughters of the American Revolution's President General.

Michael and Jessica have one child, Eric Michael Weber, born December 30, 2000, at Holzer Hospital, Gallipolis, Ohio. Eric enjoys attending story time at the Bossard Memorial Library in Gallipolis. Eric also enjoys spending time with all of his grandparents.

Michael, Jessica and Eric currently reside at 62 Myrtle Avenue, Addison Township, Gallipolis, Ohio.

Michael's family line includes: Spencer, Weber, Larkins, Branch, Meadows, Harper, Young, Keaton, Downey, Andrews and Mack. Jessica's family lines include: Gatewood, Gilliam, Lakin, Pickens, Turner, Williams, Watts, Sims, Trowbridge, Caldwell, Sheets, Ferrier, Lowery, Cole, Nickell and Fraley, Many of Jessica's family lines can be found in other histories within this book.

*Submitted by: Michael and Jessica Wood Weber*

**WEED -** My grandmother, Cynthia Weed, was born May 29, 1872, to William B Weed and Josephine Topping of Gallia County, Ohio; he the son of Tracy Hoyt Weed and Cynthia Cherrington of that county. What I remember about her is from living in her house in Colorado as a boy from the age of 5 until her death in 1965 at the age of 93.

She was one of five girls, and upon the death of her mother and the subsequent 2nd marriage of her father in 1881, which produced three more girls and one boy. She went out of her house at (abt) 14 years of age to work as a housekeeper/baby sitter for neighboring families.

Correspondence with a sister living in Colorado led her, at the age of 16, to board a train for the West and a new life.

True enough. There she met Charles Steele, a cowboy, and friend of Charles Russell (the painter and sculptor of the old west). Charles had come west from New York State as a teenager, some 20 years before, to seek his fortune. She, and this dashing young man of her dreams married, January 1, 1893, in Hinsdale County, Colorado, near the town of Lake City; he 42 years of age and she 20 years old.

He divided his time between raising horses and providing ties for the railroad. She managed the household and a large vegetable garden from which she sold "carrots and peas" to the residents of Lake City. They began a family and in 1897 completed homestead of the Alta Vista Ranch in that county.

The marriage produced eight children, Lee (b. 1894), Edna (b. 1896), Mabel (b. 1898), Mary (b. 1901), Nell (b. 1904), Herbert (b. 1907), Charles Merlin (b. 1910) and Elizabeth (b. 1913). Two of the children perished at early ages, of scarlet fever. One purportedly shot herself. The others survived to have families of their own. My mother, Elizabeth Virginia, born May 23, 1913, was the last child of my grandmother—the "baby" of the family.

The children were schooled at home by a live-in teacher. They attended high school at Lake City, about 8 miles from the ranch. The house contained the works of Dickens, Shakespeare, Chaucer, Balzac and a musical organ.

A stroke left Charles bedridden in 1916. The family continued to live at the ranch. In 1923 they sold it, moving to a house in Gunnison, Colorado. Charles died in Gunnison in 1926.

In Gunnison, the children attended public schools. My mother received her Masters Degree in English and taught English at the Gunnison County High School for 22 years. She wrote and published four books of the history of Gunnison County. She married Andrew Saunders of Palisade, Colorado in 1931, raised three boys, Norman, Kraig and Ray L. and one girl, Sue Ellen, by a second marriage. She died in Gunnison in 1992.

Mabel became the wife of Raymond Wright, a Mineral County, Colorado rancher, until her death in 1991. Herbert retired from work at the Hanford nuclear facility in Washington State (1978?) to live in Alaska and Charles Merlin and his wife Dorothy presently live in Mineral County, Colorado as rancher and resort owners.

My grandmother continued to write to her sisters throughout her life, never failed to read the Rocky Mountain News, darned socks for us using a light bulb, filled in for my mother when my mother was out of the house, and loved music. She kept a Whitehouse cookbook on the stairs, had a stereoscope with hundreds of cards from WWI and various scenic sites and subscribed to the National Geographic.

She tended her traditional vegetable garden (including horseradish and rhubarb), several flower beds (Peonies, Babies Breath, Bachelor's Buttons, Lilacs). She weighed about 110 pounds and was about 5' 2" tall, fought Mountain Lions and Bears, drove teams of horses through the river to Lake City with vegetables, and took an airplane trip at 80 years of age to visit her son, Herbert, in Washington State. She was paid a visit at Alta Vista in 1910 by her father who had come from Ohio by train. She died in 1965 in Gunnison, Colorado.

*Footnote:*

*I had the pleasure of meeting my grandmother's half-sisters, Bertha and Eva, at chicken dinners, at their home in Columbus, Ohio in 1953-54. I was a graduate student at The Ohio State University at the time. They had retired to Columbus from public school teaching. Submitted by: Norman Saunders*

**CHARLES A. AND BEULAH (BLAKE) WEED FAMILY -** The Rev. Dr. Charles Allison Weed was born, Bristol, NH, March 9, 1896. He was the great-grandson of William Weed and Olive (Branch) who entered Gallia County, 1812. He was the grandson of Tracy Hoyt Weed and Cynthia (Cherrington) and son of the Rev. Simeon J. Weed and Lutitia Caroline (Allison). Charles died November 17, 1981, Holzer Medical Center, Gallipolis, Ohio. Internment was at Calvary Cemetery, Rio Grande, Ohio. Charles married Beulah Blake, March 23, 1918. Beulah was born September 18, 1898, Lawrence County, Ohio, daughter of Milroy R. Blake and Sarah Ellen (Earles). Beulah entered Rio Grande College and graduated the two-year normal curriculum, 1918. She taught at Proctorville and Freedom, Ohio and received the B.Sc. in Ed., Rio Grande College, 1940. She died, November 24, 1972, Holzer Medical Center, Gallipolis, Ohio. Internment was at Calvary Cemetery, Rio Grande, Ohio.

*Beulah (Blake) And Charles A. Weed*

Following high school Charles taught in a one-room school one year. He entered Rio Grande College, 1915, volunteered for the U.S. Army, (WWI); six weeks after discharge lost his right arm working at the American Car and Foundry Company, Huntington, WV. Charles was awarded a cash settlement of $1,085, he returned to Rio Grande College and received the following degrees: A.B., Rio Grande College; M.A., Colgate University; B.D., Th.M., Crozer Theologicol Seminary; D.D., Alderson-Boraddus College; Ph.D., Webster University. He was on the faculty: Baptist Institute for Christian Workers, Philadelphia, PA; Rio Grande College, Ohio; Alderson-Broaddus College, West Virginia. He served Ohio and Pennsylvania churches as pastor. Charles and Beulah retired 1966, and purchased a house at Rio Grande, Ohio. He served Calvary Baptist Church, Rio Grande, Ohio, as interim pastor. May 24, 1981, elected Fellow of Rio Grande College. Children: Gilbert, Roy, and Helen.

Orel Gilbert Weed, born, July 10, 1921, in Proctorville, Ohio. Orel graduated from Rio Grande high school and entered Rio Grande College, 1939. He volunteered for the U.S. Marine Corps, (WWII). Orel married Janet George, March 13, 1943. He remained in the Marine Reserves until 1961 and attained the rank of Major. Gilbert became an insurance agent. He resided at North Carolina, Kentucky and Tennessee. Janet died August 15, 1971. Gilbert married Ruth Lane Wheeler, Durham, NC, December 19, 1971. Gilbert died June 6, 1996, Franklin, TN. Internment Pearl Webb Cemetery, Canmer, Hart County, KY.

The Rev. Roy Simeon Weed, born, Proctorville, Lawrence County, OH, March 27, 1923, volunteered for the U.S. Navy, (WWII). He married Jane Curle, Cleveland, OH, and April 7, 1945. He has degrees in the following: B.B.A., Case Western Reserve University; B.D./M. Div., Crozer Theological Seminary; M.B.A., Temple University. Children: Margaret Elaine, born October 7, 1946; Charles Roy, born August 27, 1948; Barbara Jane, born October 4, 1960.

Helen Judith Weed, born Jenner Township, Somerset County, PA, January 12, 1926, entered Rio Grande College, 1944; married Glenn Daun "Dick" Lanier, June 22, 1945. A brain tumor caused Dick's death at age 54. Internment was at Calvary Cemetery, Rio Grande, OH. Children: Patricia Lee, born March 15, 1949; Sheila Louise, born October 13, 1959; Brenda Gay, born August 21, 1962. Helen married Richard Granville Sayre, April 13, 1987. Helen died February 20, 1989, at Holzer Medical Center, Gallipolis, OH. Internment was at Calvary Cemetery, Rio Grande, OH.

*Submitted by Roy S. Weed*

**DR. WILLIAM A. AND JANE F. (HASKINS) WELKER FAMILY -** William Allison Welker was born July 21, 1930, in Rio Grande, Ohio. His fifth great-grandfather, Andreas Welker, came to this country from Germany on the ship Albany arriving at Philadelphia in 1749. He settled first in Berks County, PA, where he and his wife, Anna Catherine, had five children, the second son being Jacob Andrew Welker, William A's fourth great-grandfather, born November 18, 1760. Jacob Andrew migrated from PA to Columbiana County, Ohio, where he married Margaret Grate, and they had ten children of which William Welker was the second son. He was born October 21, 1795. He took as his wife Elizabeth Might and this union produced ten children, one of which was William M. Welker, who at age 20 came to Gallia County where he married Taphena Holcomb, granddaughter of Gen. Samuel R.

Holcomb. One of their sons, Samuel H. Welker, born May 5, 1847, in Vinton, Ohio, married Isabel Huntley; they were William A. Welker's great grandparents. Their oldest son, William Edgar Welker, was born May 31, 1871, near Rio Grande, Ohio. He married Nancy Malaby and their son, William Kenneth Welker, was born February 3, 1906, in Rio Grande, Ohio. He married Florence Mildred Allison, William A. Welker's parents. William Kenneth served in WWII as a dentist in the Ohio 37th Division. He earned the nickname of "The Fighting Dentist" as well as the Silver Star for gallantry in action in the Solomon Islands.

William A. attended Gallia Academy High School where he was a member of the "Golden Era" football team, graduating in 1948. He entered the Ohio State University College of Dentistry in 1955 and earned his DDS degree in 1959. He went on active duty in the USAF and served a year in Vietnam earning the Bronze Star.

In September of 1977, William retired as a colonel from active duty in the Air Force and began teaching at the Ohio State University College of Dentistry, serving eight years as Chairman, Department of Prosthodontics. He retired from the College of Dentistry and active dental practice in 1992.

Jane Frances (Haskins) Welker was born December 11, 1930, in Gallipolis, Ohio, the daughter of Lawrence Paul and May (Phillips) Haskins. She attended grade school in the Gallipolis public schools and graduated from Gallia Academy High School in 1948. In the fall of 1948, Jane entered the Conservatory of Music, Cincinnati, Ohio, to study piano. Bill and Jane married June 24, 1951, at Gallipolis.

William A. and Jane have two children, William Paul born February 19, 1953, in Auora County and Rebecca Jane born October 23, 1960, in Colorado Springs, Colorado. William Paul is married to Shelly Lynn Weyand and they have one daughter, Elizabeth Rose, born October 17, 1997, in Dayton, Ohio. Rebecca Jane is married to William Lee Burke and they have three children: Molly Jane born August 18, 1985, Amanda Pearl born January 17, 1987, and Kenneth Edward born May 23, 1988.

*Submitted by Dr. William Allison Welker*

**WILLIAM EDWARD AND NANCY (MALABY) WELKER FAMILY -** William Edward Welker was born May 31, 1871, in Gallia County, Ohio. His great-great-great-grandfather, Andreas Welker, born 1720 in Germany, came to this country on the ship Albany in 1749, arriving at Philadelphia and settling in Berks County, PA, where he and his wife, Anna Catherine, had five children: John Paul, Anna Catherine, Jacob Andrew, Anna Christina and Elizabeth. In the late 1760's Andreas started his migration west. They migrated through and stopped, at times, in Maryland and Pennsylvania for the next fifteen years, finally settling in Columbiana County, Ohio.

William Edward great-great-grandfather, Jacob Andrew Welker, born November 18, 1760, married Margaret Grate in Columbiana County, Ohio; they had eleven children: Sara, George, William, Abraham, John, Isaac, Solomon, Jacob, Hanna, Margaret and Andrew. Jacob Andrew died in Columbiana County and is buried there.

William Welker, William Edward's great grandfather, born October 21, 1795, in Columbiana County, Ohio, took as his wife Elizabeth Might and this union produced ten children: Silas, Samuel, Andrew, Hanna, William M., Isaac, Might, Jacob and David. William served the entire War of 1812. William and Elizabeth both died in Meigs County, Ohio, and are buried in the Barton-Bing Cemetery there.

William Edward's grandfather, William M. Welker, born August 29, 1822, in Columbiana County, Ohio, came to Gallia County, Ohio, about 1840 and there he married Taphena Holcomb on July 19, 1846. They had the following children: Samuel Holcomb, Ann S., Elizabeth, William S., Abner Johnson, Might S., Laura J., Ansel Elsworth, Adelbert, and Ansil. William M. and Taphena are buried in Mt. Tabor Cemetery, Gallia County, Ohio.

Samuel Holcomb Welker, William Edward's father, was born in Vinton, Ohio, May 5, 1847. After serving on the Union side in the Civil War, Samuel lived his life in Rio Grande, Ohio, and was postmaster there. On October 17, 1867, in Gallipolis, Ohio, he married Isabel Huntley and they had six children: Stephen H., William Edward, Elizabeth, Adril and Mathew. Samuel H. and Isabel are buried in Calvary Baptist Cemetery at Rio Grande, Ohio.

William Edward Welker was born May 31, 1871, near Rio Grande, Ohio. On June 11, 1892, he married Nancy Lodice Malaby and they had the following children: Laura Pearl who married first August Kraus who died in the flu epidemic in 1918 and second Everett G. Lewis; Lora Lucille who married Irwin R. McCarley; Ruby Lenore who married Charles N. Houck; and William Kenneth who married Florence Mildred Allison. William E. was a teacher in Gallia, Meigs, and Athens Counties. He also served as clerk of courts in Gallia County. For a time in the 1920's, he operated a country store in Porter, Ohio, that was part of the Underground Railroad at one time. He died in 1944 at the age of 73. He and Nancy are buried in the Calvary Baptist Cemetery at Rio Grande, Ohio.

*Submitted by William A. Welker*

**BOYD EUGENE (GENE) AND ELEANOR MARIE (ANGELL) WELLINGTON FAMILY -** Boyd E. was born at Cedarville, Ohio, near Springfield on February 20, 1928, to Meredith Claire and Elsie Blanche (Harmon) Wellington. They moved to Gallia County when Gene was 3 years old to live and take care of his grandparents, David and Mary Harmon, who lived along Raccoon Creek near the Hively Farm. At the age of 6 years old, they moved to Vinton where he attended Vinton School along with his brothers and sister. Gene graduated from Vinton High School at the age of 16 years old. He is a veteran of the Korean (Conflict) War.

Gene met Eleanor Marie, the daughter of Lloyd and Emma Eloise (Lambert) Angell, in 1953, and they were married on December 24, 1953, at Porter, Ohio. Eleanor was born on January 30, 1937, at Yellowtown, Ohio. She is the middle of three children and has resided in Gallia County all her life.

After marrying, Gene and Eleanor lived in many Gallia County locations before settling at Bidwell in 1960 at their present home at 524 Woodsmill Road. They have six children: Sherry Ann (Ralph) Fellure, Blanche Eloise (Guillott) Wellmeyer, Steven Eugene Wellington, Sandra Jo (Steve) Eddy, Laura Marie (Wayne) Eddy, and Tammie Sue (Mark) Mayes.

Gene worked at Jenkins Concrete for 31 years and retired in 1990 to travel and see the United States. They have visited over thirty states and have spent many winters in Georgia.

Sherry married Ralph on May 26, 1984, at Gallipolis, Ohio. They have one daughter, Christina Ann Wellington, who is a senior at the University of Rio Grande.

Blanche was married to Alan Guillott in 1973 and they have two children: Danielle Marie (Matthew) Sugg (parents of Matthew, Talia, and Anthony) and Timothy (Brittany) (parents of Gage). Blanche and Alan divorced. She then married Eric Wellmeyer and they have one son, Jonathan.

Steven married Paula Morris in 1975 and they have one daughter, Stacy Lynn (Roger) Schartiger, she has two sons, Levi Alexander Ai and Dalton Bradley. They then divorced and he married Kindra Delille and they divorced. He later married Debbie and they have one daughter, Cyndal Marie. Steven and Debbie are now divorced.

Sandra married Steve Franklin Eddy in February 1975 and they have two children: Steve Franklin II (Lethsia) and Robert Joseph who is the father of Amanda Michelle. Steve went to be with Our Lord in February 2001 where he doesn't have to suffer anymore with cancer.

Laura married Harry Wayne Eddy on May 31, 1977. They have three children: Terri Mae (Cory) Camden; Traci Marie, and Joshua Eugene. They live on Creek Road just two miles from where Laura grew upon Woodsmill Road.

Tammie married Mark in December 1986 and they live on Williams Hollow Road, Gallipolis. Tammie is the first assistant at McDonalds in Gallipolis. Mark is with Burger King as traveling manager. They had one child Craig, who died of cancer in 1997. Tammie has five dogs and many cats that she has saved over the years.

Eleanor had an accident in May where she fell down the basement stairs and injured her spinal cord. She is recovering at home and can walk with her cane for short distances and with her walker for longer distances. She's come a long way with prayers from local and distant families, friends, and churches.

Gene found out in August 2001 that he has lung cancer. He is doing well with chemo and the prayers of everyone both far and near.

*Submitted by Sherry Fellure*

**WETHERHOLT -** The name Wetherholt dates to the 1860 in Gallia County. Elias Wetherholt Sr., a cabinetmaker from Upshur County, Virginia, now West Virginia, moved to the Kerr area where his children were born to Carolyn Clark Wetherholt and later Hettie Pringle Wetherholt.

Of his entire family Elias Wetherholt Sr., only had two sons who remained in Gallia County: George J. and Elias Jr. Both became funeral directors.

Of George J.'s sons, Frank remained in Gallipolis and followed his father in the funeral business and Paul went into the military and moved to Washington State.

*Doug and Janet Wetherholt*

Frank had one son, Frank Clark who has two sons and a daughter, and one daughter, Julia Ann Smeltzer who has one daughter and two boys. A second son died in infancy.

Elias Jr. had two sons: Harold Watts and Dwight Clinton.

Harold Wetherholt married Coell Jividen from Racine to whom were born two sons, Manning and Douglas. Manning married Pauline Beard and they had three daughters, none of whom live in Gallipolis. Douglas married Janet Brown and they have no children.

Harold owned and operated the Gallipolis Tribune for nearly three decades and was responsible for its growth and development. After selling the Tribune he served as secretary of the Gallipolis Savings and Loan until his retirement.

Manning, now deceased, followed his father in the printing business by establishing the French City Press which still functions in Gallipolis today.

Douglas followed his father in the journalism field and worked for newspapers and universities in five states before retiring back to Gallipolis.

Dwight Wetherholt's wife, Alberta Junod (Judy), was from Athens. They had one daughter, Carolyn, who married Evan Roderick, a dentist in Gallipolis. They have two daughters but none of the family resides today in Gallia County. The Rodericks now live in North Carolina.

**JEFFREY THOMAS, MELISSA DAWN MC DADE AND BEAU JACOB WHALEY FAMILY** - Jeffrey Thomas Whaley was born July 5, 1960, in Springfield, OH, to Charles (Chuck) and Kathleen Fisher Whaley. Chuck and Kathy moved to Gallia County in 1973 along with their seven children - Kim, Karen, Chris, Rick, Andy, Lisa and Jeff. Kim is married to Brad Painter, Karen to Don Carter, Chris to Cathy Price and Lisa to Tim Tawney. Jeff married Melissa Dawn McDade June 18, 1987, in Gallia County. She was born December 7, 1965, to Mary Lee Davis Marchi of Gallipolis and Donald Ray McDade of Little Kyger, Cheshire Township (formerly of Meigs County, OH). Both Jeff (1978) and Melissa (1984) graduated from Gallia Academy High School. Jeff attended school at St. Mary's Hospital in Huntington, WV, and in Cincinnati, OH. He is currently employed at Holzer Medical Center in Gallipolis as a Certified MRI Technician. He is also certified as a Computed Tomography Tech and X-Ray Technician. Melissa (Missy) has one brother, Brian Kelly McDade. He and his wife, Karen, live at Little Kyger, Cheshire Township. OH. Missy graduated from Rio Grande College in 1986 with an Associate Degree in Nursing, Ohio University, Athens, OH, in 1988 with a BSN, and has been employed for the last thirteen years as a registered nurse with the Gallipolis City Schools. Jeff and Missy have one son, Beau Jacob Whaley, born April 18, 1991. They live in Northup, Green Township, OH. Beau attends Green Elementary School and participates in the Academically Gifted Program. He is an avid sports fan in both watching and participating in baseball, basketball and football. In 2001 Beau participated in Track and Field and advanced to the Junior Olympics district, regional, state and then placed 5th in a five-state area competition.

*Melissa Dawn, Jeffrey Thomas And Beau Jacob Whaley*

Both Missy and Beau are members of First Families of Gallia County. Missy is 9th generation and Beau is 10th generation Gallia Countians through Missy's mother, Mary Lee Davis Marchi. Their many family lines that date back to the early 1800's in Huntington, Addison, Cheshire, Gallipolis, Morgan, Springfield, and Raccoon Townships of Gallia County. Direct line surnames from Gallia County include: Davis, Smith, Walker, Roush, Glenn, Robins, Harrison, Bunce, Warner, Beard, Ward, Cramer, Curry, Young, Edwards, Kelcher, Knapp, Phlum, Richards, Schler, Tharp and Wise. "Our family is proud to be Gallia Countians and hope to be able to contribute back to the county and its people."

*Submitted by Mary Lee Davis Marchi*

**ROBIN LEAH (BURNETT) AND GEORGE JACKMAN WHARTON FAMILY** - Robin Leah Burnett Wharton was born September 28, 1962, in Gallipolis, Ohio, to Clyde and Freeda Burnett. Freeda was born in Kaylong, WV, to Miriam May and William James Dunn. William was the son of James Adams Dunn and the grandson of William Dunn. Freeda's great grandfather, William Dunn (1817-1900) came to America in 1831 from County Derry, Londonberry, Ireland. In 1942 Freeda's family moved from Kaylong to Kanauga, Ohio, because the government took over the family farm to make the TNT area. Clyde D. Burnett was born and raised in Kanauga on his family's dairy farm. His parents were Stella Smith and Truman Fulton Burnett, and were both born and raised in the Mercerville area. Truman's parents were America Francis Sheets and Richard W. Burnett. Stella's parents were Laura Porter and Wilson Rolandus Smith. Wilson was the son of Nancy L. Dickey and Brice Smith. Brice Smith (1821-1896) served in the army during the Civil War. During Morgan's Raids he helped capture 82 men at Old Town and 30 men at Crown City, Ohio.

Freeda and Clyde married in 1950. They have four children: Jo Ellen (and Bob) Garbesi; John Burnett; Tom (and Tonia) Burnett; and Robin (and George) Wharton.

Robin graduated from Gallia Academy High School in 1980 and from Ohio State University in 1984 with a B.S. in Elementary Education. At OSU she met George Jackman Wharton. George was born November 26, 1960, to Kathleen and Frank Wharton, in Rocky River, Ohio. George also graduated from OSU in 1984 with an M.S. in Mechanical Engineering. George and Robin married August 11, 1984, in Gallipolis and moved to Rocky River, Ohio. Robin taught middle school science for seven years at Lakewood City Schools before deciding to be a full-time mom. George is currently Vice President of Nutro Corporation in Strongsville, Ohio. George and Robin have two children: Daniel Burnett, born March 10, 1987, and Taylor Colleen, born November 10, 1988. Dan is a freshman at Rocky River High School and participates in football, wrestling and track. Taylor is in seventh grade at Rocky River Middle School and participates in basketball and track. She also enjoys playing trumpet in the Jazz Band and taking horseback riding lessons. Dan and Taylor enjoy traveling to Gallia County to visit their grandparents and cousins.

*Submitted by Robin Wharton*

**WHITE FAMILY** - Great, great grandfather, John W. White, is first found in Gallia County in the Census of 1850. He was listed as a farm laborer living in Harrison Township. No proof has yet been discovered of his parentage. Census indicates a birthplace of either Virginia or Ohio.

John was born about 1825-1828 and died May 12, 1888. He married Nancy Annette Shoemaker, daughter of John Shoemaker and Nancy Carter, on October 15, 1848. Nancy was born October 2, 1830, in Ohio and died April 18, 1903. They were the parents of thirteen children, all born in Harrison Township: William Harvey, John F., Harrison, Jacob, Guy, Ephram, Henry, Mary, Emma, Marion, Dora, Leslie and Nancy. John and Nancy are buried in White Cemetery, Harrison Township.

John's eldest son, great grandfather William Harvey White, was born September 6, 1849, and died January 28, 1884. He married Mary Mildred Tope, daughter of George Tope and Elizabeth Donaldson, on October 20, 1870. Six children were born to them: Alla Florence, Laura Annette, John Franklin, Barkley Fred, Luther Birch and Mary Kittie. After Mary Mildred's death in 1884, Harvey married her sister, Nancy Catherine Tope. To this union seven children were born at the home farm near Patriot. They were: William Clarence, Harry Otis, Mabel May, Lillie Myrtle, Lydia Ethel, Chloe Ines and Roy Curtis.

Grandfather John Franklin White, born December 2, 1875, married Ella Thornton, daughter of John Henry Thornton and Elizabeth Short, on Christmas Day 1898. John was a farmer, carpenter and a long-time member of the Green Township School Board. A daughter, Clara Goldie, was born January 20, 1900, followed by the birth of son, John Merrill, January 8, 1910. Clara married Arthur Cooper September 12,

1916, and had one son, John Paul Cooper. Clara died August 29, 1994, and is buried in Mountain Home, Arkansas. Both John White who died June 11, 1944, and Ella, who died April 13, 1960, are buried at Mound Hill Cemetery, Gallipolis.

*1944 Three Generations of the White family L: to R: Front: J. Paul Cooper, Clara White Cooper, Marjorie White, Bessie Mc Call White. Rear: John Franklin White, Ella Thornton White, John Merrill White*

Father John Merrill White, known as Merrill, attended Gallia Academy High School but left before graduating to become a mechanic. On June 5, 1929, Merrill married his high school sweetheart, Bessie Lucinda McCall, daughter of Arthur McCall and Ruey Baker. In 1937, Merrill and Bessie founded the White Implement Company at 218 Third Avenue, Gallipolis. Their only child, Marjorie, is married to A. James Gigante. One grandchild, Lisa Marie Gigante, is married to Steven D'Amico. Bessie died April 30, 1998; Merrill died March 23, 2000, in Fort Myers, Florida. Both are buried in the family plot at Mound Hill Cemetery.

*Submitted by Marjorie White Gigante*

**ABSALOM WHITE** - Absalom White was born about 1776 in Virginia. He and his family moved to Gallia Co. sometime before 1830 His son Nicholas was born about 1801 in Virginia. He married Mary A. Angel on 9 Nov. 1826 in Gallia Co. She was born in 1805 also in Virginia. Their daughter Elizabeth was born on 4 Apr 1836 (or 1837) in Gallia Co. Jonathon and Nancy Williams, both born about 1772 in North Carolina, moved to Gallia Co. along with their daughter Mary. Mary Williams was born around 1805 in North Carolina. She and George Waugh are the parents of George Washington Williams who was born on 4 Jul 1829 in Gallia Co. and died on 7 Jan 1920. He married Elizabeth White on 27 Sep 1855 in Gallia Co. Their son Lorenzo Dow Was born on 15 Aug 1856 in Gallia Co. and died on 4 Dec 1926 in Bladen, Gallia Co. He married Phebe Ann Haslett on 1 Dec 1877 in Gallia Co.

John Gilmore was born about 1793 in Pennsylvania. His daughter Elizabeth Gilmore was born in 1829 in Ohio. She married Robert C. Haslett (or Hazle) on 17 Mar 1851. Robert C. was born on 28 Mar 1828 in Ohio. He died on 24 Feb 1892 in Gallia Co. He was a farm laborer. Their daughter Phebe Ann Haslett was born on 29 Apr 1851 in Gallia Co. Ohio and died on 23 Jun 1921 in Gallia Co.

Phebe Ann and Lorenzo Dow Williams son, John L., was born on 9 July 1878 (or 1879) in Gallia Co. He died on 8 Mar. 1962 in Gallipolis due to a burst appendix, living one month later than his wife, Rebecca Laura Morrison, whom he married on 29 October 1903 in Gallia co. Rebecca Laura was born On 30 Apr 1887 and died on 12 Dec 1961 in Gallipolis. She was described as a gardener and a quilter. John was a farm laborer. He wore overalls with the left leg always turned up a little higher than the right.

He was a quite, solitary man who didn't like noise or crowds. Their daughter Pluma Pearl Williams was born on 19 Oct. 1920 in Bladen, Gallia Co. She married Richard Louis Haack on 10 May 1947 in Dayton. They are currently living in Union City, California. They have three children, six grandchildren, and two great grandchildren.

*Submitted by: Christine Curry*

**ALMON WHITE** - This relic, Record of Almon Whites Fathers Family Ages, gives birth dates for the couple and their ten children: Alfred White, Jan 18th 1778; Mary Perry, his wife, Sept 20, 1785; Amalphis, Nov 1st 1803; Armenia, Augst 30th 1805; Amanda, June 25th 1807; Sarah, March 15th 1809; Rufus, Oct 29th 1811; Almon, June 14th [1814]; Cyntha, August 9th 1816; George H., Augst 5th 1819; Isaac, July 18th 1821; and Rachel, July 10th 1823. Another family document gives Alfred the middle name of" Talmon". Although unproven, descendants contend Alfred was a son of Isaac White of Otsego County, NY. Isaac did have a son named Alfred, about whom nothing is found. Mary Perry's ancestry is yet unsolved.

*Family of Alfred White and Mary Perry*

Alfred came down the Ohio River to Millersport in 1809 on a raft made of white pine lumber. The lumber was sawed on the Brokenstraw, a branch of the Allegheny River.... The Brokenstraw Creek runs predominantly through Warren County, Pennsylvania, where an Alfred White appears on the tax rolls for 1806 and 1809 in Brokenstraw Township (100 acres, chattel)

Alfred first appears in the Gallia records in 1812 (Chattels List, Ohio Township). He witnessed a deed for his "neighbor", Jacob Miller of Lawrence County, on 16 June 1812 in Cabell County, West Virginia. The earliest extant deed for Alfred is in 1821 (80a, Perry Township). Alfred continued to accumulate property, even in Lawrence County. He received Patent Land in Symmes Township (Lawrence) in 1835 and in Perry Township in 1838. His last Gallia purchase was in 1845 from his son, George, who had moved to Iowa. Alfred sold six parcels (246.5a) around Raccoon Creek to Thomas Pierce in November 1846, following George into Iowa the following month.

In 1850, Alfred and two sons, George and Isaac, were consecutively enumerated in Jones County. Alfred's household: Alfred White, 72, Farmer, Mass., Mary, 66, VT; William Burk, 13, IL; Mary White, 20, OH. Alfred sold out in 1850-51, soon leaving for Oregon Territory. An Alfred White (described elsewhere as an old man) signed the December 1853 petition for the creation of Tillamook County, Oregon; an Alf White was present at the first election 5 June 1854. Alfred is said to have died in Oregon later that year and was "buried upon the plains".. ."the first white man buried in that State".

Mary may have gone with Alfred, however in 1860 she appears in the household of George and Sarah Carter in Patriot: . . .Mary White, 78, VT.... Sarah Carter's will (1865) makes bequests to sisters Rachael wife of Thomas Thompson, Armenia widow of John "Sherlock", Cynthia widow of Andrew Burke and to sisters-in-law Lucinda wife of Rufus White and Mary widow of"Amalthis" White. On 6 December 1867 Stephen Keller, executor, pays in full of the bequest of the last-will of said Sarah Carter and for the taking care of their mother Mary White the wife of Alfred White.... The receipt, signed by Cynthia Burk, Lucinda White and Arminia Scurlock, seems to imply Mary was still living on that date. Neither death nor burial records have been found for Mary (Hardesty's account says she died 1868).

**AMALPHIS "MALPHUS" WHITE** - Amalphis "Malphus" White of Perry Township was born 1 November 1803, eldest child of Gallia County First Family Alfred and Mary (Perry) White. Family lore states Alfred and Mary had a son named Alfred-Amalphis appears on the 1850 Census as "Alfred White." Where Malphus was born is subject to debate, but Census records indicate he was born in a portion of Virginia now West Virginia.

"Amalpher" White married Christianna Hammon 9 April 1829. "Malfus" appears in Perry Township in 1830 with a wife and no children. What became of Christianna is unknown, but it's believed the couple had a daughter. A 20-year-old Mary White, born Ohio, is living in the household of Alfred and Mary (Perry) White in 1850. She was not their daughter but probably a granddaughter-Malphus and Christianna are the only viable candidates for parents.

"Amalphus" married, second, Mary Carson on 15 August 1836. Mary was born in Scotland 8 June 1810 and may have come to America with her sister Catherine and husband, John Craig, about 1832. Carson researchers believe the women were born in Closeburn Parish, Dumfrieshire, to James and Mary (Kirkpatrick) Carson.

Malphus and Mary had eight children. Twins Armenia and Christena were born 14 March 1837. Armenia married James O. Henshaw s/o James G. and Elizabeth A. (Kridler). Christena married John Perry White s/o John and Susannah (Wigner). Amanda, born about 1840, married John Asher/Archer. Twins Thomas and John were born in 1843. Thomas married Christian Wise in Delaware County, Ohio. Isaac, born 30 October

1844, married Viola A. Sprague d/o David A. and Julia (Hannan); his second wife, Anna Eliza Roy, married first George Betz and third Charles H. Mills. Alfred, born about 1847, and Margaret, March 1850, may have died young. Mary had two sons born in Scotland:

James, about 1832; and William, 5 June 1833, who married Mary A. Wright. James went by the surname White and went to California in 1852.

Three sons served in the Civil War. John (Co. F, 33RD Regiment, Gen. Mitchels Division, J. B. Montgomery, Capt.) wrote from Huntsville, Alabama, 23 April 1862 to "brother" William Carson saying, "it is a hard life. The soldier's life is." He was killed at Flat top Mountain on 9 May 1864. Almon White wrote 9 June 1864 that "Mary's Son John is kid... Shot above the right eye and the ball went plum thro his head killing him instantly". Thomas (Pvt., Cpl., Co. L, 7th.' Regiment OH Cav.) enlisted 30 August 1862 at Gallipolis; was wounded at the battle of Ebenezer Church n;ar Selma, Alabama; discharged 31 May 1865 at Mound City, Illinois. Isaac White (Pvt., Co. E, 28th " Regiment OH Vet. Vol. Inf.) enlisted 27 March 1864; discharged 26 July1865 at Cumberland, Maryland.

Malphus died at Patriot in 1861 and is buried at White Cemetery. Mary died 30 January 1882 and is buried at Pine Street Cemetery in Gallipolis. Mary's will names daughters Armenia Henshaw, Christiana White; sons William Carson, Thomas White and Isaac White "my own living heirs"; grandson Alfred White; Thomas Ramsey and David Sprague, executors.

*Submitted by: Linda Gaylord-kuhn*

**GEORGE HENRY WHITE** - George Henry White was the fourth son of Gallia County First Family Alfred and Mary (Perry) White. George was born 5 August 1819 (according to the account of his brother, Almon) in Perry Township.

George White of Gallia County received a U.S. Patent for 39.69 acres in Perry Township (SE 1/4 of SE 1/4 Section 23) on 25 June 1841. He married Nancy Eleanor Gibson on 2 June 1842. Nancy, a native of Gallia County, was born 22 June 1822. Her parents have not been identified.

On 12 March 1845 George H. White of Cedar County, Iowa, and Nancy, his wife, sold the patent land to his father, Alfred White.

The 1879 History of Jones County provides a biographical sketch: G. H. White, beekeeper and retired farmer, Monticello.. .born in Gallia Co., Ohio, Aug. 5, 1818; grew up to manhood in that State; in 1842, he came to Iowa, stopped in Cedar Co. over one year, then came to Jones Co. and located on Bowen's Prairie in March, 1844, and commenced making a farm and entered the land when it came into market. He was one of the early settlers in this county; when he came here, he had nothing and was $9 in debt, and his neighbors predicted that he would starve out on the prairie, but he did not starve, and now owns 400 acres of good land.. .he has from 75 to 100 stands of bees which make from 75 to 125 pounds of honey yearly, from each hive....

Nancy died 7 September 1874 aged 52y-2m-16d and was buried at Monticello. She and George had at least eight children, six of whom survived her.

Joseph L. (Co. D., 9th Iowa) was born about 1843 in Gallia County and died unmarried 24 April 1862 of wounds received at the battle of Pea Ridge. Joseph's uncle, Isaac White, brought him home from the battle just seven days prior.

Mary J., born about 1845 in Iowa, and died before her mother.

Alfred was born about 1847/48. Records indicate he first married Mary Ross on 27 December 1874. He later married his cousin, Mahala Jane White daughter of Rufus and Lucinda (Childers) about 1883 and removed to Nez Perce County, Idaho where he died on 2 September 1918. He was buried at Gilbert Cemetery in Orofino, Idaho.

Lucinda, born about 1849, lived in Oakland, California 1879.

Amanda S. White was born in Iowa about 1851; married 23 January 1877 Henry E. Smith and removed to Nebraska.

Amelia, born about 1853, also lived in Oakland 1879.

John L., born about 1855, married Jennie M. White daughter of John W. and Elizabeth A. (Elmore) 17 October 1876 in Monticello. She was no relation to John.

Rozetta, born about 1863, lived in Nebraska 1879.

George next married Mrs. Eleanor R. Leamon who came to Iowa in 1857 and owned a farm of eighty acres. Eleanor was born in March 1827; her maiden name is still unknown. When and where George and Eleanor died is not yet known.

*Submitted by: Linda Gaylord-Kuhn*

**ISAAC ABRAHAM WHITE** - Isaac Abraham White, fifth son and youngest child of Gallia County First Family Alfred and Mary (Perry) White, was born 18 July 1821 (probably in Perry Township). He married Barbara Ann McCulley 9 April 1843 in Ross County, Ohio. Barbara was born 11 October 1825 in Rockingham County, Virginia, the daughter of Raulley and Nancy who came to Ohio about 1828. The couple removed with Isaac's family to Jones County, Iowa, in December 1846 where be engaged in farming until the outbreak of the Rebellion.

*Isaac Abraham White*

An interesting anecdote was recounted in the Jones County Historical Review, Vol. 1, No. 3, Summer 1975 which reads: Among those interred at Bowen's Prairie are ... Curtis Stone ... This was the Curtis Stone, who, on a fine horse, rode up to a group of men who were enlisting during the Civil War. Isaac White had not volunteered, but seeing Mr. Stone, he remarked, "If I had that horse, I would go too". "Take it," was Mr. Stone's reply. "It is yours." No sooner said than done. Mr. White vaulted into the saddle and started to fight for his country.

Isaac enlisted 16 August 1861 (Pvt., Co. D, 9th ' Iowa Volunteers). He and his nephew, John L. White, fought at the Battle of Pea Ridge in April 1862. John was mortally wounded during the battle and it was Isaac who brought the lad back home to die. Isaac returned to his command and was discharged for general disability 3 July 1862. He reenlisted 28 February 1864 in the same company and regiment, was with Sherman on his march to the sea, and at the grand review at Washington. Isaac served until the end of the war, being discharged at Clinton, Iowa. Isaac's granddaughter, Mildred White, said Isaac was always troubled by the savagery of Sherman's scorched earth march to the sea.

In the fall of 1868, Isaac and Barbara sold out and removed to Cerro Gordo County for one year then on to Worth County where he farmed 160 acres in Section 33. Isaac and Barbara had seven known children:

Edward, born about 1843 Ohio; died 30 March 1855 is buried Bowen's Prairie Cemetery in Jones County, Iowa.

Nancy J., born 8 February 1844 Ohio, married Henry Harrison Shields 4 October 1863 in Monticello, Iowa.

Almira, born 6 November 1845 Ohio; married William H. McVay 4 October 1863 in Monticello removed to Fairbury, Nebraska.

Jackson "Jack", born 31 May 1850 Iowa; married Alice Laura Owen removed to Philomath, Oregon.

Isaac Marion, born 13 October 1863 Iowa; died 9 July 1865, is buried Bowen's Prairie Cemetery.

Edith Melissa, born 13 September 1866, Iowa, married William Henry Humphrey, son of Squire Samuel and Semildah (Conner) 13 September 1883 in Mason City, Iowa.

Elmer Ellsworth, about 1871 Worth County; married Rena Isabell Fankell daughter of William and Rachel 9/10 March 1898 in Albert Lea, Minnesota.

Barbara (McCulley) White paralyzed about seven years earlier, died on 28 July 1894 and was buried at Lincoln Cemetery in Cerro Gordo County, Iowa. Isaac White died 1 April 1903, aged 81y-9m-13d, and was buried beside his wife.

*Submitted By: Linda Gaylord-Kuhn*

**RUFUS WHITE** - Although Hardesty's 1882 History of Gallia County provides an informative sketch of Rufus White, more details can now be added.

Rufus was the second son of Gallia County First Family Alfred and Mary (Perry) White, born in Millersport, Lawrence County. The record of his brother, Almon, states Rufus was born 29 October 1811 but the date varies from record to record (being seen in aggregate as 29/30/3 1 October 1811/1812).

Rufus married Lucinda Childers on 13 January 1839. She was the daughter of First Family Abraham and Rachel (Rickabaugh), born 26 December 1822. Twelve children resulted from this marriage.

Abraham B. White (Co. F, 1 Battalion, 15th US Infantry), born 24 December 1839 in the town of Wales; died 24 November 1916 Granger, Missouri, twice married Mary A. Parkins-first on 15 October 1865 in Gallia County and again 13 December 1913 in Luray, Missouri.

Levi A., born 24 July 1841. Levi was living 5 February 1920 in Idaho County, Idaho. Levi apparently never married.

Alfred, born 9 December 1843; died 9 October 1858; buried Old Pine Cemetery in Raccoon Township.

Julia A., born 4 February 1846; died 5 March 1847; buried Old Pine.

Sarah Louisa, born 5 January 1848; died 27 August 1864; buried Old Pine.

Mary Etta, born 7 May 1850. She married 5 July 1868 Charles C. [aka Rollins Cherrington] Prose who died of a gunshot wound 8 August 1869. She then married Lyman H. Bingham 29 December 1870 and removed to Jackson County.

Martha Ellen, born 22 September 1852; died 13 May 1923 [Norris City], Illinois, married Nelson Redfern (Co. C, 148 Regiment, OH N.G.I. Volunteers) 27 March 1870 in Bentonville, Arkansas.

John Riley, born 14 November 1854; died 28 May 1937; buried Old Pine. John married Lillie Belle Norman daughter of William and Rhodah (Pauley) 29 June 1886. Their grandson, John "Jack" Hansen was living on the Rufus White property in Patriot in 1994.

Mahala Jane, born 16 April 1858; died 1947; buried Idaho. Mahala married her cousin Alfred White, son of George and Nancy (Gibson), about 1883 and the couple removed to Nez Perce County, Idaho.

Charles Lewis, born 15 June 1860. Living 1904 in Santa Monica, California.

Rachel M., born 20 April 1863; died 27 February 1864; buried Old Pine.

Emma L., born 5 April 1866. She married James F. Norman (brother of Lillie Belle) 10 January 1889. She's listed as divorced in the 1900 household of her brother, Levi, in Idaho County, Idaho.

Lucinda (Childers) White died 26 January 1868. Rufus remarried 27 January 1869 to Mrs. Margaret Daniels. Margaret, born 20 September 1835 in Greenbrier County, West Virginia, was the daughter of Fredric Jacot. Her first husband was David Daniels, whom she married 10 May 1858 in Jackson County, Ohio.

Rufus White died 3 March 1886 and was buried at Old Pine beside his first wife. His will (dated 3 March 1886, proved 18 May) names wife Margaret; sons A.B., John and Charles; daughter Emma and granddaughter Orie Redfern of the home. Margaret (Jacot) White died 28 February 1907 and was also buried at Old Pine.

**WILLIAM ALMON WHITE -** William Almon White (known as "Almon') was the third son of Gallia County First Family Alfred and Mary (Perry) White, born 14 June 1814 in Lawrence County. His parents moved to Gallia County, settling along the banks of Raccoon Creek in Perry Township. He married Mary Burk 18 February 1835 in Lawrence County, a daughter of William and Mary (Neal) Burk of that county, born 5 February 1818. Twelve children were recorded in their Bible: Sarah L., 29 Jan 1836 (married James W. McVay); Alfred, 20 Feb 1837 (married Elizabeth Trussell); Mary Ann, 2 Feb 1839 (married Benjamin Abbott Atwell); Isaac N., 27 Dec 1840 (married Emily Trussell); Samuel J., 22 Apr 1843; Lucinda J., 22 May 1845 (married Wilson Shannon Lear ); Talmon R., 10 Jan 1848 (married Mary E. Richmond); Nancy E. C., 28 Jul 1850 (married William McConnell); David Curtis, 12 Sept 1852 (married Anna Delphine Brewer); Eliza Howel, 5 Sept 1855 (m. first James David Smith and second Henry Perrier Macaulay); James Pascal, 2 Sept 1857, died 17 Nov 1857; William Almon Oterbein, 27 Nov 1858 (married Bertha Elizabeth Gard).

*William "Almon" White*

The family lived in Waterloo, not far from Almon's Gallia kin, until c1849. Following a brief stay in Missouri during 1850, Almon purchased his father's farm in Jones County, Iowa. Early in 1856, the family headed for Kansas, getting as far as Davies County. Missouri, when several family members contracted the measles. That summer, Almon purchased a farm near the county seat of Gallatin and a gristmill in Harrison County, thirty miles away.

Almon served in the Civil War (Pvt, Co. B, 1st. Regiment MO SM Cav), being discharged 2 December 1862 for a disability described in the minor's claim as lung disease. Later, Almon returned to Gallia County and wrote:

Wales Gallia Co. Ohio May 31st 1864. Dear family. I rote you when in Cincinnati.. .I was very weak... and would start in a few days to Gallia County ,I continued getting worse... Sam said he would come with me for fear I would fall by the way amongst Strangers, so we Started on Thursday the 19 and got to Gallipolis on Saturday morning, hired a horse and buggy to ride 8 miles out to Sister Rachel's [in Rodney] paid $4.00.. .They sent to [my brother] Rufus on Sunday and he was gone from home to see a woman leave this world so he came down to Rachel's on Monday morning and Sam and me went home with him.. .I continued to get worse and weaker... finally I began to feel better... at Saint Louis. I took the disease using the river water ,came round all the way to Gallipolis by water.

June 9 1864 I am gaining strength daily. I may not get home until fall, my cough is returning.. .my common weight when well was 155 now it is 130.

Almon made it home to Gallatin before he died on 7 October 1864. Circumstances for his widow and five minor children worsened when raiders burned the homestead. Destitute, Mary fled to Jasper County, Iowa, where some of her older children were living. She died there on 15 March 1874.

*Submitted By: Linda Gaylord-Kuhn*

**WHITE, CLARY, GLENN FAMILY -** Job Hamilton White was born October 26, 1871, on White Hollow Road in Walnut Township, Gallia County, OH, to William H. White (born September 19, 1824 in Maryland-died December 9, 1902, Gallia County, OH) and Sarah Luman (born September 27, 1836, Muskingum County, OH-died March 22, 1902, Gallia County, OH).

*Arlene Glenn (1936) And Job White (1871-1948)*

On December 14, 1899, Job married Rebecca Jane Clary (born December 20, 1871, Gallia County-died July 7, 1909, Gallia County). Rebecca was the daughter of John James Clary (born December 14, 1837, Noble County, OH-died March 26, 1909, Gallia County) and Avis Galloway (born June 25, 1846, Guernsey County, OH - died September 1, 1904, Gallia County).

Three daughters were born in Gallia County to Job and Rebecca. They were Anna May (born October 13, 1900-died May 21, 1979, Jackson County, OH), Mamie Marie (born August 16, 1902-died 1988 Jackson County, OH) and Priscilla Jane (born August 22, 1905-died 1976 Washington Court House, OH).

Rebecca died in 1909. Job never remarried and raised the girls himself. Their three daughters graduated from Rio Grande College in 1929. Job died January 27, 1948, in Washington Court House and is buried in Vinton Memorial Park. Rebecca is buried in Lawrence Chapel Cemetery, Lawrence County, OH.

On May 3, 1934, Anna married Harry McKinley Glenn (born November 10, 1891, Springfield Township, Gallia County-died February 21, 1952, Vinton, OH) son of Elza Armstrong Glenn and Anise Victoria Ewing.

Harry had a barber shop in Vinton. Anna returned to teaching school in 1946. She retired from the Highland County, Ohio, School system in 1970. They are buried in Vinton Memorial Park, Vinton, OH.

Harry and Anna had five children born in Gallia County.

1. Ewing Fredrick (August 2, 1935-August 3, 1935).

2. Arlene Marie (July 29, 1936) married Buddy Charles Uldrich (October 2, 1932), son of Icie Mae Uldrich and Isaac Hannon Sheets. They have five children:

Renee and husband, John Lamont. She has two children: Angela and Vincent.

Dennis Alan (July 27, 1955, Gallipolis, OH-December 21, 2000, New Jersey), married Trudy Griffin. Children: Emily, Dennis Jr., and John.

Ronald Eugene married Karen Rentz. Children: Stephanie and Brittany.

Gregory Charles married Debra Rauch. Son: Dylan. Lynne Kristine married Donald Hock. Daughter: Caitlin.

3. Howard Eugene (October 12, 1938-January 31, 2001, Pike County, OH) married Judy Argabright. Children: Jeffrey (1961-1988), Timothy and Susan. Grandchildren: Natilie and Madison.

4. Irene Victoria (May 11, 1940) married Daryl Petrie. Children: Terry, James, Robin and Steven. Grandchildren: Natalie, Christopher, Rebekah, Travis, Haley, Tyler, and Sara.

5. Clara Belle (December 5, 1941) married Herbert Montgomery. Children: Lori and Brian.

Arlene and Buddy moved from Gallia County to Kettering, OH, in 1955.

*Submitted by Arlene Glenn Uldrich*

**CHRISTOPHER BARRY AND KIMBERLY KAY (BARNHILL) WILCOXON** - Christopher Barry Wilcoxon was born December 22, 1973, in Gallipolis, Ohio, to Merrill and Judy (Thomas) Wilcoxon. Merrill, born to Dewey and Helen (Halley) Wilcoxon on September 28, 1939, is a native of Gallia County as is Judy, daughter of Marvin and Grace (Sisson) Thomas. Judy was born January 9, 1942. Merrill and Judy were married on November 4, 1961, in Chillicothe, Ohio.

They have three sons—Joey David, Stephen Lee, and Christopher Barry. Joey is married to Rebecca Hoafat and Steve to Portia Hensley. Joey and Rebecca have five children—Lauren Morrison, Brittany Wilcoxon, Alex Morrison, Adriana Wilcoxon, and Joseph (Pierce) Wilcoxon. Stephen and Portia have one child, Natalie Wilcoxon. Christopher married Kimberly Kay Barnhill on May 4, 2001, in Gatlinburg, Tennessee. She was born May 22, 1973, to George Perry Barnhill and Violet Kay (Mathers) Barnhill in Brewster, Washington. George (Perry) born to George and Jane (Fournier) Barnhill on December 14, 1944, in Carson City, Nevada, met Violet (Kay) while living in California. Kay was born March 30, 1948, in Wenatchee, Washington, to Lowell Donald (Jack) Mathers and Violet (Pidcock) Mathers. Perry and Kay Barnhill were married January 28, 1970, in Las Vegas, Nevada. They have two children—Perry Eugene and Kimberly Kay. Perry lives in Kennewick, Washington, and is married to Amy Forsht. They have three children—Justin, Jordan, and Caitlyn.

Christopher attended Gallipolis city schools and graduated from Gallia Academy in 1992. He attended the University of Rio Grande. He then went on to attend Palmer College of Chiropractic in Davenport, Iowa, and graduated with a Doctor of Chiropractic degree in 1997. While in college, he met his wife, Kimberly Kay Barnhill.

Kimberly was born and raised in Washington State. She grew up in Prosser, Washington. She attended local elementary schools and graduated from Prosser Senior High School in 1991. Kimberly's first introduction to Gallia County was in 1998 when she moved to Gallipolis and enrolled at the University of Rio Grande.

Christopher and Kimberly now live in Gallipolis, Ohio. Christopher is enjoying his professional life as a Doctor of Chiropractic. He is the owner of French City Chiropractic in Gallipolis. Kimberly is employed by Bossard Memorial Library in Gallipolis.

*Submitted by Chris Wilcoxon*

**MERRILL L. WILCOXON FAMILY** - Merrill Lee Wilcoxon was born September 28, 1939 to Dewey and Helen (Halley) Wilcoxon in the area of Centenary. Merrill is the youngest of eight children. In 1957, Merrill graduated from Gallia Academy High School and went on to graduate from the Huntington Barber College. Wedding bells rang in Chillicothe when he married Judy Thomas on November 4, 1961. Judy was born January 9, 1942 to Marvin and Grace (Sisson) Thomas of Cheshire. Judy's younger brother was born into the family on January 25, 1944, David Lee, who grew up to become a well-respected chiropractor in the Gallipolis area.. In 1959, Judy graduated from Kyger Creek High School.

*Merrill And Judy Wilcoxon*

Merrill and Judy set up housekeeping in Gallipolis, Ohio. Merrill worked in Gallipolis in the banking industry for 25 years and also raised cattle on his farms in Gallia County. Judy was a homemaker for 20 years before beginning employment in 1982 with the Gallia County District Library. Judy is currently the Deputy Director of the Gallia County District Library. Three children were born to Merrill and Judy. The eldest son is Joey David, born August 11, 1962. Joey graduated from Palmer College of Chiropractic in 1985 and began practicing as a Chiropractic Physician with his uncle, Dr. David Thomas. Joey has a daughter from a previous marriage, Brittany Nicole, born June 16, 1986. In 1991, Joey began his own practice, the Gallipolis Chiropractic Center. In 1992, Joey married Rebecca Hoafat Morrison. Rebecca has two daughters from a previous marriage, Lauren and Alexandra. Two children were born to Joey and Rebecca: Adrianna Juliette, born December 5, 1997 and Joseph Pierce, born July 25, 1999. Rebecca is office manager of the Gallipolis Chiropractic Center. In 2001, Joey performed at the Gallia County Junior Fair and promoted his newest CD, "Bitter Side of Sweet".

The second of Merrill and Judy's sons is Stephen Lee, born November 16, 1967. Steve married Portia Hensley on June 18, 1994. Portia is the daughter of James and Brenda (Wheeler) Hensley of Gallipolis. In December 1990, Portia obtained a bachelor's degree in journalism from Morehead State University. Steve graduated from Palmer College of Chiropractic in 1997 and began practicing as a Chiropractic Physician along with his brother, Dr. Christopher Wilcoxon. Both Steve and Chris were proud to name their new chiropractic center "French City Chiropractic", in memory of their uncle, Dr. David Thomas. On February 7, 1999, a daughter, Natalie Grace, was born to Steve and Portia.

Christopher Barry Wilcoxon is the youngest of Merrill and Judy's sons. Chris was born December 22, 1973. In 1997, Chris graduated from the Palmer College of Chiropractic and began practicing as a Chiropractic Physician with his brother Steve at the French City Chiropractic.

Chris married Kimberly Barnhill on May 4, 2001 in Gatlinburg, TN, Kim was born to Perry and Kay Barnhill of the state of Washington. Kim is employed as a circulation clerk at the Gallia County District Library.

Merrill and Judy enjoy a rich family life filled with Sunday dinners and croquet matches in the backyard. They agree that there is nothing greater than spending time with their grandchildren.

*Submitted by: Judy Wilcoxon*

**DR. STEPHEN LEE, PORTIA LOUISE (HENSLEY) WILCOXON FAMILY** - Stephen Lee, born November 16, 1967 in Gallipolis, Ohio, is the son of Merrill Lee Wilcoxon and Judy Ann (Thomas) Wilcoxon. Merrill, born September 28, 1939 in Centenary is the son of Dewey Joseph and Helen (Halley) Wilcoxon, both deceased.

*Stephen, Portia, & Natalie Wilcoxon*

Judy, born January 9, 1942 in Cheshire, is the daughter of the late Marvin Warren and Grace Marie (Sisson) Thomas. Merrill and Judy were married on November 4, 1961 in Chillicothe, Ohio. Stephen has two brothers, Dr. Joey D. Wilcoxon and Dr. Christopher B. Wilcoxon.

Portia Louise (Hensley) Wilcoxon, born October 30, 1967, in Minot, North Dakota, is the only child of James Monroe and Brenda Mae (Wheeler) Hensley. Jim, born December 13, 1940 in Covington, Kentucky, is the seventh son of

*Christopher Barry And Kimberly Kay (Barnhill) Wilcoxon*

Starling and Minnie Belle (Patton) Hensley, both deceased. Brenda, born June 4, 1945, in Cincinnati, Ohio is the youngest daughter of the late David Jr. and Stella Mae (Money) Wheeler. Jim and Brenda were married June 27, 1964 in Hebron, Kentucky. The Hensleys moved to Gallipolis in 1980.

Stephen is a 1986 graduate of Gallia Academy High School. In 1990, Stephen obtained a B.S. in Mathematics with a double minor in Chemistry and Computer Science from University of Rio Grande. Stephen was employed as a Chemist for the American Electric Power Central Laboratory from 1991-93. He graduated from Palmer College of Chiropractic in Davenport, Iowa on June 13, 1997 and opened French City Chiropractic on February 2, 1998, along with his younger brother, Dr. Christopher B. Wilcoxon.

Portia is a 1986 graduate of Ohio Valley Christian School. In 1990, Portia obtained a B.A. in Journalism from Morehead State University in Morehead, Kentucky. Stephen and Portia were married on June 18, 1994 in Gallipolis. Their family includes one daughter, Natalie Grace, born February 7, 1999 in Huntington, West Virginia. Stephen, Portia and Natalie are members of Vinton Baptist Church in Vinton, Ohio.

Both Stephen and Natalie are members of the First Families of Gallia County. Stephen is 7th generation and Natalie is 8th generation Gallia Countians through Stephen's mother Judy Ann Thomas Wilcoxon.

**WILCOXON'S BARBER SHOP** - The owner, Willis G. Wilcoxon, is a Gallia Countian who graduated from Gallia Academy. He attended Andrews Barber College, Columbus, Ohio, in 1954. He did his 18 months barbering apprenticeship at Helman's Barber Shop, Waverly, Ohio, and Fletcher's Barber Shop, Ironton, Ohio. Af-

*Willis Wilcoxon*

ter completing his apprenticeship and receiving his master barber licenses, he was drafted into the Army for a period of 2 years. He took basic training at Fort Smith, Arkansas, and after basic was sent to Fitzsimmons Army Hospital, Denver, Colorado; there he spent the remainder of his 2 years. As quickly as he was discharged from the Army, he returned to his home (Gallipolis, Ohio) to open a business of his own, being Wilcoxon's Barber Shop. He rented a room in the Lafayette Hotel at 44 Court Street, Gallipolis, Ohio. The barber shop was opened for business in 1958 and remained at 44 Court Street until 1973 when property at 37 Court Street (the current location of the barber shop) was purchased from Ben and Madge Eachus. The Eachus property at 37 Court Street has been used for a barber shop in earlier years. When the business opened in 1958, regular haircuts were $1, and the barber shop was open Monday through Saturday. Business was booming even though there were several other barber shops in Gallipolis. After 43 years, the barber shop is open three days a week with haircuts by appointment. A regular haircut now costs $12. You can always view interesting photographs and pictures in the windows of the barber shop. Quite often you will see visitors to Gallipolis stop and view them.

*Submitted by Phyllis P. Wilcoxon*

**ROBERT WILLEY FAMILY** - I was born in Gallia County in June of 1958 at the old Holzer Hospital, the firstborn child of Robert and Joy (Saunders) Spencer. A sister, Melinda, and two brothers, Joel and Jeremy later joined me. I attended Clay Elementary from first to sixth grade, then Gallia Academy, from where I graduated in 1976, wearing a red, white and blue tassel on my mortarboard to commemorate the nation's bicentennial. I continued my education at Rio Grande College, where I received my B.S. in Elementary Education. While there, I met and married my husband, Robert Willey, son of W.K. "Huck" and E. Eileen Willey of Newark, Ohio. Bob was a college instructor and coach of the men's track and cross-country teams. In the winter of 1979, Bob was hired at Morehead State University to coach, so we moved to Morehead, Kentucky. While at Morehead, I completed my M.Ed. in Education, and was employed at the university to teach in their Head Start program. Our oldest child, Kelsey, was born at Good Samaritan Hospital in Lexington, Kentucky in July of 1983. In 1985, Bob had the opportunity to return to Rio Grande, so we moved back to Gallia County, into a small white house on Mabeline Drive. In March of 1986, our second daughter, Kali, was born at Holzer Hospital. During the fall of that same year, I was hired at Rio Grande College to oversee the Department of Early Field Experiences, a job I held for two years. In the fall of 1988, I was hired as a kindergarten teacher in the Gallia County

*The Willey Family: Bob, Carla, Kelsey, Kali & Kacie.*

Local Schools, for whom I continue to work. Our third daughter, Kacie, was born in August of 1989.

Although time has passed and our family has endured some changes, some things remain the same. Bob is still coaching both the men's and women's cross-country and track teams at The University of Rio Grande, as well as teaching health courses, serving as a positive influence in the lives of the young men and women he serves. I am currently teaching kindergarten at Vinton Elementary School, where I continue to learn from the children as well as teaching them. Kelsey is a freshman at the University of Rio Grande, Kali is a sophomore at Gallia Academy High School and Kacie is a seventh grader at Kyger Creek Middle School. In the winter of 1989 we moved to a larger home on Second Avenue to accommodate our growing family, and still live there today. We are owned by a miniature poodle named "Frisky" and a cat "Pumpkin" (who adopted us). Life (and God) has been good to us, and we are continually thankful for all we have in our lives today.

*Submitted by Carla (Spencer) Willey*

**CLARA WILLIAMS** - Clara was the daughter of William Preston Williams and his wife, Rebecca (Tagg). She was born ca March 18, 1878-79 in Gallia County, probably in the Crown City area. She had several siblings.

Clara was married twice. Her first husband was William H. Caldwell. They married July 25, 1896 in Gallia County. They had two daughters, Clymenia, born ca April 18, 1897. Rebecca was born ca June 1899 and died at a young age.

"Will" died December 11, 1898. Clara's second husband was Jesse A. Woodyard. She married him August 3, 1901 in Gallia County. Their children were William L. ("Uncle Lem"), Ernie, Fred, Earl, Kenneth, Stella and Walter. Kenneth was young; maybe a young teen-ager when he died. Stella married and had a daughter. Stella and Kenneth were not listed as survivors. They had to have died first. Jesse, I believe, died between 1926 - 29 in Columbus, Oh. I'm sure he is buried there.

According to the 1915 Huntington City Directory, Jesse A. and Clara lived at 3016 6th Avenue.

Clara died on May 25, 1961; her funeral was held May 29th by Reverend Boyd Rice at the Cook & Son Funeral Chapel.

*Submitted by Joyce Ann (Byrd) Saunders - great granddaughter at South Elgin, IL. Written by Carole Clagg by Joyce's permission*

**JOHN WILLIAMS FAMILY** - John Williams, born February 20,1796 and died February 18,1879, came to Gallia County from Greenbrier County, Virginia. In March 2, 1818, he married Lucy Tilman Sartain in Gallia County, Ohio. John and Lucy were among the first settlers of Guyan Twp, Gallia County that is the extreme southern township in the county. John and Lucy had the following children: Elijah, John, William, James, Jesse, Sarah, Lewis, George, Clarassa, Ellen, Leatha and Ann. John, William and James were in the Civil War. John died in his second year of service after contracting the measles. William and James both served three years with James dying in Washington after the war had closed.

Elijah, born in Guyan Twp., November 4, 1820, died July 3, 1903, married Eliza Griffith in Lawrence County, Ohio, June 1, 1853. Elijah was engaged in farming in Guyan Twp. Eliza was born in Lawrence County, February 10, 1835 to John and Mary Gwinn Griffith. Elijah and Eliza had the following children: Angaline, John, James, Lucy, Louis B. Mary, Elijah, Murtie, Albert, Letha and Charles.

Louis Benjamin Williams, born January 12, 1864, died August 13, 1940, was married to Rebecca A. Watts, daughter of Michael and Alvira Drummond Watts. Lewis was a farmer in the Crown City, Guyan Township. He and Rebecca are buried in the Crown City Cemetery. They had the following children: Elijah Michael, Carrie, Cornie, Irvin and Clarence.

*Lewis Benjamin (Ben) and Rebecca (Becky) Watts William*

Elijah Michael, born 1893, Crown City, Ohio died June 25, 1975, Gallipolis, Ohio, married Effie Viola Sims in June of 1911. Elijah (Lige) retired from the Gallipolis State Institute and Effie was a homemaker. They resided for many years at 517 Fourth Avenue, Gallipolis. They had the following children: Marjorie, Mildred, Clarence, Alva and Dwight.

Marjorie Agnes, born December 8, 1912, Crown City, died December 7, 1990, Gallipolis, Ohio, married Ernest Monroe Gatewood on January 11, 1934. Marjorie was a homemaker and very active in church work at Grace United Methodist Church. Marjorie and Monroe had the following children: Eleanor and Charles. Eleanor was married to James (Jim) Gilliam and had the following children: James Randall (Randy), Marjorie Lynn, and Margaret Gwen. Marjorie and Monroe are buried Memorial Gardens Cemetery, Gallipolis, and Ohio along with daughter and son-in-law, Eleanor and Jim. Charles has been married three times, first, Sandra Hughes and they had the following children: Thomas Michael, Wendy Renee and Amy Marie. He was second married to Charlene Carter and presently to Deborah Guinther.

Mildred Gertrude was twice married, first to Howard Hardway and second to William Jenkins. Mildred and Howard had the following children: Ann, Charles, (died in infancy), Mickey and Karen.

Clarence married Lillian Shaw, after marriage they moved to Washington County, Ohio but both are buried in Ridgelawn Cemetery, Mercerville, Gallia County. They had the following children: Richard, Roger and Jerry (deceased).

Alva married Belle Patterson, after marriage they moved to Summit County, Ohio. Alva and Belle have the following children: Robert, Jean and Steven. Dwight was married twice, first to Suzie Gay and they adopted a daughter, Victoria, (Vicky). He was married second to Glenna and they reside in Columbus, Ohio.

*Submitted by: Marjorie Gilliam Wood*

**WILLIAM PRESTON WILLIAMS** - William was born December 11, 1839; probably in Gallia County. He was the son of John and Lucy (Sarfain) Williams. He had several siblings.

*Bill Williams, William Preston Williams, born 1839-died 1910. Buried at Goodhope Cemetery in Gallia Co., Ohio*

While in his early 20's, he joined up as a private with the Company G, 3rd WV Cav. U.S.A. (3rd Regiment). He enlisted Oct. 10, 1862 and was discharged on June 30, 1865.

William was united in marriage with Rebecca Tagg March 12, 1869 in Gallia County. He was ca. 29 years old; she was ca. 19-20 years old. She was the daughter of James Tagg and Sarah McComas. William and Rebecca had several children. Among them was Clara A. Williams.

For several years before his death, he received a pension check. According to military records, he received his last check on June 4, 1910. It was for the amount of $30.00. His military records give the death date as June 20, 1910. Gallia County Courthouse records give his death date as June 24, 1910.

William and Rebecca are buried in the Goodhope Cemetery, Guyan Township, Gallia County, Ohio. She died 1897.

*Submitted by Jeffery Thomas Clagg, great,great,great grandson*

**MATTHEW RAY AND LETTY JO (WALKER) WILLIS FAMILY** - Matthew Ray was born May 29, 1962 in Gallipolis, Ohio to Cleeland Ray and Wanda Lou Saunders Willis. Matt was greeted by one sister, Lou Ann who is now married to Kent Shawver. Matt married Letty Jo Walker on May 21, 1983 in Gallipolis, Ohio. Letty was born on September 21, 1960 to Harold Lloyd and Betty Evelyn Roush Walker. Letty was greeted by one sister Paula Sue who is now Polly Salisbury.

Both Matt (1980) and Letty (1978) graduated from Gallia Academy High School. Matthew attended Rio Grande College. Matt then graduated from the Cincinnati College of Mortuary Science in 1982 when he received an Associate Degree in Applied Science. After serving his apprenticeship and passing his state board examinations, Matt became a licensed embalmer and funeral director. He is currently working at Willis Funeral Home on Garfield Avenue and Portsmouth Road in Gallipolis, Ohio. Matt is the president of Willis Funeral Home, which has served Gallia County for twenty-eight years. Having previously co-owned Foglesong Funeral Home in Mason, West Virginia for ten years, Matt is also a licensed embalmer and funeral director in the state of West Virginia. He is a volunteer for the Central Ohio Lions Eye Bank as a certified eye enucleator and a volunteer on the human rights committee for Gallipolis Developmental Center (GDC). Matt has held an Ohio life insurance license since 1987. In 1997, Matt earned his Bachelor of Science in Business with an emphasis in Accounting from Liberty University.

*The Matthew Ray And Letty Jo (Walker) Willis Family*

Letty graduated from Cedarville College in 1982 with a Bachelor of Arts in English Education. In 1986, Letty earned her Master of Science in Education (School Counseling) from the University of Dayton. Letty has been employed by Gallipolis City Schools for eighteen years. Teaching Senior English (college preparatory, practical, and honors English) at Gallia Academy has been an enjoyable and rewarding experience for Letty. Letty is currently serving as English department chair, senior activities advisor, and co-chair for the North Central internal team. In the past, Letty has served as the Gallian yearbook business and editorial advisor. After Pathwise training, Letty has also mentored new teachers to the English department. Participating in two School to Work internship programs, Letty has been afforded the opportunity of meeting and working with several Gallipolis area employers and business owners. In 1990 and 1996, Ashland Oil Inc. awarded Letty the Golden Apple Achiever Award to recognize and reward excellent teachers.

Matthew and Letty have two daughters, Brianne Rae Willis and Brooke Joelle Willis. Brianne was born on June 10, 1986 at Holzer Medical Center. Brianne attended Washington Elementary and is now a sophomore at Gallia Academy High School. Earning recognition on the honor roll every nine weeks, Brianne is enrolled in a college preparatory curriculum with advancement in math and Spanish (Algebra I and Spanish I in eighth grade). Starting her volleyball career in junior high, Brianne has polished her skills through summer camp at Cedarville University. During the 2001 season, Brianne was a member of the Junior Varsity League Championship team. Brianne actively participates in ProTeens where she has earned the rank of Pro III. Brooke was born on July 2, 1991 at Holzer Medical Center. Brooke currently attends Washington Elementary where she is in the fifth grade. Earning recognition on the honor roll every nine weeks, Brooke has participated in the Elks Foul Shooting competition both locally and in New Lexington. During the 2001-2002 season, Brooke participated in Rinky Dink basketball and tournament team play. Brooke participates in Awana. Both Brianne and Brooke actively participate in Gallia County's 4-H program and show market hogs at the Gallia County Junior Fair.

Matt and Letty met at First Baptist Church where Matt is now serving as a van driver and a deacon. Active in the Gallipolis Rotary Club, Matt is a director who has chaired many community activities such as the farm festival booth and the wrestling tournament at Gallia Academy. Desiring to return to the community the love and support they have received, Matt proudly serves the community of Gallia County while Letty proudly serves its youth.

**MARGARET BESS WILSON -** I was born on July 11, 1920 on a farm one mile from Vinton, Ohio, in Gallia County.

My Mother, Cecile Pauline Wallace, was the youngest daughter of Frank and Cathrine Wallace.

*Margaret Bess Wilson And William H. Wilson*

I started elementary school in Vinton, Ohio, in 1926 Since buses didn't come to the farm at that time, I walked across the hill through the woods each school day. In one week, I was promoted to second grade, because my grandparents had taught me to count and read.

In 1932, my grandmother died and I moved to Alice, Ohio, to live with my mother and stepfather, Vonley C. Thompson.

When I started to High School, I was legally adopted, and my name was changed to Thompson.

In May, 1937, I graduated from Vinton High School, and attended Bliss College in Columbus, Ohio, until the Spring of 1938.

On June 22nd, 1939, I married William H. Wilson, who lived in Gallipolis, Ohio. We were married for 53 years, and have one son, Jack Allen, born August 14th 1942.

My husband was a very talented athlete and was awarded two football scholarships.

The first was from Rio Grande College in 1937, and the second from Eastern Kentucky State College in Richmond.

In 1940, we bought a rolling store, which my husband drove through the country; selling merchandise to customers living in secluded areas. Some people were so needy they traded chickens for groceries!

World War II caused rationing so severe we had to sell the store.

My husband was in the U. S. Navy until 1945. He was a Radar Man Third Class.

After the service he attended Boston University and received his B. S. and Master's Degrees in 1948.

We moved from Boston, Massachusetts, and my husband was Athletic Director at the Reynoldsburg, Ohio, High School until 1961.

Our son graduated from Denison University in Granville, Ohio, in 1964, and married Patty Helbling in September of that year. Their daughter, Gwen, was born July 2, 1965, and married William Kline on March 21, 1987. They have one son, Evan Maxwell, born May 26, 1991, and a daughter, Emma Kate, born April 30th, 1994.

Jack and Patty were blessed with another daughter, Stacie Renee, born May 18th, 1970.

Stacie married Jonathan Brooks on February 17, 1996. They live in Rocklin, California, and have a son, Jack Riley, born September 14, 1996, and a daughter, Abagail, born September 8th, 1997.

My husband attended Ohio State University part time during the 50's and received his administrative degree in 1961. He was principal and superintendent in Ohio High Schools until 1971 when we moved to Stuart, Florida, to enjoy retirement. However, he decided to teach again, and was hired at the Martin County High School to teach work experience to slow learners.

In 1977, a stroke prevented my husband from continuing his teaching career.

He died on March 25th, 1993. On June 22, 1993 we would have celebrated our 54th year of marriage.

I still live in Florida, but spend summers in Ohio.

**MARY AGNES WILSON -** Mary Agnes Wilson was a slave in Virginia. She was going to be sold, but as she was crying near her cabin, a young white soldier saw her and asked the reason for her tears. She told him her plight. He said, NO, he would help her, which he did. He brought her to safety across the Ohio River. His name was Joseph Smith, referred to by his descendants as "Pennsylvania Dutch" or The "German Soldier". He stayed with Mary Agnes and they lived on what was and is known as Buck Ridge. (because of the large quantity of deer).

*Mary Agnes Wilson Smith and sons Charles and Christopher*

Joseph was a member of the "Squirrel Hunter" unit during the Civil War. He died December 25, 1882 according to Record of Registration of War Veterans Graves, Gallipolis Courthouse Verification, Springfield Township 4.

Mary Agnes and Joseph were parents of twelve children, 1. Granville born 1850 died 1917, married 1st wife, Mary Mayo (2 children), 2nd wife, Sally Lewis - no children, 2. Alexander, born February 25, 1851, died August 7, 1930, 9 children, 3. Madeline, born 1855, married John Robert Mayo and there were eleven children, 4. John, born 1857, died June 2, 1950, married Martha Carter there were seven children, 5. Barbara, born 1859, married Phillip G. Colston and there were three children, 6. Henry, born August 2, 1860, died September 20, 1883, never married, 7. Jophannis, born 1861, no information, 8. Jerome, born 1863, died January 2, 1960 married Fannie Cordell and there were ten children, 9. Hattie, born January 16, 1870, died November 4, 1940, married John Garner and there were twelve children, 10. Mary (Mollie) age 6 months, 1870 census - married Henry Guthrie and there were four children, 11. Christopher, born February 24, 1874, married Hettie Brindley and they had one son, 12, Charles, birth date unknown, married Rosa Garnes and they had one son.

Mary Agnes Wilson and Joseph Smith descendants cover a time period beginning in 1830 until now.

Her life was rich and full. She has history of being a loving and caring person, an excellent cook and the best maker of homemade light bread said her grandson, Alexander "Cap" Smith" in the area. He would leave his mother's home-cooked meal and go to "Grandma's" house and eat huge slabs of bread and homemade jelly.

Mary Agnes and Joseph were married March 22, 1879, three years before his death.

Mary Agnes's death certificate says her father was W. H. Wilson and her mother was Polly Hill. She died January 9, 1916 of valvular heart disease and is buried in Buck Ridge Cemetery.

She and her family were some of the organizers of the Providence Baptist Church. Her son, Jerome, helped to build the church building that stands under the remodeled section of today 2002.

Records show that she had a brother named Daniel Wilson and a half-brother named Jim Johnson. They all lived in the same area.

*Submitted by Barbara M. Smith Scott*

**LOTTIE (DEWITT) WODA -** Lottie (DeWitt) Woda was born on September 20, 1901 at Rodney, Ohio to Abraham Lincoln and Dora (Erwin) DeWitt. She died on September 13, 1994 after spending most of her adult life in Grove City, Ohio. The following is an article written for the Grove City Record by writer Barb Albert:

"I'm only halfway to 92," smiled 91-year-old Lottie Woda, a Grove City resident and former teacher, "but I feel better than I did when I was 40, so I'm thankful every day."

The energetic senior stays busy "every day but Saturday" with activities at the Evans Senior Center in Grove City, with quilting and reminiscing, about old times with her grandson Fred. Woda has four grandchildren and seven great-grandchildren.

"I started teaching September of 1919 when I was just 18 years old," remembers Woda. "I started in a one-room school in Gallia County in southern Ohio," she said.

"I got my teacher training at Rio Grande College in two years," Woda said, "and I tell you, in the two years, we got more of what you need in a classroom than you get in four years of school now."

Woda remembers training that focused on real experiences rather than theory. "One class was observation and conference," she said. "For two days, we had to watch the teacher, and then we met with her two other days of the week to find out why she did the things she did in the classroom," she said.

"Teachers were supposed to have high conduct and set an example," Woda said. "There were a lot of old maids who were teachers, because you couldn't be married and teach," she said. "In that first classroom, I had all eight grades, with an average of about 25 children," she said. "We had a schedule to follow. The smaller desks were in the front, and there was a long recitation seat along one side."

"One class would come up and do recitation work and get their assignments and the little ones would listen, then the next class would come up and do the same," said Woda. "There was order, and the younger ones would learn a lot from the older children."

"The children were there to learn, and the parents expected them to make the best of it," she said."

Discipline problems were few. "They respected their teachers back then," said Woda. "They knew if they were disciplined at school, their parents would do it again at home, so they kept out of trouble," she laughed.

Woda recalled thinking that her increase in salary from $65 to $100 a month for teaching would make her rich. "I got more if I did my own custodial work after the kids left school, so I did," said Woda. That work included cleaning, taking care of the wood floors and stoking the coal furnace each morning.

Recess time was spent making up amusements, as there was no playground at the school. "We would play jump rope or tag or some other game," she said. "Kids were happy making up things to do then."

A water bucket and tin cup was filled each day by willing volunteers after a long trek to a neighbor's house, and the bathroom facilities were outdoors. Woda taught in the one-room school for three years, and then moved to fifth grade in an elementary school building. She married shortly thereafter and said good-bye to teaching.

"Later, I taught special education classes for 20 years, until I had to retire at 70," said Woda. Woda's classes were at what was then called Orient State Institute. "We learned more from them than they learned from us," she said of her mentally handicapped students."

During that time, Woda decided to go back to college. She finished her education at Capital University, receiving her degree at 60 years of age.

"Right now, I get up every day and get dressed, just like I am getting ready for work, and I go somewhere," said Woda. "I go to get around other people and that keeps me going."

**ELLA LOUISE EWING THOMPSON WOLTZ -** In 1810 William and Mary Ewing settled in the wilderness of Gallia County, Ohio. In 1852 their son, George, laid out the town of Ewington. In 1879 George's grandson Isaac Lafayette Ewing married Ella Salome Jones. They owned a farm near Ewington and had six children, the youngest being Ella Louise Ewing, born in January 31, 1901, in Gallia County. Louise, as she was known, lost her mother in 1905, and her father in 1910, whereupon her sister Grace undertook to raise her. Grace and Louise moved to Wilkesville, where the elder sister worked as a milliner and seamstress while Louise attended school.

*Louise Woltz And Great-grandson Jay Kahn*

On August 2, 1919, Louise married Carney Harold Thompson. They lived in Salem Center where Carney ran a small coal mine for his father. The couple had three children: Ellen Louise, Edythe Arita, and Harry Ewing Thompson. In 1927 the family moved north to Akron where Carney worked at the Goodyear Tire Factory for two years, then they returned to southern Ohio, where he managed a small coal mine in Clarion. Carney died May 7, 1931, in Gallipolis and was buried in Salem Center, Ohio.

Louise and the children moved to a house in Wilkesville. Both mother and children attended school, Louise soon completing her high-school education. In 1933 a new minister, Russell Harrison Woltz, came to town to take charge of the Presbyterian Church that Louise attended.

Rev. Woltz was a widower with a daughter, Mary, nearly the same age as Harry. On September 5, 1934, Louise and Russell were joined in marriage. After continuing his education at Ohio University, Russell taught school in Wilkesville, in addition to being minister of the church.

Louise worked as Township Clerk in Wilkesville and clerked in a local store.

In 1957 Louise and Russell retired to Wellston, leading a contented life. Louise enjoyed the Wellston Study Club and belonged to the DAR in Gallipolis. An active churchwoman, she was the Treasurer of the Lena Osier Circle at the Presbyterian Church in Wellston. Louise is remembered as a superb quilter, an avid bridge player, and a good friend.

Russell died April 28, 1980. Louise moved to Seton Square. senior housing in Wellston, where she lived to be 88 years old, passing away April 29, 1989. She is buried next to Russell in Hamden Cemetery in Hamden, Ohio. Louise was proceeded in death by her son, Harry Thompson, who died September 3, 1981. As for her daughters, Edythe Kahn passed on March 3, 1998; Ellen Metheney lives near Cincinnati, close to Harry's two sons; and Mary Shrader resides in Philo, near Zanesville. Louise was blessed with nine grandchildren: Roger, Louise, and Wilma Kahn; Benjamin, Russell, and Ellen Thompson; and Stephen, Susanne, and Michael Shrader.

Many great-grandchildren and several great-great-grandchildren have joined Louise Woltz's branch of the Ewing family tree. Although these kin currently reside outside Gallia County, Ellen Thompson, an R.N., lived in Gallipolis for several years.

*Submitted by Wilma J. Kahn, granddaughter of Louise Woltz, on behalf of Ellen Metheney, daughter of Louise Woltz*

**FAMILY OF ELIJAH & LOUIE WOOD -** Elijah Lewis Wood Born: 9-8-1874 Died: 12-7-1954, Louis Elizabeth Ellison Born: 6-5-1878 Died: 9-19-1975, Married on March 20, 1900 Parents of 11 Children

SURVIVING CHILDREN

Virgie Wood Rogers Born: 9-6-1902 Died: 3-13-1992, Married Jesse Rogers Born: 10-11-1909 Died: 1-16-1958.

*Louie & Elijah Wood*

Children: Abby Tucker, Don Rogers, Maxine Rogers, Wanda Blair & Buddy Rogers Deceased: Don-1963, Maxine-1927, Wanda-1990 & Buddy-1998 Granddaughter Joyce Rogers Petry-1992 & Great-Grandson Jeffrey Don Rogers 1997 Carmel Wood Born: 4-17-1904 Died: 4-17-1968, Married Hettie Kennison Born: 8-1-1908 Died: 6-1-2001.

Children: Mary Reese, Dale Wood, Gnelda Workman, Debra Ratliff & Carmel Wood Jr. Deceased: Dale-1988 Grandson Randy Ratliff-1983 Thelma Wood Kirkpatrick Born: 2-17-1907 Died: 8-2-1995, Married Jim Kirkpatrick Born: 1-26-1898 Died: 8-16-1985.

Children: Phyllis Curry, Kenneth Kirkpatrick & Yulonda Gancs Deceased: Children Charlene, Shirley & James Corbet Beulah Wood Stone Born: 6-23-1908, Married Orville Stone Born: 8-10-1907 Died: 11-8-1994.

Children: Donald Stone, Jewel Eddy, Ed Stone, Libby Mitchell, Ronnie Stone, Gary Stone, Gail White, Naomi DeBoard & Larry Stone.

Deceased: Donald-1944, Larry-1998, Grandson Steve Eddy-2001 & Great-Granddaughter Krystal Karol Wallace-1979 Dana Wood Born: 10-31-1910 Died:9-22-1972 Married Mattie Platt Born: 1-31-1916 Died: 5-18-1979.

Children: Janet Gilbert, Roger Wood & Alice Perry Deceased: Twin Granddaughters Reda & Freda Perry-1968 Born: 9-8-1915 Garnet Wood Born: 9-8-1915 Died: 5-18-1931 Never Married Eldion Wood Born:4-23-1919 Married Clara Pauley Born: 1-27-1928 Died: 12-3-1992.

Children: Jerry Wood, Connie Robinson, Rita Devins, Bobby Wood, Sandi Wymer, Steve

Wood, Randy Wood & Kaye Tyler Deceased: Bobby-1971, Sandi-1999 & Granddaughter Kristi Lynn Tyler-1977.

**ROBERT WOODWARD FAMILY** - Robert Lee Woodward, the son of George Edward and Nona Lee Henderson Woodward, was born on December 6, 1948. He has five siblings, Kay Lynn Maciag, Nona Kimberly Canaday, George Edward Woodward, Jr., Gregory Scott Woodward, and Daniel Fox Woodward. Bob grew up on the family farm located on State Route 775. He graduated from Gallia Academy High School in 1966 and then moved to Columbus where he attended Franklin University and then received his degree in Civil Engineering from Columbus State University. Bob is currently employed by a Columbus based engineering firm as a Field Representative.

*L: To R: Angela Steger, Robert Woodward, Jr. And Kimberly Woodward.*

Marjorie Jane Robinson was born on June 17, 1948, the daughter of Ralph O'Dell and Marjorie Louise Moore Robinson. She has two sisters, Martha Louise Schmick and Sylvia Anne Robinson. Jane grew up in Gallipolis, Ohio, and graduated from Gallia Academy High School in 1966. She received her B. S. in Elementary Education from the University of Rio Grande and her MA. in Elementary Education from Marshall University. She has been employed by the Mason County Board of Education for 32 years.

Robert and Jane were united in marriage by Pastor James Frazier on November 4,1978, at the Grace United Methodist Church in Gallipolis, Ohio. They are the parents of three children, Angela Jane Elliott Steger, born October 18, 1970, Kimberly Roberta Woodward, born December 12, 1981, and Robert Lee Woodward, Jr., born August 21, 1983.

Angela is a medical secretary in the Orthopedic Department at Holzer Clinic. She graduated from Gallia Academy in 1988 and received her degree with honors in Computers and Business Management from the University of Rio Grande. Angela has a darling four year old son, Colton Eryk Steger.

Kimberly graduated from Gallia Academy High School in 2000. She is currently attending the Cape Fear Community College Nursing Program in Wilmington, North Carolina. She is a member of Phi Theta Kappa Honor Society.

Robert, Jr. is a senior at the prestigious preparatory school, Western Reserve Academy, located in Hudson, Ohio. He is an honor student and has lettered in football and wrestling. He was named Defensive Lineman of the Year for the 2001 Western Reserve Academy Pioneer Football team. Prior to attending Western Reserve, Robert was an honor student at Gallia Academy High School.

Bob and Jane currently live on the beautiful Ohio River on State Route 7 South. They also have a farm where Bob raises Charolais cattle. They are both members of Grace United Methodist Church.

Special memories for Angela, Kimberly, and Robert, Jr. have been having the opportunity to grow up in close proximity to their grandparents. George and Nona lived just a few miles away and the children have many memories of their visits to the farm. Ralph and Marjorie lived just three houses away. They were both always there for the children whenever they needed anything. Ralph always saw that they got on the bus or he took them to school each morning. He made birthdays and holidays very special times for the children. They lost him on December 31, 2000, but the memories of their special "Papa" will always be held in their hearts.

**ANDERSON WOOTEN, JR.** - Anderson Wooten was born in Gallia County, Ohio June 7, 1821. His parents were John Wooten, Jr. and second wife Mary Russell Wooten, who were married December 24, 1820 in Gallia County. John Jr. was born October 22, 1775 in Surrey Co., NC and died December 22, 1859 in Clay Twp., Gallia County. Mary Russell Wooten, "Polly", was the widow of John's brother, Thomas Wooten. Mary and Thomas had married in Gallia County November 23, 1808 and had 2 sons, who were Marshall and Littleton. Thomas died August 30, 1818. She was born November 29, 1791 in North Carolina and died April 5, 1863 in Gallia County. Both John and Mary (Russell) Wooten Jr. are buried in Providence Cemetery, Clay Twp., Gallia County. The first wife (name unknown) of John Wooten, Jr died about 1818 in Green River, Kentucky.

Anderson Wooten first married Sarah Ann Halley on April 3, 1849, who was born March 1829 and who died May 23, 1851 in Gallia Co.. Sarah Ann is buried at Mercerville, Ohio.

Anderson then married Eustatia Martindale, daughter of James Alexander & Julia Anne (Cottrell) Martindale in late 1851. Eustatia was born August 3, 1833 in Gallia County and died July 15, 1903. Anderson died April 3, 1897. Both Anderson and Eustatia are buried in Providence Cemetery, Gallia Co., Ohio.

The twelve children of Anderson and Eustatia Wooten all born in Gallia County were: Julia Ann, born October 31, 1852, who married Jasper Newton Cox January 28, 1874 in Gallia Co. Ohio. Jasper and Julia left Ohio and settled on homesteaded land claimed in the 1893 "Run" of Oklahoma Territory. Julia died September 10, 1928 and Jasper died April 1931 in Noble Co., OK.: Missouri, born May 21, 1854, married Win. Sylvester Ashley October 8, 1871 in Gallia Co., and died August 3, 1928 in Meigs, County, Ohio: Caroline, born April 4, 1856, married Charles Thornley August 28, 1875 in Gallia County: James A. was born May 20, 1858 and died July 3, 1876 in boating accident: Mary E., born December 14, 1860, married Frank R. Swigert May 15, 1878 in Gallia Co. and died in California: John Anderson, born February 28, 1863, married Savannah Johnson August 28, 1898 and died August 29, 1944 in Gallipolis, Ohio:

Wesley Paul, born April 30, 1865, married Annie Lee Houck July 9, 1887 in Gallia Co. and died November 16, 1922 in Caddo Co., Oklahoma: Emily Frances, born November 4, 1867, married William D. Boston January 11, 1885 and died December 1940, Gallia County. Charles Irwin, born October 29, 1869, married first Donie Cox August 5, 1892, who died 1894, then married Anna Belle Pritchard July 4, 1904. Charles died March 23, 1934 in Pickaway County, Ohio:

Myrtie Alice, born February 23, 1871, who died July 21, 1891: Unnamed infant born 1874 lived 9 days: and William A., born June 19, 1875, married Ida Slayton November 8, 1895. William fell from riverboat and drowned 1905/06.

*Submitted by: Dorothy J. Gum*

**ARTHUR & RUTH WROBLEWSKI** - Arthur and I came to Gallipolis with our two sons from Pittsburgh, Pennsylvania in February, 1952. Our third son was born the following August at Point Pleasant Clinic. We lived in the East End for some years before moving to First Avenue, overlooking the beautiful Ohio River.

*Arthur & Ruth Wroblewski*

Arthur's first job was at Evans Supermarket, where he was produce manager. He got to know a lot of the Gallia County farmers, as they brought their produce to the store in those days. He worked at several jobs after that but finally ended up at the Post Office delivering mail in the city from where he retired after twenty-three years. He was an Army veteran of World War II. He was a life member of the VFW and American Legion. He was also a member of the Elks, Moose, French City Campers and Pomeroy Dance Club.

We started camping in 1956 traveling and camping throughout the eastern United States. We enjoyed camping in our beautiful state parks. We often fished in a little body of water called Evans Lake near Gallia, Sometimes we would take a frying pan and bread and have our dinner of catfish right on the spot. He also fished in Tycoon Lake and many of the large lakes in our state.

Every time anyone came to visit us we would take them to Fortification Hill with its fantastic view. We made sure they saw our beautiful downtown park with its lovely bandstand. We loved showing off our beautiful little city. We found a grave in Mound Hill Cemetery of a person who went down on the Titanic and we always made sure our visitors saw that. I don't think too many of our townspeople even know about that.

Our two older sons went to school in the little two-room schoolhouse where Mrs. Thompson and Mrs. Wood were teachers. They later attended Washington School where our third son started first grade.

Graduating from Gallia Academy High School, one son went on to graduate from Rio Grande College, becoming an accountant and one attended Marshall University. Our oldest son worked for 23 years as Assistant Engineer on towboats on the Ohio and Mississippi Rivers.

When our sons were growing up, we often went swimming at Vinton, Cora Mills and other swimming holes on Raccoon Creek. We enjoyed going with our family to Columbus to the Center of Science and Industry and the Cinerama Theater.

Arthur passed away in January 1992 while we were vacationing in Florida.

I am proud to be a Gallia County resident and always loved living in this beautiful little city. I can't imagine living anywhere else in the world.

*Submitted by Ruth Wroblewski*

## CAPTAIN CHARLES MONROE YOUNG

**1891-1978** - Charles Monroe Young was born on a hilltop farm near Evergreen, in Putnam County, West Virginia. His parents were John Riley and Mattie Parsons Young. His grandparents were Hezekiah and Emily Jane Ober Young of German descent. Charlie was the second oldest of 17 children. When he was seven, his family moved to Lock 10 on the Kanawha River. In his own words, "I have been near, on, and sometimes under the water ever since". He started his long career on the river at age 15 in 1906. His first job was as a cabin boy earning $.50 a day on the steamboat Robert P. Gillham. He worked his way up to deck hand, mate, pilot, and earned his Master's license in 1923 at age 32. The Gillham was renamed Henry C. Yeiser, Jr. in 1925; Charlie was the only master of the Yeiser until it sank in high water while laid up for repairs in 1940. Weather and high water were major problems as they towed tons of coal up and down the river so many years ago.

*February 1937 Flood, Gallipolis Bandstand*

Through the years, my father, Captain Young, was featured in many newspaper and magazine articles. He was listed in "Who's who on the Ohio River" in the 1930's; included in an episode as mate in Frederick Way's 1943 book, "Pilotin Comes Natural"; and was the captain of the winning sternwheeler, J. T. Hatfield, in the "last steamboat race" which was televised on Wide, Wide World in 1956. Recently I was pleased to see a genealogy page on the internet referring to him as a "famous riverboat captain". He was proud of the fact that he had never lost a life nor had a serious injury on "his watch".

Charlie raised 6 children with thoughtfulness and generosity. His first children were sons, Charles Lane and Dana Young (who were also riverboat captains) and a daughter, Helen Young Eakle; his second family included his wife, Goldie Eulett Abbott (from Kentucky), their twins, Charles Monroe Young 11 (who retired from the U.S. Army after serving in Vietnam twice) and Mrs. Dwight (Gloria Young) Stevers, and Goldie's daughter from a previous marriage, Mrs. Donald (Mary Abbott) Paynter.

On February 14, 1942, we moved to a big red, brick house known as the Menager house (built in 1865) located at 218 First Avenue, Gallipolis, Ohio. Charlie and Goldie had admired this little town for years as they passed by on the Yeiser. Gallipolis was always "lit up like a Christmas tree"; it was one of the prettiest towns along the Ohio River and this impressive old house had a beautiful view of the river.

Because Charlie had to leave home and school at an early age to help support his family, he became an avid reader and was a "self-made, self-educated" man. He was very intelligent and could relate history as if he had been there. He loved to tell stories, especially about the river. I can remember listening to the "river stories" he shared with my mother when he was home from the boat. Goldie had been a cook on the Yeiser in the 1930's and enjoyed hearing all the "goings on" as much as he enjoyed telling her about it. My earliest memories of my dad are of standing on the porch with my brother and mother waving to him as he passed by on the boat. He always blew the whistle as he came around the bend so we would know he was passing by. Goldie and Charlie were a sweet, old-fashioned couple. As those who knew Charlie will remember, he always tipped his hat to the ladies when he took his walk up the street to sit in the park. I remember seeing him head off to the park when he was 84 carrying a hammer, nails and a piece of wood to repair the park bench he sat on. As I type these words, I can still hear a soft-spoken old fellow, wearing gold-rimmed glasses and smoking his ever-present cigar. I never heard him raise his voice in anger. There are many things to be said about these two wonderful people, but it can't be done in 500 words or less.

Goldie passed away in 1976. Charlie spent his remaining years sitting by the window watching his old friend, the river, roll by and listening for friends in the pilothouses of passing boats to blow their whistles and say hello. He still loved to tell "river stories", wave at the boats, and reminisce about his 53 years of adventure on the river.

Charlie and Goldie are remembered by daughter and son-in-law, Dwight and Gloria Stevers with love and a smile. They are remembered by their granddaughters, Christine (Wes) Reynolds, Deborah (Tim) Adams, and Judy (Bart) Bradshaw, as probably the most important influence in their lives because of the quiet strength, kindness and love they showed my girls as they grew up.

Capt. Charlie Young should be noted as one of Gallipolis' most memorable characters. Submitted by their daughter and son-in-law, Gloria (Young) and Dwight N. Stevers, Gallipolis, Ohio.

# Index

## A

Aaron 167
Abbott 331
Ables 161
Abrams 187
Adams 22, 57, 68, 135, 146, 210, 230, 240, 256
Adcock 211
Adella 309
Adkins 8, 19, 22, 92, 146, 157, 221, 225, 240, 242, 282
Adkinson 55
Adney 16, 227
Agee 29
Ager 151
Agnes 328
Agustin 66
Ahaz 257
Ahlborn 79
Ailiff 238
Ainsworth 248
Akers 22, 157
Alberchinski 66
Albert 272, 328
Albrinck 48, 54
Alcorn 43
Alden 217
Alderman 267
Aldridge 248
Aleshire 39, 55, 77, 241, 246
Alexander 45, 70, 89
Alf 180
Alfred 187
Allance 161
Allbright 258
Allen 8, 9, 65
Allensworth 31, 36
Alley 193
Allie 22
Allinder 118
Allison 22, 59, 62, 146, 147, 173, 196, 206, 319, 320
Alloway 290
Alonzo 91
Altizer 22, 147
Amolia 271
Amos 22, 29, 36
Amsbary 92
Amsbury 256
Anderson 18, 21, 22, 30, 44, 67, 77, 83, 118, 190, 227, 231, 272, 287, 330
Angel 7, 13, 14, 15, 64, 148, 223, 322
Angell 148, 320
Ankrom 180, 279
Apple 22
Arbaugh 287
Archer 160, 283
Arden 45
Arendall 170
Armsby 256
Armstead 22
Armstrong 22, 26, 59, 62, 72, 83, 118, 147, 150, 162, 290, 295
Arnett 71
Arnold 232, 276
Arnoldussen 50, 51, 54
Arnot 260
Arrington 206, 208, 256
Arthur 146
Asbury 159
Asher 166
Ashley 22, 112
Ashworth 22, 276
Aston 221
Atchinson 94
Atha 22, 132
Athey 32, 161, 210, 243, 278, 289
Atkins 100
Atkinson 64, 160, 234, 235, 275
Augusta 271
Augustus 206
Ault 92
Austens 158
Austin 124
Austin-Braxton 163
Averell 180
Avery 228
Avner 87
Axline 111
Ayres 131

## B

Badin 48, 54
Bailey 14, 15, 39, 118, 148, 149, 271, 291, 308
Bair 223
Baird 20, 149, 150, 151, 152, 175, 177, 210, 247
Baird-Casto 150
Baird-Cheney 150
Baird-Cormick 150
Baisnautier 48
Baker 22, 52, 54, 70, 79, 83, 85, 88, 152, 153, 176, 202, 221, 241, 244, 245, 259, 273
Baldwin 22, 79, 153, 173, 252
Ball 10, 87, 100, 153, 162, 180, 181, 279
Ballard 146
Baly 147
Bane 8, 14, 64, 67, 224, 225
Banks 231
Banner 225
Barber 22
Barckhoff 58
Barcus 8, 132, 221, 225
Barger 26
Barker 22, 174, 222
Barlow 9, 100, 242, 256, 267
Barnes 4, 85, 269
Barnett 83
Barnette 22, 45
Barnhart 275
Barnhill 325
Barr 170
Barret 285
Barrett 295
Barrieres 54
Barry 22, 153, 154, 157, 255
Bartholomew 239
Bartko 264
Barton 124
Bass 21, 72, 281
Bateman 10
Bates 179
Baughman 157
Baxter 22
Bay 11, 12
Bayman 197
Bays 12, 154
Beach 216
Beall 36, 37, 273
Bean 43, 124, 133
Beard 37, 89, 206, 242, 256, 265, 321
Bearden 73
Beardsley 22, 273
Beattie 123, 146, 265
Beaver 22, 64, 100, 141, 153, 154
Beck 8, 22, 155, 156, 157, 177, 209, 228, 271
Beegle 79
Belcher 68, 248
Belier 132
Bell 22, 71, 82
Belle 150, 266
Beller 174
Belville 87, 92, 137, 166, 282, 306
Beman 9, 22
Benglog 147
Bennett 143, 198, 234
Benson 228
Bently 68
Benton 97, 178
Berent 22
Bernadine 135
Bernhardt 129
Berridge 64, 167
Berry 79, 154, 157, 202
Bert 224
Berthelot 135
Bertholf 191, 212, 213
Bess 22, 53
Betz 8, 38, 77, 137, 275, 323
Betzes 60
Beulah 329
Bevins 250
Bias 223
Bickel 13, 157, 158, 162, 305
Bickerstaff 43
Biddle 37, 83, 124, 223
Bidinger 293
Bidwell 24, 244
Biedler 282
Bigham 179
Billings 89
Bills 13
Binder 272
Bing 29, 30, 35, 94, 158, 197, 216, 304
Birchard 313
Birchfield 154
Bird 249
Birkle 123
Bisch 227
Bish 160
Bishop 183
Black 22, 25, 39, 71, 77, 136, 159, 279, 280
Blackaller 110
Blackburn 34, 35, 154
Blackhurst 314
Blackwell 83
Blagg 39, 269
Blair 22, 241, 329
Blake 11, 132, 158, 159, 160, 227, 252, 259, 274, 309, 319
Blank 118
Blankenship 11
Blauser 22
Blazer 43, 63, 79, 85, 147, 160, 161, 227, 238, 291, 308
Blessing 22
Bletner 314
Blevins 22, 76
Bloebraum 268
Bloomer 22, 183
Blosser 91
Blowers 92
Blum 221
Boardman 270
Boatman 256
Bobien 140
Bobine 223
Bobo 19
Bodkins 154
Boehm 52
Boggess 26, 150, 249, 264, 293
Boggs 8, 22, 25, 59, 87, 125, 161, 201, 246, 256, 279
Boice 31, 161
Boisnantier 48
Boister 161
Bolles 89
Bomberger 273
Bonaparte 140
Bond 242
Bonice 22
Bookman 306
Boomer 309
Boone 159, 253
Booten 59
Bootens 60
Booth 20, 118
Booton 89
Borden 25, 72, 83
Born 22
Bosley 209
Boster 13, 51, 53, 137, 152, 153, 161, 162, 174, 245, 271
Bostic 38, 148, 153, 162, 180, 192
Bostick 79, 260
Boston 330
Bosworth 26, 38
Botts 280
Bovie 238
Bowen 69, 177, 212, 246
Bowers 8
Bowles 21
Bowman 22, 56, 161, 166, 316
Boyce 228
Boyd 22, 148, 185, 186
Boyer 92
Brackenridge 286
Bradbury 9, 27, 36, 40, 136, 153, 161, 162, 163, 278, 288, 295
Bradford 217
Brading 55, 238
Bradley 203, 320
Bradshaw 92, 164, 331

Brammer 281
Brandeberry 10, 198, 208
Branham 22
Brannen 22
Brant 229
Braxton 4, 74, 88, 148, 163, 190, 231
Bray 24
Breech 91
Breedlove 230
Brennan 176
Brenneman 135
Brewer 59, 324
Brickle 234
Brickles 141
Bridger 215
Brierly 230
Briggs 40, 85, 163, 231, 295
Bright 304
Briley 84
Brink 84
Brock 229
Broderick 304
Brookmans 24
Brooks 209, 328
Brothers 64, 160
Broughman 189, 312
Browing 19
Brown 4, 22, 26, 41, 55, 66, 68, 70, 90, 92, 132, 154, 158, 164, 165, 173, 202, 219, 247, 281, 284, 296, 311
Brownell 267
Browner 21
Browning 118, 143, 267
Broyles 220, 226
Brucker 64, 271
Brumbach 272
Brumback 221
Brumfield 11, 13, 79, 112, 118, 165, 177, 186, 230, 286, 305
Brumfleld 284
Brunicardi 165, 166
Bryan 22, 68, 250
Bryant 21, 22, 65, 72, 83
Buchonich 177
Buck 23
Buckle 245, 279
Buckley 273
Buell 94
Buffington 72
Bufford 88
Bullock 246
Bumgardner 268
Bunce 21, 242, 321
Bunch 18, 288
Bunning 121
Bunside 22
Buonamici 241
Burcham 166, 282, 305
Burchett 36, 225
Burdue 290
Bureau 57, 94
Burger 85, 216, 310
Burgert 158
Burgess 22, 234, 299
Burgett 290
Burk 166, 322
Burke 19, 20
Burkhart 49, 54
Burkit 268
Burks 21

Burleson 22, 40, 100
Burnem 73
Burner 244
Burnett 8, 22, 56, 60, 62, 65, 125, 166, 167, 168, 321
Burnette 160
Burns 22, 87, 167, 184, 210, 225, 274
Burris 269, 290
Burt 234
Burton 132, 231
Burwell 295, 304
Bush 22, 42, 54, 66, 86, 167, 168, 169, 276, 280
Butcher 30, 36, 42, 169, 171, 208, 211, 212, 222, 278, 284
Butler 38, 109, 150, 246
Buttricks 35
Buys 161
Buzz 220
Byas 223
Byer 22
Byers 233

## C

Cable 22
Cade 182, 297
Cadot 110
Cain 220
Caldwell 15, 22, 40, 56, 75, 90, 148, 167, 169, 179, 204, 239, 259, 271, 290, 307, 326
Calhoun 20, 59, 90, 136
Call 66, 90, 152, 221, 269
Callahan 89, 225, 277
Callihan 118
Calloway 22, 72, 190
Calohan 39, 173
Calvert 304
Calvin 219
Cambell 48
Camden 22
Cameron 89, 169, 170
Campbell 22, 37, 53, 54, 73, 87, 92, 121, 131, 141, 148, 170, 182, 225, 226, 229, 271, 281, 289
Canaday 90, 275, 330
Cannaday 178
Canterbury 224
Cantrell 18, 20, 42, 45, 170, 171, 208
Cantrells 169
Caraway 211
Carder 177
Cardwell 230
Carel 94
Carey 164
Carl 34, 35
Carleton 272
Carman 56, 100
Carmen 233
Carnes 82
Caroll 79
Carpenter 22, 189, 246, 277, 278
Carr 22, 186, 245, 254, 269
Carrier 35
Carroll 48, 118, 155, 157, 270, 271, 279
Carsey 273
Carson 147, 322
Cart 12
Carter 8, 13, 22, 25, 26, 59, 60, 62, 79, 87, 92, 109, 118, 137, 141, 147, 154, 171, 172, 173, 174, 181, 224, 226, 245, 269, 272, 286, 321
Carver 224, 225, 309
Casey 88, 174, 201, 231
Cassidy 92
Casto 18, 33, 59, 60, 63, 73, 141, 151, 174, 175, 176, 210, 216, 232, 254
Caudill 89
Cawthorn 287
Ceiphy 89
Cemini 22
Chadwick 274
Chaflen 240
Chamberlain 85
Chamberlin 271
Chambers 22, 148, 176, 177
Champer 177
Chancelor 158
Chandler 148, 257
Chapel 64
Chapman 11, 45, 56, 68, 70, 118, 135, 177, 209, 226
Chappeli 157, 305
Chappell 157, 158, 209
Chase 11, 30, 304
Chasteen 278, 279
Cheatham 258, 267
Cheesebrew 22
Cheney 55, 149, 150, 151, 177, 210
Cherrington 19, 20, 23, 37, 77, 84, 110, 116, 131, 177, 178, 195, 197, 227, 236, 252, 257, 324
Cherringtons 24
Chich 59
Chick 22, 185
Childers 22, 178, 277, 282, 323
Chrichfield 211
Christensen 98, 213
Christian 22
Church 87
Circle 230
Clagg 22, 153, 155, 327
Clara 271
Clarey 275
Clark 4, 11, 18, 22, 25, 26, 32, 43, 59, 79, 83, 90, 140, 147, 157, 160, 172, 174, 178, 179, 180, 202, 209, 230, 244, 258, 290, 291, 292, 312, 313
Clark 27
Clarke 9, 36, 76, 77, 90, 91
Clarkson 117, 118
Clary 22, 259, 324
Clay 56, 270
Claypool 310
Clayton 176
Clendenen 73
Clendenin 77, 94, 95, 136, 148, 308
Clifford 127, 316
Cline 22, 195
Clonch 22
Cloud 19, 39
Clyse 214, 280
Cobb 221, 227, 256
Coburn 69
Cochran 22, 60, 89, 118, 156
Cocke 269

Coddington 26
Coder 268
Cofer 12
Coffee 8, 277
Coffey 247
Coffman 89
Cogar 4
Cogswell 246
Cohen 234
Colburn 22
Cole 56, 238, 268
Coleman 25, 28, 29, 123, 270
Colgrove 308
Colley 22
Collier 273
Collins 19, 67, 153, 162, 180, 233, 275
Colson 238, 253
Colston 328
Columbus 52, 53, 218
Colvin 68
Colwell 211, 259
Compton 152, 153
Condee 4, 82
Conkle 8
Conklin 87
Conley 9, 17, 67
Conn 56, 100
Connelley 66
Connolly 49, 54
Conzolina 266
Cook 79, 112, 229, 252, 266
Cooley 72
Coonen 180
Cooper 20, 22, 146, 161, 321
Copeland 22
Copenhaver 250
Coply 277
Coppin 71
Corbin 152, 264
Cordell 328
Coriell 299
Cornelius 9, 92
Cornett 37, 50, 53, 91, 263
Cornwell 249
Corrine 152
Cosette 53
Costello 234
Cothen 157
Cotterill 278
Cotton 37
Cottrell 23, 64, 83, 268, 278, 279, 316
Cottrill 39, 180, 181, 279
Coughenour 40, 100, 240
Counts 274
Courcelle 179, 312
Coury 22
Coverston 23
Cowden 160
Cox 8, 15, 22, 100, 146, 180, 181, 182, 183, 212, 229, 252, 260, 269, 274, 288, 297, 330
Crabtree 146, 273
Craft 64, 87, 97
Crago 22
Craig 88, 159
Cramer 242, 295, 321
Crance 37, 142
Crane 304
Crawford 66, 177, 219
Creech 233, 235

333

Cregg 30
Creighton 158
Cremeans 231, 232, 274, 278
Cremeens 8, 13, 92, 111, 309
Creuzet 39, 77, 135
Creviston 218
Crews 22, 60, 284
Criner 42, 143, 212, 223
Croe 160
Croft 155
Cromlish 183, 184
Cron 157
Crook 109, 111
Crouch 225
Crouse 15, 22, 148, 280
Crowell 169, 253
Crum 318
Cubbage 212, 227
Cuer 235
Cull 54
Culp 156
Cunningham 92, 155
Curnutte 118, 146
Curry 227, 242, 321, 322, 329
Curtis 9, 311, 324
Cushing 57, 77, 140
Cutler 9
Cypher 303

# D

Dabney 215, 314
Daft 22, 167, 184
Dages 91
Daggett 238
Dailey 22, 66, 79, 166, 282
Dais 22
Dale 151
Daley 12
Dallas 298
Dalton 142, 269
D'Amico 245, 322
Daniel 12, 66
Daniels 9, 18, 45, 84, 158, 167
Danner 8, 22, 40, 67, 259, 277
D'Arcy 48, 54
Darling 270
Darnborough 91
Darnell 239
Darrell 163
Darst 22, 64, 161, 184, 232, 246,
  247, 278, 285, 288, 289, 295
Dauber 269
Dauer 226, 227
Daugherty 152
Davenport 212
Davidson 230
Davies 22, 92, 142, 184, 225, 239,
  253
Davis 7, 22, 26, 37, 38, 45, 55, 59,
  66, 77, 83, 87, 90, 92, 109,
  116, 124, 125, 143, 146, 157,
  159, 184, 185, 186, 189, 209,
  211, 224, 228, 234, 241, 242,
  256, 273, 280, 309, 315, 321
Davises 60
Davison 22, 48, 49, 50, 53, 54
Day 132, 149, 150, 186, 225, 259
De Board 186
De Graff 161
De Lille 188
De Mille 129
De Soisson 9

De Trieux 161
Dear 300
Deardorff 37, 70, 279
DeBoard 300, 301, 329
Deboard 22, 187
DeCamp 227
Deckard 283
Deem 65
Deer 187, 309
Deeter 155
Defore 187, 188
Degering 49
Deitrick 189
Del Carlo 269
Delaney 248, 268
Delaux 49
Delbert 163
Deletombe 39, 40
DeLille 76, 188, 189, 268
Delille 89, 124
Dellarco 22
Delman 218
Delmond 298
Demko 191
Dempsey 17
Denney 19, 23, 24, 42, 149, 155,
  189, 204, 209, 228, 247, 253,
  254, 262, 310, 311
Denneys 24
Dennis 137
Denny 20, 157, 246
Denson 233
Depree 18
Derifield 143
Derr 277
Derry 82
Detalante 154
Detillion 154
Devacht 48, 185
Devine 71
Devins 329
Devold 153
DeWitt 9, 13, 17, 75, 162, 164,
  189, 190, 214, 215
DeWoody 253
Dexter 143, 147, 148, 163, 190,
  231, 276, 289
Dey 91, 123
Dickerson 18, 20, 289
Dickey 158, 190, 191, 212
Dickinson 96
Diddle 90, 264
Didier 48, 52, 54
Didur 48
Dieter 289
Diffenbach 231
Diggens 248
Diggins 252
Dillbone 199
Dille 276
Dilley 147
Dillion 111
Dillman 190
Dillon 9, 22, 90, 255
Dinay 94
Dingess 266
Dingus 142
Dixon 56
Dodd 195
Dodge 221
Dodrill 18, 176, 191, 275, 309
Doll 83

Donahue 156
Donaldson 62
Donley 277
Donnally 10, 24, 162, 252, 261,
  267
Donnelly 18
Donohue 60
Dooley 275
Doolittle 38
Doronila 123
Dorsey 48, 99
Doss 83
Doster 230
Dotson 22, 127
Doty 307
Double 22
Doubleday 22, 77
Dougherty 227
Doughty 267, 268
Douglas 96, 163
Dowd 49, 54
Dowden 166
Dowler 86
Dowling 265
Downard 85
Doyle 22
Drake 22, 35, 202, 303
Draper 162
Dray 274
Drouillard 77
Drummond 26, 62, 162, 190, 191,
  192, 218, 283, 316
Duc 94
Dudik 161
Due 135
Dufoe 188
Dufoot 188
Dufoor 188
Dufour 187, 188
Duke 22
Dulaney 146, 230
Duncan 22, 165, 192
Dunkle 153, 162, 198
Dunlap 28
Dunlop 285
Dunn 49, 54, 85, 166, 189, 245,
  268, 321
Dunnmore 15
Durose 92
Dursose 92
Durst 9, 265
Dusen 58
Dustin 25
Duty 274
Dwight 191
Dyas 269
Dye 256
Dyer 72, 238, 275
Dyers 24

# E

Elliott 63
Eaches 59
Eagle 36, 37, 192, 193, 289, 315
Eakins 36, 37, 271
Eakle 331
Ealy 72
Earwood 64, 87
Easter 8, 19
Eaton 77
Eberhardt 118

Ebersbach 36, 256
Eblin 36, 225, 246
Ebman 22
Ecker 37, 193, 305
Eckhardt 307
Eddy 194, 320
Edelblute 100, 194, 195, 297
Edelmann 52
Edgar 206
Edison 254
Edlers 60
Edminston 19
Edmiston 195
Edmondson 18
Edmundson 313
Edward 225
Edwards 19, 22, 60, 65, 92, 142,
  189, 242, 321
Ehman 195, 260
Eisel 92
Elliott 26
Elardo 69
Elbin 155
Elkins 230
Ellette 231
Ellifritz 51
Elliott 22, 66, 86, 146, 148, 192,
  195, 196, 206, 218, 239, 242,
  252, 275
Ellis 22, 132, 196, 233
Ellison 22
Ellsworth 226
Elmer 217
Ely 29, 278
Emeritus 72
Emerson 104
Emmett 129
Engel 252
Enochs 111
Entsminger 158, 197
Entsrninger 304
Ephriam 248
Epling 86, 87, 141, 275
Epperson 72
Erit 22
Erwin 230, 276, 278
Eshelman 281
Eshenaur 205
Estep 159, 270, 301
Estes 230
Etienne 94
Evans 6, 7, 8, 12, 22, 25, 26, 38,
  57, 66, 72, 84, 87, 100, 102,
  103, 104, 106, 130, 131, 137,
  141, 142, 153, 159, 162, 164,
  171, 172, 179, 189, 197, 198,
  219, 226, 244, 250, 253, 257,
  268, 269, 276, 277, 295
Everton 198, 199, 296
Ewing 18, 19, 20, 30, 64, 154,
  175, 199, 324, 329
Ewings 24
Eyre 76

# F

Fadely 240
Fadley 22
Fallon 8, 22, 60, 200, 253
Fargo 29
Farley 230, 252, 314
Farmer 267
Farnsworth 190

Farren 248
Faulkner 154, 226
Feathers 275
Fee 23, 193, 254, 281
Fellure 4, 22, 73, 146, 153, 162, 200, 206, 230, 281, 282, 320
Feltmans 17
Felts 100
Felty 274
Fendel 278
Fenderbosch 9, 10
Fennell 22
Fenwick 54
Ferguson 22, 155
Ferrard 94
Ferrell 22, 200, 201, 246, 276
Ferris 72
Ferry 193
Fetters 275
Feustel 159
Field 129
Fife 22, 30, 36, 201, 218, 219, 225, 229, 232, 295
Figgins 300
Fillinger 79, 146
Finney 132
Finnicum 149, 150
Fish 214, 292
Fisher 22, 277, 321
Fitzpatrick 289
Fitzwater 178, 257
Flaget 52
Fleming 84, 166
Flemington 277
Fleshman 246
Fletcher 23, 37, 72, 92, 94, 155, 168, 209, 228, 272
Flethcher 157
Flint 225
Flobert 34
Flowers 22, 254
Fogelsong 231
Fogelstrom 141
Folden 168, 253
Follies 129
Fontana 269
Foraker 111, 163
Forbus 306
Ford 21, 72, 112, 142
Forsythe 229
Foster 8, 92, 94, 201, 217, 238, 258, 303
Foudy 67
Fountain 22
Fourman 76
Fournier 66, 123
Fowler 11, 12, 13, 14, 90, 148, 201, 202, 276, 281
Fox 10, 202, 242, 259, 260, 272, 273
Fraley 22, 222, 258
Fralix 259
France 77, 118
Frances 190, 330
Francis 169, 202, 249, 296
Frank 147
Frankhammer 277
Franklin 151, 197, 202, 206, 208, 242, 249, 254, 262, 275, 320
Frantom 22
Fraser 200, 288
Frasier 229

Frasure 290
Frazee 22
Frazier 35, 234, 241
Frederick 24, 34
Fredrick 24
Freeman 152, 160, 310
Friend 22, 59
Frisby 177
Frogale 89
Fry 11, 22, 60
Fryar 273
Frye 230, 236
Fueston 59
Fulks 13, 22, 146
Fuller 152, 157, 158, 159, 206, 225
Fulton 29, 73, 83, 152, 158, 202, 240, 278, 279

## G

Gaither 22
Galiton 182
Gallaugher 146
Galloway 159
Gamber 48, 54
Gamble 317
Games 21
Gancs 329
Gandee 233
Garbesi 166, 203, 321
Garcia 234
Gard 314, 324
Gardner 33, 70, 82, 227, 256, 270, 277, 288
Gardt 314
Garfield 96
Garlic 132, 272, 282
Garlick 11
Garner 328
Garnes 4, 83
Garrett 65, 203, 278, 299
Garrison 32, 33
Gast 247
Gates 22, 57, 58, 62, 94
Gatewood 82, 85, 89, 169, 204, 207, 238, 254, 290, 291, 295, 327
Gavin 128
Gay 267
Gaylord 158, 289
Gaylord-Kuhn 173, 209, 305, 306, 323, 324
Gear 55
Gee 29, 71, 74, 83, 86, 241
Gells 54
Gelder 162
Gells 48
George 34, 35, 85, 152, 204, 205, 215, 233, 274
Gertraudt 272
Gettles 205
Ghrist 37, 64
Giannamore 51
Gibbins 76
Gibbons 221
Gibbs 141
Gibson 13, 148, 298, 324
Gierhart 99
Gigante 322
Gilbert 22, 64, 154, 205, 227, 297, 329
Giles 4, 56, 92, 205, 206, 266

Gilfilen 230
Gilford 62
Gilkey 92
Gill 22
Gilland 22
Gillespie 76, 146, 206
Gilliam 22, 87, 147, 204, 207, 269, 327
Gillian 273
Gillison 72, 206, 300
Gills 37, 87, 89
Gillum 207
Gilman 89
Gilmore 72, 83, 148, 228, 322
Gilpin 160, 309
Gindlesberger 22
Glandon 234
Glassburn 19, 23, 25, 41, 170, 207, 208, 268, 281
Gleason 273
Glenn 199, 226, 242, 245, 251, 315, 321, 324
Glenwood 248
Glier 217
Gloss 85, 90
Glover 153, 281
Goble 22, 84
Goddard 302
Godwin 56, 66, 100
Goetz 89
Golden 22
Golini 233
Golubiewski 49, 53, 54
Gombis 298
Gonzalez 199
Gooch 92, 273, 280
Good 29
Goodall 42, 170, 208
Goode 141
Goodwin 77
Goody 22
Gordon 9, 10, 30, 36, 83, 216, 229, 231, 282, 288, 309
Gore 229
Gothard 203
Gould 57, 295
Gower 307
Grace 198
Graf 230
Graham 10, 23, 37, 63, 66, 79, 85, 208, 221, 252, 261, 274, 277, 283
Grant 87, 92, 96, 176, 190, 224, 231, 256
Grape 32
Grapes 36
Grate 22, 249, 289
Gray 22, 72, 223, 246
Green 8, 22, 83, 163, 297
Greenberg 268
Greene 9, 22, 97, 190, 303
Greenlee 188
Greer 250, 305
Gregg 117
Gregory 8, 22
Gressel 49, 54
Grey 83
Griffin 141, 255, 256, 311
Griffith 22, 147, 178, 277, 326
Griggs 19
Grimes 260
Grimmer 54

Griner 148
Groover 227
Grose 209, 302
Groseclose 209, 305
Grossi 209
Grove 22, 84
Grover 21, 24, 30, 36, 40, 64, 222, 271, 284
Groves 132, 155, 157, 209
Grow 228
Grube 79
Grueser 161
Guillott 320
Guinther 241
Gum 181, 183, 330
Gunnoe 118
Gustin 266
Guthrie 27, 30, 65, 328
Guv 89
Guy 158, 240, 281, 321

## H

Hackley 28, 300
Haffelt 37
Haffleld 87
Hafflet 13
Hagans 4, 66
Hageman 230
Hager 8, 22
Haislop 22
Hakes 56
Halbert 267
Hale 268
Halfhill 30, 149, 150, 150, 151, 152, 184, 209, 210, 211, 285, 295
Hall 13, 19, 22, 36, 40, 59, 62, 68, 75, 124, 201, 211, 245, 246, 250, 270, 271
Halleck 154
Halley 8, 22, 42, 56, 64, 137, 141, 159, 169, 174, 211, 218, 285, 305, 314
Halliday 40, 82, 116, 125, 223, 276, 313
Halsted 160
Ham 161
Hamilton 89, 111, 176, 202, 239, 290
Hammon 322
Hammond 8, 9, 22, 27, 36, 39
Hampton 89, 148, 171
Hamrick 87, 263, 273
Hams 310
Hancock 109
Hand 86, 268
Haner 8
Haning 109
Hanks 24, 158
Hanna 151, 276
Hannan 55, 82, 215
Hansen 22
Hanson 22, 135, 311
Hantz 152, 153
Haptonstall 31
Harbour 22, 159, 181, 182, 186, 190, 212, 213
Harder 22, 76, 91, 213
Hardesty 11, 66, 213, 214
Harding 162, 281
Harkness 225
Harless 154, 230

335

Harmon 73, 320
Harnetty 22
Harney 279
Harnsberger 244
Harper 39, 229
Harriger 22
Harrington 77, 157, 176, 274
Harris 22, 71, 76, 147, 224, 225, 231, 272, 298, 310
Harrison 9, 22, 27, 36, 92, 136, 147, 195, 227, 232, 238, 239, 242, 262, 315, 321
Hart 74, 152, 154
Hartinger 295
Hartley 49, 237
Hartman 268, 304
Hartnedy 48, 54
Hartney 48, 54
Harvey 56
Hash 8, 214, 279
Hashrarger 22
Haskell 75
Haskins 37, 56, 129, 166, 259, 282
Haslett 322
Hatfield 22, 194, 247, 248, 331
Hatzenbuhler 221
Hawk 273, 298
Hawks 18
Hawley 36
Hawver 221
Haycraft 87
Hayes 26, 57, 157, 270, 277
Haynes 22, 275
Hayward 227, 238
Hazlett 291, 308
Heald 142
Healey 116
Heape 279
Heard 202
Heatly 24
Heaton 89
Heidari 22
Heidorn 249
Heinke 22
Heiskell 92
Heissenbuttle 147
Heister 159, 189
Hemphill 87
Henderson 22, 75, 206, 330
Hendrix 317
Henness 149
Hennessey 132
Hennesy 90
Hennis 15, 148
Henry 11, 13, 83, 118, 215, 218, 271, 292, 309
Henshaw 322
Hensley 141, 325
Herchelroth 222
Herdman 118
Hereford 215, 314
Hern 32
Herrell 273
Herrington 25
Herrmann 266
Herron 230
Hershberger 22
Hershman 149
Hersman 150
Hesse 268
Hesson 12
Hetrick 221, 227, 272

Hetzer 256
Heydt 215
Hibbard 96
Hibbs 222
Hicks 40
Higgins 246
Hiland 309
Hill 22, 44, 76, 89, 146, 148, 161, 162, 174, 189, 190, 225, 238, 254, 256
Hillman 216
Hilton 187
Hinds 312
Hine 194
Hineman 12, 87, 230, 255
Hinkle 79
Hinsch 37
Hite 159, 221
Hively 8, 37, 155, 156, 215, 230, 307
Hix 30
Hixon 79
Hobbs 11, 22
Hock 325
Hockaday 288
Hodge 92, 290, 298
Hodges 226
Hoelle 67
Hoffman 22, 77, 230, 233, 277, 299
Hofsetter 275, 277
Hogan 21, 72, 83, 111
Hogue 295
Holbrook 76, 216
Holcomb 15, 16, 17, 18, 19, 22, 100, 111, 216, 246, 267, 304, 319
Holland 8
Holley 11, 13, 64, 148, 155, 221, 232
Hollingsworth 225
Hollinshed 190
Hollow 174, 258
Holloway 82
Holman 85
Holstein 22, 230
Holston 155, 194, 211, 229
Holyoke 96
Holzer 7, 10, 37, 77, 84, 86, 91, 106, 123, 124, 125, 133, 138, 140, 142, 167, 174, 180, 182, 183, 207, 210, 213, 216, 217, 218, 219, 239, 241, 242, 247, 251, 265, 278, 303, 304, 310, 314, 316, 330
Homer 90
Hood 4, 29, 56, 100, 218, 232, 269
Hoof 260
Hooper 28
Hoose 67
Hoover 20, 22, 220
Hopkins 22, 89
Horan 218, 219, 276
Horgers 24
Horn 45
Horner 230
Hott 89
Hotzenbella 227
Houck 40, 75, 183, 189, 213, 219, 259, 268, 307, 320
House 9, 314
Howard 22, 26, 36, 74, 201, 216,

244, 276, 278, 300, 305
Howe 124, 198, 226, 272
Howel 324
Howell 8, 13, 59, 62, 83, 92, 195, 227
Hoy 84
Hoyt 219, 306, 319
Hubbard 232, 243
Hubbell 161
Huber 219, 286
Hudson 77, 84, 146, 164, 230
Huffman 22, 162, 221, 230
Hufford 228
Huggins 92
Hughes 8, 22, 32, 38, 40, 89, 152, 216, 219, 234, 278, 327
Hull 82, 220, 314
Hulshorst 63, 245
Humbert 228
Hummerich 245
Humphrey 22, 229, 289, 315, 323
Hundley 183
Hunt 22, 39, 60
Hunter 22, 238
Huntley 18
Hurgo 74
Hurlow 220
Hurst 111
Hutcheson 156
Hutchins 22
Hutchinson 146, 206, 220, 224, 273
Hutsinpillar 87, 227
Hutsinpiller 39, 83, 220, 221, 272
Hyde 233
Hylton 149
Hysell 33, 35, 233

**I**

Ihle 29
Imogene 283
Ingles 8, 85
Ingram 118
Irion 36
Iron 13
Irwin 22, 94, 195
Issacs 22
Ivey 22

**J**

Jablinski 51
Jackson 22, 28, 39, 83, 181, 221, 231, 239, 248, 268, 274
Jacob 244
Jacobi 221, 222
Jacobin 221
Jacobs 30, 227, 267
James 17, 18, 22, 86, 171, 221, 222, 232, 252, 276
Jamison 66, 135
Jamora 66, 100
Janko 50, 53
Janson 11
Jarred 275
Jarrell 22
Jarson 23
Jarvis 56, 100, 135
Jeeters 269
Jeffers 22, 23, 148, 222
Jefferson 160, 225
Jenkins 22, 36, 67, 85, 89, 91, 100,

118, 137, 162, 222, 223, 274, 280, 296, 297, 303
Jesseng 48
Jessing 54
Jett 65
Jeviett 216
Jividen 15, 22, 278
Johnson 9, 11, 13, 22, 40, 50, 51, 53, 56, 73, 83, 89, 91, 92, 94, 116, 118, 137, 141, 147, 161, 163, 186, 211, 215, 221, 223, 225, 243, 255, 262, 269, 283, 284, 300, 304
Jones 4, 21, 22, 67, 70, 73, 76, 111, 112, 116, 132, 137, 147, 151, 152, 155, 156, 157, 161, 170, 185, 204, 209, 224, 225, 226, 232, 236, 237, 238, 246, 252, 254, 271, 276, 278, 289, 290, 303, 329
Jordan 22, 83
Jordon 318
Judson 55, 147
Justice 73, 253
Justus 8

**K**

Kabish 224
Kahn 329
Kail 30, 31, 32, 40, 85
Kaiser 50, 51, 54
Kallenberg 48, 54
Kaloust 22
Kane 159, 295
Kaufman 129
Kautz 243
Keefer 22, 176
Keels 83, 88, 300
Keenan 56, 100
Keesee 155
Keeton 247
Kegan 161, 268
Kegley 305
Kelcher 242, 321
Keller 22, 55, 173, 186, 250
Kelley 235
Kellogg 125
Kellum 252
Kelly 9, 16, 17, 20, 40, 48, 54, 158
Kelsey 248
Kelton 225, 226
Kemp 67
Kemper 8
Kems 82
Kenney 22
Kennison 329
Kent 18, 26, 146, 161, 170, 226, 257, 314
Kenton 166, 253
Kents 24
Kern 238
Kerns 70, 82, 160, 164, 204, 205, 227, 238, 297, 316
Kerr 23, 24, 36, 82, 94, 136, 221, 227, 244, 272
Kerrs 24
Kessel 260
Kessler 49
Kidwell 274
Kimball 87
Kinard 285
Kincaide 284

Kinder 174, 271
Kinemond 314
Kineon 123
King 22, 67, 76, 89, 92, 164, 231, 285
Kingery 157
Kinghorn 89
Kinker 277
Kinney 70
Kirby 30, 31, 85, 141
Kirk 158
Kirkhart 22
Kirkpatrick 246, 322, 329
Kiser 20, 22, 233
Kiskis 132
Kite 273
Kitrell 174
Kitter 157
Klages 79, 227, 259, 271
Klaubauf 50, 51, 54
Klein 142
Klicker 156
Kline 328
Klinger 9
Klooz 246
Knapp 22, 321
Knight 12, 228, 253, 315
Knotter 287
Knotts 132
Knowlton 166
Koby 52, 91, 228
Kocher 22
Koepp 228, 315
Kollar 226
Koon 273
Koontz 10, 22, 24, 59, 251, 277, 304, 315
Kostenzin 221
Kramer 48, 54
Kraus 164
Kreider 237
Kreuger 295
Kridler 322
Krump 268
Kruskamp 20
Kuhn 143, 155, 158, 228, 271
Kyger 9, 97

## L

La Font 48, 54
Lacey 84
Lafferty 72
Lakin 22, 196, 269
LaMay 182
Lambert 14, 20, 21, 22, 23, 60, 117, 192, 229, 249, 250, 277, 305
Landrum 275
Lane 9, 12, 45, 152, 269
Lang 252
Langdon 75, 214
Langford 189, 305, 316
Langham 310
Langley 55, 77, 95, 154, 272
Lanham 152
Lanier 66, 155, 157, 319
Lanthorn 184
Lanthorne 152
Lapille 266
Larkins 170
Larson 148
Lasley 116, 278, 281

Lauriseh 124
Laux 237
Law 174
Lawery 160
Lawless 229
Lawrence 22, 200, 202, 229
Lawson 141, 186, 227, 234
Layfield 276
Layne 92, 179, 183, 262
Layton 9
Leach 273
Leadingham 90
Leamon 323
Leaper 64, 109, 112, 160, 271
Lear 22, 79, 155, 230, 274, 324
LeClerc 230
LeClercq 39, 77
Lee 13, 26, 71, 72, 75, 83, 147, 152, 171, 231, 315, 325
Leedy 250
Leffier 277
Leffingwell 22
Leftwiches 21
Legget 155
Leggett 292
Leigh 242
Leith 86
Lemley 36, 63, 141, 151, 209, 211, 218, 225, 231, 232
Lemming 246
Lemnitzer 204
Lent 281
Leonard 149, 167, 240, 275, 278
Leota 316
Leport 146
Leppert 189
Lesene 226
Lester 22, 92, 146
Lewis 8, 12, 15, 22, 26, 38, 64, 68, 74, 75, 83, 85, 92, 94, 154, 188, 218, 232, 248, 259, 270, 300, 320
Lincoln 22, 39, 83, 96, 204, 250
Lindsay 174
Lintala 42
Lionberger 277
Lipton 36
Little 31, 32, 34, 35, 92, 232, 233, 234, 235, 240, 302
Little-Creech 36
Littleton 13
Lively 22
Livesay 255
Livingood 210
Lizon 128
Lloyd 22, 26, 174, 180, 236
Lobdell 237
Lockridge 281
Loedig 48, 54
Logue 278
Lollis 229, 236, 237
Long 17, 18, 19, 25, 36, 141, 160, 231, 233, 237, 247, 248, 288, 289, 294, 311
Looney 225
Loria 271
Loucks 13, 162, 227, 237, 238
Louis 25, 52
Lounds 25
Love 22
Lovelace 22, 201
Lovell 131, 178

Lovell- Cherrington 197
Lowery 157, 160, 238, 308
Lowks 283
Lucas 22, 27, 36
Luckenbach 180
Luckey 30
Lucky 278
Luellen 232
Luis 234
Luman 26, 238, 239, 253, 260, 273
Lupton 36, 37, 57
Lusher 64, 162, 183
Luther 271
Lutz 237
Lykins 239
Lyle 239
Lyles 22
Lynch 22, 35, 50, 52, 263
Lynn 69, 145, 175
Lyon 109, 118
Lyons 84, 222

## M

Maag 31
Mabe 22
Macaulay 324
MacFarlin 295
Maciag 330
Macias 150
Mack 27, 30, 31, 32, 33, 35, 36, 240
Mackamul 305
MacKenzie 38, 86
Mackenzie 77
Mackinson 188
Macomber 19
Macoubrie 201
Maddox 264
Maddy 36, 65, 292
Madison 73, 174, 204, 238
Mager 125
Mahan 26, 56
Maher 258
Mahor 258
Malaby 240, 278, 320
Malcolm 92
Mandat 189
Mangum 162
Manley 34, 233, 240, 241
Mann 148, 152
Mannering 256
Mansfield 318
Mapes 34
Marchi 4, 9, 10, 166, 209, 241, 282, 306, 321
Marcum 224
Margoles 269
Marhoover 20
Marie 314
Marion 261
Marley 58
Marple 97
Marr 19, 56, 79, 100, 146, 242
Marrs 258
Marshall 235
Martin 8, 13, 14, 17, 22, 36, 38, 56, 89, 90, 105, 118, 133, 146, 147, 148, 154, 177, 183, 188, 189, 205, 218, 249, 250, 252, 268, 313
Martindale 156, 157, 182, 209, 226, 278
Martt 43
Maslen 184, 278
Mason 159, 235
Masser 219
Massey 22, 128
Massie 22, 142, 145, 242, 243, 270
Masterson 213
Materne 118
Mathers 325
Mathews 246
Matthews 17, 18, 19, 21, 32, 63, 100, 111, 158, 195, 202, 216, 243, 277, 290
Matthias 272
Mattingly 49, 54
Matura 118, 123
Mauck 28, 29, 30, 39, 111, 161, 243, 244
Maud 254
Maureen 180
Maxon 77, 116
Maxwell 283, 328
Mayer 258
Mayes 22, 151, 320
Mayle 67
Maynard 189, 216
Mayo 72, 92, 244, 245, 328
Mays 310
McAlister 26
McAllister 198
McAlpin 161
McAtee 314
McBrayer 205
McBride 177, 288, 302, 303
McCall 63
McCarley 279
McCafferty 86
McCafferty 197
McCall 13, 14, 22, 245, 252, 261, 262, 274, 277, 322
McCallister 316
McCann 49, 54
McCarley 17, 18, 19, 20, 199, 201, 245, 246, 256, 280, 320
McCarly 85
McCarty 8, 20, 32, 36, 246, 278, 285
McClaskey 89, 257, 279, 311
McCleary 69
McClellan 22
McClintock 239
McClurg 77, 215, 314
McColm 224
McComas 286
McCombs 22, 62
McConnell 22, 55, 324
McCook 112
McCordock 226
McCorkle 167
McCormick 11, 36, 37, 63, 86, 87, 89, 91, 111, 123, 247, 275, 298, 303, 304
McCormicks 10
McCoy 19, 20, 92, 150, 189, 229, 247, 248, 254, 255, 277, 316
McCrary 224
McCreedy 22
McCue 149
McCulley 323
McCulty 189

337

McCumber 191
McDade 209, 241, 321
McDaniel 18, 22, 25, 26, 43, 59, 62, 72, 75, 100, 129, 166, 173, 187, 188, 248, 249, 250, 277, 300
McDonald 212
McDonough 67
McDowell 246, 268
McElyea 147
McFarland 89
McGath 22
McGhee 8, 17, 18, 90, 103, 136, 195, 274, 289, 290, 315
McGinnis 22
McGovern 22
McGraw 90
McGuire 22, 118, 148, 183, 207, 225, 274, 295, 298
McHaus 174
McIntyre 55, 137, 215, 231
McKean 15, 160, 222, 267, 272, 308
McKenzie 103, 250, 251, 280
Mckibbon 20
McKiernan 48, 54
McKinley 111, 148, 204, 227, 256, 324
McKnight 18, 87, 239, 248
McLaughlin 222
McLoud 22
McMahon 87, 90, 92
McMillin 281, 304
McNeal 16, 18, 22, 267
McNealey 37
McNeally 227
McNeil 18, 229, 236
McNeill 199
McNeir 254
McNerlin 178
McPherson 220
McQuaid 42
McVey 252
Meade 9, 17, 261
Meadows 7, 22, 194
Meaige 241
Meal 64
Means 240, 267
Meara 49, 54, 140
Medley 8
Meek 84, 92
Mefford 155
Meigs 264
Meir 258
Meirers 258
Meirs 258
Melia 53
Melton 64
Menager 39, 77, 94, 140, 223
Mendieta 91
Menshouse 87
Menzer 224, 252, 314
Menzers 251, 261
Mercer 94
Merlin 319
Merrick 274
Merrifield 168
Merriken 229
Merrill 185, 186
Merriman 86, 179
Merrow 249
Mershon 22

Metcalf 111
Metzger 22
Metzler 8
Meyer 22
Meyers 258
Michael 22, 68
Michelfelder 77
Middleton 252, 317
Middlewarth 43
Midkiff 273
Miers 258
Might 281, 284, 295
Milam 85
Miles 22, 268
Milford 180
Miller 8, 9, 11, 20, 22, 30, 42, 56, 59, 60, 66, 68, 72, 79, 86, 92, 100, 110, 161, 164, 200, 214, 218, 219, 223, 226, 235, 236, 249, 250, 252, 253, 277, 285, 300
Millers 21
Millhone 8
Mills 23, 27, 82, 86, 89, 92, 116, 221, 222, 227, 253, 276, 323
Milstead 92, 155, 228, 271
Milton 164, 165
Mink 230
Minkler 257
Minnis 21, 22
Minnises 21
Minor 59, 285
Minturn 89
Mire 258
Mires 258
Mitchell 22, 181, 216, 230, 254, 266, 300, 301
Mitchels 323
Mitilida 251
Miyazaki 226
Moats 22
Mobley 22
Moch 40
Mock 100
Moeller 49
Moffitt 24
Mohler 22, 152
Moirs 258
Moline 264
Monroe 204, 206
Montgomery 20, 111, 158, 259, 297, 323
Moody 284
Mooney 8, 274
Moore 9, 10, 42, 55, 69, 82, 92, 118, 135, 153, 184, 189, 204, 219, 254, 255, 256, 279
Morando 228
Morehouse 70, 125, 226, 227, 256, 257
MORGAN 184
Morgan 6, 16, 22, 77, 86, 111, 147, 158, 180, 184, 185, 212, 236, 243, 273, 296, 300, 307, 312
Morris 22, 125, 170, 277, 283, 320
Morrison 24, 55, 118, 227, 251, 272, 322, 325
Morrisons 24
Morse 137, 243
Mortimer 71
Morton 109, 110, 238, 267

Mosby 44
Moshier 84
Mosier 26
Mossbarger 22
Mossman 55, 299
Mossmans 24
Moulton 4, 8, 86, 88, 92, 131, 137, 197, 257
Mount 154, 157
Mounts 267
Mowery 118
Mowyer 258
Moyer 258
Moyers 258
Mulford 33, 35, 36, 230, 293, 295
Mulholand 190, 213, 257
Muller 79
Mullineaux 55, 82
Mullineauz 89
Mullineux 238
Mullins 9, 22, 84, 97, 135
Mundell 20, 72
Murawski 77
Murphy 29, 42, 43, 49, 54
Murray 4, 6, 20, 56, 100, 201, 258
Mussio 49
Myer 258
Myers 4, 22, 26, 37, 50, 51, 52, 53, 54, 59, 62, 79, 85, 92, 132, 154, 156, 157, 159, 189, 200, 202, 218, 238, 258, 259, 267, 268, 269, 270, 271
Myres 258

**N**

Nagy 87
Nance 62
Napier 278, 279
Napper 71
Naret 77
Nash 77, 91, 315
Neal 8, 9, 19, 22, 25, 26, 27, 32, 33, 36, 59, 82, 87, 92, 96, 166, 168, 231, 239, 248, 249, 260, 261, 272, 273, 281, 282
Nebert 162
Needham 282
Nelson 193
Nemeth 171
Neuman 175
Neuschwanger 262
Newberry 22
Newell 226
Newman 111, 223
Newport 168
Newsom 94, 223
Newsome 71, 225
Newton 55, 157
Nibert 162
Nichols 221
Nicholson 199
Nida 261
Niday 62, 142, 147, 224, 230, 251, 252, 261, 262, 314
Niehm 123
Nisewanger 227, 272
Noble 33, 190, 226, 227, 292, 304
Noe 90
Noel 22
Nolan 22, 262
Noland 285
Norman 21, 22

Norris 215, 286
North 84, 100, 112, 141
Northup 13, 63, 66, 92, 205, 245, 262, 266, 274
Norwick 50, 51, 52, 54
Notter 79, 146, 195, 242, 293
Nuby 72
Nugent 54
Null 22, 25, 26, 218, 238, 262, 263, 276
Nutter 22

**O**

Oberholzer 296
O'Brien 82, 135
Odell 275
O'Dell 89, 175, 205, 241, 245, 330
Odessa 189
O'Donnell 90, 263
Oeink 54
Ohlamacher 123
Oiler 18, 233, 264, 279
Oilers 263
Oilman 22
Oliver 4, 85, 146, 167, 264
Olson 256
Ondejko 234
O'Neal 256
O'Neil 217
Oney 308
O'Rourke 4, 264
Orr 91, 118
Orsbon 200
Osborn 295
Osterhout 220
Osterle 125
Oterbein 324
Ottenweller 50, 51, 52
Ours 166
Overby 143
Overstreet 232
Overturf 265
Owen 10, 22, 173, 257
Owens 22, 92
Oxyer 22
Oyler 263

**P**

Pade 231
Paine 23
Painter 321
Pake 29
Palk 267
Palmer 30, 32, 201, 258
Palsley 20
Parker 22, 70, 257
Parkins 22, 222
Parks 161
Parsons 150, 154, 260
Pasquale 89, 206, 265
Passen 180, 181
Patrick 22, 69, 267
Patro 22
Patterson 22, 227, 236, 250, 327
Patton 195
Paul 50, 52, 53
Pauley 22, 253
Paulins 210
Pavey 277
Pavilion 120

Payne 8, 21, 22, 71, 72, 79, 83, 227, 231, 267
Paynes 60
Paynter 331
Payton 97
Pearl 310
Peden 19
Peeps 105
Pegg 66, 267
Peirce 220
Pellegrinon 4, 126, 140
Pemberton 249
Pendleton 19
Penick 300
Pennington 153
Penrod 311
Penwell 22
Peoples 25
Perkey 188
Perkins 14, 17, 18, 87, 90, 100, 148, 198, 212, 227
Perovish 249
Perroud 9
Perry 22, 39, 166, 173, 220, 288, 323, 329
Persch 221
Peterkowski 90
Peters 36, 227, 296, 305
Peterson 273
Petrie 8, 19, 22
Pettibone 216
Pettit 231
Pettus 161, 268
Petty 26
Pflum 242
Pfoloun 184
Phelps 83, 89, 245, 252, 274
Philhis 264
Phillip 188
Phillips 22, 24, 41, 85, 147, 169, 177, 205, 252, 259, 261, 268, 269, 275, 277
Phipps 188
Phlegar 128
Phlum 321
Pickens 230, 255, 269
Pidcock 325
Pierce 22, 266, 268
Pierotti 269
Pierson 264
Pigote 45
Piles 269
Pillow 224, 225, 270, 271
Pinkerman 22, 274
Pinson 68
Pirce 232
Pitchford 22
Pittard 146
Pius 48
Plants 33, 112, 143, 281, 286
Plantz 220
Platt 273
Playfair 9
Pleasant 42
Pleasants 87
Plumley 69
Plybon 273
Plymale 7, 64, 155, 219, 228, 271, 316
Polcyn 8, 288
Pollard 56, 100, 215
Pollitt 317

Pollock 87
Polly 268
Pollyanna 192
Polsley 39
Poole 264
Pope 8, 22, 26, 79, 137, 142, 218, 221, 258, 259, 267, 271
Poppe 271
Poppoe 79
Porter 18, 22, 64, 66, 86, 92, 105, 148, 157, 158, 244, 250, 271, 272, 296
Poston 296
Potts 22
Poulton 163
Pound 21
Pounds 18, 21
Powell 4, 24, 29, 55, 69, 72, 132, 189, 221, 227, 248, 249, 262, 272, 273, 290, 303
Powers 277
Pratt 22, 262, 314
Preston 31, 32, 33, 36, 85, 92, 239
Prevo 311
Price 15, 38, 79, 149, 161, 232, 284, 307
Prichard 123
Prickett 20
Priestley 220, 273
Priestly 11, 43, 89, 273
Pritchard 222, 330
Pritchet 89
Pritchett 89, 160
Prose 22, 59, 249, 250, 269
Provens 22, 62, 146
Pry 22
Puckett 22
Pugh 18
Pullins 273
Purcell 48
Purvis 154
Putnam 131, 197, 243, 246
Pyles 157, 259, 260, 270, 273

# Q

Qeink 49
Quamme 273
Queen 9, 22, 59, 100, 141, 156, 159, 274, 283, 297
Questel 167, 184
Questrell 167
Quinn 54
Quirk 48, 54

# R

Rader 32, 221, 281
Radford 11
Radigab 282
Raider 272
Raike 32, 153, 186, 275
Raines 247
Rainey 67
Ralph 30, 45, 89, 231, 232
Ralston 30, 40
Ramey 22
Raming 212
Ramsay 40
Ramsey 216
Randall 204
Randolph 22, 118, 154
Randolphs 21

Rankin 12, 199, 268, 273, 282
Rathburn 89, 201, 295
Ratliff 329
Raulf 253
Rausch 224
Rawlins 22
Rawson 312
Ray 26
Rayburn 65, 314
Rea 221
Ream 264
Reapp 226, 260
Rectenwald 51
Reece 309
Reed 29, 84, 281
Reeds 21
Rees 8, 22, 45, 85, 94, 141, 158
Reese 9, 24, 27, 36, 280, 329
Reeves 111, 295
Regan 8, 275
Reimsnyder 283
Reiter 299
Reitmire 200
Rentz 324
Resener 28, 29, 37
Rettberg 271
Reynolds 22, 36, 83, 85, 92, 154, 159, 185, 201, 216, 240, 256, 268, 273, 275
Rhodes 274
Rhoses 276
Rice 12, 22, 33, 35, 36, 147, 164
Richards 22, 45, 77, 85, 87, 124, 173, 217, 263, 276, 321
Richardson 41, 173, 198, 281
Richie 22, 276, 277
Richter 132
Rickabaugh 178, 277, 323
Rickards 273
Rickeft 157
Rickets 158
Ricketts 111
Rickman 72
Riddle 72, 83
Ridenour 246, 273
Ridge 249, 277
Riedel 311
Rife 7, 29, 30, 32, 36, 40, 60, 157, 158, 184, 209, 216, 226, 237, 243, 246, 277, 278, 310
Riffle 89
Riggenbacher 277
Rigney 188
Riley 8, 79, 277, 328
Rimmey 201
Rinehart 84
Ripley 22, 76, 224, 261
Ripleys 60
Rippey 132, 231
Rippley 59, 75
Riser 280
Roach 22, 42, 89, 143, 188, 262
Roadamour 13, 22, 227
Roadarmour 180, 279, 307
Robbins 132, 189, 233
Roberts 15, 20, 21, 22, 26, 77, 89, 123, 143, 154, 158, 216, 262, 277, 279, 280, 281, 301
Robertson 32
Robins 321

Robinson 20, 37, 41, 94, 163, 202, 216, 220, 246, 247, 272, 278, 281, 329, 330
Rockerfeller 55
Roderick 86, 304
Rodgers 22, 94, 185, 200, 213, 227, 229, 253, 273, 281, 282, 287
Rogers 129, 228, 329
Rohrs 253
Roland 215, 314
Rolland 318
Rollert 312
Rolston 252
Romaine 64
Romine 246
Roosevelt 111, 204, 250
Ropeter 79
Rose 9, 12, 13, 15, 22, 62, 63, 79, 87, 175, 229, 232, 255, 282
Roses 60
Ross 181, 230, 284, 288, 289, 323
Rossiter 153
Roth 84
Rothgeb 8, 29, 30, 31, 32, 36, 40, 65, 85, 92, 106, 155, 157, 161, 178, 209, 226, 228, 244, 278, 282
Rothgels 34
Rott 283, 287
Rouse 85
Roush 4, 30, 40, 92, 209, 224, 237, 240, 242, 249, 253, 276, 278, 283, 284, 293, 314, 321
Rowena 309
Rowland 311
Rowley 201, 246, 277
Rowsey 268
Rowson 155
Roy 323
Rucker 12, 22, 36, 118
Rude 73
Rue 37
Ruff 22, 222
Ruffner 244
Rufus 250
Rumfield 284
Rumfleld 278
Rumley 218
Runyan 66
Rupe 22, 33, 56, 153, 163, 211, 275, 282, 284, 285, 288, 295
Ruppert 249
Rushie 262
Rusk 49, 66, 202
Russell 18, 22, 23, 24, 32, 36, 40, 63, 73, 87, 131, 146, 158, 161, 206, 239, 243, 248, 282, 285, 286
Rustemeyer 22
Rutan 256
Ruth 273
Rutherford 22, 100, 216
Rutt 79, 283, 287
Rutter 123
Ryal 87
Ryan 49, 54, 90
Ryther 152, 237

# S

Safford 57, 89, 94, 158, 177, 212, 290

Sagan 56
Sailey 125
Sales 19, 21
Salisbury 22, 56, 163
Sallee 9, 17
Salmons 223
Salser 242
Samples 267
Samuals 22
Sanders 22, 79, 155, 157, 209, 230, 267, 286, 287, 290
Sands 83, 125, 279, 286
Sanford 183
Sargant 9
Sargeant 18
Sass 256
Sattler 239
Saunders 8, 15, 22, 41, 60, 92, 143, 146, 148, 153, 164, 183, 220, 225, 272, 281, 283, 286, 287, 326
Savage 92, 171, 246
Sawyer 23, 158
Sawyers 256, 281
Saxton 253
Sayre 265
Sborgia 234
Scarberry 22, 215
Schenk 247
Scherer 287
Schiele 49, 54
Schlecht 233
Schler 321
Schlern 224
Schmeisser 240
Schmidt 132
Schneider 49, 54
Schoonfeld 40
Schoonover 152
Schriber 227
Schuffer 22
Schuldt 22
Schultz 174, 272
Schwartz 123
Scott 4, 17, 20, 22, 32, 33, 39, 40, 68, 71, 73, 74, 85, 88, 159, 163, 206, 223, 229, 231, 232, 234, 246, 256, 257, 268, 277, 278, 288, 289, 300, 328
Scouten 100
Scurlock 252, 289
Searls 288
Sears 94
Seashole 281
Seaver 204
Sebert 66
Seeds 204
Selina 309
Selleck 256
Selover 161
Serra 52
Serriere 64
Sessions 194
Sessor 66
Seton 52
Settle-Young, 131
Settlemire 256
Setzer 209
Sexton 22, 151, 187, 189
Shack 17, 193, 289, 290
Shade 18
Shadenck 19

Shadwick 8
Shafer 73, 189
Shaffer 18, 234
Shain 251
Shallcross 82
Shamblin 32
Shane 147
Shank 89, 310
Shato 22
Shaver 40, 85, 154, 157, 161, 226, 232, 278, 290
Shaw 82, 87, 145, 232
Shawver 56, 327
Sheets 11, 13, 22, 65, 85, 89, 155, 157, 160, 161, 169, 204, 209, 214, 229, 230, 238, 248, 262, 287, 290, 291, 292, 308, 321
Sheldon 50, 53, 54
Sheline 8, 266
Shellenberger 158
Shelton 22, 92, 256, 277
Shemik 238
Shenefield 109
Shepard 65, 70, 121, 246, 292, 305
Shephard 221
Shepherd 213
Sheppard 65
Sherman 260
Sherow 92
Shields 323
Shively 289
Shober 36, 37
Shockely 12
Shockley 87, 213
Shoemaker 22, 85, 210, 218, 225, 231, 232, 293, 295, 321
Shondel 90, 293
Shong 118
Short 238
Shrader 329
Shriver 10, 22, 151, 153, 162, 180
Shuck 202
Shuler 22, 29, 32, 109, 223, 277, 278, 293, 294
Shumate 249, 250
Shupe 118
Shurtz 289
Siders 24, 208, 225
Sigler 164, 167, 184, 274
Silleck 256
Silverman 37
Simmerman 59
Simmermans 60
Simmons 10
Simon 294
Simonich 50, 51, 54
Simonin 230
Simpkins 218
Simpson 96, 233, 305, 306
Sims 150, 238, 294, 327
Singer 92
Singleton 45
Sirdefield 180
Sisson 23, 100, 109, 163, 227, 256, 257, 295, 325
Sivisher 34
Skaggs 9, 22, 45, 293
Skeen 132
Skidmore 22, 95, 256, 314
Skidmores 24
Skinner 9, 10, 22, 40, 45, 295, 296, 304

Skirvin 268
Slack 22
Slagle 22, 26
Slater 164, 246
Slaton 85
Slaven 22, 89
Slavin 84
Slaymaker 129
Slayton 330
Sloan 22, 181
Sloane 22
Slone 8, 118, 274, 297, 317
Small 204, 238
Smelter 227
Smeltzer 92, 160, 243, 261
Smith 4, 8, 15, 22, 26, 37, 50, 51, 52, 54, 56, 63, 64, 66, 67, 72, 85, 88, 100, 118, 138, 141, 148, 162, 166, 173, 174, 176, 183, 198, 206, 233, 242, 244, 245, 246, 256, 260, 262, 268, 271, 273, 275, 285, 288, 289, 297, 298, 299, 300, 302, 308, 321, 328
Smyth 40
Snedaker 56, 84, 90
Sneed 284
Snodgrass 22, 156, 222
Snowden 9, 10, 92
Snyder 19, 90, 92, 213, 299, 314
Soles 53
Somerville 150
Sommer 87
Sopp 275
Soupene 245
Souverain 89
Sow 83
Sowards 9, 17, 22, 177, 305
Spars 18
Spear 22, 37
Spears 74, 249
Speiss 123
Spencer 132, 188, 189, 229, 231, 299, 326
Spicer 212
Spiers 22
Spires 20, 36
Splete 84
Sprague 23, 256, 299, 300
Springer 42
Sprinkles 26
Sprouse 22, 279, 280
Spurlock 22, 56, 229
Staats 205
Stackhouse 66
Stafford 63
Staley 22, 132
Standish 92, 217
Stanford 183
Stanley 8, 22, 269
Stansberry 68
Stapelton 63
Stapleton 76, 143
Starcher 45
Starkey 209
Statzer 177
Stauffer 22
Stauss 189
Stayer 22
Stebbins 226
Stedman 246, 278
Steele 65, 90

Steenbergen 94, 300
Steger 64, 152, 195, 330
Steiger 227
Steinbrink 202
Steivers 174
Stephens 24, 183
Sterling 55
Sterrett 273
Stevens 17, 22, 162, 274
Stevenson 239, 267
Stevers 136, 146, 331
Steward 74
Stewart 26, 39, 65, 71, 79, 100, 111, 145, 168, 218, 249, 267, 302
Stillings 261
Stillwell 225, 226
Stiltner 183
Stinson 266
Stockhoff 40, 116
Stocksdale 45
Stollings 262
Stone 56, 63, 65, 186, 194, 219, 253, 300, 301, 323, 329
Stoney 88
Story 30
Stout 45, 189, 268, 294, 310
Stover 212, 215, 220
Strafford 142
Straight 146
Strait 14, 53, 64, 154, 272, 274
Stratton 285
Straub 22
Strausbaugh 301
Street 22
Streibig 84
Streicher 234
Stringfellow 305
Strong 94, 157, 287
Strunk 137
Stuart 187
Stuber 220
Stumbo 22, 118
Stump 69
Sturgills 281
Suiter 86, 87
Sullivan 135
Summers 70, 89, 303
Surdyka 22
Sutherland 282
Swain 8, 173
Swander 278
Swanson 28, 35, 85, 89, 152
Swartz 273
Swett 43
Swick 277
Swigart 304
Swindler 11, 13, 22, 183, 213, 259
Swisher 30, 31, 32, 34, 36, 40, 85, 87, 112, 151, 214, 216, 221, 233, 288, 301, 302
Switzer 208, 215
Swope 293
Sydenstricker 160
Syler 227, 316
Symmes 28, 29

**T**

Tabor 204
Tackett 59, 60, 253, 273
Taft 197
Tandy 147, 314

Tanner 22, 37, 94
Tap 54, 86
Tarr 90
Tate 29, 240, 278
Tawney 87, 90, 223, 288, 302, 303
Taylor 8, 15, 22, 56, 83, 92, 100, 134, 157, 158, 183, 194, 210, 219, 222, 249, 254, 279, 281, 316
Teal 279
Terre-Blanche 100
Terry 9, 22
Thabet 269
Thacker 22, 32
Thaler 84, 303, 304
Thaney 311
Tharp 242, 321
Thaxton 150, 163, 276, 278
Theiss 154
Thevinen 64
Thierry 190, 191
Thivener 155
Thivenin 146
Thomas 22, 33, 36, 40, 56, 66, 70, 90, 100, 133, 137, 154, 161, 198, 201, 210, 211, 229, 272, 273, 277, 278, 284, 292, 296, 304, 305, 325
Thommen 277
Thompson 2, 4, 8, 20, 23, 30, 32, 34, 35, 36, 39, 40, 62, 85, 87, 90, 92, 136, 157, 166, 169, 175, 209, 232, 238, 265, 266, 267, 268, 285, 290, 292, 304, 305, 306, 309, 313, 315, 329
Thorn 310
Thornton 154, 238, 259, 260, 263
Thrapp 92
Thurman 157
Tibbs 266
Tilden 19
Tilder 20
Tillis 100
Tinsley 206
Tippens 89
Tipple 90
Tipton 30, 305
Tirpak 23
Tisdale 23
Toler 158
Tolliver 71
Tompkins 191
Toney 71
Tope 23, 100, 189, 218, 263
Topping 225, 305
Torrance 162
Totten 246
Towle 184
Townsend 111
Townshend 208
Tracewell 32
Tracy 85, 92
Traux 161
Travis 23
Trawick 128
Treat 234
Trewartha 118
Triplett 23
Trotter 13, 15, 42, 148, 149, 160, 181, 228, 279, 291, 307, 308
Trout 23, 87, 89, 315
Trowbridge 112, 147, 252, 259, 309

Troyman 19
Trueblood 219
Truesdale 260
Truex 161
Trumbo 31
Truslow 48
Trussell 324
Tuck 171
Tucker 8, 23, 229, 329
Tudor 250
Tulloss 159
Tupper 94
Turner 2, 18, 20, 25, 90, 111, 269
Turney 157
Twyman 20, 85, 196, 309, 310
Tye 271
Tyler 18, 20, 191, 227, 296, 310, 317, 330

## U

Uebing 314
Ulderich 310, 311
Uldrich 310, 325
Ulrick 243
Ummensetter 273
Underwood 33, 36, 311
Unroe 9, 297
Utterback 73

## V

Vacchetta 228
Vale 20
Valiance 308
Vallance 187, 291, 309
Van Dyke 273
Van Kirk 223, 225
Vanbibber 23
Vance 20, 40, 65, 77, 99, 110, 111, 121, 161, 250, 256, 270, 275, 311
Vanco 298, 301
Vanden 89, 91, 116, 117, 227
Vandusen 253
VanMatre 100
Vanmeeter 246
VanMeter 56
VanSickle 222, 246
Vanzant 30
Vare 66
Varian 23
Varney 45, 312
Vaughn 59, 312
Vaught 62
Veith 233
Veley 154
Venz 67
Vernon 224, 270, 271
Viers 199, 225
Vigue 23
Vimont 94
Viney 21, 72, 74
Vining 247
Vinton 16, 86
Virginia 314
Volborn 251, 315
Volga 247
Von Schritz 312
Von Schritzz 94
Von Thompson 290
Vorhees 265
Vornholt 86, 124, 133, 217, 218

Voss 67
Vyszenski 50, 51, 54

## W

Waddell 173, 216, 224, 226
Wade 23, 68, 162
Wafts 22
Wagner 23, 65, 125, 126, 154, 256
Wagoneer 246
Wagoner 171, 313
Wahl 56, 100
Waid 295
Wailer 161
Wakefield 316
Walford 159
Walker 9, 23, 37, 42, 66, 82, 88, 90, 147, 198, 209, 215, 220, 224, 227, 238, 242, 252, 266, 313, 314, 321
Walker-Marguerite 215
Walkup 23
Wallace 18, 23, 201, 228, 246, 255, 290, 306, 314, 315, 328, 329
Waller 161
Wallis 314
Walls 306
Walp 224, 245
Walter 23, 155, 243
Walters 22, 64, 189, 255, 315, 316
Walton 146
Wamsley 56
Ward 13, 23, 25, 31, 32, 33, 36, 74, 87, 89, 159, 162, 232, 242, 268, 278, 321
Ware 87
Warehime 92
Warfuel 200
Warner 29, 31, 32, 34, 232, 242, 321
Warren 75, 247, 248, 268, 291, 292, 316, 317
Warsham 216
Wash 32
Washington 48, 96, 178, 216, 290, 309
Waters 214, 304, 315
Watkins 23, 28, 318
Watson 8, 45, 72, 92, 154, 253, 254, 255, 285
Watterson 48, 125
Watts 23, 215, 297
Waugh 8, 13, 23, 76, 125, 178, 181, 182, 208, 252, 317, 318, 322
Waugh-Hendrix 317
Waver 231
Wax 220
Wayne 45, 295, 318
Weatherford 26
Webb 23, 79, 205, 229
Weber 100, 207, 295, 318
Weberly 201
Webster 111, 161, 215, 296
Wedemeyer 23, 79, 227, 271
Weed 28, 29, 86, 319
Weese 240
Weiderman 224
Weis 22
Weize 45
Welch 231
Weldon 201

Welker 92, 147, 164, 240, 275, 281, 319, 320
Well 17
Wellington 23, 76, 254
Wellman 146, 189
Wellmeyer 320
Wells 23, 183, 201, 230
Wemyss 23
Wendell 189
Wenneyer 59
Wentling 247
Werner 184
Wese 227
Wesley 248, 249, 296
West 37, 161
Westfall 168
Westover 148
Wetherholt 4, 9, 41, 64, 82, 86, 87, 160, 161, 279, 291, 308, 309, 320, 321
Wetzel 159, 253
Weygandt 272
Whaley 241, 302, 321
Wharton 321
Wheaton 220, 273, 288
Wheeler 29, 129, 220, 274, 325
Wheelock 221
Whelchel 211
where 29
Whipple 125
White 22, 26, 45, 59, 63, 68, 85, 87, 103, 121, 125, 142, 162, 166, 173, 186, 199, 209, 223, 230, 233, 252, 276, 282, 288, 289, 302, 305, 321, 322, 323, 324
Whiteley 8
Whittaker 23
Whitted 295
Whittington 20, 23
Wickline 22, 26, 79, 195, 196
Wickman 160
Wideck 282
Wigner 22, 224
Wilburn 23
Wilcox 36, 199, 251, 315
Wilcoxen 155, 291, 292, 295
Wilcoxon 118, 155, 156, 157, 209, 325, 326
Wilhelm 217, 282
Wiliams 218
Wilkins 280
Wilkinson 189, 232
Willams 100
Willem 231
Willey 299, 326
William 169, 238, 290
Williams 11, 12, 13, 23, 25, 56, 59, 62, 72, 79, 100, 141, 146, 153, 154, 155, 163, 173, 189, 192, 198, 217, 221, 227, 236, 273, 277, 300, 306, 322, 326
Williamson 242, 263
Williass 89
Willis 26, 56, 155, 159, 233, 314, 327
Willock 186, 289
Wills 159
Willson 271
Wilmer 206
Wilmot 247
Wilson 22, 56, 66, 67, 90, 92, 94,

341

104, 112, 124, 153, 154, 240, 251, 265, 275, 282, 291, 300, 315, 317, 318, 328
Wilt 225
Windland 273
Winegar 31
Wingfield 20
Wingflelds 21
Winkel 203
Winroth 235
Winslow 252
Winsor 221, 272
Winston 32, 72
Wion 251, 307, 313, 315
Wirhbarger 277
Wise 87, 157, 158, 202, 233, 242, 281, 321
Wisecarver 280
Wiseman 22, 23, 26, 59, 249, 250, 260, 266, 273, 280
Wisner 147
Witham 275
Withers 314
Witherspoon 58
Woda 189, 190, 328
Woerner 141
Wojack 314
Wolfe 118, 293
Wolford 9, 19, 159
Woltz 329
Womeldorf 227
Womeldorff 22, 23
Wood 4, 18, 22, 23, 26, 37, 55, 56, 68, 70, 82, 87, 90, 100, 141, 186, 191, 194, 207, 221, 227, 238, 239, 253, 254, 269, 295, 300, 301, 305, 318, 327, 329, 331
Wooda 79
Woodall 150
Woodard 72
Woodruff 18, 292
Woods 36, 215, 227, 246, 311
Woodward 8, 159, 198, 304, 330
Woody 71
Woodyard 9
Woofter 160, 161, 309
Woolem 249
Woolum 90
Wooten 23, 153, 182, 221, 253, 330
Workman 221, 277, 329
Worman 57
Worthington 238, 239
Wothe 9
Wright 8, 22, 38, 55, 72, 132, 159, 246, 323
Wroblewski 330, 331
Wymer 329

## Y

Yates 281

Yeager 153, 225
Yeaguer 232
Yeauger 36, 285, 288
Yeiser 331
Yinger 174
Yoder 23
Yoho 23
Yokokawa 274
Yonis 175
Yonts 277
Yost 121
Young 87, 89, 152, 321, 331
Yvonne 202

## Z

Zenk 204
Zerkle 32, 36
Zimmerman 59, 123
Zink 22
Zirille 100
Zirkle 246

# Family Tree

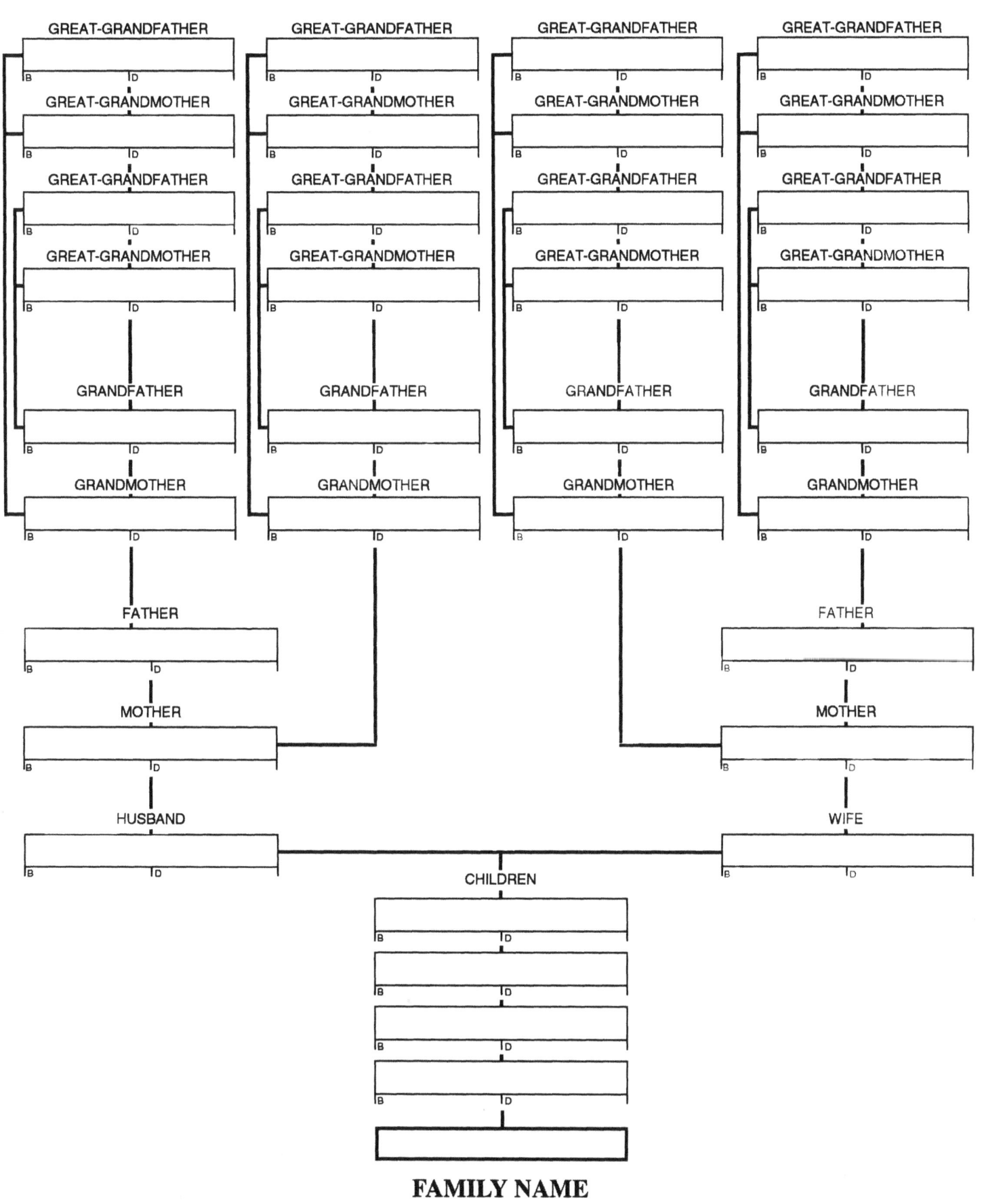

**Family Name**

# Notes

# Gallia County, Ohio

*Gallipolis Bicentennial Commemorative Statue "La Vue Premiere" Gallipolis, Ohio*

*Hutchinson Hardware Store, 50 Court Street, Gallipolis, Ohio*

*June 12, 1938*

*Gallipolis Ferry*

# Gallia County, Ohio

www.ingramcontent.com/pod-product-compliance
Lightning Source LLC
Chambersburg PA
CBHW081826170426
43202CB00019B/2967